Frommer's®

Mexico

D1330645

Here's what the critics say about Frommer's:

"Amazingly easy to use. Very portable, very complete."
—*Booklist*

♦

"Complete, concise, and filled with useful information."
—*New York Daily News*

♦

"Hotel information is close to encyclopedic."
—*Des Moines Sunday Register*

♦

"The only mainstream guide to list specific prices. The Walter Cronkite of guidebooks—with all that implies."
—*Travel & Leisure*

Frommer's® 99

Mexico

by David Baird & Lynne Bairstow

MACMILLAN • USA

ABOUT THE AUTHORS

David Baird (chapters 1, 2, 6, 7, 8, 11, 14, and 16) is a writer, editor, and translator based in Austin, Texas. He spent part of his childhood in Morelia, Mexico, and later lived for 2 years among the Mazatec Indians in Oaxaca, while he was doing graduate fieldwork.

Lynne Bairstow (chapters 1, 3, 4, 5, 9, 10, 12, 13, 15, and 17) is a travel writer and Web site developer who has lived in Puerto Vallarta, Mexico, at least part time for the past 7 years. She now lives there year-round. In a previous professional life, she was a VP for Merrill Lynch in Chicago and New York.

They are also the authors of Frommer's Cancún, Cozumel & the Yucatán.

MACMILLAN TRAVEL

A Simon & Schuster Macmillan Company
1633 Broadway
New York, NY 10019

Find us on-line at **www.frommers.com**

ISBN 0-02862305-3
ISSN 1042-8399

Editor: Neil E. Schlecht
thanks to Dan Glover
Production Editor: Suzanne Snyder
Photo Editor: Richard Fox
Design by Michele Laseau
Digital Cartography by Ortelius Design
Page Creation by Lissa Auciello, Troy Barnes, Jerry Cole, Bob LaRoche, and Linda Quigley

SPECIAL SALES

Bulk purchases (10+ copies) of Frommer's and selected Macmillan travel guides are available to corporations, organizations, mail-order catalogs, institutions, and charities at special discounts, and can be customized to suit individual needs. For more information write to: Special Sales, Macmillan General Reference, 1633 Broadway, New York, NY 10019.

Manufactured in the United States of America

Contents

List of Maps

AN INVITATION TO THE READER

In researching this book, we discovered many wonderful places—resorts, inns, restaurants, shops, and more. We're sure you'll find others. Please tell us about them, so we can share the information with your fellow travelers in upcoming editions. If you were disappointed with a recommendation, we'd love to know that, too. Please write to:

Frommer's Mexico '99
Macmillan Travel
1633 Broadway
New York, NY 10019

AN ADDITIONAL NOTE

Please be advised that travel information is subject to change at any time—and this is especially true of prices. We therefore suggest that you write or call ahead for confirmation when making your travel plans. The authors, editors, and publisher cannot be held responsible for the experiences of readers while traveling. Your safety is important to us, however, so we encourage you to stay alert and be aware of your surroundings. Keep a close eye on cameras, purses, and wallets, all favorite targets of thieves and pickpockets.

A FEW WORDS ABOUT PRICES

The peso's value continues to fluctuate—at press time it was slightly more than 8 pesos to the dollar. Prices in this book (which are always given in U.S. dollars) have been converted to U.S. dollars at 8 pesos to the dollar. Most hotels in Mexico—with the exception of places that receive little foreign tourism—quote prices in U.S. dollars. Thus, currency fluctuations are unlikely to affect the prices charged by most hotels.

Mexico has a **value-added tax** of 15% (Impuesto de Valor Agregado, or IVA, pronounced "ee-bah") on most everything, including restaurant meals, bus tickets, and souvenirs. (Exceptions are Cancún, Cozumel, and Los Cabos, where the IVA is 10%; as ports of entry, they receive a special 5% break on taxes.) Hotels charge the usual 15% IVA, plus a locally administered bed tax of 2% (in many but not all areas), for a total of 17%. In Cancún, Los Cabos, and Cozumel, hotels charge the 10% IVA plus 2% room tax. IVA will not necessarily be included in the prices quoted by hotels and restaurants. You may find that upper-end properties (three or more stars) quote prices without IVA included, while lower-priced hotels include IVA in their quotes. Always ask to see a printed price sheet and always ask if the tax is included.

WHAT THE SYMBOLS MEAN

✪ Frommer's Favorites

Our favorite places and experiences—outstanding for quality, value, or both.

The following abbreviations are used for credit cards:

AE	American Express	JCB	Japan Credit Bank
CB	Carte Blanche	MC	MasterCard
DC	Diners Club	V	Visa
DISC	Discover		

The Best of Mexico

Across Mexico, in small villages and large cities, and in jungle, mountain, and tropical coastal settings, delightful surprises await travelers. These might take the form of a fantastic small-town festival, delightful evening dining in a wonderful restaurant, or even a stretch of road through beautiful countryside. Below is a starter list of our Mexico favorites, to which you'll have the pleasure of adding your own discoveries.

1 The Best Beach Vacations

Almost as valuable as knowing the best beaches is knowing which beaches are not so inviting, such as San Blas, south of Mazatlán, and most of the coast of Veracruz. In both places, the hard-packed sand is likely to be a disappointment to those in search of a dream beach.

- **Puerto Vallarta.** The spectacularly wide Banderas Bay offers 26 miles of beaches in various shapes, sizes, and appeal. Some, like Playa Los Muertos—the popular public beach in town—is packed with palapa restaurants, beach volleyball, and parasailing. Others are nestled in coves, accessible only by boat. Puerto Vallarta itself offers the only place in Mexico with an authentic ambiance of colonial Mexico mixed in with true resort amenities. See chapter 9.
- **Tenacatita Bay & Barra de Navidad.** The entire Costa Alegre offers secluded hotels and resorts tucked into pristine coves and secluded shorelines, but Tenacatita Bay stands out among them. Its main beach offers a choice of two all-inclusive resorts, plus gentle waters that are a playground for the abundance of dolphins that make this bay their home. Nearby, a number of almost uninhabited beaches are accessible by taxi or boat. The golden sands of Barra de Navidad Bay spread to the neighboring village of Melaque. The best choice for those in search of inexpensive hotels right on the beach (or very nearby) and a relaxed pace of life. See chapter 9.
- **Puerto Escondido.** The best overall beach value in Mexico is principally known for its world-class surfing beach, Playa Zicatela. The surrounding beaches all have their own unique appeal; the central town beach is dotted with colorful fishing *pangas* parked under the shade of palms leaning so far over they almost touch the ground. Puerto Escondido offers unique accommodations at excellent prices, with exceptional budget dining and nightlife as well. It defines the term "laid-back." See chapter 10.

- **Ixtapa/Zihuatanejo.** This resort duo packs a punch of good beaches into a relatively small area. The best and most beautiful of those close to Zihuatanejo is Playa La Ropa. The wide beach at Playa Las Gatas, with its beachside restaurants and snorkeling sites, is also a great place to play. The luxury hotels in Ixtapa, on the next bay over from Zihuatanejo, front Playa Palmar, a fine, wide strip of beach. Just offshore, Isla Ixtapa offers a good beach and snorkeling area and lots of palapa restaurants serving just-caught fish. See chapter 10.
- **Cancún.** Mexico's best beaches are in Cancún and along the Yucatán's Quintana Roo coast, extending almost all the way to Chetumal on the border with Belize. The powdery, white-sand beaches front water the color of a Technicolor dream, so clear you can see right through to the coral reefs below. Cancún also offers the widest assortment of luxury beachfront hotels, with more restaurants, nightlife and activities than any other resort destination in the country. See chapter 12.
- **Playa del Carmen.** Not only is the town currently the hottest, hippest place in the county for adventurous travelers looking for original rather than manufactured appeal, but the beaches here are of the pure-white, soft-sand variety. The water is crystal clear and turquoise, and the swimming is safe right offshore. With a strong influx of Europeans, topless sunbathing is permitted, even encouraged, despite its taboo throughout the rest of Mexico. "Playa," as it's known, is not far from the ruins of Tulum and Cobá, and a mere 45-minute ferry ride over to Cozumel, giving you two beach vacations in one. See chapter 13.
- **Isla Mujeres.** There's only one small excellent beach here—Playa Norte—but it's superb. From this island you can dive in the cave of the sleeping sharks, snorkel right off shore, and take a boat excursion to the Isla Contoy National Park, which features great bird life and a fabulous, uninhabited beach. See chapter 13.
- **Los Cabos.** Beaches with dramatic rock formations and crashing waves are interspersed with wide stretches of soft sand and a rolling break. Start at Pueblo la Playa just north of San José del Cabo and work your way down the Cabo Corridor to the famed Playa de Amor at Land's End. Some beaches are more appropriate for meaningful contemplation than safe swimming, which isn't all bad. See chapter 17.

2 The Best Cultural Experiences

We all have at least some curiosity about how people live in a different culture; here are some windows onto the different world south of the Rio Grande.

- **Hanging Out in the Plazas.** All the world may be a stage, but some parts have richer backdrops than others. Town plazas in Mexico are the perfect settings for watching everyday life unfold: There's a stateliness and serenity in the colonial architecture that help you slow down and take time to observe. Alive with people, these open spaces are no modern product of urban planners, but are rooted in the traditional Mexican view of what society is all about. Several plazas are standouts: **Veracruz's Plaza de Armas** (see chapter 15) features nearly nonstop music and the tropical gaiety that has made it famous. At first glance, it's obvious how important **Oaxaca's zócalo** (see chapter 11) is to the local citizenry; the plaza is remarkably beautiful, grand, and intimate all at once. **Mexico City's Alameda** (see chapter 4) has a dark, dramatic history—heretics were burned at the stake here during the colonial period—but today it's a people's park in the heart of the Centro Histórico, where lovers sit, cotton-candy vendors spin out their pink treats, and the sound of organ grinders drifts over the changing crowd. **San Miguel de Allende's Jardín** (see chapter 6) is the focal point for meeting, sitting, painting, and sketching. During festivals, it fills with dancers, parades, and elaborate fireworks. **Guanajuato** and **Querétaro** (see chapter 6) have the coziest of plazas, while **Mérida's "Centro"** (see chapter 14) on a Sunday can't be beat.

- **Música Popular.** Nothing reveals the soul of a people like their music, and in Mexico there are many kinds being played in many different settings. You can find brassy, belt-it-out **mariachi** music in the famous Plaza Garibaldi in Mexico City (see chapter 4), or under the portals of El Parián in Tlaquepaque and in other parts of Guadalajara (see chapter 8). Or perhaps you want to hear romantic **boleros** about love's betrayal sung to the strumming of a Spanish guitar. Or what Mexicans call *música tropical* and related Mexican-style cumbias, mambos, and cha-cha-chas (see chapters 14 and 15).

- **Regional Folk Dancing.** Be it the Ballet Folklórico in Mexico City or Guadalajara (see chapters 4 and 8), the almost-nightly park performances in Mérida (see chapter 14), or celebrations countrywide, these performances are diverse and colorful expressions of Mexican traditions.

- **Fireworks.** Mexicans have such a passion for fireworks and such a cavalier attitude towards them that it's a good thing the buildings are made of stone and cement or the whole country would have burned down long ago. There are many local traditions surrounding fireworks, and just as many theories as to why they are so popular; every festival has some sort of display. The most lavish of these are the large fireworks constructions known as *castillos,* and the wildest are the *toros* that men carry over their shoulders while running through the streets, causing festival-goers to dive for cover.

- **The Callejoneada in Zacatecas.** Nothing compares to the exhilaration of following a band of horns and drums, a burro laden with barrels of fiery mezcal (from which you imbibe frequently using a cup hung around your neck), and a group of merry celebrants swinging hands and dancing through the narrow streets (*callejones*) of Zacatecas—legally disturbing the peace until the wee hours. See chapter 6.

- **Estudiantinas in Guanajuato.** University students (*estudiantes*) dressed in medieval garb sing their way through the streets of Guanajuato accompanying a burro laden with plenty of tequila for onlookers. Crowds follow the parade drinking, dancing, and singing along until exhaustion sets in. Often, especially during the **Cervantino Festival,** the students appear spontaneously in restaurants. See chapter 6.

- **Strolling the Malecón.** Wherever there's a seafront road, you'll find the malecón bordering it. This is generally a wide sidewalk for strolling that in some cases has supplanted the town plaza as a centerpiece of town life, complete with strolling vendors selling pinwheels and cotton candy. The best examples are found in **Puerto Vallarta,** with its impressive display of public sculpture, **Mazatlán** (see chapter 9), and **Cozumel** (see chapter 13).

3 The Best Festivals & Celebrations

If you're in Mexico any length of time at all, you are likely to happen upon a celebration of some sort. Some of the country's most memorable celebrations, such as Holy Week, are solemn religious events that employ elaborate and colorful pageantry. Others are the kind of nonstop revelry endemic to a country that knows how to put on a whale of a fiesta. Festivals are as much a part of Mexico as tortillas and frijoles. You can discover some perfectly charming festivals in small towns, but here is a short list of some of the big ones.

- **Festival de Nuestra Señora de Guadalupe.** This annual celebration leads up to Día de Nuestra Señora de Guadalupe, celebrated throughout Mexico on December 12. The Virgin of Guadalupe is the patron saint of Mexico, and is also identified with the Aztec earth goddess and mother of humankind. The importance of this day stems from the intermingling of ancient Indian beliefs with the new culture and religion brought to Mexico by the Spaniards. Although the basilica just outside of **Mexico City** features the largest celebration and the most impressive crowd of impassioned believers, perhaps the best place to view the festivities is in Puerto Vallarta, where they continue around the clock for 12 straight days. It is a visual delight, especially for photographers. See chapters 4 and 9.

- **Days of the Dead.** *Los Días de los Muertos* (Oct 31 to Nov 2) are celebrated across the country; it is the general custom to erect altars for the dead, with marigolds (the flower of the dead) and offerings of food and drink. But the most popular celebrations happen in the villages around **Pátzcuaro** (see chapter 7) and in the valley of **Oaxaca** (see chapter 11). People head out to the cemetery for all-night vigils and sing and pray for the souls of the dearly departed. During the day, markets sell crafts and special items made just for the festival.

- **Carnaval.** Throughout the world, certain cities have a conspicuously festive way of indulging prior to the pious period of Lent. In Mexico, the two most notable celebrations of Carnaval take place in Veracruz and Mazatlán. Festivities in **Veracruz** take place during the 3 days before Ash Wednesday, with fabulous floats, dancing in the plaza, and live entertainment. See chapter 15. **Mazatlán's** party lasts a full week before Lent, with parades, strolling musicians, and crowds of revelers along the entire stretch of the malecón. See chapter 9.

- **Holy Week.** The silver city of **Taxco** hosts one of the most compelling Holy Week commemorations in the country, beginning the Friday before Palm Sunday with nightly processions and several during the day. On the evening of Holy Thursday, villagers carrying saints from the surrounding area are followed by hooded members of a society of self-flagellating penitents. Others are chained at the ankles and still more carry huge wooden crosses and bundles of penetrating thorny branches. On the Saturday morning before Easter, the Plaza Borda fills for the Procession of Three Falls, which reenacts the three times Christ stumbled and fell while carrying his cross. See chapter 5. In **San Miguel Allende, Pátzcuaro** and surrounding communities, and in **Oaxaca,** this solemn weeklong commemoration involves nightly candlelit processions through the streets and daily masses and other religious events. See chapters 6, 7, and 11.

- **La Fiesta de los Locos.** In **San Miguel de Allende,** a town known for celebrating a remarkable number of holidays, this one is the most fun for visitors to attend. Young and old alike dress in grotesque costumes and parade around the center of town or in dressed up carts to the accompaniment of instruments. Keep an eye open for practical jokes being played. See chapter 6.

- **Guelaguetza.** On the last 2 Mondays in July, Oaxaca puts on a big show. Dance groups from communities across the state perform in the amphitheater on the hillside above the city. See chapter 11.

- **Christmas: "Night of the Radishes".** Unique in the country, December 23 in **Oaxaca** is when the Oaxaqueños build fantastic sculptures out of radishes (the most prized vegetable cultivated during the colonial period), flowers, and dried corn husks. They are displayed on the zócalo. On December 24, each Oaxacan church organizes a procession with music, floats, and crowds bearing candles that parade to the zócalo before returning to parish churches. See chapter 11.

4 The Best Archaeological Sites

- **Teotihuacán.** So close to Mexico City, yet centuries away. You can feel the majesty of the past in a stroll down the pyramid-lined Avenue of the Dead, from the Pyramid of the Sun to the Pyramid of the Moon. Imagine what a fabulous place this must have been when the walls were stuccoed and painted in brilliant colors. See chapter 5.
- **Monte Albán.** A grand ceremonial city built on a mountaintop overlooking the valley of Oaxaca, Monte Albán offers the visitor panoramic vistas; a fascinating view of a society in transition, reflected in the contrasting methods for building the pyramids; and intriguing details in ornamentation. There is much to ponder. See chapter 11.
- **Palenque.** Like the ancient pharaohs, the rulers of this city built tombs for themselves deep within their pyramids. Imagine the magnificent ceremony in 683 A.D. when King Pacal was buried below ground in a secret pyramidal tomb—unspoiled until its discovery in 1952. For any further understanding, we must depend on the city they left behind and its mysterious and beautiful artistic expressions—whose style is as dense as the surrounding jungle. See chapter 11.
- **Uxmal.** No matter how many times you see Uxmal, the splendor of its stone carvings is awe-inspiring. A stone rattlesnake undulates across the facade of the Nunnery complex, and 103 masks of Chaac—the rain god—project from the Governor's Palace. See chapter 14.
- **Chichén-Itzá.** Stand beside the giant serpent head at the foot of El Castillo pyramid and marvel at the architects and astronomers who positioned the building so precisely that shadow and sunlight form a serpent's body slithering from the peak to the earth at each equinox (Mar 21 and Sept 21). See chapter 14.

5 The Best Active Vacations

- **Biking in the Sierra Madre Foothills.** In Puerto Vallarta, professional mountain-bike trips are offered into the mountains surrounding this picturesque village. Trips range from half-day trips up the Cuale canyon to overnight trips to the mountain villages of San Sebastian, Talpa, and Mascota. See chapter 9.
- **Scuba Diving in Cozumel.** The coral reefs off the island of Cozumel are Mexico's premier diving destination, considered among the top-10 dive spots in the world. An easy journey over to the Yucatán mainland offers a completely different dive experience, into the deep, clear *cenotes* (sinkholes or natural wells). See chapter 13. Other excellent dive sites are found in and around **Puerto Vallarta's** Banderas Bay and in the Sea of Cortés at Cabo Pulmo off **Los Cabos.** See chapters 9 and 17.
- **Fly-Fishing off the Punta Allen Peninsula.** Serious fishers will enjoy the challenge of fly-fishing the saltwater flats and lagoons of Ascención Bay for bonefish, permit, and snook, near Punta Allen, where they can stay at the Cuzan Guest House. See chapter 13.
- **Hiking and Mountaineering in the Copper Canyon.** Miles and miles of beautiful, remote, and challenging canyon lands are paradise for the serious hiker or rider. For hikers, **Columbus Travel** (☎ 800/843-1060) can set you up with one of their Tarahumara Indian guides who can take you deep into the canyons to places rarely viewed by tourists. Doug Rhodes of the **Paraíso del Oso** (☎ 14/21-3372) leads tours of experienced horseback riders on a 12-day ride that tests a rider's skill in mountainous terrain and has to be the most challenging ride in North America. See chapter 16.

- **Golfing in Los Cabos.** More than "up-and-coming," the Corridor between San José del Cabo and Cabo San Lucas is now known as one of the world's premier golf destinations, with four championship courses open and a total of 207 holes slated for the area. See chapter 17.
- **Surfing Zicatela Beach in Puerto Escondido.** This world-class break is a lure for surfers around the globe. The best in the sport are challenged each September and October, when the waves peak and the annual surf competition is held. See chapter 10. Other noted surf breaks in Mexico include Las Islitas Beach near **San Blas** (north of Puerto Vallarta), and Playa Costa Azul, on the outskirts of **San José del Cabo.** See chapters 9 and 17.
- **Sportfishing in Cabo San Lucas.** Billfishing for magnificent marlin and sailfish is a popular sport in Los Cabos, where catch and release is widely practiced. See chapter 17. Fishing is also excellent in La Paz, Mazatlán, Manzanillo, and Zihuatanejo. See chapters 9 and 10.

6 The Best of Natural Mexico

- **Michoacán's Million Monarch March.** Mexico is an exotic land, and nowhere is this driven home more forcefully than when you're standing in a mountain forest surrounded by millions of migrating monarch butterflies—it's like being in a fairy tale. The setting is the rugged highlands of Michoacán (some of the most beautiful country in Mexico) between November and February. See chapter 7.
- **Whale Watching.** Each winter, between December and April, magnificent humpback and gray whales return to breed and instruct their young in the waters offshore in Banderas Bay, fronting **Puerto Vallarta,** and in **Los Cabos.** Photograph these majestic mammals breaching and slapping their tails in their natural habitat. See chapters 9 and 17.
- **Sea-Turtle Nesting Beaches.** Between June and November, sea turtles return to the beaches of their birth to lay their eggs, which they deposit in nests on the sand. With poaching and natural predators threatening the continuation of these species, local communities along Mexico's Pacific coastlines have established protected nesting areas. Many are open for public viewing and participation of the egg collection and baby-turtle release processes. Turtles are found in Baja Sur, the Oaxaca coast, Puerto Vallarta, and Costa Alegre. See chapters 9, 10, and 17.
- **Cozumel's Coral Reefs.** Known as some of the most diverse, extensive reef formations in the world, the coral-reef systems offshore Cozumel Island have made this a world-favorite diving destination. See chapter 13.
- **Lago Bacalar** (Yucatán Peninsula): The waters of this crystal-clear, spring-fed lake—Mexico's second largest—empty into the Caribbean and are noted for their vibrant variations of colors, ranging from pale blue to deep blue-green and turquoise. The area surrounding the lake is noted for bird watching, with over 130 species identified. See chapter 13.
- **The Rugged Copper Canyon.** The group of canyons known collectively as the Copper Canyon are beautiful, remote, and unspoiled. The entire network is more vast than the Grand Canyon, and it includes high waterfalls, vertical canyon walls, and sharp contrasts in vegetation from mountain forests in the canyon-rim country to semi-arid desert inside the canyons. This is the land of the Tarahumara Indians, whose legendary endurance was gained from living in this wild land. See chapter 16.
- **Desert Landscapes in Baja Sur.** The painted desert colors and unique plant life are a natural curiosity in **Los Cabos,** with horseback, hiking, and ATV trips available

for exploring the area. The region is noted for the sharp contrasts of the arid desert bordered by the intense blue of the strong sea surrounding this peninsula. See chapter 17.

7 The Best Places to Get Away from It All

A few places in Mexico come to mind as total escapes for a moment, a day, a week, or more. Some of these could double as romantic escapes.

- **Costa Alegre.** Between Puerto Vallarta and Manzanillo, a number of superexclusive hotels cater to those with both time and money. These resorts—Las Alamandas, Hotel Bel-Air Costa Careyes, and El Tamarindo—are miles from civilization and boast their own private beaches. The rustic yet luxurious Hotelito Desconocido is an ecological retreat set on a lagoon, a short stretch from the Pacific Ocean. See chapter 9.

- **Troncones.** Twenty miles northwest of Ixtapa, this Pacific Coast hideaway started out as a simple-but-wonderful place to have a delicious lobster or shrimp lunch, a swim in the ocean, and a stroll on the beach without bumping into a soul. Now, five small inns on the beach offer comforts without the crowds. With rooms for only a few guests, it's a complete getaway that's hard to beat for simplicity and tranquillity. See chapter 10.

- **Costa Turquesa & Punta Allen Peninsula.** Away from the popular resort of Cancún, the Turquoise Coast's string of heavenly quiet getaways, including Capitán Lafitte, Paamul, Akumal, and a portion of Xpuha, offer tranquillity at low prices on beautiful palm-lined beaches. South of the Tulum ruins, Punta Allen's beachside budget inns offer some of the most peaceful getaways in the country. Life here among the birds and coconut palms has never been anything but leisurely. See chapter 13.

- **Lago Bacalar.** The spring-fed waters of Lake Bacalar—Mexico's second largest lake—make an ideal place to unwind. Located south of Cancún near Chetumal, there's nothing around for miles. But if you want adventure, you can take a kayak out on the lake, follow a birding trail, or take excursions to Belize or to the nearby Maya ruins on the Río Bec ruin route. See chapter 13.

- **Batopilas.** Batopilas is a near–ghost town, left over from 18th- and 19th-century silver-mining booms. Preserved as though someone sealed it for safekeeping, the town's feel of yesteryear is indelibly imprinted on its stuccoed walls and cobbled streets. This outpost has no telephones or newspapers. Electricity, a recent installation, makes the one or two TVs operable. See chapter 16.

- **Todos Santos.** Purportedly home of the original Hotel California. You can check out any time, but you may not want to leave, once you unwind for a while in this artists" outpost, also known as "Bohemian Baja." See chapter 17.

8 The Best Art, Architecture & Museums

With a history spanning over 2,000 years, Mexico is a living museum of art, architecture, and culture. Mexico City has a concentration of some of the world's finest museums, as well as examples of architectural styles from ancient to contemporary. Many museums or structures showcasing cultural treasures are works of art in themselves.

- **Museo Nacional de Antropología.** Counted among the world's most outstanding museums, the Museum of Anthropology in Mexico City contains many riches representing 3,000 years of Mexico's past. Also on view are fabulous examples of rich and still-thriving indigenous cultures. The building itself is stunning, designed by architect Pedro Ramírez Vázquez. See chapter 4.

- **Frida Kahlo House and Museum (Museo Frida Kahlo).** While perhaps not a world-class collection of works by Mexico's first couple of art, Frida Kahlo and Diego Rivera, this museum in Mexico City does offer a strong sampling of their works, plus their fascinating private collection. With rooms intact as they were when the couple lived here, it also allows visitors the chance to peek into the lives of these two creative masters. See chapter 4.

- **The Capital's Palacio Nacional.** Mexico's center of government and presidential office was originally built in 1692 on the site of Moctezuma's "new" palace, to be the home of Hernán Cortés. In the late 1920s, the top floor was added, which is decorated by a series of stunning Diego Rivera murals depicting the history of Mexico. See chapter 4.

- **Palacio de Bellas Artes in Mexico City.** The premier venue for the performing arts in Mexico, this fabulous building is the combined work of several masters, including the Italian architect Adamo Boari and Mexican painter Gerardo Murillo, who designed the glass curtain that was constructed in the Tiffany Studios of New York. The theater's exterior is turn-of-the-century art nouveau, covered in marble, while the interior is 1930s art deco. See chapter 4.

- **The Templo Mayor's Aztec Splendor.** The Templo Mayor and Museo del Templo Mayor, in Mexico City, are an archaeological excavation and a museum with 6,000 objects displayed, showcasing the variety and splendor of the Aztec Empire, as it existed in the center of what is now Mexico City. See chapter 4.

- **Cathedral Metropolitana.** This impressive, towering cathedral, begun in 1573 and finished in 1788, blends baroque, neoclassic, and Mexican churrigueresque architecture, and was constructed primarily from the stones of destroyed Aztec temples. See chapter 4.

- **Puebla's Popular Art Museum.** Located in a two-story convent, the Museo de Artes Populares houses a huge collection of the state's regional costumes, pottery, and everyday utensils. Plus, there are cavernous rooms showing works in clay, leather, straw, and papier-mâché from villages statewide. See chapter 5.

- **Santa Prisca y San Sebastián Church.** One of Mexico's most impressive baroque churches, completed in 1758, this church in Taxco, has an intricately carved facade, with an interior decorated with gold-leafed saints and angels, as well as paintings by Miguel Cabrera, one of Mexico's most famous colonial-era artists. See chapter 5.

- **Mexican Masks in Zacatecas.** Masks are a ubiquitous feature in Mexican festivals and folk art, and the Museo Rafael Coronel in Zacatecas has perhaps the greatest collection in the country. See chapter 6.

- **Colonial-era Civil & Religious Art in Guanajuato.** The Museo del Pueblo de Guanajuato contains a priceless collection of more than 1,000 pieces gathered by the muralist José Chávez Morado. See chapter 6.

9 The Best Shopping

Mexico abounds with colorful, memorable artistry, much of it utilitarian and all attractively priced. Superior shopping is found in more than a half dozen cities and villages.

- **Bazar Sábado in San Ángel.** This festive weekly market in a colonial neighborhood south of Mexico City offers exceptional crafts, of a more sophisticated nature than in most mercados. Furnishings, antiques, and collectibles are also easy to find in sur-rounding garages and street plazas. See chapter 4.

- **Zona Rosa in Mexico City.** This fashionable neighborhood in the nation's capital is noted for its designer boutiques, cigar shops, fine jewelers, and leather-goods offerings. See chapter 4.
- **Contemporary Art.** Latin American art is surging in popularity and recognition. Mexico's masters and emerging stars are featured in galleries in Mexico City, with San Miguel de Allende and Puerto Vallarta galleries also offering excellent selec-tions. See chapters 4, 6, and 9.
- **Taxco Silver.** Mexico's silver capital, Taxco has more than 200 stores featuring fine jewelry and decorative objects. See chapter 5.
- **Talavera Pottery in Puebla & Dolores Hidalgo.** A pottery center even before the Conquest of Mexico, Puebla is the point of origin for the painted ceramics and tiles that adorn building facades and church domes throughout the area. Factories pro-duce highly collectible tile and colorful tableware with unique motifs. See chapter 5. A few miles north of San Miguel de Allende, Dolores Hidalgo is fast becoming the best-known pottery-producing village in Mexico. Almost every block has facto-ries or store outlets offering at low prices the colorful Talavera-style pottery that the town is known for. See chapter 6.
- **San Miguel de Allende's Diverse Crafts.** Perhaps it's the influence of the Instituto Allende art school, but something has given storekeepers here a real savvy about choosing their merchandise. The stores here have fewer of the typical articles of Mexican handcrafts and more interesting and eye-catching works than what you'll find in shopping other Mexican towns. The shopping experience here is quite pleasant. See chapter 6.
- **Pátzcuaro's Fine Crafts.** Michoacán is known for its crafts, and Pátzcuaro is at the center of it all. You can find beautiful cotton textiles, wood carving, pottery, lac-querware, straw weaving, and copper items in the market, or you can track the item to its source in one of the nearby villages. See chapter 7.
- **Decorative Arts in Tonalá and Tlaquepaque.** These two neighborhoods of Guadalajara offer perhaps the most enjoyable shopping in Mexico. Tlaquepaque has attracted many sophisticated and wide-ranging shops selling an incredible variety of decorative art pieces. People are relaxed and friendly, and the community has a very pleasant feel about it. In Tonalá, more than 400 artisans have workshops, and you can visit many of these on regular days, and on market days you can wander through blocks and blocks of market stalls seeking that one piece that has eluded you. See chapter 8.
- **Huichol Art in Puerto Vallarta.** One of the last indigenous cultures to remain faithful to their customs, language, and traditions, the Huichol Indians come down from the Sierra Madre mountains to sell their unusual works of art to Puerto Val-larta galleries. Inspired by visions received during spiritual ceremonies, the Huichols create their art with colorful yarn or beads pressed into wax. See chapter 9.
- **Oaxacan Textiles.** This area has the best weavings and naturally dyed textiles in Mexico; it's also famous for its pottery (especially the black pottery), and colorful, imaginative wood carvings. See chapter 11.
- **The Markets of San Cristóbal de las Casas.** This city, located deep in the heart of the Maya highlands, has shops, open plazas, and markets featuring distinctive waist-loomed wool and cotton textiles, as well as leather shoes, handsomely crude pottery, genre dolls, and Guatemalan textiles. See chapter 11.

10 The Hottest Nightlife

In Mexico, nightlife can mean a cold *cerveza* at a funky cantina on the beach or one of the most elaborate discos you've ever encountered. These flamboyant 1970s-style clubs may be passé in the rest of the world, but in Mexico *dees-cohs* are more than alive and well: They have a thriving life of their own. Most nightspots get going around 10pm and close down somewhere toward sunrise.

- **Guadalajara's Sophisticated Scene.** The nightlife in Guadalajara extends to theater and classical-music concerts, virtuoso performances of jazz, and salsa, never forgetting mariachi music (which when done properly, requires vocalists to really flaunt their talent). The city also has a fun discotheque situated in the colonial ex-convent of capuchin nuns where circus acts please the crowd from an elevated stage in the convent's courtyard. See chapter 8.
- **Puerto Vallarta's Live Music.** Puerto Vallarta has an excellent selection of small clubs featuring jazz, blues, and good old rock 'n' roll. Notable is Club Roxy, with an excellent house band. You'll also find mariachi, pre-Columbian, and traditional Mexican ballads played in clubs and restaurants around town. See chapter 9.
- **Valentino's in Mazatlán.** Though this clean beachside city doesn't have the breadth of nightlife of other resorts, it does have Valentino's, one of the best known and most popular discos in the country. The white, Moorish-looking building is dramatically perched on a rocky outcropping overlooking the sea. See chapter 9.
- **Acapulco Discos.** Nightlife couldn't possibly get as lavish, extravagant, or flashy as it is in Acapulco, the diva of Mexico. This city's main cultural attraction is the collection of clubs that rock till sunrise, several of which have walls of windows overlooking the bay. See chapter 10.
- **The Lively Offerings of San Cristóbal de las Casas.** Small though it may be, this city has a live-music scene that can't be beat for sheer fun, casual atmosphere, and friendly nightlife. It's inexpensive, too. This is the perfect place to do some barhopping: there's variety, no covers, and everything is within walking distance. See chapter 11.
- **Cancún's Clubs-in-Malls.** Second to Acapulco, Cancún's wide-ranging hot spots include most of the name-brand nightlife, concentrated in entertainment malls, as well as hotel-lobby bars with live music and sophisticated discos. There are plenty of options in Cancún for staying out until the sun comes up. See chapter 12.
- **Mérida's Tropical Latin Flavor.** Mérida offers a combination of entertainment that can't be matched elsewhere in Mexico: from skimpily clad Cuban dancers in colorful headdresses performing rumbas before a background of replicas of Maya pyramids; to dark, cozy dens where trios croon romantic *boleros* punctuated by elegant guitar solos; to Latin jazz and pop, to Caribbean-style *música tropical*. See chapter 14.
- **Cabo San Lucas Beach Bars.** The nightlife capital of Baja California, after-dark fun here is centered around the casual bars and restaurants that line the main drag, as well as those on the town's public beach, Playa Medano. There's still a rowdy, outlaw feel to the place, despite the influx of tony clubs. See chapter 17.

11 The Best Luxury Hotels

- **Hotel Four Seasons** (Mexico City; ☎ **800/332-3442** in the U.S., or 800/ 268-6282 in Canada). The standard of excellence in service and amenities throughout Mexico, this hotel manages to capture both serenity and elegance in its hacienda-styled building surrounding a picturesque courtyard. The gracious staff and offerings of unique cultural tours are added bonuses to this cool oasis in the midst of the largest city in the world. See chapter 4.

- **Las Mañanitas** (Cuernavaca; ☎ **73/14-1466** or 73/12-4646). This small hotel is elegant in every way, exclusive without being snobby. Everything here is polished, from the brass and mahogany to the top-notch service. Even the peacocks strolling in the garden are well groomed. See chapter 5.

- **Casa de Sierra Nevada** (San Miguel de Allende; ☎ **800/223-6510** in the U.S.). This luxury hotel has all the flavor of colonial Mexico; it's a collection of eight elegantly outfitted manor houses in one of the country's most appealing colonial towns. The owner keeps a stable of horses and a large ranch for the use of his guests. See chapter 6.

- **Villa Montaña** (Morelia; ☎ **800/223-6510** in the U.S., or 800/44-UTELL in Canada). The Villa Montaña defines perfection. In the layout of the grounds and the decoration of the rooms, every detail has been skillfully handled. The hotel is perched on a ridge overlooking Morelia; from its terraces guests can survey the city below as if from an ivory tower. The restaurant is one of the city's best. See chapter 7.

- **Grand Bay Hotel** (Puerto de la Navidad; ☎ **888/80-GRAND** in the U.S.). This hotel, which opened in 1997 next to a challenging 27-hole golf course, manages to combine warm hospitality with lavishly furnished quarters. It's situated on a peninsula across a narrow inlet from the laid-back village of Barra de Navidad—only 25 minutes north of the Manzanillo airport. See chapter 9.

- **Hotel Bel-Air Costa Carayes** (between Manzanillo and Puerto Vallarta; ☎ **800/457-7676** in the U.S. and Canada). Big-time exclusive, the luxurious hotel in a dense coastal jungle setting offers a full-service, state-of-the-art spa as well as spacious, gracious rooms. Activities include sportfishing, horseback riding, and midnight turtle-nesting watches (seasonal). It's closer to Manzanillo than Puerto Vallarta. See chapter 9.

- **Quinta Real** (Bahías de Huatulco; ☎ **888/561-2817** or 800/445-4565 in the U.S.). A tranquil, elegant retreat, with small groupings of cream and white adobe buildings offering complete privacy. Well-appointed suites, most with their own private pools, overlook the natural beauty of Tangolunda Bay. Attentive service is emphasized. See chapter 10.

- **Hotel Camino Real** (Oaxaca; ☎ **800/722-6466** in the U.S.). A magnificent hotel built inside a 16th-century convent in the middle of the best part of Oaxaca City. The hotel is quite spacious, with several beautiful and tranquil courtyards where renovation efforts have carefully preserved the marks of time. No other hotel in Mexico captures the sense of antiquity as well as this one. The rooms are finely furnished, and the restaurant does credit to Oaxacan cooking. See chapter 11.

- **Ritz-Carlton Hotel** (Cancún; ☎ **800/241-3333** in the U.S. and Canada). In a resort known for high-rise luxury, this hotel is in a class apart, with spectacular facilities fronting a perfect Caribbean beach. You'll find spacious, beautifully furnished rooms; gleaming marble floors; elegant dining; and exceptional service. See chapter 12.

- **Las Ventanas al Paraíso** (Los Cabos; ☎ **888/525-0483** in the U.S.). Completed in late 1997, this is currently Mexico's most luxurious property, complete with a deluxe European spa, excellent gourmet restaurant, and elegantly appointed rooms and suites—every detail has been carefully considered. With fireplaces and telescopes to private pools and rooftop terraces, each suite is a private slice of heaven. See chapter 17.

- **Hotel Palmilla** (San José del Cabo; ☎ **800/637-2226** in the U.S.). Perched on a cliff above the sea, this is one of the most luxurious yet relaxed hotels in Mexico, with it's own championship golf course and a collection of room amenities designed to provide for every imaginable comfort. The original luxury hotel in Baja, a recent renovation has taken it to a new standard of excellence. See chapter 17.

12 The Best Unique Inns

- **Casa de los Espíritus Alegres** (Guanajuato; ☎ **473/3-1013**). Folk art and atmosphere abound in this idiosyncratic "house of happy spirits," just outside the lovely mining town of Guanajuato in the heart of Mexico. It's surely the quirkiest 16th-century hacienda you'll ever see. The individually named rooms are all uniquely and colorfully decorated, and each has its own fireplace. The owners also have a small folk-art shop downstairs. See chapter 6.
- **Quinta María Cortez** (Puerto Vallarta; ☎ **888/640-8100** in the U.S.). This is one of the most original places to stay in Mexico, an eclectic B&B on the sea with six suites, all uniquely decorated in antiques, capricious curios, and original art. Located on a beautiful cove on Conchas Chinas beach, this intimate inn has been recently renovated, yet retains the honed charm that has welcomed celebrity guests and movie sets. See chapter 9.
- **Las Alamandas** (between Manzanillo and Puerto Vallarta; ☎ **800/223-6510** in the U.S.). Easily the most exclusive remote resort in Mexico, this inn, with only five large *casitas* facing the Pacific, hosts Hollywood celebrities and the well-to-do from around the world. It's just about equidistant between Manzanillo and Puerto Vallarta. See chapter 9.
- **La Casa Que Canta** (Zihuatanejo; ☎ **800/432-6075** or 800/448-8355 in the U.S.). This architecturally dramatic hotel harmonizes wonderful Mexican adobe and folk art in grandly scaled rooms. It's a delightful place to unwind, read books on the terrace overlooking the bay, and order room service. See chapter 10.
- **Hotel Santa Fe** (Puerto Escondido; ☎ **958/2-0170**). A unique Spanish-colonial styled inn, with a welcoming staff and clean, comfortable rooms decorated in simple, rustic wood furnishings. The three-story, hacienda-style buildings, with archways and blooming bougainvillea, surround two courtyard swimming pools, and are across the street from the famed surfing beach, Zicatela. An added bonus is the Santa Fe Restaurant, one of the best on the southern Pacific coast. See chapter 10.
- **El Jacarandal** (San Cristóbal de las Casas; ☎ **967/8-1065**). This is really not so much like being at an inn, but more like staying at someone's house who has invited you down for a visit and to see the sights. The owners are gracious and informed folks whose society is engaging. They can take you on a horseback ride through the countryside or on a visit to the nearby Indian villages. See chapter 11.
- **Hotel Jungla Caribe** (Playa del Carmen; ☎ **987/3-0650**). Located right in the heart of Playa's pedestrian-only 5th Avenue, this inventive inn has a high-styled decor that mixes neoclassical with Robinson Crusoe. All rooms are spacious, with whimsical touches. Just 2 blocks from the beach, and in the heart of action in this ultrahip town. See chapter 13.
- **La Casa de los Sueños** (Isla Mujeres; ☎ **800/551-2558** in the U.S.). A private home turned upscale B&B, this stunning inn offers complete relaxation and luxury amenities for nonsmoking adults. A large, open interior courtyard, tropical gardens, infinity pool, small beach, and palapa-shaded lounge area are just a few of the very

"un-common" areas shared by guests. It's geared for those looking for a healthful, stress-free vacation. See chapter 13.

- **Casa Mexilio Guest House** (Mérida; ☎ **800/538-6802** in the U.S., or 99/ 28-2505). An imaginative arrangement of rooms around a courtyard features a pool surrounded by a riot of tropical vegetation. The rooms are divided among different levels for the sake of privacy, and connected by stairs and catwalks. Breakfast here provides an extra incentive for getting out of bed. See chapter 14.

13 The Best Inexpensive Inns

Some inns stand out for their combination of hospitality and simple but colorful surroundings. These are places guests return to again and again.

- **Hotel Gillow** (Mexico City; ☎ **5/518-1440**). The secret? You get a lot for your money here—a modern hotel, a perfect location between the zócalo and Alameda, comfortable beds, excellent lighting, a good restaurant, and a staff likely to remember you from one visit to the next. See chapter 4.
- **Hotel Rancho Taxco Victoria** (Taxco; ☎ **762/2-0004**). With its pristine 1940s decor and fabulous hillside setting overlooking all of Taxco, this hotel gets special marks as an inexpensive inn that exudes all the charm of old-fashioned Mexico. See chapter 5.
- **Hotel Mansión Iturbe Bed and Breakfast** (Pátzcuaro; ☎ **434/2-0368**). Few budget hotels offer more free perks for guests than this 17th-century town house on Pátzcuaro's Plaza Grande—a welcome drink; hot water for instant coffee in the lobby early each morning; full breakfast in Doña Paca, the hotel's great little restaurant; free daily paper; 2 hours of free bicycle rental; and the 4th night free. See chapter 7.
- **Hotel Posada de la Basílica** (Pátzcuaro; ☎ **434/2-1108**). A mansion turned hotel, this appealing colonial-style inn has comfortable rooms with fireplaces. The rooms are built around a lovely patio with a view of the village. See chapter 7.
- **Los Cuatro Vientos** (Puerto Vallarta; ☎ **322/2-0161**). A quiet, cozy inn set on a hillside overlooking Banderas Bay, it features colorfully decorated rooms built around a small pool and central patio, daily continental breakfast, and the absolute best venue for sunsets in Puerto Vallarta. See chapter 9.
- **Hotel Flor de María** (Puerto Escondido; ☎ **958/2-0536**): This hotel is charming in every way, from the hospitable owners Lino and María Francato to the guest rooms individually decorated with Lino's fine artistic touches. The restaurant is the best in town. See chapter 10.
- **Las Golondrinas** (Oaxaca; ☎ **951/4-3298**). We receive more favorable letters about this hotel than any other in the country. Small and simple, but colorful, with homey touches of folk art and pathways lined with abundant foliage. See chapter 11.
- **Cuzan Guest House** (Punta Allen; ☎ **983/4-0358** in Felipe Carrillo Puerto). Getting to the isolated lobster fishing village of Punta Allen is half the adventure. You nest in a hammock, dine on lobster and stone crabs, and absolutely forget the outside world; there are no phones, TVs, or newspapers, and "town" is 35 miles away. Nature trips and bonefishing are the activities of choice. See chapter 13.
- **Villa Catarina Rooms & Cabañas** (Playa del Carmen; ☎ **987/3-0970**). Budget prices for stylishly rustic rooms and cabañas, with high-quality furnishings and folk-art accents, nestled in a grove of palms and fruit trees. One block from Playa del Carmen's exquisite beach. See chapter 13.

- **Hotel Mucuy** (Mérida: ☎ **99/28-5193**). Alfredo and Ofelia Comín, owners of one of the most hospitable budget hotels on the peninsula, strive to make guests feel at home with cheery, clean rooms, comfortable outdoor tables and chairs, a communal refrigerator in the lobby, and laundry facilities. See chapter 14.
- **Cabo Inn** (Cabo San Lucas; ☎/fax **114/3-0819**). This is the best budget inn in the area; a former bordello, the small but extra-clean rooms are invitingly decorated with lots of extra amenities and friendly, helpful managers/owners. Ideally located, close to town and near the marina, it caters to sportfishers. See chapter 17.

14　The Best Mexican Food & Drink

- **Fonda El Refugio, for Traditional Mexican Food** (Mexico City; ☎ **5/ 207-2732**). This elegantly casual place prepares specialties from all over the country, including *manchamanteles* ("tablecloth stainers") on Tuesday and *albóndigas en chile chipotle* (meatballs in chipotle sauce) on Saturday. See chapter 4.
- **Fonda Santa Clara, for Mexican Culinary Specialties** (Mexico City and Puebla; ☎ **5/557-6144** in Mexico City, or **22/42-2659** in Puebla). The menu here features such traditional dishes as *pollo mole poblano, mixiotes,* and *tinga* (a great beef stew). The real highlight here are the culinary, seasonal specialties of the country that include fried grasshoppers in October and November, maguey worms in April and May, *huitlacoche* in June, and *chiles en nogada* July through September. See chapters 4 and 5.
- **Los Almendros, for Yucatecan Specialties** (Mexico City, Cancún, Mérida, and Ticul). This family-owned restaurant chain features Yucatecan specialties, such as *poc chuc,* a marinated and grilled pork dish. Yucatecan cuisine is based on ancient Mayan recipes. See chapters 12 and 14.
- **El Estribo Bar, for Premium Tequilas** (Mexico City; ☎ **5/281-4554**). No longer is tequila relegated to salt-and-lime shooters; it's being recognized for its unique properties and subtle taste variations, equal in sophistication to a fine scotch whiskey. Premium-tequila tastings are the rage; El Estribo is among the best of the new places for sampling. Over 480 different types of tequila are available, most of which are 100% blue agave, the mark of a fine tequila. See chapter 4.
- **La Lola, for Nouvelle Cuisine in Mexico's Heartland** (San Miguel de Allende; ☎ **415/2-4050**). The town of San Miguel might seem like a strange place to be trying international nouvelle cuisine, but it's a different sort of place, and so is La Lola. The food here would be thought exceptional anywhere. But it is difficult to point to particular dishes since the menu is forever changing. The chef would have it no other way. See chapter 6.
- **El Mirador, for Margaritas** (Acapulco; in the Hotel Plaza Las Glorias; ☎ **800/ 342-AMIGO** in the U.S.). You can enjoy a great margarita many places in Mexico, but this is the only place that serves them accompanied by the view of the spectacular La Quebrada cliff divers. See chapter 10.
- **El Naranjo, for Traditional Oaxacan Cuisine** (Oaxaca; ☎ **951/4-1878**). Oaxacan cooking is a wonderful regional variety of Mexican cuisine, and I am delighted by what the chef at El Naranjo has done with some of the traditional dishes. Each day offers a different kind of mole in addition to several uncommon dishes. This is a wonderful place for throwing caution to the wind—the owner is meticulous about cleaning and sterilizing foods. See chapter 11.

- **100% Natural, for Licuados.** *Licuados,* drinks made from fresh fruit mixed with water or milk, are standard fare in Mexico, and much more popular than soft drinks. This restaurant chain offers the widest selection, including innovative mixtures like the Cozumel (spinach, pineapple, and orange) or the Caligula (orange, pineapple, beet, celery, parsley, carrot, and lime juices). A healthy indulgence. Branches in Puerto Vallarta, Acapulco, and Cancún.
- **Virrey de Mendoza, for Yucatecan specialties** (Mérida; ☎ **99/25-3082**). If you're in Mérida and feel like splurging for a night, this is the place. It specializes in highly refined versions of Mexican cooking's most elaborate dishes. The Yucatecan specialties are superb, especially the seafood. The setting, lighting, and background music are first-rate. See chapter 14.

2

Getting to Know Mexico

Mexico is an exotic and adventurous land inhabited by a vivacious and colorful people. That it is so close to the United States and yet so vastly different amazes many first-time visitors. Those who fly into Mexico City might immediately perceive this difference: From the plane's window you catch a glimpse of majestic snowcapped volcanoes with the strange-sounding names "Popocatépetl" and "Ixtaccihuatl." Travelers to Mexico enter a land of volcanoes and pyramids, mountains and jungles, from which rise the ruins of ancient civilizations. Those civilizations have left more of a mark on Mexico than just a handful of ruins and a few strange-sounding place names, however. Spoken by millions of Mexicans, their languages—Náhuatl (Aztec), Maya, Zapotec, and others—customs, and beliefs have shaped Mexico's national culture, making it different from any other in the Spanish-speaking world.

Mexicans are famous for their warmth, the breadth and power of their arts, their playful and melodic take on the Spanish language, and their willingness to celebrate at the least provocation. By comparison, the speech and gestures of many other Spanish-speakers are dry, understated, and monotonic. Mexican food, music, and dance have spread throughout the world, but the best of this vibrant culture is still to be found in the mountains and beaches of home.

1 The Land & Its People

Mexico stretches nearly 2,000 miles from east to west and more than 1,000 miles north to south. Only one-fifth the size of the United States, Mexico contains its variety in a compact space. The country includes trackless deserts in the north, dark jungles in the south, and thousands of miles of lush seacoast that abound with virtually any kind of beach you would want. Highlands, where the air is crisp and cool and the weather is as close to perfection as you're likely to find, run the length of the country.

Mexico is bounded to the north by the United States; to the southeast by Belize, Guatemala, and the Caribbean; to the east by the Gulf of Mexico; and to the west by the Sea of Cortés and the Pacific Ocean.

THE REGIONS IN BRIEF

BAJA CALIFORNIA A peninsula longer than Italy, Baja stretches 876 miles from its border with California and Mexico's northernmost city of Tijuana to **Cabo San Lucas** at its southern tip. On one side is the Pacific Ocean, on the other, the **Sea of Cortés.** The peninsula was formed by volcanic uplifting, creating the craggy desertscape you see today. Culturally and geographically, Baja is set apart from mainland Mexico—and it remained isolated until very late. Now the state of Baja California del Sur, it has developed into a vacation haven that offers fishing, diving, and whale watching amidst beautiful settings and posh resorts.

THE COPPER CANYON   The Copper Canyon is the common name given a region of roughly 6,500 square miles in the northern state of Chihuahua, located midway between the state's capital city and the Pacific coast. Here you'll find a network of canyons deeply etched into the volcanic rock of the **Sierra Tarahumara.** The canyons, beautiful and very dramatic, are one of those few places that evoke a sense of the earth's creation. To get there, you take a ride on the famous *Chihuahua al Pacífico* railroad, which took several entrepreneurs from 1863 to 1928 to complete. It starts at the seaport of Topolobampo just outside of **Los Mochis** and travels 390 miles to **Chihuahua City,** climbing above an altitude of 9,000 feet in the process. The train skirts the edge of more than 20 canyons, and the vistas are beautiful, but to see the canyon area, you have to stay in one of the towns along the way. Tours here are arranged to accommodate any kind of traveler, from primitive camper to modern-hotel–goer.

THE PACIFIC COAST   The Pacific coast has every kind of beach and surroundings. You can stay in modern resorts that offer an inexhaustible array of amenities and activities—from sailing to scuba diving to parasailing, capped off by exuberant nightlife. Or you could stay in a sleepy coastal town where the scenery is loaded with rustic charm, life is slower, and the beaches are quieter. At the northern extreme is **Puerto Peñasco,** an offbeat holiday beach town. By **Mazatlán** the desert disappears, replaced by tropical vegetation with plantations of coconut and other fruit. At **Puerto Vallarta,** forest-covered mountains meet the sea along the beautiful and wide Banderas Bay. For many this is the most delightful place on the coast; the town is a wonderful combination of natural beauty, modern sophistication, and small-town charm. From here it's only a 5-hour car ride inland to **Guadalajara,** Mexico's most Mexican of cities and a wonderful place for shopping, especially for decorative arts. Tropical forests interspersed with horizon-to-horizon banana, mango, and coconut palm plantations cover the coast from here to **Manzanillo.** Well south of Manzanillo, in the state of Guerrero, are the beach towns **Zihuatanejo/Ixtapas.** Tree-covered mountains still remain around **Acapulco,** though hillside development has marred them some. From Acapulco there is a road inland to **Taxco,** a colonial city that clings to the side of a mountain and is famed for its hundreds of silver shops. Farther south along the coast from Acapulco are the nine gorgeous bays of **Huatulco.**

THE NORTH-CENTRAL REGION   This funnel-shaped region stretches from the northern border with Texas and New Mexico all the way to **Mexico City** and includes the beautiful colonial silver cities, all of which were founded within 50 years of the Conquest. The majority of this territory lies in the vast Chihuahua/Coahuila desert of the north, bordered on the east and west by the **Sierra Madre.** The **colonial cities** are nestled in the mountains not far to the north and west of Mexico City. Here, in the cool mountain air and amid an elegant backdrop of cut stone and wrought iron, people go about their business and pleasure in the relaxed rhythms that gently induce the visitor to kick back and slow down.

THE GULF COAST   Of all Mexico, this region is probably the least known, but this whole coast, which includes the long, skinny state of Veracruz, has marvelous pockets of scenery and culture. Highway 180 leads down from **Matamoros** at the Texas border and offers a few glimpses of the Gulf, which in some places is the same

Mexico

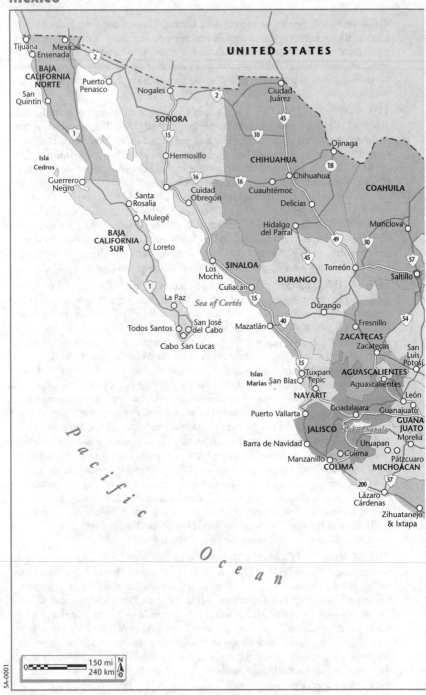

UNITED STATES

Tijuana
Ensenada
Mexicali

BAJA CALIFORNIA NORTE

San Quintin

Puerto Penasco

Nogales

Ciudad Juárez

SONORA

Isla Cedros

Guerrero Negro

Santa Rosalia

Mulegé

Hermosillo

Cuidad Obregón

Cuauhtémoc

CHIHUAHUA

Chihuahua

Ojinaga

Delicias

COAHUILA

BAJA CALIFORNIA SUR

Loreto

Hidalgo del Parral

Monclova

Los Mochis

SINALOA

DURANGO

Torreón

Saltillo

La Paz

Sea of Cortés

Culiacán

Durango

Fresnillo

Todos Santos

San José del Cabo

Cabo San Lucas

Mazatlán

ZACATECAS

Zacatecas

San Luis Potosí

Islas Marias

San Blas

Tuxpan
Tepic

AGUASCALIENTES

Aguascalientes

León

NAYARIT

Puerto Vallarta

Guadalajara

Guanajuato

GUANA JUATO

Barra de Navidad

JALISCO

Lake Chapala

Uruapan

Morelia

Manzanillo

Colima

Pátzcuaro

COLIMA

MICHOACAN

Lázaro Cárdenas

Zihuatanejo & Ixtapa

Pacific Ocean

0   150 mi
       240 km

N

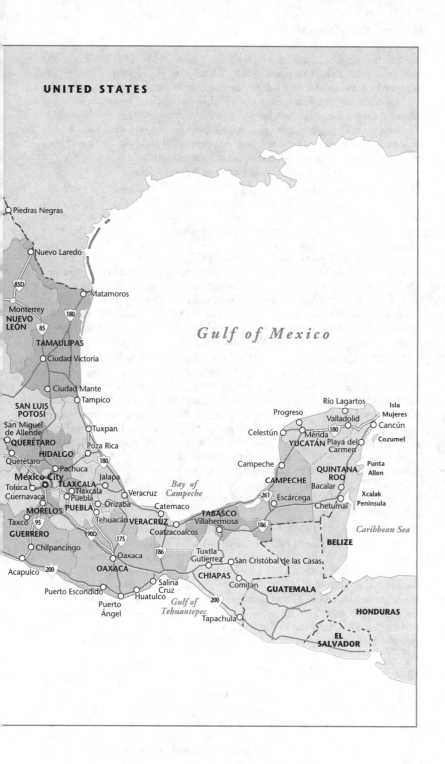

UNITED STATES

Piedras Negras

Nuevo Laredo

85D

Matamoros

Monterrey
NUEVO
LEÓN
TAMAULIPAS

180

85

Ciudad Victoria

Ciudad Mante

Tampico

SAN LUIS
POTOSÍ

San Miguel
de Allende

Tuxpan

QUERÉTARO

Poza Rica

Querétaro

HIDALGO

180

Pachuca

Mexico City

Jalapa

Toluca

TLAXCALA

Cúernavaca

Tlaxcala

Veracruz

Puebla

MORELOS

PUEBLA

Orizaba

Taxco

95

Tehuacán

VERACRUZ

Catemaco

GUERRERO

190D

175

Coatzacoalcos

Chilpancingo

Oaxaca

186

Acapulco

200

OAXACA

Puerto Escondido

Salina
Cruz

Huatulco

Puerto
Ángel

Gulf of
Tehuantepec

200

Gulf of Mexico

Río Lagartos

Isla
Mujeres

Progreso

Valladolid

Celestún

Mérida

180

Cancún

YUCATÁN

Playa del
Carmen

Cozumel

Campeche

QUINTANA
ROO

Punta
Allen

CAMPECHE

Bacalar

Bay of
Campeche

261

Escárcega

Chetumal

Xcalak
Peninsula

TABASCO

Villahermosa

186

Tuxtla
Gutierrez

San Cristóbal de las Casas

Caribbean Sea

BELIZE

CHIAPAS

Comitán

GUATEMALA

Tapachula

HONDURAS

EL
SALVADOR

19

cerulean blue as the Caribbean. The mostly two-lane road is paved and flat almost until you reach **Lake Catemaco.** There it undulates gently among grassy fields humped with unexplored mounds left by the Olmecs more than 3,000 years ago. Highlights of this region are the ruins of **El Tajín** near the mountain village of Papantla; the mountain town of **Jalapa,** Veracruz's capital and home of the magnificent Museo de Antropología; and the lively, colorful port of **Veracruz.** You'll see sugarcane fields along most of the coast. Near Santiago Tuxtla and Lake Catemaco, you'll see roadside stands with pyramidal mounds of fruit in colorful displays. This is a good region to visit if you're longing for the Mexico of yesteryear.

TARASCAN COUNTRY This region, in the state of Michoacán, presents two quite distinct visions of colonial architecture: **Pátzcuaro,** with its tile roofs and adobe walls stuccoed and painted in the traditional white with red along the bottom; and **Morelia,** with its views of stately palaces built of stone, broad plazas, and impressive cathedral. Michoacán is considered by many to be the most beautiful state in the country. The eastern part of the state consists of high mountains with large tracts of pine and fir forests. This area is the destination of millions of **monarch butterflies,** which congregate in a small part of the forest there. The central part of the state is a land of lakes and is the homeland of the Purepechan or Tarascan Indians. The villages throughout this area specialize in particular crafts for which the region is well known. Farther west lie the hotlands and the coast. Tarascan Country is not overrun by tourists except during the Days of the Dead.

SOUTHERNMOST MEXICO: OAXACA, CHIAPAS & TABASCO This is the land of the Zapotec, Mixtec, and Maya cultures. Most people don't drive from one area to the other in this region (they usually fly), but a new toll highway from near Puebla to **Oaxaca City** makes the area more accessible by car. The valley of Oaxaca is one of the grandest places in Mexico: fascinating Indian villages everywhere, beautiful ruins, and a wonderful colonial city in the middle of it all. **San Cristóbal de las Casas,** in Chiapas, is harder to get to, but definitely worth it and entirely different from Oaxaca. Cooler and set amongst greener mountains, it is more in the mold of a provincial, colonial town. As you approach San Cristóbal from any direction, you see small plots of corn tended by colorfully clad Maya. Oaxaca and Chiapas are both rich in crafts, from wood carvers to potters and weavers. Of the three states, Tabasco is the least interesting.

THE YUCATÁN PENINSULA Travelers to the peninsula will have an opportunity to see pre-Hispanic ruins—such as **Chichén-Itzá, Uxmal,** and **Tulum**—and the living descendants of the cultures who built them, as well as the ultimate in resort Mexico: **Cancún.** The peninsula is edged by the dull aquamarine Gulf of Mexico on the west and north, and the Caribbean Sea on the east. It covers almost 84,000 square miles, with nearly 1,000 miles of shoreline. Natural wells called *cenotes,* or collapsed caves, dot the region. The only sense of height comes from the hills rising from the western shores of **Campeche** inland to the border with Yucatán state. This rise, called the **Puuc hills,** is the Maya "Alps," a mighty 980 feet high. Locally the hills are known as the Sierra de Ticul or Sierra Alta.

The interior of the peninsula is dotted with lovely rock-walled Maya villages and crumbling *henequén* haciendas. In contrast to the placid interior is the hubbub of the Caribbean Coast. From Cancún south to **Chetumal,** the jungle coastline is spotted with development of all kinds, from posh to budget, but it also hosts an enormous array of wildlife, including hundreds of species of birds. The western side of the peninsula fronts the Gulf Coast, and the beaches there, while good enough, don't compare to those on the Caribbean. National parks near **Celestún** and **Río Lagartos** on the Gulf Coast are home to amazing flocks of flamingos.

THE MEXICAN PEOPLE

There are 93 million Mexicans, 23 million of them live in the capital, Mexico City—a good illustration of just how centralized Mexico is. The next largest town is Guadalajara, with a much more easily manageable 5 million. But things are changing in Mexico. The rate of population growth has been steadily declining, from 3.5% per year in the 1970s to 2% at present. Mexico City's Federal District now has the slowest growth rate of any state in Mexico: less than 1% per year.

Today, 4½ centuries after the Conquest, five million Mexicans speak a native language; of these, 800,000 do not speak Spanish. The states with the highest populations of Indians are Oaxaca, Chiapas, Yucatán, Michoacán, and Puebla.

By most measurements, the disparity between rich and poor has increased in the last 30 years. Cycles of boom-and-bust seem to weigh heavier on the poor than on the rich. The middle class also seems to have had a rough ride of it, especially during the monetary crisis of 1994, due to the steep increases in interest rates. Depending on how you define it, the middle class is presently 15% to 32% of the population, though certainly not a majority.

But in the face of all of this, Mexican society maintains its cohesiveness. It is amazingly resilient, due in some part to the way Mexicans live. They haven't lost their knack for having a good time, and they value social gatherings over other concerns. There is always time to meet with friends for a drink or a cup of coffee, or attend a family celebration. The many high-spirited public celebrations are just another manifestation of this.

Although Mexico is part of North America, its culture is dramatically different from its neighbors to the north. It has often been observed by American and English travelers that life in Mexico obeys slower rhythms: Mexicans simply have a different conception of time. Yet few of these observers go on to explain more than superficially what the consequences of this are for the visitor to Mexico. This is a shame, because an imperfect comprehension of this difference causes a good deal of misunderstanding between the tourist and the native Mexican.

SOCIAL MORES   Americans, in addition to many Canadians and northern Europeans, tend to do things at a faster pace and skip some of the niceties of social interaction. One of the most important pieces of advice I can give the traveler is always to give a proper greeting when addressing Mexicans; don't try to abbreviate social intercourse. When walking into a store, many Americans simply smile at a clerk and launch right into a question or demand. The smile, in effect, replaces the greeting. In Mexico, it doesn't work that way. Smiles, when there is no context, can be ambiguous; they can convey amusement, smugness, superiority, etc.

On several occasions, I have been asked by Mexican acquaintances why Americans grin all the time. I didn't know what to make of the question the first time I heard it; it was only gradually that I began to appreciate what was at issue. Mexican culture places a higher value on proper social form than on saving time. For Mexicans, civil society requires individuals to show that they recognize and treat people as fellow persons and not simply as a means to their ends. A Mexican must at least say *"¡Buenos días!"* or a quick *"¿Qué pasó?"* (or its equivalent) even to total strangers—a show of proper respect. And when an individual meets a group of people, he or she will greet each member of the group by shaking hands, kissing, or whatever is proper for the occasion. This can take a while, depending on the size of the party. We might consider such behavior obtrusive and presumptuous; for us the polite thing would be to keep our interruption to a minimum, and give a general greeting to all.

Mexicans, like most people, will consciously or subconsciously make quick judgments about someone they meet. Most divide the world into well-raised and cultured (*bien educado*) on the one hand, and poorly raised (*mal educado*) on the other. Unfortunately, many visitors are reluctant to try out their Spanish, preferring to keep exchanges to a minimum. Don't do this. To be categorized as a foreigner isn't a big deal. What's important in Mexico is to be categorized as one of the cultured foreigners and not one of the barbarians. This makes it easier to get the attention of waiters, hotel desk clerks, and people on the street.

When it comes to foreigners, Mexicans want visitors to know, love, and enjoy their country; they will extend many thoughtful courtesies. They'll invite visitors to share a table in a crowded restaurant, go out of their way to give directions, help with luggage, and see stranded travelers safely on their way.

2 A Look at the Past

Dateline

- **10,000–2,300 B.C.** Prehistoric period: Cultivation of chilies, corn, beans, avocado, amaranth, and pumpkin. Mortars and pestles in use. Stone bowls and jars, obsidian knives, and open-weave basketry developed.
- **1500–300 B.C.** Preclassic period: Olmec culture spreads and develops over Gulf Coast, southern Mexico, Central America, and lower Mexican Pacific Coast and is eventually linked to the development of the Maya culture.
- **1000–900 B.C.** Olmec San Lorenzo center is destroyed; they begin anew at La Venta.
- **600 B.C.** La Venta Olmec cultural zenith. Zapotec culture emerges near Monte Albán Oaxaca.
- **500–100 B.C.** The Zapotec flourish and invent the Calendar Round, which is later used near the end of the Olmec period and later by Maya. Olmec culture disintegrates. Teotihuacán settlement is started in central Mexico.
- **A.D. 100** Building begins on Sun and Moon pyramids at Teotihuacán; Palenque dynasty emerges in Yucatán.
- **300–900** Classic period begins: Xochicalco estab-

continues

PRE-HISPANIC CIVILIZATIONS

The earliest "Mexicans" were Stone Age hunter-gatherers coming from the north, descendants of a race that had crossed the Bering Strait and reached North America before 12,000 B.C. They arrived in what is now Mexico by 10,000 B.C. Sometime between 5200 and 1500 B.C., in what is known as the **Archaic period,** they began practicing agriculture and domesticating animals. They wove baskets; grew corn, beans, squash, and tomatoes; and kept turkeys and dogs for food. By 2400 B.C., the art of pottery had been discovered. We find evidence of artists who made clay figurines for use as votive offerings or household gods and goddesses.

THE PRECLASSIC PERIOD (1500 B.C. to A.D. 300) Eventually, agriculture improved to the point that it could provide enough food to support large communities and enough surplus to free some of the population from agricultural work. A civilization emerged that we call the **Olmec**—an enigmatic people who settled the lower Gulf Coast in what is now Tabasco and Veracruz. Anthropologists regard them as the mother culture of Mesoamerica, since they established a pattern for later civilizations in a wide area stretching from northern Mexico into Central America. The Olmec developed the basic calendar used throughout the region, established the predominance of a 52-year cycle and used it to schedule the construction of pyramids, established principles of urban layout and architecture, and originated the cult of the jaguar and the sacredness of jade. They may also have bequeathed the sacred ritual of "the ball game"—a universal element of Mesoamerican culture.

The Olmec also left behind colossal stone heads—one habit that seems to have died out in later cultures. We still don't know what purposes these heads served, but they were immense projects; the basalt stone from which they were sculpted was mined miles inland and transported to the Olmec cities on the coast, probably by river rafts. The heads share a rounded, baby-faced look, marked by the peculiar "jaguar mouth"—a high-arched lip that is an identifying mark of Olmec sculpture.

The **Maya** civilization began developing in the late Preclassic period, around 500 B.C. Our understanding of this period is only sketchy, but Olmec influences are apparent everywhere. Somewhere along the way the Maya perfected the Olmec calendar and developed their ornate system of hieroglyphic writing and their early architecture. Two other civilizations also began their rise to prominence around this time: the people of **Teotihuacán,** just north of present-day Mexico City, and the **Zapotec** of Monte Albán in the valley of Oaxaca.

THE CLASSIC PERIOD (A.D. 300 to 900)   The flourishing of these three civilizations marks the boundaries of this period—the heyday of pre-Columbian Mesoamerican artistic and cultural achievements. These include the pyramids and palaces in Teotihuacán; the ceremonial center of Monte Albán; and the stelae and temples of Palenque, Bonampak, and the Tikal site in Guatemala. Beyond their achievements in art and architecture, the Maya made significant discoveries in science, including the use of the zero in mathematics and a complex calendar with which the priests could predict eclipses and the movements of the stars for centuries to come.

The Maya were warlike, raiding their neighbors to acquire slaves and land and to take captives for their many blood rituals. Recent studies, notably *Blood of Kings* (Braziller, 1986) by Linda Schele and Mary Ellen Miller, have debunked the long-held theory that the Maya were a peaceful people. Scholars continue to decipher the Maya hieroglyphs, murals, and relief carvings to reveal a Maya world based on the belief that blood sacrifice was necessary for dynastic survival.

The inhabitants of **Teotihuacán** (100 B.C. to A.D. 700—near present-day Mexico City) built a city that at its zenith is thought to have had 100,000 or more inhabitants covering 9 square miles. It was an extremely well organized city, built on a grid with streams channeled to follow the city's plan. Different social classes such as artisans and merchants were assigned to specific neighborhoods. At its height, Teotihuacán was the greatest cultural center in Mexico, with tremendous influence as far as Guatemala and the Yucatán Peninsula. The ceremonial

lished where pyramids bearing Maya-like figures are eventually built; Maya civilization develops in Yucatán and Chiapas.

- **500–650** Teotihuacán culture from central Mexico exerts strong influence in the Maya world, including intermarrying with the Maya.

- **683** Maya Lord Pacal is buried in an elaborate tomb below the Palace of the Inscriptions at Palenque.

- **650–800** Teotihuacán burns and is deserted. Cacaxtla, in central Mexico, is at its zenith with brilliantly colored murals of Maya warriors splashed across its walls.

- **750** Zapotecs conquer the Valley of Oaxaca and invent first Mesoamerican writing system.

- **800** Bonampak battle/victory mural painted.

- **900** Postclassic period begins: Toltec culture emerges at Tula and spreads to Chichén-Itzá on the Yucatán Peninsula by 978.

- **909** A small monument at Toniná (near San Cristóbal de las Casas) has this as the last Long Count date discovered so far, symbolizing the end of the Classic Maya era.

- **1156–1230** Tula, the Toltec capital, is abandoned.

- **1290** Zapotec decline and Mixtec emerge at Monte Albán; Mitla becomes refuge of Zapotecs.

- **1325–45** Aztec capital Tenochtitlán founded; Aztecs begin to dominate Mexico but not Chiapas or the Yucatán Peninsula.

- **1443** Calkaní founded after destruction of Mayapán.

- **1511** Santo Domingo–bound Spanish sailors sailing

continues

from the Darien Gap near Panama are shipwrecked off the coast of what is today Quintana Roo, and two passengers survive. One survivor is a clergyman, Jerónimo de Águilar, who learns to speak Yukatek Maya and later becomes Cortés's translator. The other, Gonzalo Guerrero, adopts the Maya culture, marries a Maya woman, and has a family. Guerrero eventually leads Maya in battle against Spaniards.

- **1516** Gold found on Cozumel in aborted Spanish expedition of Yucatán Peninsula arouses interest of Spanish governor in Cuba, who sends Juan de Grijalva on an expedition, followed by another, led by Hernán Cortés.
- **1517** Cortés arrives in Cozumel and rescues Águilar but Gonzalo Guerrero prefers to remain with his family and adopted culture.
- **1518** Spaniards first visited what is today Campeche.
- **1519** Conquest of Mexico begins: Hernán Cortés and troops arrive near present-day Veracruz.
- **1521** Conquest is complete after Aztec defeat at Tlatelolco in 1521.
- **1521–24** Cortés organizes Spanish empire in Mexico and begins building Mexico City on the ruins of Tenochtitlán.
- **1524** First Franciscan friars arrive from Spain.
- **1524–35** Cortés removed from leadership. Spanish King sends officials, judges, and finally an *audiencia* to govern.
- **1526** Francisco Montejo permitted by King of Spain to colonize the Yucatán.

continues

center is so large that it was thought by the Aztecs to have been built by gods. Its feathered serpent, later known as **Quetzalcóatl,** became part of the pantheon of many succeeding cultures. The ruling classes were industrious, literate, and cosmopolitan; their trading posts extended into the Maya and Zapotec heartlands. The beautiful sculpture and ceramics of Teotihuacán display a highly stylized and refined aesthetic whose influences can be seen clearly in objects of Maya and Zapotec origin. Around the 7th century, the city was abandoned for unknown reasons. Who these people were and where they went remains a mystery.

Further south, the **Zapotecs,** influenced by the Olmecs, raised an impressive culture in the region of Oaxaca. Their two principal cities were **Monte Albán,** inhabited by an elite of merchants and artisans, and **Mitla,** reserved for the high priests.

THE POSTCLASSIC PERIOD (A.D. 900 to 1521)

Warfare becomes a more conspicuous activity of the civilizations that flourished in this period. Social development was impressive, but not as cosmopolitan as the Maya, Teotihuacán, and Zapotec societies. In central Mexico, a people known as the **Toltecs** established their capital at Tula in the 10th century. They were originally one of the barbarous hordes of Indians that periodically migrated from the north. At some stage in their development, the Toltec were influenced by remnants of Teotihuacán culture and adopted the feathered serpent Quetzalcoatl as their god, but they also revered a god known as **Tezcatlipoca,** or "smoking mirror," who later became god of the Aztec. The Toltecs maintained a large military class divided into orders symbolized by animals. At its zenith, Tula may have had 40,000 people, and it spread its influence across Mesoamerica. By the 13th century, however, the Toltec had exhausted themselves, probably in civil wars and in battles with the invaders from the north.

Of those northern tribes, the **Aztecs** were the most warlike. At first they occupied themselves as mercenaries for the established cities in the valley of Mexico—one of which allotted to them an unwanted marshy piece of land in the middle of Lake Texcoco for their settlement. This eventually grew into the island city of Tenochtitlán. Through aggressive diplomacy and military measures, the Aztec soon conquered all of central Mexico and extended their rule east to the Gulf Coast and south to the valley of Oaxaca.

After the Classic period, the Maya migrated from their historic homelands in Guatemala and Chiapas into the lowlands of the Yucatán (roughly the modern states of Yucatán and Campeche), where they spent the centuries, from A.D. 900 to 1500, trying to recover their former greatness.

During this period, the cities near the Yucatán's low western Puuc hills were built. The region's architecture, called **Puuc style,** is characterized by elaborate exterior stonework appearing above door frames and extending to the roofline. Examples of this architecture, such as the Codz Poop at Kabah and the palaces at Sayil and Labná, are beautiful and quite impressive.

The Yucatán was profoundly affected by strong influences from central Mexico; the great city of **Chichén-Itzá** is clearly a melding of Toltec and Maya styles, but the nature of this Toltec influence is a subject of great debate. Most prominent are the depictions of a feathered serpent, Kukulcan. In central Mexico there is an intriguing story told in mythographic shorthand of a civil war in Tula between the followers of Tezcatlipoca and those of Quetzalcoatl, the plumed serpent. The followers of Quetzalcoatl lost and fled to the Gulf Coast from whence they sailed east toward the morning star, vowing to return. Did they arrive in the Yucatán and become involved in the building of Chichén-Itzá? In the language of myth, the head priest would naturally have been identified with the god Quetzalcoatl so, when read literally, it was the god, not the priests, who would return one day. This myth became in the hands of the Spanish, a powerful weapon of conquest.

Some theories claim that a distantly related branch of the Maya people, called the **Putun Maya,** came from the borders of the Yucatán Peninsula between mainland Mexico and the Classic Maya lands in Péten and Chiapas. They spoke the Maya language poorly and used many Náhuatl (Aztec) words.

When the Putun Maya left their ships and moved inland, they became known as the **Itzáes** and settled in what eventually became known as Chichén-Itzá (Well of the Itzá). They brought with them years of experience in trading with distant cultures, which could explain the Toltec influence at Chichén-Itzá.

Uxmal was inhabited during this same period (around A.D. 1000), by the tribe known as the **Tutul Xiú,** who came from the region of Oaxaca and Tabasco. Some scholars think that the Xiú took the city from earlier builders, since archaeological evidence shows that the region around Uxmal was inhabited as early as 800 B.C.

- **1530** Territory of Tabasco conquered by Francisco Montejo.
- **1535–1821** Viceregal period: Mexico governed by 61 viceroys appointed by King of Spain. Landed aristocracy, a small elite class owning huge portions of land (haciendas) emerges. Yucatán is led by a governor who reports to the king rather than to viceroys.
- **1540** Campeche, Mérida, and Valladolid are founded.
- **1542** Mérida established as capital of Yucatán Peninsula.
- **1546** Maya rebel and take control of peninsula.
- **1559** French and Spanish pirates attack Campeche.
- **1562** Friar Diego de Landa destroys 5,000 Mayan religious stone figures and burns 27 hieroglyphic painted manuscripts at Maní, Yucatán. Widespread torture and death are meted out to Maya believed to secretly practice pre-Hispanic beliefs.
- **1563–66** Diego de Landa forced to return to Spain to answer for his actions. In defense of himself he writes his now-famous and invaluable "Yucatán Before and After the Conquest," which was published 298 years later.
- **1579** Diego de Landa dies in the Yucatán.
- **1739** What became known as the *Dresden Codex,* a lost Maya calendar text, is purchased in Vienna by the Royal Library of Dresden, where it languishes for more than a century.
- **1767** Jesuits expelled from New Spain.
- **1810–21** War of Independence: Miguel Hidalgo starts movement for Mexico's

continues

independence from Spain, but is executed within a year; leadership and goals change during the war years, but a compromise between monarchy and a republic is outlined by Agustín de Iturbide.

- **1821** Independence from Spain achieved. The Spanish governor of Yucatán resigns and the Yucatán Peninsula becomes an independent country.
- **1822** First Empire: Iturbide ascends throne as Emperor of Mexico.
- **1823** The Yucatán Peninsula decides to become part of Mexico.
- **1824** Iturbide is expelled, returns, and is executed by firing squad.
- **1824–55** Federal Republic period: Guadalupe Victoria is elected first president of Mexico in 1824; he is followed by 26 presidents and interim presidents, among them José López de Santa Anna.
- **1828** Slavery abolished.
- **1829** Dresden Codex is faithfully reproduced in watercolor and a few copies are published.
- **1836** Santa Anna defeats Texans at Battle of the Alamo, at San Antonio, Texas, but is later defeated and captured at the Battle of San Jacinto outside Houston, Texas.
- **1838** France invades Mexico at Veracruz.
- **1839–41** Americans John L. Stephens and Frederick Catherwood whack their way to Yucatecan ruins in two journeys that were to become the talk of the literary world.
- **1841–43** Stephens publishes his three volumes of

continues

The three great Maya centers of Chichén-Itzá, Mayapán, and Uxmal lived in peace under a confederation: The Itzá ruled in Chichén-Itzá, the Cocom tribe in Mayapán, and the Xiú in Uxmal. Authorities don't agree on the exact year, but sometime during the 12th century A.D. the people of Mayapán overthrew the confederation, sacked Chichén-Itzá, conquered Uxmal, and captured the leaders of the Itzá and the Xiú. Held in Mayapán, the Itzá and the Xiú princes reigned over but did not rule their former cities. **Mayapán** remained the seat of the confederation for over 200 years.

The Xiú took their revenge in 1441 when they marched from Uxmal on Mayapán, capturing and destroying the city, and killing the Cocom rulers. They founded a new city at Maní. Battles and skirmishes continued to plague the Maya territory until conquered by the Spanish conquistadors.

THE CONQUEST

In 1517, the first Spaniards to arrive in what is today known as Mexico skirmished with Maya Indians off the coast of the Yucatán Peninsula. One of these fledgling expeditions ended in shipwreck, leaving several Spaniards stranded as prisoners of the Maya. The Spanish sent out another expedition, under the command of **Hernán Cortés,** which landed on Cozumel in February of 1519. Cortés inquired about the gold and riches of the interior, and the coastal Maya were happy to describe the wealth and splendor of the Aztec empire in central Mexico. Cortés promptly decided to disobey all orders of his superior, the governor of Cuba, and sail to the mainland where he rescued the Spaniard Jerónimo de Águilar, one of the shipwrecked Spaniards.

Cortés arrived when the Aztec empire was at the height of its wealth and power. **Moctezuma** ruled over the central and southern highlands and extracted tribute from lowland peoples. His greatest temples were literally plated with gold and encrusted with the blood of sacrificial captives. Moctezuma himself was a fool, a mystic, and something of a coward. Despite his wealth and military power, he dithered in his capital at Tenochtitlán, sending messengers with gifts and suggestions that Cortés leave while Cortés blustered and negotiated his way into the highlands, always cloaking his real intentions. Moctezuma, terrified by the military tactics and technology of the Spaniard, convinced himself that Cortés was in fact the god **Quetzalcoatl** making his long-awaited return. In November of 1519, Cortés confronted Moctezuma and took him hostage in an effort to leverage from him control of the empire.

In the middle of Cortés's dangerous game of manipulation, another Spanish expedition arrived with orders to end Cortés's authority over the mission. The Spaniard hastened to meet the rival's force and persuade them to join his own. In the meantime, the Aztecs chased the garrison out of **Tenochtitlán,** and either they or the Spaniards killed Moctezuma. For the next year and a half, Cortés planned and executed the siege of Tenochtitlán with the help of rival Indians and a decimating epidemic of small pox, to which the Indians had no resistance. In the end, the Aztec capital fell, and when it did, it lay all of central Mexico at the feet of the conquistadors.

The Spanish conquest started out as a pirate expedition by Cortés and his men, unauthorized by the Spanish crown or its governor in Cuba. The Spanish king legitimized Cortés following his victory over the Aztec and ordered the forcible Christianization of this new colony, to be called **New Spain.** Guatemala and Honduras were explored and conquered, and by 1540 the territory of New Spain included Spanish possessions from Vancouver to Panama. In the two centuries that followed, Franciscan and Augustinian friars converted millions of Indians to Christianity, and the Spanish lords built up huge feudal estates on which the Indian farmers were little more than serfs. The silver and gold that Cortés looted made Spain the richest country in Europe.

The conquest of the Yucatán Peninsula, occurred after Cortés had subjugated the highlands. In 1526, the king of Spain granted permission to **Francisco Montejo** to conquer the Yucatán Peninsula—and the Maya fought desperately up to their decisive defeat 20 years later. The Maya never quite accepted the rule of Europeans; when their opportunity to rebel came in the 1840s, a civil war broke out that allowed them to gain control of most of the peninsula. This is known as the **Caste War.** The Maya eventually lost, but the southern and eastern half of the peninsula remained a virtual no-man's-land (to outsiders); the Maya resided almost untouched by the outside world until coastal development began in the late 1960s.

THE COLONIAL PERIOD

Hernán Cortés set about building a new city and the seat of government of New Spain upon the ruins of the old Aztec capital. For indigenous peoples (besides the Tlaxcaltecans, Cortés's Indian allies), heavy tributes once paid to the Aztecs were now rendered

Incidents of Travel illustrated by Catherwood, which stimulate interest in the Yucatán.

- **1845** United States annexes Texas.
- **1846–48** War with the United States: For $15 million Mexico relinquishes half of its national territory to the United States in Treaty of Guadalupe Hidalgo.
- **1847–66** War of the Castes: Degrading segregationist policies by Yucatán leaders against the Maya cause revolt, upheaval, and decimation of half the Maya population. Strife lasts well into 20th century. Exportation of *henequén* (agave plant) products, such as hemp for rope, and *chicle* (for gum) bring Yucatán into the world economy.
- **1855–72** Reform years: Includes a 3-year war in Mexico, pitting cities against villages and rich against poor in search for ideology, stability, and political leadership. Benito Juárez is president in fact and in exile off and on between Reform Wars and during reign of Emperor Maximilian. Juárez nationalizes church property and declares separation of church and state.
- **1858** Campeche and Yucatán become territories.
- **1862** England, Spain, and France send troops to Mexico to demand debt payment, and all except France withdraw. Diego de Landa's 1566 account of *Yucatán Before and After the Conquest* is discovered in the Royal Academy of History in Madrid.
- **1863** Campeche gains statehood.

continues

- **1864–67** Second Empire: French Emperor Napoleon Bonaparte III sends Maximilian of Hapsburg to be Emperor of Mexico.
- **1867** Juárez orders execution of Maximilian at Querétaro and resumes presidency in Mexico City until his death in 1872.
- **1872–84** Postreform period: Four presidents hold office but country is nearly bankrupt.
- **1876–1911** Porfiriato: Porfirio Díaz is president/dictator of Mexico for 35 years, leads country to modernization at the expense of human rights. Díaz opponents, including Yaqui Indians from northern Mexico, are exiled to the Yucatán Peninsula to suffer and die as slaves.
- **1902** Quintana Roo becomes Mexican territory.
- **1911–17** Mexican Revolution: Francisco Madero drafts revolutionary plan. Díaz resigns. Leaders jockey for power during period of great violence, national upheaval, and tremendous loss of life.
- **1913** President Madero assassinated.
- **1914** and **1916** United States invades Mexico.
- **1915** Payo Obispo becomes capital of territory of Quintana Roo.
- **1917–40** Reconstruction: Present constitution of Mexico signed; land and education reforms are initiated, and labor unions strengthened; Mexico expels U.S. oil companies and nationalizes all natural resources and railroads. Pancho Villa, Zapata, and presidents Obregón

continues

in forced labor to the Spanish. Diseases carried by the Spaniards, against which the Indian populations had no natural immunity, wiped out most of the native population.

Over the three centuries of the colonial period, 61 viceroys appointed by the king of Spain governed Mexico. Spain became rich from New World gold and silver, chiseled out by backbreaking Indian labor. The colonial elite built lavish homes both in Mexico City and in the countryside. They filled their homes with ornate furniture, had many servants, and adorned themselves in velvets, satins, and jewels imported from abroad. A new class system developed: Those born in Spain considered themselves superior to the *criollos* (Spaniards born in Mexico). Those of other races and the *castas* (mixtures of Spanish and Indian, Spanish and Negro, or Indian and Negro) occupied the bottom rung of society.

It took great cunning to stay a step ahead of the avaricious crown, which demanded increasingly higher taxes and contributions from its fabled foreign conquests. Still, wealthy colonists prospered grandly enough to develop an extravagant society. However, discontent with the mother country simmered for years over social and political hot points: taxes, the royal bureaucracy, Spanish-born citizens' advantages over Mexican-born subjects, and restrictions on commerce with Spain and other countries. Dissatisfaction with Spain found an opportune moment in 1808 when Napoléon invaded Spain and crowned his brother Joseph king in place of Charles IV. To many in Mexico, allegiance to France was out of the question; Mexico, discontent with the mother country, reached the level of revolt.

INDEPENDENCE

The rebellion began in 1810, when a priest, **Father Miguel Hidalgo** gave the *grito,* a cry for independence from his church in the town of Dolores, Guanajuato. The uprising soon became a full-fledged revolution, as Hidalgo and Ignacio Allende gathered an "army" of citizens and threatened Mexico City. Although Hidalgo was executed, he is honored as "the Father of Mexican Independence." Another priest, **José María Morelos** kept the revolt alive with several successful campaigns through 1815, when he, too, was captured and executed.

Rebel prospects for independence were rather dim until the Spanish king who replaced Joseph Bonaparte decided to make social reforms in the colonies, which convinced the conservative powers in Mexico that they didn't need Spain after all. With their tacit approval, **Agustín de Iturbide,** then commander of royalist forces, declared Mexico independent and himself emperor. It was not long, however, before internal dissension brought about the fall of the emperor, and Mexico was proclaimed a republic.

The young Mexican republic was inflamed by political instability and ran through a dizzying succession of presidents and dictators as struggles between federalists and centralists and conservatives and liberals divided the country and consumed its energy. Moreover, there was a disastrous war with the United States in which Mexico lost half its territory. A central figure was **Antonio López de Santa Anna,** who assumed the leadership of his country no fewer than 11 times and was flexible enough in those volatile times to portray himself variously as a liberal, a conservative, a federalist, or a centralist. He probably holds the record for frequency of exile; by 1855 he was finally left without a political comeback and remained the rest of his days in Venezuela.

Political instability persisted, and the conservative forces, with some encouragement from Napoléon III, lit upon the bright idea of inviting in a Hapsburg (as if that strategy had ever worked for Spain). They found a willing Hapsburg in Archduke Maximilian of Austria, who, being at the time unemployed in ruling anyone, accepted the position of Mexican emperor with the support of French troops. The first French forces—a modern, well-equipped army—was defeated by the rag-tag Mexican forces in a battle near Puebla (now celebrated annually as **Cinco de Mayo**). The second attempt was more successful, and Ferdinand Maximilian Joseph of Hapsburg became emperor for 3 years of civil war in which the French were finally induced to abandon the emperor's cause. **Maximilian** was captured and executed by a firing squad near Querétaro in 1867. His adversary and successor (as president of Mexico) was **Benito Juárez,** a Zapotec Indian lawyer and one of the great heroes of Mexican history. Juárez did his best to unify and strengthen his country before dying of a heart attack in 1872; his effect on Mexico's future was profound, and his plans and visions bore fruit for decades.

THE PORFIRIATO & THE REVOLUTION

A few years after Juárez's death, one of his generals, **Porfirio Díaz,** assumed power in a coup and ruled Mexico from 1877 to 1911, a period now called the

and Carranza are assassinated.

- **1931** Citizens of Yucatán Peninsula protest division of Quintana Roo territory between the states of Yucatán and Campeche.

- **1935** Quintana Roo is restored to territorial status.

- **1940** Mexico enters period of political stability and makes tremendous economic progress and improvement in the quality of life, although problems of corruption, inflation, national health, and unresolved land and agricultural issues continue.

- **1946** Locals living in the jungle show Giles Healy the magnificent Maya murals at Bonampak, which he reports to the world.

- **1950** The first train links Campeche with Coatzacoalcos.

- **1952** Dr. Yuri Valentinovich Knorosov, a Russian scholar who had never seen a Maya ruin, publishes the modern-day key to deciphering Maya hieroglyphics; it is not fully accepted for at least 20 years. Mexican archaeologist Alberto Ruíz Lhuller uncovers King Pacal's tomb in the Temple of the Inscriptions at Palenque—one of the greatest discoveries of the Maya world.

- **1974** Quintana Roo achieves statehood and Cancún opens to tourism.

- **1982** President Echeverría nationalizes the country's banks.

- **1988** Mexico enters the General Agreement on Trade and Tariffs (GATT).

- **1991** Mexico, Canada, and the United States begin Free Trade Agreement negotiations. Mexico begins massive

continues

push to excavate "new" Maya sites and re-excavate and conserve others.

- **1992** Sale of *ejido* land (peasant communal property) to private citizens is allowed. Mexico and the Vatican establish diplomatic relations after an interruption of 100 years.

- **1993** Mexico deregulates hotel and restaurant prices; New Peso currency begins circulation.

- **1994** Mexico, Canada, and the United States sign the North American Free Trade Agreement (NAFTA). An Indian uprising in Chiapas sparks protests countrywide over government policies concerning land distribution, bank loans, health, education, and voting and human rights. In an unrelated incident, PRI candidate Luis Donaldo Colossio is assassinated 5 months before the election; replacement candidate Ernesto Zedillo Ponce de Leon is elected and inaugurated as president in December. Within weeks, the peso is devalued, throwing the nation into turmoil.

- **1995** The peso loses half its value within the first 3 months of the year. The government raises prices on oil and utilities. Interest on debt soars to 140%; businesses begin to fail; unemployment rises. The Chiapan rebels threaten another rebellion, which is quickly quashed by the government. Former president Carlos Salinas de Gortari, with the devaluation having left his reputation for economic leadership in shambles, leaves Mexico for the United States. Salinas's brother is accused of

continues

"Porfiriato." He stayed in power through brutal repression of the opposition and by courting the favor of the powerful nations of the time. Generous in his dealings with foreign investors, who were grateful in return, Díaz became, in the eyes of most Mexicans, the archetypal *entreguista* (one who sells out his country for private gain). With foreign investment came the concentration of great wealth in few hands. Social conditions worsened.

In 1910, Francisco Madero called for an armed rebellion that became the **Mexican Revolution** ("La Revolución" in Mexico; the revolution against Spain is called the "Guerra de Independencia"). Díaz was sent into exile; while in London he became a celebrity at the age of 81 when he jumped into the Thames to save a drowning boy. Díaz is buried in Paris. Madero became president but was promptly betrayed and executed by a heavy straight out of the Hollywood school of villains—the despicable **Victoriano Huerta.** Those who had answered Madero's call responded again—the great peasant hero **Emiliano Zapata** in the south and the seemingly invincible **Pancho Villa** in the central north, with Álvaro Obregón and Venustiano Carranza flanking him. They eventually put Huerta to flight and began hashing out a new constitution.

For the next few years, the revolutionaries Carranza, Obregón, and Villa fought amongst themselves; Zapata did not seek national power, though he fought tenaciously for land for peasants. He was betrayed and assassinated by Carranza, who at that time was president. Obregón finally consolidated power and executed Carranza, but was assassinated when he tried to break one of the tenets of the Revolution—no reelection. His protégé, Plutarco Elías Calles, learned the lesson and installed one puppet president after another until **Lázaro Cárdenas** severed the puppeteer's strings and banished him to exile.

Until Cárdenas's election in 1934, the eventual outcome of the Revolution remained in doubt. There had been some land redistribution, but other measures took a back seat to political expediency. Cárdenas changed all that. He implemented a massive redistribution of land and nationalized the oil industry. He instituted many reforms and gave shape to the ruling political party (now the **Partido Revolucionario Institucional,** or PRI) by bringing under its banner a broad representation of Mexican society and establishing the mechanisms for consensus building. Cárdenas is practically canonized by most Mexicans.

MODERN MEXICO

The presidents that followed are more noted for graft than leadership. The party's base narrowed when many of the reform-minded elements were marginalized. Progress, a lot of it in the form of large development projects, became the PRI's main basis for legitimacy. In 1968, the government violently repressed a democratic student movement at a massacre in Tlatelolco, a section of Mexico City. Though the PRI maintained its grip on power, it lost all semblance of being a progressive party. In 1985 there was a devastating **earthquake in Mexico City** that brought down many of the government's new, supposedly earthquake-proof buildings, thus exposing shoddy construction and the widespread government corruption that fostered it. There was heavy criticism, too, for how it handled the relief efforts. In 1994, a political/military **uprising in Chiapas** brought Mexico's great social problems to the world's attention. A new political force, the Zapatista National Liberation Army (EZLN, for Ejército Zapista de Liberación Nacional), has skillfully publicized the plight of the peasant in today's Mexico. The government was forced into negotiations with the EZLN, a position that can bring it little if any political capital. Its tactics have been to make some easy concessions and to stall on other demands.

In recent years, opposition political parties have grown in power and legitimacy. Facing enormous pressure and scrutiny from national and international organizations, and widespread public discontent, the PRI has had to concede electoral defeats for state governors and congresspersons. But the power structure within the party is inflexible; the party cannot adapt to changing situations and is in an internal crisis of its own, manifested in the several political assassinations that have occurred in the last few years. For the first time ever, the PRI has had to concede the loss of the mayorship of Mexico City, the second most powerful position in the country. The new opposition mayor is **Cuauhtémoc Cárdenas,** son of the PRI's brightest star, Lázaro. What will happen now is anyone's guess.

plotting the assassination of their brother-in-law, the head of the PRI. The United States extends Mexico $40 billion in loans to stabilize the economy following the peso crisis.

- **1996** Effects of the devaluation continue as in 1995, but many businesses without debt expand and prosper. Mexico begins repaying the loan from the United States extended in 1995; the wife of the president's brother is arrested attempting to remove millions of dollars from a Swiss Bank—drug ties are alleged; former president Salinas's whereabouts unknown, though he speaks out occasionally; the Chiapan crisis remains unsettled, but some progress has been made.

- **1997** Mexico continues early repayment of its debt to the United States; Mexico's economy shows signs of improving, but the people struggle under effects of inflation, low pay, and lack of jobs. The Chiapas issue flares up again when 45 villagers are massacred in Acteal. The fourth Chiapanecan governor in 4 years is forced to resign, and the government makes arrests.

- **1998** Cuauhtemoc Cárdenas becomes the first opposition candidate to become mayor of Mexico City, the second most powerful office in the country.

3 Food & Drink

Authentic Mexican food differs quite dramatically from the versions and derivatives served in the United States. For many travelers, then, Mexico will be new and exciting culinary territory. Even grizzled veterans will find much that is new to them when they visit different parts of the country, because each region has its own specialties.

There are some general rules. Mexican food usually isn't pepper-hot when it arrives at the table (though many dishes must have a certain amount of piquancy, and some home cooking can be very spicy, depending on a family's or chef's tastes). Generally, the *picante* flavor is added with *chiles* and sauces after the food is served; you'll never see a table in Mexico without one or both of these condiments. Mexicans don't drown their cooking in cheese and sour cream, à la Tex-Mex, and they use a greater variety of ingredients than most people believe. But the basis of Mexican food is simple—tortillas, beans, chilies, squash, and tomatoes—the same as it was centuries ago, before the arrival of the Europeans.

THE BASICS

TORTILLAS Traditional tortillas are made from corn that's been soaked and cooked in water and lime, then ground into *masa* (a grainy dough), patted and pressed into thin cakes, and cooked on a hot griddle known as a *comal*. In many households the tortilla takes the place of fork and spoon; Mexicans merely tear them into wedge-shaped pieces, which they use to scoop up their food. Restaurants often serve bread rather than tortillas because it's easier, but you can always ask for tortillas. A more recent invention from northern Mexico is the flour tortilla, which is seen less frequently in the rest of Mexico.

ENCHILADAS The tortilla is the basis of several Mexican dishes, but the most famous of these is the enchilada. The original name for this dish would have been tortilla enchilada, which simply means a tortilla dipped in a chile sauce. In like manner, there's the *entomatada* (tortilla dipped in a tomato sauce) and the *enfrijolada* (in a bean sauce). The enchilada began as a very simple dish. A tortilla is dipped in chile sauce (usually with ancho chile) and then into very hot oil, then quickly folded or rolled on a plate and sprinkled with chopped onions and a little *queso cotija* (crumbly white cheese). You can get this basic enchilada in food stands across the country. I love them, and if you come across them in your travels, give them a try. In restaurants you get the more elaborate enchilada, with different fillings of cheese, chicken, or pork or even seafood, and sometimes prepared as a casserole. These are often a restaurant's best dish.

TACOS Another food based on the tortilla is the famous taco. A taco is anything folded or rolled into a tortilla, and sometimes a double tortilla. The tortilla can be served either soft or fried. *Flautas* and quesadillas (except in Mexico City where they are something quite different) are species of tacos. For Mexicans, the taco is the quintessential fast food and the taco stand (*taquería*)—a ubiquitous sight—is a great place to get a cheap, good, and filling meal. See the section below, "Eating Out: Restaurants, Taquerías & Tipping," for information on taquerías.

FRIJOLES An invisible "bean line" divides Mexico: It starts at the Gulf Coast in the southern part of the state of Tamaulipas and moves inland through the eastern quarter of San Luis Potosí and most of the state of Hidalgo, then straight through Mexico City and Morelos and into Guerrero, where it curves slightly westward to the Pacific. To the north and west of this line, the pink bean known as the *flor de mayo* is the staple food; to the south and east, the standard is the black bean. (Curiously enough, this line also roughly determines whether a taco will come with one or two tortillas; to the north and west, you get two tortillas, to the south and east, only one.)

In private households, beans are served at least once a day; with every meal among the working class and peasantry if the family can afford it. Mexicans almost always prepare beans with a minimum of condiments, usually just a little onion and garlic and perhaps a pinch of herbs. They want their beans to serve as a quiet contrast to the other heavily spiced foods in a meal. Sometimes they are served at the end of a meal with a little Mexican-style sour cream.

Mexicans often fry leftover beans and serve them on the side as *frijoles refritos*. "Refritos" is usually translated as refried, but this is a misnomer—the beans are fried only once. The prefix "re" actually means "well," and what Mexicans mean is "well fried."

TAMALES You make a *tamal* by mixing corn masa with a little lard, adding one of several fillings—meats flavored with chiles (or no filling at all)—then wrapping it in a corn shuck or banana leaf, and steaming it. Every region in Mexico has its own traditional way of making tamales. In some places, a single *tamal* can be big enough to feed a family, while in others they are only 3 inches long and an inch thick.

CHILES There are many kinds of chiles and Mexicans call each of them by one name when they're fresh and another when they're dried. Some are blazing hot with only a mild flavor; some are mild but have a rich, complex flavor. They can be pickled, smoked, stuffed, stewed, chopped, and used in an endless variety of dishes.

MEALTIME

MORNING The morning meal, known as *el desayuno,* can be something very light, such as coffee and sweet bread, or something more substantial: eggs cooked in a Mexican fashion, beans, tortillas, bread, fruit, and juice. It can be eaten early or late and is always a sure bet in Mexico. The variety and sweetness of the fruits is remarkable, and you can't go wrong with Mexican egg dishes.

MIDAFTERNOON The main meal of the day, known as *la comida,* is eaten between 2 and 4pm. Stores and businesses close, and most people will go home to eat and perhaps take a short afternoon siesta before going about their business. The first course is the *sopa,* which can be either soup (*caldo*) or rice (*sopa de arroz*) or both; then comes the main course, which ideally would be a meat or fish dish prepared in some kind of sauce and probably served with beans, followed by dessert.

EVENING Between 8 and 10pm most Mexicans will have a light meal called *la cena.* If eaten at home, it will be something like a sandwich or bread and jam or perhaps a couple of tacos made from some of the day's leftovers. At restaurants, the most common thing to eat is *antojitos* (literally, "little cravings"), a general label for light fare. Antojitos include *tostadas,* tamales, tacos, and simple enchiladas, and are big hits with travelers. Large restaurants will offer complete meals as well.

EATING OUT: RESTAURANTS, TAQUERÍAS, & TIPPING

First of all, I feel compelled to debunk the prevailing myth that the cheapest place to eat in Mexico is in the market. Actually, this is almost never the case. You can usually find better food at a better price without going more than 2 blocks out of your way. Why? Food stalls in the marketplace pay high rents, they have a near-captive clientele of market vendors and truckers, and they get a lot of business from many Mexicans for whom eating in the market is a traditional way of confirming their culture.

On the other side of the spectrum, avoid eating at those inviting sidewalk restaurants that you see beneath the stone archways that border the main plazas. These places usually cater to tourists and don't need to count on getting any return business. But they are great for getting a coffee or beer and watching the world turn.

In most nonresort towns, there are always one or two restaurants (sometimes its a coffee shop) that are social centers for a large group of established patrons. These establishments over time become virtual institutions, and change comes very slowly to them. The food is usually good standard fare, cooked as it was 20 years ago; the decor is simple. The patrons have known each other and the staff for years, and the *charla* (banter), gestures, and greetings are friendly, open, and unaffected. If you're curious about Mexican culture, these places are great fun to eat in and observe the goings on.

On your trip you're going to see many *taquerías* (taco joints). These are generally small places with a counter or a few tables set around the cooking area; you get to see exactly how they make their tacos before deciding whether to order. Most tacos come with a little chopped onion and cilantro, but not with tomato and lettuce. Find one that seems popular with the locals and where the cook performs with brio (a good sign of pride in the product). Sometimes there will be a woman making the tortillas right there (or working the masa into *gorditas, sopes,* or *panuchos* if these are also served). You will never see men doing this—this is perhaps the strictest gender division in Mexican society. Men do all other cooking and kitchen tasks, and work with already-made tortillas, but will never be found working masa.

For the main meal of the day, many restaurants offer a multicourse blue-plate special called **comida corrida** or **menú del día.** This is the most inexpensive way to get a full dinner. In Mexico, you need to ask for your check; if you're in a hurry to get somewhere, ask for the check when your food arrives; otherwise it can be slow in coming.

Tips are about the same as in the United States. You'll find a 15% **value-added tax** on restaurant meals, which shows up on the bill as "IVA." This is a boon to arithmetically challenged tippers, saving them from undue exertion.

To summon the waiter, wave or raise your hand, but don't motion with your index finger, which is a demeaning gesture that may even cause the waiter to ignore you. Or if it's the check you want, you can motion to the waiter from across the room using the universal pretend-like-you're-writing gesture.

Most restaurants do not have **nonsmoking sections;** when they do, we mention it in the reviews. But Mexico's wonderful climate makes for many open-air restaurants, usually set inside a courtyard of a colonial house, or in rooms with tall ceilings and plenty of open windows.

DRINKS

All over Mexico you'll find shops selling **juices** and **smoothies** from several kinds of tropical fruit. They're excellent and refreshing; while traveling I take full advantage of them. You'll also come across *aguas frescas*—water flavored with hibiscus, melon, tamarind, or lime. Soft drinks come in more flavors than in any other country I know. Pepsi and Coca-Cola taste the way they did in the United States years ago, before the makers started adding corn syrup. The coffee is generally good, and **hot chocolate** is a traditional drink, as is *atole*—a hot, corn-based beverage that can be sweet or bitter.

Of course, Mexico has a proud and lucrative **beer**-brewing tradition. A less-known brewed beverage is **pulque,** a pre-Hispanic drink: the fermented juice of a few species of maguey or agave. Mostly you find it for sale in *pulquerías* in central Mexico. It is an acquired taste, and not every gringo acquires it. **Mezcal** and **tequila** also come from the agave. Tequila is a variety of mezcal produced from the a. tequilana species of agave in and around the area of Tequila, in the state of Jalisco. Mezcal comes from various parts of Mexico and from different varieties of agave. The distilling process is usually much less sophisticated than that of tequila and, with its stronger smell and taste, mezcal is much more easily detected on the drinker's breath. In some places like Oaxaca it comes with a worm in the bottle; you are supposed to eat the worm after polishing off the mezcal. But for those teetotalers out there who are interested in just the worm, I have good news—you can find these worms for sale in Mexican markets when in season. *Salud!*

4 Recommended Books & Recordings

BOOKS

HISTORY & CULTURE   *Ancient Mexico: An Overview* (University of New Mexico Press, 1985), by Jaime Litvak, is a short, very readable history of pre-Hispanic Mexico. *The Wind That Swept Mexico* (University of Texas Press, 1971), by Anita Brenner, is a classic illustrated account of the Mexican Revolution. *Barbarous Mexico,* by John Kenneth Turner (University of Texas Press, 1984), was written in the early 1900s as a shocking exposé of the atrocities of the Porfirio Díaz presidency. A good, but controversial, all-around introduction to contemporary Mexico and its people is *Distant Neighbors: A Portrait of the Mexicans* (Random House, 1984), by Alan Riding. In a more personal vein is Patrick Oster's *The Mexicans: A Personal Portrait of the Mexican People* (Harper & Row, 1989), a reporter's insightful account of ordinary Mexican people. A novel with valuable insights into the Mexican character is *The Labyrinth of Solitude* (Grove Press, 1985), by Octavio Paz.

ART & ARCHITECTURE   *Mexico: Splendors of Thirty Centuries* (Metropolitan Museum of Art, 1990), the catalog of the 1991 traveling exhibition, is a wonderful resource on Mexico's art from 1500 B.C. through the 1950s. Another superb catalog, *Images of Mexico: The Contribution of Mexico to 20th Century Art* (Dallas Museum of Art, 1987), is a fabulously illustrated and detailed account of Mexican art gathered from collections around the world. *Casa Mexicana* (Stewart, Tabori & Chang, 1989), by Tim Street-Porter, takes readers through the interiors of some of Mexico's finest homes-turned-museums, public buildings, and private homes.

Mexican Masks (University of Texas Press, 1980), by Donald Cordry, based on the author's collection and travels, remains the definitive work on the subject. *Folk Treasures of Mexico* (Harry N. Abrams, 1990), by Marion Oettinger, is the fascinating illustrated story behind the 3,000-piece Mexican folk-art collection amassed by Nelson Rockefeller over a 50-year period, as well as much information about individual folk artists.

NATURE   *A Naturalist's Mexico* (Texas A&M University Press, 1992), by Roland H. Wauer, is a fabulous guide to birding in Mexico. *A Hiker's Guide to Mexico's Natural History* (Mountaineers, 1995), by Jim Conrad, covers Mexican flora and fauna and tells how to find the easy-to-reach as well as out-of-the-way spots he describes. *Peterson Field Guides: Mexican Birds* (Houghton-Mifflin, 1973), by Roger Tory Peterson and Edward L. Chalif, is an excellent guide to the country's birds.

RECORDINGS

Mexicans take their music very seriously—notice the tapes for sale almost everywhere, ceaseless music in the streets, and the bus drivers with collections of tapes to entertain passengers. For the collector, choices range from contemporary rock to revolutionary ballads, ranchero, salsa, and romantic trios.

Mariachi music is played and sold all over Mexico. Among the top recording artists is Mariachi Vargas. No mariachi performance is complete without "Guadalajara," "Las Mañanitas," and "Jarabe Tapatío." For **trio music,** some of the best are by Los Tres Diamantes and Los Tres Reyes. If you're requesting songs of a trio, good ones to ask for are "Sin Ti," "Usted," "Amor de la Calle," and "Cielito Lindo."

"Rock en Español" is growing tremendously in influence in Mexico, throughout Latin America, and in the United States. Some of the best-known Mexican pop-rock bands, which incorporate traditional folk with reggae, ska, and metal, are Café Tacuba, Maná, and Maldita Vecindad.

3

Planning a Trip to Mexico

A little advance planning can make the difference between a good trip and a great trip. When should you go? What's the best way to get there? How much should you plan on spending? What festivals or special events will be taking place during your visit? We'll answer these and other questions for you in this chapter.

1 Visitor Information, Entry Requirements & Money

SOURCES OF INFORMATION

The **Mexico Hotline** (☎ 800/44-MEXICO) is a good source for very general informational brochures on the country and for answers to the most commonly asked questions. If you have a fax, Mexico's Ministry of Tourism also offers **FaxMeMexico** (☎ 541/385-9282). Call, give them your fax number, and select from a variety of topics from accommodations (the service lists 400 hotels) to shopping, dining, sports, sightseeing, festivals, and nightlife. They'll then fax you the materials you're interested in.

More information (15,000 pages worth, they say) about Mexico is available on the Mexico Ministry of Tourism's Web site: **mexico-travel.com.**

The **U.S. State Department** (☎ 202/647-5225 for travel information and Overseas Citizens Services) offers a **Consular Information Sheet** on Mexico, with a compilation of safety, medical, driving, and general travel information gleaned from reports by official U.S. State Department offices in Mexico. You can also request the Consular Information Sheet by fax (☎ 202/647-2000). The State Department is also on the Internet; check out **travel.state.gov/mexico.html** for the Consular Information Sheet on Mexico; **travel.state.gov/travel_warnings.html** for other Consular Information sheets and travel warnings; and **travel.state.gov/tips_mexico. html** for the State Department's *Tips for Travelers to Mexico.*

The **Center for Disease Control Hotline** (☎ 404/332-4559) is another source for medical information affecting travelers to Mexico and elsewhere. The center's Web site, **www.cdc.gov/,** provides lengthy information on health issues for specific countries.

MEXICAN GOVERNMENT TOURIST OFFICES Mexico's foreign tourist offices (MGTO) throughout the world—with the exception of the United States and Canada—were closed effective January 1997. Those operating in North America include the following:

United States: Chicago, IL (☎ **312/606-9252**); Houston, TX (☎ **713/ 629-1611**); Los Angeles, CA (☎ **310/203-8191**); Miami, FL (☎ **305/443-9160**); New York, NY (☎ **212/421-6655**); and the Mexican Embassy Tourism Delegate, 1911 Pennsylvania Ave., Washington, DC 20005 (☎ **202/728-1750**). At publication time, the MGTO offices were being combined with Mexican Consulate offices in the same cities, but this was still up for confirmation. The telephone numbers should still be operational, but if not, check with your nearest Mexican Consulate.

Canada: 1 Place Ville-Marie, Suite 1526, Montréal, QUEB, H3B 2B5 (☎ **514/871-1052**); 2 Bloor St. W., Suite 1801, Toronto, ON, M4W 3E2 (☎ **416/ 925-2753**); 999 W. Hastings, Suite 1610, Vancouver, BC, V6C 2W2 (☎ **604/ 669-2845**).

STATE TOURISM DEVELOPMENT OFFICES   Two Mexican states have tourism and trade development offices in the United States: **Guerrero State Convention and Visitors Bureau,** 5075 Westheimer, Suite 980 West, Houston, TX 77056 (☎ **713/339-1880;** fax 713/339-1615); and **Casa Nuevo León State Promotion Office,** 100 W. Houston St., Suite 1400, San Antonio, TX 78205 (☎ **210/ 225-0732;** fax 210/225-0736).

OTHER SOURCES   The following newsletters may be of interest to readers: *Mexican Meanderings,* P.O. Box 33057, Austin, TX 78764, aimed at readers who travel to off-the-beaten-track destinations by car, bus, or train (six to eight pages, published six times annually; subscription $18); *Travel Mexico,* Apdo. Postal 6-1007, 06600 Mexico, D.F., from the publishers of the *Traveler's Guide to Mexico,* the book frequently found in hotel rooms in Mexico, covers a variety of topics from archaeology news to hotel packages, new resorts and hotels, and the economy (six times annually; subscription $18).

For other newsletters, see "For Seniors" under "Tips for Travelers with Special Needs," below.

ENTRY REQUIREMENTS

DOCUMENTS   All travelers to Mexico are required to present **proof of citizenship,** such as an original birth certificate with a raised seal, a valid passport, state issued driver's license or official ID, or naturalization papers. Those using a birth certificate should also have a current photo identification such as a driver's license. Those whose last name on the birth certificate is different from their current name (women using a married name, for example) should also bring a photo identification card *and* legal proof of the name change such as the *original* marriage license or certificate. This proof of citizenship may also be requested when you want to reenter either the United States or Mexico. Note that photocopies are *not* acceptable.

You must also carry a **Mexican Tourist Permit,** which is issued free of charge by Mexican border officials after proof of citizenship is accepted. The tourist permit is more important than a passport in Mexico, so guard it carefully. If you lose it, you may not be permitted to leave the country until you can replace it—a bureaucratic hassle that takes several days to a week at least. (If you do lose your tourist permit, get a police report from local authorities indicating that your documents were stolen; having one *might* lessen the hassle of exiting the country without all your identification.)

A tourist permit can be issued for up to 180 days, and although your stay south of the border may be shorter than that, you should ask for the maximum time, just in case. Sometimes officials don't ask—they just stamp a time limit, so be sure to say "6 months" (or at least twice as long as you intend to stay). If you should decide to extend your stay, you'll eliminate hassle by not needing to renew your papers.

Note that children under age 18 traveling without parents or with only one parent must have a notarized letter from the absent parent or parents authorizing the travel.

Lost Documents   To replace a **lost passport,** contact your embassy or nearest consular agent (see "Fast Facts: Mexico," below). You must establish a record of your citizenship and also fill out a form requesting another Mexican Tourist Permit (assuming it, too, was lost). Without the **tourist permit** you can't leave the country, and without an affidavit affirming your passport request and citizenship, you may have problems at Customs when you get home. So it's important to clear everything up *before* trying to leave. Mexican Customs may, however, accept the police report of the loss of the tourist permit and allow you to leave.

CUSTOMS ALLOWANCES   When you enter Mexico, Customs officials will be tolerant as long as you have no illegal drugs or firearms. You're allowed to bring in two cartons of cigarettes, or 50 cigars, plus a kilogram (2.2 lb.) of smoking tobacco; the liquor allowance is two 1-liter bottles of anything, wine or hard liquor; you are also allowed 12 rolls of film. A laptop computer, camera equipment, and sporting equipment (golf clubs, scuba gear, a bicycle) that could feasibly be used during your stay are also allowed. The underlying guideline is that they will disallow anything that appears as if you will be attempting to resell it in Mexico.

When you reenter the **United States,** federal law allows you to bring in up to $400 in purchases duty-free every 30 days. The first $1,000 over the $400 allowance is taxed at 10%. You may bring in a carton (200) of cigarettes or 50 cigars or 2 kilograms (4.4 lb.) of smoking tobacco, plus 1 liter of an alcoholic beverage (wine, beer, or spirits).

Canadian citizens are allowed $20 in purchases after a 24-hour absence from the country or $100 after a stay of 48 hours or more.

British travelers returning from outside the European Union are allowed to bring in £145 worth of goods, in addition to the following: up to 200 cigarettes, 50 cigars or 250 grams of tobacco; 2 liters of wine; 1 liter of liqueur greater than 22% alcohol by volume and 60cc/milliliters of perfume. If any item worth more than the limit of £45 is brought in, payment must be made on the full value, not just on the amount above £145.

Citizens of **New Zealand** are allowed to return with a combined value of up to NZ$700 in goods, duty-free.

GOING THROUGH CUSTOMS   Mexican Customs inspection has been streamlined. At most points of entry, tourists are requested to punch a button in front of what looks like a traffic signal, which alternates on touch between red and green signals. Green light and you go through without inspection; red light and your luggage or car may be inspected briefly or thoroughly. If you have an unusual amount of luggage or an oversized piece, you may be subject to inspection despite the traffic signal routine.

MONEY
CASH/CURRENCY   The currency in Mexico is the Mexican **peso.** Paper currency comes in denominations of 10, 20, 50, 100, 200, and 500 pesos. Coins come in denominations of 1, 2, 5, and 10 pesos and 20 and 50 **centavos** (100 centavos equal 1 peso). The current exchange rate for the U.S. dollar is around 8 pesos; at that rate, an item that costs 10 pesos would be equivalent to US$1.25.

Getting **change** continues to be a problem in Mexico. Small-denomination bills and coins are hard to come by, so start collecting them early in your trip and continue as you travel. Shopkeepers everywhere seem always to be out of change and small bills; that's doubly true in a market.

Note: The **universal currency sign ($)** is used to indicate pesos in Mexico. The use of this symbol in this book, however, denotes U.S. currency.

Many establishments dealing with tourists, especially in coastal resort areas, quote prices in dollars. To avoid confusion, they use the abbreviations "Dlls." for dollars and "M.N." (*moneda nacional,* or national currency) for pesos. All dollar equivalencies in this book were assuming an exchange rate of 8 pesos per dollar.

EXCHANGING MONEY   The rate of exchange fluctuates a tiny bit daily, so you probably are better off not exchanging too much of your currency at once. Don't forget, however, to have enough pesos to carry you over a weekend or Mexican holiday, when banks are closed. In general, avoid carrying the U.S. $100 bill, the bill most commonly counterfeited in Mexico, and therefore the most difficult to exchange, especially in smaller towns. Since small bills and coins in pesos are hard to come by in Mexico, the U.S. $1 bill is very useful for tipping.

The bottom line on exchanging money of all kinds: It pays to ask first and shop around. Banks pay the top rates.

Exchange houses (*casas de cambio*) are generally more convenient than banks since they have more locations and longer hours; the rate of exchange may be the same as a bank or slightly lower. *Note:* Before leaving a bank or exchange-house window, always count your change in front of the teller before the next client steps up.

Large airports have currency-exchange counters that often stay open whenever flights are arriving or departing. Though convenient, these generally do not offer the most favorable rates.

A hotel's exchange desk almost always pays less favorable rates than banks.

BANKS & ATM'S   Banks in Mexico are rapidly expanding services. New hours tend to be from 9am until 5 or 6pm, with many open for at least a half day on Saturday, and some even offering limited hours on Sunday. The exchange of dollars, which used to be limited until noon, can now be accommodated anytime during business hours. Some, but not all, banks charge a service fee of about 1% to exchange traveler's checks. However, most purchases can be paid for directly with travelers checks at the stated exchange rate of the establishment. Personal checks may be cashed but not without weeks of delay—a bank will wait for your check to clear before giving you your money.

Travelers to Mexico can also access money from **automatic teller machines (ATMs),** now available in most major cities and resort areas in Mexico. Universal bank cards (such as the Cirrus and PLUS systems) can be used, and this is a convenient way to withdraw money from your bank and avoid carrying too much with you at any time. There is generally a service fee charged by your bank for each transaction. Most machines offer Spanish/English menus and dispense pesos. For Cirrus locations abroad, call ☎ **800/424-7787,** or check out MasterCard's Web site (**www.mastercard.com**). For PLUS usage abroad, visit Visa's Web site (**www.visa.com**).

TRAVELER'S CHECKS   Traveler's checks are readily accepted nearly everywhere, but they can be difficult to cash on a weekend or holiday or in an out-of-the-way place. Their best value is in replacement in case of theft. Frequently in Mexico, a bank or establishment will pay more for traveler's checks than for cash dollars.

CREDIT CARDS   You'll be able to charge most hotel, restaurant, and store purchases, as well as almost all airline tickets, on your credit card. You can get cash advances of several hundred dollars on your card, but there may be a wait of 20 minutes to 2 hours. You can't charge gasoline purchases in Mexico. Visa ("Bancomer" in Mexico), MasterCard ("Carnet" in Mexico), and American Express are the most accepted cards.

Credit-card bills will be billed in pesos, then later converted into dollars by the bank issuing the credit card. Generally you receive the favorable bank rate when paying by credit card.

CRIME, BRIBES & SCAMS

CRIME   Crime in Mexico has received much attention in the North American press over the past year (1997 to 1998). Some in Mexico feel this unfairly reflects the real dangers of traveling there, but it should be noted that crime is in fact on the rise, especially taxi robberies, kidnappings, and highway carjackings. From December 1997 to April 1998, six foreigners were murdered while traveling in Mexico—from Baja and Mexico City to Zihuatanejo and even the tranquil fishing village of Puerto Escondido.

So precautions are necessary, but travelers should be realistic. When traveling any place in the world, common sense is essential. I have lived in and traveled throughout Mexico for 8 years now, without serious incident. The crime rate is on the whole much lower in Mexico than in most parts of the United States, and the nature of crimes in general is less violent. You are much more likely to meet kind and helpful Mexicans than you are to encounter those set on thievery and deceit. A good rule of thumb is that you can generally trust people whom you approach for help, assistance, or directions—but be wary of anyone who approaches you offering the same. The more insistent they are, the more cautious you should be.

Although these general comments on crime are basically true throughout Mexico, the one notable exception is in **Mexico City,** where violent crime is seriously on the rise. Do not wear fine jewelry, expensive watches, or any other obvious displays of wealth. Muggings—day or night—are common. Avoid the use of the **green Volkswagen taxis** as many of these have been involved in "pirate" robberies, muggings, and even kidnappings. Car theft and carjackings are also a common occurrence. Despite the rise in Mexico City's crime, you should be fine if you avoid ostentatious displays of wealth, follow commonsense precautions, and take taxis only dispatched from official sites ("sitios"). Mexico City is a worthwhile destination, with a wealth of cultural offerings—it's unfortunate that, like many major cities in the world, it has problems with violence and crime. More specific precautions can be found in chapter 4, "Mexico City." (See also "Emergencies" under "Fast Facts: Mexico," later in this chapter.)

BRIBES & SCAMS   As is the case around the world, there are the occasional bribes and scams, targeted at people believed to be naive in the ways of the place—i.e., obvious tourists. For years Mexico was known as a place where bribes—called *propinas* (tips) or *mordidas* ("bites")—were expected; however, the country is rapidly changing. Frequently, offering a bribe today, especially to a police officer, is considered an insult, and it can land you in deeper trouble.

If you believe a bribe is being requested, here are a few tips on dealing with the situation. Even if you speak Spanish, don't utter a word of it to Mexican officials. That way you'll appear innocent, all the while understanding every word.

When you are crossing the border, should the man who inspects your car ask for a tip, you can ignore this request—but understand that the official may suddenly decide that a complete search of your belongings is in order. If faced with a situation where you feel you're being asked for a *propina,* how much should you offer? Usually $3 to $5 or the equivalent in pesos will do the trick. There's a number to

report irregularities with Customs officials (☎ **01/800-0-0148** in Mexico). Your call will go to the office of the Comptroller and Administrative Development Secretariat (SECODAM); however, be forewarned that most personnel do not speak English. Be sure you have some basic information—such as the name of the person who requested a bribe or acted in a rude manner, as well as the place, time, and day of the event.

Whatever you do, avoid impoliteness; under no circumstances should you insult a Latin American official. Mexico is ruled by extreme politeness, even in the face of adversity. In Mexico, *gringos* have a reputation for being loud and demanding. By adopting the local custom of excessive courtesy, you'll have greater success in negotiations of any kind. Stand your ground, but do it politely.

As you travel in Mexico, you may encounter several types of **scams,** which are typical throughout the world. One involves some sort of a **distraction** or feigned commotion. While your attention is diverted, a pickpocket makes a grab for your wallet. In another common scam, an **unaccompanied child** pretends to be lost and frightened and takes your hand for safety. Meanwhile the child, or an accomplice, manages to plunder your pockets. A third involves **confusing currency.** A shoe-shine boy, street musician, guide, or other individual might offer you a service for a price that seems reasonable—in pesos. When it comes time to pay, they tell you the price is in dollars, not pesos, and become very hostile if payment is not made. Be very clear on the price and currency when services are involved.

2 When to Go

SEASONS   Mexico has two principal travel seasons: high and low. **High season** begins around December 20 and continues to Easter, although in some places high season can begin as early as mid-November. **Low season** begins the day after Easter and continues to mid-December; during low season, prices may drop 20% to 50%, especially in beach destinations. Prices in inland cities seldom fluctuate from high to low season, but may rise dramatically during **Easter** and **Christmas** weeks. Taxco and Pátzcuaro raise prices during Easter week due to the popularity of their Easter-week celebrations. In Isla Mujeres and Playa del Carmen, both on the Yucatán Peninsula, high season starts earlier than in the rest of the country and includes the month of August, when many European visitors arrive. Another exception to the typical high and low seasons is Veracruz, where prices rise for Mexican holidays, especially in summer when children are out of school. All of these exceptions and others are mentioned in the appropriate chapters that follow.

Mexico has two main climate seasons as well: **rainy** (May to mid-Oct) and **dry** (mid-Oct through Apr). The rainy season can be of little consequence in the dry, northern region of the country. Southern regions typically receive tropical showers, which begin around 4 or 5pm and last a few hours. Though these rains can come on suddenly and be quite strong, they usually end just as fast and cool off the air for the evening. **Hurricane season** particularly affects the Yucatán Peninsula, especially from June through October. However, if no hurricanes strike, the light, cooling winds, especially from September through November, can make it a perfect time to more comfortably tackle the pre-Hispanic ruins that dot the interior of the peninsula.

June, July, and August are unrelentingly hot on the Yucatán Peninsula, though temperatures rise only into the mid-80s to 90°F. Most of coastal Mexico experiences temperatures in the 80s in the hottest months. Very high summer temperatures are reserved for Mexico's northern states that border the United States.

Elevation is another important factor affecting climate. High-elevation cities such as Mexico City, San Cristóbal de las Casas, Real de Catorce, or the joint volcano park of Popo-Ixta east of Mexico City can be surprisingly cold. Temperatures can drop close to freezing at night in winter even in San Miguel de Allende and Guanajuato, which are at lower elevations than those cities mentioned above. In December 1997, snow fell in Guadalajara for the first time in some 80 years. *Viva El Niño!*

MEXICO CALENDAR OF EVENTS

January

- **New Year's Day (Año Nuevo).** National holiday. Parades, religious observances, parties, and fireworks welcome in the new year everywhere. In traditional indigenous communities, new tribal leaders are inaugurated with colorful ceremonies rooted in the pre-Hispanic past. January 1.
- **Three Kings Day,** nationwide. Commemorates the Three Kings' bringing of gifts to the Christ Child. On this day, the Three Kings "bring" gifts to children. Friends and families gather to share the *Rosca de Reyes,* a special cake. Inside the cake there is a small doll representing the Christ Child; whoever receives the doll in his or her piece must host a tamales-and-*atole* party the next month. January 6.
- **Regional Fair,** Leon, Guanajuato. One of Mexico's largest fairs celebrates the founding of this shoemaking/leather craft city. Parades, theater, craft exhibits, music, and dance. January 9 to February 5.
- **Feast of San Antonio Abad,** Mexico City. Blessing of the Animals at the Santiago Tlatelolco Church on the Plaza of Three Cultures, at San Juan Bautista Church in Coyoacán, and at the Church of San Fernando, 2 blocks north of the Juárez/Reforma intersection. January 17.

February

- **Candlemas,** nationwide. Music, dances, processions, food, and other festivities lead up to a blessing of seed and candles in a tradition that mixes pre-Hispanic and European traditions marking the end of winter. All those who attended the Three Kings Celebration reunite to share *atole* and tamales at a party hosted by the recipient of the doll found in the Rosca. February 2.
- ✪ **Carnaval.** Carnaval takes place the 3 days preceding Ash Wednesday and the beginning of Lent. It is celebrated with special reverence in the cities of Tepoztlán, Huejotzingo, Chamula, Veracruz, Cozumel, and Mazatlán. In some places, such as Veracruz, Mazatlán, and Cozumel, the celebration resembles New Orleans's Mardi Gras, with a festive atmosphere and parades. In Chamula, however, the event harks back to pre-Hispanic times with ritualistic running on flaming branches. On the Tuesday before Ash Wednesday in Tepoztlán and Huejotzingo, masked and brilliantly clad dancers fill the streets. In some towns there will be no special celebration, while in others there will be a few parades.

  Transportation and hotels are packed, so it's best to make reservations 6 months in advance and arrive a couple of days ahead of the beginning of celebrations. February 17 to 25.
- **Ash Wednesday.** The start of Lent and time of abstinence. It's a day of reverence nationwide, but some towns honor it with folk dancing and fairs. The date varies from year to year.

March

- **Annual witches conference,** Veracruz. At Lake Catemaco. Shamans, white witches, black witches, and practitioners of macumba, Caribbean, Afro, and Antillian ritualistic practices gather on the shores of Lake Catemaco (a region whose spiritual community dates back to pre-Columbian times). Tourists can witness the spectacle and pick up a good luck charm. March 12 to 15.

- **Benito Juárez's Birthday.** National Holiday. Small hometown celebrations countrywide, especially in Juárez's birthplace—Guelatao, Oaxaca. March 21.
- **Spring Equinox,** Chichén-Itzá. On the 1st day of spring, the Temple of Kukulcan—Chichén-Itza's main pyramid—aligns with the sun and the shadow of the plumed serpent moves slowly from the top of the building down. When the shadow reaches the bottom, the body joins the carved stone snake's head at the base of the pyramid. According to ancient legend, at the moment that the serpent is whole, the earth is fertilized to assure a bountiful growing season. Visitors come from around the world for the spectacle, so advance arrangements are advisable. March 21. (The shadow can be seen from Mar 19 to 23.)
- ✪ **Holy Week.** Celebrates the last week in the life of Christ from Palm Sunday through Easter Sunday with somber religious processions almost nightly, spoofing of Judas, and reenactments of specific biblical events, plus food and craft fairs. Among the Tarahumara in the Copper Canyon, celebrations have pre-Hispanic overtones. Special celebrations are also held in Pátzcuaro, Taxco, and Malinalco. Businesses close during this traditional week of Mexican national vacations.
  If you plan on traveling to or around Mexico during Holy Week, make your reservations early. Airline seats on flights into and out of the country will be reserved months in advance. Buses to these towns or to almost anywhere in Mexico will be full, so try arriving on the Wednesday or Thursday before Good Friday. Easter Sunday is quiet. March or April (dates vary).

April

- **Cuernavaca Flower Fair.** Exhibits and competition in floriculture and gardening, plus a sound-and-light show. Popular entertainers. April 3 to 7.
- **San Marcos National Fair,** Aguascalientes. Mexico's largest fair was first held in 1604 and begins the 3rd week in April and lasts 22 days. About a million visitors come for nationally famous bullfights and rodeos as well as ranchera music and mariachis. Craft and industrial exhibits, markets, fireworks, and folk dancing. April 12 to May 4.

May

- **Labor Day,** nationwide. Workers' parades countrywide and everything closes. May 1.
- **Holy Cross Day** (Día de la Santa Cruz). Workers place a cross on top of unfinished buildings and celebrate with food, bands, folk dancing, and fireworks around the work site. Celebrations are particularly colorful in Valle de Bravo, in the state of Mexico, and Paracho, Michoacán. May 3.
- **Cinco de Mayo.** Puebla and nationwide. A national holiday that celebrates the defeat of the French at the Battle of Puebla. May 5.
- **Feast of San Isidro.** The patron saint of farmers is honored with a blessing of seeds and work animals. May 15.
- **Cancún Jazz Festival.** Under new management. For dates call ☎ **800-44-MEXICO.** TBA.

June

- ✪ **Corpus Christi,** celebrated nationwide. Honors the Body of Christ (the Eucharist) with religious processions, masses, and food. Festivities include performances of *voladores* (flying pole dancers) beside the church and at the ruins of El Tajín. In Mexico City, children dressed as Indians and carrying decorated baskets of fruit for the priest's blessing gather, along with their parents, before the National Cathedral on the zócalo. *Mulitas* (mules) handmade from dried corn husks and painted, often with a corn-husk rider, and sometimes accompanied by pairs of corn-husk dolls, are traditionally sold there on that day. Dates vary (66 days after Easter).

- **National Ceramics Fair and Fiesta,** Tlaquepaque, Jalisco. This pottery center on the outskirts of Guadalajara offers craft demonstrations and competitions as well as mariachis, dancers, and colorful parades. June 14.
- **Día de San Pedro** (St. Peter and St. Paul's Day), nationwide. Celebrated wherever St. Peter is the patron saint, and honors anyone named Pedro or Peter. It's especially festive at San Pedro Tlaquepaque, near Guadalajara, with numerous mariachi bands, folk dancers, and parades with floats. In Mexcatitlan, Nayarit, shrimpers hold a regatta to celebrate the season opening. June 29.

July

- **The Guelaguetza Dance Festival,** Oaxaca. One of Mexico's most popular events. Villagers from the seven regions around Oaxaca gather in the city's amphitheater. All dress in traditional costumes, and many wear colorful "dancing" masks. The celebration goes back to pre-Hispanic times when a similar celebration was held to honor the fertility goddess who would, in exchange, grant a plentiful corn harvest. Make advanced reservations as this festival gathers visitors from around the world in Oaxaca to witness the celebration. June 21 to 28.

August

- **International Chamber Music Festival,** San Miguel de Allende. Held for the last 19 years in this beautiful town, the festival features international award-winning classical-music ensembles. August 1 to 15.
- **Fall of Tenochtitlán,** Mexico City. The last battle of the Spanish Conquest took place at Tlatelolco, ruins that are now part of the Plaza of Three Cultures. Wreath-laying ceremonies there and at the Cuauhtémoc monument on Reforma commemorate the event when the last Aztec king, Cuauhtémoc, surrendered to Hernán Cortés and thousands lost their lives. August 13.
- ✪ **Assumption of the Virgin Mary.** Celebrated throughout the country with special masses and in some places with processions. In Huamantla, streets are carpeted in flower petals and colored sawdust. At midnight on the 15th, a statue of the Virgin is carried through the streets; the 16th is a running of the bulls. On August 15 in Santa Clara del Cobre, near Pátzcuaro, Our Lady of Santa Clara de Asis and the Virgen de la Sagrado Patrona are honored with a parade of floats, dancers on the main square, and an exposition of regional crafts, especially copper. Buses to Huamantla from Puebla or Mexico City will be full, and there are few hotels in Huamantla. Plan to stay in Puebla and commute to the festivities. August 20 to 22.

September

- **Mariachi Festival.** Guadalajara, Jalisco. Public concerts of mariachi music, includ-ing visiting mariachi groups from around the world (including Japan!). Workshops and lectures are given on the history, culture, and music of the mariachi in Mexico. September 1 to 15.
- **Independence Day.** Celebrates Mexico's independence from Spain. A day of parades, picnics, and family reunions throughout the country. At 11pm on September 15, the president of Mexico gives the famous independence *grito* (shout) from the National Palace in Mexico City. At least half a million people are crowded into the zócalo, and the rest of the country watches the event on TV. The

enormous military parade on September 16 starts at the zócalo and ends at the Independence Monument on Reforma. Tall buildings downtown are draped in the national colors—red, green, and white—and the zócalo is ablaze with lights; it's popular to drive downtown at night to see the lights. It's also elaborately celebrated in Querétaro and San Miguel de Allende, where Independence conspirators lived and met, but the schedule of events is exactly the same in every village, town, and city across Mexico. September 15 to 16.

• **Fall Equinox,** Chichén-Itzá. The same shadow play that occurs during the spring equinox repeats itself for the fall equinox. September 21 to 22.

October

✪ **Cervantino Festival,** Guanajuato. Begun in the 1970s as a cultural event bringing performing artists from all over the world to this picturesque village northeast of Mexico City. Now the artists travel all over the republic after appearing in Guanajuato. Check local calendars for appearances. Early to mid-October.

• **Fiestas de Octubre** (October Festivals), Guadalajara. This "most Mexican of cities" celebrates for a whole month with its mariachi music trademark. A bountiful display of popular culture and fine arts, a spectacular spread of traditional foods, Mexican beers and wines. All month.

• **Día de la Raza** ("Ethnicity Day" or Columbus Day). Commemorates the fusion of the Spanish and Mexican peoples. October 12.

November

✪ **Day of the Dead.** What's commonly called the Day of the Dead is actually 2 days, All Saints' Day—honoring saints and deceased children—and All Souls' Day, honoring deceased adults. Relatives gather at cemeteries countrywide, carrying candles and food, often spending the night beside graves of loved ones. Weeks before, bakers begin producing bread formed in the shape of mummies or round loaves decorated with bread "bones." Decorated sugar skulls emblazoned with glittery names are sold everywhere. Many days ahead, homes and churches erect special altars laden with Day of the Dead bread, fruit, flowers, candles, and favorite foods and photographs of saints and of the deceased. On the 2 nights, children dress in costumes and masks, often carrying mock coffins and pumpkin lanterns, into which they expect money will be dropped, through the streets.
The most famous celebration is on Janitzio, an island on Lake Pátzcuaro, Michoacán, west of Mexico City, but it has become almost too well known. Mixquic, a mountain village south of Mexico City, hosts an elaborate street fair, and around 11pm on both nights, solemn processions lead to the cemetery in the center of town where villagers are already settled in with candles, flowers, and food. Cemeteries around Oaxaca City are well known for their solemn vigils and some for their Carnaval-like atmosphere. November 1 to 2.

• **Fiesta del Mar,** Puerto Vallarta. A monthlong calendar of activities including art festivals, sports competitions, boat show, and a gourmet dining festival, ending with fireworks on the 30th. November 10 to 30.

• **Revolution Day.** Commemorates the start of the Mexican Revolution in 1910 with parades, speeches, rodeos, and patriotic events. November 20.

• **National Silver Fair,** Taxco. A competition of Mexico's best silversmiths and some of the worlds finest artisans. Features exhibits, concerts, dances, and fireworks. November 29 to December 6.

December

✪ **Feast of the Virgin of Guadalupe.** Throughout the country the patroness of Mexico is honored with religious processions, street fairs, dancing, fireworks, and masses. It is one of Mexico's most moving and beautiful displays of traditional culture. The Virgin of Guadalupe appeared to a young man, Juan Diego, in December 1531, on a hill near Mexico City. He convinced the bishop that he had seen the apparition by revealing his cloak, upon which the Virgin was emblazoned. It's customary for children to dress up as Juan Diego, wearing mustaches and red bandannas. One of the most famous and elaborate celebrations takes place at the Basílica of Guadalupe, north of Mexico City, where the Virgin appeared. But every village celebrates this day, often with processions of children carrying banners of the Virgin and with *charreadas* (rodeos), bicycle races, dancing, and fireworks. December 12.

In Puerto Vallarta, the celebration begins on December 1 and extends through December 12, with traditional processions to the church for a brief *misa* (mass) and blessing. In the final days, the processions and festivities take place around the clock. There's a major fireworks exhibition on December 12 at 11pm.

- **Christmas Posadas.** On each of the 12 nights before Christmas, it's customary to reenact the Holy Family's search for an inn, with door-to-door candlelit processions in cities and villages nationwide. You may see them especially in Querétaro and Taxco. These are also hosted by most businesses and community organizations, taking the place of the northern tradition of a Christmas party. December 15 to 24.

- **Christmas.** Mexicans extend this celebration and leave their jobs often beginning 2 weeks before Christmas all the way through New Year's. Many businesses close, and resorts and hotels fill up. On December 23 there are significant celebrations. Querétaro has a huge parade. In Oaxaca it's the "Night of the Radishes," with displays of huge carved radishes, as well as elaborate figures made of corn husks and dried flowers. On the evening of December 24 in Oaxaca, processions culminate on the central plaza. On the same night, Santiago Tuxtla in Veracruz celebrates by dancing the *huapango* and with *jarocho* bands in the beautiful town square. In Quiroga, Michoacán, villagers present *Pastorelas* (Nativity plays) at churches around the city on the evenings of December 24 and 25.

- **New Year's Eve.** As in the rest of the world, New Year's Eve in Mexico is celebrated with parties, fireworks, and plenty of noise. Special festivities take place at Santa Clara del Cobre, with its candlelit procession of Christ, and at Tlacolula near Oaxaca, with commemorative mock battles for good luck in the new year. December 31.

3 Active Vacations in Mexico

Mexico has over 130 **golf** courses in the country, concentrated in the resort areas, with excellent ones in Mexico City and Guadalajara as well. Los Cabos, in Baja Sur, has become the preeminent golf destination in Mexico, where several annual championship tournaments are held each year. For details on courses and events, see chapter 17, "Los Cabos & Baja California Sur." **Tennis, racquetball, squash, waterskiing, surfing, bicycling,** and **horseback riding** are all sports visitors can enjoy in Mexico. **Scuba diving** is excellent in Mexico, not only off the Yucatán's Caribbean coast (especially Cozumel), but also on the Pacific Coast at Puerto Vallarta and Manzanillo and off Baja in the Sea of Cortez. **Mountain and volcano climbing** is a rugged sport where you'll meet like-minded folks from around the world. The top peaks are just 50 miles south of Mexico City—the snowcapped volcanoes Popocatépetl (17,887 ft.) and Ixtaccihuatl (17,342 ft.). For helpful information on visiting and climbing the volcanoes, contact the **Club de Exploraciones de México** in Mexico City (☎ 5/ 740-8032).

PARKS   Most of the national parks and nature reserves are understaffed or unstaffed. In addition to the reliable Mexican companies offering adventure trips (such as the AMTAVE members; see below), many U.S.-based companies also offer this kind of travel, with trips led by specialists.

OUTDOORS ORGANIZATIONS & TOUR OPERATORS   There's a new association in Mexico of eco- and adventure tour operators called **AMTAVE** (Asociación Mexicana de Turismo de Aventura y Ecoturismo, A.C.). They publish an annual catalog of participating firms and their offerings, all of which must meet certain criteria for security, quality and training of the guides, as well as for sustainability of natural and cultural environments. For more information, contact them (in Mexico City) at ☎ 5/255-4400; ask for Agustín Arroyo.

The American Wilderness Experience, P.O. Box 1486, Boulder, CO 80306 (☎ 800/444-0099 or 303/444-2622), leads catered camping, kayaking, biking, and hiking trips in Baja California, the Copper Canyon, and the Yucatán Peninsula.

The Archaeological Conservancy, 5301 Central Ave. NE, Suite 1218, Albuquerque, NM 87108-1517 (☎ 505/266-1540), presents one expert-led (usually an archaeologist) trip to Mexico per year. The trips change from year to year and space is limited, so you must make reservations early in the year.

ATC Tours and Travel, calle 16 de Septiembre 16, 29200 San Cristóbal de las Casas, Chiapas (☎ 967/8-2550 or 967/8-2557; fax 967/8-3145), a Mexico-based tour operator with an excellent reputation, offers specialist-led trips primarily in southern Mexico. In addition to trips to the ruins of Palenque and Yaxchilán (extending into Belize and Guatemala by river, plane, and bus if desired), they also offer horseback tours and day-trips to the ruins of Toniná around San Cristóbal de las Casas, Chiapas; birding in the rain forests of Chiapas and Guatemala (including in the El Triunfo Reserve of Chiapas where you can see the rare quetzal bird and orchids); hikes out to the shops and homes of native textile artists of the Chiapas highlands; and walks from the Lagos de Montebello in the Montes Azules Biosphere Reserve, with camping and canoeing.

Baja Expeditions, 2625 Garnet Ave., San Diego, CA 92109 (☎ 800/843-6967 or 619/581-3311; www.bajaex.com; E-mail: travel@bajaex.com), offers natural-history cruises, whale watching, sea kayaking, and scuba-diving trips out of La Paz, Baja California. One trip retraces John Steinbeck's journey as he wrote it in "Log from the Sea of Cortez."

Bike Mex Adventures, calle Guerrero s/n, 48300 Puerto Vallarta, Jalisco (☎ 322/ 3-2718; www.bikemex.com; E-Mail: bikemex@zonavirtual.com.mx), offers day or overnight mountain-biking excursions in the Sierra Madre foothills near Puerto Vallarta. One overnight trip travels to the old mountain mining towns of Mascota, Talpa de Allende, and San Sebastian. Combination of van transport and biking between towns, with stays in old haciendas.

The California Native, 8701 W. 87th Place, Los Angeles, CA 90045 (☎ 800/ 926-1140 or 310/642-1140), offers either escort-led or individual Copper Canyon trips for backpackers, photographers, mountain bikers, four-wheelers, and birders, as well as a side trip to Mennonite lands near Chihuahua.

Cloud Forest Adventure, 4926 Strass Dr., Austin, TX 78731 (☎ 512/451-1669), offers once- or twice-a-year weeklong trips (usually in June) to America's northernmost tropical cloud forest and the Rancho El Cielo in the remote El Cielo Biosphere

Reserve 50 miles south of Ciudad Victoria, Tamaulipas, in northern Mexico. The trips are sponsored by the Gorgas Science Foundation of Texas Southmost College. The area is rich in birds, orchids, and bromeliads and is home to endangered black bear, jaguar, and ocelot. Two nature movies explaining the region are available from the foundation—*At a Bend in a Mexican River* about birds and nature along the Río Sabinas, and *El Cielo, Forest in the Clouds,* exploring the adjacent mountain range and what visitors may see.

Columbus Travel, 900 Rich Creek Lane, Bulverde, TX 78163-2872 (☎ **800/ 843-1060** in the U.S. and Canada, or 830/885-2000), has a variety of easy-to-challenging adventures, specializing in the Copper Canyon. They can design trips for special-interest groups of agriculturists, geologists, rock hounds, and bird-watchers. They can also design custom trips to the Copper Canyon. The owner works with the Tarahumara Indians and believes more in "responsible tourism" than the often misused term ecotourism.

Culinary Adventures, 6023 Reid Dr. NW, Gig Harbor, WA 98335 (☎ **206/ 851-7676;** fax 206/851-9532), specializes in a short but special list of cooking tours in Mexico featuring well-known cooks and traveling to particular regions known for excellent cuisine. The owner, Marilyn Tausend, is the coauthor of *Mexico the Beautiful Cookbook.*

Far Flung Adventures, P.O. Box 377, Terlingua, TX 79852 (☎ **800/359-4138** or 915/371-2489), takes clients on specialist-led river trips to the Antigua River in Veracruz and the Río Usumacinta that runs between Mexico and Guatemala.

Intercontinental Adventures, Georgia 120-9 (A), 03810 México, D.F. (☎ **5/ 255-4400**), under the leadership of Augustín Arroyo, offers a new tour covering the original route of Cortés, though unlike Cortés and his henchmen, you're not on horseback or foot. Highlights include the ruins of Zempoala; the cities of Veracruz (where you learn the local dance, "danzon"), Jalapa and the excellent Museo de Antropología there, Puebla, Tlaxcala, and Mexico City; river rafting (if you desire); plus cultural experiences in food, history, and literature along the way. Trips can be customized.

Mexico Sportsman, 202 Milam Building, San Antonio, TX 78205 (☎/fax **210/494-9916**), is sportfishing central for anyone interested in advance arrangements for fishing in Cancún, Cozumel, Puerto Vallarta, Ixtapa/Zihuatanejo, Cabo San Lucas, or Mazatlán. The company offers complete information, from the cost to the length of a fishing trip; kind of boat, line and tackle used; and whether or not bait, drinks, and lunch are included. Prices are as good as you'll get on-site in Mexico.

Mountain Travel Sobek, 6420 Fairmount Ave., El Cerrito, CA 94530 (☎ **800/ 227-2384** or 510/527-8100), leads groups for kayaking in the Sea of Cortez.

Natural Habitat Adventures, 1696 F Ocean Dr., McKinleyville, CA 95521 (☎ **800/543-8917**), offers naturalist-led natural-history and adventure travel. Expeditions change every year, so call to find out if they are scheduling anything to Mexico.

Naturequest, 934 Acapulco St., Laguna Beach, CA 92651 (☎ **800/369-3033** or 714/499-9561), specializes in the natural history, culture, and wildlife of the Copper Canyon and the remote lagoons and waterways off Baja California. A 10-day hiking trip ventures into rugged areas of the Copper Canyon, but they offer a less strenuous trip to Creel and Batopilas in the same area. Baja trips get close to nature with special permits for venturing by two-person kayak into sanctuaries for whales and birds, slipping among mangroves and into shallow bays, estuaries, and lagoons.

One World Workforce, P.O. Box 3188, La Mesa, AZ 91944 (☎ **800/451-9564**), has "hands-on conservation trips" that offer working volunteers a chance to help with sea-turtle conservation at Bahía de Los Angeles, Baja (spring, summer, and fall), and along the Majahuas/Mismaloya beach 60 miles south of Puerto Vallarta (summer and fall). Overnight visits (2 days and 1 night) from Puerto Vallarta to the Majahuas reserve can also be arranged.

San Juan Kayak Expeditions, P.O. Box 2041, San Juan Harbor, WA 98250 (☎ **360/378-4436**), takes travelers kayaking between Loreto and Mulege from November through April.

Trek America, P.O. Box 189, Rockaway, NJ 07866 (☎ **800/221-0596** or 201/ 983-1144; fax 201/983-8551), organizes lengthy, active trips that combine trekking, hiking, van transportation, and camping in the Yucatán, Chiapas, Oaxaca, the Copper Canyon, and Mexico's Pacific coast, and touching on Mexico City and Guadalajara.

Veraventuras, Santos Degollado 81-8, 91000 Jalapa, Veracruz (☎ **28/18-9579,** or 01-800/712-6572 within Mexico; fax 28/18-9680), uses specially trained leaders on well-organized and outfitted adventures into the state of Veracruz, including rafting the rapids of the Antigua, Actopan, and Filo Bobos rivers.

Wildland Adventures, 3516 NE 155th St., Seattle, WA 98155 (☎ **800/ 345-4453**), offers an interesting mix of nature- and history-oriented tours in Mexico. They include the "Belize-Yucatán Adventure," which uses Rancho Encantado on Lake Bacalar as a base for forays into the Río Bec ruin route of the southern Yucatán Peninsula and Lamanai in nearby Belize. Trekking the Copper Canyon is a more rugged adventure, with options to stay in Batopilas, Chihuahua, or Los Mochis at the trip's end. There's also a trip to the Monarch Butterfly Refuge.

Zapotec Tours, 5121 N. Ravenswood, Suite B, Chicago, IL 60640 (☎ **800/ 44-OAXACA** outside Ill., or 773/506-2444), offers a variety of tours to Oaxaca City and the Oaxaca coast (including Puerto Escondido and Huatulco), and two specialty trips: Day of the Dead in Oaxaca, and the Food of the Gods Tour of Oaxaca. Coastal trips emphasize nature. Oaxaca City tours focus on the immediate area with visits to weavers, potters, and markets and archaeological sites. They are also the U.S. contact for several hotels in Oaxaca City and for the Oaxaca State route of Aerocaribe (serving the Oaxaca coast and Oaxaca City). Call them for information, but all reservations must be made through a travel agent.

4 Health, Safety & Insurance

STAYING HEALTHY

COMMON AILMENTS   Travelers to certain regions of Mexico occasionally experience **elevation sickness,** which results from the relative lack of oxygen and the decrease in barometric pressure that characterizes high elevations (over 5,000 ft./1,500m). Symptoms include shortness of breath, fatigue, headache, insomnia, and even nausea. Mexico City is at an elevation of more than 7,000 feet, as are a number of other central and southern Mexican cities, such as the Ixta-Popo Park outside Mexico City (13,000 ft.) and San Cristóbal de las Casas (more than 7,000 ft.). At high elevations it takes about 10 days to acquire the extra red blood corpuscles you need to adjust to the scarcity of oxygen.

Over-the-Counter Drugs in Mexico

Over-the-Counter Drugs: Antibiotics and other drugs that you'd need a prescription to buy in the States are sold over-the-counter in Mexican pharmacies. Mexican pharmacies also have common over-the-counter sinus and allergy remedies, although perhaps not the broad selection we're accustomed to finding easily.

Turista on the Toilet: What to Do if You Get Sick

It's called "travelers' diarrhea" or *turista,* the Spanish word for "tourist": the persistent diarrhea, often accompanied by fever, nausea, and vomiting, that used to attack many travelers to Mexico. Some in the United States call this "Montezuma's revenge," but you won't hear it referred to this way in Mexico. Widespread improvements in infrastructure, sanitation, and education have practically eliminated this ailment, especially in well-developed resort areas. Most travelers make a habit of drinking only bottled water, which also helps to protect against unfamiliar bacteria. In resort areas, and generally throughout Mexico, only purified ice is used. Doctors say it's not caused by just one "bug," but by a combination of consuming different foods and water, upsetting your schedule, being overtired, and experiencing the stresses of travel. A good high-potency (or "therapeutic") vitamin supplement, and even extra vitamin C, is a help; yogurt is good for healthy digestion. If you do happen to come down with this ailment, nothing beats Pepto Bismol, readily available in Mexico.

How to Prevent It: The U.S. Public Health Service recommends the following measures for preventing travelers' diarrhea:

- *Drink only purified water.* This means tea, coffee, and other beverages made with boiled water; canned or bottled carbonated beverages and water; or beer and wine. Most restaurants with a large tourist clientele use only purified water and ice.
- *Choose food carefully.* In general, avoid salads, uncooked vegetables, and unpasteurized milk or milk products (including cheese). However, salads in a first-class restaurant, or one serving a lot of tourists, are generally safe to eat. Choose food that is freshly cooked and still hot. Peelable fruit is ideal. Don't eat undercooked meat, fish, or shellfish.

In addition, something so simple as clean hands can go a long way toward preventing *turista.*

Since **dehydration** can quickly become life-threatening, the Public Health Service advises that you be especially careful to replace fluids and electrolytes (potassium, sodium, and the like) during a bout of diarrhea. Do this by drinking Pedialyte, a rehydration solution available at most Mexican pharmacies, or glasses of natural fruit juice (high in potassium) with a pinch of salt added, or you can also try a glass of boiled pure water with a quarter teaspoon of sodium bicarbonate (baking soda) added.

Take it easy for the first few days after you arrive at a high elevation. Drink extra fluids but avoid alcohol. If you have heart or lung problems, talk to your doctor before going above 8,000 feet.

Mosquitoes and **gnats** are prevalent along the coast and in the Yucatán lowlands. Insect repellent (*repelente contra insectos*) is a must, and it's not always available in Mexico. If you'll be in these areas, and are prone to bites, bring a repellent along that contains the active ingredient DEET. Avon's "Skin So Soft" also works extremely well. If you're sensitive to bites, pick up some antihistamine cream from a drugstore at home.

Most readers won't ever see a scorpion (*alacrán*). But if you're stung, go immediately to a doctor.

MORE SERIOUS DISEASES   You shouldn't be overly concerned about tropical diseases if you stay on the normal tourist routes and don't eat street food. However, both dengue fever and cholera have appeared in Mexico in recent years. Talk to your doctor, or a medical specialist in tropical diseases, about any precautions you should take. You can also get medical bulletins from the U.S. State Department and the Centers for Disease Control (see "Sources of Information," above). You can protect yourself by taking some simple precautions. Watch what you eat and drink; don't swim in stagnant water (ponds, slow-moving rivers, or wells); and avoid mosquito bites by covering up, using repellent, and sleeping under mosquito netting. The most dangerous areas seem to be on Mexico's west coast, away from the big resorts (which are relatively safe).

EMERGENCY EVACUATION   For extreme medical emergencies, there's a service from the United States that will fly people to American hospitals: **Air-Evac,** a 24-hour air ambulance (☎ **800/854-2569,** or call collect 510/293-5968). You can also contact the service in Guadalajara (☎ **01-800/305-9400** or 3/616-9616 or 3/615-2471).

SAFETY

I have lived and traveled in Mexico for over 8 years, have never had any serious trouble, and rarely feel suspicious of anyone or any situation. You will probably feel physically safer in most Mexican cities and villages than in any comparable place at home. See "Crime, Bribes & Scams," and "Sources of Information," above, for more information and how to access the latest **U.S. State Department advisories.** They urge travelers to contact them for security information before traveling to Chiapas. And they caution travelers *not to use* any roaming VW Beetle taxis in Mexico City and to use only radio-dispatched taxis or taxis at a *sitio* from your hotel. See also "Crime, Bribes & Scams," earlier in this chapter.

INSURANCE

HEALTH/ACCIDENT/LOSS   Even the most careful of us can still experience a traveler's nightmare: You discover you've lost your wallet, your passport, your airline ticket, or your tourist permit. Always keep a photocopy of these documents in your luggage—it makes replacing them easier. To be reimbursed for insured items once you return, you'll need to report the loss to the Mexican police and get a written report. If you don't speak Spanish, take along someone who does. If you lose official documents, you'll need to contact both Mexican and U.S. officials in Mexico before you leave the country.

   Health Care Abroad, Wallach and Co. Inc., 107 W. Federal St. (P.O. Box 480), Middleburg, VA 22117 (☎ **800/237-6615** or 540/687-3166), and **World Access,** 6600 W. Broad St., Richmond, VA 23230 (☎ **800/628-4908** or 804/285-3300), offer medical and accident insurance as well as coverage for luggage loss and trip cancellation. Always read the fine print on the policy to be sure that you're getting the coverage you want.

5 Tips for Travelers with Special Needs

FOR FAMILIES   Children are considered the national treasure of Mexico, and Mexicans will warmly welcome and cater to your children. Hotels can often arrange for a baby-sitter. Some hotels in the moderate-to-luxury range have small playgrounds and pools for children and hire caretakers with special activity programs during the day. Few budget hotels offer these amenities.

Before leaving, you should check with your doctor to get advice on medications to take along. Disposable diapers cost about the same in Mexico but are of poorer quality. You can get Huggies Supreme and Pampers identical to the ones sold in the United States, but at a higher price. Gerber's baby foods are sold in many stores. Dry cereals, powdered formulas, baby bottles, and purified water are all easily available in midsize and large cities.

Cribs, however, may present a problem. Only the largest and most luxurious hotels provide cribs. However, rollaway beds to accommodate children staying in the room with parents are often available. Child seats or high chairs at restaurants are common, and most restaurants will go out of their way to accommodate the comfort of your child.

FOR GAY & LESBIAN TRAVELERS   Mexico is a conservative country, with deeply rooted Catholic religious traditions. As such, public displays of same-sex affection are rare and still considered shocking, for men especially. Women in Mexico frequently walk hand in hand, but anything more would cross the boundary of acceptability. However, gay and lesbian travelers are generally treated with respect and should not experience any harassment, assuming the appropriate regard is given to local culture and customs. Puerto Vallarta is perhaps the most welcoming and accepting destination in Mexico, with a selection of accommodations and entertainment oriented especially for gay and lesbian travelers.

The International Gay and Lesbian Association (☎ 506/234-2411) can provide helpful information and additional tips.

FOR PEOPLE WITH DISABILITIES   Mexico may seem like one giant obstacle course to travelers in wheelchairs or on crutches. At airports, you may encounter steep stairs before finding a well-hidden elevator or escalator—if one exists. Airlines will often arrange wheelchair assistance for passengers to the baggage area. Porters are generally available to help with luggage at airports and large bus stations, once you've cleared baggage claim.

In addition, escalators (there aren't many in the country) are often out of operation. Few rest rooms are equipped for travelers with disabilities, or when one is available, access to it may be via a narrow passage that won't accommodate a wheelchair or someone on crutches. Many deluxe hotels (the most expensive) now have rooms with baths for people with disabilities. Those traveling on a budget should stick with one-story hotels or those with elevators. Even so, there will probably still be obstacles somewhere. Stairs without handrails abound in Mexico. Generally speaking, no matter where you are, someone will lend a hand, although you may have to ask for it.

Few airports offer the luxury of boarding an airplane from the waiting room. You either descend stairs to a bus that ferries you to the waiting plane that's boarded by climbing stairs, or you walk across the airport tarmac to your plane and ascend the stairs. Deplaning presents the same problem in reverse.

FOR SENIORS   Mexico is a popular country for retirees. For decades, North Americans have been living indefinitely in Mexico by returning to the border and recrossing with a new tourist permit every 6 months.

Some of the most popular places for long-term stays are Guadalajara, Lake Chapala, Ajijic, and Puerto Vallarta—all in the state of Jalisco; San Miguel de Allende and Guanajuato in the state of Guanajuato; Cuernavaca and Morelos; Alamos and Sinaloa; and to a lesser extent Manzanillo, Colima, and Morelia in Michoacán. Crowds don't necessarily mean there are no other good places: Oaxaca, Querétaro, Puebla, Guanajuato, Tepoztlán, and Valle de Bravo have much to offer, even though Americans have yet to collect there in large numbers.

The following newsletter is written for prospective retirees: *AIM,* Apdo. Postal 31–70, 45050 Guadalajara, Jalisco, Mexico, is a well-written, candid, and very informative newsletter on retirement in Mexico. Recent issues evaluated retirement in Aguascalientes, Puebla, San Cristóbal de las Casas, Puerto Ángel, Puerto Escondido and Huatulco, Oaxaca, Taxco, Tepic, Manzanillo, Melaque, and Barra de Navidad. Subscriptions cost $18 to the United States and $21 to Canada. Back issues are three for $5.

Sanborn Tours, 1007 Main St., Bastrop, TX 78602 (☎ **800/395-8482**), offers a "Retire in Mexico" Guadalajara orientation tour. American Express, Discover, Master-Card, and Visa are accepted.

FOR SINGLES Mexico may be an old favorite for romantic honeymoons, but it's also a great place to travel on your own without really being or feeling alone. Although offering an identical room rate regardless of single or double occupancy is slowly becoming a trend in Mexico, many of the hotels mentioned in this book still offer singles at lower rates.

Mexicans are very friendly, and it's easy to meet other foreigners. But if you don't like the idea of traveling alone, then try **Travel Companion Exchange,** P.O. Box 833, Amityville, NY 11701 (☎ **800/392-1256** or 516/454-0880; fax 516/454-0170), which brings prospective travelers together. Members complete a profile, then place an anonymous listing of their travel interests in the newsletter. Prospective traveling companions then make contact through the exchange. Membership costs $99 for 6 months or $159 for a year. They also offer an excellent booklet on avoiding theft and scams while traveling abroad, for $3.95. Order through the same number listed above.

For Women As a female traveling alone, I can tell you firsthand that I feel safer traveling in Mexico than in the United States. But I use the same commonsense precautions I use traveling anywhere else in the world and am alert to what's going on around me.

Mexicans in general, and men in particular, are nosy about single travelers, especially women. If taxi drivers or anyone else with whom you don't want to become friendly asks about your marital status, family, etc., my advice is to make up a set of answers (regardless of the truth): "I'm married, traveling with friends, and I have three children."

Saying you are single and traveling alone may send out the wrong message about availability. Movies and television shows exported from the United States have created an image of sexually aggressive North American women. If bothered by someone, don't try to be polite—just leave or head into a public place.

FOR STUDENTS Because higher education is still considered more of a luxury than a birth right in Mexico, a formal network of student discounts and programs does not exist in this country. Also, most students within the country travel with their families, rather than with other students—thus student discount cards are not commonly recognized here.

For those wishing to study in Mexico, however, there are a number of university-affiliated and independent programs geared for intensive Spanish-language study. Frequently, these will also assist with accommodations, usually living with a local family in their home. One such program is **KABAH Travel and Education Tourism,** based in Guadalajara, which offers study and travel programs throughout the country. You can get faxed information at: **800/596-4768.** More information is available at their Web site: **http://mexplaza.com.mx/kabah/.**

The **Council on International Educational Exchange (CIEE),** 205 E. 42nd St. New York, NY 10017 (☎ **212/661-1414** or 212/661-1450), can assist students interested in a working vacation in Mexico. They also issue official student identity cards and have offices across the United States.

6 Getting There

BY PLANE

The airline situation in Mexico is changing rapidly, with many new regional carriers offering scheduled service to areas previously not served. In addition to regularly scheduled service, charter service direct from U.S. cities to resorts is making Mexico more accessible.

THE MAJOR INTERNATIONAL AIRLINES The main airlines operating direct or nonstop flights from the United States to points in Mexico include **Aerocalifornia** (☎ 800/237-6225), **Aeromexico** (☎ 800/237-6639), **Air France** (☎ 800/ 237-2747), **Alaska Airlines** (☎ 800/426-0333), **America West** (☎ 800/235-9292), **American** (☎ 800/433-7300), **Aspen Mountain Airlines** (☎ **800/877-3932**), **Continental** (☎ 800/231-0856), **Lacsa** (☎ 800/225-2272), **Mexicana** (☎ 800/ 531-7921), **Northwest** (☎ 800/225-2525), **United** (☎ 800/241-6522), and **US Airways** (☎ 800/428-4322). **Southwest Airlines** (☎ 800/435-9792) serves the U.S. border.

The main departure points in North America for international airlines are Atlanta, Chicago, Dallas/Fort Worth, Denver, Houston, Los Angeles, Miami, New Orleans,

---

Take a Luxury Bus Direct to Your Destination from the Mexico City Airport

This new airport-to-destination service takes the hassle out of travel to a number of the most alluring cities in central Mexico. Buses serving these routes are deluxe, air-conditioned, and have video movies and a rest room. In most cases there's complimentary soft-drink service.

If you're going to **Puebla,** Estrella Roja and Pullman Plus buses depart from the airport hourly (beginning at 6 or 7:30am), from in front of the airport at the Sala (gate) D exit.

If your destination is **Cuernavaca,** Suburban takes up to seven passengers in a (guess what) Suburban, leaving approximately every 2 hours between 6am and 9pm daily. It's affiliated with the Pullman de Morelos bus line. The Suburban ticket kiosk is near Sala A. Pullman de Morelos also runs almost-hourly buses from the airport to Cuernavaca.

Estrella Roja/Flecha Amarillo and **TMT Caminante** buses (☎ 5/277-2746, or 5/271-1433 in Mexico City) also go to **Toluca** and **Querétaro** with schedules similar to that of Puebla. This is the bus to take if your destination is **San Miguel de Allende;** from Querétaro you take one of the frequent buses to San Miguel.

Buses for all of these lines are found in front of the covered concourse outside the terminal between exit doors for Gates C and D. If you have trouble locating any of these, ask for help at one of the information desks on the airport's main concourse. Most importantly, since this airport bus transportation service is new and could change, and/or if precise scheduling is essential to your trip, you might want to call the **Airport Information Office** (☎ 5/728-4811 or 5/571-3600) to verify names of buses, the place to find them, and current schedules.

CyberDeals for Net Surfers

A great way to find the cheapest fare is by using the Internet to do your searching for you. There are too many companies to mention them all, but a few of the better-respected ones are **Travelocity** (**www.travelocity.com**), **Microsoft Expedia** (**www.expedia.com**), and **Yahoo's Flifo Global** (**travel.yahoo.com/travel**). Each has its own little quirks—Travelocity, for example, requires you to register with them—but they all provide variations of the same service. Just enter the dates you want to fly and the cities you want to visit, and the computer looks for the lowest fares. The Yahoo site has a feature called "Fare Beater," which will check flights on other airlines or at different times or dates in hopes of finding an even cheaper fare. Expedia's site will E-mail you the best airfare deal once a week if you so choose. Travelocity uses the SABRE computer reservations system that most travel agents use, and has a "Last Minute Deals" database that advertises really cheap fares for those who can get away at a moment's notice.

Great last-minute deals are also available directly from the airlines themselves through a free E-mail service called **E-savers.** Each week, the airline sends you a list of discounted flights, usually leaving the upcoming Friday or Saturday, and returning the following Monday or Tuesday. You can sign up for all the major airlines at once by logging on to **Epicurious Travel** (**travel.epicurious.com/travel/c_planning/02_airfares/email/signup.html**), or go to each individual airline's Web site:

- **American Airlines:** www.americanair.com
- **Continental Airlines:** www.flycontinental.com
- **Northwest Airlines:** www.nwa.com
- **US Airways:** www.usairways.com
- **Aeromexico**: www.aeromexico.com
- **Mexicana:** www.mexicana.com
- **America West:** www.americawest.com
- **Alaska Airlines:** www.alaskaair.com

One caveat: Charter airfares and those offered through wholesalers (like Apple Vacations, Funjet, etc.) are generally not included in these on-line services, meaning you still may want to check with a travel agent to ensure you have the best all-around package price.

New York, Orlando, Philadelphia, Raleigh/Durham, San Antonio, San Francisco, Seattle, Toronto, Tucson, and Washington, D.C.

BY CAR

Driving is not the cheapest way to get to Mexico, but it is the best way to see the country. Even so, you may think twice about taking your own car south of the border once you've pondered the many bureaucratic requirements that affect foreign drivers here. One option would be to rent a car, for touring around a specific region, once you arrive in Mexico. Rental cars in Mexico are now generally new, clean, and very well maintained. Although pricier than in the United States, discounts are often available for rentals of a week or longer, especially when arrangements are made in advance from the United States. (See "Car Rentals," below, for more details).

Carrying Car Documents

You must carry your temporary car-importation permit, tourist permit (see "Entry Requirements," above), and, if you purchased it, your proof of Mexican car insurance (see below) in the car at all times. The temporary car-importation permit papers will be issued for 6 months and the tourist permit is usually issued for 180 days, but they might stamp it for half that, or even 30 days, so state your preference *before* the official stamps your papers. It's a good idea also to overestimate the time you'll spend in Mexico, so that if something unforeseen happens and you have to (or want to) stay longer, you'll have avoided the long hassle of getting your papers renewed. Whatever you do, don't overstay either permit. Doing so invites heavy fines and/or confiscation of your vehicle, which will not be returned. Remember also that 6 months does not necessarily work out to be 180 days— be sure that you return before whichever expiration date comes first.

If, after reading the section that follows, you have any additional questions or you want to confirm the current rules, call your nearest Mexican consulate, Mexican Government Tourist Office, AAA, or **Sanborn's** (☎ **800/395-8482**). To check on road conditions or to get help with any travel emergency while in Mexico, call ☎ **01800/903-9200,** or 5/250-0151 in Mexico City. Both numbers are staffed by English-speaking operators.

In addition, check with the **U.S. State Department** (see "Sources of Information," at the beginning of this chapter) for their warnings about dangerous driving areas.

CAR DOCUMENTS   To drive your car into Mexico, you'll need a **temporary car-importation permit,** which is granted after you complete a long and strictly required list of documents (see below). The permit can be obtained either through Banco del Ejército (*Banjercito*) officials, who have a desk, booth, or office at the Mexican Customs (*Aduana*) building after you cross the border into Mexico. Or, you can obtain the permit before you travel through Sanborn's Insurance or the American Automobile Association (AAA), each of which maintains border offices in Texas, New Mexico, Arizona, and California. These companies may charge a fee for this service, but it will be worth it to avoid the uncertain prospect of traveling all the way to the border without proper documents for crossing. However, even if you go through Sanborn's or AAA, your credentials *may* be reviewed again by Mexican officials at the border—you must take them all with you since they are still subject to questions of validity.

The following requirements for border crossing were accurate at press time:

- *A valid driver's license,* issued outside of Mexico.
- *Current, original car registration and a copy of the original car title.* If the registration or title is in more than one name and not all the named people are traveling with you, then a notarized letter from the absent person(s) authorizing use of the vehicle for the trip is required; have it ready just in case. The car registration and your credit card (see below) must be in the same name.
- *A valid international major credit card.* Using only your credit card, you are required to pay a $12 car-importation fee. The credit card must be in the same name as the car registration.
- *A signed declaration promising to return to your country of origin with the vehicle.* This form is provided by AAA or Sanborn's before you go or by Banjercito officials at the border. There's no charge. The form does not stipulate that you return through the same border entry you came through on your way south.

If you receive your documentation at the border (rather than through Sanborn's or AAA), Mexican border officials will make two copies of everything and charge you for the copies.

Important reminder: Someone else may drive the car, but the person (or relative of the person) whose name appears on the car-importation permit must *always* be in the car at the same time. (If stopped by police, a nonregistered family member driver driving without the registered driver, must be prepared to prove familial relationship to the registered driver—no joke.) Violation of this rule makes the car subject to impoundment and the driver to imprisonment and/or a fine. You can only drive a car with foreign license plates if you have an international (non-Mexican) driver's license.

MEXICAN AUTO INSURANCE   Auto insurance is not legally required in Mexico. U.S. insurance is invalid in Mexico; to be insured in Mexico, you must purchase Mexican insurance. Any party involved in an accident who has no insurance is automatically sent to jail and his or her car is impounded until all claims are settled. This is true even if you just drive across the border to spend the day, and it may be true even if you're injured.

Car insurance can be purchased through **Sanborn's Mexico Insurance,** P.O. Box 310, Dept. FR, 2009 S. 10th, McAllen, TX 78505-0310 (☎ **210/686-0711;** fax 210/686-0732 in Tex. or 800/222-0158 elsewhere in the U.S.). The company has offices at all of the border crossings in the United States. Its policies cost the same as the competition's do, but you get legal coverage (attorney and bail bonds if needed) and a detailed mile-by-mile guide for your proposed route. Most of Sanborn's border offices are open Monday through Friday, and a few are staffed on Saturday and Sunday. **AAA** auto club also sells insurance.

RETURNING TO THE UNITED STATES WITH YOUR CAR   The car papers you obtained when you entered Mexico *must* be returned when you cross back with your car or at some point within the time limit of 180 days. (You can cross as many times as you wish within the 180 days.) If the documents aren't returned, heavy fines are imposed ($250 for each 15 days late), and your car may be impounded and confiscated or you may be jailed if you return to Mexico. You can only return the car documents to a Banjercito official on duty at the Mexican Customs (*Aduana*) building *before* you cross back into the United States. Some border cities have Banjercito officials on duty 24 hours a day, but others do not; some also do not have Sunday hours. On the U.S. side, customs agents may or may not inspect your car from stem to stern.

BY SHIP

Numerous cruise lines serve Mexico. Possible trips might cruise from California down to the Baja Peninsula (including specialized whale-watching trips) and ports of call on the Pacific Coast or from Houston or Miami to the Caribbean (which often includes stops in Cancún, Playa del Carmen, and Cozumel). If you don't mind taking off at the last minute, several cruise-tour specialists arrange substantial discounts on unsold cabins. One such company is **The Cruise Line,** 4770 Biscayne Blvd., Penthouse 1–3, Miami, FL 33137 (☎ **800/777-0707,** 800/327-3021, or 305/576-0036).

BY BUS

Greyhound-Trailways (or its affiliates) offers service from around the United States to the Mexican border, where passengers disembark, cross the border, and buy a ticket for travel into the interior of Mexico. At many border crossings there are scheduled buses from the U.S. bus station to the Mexican bus station.

7 The Pros & Cons of Package Tours

Say the word "package tour" and many people automatically feel as though they're being forced to choose: your money or your lifestyle. This isn't necessarily the case. Most Mexican packages let you have both your independence *and* your in-the-black bank-account balance. Package tours are not the same thing as escorted tours. They are simply a way of buying your airfare, accommodations, and other pieces of your trip (usually airport transfers, and sometimes meals and activities) at the same time.

For popular destinations like Mexico they're often the smart way to go, because they can save you a ton of money. In many cases, a package that includes airfare, hotel, and transportation to and from the airport will cost you less than just the hotel alone if you booked it yourself. That's because packages are sold in bulk to tour operators, who resell them to the public.

You can buy a package at any time of the year, but the best deals usually coincide with low season—May to early December—when room rates and airfares plunge. But packages vary widely. Some offer a better class of hotels than others. Some offer the same hotels for lower prices. Some offer flights on scheduled airlines while others book charters. In some packages, your choices of accommodations and travel days may be limited. Each destination usually has some packagers that are better than the rest because they buy in even bigger bulk. Not only can that mean better prices, but it can also mean more choices—a packager that just dabbles in Mexico may only have a half-dozen or so hotels for you to choose from, while a packager that focuses much of its energy on south-of-the-border vacations may have dozens of hotels for you to choose from, with a good selection in every price range.

WARNINGS

- **Read the fine print.** Make sure you know *exactly* what's included in the price you're being quoted, and what's not.
- **Don't compare Mayas and Aztecs.** When you're looking over different packagers, compare the deals that they're offering on similar properties. Most packagers can offer bigger savings on some hotels than others.
- **Know what you're getting yourself into—and if you can get yourself out of it.** Before you commit to a package, make sure you know how much flexibility you have.
- **Use your best judgment.** Stay away from fly-by-nights and shady packagers. Go with a reputable firm with a proven track record. This is where your travel agent can come in handy.

WHERE TO BROWSE

- For one-stop shopping on the Web, go to **www.vacationpackager.com,** an extensive search engine that'll link you up with more than 30 packagers offering Mexican beach vacations—and even let you custom design your own package.
- Check out **www.2travel.com** and find a page with links to a number of the big-name Mexico packagers, including several of the ones listed here.

PACKAGERS PACKIN' A PUNCH

- **Aeromexico Vacations** (☎ 800/245-8585; www.aeromexico.com): Year-round packages for Acapulco, Cancún, Cozumel, Ixtapa/Zihuatanejo, Los Cabos, and Puerto Vallarta. Aeromexico has a large selection of resorts in these destinations (39 in Cancún, 11 in Cozumel, 12 in Ixtapa/Zihuatanejo, 14 in Los Cabos, 21 in

Puerto Vallarta) in a variety of price ranges. The best deals are from Houston, Dallas, San Diego, Los Angeles, Miami, and New York, in that order. Aeromexico's **Sun-Brero** packages give you 3 nights in Mexico City and your choice of 4 nights in Acapulco, Cancún, Puerto Vallarta, or Ixtapa/Zihuatanejo plus a half-day city tour of Mexico's major city. You get to choose the hotel category—standard, superior, and deluxe—but have no options within those parameters.

- **American Airlines Vacations** (☎ 800/321-2121; www.americanair.com): American has seasonal packages to Acapulco and year-round deals for Cancún, Cozumel, Los Cabos, and Puerto Vallarta. You don't have to fly with American if you can get a better deal on another airline; land-only packages include hotel, airport transfers, and hotel room tax. American's hubs to Mexico are Dallas/Fort Worth, Chicago, and Miami, so you're likely to get the best prices—and the most direct flights—if you live near those cities.

- **Apple Vacations** (☎ 800/365-2775): Apple offers inclusive packages to all the beach resorts, and has the largest choice of hotels: 16 in Acapulco, 48 in Cancún, 17 in Cozumel, 13 in Ixtapa, 14 in Los Cabos, 6 in Manzanillo, 12 in Mazatlán, and 31 in Puerto Vallarta. Scheduled carriers booked for the air portion include American, United, Mexicana, Delta, TWA, US Airways, Reno Air, Alaska Airlines, AeroCalifornia, and Aeromexico. Apple perks include baggage handling and the services of an Apple representative at the major hotels.

- **Continental Vacations** (☎ 800/634-5555; www.flycontinental.com): With Continental, you've got to buy air from the carrier if you want to book a room. The airline has year-round packages available to Cancún, Cozumel, Puerto Vallarta, Cabo San Lucas, Acapulco, Ixtapa, and Mazatlán, and the best deals are from Houston; Newark, New Jersey; and Cleveland.

- **Friendly Holidays** (☎ 800/344-5687; www.2travel.com/friendly/mexico.html): This major player in the Mexico field is based in upstate New York, but also has offices in California and Houston, so they've got their bases covered. They offer trips to all the resorts: Los Cabos, Mazatlán, Puerto Vallarta, Ixtapa, Manzanillo, Cancún, Cozumel, and Acapulco. Although they don't have the largest variety of hotels from which to choose, the ones they work with are high quality. In addition, their Web site is very user-friendly, listing both a starting price for 3 nights' hotel room and a figure for air add-ons, so at least you have a rough idea of what your trip is likely to cost you.

- **Funjet Vacations** (bookable through travel agents or on-line at **www.funjet.com**): One of the largest vacation packagers in the United States, Funjet has packages to Cancún, Cozumel, Los Cabos, Mazatlán, Ixtapa, and Puerto Vallarta. You can choose a charter or fly on American, Continental, Delta, Aeromexico, US Airways, Alaska Air, TWA, or United.

GOING WITH THE AIRLINES

Alaska Airlines Vacations (☎ 800-396-4371; www.alaskair.com) sells packages to Los Cabos, Puerto Vallarta, and, in high season, to Ixtapa/Zihuatanejo. Alaska flies direct to Mexico from Los Angeles, San Diego, San Jose, San Francisco, Seattle, Vancouver, Anchorage, and Fairbanks.

America West Vacations (☎ 800-356-6611; www.americawest.com) has deals to Mazatlán, Manzanillo, Los Cabos, and Puerto Vallarta, mostly from its Phoenix gateway.

Delta Vacations (☎ 800/872-7786; www.delta-air.com) has year-round packages to Acapulco, Cancún, Cozumel, and Ixtapa/Zihuatanejo. Atlanta is the hub, so expect the best prices from there.

Mexicana Vacations (or MexSeaSun Vacations) (☎ 800/531-9321; www. mexicana.com) offers getaways to all the resorts except Manzanillo, buttressed by Mexicana's daily direct flights from Los Angeles to Los Cabos, Mazatlán, Cancún, Puerto Vallarta, and Ixtapa/Zihuatanejo.

TWA Vacations (☎ 800/438-292; www.twa.com) runs seasonal deals to Puerto Vallarta and year-round packages to Cancún.

US Airways Vacations (☎ 800/455-0123; www.usairways.com) features Cancún in its year-round Mexico packages, departing from most major U.S. cities.

REGIONAL PACKAGERS
From the East Coast: Liberty Travel (lots of offices but no central number) frequently runs Mexico specials. Here, the best bet is to check the ads in your Sunday travel section or go to a Liberty rep near you.

From the West Coast: Sunquest Holidays (☎ 800/357-2400 or 888/888-5028 for departures within 14 days) is one of the largest packagers for Mexico on the West Coast, arranging regular charters to Cancún, Cozumel, Los Cabos, and Puerto Vallarta from Los Angeles paired with a large selection of hotels.

From the Southwest: Town and Country (bookable through travel agents) packages regular deals to Los Cabos, Mazatlán, Puerto Vallarta, Ixtapa, Manzanillo, Cancún, Cozumel, and Acapulco with America West from the airline's Phoenix and Las Vegas gateways.

Resorts The biggest hotel chains and resorts also sell packages. The Mexican-owned Fiesta Americana/Fiesta Inns, for example, run **Fiesta Break** deals that include airfare from New York, Los Angeles, Dallas, or Houston, airport transfers, optional meal plans, and more. In 1998, a high-season Fiesta Break package from Dallas to Cozumel cost $677 per person, including airfare, transfers, and 3 nights' room in the Fiesta Americana Cozumel Reef. Call ☎ 800-9-BREAK for details.

8 Getting Around

An important note: If your travel schedule depends on an important connection, say a plane trip between points, or a ferry or bus connection, use the telephone numbers in this book or other information resources mentioned here to find out if the connection you are depending on is still available. Although we've done our best to provide accurate information, transportation schedules can and do change.

BY PLANE
To fly from point to point within Mexico, you'll rely on Mexican airlines. Mexico has two privately owned large national carriers: **Mexicana** (☎ 800/531-7921) and **Aeromexico** (☎ 800/237-6639), in addition to several up-and-coming regional carriers. Mexicana and Aeromexico both offer extensive connections to the United States as well as within Mexico.

Several of the new regional carriers are operated by or can be booked through Mexicana or Aeromexico. Regional carriers are **Aero Cancún** (see Mexicana); **Aerocaribe** (see Mexicana); **Aerolitoral** (see Aeromexico); and **Aero Monterrey** (see Mexicana). For points inside the state of Oaxaca only—Oaxaca City, Puerto Escondido, and Puerto Ángel—contact **Zapotec Tours** (☎ 800/44-OAXACA, or 773/506-2444 in Ill.). The regional carriers are expensive, but they go to difficult-to-reach places. In each applicable section of this book, we've mentioned regional carriers with all pertinent telephone numbers.

Because major airlines can book some regional carriers, read your ticket carefully to see if your connecting flight is on one of these smaller carriers—they may leave from a different airport or check in at a different counter.

AIRPORT TAXES Mexico charges an airport tax on all departures. Passengers leaving the country on an international departure pay $12—in dollars or the peso equivalent. It has become a common practice to include this departure tax in your ticket price, but double-check to make sure so you're not caught by surprise at the airport upon leaving. Taxes on each domestic departure you make within Mexico cost around $8, unless you're on a connecting flight and have already paid at the start of the flight; you shouldn't be charged again if you have to change planes for a connecting flight. These taxes are usually included in the price of your ticket.

RECONFIRMING FLIGHTS Although airlines in Mexico say it's not necessary to reconfirm a flight, it's still a good practice. To avoid getting bumped on popular, possibly overbooked flights, check in for an international flight the required hour and a half in advance of travel.

BY CAR

Most Mexican roads are not up to U.S. standards of smoothness, hardness, width of curve, grade of hill, or safety marking. Driving at night is dangerous—the roads aren't good enough and are rarely lit; the trucks, carts, pedestrians, and bicycles usually have no lights; and you can hit potholes, animals, rocks, dead ends, or bridges out with no warning.

The "spirited" style of Mexican driving sometimes requires super vision and reflexes. Be prepared for new procedures, as when a truck driver flips on his left-turn signal when there's not a crossroad for miles. He's probably telling you the road's clear ahead for you to pass—after all, he's in a better position to see than you are. Another custom that's very important to respect is how to make a left turn. Never turn left by stopping in the middle of a highway with your left signal on. Instead, pull off the highway onto the right shoulder, wait for traffic to clear, then proceed across the road.

GASOLINE There's one government-owned brand of gas and one gasoline station name throughout the country—**Pemex** (Petroleras Mexicanas). There are three types of gas in Mexico: *nova,* an 82-octane leaded gas; *magna sin,* an 87-octane unleaded gas (slowly disappearing from the market); and the newer premium 92-octane. In Mexico, fuel and oil are sold by the liter, which is slightly more than a quart (40 liters equals about 10½ gal.). *Important note:* No credit cards are accepted for gas purchases.

TOLL ROADS Mexico charges among the highest tolls in the world for its network of new toll roads. As a result, they are little used. Generally speaking, using the toll roads will cut your travel time between destinations. Older toll-free roads are generally in good condition but travel times tend to be longer, since they tend to be mountainous and clotted with slow-moving trucks.

BREAKDOWNS Your best guide to repair shops is the Yellow Pages. For specific makes and shops that repair cars, look under "Automoviles y Camiones: Talleres de Reparación y Servicio"; auto-parts stores are listed under "Refacciones y Accesorios para Automoviles." To find a mechanic on the road, look for a sign that says TALLER MECÁNICO.

If your car breaks down on the road, help might already be on the way. Radio-equipped green repair trucks operated by uniformed English-speaking officers patrol the major highways during daylight hours to aid motorists in trouble. These **"Green Angels"** will perform minor repairs and adjustments for free, but you pay for parts and materials.

MINOR ACCIDENTS When possible, many Mexicans drive away from minor accidents to avoid hassles with police. If the police arrive while the involved persons are still at the scene, everyone may be locked in jail until blame is assessed. In any case, you have to settle up immediately, which may take days of red tape. Foreigners who don't speak fluent Spanish are at a distinct disadvantage when trying to explain their side of the event. Three steps may help the foreigner who doesn't wish to do as the Mexicans do: If you're in your own car, notify your Mexican insurance company, whose job it is to intervene on your behalf. If you're in a rental car, notify the rental company immediately and ask how to contact the nearest adjuster. (You did buy insurance with the rental, right?) Finally, if all else fails, ask to contact the nearest Green Angel, who may be able to explain to officials that you are covered by insurance.

See also "Mexican Auto Insurance" in "Getting There," above.

CAR RENTALS You'll get the best price if you reserve a car a week in advance in the United States. U.S. car-rental firms include **Avis** (☎ **800/331-1212** in the U.S., 800/TRY-AVIS in Canada), **Budget** (☎ **800/527-0700** in the U.S. and Canada), **Hertz** (☎ **800/654-3131** in the U.S. and Canada), and **National** (☎ **800/ CAR-RENT** in the U.S. and Canada). For European travelers, **Kemwel Holiday Auto** (☎ **800/678-0678**) and **Auto Europe** (☎ **800/223-5555**) can arrange Mexican rentals, sometimes through other agencies. These and some local firms have offices in Mexico City and most other large Mexican cities. You'll find rental desks at airports, all major hotels, and many travel agencies.

Cars are easy to rent if you have a major credit card, are 25 or over, and have a valid driver's license and passport with you. Without a credit card you must leave a cash deposit, usually a big one. Rent-here/leave-there arrangements are usually simple to make but more costly.

Car-rental costs are high in Mexico, because cars are more expensive here. The condition of rental cars has improved greatly over the years, however, and clean, comfortable, new cars are the norm. The basic cost of a 1-day rental of a Volkswagen Beetle, with unlimited mileage (but before 17% tax and $15 daily insurance), was $44 in Cancún, $48 in Mexico City, $40 in Puerto Vallarta, $48 in Oaxaca, and $27 in Mérida. Renting by the week gives you a lower daily rate. Avis was offering a basic 7-day weekly rate for a VW Beetle (before tax or insurance) of $190 in Cancún and Puerto Vallarta, $160 in Mérida, and $225 in Mexico City. Prices may be considerably higher if you rent in these same cities around a major holiday.

Car-rental companies usually write up a credit-card charge in U.S. dollars.

Deductibles Be careful—these vary greatly in Mexico; some are as high as $2,500, which comes out of your pocket immediately in case of car damage. Hertz's deductible is $1,000 on a VW Beetle; Avis's is $500 for the same car.

Insurance Insurance is offered in two parts: **Collision and damage** insurance covers your car and others if the accident is your fault, and **personal accident** insurance covers you and anyone in your car. Read the fine print on the back of your rental agreement and note that insurance may be invalid if you have an accident while driving on an unpaved road.

Travel Tip

There's little English spoken at bus stations, so come prepared with your destination written down, then double-check the departure.

Bus Hijackings

The U.S. State Department notes that bandits target long-distance buses traveling at night, but there have been daylight robberies as well. This is especially true on Highway 200 south from Acapulco to Huatulco. Avoid this route if at all possible.

Damage Always inspect your car carefully and note every damaged or missing item, no matter how minute, on your rental agreement, or you may be charged.

Trouble Number It's advisable to carefully note both the rental company's trouble number, as well as the direct number of the agency where you rented the car.

BY TAXI

Taxis are the preferred way to get around in almost all of the resort areas of Mexico, and also around Mexico City. Short trips within towns are generally charged by preset zones, and are quite reasonable compared with U.S. rates. Los Cabos would be an exception because of the higher price of taxi service and the distance between Cabo San Lucas and San José del Cabo. For longer trips, or excursions to nearby cities, taxis can generally be hired for around $10 to $15 per hour, or for a negotiated daily rate. Even drops to different destinations, say between Cancún and Playa del Carmen, or Huatulco and Puerto Escondido, can be arranged. A negotiated one-way price is usually much less than the cost of a rental car for a day, and service is much faster than traveling by bus. For anyone who is uncomfortable driving in Mexico, this is a convenient, comfortable route. An added bonus is that you have a Spanish-speaking person with you in case you run into any car or road trouble. Many taxi drivers speak at least some English. Your hotel can assist you with the arrangements.

BY BUS

Except for the Baja and Yucatán peninsulas, where bus service is not as well developed as in other parts of the country, Mexican buses are frequent, readily accessible, and can get you to almost anywhere you want to go. They're often the only way to get from large cities to other nearby cities and small villages. Don't hesitate to ask questions if you're confused about anything.

Dozens of Mexican companies operate large, air-conditioned, Greyhound-type buses between most cities. Travel class is generally labeled first (*primera*), second (*segunda*), and deluxe, which is referred to by a variety of names. The deluxe buses often have fewer seats than regular buses, show video movies en route, are air-conditioned, and have few stops; some have complimentary refreshments. Many run express from origin to the final destination. They are well worth the few dollars more that you'll pay. In rural areas, buses are often of the school-bus variety, with lots of local color.

Whenever possible, it's best to buy your reserved-seat ticket, often via a computerized system, a day in advance on many long-distance routes and especially before holidays. Schedules are fairly dependable, so be at the terminal on time for departure. Current information must be obtained from local bus stations.

See the Appendix for a list of helpful bus terms in Spanish.

FAST FACTS: Mexico

Abbreviations Dept. (apartments); Apdo. (post office box); Av. (Avenida; avenue); c/ (calle; street); Calz. (Calzada; boulevard). "C" on faucets stands for *caliente* (hot), and "F" stands for *fría* (cold). PB (*planta baja*) means ground floor.

Business Hours   In general, businesses in larger cities are open between 9am and 7pm; in smaller towns many close between 2 and 4pm. Most are closed on Sunday. Bank hours are Monday through Friday from 9 or 9:30am to 5 or 6pm. Increasingly, banks are offering Saturday hours for at least a half day.

Cameras/Film   Film costs about the same as in the United States. Tourists wishing to use a video or still camera at any archaeological site in Mexico and at many museums operated by the Instituto de Antropología e Historia (INAH) may be required to pay $4 per video camera and/or still camera in their possession at each site or museum visited. Such fees are noted in the listings for specific sites and museums. Also, use of a tripod at any archaeological site in Mexico requires a permit from INAH. It's courteous to ask permission before photographing anyone. In some areas, such as around San Cristóbal de las Casas, there are other restrictions on photographing people and villages. Such restrictions are noted in specific cities, towns, and sites.

Customs   See "Visitor Information, Entry Requirements & Money," earlier in this chapter.

Doctors/Dentists   Every embassy and consulate is prepared to recommend local doctors and dentists with good training and modern equipment; some of the doctors and dentists even speak English. See the list of embassies and consulates under "Embassies/Consulates," below. Hotels with a large foreign clientele are often prepared to recommend English-speaking doctors. Almost all first-class hotels in Mexico have a doctor on call.

Drug Laws   To be blunt, don't use or possess illegal drugs in Mexico. Mexican officials have no tolerance for drug users, and jail is their solution, with very little hope of getting out until the sentence (usually a long one) is completed or heavy fines or bribes are paid. Remember—in Mexico the legal system assumes you are guilty until proven innocent. (*Important note:* It isn't uncommon to be befriended by a fellow user, only to be turned in by that "friend"—he's collected a bounty for turning you in.) Bring prescription drugs in their original containers. If possible, pack a copy of the original prescription with the generic name of the drug.

U.S. Customs officials are also on the lookout for diet drugs sold in Mexico, possession of which could also land you in a U.S. jail because they are illegal here. If you buy antibiotics over the counter (which you can do in Mexico)—say, for a sinus infection—and still have some left, you probably won't be hassled by U.S. Customs.

Drugstores   Drugstores (*farmacias*) will sell you just about anything you want, with a prescription or without one. Most drugstores are open Monday through Saturday from 8am to 8pm. There are generally one or two 24-hour pharmacies now located in the major resort areas. If you are in a smaller town and need to buy medicines after normal hours, ask for the *farmacia de turno;* pharmacies take turns staying open during off-hours.

Electricity   The electrical system in Mexico is 110 volts AC (60 cycles), as in the United States and Canada. However, in reality it may cycle more slowly and overheat your appliances. To compensate, select a medium or low speed for hair dryers. Many older hotels still have electrical outlets for flat two-prong plugs; you'll need an adapter for using any modern electrical apparatus that has an enlarged end on one prong or that has three prongs. Many first-class and deluxe hotels have the three-holed outlets (*trifácicos* in Spanish). Those that don't may have loan adapters, but to be sure, it's always better to carry your own.

Embassies/Consulates   They provide valuable lists of doctors and lawyers, as well as regulations concerning marriages in Mexico. Contrary to popular belief, your embassy cannot get you out of a Mexican jail, provide postal or banking services, or fly you home when you run out of money. Consular officers can provide you with advice on most matters and problems, however. Most countries have a representative embassy in Mexico City and many have consular offices or representatives in the provinces.

The Embassy of **Australia** in Mexico City is at Jaime Balmes 11, Plaza Polanco, Torre B (☎ **5/395-9988** or 5/566-3053); it's open Monday through Friday from 8am to 1pm.

The Embassy of **Canada** in Mexico City is at Schiller 529, in Polanco (☎ **5/254-3288**); it's open Monday through Friday from 9am to 1pm and 2 to 5pm (at other times the name of a duty officer is posted on the embassy door). In Acapulco, the Canadian consulate is in the Hotel Club del Sol, Costera Miguel Alemán, at the corner of Reyes Católicos (☎ **74/85-6621**); it's open Monday through Friday from 8am to 3pm.

The Embassy of **New Zealand** in Mexico City is at Homero 229, 8th floor (☎ **5/540-7780**); it's open Monday through Thursday from 9am to 2pm and 3 to 5pm and Friday from 9am to 2pm.

The Embassy of the **United Kingdom** in Mexico City is in Bosques de las Lomas (☎ **5/596-6333**); it's open Monday through Friday from 9am to 2pm.

Irish and **South African** citizens must go to the British Consulate.

The Embassy of the **United States** in Mexico City is next to the Hotel María Isabel Sheraton at Paseo de la Reforma 305, at the corner of Río Danubio (☎ **5/557-2238** or 5/209-9100). There are U.S. Consulates General in Ciudad Juárez, López Mateos 924-N (☎ **16/13-4048**); Guadalajara, Progreso 175 (☎ **3/825-2998**); Monterrey, Av. Constitución 411 Poniente (☎ **83/45-2120**); and Tijuana, Tapachula 96 (☎ **66/81-7400**). In addition, consular agencies are in Acapulco (☎ **74/84-0300** or 74/69-0556); Cabo San Lucas (☎ **114/3-3566**); Cancún (☎ **98/83-0272**); Hermosillo (☎ **621/7-2375**); Matamoros (☎ **88/12-4402**); Mazatlán (☎ **69/13-4444**, ext. 285); Mérida (☎ **99/25-5011**); Nuevo Laredo (☎ **871/4-0512**); Oaxaca (☎ **951/4-3054**); Puerto Vallarta (☎ **322/2-0069**); San Luis Potosí (☎ **481/2-1528**); and San Miguel de Allende (☎ **465/2-2357** or 465/2-0068).

Emergencies   The 24-hour **Tourist Help Line** in Mexico City is ☎ **5/250-0151.**

Legal Aid   International Legal Defense Counsel, 111 S. 15th St., 24th Floor, Packard Building, Philadelphia, PA 19102 (☎ **215/977-9982**), is a law firm specializing in legal difficulties of Americans abroad. See also "Embassies/Consulates" and "Emergencies," above.

Newspapers/Magazines   Two English-language newspapers, the *News* and the *Mexico City Times,* are published in Mexico City, distributed nationally, and carry world news and commentaries, plus a calendar of the day's events, including concerts, art shows, and plays. Newspaper kiosks in larger Mexican cities will carry a selection of English-language magazines.

Pets   Taking a pet into Mexico is easy, but requires a little preplanning. For travelers coming from the United States and Canada, your pet needs to be checked for health within 30 days of arrival into Mexico. Most veterinarians in major cities have the appropriate paperwork—an official health certificate, to be presented to Mexican Customs officials, which they will give you at the time of their check up and which ensures the pet is up-to-date on its vaccinations. When you and your pet return from Mexico, the same type of paperwork will be required by U.S. Customs officials. If your stay extends beyond the 30-day time frame of your U.S.-issued certificate, you'll need to get an updated Certificate of Health issued by a veterinarian in Mexico that also states the condition of your pet, and the status of its vaccinations. To be certain of any last-minute changes in requirements, consult the Mexican Government Tourist Office nearest you (see "Visitor Information, Entry Requirements & Money," earlier in this chapter).

Police   In Mexico City, police are to be suspected as frequently as they are to be trusted; however, you'll find many who are quite honest and helpful. In the rest of the country, especially in the tourist areas, the majority are very protective of international visitors. Several cities, including Puerto Vallarta and Acapulco, have gone as far as to set up a special corps of English-speaking Tourist Police to assist with directions, guidance, and more.

Taxes   There's a 15% IVA tax on goods and services in most of Mexico, and it's supposed to be included in the posted price. This tax is 10% in Cancún, Cozumel, and Los Cabos. There is an exit tax of around $2 imposed on every foreigner leaving the country, included in the price of airline tickets.

Telephone/Fax   Telephone area codes are gradually being changed all over the country. The change may affect the area code and first digit or only the area code. Some cities are even adding exchanges and changing whole numbers. Courtesy messages telling you that the number you dialed has been changed do not exist. You can call operator assistance for difficult-to-reach numbers. Many fax numbers are also regular telephone numbers; you have to ask whoever answers your call for the fax tone (*"tono de fax, por favor"*).

The **country code** for Mexico is **52.** For instructions on how to call Mexico from the United States, call the United States from Mexico, place calls within Mexico, or use a pay phone, consult "Telephones & Mail" in the Appendix.

Time Zone   Central standard time prevails throughout most of Mexico. The west-coast states of Sonora, Sinaloa, and parts of Nayarit are on mountain standard time. The state of Baja California Norte is on Pacific time, but Baja California Sur is on mountain time. Mexico observes **daylight saving time.**

Water   Most hotels have decanters or bottles of purified water in the rooms, and the better hotels have either purified water from regular taps or special taps marked *agua purificada.* Some hotels will charge for in-room bottled water. Virtually any hotel, restaurant, or bar will bring you purified water if you specifically request it, but you'll usually be charged for it. Bottled purified water is sold widely at drugstores and grocery stores.

Mexico City 4

Monumental Mexico City, steeped in history and culture, is timeless. Located at the heart of the Americas, it has been a center of life and commerce for over 2,000 years. Teotihuacans, Toltecs, Aztecs, and European conquistadors have all contributed to the city's fascinating evolution, art, and heritage. Although residents refer to their city as simply México (*meh*-hee-koh), its confluence of ancient ruins, colonial masterpieces, and modern architecture has prompted others to call it "The City of Palaces."

Mexico's grandest city should be the starting point for anyone serious about getting to know the country. The central downtown area is much like that of a European city, dominated by adorned buildings and broad boulevards, and interspersed with public art, parks, and gardens. Though this sprawling city is thoroughly modern and in places unsightly and chaotic, you'll never stray far from its historical roots. In the center are the partially excavated ruins of an Aztec temple; pyramids loom just beyond the city. The geography of Mexico City is as impressive as its history. Surrounded by towering mountains, the city sits on an enormous dry lake bed in a highland valley, at an elevation of 7,400 feet.

Mexico City is the most populated city in the world, with over 23 million inhabitants. The sheer number of residents trying to survive here, combined with continued economic malaise, high unemployment, and government corruption, have created a city where petty crime, such as muggings and purse-snatchings, is on the rise. Violent crime in Mexico is largely concentrated among drug traffickers and politicians, but kidnappings and murders of businesspeople, both Mexican and foreign, alarmingly are on the rise. Mexico City has many treasures to enjoy, but safety concerns almost demand that you dress and behave modestly as you explore the city. Leave all jewelry of value at home or in the safe-deposit box of your hotel. Don't carry more cash or credit cards than are necessary and use extra caution when in doubt. Mexico City is a remarkable city and well worth exploring—just do so cautiously.

Technically, Mexico City is a "Federal District," called the *Distrito Federal*, or D.F. for short (similar to the designation of Washington, D.C.). True to the city's status, one finds here a microcosm of all that is happening in the rest of the country—it's not only the seat of government but in every way the dominant center of Mexican life.

Mexico continues to become further immersed in the modern global economy, and the capital is the stage on which this exciting new chapter in the country's history is being played out. All important government and private business flows through the capital; the streets, coffeehouses, and executive suites of Mexico City are where the nation's political and economic directions are set. Foreign businesspeople fill to capacity the best hotels in the city.

Though immense, Mexico City is easily walkable and enjoyable on foot. And it's not the impersonal place you might expect. It's easy to make eye contact and exchange pleasantries with strangers. Residents usually take time to help tourists—they will go out of their way to help you with directions or tell you when your bus stop is approaching.

You've undoubtedly heard about Mexico City's pollution. Major steps to improve the air quality (restricted driving, factory closings, emission-controlled buses and taxis) have worked wonders, but the problem persists. For the visitor, dealing with the pollution is a matter of luck and perseverance. On some days you won't notice it; on other days it will make your nose run, eyes water, and throat rasp. One positive note: In the evenings the air is usually deliciously cool and relatively clean. If you have respiratory problems, be very careful; the city's elevation makes matters even worse. Minimize your exposure to the fumes by refraining from walking busy streets during rush hour. Sunday, when many factories are closed and many cars escape the city, should be your prime outdoor day. (See also "Pollution" under "Fast Facts: Mexico City" later in this chapter.)

If you enjoy urban energy, culture, dining, and shopping, Mexico is a feast of discoveries. The city has sidewalk cafes and cantinas; bazaars and boutiques; pyramids, monuments, and museums; and a multitude of entertainment Options. And when you've had your fill of the metropolis, trips only a couple of hours in all directions take you to memorable towns and historic national landmarks.

1 Orientation

The thought of tackling one of the world's most enormous cities is enough to daunt even the most experienced traveler, but fortunately Mexico City is quite well organized. Almost all of the important sites are grouped in several key areas that are easily walkable and easy to reach.

ARRIVING & DEPARTING

BY PLANE   For information on carriers serving Mexico City from the United States, reconfirmation of flights, and so on, see chapter 3.

Mexico City's **Benito Juárez International Airport** is something of a small city, where you can grab a bite, have an espresso, or buy a wardrobe, books, gifts, and insurance, as well as exchange money or arrange a hotel room.

Near Gate A is a guarded **baggage-storage area** (another is near Gate F). The key-locked metal storage lockers measure about 2 feet by 2 feet by 18 inches and cost $3 daily. Larger items are stored in a warehouse; cost for each 24 hours is $3.50 to $8.50, depending on the size; they'll hold your items up to a month.

The Mexico City Hotel and Motel Association offers a **hotel-reservation service** for its member hotels. Look for its booths before you leave the baggage-claim area or near Gate A on the concourse. Representatives will make the call according to your specifications for location and price. If they book the hotel, they require 1 night's advance payment and will give you a voucher showing payment, which you must present at the hotel. Ask about hotels with special deals. Special low-cost **long-distance telephones** (Ladatel) are strategically placed all along the public concourse (for instructions on how to use them, see chapter 3 and the Appendix).

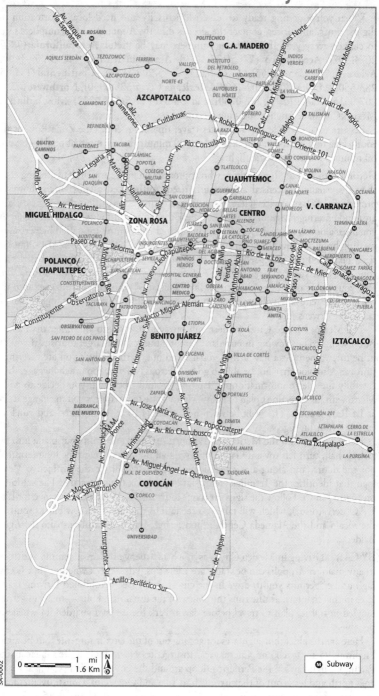

Av. Parque
Vía Esperanza
EL ROSARIO M
AQUILES SERDÁN M TEZOZOMOC M FERRERIA M
AZCAPOTZALCO M
NORTE 45 M
POLITÉCNICO M
G.A. MADERO
INSTITUTO
DEL PETRÓLEO
VALLEJO M LINDAVISTA M
INDIOS
VERDES
MARTÍN
CARRERA
San Juan de Aragón
BASÍLICA M
LA VILLA M
TALISMAN M
AUTOBUSES
DEL NORTE M
CAMARONES M
AZCAPOTZALCO
REFINERIA M
Calz. Camarones
Calz. Cuitláhuac
Av. Roblet
Dominguez Av. Oriente 101
POTRERO M
LA RAZA M
MISTERIOS M
VALLE
GÓMEZ M
BONDOJITO M
RÍO CONSULADO M
S. MOLINA M
ARAGÓN M
QUATRO
CAMINOS
PANTEONES M TACUBA M
CUITLÁHUAC M
POPOTLA M
COLEGIO
MILITAR M
SAN
JOAQUÍN M
NORMAL M
TLATELOLCO M
Calz. Melchor Ocam. Av. Río Consulado
Anillo Periférico
Calz. Legaria
Av. Marina Nacional
Calz. M. Escobedo
Av. Presidente
MIGUEL HIDALGO
POLANCO M
ZONA ROSA
AUDITORIO M
CHAPULTEPEC M
Av. Nuevo León
SAN COSME M
REVOLUCIÓN M
HIDALGO M BELLAS
ARTES M
JUÁREZ M SAN JUAN
BALDERAS M DE LETRÁN
LA CATÓLICA M
SALTO
DEL AGUA M ISABEL
NIÑOS M DOCTORES M
HÉROES
HOSPITAL GENERAL M
GUERRERO M
GARIBALDI M
CUAUHTÉMOC
CANAL
DEL NORTE M
OCEANIA M
MORELOS M
V. CARRANZA
TERMINAL AÉREA M
CENTRO
ZÓCALO M CANDELARIA M
PINO SUÁREZ M SAN LÁZARO M
MERCED M
MOCTEZUMA M
BALBUENA M
AEROPUERTO M
HANGARES M
Río de la Loza
SAN
ANTONIO
ABAD M
FRAY
SERVANDO M
JAMAICA M GÓMEZ FARÍAS M
PANTITLÁN M
ZARAGOZA M
Calz. Ignacio Zaragoza
**POLANCO/
CHAPULTEPEC**
CONSTITUYENTES
Av. Observatorio
JUANACATLÁN M
Av. Molino del Rey
Paseo de la Reforma
INSURGENTES M
SEVILLA M
CENTRO
MÉDICO M
OBRERA M
LÁZARO
CÁRDENAS M
LA VIGA M
MIXIUHCA M
SANTA
ANITA M
VELÓDROMO M
CD. DEPORTIVA M
PUEBLA M
Av. Constituyentes
TACUBAYA M
PATRIOTISMO M
Viaducto Miguel Alemán
CHILPANCINGO M
ETIOPIA M
XOLA M
COYUYA M
IZTACALCO M
Calz. Río Consulado
OBSERVATORIO M
SAN PEDRO DE LOS PINOS M
BENITO JUÁREZ
EUGENIA M VILLA DE CORTÉS M
NATIVITAS M
IZTACALCO
Av. Insurgentes Sur
Calz. Tacubaya
Patriotismo
SAN ANTONIO M
MIXCOAC M
DIVISIÓN
DEL NORTE M
Av. de la Viga
APATLACO M
ZAPATA M
PORTALES M
CULHUACÁN M
ESCUADRÓN 201 M
IZTAPALAPA M CERRO DE
LA ESTRELLA M
ATLALILCO M
Calz. Ermita Ixtapalapa
LA PURÍSIMA M
BARRANCA
DEL MUERTO M
Av. José María Rico
Av. División Av. Popocatéptl
COYOACÁN M
ERMITA M
GENERAL ANAYA M
TASQUEÑA M
Av. Río Churubusco
del Norte
Av. Revolución
M.M. Ponce
Av. Universidad
VIVEROS M
Av. Miguel Ángel de Quevedo
M.A. DE QUEVEDO M
COYOCÁN
COPILCO M
Av. Moctezuma
Av. San Jerónimo
Anillo Periférico
UNIVERSIDAD M
Av. Insurgentes Sur
Anillo Periférico Sur
Calz. de Tlalpan

0   1   mi
1.6 Km
N

Ⓜ Subway

SA-0002

When you're getting ready to leave Mexico City and need local information on flights, times, and prices, contact the airlines directly. Although airline numbers seem to change every year, the following numbers may be useful: **Aerocalifornia** (☎ 5/207-1392), **Aeromexico** (☎ 5/133-4010), **American Airlines** (☎ 5/209-1400), **Aviacsa** (☎ 5/559-1955), **Canadian** (☎ 5/208-1883), **Continental** (☎ 5/283-5500), **Delta** (☎ 5/202-1608), **Mexicana** (☎ 5/325-0990), **Northwest** (☎ 5/207-0515), **Taesa** (☎ 5/227-0700), and **United** (☎ 5/627-0222). Most airlines in Mexico City have English-speaking personnel.

Be sure to allow at least 45 minutes travel time from either the Zona Rosa or the zócalo area to the airport. Check in at least 90 minutes before international flights and 60 minutes before domestic flights.

Getting Into Town   Ignore those who approach you in the arrivals hall offering taxis; they are usually unlicensed and unauthorized. **Authorized airport taxis,** however, provide good, fast service. Here's how to use them: After exiting the baggage-claim area and entering the public concourse, near the far end of the terminal near Gate A, you'll see a booth marked TAXI. These authorized taxi booths are staffed by personnel wearing bright-yellow jackets or bibs emblazoned with "TAXI AUTORIZADO" (authorized taxi). Tell the ticket-seller your hotel or destination, as the price is based on a zone system. Expect to pay around $7.50 for a *boleto* (ticket) to the Zona Rosa. Present your ticket outside to the driver. Taxi "assistants" who lift your luggage into the waiting taxi naturally will expect a tip for their trouble. Putting your luggage in the taxi is the driver's job.

The **Metro,** Mexico City's modern subway system, is cheap and faster than a taxi. But it seems to be growing in popularity among thieves who target tourists. If you try it, be forewarned: As a new arrival you'll stand out, particularly if you are carrying a suitcase. Also, you may not be able to go by Metro if you have too much luggage. Read carefully the Metro information in "Getting Around," below. If you decide to go by Metro with luggage, don't plan to take a Metro route that requires you to change trains at **La Raza** station. The walk between lines there is 10 to 15 minutes, and you'll be carrying your luggage.

Here's how to find the Metro at the airport: As you come from your plane into the arrivals hall, turn left toward Gate A and walk all the way through the long terminal, out the doors, and along a covered sidewalk. Soon, you'll see the distinctive Metro logo that identifies the Terminal Aérea station, down a flight of stairs. The station is on Metro Line 5. Follow the signs for trains to Pantitlán. At Pantitlán, change for Line 1 ("Observatorio"), which will take you to stations that are just a few blocks south of the zócalo and the Alameda Central: Piño Suárez, Isabel la Católica, Salto del Agua, Balderas.

BY CAR   Driving in Mexico City is as much a challenge and an adventure as driving in any major metropolis can be. Here are a few tips. First, check whether your license tag number permits you to drive in the city that day (see "Prohibited Driving Days" later in this chapter). Traffic runs the course of the usual rush hours—to avoid getting tangled in traffic, plan to travel before dawn. Park the car in a guarded lot whenever possible.

Here are the chief thoroughfares for getting out of the city: Insurgentes Sur becomes Highway 95 to Taxco and Cuernavaca. Insurgentes Norte leads to Teotihuacán and Pachuca. Highway 57, the Periférico (loop around the city), is called "Camacho" as it goes north and leads out of the city north to Tula and Querétaro. Constituyentes leads west out of the city past Chapultepec Park and connects with Highway 15 to Toluca, Morelia, and Pátzcuaro. Zaragoza leads east to Highway 150 to Puebla and Veracruz.

Important Taxi Safety Precautions in Mexico City

There has been a marked increase in violent crime against both residents and tourists using taxis for transportation in Mexico City, concentrated among users of Volkswagen "bug" taxis. Robberies of taxi passengers have become increasingly violent, with beatings and even murders not uncommon. A U.S. citizen was shot and killed in an apparent taxi robbery in December 1997. These occurrences have become so common and so severe that, as of the time of this update, the United States State Department had issued a standing **travelers' advisory** concerning taxi-cab travel in Mexico City.

If you plan to use a **taxi from the airport or bus stations,** use only an authorized airport cab with all the familiar markings: yellow car, white taxi light on the roof, and TRANSPORTACIÓN TERRESTRE painted on the doors. Buy your ticket from the clearly marked taxi booth inside the terminal—nowhere else. After purchasing your ticket, go outside to the line of taxis where an official taxi "chief" will direct you to the next taxi in line. Don't follow anyone else.

In Mexico City *do not hail a passing taxi on the street.* Most hotels have official taxi drivers who are recognized and regulated by the terminal and city; they are considered "safe" taxis to use. These are known as authorized or *sitio* taxis. Hotels and restaurants can call the radio-dispatched taxis. **Official Radio Taxis** (☎ 5/271-9146, 5/271-9058, or 5/272-6125) are also considered safe. You can also hire one of these taxis for an hourly or negotiated fee; the driver will frequently act as your personal driver, and escort you through your travels in the city. This is a particularly advisable option at night.

All official taxis, except the expensive "Turismo" cabs, are painted predominantly yellow, orange, or green, have white plastic roof signs bearing the word *Taxi,* have "TAXI" or "SITIO" painted on the doors, and are equipped with meters. Look for all of these indications, not just one or two of them. Even then, be cautious. The safest cars to use are the sedan taxis (luxury cars without markings) that are dispatched from four- and five-star hotels. They are the most expensive, but the taxi crime in Mexico City is very real.

Do not use VW Beetle taxis, which are frequently involved in robberies of tourists. Even though they are the least expensive taxis, you could be taking your life into your hands should you opt to use one. In any case, never get in a taxi that does not display a large 5-by-7–inch laminated **license card** with a picture of the driver on it; it's usually hanging from the door chain or glove box, or stuck behind the sun visor. *If there is no license, or if the photo doesn't match the driver, don't get in.* It's illegal for a taxi to operate without the license in view. No matter what vehicle you use for transportation, lock the doors as soon as you get in. Do not carry credit cards, large sums of cash, or wear expensive jewelry when taking taxis.

The U.S. State Department advisory also specifies that taxis parked in front of the **Bellas Artes Theater** and in front of nightclubs, restaurants, or cruising tourist areas should be avoided.

BY BUS   Mexico City has a bus terminal for each of the four points of the compass: north, east, south, and west. You can't necessarily tell which terminal serves which area of the country by looking at a map, however. (Some buses leave directly from the Mexico City airport.) If you're in doubt about which station serves the destination you're considering, ask any taxi driver—they know the stations and the routes they serve. All stations have restaurants, money-exchange booths or banks, post offices, luggage storage, and long-distance telephone booths where you can also send a fax.

Taxis from bus stations: Each station has a taxi system based on fixed-price tickets to various zones within the city, operated from a booth or kiosk in or near the entry foyer of the terminal. Locate your destination on a zone map or tell the seller where you want to go, and buy a *boleto* (ticket). See also the "Important Taxi Safety Precaution in Mexico City" box, above.

For bus riders' terms and translations, see the Appendix.

Terminal Central de Autobuses del Norte Called "Camiones Norte," "Terminal Norte," "Central del Norte," or even just **"CN,"** this is Mexico's largest bus station, on avenida de los 100 ("Cien") Metros. It handles most buses coming from the U.S.-Mexico border. Buses that arrive and depart from here include those: to/from the Pacific Coast as far south as Puerto Vallarta and Manzanillo; to/from the Gulf Coast as far south as Tampico and Veracruz; and to/from such cities as Guadalajara, San Luis Potosí, Durango, Zacatecas, Morelia, and Colima. You can also get to the pyramids of San Juan Teotihuacán and Tula from here.

To get downtown from the Terminal Norte, you have a choice: The **Metro** has a station (Terminal de Autobuses del Norte, or **TAN**) right here, so it's easy to hop a train and connect for all points. Walk to the center of the terminal, go out the front door, down the steps, and to the Metro station. This is Línea 5. Follow the signs that say DIRECCIÓN PANTITLÁN. For downtown, you can change trains at either La Raza or Consulado (see the Mexico City Metro map on the inside back cover). Be aware that if you change at La Raza, you'll have to walk for 10 to 15 minutes and will encounter stairs. The walk is through a marble-lined underground corridor, but it's a long way with heavy luggage.

Another way to get downtown is by **trolleybus.** The stop is on avenida de los Cien Metros, in front of the terminal. The trolleybus runs right down avenida Lázaro Cárdenas, the "Eje Central" (Central Artery). Or try the "Central Camionera del Norte–Villa Olímpica" buses, which go down avenida Insurgentes, past the university.

Terminal de Autobuses de Pasajeros de Oriente (TAPO) The terminal is known by all as **TAPO.** Buses going east (Puebla, Pachuca, Cholula, Amecameca, the Yucatán Peninsula, Veracruz, Jalapa, San Cristóbal de las Casas, and others) arrive and depart from here. Buses originating in Oaxaca arrive and depart from here as well, since they pass through Puebla, east of Mexico City.

To get to TAPO, take a "Hipodromo-Pantitlán" bus east along Alvarado, Hidalgo, or Donceles; if you take the Metro, go to the San Lázaro station on the eastern portion of Line 1 (DIRECCIÓN PANTITLÁN).

Terminal Central de Autobuses del Sur Mexico City's southern bus terminal is located at avenida Tasqueña 1320, right next to the Tasqueña Metro stop, the last stop on Line 2. The Central del Sur handles buses to/from Cuernavaca, Taxco, Acapulco, Zihuatanejo, and intermediate points. The easiest way to get to or from the Central del Sur is on the Metro. To get downtown from the Tasqueña Metro station, look for signs that say DIRECCIÓN CUATRO CAMINOS. Or take a trolleybus on avenida Lázaro Cárdenas.

Terminal Poniente de Autobuses The western bus terminal is conveniently located right next to the Observatorio Metro station at Sur 122 and Río Tacubaya. This is the station where you'll arrive if you're coming from Acapulco, Cuernavaca, Ixtapa, Taxco, Zihuatanejo, or Morelia.

This is the smallest terminal; it mainly serves the route between Mexico City and Toluca. But other cities to the west and northwest are served also, including Ixtapan

✪ Frommer's Favorite Mexico City Experiences

Breakfast, Lunch, or Dinner at the Hotel Majestic Rooftop Restaurant. Enjoy a meal or drinks under one of the colorful umbrellas overlooking the historic downtown and the zócalo. If you arrive just before sunset, you can watch soldiers file out of the Palacio Nacional and perform the flag-lowering ceremony on the zócalo.

The Ethnography Section of the Museo Nacional de Antropología. Overlooked by many visitors, the second-floor Ethnography section is the perfect introduction to Mexican life, far from the beaches, resorts, and cities. Fine, unusual weavings, pottery, handcrafts, furniture, huts, plows, and canoes are presented in the context of everyday life. It's a must for those about to visit the interior of the country, those who are curious about the villagers seen on the capital's streets, and those who expect their Mexico journeys to be off the beaten path.

The Sunday Lagunilla Market. The best flea market in Mexico, this one spreads out for blocks with vendors selling santos, jewelry, antiques, pottery, miniatures, brass, glass, and oddities such as old locks and keys, an armadillo purse complete with head and feet, a piece of Spanish armor, a 16th-century religious sculpture, an elk-horn earring, and much more.

Shopping in the Zona Rosa and Polanco. The dozens of fashionable shops lining the streets of these attractive areas sell designer clothing, jewelry, and antiques; there are lots of tempting restaurants in between.

The Saturday Bazaar in San Ángel. Only on Saturdays (hence the name, Bazar Sábado) is this colonial-era suburb of mansions near Parque San Jacinto invigorated with hundreds of artists, antique dealers, street vendors, and sellers of popular art; the area restaurants consequently are packed—and are excellent.

Afternoon Tea at the Salón de Thé Duca d'Este. In Mexico, tea and coffee breaks are taken seriously. This cheerful Zona Rosa restaurant and pastry shop is great for sipping a frothy cappuccino and whiling away some time watching passersby through the huge windows facing the street.

The Ballet Folklórico de México. Among the best folkloric ballet groups in Mexico are those that perform in Mexico City either at the Teatro Bellas Artes or at the Teatro de la Ciudad. At the Bellas Artes you'll get to see the famed Tiffany glass curtain, which is usually (but not always) shown before each performance.

The Centro Histórico. Stroll the streets fanning out from the zócalo and stretching to the Alameda. Almost every step reveals amazing architecture constructed over the centuries of this historic city. Hundreds of buildings have been restored or are in the process of restoration. You'll notice that each block seems to have a particular commercial concentration—whether used and rare books, wedding dresses, or stereo equipment.

The Ruins of Teotihuacán. There's nothing to compare with walking down the wide Avenue of the Dead, with the Pyramid of the Moon at one end and pyramidal structures on both sides, imagining what it must have looked like when the walls were embellished with murals on brilliantly colored stucco. See chapter 5, "Side Trips from Mexico City."

de la Sal, Valle de Bravo, Morelia, Uruapan, and Guadalajara. In general, if your chosen destination is also served from the Terminal Norte, you'd be better off going there. The Terminal Norte simply has more buses and better bus lines.

VISITOR INFORMATION

The Federal District Department provides several information services for visitors. **Infotur** offices offer information in English and Spanish, including maps, a wide selection of brochures, and access to information from the Mexico Secretary of Tourism Web site. The most convenient of these is in the Zona Rosa at Amberes 54, at the corner of Londres (☎ **5/525-9380**). Others are at the TAPO bus terminal and at the airport. They're open daily from 9am to 9pm.

The **Mexico City Chamber of Commerce** (☎ **5/592-2665**) maintains an information office with a very friendly, helpful staff who can sell you detailed maps of the city or country and answer your questions. It's conveniently located at Reforma 42— look for the Cámara Nacional de Comercio de la Ciudad de México. It's open Monday through Thursday from 9am to 2pm and 3 to 6pm; Friday from 9am to 2pm and 3 to 5:30pm.

CITY LAYOUT

FINDING AN ADDRESS   Despite its size, Mexico City is not outrageously hard to get a feel for. The city is divided into 350 *colonias,* or neighborhoods. Taxi drivers are notoriously ignorant of the city, including even the major tourist sights and popular restaurants. Before getting into a taxi, always give them, in addition to a street address and colonia, cross streets as a reference and locate your destination on a map that you carry with you. Some of the most important colonias are *Colonia Centro* (historic city center); Zona Rosa (*Colonia Juárez*); Polanco (*Colonia Polanco*), a fashionable neighborhood immediately north of Chapultepec Park; *colonias Condesa* and *Roma,* south of the Zona Rosa, where there are many restaurants in quiet neighborhoods; and all the Lomas—Lomas de Chapultepec, Lomas Tecamachalco, etc.—very exclusive neighborhoods west of Chapultepec Park. In addresses, the word is abbreviated *Col.,* although the full colonia name is vital in addressing correspondence.

STREET MAPS   Should you want more detailed maps of Mexico City than the ones included in this guide, you can obtain them easily. The **Infotur** office (see "Visitor Information," above) generally has several maps available for free. A few bookstores carry a local map-guide entitled **Mexico City Trillas Tourist Guide,** a softbound book of gorgeous block-by-block pictorial maps covering most areas of the city that are of interest to visitors. The English text includes interesting facts and statistics on Mexico City and its sights. More readily available are maps published by **Guía Roji** in both sheet and softbound book form. Quite detailed, they are valuable if you plan to venture much out of the Centro Histórico or the Zona Rosa.

NEIGHBORHOODS IN BRIEF

Centro Histórico   Centro Histórico refers to the heart of Mexico City, its business, banking, and historic center, including the areas in and around the Alameda Central and the zócalo. The Spaniards built their new capital city on top of the destroyed capital of the conquered Aztecs. This is where you'll find the historic landmarks, the most important public buildings, the partially unearthed Aztec ruins of the Temple Major, and numerous museums. There's dining, shopping, and hotels in this area as well. The streets are very active during business hours during the week, then empty out a bit in the evenings and weekends.

Chapultepec Park and Polanco   A large residential area west of the city center and Zona Rosa, it centers around Chapultepec Park, the largest green area in Mexico City, dedicated as a park in the 15th century by the Aztec ruler Netzahualcoytl. Together with the neighboring colonia of Polanco to the immediate north of the park, this is currently Mexico City's most exclusive address. With its zoo, many notable museums, antique shops, fashionable shopping and dining, and upscale hotels, it's an ideal place for discovering the culture of Mexico. **Presidente Mazaryk** is the main artery running through it.

Coyoacán   Five miles from the city center, east of San Ángel and north of the Ciudad Universitaria, Coyoacán is a colonial-era suburb noted for its beautiful town square, cobblestone streets lined with fine old mansions, and several of the city's most interesting museums. This was the former home of Frida Kahlo and Diego Rivera, as well as where Leon Trotsky lived following his exile from Stalin's Russia. It's a wonderful place to spend the day, but there are limited accommodations for overnight. Attractions in Coyoacán are located in the designation "Southern Neighborhoods."

San Ángel   Five miles south of the city center, San Ángel was once a distinct village but is now absorbed by the city. Yet the neighborhood remains a beautiful suburb of cobbled streets and beautiful colonial-era homes. This is where the renowned Bazar Sábado (Saturday Bazaar) is held. It's full of artistic and antique treasures, with excellent restaurants as well—a good place to spend a day. Attractions in San Ángel are located in the designation "Southern Neighborhoods."

Xochimilco   Fifteen miles south of town center, Xochimilco is noted for its famed canals and "Floating Gardens," which date from pre-Hispanic times. Attractions in Xochimilco are located in the designation "Southern Neighborhoods."

Zona Rosa   West of the Centro, the "Pink Zone" was once the city's most exclusive residential neighborhood, but it has given way to the countless tourists that visit, with a dazzling array of luxury hotels, designer boutiques, fine dining, and nightlife. Many of the streets are pedestrian-only, making it an inviting place for shopping or taking in the sights over a cappuccino or aperitif at one of the numerous cafes. It's the most popular place to stay, despite the fact that it has fewer real historic or cultural attractions than other parts of the city.

2 Getting Around

Luckily for budget travelers, Mexico City has a highly developed and remarkably cheap public transportation system. The Metro, first- and second-class buses, minibuses (colectivos), and yellow or green VW taxis will take you anywhere you want to go for very little money—but the recent, sharp increase in crime has led to visitor warnings about the use of public transportation. However, even *sitio* taxis (official taxis registered to a specific locale or hotel) are relatively inexpensive, and are the safest way to travel today within the city.

BY TAXI   Taxis operate under several distinct sets of rules, established in early 1991:

Metered Taxis   Yellow or green VW Beetle and *"sitio"* (radio-dispatched) Datsun cabs provide for low-cost service. *Please read the cautionary box, "Important Taxi Safety Precaution in Mexico City," above, before using any taxi.* Though you will often encounter a gouging driver ("Ah, the meter just broke yesterday; I'll have it fixed tomorrow!"), or one who advances the meter or drives farther than necessary to run up the tab, most service is quick and adequate. As of early 1991, these taxis began operating strictly by the meter. If the driver says his meter isn't working, find another taxi.

Downtown Mexico City

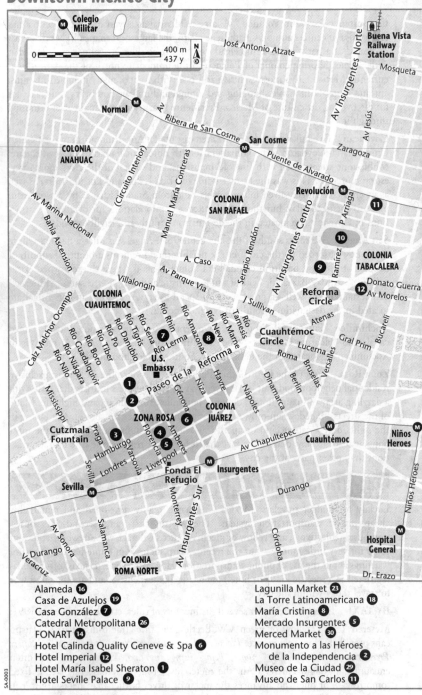

Colegio Militar
José Antonio Atzate
Buena Vista Railway Station
Mosqueta

0   400 m
     437 y
N

Normal
Av Ribera de San Cosme
San Cosme
Puente de Alvarado
Zaragoza

COLONIA ANAHUAC

Av Insurgentes Norte
Av Jesús

COLONIA SAN RAFAEL

Revolución
Museo de San Carlos 11

COLONIA TABACALERA
Donato Guerra
Av Morelos

Av Marina Nacional
Bahia Ascension
Manuel María Contreras
A. Caso
Serapio Rendón
Villalongin
Av Parque Via
J Sullivan

Av Insurgentes Centro
I Ramírez
P Arriaga

Reforma Circle

COLONIA CUAUHTEMOC

Calz Melchor Ocampo
Río Nilo
Río Niágara
Río Guadalquivir
Río Boro
Río Tiber
Río Po
Río Danubio
Río Tigris
Río Sena
Río Rhin
Río Lerma
Río Amazonas
Río Neva
Río Marne
Río Tamesis
Río Rhin

U.S. Embassy
Paseo de la Reforma
Génova
Niza
Havre
Nápoles

Cuauhtémoc Circle
Atenas
Lucerna
Roma
Bruselas
Versalles
Berlin
Dinamarca
Gral Prim
Bucareli

Mississippi
Cutzmala Fountain

ZONA ROSA
Florencia
Amberes

COLONIA JUÁREZ

Praga
Varsovia
Hamburgo
Sevilla
Londres
Liverpool

Fonda El Refugio
Insurgentes
Av Chapultepec
Cuauhtémoc
Niños Heroes
Niños Heroes

Sevilla
Monterrey
Durango
Salamanca
Av Insurgentes Sur

COLONIA ROMA NORTE
Av Sonora
Durango
Veracruz
Córdoba

Hospital General
Dr. Erazo

Alameda 16
Casa de Azulejos 19
Casa González 7
Catedral Metropolitana 26
FONART 14
Hotel Calinda Quality Geneve & Spa 6
Hotel Imperial 12
Hotel María Isabel Sheraton 1
Hotel Seville Palace 9

Lagunilla Market 23
La Torre Latinoamericana 18
María Cristina 8
Mercado Insurgentes 5
Merced Market 30
Monumento a las Héroes
   de la Independencia 2
Museo de la Ciudad 29
Museo de San Carlos 11

SA-0003

76

"Turismo" Taxis   These unmarked cabs have special license plates, bags covering their meters, and are usually well-kept luxury cars, assigned to specific hotels. Though more expensive than the VW or Datsun taxis, they, along with radio-dispatched taxis, are the safest ones to use. The drivers negotiate rates with individual passengers for sightseeing, but rates to and from the airport are established. Ask the bell captain what the airport rate should be and establish the rate before taking off. These drivers are often licensed English-speaking guides and can provide exceptional service. In general, expect to pay around $10 per hour for guided service, and about 15% more than metered rates for normal transportation. Often, these drivers will wait for you while you shop or dine, to take you back to the hotel, or can be called to come and pick you up. These are by far *the safest way to travel* within Mexico City.

BY METRO   The subway system in Mexico City offers a smooth ride for one of the lowest fares anywhere in the world (1.5 pesos, or 20¢ per ride). Ten lines crisscross the sprawling city. Each train usually has nine cars, each seating 39 people. Another 50 or more can be accommodated standing.

As you enter the station, buy a *boleto* (ticket) at the glass *taquilla* (ticket booth). Insert your ticket into the slot at the turnstile and pass through; inside, you'll see two large signs showing the line's destination (for example, for Line 1, it's OBSERVATORIO and PANTITLÁN). Follow the signs in the direction you want and *know where you're going*, since there is usually only one map of the routes, at the entrance to the station. There are, however, two signs you'll see everywhere: **SALIDA,** which means "exit," and **ANDENES,** which means "platforms." Once inside the train, you'll see above each door a map of the station stops for that line, with symbols and names.

Transfer of lines is indicated by **Correspondencias.** The ride is smooth, fast, and efficient (although hot and crowded during rush hours). The stations are clean and beautifully designed and have the added attraction of displaying several archaeological ruins unearthed during construction. There is also a subterranean passage that goes between the Piño Suárez and Zócalo stations so you can avoid the crowds and the rain along Piño Suárez. The Zócalo station features dioramas and large photographs of the different periods in the history of the Valley of Mexico, while at Piño Suárez you'll find the foundation of a pyramid from the Aztec Empire.

Metro travel is crowded during daylight hours on weekdays and consequently pretty hot and muggy in summer. In fact, you may find that between 4 and 7pm on week-days, the Metro is virtually unusable downtown because of Tokyo-like sardine-can conditions. At some stations, there are even separate lanes roped off for women and children; the press of the crowd is so great that someone might get molested. Buses,

The Subway Skinny

The Metro system runs workdays from 5am to 12:30am, Saturday from 6am to 1:30am, and Sunday and holidays from 7am to 1:30am. Large baggage is not allowed into the system. In practice, this means that bulky suitcases or backpacks sometimes will make you a persona non grata. On an average day Mexico City's Metro handles more than five million riders—leaving precious little room for bags! But, in effect, if no one stops you as you enter, you're in.

Watch your bags and your pockets, however. Metro pickpockets prey on the unwary (especially foreigners) and are very crafty—on a crowded train they've been known to empty a fanny pack from the front. Be careful and carry valuables inside your clothing.

Pollution Control

To control pollution in the capital, regulations for car use according to day of the week, tag number, and color are in force as shown here:

Prohibited Driving Days

	Mon	Tues	Wed	Thurs	Fri
Tag color	Yellow	Pink	Red	Green	Blue
Tag ends in	5 or 6	7 or 8	3 or 4	1 or 2	9 or 0

This means that if your car tag is yellow and ends in a 5 or 6, you are prohibited from driving in Mexico City on Monday, but you can drive any other day of the week. Note that this applies to rental cars and to tourist cars (for foreign license plates, it's the last digit that counts), but it is not in effect on Saturday or Sunday. There's a stiff fine for violating this regulation.

colectivos, and taxis are all heavily used during these hours. You can sometimes beat the mob scene by choosing one of the fore or aft cars—they seem to be less crowded. Or wait a few minutes for the next train.

BY BUS   Moving millions of people through this sprawling urban mass is a gargantuan task, but the city officials do a pretty good job of it. Still, they tend to change bus numbers and routes frequently. Maps of the entire system are impossible to find. However, bus stops on the major tourist streets usually have a map posted with the full route description.

The large buses that ran on the major tourist routes (**Reforma** and **Insurgentes**) tended to become overpacked and have been phased out in favor of small buses, and more of them. Thus, crowding is uncommon except perhaps during peak hours. The cost in pesos is the U.S. equivalent of around 10¢ to 25¢. Although the driver usually has change, try to have exact fare when you board.

One of the most important bus routes is the one that runs between the zócalo and the Auditorio (National Auditorium in Chapultepec Park) or the Observatorio Metro station. The route is via avenida Madero or Cinco (5) de Mayo, avenida Juárez, and Paseo de la Reforma. Buses marked ZÓCALO run this route.

Another important route is **"Indios Verdes–Tlalpan,"** which runs along avenida Insurgentes connecting the northern bus terminal (Terminal Norte), Buenavista railroad station, Reforma, the Zona Rosa, and, far to the south, San Ángel and University City.

BY COLECTIVO   Also called *peseros,* these are sedans or minibuses, usually green and gray, that run along major arteries. They pick up and discharge passengers along the route, charge established fares, and provide more comfort and speed than the bus. Routes are displayed on cards in the windshield; often a Metro station will be the destination. One of the most useful routes for tourists runs from the **zócalo** along **avenida Juárez,** along **Reforma** to **Chapultepec,** and back again. Get a colectivo with a sign saying ZÓCALO, not VILLA. A "Villa" bus or pesero goes to the Basílica de Guadalupe.

Some of the minibuses on this route have automatic sliding doors—you don't have to shut them, a motor does.

Rent a Car? In Mexico City?

If you're planning on traveling to Puebla or a surrounding area, a rental car might come in handy. Driving in Mexico City is really not *that bad* for a giant city, but using taxis and the Metro eliminates the risk of getting lost in an unsavory area. Due to high rates of auto theft, unless it's truly needed, I wouldn't recommend renting a car.

As the driver approaches a stop, he may put his hand out the window and hold up one or more fingers. This is the number of passengers he's willing to take on (vacant seats are difficult to see if you're outside the car).

RENTAL CARS   The least-expensive rental car is the (old-style) manual-shift Volkswagen Beetle, manufactured in Mexico. The price jump is considerable beyond the VW Beetle, and you pay more for automatic transmission and air-conditioning in any car. Hertz, Budget, National, and Avis car rentals, among others, are represented at the airport, and each has several city offices as well. Daily rates and deductibles vary considerably. It's more economical to arrange the rental from your home country than to wait to rent one upon arrival. (See also "Getting Around," in chapter 3.)

FAST FACTS: Mexico City

In "Fast Facts: Mexico" in chapter 3 you'll find the answers to all sorts of questions about daily life in Mexico City. But here are a few essentials for getting along in this metropolis:

American Express   The Mexico City office is at Reforma 234 (☎ **5/207-7282** or 5/514-0629) in the Zona Rosa. It's open for banking, the pickup of American Express clients' mail, and travel advice Monday through Friday from 9am to 6pm and Saturday from 9am to 1pm.

Area Code   The telephone area code for Mexico City is **5.**

Banks   Banks are usually open Monday through Friday from 9am to 5pm; many now offer Saturday and even Sunday business hours. Bank branches at the airport are open whenever the airport is busy, including weekends. They usually offer ATM machines and good rates of exchange. avenida Reforma is lined with banks and money-exchange places. The Historic Center downtown also has banks and money-exchange booths on almost every block, as does the Zona Rosa.

Bookstores   In Mexico City, **Sanborn's** always has a great selection of books in English, as well as magazines and newspapers.

About the most convenient foreign- and Spanish-language bookstore in Mexico City, with a good selection of guidebooks and texts on Mexico, is **Librería Gandhi** (formerly Librería Mizrachi), Juárez 4, near avenida Lázaro Cárdenas (☎ **5/510-4231**), right across from the Bellas Artes. It's open Monday through Saturday from 10am to 7:45pm and Sunday from 11am to 7:45pm. Another nearby shop, the **Librería Británica,** Madero 40-B (☎ **5/521-0180**) at Isabel la Católica, also has a small coffee bar. It's open Monday through Friday from 10am to 7pm and Saturday from 10am to 6pm. The **Museo Nacional de Antropología,** in Chapultepec Park (☎ **5/553-6266**), also has a fair selection of books on Mexico, particularly special-interest guides.

Currency Exchange   The alternative to a bank is a currency-exchange booth, or *casa de cambio.* These often offer extended hours, with greater convenience to hotels and shopping areas, and rates similar to bank exchange rates. Usually, their rates are much better than those offered by most hotels.

Drugstores   The drug departments at Sanborn's stay open late. Check the phone directory for the location nearest you. After hours, check with your hotel staff, which can usually contact the on-call drugstore (*de turno*).

Elevation   Remember, you are now at an elevation of 7,240 feet—almost a mile and a half in the sky. There's a lot less oxygen in the air than you're used to. If you run for a bus and feel dizzy when you sit down, it's the elevation; if you think you're in shape but huff and puff getting up Chapultepec hill, it's the elevation. If your food isn't digesting, again, it's the elevation. It takes about 10 days or so to adjust to the scarcity of oxygen. Go easy on food and alcohol the first few days in the city.

Emergencies   A government-operated service, **Locatel** (☎ **5/658-1111**), is most often associated with finding missing persons anywhere in the country. With a good description of a car and its occupants, they'll search for motorists who have an emergency back home. **SECTUR** (Secretaría de Turismo) staffs telephones 24 hours daily (☎ **5/250-0123,** 5/250-0493, 5/250-0027, 5/250-0151, 5/250-0292, or 5/250-0589) to help tourists in difficulty. The police number is hard to reach, so have a local help you. **Dialing** ☎ 06 is similar to dialing ☎ 911 in the United States, but the emergency number is only valid for subscribing users. Thus *if the phone you are using isn't a subscriber,* ☎ 06 gets you nowhere.

Hospitals   Catering to foreigners, the **American-British Cowdray (ABC) Hospital** is located at calle Sur 132 no. 136, at the corner of avenida Observatorio, Colonia las Américas (Sur 132 is the name of the street; ☎ **5/230-8000**).

Hot Lines   If you think you've been ripped off in a purchase, try calling the **consumer protection office,** the Procuraduría Nacional del Consumidor (☎ **5/568-8722**). They also have a 24-hour tourist-assistance line (☎ **5/250-0123** or 5/205-0493).

Luggage Storage/Lockers   There are *guarda equipaje* rooms at the airport and bus stations. Most hotels have a key-locked storage area for guests who want to leave possessions for a few days.

Newspapers/Magazines   The *Mexico City News* and the *Mexico City Times* are the country's principle English-language daily newspapers and carry an extensive section of international news. See also "Bookstores," above.

Photographic Needs   There are many small photo stores offering film and other supplies throughout town. Be discrete with expensive cameras and try to conceal them when not in use. Film costs are similar to prices in the United States.

Pollution   September and October seem to be light months for pollution, while mid- to late November, as well as December and January, are months noted for heavy pollution. During January, schools may even close because of it, and restrictions on driving usually imposed only on weekdays may be imposed on weekends during heavy pollution; be sure to check before driving into or around the city. (See "Rental Cars" under "Getting Around," earlier in this chapter). Be careful if you have respiratory problems; being at an altitude of 7,240 feet will make your problems even worse. Just before your planned visit, call the Mexican Government Tourist Office nearest you (see "Visitor Information, Entry Requirements & Money" in chapter 3 for the address) and ask for the latest information on pollution in the capital. Minimize your exposure to the fumes by refraining from walking busy streets during rush hour. Make Sunday, when many factories are closed and many cars escape the city, your prime sightseeing day.

Post Office   The city's main post office, the **Correo Mayor,** is a block north of the Palacio de Bellas Artes on avenida Lázaro Cárdenas, at the corner of Tacuba.

If you need to mail a package in Mexico City, take it to the post office called Correos Internacional no. 2, calle Dr. Andrade and Río de la Loza (Metro: Balderas or Salto del Agua), open Monday through Friday from 8am to noon. Don't wrap up your package securely until an inspector examines it. Keep in mind, though postal service is improving, your package may never arrive at its destination. (For a glossary of mail terms, see the Appendix.)

Alternatively, packages may be sent via the familiar UPS, Federal Express, MexPost, or DHL, for a greater assurance that it may make it to its destination.

Rest Rooms   There are few public rest rooms. Use those in the larger hotels, and in cafes, restaurants, and museums. Seasoned travelers frequently carry their own toilet paper and hand soap.

Safety   Read the "Safety" section under "Health, Safety & Insurance" and "Crime, Bribes & Scams" in chapter 3, and the "Important Taxi Safety Precaution in Mexico City" box, above. In response to rising crime, Mexico City has added hundreds more foot and mounted police, and there's a strong military presence. But they can't be everywhere. Watch for pickpockets. Mexico City is unique in many ways, but in one matter it resembles any big city anywhere—pickpockets. Crowded subway cars and buses provide the perfect workplace for petty thieves, as do major museums (inside and out), thronged outdoor markets and bullfights, and indoor theaters. The "touch" can range from light-fingered wallet lifting or purse opening to a fairly rough shoving by two or three petty thieves. Sometimes the ploy is this: Someone drops a coin, and while everyone is looking, pushing, and shoving, your wallet disappears. Another trick is a child who takes your hand on a crowded bus or the Metro. While you kindly steady this child, someone else is pilfering your fanny pack, wallet, purse, and so on. Watch out for any place tourists go in numbers: on the Metro, in Reforma buses, in crowded hotel elevators and lobbies, at the Ballet Folklórico, and at the Museo de Antropología.

Until the peso crisis of 1994, muggings were pretty infrequent in Mexico City. But people of all walks of life have become desperate and some have resorted to theft. Robberies now happen in broad daylight on crowded streets in "good" parts of town, outside major tourist sights, and in front of posh hotels. The best way to avoid being mugged is not to wear any jewelry of value, especially expensive watches. If you find yourself up against a handful of these guys, the best thing to do is give up the demanded possession, flee, and then notify the police. (You'll need the police report to file an insurance claim.) If you're in a crowded place, you could try raising a fuss—no matter whether you do it in Spanish or in English. Just a few shouts of *"¡Ladrón!"* ("Thief!") might put them off. But that could also be risky. Overall, it's wise to leave valuables in the hotel safe and to take only the cash you'll need for the day, and no credit cards. Conceal a camera in a shoulder bag draped across your body and hanging in front of you, not on the side.

Taxes   Mexico's 15% sales tax is generally included in posted prices, however it may be added to a posted price. If in doubt, ask *"¿Más IVA?"* (plus tax?) or *"¿Con IVA?"* (with tax?). There are also airport taxes for domestic and international flights, but these are usually included in the price of your ticket. (See "Getting Around" in chapter 3.)

Telephones   Generally speaking, Mexico City's telephone system is in bad shape, although new digital lines are gradually replacing the old ones, offering much-improved service. Some of this improvement is resulting in numbers being changed.

As elsewhere in the country, the telephone company changes numbers without informing the telephone owners or the information operators. Business telephone numbers may be registered in the name of the corporation, which may be different than the name of a hotel or restaurant owned by the corporation. A telephone number is accessed by the operator under the corporate name unless the corporation pays for a separate listing. The local number for **information** is ☎ **04,** and you are allowed to request three numbers with each information call.

Coin-operated phones are prone to vandalism and so have mostly been replaced by **card-only Ladatel phones.** Ladatel cards are usually available for purchase at pharmacies and newsstands near public phones. They come in denominations of 20, 50, and 100 pesos. **Long-distance calls** within Mexico and to foreign points can be surprisingly expensive. Consult "Telephones & Mail" in the Appendix for how to use phones. Hotels are beginning to charge for local calls, but budget-priced hotels are less likely to do this because they lack the equipment to track calls from individual rooms.

Television   "Cablevision" provides CBS, ABC, NBC, and 13 variety channels, as well as Arts & Entertainment, The Movie Channel, and Sports Channel, 24 hours a day. Many first-class and several budget-category hotels receive these channels. New satellite-television services carry more than 100 channels with both national and international programming.

Weather/Clothing   Mexico City's high altitude means you'll need a warm jacket and sweater in winter. The southern parts of the city, such as the university area and Xochimilco, are much colder than the central part of the city. In summer, it gets warm during the day and cool, but not cold, at night. The rainy season runs between May and October (this is common all over Mexico)—take a raincoat or rain poncho. The showers may last all day or for only an hour or two.

3 Where to Stay

Not only is Mexico City one of the most exciting cities in the world, it can also be one of the most affordable when it comes to accommodations. For $20 to $40 you can find a double room in a fairly central hotel, complete with a bathroom and often such extras as air-conditioning and TV. Many hotels have their own garages where guests can park free.

The best values in hotel rooms are concentrated in the downtown **Historic district,** currently in the midst of a dining and nightlife renaissance. Luxury hotels are mostly located in the Zona Rosa or Chapultepec Park/Polanco neighborhoods, which are the most popular areas for mainstream tourism in Mexico City. The **Zona Rosa** seems to attract predominantly those in the city for business or shopping, whereas the **Chapultepec/Polanco** location is ideally located near museums and other cultural attractions.

Hotels in these zones not only offer more deluxe accommodations and amenities, but also generally have their own fleets of taxis and secured entrances for guests. Given the current increase in crime, including violent crime, visitors should consider staying in the most secure accommodations they can afford.

CHAPULTEPEC PARK & POLANCO
VERY EXPENSIVE

✪ **Hotel Camino Real.** Mariano Escobedo 700, 11590 México, D.F. ☎ **800/ 722-6466** in the U.S. and Canada, or 5/203-2121. Fax 5/250-6897. 711 units. A/C MINIBAR TV TEL. $239–$299 double; $339–$600 suite; $299 Executive Club rooms. AE, DC, MC, V. Metro: Chapultepec.

Long one of the capital's leading hotels, the Camino Real continues to be so popular that often every room is booked. No expense is being spared as the Camino Real vies to remain one of the capital's hot spots for business and social entertaining. A Rufino Tamayo mural, *Man Facing Eternity,* greets visitors as they enter the front doors, and a mural by José Luis Covarrubias graces the hotel's La Huerta restaurant. The spacious rooms, all with brightly colored, modern decor and a sitting and desk area, come with armoires that conceal the TV and minibar, in-room safe-deposit boxes, bathtubs, hair dryers, remote-control TVs, electronic-card door locks, fax connections, and direct-dial phones with voice mail. The entire second floor is reserved for nonsmokers. Five rooms are outfitted for guests with disabilities. Executive Club rooms come with bathrobes, continental breakfast and evening cocktail hour, and daily newspaper.

Dining: Fouquet's de Paris is the hotel's best restaurant and one of the capital's top dining establishments (see "Where to Dine," below). The hotel has two other, more informal restaurants.

Amenities: Full-service business center, private conference rooms, complete gym, massage, sauna, steam room, four tennis courts, pool, laundry and dry cleaning, car rental, travel agency, barber and beauty shop, concierge, boutiques, book and gift shop, jewelry store.

✪ **Hotel Four Seasons.** Reforma 500, Col. Juárez, 06600 México, D.F. ☎ **800/ 332-3442** in the U.S., 800/268-6282 in Canada, or 5/230-1818. Fax 5/230-1808. 240 units. A/C MINIBAR TV TEL. $260 double; $370–$2,310 suite. Special weekend packages frequently available. AE, CB, DC, MC, V. Valet parking. Metro: Sevilla.

One of the finest hotels in all of Mexico, and my personal favorite, the Four Seasons sets the standard for service with a staff noted for their gracious manners. Built in the style of an elegant Mexican hacienda, the hotel's rooms surround a beautiful interior courtyard—a veritable sanctuary in this busy city. Though you're only steps from the busy Paseo de la Reforma, the grounds of the eight-story hotel seem more like the quiet countryside surrounding a gracious manor house. On one side of the large and inviting outdoor courtyard there's umbrella-covered alfresco dining with colonnaded walkways all around; other dining rooms and bars face this pleasant scene.

The airy, huge rooms have high ceilings and are resolutely sumptuous. Each has plush, thick bedspreads, beautiful Talavera-pottery lamps and bathroom accessories, Indonesian tapestries, and rich dark-wood furnishings, including a working desk. All rooms have twice-daily maid service (with ice refills), complimentary daily newspaper, hair dryer, remote-control TV, safe-deposit box, fax outlet, separate shower and tub, robes, and illuminated makeup mirrors. Most rooms face the interior courtyard, two deluxe suites have patios facing the courtyard, and most Executive Suites (with one or two separate bedrooms) overlook Reforma. About 100 rooms are reserved for nonsmokers and there are two rooms equipped for guests with disabilities. The Four Seasons is located at the western end of the Zona Rosa, near Chapultepec Park and Polanco and opposite the Hotel Marquis Reforma.

Dining/Diversions: The fine-dining spot here (known simply as "the Restaurant") features low-key, live entertainment. **Cafe Four Seasons** is a more informal dining option, brightly lit and open for all three meals. Fridays feature a seafood buffet.

Weekend Deals

The top hotels often lower rates substantially Friday through Sunday, as the majority of their business comes from traveling business professionals.

Polanco/Chapultepec Area

El Salón is a cozy bar with an excellent selection of premium tequilas, and the **Lobby Lounge,** open from 4pm to midnight, is like a series of gracious living rooms with comfortable couch-and-chair groupings and an excellent atmosphere for conversation.

Amenities: Spa with completely equipped gym, massage services, sauna, whirlpool, and rooftop swimming pool. The complete business center offers computers, secretarial and multilingual translation services, and private meeting rooms. Laundry, dry cleaning, 1-hour pressing service, room service, boutiques, beauty and barber shop, facials, pedicure, manicure. Expert-led private tours to many of the city's historic sites and museums are a unique offering of this hotel to its guests. Weekend guests have the option of one or two of these tours included in the price of the room—a true value.

Hotel Marquis Reforma. Reforma 465, Col. Cuauhtémoc, 06500 México, D.F. ☎ **800/ 235-2387** in the U.S., 5/211-3600, or 5/211-0577. Fax 5/211-5561. 209 units. A/C MINIBAR TV TEL. $235 double; $370–$480 suite. AE, DC, MC, V. Metro: Sevilla.

With a faux art deco exterior and an overdone combination of glass, marble, and dark mahogany within, the Marquis Reforma opened in 1991 and has been billed as one of the city's state-of-the-art luxury hotels. If superfluity is your style, you'll be thrilled here. If you prefer understated elegance, try another choice—you'll feel imposed upon here. It does have an excellent location, however, at the eastern end of Chapultepec Park opposite the Four Seasons and western end of the Zona Rosa, almost equidistant between the U.S. Embassy and the Chapultepec/Polanco area. Rooms are quite varied in shape and size. Some have terraces; some separate living rooms, dining rooms, and bedrooms; some an attached meeting room. Standard double rooms have king-size beds and small sitting areas. The rooms billed as business rooms, however, lack a suitable desk and all are smaller than normal for the type and price. The fourth floor is for nonsmokers. Guests staying in first- or second-floor Diamond Floor rooms have separate check-in and checkout and receive complimentary continental breakfast as well as late-afternoon cocktails and appetizers. The hotel reserves Diamond Floor rooms directly, rather than through its toll-free number.

Dining/Diversions: There are two restaurants: **La Jolla** specializes in northern Italian food, and the more casual coffee shop is called **Café Royal.** An elegant musical quartet entertains nightly in the lobby **Caviar Bar,** the highlight of the hotel, where tea, drinks, and light meals are served.

Amenities: Complete business center, fitness center with workout equipment, massage service, three whirlpools and sauna and steam rooms, free parking adjacent to hotel. Laundry and room service; hair salon; car rental; travel agency; video recorders, computers, cellular phones, and fax machines for rent; electric adapters and converters on request. Golf privileges at a local course.

Hotel Nikko. Campos Eliseos 204, Col. Polanco, 11560 México, D.F. ☎ **800/NIKKO-US** in the U.S., or 5/280-1111. Fax 5/280-8965 or 5/280-9191. 750 units. A/C MINIBAR TV TEL. $260 deluxe; $295 Nikko Floors; $550–$1,300 suite. AE, MC, V. Metro: Auditorio.

One of the largest hotels in the city, the Nikko has 38 floors of pragmatically decorated rooms, with an ideal location opposite Chapultepec Park and the Auditorio Nacional, near all the Chapultepec Park museums. It blends modern comfort and convenience with traditional Asian decorating styles. The hotel lacks the warmth of many properties in Mexico City, partly due to its size, partly due to the influence of the stark decor. Rooms, which are quiet but small, are accessed with electronic keys. Security boxes and remote control for the TV are available at the front desk, and electric-plug adapters are found at the concierge desk. Bathrooms are also small in size with a combination shower/tub. One of the best parts of the standard rooms are the views: Large picture windows overlook the expanse of city in the valley. Nonsmokers have three floors reserved for them. Travelers with disabilities will find four specially equipped rooms. The four top floors are "Nikko Floors," with special check-in and checkout, concierge service, and a lounge for continental breakfast and evening cocktails.

Dining/Diversions: Of the hotel's four restaurants, two offer Japanese cuisine, one offers French, and another is international with a Mexican and American slant. **Shelty Bar,** with an English theme, often features live music; there's also a lobby bar and a disco.

Amenities: Indoor glass-topped pool, three tennis courts, practice court, fitness center, steam and sauna, whirlpool, massage, jogging track, laundry and dry cleaning, room service, beauty and barber shop, boutiques, art gallery, jewelry shop, car rental, and travel agency.

ZONA ROSA & SURROUNDING AREAS
VERY EXPENSIVE

Hotel María Isabel Sheraton. Reforma 325, at Río Tiber, 06500 México, D.F. ☎ **800/ 325-3535** in the U.S., or 5/207-3933. Fax 5/207-0684. 819 units. A/C MINIBAR TV TEL. $255–$325 double, standard room; $310–$355 Tower. AE, DC, Vc MC. Covered parking available. Metro: Insurgentes (6 blocks away).

The María Isabel Sheraton set the original standard for luxury hotels in Mexico City, and it continues to hold its own against newer competition. Its location in front of the *Monumento de la Independencia* is ideal: It's next to the U.S. Embassy and across Reforma from the heart of the Zona Rosa. The plush marble lobby hums with the comings and goings of foreign guests and the efficient activity of hotel personnel. In all its rooms, the hotel offers amenities such as card-activated door locks, hair dryers and magnifying makeup mirrors, in-room safes, purified tap water, three-pronged electrical outlets, and telephone voice mail. Three floors are reserved for nonsmokers, and seven rooms are outfitted for travelers with disabilities. Tower suites, the most deluxe in the hotel, occupy the fourth floor and have private check-in, butler service, and continental breakfast and evening canapés.

Dining/Diversions: The hotel offers three restaurants: The **Cafe Pavillon** serves international selections for breakfast, lunch, and dinner in a colonial-styled atmosphere. **Cardinale** serves specialty Italian cuisine, while the **Veranda** offers Mexican specialties; both are open for lunch and dinner. The **Jorongo Bar,** a Mexico City entertainment institution, offers live entertainment nightly from 7pm to 1am. (See "Mexico City After Dark," below, for more on the Jorongo.) The lobby bar also has live music nightly and is a popular place for enjoying a cocktail in a sophisticated atmosphere. Room service is available 24 hours.

Amenities: Complete business center with computers, modern full-service fitness center, two tennis courts, open-air pool and nearby golf-course privileges, laundry, dry cleaning, room service, travel agency, beauty and barber shop, boutiques, art galleries, jewelry stores.

✪ **Westin Galería Plaza.** Hamburgo 195, 06600 México, D.F. ☎ **800/WESTIN-1** in the U.S., or 5/230-1717. Fax 5/207-5867. 439 units. A/C MINIBAR TV TEL. $211 double. AE, DC, MC, V. Metro: Insurgentes.

Located in the heart of the Zona Rosa, the Westin Galería Plaza has earned a reputation as one of the highest-quality hotels in Mexico City. It's immensely popular with business travelers. The large and bright rooms have light-colored wood and wicker furniture with beds and drapes of elegant fabrics. All rooms come with direct-dial phones, voice mail, purified tap water, coffeemaker, iron, ironing board, and in-room safe-deposit box. Marble bathrooms have hair dryers, make-up mirrors, and a telephone extension. Universal outlets accommodate a fax or computer, and electrical adapters are available from the concierge. Executive Floor guests enjoy free local calls, parking privileges, and complimentary continental breakfast and afternoon cocktails served daily in the Executive Lounge. Special Guest Office rooms have a nearly complete office set up, including printer/fax/copier, desk, speakerphone with data port and special telephone rates that include free local calls and long-distance access, plus in-room faxing without a surcharge. Nonsmoking floors and rooms for travelers with disabilities are also available. The staff is professional, efficient, and accommodating.

Dining/Diversions: Of the hotel's four restaurants, the finest is **Il de France,** featuring elegant continental cuisine. **Cava Baja Bontana Bar** serves home-style Mexican dishes, the **Plaza Restaurant** offers international cuisine in an informal setting, and **Cafe Plaza** serves coffee and pastries. The sleek lobby bar overlooks a key intersection of the Zona Rosa and features an excellent selection of premium tequilas.

Amenities: Full-service business center with computers, fax, copier, meeting rooms, Internet access, bilingual secretarial assistance and presentation equipment; heated rooftop swimming pool; sundeck and fully equipped fitness center; laundry and dry cleaning; room service; 24-hour concierge travel agency; car rental; boutiques.

EXPENSIVE

Hotel Calinda Quality Geneve & Spa. Londres 130, 06600 México, D.F. ☎ **800/ 221-2222** in the U.S., 5/211-0071, or 5/221-2222. Fax 5/208-7422. 320 units. MINIBAR TV TEL. $155 double. AE, CB, DC, MC, V. Metro: Insurgentes.

One of the capital's most popular hotels, the Geneve has been receiving guests for more than 90 years. The lobby is always busy with travelers who've chosen it for its comfort and convenience—the location is top-notch. It's just steps from all the Zona Rosa restaurants and shops. Rooms are fresh and modern with colonial-style furniture, though you may want to request one on the upper floors; lobby noise has a way of traveling in this hotel. One hundred of the rooms have air-conditioning. There's a casual restaurant to the left of the lobby after you enter, but the hot spot here is El Jardín, a restaurant/bar with gorgeous stained-glass walls in the back of the lobby. The hotel is between Génova and Amberes.

Dining: A branch of the ever-present Sanborn's is located to the left of the lobby entrance, with the renowned **El Jardín** restaurant (now also operated by Sanborn's) located in the back of the lobby. Both are open for breakfast, lunch, and dinner, with full bar service.

Amenities: Modern spa facilities including fitness center and massage service; business center with computers, fax, secretarial services and meeting rooms; tobacco shop, gift shop, laundry service, travel agency.

Hotel Sevilla Palace. Reforma 105, 06030 México, D.F. ☎ **800/732-9488** in the U.S., or 5/566-8877. Fax 5/703-1521. 434 units. A/C MINIBAR TV TEL. $100 double; $150–$239 suite. MC, V. Free parking available. Metro: Revolución.

Although the Sevilla Palace is top quality in every way, it's mainly overlooked by foreigners. Its soaring lobby is embellished with teak-stained wood and burgundy marble and has four glass elevators whizzing up and down. Rooms are large, handsomely furnished, and all have voice mail, in-room safe-deposit boxes, electronic-card locks, and hair dryers. Most rooms have large showers and couches with sitting/table areas. Three-prong electrical adapters are available at the reception desk. The 20th and 21st floors are reserved for nonsmokers.

Dining/Diversions: There's a fine-dining restaurant (**El Lepanto**), a coffee shop (**Los Naranjos**), and a lobby bar with evening piano entertainment.

Amenities: Business center, workout room with enclosed swimming pool and whirlpool, laundry and room service, ice machines on each floor, travel agency, beauty and barber shop, gift shop, newsstand.

✪ La Casona Hotel-Relais. Durango 280 (corner of Cozumel), Col. Roma, 06700 México, D.F. ☎ **800/223-5652** in the U.S., or 5/286-3001. Fax 5/211-0871. E-mail: casona@mailer.data.net.mx. 30 units. TV TEL. $150 double. AE, CB, DC, MC, V. Metro: Sevilla (4 blocks away).

Reminiscent of a small European luxury hotel, this exquisite new hotel opened in 1996 after restoring a dilapidated 1923 building. It has since been designated an artistic monument by Mexico's National Institute of Fine Arts. Each luxuriously decorated room is unique; all have antique furniture. Tall interior shutter doors (some of them originals) on windows in each room keep out sound and light at night, and thick window glass mutes street noise by day. Oriental-style rugs warm the hardwood floors throughout hallways and rooms.

The hotel is 3 blocks south of the Diana Circle on Reforma and 4 longish blocks west of the western edge of the Zona Rosa. Chapultepec Park is about a 20-minute walk to the northwest. More important than decor or location is the excellence of service here—truly capable of leaving you with a pampered feeling.

Dining/Diversions: The small cheery restaurant, where all three moderately priced meals are served, is a cozy place. A small wine cellar/bar below the lobby is a popular gathering place with guests for drinks and conversation.

Amenities: Luxurious services and facilities include concierge, room service, complimentary daily newspaper, a small gym with a steam room, a solarium, and small meeting facilities.

MODERATE 888-412-9054

✪ Hotel Imperial. Paseo de la Reforma 64, 06600 México, D.F. ☎ **5/705-4911.** Fax 5/703-3122. 65 units. A/C MINIBAR TV TEL. $88 double; $123–$158 suite. AE, DC. Free parking. Metro: Revolución or Juárez.

This classic hotel, which dates to 1904 and is designated a Historic Monument, is one of the most memorable buildings along the avenida Reforma. With a legacy that includes serving as the home of one Mexican president, the site of the assassination of a second president, and for years the former location of the U.S. embassy, the Imperial had several changes in its operations before returning to its original name and status as a five-star hotel in 1989. Popular with foreign—especially European—guests, it's one of the best values in the area. Rooms are extra large and clean with high ceilings and carpeting, although the traditional-style furnishings are a bit dated. All rooms have either king or two double beds plus in-room safe-deposit boxes, and desk and sitting areas. Bathrooms are very large with separate vanity, tub, and hair dryers. The five Master Suites are the rooms located at the top of the five floors of the building, with a unique triangular bedroom overlooking avenida Reforma. These suites also feature a living/dining room, bar, and Jacuzzi in the bathroom. All rooms are entered from a central atrium with staircase.

The hotel offers laundry and dry cleaning, room service, concierge, and business center, and the noted Spanish restaurant and bar **Baudi** features live music nightly. Located where Reforma intersects with Morelos.

INEXPENSIVE

✪ Casa González. Río Sena 69, 06500 México, D.F. ☎ **5/514-3302.** 22 units. $24–$30 double; $50 suite for 4. No credit cards. Metro: Insurgentes (4 blocks away).

Casa González is a two-story hostelry made up of two mansions that have been converted into guest rooms. The houses, with little grassy patios out back and a huge shade tree, make a pleasant and quiet oasis in the middle of the city. Rooms are charming and homey—and heated for those chilly mornings. Each is unique, and some have a terrace or balcony. Meals (optional) are taken in a dining room bright with stained glass and international conversation. Casa González is especially good for women traveling alone, although there are only three single rooms. The warm, caring, management assures each guest feels like more than the passing visitor, but a part of a shifting, growing family. There's limited parking in the driveway. The hotel is between Río Lerma and Río Panuco.

María Cristina. Río Lerma 31, 06030 México, D.F. ☎ **5/703-1212** or 5/566-9688. Fax 5/566-9194. 189 units. MINIBAR TV TEL. $39 double; $55–$69 suite. AE, DC, MC, V.

This classic choice for budget travelers is conveniently located: just a 10-minute walk to the Zona Rosa. Rooms are bright and have one king or two double beds, ample closets, modern bathrooms, and come equipped with in-room safes. The large lobby with overstuffed couches and a fireplace makes a comfortable meeting place. A coffee shop is adjacent to the lobby, and a grassy courtyard offers lounge chairs for reading or relaxing. The hotel is at Río Neva, on the north side of Reforma.

CENTRO HISTÓRICO & SURROUNDING AREAS
MODERATE

✪ Best Western Hotel de Cortés. Av. Hidalgo 85, 06300 México, D.F. ☎ **800/ 528-1234** in the U.S., or 5/518-2184. Fax 5/521-0234. 29 units. MINIBAR TV TEL. $85 double; $152 suite. AE, DC, MC, V.

This baroque-style hotel offers clean, comfortable, modern accommodations in a fascinating historic building—a former home for Augustinian friars. The 18th-century stone structure features rooms on two floors surrounding a central colonial courtyard with a graceful fountain and Mexican restaurant. It's located on Alameda Park, a short distance from the Palace of Fine Arts and the Franz Mayer Museum. Rooms vary in size and features, but all are clean with handwoven bedspreads, carpeting, desk and newly remodeled bathrooms with modern sinks, 3-prong plugs, and tile accents. Security boxes are available in the reception area.

○ **Best Western Hotel Majestic.** Av. Madero 73, 06000 México, D.F. ☎ **800/ 528-1234** in the U.S., or 5/521-8600. Fax 5/512-6262. www.majestic.com.mx. 85 units. A/C MINIBAR TV TEL. $85 double; $125 suite. AE, MC, V. Metro: Zócalo.

This places earns its star for its prime location—facing the zócalo, the impressive central plaza of Mexico City. The Majestic is somewhat of a Mexico City institution that visitors should experience at least once. Rooms that don't look onto Mexico City's main square overlook avenida Madero or the hotel's own inner court. From the lobby, which is decorated with stone arches, beautiful tiles, and stone fountains, take the elevator to the second floor and its courtyard. There, you'll find a floor of glass blocks— ideal for gazing all the way up to the glass roof six stories above. Each doorway has a border of blue-and-white tiles.

The only adequately furnished rooms have dated furniture and tile bathrooms with tubs. In lower-floor rooms facing avenida Madero, noise from the street may be a problem—you may choose the quieter rooms that look out onto the interior court—or the upper floors. Occupants of rooms facing the zócalo will get an unexpected jolt from the early-morning flag-raising ceremony, complete with marching feet, drums, and bugle. The finishing touch to the Majestic is a popular rooftop cafe/restaurant where umbrella-shaded tables welcome patrons for all three meals. Additional services include room service, travel agency, and baby-sitting. You can save quite a few dollars by booking direct with the hotel and by asking for promotional rates or current discounts.

INEXPENSIVE

○ **Hotel Catedral.** Calle Donceles 95, 06020 México, D.F. ☎ **5/518-5232.** Fax 5/512-4344. 116 units. TV TEL. $33 double. AE, MC, V. Free parking. Metro: Zócalo.

This modern hotel with a stellar location is also an excellent value. One block north of calle Tacuba is the tree-shaded calle Donceles, where you'll find the eight-story (with elevator) Hotel Catedral, half a block from the Templo Mayor and a block from the Museo San Ildefonso. In front of the big marble-embellished lobby is the restaurant, bustling with white-jacketed waiters. The bar beyond the reception desk is cozy with cloth-clad tables and food service as well. The handsomely remodeled rooms are modern; some have tub/shower combinations, some have Jacuzzis, while all have purified drinking water from a special tap, good over-bed reading lights, and TV with U.S. cable channels. Rooms on the upper floors have views of Mexico City's mammoth cathedral. On the seventh floor, a terrace with small tables and chairs offers great views. Its location is ideal for sightseeing, and the central downtown district is experiencing a revival in its offerings of trendy restaurants and chic clubs. Due to the heavily trafficked streets that surround it, add an extra 45 minutes on to your departure time if you go to the airport from here. The hotel is between the streets Brasil and Argentina.

○ **Hotel Gillow.** Isabel la Católica 17, 06000 México, D.F. ☎ **5/518-1440.** Fax 5/ 512-2078. 103 units. TV TEL. $38 double. AE, MC, V. Metro: Zócalo.

Personal friends and many readers give this hotel high praise, as do I. The dignified looking, seven-story Gillow is a modern hotel with six stories of rooms grouped around a long, glass-canopied, rectangular courtyard with a colonial fountain. Were it in the Zona Rosa, the Gillow could easily cost three times the price. Clean, well-kept, newly carpeted rooms with comfortable beds, a tub/shower combination, excellent lighting, and remote-control TV (in most rooms) are among the best features in each room. Some rooms are small, with one double bed and enough room for one person's luggage. Others are quite spacious with a long carpeted bench for suitcases. Interior room windows open to an air shaft, exterior rooms have small terraces with wrought-iron furniture. Ice machines are on several floors. An excellent restaurant on the first floor offers long hours, good food, friendly service, and an excellent comida corrida. The hotel is on the west side of the street between Cinco de Mayo and Madero—a hard-to-beat downtown location.

NEAR THE AIRPORT

Marriott Hotel. Puerto 80, 15520 México, D.F. ☎ **800/228-9290** or 5/230-0505. Fax 5/230-0555. 600 units. A/C MINIBAR TV TEL. $105 double. AE, DC, MC, V. Wait for the courtesy van near the Gate A exit in front of the airport.

This hotel is directly opposite the airport, actually on-site; to get there, exit the terminal near Gate A and look for the hotel sign by the curb; a courtesy van makes continuous rounds to take arriving guests to the hotel without charge. The staff is attentive and the rooms are nicely furnished, each with color TV with U.S. channels and pay-per-view movies, plus purified water from the tap. You'll find several restaurants, a bar, a disco, 24-hour business center and a health club with pool, steam room, massage services, beauty salon, and workout facilities. The hotel also provides a 24-hour concierge service, room service, laundry and pressing service, and courtesy van to the airport. There's also a convenient walkway directly to the airport.

4 Where to Dine

Dining in Mexico City can be every bit as sophisticated as other principal cities in the world, with cuisines that span the globe. From high chic to the Mexican standard of comida corrida, the capital of Mexico offers something for every taste and budget. The **Polanco area** in particular has become a place of exquisite dining options, with new restaurants rediscovering and modernizing classic Mexican dishes. The **Centro Histórico** has seen a resurgence of restaurants and clubs open for late night and ultrahip dining and nightlife. Cantinas, until not so long ago the privilege of men only, offer some of the best food and colorful local atmosphere.

Everybody eats out in Mexico City, regardless of social strata. Consequently, you can find restaurants of every type, size, and price range scattered across the city. Mexicans take their food and dining seriously, so wherever you see a full house is generally recommendation enough. But those same places may be entirely empty if you arrive early—remember, here, lunch is generally eaten at 3pm, with dinner not even considered before 9pm.

Although there exists the presence of American-type chains such as McDonald's, Subway, Burger King, Pizza Hut, VIP's, Denny's, and the Hard Rock Cafe affiliates, I feel no need to describe them—you'll run across them frequently. With so many unique and wonderful choices at your disposal in every price range, why fall back on the familiar? Venture out, dig in, and enjoy!

CHAPULTEPEC PARK & POLANCO
VERY EXPENSIVE

Chez Wok. Tennyson 117, at Mazaryk. ☎ 5/281-3410 or 5/281-2921. Reservations recommended. Main courses $21–$55. AE, MC, V. Mon–Sat 1:45–4:45pm and 7:30–11:45pm. Valet and free parking available. Metro: Polanco. HAUTE CHINESE.

Opened in the fashionable Polanco area in 1992 with five chefs from Hong Kong and their incredible recipes, Chez Wok immediately became *the* place to feast on Chinese food. Located on the second floor, it's packed at every hour. Prices are high, though most dishes serve two or three people. The dining area, with large and small sections, has a combination of booths and tables with an elegant but simple yellow, black, and beige decor. Lettuce rolls come stuffed with minced quail and vegetables, and authentic shark-fin soup is the most expensive item on the menu. Main courses include steamed red snapper with white-wine sauce, chicken in a shrimp paste with sesame and crab sauce, and the house specialty of Peking duck. To beat the crowd, plan to be there when it opens, before the locals arrive. *Note:* Jacket and tie are required evenings. The place is usually filled with businessmen at lunchtime and families at night.

✪ Fouquets de Paris. In the Hotel Camino Real, Mariano Escobedo 700. ☎ 5/203-2121, ext. 8500. Reservations recommended for dinner. Jacket/tie required for men. Main courses $24–$35. AE, DC, MC, V. Mon–Fri 7:30–11:30am and 1:30–5pm; Mon–Sat 7:30–11:30pm. Valet parking and covered parking available at $1.50 per hr. Metro: Chapultepec. INTERNATIONAL.

Dining at Fouquets de Paris is a culinary experience of the first order, made all the better by the elegant atmosphere and refined service. Government ministers, senators, and visiting dignitaries often dine here. And this is a popular place for those trendy power breakfasts; the morning menu mixes creative combinations of Mexican and international cuisines—for example, crepes with *machaca* (dried beef) and eggs, huitlacoche omelets, or omelets with morel mushrooms and artichokes—with traditional breakfast fare such as hotcakes. For other meals you might consider lobster bisque, asparagus and crawfish in a puff pastry, rack of lamb, beef tenderloin, or veal in morel mushrooms. Highly recommended.

Hacienda de los Morales. Vázquez de Mella 525. ☎ 5/281-4554 or 5/281-4703. Reservations required. Jacket/tie required for men in the evening. Main courses $18–$40. AE, MC, V. Daily 1pm–1am. Valet parking. INTERNATIONAL.

The Hacienda de los Morales, which resides in a great Spanish colonial house not far from Chapultepec Park, has been a favorite of visitors and locals for years. Within the house are a cocktail lounge with entertainment, numerous richly decorated dining rooms, and a plant-filled inner courtyard. The service is polished, the food delicious. Among their specialties are seafood soup and *tampiqueña* steak. The restaurant is northwest of Chapultepec Park at the corner of avenida Ejercito Nacional.

La Galvia. Campos Eliseos 247. ☎ 5/281-2310. Reservations suggested. Main courses $12–$25. AE, DC, MC, V. Mon–Fri 1:30–11pm; Sat 2–11pm; Sun 2–5pm. Metro: Auditorio. MEXICAN HAUTE CUISINE/INTERNATIONAL.

A top dining address, La Galvia seats its guests in a large window-framed room and treats them to impeccable service and refined food from a short but select menu. There's both a cold and a hot appetizer menu that includes black-bean soup with *nopalitos* (baby cactus). Entrees include salmon in soy sauce and *róbalo* (bass) in three-chile sauce. The menu changes every 3 months. For dessert try the Helena chocolate torte. You'll find the restaurant in Polanco immediately behind the Hotel Presidente Inter-Continental at the corner of Eugenio Sur.

EXPENSIVE

✪ **Fonda Santa Clara.** Homero 1910, Col. Polanco; ☎ **5/557-6144.** Av. San Jerónimo 775, Col. San Jerónimo Lídice; ☎ **5/683-0730.** Main courses $8–$18. AE, DC, MC, V. Mon 7:30am–6pm; Tues–Fri 7:30am–midnight; Sat 8:30am–midnight; Sun 8:30am–6pm. TRADITIONAL MEXICAN/PUEBLA.

Another of the city's fine dining establishments, this one presents the best of Puebla's cuisine to a full dining room daily. The menu lists a full range of specialties that are offered daily and others that are seasonal. The large serving of *manchamantel* (literally, "tablecloth stainer") is a sweet, smooth mole made by blending chiles, apricots, pears, apples, and bananas and served over pork or chicken—it's fabulous. The *sartenada ranchera* is enough to fill two diners. The feast is a combination plate of superbly seasoned and grilled meats with sausage and bacon served with onions, salsa, and avocado. Service is refined and attentive. Arrive early, since every seat in its several dining areas will be filled, especially at lunch. If you happen to be visiting this restaurant between late July and September, you must try the chiles en nogada, a delicious blend of hot chiles stuffed with meat and fruit and covered in a walnut sauce. This is one of the most baroque dishes in Mexican cuisine. This restaurant is a more expensive cousin of the Santa Clara in Puebla, but the menus are almost identical. Mexico City has two branches: One is in Polanco, between the Pereférico Norte and Blas Pascal, and the other is on the south side, in San Jerónimo—take a taxi.

La Fonda del Recuerdo. Bahía de las Palmas 37, Col. Verónica Anzures. ☎ **5/260-0545.** Main courses $7–$21. AE, DC, MC, V. Daily noon–midnight. MEXICAN/SEAFOOD.

For an all-out good time, no other restaurant in the city compares to this one. Diners at Fonda del Recuerdo enjoy their platters of Mexican food amid a glorious din created by *jarocho* musicians from Veracruz (there will be several groups roving around the restaurant at once). Come here if you want to immerse yourself in Mexico and join people eating, drinking, and singing, having the time of their lives. The menu is authentically Mexican, with an emphasis on seafood; specials match the culinary traditions of whichever Mexican holiday is closest on the calendar. Arrive before 1:30pm for lunch or you'll have to wait in a long line, which nonetheless will be worth it if you have all afternoon. At night it's just as festive, but try to make it before 9pm, when it begins to get crowded. It's near the corner of Bahía de Santa Bárbara—take a taxi.

✪ **La Valentina.** Mazaryk 393, Col. Polanco. ☎ **5/282-2656** or 5/282-2514. Main courses $10–$15. AE, DC, MC, V. Daily 2pm–2am. Valet parking $2. Metro: Polanco. MEXICAN NOUVELLE CUISINE.

In the midst of posh Polanco, on the second floor of a small boutique-filled shopping center, is this dignified restaurant with an elegantly casual flair. Pale-apricot stucco walls, shiny wood floors, and wood-beamed ceilings set off the cozy nooks of immaculately set tables. The menu features specialties from some of the country's best Mexican cooks. For example, there's Marta Chapa's breaded shrimp with sesame, lettuce, herbs, and chiles; cilantro soup by Suzanna Palanzuelos; and Patricia Quintana's fillet in butter and salsa. Other selections include changing daily specials and mole with the flavor of tamarind. Their ample-sized bar is worth a visit on its own, with an impressive selection of premium tequilas, a selection of fine art, and an upscale cantina-style atmosphere. The restaurant is near the corner of Lafontaine.

MODERATE

Nautilus. Mazarik 360-4. ☎ **5/280-2283** or 5/2802-1320. Main courses $10–$20. AE, MC, V. Mon–Sat 8am–11pm; Sun 9am–7pm. Valet parking $1.25. Metro: Polanco. SEAFOOD/INTERNATIONAL.

An outdoor restaurant on Polanco's main drag, this is a popular place to grab an umbrella-shaded sidewalk table and feast while watching the passing scene. The menu choices feature seafood, pasta, and steak. The Fillet Oaxaca comes breaded with Oaxaca cheese and cream sauce. The Fillet Moctezuma is accompanied with huitlacoche and flor de calabaza. Plus, there's a full lineup of special tacos—try the lobster tacos. The restaurant is located on Mazaryk between Oscar Wilde and Muset, near the Polanco or Auditorio Subway stations.

ZONA ROSA & SURROUNDING AREAS
EXPENSIVE

✪ **Cicero Centenario.** Londres 195. ☎ **5/533-3800.** Reservations recommended. Main courses $10–$30. AE, DC, MC, V. Mon–Sat 1pm–1am. Valet parking available. Metro: Insurgentes. INTERNATIONAL/NOUVELLE MEXICAN.

Cicero Centenario is the epitome of Mexico's elegant cafe society and one of the most noted restaurants in the country. Stylish, eccentric, artistic, and whimsical all at once, this place offers more than excellent food but a complete dining experience *a la mexicana.* Tables in the intimate nooks of the restaurant's smart salons look out on a backdrop of stained glass, antiques, and flickering candlelight. Among the highlights on the menu are starters such as a delectable cream of cilantro soup, and crepes stuffed with squash flower blossoms and Gruyère cheese in a mild poblano chile sauce. Main dishes include recipes developed for the restaurant by noted chef and author Patricia Quintana, such as chicken in a rich almond sauce and her renowned mole poblano. The restaurant is between Florencia and Amberes. There is another branch of the restaurant in the Historic Center of the city (see below).

Restaurant Angus. Copenhague 31, at the corner of Hamburgo. ☎ **5/208-2828** or 5/511-8633. Reservations recommended. Main courses $8–$16; steaks $14–$25. AE, DC, MC, V. Daily 1pm–1am. Valet parking available. Metro: Insurgentes. STEAKS.

Restaurant Angus is the place to go in the D.F. when you want nothing so much as a good, juicy steak. The interior features Old West decor with fashionable details, and there's outdoor dining under a green awning with brass rails on cafe-lined, pedestrian-only Copenhague (the outdoor portion of Angus expanded to take up half the street). The clientele is a mix of business types clad in suits and others dressed a bit more casually. All varieties of steaks are served here, and there's prime rib and fajitas as well. A few shrimp selections may satisfy those who don't want beef.

Restaurant Passy. Amberes 10. ☎ **5/208-2087.** Reservations recommended. Main courses $18–$25. AE, MC, V. Mon–Sat 1–11pm. Valet parking available. Metro: Insurgentes. INTERNATIONAL.

The Restaurant Passy is an elegant old favorite of locals and tourists alike. The attractive, classic, and restrained decor features low lights, antiques, linen, and candles. The service is polished and polite, and the menu is traditional French: Oysters Rockefeller, onion or oyster soup, chicken cordon bleu, canard (duck) à l'orange, and coq au vin are among the continental favorites. There's also a good selection of fish. It's between Reforma and Hamburgo.

MODERATE

Chalet Suizo. Niza 37. ☎ **5/511-7529.** Main courses $5.25–$12. V, MC. Daily 12:30pm–midnight. Metro: Insurgentes. INTERNATIONAL.

Founded in 1950 and still one of the most dependable and cozy restaurants around, Chalet Suizo features, logically, Swiss decor: checkered tablecloths, pine walls, beamed ceilings, and Alpine landscapes. The menu features hearty French onion soup and a wide range of interesting main dishes, some of which are changed daily. Among these are veal with morel mushrooms, smoked pork chops, German-style pot roast, chicken tarragon, veal goulash, sauerbraten, and excellent fondue. The food is delicious, the portions large, and the service friendly and quick. The restaurant is on the west side of the street between Hamburgo and Londres.

✪ **Fonda El Refugio.** Liverpool 166. ☎ **5/207-2732** or 5/525-8128. Main courses $7–$15. AE, MC, V. Mon–Sat 1pm–midnight; Sun 1–10pm. Valet parking available. Metro: Insurgentes. MEXICAN.

The service, food, and atmosphere at Fonda El Refugio have been shaped by more than 40 years of tradition, making it a very special place for authentic Mexican dining. Although small, it's unusually congenial, with a large fireplace decorated with gleaming copper pots and pans. Rows and rows of culinary awards and citations hang behind the desk. The restaurant manages the almost impossible task of being both elegant and informal. The menu runs the gamut of Mexican cuisine, from *arroz con plátanos* (rice with fried bananas) to enchiladas con mole poblano, topped with the rich, thick, spicy chocolate sauce of Puebla. There's a daily specialty. Try the chiles stuffed with ground beef or cheese and for dessert have some coconut candy. Fonda El Refugio is very popular, especially on Saturday night, so get there early. It's between Florencia and Amberes.

CENTRO HISTÓRICO & SURROUNDING AREAS
EXPENSIVE

✪ **Cicero Centenario.** Cuba 79. ☎ **5/521-2934** or 5/521-7866. Reservations recommended. Main courses $10–$30. AE, DC, MC, V. Mon–Sat 1pm–1am. Metro: Allende. INTERNATIONAL/NOUVELLE MEXICAN.

This Cicero shares the same ambiance of magical realism as its sister restaurant in the Zona Rosa. Tucked in the historic zone in an elegant two-story 19th-century mansion, it is among the most popular eating establishments in the city. At every meal all the tables have reservation cards bearing the name of a client. The menu is essentially the same as the other Cicero's—fish, beef, and chicken served with great sauces and seasonings. Each day there's a different special: Friday brings whitefish from Pátzcuaro, while on Saturday it's manchamanteles—both gourmet delights. June through September they offer chiles en nogada; during April and May, *gusanos de maguey.* The latter is a seasonal "worm dish": worms that live on the maguey leaves (the tequila plant), considered a delicacy. They're served fried, accompanied with guacamole and tortillas. The restaurant is 5 blocks northeast of the Alameda, between República de Chile and Palma, not far from the Santo Domingo Plaza and Church.

MODERATE

✪ **Café Tacuba.** Tacuba 28. ☎ **5/512-8482.** Breakfast $4–$8.25; main courses $6–$9.50; comida corrida $9–$13. AE, MC, V. Daily 8am–11:30pm. Metro: Allende. MEXICAN.

One of the city's best-established and popular restaurants, Café Tacuba dates to 1912, with a handsome colonial-era atmosphere. Guests are welcomed into one of two long dining rooms, with brass lamps, dark and brooding oil paintings, and a large mural of nuns working in a kitchen. The menu is authentic Mexican with traditional recipes, including tamales, enchiladas, chiles rellenos, mole, and pozole. Thursday through Sunday from 6pm until closing, a wonderful group of medieval-costumed singers entertains; their sound is like the melodious *estudiantina* groups of Guanajuato accompanied by mandolins and guitars. The cafe is between República de Chile and Bolívar.

Hosteria de Santo Domingo. Domínguez 72. ☎ **5/510-1434.** Breakfast $3–$4.50; main courses $4–$10; specialties of the day $9. AE, MC, V. Daily 9am–11pm. Metro: Allende. MEXICAN.

Established in 1860, the Hostería de Santo Domingo is said to be the oldest restaurant in the city still in operation. A mural at one end of the main dining room shows the Plaza Domingo during colonial times. The player piano will fool you into thinking a pianist is playing nonstop—then again, a pianist may in fact be playing. The food is excellent, with large portions. At lunchtime the place is generally packed, so arrive early. Try the stuffed peppers with cheese, the pork loin, or the unusual bread soup. The restaurant is north of the zócalo, between República de Brazil and República de Chile, near Palma.

Restaurant Danúbio. Uruguay 3. ☎ **5/512-0912.** Main courses $9–$15. AE, MC, V. Daily 1–10pm. Metro: Bellas Artes or Salto del Agua. SEAFOOD/SPANISH.

This place has been a Mexico City tradition since 1938, and it remains an excellent choice for lunch. Locals enjoy this restaurant on weekends with their families. The house specialty is *langostinos* (baby crayfish), and the menu offers a range of selections emphasizing seafood. Danúbio is noted for its excellent wine cellar. The restaurant is south of the Alameda near the corner of Lázaro Cárdenas.

INEXPENSIVE

Café Cinco de Mayo. Cinco de Mayo no. 57. ☎ **5/510-1995.** Breakfast $1.75–$3; main courses $2.50–$6.50; comida corrida $2.75–$4. AE, DISC, MC, V. Daily 7am–11pm. Metro: Zócalo. MEXICAN.

Less than a block west of the cathedral on the south side of the street, this Mexican-style lunchroom is bright with fluorescent lights and loud with conversation. Regulars take their places at the long counter. Waiters scurry here and there bearing enormous glasses of fresh orange juice, cups of hot coffee, baskets of pan dulce, sandwiches, pork chops—just about anything you can imagine. If you order café con leche, a waiter will approach with a big copper coffeepot, pour an inch of thick, bitter coffee into the bottom of your glass, and then fill it up with hot milk. The restaurant is between the zócalo and Palma.

Sanborn's Casa de Azulejos. Madero 4. ☎ **5/518-6676.** Main courses $3.25–$8; dessert and coffee $2–$4. AE, V, MC, DC. Daily 7am–1am. Metro: Bellas Artes. MEXICAN/AMERICAN.

Known today as Sanborn's House of Tiles (for the tiles covering the outside walls), this gorgeous antique building was once the palace of the counts of the Valley of Orizaba. For many years now it has housed a branch of the Sanborn's restaurant and variety-store chain. Dining tables are set in an elaborate covered courtyard complete with carved pillars, tiles, and peacock frescoes. The second floor has lovely secluded dining areas and a handsome bar. It's directly across Madero from the San Francisco church and diagonally across from the Latin American Tower. Food is standard shop fare, found throughout the Sanborn's chain everywhere in Mexico. You go to the House of Tiles for the building, not the food.

CANTINAS

Cantina La Guadalupana. Higuera 14, Coyoacán. ☎ **5/554-6253.** Main courses $3.25–$10; mixed drinks $2.75–$6. AE, MC, V. Mon–Sat 1pm–midnight. INTERNATIONAL.

Opened in 1928, this cantina is located in Coyoacán, the southern neighborhood that was once the home of the artists Diego Rivera and Frida Kahlo and the revolutionary Leon Trotsky. From the entrance—off a narrow, cobblestone, colonial street—to the antiquated bar, a sense of nostalgia permeates the atmosphere here. The operation of this cantina is as traditional as its menu, and it has a comfortable, jovial air about it. For those who are only drinking, waiters bring the customary small plates of complimentary snacks that range from crisp jícama slices with lime and chile to pigs feet in a red sauce. Located 1 block from the central plaza.

La Ópera Bar. Cinco de Mayo 10. ☎ **5/512-8959.** Reservations recommended at lunch. Main courses $4.25–$9; mixed drinks $2.75–$6. AE, MC, V. Mon–Sat 1pm–midnight. Metro: Bellas Artes. INTERNATIONAL.

La Ópera Bar, 3 blocks east of the Alameda, is the most opulent of the city's cantinas. Slide into one of the dark wood booths, below gilded baroque ceilings, patches of beveled mirror, and exquisite small oil paintings of pastoral scenes. Or grab a linen-covered table with a basket of fresh bread. La Ópera is the Mexican equivalent of a London gentlemen's club, although it has become so popular for dining that fewer and fewer men play dominoes. In fact, you see more and more people enjoying romantic interludes in one of the cavernous booths—but tables of any kind are hard to find. Service is best if you arrive for lunch when it opens or go after 5pm when the throngs have diminished; waiters cater to regulars at the expense of diners that are unknown to them. The Spanish and Mexican menu is sophisticated and extensive, and the atmosphere for lunch and dinner is excellent. Try the incredible "Aperital Batido," the bartender's special aperitif. While you wait for one of the jacketed waiters to bring your meal, look to the ceiling for the bullet hole that legend says Pancho Villa left when he galloped in on a horse. It's half a block toward the zócalo from Sanborn's House of Tiles.

A TEAHOUSE

Salón de Thé Duca d'Este. Hamburgo 164b. ☎ **5/525-6374** or 5/514-0566. Breakfast $3–$4; ice cream or pastry $1.75–$2.35; salads $3–$4; soups $2.50. AE, DC, MC, V. Sun–Thurs 8am–11pm; Fri–Sat 8am–midnight. Metro: Insurgentes. CONTINENTAL.

You may not immediately think "tea!" in Mexico City, but Duca d'Este is a good place for it and simple meals. Small tea tables draped in apricot cloths look out onto the bustle of pedestrian traffic in the Zona Rosa. There's a good selection of coffees, teas, and hot chocolates, to accompany pastries, fresh and candied fruits, ice creams, and other fare. You can have a light lunch or supper by ordering soup, salad, or salmon. It's at the corner of Florencia and Hamburgo.

5 Exploring Mexico City

The diverse attractions in Mexico City rival its complex layers of history. From the simple pleasure of a stroll through a bustling mercado to museums filled with treasures of artistic and historic significance, Mexico City has much to explore.

Mexico City was built on the ruins of the ancient city of Tenochtitlán. A downtown portion of the city, comprising almost 700 blocks and 1,500 buildings, has been designated a Historical Zone (Centro Histórico). The area has surged in popularity, and neglected buildings are rapidly being converted into chic clubs and trendy restaurants, reminiscent of its former colonial charm.

Remember that this is a city, and a major one at that; dress is more professional and formal here than in other parts of the country. The altitude makes temperatures much cooler, which is often a surprise for travelers with preconceptions that Mexico is perpetually hot. In summer, always be prepared for rain, which comes almost daily. In winter, carry a jacket or sweater—stone museums are cold inside, and when the sun goes down, the outside air gets chilly.

MEXICO CITY NEIGHBORHOODS
CENTRO HISTÓRICO

At least 1,500 buildings and an area of almost 700 acres of historic downtown Mexico City around the Alameda and zócalo have been earmarked for preservation. Much of the history of Mexico from the 16th to the 20th centuries is reflected in the grand palaces and buildings in these two areas.

COYOACÁN

Coyoacán (koh-yoh-ah-*kahn*) is a pretty and wealthy colonial suburb boasting many old houses and cobbled streets dating from the 16th century. At its center are two graceful large plazas, the Plaza Hidalgo and Jardín Centenario, and the Church of San Juan Bautista (1583). Once the capital of the Tepanec kingdom, Coyoacán was later conquered by the Aztecs and then by Cortés, who lived here during the building of Mexico City.

From downtown, the Metro Line 3 can take you to the Coyoacán or Viveros station, within walking distance of Coyoacán's museums. Or "Iztacala–Coyoacán" buses will get you from the center to this suburb.

If you're coming from San Ángel, the quickest and easiest way is to take a cab for the 15-minute ride to the Plaza Hidalgo. Sosa, a pretty street, is the main artery into Coyoacán from San Ángel. Or you can catch the "Alcantarilla–Col. Agrarista" bus heading east along the Camino al Desierto de los Leones or avenida Altavista, near the San Ángel Inn. Get off when the bus gets to the corner of avenida Mexico and Xicoténcatl in Coyoacán.

SAN ÁNGEL

San Ángel (sahn *ahn*-hail) is a fashionable colonial-era suburb of cobblestone streets with several worthwhile museums. The nearest Metro station is M.A. Quevedo (Line 3). From downtown, take a colectivo (marked "SAN ÁNGEL") or bus ("marked INDIOS VERDES–TLALPAN" or "CENTRAL NORTE–VILLA OLÍMPICA") south along Insurgentes near the Zona Rosa. Ask to get off at La Paz. To the east is a pretty park, the Plaza del Carmen, and on the west side of Insurgentes is a Sanborn's store/restaurant. Saturday is a good day to go because you can combine museum visits with the wonderful Bazar Sábado Market (see "Shopping," below), which occurs only on Saturday (Sábado).

XOCHIMILCO

Naturally flowing shallow canals have existed here since the time of the Aztecs. Today, the most well-known attractions of Xochimilco (so-chee-*meel*-co) are the more than 50 miles of canals known as the "Floating Gardens" (see "Parks/Gardens," below for details).

Xochimilco itself is a colonial-era gem: With its bricked streets and light traffic, it seems small despite its sizable population of 300,000. Restaurants are at the edge of the canal and shopping area, and historically significant churches are within easy walking distance of the main square. When you get to the town of Xochimilco, you'll find a busy market in operation, specializing in rugs, ethnic clothing, and brightly decorated pottery.

Xochimilco hosts an amazing 422 festivals annually, the most famous of which celebrate the **Niñopa,** a figure of the Christ Child that since 1875 has been believed to possess miraculous powers. The figure is venerated on January 6 (Three Kings Day), February 2 (changing of the Niñopa's custodian), December 16 through 24 (posadas for the Niñopa), and April 30 (Day of the Child). Caring for the Niñopa is a coveted privilege which lasts a year, and the schedule of approved caretakers is filled through the year 2031. March 28 through April 4 (it varies slightly) is the *Feria de la Flor Más Bella del Ejido,* a flower fair when the most beautiful girl with Indian features and costume is selected. For more information and exact dates, contact the **Xochimilco Tourist Office** (Subdirección de Turismo), Piño no. 36 (☎ **5/676-5844;** fax 5/676-0978), 2 blocks from the main square. It's open Monday through Saturday from 8am until 3pm and 6 to 9pm.

To reach Xochimilco, take the Metro to Tasqueña, then the *tren ligero,* which stops at the outskirts of Xochimilco. From there, take a taxi to the main plaza of the town of Xochimilco. Buses run all the way across the city from north to south to end up at Xochimilco, but they take longer than the Metro. Of the buses coming from the center, the most convenient is "La Villa–Xochimilco," which you catch going south on Correo Mayor and Pino Suárez near the zócalo; or near Chapultepec on avenida Vasconcelos, avenida Nuevo León, and avenida Division del Norte.

THE TOP ATTRACTIONS

✪ **Basílica de Nuestra Señora de Guadalupe.** Villa de Guadalupe. No phone. Free admission; museum 50¢. Tues–Sun 10am–6pm. Metro: Basílica or La Villa. From Basílica, take the exit marked SALIDA AV. MONTIEL; walk a block or so north of the Metro station to a major intersection (Montevideo; you'll know it by the VIP's and Denny's across the street to the left); turn right onto Av. Montevideo and cross the overpass; after about 15-min. walk, you'll see the great church looming ahead. From La Villa, walk north on Calzada de Guadalupe.

Within the northern city limits is the famous Basilica of Guadalupe, located on the site where, on December 9, 1531, a poor Indian named Juan Diego is reputed to have seen a vision of a beautiful lady in a blue mantle. The local bishop, Zumarraga, was reluctant to confirm that Juan had indeed seen the Virgin Mary, so he asked the peasant for some evidence. Juan saw the vision a second time, on December 12, and when he asked her for proof, she instructed him to collect the roses that began blooming in the rocky soil at Juan Diego's feet. He gathered the flowers in his cloak and returned to the bishop. When he unfurled his cloak, the flowers dropped to the ground and the image of the Virgin was miraculously emblazoned on the rough-hewn cloth. The bishop immediately ordered the building of a church on the spot, and upon its completion the image was hung in a place of honor, framed in gold. Since that time, millions of the devout and the curious have come to view the miraculous image that experts, it is said, are at a loss to explain. The blue-mantled Virgin of Guadalupe is the patron saint of Mexico.

So heavy was the flow of visitors—many approached for hundreds of yards on their knees—that the old church, already fragile, was insufficient to handle them. An audacious New Basilica was built, designed by Pedro Ramírez Vazquez, the same architect who did the breathtaking Museo Nacional de Antropología.

The miracle cloak hangs behind bullet-proof glass above the altar. Electric people-movers going in two directions move the crowds a distance below the cloak. If you want to see it again, take the people mover going in the opposite direction; you can do it as many times as you wish.

To the right of the modern basilica is the Old Basilica, actually the second one built to house the cloak—the first one is higher up on the hill. Unfortunately, the Old Basilica is tilting precariously, and is not open to visitors. Restoration has been ongoing for at least 10 years, but is moving more rapidly now. To the back of it is the entrance to the Basilica Museum, with a very good display of religious art in restored rooms. One of the side chapels, with a silver altar, is adjacent to the museum and nearing completion of restoration; check to see if it has reopened.

Outside the museum is a garden commemorating the moment Juan Diego showed the cloak to the archbishop. Numerous photographers with colorful backdrops gather there to capture your visit on film. At the top of the hill, behind the basilica, is the **Panteón del Tepeyac,** a cemetery for Mexico's more infamous folk (Santa Anna among them), and several gift shops specializing in religious objects and other folk art. The steps up this hill are lined with flowers, shrubs, and waterfalls, and the climb, although tiring, is worthwhile for the view from the top.

If you visit Mexico City on **December 12,** you can witness the grand festival in honor of the **Virgin of Guadalupe.** The square in front of the basilica fills up with the pious and the party-minded as prayers, dances, and a carnival atmosphere attract thousands of the devout. Many visitors combine a trip to the basilica with one to the **ruins of Teotihuacán,** since both are out of the city center in the same direction. It is virtually impossible to understand Mexico and its culture without appreciating the national devotion for the Virgin of Our Lady of Guadalupe.

✪ **Museo Frida Kahlo.** Londres 247, Coyoacán. ☎ **5/554-5999.** Admission $1.50. Tues–Sun 10am–6pm. Note that no cameras are allowed. Metro: Coyoacán.

Although during her lifetime Frida Kahlo was known principally as the muralist Diego Rivera's wife, today her own art now surpasses his in popularity. Kahlo's life was dedicated both to her painting and her passionate, tortured love for her husband. Her emotional and physical pain—her spine was pierced during a serious streetcar accident in her youth—were the primary subjects of her canvases, many of which are self portraits. These paintings are now acknowledged as not only exceptional works of Latin American art, but some of the purest artistic representations of female strength and struggle ever created. As her paintings have surged in renown and price, so has an interest in the life of this courageous, provocative, and revolutionary woman.

Kahlo was born in this house on July 7, 1910, and lived here with Rivera from 1929 to 1954. During the 1930s and 1940s it was a popular gathering place for intellectuals. As you wander through the rooms of this cornflower-blue house you'll get a glimpse of the life they led. Most of the rooms remain in their original state, with mementos everywhere. Tiny clay pots hang about; the names Diego and Frida are painted on the walls of the kitchen. In the studio upstairs, a wheelchair sits next to the easel with a partially completed painting surrounded by paintbrushes, palettes, books, photographs, and other paraphernalia of the couple's art-centered lives.

Frida and Diego collected pre-Columbian art, and many of the rooms contain jewelry and terra-cotta figurines from Teotihuacán and Tlatelolco. Kahlo even had a mock-up of a temple built in the garden to exhibit her numerous pots and statues. On the back side of the temple are several skulls from Chichén-Itzá. A cafe on the first floor serves light snacks, and the adjacent bookstore offers a full range of Kahlo and Rivera books and other commercialized memorabilia of this famous couple.

To learn more about their remarkable lives, I recommend Bertram D. Wolfe's *Diego Rivera: His Life and Times* and Hayden Herrara's *Frida: A Biography of Frida Kahlo.*

✪ **Museo Nacional de Antropología.** Chapultepec Park. ☎ **5/553-6381.** Admission $2.25; free Sun. There is a $1.50 fee for still cameras, $3.50 for amateur video cameras; no tripods permitted. Tues–Sat 9am–7pm; Sun 10am–6pm. Metro: Auditorio.

Occupying 44,000 square feet, Mexico City's anthropology museum is regarded as one of the top museums in the world. The museum offers the single best introduction to the culture of Mexico. First-floor rooms are devoted to the pre-Hispanic cultures of Mexico. Second-floor rooms cover contemporary rural cultures through their crafts and everyday life.

Chapultepec Park

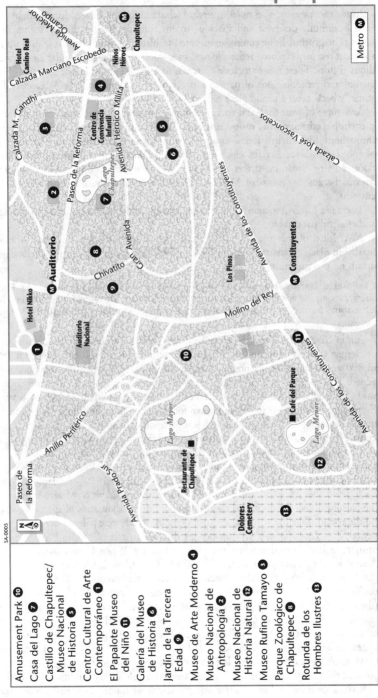

Amusement Park **10**

Casa del Lago **7**

Castillo de Chapultepec/
Museo Nacional
de Historia **5**

Centro Cultural de Arte
Contemporáneo **1**

El Papalote Museo
del Niño **11**

Galería del Museo
de Historia **6**

Jardín de la Tercera
Edad **9**

Museo de Arte Moderno **4**

Museo Nacional de
Antropología **2**

Museo Nacional de
Historia Natural **12**

Museo Rufino Tamayo **3**

Parque Zoológico de
Chapultepec **8**

Rotunda de los
Hombres Ilustres **13**

Metro **M**

SA-0005

Inside the museum is an open courtyard (containing the Chávez Morado fountain) with beautifully designed and spacious rooms running around three sides on two levels. The **ground-floor rooms** are devoted to history—from prehistoric days up to the most recently explored archaeological sites—and are the most popular among studious visitors. These rooms include dioramas of Mexico City when the Spaniards first arrived and reproductions of part of a pyramid at Teotihuacán. The Aztec calendar stone "wheel" takes a proud place here.

Save some of your time and energy, though, for the livelier and more readily comprehensible **ethnographic rooms upstairs.** This section is devoted to the way people throughout Mexico live today, complete with straw-covered huts, tape recordings of songs and dances, crafts, clothing, and lifelike models of village activities. This floor, a living museum, strikes me as vital to the understanding of contemporary Mexico because so much of Mexican village life remains swathed in pre-Hispanic customs.

There is a lovely restaurant in the museum with moderate prices, air-conditioning, and cheerful patio tables.

Note: Most of the museum is wheelchair accessible; however, assistance will be needed in places. Signs are in Spanish only. (See "Museum Walking Tour," below, for details on this museum.)

✪ **Palacio Nacional and the Diego Rivera Murals.** Palacio Nacional, Av. Pino Suárez, facing the zócalo. Admission is free, but visitor tags are required; be prepared to leave some form of photo identification in exchange. Mon–Sat 9am–5:30pm. Metro: Zócalo.

Begun in 1692 on the site of Moctezuma's "new" palace, this building became the site of Hernán Cortés's home and the residence of colonial viceroys. It has changed much in 300 years, taking on its present form in the late 1920s when the top floor was added. This complex of countless rooms, wide stone stairways, and numerous courtyards adorned with carved brass balconies is where the president of Mexico works. Even so, to most visitors it's better known for the fabulous second-floor Diego Rivera murals depicting the history of Mexico. Just 30 minutes here with an English-speaking guide provides essential background for an understanding of Mexican history. The cost of a guide is negotiable: $8.25 or less, depending on your haggling ability.

Enter by the central door, over which hangs the bell rung by Padre Miguel Hidalgo when he proclaimed Mexico's independence from Spain in 1810—the famous *grito.* Each September 15, Mexican Independence Day, the president of Mexico stands on the balcony above the door to echo Hidalgo's cry to the thousands of spectators that fill the zócalo. Take the stairs to the Rivera murals, which were painted over a 25-year period. The *Legend of Quetzalcoatl* depicts the famous tale of the feathered serpent bringing a blond-bearded white man to the country. When Cortés arrived, many Aztecs, recalling this legend, believed him to be Quetzalcoatl. Another mural tells of the American Intervention when American invaders marched into Mexico City during the War of 1847. It was on this occasion that the military cadets of Chapultepec Castle (then a military school) fought bravely to the last man. The most notable of Rivera's murals is the *Great City of Tenochtitlán,* a study of the original settlement in the Valley of Mexico. The city is but a small part of the mural; the remainder is filled with what appear to be four million extras left over from a Hollywood epic. Diego Rivera, one of Mexico's legendary muralists, left an indelible stamp on Mexico City, his painted political themes affecting the way millions view Mexican history. Additional examples of Rivera's stunning and provocative interpretations are found at the Bellas Artes, the National Preparatory School, the Department of Public Education, the National School of Agriculture at Chapingo, the National Institute of Cardiology, and the

Museo Mural Diego Rivera (housing the mural formerly located in the now razed Hotel del Prado).

✪ **Templo Mayor and Museo del Templo Mayor (Great Temple).** Off the zócalo. ☎ **5/542-0606.** Fax 5/542-1717. Admission $2.25 (valid for both ruins and museum); free Sun. Use of still camera $1.50; personal video camera $4. Tues–Sun 9am–6pm (last ticket sold 5pm). Metro: Zócalo.

In 1978, workmen digging on the east side of the Metropolitan Cathedral, next to the Palacio Nacional, unearthed an exquisite Aztec stone of the moon goddess Coyolxauhqui. Mexican archaeologists followed up the discovery with major excavations, and what they uncovered were interior remains of the Pyramid of Huitzilopochtli, also called the Templo Mayor (Great Temple)—the most important religious structure in the Aztec capital. What you see are the remains of pyramids that were covered by the great pyramid the Spaniards saw upon their arrival in the 16th century.

At the time of the 1521 Conquest, the site was the center of religious life for the city of 300,000. No other museum displays the variety and splendor of the Aztec Empire the way this one does. All 6,000 pieces came from the relatively small plot of excavated ruins just in front of the museum. Strolling along the walkways built over the site, visitors pass a water-collection conduit constructed during the presidency of Porfirio Díaz (1877–1911), as well as far earlier constructions. Shelters cover the ruins to protect traces of original paint work and carving. Note especially the Tzompantli, or Altar of Skulls, a common Aztec and Maya design. Explanatory plaques with building dates are in Spanish.

The Museo del Templo Mayor (Museum of the Great Temple) opened in 1987. To enter it, take the walkway to the large building in the back portion of the site, which contains fabulous artifacts from on-site excavations. Inside the door, a model of Tenochtitlán gives a good idea of the scale of the vast city of the Aztecs. The rooms and exhibits are organized by subject on many levels around a central open space. You'll see some marvelous displays of masks, figurines, tools, jewelry, and other artifacts, including the huge stone wheel of the moon goddess Coyolxauhqui ("she with bells painted upon her face") on the second floor. The goddess ruled the night, the Aztecs believed, but died at the dawning of every day, slain and dismembered by her brother, Huitzilopochtli, the sun god.

Look also for the striking jade-and-obsidian mask and the full-size terra-cotta figures of the *guerreros águilas,* or eagle warriors. A cutaway model of the Templo Mayor shows the layers and methods of construction.

Here's a quick guide to the exhibit rooms: **Sala 1,** "Antecedentes," contains exhibits about the early days of Tenochtitlán. **Sala 2,** "Guerra y Sacrificio," addresses the details of the Aztec religious duties of war and human sacrifice. **Sala 3,** "Tributo y Comercio," deals with Aztec government and its alliances and commerce with tributary states. **Sala 4,** "Huitzilopochtli," treats this most important of Aztec gods, a triumphant warrior, the son of Coatlicue, who bore him without losing her virginity. Huitzilopochtli, the "hummingbird god,"(other manifestations of Huitzilopochtli are the god of war, and the sun god) was the one who demanded that human sacrifices be made to sustain him. In **Sala 5,** "Tlaloc," exhibits explain the role of the Aztec rain god in daily and religious life. **Sala 6,** "Faunas," deals with the wild and domesticated animals common in the Aztec Empire at the time when the capital flourished. **Sala 7,** "Religion," explains Aztec religious beliefs, amazingly complex and sometimes confusing because they are so different from the familiar religions of Europe and the Middle East. **Sala 8,** "Caída de Tenochtitlán," recounts the fall of the great city and its last emperors, Moctezuma and Cuauhtémoc to Hernán Cortés and his conquistadors.

ARCHITECTURAL HIGHLIGHTS

Casa de Azulejos. Madero 4, Centro Histórico. ☎ **5/518-6676.** Daily 7:30am–11pm. Metro: Bellas Artes.

This "House of Tiles" is one of Mexico City's most precious colonial gems and popular meeting places. It's covered in gorgeous blue-and-white tiles, and dates from the end of the 1500s, when it was built for the count of the Valley of Orizaba. According to the oft-told story, during the count's defiant youth his father proclaimed: "You will never build a house of tiles." (A tiled house was a sign of success at the time—the father was sure his son would amount to nothing.) So when success came, the young count covered his house in tiles, a fine example of Puebla craftsmanship. Today the tile-covered house is a branch of Sanborn's restaurant/newsstand/gift shop/drugstore chain. You can stroll through to admire the interior and have a refreshing drink or a full meal. Pause to see the Orozco mural, *Omniscience,* on the landing leading to the second floor (where the rest rooms are).

Gran Hotel Ciudad de México. Palma and Piedad, facing the zócalo, Centro Histórico. Daily, 24 hours. Free admission to view the lobby. Metro: Zócalo.

Originally a department store and later converted to a hotel, the Gran Hotel is now operated by the Howard Johnson chain. It boasts one of the most splendid interiors of any downtown building. Step inside to see the lavish lobby, with gilded open elevators on both sides and topped with its breathtaking 1908 stained-glass canopy by Jacques Graber.

✪ Palacio de Bellas Artes. Calle Lopez Peralta, east end of the Alameda, Centro Histórico. ☎ **5/512-2592,** ext. 152. Free admission to view building, when performances are not in progress. Tues–Sat 11am–7pm; Sun 9am–7pm. Metro: Bellas Artes.

The theater's exterior is turn-of-the-century art nouveau, built during the Porfiriato and covered in Italian Carrara marble. Inside, it's completely 1930s art deco. Since construction began in 1904 (it was opened in 1934), the theater has sunk some 12 feet into the soft belly of Lake Texcoco. The palacio is the work of several masters: Italian architect Adamo Boari, who made the original plans; Antonio Muñoz and Federico Mariscal, who modified Boari's plans considerably; and Mexican painter Gerardo Murillo ("Doctor Atl"), who designed the fabulous art-nouveau glass curtain that was constructed by Louis Comfort Tiffany in the Tiffany Studios of New York. Made from nearly a million iridescent pieces of colored glass, the curtain portrays the Valley of Mexico with its two great volcanoes. You can see the curtain before important performances at the theater and on Sunday mornings.

In addition to being the concert hall, the theater houses permanent and traveling art shows. On the third level are the famous murals by Rivera, Orozco, and Siqueiros. The controversial Rivera mural *Man in Control of His Universe* was commissioned in 1933 for Rockefeller Center in New York City. He completed the work there just as you see it: A giant vacuum sucks up the riches of the earth to feed the factories of callous, card-playing, hard-drinking white capitalist thugs, while the noble workers of the earth, of all races, rally behind the red flag of socialism and its standard-bearer, Lenin. Needless to say, the Rockefellers weren't so keen on their new purchase. Much to their discredit, they had it painted over—destroyed. Rivera duplicated the mural here as *Man at the Crossing of the Ways* to preserve it. For information on tickets to performances of the **Ballet Folklórico,** see "Mexico City After Dark" later in this chapter.

A note of caution: The U.S. State Department advisory specifies that taxis parked in front of the Bellas Artes Theater should be avoided.

Palacio de Iturbide. Madero 17, Centro Histórico. Free admission. Daily 10am–7pm. Metro: Zócalo.

This ornate stone palace with huge, hand-carved wooden doors and a wildly baroque, 40-foot-high, carved stone archway was built in 1780 for the Conde de San Mateo de Valparaíso as a gift for his daughter. In 1821, the palace became the residence of Agustín de Iturbide, who later proclaimed himself emperor of Mexico (1822–23). His reign lasted only a matter of months, for although he was a partisan of Mexican independence, his political outlook was basically royalist and conservative. Iturbide was exiled; later, upon his unauthorized return, he was executed in Padilla, Tamaulipas, and buried there. Years later his contribution to Mexican independence was recognized, and his body was reburied in the Metropolitan Cathedral, where it remains today.

In 1847, the palace briefly served as a garrison for American soldiers during the U.S. invasion of Mexico. From 1855 until 1928, it was the prestigious Hotel Iturbide. Banamex, the present owner of the building, restored the palace in 1972, and the result is beautiful. Enter a courtyard with three tiers of balconies: The ground floor is a banking office and has a temporary art exhibition area; the upper floors have executive offices. Period paintings and statues grace walls and corners, and the second-floor chapel has been beautifully restored. Banamex has a brief (but free) printed guide to the building; ask the guard for one and come in and have a look at any time during normal business hours. A bookstore is to the right after you enter the building.

Palacio de Minería. Tacuba 11, Centro Histórico. Free admission. Tues–Sun 9am–5:30pm. Metro: Bellas Artes.

Built in the 1800s, this "mining palace" is one of architect Manuel Tolsá's finest works and one of the capital's most handsome buildings. Formerly the school of mining, it's occasionally used today for concerts and cultural events. If it's open, step inside for a look at the several patios and fabulous stonework.

CEMETERIES

Plaza and Cemetery of San Fernando. Puente de Alvarado and Vicente Guerrero, near Alameda Park. Free admission. Daily 8am–3pm. Metro: Hidalgo.

At one end of the plaza is the 18th-century San Fernando Church and next to it, 2½ blocks west of the Alameda, is a small cemetery by the same name where a few of Mexico's elite families are buried. It's the only cemetery remaining in the city from the 19th century, and President Benito Juárez was the last person buried here, on July 23, 1872.

Rotonda de los Hombres Ilustres. Constituyentes and Av. Civil Dolores; Dolores Cemetery, Chapultepec Park. Free admission. Daily 6am–6pm. Metro: Constituyentes.

The din of traffic recedes in the serene resting place where Mexico's illustrious military, political, and artistic elite are buried. It's more like an outdoor monument museum than a cemetery; the stone markers are grouped in a double circle around an eternal flame. A stroll here is a trip through who's who in Mexican history. Among the famous buried here are the artists Diego Rivera, David Alfaro Siqueiros, José Clemente Orozco, and Gerardo Murillo; presidents Sebastian Lerdo de Tejada, Valentín Gómez Farías, and Plutarco Calles; musicians Jaime Nuño (author of the Mexican national anthem), Juventino Rosas, and Agustín Lara; and outstanding citizens such as the philanthropist and writer Carlos Pellicer. Stop in the entrance building and the guard will give you a map with a list of those buried here, which includes biographical information.

CHURCHES

⚙ **Catedral Metropolitana.** The zócalo, on Cinco de Mayo, Centro Histórico. Free admission. Daily 7am–7pm. Metro: Zócalo.

An impressive, towering cathedral, begun in 1573 and finished in 1788, it blends baroque, neoclassic, and Mexican churrigueresque architecture. As you look around the cathedral and the Sagrario next to it, note how the building has sunk into the soft lake bottom beneath. The base of the facade is far from level and straight, and when one considers the weight of the immense towers, it's no surprise. Permanent scaffolding is in place to stabilize the building.

In Mexico, the sacred ground of one religion often becomes the sacred ground of its successor. Cortés and his Spanish missionaries converted the Aztecs, tore down their temples, and used much of the stone to construct a church on this spot. The church they built was pulled down in 1628 while the present Metropolitan Cathedral was under construction. The building today has 5 naves and 14 chapels. As you wander past the small chapels, you may hear guides describing some of the cathedral's outstanding features: the tomb of Agustín Iturbide, placed here in 1838; a painting attributed to the Spanish artist Bartolomé Esteban Murillo; and the fact that the stone holy-water fonts ring like metal when tapped with a coin. Like many huge churches, it has catacombs underneath. The much older–looking church next to the cathedral is the chapel known as the Sagrario, another tour de force of Mexican baroque architecture built in the mid-1700s.

As you walk around the outside of the cathedral, you will notice a reminder of medieval trade life. The west side is the gathering place of carpenters, plasterers, plumbers, painters, and electricians who have no shops. Craftspeople display the tools of their trades, sometimes along with pictures of their work.

Convent of San Bernardino de Siena. Pino and Hidalgo, in Xochimilco. Free admission. Daily 8am–8pm. *Tren ligero:* Xochimilco.

This 16th-century building is noted for its flower petals carved in stone—a signature of the Indians who did most of the work—on 16th-century retablos, including one of the country's three such retablos that has miraculously been preserved for more than 400 years. The last Indian governor of Xochimilco, Apoxquiyohuatzin, is buried here. Inside and to the right, the skull over the font is from a pre-Hispanic skull rack signifying an Indian/Christian mixture of the concept of life and death. Eight lateral retablos date from the 16th to the 18th centuries. The fabulous gilt main altar, also from the 16th century, is like an open book with sculpture and religious paintings. A profusion of cherubic angels decorates columns and borders. Some of the altar paintings are attributed to Baltasar Echave Orio the Elder. Over the altar, above the figure of Christ, is San Bernardino with the *caciques* (local authorities) dressed in clothing with Indian elements and without shoes. It's located facing the main square.

Iglesia y Hospital de Jesús Nazareño. Piño Suárez and El Salvador, Centro Histórico. Free admission. Mon–Sat 7am–8pm; Sun 7am–1pm and 5–8pm. Metro: Zócalo.

This church was founded by Hernán Cortés soon after the Conquest. A stone marker on Piño Suárez marks it as the spot where Cortés and Moctezuma reportedly met for the first time. Cortés died in Spain in 1547, but his remains are in a vault inside the chapel (entered by a side door on República del Salvador). Vaults on the opposite wall store the remains of Cortés's relatives. Notice the Orozco mural, *The Apocalypse*, on the choir ceiling.

HISTORIC BUILDINGS & MONUMENTS
CHAPULTEPEC PARK & POLANCO

Castillo de Chapultepec/Museo Nacional de Historia. Chapultepec Park. ☎ **5/553-6224** or 5/553-6396. Admission $2.50; free Sun. Tues–Sun 9am–5pm (tickets sold until 4pm). Metro: Chapultepec.

This site had been occupied by a fortress since the days of the Aztecs; the present palace wasn't built until the 1780s. The castle offers a beautiful view of Mexico City. During the French occupation of the 1860s, Carlota (who designed the lovely garden surrounding the palace) could sit up in bed and watch her husband, Maximilian, proceeding down Reforma on his way to work. Later, this became the official home of Mexico's president, until 1939. Today, the castle houses a variety of historical artifacts covering the period between 1521 and 1917. You'll see murals by Orozco, Siqueiros, and others; elaborate European furnishings brought here by Maximilian and Carlota; and jewelry and colonial art objects.

ZONA ROSA & SURROUNDING AREAS

✪ **Monumento a los Héroes de la Independencia.** Paseo de la Reforma, Florencia, and Río Tiber intersection. Reforma/Zona Rosa. Metro: Insurgentes.

Without a doubt, the Monument to the Heroes of Independence is the most noted of Mexico City's exceptional public sculptures and monuments. The "Angel" is both a landmark and homage to those who lost their lives fighting for independence. Set upon a tall marble shaft, the golden angel is an important and easily discerned guidepost for travelers. A creation of Antonio Rivas Mercado, the 22-foot-high, gold-plated, bronze angel, cast in Florence, Italy, was completed in 1906 at a cost of $2.5 million. With its base of marble and Italian granite, the monument's total height is 150 feet.

CENTRO HISTÓRICO & SURROUNDING AREAS

Monumento a la Revolución and Museo Nacional de la Revolución. Av. Juárez and La Fragua. ☎ **5/546-2115** or 5/566-1902. Free admission. Tues–Sat 9am–5pm; Sun 9am–3pm. From the Colón Monument on Reforma, walk 2 blocks north on I. Ramírez; the monument looms ahead. Metro: Revolución.

The stocky art-deco Monument to the Revolution, set in the large **Plaza de la República,** has a curious and ironic history. The government of Porfirio Díaz, perennially "reelected" as president of Mexico, began construction of what was intended to be a new legislative chamber. However, only the dome was raised by the time the Mexican Revolution (1910) put an end to his plans, not to mention his dictatorship. In the 1930s, after the revolutionary turmoil had died down, the dome was finished as a monument. The mortal remains of two revolutionary presidents, Francisco Madero and Venustiano Carranza, were entombed in two of its pillars, and it was dedicated to the Revolution. Later, the bodies of presidents Plutarco Elías Calles and Lázaro Cárdenas were buried there.

Beneath the Monument to the Revolution is the **Museo Nacional de la Revolución** (entry directly across from the Frontón). The tumultuous years from 1867 through the Revolution (which started in 1910) to 1917, when the present constitution was signed, are chronicled in excellent exhibits of documents, newspaper stories, photographs, drawings, clothing, costumes, uniforms, weapons, and furnishings.

Secretaría de Educación Pública. República de Cuba, between República de Brazil and República de Argentina. Free admission. Mon–Fri 9:30am–5:30pm. Metro Allende.

The Secretariat of Public Education was built in 1922 and decorated with a great series of more than 200 Diego Rivera murals dating from 1923 and 1928. Other artists did a panel here and there, but the Rivera murals are the most outstanding.

Suprema Corte de Justicia. Pino Suárez and Corregidora, Centro Histórico. Free admission. Mon–Fri 9am–5:30pm. Metro: Zócalo.

The Supreme Court of Justice, built between 1935 and 1941, is the highest court in the country. Inside, on the main staircase and its landings, are Orozco murals depicting a theme of justice.

OTHER MUSEUMS & GALLERIES

Mexico City boasts over 90 museums that celebrate the several thousand years of its existence as a hemispheric cultural center. Following is a selection of the most notable, listed by area of location.

CHAPULTEPEC PARK/POLANCO

Galería de la Museo de Historia. Chapultepec Park. Admission $1; free Sun. Tues–Sat 9am–4:30pm; Sun 10am–3:30pm. Metro: Chapultepec.

About 200 yards below Chapultepec Castle is this circular glass building, also known as the Museo Caracol (Snail Museum) for its spiral shape and the Museo de la Lucha del Pueblo Mexicano por su Libertad (Museum of the Mexican People's Fight for Their Liberty) for its content. It's a condensed chronological history of Mexico from 1800 to 1917, complete with portraits, reproductions of documents, and dramatic dioramas. The more recent years are also represented, with large photographic blowups. Some scenes, such as Maximilian's execution, are staged with great drama and imagination. In many ways, this museum is more riveting than the Museo Nacional de Historia on the hill above.

✪ **Museo de Arte Moderno.** Chapultepec Park. ☎ **5/553-6233.** Admission $1.50; free Sun. Tues–Sun 10am–5:30pm. Metro: Chapultepec.

The Museum of Modern Art is known for having the best permanent exhibition of Mexican painters and sculptors from the modern Mexican art movement. The Mexican muralist movement is represented with significant works by the three greats: Diego Rivera, José Clemente Orozco, and David Alfaro Siqueiros. The main building itself is a round, two-story structure with a central staircase. Two of the museum's four permanent spaces are dedicated to their permanent collection, which also contains works by Mexico's other modern masters—Tamayo, José Luis Cuevas, Alejandro Colunga, Francisco Toledo, and Vladamir Cora. The remaining two exhibition spaces house visiting exhibitions. The museum is recognized for featuring some of the most important temporary exhibitions of national and international modern art in the world. Large-scale public sculptures are exhibited in the museum's surrounding gardens.

Museo Nacional de Historia Natural. Chapultepec Park, Section 2. ☎ **5/515-2222.** Admission 50¢; free Sun. Tues–Sun 10am–5pm. Metro: Constituyentes.

The 10 interconnecting domes that form the Museum of Natural History contain stuffed and preserved animals and birds; tableaux of different natural environments with the appropriate wildlife; and exhibits on geology, astronomy, biology, the origin of life, and more. It's a fascinating place for anyone with the slightest curiosity about nature and is totally absorbing for youngsters.

✪ **Museo Rufino Tamayo.** Chapultepec Park. ☎ **5/286-5889** or 5/286-5939. Admission $2.25; free Sun. Tues–Sun 10am–6pm. Free guided tours Sat–Sun 10am–2pm. Metro: Chapultepec.

Oaxaca-born painter Rufino Tamayo not only contributed a great deal to modern Mexican painting, but he also collected pre-Hispanic, Mexican, and foreign works, including pieces by de Kooning, Warhol, Dalí, and Magritte. Tamayo's pre-Hispanic collection is in Oaxaca, but here you can see a number of his works and the remainder of his collection, unless they are temporarily displaced by a special exhibit.

✪ **El Papalote, Museo del Niño.** Av. de los Constituyentes 268, Chapultepec Park, Section 2. ☎ **5/224-1260** or 5/160-6060. Admission $3 adults ($5 including IMAX show); $2.50 children ($3.50 including IMAX show). Mon–Fri 9am–1pm and 2–6pm; Sat–Sun and holidays 10am–2pm and 3–7pm. Metro: Constituyentes.

This interactive children's museum opened in 1993 in three separate buildings. The Building of the Pyramids holds most of the exhibits, while in the IMAX building two films alternate (10 shows daily). There's virtually nothing here that children can't touch; once they discover this, they'll want to stay a long time. Children must be accompanied by an adult.

CENTRO HISTÓRICO & SURROUNDING AREAS

Museo de la Ciudad de México. Pino Suárez 30, Centro Histórico. ☎ **5/542-8356** or 5/542-0487. Free admission. Tues–Sun 10am–6pm. Metro: Pino Suárez.

Before you enter the Museum of Mexico City, go to the corner of República del Salvador and look at the enormous stone serpent head, a corner support at the building's base. The stone was once part of an Aztec pyramid. At the entrance, a stone doorway opens to the courtyard of this mansion built in 1778 as the House of the Counts of Santiago de Calimaya. This classic old building was converted into the Museum of the City of Mexico in 1964 and should be visited by anyone interested in the country's past. Dealing solely with the Mexico Valley, where the first people arrived around 8000 B.C., the museum contains some fine maps and pictographic presentations of the initial settlements and outlines of the social organization as it developed, as well as models of several famous buildings of the city. Upstairs is the studio of Mexican impressionist Joaquín Clausell (1866–1935). There's a good bookstore to the left after you enter.

✪ **Museo Franz Mayer.** Hidalgo 45, facing the Alameda. ☎ **5/518-2265.** Admission $1.25; free Sun. Tues–Sun 10am–5pm. Guided tours Mon–Sat 10:30am, 11:30am, and 12:30pm. Metro: Hidalgo or Bellas Artes.

One of the capital's foremost museums, the Franz Mayer Museum opened in 1986 in a beautifully restored 16th-century building on Plaza de la Santa Veracruz on the north side of the Alameda. The extraordinary 10,000-piece collection of antiques, mostly from Mexico's 16th through 19th centuries, was amassed by one man: Franz Mayer. A German immigrant, he adopted Mexico as his home in 1905 and grew rich there. Before his death in 1975, Mayer bequeathed the collection to the country and arranged for its permanent display through a trust with the Banco Nacional. The pieces, mostly utilitarian objects (as opposed to pure art objects), include inlaid and richly carved furniture; an enormous collection of Talavera pottery; gold and silver religious pieces; sculptures; tapestries; rare watches and clocks (the oldest is a 1680 lantern clock); wrought iron; old-master paintings from Europe and Mexico; and 770 Don Quixote volumes, many of which are rare editions or typographically unique. There's so much here it may take two visits to absorb it.

Museo Mural Diego Rivera. Plaza de la Solidaridad, Balderas, and Colón, Centro Histórico–Alameda. ☎ **5/510-2329.** Admission $1.25; free Sun. Tues–Sun 10am–7pm. Metro: Hidalgo.

This museum houses Diego Rivera's famous mural *Dream of a Sunday Afternoon in Alameda Park,* which was painted on a wall of the Hotel Prado in 1947. The hotel was demolished after the 1985 earthquake, but the precious mural, perhaps the best known of Rivera's works, was saved and transferred to its new location in 1986. The huge picture, 50 feet long and 13 feet high, chronicles the history of the park from the time of Cortés onward. Portrayed in the mural are numerous historical figures who have left their mark on Mexican history. More or less from left to right, but not in chronological order, they include: Cortés; a heretic suffering under the Spanish Inquisition; Sor Juana Inés de la Cruz, a brilliant and progressive woman who became a nun in order to continue her scholarly pursuits; Benito Juárez, seen putting forth the laws of Mexico's great Reforma; the conservative Gen. Antonio López de Santa Anna, handing the keys to Mexico to the invading American Gen. Winfield Scott; Emperor Maximilian and Empress Carlota; José Martí, the Cuban revolutionary; Death, with the plumed serpent (Quetzalcoatl) entwined about his neck; Gen. Porfirio Díaz, great with age and medals, asleep; a police officer keeping the Alameda free of "riffraff" by ordering a poor family out of the elitists' park; and Francisco Madero, the martyred democratic president who caused the downfall of Díaz, whose betrayal and alleged murder by Gen. Victoriano Huerta (pictured on the right) resulted in years of civil turmoil in Mexico.

Museo Nacional de Arte. Tacuba 8, Centro Histórico. ☎ **5/512-3224** or 5/521-7320. Admission $1.50; free Sun. Tues–Sun 10am–5:30pm. Metro: Tacuba.

The National Art Museum's palacelike building, designed by Italian architect Silvio Contri and completed in 1911—another legacy of the years of Europe-loving Porfirio Díaz—was built to house the government's offices of Communications and Public Works. Díaz occupied the opulent second floor salon, where he welcomed visiting dignitaries. The National Museum of Art took over the building in 1982. Wander through the immense rooms with polished wooden floors as you view the wealth of paintings showing Mexico's art development, primarily covering the period from 1810 to 1950. There's a nice cafe on the second floor.

Museo Nacional de la Estampa. Hidalgo 39 (next door to the Museo Franz Mayer), Centro Histórico–Alameda. ☎ **5/521-2244**. Admission $1.25; free Sun. Tues–Sun 10am–6pm. Metro: Hidalgo.

Estampa means "engraving" or "printing," and the museum is devoted to understanding and preserving the graphic arts. Housed in a beautifully restored 16th-century building, the museum has both permanent and changing exhibits. Displays include those from pre-Hispanic times when clay seals were used for designs on fabrics, ceramics, and other surfaces. But the most famous works here are probably those of José Guadalupe Posada, Mexico's famous printmaker, who poked fun at death and politicians through his skeleton figure drawings. If your interest in this subject is deep, ask to see the video programs on graphic techniques—woodcuts, lithography, etchings, and the like.

Museo de San Carlos. Puente de Alvarado 50. ☎ **5/566-8522** or 5/592-3721. Admission $1; free Sun. Tues–Sun 10am–6pm. Walk 5½ blocks west of the Alameda (2½ blocks west of San Fernando Plaza); it's at the corner of Arizpe. Metro: Revolución.

The San Carlos Museum exhibits 15th- to 19th-century European paintings. The museum was once the Academy of San Carlos, an art school that some of the country's great painters—Rivera and Orozco among them—counted as their alma mater. The beautiful converted mansion that houses the museum was built in the early 1800s by architect Manuel Tolsá; it was later the home of the Marqués de Buenavista.

Coyoacán

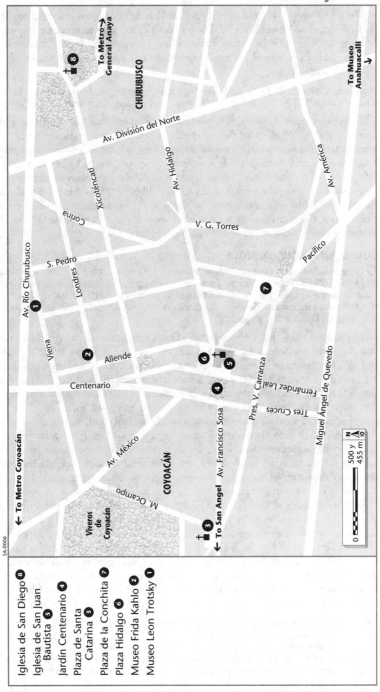

Iglesia de San Diego **8**
Iglesia de San Juan Bautista **5**
Jardín Centenario **4**
Plaza de Santa Catarina **3**
Plaza de la Conchita **7**
Plaza Hidalgo **6**
Museo Frida Kahlo **2**
Museo Leon Trotsky **1**

SA-0006

The rooms on the first and second floors hold some of Mexico's best paintings, by both Mexican and European artists. There is also a gallery with prints and engravings. In the mansion's elliptical court are displays of the 19th-century Mexican statuary and busts by Manuel Vilar and his pupils, and off to one side is a pretty garden court shaded by rubber trees.

Pinacoteca Virreinal de San Diego. Dr. Mora 7, Centro Histórico–Alameda. ☎ **5/ 510-2793** or 5/512-2079. Admission $1.25; free Sun. Tues–Sun 10am–5pm. Metro: Hidalgo.

This former church is now a gallery of paintings, most from the 16th and 17th centuries and ecclesiastical in theme. Highlights are apparent immediately: In the wing to the right of where the altar would have been is a room featuring a gorgeous blue-and-gilt ceiling with gleaming rosettes and a striking mural by Federico Canto (1959), one of the few modern works. Upstairs in a cloister are many small paintings by Hipolito de Rioja (who worked in the second half of the 17th century), Baltázar de Echave Ibia (1610–40), and others. By the way, the tremendous painting on the cloister wall, *Glorificación de la Inmaculada* by Francisco Antonio Vallejo (1756–83), should be viewed from upstairs—the lighting is better.

SOUTHERN NEIGHBORHOODS

✪ **The Anahuacalli (Diego Rivera Museum).** Calle Museo 150, Col. Tepetlapa. ☎ **5/677-2873.** Free admission. Tues–Sun 10am–2pm and 3–6pm. Take the Metro (Line 2) to the Tasqueña terminal and change to the *tren ligero* (Light Train). Get off at the Xotepingo station and go west on Xotepingo (Museo) 3 short blocks; cross División del Norte and go another 6 blocks.

Not to be confused with the Museo Estudio Diego Rivera near the San Ángel Inn, this is probably the most unusual museum in the city. Designed by Rivera before his death in 1957, it's devoted to his works as well as his extensive collection of pre-Columbian art. Called the Anahuacalli ("House of Mexico") Museum and constructed of pedregal (the lava rock in which the area abounds), it resembles Maya and Aztec architecture. The name *Anahuac* was the old name for the ancient Valley of Mexico.

In front of the museum is a reproduction of a Toltec ball court, and the entrance to the museum itself is via a coffin-shaped door. Light filters in through translucent onyx slabs and is supplemented by lights inside niches and wall cases containing the exhibits. Rivera collected nearly 60,000 pre-Columbian artifacts, and the museum showcases thousands of them, in 23 rooms in chronological order, stashed on the shelves, tucked away in corners, and peeking from behind glass cases.

Upstairs, a replica of Rivera's studio has been constructed, and there you'll find the original sketches for some of his murals and two in-progress canvases. His first sketch (of a train) was done at the age of three, and there's a photo of it, plus a color photograph of him at work later in life in a pair of baggy pants and a blue denim jacket. Rivera (1886–1957) studied in Europe for 15 years and spent much of his life as a devoted Marxist. Yet, he came through political scrapes and personal tragedies with no apparent diminution of creative energy, and a plaque in the museum proclaims him "a man of genius who is among the greatest painters of all time."

Archaeological Museum of Xochimilco. Av. Tenochtitlán and Calle La Planta in the town of Santa Cruz Acalpixcan. ☎ **5/675-0168** or 5/675-0426. Free admission. Tues–Sun 10am–5pm. Metro: to the Taxqueña stop, and from there take the light train (*tren ligero*) to Xochimilco; you'll arrive at the main square in Xochimilco. Take a cab or a microbus that goes to Tulyehualco. The Museum is on the corner of Tenochtitlán and La Planta on the left side.

The building dates from 1904, when it was the pump house for the springs. It houses artifacts from the area, many of them found when residents built their homes— 10,000-year-old mammoth bones; figures dating from the Teotihuacán period,

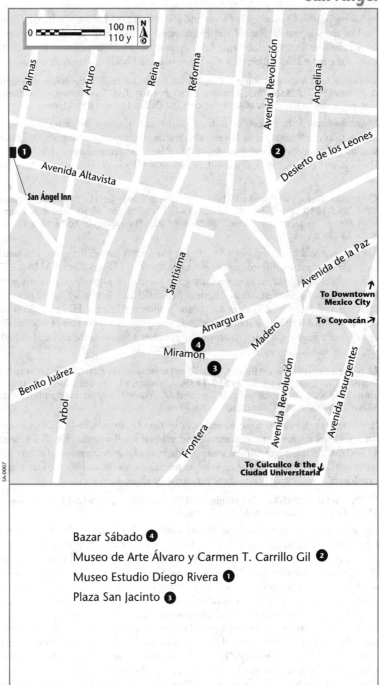

Bazar Sábado ❹

Museo de Arte Álvaro y Carmen T. Carrillo Gil ❷

Museo Estudio Diego Rivera ❶

Plaza San Jacinto ❸

including figures of Tlaloc (god of water and life), Ehecatl (god of the wind), Xipe Totec (god of renewal and of plants), and Huehueteotl (god of fire); polychrome pottery; carved abalone; and tombs showing funerary practices of 23 Teotihuacán inhabitants. One of the most unique pieces is a clay figure of a child holding a bouquet of flowers.

Museo de Arte Alvar y Carmen T. Carrillo Gil. Revolución 1608, at the corner of Desierto de los Leones. ☎ **5/550-3983.** Admission $1.50; free Sun. Tues–Sun 10am–6pm. No Metro service. Located at the corner of Av. Revolución and Calz. al Desierto de los Leones.

Sometimes called the Museo de la Esquina (Corner Museum) since it's at a major intersection on avenida de la Revolución, this modern gallery features a collection that includes rooms dedicated to the works of José Clemente Orozco (1883–1949), Diego Rivera (1886–1957), David Alfaro Siqueiros (1896–1974), and other Mexican painters.

⚫ **Museo Dolores Olmedo Patiño.** Av. México 5843, Col. La Noria, Xochimilco. ☎ **5/555-1016** or 5/555-0891. Fax 5/555-1642. Admission $1.50. Tues–Sun 10am–6pm. Metro: Taxqueña; from there, take the light train (*tren ligero*) to Xochimilco. Get off at the La Noria station.

Art collector and philanthropist Olmedo left her former home, the grand Hacienda La Noria, as a museum featuring the works of her friend Diego Rivera. At least 137 of his works are displayed here, including his portrait of Olmedo, 25 paintings of Frida Kahlo, and 37 creations of Angelina Beloff (Rivera's first wife), many of them drawings and engravings. Besides the paintings there are fine pre-Hispanic pieces on display, colonial furniture and other hacienda artifacts, and a collection of folk art. An excellent gift shop and a cafeteria are on the premises. Olmeda is the executor of both the Rivera and Kahlo estates.

⚫ **Museo Estudio Diego Rivera.** Calle Diego Rivera and Av. Altavista (across from the San Ángel Inn), San Ángel. ☎ **5/550-1139.** Admission $1; free Sun. Tues–Sun 10am–5pm. No Metro station close by. It's located on Altavista. Go up Insurgentes Sur to Altavista and make a left. Easiest to reach by taxi.

It was here, in the studio designed and built by Juan O'Gorman in 1928, that Rivera drew sketches for his wonderful murals and painted smaller works. He died here in 1957. Now a museum, the Rivera studio holds some of the artist's personal effects and mementos, and there are changing exhibits relating to his life and work. (Don't confuse Rivera's studio with his museum called the Anahuacalli; see above.)

⚫ **Museo Leon Trotsky.** Río Churubusco 410, Coyoacán. ☎ **5/658-8732.** Admission $1.50. Tues–Sun 10am–5pm. Metro: Coyoacán.

During Lenin's last days, Stalin and Trotsky fought a silent battle for leadership of the Communist party in the Soviet Union. Trotsky stuck to ideology, while Stalin took control of the party mechanism. Stalin won, and Trotsky was exiled to continue his ideological struggle elsewhere. Invited by Diego Rivera, he settled here on the outskirts of Mexico City to continue his work and writing on political topics and Communist ideology. His ideas clashed with those of Stalin in many respects, and Stalin, wanting no opposition or dissension in world Communist ranks, set out to have Trotsky assassinated. A first attempt failed, but it served to give a warning to Trotsky and his household, and from then on the house became a veritable fortress with watchtowers, thick steel doors protecting Trotsky's bedroom, and round-the-clock guards, several of whom were Americans who sympathized with Trotsky's philosophies. Finally, a man thought to have been paid, cajoled, or blackmailed by Stalin, directly or indirectly, was able to get himself admitted to the house by posing as a friend of Trotsky's and of his political views. On August 20, 1940, he put an ice pick into the philosopher's head.

Xochimilco

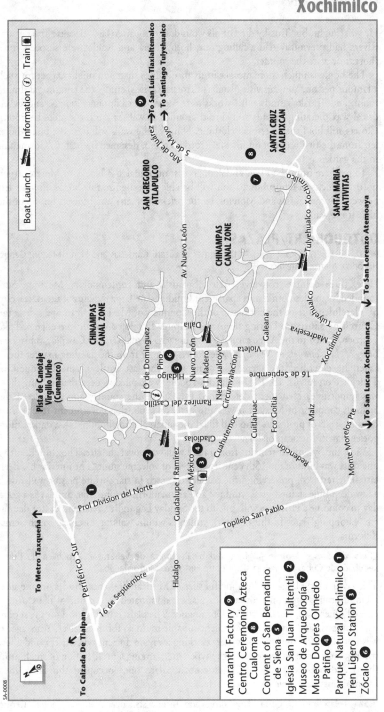

Boat Launch · Information ⓘ · Train ▣

CHINAMPAS CANAL ZONE

Pista de Canotaje Virgilio Uribe (Cuemanco)

CHINAMPAS CANAL ZONE

SAN GREGORIO ATLAPULCO

SANTA CRUZ ACALPIXCAN

SANTA MARIA NATIVITAS

To San Luis Tlaxialtemalco
To Santiago Tulyehualco
To San Lorenzo Atemoaya
To San Lucas Xochimanca
To Metro Taxqueña
To Calzada De Tlalpan

Av Nuevo León
Año de Juárez
5 de Mayo
Tulyehualco Xochimilco
Madreselva
Xochimilco
Tulyehualco
Galeana
Violeta
Dalia
Nuevo León
F I Madero
Netzahualcoyot
Circunvalación
Ramirez del Castillo
Hidalgo
Pino
O de Dominguez
Cuitlahuac
Fco Goitia
Maiz
16 de Septiembre
Monte Morelos Pte
Redención
Cuauhtemoc
Gladiolas
Av México
Guadalupe I Ramirez
Prol Division del Norte
Topilejo San Pablo
Periférico Sur
Hidalgo
16 de Septiembre

Amaranth Factory ❾
Centro Ceremonio Azteca Cualoma ❽
Convent of San Bernardino de Siena ❺
Iglesia San Juan Tlaltentli ❷
Museo de Arqueología ❼
Museo Dolores Olmedo Patiño ❹
Parque Natural Xochimilco ❶
Tren Ligero Station ❸
Zócalo ❻

SA-0008

He was caught, but Trotsky died of his wounds shortly afterward. Because Trotsky and Rivera had previously had a falling out, both Rivera and Kahlo were suspects for a short time after the murder.

The home is much more meager in its furnishings than you might expect for such a famous person. You can visit Natalia's (Trotsky's wife's) study; the communal dining room; and Trotsky's study with worksheets, newspaper clippings, books, and cylindrical wax dictating records still spread around; as well as the fortresslike bedroom. Closets still hold their personal clothing. Some of the walls still bear the bullet holes left from the first attempt on his life. Trotsky's tomb, designed by Juan O'Gorman, is in the garden.

To get here from the Plaza Hidalgo, go east on Hidalgo 3 blocks to Morelos, then north 8 blocks to Churubusco. You will be able to recognize this house, to your left between Gómez Farías and Morelos, by the brick riflemen's watchtowers on top of the high stone walls.

OUTDOOR ART/PLAZAS

Plaza de las Tres Culturas. At the corner of Lázaro Cárdenas and Flores Magón, Centro Histórico. Metro: Tlatelolco.

Here, three cultures converge: Aztec, Spanish, and contemporary Mexican. Surrounded by modern office and apartment buildings are large remains of the **Aztec city of Tlatelolco,** site of the last battle of the Conquest of Mexico. Off to one side is the **Church of Santiago.** During the Aztec Empire, Tlatelolco was on the edge of Lake Texcoco, linked to the Aztec capital by a causeway. Bernal Díaz de Castillo, in his *True Story of the Conquest of New Spain,* described the roar from the dazzling market there. Later, he described the incredible scene after the last battle of the Conquest in Tlatelolco on August 13, 1521—the dead bodies were piled so deep that walking there was impossible. That night determined the fate of the country and completed the Spanish conquest of Mexico. It was also here, in 1968, that government troops fired on thousands of protesters who had filled the square, killing hundreds—a dark, unforgotten day in Mexican history.

View the pyramidal remains from raised walkways over the site. The church, off to one side, was built in the 16th century entirely of volcanic stone. The interior has been tastefully restored, preserving little patches of fresco in stark-white plaster walls, with a few deep-blue stained-glass windows and an unadorned stone altar. Sunday is a good day to combine a visit here with one to the Sunday Lagunilla street market (for details, see "Shopping" later in this chapter), which is within walking distance, south across Reforma.

Plaza de Santo Domingo. Bordered by República de Venezuela, República de Brazil, República de Cuba, and Palma sts., Centro Histórico. Metro: Tacuba.

This fascinating plaza—and wonderful slice of Mexican life—has arcades on one side, a Dominican church on another. The plaza is dominated by a statue of the Corregidora of Querétaro, Josefa Ortiz de Domínguez. The plaza is best known for the scribes who compose and type letters for clients unable to do so for themselves. Years ago, it was full of professional public writers clacking away on ancient typewriters, and a few still ply their trade on ancient electric typewriters among a proliferation of small print shops and presses. Emperor Cuauhtémoc's palace once occupied this land, then Dominicans built their monastery here.

Plaza Tolsá and El Caballito. Correo and Tacuba sts., near Alameda Central, Centro Histórico. Metro: Bellas Artes.

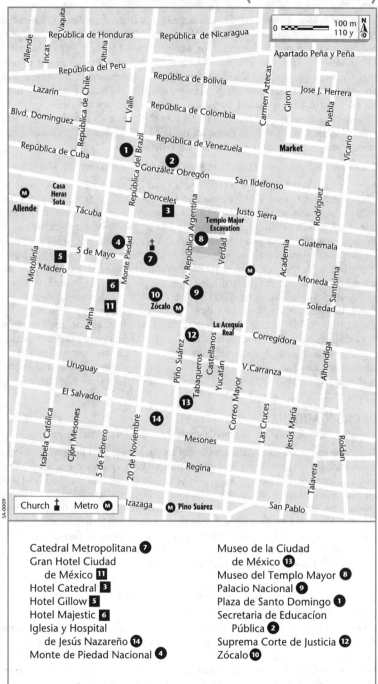

Catedral Metropolitana **7**
Gran Hotel Ciudad
 de México **11**
Hotel Catedral **3**
Hotel Gillow **5**
Hotel Majestic **6**
Iglesia y Hospital
 de Jesús Nazareño **14**
Monte de Piedad Nacional **4**

Museo de la Ciudad
 de México **13**
Museo del Templo Mayor **8**
Palacio Nacional **9**
Plaza de Santo Domingo **1**
Secretaria de Educacíon
 Pública **2**
Suprema Corte de Justicia **12**
Zócalo **10**

This plaza is known for the huge equestrian statue in front of the Museo Nacional de Arte. The gallant statue of King Carlos IV of Spain (1788–1808) atop a high-stepping horse was crafted by Mexican sculptor Manuel Tolsá. Mexicans call the statue El Caballito ("The Little Horse"), and the name reveals a lot: They prefer not to mention Carlos, who was king shortly before Mexico's independence movement from Spain began in 1810. Despite the subject's unpopularity, the statue remains one of the largest and most finely crafted equestrian statues in the world. Erected first in the zócalo, it was moved in 1852 to a traffic circle in the Paseo de la Reforma. A few years ago El Caballito was moved to this more dignified and appropriate position in front of the museum opposite the handsome Palacio de Minería.

Zócalo. At the intersection of Juárez and 20 de Noviembre, Centro Histórico. Metro: Zócalo.

Every Spanish colonial city in North America was laid out according to a textbook plan, with a plaza at the center surrounded by a church, government buildings, and military headquarters. Since Mexico City was the capital of New Spain, its zócalo is one of the grandest and is graced on all sides by stately 17th-century buildings.

Zócalo actually means "pedestal" or "plinth." A grand monument to Mexico's independence was planned and the pedestal built, but the project was never completed. Nevertheless, the pedestal became a landmark for visitors, and soon everyone was calling the square for the pedestal, even after the pedestal was removed. Its official name, which you will rarely hear, is Plaza de la Constitución. It covers almost 10 acres and is bounded on the north by Cinco de Mayo, on the east by Piño Suárez, on the south by 16 de Septiembre, and on the west by Monte de Piedad. The downtown district, especially to the north of the Templo Mayor, one of the oldest archaeological sites in the city, has suffered long neglect, but a restoration project is slowly renewing much of its colonial charm. Occupying the entire east side of the zócalo is the majestic, red tezontle stone Palacio National, seat of the Mexican national government.

PARKS/GARDENS

Alameda Park. Av. Juárez and Lázaro Cárdenas. Free admission. Metro: Belles Artes.

Today, the lovely tree-filled Alameda Central Park is a magnet for pedestrians, cotton-candy vendors, strollers, lovers, and organ grinders. Long ago, the site of the Alameda was an Aztec marketplace. When the conquistadors took over in the mid-1500s, heretics were burned at the stake there under the Spanish Inquisition. In 1592, the governor of New Spain, Viceroy Luis de Velasco, converted it to a public park. Within the park is the **Juárez Monument,** sometimes called the **Hemiciclo** (hemicycle or half-circle), facing avenida Juárez. Enthroned as the hero he was, Juárez assumes his proper place here in the pantheon of Mexican patriots. Most of the other statuary in the park was done by European sculptors (particularly French) in the late 19th and early 20th centuries.

Chapultepec Park. Between Paseo de la Reforma, Circuito Interior, and Av. Constituyentes. Free admission. Daily 5am–5pm. Metro: Chapultepec.

One of the biggest city parks in the world, the 551-acre Chapultepec Park is more than a playground. Besides accommodating picnickers on worn-away grass under centuries-old trees, it boasts canoes on the lake; jogging and bridle paths; vendors selling balloons, trinkets, and food; a miniature train; an auditorium; and **Los Pinos,** home of Mexico's president. The park is also home to the **City Zoo** and **La Feria** amusement park. Most important for tourists, it contains a number of interesting museums, including the Museo Nacional de Antropología (see the "Walking Tour" later in this chapter for information on this most famous of park attractions).

In case you want to see the world.

At American Express, we're here to make your journey a smooth one. So we have over 1,700 travel service locations in over 120 countries ready to help. What else would you expect from the world's largest travel agency?

do more

Travel

http://www.americanexpress.com/travel

In case you want to be welcomed there.

We're here to see that you're always welcomed at establishments everywhere. That's why millions of people carry the American Express® Card – for peace of mind, confidence, and security, around the world or just around the corner.

do more

Cards

In case you're running low.

We're here to help with more than 118,000 Express Cash locations around the world. In order to enroll, just call American Express before you start your vacation.

do more

Express Cash

And just in case.

We're here with American Express® Travelers Cheques and Cheques *for Two*.® They're the safest way to carry money on your vacation and the surest way to get a refund, practically anywhere, anytime. Another way we help you...

do more

Travelers Cheques

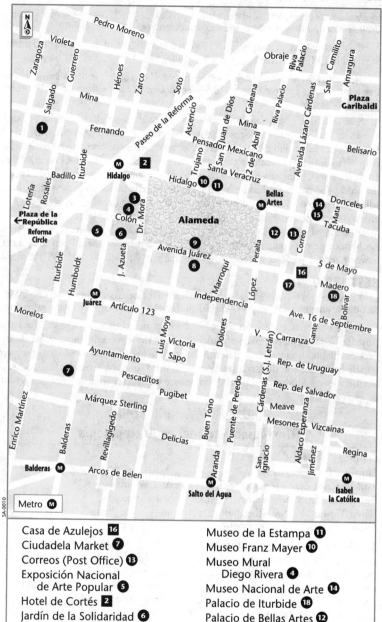

Metro **M**

Casa de Azulejos **16**
Ciudadela Market **7**
Correos (Post Office) **13**
Exposición Nacional
de Arte Popular **5**
Hotel de Cortés **2**
Jardín de la Solidaridad **6**
Juárez Monument **9**
La Torre Latinoamericana **17**
Museo de Artes e
Industrias Populares **8**

Museo de la Estampa **11**
Museo Franz Mayer **10**
Museo Mural
Diego Rivera **4**
Museo Nacional de Arte **14**
Palacio de Iturbide **18**
Palacio de Bellas Artes **12**
Pinacoteca Virreinal
de San Diego **3**
Plaza Tolsá and El Caballito **15**
Plaza San Fernando **1**

Jardín de la Solidaridad. Av. Juárez, across from Calle J. Azueta, near the Alameda Central, Centro Histórico–Alameda. Metro: Hidalgo. Admission free.

The "Solidarity Garden" was built in 1986 in remembrance of those who died during the terrible 1985 earthquake.

Floating Gardens of Xochimilco. Southern neighborhood of Xochimilco. Admission to the area is free; charge for boat rides is $16.50 per boat; boats can be shared by 8–10 people. Daily morning–dusk.

In the southern neighborhood of Xochimilco, there are more than 50 miles of canals known as the "Floating Gardens." Segregated into two main parts, the first is the tourism-oriented area in the historic center of town, where colorful boats take loads of tourists (some of them picnicking along the way) through a portion of the canals. Lively music is a staple, some of it provided by mariachi and trio musicians for hire who board the boats. The area is flanked by historic buildings, restaurants, souvenir stands, curio sellers, and boat vendors. The other section, north of the center of town, is the ecology-oriented area: Parque Natural Xochimilco. On Sunday, Xochimilco (especially the tourist-oriented section) is jammed; on weekdays, it's nearly deserted. As you enter Xochimilco proper you will see many places to board boats. Should you miss them, however, turn along Madero and follow signs that say LOS EMBARCADEROS (the piers).

BEST VIEW

La Torre Latinoamericana. Madero and Lázaro Cárdenas, Centro Histórico. ☎ 5/521-0844. Admission $2.50 adults, $2 children. 10am–11pm. Open daily. Metro: Bellas Artes.

From the observation deck on the 42nd floor of this soaring skyscraper, the Latin American Tower, you can take in fabulous views of the whole city. Buy a ticket for the deck at the booth as you approach the elevators. Tokens for the telescope up top are on sale here, too. You then take an elevator to the 37th floor, cross the hall, and take another elevator to the 42nd floor. An employee will ask for your ticket as you get off.

MUSEUM WALKING TOUR
The Museo Nacional de Antropología

Start: Sala (Room) 1
Finish: Sala (Room) 22
Time: At least 2 or 3 hours, even if you're a dedicated museum-rusher.
Best Times: Early any weekday, or Sunday, when it's free.
Worst Times: Monday—the absolute worst time—when the museum is closed, or a national holiday, when it's crowded.

The **Museo Nacional de Antropología** (☎ 5/553-6381) is breathtaking in its splendor, with a tall fountain designed by José Chávez Morado. It's open Tuesday through Saturday from 9am to 7pm and Sunday from 10am until 6pm. Admission costs $2.25 (free on Sun). Free tours are available on request (for a minimum of five people) in English, French, or Spanish, Tuesday through Saturday from 10am to 5pm. An audio tape for a guided tour is available for $4.

The museum has three sections. First is the entrance hall, with a checkroom on the right and the museum bookstore on the left. The bookstore has a superior collection of guides to cultural, culinary, and archaeological attractions in Mexico. See "The Top Attractions," above, for a general description of the museum.

Note: Most of the museum is wheelchair accessible; however, assistance will be needed in places. Signs are in Spanish only. A systematic room-at-a-time renovation and reorganization started in 1995, so a room or portion of one may be closed during your visit.

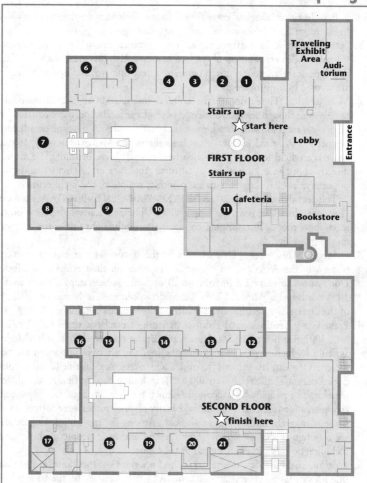

Museo Nacional de Antropología

FIRST FLOOR:

1. Introducción a la Antropología
2. Mesoamérica
3. Orígenes
4. Preclásica y Teotihuacana
5. Teotihuacán
6. Tolteca
7. Mexica
8. Oaxaca
9. Golfo de México
10. Maya
11. Norte y Occidente

SECOND FLOOR:

12. Introductoría
13. Los Coras y Huicholes
14. Purepecha
15. Otomianos
16. Sierra Norte de Puebla
17. Oaxaca
18. Costa Golfo
19. Maya
20. Noroeste de México
21. Las Nahuas

Pass the ticket taker and enter the courtyard. Following are the museum's highlights, room (sala) by room, beginning on your right:

1. **Introducción a la Antropología.** The entrance mural by Jorge González Camarena depicts women of various nations. Exhibits deal with humanity throughout the world, groups' progress and development, and how these aspects are studied by anthropologists.

2. **Mesoamérica.** Here you see the cultural interrelation of the Mesoamerican people even though they are dispersed over a large landscape, demonstrated by a large color map showing locations of the great cultures. A timeline puts them in perspective. A mural by Raul Anguiano shows the Maya cosmogony: thirteen heavens are held up by a giant ceiba tree; nine hells are beneath. The mural is directly above an exhibit of burial customs. You'll see other fascinating displays of pottery, jewelry, skeletal remains, painting, sculpture, and architecture.

The next sign you'll see, SALAS DE ETNOGRAFÍA, EN LA PLANTA ALTA, means "Ethnographic Rooms on the Upper Floor." There's a stairway here so you can reach those rooms. But, for now, continue around the right side of the courtyard on the main level to:

3. **Orígenes.** This room, "Origins," traces the history of the earliest men and women in the Americas, with specific emphasis on their remains in Mexico. Don't miss the *mamut* 2 (mammoth 2) of Santa Isabel Ixtapan, discovered in 1954 northwest of Mexico City. Of considerable interest is the miniature display of the diverse architectural styles evidenced in Mexico's pyramids.

4. **Preclásica y Teotihuacána.** Exhibits here are of Preclassic times (2000 B.C. to A.D. 300), just before the Mesoamerican cultures reached their zenith. Religion, agriculture, hieroglyphic writing, numbering, and art were important facets of society. One display shows a reconstructed archaeological site found in place during digs at Tlatilco (1300 to 800 B.C.), including pottery, figures, and skeletal remains. The people of Tlatilco were known for their appliqué technique using clay pieces for figure decoration, and many of their pieces were formed in the shape of animals, birds, frogs, and squash. Among the most interesting displays are clay figures that effectively show the appearance of people in those times, including pottery pieces attributed to the Olmecs.

5. **Teotihuacán.** First view the model of this important site that flourished just outside Mexico City between 200 B.C. and A.D. 900. Outside on the back patio is another mockup view of the site at eye level. This sala will prepare you for seeing the ruins in person. Chronologically displayed pottery gives a clear picture of the development of this utilitarian art at Teotihuacán. Other exhibits show tools for building, sculpture, fresco painting, jewelry making, and weaving. There's a reproduction of the mural *Paradise of the God Tlaloc,* and visitors are dwarfed beside the life-size replica of a portion of the Temple of Quetzalcoatl.

6. **Tolteca.** Toltec, Chichimec, and Cholulan cultures are preserved here, but the exhibit begins at Xochicalco, a site between Cuernavaca and Taxco that was both a crossroads of many cultures and perhaps a bridge between Teotihuacán and the Toltecs at Tula, north of Mexico City. Xochicalco building and pottery show a cross-cultural mix with the Maya, Teotihuacán, and the Toltecs. The artistic elements of the Toltecs influenced those of many groups that followed them: They were the developers of serpentine columns, *chac-mools,* Atlantean figures, the eagle motif, and pilasters of war figures. Also here is one of the huge Atlantean-men statues from the Temple of Tlahuizcalpantecutli at Tula, as well as other great monoliths and pottery. A model shows what the site of Tula looked like, and another shows how it may have been constructed. A model of the pyramid

site at Cholula, by volume the largest pyramid in the world, displays its three superimpositions (buildings one on top of another). Cholulan pottery was especially accomplished, so don't miss the displays of it here.

7. Mexica. At the far end of the courtyard, lettering on the lintel reads CEM-ANAHUAC TENOCHCA TLALPAN, and beneath it is the entrance to one of the most important rooms in the museum. This room is an excellent one to see before visiting the Templo Mayor site and museum near the zócalo in the historical zone of Mexico City. Among the amazing stone carvings are the Aztec Calendar Stone, which bears symbols for all the ages of humankind (as the Aztecs saw them); the Piedra de Tizoc; Xiuhcoatl, the fire serpent; a Tzompantli, or wall of skulls; the terrifying headless monolith of Coatlicue, goddess of earth and death, with two serpent heads coming from her neck, a necklace of hands and hearts, and a skirt of serpents; and the stone head of the moon goddess, Coyolxauhqui, with bells on her cheeks, sun disks in her earlobes, and a nose ring.

Amid all this ominous dark volcanic rock, the iridescent feathered headdress of Moctezuma (a copy) blazes away, as impressive today as when the Aztec emperor proceeded regally through the streets of Tenochtitlán. Near the glass case holding the headdress is a large model of Moctezuma's rich capital city; a mural echoes the city's grandeur as well. A popular display is the enormous diorama of the thriving market at Tlatelolco, which brings to life the description of it by Bernal Díaz de Castillo. (The remains of Tlatelolco are north of the zócalo in the Plaza of Three Cultures.)

8. Oaxaca. After the Mexica room comes that of Oaxaca, with its Zapotec and Mixtec cultures, Olmec influences, and priceless artifacts from the Monte Albán excavations. The huge display of pottery is arranged chronologically to show its evolution, and a deerskin Mixtec codice exemplifies picture writing. The Mixtecs were accomplished metalworkers, gemsmiths, and wood-carvers, and you'll see fine examples of their work. Take time to admire the reproduction of Tomb 105 from Monte Albán. Go down the stairs to a reproduction of Tomb 104, complete with wall frescoes and burial figures surrounded by offerings. A huge mural shows how the mountaintop ruins of Monte Albán looked at their apogee.

9. Golfo de México. Divided into four sections, this hall covers the rich cultures of the Huastecas from the northern part of Veracruz and Tamaulipas; the Remojadas and Totonacs, who occupied the middle portion of the region; and the Olmec, who occupied southern Veracruz and northern Tabasco but whose influence was felt far away. Certainly the most visible highlight here is an enormous multiton, basaltic rock head, though one of the finest is the graceful and beautifully sculpted "wrestler," both by Olmec master stone-carvers. The Huastecas were known for their exquisite polychrome pottery with anthropomorphic and zoomorphic forms, and the pottery display does justice to the culture. But the tall, slender stone-carved figure of the "Huastec Adolescent," with a baby on its back, is one of Mesoamerica's most graceful. There are models of the archaeological sites at El Tajín, near Papantla, and Zempoala, near Veracruz.

10. Maya. This is one of the most stunning exhibitions in this grand museum. Maya art and culture have tremendous intrinsic interest, and the exhibits in this section are wonderful. Displays here include a fine collection of well-preserved, beautiful Maya carvings, not just from Mexican territory but from other parts of Mesoamerica (Central America) as well.

Models of ancient cities include Copan (Honduras), Yaxchilán (Chiapas), Tulum (Quintana Roo), and Uaxactun (Guatemala). Downstairs is a model of the fabulous tomb discovered in the Temple of the Inscriptions at Palenque, complete with a rich jade mask for the deceased monarch. Outside the exhibit room is a full-scale replica of a temple at Hochob (Campeche) and another of the Temple of Paintings at Bonampak, plus replicas of stele from Quirigua (Guatemala). In all these examples, notice especially the fineness of the carving. In the Tablero de la Cruz Enramada, from Palenque, note the fine work in the glyphs.

⏺ **TAKE A BREAK**   After touring the Maya room, descend a wide staircase to reach the reasonably priced **Cafetería Museo.** Beer and mixed or soft drinks are served, as well as breakfast, soups, salads, sandwiches, and more substantial main courses. It's open Tuesday through Saturday from 9am to 7pm and Sunday from 9am to 6pm.

11. **Norte y Occidente.** These rooms deal with the "culture of the desert" from northern and western Mexico. If you're familiar with the cultures of the Indians of the southwestern United States, you'll notice numerous similarities here. Many of the artifacts are from the Casas Grandes pueblo in the state of Chihuahua, where the people lived in adobe pueblos and crafted pottery very much like that of New Mexico and Arizona.

    The occidental exhibits hold echoes of the great civilization of the Valley of Mexico, mostly from such sites as Tzintzuntzán (Michoacán), Ixtlán (Nayarit), Ixtepete (Jalisco), and Chupicuaro (Guanajuato), but they also include objects from San Miguel de Allende and San Luis Potosí. The *chac-mool* from Ihuatzio looks like a bad copy or a stylized rendering of the great *chac-mools* of Tula and Chichén-Itzá. There's also a model of a *yácata,* a vast, stepped ceremonial platform, as found in the western zone.

    From here, cross to the end of the patio next to the Sala de Orígenes and take the stairs up to the splendid displays of daily life in the **Ethnographic Section.** Begin in the first room on the right:

12. **Introductoría.** Murals, maps, photographs, textiles, jewelry, and other objects provide perspective on Mexico's daily life from pre-Hispanic times to the present.

13. **Cora y Huichol.** Devoted to inhabitants of the west-coast states of Nayarit and Jalisco, this room displays lifelike figures, clad in traditionally embroidered clothing and seated on *equipale* stools before an authentic indigenous hut. Particularly note the pottery and *morales* (woven bags), all of which are in use in villages today.

14. **Purépecha.** The Purépecha, more generally known as Tarascans, live in the state of Michoacán and carry on crafts learned centuries ago under the influence of the first bishop of Pátzcuaro, Vasco de Quiroga. The main calling card of this display is the enormously long dugout canoe at the entrance. You'll see examples of guitars from Paracho, copper objects from Santa Clara del Cobre, and samples of fine dinnerware from potters around Lake Pátzcuaro. Occasionally on display is an example of the exquisite reversible black-and-white serape trimmed with stylized quetzal bird designs that is produced by weavers from Angahuan, a village near the Paricutín volcano.

15. **Otomianos.** Otomi Indians, who speak several languages within the Otomangue language group, live in the states of Hidalgo, México (which almost surrounds Mexico City), San Luis Potosí, and Querétaro. This group of Indians includes the Nahua, Azteca, Mazahua, and Matlatzinca, all of which are believed to be descendants of the Toltec. Here you see figures weaving *ixtle* fibers of the maguey plant.

There are also cases of products made for everyday use and trade, such as baskets, belts, jars, blouses, and serapes.

16. **Sierra Norte de Puebla.** The northern part of the state of Puebla is one of the country's most interesting areas, yet it's little visited by tourists. Note the villagers of San Pablito pounding bark into paper, the unfinished pink and black *quechquemitl* on an unusual loom that rounds corners, and the finely embroidered blouses with flower and animal designs.

17. **Oaxaca.** The southern state of Oaxaca is one of the most interesting in the country, due in part to the numerous varieties of colorful *huipils* (loose garments) worn by women from different indigenous groups. A full-size hut is complete with furnishings, weaving looms, and pottery, plus an oxcart outside. Another section shows the different styles of huts used along the coast of Oaxaca, and men and boys weaving palm.

18. **Costa Golfo.** This region is composed of indigenous groups of Huastecas, Totonacas, and Nahuas. The Huasteca Indians speak a language related to Maya. Inside the hut, women wearing embroidered blouses and ribbons twisted through their braided hair are surrounded by pottery and frozen in the motion of decorating and forming clay by hand.

19. **Maya.** The land of the Maya comprises the states of Tabasco, Chiapas, Yucatán, Campeche, and Quintana Roo; of these, the most colorful is Chiapas. Besides the cases of costumes and pottery, there are examples of musical instruments and furnished huts showing life today. A market scene from the Chiapas highlands shows men and women in regional attire—heavy wool tunics and colorful, richly brocaded loomed *huipils*. In another scene, a woman from the Yucatán weaves henequen fiber on a stick loom.

20. **Noroeste de México.** Seri, Tarahumara, and Yaqui Indians live in northwestern Mexico in the states of Sonora, Chihuahua, and Sinaloa, as well as in Baja California. Among the unusual items you'll see are beautiful basketry that's quite similar to some made in the southwestern United States. A painting shows how the Seri women decorate their faces.

21. **Las Nahuas.** The last room is devoted to this Indian group in modern Mexico who live in central Veracruz, Hidalgo, Guerrero, Morelos, Durango, Tlaxcala, Jalisco, and the state of México. It portrays them in various acts of their daily life, which is based on the corn culture. A written narrative states that this group is in a precarious situation due to poor health care, unemployment, illiteracy, injustice, and oppression.

6 Organized Tours

Mexico City is a great place for looking around on your own, and in general this is the easiest and least expensive way to see whatever you like. However, if your time is limited, you may wish to acclimate yourself quickly by taking a tour or two.

Among the noncommercial offerings are **free guided tours** sponsored by the **Mexico City Historical Center** (☎ **5/510-2541** or 5/510-4737, ext. 1499), which is housed in the 18th-century home of Don Manuel de Heras y Soto, at Donceles and República de Chile. Groups meet each Sunday at 10:45am at a central gathering place for that day's tour, which varies from week to week. These tours might explore a historic downtown street, cafes and theaters, cemeteries, or the colonial churches of Xochimilco. Most tours, which last about 2 hours, are in Spanish; as many as 300 people may be divided among 10 guides. However, visitors with other language requirements can ask a day in advance for a guide who speaks their language. Since the

Tours: The Downside

Many readers have written to say they were unhappy with the sightseeing tours of this or that company. The reasons are myriad: The tour was too rushed; the guide knew nothing and made up stories about the sights; the tour spent most of its time in a handcrafts shop (chosen by the tour company) rather than seeing the sights. Do tour companies get a kickback from souvenir shops? You bet they do! If you meet someone who has recently taken a guided tour and liked it, go with the same company. Otherwise, you might do well to see the sights on your own, following the detailed information in this book. Your hotel can arrange a private car by the hour or day—and generally these drivers are also English-speaking guides. This can often be less expensive or only slightly more than the cost of an organized tour, with greater flexibility and personalized service.

center's phone is almost always busy, you'll have to visit the office in the far back of the building, on the right and up a spiral staircase, to obtain a list of upcoming tours and gathering locations. Office hours are Monday through Friday from 9am to 3pm and 6 to 9pm.

A 1-hour **trolleybus tour** of the Centro Histórico is sponsored by the Chamber of Commerce Tourism Services (☎ **5/512-1012**) Tuesday through Sunday. Buses load across Piño Suárez from the Museo de la Ciudad, and leave every 30 minutes between 10am and 4pm. Cost is $3.

Many commercial tours are offered, such as a 4-hour city tour including such sites as the **Metropolitan Cathedral,** the **Nacional Palace,** and **Chapultepec Park and Castle;** a longer tour to the **Shrine of Guadalupe** and nearby pyramids at **Teotihuacán;** and the Sunday tour that begins with the **Ballet Folklórico,** moves on to the **Floating Gardens of Xochimilco,** and may or may not include lunch and the afternoon bullfights. Almost as popular are the 1-day and overnight tours to Puebla, Cuernavaca, Taxco, and Acapulco. There are also several nightclub tours.

7 Shopping

From handcrafts to the finest in designer goods, Mexico City, like any major metropolitan area, is a marvelous place for shopping. From malls to mercados, there are numerous places displaying fascinating native products and sophisticated goods.

The two best districts for browsing are on and off **avenida Juárez** facing the Alameda; **avenida Madero** and the streets parallel to it; and in the **Zona Rosa** (for jewelry, calle Amberes is the place, for instance). A few unique shops deserve particular mention.

Several government-run shops and a few excellent privately run shops have exceptionally good collections of Mexico's arts and crafts. Here's the rundown on the best places to shop, from small, selective crafts shops to vast general markets.

SHOPPING A TO Z
ART

Arvil. Cerrada de Hamburgo 7 and 9, Reforma/Zona Rosa. ☎ **5/207-2647** or 5/207-3994. By appointment only. AE, MC, V. Metro: Insurgentes.

Collectible works of art by Mexican masters—auction-quality pieces.

López Quiroga Gallery. Presidente Masaryk 379 and Seneca, Polanco. ☎ **5/280-1247.** Fax 5/280-4053. Mon–Fri 10am–5pm. AE, CB, DC. No Metro station.

Auction-quality works of art by contemporary Latin American masters including Toledo and Tamayo.

O.M.R. Gallery. Plaza Río de Janeiro 54. Plaza Río de Janeiro (Roma). ☎ **5/525-4368;** 5/511-1179. Mon–Fri 10am–6pm; Sat 10am–2pm. AE, MC, V.

This gallery has earned a reputation for discovering and introducing emerging talents and new artists. Its specialization is Latin America.

Sergio Bustamante. Amberes 13. Hotel Nikko, Polanco. ☎ **5/525-9059.** Mon–Fri 10am–7:30pm; Sat 10am–7pm. AE, DC, MC, V. Metro: Insurgentes.

One of Mexico's best-known contemporary sculptors and artists, his Zona Rosa store has a broad selection of his surrealistic and very collectible work. Each piece is signed. Showcases in the front of the store hold his jewelry designs fashioned in gold, many of them miniatures of his sculpture. There's another Bustamante outlet in the lobby of the Hotel Nikko. The store is between Hamburgo and Reforma.

CIGARS

Humo en la Boca. Amberes 15, Zona Rosa. ☎**5/525-2922** or 5/514-6974. Mon–Sat 10am–6pm. AE, MC, V. Metro: Insurgentes.

This cozy, elegant shop ("Smoke in the Mouth") has an outstanding selection of premium Cuban and Caribbean cigars, along with cutters, humidors, and other accessories. This is Mexico City's finest cigar outfitter.

CRAFTS

Artesanías de México. Londres 117, Zona Rosa. ☎ **5/514-2025** or 5/514-7455. Mon–Fri 10am–7pm; Sat 10am–3pm. AE, MC, V. Metro: Insurgentes.

This shop in the Zona Rosa sells crafts from all over Mexico. It isn't large, but it's a good place to see handsome displays of pottery, textiles, and original art.

Exposición Nacional de Arte Popular (FONART). Juárez 89, Centro Histórico. ☎ **5/ 521-6681** or 5/518-3058. Daily 10am–6pm. MC, V. Metro: Hidalgo or Juárez.

This government-operated store is usually loaded with crafts: papier-mâché figurines, textiles, earthenware, colorfully painted candelabra, hand-carved wooden masks, straw goods, beads, bangles, and glass. It is operated by the Fonda Nacional para el Fomento de las Artes (FONART), a government organization that helps village craftspeople.

FONART. Londres 136A, Zona Rosa. ☎ **5/525-2026.** Mon–Sat 10am–7pm. MC, V. Metro: Insurgentes.

Another branch of the government-operated store (see above) is in the heart of the Zona Rosa. Though in small, narrow upstairs quarters, it is chock full of folk art, much of it not duplicated at the larger store on Juárez.

Museo Nacional de Artes e Industrias Populares. Juárez 44, Centro Histórico. ☎ **5/ 521-6679.** Daily 10am–6pm. Metro: Bellas Artes.

The Forbidden Fruits of Cuban Cigars

Cuban cigars are available for sale in Mexico and can be enjoyed by Americans while in Mexico, but cannot be brought back into the United States—the purchase of Cuban goods is a violation of the country's embargo against this island nation. As an alternative, cigars made in Veracruz are also excellent, many made by former Cuban master cigar-rollers who left the island during the revolution.

Folk-art enthusiasts will delight in this excellent government-operated craft shop. The building was once the Corpus Christi Convent, built during the 18th century. This store with a museum is located across from the Benito Juárez statue in Alameda Park, and it has an enormous selection of high-quality Mexican crafts for sale. Because the prices are fixed, you can get an idea of quality versus cost for later use in market bargaining.

Victor Artes Populares Mexicanas. Madero 10, 2nd floor, Room 305, Centro Histórico. ☎ **5/512-1263.** Mon–Fri 12:30–7pm. AE, MC, V. Metro: Zócalo.

Owned by the Fosado family, which has been in the folk art business for more than 60 years, Victor, near the Alameda, is a shop for serious buyers and art collectors. The Fosados buy most of their crafts from Indian villages near and far, and supply various exhibits with native crafts.

GLASS

Avalos Brothers. Carretones 5, Centro Histórico. ☎ **5/522-5311.** Fax 5/522-6420. Mon–Fri 10am–5pm; Sat 10am–2pm. Metro: La Merced.

For more than 100 years, blown glass has come from this run-down location in the old section of town. You can watch men and women scurry around with red-hot glass in various stages of shaping until it cools. A sales showroom to the left of the entrance holds shelves full of glass objects—pitchers, vases, plates, glasses, flowers, cream and sugar containers, and the like, in various colors. Few tourists seem to find their way here, but among locals this is the store of choice for selection and price. It is near the La Merced market where Carretones dead-ends into Tapacio, a short block south of San Pablo.

JEWELRY

Besides the shops mentioned below, there are dozens of jewelry stores and optical shops on Madero from Motolinia to the zócalo, in the portals facing the National Palace. **Monte Piedad/National Pawn Shop,** also opposite the National Palace, has an enormous jewelry selection, and the sculptor **Sergio Bustamante** also designs jewelry (see "Art," above).

Bazar del Centro. Isabel la Católica 30, Centro Histórico. No phone. Mon–Fri 10am–7pm; Sat 10am–3pm. Metro: Zócalo.

Located between the Alameda and the zócalo, this colonial-era building was the palace of the Counts of Miravale. Now it houses shops selling jewelry, precious stones, and silver.

Los Castillo. Amberes 41, Zona Rosa. ☎ **5/511-6198** or 5/511-8396. Mon–Fri 10am–7pm; Sat 10am–3pm. Metro: Insurgentes.

This Zona Rosa branch of the famous Taxco silversmith family houses some of their best work—pieces you won't see at their shop in Taxco, for example. Besides handsome silver jewelry, you'll find decorative bowls made of porcelain fused with silver, napkin rings, and furniture with silver and porcelain tops.

Tane. Amberes 70. Reforma/Zona Rosa. ☎ **5/207-8202** or 5/510-9429. Mon–Fri 10am–7pm; Sat 11am–2:30pm. Metro: Insurgentes.

Tucked in the Zona Rosa, this is the original store of one of the top silver designers in Mexico, with branches only in the best hotels and shopping centers. The quantity and quality of silver work is enormous, from jewelry to platters, pitchers, dinner plates, cutlery, frames, candlestick holders and even their own china by Limoges. There are also branches in the Hotel Presidente Inter-Continental and in the neighborhoods of Polanco and San Ángel and at the airport.

MARKETS

✪ **Bazar Sábado.** Plaza de San Jacinto, San Ángel. Sat 9am–6pm.

A festive and unique shopping experience, the Bazar Sábado is held every Saturday, as its name indicates—and only on Saturday. Located in an expensive colonial-era suburb of cobbled streets, mansions, and parks a few miles south of the city, it's my top recommendation for passing a Saturday afternoon in Mexico City. You don't have to even like shopping to enjoy a day here. The actual bazaar building is an elegant two-story mansion built around a courtyard.

The central area now houses an excellent, authentic Mexican cafe, whose atmosphere is hectic as waiters hustle to serve tacos hot off the grill and frosty margaritas, plus *antojitos* and traditional main dishes like enchiladas. Marimba music serenades in the background. Dozens of small rooms surrounding the courtyard serve as permanent stalls featuring original works of high-quality decorative art. Among the one-of-a-kind treasures, you'll find blown glass, original fine-jewelry designs, papier-mâché figures, masks, and embroidered clothing. The prices are on the high side, but the quality is equally high, and the designs are sophisticated. On adjacent plazas, hundreds of easel artists display their paintings, with surrounding homes filled with antiques, fine rugs, and hand-carved furniture for sale. Members of indigenous groups from Puebla and elsewhere bring their folk art—baskets, masks, pottery, textiles, and so on—to display in the parks. Restaurants (some in mansions) lining the streets play host to leisurely diners seated at umbrella-shaded tables. Plan to spend all Saturday touring the attractions on the southern outskirts of the city. (See also "San Ángel" under "Southern Neighborhoods," earlier in this chapter.)

Centro Artesanal (Mercado de Curiosidades). At the corner of Ayuntamiento and Dolores, Reforma North. Mon–Sat 10am–5:30pm. Metro: Guerrero.

This rather modern building set back off a plaza is composed of a number of stalls on two levels, selling everything from leather to tiles. They have some lovely silver jewelry and, as in most non–fixed-price stores, the asking price is high but the bargained result is often very reasonable.

Lagunilla Market. 3 blocks east of Plaza de Garibaldi. Daily 9am–5pm. Metro: Allende.

This is one of the most interesting and unusual markets in Mexico—but watch out for pickpockets. The best day is Sunday, when the Lagunilla becomes a colorful outdoor market filling the streets for blocks. Arrive around 9am. Vendors sell everything from axes to antiques. The two enclosed sections are open all week and are separated by a short street, calle Juan Álvarez. They have different specialties: The one to the north is noted for clothes, rebozos, and blankets; the one to the south for tools, pottery, and household goods, such as attractive hanging copper lamps. This is also the area to find old and rare books, many at a ridiculously low cost, if you're willing to hunt and bargain.

Mercado Insurgentes. On Londres between Florencia and Amberes, Zona Rosa. Mon–Sat 9am–5:30pm. Metro: Insurgentes.

Mercado Insurgentes is a full-fledged crafts market tucked in the Zona Rosa. Because of its address you might expect exorbitant prices, but vendors in the maze of stalls are eager to bargain, and good buys aren't hard to come by.

Merced Market. Circunvalación between General Anaya and Adolfo Gurrión. Mon–Fri 8am–4pm; Sat 8am–2pm. Metro: Merced.

This is the biggest market in the city and among the most fascinating in the country, with intense activity and an energy level akin to the Abastos Market in Oaxaca. Officially it consists of several modern buildings, but shops line tidy but crowded streets all the way to the zócalo.

The first building is mainly for fruits and vegetables; the others contain just about everything you would find if a department store joined forces with a discount warehouse—a good place to shop especially for housewares such as hand-held citrus juicers of all sizes, tinware, colorful spoons, decorative oil cloth, and so on. The main market is east of the zócalo on Circunvalación between General Anaya and Adolfo Gurrión and is the place to stock up on Mexican spices. It's easy to walk the 13 blocks from the zócalo, zigzagging your way past many shops en route. Or take the Metro to the Merced stop right outside the market.

Monte de Piedad Nacional (National Pawn Shop). Corner of Monte de Piedad and Cinco de Mayo, Centro Histórico. ☎ **5/597-3455.** Mon–Fri 8:30am–6pm; Sat 8:30am–3pm. Metro: Zócalo.

This could be described as the world's largest and most elegant thrift store. Electric power tools, jewelry, antique furniture, heavy machine tools, sofa beds, and a bewildering array of other things from trash to treasure are all on display. Buying is not required, but taking a look is recommended. Be sure to see the "Sala de Arte y Regalos" (art and gift shop); it's a hodgepodge of items ranging from the ridiculous to the exquisite. The building is on the site of Moctezuma's old Axayácatl palace, where the captive emperor was accidentally killed. Cortés used the site to build a viceregal palace. The present building was given by Pedro Romero de Terreros, the Count of Regla, an 18th-century silver magnate from Pachuca, so that Mexican people might obtain low-interest loans.

MUSIC

Mercado De Discos. Eje Central/Cárdenas 10, Centro Histórico. ☎ **5/521-5853.** Mon–Sat 10am–8pm; Sun 11am–8pm. AE, DC, MC, V. Metro: Lázaro Cárdenas.

This may not be the most upscale-looking place, but the selection of national and international records and tapes is immense. It's between Madero and 16 de Septiembre, only 2 blocks from the Palacio de Bellas Artes.

RUGS

Temoaya Tapetes Mexicanos. S. A. Hamburgo 235, Col. Juárez. ☎ **5/511-0069.** Fax 5/5633-6420 or 5/533-3851 5/207-4991. Mon–Fri 10am–6pm; Sat 10am–2pm. CB, DISC, MC, V. Metro: Insurgentes.

A full selection of the Persian-style rugs made in Temoaya (outside of Toluca) are found at this outlet of the rug-maker's cooperative. These sought-after works of art are made using hooked-rug techniques taught by Iranian rug makers and design motifs from the indigenous groups of Mexico. Color combinations can make the same design appear to be completely different. You can also select colors and designs to your liking from their catalog and have a rug made to order. Completion takes several months and they don't ship. A 6-by-9-foot rug costs around $1,600. Manager Isaac Garci Dueñas y Rodriguez has a good command of the motifs and their meanings.

8 Mexico City After Dark

From mariachis, reggae, and opera to folkloric dance, classical ballet, and dinner shows, the choice of nighttime entertainment in Mexico City is enormous and sophisticated. Prices here are much lower than comparable entertainment in most of the

Crime at Night

Due to the escalation of crime, make sure to leave valuables—especially watches and jewelry—at your hotel, and bring only the cash or credit cards you will need. While I list Metro stops, these should probably be used only for orientation; take only authorized *sitio* taxis (see advisory, "Important Taxi Safety Precaution in Mexico City," at the beginning of this chapter) or hire a private taxi by the hour and enjoy an escort waiting for you as you sample the festivities of the city. Your hotel can help with these arrangements.

world's major cities. On the other hand, if you're willing to let *la vida mexicana* put on its own fascinating show for you, the bill will be much less. People watching, cafe sitting, music, and even a dozen mariachi bands all playing at once, can be yours for next to nothing.

THE ENTERTAINMENT SCENE

There's a very impressive club scene in Mexico City, with great places for dancing to music ranging from salsa to techno. The **Historic Center** downtown has the broadest range of hip clubs concentrated within walking distance from one another. The **Zona Rosa** remains a highly popular place for nightlife, and may be a more comfortable place for tourists. The music tends to be more English-language than Spanish, and the masses of people strolling the sidewalks gives the area a festive, friendly feel. Clubs and dinner-dance establishments tend to get going around 10 or 11pm and last until at least 3am. Many clubs operate only Thursday through Saturday.

Fiesta nights give visitors a chance to dine on typical Mexican food and see Mexico's wonderful regional dancing, which seems always to be a treat no matter how many times you've seen them.

For lower-key nightlife and people watching, outdoor cafes remain a popular option here. Those on **Copenhague Street** are among the liveliest for being in the thick of the Zona Rosa scene, but with one or two exceptions, they have become more expensive than they are good. Another tradition is **Garibaldi Square,** where mariachis tune up and wait to be hired—*but street crime in this area, both day and night, has made this a place I can no longer recommend.* Restaurants and drinking establishments here feature mariachis in a typical Mexican atmosphere. It's a slice of Mexican life that's tempting to travelers—if you check it out, do so with caution and preferably with a group.

Hotel lobby bars tend to have live entertainment of the low-key type in the late afternoon and on into the evening.

THE PERFORMING ARTS

Mexico City's offering of performing arts is among the finest and most comprehensive in the world. Opera, theater, ballet and dance, along with concerts of symphonic, rock, and popular music, are presented with a changing schedule of performances.

For current information on cultural offerings, the best source is the Sunday edition of the English-language daily newspapers, the *News* or the *Times,* both of which have full listings of cultural events. A limited number of events are printed other days. *Donde* and *Concierge,* free magazines found in hotels, are other good sources for locating the newest places, but they don't have complete listings of changing entertainment or current exhibits. For performances of major attractions, tickets can usually be obtained through **TicketMaster** (☎ **5/325-9000**).

The **Folkloric Ballet of Mexico** is perhaps the city's most renowned entertainment for visitors here, with its stunning presentation of regional dance.

Note: The majority of the theatrical performances at the Palacio de Bellas Artes and in other theaters around the city are presented in Spanish.

FOLKLORIC BALLET

Palacio de Bellas Artes. Calle López Peralta, east end of the Alameda, Centro Histórico–Alameda. ☎ **5/512-2592**, ext. 152. Tickets $15–$30. Metro: Bellas Artes.

Although various groups perform around the city, the finest is at the Palacio de Bellas Artes, where performances of Mexico's famed **Ballet Folklórico de México** are held here several times a week. The Ballet Folklórico is a celebration of pre- and post-Hispanic dancing in Mexico. A typical program includes Aztec ritual dances, agricultural dances from Jalisco, a fiesta in Veracruz, a wedding celebration—all wedded together with mariachis, marimba players, singers, and dancers.

Since many other events are held in the Bellas Artes—visits by foreign opera companies, for instance—the Ballet Folklórico is occasionally moved. Usually, it reappears in the **National Auditorium** in Chapultepec Park. Check at the Bellas Artes box office. The show is popular and tickets are bought up rapidly (especially by tour agencies at twice the cost). The box office is on the ground floor of the Bellas Artes, main entrance. *Note:* The theater tends to be very cold, so you may want to bring a sweater. The box office is open Monday through Saturday from 11am to 7pm and Sunday from 8:30am to 7pm; Ballet Folklórico performances are held on Sunday at 9:30am and Wednesday at 8:30pm.

The Fine Arts theater not only offers the finest in performing arts, but is architecturally worth a visit on its own (see "Exploring Mexico City," above).

Teatro de la Ciudad. Donceles 36, Centro Histórico. ☎ **5/521-2355**. Tickets $7–$17 to the Ballet Folklórico; call about other performances. Shows Sun 9:30am and Tues 8:30pm. Metro: Tacuba.

An alternative to the Ballet Folklórico de México is the **Ballet Folklórico Nacional Aztlán,** in the beautiful turn-of-the-century Teatro de la Ciudad, a block northeast of the Bellas Artes between Xicoténcatl and Allende. Performances here are as good as the better-known ones in the Bellas Artes, but tickets are less expensive and much easier to obtain. Other major performances of ballet, concerts, and the like also appear here.

THE CLUB & MUSIC SCENE

This warning probably can't be reiterated enough: *Take an authorized sitio taxi to all nightspots. Metro stops are given merely as a point of reference.*

MARIACHIS

Mariachis play the music of Mexico. Although the songs they play may be familiar—ranging from Mozart to the Beatles, along with traditional *boleros*—their style and presentation are unique to Mexico. Known for their distinctive dress, strolling presentation, and mix of brass and guitars, they epitomize the romance and tradition of the country. They look a little like Mexican cowboys dressed up for a special occasion—tight trousers studded with silver buttons down the outside of the legs, elaborate cropped jackets, embroidered shirts with big bow ties, and grandiose sombrero hats. The dress dates back to the French occupation of Mexico in the mid-19th century, as does the name. *Mariachi* is believed to be an adaptation of the French word for marriage; this was the type of music commonly played at weddings in the 15th and 16th centuries. The music itself is a derivative of *fandango*, which was the most

A Note of Caution in Garibaldi Square

Plaza de Garibaldi, *both day and night*, is increasingly populated by thieves looking to separate tourists from their valuables, and I can no longer recommend that individual tourists go there, unless by private taxi. If you choose to go, don't take credit cards or excess money with you. Go with a crowd of friends rather than alone, or take one of the Garibaldi tours.

popular dance music of the elite classes in 16th-century Spain. In Mexico, fandango became the peasant's song and dance.

In Mexico City, the mariachis make their headquarters around the **Plaza de Garibaldi,** 5 blocks north of the Palacio de Bellas Artes—up avenida Lázaro Cárdenas, at avenida República de Honduras. Mariachi players are everywhere in the plaza. At every corner, guitars are stacked together like rifles in an army training camp. Young musicians strut proudly in their outfits, on the lookout for señoritas to impress. They play when they feel like it, when there's a good chance to gather in some tips, or when someone orders a song—the going rate is from $1.50 to $3.25 per song.

Should you want to enjoy mariachi music in a more tourist-friendly venue, I can recommend:

Jorongo Bar. Hotel María Isabel-Sheraton, Reforma 325 (Zona Rosa). ☎ **5/207-3933.** Cover $8.25. AE, MC, V. Metro: Insurgentes.

For wonderful mariachi and trio music in plush surroundings, make your way to the Hotel María Isabel-Sheraton, facing the Ángel Monument. The reputation for this bar's mariachi music has been intact for decades—it's an institution. Nightly from 7pm to 1am, you can enjoy the smooth and joyous sounds for the price of a drink ($2.50 to $5) plus cover.

CLUBS & MUSIC BARS

✪ **Bar Fly.** Mazaryk 393, Polanco. ☎ **5/282-2906.** No cover; 2-drink minimum. Nightly 9pm–2am.

The talented house band—direct from Cuba—makes this small but stylish bar sizzle. By midnight the tiny dance floor is overflowing. Located on the second floor of an upscale shopping center, it has become one of the hottest clubs in Polanco.

Bar León. Brasil 5, Centro Histórico. ☎ **5/510-3093.** Mon–Sat 9pm–3am. Cover varies with live music availability. MC, V. Metro: Zócalo.

An outstanding choice for dancing merengue and salsa, with live groups frequently featured.

Bar Mata. Filomeno Mata 11, 3rd floor, Centro Histórico. ☎ **5/518-0237.** Tues–Sat 8pm–2am. Cover varies with live music; call ahead. MC, V. Metro: Bellas Artes.

An art-deco ambiance in a 19th-century historic building sets the backdrop for this very hip dance club. Live music—generally jazz, blues, and rock—on Wednesday and Sunday.

Casa de Paquita la del Barrio. Zarco 202, Col. Guerrero. ☎ **5/583-8131.** Nightly 9pm–3am. Cover $6 or more, depending on performers. AE, MC, V. Guerrero

This nightclub features its namesake and star performer, Paquita la del Barrio, famous for her resonant voice and interpretation of traditional ballads. Paquita takes the stage solo, or other performers may join her, making this a top choice for rousing Mexican music.

Gypsy's. Florencia 32, Col. Juárez, Zona Rosa. ☎ **5/514-1698.** Thurs–Sat 9pm–2am. No cover. MC, V. Metro: Insurgentes.

One of the longest-standing discos in the Zona Rosa, Gypsy's continues to pack in a young, upbeat crowd. The club features two dance floors, recorded rock music, and occasional live salsa bands. A cover charge is in effect when live music is featured, but the cover varies with the acts.

La Boom. Rodolfo Gaona 3, Col. Lomas de Sotelo (Chapultepec/Polanco). ☎ **5/580-6473.** Wed–Sat 9pm–4am. Cover $5–$10. AE, DC, MC, V. Metro: Toréo.

The most popular disco and dance club in town frequently has live bands. Techno and hip-hop are prominently spun, with a strong mix of Mexican rock as well. Additional cover charge applies for concert performances.

⭐ **La Llorona.** Mesones 87, Centro Histórico. ☎ **5/709-8121.** Cover $8. Thurs–Sat 9:30pm–3:30am. AE, DC, MC, V. Metro: Zócalo.

There's a line out the door and down the street on weekends to enter the ultimate (at least at press time) downtown club. Recorded techno, hip-hop, disco, and rock are what you'll hear—with an emphasis on dance-ability. Located in an elegant 18th-century building.

Luna Café. Plaza Constitución (zócalo) 13, Centro Histórico. ☎ **5/512-6161.** No cover. MC, V. Metro: Zócalo.

This bar and dance club is mostly noted for its location and view—it's found between the terraces of the Majestic Hotel and Grand Hotel, facing the zócalo. It sports classical Mexican decor and an ample dance floor, and it also serves a full dining menu.

Salon Q. Paseo de la Reforma 169, Col. Guerrero. ☎ **5/529-3495.** Wed–Sat 10pm–dawn. Cover varies; call ahead. MC, V. Metro: Guerrero.

Transport yourself to the tropics! This dance clubs features hot rhythms for dancing salsa, marimba, merengue, and other afro-Caribbean beats. Also offers an excellent snack menu.

Salon Tropicana. Eje Centro Lázaro Cárdenas 43, Centro Histórico. ☎ **5/529-7316.** Tues–Sun 8pm–4am. No cover. AE, DC, MC, V. Metro: Salto del Agua.

Dance club and bar featuring Mexican romantic, mariachi, and salsa music.

BARS

Bar Museo Frida. Hamburgo 32, Col. Juárez, Reforma/Zona Rosa. ☎ **5/511-8353** or 5/525-3049. Mon–Thurs 2pm–2am; Fri 2pm–3am; Sat 9pm–3am. No cover. AE, DC, MC, V. Metro: Insurgentes.

Capitalizing on the popularity of this Mexican master artist, this bar allows you to indulge in Frida fantasies over a premium tequila or cold beer. Great location, and wonderful ambiance for Frida fans.

La Llorona of the Night

La Llorona, the name of a prominent Mexico City nightclub, is a character from a traditional Mexican horror story: a woman who went mad and killed her own children. For this she was cursed to wander around howling for her lost children, weeping in a ghostly manner *"¡Ay mis hijos!"* ("Oh my children!") until she found them. In order to ease her pain, every once in a while she takes a small child into her ghostly realm but to no avail—she will always come back and haunt the nightmares of many for all eternity. Mexican children are terrified of La Llorona.

Caviar Bar. Hotel Marquís Reforma, Reforma 465, Col. Cuauhtémoc. ☎ **5/211-3600.** Daily 1pm–1am. AE, DC, MC, V. Metro: Insurgentes.

While guests enjoy light meals and drinks in this stylish hotel's lobby bar, a string quartet plays in the evening hours. It's elegant and wonderfully soothing.

El Estribo. La Hacienda de los Morales, Basques de Mella (Chapultepec). ☎ **5/281-4554.** No cover.

This small but swank bar serves premium tequilas—and a lot of 'em. Some 480 types in all, including very rare and collectible tequilas. Before you head there with a plan to try them all, however, you should know that nearly a third are so rare that they're not even for sale. El Estribo, which occupies a corner of the elegant 16th-century mansion La Hacienda de los Morales, opened in 1996. About 90% of its tequilas on hand are fully distilled from blue agave, which produces much higher quality tequilas than the inexpensive blends most of us are accustomed to. This is the perfect place to sample aged *reposado* and *añejo* tequilas—these are smooth, complex, and Mexico's answer to fine single malt whisky. You can try some of the house specialties, including the tequila Estribo (concocted with apple juice, cassis, and cream), or simply have a perfect margarita.

La Casa de las Sirenas. Guatemala 32, Centro Histórico, behind the cathedral. ☎ **5/704-3273** or 5/704-3225. Daily 8am–11pm. No cover. AE, MC, V. Metro: Zócalo.

This bar serves 146 types—one of the widest selections available anywhere—of premium tequilas, in a stylish atmosphere. Although they serve breakfast, lunch, and dinner here, it's best known for its bar crowd and ambiance. It becomes a popular club, playing recorded rock music, Thursday through Saturday evenings. It's located in an 18th-century colonial building with a courtyard filled with flowering plants and trees.

La Nueva Ópera Bar. Cinco de Mayo 19, Centro Histórico. ☎ **5/512-8959.** Mon–Sat 1pm–midnight; Sun 1–6pm. No cover. AE, DC, MC, V. Metro: Bellas Artes.

The classic cantina in Mexico City since 1870, with a magnificent bar. Opulent in atmosphere, rich in historic significance. (See also "Cantinas" under "Dining," above).

Museo El Bar. Madero 6, 1st floor, Centro Histórico. ☎ **5/510-4020.** Thurs–Sat 9pm–3am. No cover. MC, V. Metro: Zócalo.

A classically elegant atmosphere for enjoying a cocktail, cognac, or premium tequila. Recorded Nuevo Mexican rock and Latin jazz.

Strip Clubs

The Men's Club Mexico City. Varsovia 54, Col. Juárez, Zona Rosa. ☎ **5/533-2224.** www.mensclub.com.mx. Mon–Fri 2pm–2am; Sat 10pm–2am. Cover $12.50 ($20 cover package includes buffet and national wine from 2–5pm). AE, MC, V.

Entertainment for men, including erotic shows and private dancing. Special parties also featured; call for details.

5 | Side Trips from Mexico City

The small towns that surround Mexico City are every bit as fascinating as the city itself, and vary in character from sophisticated suburbs to relaxed rural settings with archaeological and colonial-era attractions. All can easily be reached by private car or taxi, or by inexpensive bus ride, in under a few hours. Most visitors consider the ancient pyramids of Teotihuacán the first choice for a side trip from Mexico City. In addition to being a popular organized daylong tour, the pyramids can also be reached independently for more leisurely exploration.

Puebla, the "City of Tiles," is a town of historical importance whose architectural and artistic traditions reflect the European influences evident in Mexico. Along with the ruins at neighboring Tlaxcala, both can be visited in a day, but are intriguing enough to entice you into a longer stay.

Traveling about 2½ to 3½ hours from Mexico City southwest over the mountains, you'll reach the thermal spas and elegant golf courses at Ixtapan de la Sal and Valle de Bravo. Cuernavaca, known as the land of eternal spring, is a popular second home for Mexico City professionals and ex-pats from the United States. The legendary silver city of Taxco, on the road to Acapulco, is renowned for its museums, picturesque hillside colonial-era charm, and, of course, its silver shops.

1 The Pyramids of San Juan Teotihuacán

30 miles NE of Mexico City

The ruins of Teotihuacán are among the most remarkable in Mexico—indeed, they are among the most important ruins in the world. Mystery envelops this former city of 200,000; though the epicenter of culture and commerce for ancient Mesoamerica, its inhabitants vanished without a trace. *Teotihuacán* means "place where gods were born," reflecting the Aztecs' belief that the gods created the universe here.

Occupation of the area began around 500 B.C., but it wasn't until after 100 B.C. that construction of the enormous Pyramid of the Sun commenced. Teotihuacán's rise coincided with the classical Romans' building of their great monuments on the other side of the world, and with the beginning of cultures in Mexico's Yucatán Peninsula, Oaxaca, and Puebla. Teotihuacán's magnificent pyramids and palaces covered 12 square miles. At its zenith around A.D. 500, the city counted more inhabitants than in contemporary Rome. Through trade and other contact, Teotihuacán's influence was known in other parts of Mexico and as far south as Yucatán and Guatemala. Still, little is known about the city's inhabitants: what language they spoke, where they came from, or why they abandoned the place around A.D. 700. It is known, however, that at the beginning of the first century A.D., the Xitle volcano erupted near Cuicuilco (south of Mexico City) and decimated that city, which was the most prominent city of the time. Those inhabitants migrated to Teotihuacán. Scholars believe that Teotihuacán's decline, probably caused by overpopulation and depletion of natural resources, was gradual, perhaps occurring over a 250-year period. In the last years it appears that the people were poorly nourished and that the city was deliberately burned.

Ongoing excavations have revealed something of the culture. According to archaeoastronomer John B. Carlson, the cult of the planet Venus that determined wars and human sacrifices elsewhere in Mesoamerica was prominent at Teotihuacán as well. (Archaeoastronomy is the study of the position of stars and planets in relation to archaeology.) Ceremonial rituals were timed with the appearance of Venus as the morning and evening star. The symbol of Venus at Teotihuacán (as at Cacaxtla, 50 miles away, near Tlaxcala) appears as a star or half star with a full or half circle. Carlson also suggests the possibility that Teotihuacán was conquered by people from Cacaxtla, since name glyphs of conquered peoples at Cacaxtla show Teotihuacán-like pyramids. Numerous tombs with human remains (many of them either sacrificial inhabitants of the city or perhaps war captives) and objects of jewelry, pottery, and daily life have been uncovered along the foundations of buildings. It appears that the primary deity at Teotihuacán was a female, called "Great Goddess" for lack of any known name.

Today, what remains are the rough stone structures of the three pyramids and sacrificial altars, and some of the grand houses, all of which were once covered in stucco and painted with brilliant frescos (mainly in red). The Toltecs, who rose in power after the city's decline, were fascinated with Teotihuacán and incorporated its symbols into their own cultural motifs. The Aztecs, who followed the Toltecs, were fascinated with the Toltecs and with the ruins of Teotihuacán; they likewise adopted many of their symbols and motifs. For more information on Teotihuacán and its influence in Mesoamerica, see also chapter 2, "Getting to Know Mexico." Fascinating articles about the ruins have appeared in *National Geographic* (December 1995) and *Archeology* (December 1993). The murals of Teotihuacán are the focus of an article in *Arqueología* (vol. 3, no. 16, 1995), published in Spanish in Mexico by the Instituto Nacional de Antropología e Historia.

ESSENTIALS

GETTING THERE & DEPARTING   By Car   Driving to San Juan Teotihuacán on either the toll Highway 85D or the free Highway 132D will take about an hour. Head north on Insurgentes to get out of the city. Highway 132D passes through picturesque villages and the like but can be slow, due to the surfeit of trucks and buses; Highway 85D, the toll road, is less attractive, but faster.

By Private Sedan or Taxi   If you prefer to explore solo or want more or less time than an organized tour commands, consider renting a private car and driver for the trip. These can easily be arranged through your hotel or at the Secretary of Tourism (SECTUR) information module in the Zona Rosa, and cost about $10 to $15 an hour. The higher price is generally for a sedan with an English-speaking driver who doubles as a tour guide. Rates can also be negotiated for the entire day.

By Bus   Buses leave daily every half hour (from 5am to 10pm) from the Terminal Central de Autobuses del Norte; the trip takes 1 hour. When you reach the Terminal

Side Trips from Mexico City

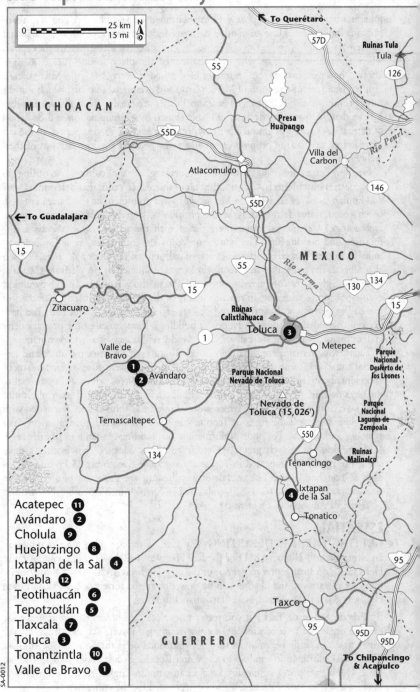

Acatepec ⑪
Avándaro ②
Cholula ⑨
Huejotzingo ⑧
Ixtapan de la Sal ④
Puebla ⑫
Teotihuacán ⑥
Tepotzotlán ⑤
Tlaxcala ⑦
Toluca ③
Tonantzintla ⑩
Valle de Bravo ①

SA-0012

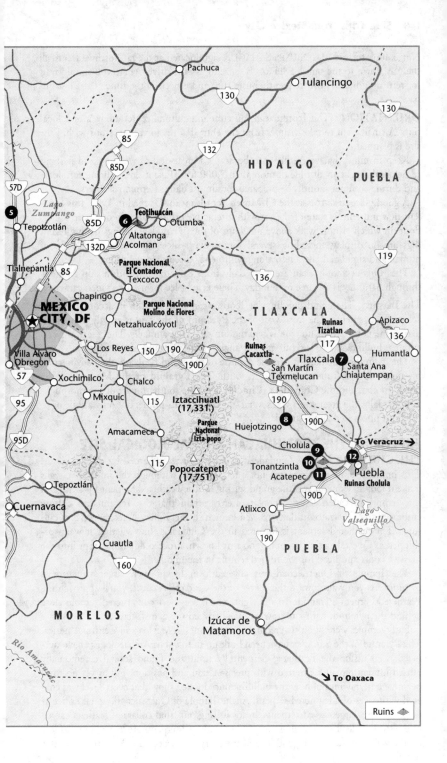

Norte, look for the AUTOBUSES SAHAGUN sign located at the far northwest end, all the way down to the sign 8 ESPERA. Be sure to ask the driver where you should wait for returning buses, how frequently buses run, and especially the time of the last bus back.

ORIENTATION   The Teotihuacán museum and cultural center are in a new location. A small train to take visitors from the entry booths to various stops within the site is planned.

Keep in mind that you're likely to be doing a great deal of walking, and perhaps some climbing, at an altitude of more than 7,000 feet. Take it slowly, bring sunblock, and during summer months be prepared for almost daily afternoon showers.

A good place to start is at the ✪ **Museo Teotihuacán.** Opened in 1995, this excellent new museum is state-of-the-art with interactive exhibits and, in one part, a glass floor on which visitors walk above mockups of the pyramids. Findings during recent digs are on display, including several tombs, with skeletons wearing necklaces of human and simulated jawbones, along with newly discovered sculptures.

The ruins of Teotihuacán are open daily from 8am to 5pm. Admission Monday through Saturday is $4; free on Sunday. There is a $4 fee for use of a video camera.

The Layout   The grand buildings of Teotihuacán were laid out in accordance with celestial movements. The front wall of the **Pyramid of the Sun** is exactly perpendicular to the point on the horizon where the sun sets twice annually. The rest of the ceremonial buildings were laid out at right angles to the Pyramid of the Sun.

The main thoroughfare, called the **Avenue of the Dead (Calzada de los Muertos)** by archaeologists, runs roughly north-south. The **Pyramid of the Moon** is at the northern end, and the **Ciudadela (Citadel)** is on the southern part of the thoroughfare. Actually, the great street was several miles long in its prime, but only a mile or so has been uncovered and restored.

EXPLORING THE TEOTIHUACÁN ARCHAEOLOGICAL SITE

THE CIUDADELA   The Ciudadela, or Citadel, was so named by the Spaniards. This immense sunken square was not a fortress at all, although the impressive walls make it look like one. It was the grand setting for the Feathered Serpent Pyramid and the Temple of Quetzalcoatl. Scholars aren't certain that the Teotihuacán culture embraced the Quetzalcoatl deity so well known in the Toltec, Aztec, and Maya cultures. The feathered serpent is featured in the Ciudadela, but whether it was worshipped as Quetzalcoatl or a similar god isn't known. Proceed down the steps into the massive court and head for the ruined temple in the middle.

The Temple of Quetzalcoatl was covered over by an even larger structure, a pyramid. As you walk toward the center of the Ciudadela's court, you'll approach the Feathered Serpent Pyramid. To the right, you'll see the reconstructed temple close behind the pyramid, with a narrow passage between the two structures.

Early temples were often covered over by later ones in Mexico and Central America. The Pyramid of the Sun may have been built up in this way. Archaeologists have tunneled deep inside the Feathered Serpent Pyramid and found several ceremonially buried human remains, interred with precise detail and position, but as yet no royal personages. Drawings of how the building once looked show that every level was covered with faces of a feathered serpent. At the Temple of Quetzalcoatl, you'll notice at once the fine, large carved serpents' heads jutting out from collars of feathers carved in the stone walls; these weigh 4 tons. Other feathered serpents are carved in relief low on the walls. You can get a good idea of the glory of Mexico's ancient cities from this temple.

Teotihuacán

SAN MARTÍN

- La Cueva
- Villas Arqueológicas
- Entrance
- Parking
- Parking
- Peripheral Highway
- Peripheral Highway
- Rio San Juan
- Avenue of the Dead
- Avenue of the Dead
- Parking
- Parking
- Parking
- Entrance
- Roadside Cookshops
- Entrance
- Parking
- Pyramid Charlie's
- To San Juan Teotihuacán
- Terraced Road
- To Mexico City
- Parking

1 Tepantitla
2 Pyramid of the Moon
3 Palace of Quetzalpapálotl
4 Palace of the Jaguars
5 El Corso
6 Pyramid of the Sun
7 The High Priest's Home
8 New Museum Location
9 The Viking Group
10 The Temple of Quetzlcoatl
11 The Citadel
12 Old Museum Building
13 La Ventilla
14 Atetelco
15 Tetitla
16 Zacuala
17 Yayahuala

SA-0013

AVENUE OF THE DEAD   The Avenue of the Dead got its strange and forbidding name from the Aztecs, who mistook the little temples that line both sides of the avenue for tombs of kings or priests.

As you stroll north along the Avenue of the Dead toward the Pyramid of the Moon, look on the right for a bit of wall sheltered by a modern corrugated roof. Beneath the shelter, the wall still bears a painting of a jaguar. From this fragment, you might be able to build a picture of the breathtaking spectacle that must have been visible when all the paintings along the avenue were intact.

PYRAMID OF THE SUN   The Pyramid of the Sun is located on the east side of the Avenue of the Dead, and is the third largest pyramid in the world. (The Great Pyramid of Cholula, near Puebla, is the largest structure ever built; second largest is the Pyramid of Cheops on the outskirts of Cairo, Egypt.) Teotihuacán's Pyramid of the Sun at its base is 730 feet per side—almost as large as Cheops. But at 210 feet high, the Sun pyramid is only about half as high as its Egyptian rival. No matter. It's still the biggest restored pyramid in the western hemisphere, and an awesome sight. Although the Pyramid of the Sun was not built as a great king's tomb, it is built on top of a series of sacred caves, but they aren't open to the public.

The first structure of the pyramid was probably built a century before Christ, and the temple that used to crown the pyramid was finished about 400 years later (A.D. 300). By the time the pyramid was discovered and restoration was begun (early in our century), the temple had completely disappeared, and the pyramid was just a mass of rubble covered with bushes and trees.

It's a worthwhile 248-step climb to the top. The view is extraordinary and the sensation exhilarating.

PYRAMID OF THE MOON The Pyramid of the Moon faces a plaza at the northern end of the avenue. The plaza is surrounded by little temples and by the Palace of Quetzalpapalotl or Quetzal-Mariposa (Quetzal-Butterfly) on the left (west) side. You have about the same range of view from the top of the Pyramid of the Moon as you do from its larger neighbor, because the moon pyramid is built on higher ground. The perspective straight down the Avenue of the Dead is magnificent.

PALACE OF QUETZALPAPALOTL The Palace of Quetzalpapalotl lay in ruins until the 1960s, when restoration work began. Today it reverberates with former glory, as figures of Quetzal-Mariposa (a mythical, exotic bird-butterfly) appear painted on walls or carved in the pillars of the inner court.

Behind the Palace of Quetzalpapalotl is the Palace of the Jaguars, complete with murals showing a lively jaguar musical combo, and some frescoes.

WHERE TO DINE

Vendors at the ruins sell drinks and snacks. In addition, many visitors choose to pack a box lunch to take with them—almost any hotel or restaurant in the city can prepare one for you. A picnic in the shadow of this impressive ancient city allows extended time and perspective to take it all in. There is a **restaurant** in the new Museo Teotihuacén, which is the most convenient place for a snack or a meal.

La Gruta. Peripheral Hwy. ☎ **595/6-0127** or 595/6-0104. Main courses $6–$11. AE, DC, MC, V. Daily 11am–7pm. A bit northwest of Gate 5 on the Peripheral Hwy. MEXICAN.

La Gruta is a huge, delightfully cool, natural grotto. You have the option of ordering a five-course set-price lunch or choosing your own combination—perhaps a hamburger and a soft drink or beer. It's a spirited place to end a day of exploration.

2 Puebla: Museums & Architecture

80 miles E of Mexico City

Puebla dates back to the early 1500s; it was founded as a safe haven in the historic heartland, linking Mexico's Gulf Coast with its capital. Blessed with a wealth of preserved architectural beauty dating from colonial times, it's been named a UNESCO World Heritage Site. Its fame for building facades embellished with richly colored tiles and church domes glistening with bright tiles has attracted generations of tourists.

Mansions and public buildings were built by those who passed through on their way to and from the capital. Already known for pottery making before the Conquest, Talavera artisans from Toledo, Spain, blended their talents with those of the native population to create a wonderful tradition of hand-painted pottery and tile that's still practiced today. Exploring Puebla's Talavera pottery workshops in search of hand-painted tiles or ceramic dinnerware made from local clay is a principal reason many travelers visit Puebla.

Catholicism was pervasive in New Spain and it flourished throughout the country until 1857, when an anti-Catholic movement closed (but did not destroy) many churches and convents. Of these, at least 99 churches survived, along with many grand monasteries, convents, and a magnificent Bishop's Palace next to the cathedral. The church chose Puebla as a major center, along with San Luis Potosí and Oaxaca. To this day it retains a strong conservative and religious influence.

Puebla is a city of three million of indigenous roots and European influence. Set at an elevation of over 7,000 ft. in a valley between snow-capped volcanoes, it remains

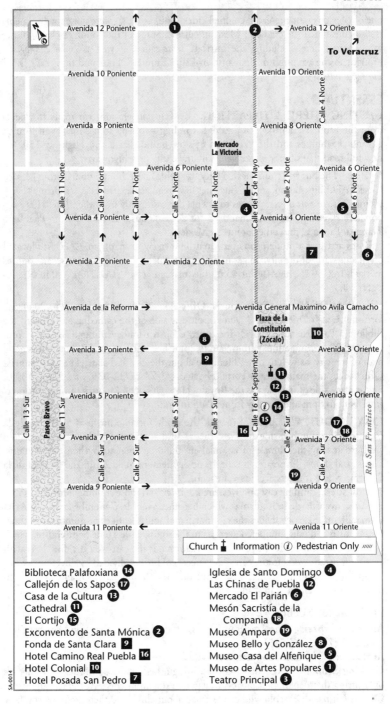

Puebla

To Veracruz

Avenida 12 Poniente — Avenida 12 Oriente
Avenida 10 Poniente — Avenida 10 Oriente
Avenida 8 Poniente — Avenida 8 Oriente

Mercado La Victoria

Avenida 6 Poniente — Avenida 6 Oriente
Avenida 4 Poniente — Avenida 4 Oriente
Avenida 2 Poniente — Avenida 2 Oriente

Avenida de la Reforma — Avenida General Maximino Avila Camacho

Plaza de la Constitución (Zócalo)

Avenida 3 Poniente — Avenida 3 Oriente
Avenida 5 Poniente — Avenida 5 Oriente
Avenida 7 Poniente — Avenida 7 Oriente
Avenida 9 Poniente — Avenida 9 Oriente
Avenida 11 Poniente — Avenida 11 Oriente

Calle 13 Sur · Calle 11 Sur · Paseo Bravo · Calle 11 Norte · Calle 9 Norte · Calle 7 Norte · Calle 5 Norte · Calle 3 Norte · Calle del 5 de Mayo · Calle 2 Norte · Calle 4 Norte · Calle 6 Norte
Calle 13 Sur · Calle 11 Sur · Calle 9 Sur · Calle 7 Sur · Calle 5 Sur · Calle 3 Sur · Calle 16 de Septiembre · Calle 2 Sur · Calle 4 Sur

Río San Francisco

Church ✝ Information ⓘ Pedestrian Only ▨

Biblioteca Palafoxiana **14**
Callejón de los Sapos **17**
Casa de la Cultura **13**
Cathedral **11**
El Cortijo **15**
Exconvento de Santa Mónica **2**
Fonda de Santa Clara **9**
Hotel Camino Real Puebla **16**
Hotel Colonial **10**
Hotel Posada San Pedro **7**

Iglesia de Santo Domingo **4**
Las Chinas de Puebla **12**
Mercado El Parián **6**
Mesón Sacristía de la Compania **18**
Museo Amparo **19**
Museo Bello y González **8**
Museo Casa del Alfeñique **5**
Museo de Artes Populares **1**
Teatro Principal **3**

SA-0014

143

one of Mexico's best-preserved colonial cities. And, as if that were not enough, Puebla is also considered the cradle of Mexican cuisine. Some of the country's classic dishes were created here, including the intricate *mole* sauce, as well as *chiles en nogada,* brought to the attention of the world in Laura Esquival's book and film, *Like Water For Chocolate.*

ESSENTIALS

GETTING THERE & DEPARTING **By Car** There are two roads to Puebla from the capital: Highway 190, an old, winding two-lane scenic road with limited passing capabilities and the likelihood of slow traffic ahead; and Highway 150D, a new toll road that's faster. Buses generally travel the new highway.

By Bus The bus trip from Mexico City to Puebla takes about 2 hours. From Mexico City's TAPO bus station, several bus lines have regular departures as frequent as every 15 minutes. *Important note:* Buses to Puebla depart directly from the Mexico City airport (see "Getting There" in chapter 3 for details). Buses also travel from Puebla to Tlaxcala, Pachuca, and other points in Mexico.

Buses arrive at a modern **bus terminal,** known by its acronym, CAPU; it's located on the outskirts of the city. To get to downtown Puebla, look for one of several booths marked TAXI AUTORIZADO or a city bus marked "CAPU CENTRAL CAMIONERA–CENTRO.

INFORMATION The **State Tourist Office** (☎ 22/46-1285; fax 22/46-2044, ask for tone) is at 5 Oriente no. 3, across from the side of the cathedral and next to the Biblioteca Palafoxiana (Library); the office is open Monday through Saturday from 9am to 8:30pm, and Sunday from 9am to 2pm. The staff can provide you with a good map of the city, as well as other literature about the city and state. The **City Tourist Office** faces the main plaza at Portal Hidalgo 14 (☎ 22/32-0357; fax 22/32-1399), on the same side of the plaza as the Royalty Hotel. It's open Monday through Saturday from 9am to 8pm and Sunday from 10am to 4pm.

CITY LAYOUT The heart of town is the shady zócalo, known as the **Plaza de la Constitución.** On one side are the cathedral and avenida 3 Oriente. The other sides are bordered by the *portales* of colonial-era buildings that today house restaurants, hotels, and shops. These are on calle 16 de Septiembre, calle 2 Sur, and avenida de la Reforma where it meets avenida Camacho.

Most streets running east and west are *avenidas,* and those running north and south are *calles.* **avenida de la Reforma** (which becomes **avenida General Maximino Avila Camacho** on the east) divides the city north and south, with even-numbered avenues to the north and odd-numbered avenues to the south. **calle 16 de Septiembre,** which becomes **calle Cinco de Mayo** north of Reforma, is the east-west dividing line, with even-numbered streets to the east. City streets are further divided by direction: North "Norte" (Nte.), South "Sur," West "Poniente" (Pte.), and East "Oriente" (Ote.). In practice, the "avenida" and "calle" are often dropped.

FAST FACTS: PUEBLA

American Express The American Express office is on calle Cinco de Mayo, at Plaza Dorada 2 (☎ 22/37-5551).

Area Code The telephone area code is **22.**

Cooking School Since Puebla is the distinguished cradle of Mexican cuisine, it's only fitting that cooking lessons be available to the uninitiated. At the restaurant/bar ✪ **Las Chinas de Puebla,** you can learn all about chiles and their use in sauces, how a good *mole poblano* and *mixiotes* should taste and how to fix them, and much more

"Cinco de Mayo" and the Battle of Puebla

Within the United States, the Mexican holiday "Cinco de Mayo" is often compared to the Fourth of July—a Mexican Independence Day. In truth this date commemorates the Battle of Puebla, which took place on May 5, 1862, and resulted in a brief but memorable victory against foreign invasion.

At the time, Napoleon III of France was scheming to occupy Mexico. A well-trained and handsomely uniformed army of 6,000, under the command of General Laurencez, was given orders to occupy Mexico City. On his path to the capital was Puebla, defended by 4,000 Mexicans armed with antiquated guns and a fervent sense of nationalism. Despite the odds, the Mexicans won a resounding victory. The French were humiliated, handed their first defeat in nearly half a century at the hands of the penniless, war-torn republic of Mexico.

For Mexico, it marked the nation's first victory against foreign attack, and the battle remains a matter of intense national pride. Never mind that by the following year the French were vindicated by taking both Puebla as well as the capital city. Today the Cinco de Mayo holiday is an enduring symbol of Mexico's sense of nationalism.

On a visit to the Puebla area, you can visit the forts of Guadalupe and Loreto, where the battles took place, just north of the city.

in even a short class of around 3 hours. Classes are simple but extremely informative, with the excellent restaurant cook Trinidad Becerra. Classes are held from Monday through Saturday, after 6pm, and the cost is $9.40 per hour. Reservations are required. For details, see "Where to Dine," below.

Population   Puebla has three million residents.

Post Office   The Correo (post office) is in the Archbishop's Palace next to the cathedral, at the corner of avenida 5 Oriente and calle 16 de Septiembre.

EXPLORING PUEBLA
A WALK THROUGH THE DOWNTOWN AREA

The **zócalo,** or **Plaza de la Constitución,** is the heart of downtown Puebla. On one side of it is the cathedral, completed in 1649, with towers that are the tallest in Mexico. Bells hang in the tower closer to the zócalo (the other tower is empty). The other sides of the zócalo are the *portales* (arcades) filled with restaurants, hotels, and shops.

Across the street from the cathedral, on the corner of avenida 5 Oriente and calle 16 de Septiembre, is the old Archbishop's Palace, which now houses the post office, the **Casa de la Cultura,** and the **Biblioteca Palafoxiana.** This exquisite library, the oldest in the Americas, was built in 1646 by Juan de Palafox y Mendoza, then archbishop and founder of the College of Saints Peter and Paul. It's a testament to the glory of this period, with its elegant tile floor, hand-carved wood walls and ceiling, inlaid tables, and gilded wooden statues. Bookcases are filled with 17th-century books and manuscripts in Spanish, Creole, French, and English.

The Iglesia de Santo Domingo, on the corner of Cinco de Mayo and 4 Poniente, was originally part of a monastery, completed in 1611. In 1690 the Capilla del Rosario was built, a symphony of gilt and stone dedicated to the Virgin of the Rosary. Puebla has many other churches and convents that date from the 17th and 18th centuries.

MUSEUMS

Museo Amparo. Calle 2 Sur 708. ☎ **22/46-4200.** Admission $2 adults; $1 children 3–12 and students; free Mon. Wed–Mon 10am–6pm.

Opened in 1991 and dedicated to Amparo Rugarcia de Espinoza by her husband, this is among the top archaeological museums in the country. Housed in a colonial-era building, it was first a hospital in 1534, later the Colegio San José de Gracia for married women, and lastly the Colegio Esparza before its adaptation as a museum. Audio tours on headsets can be rented to guide you through.

Sala "Arte Rupestre" contains examples of cave paintings from around the world, and in the Sala "Códice del Tiempo" a wonderful wall-size timeline marks important world cultures and events from 2500 B.C. to A.D. 1500. Other salas (rooms) include information on the importance of corn in Mexican culture, techniques for the production of art, and the function of art in society. Upstairs is a notable collection of pre-Hispanic art covering the Pre- to Postclassic periods, including an impressive collection of clay figures from Nayarit and Colima states. Signs are in Spanish and English; no cameras are permitted. The museum is located 3 blocks south of the zócalo near the corner of avenida 9 Poniente.

Museo Bello y González. Av. 3 Pte. no. 302. ☎ **22/32-9475.** Admission $1.25; free Tues. Tues–Sun 10am–5pm.

Located near the corner of calle 3 Sur and avenida 3 Poniente, a block west of the zócalo, this museum houses a collection of fine 17-, 18th-, and 19th-century art. José Luis Bello y González made his fortune in tobacco and began to collect art from all over the world, though he personally never traveled. Later, Bello, who was a fine artist and an accomplished organist, founded a museum, which he willed to the state. Personal decorative objects fill the house, including velvet curtains, French porcelain, beautiful hand-carved furniture, several very fine organs, and numerous paintings. A guided tour (in English or Spanish) is included in the price of admission.

✪ **Museo Casa del Alfeñique.** Av. 4 Ote. 416. ☎ **22/32-4296.** Admission 75¢; free Tues. Tues–Sun 10am–4:30pm.

One of the most interesting parts of this museum is the building itself, the Casa del Alfeñique. The 18th-century house resembles an elaborate wedding cake; in fact, the name means "sugar-cake house." Inside, it's architecturally embellished with an elaborate plaster doorway and brick-and-beam ceilings. The exhibits include a good collection of pre-Hispanic artifacts and pottery, displays of regional crafts, colonial-era furniture, and a sizable collection of *china poblana* costumes. The museum is 4 blocks northeast of the zócalo, between calles 4 and 6 Norte.

Exconvento de Santa Mónica. Av. 18 Pte. no. 103. ☎ **22/32-0178.** Admission $1; free Sun and holidays. Tues–Sun 9am–5:30pm.

When the convents of Puebla were closed in 1857, this one and two others operated secretly, using entrances through private homes, which hid the convent from public view. Very few people knew this convent existed before it was rediscovered in 1935 by a tax collector. Today, it's a museum, maintained as it was found. It's some 10 blocks north of the zócalo near the corner of avenida 18 Poniente and Cinco de Mayo, at Callejón de la av. 18 Poniente.

✪ **Museo de Artes Populares and the Cocina de Santa Rosa.** Calle 3 Nte. at 12 Pte. ☎ **22/46-4526.** Admission 75¢. Tues–Sun 10am–4:30pm.

The largest convent in Puebla, Santa Rosa belonged to the Dominican order. It has been beautifully restored and is worth a visit to see the cavernous, beautifully tiled kitchen (cocina) where many native Mexican dishes were created. The museum has two floors of elaborate Mexican arts and crafts, including a 6-foot earthenware candelabra, regional costumes, minute scenes made of straw and clay, and hand-tooled leather. A small shop sells local crafts. Tours of the museum and kitchen, lasting 20 minutes, are offered, the last starting at 4:30pm. The museum is 8 blocks northwest of the zócalo, between avenida 12 and avenida 14 Poniente. The front door, closed and locked, is on calle 3 Norte. Go around the corner to a public parking lot at av. 14 Poniente 305; the entry is through there.

SHOPPING

Puebla is the home of ☻ **Talavera dinnerware.** Numerous workshops produce this famous pottery, which is expensive. Operating since 1824, **Uriarte Talavera,** calle 4 Pte. 911 (☎ **22/32-1598**), is one of the most established potters in Puebla. Behind an unprepossessing doorway, the factory produces exquisite pieces, many examples of which are displayed in its sophisticated showrooms. Some are for sale, while others are samples from which to order. Tours of the factory are given Monday through Saturday at 10am, 11am, noon, and 1pm. It's open Monday through Saturday from 9am to 6:30pm and Sunday from 11am to 6pm. They can ship your purchases; American Express, MasterCard, and Visa are accepted. The **Centro Talavera Poblana,** calle 6 Ote. 11 (☎ **22/42-0848**), offers a wide range of Talaveraware from producers in Puebla as well as Tlaxcala. The huge showroom has full sets with between 6 and 12 place settings ready for you to take home. Prices are fixed. Between calle 2 Norte and calle Cinco de Mayo, it's open Monday through Saturday from 9:30am to 8pm and Sunday from 10am to 7pm. They can ship your purchases; American Express, Diners Club, MasterCard, and Visa are accepted.

The **Mercado de Artesanías,** or **El Parián** as it's also called, is a pedestrians-only, open-air shopping area just east of calle 6 Norte between Avenidas 2 and 6 Oriente. You'll see rows of neat brick shops selling crafts and souvenirs. Don't judge all Talavera pottery by what you see here, though. Artists seem to have gone overboard with design. The shops are open daily from 10am to 8pm. Bargain to get a good price. While you're in this area, you can take a look at the **Teatro Principal.**

A good selection of the better-quality Talaveraware, along with other fine crafts such as textiles, can be found under the portales at **Tienda DIF** (☎ **22/32-1017**), a government-owned shop, the proceeds from which benefit local families. Located at Portal Hidalgo 14, it's open from 10am to 8pm daily.

For some good antique browsing, go to **Callejón de los Sapos** (Alley of the Frogs), about 3 blocks southeast of the zócalo near calle 4 Sur and avenida 7 Oriente. Wander in and out, for there's good stuff both large and small. Shops are generally open daily from 10am to 2pm and 4 to 6pm. Bargain to get a good price.

WHERE TO STAY
EXPENSIVE

☻ **Hotel Camino Real Puebla.** Av. 7 Pte. 105, Centro Histórico, 72000 Puebla, Pue. ☎ **800/722-6466** in the U.S., 22/29-0909, or 22/29-0910. Fax 22/32-9251. 83 units. TV TEL. $115 double; $167–$335 suite. AE, DC, MC, V.

Puebla's most exquisite hotel opened in May 1996 in the 16th-century building that once housed the Convent of the Immaculate Conception. Courtyards spill into yet more courtyards, and remnants of the polychromed colonial-era frescos are everywhere, even in the rooms. It's a colonial gem of the first order that took 7 years to restore. Rooms are beautifully decorated with tile floors, a few antiques in some, original paintings, and handsome blue-and-yellow comforter-style bedcoverings with colors and designs inspired by Talavera pottery. The hotel is 2½ blocks south of the zócalo between calle 3 Sur and avenida 16 de Septiembre.

Dining/Diversions: Two restaurants serve all meals. The lobby bar, to the left of the reception area, is a large gathering place with comfortable groupings of tables and chairs.

Amenities: Business center, L. A. Cano jewelry store (featuring reproductions of pre-Hispanic gold jewelry), Sergio Bustamante Art Gallery, laundry, dry cleaning, room service, travel agency, car rental, 24-hour medical service.

MODERATE

Mesón Sacristía de la Compañía. Calle 6 Sur 304, Callejón de los Sapos, 72000 Puebla, Pue. ☎ **22/32-4513.** Fax 22/42-1554. 9 units. TV TEL. $100 for up to 4 people; $150 suite. Rates include breakfast. Free parking. AE, DC, MC, V.

Third-generation antique dealer Leobardo Espinosa turned his 200-year-old building and antique store into a fashionable restaurant/bar/hotel where all the furnishings are for sale, including a complete 12-place setting of Talavera pottery. That lovely four-poster brass bed with a crown on top that you got lost in while occupying the exquisitely furnished bridal suite may not be there next week, and perhaps the grandiose armoire where you stowed your clothing will find a new owner as well; but something equally exquisite will take their places. The spacious rooms are on the second floor and no two are alike. Those facing the street, with small balconies and large window/doors, are preferable to those on the back side, which have no windows. Floor fans are available for ventilation. *One caveat:* Musicians entertain diners in the courtyard until midnight nightly—if you turn in early, you may want to bring earplugs.

Señor Espinosa is readying his second all-antique hotel, the **Mesón Sacristía de Capuchinas,** with seven rooms in a 400-year-old building just half a block from the Museo Amparo. He hopes to open its doors to the public in November 1998. It, too, will have a restaurant featuring nouvelle Mexican cuisine, but without the emphasis on entertainment. The Mesón Sacristía de la Compañia is at the end of calle 6 Sur (also called Callejón de los Sapos), near where calle 6 Sur intersects with the Plaza de los Sapos, 3 blocks south of the zócalo.

INEXPENSIVE

Hotel Colonial. Calle 4 Sur no. 105, 72000 Puebla, Pue. ☎ **22/46-4199.** Fax 22/46-0818. 70 units. TEL. $34 double. AE, CB, DISC, MC, V.

The four-story hotel (with elevator) is charming in an old way, with arches and lots of tiles on the interior public areas. The rooms, too, have tile floors and are neatly furnished. It's comfortable and close to all the sights. The restaurant is popular with locals. Expensive garage parking is around the corner. The Colonial is 1 block east of the zócalo, on a pedestrian-way between Camacho and avenida 3 Oriente.

Hotel Posada San Pedro. Av. 2 Ote. no. 202, 72000 Puebla, Pue. ☎ **22/46-5077.** Fax 22/46-5376. 76 units. MINIBAR TV TEL. $56 double. Free parking. AE, DC, DISC, MC, V.

Behind a rather uninspiring front is this choice little five-story hostelry. It is much less expensive and of much higher quality than some other downtown "luxury" hotels. The rooms have high ceilings, heavily textured walls, and modern furnishings. Bathrooms are large, equipped with all the toiletry amenities, bath mats, and large towels. There is a swimming pool in the atrium, and an intimate bar discreetly located on the mezzanine floor. This is a family hotel, with afternoon videos for the kids and child care by prior arrangement. It's conveniently located between calles 2 and 4 Norte, only 2 blocks from the zócalo.

WHERE TO DINE

Puebla is known throughout Mexico for *mole poblano,* a sauce with more than 20 ingredients, as well as *mixiotes* (meesh-*oh*-tehs), a dish of beef, pork, or lamb in a spicy red sauce baked in maguey paper. *Dulces* (sweets) shops are scattered about, with display windows brim-full of marzipan crafted into various shapes and designs, candied figs, guava paste, and camotes, which are little cylinders of a fruity sweet-potato paste wrapped in waxed paper.

"**El Cortijo.** Calle 16 de Septiembre no. 506. ☎ **22/42-0503.** Main courses $6.25–$12; comida corrida $6.25. AE, MC, V. Sat–Thurs 1–6pm; Fri 1pm–2am (comida corrida served 1–3pm). MEXICAN.

This enclosed patio restaurant has a comfortable atmosphere and tasty food. Dishes range from pork chops to delicious jumbo shrimp or paella. The *cubierto* (or comida corrida) starts with a fruit cocktail, followed by a choice of two soups, a midcourse of perhaps paella or spaghetti, and then the main course, which might include a choice of pork leg, mole, fish, or chicken. This is a good place for that large afternoon meal and a bottle of wine. The restaurant is 2½ blocks south of the zócalo, between avenidas 5 and 7 Oriente.

✪ **Fonda de Santa Clara.** Av. 3 Pte. no. 307. ☎ **22/42-2659.** Lunch $4–$9; dinner $4–$8. AE, DC, DISC, MC, V. Daily 9am–10pm. REGIONAL.

This is one of the city's most popular and traditional restaurants, serving regional food. It's busy but cozy and slightly formal. The menu includes such local dishes as pollo mole poblano, mixiotes, and *tinga* (a great beef stew). There are seasonal specialties as well, like fried grasshoppers in October and November, maguey worms in April and May, chiles en nogada July through September, and huitlacoche in June. The light dinner menu features such specials as *tacos de sesos* (brain tacos), tamales, pozole, *mole de panza* (mole with stomach meat), and atole. The restaurant is 1½ blocks west of the zócalo, opposite the Bello Museum.

Las Chinas de Puebla. Av. 5 Ote. 3, in the Tourism Office. ☎ **22/42-2561.** Main courses $2.75–$4. No credit cards. Daily 9am–9pm. PUEBLA CUISINE.

This restaurant in the Tourism Office replicates the look of an authentic 19th-century Puebla *pulquería* as painted by the famous Pueblan *costumbrista* artist, Augustine Arrieta (1803–74)—copies of his paintings decorate the walls. And it's an example of what the best Puebla cuisine is all about. Here you can try *cemitas* (the local name for a sandwich made with a special delicious bread), *chanclas* (a sandwich covered in a delicious red-pepper sauce), extraordinarily good mixiotes and mole poblano, plus a full range of meal-size appetizers such as *molotes,* which in Puebla is a deep-fried flour wrapper stuffed with cheese, potatoes, or meat, epazote, and jalapeño pepper—it's not picante. All the sauces are made fresh daily. Sundays, manchamantele is the off-the-menu special.

Cooking lessons can be arranged evenings Wednesday through Monday. Speak with owner María Esther Rodríguez a day or so in advance of your desired lesson time, or write to arrange it before you arrive. To find it, look to the right of the cathedral on avenida 5 Oriente in the State Tourism Office.

PUEBLA AFTER DARK

Mariachis play daily, beginning at 6pm, on **Plaza de Santa Inés,** at avenida 11 Poniente and calle 3 Sur. They stroll through the crowds that gather at the sidewalk cafes. Another square that attracts mariachis is **Plaza de los Sapos,** avenida 7 Oriente near calle 6 Sur. To get there, walk 2 blocks south from the zócalo and take a left onto avenida 7 Oriente, toward the river. The plaza will be on your left spreading out between avenida 7 and avenida 5 Oriente just past calle 4 Sur. If you use avenida 5 Oriente from the cathedral to reach the Plaza de los Sapos, you'll pass several local hangouts where students, artists, and others gather for conversation, coffee, drinks, and snacks.

But for the best evening entertainment in town, try the ✪ **Mesón Sacristía de la Compañía** at calle 6 Sur 304 (calle 6 Sur is also called Callejón de los Sapos and is known for its numerous antique shops—see "Shopping," above). Leobardo Espinosa turned his antique shop into the trendiest patio restaurant in Puebla and transformed the 200-year-old building into a small hotel. All the furniture in the nine hotel rooms is for sale, as is just about everything else you'll see in the dining areas as well. During the late afternoon, a pianist plays soft music. At 9pm a singer/guitarist entertains with popular ballads until midnight. The restaurant, which fills the inner patio and adjacent rooms, is moderately priced and serves a complete selection of Puebla specialties—you can dine or drink and enjoy the free entertainment without breaking the bank.

Teorema, Reforma 540 near calle 7 Norte (☎ **22/42-1014**), is a wonderful coffee shop/bookstore that features guitarists and folksingers every evening. This is a good place to meet young local residents. It's open daily from 9:30am to 2:30pm and 4:30pm to midnight. MasterCard and Visa are accepted.

SIDE TRIPS FROM PUEBLA: COLONIAL TLAXCALA & NEARBY CACAXTLA & XOCHITÉCATL RUINS

Tlaxcala, 25 miles north of Puebla and 75 miles east of Mexico City, is the capital of Mexico's smallest state of the same name and a colonial-era city with several unique claims to fame. Tlaxcalan warriors, who allied with Cortés against the Aztecs, were essential in Cortés's defeat of the Aztecs. Tlaxcalan chiefs were the first to be baptized by the Spaniards; the baptismal font used for them is found in the **Templo de San Francisco** (located 2 blocks from the main plaza and just above the bullring). The church is noted for its elaborately inlaid Moorish ceiling below the choir loft. A painting inside the Chapel of the Third Order shows the baptism of the chiefs.

To the right of the Templo is the **Exconvento,** now a museum containing early paintings and artifacts from nearby archaeological sites. The **Government Palace,** on the handsome, tree-shaped central zócalo, is painted inside with vivid murals showing Tlaxcala history by a local artist, Desiderio Hernández Xochitiotzin. The expanded **Museo de Artesanías,** on Sanchez Piedras between Lardizabal and 1 de Mayo, show-cases the state's wide-ranging crafts and customs. Here, local artisans give visitors demonstrations in such crafts as embroidery, weaving, and pulque making. Don't plan to breeze through; tours are mandatory, rather structured, and take an hour or more—but are very interesting. The museum is open Tuesday through Sunday from 10am to 6pm; admission is $1 (includes tour).

A bit over half a mile from the town center is the famed **Ocotlán Sanctuary,** con-structed after Juan Diego Bernardino claimed to have seen an apparition of the Virgin Mary on that site in 1541. Baroque inside and out, the elaborate interior decorations of carved figures and curling gilded wood date from the 1700s. These carvings are attributed to Francisco Miguel Tlayotehuanitzin, an Indian sculptor who labored for more than 20 years to create them. Santa Ana, a wool-weaving village, is only 1½ miles east of Tlaxcala. Shops selling large rugs, serapes, and sweaters woven locally line the main street. Huamantla, 30 miles southeast of Tlaxcala, is a small village noted for its commemoration of the Assumption of the Virgin on August 14 and 15. Tlaxcala's

(go down in history)

Don't drop down to Mexico without an **AT&T Direct**® Service wallet guide. It's a list of access numbers you need to call home fast and clear from around the world, using an AT&T Calling Card or credit card. What an amazing culture we live in.

For a list of **AT&T Access Numbers,** take the attached wallet guide.

It's all within your reach.

For Travelers who want more than the Official Line

For Travelers Who Want More Than the Official Line

the Unofficial Guide to New Orleans

The Series with More Than 2.5 Million Copies Sold!

♦ Save Time & Money
♦ Hotels & Restaurants Candidly Rated & Ranked
♦ Insider Tips & Warnings

Eve Zibart with Bob Sehlinger

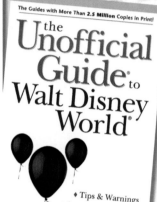

The Guides with More Than 2.5 Million Copies in Print!

the Unofficial Guide to Walt Disney World®

♦ Tips & Warnings
♦ Save Money & Time
♦ All Attractions Ranked & Rated
♦ Plus Disney's New Animal Kingdom

Bob Sehlinger

For Travelers Who Want More Than the Official Line

the Unofficial Guide to Las Vegas

The Series with More Than 2.5 Million Copies Sold!

♦ Save Time & Money
♦ Insider Gambling Tips
♦ Casinos & Hotels Candidly Rated & Ranked

Bob Sehlinger

Macmillan Publishing USA

Also Available:

- The Unofficial Guide to Branson
- The Unofficial Guide to Chicago
- The Unofficial Guide to Cruises
- The Unofficial Disney Companion
- The Unofficial Guide to Disneyland
- The Unofficial Guide to the Great Smoky & Blue Ridge Mountains
- The Unofficial Guide to Miami & the Keys
- Mini-Mickey: The Pocket-Sized Unofficial Guide to Walt Disney World
- The Unofficial Guide to New York City
- The Unofficial Guide to San Francisco
- The Unofficial Guide to Skiing in the West
- The Unofficial Guide to Washington, D.C.

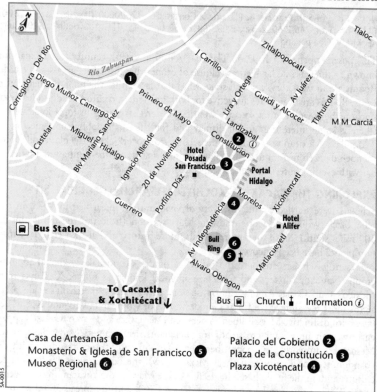

Tlaloc

Corregidora Del Río

Río Zahuapan

J Carrillo

Zitlalpopocatl

Diego Muñoz Camargo

Primero de Mayo

Lira y Ortega

Guridi y Alcocer

Av Juárez

Tlahuicole

M M Garciá

J Castelar

Miguelno Sanchez

Blv Mariano Hidalgo

Ignacio Allende

20 de Noviembre

Constitución

Lardizabal

Hotel Posada San Francisco

Portal Hidalgo

Morelos

Xicohtencatl

Hotel Alifer

Guerrero

Porfirio Diaz

Av Independencia

🚌 **Bus Station**

Bull Ring

Matlacueyetl

Alvaro Obregon

To Cacaxtla & Xochitécatl ↓

| Bus 🚌 | Church ✝ | Information ⓘ |

Casa de Artesanías ❶
Monasterio & Iglesia de San Francisco ❺
Museo Regional ❻

Palacio del Gobierno ❷
Plaza de la Constitución ❸
Plaza Xicoténcatl ❹

SA-0015

main attractions, however, are **Cacaxtla** (kah-*kahsh*-tlah) and the recently opened **Xochitécatl** (soh-she-*teh*-kahtl), unique pre-Hispanic hilltop sites 12 miles southwest of the city of Tlaxcala. This wonderfully pleasant city generally hosts few tourists and, because of that, retains its small-town atmosphere and overall low prices. If you are there on a weekend, the State Tourism Office sponsors a Saturday tour of the city and a Sunday tour of the Cacaxtla-Xochitécatl sites. Tours leave from the front of the Posada San Francisco Villas Arqueológicas at 10am both mornings. Board the bus; the guide will collect the $1.75 fee as you go.

WHERE TO STAY & DINE IN TLAXCALA

Tlaxcala has several good restaurants beneath the portal on the east side of the zócalo (some with live music in the evening), and budget hotels are nearby and along the road to Apizaco.

Hotel Alifer. Morelos 11, 90000 Tlaxcala, Tlax. ☎ **246/2-5678.** 18 units. TV TEL. $23 double. MC, V. Free parking.

The Alifer's clean rooms, with a black-and-red Spanish colonial decor, are carpeted and come with tile-and-marble bathrooms with showers. To get there from the Plaza Constitución, with your back to the Posada San Francisco, walk to the right 2 blocks; you'll reach the hotel entrance, just before the street turns to the right. The parking lot is next to the lobby entrance. The restaurant is open from 7am to 10pm. Laundry service is available.

Hotel Posada San Francisco. Plaza de la Constitución 17, 90000 Tlaxcala, Tlax. ☎ **800/ CLUB-MED** or 246/2-6022. Fax 246/2-6818. 68 units. TV, TEL. $65 double; $100 suite. AE, MC, V. Free parking.

This posada opened in 1992 on Tlaxcala's zócalo in a 19th-century former mansion known as the Casa de las Piedras (House of Stones) because of its gray-stone facade. Rooms are in two-story, colonial-style wings that face either the pool or small court-yards. Rooms are heated. It's attractive for both its modern comforts and its ideal loca-tion on the town's central square. Even if you don't stay, stop in for a look around (there is some interesting art on display and for sale in the lobby) or a meal at La Trasquila, a Mexican restaurant on the second story overlooking the plaza and lobby; it's open daily from 7am to 11pm. There's also a first-floor, fine-dining restaurant and bar with evening entertainment. It's operated by Club Med.

EXPLORING THE CACAXTLA-XOCHITÉCATL ARCHAEOLOGICAL SITE

Scholars were startled by the discovery of vivid murals, unearthed in 1975, in red, blue, black, yellow, and white, showing Maya warriors (from the Yucatán Peninsula, 500 miles south). Since then more murals, more history, and at least eight construc-tion phases have been uncovered.

Presently, scholars attribute the influence of the site to a little-known triethnic group (Náhuatl, Mixtec, and Chocho-popoloca) known as Olmec-Xicalanca from Mexico's Gulf Coast. Among the translations of its name, "merchant's trade pack" seems most revealing. Like Casas Grandes north of Chihuahua City and Xochicalco (also with distinctive Maya influence) between Cuernavaca and Taxco, Cacaxtla appar-ently was an important crossroads for merchants, astronomers, and others in the Mesoamerican world. Its apogee, between A.D. 650 and 900, corresponds with the abandonment of Teotihuacán (near Mexico City), the beginning of Casas Grandes culture, and, in the final phase, the decline of the Maya in the Yucatán, the emergence of the Toltec culture at Tula (also near Mexico City), and the spread of Toltec influ-ence to the Yucatán. How, or even if, those events affected Cacaxtla isn't known. Apparently the mural is a victory scene with warrior figures clothed magnificently in jaguar skins and seemingly victorious over figures dressed in feathers who were to be sacrificial victims. Some of the victims are even depicted lying on the floor, where they will undergo the ultimate humiliation of being walked on by the victors. Numerous symbols of Venus (a half star with five points) found painted at the site have led archaeoastronomy scholar John Carlson to link historical events such as wars, captive-taking, and ritual sacrifice with the appearance of Venus; all of this was likely under-taken in hopes of assuring the continued fertility of crops. These symbols of blood, along with toads and turtles (all water symbols), sacrifice, and Venus, together with others of corn stalks, and cacao trees (symbolizing fertility), were to appease the gods to ensure a productive cycle of rain, crops, and trade. The latest mural discoveries show a wall of corn and cacao trees leading to a merchant whose trade pack is laden with these symbolic crops. The murals flank a grand acropolis with unusual architectural motifs. For a lavishly illustrated account of the site, read "Mural Masterpieces of Ancient Cacaxtla" (*National Geographic*, September 1992). The grand plaza and murals are now protected by a giant steel roof.

Xochitécatl is a small ceremonial center located on a hilltop overlooking Cacaxtla, 2½ miles to the east. A curious circular pyramid stands atop this hill, 600 feet above the surrounding countryside. Beside this are two other pyramids (one of which is the fourth largest in Mexico), and three massive boulders (one about 10 ft. in diameter), which were hollowed out for some obscure reason. Hollowed boulders appear to have been restricted to the Puebla-Tlaxcala valley. Excavation of the Edificio de la Espiral (circular pyramid), dated between 1000 to 800 B.C. (middle formative period), encountered no stairways, hence access is thought to have been via its spiral walkway. Rounded boulders from the nearby Zahuapan and Atoyac rivers were used in its construction. Rounded pyramids, in this part of Mexico, are thought to have been dedicated to Ehécatl, god of the wind. The base diameter exceeds 180 feet, and it rises to a height of 50 feet.

The stepped and terraced Pyramid of the Flowers, made of rounded boulders, was begun during the middle formative period, though modifications continued into colonial times, as exemplified by faced-stone and stucco-covered adobe. Of the 30 bodies found during excavations, all but one were children. Little is known about the people who built Xochitécatl, but at least part of the time they were contemporaneous with neighboring Cacaxtla. Evidence suggests that the area was dedicated to Xochitl, goddess of flowers and fertility. There is a small site museum containing pottery and small sculpture and a garden with displays of larger sculpture.

To get to Cacaxtla from Tlaxcala, take a *combi* (collective minivan) or city bus to Nativitas (also called San Miguel Milagro), the village nearest the Cacaxtla ruins. From there, walk the paved mile or so or take a taxi to the entrance. From the parking lot it is a 100-yard climb to the archaeological site. The wooden steps can be slippery—use the handrails if wet.

To arrive at Xochitécatl, stay on the bus until you get to Xochitecatitla, then walk or take a cab to the ruins, which are another couple of miles on a blacktop road. If you're driving from Tlaxcala, take the road south to Tetlatlahuaca and turn right to Xochitecatitla or Nativitas. There are signs to the ruins in both towns.

From Puebla, take Highway 119 north to the crossroads near Zacualpan and turn left passing Tetlatlahuaca; turn right when you see signs to Nativitas and Cacaxtla. From Mexico City, take Highway 190 to San Martin Texmelucan, where you should ask directions for the road leading directly to the ruins, which are about 6 miles ahead. (This is the southern road you can use without going to Tlaxcala.)

Admission is $2.75 (one ticket is good for both sites), plus $4 for a video camera and $4 for a still camera; free Sunday and holidays. At Cacaxtla, since neither a flash nor a tripod is allowed, the site is difficult to photograph from the inside because of dust and low light caused by shading from the giant roof. Both sites are open Tuesday through Sunday from 10am to 5pm.

3 Ixtapan de la Sal: Thermal Spa Town

75 miles SW of Mexico City

Southwest of Mexico City, the whitewashed town of Ixtapan de la Sal (not to be confused with Ixtapa on the Pacific Coast) caters to the pleasures of thermal mud baths. The Balneario Ixtapan, next to the Hotel Spa Ixtapan, is the town's public spa and bathhouse. Here, you can take private thermal water baths or have a massage, facial, hair treatment, paraffin wrap, pedicure, and manicure—all of which cost between $10 and $20 each. It's open daily from 8am to 6pm.

Hotels in Ixtapan de la Sal tend to be full on weekends and Mexican holidays, as it's a popular retreat from the city. There's little to do but relax in the town. Cuernavaca, Taxco, and Toluca are all easy side trips.

ESSENTIALS

GETTING THERE & DEPARTING By Car To get here from Mexico City by car, take Highway 15 to Toluca. In Toluca, Highway 15 becomes Paseo Tollocan. Follow Tollocan south until you see signs pointing left to Ixtapan de la Sal. After the

Ixtapan de la Sal

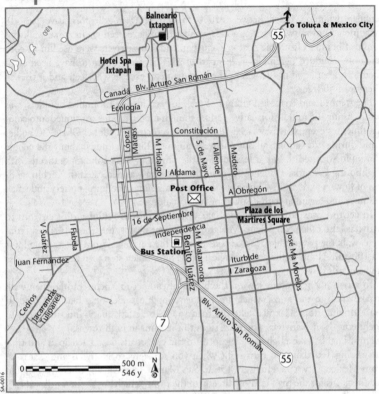

turn, continue straight for around 10 miles. Just before the town of Tenango del Valle, you have a choice of the free road to Ixtapan de la Sal or the toll road. The free road winds through the mountains and takes 1½ hours. The two-lane toll road has fewer mountain curves, is inexpensive, and takes around an hour—it's worth taking. The toll road stops about 10 miles before Ixtapan; you resume a curvy mountainous drive to reach the town.

By Bus From Mexico City's Terminal Poniente, buses leave for Ixtapan de la Sal every few minutes. Request a bus that's taking the toll road, which cuts the travel time from between 3 and 3½ hours to about 2½ hours. To return, take a bus marked "MÉXICO DIRECTO," which leaves every 10 minutes and usually stops in Toluca (confirm that yours does stop in Toluca if that's your destination). Buses from here also go to Cuernavaca and Taxco every 40 minutes.

WHERE TO STAY & DINE

✪ **Hotel Spa Ixtapan.** Bulevar San Román s/n, Ixtapan de la Sal, 51900 Edo. de México. ☎ **800/638-7950** in the U.S., or 714/3-0304. Fax 714/3-0856. 200 units, 50 villas. MINIBAR TV TEL. $135 double; $135 villa. 7-day Spa Diet package $885 per person double; 7-day Spa Relax package $985 per person double; 7-day Spa Sports package $985 per person double. (4-day and daily rates available.) Rates include 3 daily meals. AE, MC, V.

Set on several manicured and flower-filled acres, the town's only first-class hotel is also one of the country's best spa hotels, which has been in operation for more than 40 years. When you compare its comfort, weight-loss programs, good food, and relaxing pace to other spas, you'll understand its continued popularity and why it is considered the best spa value in Mexico. A typical day starts with an hour-long' hike into the surrounding hills, followed by an hour of aerobics or yoga and water exercise. A personalized treatment schedule follows, which includes massages, facials, and hair treatments; herbal wraps and salt-glow loofah scrubs; saunas, steam baths, and whirlpool tubs; and perhaps a tennis or golf lesson. A reflexologist is also available. Programs are separate for men and women, but everyone eats together. The spa week goes from Monday through Friday, with Sunday arrival preferred. Spa facilities are closed on Sunday. Hotel guests not on the spa program can use the spa facilities on a per treatment pay plan, and there's no daily admission charge. The entire property has just undergone extensive renovations. Rooms are large, comfortable, and stylishly furnished, and they come with cable TV with U.S. channels. Round-trip taxi transportation from the Mexico City airport can be arranged at the time of reservation for around $180, which can be shared by up to four people. Consider, also, the public bus from Mexico City (see "Getting There & Departing," above).

Dining: Spa dining room and hotel dining room. Food in the main (nonspa) dining room (also included in the room prices) is excellent and graciously served.

Amenities: Private 9-hole golf course; two tennis courts; full-service fitness, health, and beauty spa with fully equipped gym (opened June 1997), aerobics room and classes, steam room, solarium, three indoor whirlpools, two outdoor pools (one thermal and one freshwater), and sauna; horseback riding; mountain bikes; hiking trails; tour desk; laundry; room service. Guests provide their own workout clothes and bathrobe.

4 Valle de Bravo & Avándaro: Mexico's Switzerland

95 miles SW of Mexico City

At 6,070 feet, Valle de Bravo is one of Mexico's hidden retreats and has aptly been called the "Switzerland" of Mexico. Ringed by pine-forested mountains and set beside a beautiful man-made lake, Valle de Bravo is a 16th-century village with cobblestone streets and colonial structures built around a town plaza. Like San Miguel de Allende, Taxco, and Puerto Vallarta, Valle de Bravo is a National Monument village; new construction must conform to the colonial style of the original village.

Its neighbor Avándaro (4 miles away) is also a weekend retreat for well-to-do residents of Mexico City.

The cobbled streets, small restaurants, hotels, and shops of Valle de Bravo are full on weekends. Some shops and restaurants may be closed weekdays. The crafts market, located 3 blocks from the main square, is open daily from 10am to 5pm, and colorfully dressed Mazahua Indians sell their handmade tapestries daily around the town plaza. Fishing for bass and waterskiing are two activities centered around the lake. Possible excursions from here include a trip to the nesting grounds of the monarch butterfly between November and February. In addition to the summer rainy season, it can also be very rainy and chilly from September through December.

ESSENTIALS

GETTING THERE & DEPARTING   By Car   The quickest route from Mexico City by car is via Highway 15 to Toluca. In Toluca, Highway 15 becomes Paseo Tollocan. Follow Tollocan south until you see signs pointing left to Highway 134 and Valle de Bravo, Francisco de los Ranchos, and Temascaltepec. After the turn, continue on Highway 142 until Francisco de los Ranchos, where you bear right, following signs to Valle de Bravo. The drive from this point takes about 1½ to 2 hours.

Valle de Bravo & Avándaro

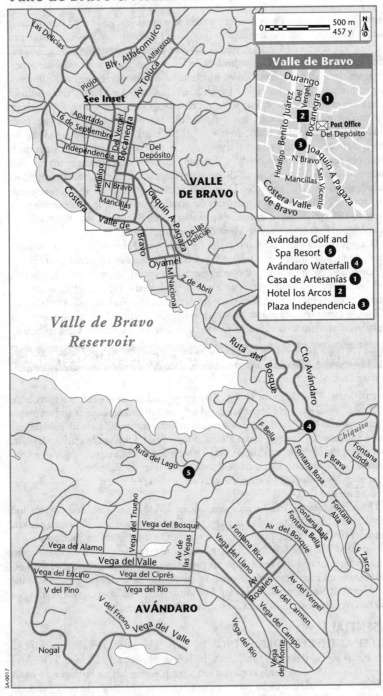

Valle de Bravo

Durango
Del Vergel
Del Vergel
Benito Juárez
Bocanegra
Post Office
Del Depósito
Joaquín A Pagaza
Hidalgo
N Bravo
San Vicente
Mancillas
Costera Valle
de Bravo

Avándaro Golf and
Spa Resort ❺
Avándaro Waterfall ❹
Casa de Artesanías ❶
Hotel los Arcos ❷
Plaza Independencia ❸

Las Delicias
Blv. Atlacomulco
Alfareros
Av Toluca
Piojo
See Inset
Apartado
16 de Septiembre
Del Vergel
Bocanegra
Del
Depósito
Independencia
Hidalgo
N Bravo
Mancillas
Costera
Valle de
Bravo
Joaquín A Pagaza
Oyamel
M Nacional
De las
Delicias
2 de Abril

**VALLE
DE BRAVO**

*Valle de Bravo
Reservoir*

Ruta del Bosque
Cto Avándaro
F Bella
❹
Chiquito
Fontana
Linda
Fontana Rosa
F Brava
Ruta del Lago
❺
Fontana
Alta
Fontana Baja
Fontana Bella
Vega del Trueno
Vega del Bosque
Vega del Alamo
Av de
las Vegas
Vega del Valle
Fontana Rica
Av del Bosque
Vega del Llano
Vega del Encino
Vega del Ciprés
V del Pino
Vega del Río
V del Fresno
AVÁNDARO
Vega del Valle
Nogal
Vega del Río
Av
Rosales
Av del Carmen
Vega del Campo
Av del Vergel
F Zarca
Vega del Monte

0 ____ 500 m
457 y

SA-0017

By Bus   From Mexico City's Terminal Poniente, buses leave every 20 minutes for the 3-hour journey. First-class buses depart hourly.

WHERE TO STAY & DINE

In addition to the restaurants at the hotels listed here, there are several fine restaurants on or near Valle de Bravo's central square.

Avándaro Golf and Spa Resort. Fracc. Avándaro, 51200 Valle de Bravo, Edo. de México. ☎ **800/ALL-SPAS** or 726/6-0366. Call Mexico City for round-trip arrangements and packages at ☎ 5/280-1532, 5/280-5532, or 5/282-0578. 87 units. TV TEL. $85 double cabana; $150–$275 deluxe suite. 7-day spa or golf package available. AE, MC, V.

Nestled on 296 acres amid large estates, lushly forested mountains, and a gorgeous, rolling 18-hole golf course, this resort has one of the loveliest settings in Mexico. Rooms come in two categories: large, beautifully furnished deluxe suites, and cabanas, which are small and less luxurious. Both kinds of room have fireplaces and terraces or balconies overlooking the grounds. Only the deluxe suites can be booked through the toll-free number mentioned above; cabanas must be booked directly with the hotel. There are two restaurants.

   Amenities: The ultramodern spa compares to the best in the United States, with a well-trained staff. A full range of services includes sauna and steam rooms, hot and cold whirlpools, and state-of-the-art weight-training equipment. A 25-meter junior Olympic-size pool overlooks the 18-hole golf course and seven tennis courts. Daily staff-led walks, plus massage, wraps, facials, aerobics, exercise classes, and numerous body treatments. Spa attire is provided and transportation can be arranged from Mexico City.

Hotel los Arcos. Bocanegra 310, 51200 Valle de Bravo, Edo. de México. ☎ and fax **726/2-0042.** 23 units. $28 double Sun–Thurs; $50 double Fri–Sat. AE, MC, V.

Close to the main square, the Hotel los Arcos has views of the village and mountains. Two stories of rooms on one side and three stories on the other are all built around a swimming pool. Nineteen rooms have fireplaces, an important feature in winter here. Some rooms have balconies, and most have glass walls with views. About half the rooms have TVs.

5 Cuernavaca: Land of Eternal Spring

64 miles S of Mexico City; 50 miles N of Taxco

Cuernavaca, capital of the state of Morelos, has been popular as a resort for people from Mexico City ever since the time of Moctezuma. Emperor Maximilian built a retreat here over a century ago. Mexicans say the town has a climate of "eternal spring," and on weekends the city is crowded with day-trippers from surrounding cities, especially the capital. On weekends, the roads between Mexico City and Cuernavaca are jammed, and restaurants and hotels may be full as well. Cuernavaca has a large American colony, plus students attending the myriad language and cultural institutes that crowd the city.

   Emperor Charles V gave Cuernavaca to Hernán Cortés as a fief, and the conquistador built a palace in 1532 (now the Museo de Cuauhnahuac), where he lived on and off for half a dozen years before returning to Spain. Cortés introduced sugarcane cultivation to the area, and Caribbean slaves were brought in to work in the cane fields. His sugar hacienda at the edge of town is now the luxurious Hotel de Cortés. The economics of large sugarcane growers failed to serve the interests of the indigenous farmers, and there were numerous uprisings in colonial times.

After independence, mighty landowners from Mexico City gradually dispossessed the remaining small landholders, converting them to virtual serfdom. It was this condition that led to the rise of Emiliano Zapata, the great champion of agrarian reform, who battled the forces of wealth and power, defending the small farmer with the cry of *"¡Tierra y Libertad!"* (Land and Liberty!) during the Mexican Revolution following 1910.

In this century, Cuernavaca has seen an influx of wealthy foreigners and of industrial capital. The giant CIVAC industrial complex on the outskirts has brought wealth to the city but also the curse of increased traffic, noise, and air pollution.

ESSENTIALS

GETTING THERE & DEPARTING   By Car   From Mexico City, take Paseo de la Reforma to Chapultepec Park and merge with the Periférico, which will take you to Highway 95D, the toll road on the far south of town that goes to Cuernavaca. From the Periférico, take the Insurgentes exit and continue until you come to signs for Cuernavaca/Tlalpan. Choose either the Cuernavaca Cuota (toll) or the old Cuernavaca Libre (free) road on the right. The free road is slower and very windy, but is more scenic.

By Bus   *Important note:* Buses to Cuernavaca depart directly from the Mexico City airport. (See "Getting There" in chapter 3 for details.) The trip takes an hour. The **Mexico City Central de Autobuses del Sur** exists primarily to serve the route Mexico City–Cuernavaca–Taxco–Acapulco–Zihuatanejo, so you'll have little trouble getting a bus. Pullman has two stations in Cuernavaca; the downtown station is at the corner of Abasolo and Netzahualcoyotl, 4 blocks south of the center of town. Their other station, Casino de la Selva, is less conveniently located near the railroad station.

Líneas Unidas del Sur/Flecha Roja, with 33 buses daily from Mexico City to Cuernavaca, has a new terminal in Cuernavaca at Morelos 505, between Arista and Victoria, 6 blocks north of the town center. Here, you'll find frequent buses to Toluca, Chalma, Ixtapan de la Sal, Taxco, Acapulco, the Cacahuamilpa Caves, Querétaro, and Nuevo Laredo.

Estrella Roja, a second-class station at Galeana and Cuauhtemotzin in Cuernavaca, about 8 blocks south of the town center, serves Cuautla, Yautepec, Oaxtepec, and Izúcar de Matamoros.

The **Autobuses Estrella Blanco** terminal in Cuernavaca is at Morelos Sur 503, serving Taxco.

VISITOR INFORMATION   Cuernavaca's **State Tourist Office** is at av. Morelos Sur 187, between Jalisco and Tabasco (☎ **73/14-3872** or 73/14-3920; fax 73/ 14-3881), half a block north of the Estrella de Oro bus station and about a 15- to 20-minute walk south of the cathedral. It's open Monday through Friday from 9am to 8pm and Saturday and Sunday from 9am to 5pm. There's also a **City Tourism kiosk** in the wall of the cathedral grounds on Hidalgo close to Morelos. It's open Monday through Friday from 9am to 4pm and Saturday from 9am to 2pm.

CITY LAYOUT   In the center of the city are two contiguous plazas. The small and more formal of the two, across from the post office, has a Victorian gazebo (designed by Gustave Eiffel of Eiffel Tower fame) at its center. This is the **Alameda.** The larger, rectangular plaza with trees, shrubs, and benches is the **Plaza de Armas.** These two plazas are known collectively as the **zócalo** and are the hub for strolling vendors selling balloons, baskets, bracelets, and other crafts from surrounding villages. It's all easy-going, and one of the pleasures is hanging out at a park bench or table in a nearby restaurant just to watch. On Sunday afternoons, orchestras play from the gazebo. At the eastern end of the Alameda is the **Cortés Palace,** the conquistador's residence that now serves as the Museo de Cuauhnahuac.

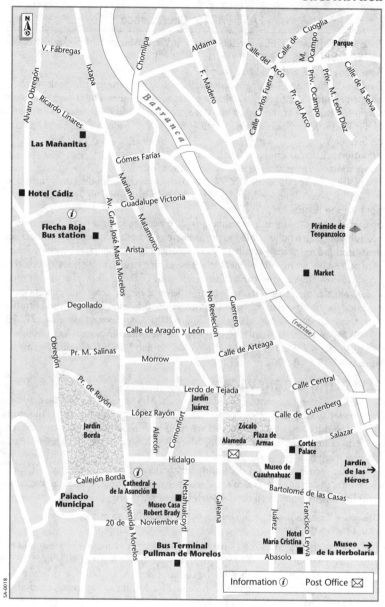

Cuernavaca

You should be aware that this city's street-numbering system is extremely confusing. It appears that the city fathers, during the past century or so, became dissatisfied with the street numbers every 10 or 20 years and imposed a new numbering system each time. Thus, you may find an address given as "no. 5" only to find that the building itself bears the number "506," or perhaps "Antes no. 5" (former no. 5). In descriptions of hotels, restaurants, and sights, the nearest cross streets will be noted so you can find your way to your chosen destination.

FAST FACTS: Cuernavaca

American Express   The local representative is **Viajes Marín,** Edificio las Plazas, Loc. 13 (☎ **73/14-2266** or 73/18-9901; fax 73/12-9297).

Area Code   The telephone area code is **73.**

Banks   Money can be changed from 9:30am to 1pm through the bank tellers, or through automatic tellers or casas de cambio at all other times. The closest bank to the zócalo is Bancomer at the corner of Matamoros and Lerdo de Tejada, catercorner to Jardín Juárez. Most banks are open until 6pm Monday through Friday, and half days on Saturday.

Elevation   Cuernavaca sits at 5,058 feet.

Population   Cuernavaca has 400,000 residents.

Post Office   The post office (☎ 73/12-4379) is on the Plaza de Armas, next door to Café los Arcos. It's open Monday through Friday from 8am to 7pm and Saturday from 9am to noon.

Spanish Lessons   As much as for its springlike weather, Cuernavaca is known for its Spanish-language schools, aimed at the foreigner. Generally the schools will help students find lodging with a family or provide a list of potential places to stay. Rather than make a long-term commitment in a family living situation, try it for a week, then decide. Below are the names and addresses of some of the schools. The whole experience, from classes to lodging, can be quite expensive, and the school may accept credit cards for the class portion. Contact the **Center for Bilingual Multicultural Studies,** San Jerónimo 304 (Apdo. Postal 1520), 62000 Cuernavaca, Morelos (☎ **73/13-0011**); or Universal Centro de Lengua y Comunicación Social A.C. (Universal Language School), J.H. Preciado 171 (Apdo. Postal 1-1826), 62000 Cuernavaca, Morelos (☎ **73/18-2904** or 73/12-4902).

EXPLORING CUERNAVACA

If you plan to visit Cuernavaca on a day-trip from Mexico City, the best days to do so are Tuesday, Wednesday, or Thursday (and perhaps Friday). On weekends the roads, the city, and its hotels and restaurants are filled with people from Mexico City. The museum, a key attraction, is closed on Monday. This makes weekends more hectic, but also more fun.

You can spend 1 to 2 days sightseeing in Cuernavaca pleasantly enough. If you've come on a day-trip from Mexico City, you may not have time to make all the excursions listed below, but you'll have enough time to see the sights in town.

Museo de Cuauhnahuac. In the Cortés Palace, Leyva 100. No phone. Admission $2; free Sun. Tues–Sun 10am–5pm.

The museum is housed in the Cortés Palace, the former home of the greatest of the conquistadors, Hernán Cortés. Begun by him in 1530 on the site of a Tlahuica Indian ceremonial center, it was finished by the conquistador's son, Martín, and later served as the legislative headquarters for the state of Morelos. It's in the town center at the eastern end of the Alameda/Plaza de Armas.

In the east portico on the upper floor, there's a large Diego Rivera mural commissioned by Dwight Morrow, U.S. ambassador to Mexico in the 1920s, depicting the history of Cuernavaca from the coming of the Spaniards to the rise of Zapata (1910).

Catedral de la Asunción. At the corner of Hidalgo and Morelos. Free admission. Daily 8am–2pm and 4–10pm. Walk 3 blocks southwest of the Plaza de Armas.

As you enter the church precincts and pass down the walk, try to imagine what life in Mexico was like in the old days. Construction on the church was begun in 1533, a mere 12 years after Cortés conquered Tenochtitlán (Mexico City) from the Aztecs.

The churchmen could hardly trust their safety to the tenuous allegiance of their new converts, so they built a fortress as a church. The skull and crossbones above the main door is not a comment on their feelings about the future, however, but a symbol for the Franciscan order, which had its monastery here in the church precincts.

Inside, the church is stark, even severe, having been refurbished in the 1960s. The most curious aspect of the interior is the mystery of the frescoes painted in Japanese style. Discovered during the refurbishing, they depict the persecution and martyrdom of St. Felipe de Jesús and his companions in Japan. No one is certain who painted them.

✪ **Museo Casa Robert Brady.** Calle Netzahualcóyotl 4. ☎ **73/718-8554.** Admission $2.50. Tues–Sun 10am–6pm.

This museum in a private home contains more than 1,300 works of art. Among them are pre-Hispanic and colonial pieces; oil paintings by Frida Kahlo and Rufino Tamayo; and handcrafts from America, Africa, Asia, and India. The collections were assembled by Robert Brady, born in Iowa with a career in fine arts at the Art Institute of Chicago. He lived in Venice for 5 years before settling in Cuernavaca in 1962. Through his years and travels he assembled this rich mosaic of contrasting styles and epochs. The wildly colorful rooms are exactly as Brady left them. Admission includes a guide in Spanish; English and French guides are available if requested in advance.

Jardín Borda. Morelos 103, at Hidalgo. ☎ **73/18-1038** or 73/18-1052. Admission 80¢. Tues–Sun 10am–5pm.

Half a block from the cathedral is the Jardín Borda (Borda Gardens). One of the many wealthy builders to choose Cuernavaca was José de la Borda, the Taxco silver magnate, who ordered a sumptuous vacation house built here in the late 1700s. The large enclosed garden next to the house was actually a huge private park, laid out in Andalusian style with little kiosks and an artificial pond. Maximilian found it worthy of an emperor and took it over as his private preserve in the mid-1800s. After Maximilian, the Borda Gardens fell on hard times; decades of neglect followed.

The gardens have been completely restored and were reopened in October 1987 as the Jardín Borda Centro de Artes. In the gateway buildings are several galleries for changing exhibits and several large paintings showing scenes from the life of Maximilian and from the history of the Borda Gardens. Scenes from the paintings include the initial meeting between Maximilian and La India Bonita, who was to become his lover.

On your stroll through the gardens you'll see the same little artificial lake on which Austrian, French, and Mexican nobility rowed in little boats beneath the moonlight. Ducks have taken the place of dukes, however, and there are rowboats for rent. The lake is now artfully adapted as an outdoor theater, with seats for the audience on one side and the stage on the other. There is a cafe for refreshments and light meals, and a bookstore.

✪ **Museo de la Herbolaría.** Matamoros 200, Acapantzingo. ☎ **73/12-5956.** Admission $2. Daily 10am–5pm.

This museum of traditional herbal medicine, in the south Cuernavaca suburb of Acapantzingo, has been set up in a former resort residence built by Maximilian, the Casa del Olindo, or Casa del Olvido. It was here, during his brief reign, that the Austrian-born emperor would come for trysts with La India Bonita, his Cuernavacan lover. Restored in 1960, the house and gardens now preserve the local wisdom of folk medicine. The shady gardens are lovely to wander through, and you shouldn't miss the 200 orchids growing near the rear of the property. However, the lovers' actual house, the little dark-pink building in the back, is closed. Take a taxi, or catch combi no. 6 at the mercado on Degollado. Ask to be dropped off at Matamoros near the museum. Turn right on Matamoros and walk 1½ blocks; the museum will be on your right.

WHERE TO STAY

Because so many residents of Mexico City come down for the day or weekend, tourist traffic at the hotels here may be heavy on weekends and holidays. Reservations during these times are recommended.

EXPENSIVE

✪ **Camino Real Sumiya.** Interior Fracc. Sumiya s/n, Col. José Parres, 62550 Jiutepec, Mor. ☎ **800/7-CAMINO** in the U.S., or 73/20-9199. Fax 73/20-9155. 169 units. A/C MINIBAR TV TEL. $123 double; $231–$265 suite. Low-season packages and discounts available. AE, DC, MC, V.

Sumiya's charm is its relaxing atmosphere, which is best midweek since escapees from Mexico City tend to fill it on weekends. About 7 miles south of Cuernavaca, this unusual resort, whose name means "the House on the Corner," was once the exclusive home of Woolworth heiress Barbara Hutton. Using materials and craftsmen from Japan, she constructed the estate in 1959 for $3.2 million on 30 beautifully wooded acres. The house is an exact replica of one in Kyoto, Japan. The main house, a series of large interconnected rooms and decks, overlooks the grounds and contains restaurants and the lobby.

The guest rooms, which are clustered in three-storied buildings flanking manicured lawns, are plain in comparison to the striking Japanese architecture of the main house. Rooms, however, have nice Japanese accents, with austere but comfortable furnishings, scrolled wood doors, and round pulls on the armoire and closet. Each room has direct-dial, long-distance phones, fax connections, three-prong electrical outlets, ceiling fans, and in-room wall safes. Hutton built a kabuki-style theater on the grounds, which is now used for special events. Hutton's life is chronicled in *Poor Little Rich Girl,* an excellent biography by C. David Heymann (Simon & Schuster, 1984).

Cuernavaca is an inexpensive taxi ride away. From the freeway, take the Atlacomulco exit and follow Sumiya signs. Ask directions in Cuernavaca if you're coming from there since the route to the resort is complicated.

Dining: There's La Arboleda, an outdoor restaurant shaded by enormous Indian laurel trees; Sumiya, with both terrace and indoor dining; and a snack bar by the pool.

Amenities: Pool, 10 tennis courts, convention facilities with simultaneous translation capabilities, room service, business center.

✪ **Las Mañanitas.** Ricardo Linares 107, 62000 Cuernavaca, Mor. ☎ **73/14-1466** or 73/12-4646. Fax 73/18-3672. www.acnet.net/empresas/las-mananitas/. E-mail: mananita@intersur.com. 22 units. TEL. $92–$247 double; $348 suite. AE. Valet parking.

Cuernavaca's best-known luxury lodging is Las Mañanitas—with good reason. Gleaming polished molding and brass accents, large bathrooms, luxurious rooms, and superior attention to detail result in an unforgettably perfect place to stay. It's one of two hotels in Mexico associated with the prestigious Relais & Château hotels. Rooms are in three sections: those in the original mansion, called terrace suites, overlooking the restaurant and inner lawn; four large rooms in the patio section, each with a secluded patio; and the luxurious and most expensive garden section, where each room has a large patio overlooking the pool and emerald lawns where peacocks and other exotic birds strut and preen, and fountains tinkle musically. Thirteen rooms have fireplaces, and the hotel also has a heated pool in the private garden. One room (the lowest price above) above the restaurant is the hotel's only standard room—but it's very nice and has an excellent view of the public garden. For decades the hotel did not accept credit cards, but now accepts American Express. It's 5½ long blocks north of the Jardín Borda.

Dining: The restaurant, overlooking the gardens, is one of the premier dining places in Mexico (see "Where to Dine," below). The restaurant is open to nonguests for lunch and dinner only.

Amenities: Swimming pool, laundry and room service, concierge. Transportation to and from the Mexico City airport can be arranged through the hotel for $180 round-trip.

MODERATE

Hotel María Cristina. Leyva 200 (Apdo. Postal 203), 62000 Cuernavaca, Mor. ☎ **73/ 18-5767.** Fax 73/12-9126. 17 units. TV TEL. $70 double; $97–$137 suite and cabana. AE, MC, V. Free parking.

Formerly La Posada de Xochiquetzal, the María Cristina's high walls conceal many delights: a small swimming pool, lush gardens with fountains, colonial-style furnishings, a good restaurant, patios, and large and small guest rooms. The hotel, under new ownership since 1994, has been remodeled into a royal-blue and natural-wood theme. Though better kept than in the past, the personality of each room vanished with the homogenized remodeling. Suites are only slightly larger than standard rooms. A pool is on the lower level of the grounds, and the bar/restaurant there is open on weekends. La Casona, the handsome little restaurant on the first floor, overlooks the gardens and serves excellent meals based on Mexican and international recipes. Even if you don't stay here, consider a meal here. It is on the southwest corner of Leyva and Abasolo, half a block from the Palacio de Cortez.

INEXPENSIVE

Hotel Cádiz. Álvaro Obregón 329, 62000 Cuernavaca, Mor. ☎ **73/18-9204.** 17 units. FAN. $30 double. Add $5 extra for TV. No credit cards.

Run by the gracious Cárdenas-Aguilar family, the Cádiz has that kind of homey charm that makes it comforting to return. Each of the fresh, simple rooms is furnished uniquely, and there's a lot of old-fashioned tile and big, old (but well-kept) freestanding sinks. The grounds, set back from the street, make a pleasant respite. There are a pool and a small inexpensive restaurant that's open from 9am to 4pm. From Morelos, turn left on Ricardo Linares and go past Las Mañanitas. Turn left at the first street, Obregón; the hotel is a block ahead on the right.

WHERE TO DINE
EXPENSIVE

✪ **Restaurant Las Mañanitas.** Ricardo Linares 107. ☎ **73/14-1466** or 73/12-4646. Reservations recommended. Main courses $9–$17. AE. Daily 1–5pm and 7–11pm. MEXICAN/INTERNATIONAL.

Las Mañanitas sets the standard for sumptuous, leisurely dining in Cuernavaca. Tables are set on a shaded terrace with a view of gardens, strolling peacocks, and softly playing violinists or a romantic trio. The ambiance and service are extremely friendly and attentive. When you arrive, you can enjoy cocktails in the cozy sala or at lounge chairs on the lawn; when you're ready to dine, a waiter will present you with a large blackboard menu listing a dozen or more daily specials. The cuisine is Mexican with an international flair, drawing on whatever fruits and vegetables are in season and offering a full selection of fresh seafood, beef, pork, veal, and fowl. Try the cream of watercress soup, the fillet of red snapper in cilantro sauce, and top it off with black-bottom pie, the house specialty. Las Mañanitas is 5½ long blocks north of the Jardín Borda.

MODERATE

Restaurant La India Bonita. Morrow 106B. ☎ **73/18-6967.** Breakfast $3–$5.75; main courses $5–$10. AE, MC, V. Tues–Fri 8am–10pm; Sat 9am–10pm; Sun 9am–8pm. MEXICAN.

Housed among the interior patios and portals of the restored home of former U.S. Ambassador Dwight Morrow (1920s), La India Bonita is gracious, sophisticated, and a Cuernavaca haven where you can enjoy the setting as well as the food. Specialties include *mole poblano* (chicken with a sauce of bitter chocolate and fiery chiles) and *fillet à la parrilla* (charcoal-grilled steak). There are also several daily specials. A breakfast mainstay is the *desayuno Maximiliano:* a gigantic platter featuring enchiladas. The restaurant is 2 blocks north of the Jardín Juárez between Matamoros and Morelos.

Restaurant Vienés. Lerdo de Tejada 4. ☎ **73/18-4044** or 73/14-3404. Breakfast $3–$4.50; main courses $5–$8. Daily 8am–10pm. AE, MC, V. VIENNESE.

A legacy of this city's Viennese immigrant heritage is the Restaurant Vienés, a tidy and somewhat Viennese-looking place a block from the Jardín Juárez between Lerdo de Tejada and Morrow. The menu also has old-world specialties such as grilled trout with vegetables and German potato salad; for dessert there's apple strudel followed by Viennese coffee. Next door, the restaurant runs a pastry/coffee shop called **Los Pasteles de Vienés.** Although the menu is identical, the atmosphere in the coffee shop is much more leisurely, and there the tempting pastries are on full display in glass cases.

INEXPENSIVE

La Parroquia. Guerrero 102. ☎ **73/18-5820.** Breakfast $2–$3; main courses $3–$6; comida corrida $4. AE, MC, V. Daily 7am–midnight. MEXICAN/PASTRIES.

This place does a teeming business, partly because of its great location (half a block north of the Alameda, opposite Parque Juárez), partly because of its Arab specialties, and partly because it has fairly reasonable prices for Cuernavaca. It's open to the street with a few outdoor cafe tables, perfect for watching the changing parade of street vendors and park life.

CUERNAVACA AFTER DARK

Cuernavaca has a number of cafes right off the Jardín Juárez where people gather to sip coffee or drinks till the wee hours of the morning. The best are La Parroquia and the Los Pasteles de Vienés (see "Where to Dine," above). There are band concerts in the Jardín Juárez on Thursday and Sunday evenings.

Harry's Grill. Gutenberg 5, at Salazar, just off the main square. ☎ **73/12-7639.**

Harry's Grill is another addition to the Carlos Anderson chain and includes its usual good food and craziness with Mexican revolutionary posters and flirtatious waiters. Although it serves full dinners, I'd recommend you go for drinks. It's open daily from 1:30 to 11:30pm. American Express, MasterCard, and Visa are accepted.

6 Taxco: Cobblestones & Silver

111 miles SW of Mexico City; 50 miles SW of Cuernavaca; 185 miles NE of Acapulco

Taxco (*tahs*-ko), famous for its silver work, has topography on its side: The town sits at nearly 5,000 feet on a hill among hills, and almost any point in the city offers fantastic views.

Taxco was discovered by Hernán Cortés as he combed the area for treasure, but the rich caches of silver weren't fully exploited for another 2 centuries, by the French prospector Joseph de la Borda. In 1751 de la Borda commissioned the baroque Santa

Prisca Church that dominates Taxco's zócalo as a way of giving something back to the town.

That Taxco has become Mexico's most renowned center for silver design, although only a small amount of the silver is still mined there, is due to an American, William Spratling. Spratling arrived in the late 1920s with the intention of writing a book; however, he soon noticed the skill of the local craftsmen and opened a workshop to produce handmade silver jewelry and tableware based on pre-Hispanic art, which were exported to the United States in bulk. The workshops flourished, Taxco's reputation grew, and today there are more than 200 silver shops.

Most are supplied by tiny one-man factories that line the cobbled streets all the way up into the hills. Whether you find bargains depends on how much you know about the quality and price of silver. But nowhere else in the country will you find the quantity and variety of silver available in Taxco. The artistry and imagination of the local silversmiths are evident in each piece.

You can get an idea of what Taxco is like by spending an afternoon here, but there's much more to this picturesque town of 87,000 than just the Plaza Borda and the shops surrounding it. You'll have to stay overnight if you want more time to wander its steep cobblestone streets, discovering little plazas and fine churches. The main part of town is relatively flat. It stretches up the hillside from the highway, and it's a steep but brief walk up. White VW minibuses, called *burritos,* make the circuit through and around town, picking up and dropping off passengers along the route. They run the route from about 7am until 9pm. Taxis in town are inexpensive.

Warning: Self-appointed guides will undoubtedly approach you in the zócalo (Plaza Borda) and offer their guide services—they get a cut (up to 25%) of all you buy in the shops they take you to. Before hiring a guide, ask to see his **Departamento de Turismo** credentials. The Department of Tourism office on the highway at the north end of town can recommend a licensed guide either using your car or on foot.

ESSENTIALS

GETTING THERE & DEPARTING By Car From Mexico City, take Paseo de la Reforma to Chapultepec Park and merge with the Periférico, which will take you to Highway 95D on the south end of town. From the Periférico, take the Insurgentes exit and merge until you come to the sign for Cuernavaca/Tlalpan. Choose either "Cuernavaca Cuota" (toll) or "Cuernavaca Libre" (free). Continue south around Cuernavaca to the Amacuzac interchange and proceed straight ahead for Taxco. The drive from Mexico City takes about 3½ hours. Gas stations are infrequent beyond Cuernavaca.

From Acapulco you have two options. Highway 95D is the new toll road through Iguala to Taxco. Or you can take the old two-lane road (95) that winds through villages and is slower, but it's in good condition.

By Bus From Mexico City, buses to Taxco depart from the Central de Autobuses del Sur station (Metro: Tasqueña) and take 2 to 3 hours, with frequent departures.

Taxco has two bus stations. Estrella de Oro buses arrive at their own station on the southern edge of town. Flecha Rojo and Futura buses arrive at the station on the eastern edge of town on avenida Kennedy. Taxis cost around 75¢ to the zócalo.

VISITOR INFORMATION The **State of Guerrero Dirección de Turismo** (☎ **762/2-6616;** fax 762/2-2274) has offices at the arches on the main highway at the north end of town, useful if you're driving into town. The office is open daily from 9am to 8pm. To get there from the Plaza Borda, take a combi ("Zócalo-Arcos") and get off at the arch over the highway. As you face the arches, the tourism office is on your right.

CITY LAYOUT   The center of town is the tiny **Plaza Borda,** shaded by perfectly manicured Indian laurel trees. On one side is the imposing twin-towered, pink-stone **Santa Prisca Church,** and the other sides are lined with whitewashed, red-tile buildings housing the famous silver shops and a restaurant or two. Beside the church, deep in a crevice of the mountain, is the **city market.** One of the beauties of Taxco is that its brick-paved and cobblestone streets are completely asymmetrical, zigzagging up and down the hillsides. Besides the silver-filled shops, the plaza swirls with vendors of everything from hammocks to cotton candy and from bark paintings to balloons.

Fast Facts: Taxco

Area Code   The telephone area code is **762.**

Post Office   The post office (correo) moved to the outskirts of Taxco on the highway heading toward Acapulco. It's in a row of shops with a black-and-white CORREO sign.

Spanish/Art Classes   In 1993, the Universidad Nacional Autónoma de México (UNAM) opened its doors in the buildings and grounds of the Hacienda del Chorillo, formerly part of the Cortés land grant. Here, students can study silversmithing, Spanish, drawing, composition, and history under the supervision of UNAM instructors. Classes are small, and courses are generally for 3 months at a time. The school will provide a list of prospective town accommodations that consist primarily of hotels. More reasonable accommodations can be found for a lengthy stay, but that's best arranged once you're there. At locations all over town are notices of furnished apartments or rooms for rent at reasonable prices. For information about the school, contact either the **Dirección de Turismo** (tourist office) in Taxco (see "Information," above) or write the school directly: **UNAM,** Hacienda del Chorillo, 40200 Taxco, Guerrero (☎ **762/2-3690**).

EXPLORING TAXCO

Since Taxco boasts more than 200 shops selling silver, shopping for jewelry and other items is the major pastime, the main reason most tourists come to town. But Taxco offers other cultural attractions. Besides the opulent, world-renowned **Santa Prisca y San Sebastián Church,** there are the **Spratling Archaeology Museum,** the **Silver Museum,** and the **Humboldt House/Museo Virreynal de Taxco.**

Malasia Tours (☎ 762/2-7983) offers daily tours to the Cacahuamilpa Caves and the ruins of Xochicalco. They also sell bus tickets to Acapulco, Chilpancingo, Iguala, and Cuernavaca. The agency is located on the Plazuela San Juan no. 5 to the left of La Hamburguesa.

SPECIAL EVENTS & FESTIVALS   Taxco's **Silver Fair** starts the last Saturday in November and continues for 1 week. It includes a competition for silver sculptures among the top silversmiths. ✪ **Holy Week** in Taxco is one of the most compelling in the country, beginning the Friday a week before Easter with nightly processions and several during the day. The most riveting procession, on Thursday evening, lasts almost 4 hours and includes villagers from the surrounding area carrying statues of saints, followed by hooded members of a society of self-flagellating penitents chained at the ankles and carrying huge wooden crosses and bundles of penetrating thorny branches. On Saturday morning, the Plaza Borda fills for the **Procession of Three Falls,** reenacting the three times Christ stumbled and fell while carrying his cross. The **Jornadas Alarconianas,** featuring plays and literary events in honor of Juan Ruíz de Alarcón (1572–1639), a world-famous dramatist who was born in Taxco, were traditionally held in the spring, but have switched to the fall in recent years.

Taxco

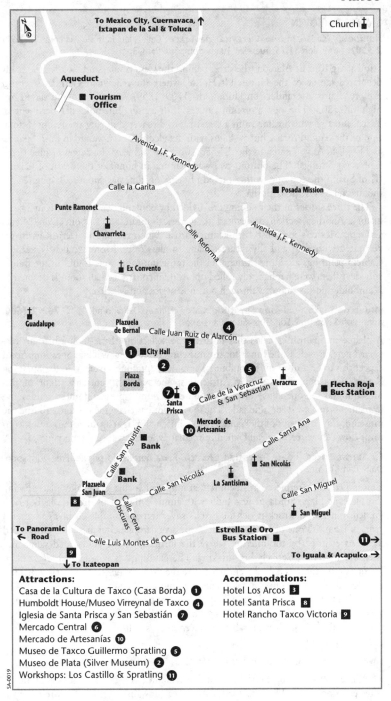

To Mexico City, Cuernavaca,
Ixtapan de la Sal & Toluca ↑

Church ✝

Aqueduct

■ Tourism Office

Avenida J.F. Kennedy

Calle la Garita

■ Posada Mission

Punte Ramonet

✝ Chavarrieta

Calle Reforma

Avenida J.F. Kennedy

✝ Ex Convento

✝ Guadalupe

Plazuela de Bernal

Calle Juan Ruiz de Alarcón

❹

❶ ■ City Hall

❸

❷

Plaza Borda

❺

❼ ✝

Santa Prisca

❻

Calle de la Veracruz & San Sebastián

✝ Veracruz

■ Flecha Roja Bus Station

Mercado de Artesanías

❿

Calle Santa Ana

Calle San Agustín

■ Bank

■ San Nicolás

■ Bank

Calle San Nicolás

✝ La Santisima

Plazuela San Juan

Calle Cena Obscuras

❽

Calle San Miguel

✝ San Miguel

To Panoramic
← Road

Calle Luis Montes de Oca

Estrella de Oro
Bus Station ■

⓫→

❾
↓ To Ixateopan

To Iguala & Acapulco →

Attractions:
Casa de la Cultura de Taxco (Casa Borda) ❶
Humboldt House/Museo Virreynal de Taxco ❹
Iglesia de Santa Prisca y San Sebastián ❼
Mercado Central ❻
Mercado de Artesanías ❿
Museo de Taxco Guillermo Spratling ❺
Museo de Plata (Silver Museum) ❷
Workshops: Los Castillo & Spratling ⓫

Accommodations:
Hotel Los Arcos ❸
Hotel Santa Prisca ❽
Hotel Rancho Taxco Victoria ❾

SA-0019

167

SIGHTS IN TOWN

Humboldt House/Museo Virreynal de Taxco. Calle Juan Ruíz de Alarcón. ☎ **762/ 2-5501.** Admission $1.75. Tues–Sat 10am–5pm; Sun 9am–3pm.

Stroll along Ruíz de Alarcón (the street behind the Casa Borda) and look for the richly decorated facade of the Humboldt House, where the renowned German scientist/ explorer Baron Alexander von Humboldt (1769–1859) visited Taxco and stayed one night in 1803. The new museum houses 18th-century memorabilia pertinent to Taxco, most of which came from a secret room discovered during the recent restoration of the Santa Prisca Church. Signs with detailed information are in both Spanish and English. As you enter, to the right are two huge and very rare *tumelos* (three-tiered funerary paintings). The bottom two were painted in honor of the death of Charles III of Spain; the top one, with a carved phoenix on top, was supposedly painted for the funeral of José de la Borda.

The three stories of the museum are divided by eras and persons famous in Taxco's history. Another section is devoted to historical information about Don Miguel Cabrera, Mexico's foremost 18th-century artist. Fine examples of clerical garments decorated with gold and silver thread hang in glass cases. More excellently restored Cabrera paintings are hung throughout the museum; some were found in the frames you see, others were haphazardly rolled up. And, of course, a small room is devoted to Humboldt and his sojourns through South America and Mexico.

Museo de Taxco Guillermo Spratling. Calle Porfirio A. Delgado no. 1. ☎ **762/2-1660.** Admission $1.50; free Sun. Tues–Sun 10am–5pm.

A plaque in Spanish explains that most of the collection of pre-Columbian art displayed here, as well as the funds for the museum, came from William Spratling. You'd expect this to be a silver museum, but it's not—for Spratling silver, go to the Spratling Ranch Workshop (see "Nearby Attractions," below). The entrance floor of this museum and the one above display a good collection of pre-Columbian statues and implements in clay, stone, and jade. The lower floor has changing exhibits. To find the museum, turn right out of the Santa Prisca Church and right again at the corner; continue down the street, jog right, then immediately left. It will be facing you.

✪ **Santa Prisca y San Sebastián Church.** Plaza Borda. No phone. Free admission. Daily 8am–11pm.

This is Taxco's centerpiece parish church, around which village life takes place. Facing the pleasant Plaza Borda, it was built with funds provided by José de la Borda, a French miner who struck it rich in Taxco's silver mines. Completed in 1758 after 8 years of labor, it's one of Mexico's most impressive baroque churches. The ultracarved facade is eclipsed by the interior, where the intricacy of the gold-leafed saints and cherubic angels is positively breathtaking. The paintings by Miguel Cabrera, one of Mexico's most famous colonial-era artists, are the pride of Taxco. The sacristy (behind the high altar) is now open and contains even more Cabrera paintings.

Guides, both boys and adults, will approach you outside the church offering to give a tour, and it's worth the few pesos to get a full rendition of what you're seeing. Make sure the guide's English is passable, however, and establish whether the price is per person or per tour.

Silver Museum. Plaza Borda. Admission 75¢. Daily 10am–5pm.

The Silver Museum, operated by a local silversmith, is a recent addition to Taxco. After entering the building next to Santa Prisca (upstairs is Sr. Costilla's restaurant), look for a sign on the left; the museum is downstairs. It's not a traditional public-sponsored museum. Nevertheless, it does a much-needed job of describing the history of silver in Mexico and Taxco, as well as displaying some historic and contemporary award-winning pieces. Time spent here seeing quality silver work will make you a more discerning shopper in Taxco's dazzling silver shops.

Casa de la Cultura de Taxco (Casa Borda). Plaza Borda. ☎/fax **762/2-6617.** Free admission. Daily 10am–3pm and 5–7pm.

Catercorner from the Santa Prisca Church and facing Plaza Borda is the home José de la Borda built for his son around 1759. It is now the Guerrero State Cultural Center, housing classrooms and exhibit halls where period clothing, engravings, paintings, and crafts are displayed. Traveling exhibits are also on display.

Mercado Central. Plaza Borda. Daily 7am–6pm.

To the right of the Santa Prisca Church, behind and below Berta's, Taxco's central market meanders deep inside the mountain. Take the stairs off the street. Among the curio stores, you'll find food stalls and cook shops, always the best place for a cheap meal.

NEARBY ATTRACTIONS

The large Grutas de Cacahuamilpa (Cacahuamilpa Grottoes) are 20 minutes north of Taxco. There are hourly guided tours daily at the grottoes, but these caves are much like any others you may have visited.

For a spectacular view of Taxco, ride the cable cars (gondola) to the Hotel Monte Taxco. Catch them across the street from the state tourism office, left of the arches, near the college campus. Take a taxi or the combi marked "LOS ARCOS" (exit just before the arches, turn left, and follow the signs to the cable cars). Daily hours are 7am to 7pm.

Spratling Ranch Workshop. 6 miles south of town on the Acapulco Hwy. No phone. Free admission. Mon–Sat 9am–5pm.

Spratling's hacienda-style home/workshop on the outskirts of Taxco still hums with busy hands reproducing his unique designs. A trip here will show you what distinctive Spratling work was all about, for the designs crafted today show the same fine work— even Spratling's workshop foreman is employed overseeing the development of a new generation of silversmiths. Prices are high, but the designs are unusual and considered collectible. There's no store in Taxco, and unfortunately, most of the display cases hold only samples. With the exception of a few jewelry pieces, most items are by order only. Ask about their U.S. outlets.

Los Castillo. 5 miles south of town on the Acapulco Hwy., and in Taxco on Plazuela Bernal. ☎ **762/2-1016** (workshop) or 762/2-3471 (store). Free admission. Workshop, Mon–Fri 9am–5pm. Store, Mon–Fri 9am–6:30pm; Sat 9am–1pm; Sun 10am–3pm.

Don Antonio Castillo was one of hundreds of young men to whom William Spratling taught the silversmithing trade in the 1930s. He was also one of the first to branch out with his own shops and line of designs, which over the years have earned him a fine name. Castillo has shops in several Mexican cities. Now, his daughter Emilia creates her own noteworthy designs, among which are decorative pieces with silver fused onto porcelain. Emilia's work is for sale on the ground floor of the Posada de los Castillo, just below the Plazuela Bernal. Another store, featuring the designs of Don Antonio, is found in Mexico City's Zona Rosa, at Amberes 41.

WHERE TO STAY

Compared to Cuernavaca, Taxco is an overnight-stop visitor's dream: charming and picturesque, with a respectable selection of well-kept and delightful hotels. Hotel prices tend to "bulge" at holiday times (especially Easter week).

MODERATE

Hacienda del Solar. Paraje del Solar s/n (Apdo. Postal 96), 40200 Taxco, Gro. ☎/fax **762/2-0323.** 22 units. $50 double; $60–$70 junior and deluxe suite.

On a beautifully landscaped hilltop with magnificent views of the surrounding valleys and the town, this hotel comprises several Mexican-style cottages. The decor is slightly different in each one, but most include lots of beautiful handcrafts, red-tile floors, and bathrooms with handmade tiles. Several rooms have vaulted tile ceilings and fine private terraces with panoramic views. Standard rooms have no terraces and only showers in the bathrooms; deluxe rooms have sunken tubs (with showers) and terraces. Junior suites are the largest and most luxurious accommodations.

The hotel is 2½ miles south of the town center off Highway 95 to Acapulco; look for signs on the left and go straight down a narrow road until you see the hotel entrance.

Dining: La Ventana de Taxco restaurant overlooking the city, is the best place to dine in the area. The restaurant has a spectacular view of the city and the cuisine is Italian. Main courses run $8 to $17. It's open for all meals.

Amenities: Heated swimming pool, tennis court, laundry, and room service.

INEXPENSIVE

Hotel los Arcos. Juan Ruíz de Alarcón 12, 40200 Taxco, Gro. ☎ **762/2-1836.** Fax 762/2-7982. 24 units. $22 double. No credit cards.

Los Arcos occupies a converted 1620 monastery. The handsome inner patio is bedecked with Puebla pottery and a cheerful restaurant area to the left, all around a central fountain. The rooms are nicely but sparsely furnished, with natural tile floors and colonial-style furniture. You'll be immersed in colonial charm and blissful quiet. To find it from the Plaza Borda, follow the hill down (with Hotel Agua Escondida on your left) and make an immediate right at the Plazuela Bernal; the hotel is a block down on the left, opposite the Posada de los Castillo (see below).

✪ **Hotel Rancho Taxco Victoria.** Carlos J. Nibbi 27 (Apdo. Postal 83), 40200 Taxco, Gro. ☎ **762/2-0004.** Fax 762/2-0210. 64 units (some with TV). $35 double standard; $44 double deluxe; $50 junior suite. AE, MC, V.

The Rancho Taxco Victoria clings to the hillside above town, with breathtaking views from its flower-covered verandas. It exudes all the charm of old-fashioned Mexico. The furnishings, beautifully kept, whisper comfortably of the hotel's heyday in the 1940s. Each standard room comes with a bedroom and in front of each is a table and chairs set out on the tiled common walkway. Each deluxe room has a bedroom and private terrace; each junior suite has a bedroom, a nicely furnished large living room, and a spacious private terrace overlooking the city. There's a lovely pool, plus a restaurant—both with a great view of Taxco. Even if you don't stay here, come for a drink at sunset, or any time, in the comfortable bar/living room, then stroll or sit on the terrace to take in the fabulous view. From the Plazuela San Juan, go up a narrow, winding cobbled street named Carlos J. Nibbi. The hotel is at the top of the hill.

Hotel Santa Prisca. Plazuela San Juan 7, 40200 Taxco, Gro. ☎ **762/2-0080** or 762/2-0980. Fax 762/2-2938. 34 units. $31 double; $34.50 superior; $55 suite. AE, MC, V.

The Santa Prisca, 1 block from the Plaza Borda on the Plazuela San Juan, is one of the older and nicer hotels in town. Rooms are small but comfortable, with newly remodeled bathrooms (showers only), tile floors, wood beams, and a colonial atmosphere. For longer stays, ask for a room in the adjacent "new addition," where the rooms are sunnier, quieter, and more spacious. There is a reading area in an upstairs salon overlooking Taxco, a lush patio with fountains, and a lovely dining room done in mustard and blue.

Posada de los Castillo. Juan Ruíz de Alarcón 7, 40200 Taxco. Gro. ☎/fax **762/2-1396.** 14 units. $18.75 double. MC, V.

Each room in this delightful small hotel is simply but beautifully furnished with handsome carved doors and furniture; bathrooms have either tubs or showers. The manager, Don Teodoro Contreras Galindo, is a true gentleman and a fountain of information about Taxco. To get here from the Plaza Borda, go downhill a short block to the Plazuela Bernal; make an immediate right, and the hotel is a block farther on the right, opposite the Hotel los Arcos (see above).

WHERE TO DINE

Taxco gets a lot of people on day-trips from the capital and Acapulco. There are not enough good restaurants to fill the demand, so prices are high for what you get. Besides those mentioned below, the top dining spot in Taxco is La Ventana de Taxco at the Hacienda del Solar, mentioned above.

VERY EXPENSIVE

Toni's. In the Hotel Monte Taxco. ☎ **762/2-1300.** Reservations recommended. Main courses $20–$35. AE, MC, V. Tues–Sat 7:30pm–1am. STEAKS/SEAFOOD.

High on a mountaintop, Toni's is an intimate and classy restaurant enclosed in a huge, cone-shaped palapa with a panoramic view of the city below. Eleven candlelit tables sparkle with crystal and crisp linen. The menu of shrimp or beef is limited, but the food is superior. Try the tender, juicy prime roast beef, which comes with Yorkshire pudding, creamed spinach, and baked potato. Lobster is sometimes available. To reach Toni's, take a taxi.

MODERATE

Cielito Lindo. Plaza Borda 14. ☎ **762/2-0603.** Breakfast $2.75–$6.25; main courses $4.50–$6.50. MC, V. Daily 10am–11pm. MEXICAN/INTERNATIONAL.

Cielito Lindo is probably the most popular place on the plaza for lunch, perhaps more for its visibility and colorful decor than for its food, which is fine, but not overwhelming. The tables, covered in white and blue and laid with blue-and-white local crockery, are usually packed, and plates of food disappear as fast as the waiters can bring them. You can get anything from soup to roast chicken, enchiladas, tacos, steak, and dessert, as well as frosty margaritas.

Sotavento Restaurant Bar Galería. Juárez 8. Main courses $3–$8. No credit cards. Tues–Sun 1pm–midnight. ITALIAN/INTERNATIONAL.

Formerly La Taberna, this restaurant's stylish decor has paintings decorating the walls and a variety of linen colors on the table. The menu features many Italian specialties—try the deliciously fresh spinach salad and the large pepper steak for a hearty meal; or the Spaghetti Barbara with poblano peppers and avocado for a vegetarian meal. To find it from the Plaza Borda, walk downhill beside the Hotel Agua Escondida, then follow the street as it bears left (don't go right on Juan Ruíz de Alarcón) about a block. The restaurant is on the left just after the street bends left.

Sr. Costilla's. Plaza Borda 1. ☎ **762/2-3215.** Main courses $4–$11. AE, MC, V. Daily 1pm–midnight. INTERNATIONAL.

The offbeat decor here at "Mr. Ribs" includes a ceiling festooned with the usual assortment of cultural flotsam and jetsam. Several tiny balconies hold a few minuscule tables that afford a view of the plaza and church (it's next to Santa Prisca, above Patio de las Artesanías), and these fill up long before the large dining room does. The menu is typical Andersonese (like the other Carlos Anderson restaurants you may have encountered in your Mexican travels), with Spanglish jive and a large selection of everything from soup, steaks, sandwiches, and spareribs to desserts and coffee. Wine, beer, and drinks are served.

INEXPENSIVE

Restaurante Ethel. Plazuela San Juan 14. ☎ **762/2-0788.** Breakfast $1.50–$2.25; main courses $2–$6; comida corrida $4.25. No credit cards. Daily 9am–10pm (comida corrida served 1–5pm). MEXICAN.

A family-run place opposite the Hotel Santa Prisca on the Plazuela San Juan, 1 block from the Plaza Borda, Restaurante Ethel is kept clean and tidy, with colorful cloths on the tables and a homey atmosphere. The hearty daily comida corrida consists of soup or pasta, meat (perhaps a small steak), dessert, and good coffee.

TAXCO AFTER DARK

Paco's is just about the most popular place overlooking the square for sipping, nibbling, mingling, and people watching, all of which continues until midnight daily. And there's Taxco's dazzling disco, **Windows,** high up the mountain in the **Hotel Monte Taxco** (☎ 762/2-1300). The whole city is on view from there, and music runs the gamut from the hit parade to hard rock. For a cover of $5, you can dance away Saturday night from 9pm to 3am.

Completely different in tone is **Berta's,** next to the Santa Prisca Church. Opened in 1930 by a lady named Berta, who made her fame on a drink of the same name (tequila, soda, lime, and honey), it's traditionally the gathering place of the local gentry and not a few tourists. Spurs and old swords decorate the walls, and a saddle is casually slung over the banister of the stairs leading to the second-floor room where tin masks leer from the walls. A Berta (the drink, of course) costs about $2; rum, the same. Open daily from 11am to around 10pm.

National drinks (not beer) are two-for-one nightly between 6 and 8pm at the terrace bar of the **Hotel Rancho Taxco Victoria,** where you can also drink in the fabulous view.

San Miguel de Allende & the Colonial Silver Cities

6

Mexico's historic silver mining cities—San Miguel, Querétaro, San Luis Potosí, Guanajuato, and Zacatecas—lie northwest of Mexico City in the rugged mountains of the Sierra Madre Occidental. The towns feature beautiful colonial settings with backdrops of high mountains, an ideal climate, a great variety of handcrafts, good food, and many memorable sites to visit. San Miguel's cobblestone streets and fanciful church reflect the mood of this casual and quirky town—which for many years has supported a resident population of artists, artisans, and expatriates. Guanajuato and Zacatecas, with their winding streets and alleys and diminutive plazas, seem more like medieval towns than colonial cities. Querétaro and San Luis Potosí, meanwhile, are impressive cities of broad plazas and monumental public buildings.

Travel through these parts is easy and relaxing, there is little crime, and the inhabitants are a very gracious people. The region is a good introduction to Mexico's interior and is well suited for a family vacation. The locals are very family-oriented; they warm up quickly when they see a family traveling together. If you go, take your swimsuit—the region is full of hot mineral springs developed into wonderful bathing spots.

The colonial silver cities are close to the capital by modern standards, but at the time of their founding this land was the frontier. The great pre-Columbian civilizations of central Mexico never established more than a tenuous sway here. Mountainous and arid, this was the land of the Chichimeca, the nomadic tribes that would periodically swoop down and attack the cities and settlements that lay to the south and east. But once the conquistadors gained control of central Mexico, they turned their attention toward this region in hopes of finding precious metals to make their fortune. They found gold in considerable quantities, but silver proved to be present in such vast amounts that it soon made Mexico world-famous for its silver mines.

For three centuries of colonial rule, much of the great wealth of these mines went to build urban centers of impressive and lasting architecture. It's wonderful to walk leisurely around in these cities and see them, not one building at a time, but viewed as a whole. Until recently, most of the region had been spared immoderate growth because many industries that otherwise would have sprung up here were drawn away by Mexico City's disproportionate influence. Life remains very civilized here, meaning it is savored and enjoyed at a relaxed pace and not lived at break-neck speed. Many people in these cities have ancestors who lived here a least a century ago. Residents maintain a broad range of kin, friends, and acquaintances. I've walked down streets with locals who would give their warmest greeting to every third or fourth person we passed. Countless times, I've had conversations in which I mention someone from a completely different context, only to hear "Oh, he's married to my cousin." This is the kind of intimate and affecting world you enter when you visit this part of Mexico.

EXPLORING THE SILVER CITIES   All of the silver cities are easily visited from Mexico City, but the order in which they are presented here does not reflect the only possible itinerary. Simply decide which, if not all, of the cities you wish to visit. Querétaro is included as a day-trip from San Miguel, not because it doesn't have plenty to offer the visitor (it has one of the most beautiful town centers in the country), but because it is so close to San Miguel and has few good hotels in its historical center.

If you are traveling by car, the roads in the region are fairly good, though mountainous. Driving within these towns, however, can be maddening due to bizarre traffic circulation (especially true of Guanajuato and Zacatecas). If you ever have difficulty navigating your way into the center of town, simply hire a cab to lead the way. Parking can also be a problem; this is why we have included, when possible, good motels where you can park and leave your car for the entire length of your visit. If you prefer to travel by bus, you are in luck. This region is blessed with good bus stations and frequent and inexpensive first-class buses connecting all these cities, which tend to be only 2 to 3 hours apart from each other. This is probably the easiest way to see the region.

As to how best to allot your time, much depends on your particular interests. As a bare minimum, I recommend 2 to 3 days each in San Miguel de Allende, Zacatecas, and Guanajuato. But these cities are best seen at a leisurely pace. Part of their considerable charm is their relaxed way of life.

1 San Miguel de Allende

180 miles NW of Mexico City; 75 miles E of Guanajuato

San Miguel de Allende delightfully mixes the best aspects of small-town life with the cosmopolitan pleasures of the big city. Still, San Miguel is quite assuredly a small town. It is the smallest of the cities included in this chapter and perhaps the most relaxed of all of them. But it offers such a variety of good restaurants, good music, and wonderful shops and galleries that urbanites can find themselves quite at home here—hence the town's escalating popularity with sophisticated international tourists. Like Taxco, it has been declared a national monument. Virtually all the buildings you see in the central part of the village date from the colonial era, and newer buildings are required by law to conform to existing architecture. Because so much of the city remains as it was during the days of silver mining, many of the hotels, restaurants, and shops along its cobbled streets are housed in beautiful mansions dating from those years.

San Miguel has a large community of Americans, some retired, some attending art or language school, and some who have come here to live simply and follow their creative muses—painting, writing, and sculpting. The center of this community is the public library in the ex-convent of Santa Ana. This is a good place to find information on San Miguel or just to sit around in the patio and read magazines and books. The little American colony gets along very well with the townsfolk and has had surprisingly little effect on the way of life here.

One of the most notable aspects of San Migueleña society is the number of festivals it celebrates; it is known far and wide for these, in a country that needs only the barest of excuses to hold a fiesta. The town celebrates so many festivals that the odds of coming upon one by accident are decidedly in the visitor's favor. Most of these celebrations are of a religious character and are the perfect opportunity for both social activity and religious expression. People still practice Catholicism with great fervor here—going on one or another religious pilgrimage, attending all-night vigils, ringing church bells at the oddest times throughout the night (something that some visitors admittedly might not find so amusing). See the short list of festivals you might come upon.

ESSENTIALS

GETTING THERE & DEPARTING   By Plane   The two major airports used by travelers to San Miguel are the Mexico City airport, which is 3½ hours away but with direct bus transportation straight from the airport to nearby Querétaro, and the León-Bajío airport, 2 hours away. There is also a small airport in Querétaro, 1 hour away.

Arriving: AeroPlus buses (☎ 5/567-8033 in Mexico City) leave the Mexico City airport for Querétaro about every 2 hours and cost $15. From there you need to take a local bus ($3) to San Miguel. When you arrive in Querétaro, go out the front door and cross to the terminal in front. Buses for San Miguel leave about every 15 minutes.

By Car   From Mexico City: You have a choice of two routes for the 3-hour trip—via a Querétaro bypass or via Celaya. The former is shorter—take Highway 57, a four-lane freeway, north toward Querétaro. Past the Tequisquiapan turnoff, there is an exit on the right marked "A [TO] SAN MIGUEL." This toll road bypasses Querétaro and crosses Highway 57 again north of town. Here it narrows to two lanes and becomes Highway 111. Some 20 miles farther is San Miguel.

From Guanajuato: The quick route is to go south from the city a short distance on Highway 110, then east on a secondary, though paved, road passing near the village of Joconoxtle. The long but scenic route is northeast on Highway 110 through Dolores Hidalgo, then south on Highway 51. If you drive the scenic route, take a break and experience a slice of rural Mexican life, especially near the small community of Santa Rosa, where small restaurants serve the local brew, mezcal de la sierra, and Mexican specialties such as chorizo, dried meat, and Mexican-style barbecue.

By Bus   To/From Mexico City: It's a 4-hour trip to San Miguel from Mexico City's Terminal Norte (ticket area 6), on a first-class bus (with one stop in Querétaro). Primera Plus, Satelite, Elite, ETN, and Omnibus de Mexico all have three to five deluxe buses per day. Flecha Amarilla and Herradura de Plata have buses that leave almost every half hour (most are first-class). Make sure that your bus is a *directo.*

To/From Guanajuato: Flecha Amarilla has nine buses a day to San Miguel.

To/From Querétaro and Dolores Hidalgo: You can choose between Satelite, Flecha Amarilla, and Herradura de Plata. Among the three of them, there is a bus leaving every 15 minutes.

To/From Nuevo Laredo: Transportes de la Frontera/Estrella Blanca has a first-class bus that leaves Nuevo Laredo at 6:30pm, arriving in San Miguel de Allende between 7 and 8am the next morning. The return bus leaves San Miguel at 7pm and arrives in Nuevo Laredo between 7 and 8am the next morning. You can buy a ticket through Greyhound.

Arriving: The bus station is 1½ miles west of town on the westward extension of calle Canal. Taxis are cheap and available at all hours.

VISITOR INFORMATION   The **tourist information office** is inside the Ayuntamiento building (☎ 415/2-0900). The English-speaking staff has maps and information about attractions in San Miguel and the surrounding region. It's open Monday through Friday from 9am to 7pm and Saturday from 10am to 2pm.

CITY LAYOUT   San Miguel's beautiful central square, **El Jardín,** is shaded by perfectly groomed Indian laurel trees. The center of city life, it's the point of reference for just about all directions and is bounded by Correo (Post Office Street), San Francisco, Hidalgo, and Reloj.

GETTING AROUND   In San Miguel there are regular inner-city buses but no colectivo minivans. Buses to outlying villages (Taboada thermal pool, for example) leave from around the **Plaza Cívica.** Taxis to places inside town should not cost more than $2 or $3.

FAST FACTS: San Miguel de Allende

American Express   The local representative is **Viajes Vertiz,** Hidalgo 1 (☎ 415/2-1856; fax 415/2-0499), open Monday through Friday from 9am to 2pm and 4 to 6:30pm, and Saturday from 10am to 2pm.

Area Code   The telephone area code is **415.**

Climate   San Miguel can be warm in summer and cold enough for wool clothing at night and early morning in winter.

Communication and Shipping Services   San Miguel has several. All offer pretty much the same services: mail boxes, telephone messages, long distance, packing and shipping, and a Laredo address. **Border Crossings** at Correo no. 19, Int. 2 (☎ 415/2-2497) is one. **Pack 'n' Mail** has sizable space at calle Jesús 2-A (☎/fax 415/2-3191). Their hours are generally weekdays from 8:30am to 5pm and Saturday from 9am to 3pm.

Currency Exchange   Two convenient places near El Jardín change money. **Divisas 2 Mil,** Correo 13, is open Monday through Friday from 8am to 6pm and Saturday and Sunday from 9am to 2pm. **Lloyds,** at San Francisco 33, is open Monday through Friday from 9am to 3pm.

Drugstore   For medicine needs try the **Farmacia Agundus** (☎ 415/1-1198), Canal 26 at Macías. It's open daily from 10am to midnight.

E-mail   Try **Estacion Internet** at Recreo 11, second floor (☎ 415/2-7312). These guys are highly competent and offer a few other computer-related services as well—open 9am to 2pm and 4 to 8pm.

Elevation   San Miguel sits at 6,143 feet.

Library   The **Biblioteca Pública** (Public Library), Insurgentes 25 (☎ 415/2-0293), is the gathering point for the American community. It has a good selection of books in Spanish and English. It's open Monday through Saturday from 10am to 2pm and 4 to 7pm.

Newspaper   The English-language paper, *Atención,* has local news as well as a full list of what to see and do.

Parking   San Miguel is congested, and street parking is scarce. *Note:* White poles and/or signs at the ends of streets mark the stopping point for parking (so that other cars can make a turn). Police are vigilant about parking order and ticket with glee.

Population   San Miguel has 60,000 residents.

Post Office   The correo (post office) and telegraph office are at calle Correo 16, open Monday through Friday from 8am to 7pm and Saturday from 9am to 1pm.

Seasons   Because of the fast freeway access from Mexico City, San Miguel is becoming popular with weekenders from the capital. Arrive early on Friday or make

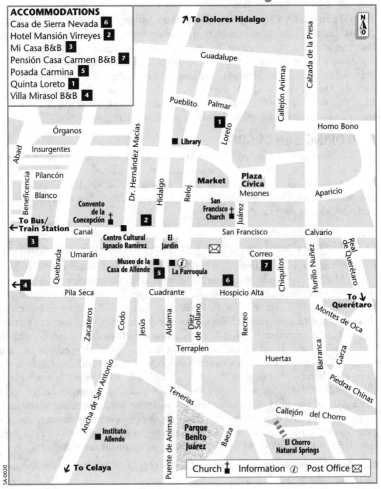

a reservation ahead of time if you're there for a weekend. There's also a squeeze on rooms around the **Christmas** and **Easter** holidays and around the feast of San Miguel's patron saint on **September 29.** October and November are slack months, as are January and February.

SPECIAL EVENTS & FESTIVALS

San Miguel celebrates between 30 and 40 festivals in the year. These are just the standouts:

January 17 is the **Blessing of the Animals.** In the morning, locals bring their decorated pets and farm animals to the town's churches to be doused with holy water. The 1st Friday in March is used to celebrate **Our Lord of the Conquest**—the day before is filled with music, fireworks, and decorated teams of oxen. After a celebratory mass, there is dancing by the *concheros.* Two weeks before Holy Week, there is the procession of **Our Lord of the Column.** Between then and Easter Sunday there are many and altars are set up in honor of **La Virgen Dolorosa.** In May there is the

Festival of the Holy Cross. In June around Saint Anthony's Day there is the ✪ **Fiesta de los Locos** ("The Madmen Festival"), when many dress up in carnavalesque costumes and go cavorting about the center of town. In August begin the preparatory festivals for the September festival of San Miguel's **patron saint,** which go on for a week. There are parades, fireworks, and bands for all of those days. In November you have the **Day of the Dead** and then there are the **Christmas fiestas.** In addition to all of this, you have the **Chamber Music Festival** in summer, **Jazz Music Festival** in the fall, and a couple of art fairs that occur on varying dates.

EXPLORING SAN MIGUEL

It's difficult to be bored in San Miguel. The shopping is excellent, and you'll run out of time before you can try all the good restaurants. San Miguel is ideally situated for side trips to Dolores Hidalgo, Querétaro, Guanajuato, and San Luis Potosí. This is also one of Mexico's most popular towns for Spanish and arts classes, just in case you find a lull during your vacation.

THE TOP ATTRACTIONS

✪ **La Parroquia.** South side of El Jardín. No phone. Free admission. Daily 6am–9pm.

La Parroquia, so different from all other Mexican churches, has become the emblem of San Miguel. The church is an object of great pride to the citizenry and a source of great discomfort for architectural purists. It was originally built in the colonial style, but in the late 19th century a local builder named Zeferino Gutiérrez reconstructed the towers and facade. Gutiérrez was supposedly unlettered, but he had seen pictures and postcards of European Gothic churches and worked from these alone, drawing his designs in the sand. I find the finished product fascinating—a very personal vision of the Gothic style that owes more to the builder's imagination and fancy than to the European churches that were its inspiration. The inside is not nearly as much fun as the outside; the church was looted on several occasions during times of social upheaval, and this kind of art criticism puts a damper on commissioning any more costly paintings and decoration. Still, there are things to see. My favorite, and one often missed, is the crypt beneath the altar. You get to it through a door on the right side. If it's locked, ask around for someone to open it (usually for a small tip).

Museo de la Casa de Allende. Southwest corner of El Jardín. No phone. Free admission. Tues–Sun 10am–4:30pm.

The birthplace of San Miguel's most famous son, the independence leader Ignacio Allende, has been converted into a museum housing colonial-era furnishings and historical documents. Inside you'll see fossils, pre-Hispanic pottery, and a biography of Allende. Exhibits also detail the fight for independence, which began in nearby Dolores Hidalgo. In 1810, Allende plotted with Padre Miguel Hidalgo of Dolores and Josefa Domínguez of neighboring Querétaro, among others, to organize for independence from Spain. Both Allende and Hidalgo were executed in Chihuahua a year later.

Centro Cultural Ignacio Ramírez (Bellas Artes/El Nigromante). Hernández Macías 75. ☎ **415/2-0289.** Free admission. Mon–Fri 9am–9pm; Sat 10am–7pm; Sun 10am–2pm.

Housed in the former Convento de la Concepción (1755), between Canal and Insurgentes, 2 blocks west of El Jardín, the center is a branch of the Palacio Bellas Artes of Mexico City. Built on two levels surrounding an enormous courtyard of lush trees, it consists of numerous rooms housing art exhibits and classrooms for drawing, painting, sculpture, lithography, textiles, ceramics, dramatic arts, ballet, regional dance, piano, and guitar. The grand mural by David Alfaro Siqueiros and memorabilia of the artist are worth seeing. A bulletin board lists concerts and lectures given at this

Learning at the Source: Going to School in San Miguel

San Miguel is known for its Spanish-language and art schools. These institutions cater to Americans and often provide a list of apartments from which to choose for long-term stays. Rates for language classes are usually by the hour and get lower the more hours you take. If you want a chance to practice, it's best to look for small classes.

Instituto Allende put San Miguel on the map back in the 1930s. It was opened by Enrique Fernández Martínez, the former governor of the state of Guanajuato, and Stirling Dickinson, an American. Today, it thrives in the 18th-century home of the former counts of Canal, a beautiful place with big grounds, elegant patios and gardens, art exhibits, and murals. You can wander past class-rooms where weavers, sculptors, painters, ceramicists, photographers, and students are at work. Much of the craft work that San Miguel is known for sprang from this institute. The language office maintains a list of local families who rent rooms for stays of a month or more. The institute offers an MFA degree, and the school's credits are transferable to at least 300 colleges and universities in the United States and Canada; noncredit students are also welcome. Instituto Allende can be found or contacted at calle Ancha de San Antonio 20, 37700 San Miguel de Allende, Guanajuato (☎ 800-319-3624 in the U.S., or 415/2-0190; fax 415/2-4538; www.ugto.mx/info_turi_gto/sma/allende/new.html).

Academia Hispano Americana has a reputation for being a comparatively tougher language school with an emphasis on grammar as well as conversation. Classes are limited to 12 people. The work is intensive, and the school is partic-ularly interested in students who plan to use Spanish in their future careers and in people who sincerely feel the need to communicate and understand the other Americas. The school has a continuous program of study of 12 4-week sessions for 35 hours a week. Private lessons cost $10 per hour. It's a member of the International Association of Language Centers. A brochure is available from the Registrar, Academia Hispano Americana, Mesones 4 (Apdo. Postal 150), 37700 San Miguel de Allende, Guanajuato (☎ 415/2-0349; fax 415/2-2333). Office hours are Monday through Friday from 8am to 1pm and 3:30 to 6:30pm.

Inter/Idiomas primarily uses a conversational method. Classes are small, usu-ally composed of three students and a teacher. Each student's level of Spanish is evaluated before placement in a class. You can begin any time and pay by the hour or week or for private lessons. Information is available from Inter/Idiomas School of Languages, 20 de Enero Sur no. 42, Col. San Antonio, 37750 San Miguel de Allende, Guanajuato (☎ 415/2-1415; http://unisono.net.mx/inter; E-mail: interid@unisono.net.mx).

Also see the **Centro Cultural Ignacio Ramírez,** in "The Top Attractions," above.

institute and elsewhere in the city. The pleasant restaurant, Las Musas, serves Mexican and Italian food daily between 10am and 8pm. Before you leave, notice the magnifi-cent dome behind the convent. It belongs to the Iglesia de la Concepción and was designed by the same unschooled architect who designed the Parroquia (see above).

MORE ATTRACTIONS

The **Centro de Crecimiento,** Zamora Ríos 6, a donation-supported school for hand-icapped children, conducts regular Saturday tours (10am to 1pm) to interesting places in the countryside around San Miguel. Donations are $15 per person; tickets are available at Casa Maxwell.

The **House and Garden Tour,** sponsored by the Biblioteca Pública, is a regular attraction in San Miguel. The tour opens the doors of some of the city's most interesting colonial and contemporary homes. Tours leave Sunday at 11:30am from the library at Insurgentes 25 (☎ 415/2-0293) and last about 2 hours. A $15 donation goes to support various library projects benefiting the youth of San Miguel.

The **Travel Institute of San Miguel,** Cuna de Allende 11 (☎ 415/2-1630 or 415/2-0078, ext. 4; fax 415/2-0121), holds walking tours, field trips to colonial and archaeological sites, adventure and nature tours, visits to artisans at work, and workshops in marketing, among other things. The office is open Monday through Saturday from 9am to 2pm and 4 to 7pm.

A couple of the most enjoyable walks in town are to the lookout point **El Mirador,** especially at sunset, which colors the whole town and the lake beyond, and to **Parque Juárez,** a lovely, spacious, and shady park.

One great way to see the mountains around San Miguel is by **Hire-a-Horse.** For $35 per person, they will provide a horse, a guide, refreshments, and a 2- to 4-hour outing. Inquire at the Casa Mexas restaurant, Canal 15 Centro, or call ☎ 415/2-3620 for information and reservations.

NEARBY ATTRACTIONS

Just outside of San Miguel are several hot mineral springs that have been made into wonderful bathing spots. The most popular of these is **La Taboada,** located just 5 miles outside San Miguel.

These mineral springs lie in the direction of the sanctuary of **Atotonilco el Grande** (9 miles away), a complex of chapels, dormitories and dining rooms, and a fascinating church. World Monuments Watch has placed it among the world's most important buildings meriting preservation, and at present it's undergoing some painstaking renovation. It was founded in 1740 in an isolated spot in the countryside by Father Luis Felipe Neri Alfaro, an austere priest and mystic. Alfaro thought the area in dire need of a religious presence, since many in the surrounding area would gather at the springs to bathe publicly and immodestly—leading to what Alfaro considered to be depraved behavior. He commissioned a local artist to paint instructive murals to illustrate verses that the father himself wrote, with much emphasis on the dangers that lie in wait for the human soul. The murals and verses cover the entire ceiling and walls and are fascinating, which adds brightness and color to an otherwise dark and severe structure. Alfaro chose this particular spot to build his sanctuary because it was here that he was granted an ecstatic vision of Christ. The location proved propitious; it was here, 70 years later, that the Virgin of Guadalupe first became a symbol of Mexican identity. In 1810, Miguel Hidalgo declared independence in Dolores and marched for San Miguel with his impromptu insurrectionist army. En route he passed by Atotonilco and used the church's image of the Virgin of Guadalupe as his banner, declaring her the protectress of the revolutionary forces.

The church and adjoining buildings still function throughout the year as a religious retreat for people who come from all over the country for a week of prayer, penance, and mortification. These spiritual exercises are conducted quietly with no public display. You can get there by taking the "El Santuario" bus at the market. It passes every hour on the hour, and goes through Taboada on its way to Atotonilco.

Querétaro and **Dolores Hidalgo** are easy day-trips from San Miguel. See "Getting There & Departing," above, for transportation information, and "Side Trips from San Miguel de Allende," below.

At least one company uses San Miguel as a base for trips to see the **monarch butterflies, which are 5 hours away** in the state of Michoacán (see chapter 7, "Tarascan Country"). The **Travel Institute of San Miguel** (see "More Attractions," above) offers this two-day trip, which involves an overnight stay at Angangueo, between November and March for $170.

SHOPPING

In general, stores in San Miguel open at 9am, close between 2 and 4pm, and reopen from 4 to 7pm. Most are closed Sunday. The town is known for its metalwork—brass, bronze, and tin—and for its textiles and pottery, especially Talaveraware (made in the nearby town Dolores Hidalgo). Shopping, however, is by no means limited to those items. Ask to see the charming children's art for sale at the public library; the proceeds help support the children's program.

The **Mercado de Artesanías** is located along the walkway below the market; here you can bargain with the vendors during most daylight hours. For metalwork try **Zacateros,** a street of shops selling pewter, tin, and ironwork.

ART

Galería San Miguel. Plaza Principal 14. ☎ **415/2-1046.**

The best local art gallery is run by a charming, stylish Mexican-American woman, a well-known art dealer. She exhibits the work (in all price ranges) of local residents as well as artists from all over Mexico. The gallery is open Monday through Friday from 10am to 2pm and 4 to 7pm, Saturday from 10am to 2pm and 4 to 8pm, and Sunday from 10am to 2pm.

CRAFTS

Casa Anguiano. Corner of Canal and Macías. ☎ **415/2-0107.**

The inventory of colorful Michoacán foot-loomed fabric by the bolt is extensive, as is the inventory of blown glass, copper, brass, and Nativity scenes. It's open Monday through Saturday from 9:30am to 8:30pm and Sunday from 9:30am to 6:30pm.

Casa Cohen/Herco. Reloj 12. ☎ **415/2-1434.**

Located half a block north of the square, this is the place to find brass and bronze bowls, plates, house numbers, doorknobs, knockers, and drawer pulls, as well as other utilitarian objects made of iron, aluminum, and carved stone. There's also hand-carved wood furniture. It's open the usual San Miguel hours (see the introduction to "Shopping," above).

Casa María Luisa. Canal 40, at Zacateros. ☎ **415/2-0130.**

If your interests are architectural or decorative, you may enjoy browsing here. Among the crowded aisles, you'll find the store's own line of furniture, as well as decorative ironwork, lamps, masks, pottery, and more. The staff will pack and ship your treasures. Hours are Monday through Saturday from 9am to 2pm and 4 to 7pm, and Sunday from 11am to 5pm.

Casa Maxwell. Canal 14. ☎ **415/2-0247.**

This is a beautiful house and garden with every imaginable craft displayed, some high-priced, others fairly reasonable. It's well worth a look around. Hours are Monday through Saturday from 9am to 2pm and 4 to 7pm.

Mesón de San José. Mesones 38. ☎ **415/2-3848.**

This lovely old mansion, across from the market between Juárez and Nuñez, houses a dozen shops and a restaurant. All are open daily from 10am to 6pm.

Veryka. Zacateros 6A. ☎ **415/2-9114.**

This small shop has a very complete collection of folk art from Mexico and the rest of Latin America, as well as fabrics, wall hangings, clothing, and jewelry. It's open standard hours (see the introduction to "Shopping," above), plus Sunday from 11am to 3pm.

MASKS

Tonatiu Metztli. Umarán 24, near Zacateros. ☎ **415/2-0869.**

This shop is a must for the mask collector. In addition to the masks hanging all over the shop walls, owner Jorge Guzman offers fine Huichol art and has a private collection of masks he shows by appointment. It is open normal San Miguel hours (see the introduction to "Shopping," above) plus Sunday from 11am to 3pm.

WHERE TO STAY

There are plenty of accommodations for visitors in San Miguel; for a long stay (more than a month), check at the instituto or the academia (see "Learning at the Source: Going to School in San Miguel," above) and other bulletin boards around town for lists of apartments or rooms to rent. Most apartments are equipped with kitchens and bedding; some come with maid service. San Miguel is becoming popular as a weekend getaway for residents from the capital, and at least one hotel raises rates on weekends. Secured parking is at a premium; if it's not provided by your hotel, you'll pay around $12 to $15 daily in a guarded lot.

VERY EXPENSIVE

✪ **Casa de Sierra Nevada.** Hospicio 35, 36600 San Miguel de Allende, Gto. ☎ **800/ 223-6510** in the U.S., 888/341-5995 (toll-free direct to hotel), or 415/2-07040. Fax 415/2-2337. 37 units. TV TEL. $190 double; $230–$351 suite. AE, CB, DISC, MC, V. Free parking. Children 16 and older accepted.

This is a handsome hotel made of several adjoining 16th-century town houses with private entrances and secluded patios, a restaurant, bar, and outdoor pool. In a hotel of this sort, details count; here they are handled masterfully. Each room has its own design, and most have private patios or secluded entrances. All have decorative antiques and beautiful tile floors with area rugs. Guests receive a fruit basket, flowers, and daily paper. The newest house, with its own restaurant, is near the Parque Juárez. The hotel, a member of the Small Luxury Hotels of the World, is 2 blocks southeast of El Jardín, between Diez de Sollano and Recreo.

Dining/Diversions: The elegant restaurant features foods from around the world (jacket and tie recommended evenings); reservations are required for dinner. Patio bar.

Amenities: Laundry and room service; concierge; tour service; limousine transportation from airports in either Mexico City or León; 60-foot heated swimming pool; full-service spa with massage, facials, body scrub, herbal wraps, manicure and pedicure, skin analysis, waxing, and other treatments. Equestrian Center, with supervised trail rides and instruction on the nearby 500-acre ranch belonging to the hotel owner. Guests can go there to walk, hike, jog, or bird-watch. Balloon rides are available.

MODERATE

Mi Casa B&B. Canal 58 (Apdo. Postal 496), 37700 San Miguel de Allende, Gto. ☎ **415/ 2-2492.** 2 units. $65 double; $85 suite. Rates include breakfast. No credit cards.

This charming colonial home is very comfortable, and in a convenient location. The hostess, a gracious expatriate named Carmen McDaniel, is an excellent source of information on San Miguel and the surroundings. Both rooms have a garden-style bathroom, and the junior suite has a sitting area and fireplace. The flower-filled rooftop patio is a wonderful place for cocktails (honor bar) or morning coffee. Breakfast includes eggs any style and fruit. This B&B is about 3 blocks west of the Jardín on calle Canal, across from Posada de las Monjas.

✪ **Pensión Casa Carmen B&B.** Correo 31 (Apdo. Postal 152), 37700 San Miguel de Allende, Gto. ☎/fax **415/2-0844.** 11 units. $62 double. Rates include breakfast and lunch. No credit cards.

This is a small, quiet pensión that gets a lot of return guests year after year. Casa Carmen is perfect for the person looking for comfortable, casual surroundings, and good food. The landlady is a most gracious hostess. The rooms, all of which have gas heaters, face a lovely colonial courtyard with plants and a fountain; meals are served in a European-style common dining room. You can reserve rooms by the day, week, or month (monthly rates are discounted). The hotel is 2½ blocks east of the Jardín near the corner of Recreo.

Villa Mirasol B&B. Pila Seca 35, 37700 San Miguel de Allende, Gto. ☎ **415/2-1564.** 8 units. TV TEL. $88–$100 double. Rates include breakfast and high tea. AE, MC, V.

This delightful bed-and-breakfast, previously known as Casa de Lujo, has individually decorated Mexican-style rooms with bright colors, private entrances, and a patio area. Short-term membership is available at a local country club for swimming, golf, and tennis. The hotel is 5½ blocks southwest of the Jardín between Quebrada and Ladrillera.

INEXPENSIVE

Hotel Mansión Virreyes. Canal 19, 37700 San Miguel de Allende, Gto. ☎ **415/2-3355** or 415/2-0851. Fax 415/2-3865. 26 units. TV TEL. Weekends $50 double; weekdays $41 double. AE, CB, DISC, MC, V.

Previously called the Hotel Central, the Mansion Virreyes has lost none of its old charm, and some judicious remodeling has improved the comfort of the 350-year-old building. It was once a private home and became the first hotel in San Miguel following the Mexican Revolution. Located half a block west of the Jardín, it is nestled among shops and restaurants. The rooms are simple but very comfortable, and the pleasant restaurant serves good, moderately priced meals. There is a TV bar behind the restaurant.

Parador San Sebastián. Mesones 7, 37700 San Miguel de Allende, Gto. ☎ **415/2-0707.** 13 units. $21 double. No credit cards. Parking $3 daily.

The San Sebastián is a colonial-era convent-turned-inn with spacious rooms that face a lovely courtyard and garden. The rooms are simple and comfortable, and the rooftop is great for enjoying morning coffee, sunning, or taking in the city views. They don't take reservations here, so you have to try your luck. The hotel is 3½ blocks northeast of the Jardín between the San Francisco Church and calle Hurillo Nuñez.

✪ **Posada Carmina.** Allende 7, 37700 San Miguel de Allende, Gto. ☎ **415/2-0458.** Fax 415/2-0135. 10 units. $42 double. No credit cards.

Located on the south side of the plaza next to the Parroquia is this charming and friendly colonial-era mansion that is over 200 years old. Rooms are nicely furnished and built around a central courtyard full of orange trees and flowering vines. Around the upstairs terrace are two comfortable living rooms, chairs, and chaise lounges. A restaurant serving good food is open in the courtyard daily from 8am to 9:30pm.

Quinta Loreto. Calle Loreto 15, 37700 San Miguel de Allende, Gto. ☎ **415/2-0042.** Fax 415/2-3616. 40 units. $30–$35 double. Weekly and monthly discounts available. AE, MC, V. Free parking.

This motel is a good place to stay whether traveling by car or not. It has a large pool, a tennis court, a lovely garden, an excellent restaurant, a friendly atmosphere, and simple but pleasant rooms, many of which come with TV and telephone. Meals are good, laundry services a bargain. Make reservations—the Loreto is very popular and is often booked months in advance. Outsiders can come for breakfast ($2 to $3) and for lunch ($6). The motel is on a small street below the market off calle Loreto, about 6 blocks from the main square.

WHERE TO DINE

Because of its large expatriate colony and popularity with Mexican tourists, San Miguel has the most varied and highest-quality restaurants of any small city in Mexico. New places open all the time, and restaurants only a few years old close down overnight. Besides those listed below, one of the city's top dining restaurants is the **Casa de Sierra Nevada** (mentioned above), serving Mexican and French cuisine; main courses are $15 to $35.

MODERATE

Casa Mexas. Canal 15 Centro. ☎ **415/2-0044.** Main courses $3.50–$12; children's plate $2.75–$3.50. AE, MC, V. Daily 1–10:30pm. MEXICAN/TEX-MEX.

A riot of baskets and colorful piñatas hang from the ceiling of this place, above white tables and chairs and white napkins stuffed into whimsical papier-mâché napkin rings. As the name suggests, it serves a blend of Mexican and Tex-Mex. Prices are moderate for the large portions of well-seasoned food. This is a place kids will like, and it offers meals with children in mind. It's across from the Casa Maxwell, half a block west of the Jardín on Canal. The room in back functions as the town's sports bar with a big-screen TV.

✪ **La Lola.** Ancha de San Antonio 31. ☎ **415/2-4050.** Main courses $10–$12. AE, MC, V. Tues–Sun 1pm–1am. INTERNATIONAL/NOUVELLE.

La Lola's owner lured away Sierra Nevada's well-known chef, Bryan Dupnik, with promises that he would be allowed free rein. It has worked out well. The menu is never the same but is always interesting and imaginative. The dish that seems to have become the de facto standard is the breast of duck with polenta and a honey-shallot vinaigrette sauce. La Lola, like so many other places in San Miguel, makes use of its wall space to display the works of local artists. You will find it just across the street from the Instituto Allende.

Mama Mía. Umarán 8. ☎ **415/2-2063.** Breakfast $1.25–$3; main courses $4–$15. AE, MC, V. Daily 9am–11:30pm (bar until 2am Thurs–Sat). ITALIAN.

This restaurant has become something of a nighttime institution in San Miguel. You can dine alfresco in a tree-shaded brick courtyard and enjoy live folkloric Latin American and flamenco music nightly. In addition to the Italian specialties, there are Mexican and American specials and a large breakfast menu. There's also a nice selection of coffee-based drinks prepared with Kahlúa or brandy. At night, it's one of the most popular spots in town (see "San Miguel After Dark," below). The restaurant is 2 blocks southwest of El Jardín between Jesús and Macías.

✪ **Restaurant/Bar Bugambilia.** Hidalgo 42. ☎ **415/2-0127.** Antojitos $3–$6; main courses $5–$12. AE, MC, V. Daily noon–10:30pm. MEXICAN TRADITIONAL.

The food and the atmosphere make this a place to linger over a meal. It's delightful, with its tree-filled patio, soft music, good service, and such specialties as *pollo en pulque* (pulque-marinated chicken) and *chiles en nogada* (pepper stuffed with meat, raisins, cream, and pomegranates). To find it from the Jardín, walk 2½ blocks north on Hidalgo.

INEXPENSIVE

✪ **Cafe Santa Ana.** Insurgentes 25 (in the rear patio of the library). ☎ **415/2-7305.** Main courses $3–$5. No credit cards. Mon–Fri 9am–6pm; Sat 9am–2pm. LIGHT/ VEGETARIAN.

This is a cool, secluded spot where you can eat well for little money. The cafe specializes in light (but not plain) meals. The menu changes weekly, but a couple of constants that are favorites include the baguette de berenjena (grilled eggplant and peppers with cheese on a baguette with pesto mayonnaise) and spinach salad with avocado and pralines and a cumin dressing. The menu always has chicken breast prepared in some fashion: a typical dish would be with green pipian, or with mushrooms and a white-wine sauce.

✪ **El Correo.** Correo 23. ☎ **415/2-0151.** Breakfast $2–$4; main courses $3–$6. MC, V. Thurs–Tues 9am–9:30pm. AMERICAN/MEXICAN.

This small restaurant has a well-conceived menu. Breakfast is very popular here; try the migas natural for a hearty breakfast with eggs, onions, tomatoes, and chile or ranchero sauce; or you can tank up on apple fritters, orange juice, or fruit with yogurt and granola. For homesick stomachs, at lunch there's fried chicken, stuffed baked potatoes, and soup. If you feel like Mexican fare, try the tortilla soup and the red enchiladas. As its name might suggest, this restaurant is just opposite the post office. half a block east of the Jardín.

✪ **El Pegaso Café and Deli.** Corregidora 6 at Correo. ☎ **415/2-13-51.** Breakfast $2.50–$5; soups, salads, sandwiches $2.75–$6.50; main courses $6–$10. MC, V. Mon–Sat 8:30am–10pm. INTERNATIONAL.

This is a popular place with many local expatriates. It's decorated in a cheerful, casual style, and people here are very friendly and helpful to travelers. There is a wide array of dishes offered, from eggs Benedict for breakfast to pad Thai for lunch to chile en nogada for dinner. This is a good place to get light fare, such as soups, salads, sandwiches, and nachos. The restaurant is 1 block east of the Jardín.

Fonda Mesón de San José. Mesones 38. ☎ **415/2-3848.** Breakfast $2.25–$3.25; soup $2.50; main courses $5–$8. MC, V. Daily 8am–10pm. INTERNATIONAL/VEGETARIAN.

Located in the midst of several interesting shops, this open-courtyard restaurant is considered the best in town by many locals. It's an excellent place, whether merely to take a break (the coffee is excellent) or to have an entire meal. The intriguing menu is so tempting it may be hard to decide between the vegetarian plate with Yucatecan tacos and vegetarian pasta or a main course of chicken curry or the pasta with chicken and spinach in a cream sauce. Everything is fresh and attractively presented.

Olé Olé. Loreto 66. ☎ **415/2-0896.** Main courses $4–$10. No credit cards. Daily 1–9pm. MEXICAN.

Festive and friendly, this small restaurant is a riot of red and yellow banners, colorful streamers, and bullfight memorabilia. The limited menu features delicious beef or chicken fajitas, shrimp brochettes, and quesadillas. The place is wildly busy at lunch. To find it, walk north from the San Francisco Plaza on Juárez and cross Mesonas; jog left then right where the street becomes Loreto and continue for 3 or 4 blocks—it's on the left with a small sign.

Villa de Ayala. Ancha de San Antonio 1. ☎ **415/2-3883.** Breakfast $2–$3.50; main courses $2.75–$5; comida corrida $3.50. No credit cards. Daily 8am–10pm (comida corrida served 1–5pm). MEXICAN.

This restaurant is a favorite with families and students from the Instituto Allende. Reached by a staircase, the place consists of one large room with the kitchen to one side and a video nook in a corner. Piñatas and balloons help dress up the plain tables and brick walls. Memelas, a house specialty, consists of large thick tortillas with beans, salsa, cheese, and a choice of meat on top. Recorded music during the day is lively but not loud; there is occasional live music on weekends. The restaurant is across the street and a few doors toward town from the Instituto; it's a long walk or short taxi ride from the Jardín.

SAN MIGUEL AFTER DARK

Local regulations make existence easier for restaurant/bars than for simple bars—so many live-music acts are found in restaurants. Clubs and discos here tend to spring up and then die off quickly. To find out which is the disco of the moment, just ask around. Also, check out a copy of the local paper, *Atención,* for other events that might be happening while you're in town. A couple of the restaurants mentioned above are very popular nightspots: part of **Mama Mía's** is a bar that has salsa and jazz bands on the weekends. There is a $4 cover. During the week people go there to enjoy the late afternoon/early evening from its rooftop terrace. **La Lola** is popular with the alternative crowd and gets some blues and jazz acts Wednesday through Sunday. If you don't feel like hearing music, how about a drink and a movie? The **Cine Bar** at the Hotel Jacaranda, calle Aldama 53, shows recently released American movies on a large screen TV and includes popcorn and a drink with the $4 price of admission. Waiters come to your table with drinks and will bring the dinner menu as well. Listed below are some of the other nightspots in San Miguel.

La Fragua. Cuna de Allende 3. ☎ **415/2-1144.** No cover.

San Miguel's artists and writers drift in and out all afternoon and evening at this popular, long-standing gathering spot. Housed in an old colonial home, the restaurant has tables around the courtyard where Mexican musicians perform every evening from 8 to 10:30pm. Several other dining rooms and a comfy bar that resembles a living room are off the courtyard. The food is standard Mexican fare and not the main attraction. This is more the kind of place you would choose when you want to have a drink and relax with some friends in an uncrowded space, and listen to acoustic music. Bar hours are daily from noon to 2am, and the restaurant serves from 1pm to midnight.

Pancho y Lefty's. Mesones 99. No phone. Cover $5 in high season, free in low season.

This longtime bar is a perennial favorite. Entertainment runs the spectrum here from reggae to rock and country to blues and jazz. It's open from 7pm to 3am Wednesday, Friday, and Saturday. Wednesday-night happy hour lasts the whole evening: two drinks for the price of one.

Tío Lucas. Mesones 103 at Macías. ☎ **415/2-4996.** No cover.

Though this is a full-service restaurant specializing in steaks (good food), it's most popular in the evenings when you can hear excellent blues, jazz, and bossa nova between 8:30pm and midnight. The restaurant opens at 1pm, and there are several cozy, dark dining rooms and a small bar with seating. Happy hour is from 6 to 8pm.

SIDE TRIPS FROM SAN MIGUEL DE ALLENDE
DOLORES HIDALGO: FINE POTTERY—AND SHRIMP ICE CREAM?

Dolores Hidalgo, often referred to as simply "Dolores" by locals, lies 25 miles to the north of San Miguel on Highway 35; from there you turn west to go to Guanajuato. It was in Dolores that Fr. Miguel Hidalgo de Costilla declared Mexico's independence, giving the famous *grito* from the steps of the parish church. It is also famous for its ice cream and pottery. Parlors around the main square sell exotic ice-cream flavors— tequila, shrimp, and alfalfa are just a few shocking examples—as well as mango, gua- nabana, and other more familiar standbys. It all started 30 years ago on a dare, and then caught on for the notoriety it gave to the parlors. Go in and ask for some impos- sibly bad flavor like cilantro-mezcal-chocolate-chip or chicken mole swirl, and, without batting an eye, they'll tell you they're fresh out and to come back tomorrow.

The **Talavera** pottery produced in Dolores is handsome and diverse. It's much cheaper, more available, and less traditional than the Talavera from Puebla. You can find all kinds of things: from sink basins to napkin rings. As you approach Dolores from San Miguel you will see some of the showroom/warehouses of the factories. Pull over and pay them a visit. Prices here are considerably lower than in San Miguel. Tiles from Dolores are also very popular. Below is a short list of Talavera factories.

The stores below are listed in the order you will find them on the road from San Miguel.

Talavera San Gabriel. 14 miles from San Miguel on the outskirts of Dolores. ☎/fax **418/ 2-0139.**

Here, you'll find a large selection of ceramic-framed mirrors and drawer knobs, tiles, sinks, candelabra, casseroles, bowls, platters, anthropomorphic jars and candlesticks, ginger jars, and tissue holders. If you get the bus to let you off here, you'll need a taxi to continue into town. Open Monday through Saturday from 8am to 5pm and Sunday from 8am to 2pm.

Talavera A. Mora. Farther along the road to Dolores and past the Talavera San Gabriel. ☎ **418/2-1884.**

This is another factory outlet; you will see this signature pottery in many San Miguel stores. Items include dinnerware with a blue-and-yellow fish motif, chicken and frog planters, and much more. Open Monday through Saturday from 9am to 6pm and Sunday from 10am to 6pm.

Talavera Cortés. Distrito Federal 8, at Tabasco. ☎ **418/2-0900.**

Homeowners in San Miguel frequent this store for sinks, tiles and knobs, towel racks, and paper holders. You can watch craftspeople at work upstairs and browse the large showroom/warehouse downstairs. Open Monday through Friday from 7am to 4:30pm and Saturday from 7am to 1pm.

Azulejos Talavera Vazquez. Puebla at Tamaulipas. ☎ **418/2-0630.**

Like the other places I've listed, this is a cornucopia of ceramics, from giant ginger jars to ashtrays and sinks. This store has good prices on colorful ceramic picture frames in many sizes. It's about 2 blocks south of the church with the gold and green tile dome. Open Monday through Saturday from 8am to 7pm and Sunday from 10am to 3pm.

Bazar El Portón. km 3.5 Calzada de los Héroes. ☎ **418/2-2229.** Fax 418/2-0894.

Located on the right side of the road as you enter Dolores, this is the place for archi- tectural antiques and new carved-wood furniture. Among the jumble are horse-head table pedestals, old wooden mining troughs, wagon wheels, rearing stallions, old and new carved doors, and carved sofas. Open Monday through Friday from 7am to 4:30pm and Saturday from 7am to 1pm.

QUERÉTARO: A HISTORIC COLONIAL CITY

If you're driving north from Mexico City, you'll pass Querétaro (altitude 5,873 ft.; population 455,000; 138 miles north of Mexico City and 63 miles from San Miguel) on your way to San Miguel. The capital of the state of Querétaro, it's a prosperous city with a fascinating history. It was here that the peace of the Mexican War was sealed with the Treaty of Guadalupe Hidalgo. Emperor Maximilian was executed here in 1866, and, finally, the present Mexican constitution was drafted here in 1916.

Arriving by bus from San Miguel, you'll be at the new bus station, south of town. Take a taxi for around $5, or catch the bus marked "CENTRO." For information on traveling directly to Querétaro from the Mexico City airport, see the feature "Take a Luxury Bus Direct to Your Destination from the Mexico City Airport" in chapter 3.

ORIENTATION　　There is a good **tourism information office** at Pasteur Norte no. 4, just off the main plaza on the north side, which is open daily from 8am to 8pm. The office offers tours of the city via trolley bus that cost $2 and last about an hour. Tours leave at 9, 10, and 11am, and 4, 5, and 6pm.

A STROLL AROUND THE HISTORIC CENTER　　Start your visit to the city from the pedestrian-only Plaza de la Independencia (also called Plaza de Armas). It's the historic heart of the city and the most beautiful plaza, graced by manicured umbrella-shaped trees, a beautiful fountain, and colonial-era stone mansions now housing government offices.

Of all the colonial-era buildings surrounding Plaza de la Independencia, the **Casa de la Corregidora/Palacio Municipal** is the most famous. It's a magnificent building, and tourists are welcome to step inside the interior courtyard. On the second floor is the Corregidora's room—where, while under lock and key, Doña Josefa Ortiz de Domínguez (the wife of the chief magistrate) managed to send a warning to Father Hidalgo that the conspiracy to declare Mexico's independence from Spain had been discovered. Hidalgo got the message and hurried to publicly shout "independence" in Dolores Hidalgo. For her actions, Domínguez was imprisoned several times between 1810 and 1817. She died impoverished and forgotten, although today she is much revered. She was the first woman to appear on a Mexican coin—the 5-centavo piece, minted from 1942 to 1946.

Across the plaza from the Corregidora's house is the **Mesón Santa Rosa,** a magnificent hotel and restaurant (see "Where to Dine," below) in a colonial-era building. Stretching out from the plaza are several flower-decorated, pedestrian-only brick streets, known as *andadores,* leading to other well-tended plazas and a few shops and restaurants.

Just west of the plaza, at Andador Libertad 52, is the **Casa Queretana de Artesanía,** run by the state (☎ **42/14-1235**). Walk through the rooms with nicely displayed weavings, regional clothing, pottery, onyx, hand-carved furniture, opals, and jewelry incorporating other semiprecious stones—all from Querétaro and all for sale. There is, as well, a nice quantity of items from other regions of Mexico. It's open Monday through Friday from 10:30am to 2pm and 3:30 to 8pm, Saturday from 10:30am to 9pm, and Sunday from 10:30am to 5pm.

Walking 2 blocks west of the Plaza Independencia on Cinco de Mayo is Querétaro's **Jardín Obregón** (also known as Jardín Benito Zenea). It's bounded by Juárez and Corregidora running north and south and by Madero and 16 de Septiembre running east and west. Across the street is a triangular-looking plaza known as the **Jardín de la**

Querétaro

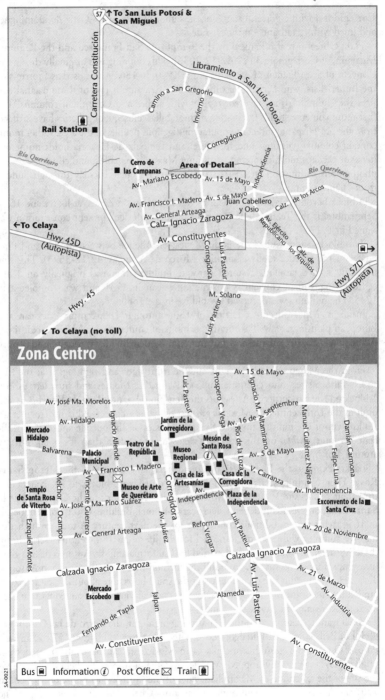

Zona Centro

Bus 🚏 Information ⓘ Post Office ✉ Train 🚆

SA-0021

189

Corregidora, with a graceful statue of the famous Doña Josefa Ortiz de Domínguez and lined with restaurants on the far side.

Plaza Obregón is also flanked by the **Templo de San Francisco** and the **Regional Museum,** at Corregidora 3 (☎ **42/12-2036**). This building was originally the Grand Convent of Saint Francis of Assisi, begun in 1540. In 1861 it was used as a fortress by the Imperialists, who backed Maximilian. The structure is one of those palatial edifices the "humble" friars favored, replete with arches and Corinthian columns. The first room you enter holds fascinating memorabilia. Subsequent galleries have artifacts from the pre-Hispanic and contemporary indigenous peoples of the area. Other rooms contain colonial paintings and furniture, and the Sala de Historia holds numerous items of perhaps morbid interest, including Maximilian's coffin and countless period photographs. Admission is $2; free on Tuesday. It's open Tuesday through Sunday from 10am to 7pm.

A block beyond the Jardín de la Corregidora and Jardín Zenea, at Juárez and 16 de Septiembre, is the **Teatro de la República,** where Mexico's present constitution was signed in 1917.

Two blocks southwest of the Jardín Zenea, on Allende between Madera and Pino Suárez, is the architecturally fascinating **Museo de Arte** (☎ **42/12-3523**). This fine museum is in a fabulous restored baroque building that was originally an 18th-century Augustinian convent. Construction began in 1731 and was completed in 1745. The building was occupied by soldiers in the 1860s.

Inside is a magnificent collection of 16th- through 18th-century Mexican and European paintings, as well as rotating exhibits of contemporary Mexican paintings. Admission is $2; free on Tuesday. The museum is open Tuesday through Sunday from 11am to 7pm.

From the Museo de Arte go right out the front door and right again at the first street, Pino Suárez, and continue for 3 blocks to E. Montes and turn left. Ahead 1 block on the left corner at Arteaga is the **Templo de Santa Rosa de Viterbo.** It was built in the 18th century by Mexico's greatest religious architect, Eduardo Tresguerras. It's known for the unusual inverted flying buttresses on the outside and the magnificent baroque *retablos* on the inside. It's closed more often than it's open, but try around 4 or 5pm.

Backtracking to the Plaza de la Independencia, take a break in the **Mesón Santa Rosa.** Then continue straight ahead on Cinco de Mayo 8 blocks to M. Najera and turn right 2 blocks to V. Carranza, where you turn left 1 block to the **Convento de la Santa Cruz,** on avenida Independencia near Carmona. Building of this convent began in 1654, with major additions continuing for the next century. A tour through this massive complex will give you some feel for the life of an 18th-century cleric. From these cloisters, Fr. Junípero Serra departed for California, and Fr. Antonio de San Buenaventura stopped on his way to found the mission that was to become San Antonio, Texas. Hours are a bit irregular, but ask at the small bookstore about fascinating tours guided by one of the brothers. Nearby is a spectacular view of the aqueduct that supplied the convent and city at that time.

You'll want to take a taxi to the final touring highlight, the **Cerro de las Campanas** ("Hill of Bells"), avenida Hidalgo, between Tecnológico and Highway 57 to San Luis Potosí. One of the most historic places in Mexico, it can be easily spotted from Highway 57 as a giant hill topped by a titanic statue of Juárez. Just below the statue is the site of the execution of Maximilian, ruler of the short-lived Empire of Mexico. In 1901 the Austrian government built an Expiatory Chapel on the side of the hill. The caretaker (who is rarely around to let you in) takes pleasure in showing you the three small columns in front of the altar, the stones that mark the exact spot where Maximilian and his generals, Miramón and Mejía, stood before the firing squad. Maximilian was in the middle, but gave that place of honor to Miramón; then he gave each member of the firing squad a gold coin so they would aim at his chest instead of his head (they complied). It's open daily from dawn to dusk.

One final place of interest is the **Lapidaria de Querétaro,** at 15 de Mayo and Peralta (☎ **42/12-0030**). Since the region is known for its opal mines, it would be a shame not to see the best in stones and mountings at this trustworthy store. Many of the stones you see here come from the family opal mine, La Catalina, 25 miles from Querétaro. But they also sell agate, turquoise, topaz, and lapis lazuli in stones or gold or silver mountings. Besides seeing craftspeople working the raw stones in the store's adjacent workshop, visitors are invited to tour the mines as well. The only charge is for gasoline. The trip starts at 9am and returns to Querétaro by around 1pm. Arrange the mine trip *a day or so in advance* of your intended visit. If you're eating at the Mariposa Restaurant, the store is only a block and a half away.

Where to Dine

Cafetería La Mariposa. Ángela Peralta 7. ☎ **42/12-1166.** Main courses $3–$5. Daily 8am–9:30pm. MEXICAN.

Look for the wrought-iron butterfly sign when you turn left on Peralta (2 blocks north of Jardín Obregón) to find one of the city's most popular restaurants. This is a good place for light lunches—enchiladas, a fruit salad, or a club sandwich—or pastries, ice cream, and coffee. Next door is a sweet shop featuring such irresistible candied figs, peaches, bananas, and papaya. You can also order these delicacies in the restaurant, as the two enterprises are under the same management.

✪ **Restaurant/Hotel Mesón Santa Rosa.** Pasteur 17. ☎ **42/14-5681.** Fax 42/12-5522. Main courses $3–$15. AE, MC, V. Daily 7:30am–11pm. MEXICAN NOUVELLE.

The state-owned Mesón Santa Rosa is the most elegant and refreshing place to eat in the historic center and also the loveliest hotel in Querétaro. Once an 18th-century stable, then quarters for Juárez's troops and later a tenement house, it became a hotel and restaurant in the late 1980s. Inside the elegant dining room to the right, the color scheme is rose and white, and the deep-rose walls are stenciled to resemble white doilies. Tables are covered with white linen, and waiters wear black jackets and bow ties. Often, there's a pianist or violinist in the adjacent bar. The international menu emphasizes Mexican cuisine.

If you want to stay overnight in this historic city, the Santa Rosa is the place—but you should make reservations *about 4 weeks in advance.* Junior suites cost $70 double and master suites run $85 to $90.

2 Guanajuato

221 miles NW of Mexico City; 35 miles SE of León; 58 miles W of San Miguel de Allende; 130 miles SW of San Luis Potosí; 102 miles N of Morelia; 175 miles SE of Zacatecas

If you're going to Mexico to lose yourself, you'll have no problem doing so on the streets of Guanajuato (gwah-na-*hwa*-toh). They seem designed to confuse and get you walking in circles. At times it seems like the Twilight Zone. A couple of times I've heard about someone passing by a lovely shop intending to return later, but never being able to find it again. And you're easily distracted, because the town is so photogenic; everywhere you look is postcard material. Most buildings are of an irregular and asymmetrical shape. None of the churches, despite the best efforts of their builders, has two matching towers, which adds to their charm.

Guanajuato is one of Mexico's hidden gems; uncovered by relatively few foreign tourists, it's a popular weekend trip for people from Mexico City. Clean and beautifully preserved, Guanajuato should be high on your list of the finest places to visit in Mexico.

Founded in 1559 around the Río Guanajuato, its narrow, winding streets reflect the past meanderings of the river. Floods plagued the town, and finally the river was diverted, leaving an excellent bed for what has now become a subterranean highway with cantilevered houses jutting over the roadway. Today, Guanajuato seems like an old Spanish city that has been dumped lock, stock, and barrel into a Mexican river valley.

During the colonial era, Guanajuato was a fabulously rich town with world-famous mines such as La Valenciana, Mineral de Cata, and Mineral de Rayas—mines that earned their owners titles of nobility. Guanajuato was one of Mexico's most important colonial cities (along with Querétaro, Zacatecas, San Miguel, and San Luis Potosí) from the 16th through the 18th centuries. Their mines produced a third of all the silver in the world; and like the gold-rush towns in the United States, they bloomed with elaborate churches and mansions, many in the Moorish style. Guanajuato remains the state's capital though it is not its largest city.

The name Guanajuato is a Spanish adaptation of the Tarascan word *guanaxuato,* meaning "hill of frogs." To the Tarascans, the rocks above town appeared to be shaped like frogs. This was especially significant since in the Tarascan culture the frog represented the god of wisdom.

ESSENTIALS

GETTING THERE & DEPARTING **By Plane** Air access to this region has improved with more frequent flights in and out of the León/Bajío airport, 17 miles from downtown Guanajuato ($15 to $20 for a taxi). American Airlines's local telephone number is ☎ **01-800/9-0460;** Continental's is ☎ **473/18-5254.** Aerolitoral (☎ **473/16-6226;** 473/14-0574 at the airport), an Aeromexico affiliate, flies to León from Guadalajara, Mexico City, Monterrey, and Tijuana. Mexicana (☎ **473/ 14-9500;** 473/13-4550 at the airport) flies in from Guadalajara, Mexico City, and Tijuana. Taesa (☎ **473/14-3660** or 473/12-3621) arrives from Morelia, Mexico City, and Tijuana.

There are airline ticket offices in León and at the León/Bajío airport. Flights can be arranged through **Viajes Frausto,** Obregón 10 (☎ **473/2-3580**) in Guanajuato, or other travel agencies.

By Car From Mexico City there are two routes. The faster route, although it may look longer, is Highway 57 north and northwest to Highway 45D at Querétaro, west through Salamanca to Irapuato, where you follow Highway 45 north to Silao and then take Highway 110 east. That route is a four-lane road almost all the way. The other route continues north on Highway 57 past Querétaro, then west on Highway 110 through Dolores Hidalgo, and continues to Guanajuato. From San Luis Potosí, the quickest way to Guanajuato is through Dolores Hidalgo.

By Bus The bus station in Guanajuato is 3½ miles southwest of town. From Mexico City's Terminal del Norte, you'll have no trouble finding a bus to Guanajuato. Flecha Amarilla, Estrella Blanca, ETN, and Primera Plus all have express buses to Guanajuato. You shouldn't have to wait more than a half hour. Make sure the bus you board is a *directo.*

From San Miguel de Allende, Flecha Amarilla makes six trips "Vía Presa" (the short route) to Guanajuato. Herradura de Plata also follows that route. Both also have service from the other silver cities, Guadalajara, Morelia, and elsewhere.

ORIENTATION   Arriving by Plane   Note that the only transportation from the León/Bajío airport, 17 miles from downtown Guanajuato, is **private taxi.** You arrange and pay for the cab ($18) inside the airport. There is no colectivo service.

Arriving by Car   Try not to lose your sanity while finding a place to park. Such a winding, hilly town as Guanajuato defies good verbal or written directions. Just be alert for one-way streets, and after winding around through the subterranean highway a bit, you'll get enough bearings to park. If in doubt, follow the signs TEATRO JUÁREZ or JARDÍN UNIÓN, which will get you to the center of town, where you can park and collect your wits. In fact, consider parking your car until you leave town, since the frustration of parking and driving in the city could spoil your visit.

Arriving by Bus   The modern station is about 3½ miles southwest of town on the road to Celaya. Cabs are easy to come by and should cost about $4.

Visitor Information   The **tourist information office** is at Plaza de la Paz 14, across from the basilica (☎ 473/2-0397). It's open Monday through Friday from 8:30am to 7:30pm and Saturday, Sunday, and holidays from 10am to 2pm. It has an English-speaking staff. Here, you can get information and a detailed free map of the city with a map of the entire state of Guanajuato on the back.

City Layout   Guanajuato is a town of narrow streets, alleys, and stairs that wend their way to small, picturesque plazas. The hilly terrain and tangle of streets are difficult to represent on a map, the one contained here or any other. You'll soon learn they aren't drawn to scale, nor is every narrow street or connecting stairway shown. The best way to get oriented to the major sights is to get the *"Mapa Turístico"* published by the state tourism office. It is a representation of the city as it would be seen from the overlook at Pípila's statue. Then, get to the overlook (see "El Pípila" among the attractions listed below) and compare what you see with the map. This will set your bearings vis-à-vis the major landmarks.

The **Jardín Unión** is the true heart of the city—the place where students, locals, and visitors gather. Facing the Jardín from the direction of El Pípila are both the **Teatro Juárez** and **Templo de San Diego.** From this plaza you are within walking distance of all the major sights.

If you're driving, an excellent way of getting to see the city is to drive the **Scenic Highway** (Carretera Panorámica) that circles the town from up above. It starts north of town off the road to Irapuato, passes El Pípila, continues south to the dam (Presa de la Olla), and finally loops around north again to the Valenciana Mine and Church.

Getting Around   Walking is the only way to really get to know this labyrinthine town. For longer stretches, taxis are reasonably priced and abundant, except between 2 and 4pm when office workers are trying to get home for the midafternoon meal. As usual, you should establish the price before setting out.

FAST FACTS: Guanajuato

Area Code   The telephone area code is **473.**

Climate   This high-elevation city has mild temperatures in summer, but in winter it can dip to freezing.

Elevation   Guanajuato sits at 6,724 feet.

Language School   Every year the positive experiences at the Instituto Falcón prompt numerous readers to write letters of commendation—more than we receive about any other place in the country. The **Instituto Falcón** (Callejón de la Mora 158, 36000 Guanajuato, Guanajuato; ☎ 473/2-3694) is directed by Jorge Barroso, who provides skilled and dedicated tutors for those wishing hourly or intensive studies at all levels. He can also arrange for boarding with local families.

Population   Guanajuato has 75,000 residents.

Post Office   The correo (post office) is located on the corner of Navarro and Carcamanes, near the Templo de la Compañía.

Seasons   Guanajuato has several high seasons during which hotel, and in some cases restaurant, prices go up and unreserved rooms are hard to find. The high seasons are Christmas, Easter Week, all of the Cervantino Festival (mid-Oct), and July and August when Mexicans and Europeans vacation.

SPECIAL EVENTS & FESTIVALS

Every year, from about October 7 to 22, the state of Guanajuato sponsors the **Festival Cervantino** (International Cervantes Festival), 2 weeks of performing arts from all over the world. In recent years the festival has featured marionettes from the Czech Republic, the Eliot Feld Ballet from New York, the Kiev Ballet, and a host of Mexican artists. The shows are held in open plazas and theaters all over town. Book rooms well in advance during the festival; if Guanajuato is full, consider staying in nearby San Miguel de Allende.

For ticket information and a schedule contact Festival Cervantino, Mineral de Cata s/n (Ex Cava), 36060 Guanajuato, Guanajuato (☎ 473/2-0959). Once you know the schedule, you can order tickets through **Ticketmaster** in Mexico City (☎ 5/325-9000). Keep your confirmation number; you'll need it to pick up your tickets in Guanajuato.

EXPLORING GUANAJUATO
THE TOP ATTRACTIONS

✪ **Iglesia de San Cayetano (Templo de la Valenciana).** Valenciana. Free admission. Daily 9am–6pm.

The magnificent church, completed toward the end of the colonial period, was built by the owner of the nearby La Valencia mine. It is the finest example of the Mexican baroque style known as *churrigueresque*. Inside is a dazzling affair filled from floor to ceiling in guilded carvings and retablos. The best time to see it is in the midafternoon, when the sunlight pours through the windows illuminating the golden carvings. The famous silver mine of the same name is said to have produced a fifth of the silver circulating in the world from 1558 to 1810. The mine was closed about 40 years ago but then reopened, and a caretaker is there to show you the eight-sided vertical shaft (1,650 ft. deep) and the once-grandiose courtyard. You can take a look down the long mine shaft (but you can't go down) where they extract silver and about 50 other minerals and metals. Silver products from this mine are sold in the adjoining silver shop. Across the road from the church is the FONART store and a wonderful restaurant called La Casa del Conde de la Valenciana. For more information on these, see "Shopping" and "Where to Dine," below.

✪ **Teatro Juárez.** Jardín de la Unión. ☎ **473/2-0183.** Admission $1.75, 50¢ additional with still camera, $2 additional with video camera. Tues–Sat 9am–1:45pm and 5–7:45pm; Sun 9am–1:45pm.

Built in 1903 during the opulent era of the Porfiriato, this theater is now the venue for many productions, especially during the Cervantino Festival. Outside are bronze sculptures of lions and lanterns, but the interior is the best part. It is done up lavishly in rich fabrics and ornate decorations. Box seats rise up four stories along the walls of the theater, and there is not a bad seat in the house.

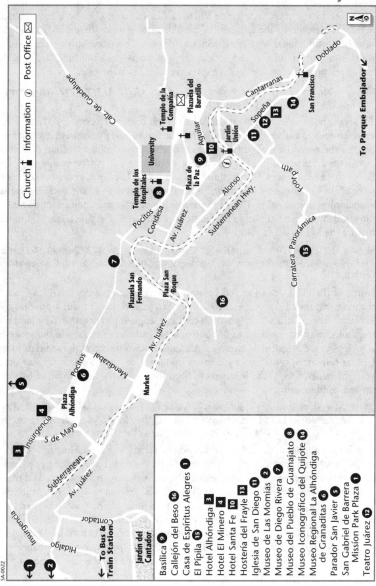

Church ✝ ■ Information ⓘ Post Office ⊠

Calz. de Guadalupe

✝ Templo de la Compañía

Plazuela del Baratillo

Doblado

Cantarranas

San Francisco

Sopeña

Aguilar

Jardín Unión

University

Plaza de la Paz

ⓘ

Templo de los Hospitales

Pocitos

Condesa

Av. Juárez

Alonso

Subterranean Hwy.

Foot Path

Carretera Panorámica

Plazuela San Fernando

Plaza San Roque

Mendizabal

Av. Juárez

Pocitos

Market

Plaza Alhóndiga

Insurgencia

5 de Mayo

Subterranean

Av. Juárez

Contador

Hidalgo

Insurgencia

To Bus & Train Station

Jardín del Cantador

To Parque Embajador ↙

List of numbered locations:

Basílica ⑨
Callejón del Beso ⑯
Casa de Espíritus Alegres ①
El Pípila ⑮
Hotel Alhóndiga ③
Hotel El Minero ④
Hotel Santa Fe ⑩
Hostería del Frayle ⑬
Iglesia de San Diego ⑪
Museo de Las Momias ②
Museo de Diego Rivera ⑦
Museo del Pueblo de Guanajuato ⑧
Museo Iconográfico del Quijote ⑭
Museo Regional La Alhóndiga de Granaditas ⑥
Parador San Javier ⑤
San Gabriel de Barrera Mission Park Plaza ①
Teatro Juárez ⑫

SA-0022

✪ **Templo de Cata.** Carretera Panorámica. Free admission. Daily 9am–5pm.

Up above the city, perched on the mountain to the north, is a small, elaborate "miners'" church. Cata is also the name of the mine nearby and the barrio that surrounds the church. A lovely baroque facade, with but one tower standing, decorates the outside, but what is most interesting are all the testimonials that line the inside walls. Most of these take the traditional form of small square sheets of metal with painted scenes (in a primitive folk style) and explanatory text describing the miracles performed by the church's Señor de Villaseca. "El Trigueñito," as he is affectionately called in reference to the darkness of his skin, is a popular figure in Guanajuato, especially with miners and truck and taxi drivers. The testimonials—examples of which you may find in craft and antique shops in town—are a touching display of the highly personal relationship these people have with "El Trigueñito."

Museum Birthplace of Diego Rivera. Calle Positos 47. ☎ **473/2-1197.** Admission $1. Tues–Sat 10am–6:30pm; Sun 10am–4pm.

This is the house where the artist Diego Rivera was born on December 8, 1886. It has been refurbished and made into a museum. The first floor is furnished as it might have been in the era of Rivera's birth. Upstairs there's a pretty good collection of Rivera's early works. He began painting when he was 10 years old and eventually moved to Paris, where he became a Marxist during World War I. The house contains sketches of some of the earlier murals that made his reputation, but most of the works on display are paintings from 1902 to 1956. On the third floor is a small auditorium where lectures and conferences are held. The house is north of the Plaza de la Paz, 1½ blocks beyond the Museo del Pueblo.

Museo del Pueblo de Guanajuato. Calle Positos 7. ☎ **473/2-2990.** Admission $1.75. Tues–Sat 10am–6:30pm; Sun 10am–2:30pm; open all day during the Cervantino Festival.

North of the Plaza de la Paz and before the Rivera Museum lies this 17th-century mansion that once belonged to the Marqués San Juan Rayas. It holds a priceless collection of more than 1,000 colonial-era civil and religious pieces gathered by local distinguished muralist José Chávez Morado. Chávez murals can be seen in this museum as well as in the Regional Museum La Alhóndiga down the street. In addition to the Chávez collection, contemporary displays upstairs show Mexican artists. Every other year, the museum hosts the Biennial of Diego Rivera, a truly fine exhibit of Mexico's up-and-coming artists.

✪ Regional Museum La Alhóndiga de Granaditas. Mendizabal 6. ☎ **473/2-1112.** Admission $2 ($4 extra for video camera), free for students with ID cards, free for all on Sun. Tues–Sat 10am–2pm and 4–6pm; Sun 10am–3pm.

Continuing a long block farther on the same street as the Rivera Museum, you'll see the huge Alhóndiga on the left (the entrance is on Positos). The Alhóndiga de Granaditas was built between 1798 and 1809 as the town granary. It was so splendid that it was called El Palacio del Maiz (the Corn Palace). The Spanish took refuge here in 1810 when El Pípila and company laid siege and burned down the doors. A year later, however, the tide had turned, and the heads of the revolutionary leaders Hidalgo, Allende, Aldama, and Jiménez were in iron cages hanging from the four corners of the building, where they remained from 1811 to 1821 to remind the populace of what happens to those who rebel. The name plaques below the cornice on the four corners of the building commemorate the four heroes.

The Alhóndinga is now one of the better museums in Mexico. There are two levels with rooms off the courtyard. You'll see numerous pre-Columbian relics, including pots, decorative seals and stamps, terra-cotta figurines, and stone implements. The lower level (on which you enter) has rooms filled with regional crafts and the pre-Hispanic art collection of José Chávez Morado—the artist responsible for the splendid murals on both stairwells (and whose colonial-era collection is in the Museo del Pueblo de Guanajuato). Mexico's most complete collection of pre-Hispanic seals was donated to the museum by American archaeologist Frederick Field. The museum contains Chupícuaro ceramics dating from A.D. 350 to 450 from the southeast part of the state; they were saved when the Solis Dam was constructed in 1949 and are a type of ceramics rarely seen in Mexico. A long corridor contains bronze masks of the revolutionary heroes as well as an eternal flame in their honor.

El Pípila. Free admission. Daily 24 hours. Go via taxi, automobile, or bus (marked "PÍPILA") or on foot up a rugged winding pathway. Walk up Calle Sopeña from the Jardín Unión and turn to the right up Callejón del Calvario. A sign on the wall reads AL PÍPILA ("To El Pípila").

This is the best vantage point in all of Guanajuato for photographs—the whole city unfolds below you with great shots at every angle. The statue is the city's monument to José de los Reyes Martínez and you can climb inside if you wish (they charge a tiny fee to climb the tiny staircase, but there is nothing to be gained by doing this). Nicknamed El Pípila, he was a brave young miner who, on Hidalgo's orders, set fire to the Alhóndiga de Granaditas, the strategically situated grain warehouse in which the Royalists were hiding during the War of Independence. On September 16, 1810, Hidalgo, a radical priest who had appealed for Mexico's independence from Spain, led an army that captured Guanajuato. In this bloody battle, 600 inhabitants and 2,000 Indians were killed, but the Revolution was on its way. Guanajuato became the rebel capital; however, its history was short—10 months later Hidalgo was captured and shot in Chihuahua, and his head was sent to Guanajuato to be exhibited.

Today, El Pípila's statue raises a torch high over the city in everlasting vigilance; the inscription at his feet proclaims AÚN HAY OTRAS ALHÓNDIGAS POR INCENDIAR— There are still other *alhóndigas* to burn."

۞ Museo de Los Momias (Mummy Museum). Calzada del Panteón. ☎ **473/ 2-0639.** Admission $2.50, $1 extra with still camera or $2 with video camera. Daily 9am–6pm. At the northwestern end of town is the Calzada del Panteón, which leads up to the municipal cemetery—a steep climb on foot. For this trip, Guanajuato's cab drivers invariably tend to charge what the traffic will bear. The bus labeled "PRESA-ESTACIÓN," which runs along the Plaza de la Paz/Sopeña, will take you to the foot of the cobbled hill.

First-time visitors find this museum either grotesque or incredibly fascinating (or both): Mummified remains of Guanajuato's residents, some of whom are garbed in tattered clothing from centuries past, are on display in tall showcases and glass caskets. Dryness, plus the earth's gases and minerals, have caused decomposition to halt in certain sections of the *panteón*. Because of space limitations, people are buried for only 5 years; then, if the relatives can't continue to pay for the graves, the bodies are exhumed to make room for more. Those on display, however, were exhumed between 1865 and 1985. The mummies stand or recline in glass cases, grinning, choking, or staring. It's impossible to resist the temptation to go up and look at them (everybody does), and this is the only graveyard I've seen with souvenir stands next to the main gate, selling sugar effigies of the mummies. If you catch a school group tour (and you know Spanish), you'll hear macabre discussions of the gruesome deaths more than a few of the residents here suffered (much of which you should probably chalk up to haunted-house hyperbole).

Museo Iconográfico del Quijote. Manuel Doblado 1. ☎ **473/2-6721.** Free admission. Tues–Sat 10am–6:30pm; Sun 10am–2:30pm.

There are only a few truly universal characters in the world of literature: Hamlet, Faust, Don Juan, and Don Quijote come to mind. Writers far and wide have taken up these characters and reworked their stories. But Don Quijote more than any other has become a favorite subject of artists. The list includes Dalí, Picasso, Miró, Raul Angiano, José Guadalupe Posada, Daumier, José Moreno Carbonero, and Pedro Coronel. This museum, a long block southeast of the Jardín Unión and past the Hostería del Frayle, holds a fascinating collection of art based upon Don Quijote—all Quijote, all the time! Particularly forceful are the sculptures and murals, but it is the sheer variety of forms that artists have used to depict Don Q that makes a stroll through this museum, constructed around a lime-green courtyard, so entertaining.

MORE ATTRACTIONS

The **Church of San Diego,** on the Jardín Unión, stands almost as it did in 1633, when it was built under the direction of Franciscan missionaries. After a 1760 flood that nearly destroyed it, reconstruction was completed in 1786; half the funds were given by the Count of Valenciana. The pink cantera-stone facade is a fine example of the Mexican churrigueresque style.

The **Plazuela del Baratillo,** just off the Jardín Unión, has a beautiful fountain (a gift from Emperor Maximilian) at its center, and you'll always find people sitting around it peacefully, some in the shade and others in the sun. It's name derives from the fact that it used to hold a weekly market (*tianguis*), and the vendors would yell *"¡barato!"* ("cheap"). The Plazuela San Fernando is larger and has a stone platform where very often there are local Mexican dances, with the younger generation decked out in bright costumes.

The magnificent **university** was founded in 1732, but its entrance was rebuilt in 1945 in a stately manner, and the building now dominates the whole town. The university is just behind Plaza de la Paz, and it's open every day. Visitors are welcome.

The **Church of the Compañía,** next to the university, was built in 1747 by the Jesuit order as the biggest of their churches at that time. It is distinctly churrigueresque on the outside, but the interior, which was restored in the 19th century, is not. This church was built as part of the Jesuit university, founded in 1732 on orders of Philip V on the site of the present university; it's the last of 23 universities built by the Jesuit order in Mexico.

NEARBY ATTRACTIONS

For a suburban outing, hop any bus marked "PRESA" (try the bus stop in the Subterranean near Jardín Unión) to the **Parque de la Acacías** and the Presa de la Olla, the artificial lake. There are several parks and lots of trees—it's a good place for a lazy afternoon.

While in the neighborhood, you might note the **Palacio del Gobierno** (Government Palace) on Paseo de la Presa with its pink-stone front and green-tile interior. The neighborhood around here is residential and will give you another glimpse of Guanajuato away from the bustle of the plazas.

Surrounding Guanajuato were more than 150 splendid haciendas of wealthy colonial mine owners. Most are now either in ruins or restored and privately owned, but one has been made into the **Museo Exhacienda San Gabriel de Barrera.** About 2 miles from town on the road to Marfil, it's a lovely place most noted for its elaborate gardens in different styles: Arab, English, Spanish, etc. The rest of the grounds are lovely as well. The hacienda house is also open to visitors and presents a good idea of 18th-century life in the grand style. As is most often the case, the hacienda has its own chapel-baroque, of course—and there you'll find a key identifying the various figures depicted in the chapel's retablo. This is quite useful if you've been going to churches and puzzling over the various figures depicted in them and are without your copy of *Who's Who in Heaven.* There is also a state-run shop displaying all the handcrafts produced in the state. You can visit it any day from 9am to 6pm; admission is $1.50, plus $1 for a still camera or $1.50 for a video camera. The store's hours are Wednesday through Sunday from 10am to 5pm.

The recommended **San Gabriel de Barrera Misíon Park Plaza** is just across the road—see "Where to Stay," below, for information on this and for directions on how to arrive here from town.

SHOPPING

Stores in Guanajuato keep the usual store hours of the rest of Mexico—10am to 2pm and 4pm to 8pm. The Mercado Hidalgo, housed in a building (1909) that resembles a Victorian railroad station, is a good place to browse or just watch the activity from the raised walkway that encircles the main floor. Aside from food and vegetable stalls there's lots of pottery and ceramic ware.

Artesanías Vazquez. Cantarranas 8. ☎ **473/2-5231.**

Outlet for factory in Dolores Hidalgo. It's small but loaded with the colorful Talavera-style pottery for which Dolores is famous; there are plates, ginger jars, frames, cups and saucers, serving bowls, and the like.

Artezano. Plazuela del Baratillo 16. ☎ **473/3-1359.**

This is a small store that shares the building with a good coffee shop—look for a sign that says "CAFE DADA." You'll find lots of pottery, wooden boxes, and art, and the store sells large (6 ft.) hot-air balloons made of paper.

FONART Store. La Casa del Conde de la Valenciana (across from the church of San Cayetano). ☎ **473/2-2550.**

Though small, it has a selection of the finest crafts from all over Mexico. It's open daily from 10am to 6pm.

The Gorky González Workshop. Calle Pastita Ex huerta de Montenegro (by the stadium). ☎ **473/2-0009.**

This famous potter has been bringing back the traditional Talavera of Guanajuato. The place keeps irregular hours, but you may be able to browse through the small showroom Monday through Friday from 9am to 2pm and 4 to 6pm.

Rincón Artesanal. Sopeña 34-A. ☎ **473/2-1094.**

Objects in carved wood, wax, papier-mâché, pewter, and ceramic produced in different workshops throughout the state of Guanajuato. The store, "Artisan's Corner," also carries items from further afield, including beautiful *catrina calaveras* (skeleton statues in fancy dress) from the state of Michoacán. The lovely mother and daughter that own and run the place are very helpful. The store is 2 blocks east of Jardín Unión.

WHERE TO STAY

During the International Cervantes Festival held in mid-October, rooms are virtually impossible to find unless you have a reservation, and even then it's good to claim your room early in the day. Some visitors have to stay as far away as Querétaro, León, or San Miguel de Allende and come to Guanajuato for the day.

EXPENSIVE

✪ **Casa de los Espíritus Alegres B&B.** La Exhacienda la Trinidad no. 1, 36250 Marfil, Gto. ☎/fax **473/3-1013.** 8 units. $88–$117 double; $175 casita. Rates include breakfast. No credit cards.

Folk art and atmosphere abound in this idiosyncratic "house of happy spirits," owned and operated by a married couple of California artists who are long-time residents of Guanajuato. Carol and Joan have incorporated 20th-century comfort into parts of a 16th-century hacienda, which they impulsively bought while on one of their folk-art hunting trips nearly two decades ago. The whole house bursts with energy and vibrant folk art. The individually named rooms follow themes: "El Mago," "Quetzal," and the newest, the "Raj Mahal" casita. All are uniquely and colorfully decorated, fulfilling the promise of "a skeleton in every closet," and each has its own fireplace.

Breakfasts, served overlooking the garden, feature Californian and Mexican cuisine, with generous helpings of fresh fruit. I had tamale pancakes and fresh-fruit smoothies. Check out the hand-painted chairs (decorated by artist friends of the owners); one pays homage to Frida Kahlo. Guests have full use of the living room, decked out in folk art and history, travel, and art books as well as paperback novels for loan. The owners also have a small folk-art shop downstairs (which they delightfully say is "open 24 hours.") The facility is sometimes used for workshops and can be rented by groups. Frequent "Marfil" buses run from the highway just outside the grounds into downtown Guanajuato some 2 miles distant (but it's just a cheap and quick 8-min. ride by taxi). Get specific directions when you make your reservations. The owners (or Betsy, the part-time manager) can get a local taxi driver, Ramón, to drive you around the area for a fixed fee.

MODERATE

Hostería del Frayle. Sopeña 3, 36000 Guanajuato, Gto. ☎ **473/2-1179.** Fax 473/2-1179, ext. 38. 37 units. TV TEL. $50 double. MC, V.

This hostería is in the center of town 1 block from the Jardín Unión. That little bit of distance makes a great deal of difference; it's a lot less noisy than the Santa Fe. The rooms tend to be larger. The building is an old colonial house, and the plumbing in the old part could be called colonial, too—nothing major, just be prepared to run the hot water for up to 5 minutes before it gets hot. The more modern rooms in the back don't have this problem. The beds are comfortable and the rooms are well furnished.

Hotel Santa Fe. Jardín Unión, 36000 Guanajuato, Gto. ☎ **473/2-0084.** Fax 473/2-0084. 50 units. TV TEL. $58 double. AE, MC, V. Limited free parking.

Right in the heart of the Jardín Unión, this is the hotel for those who want to be right in the thick of it from the moment they step out the door. The beautifully kept, comfortable rooms are furnished in dark-wood furniture. The hotel has just undergone extensive remodeling that replaced all the wiring and plumbing. The only problem here is that most rooms can be noisy due to an extremely loud disco two doors down. The hotel is putting in noise-reducing windows in an attempt to solve the problem. The tile-filled lobby holds couches perfect for cocktails, and the off-lobby restaurant and outdoor cafe are the places to be in Guanajuato.

Parador San Javier. Plaza San Javier 92, 36250 Guanajuato, Gto. ☎ **473/2-0650** or 473/2-0626. Fax 473/2-3114. 114 units. TV, TEL. $75 double. AE, CB, DISC, MC, V. Free guarded parking.

Created from a former silver-mining hacienda, the San Javier is built around lovely tree-shaded grounds about 5 blocks above the Alhóndiga. Rooms come in two sections: Those in the back section are on four floors and are carpeted, well furnished, quiet, and comfortable; there are a few in front at ground level in the older wing that are slightly larger, with vaulted brick ceilings, that are also well furnished and go for the same price. There is a lovely pool on the grounds and a restaurant next to the lobby.

San Gabriel de Barrera Misión Park Plaza. km 2.5 Camino Antiguo a Marfil, 36250 Guanajuato, Gto. ☎ **473/2-3980.** Fax 473/2-7460. 138 units. TV TEL. $90 double. AE, MC, V. Free parking.

This modern hotel is in a secluded spot next to the Hacienda San Gabriel Barrera. Much like a convent, most of the rooms look out over interior courtyards; unlike a convent, the rooms offer all the creature comforts and are large and attractive and come with either a terrace or balcony. The grounds and pool and tennis court are beautifully kept, and the staff is very helpful. The hotel offers free transportation to and from town several times daily between 10am and 8pm. Cabs are available as well. If you're driving, follow signs for the Convention Center and then look for HOTEL MISIÓN signs.

INEXPENSIVE

Hotel Alhóndiga. Insurgencia 49, 36000 Guanajuato, Gto. ☎ **473/2-0525.** 31 units. TV. $25 double. No credit cards. Free parking for 7 cars.

Located just off the Plaza Alhóndiga and half a block downhill from the Museo Alhóndiga, this hotel is within walking distance of all the downtown sights. A four-story hotel (no elevator), it has small, basic rooms, tile bathrooms, and good beds covered with garish bedspreads. Front rooms are the nicest but also the noisiest, as this is a major corner (if there is such a thing in Guanajuato). Hotel Alhóndiga has a restaurant on the premises (which I think they should call Albóndiga—"meatball").

Hotel El Minero. Alhóndiga 12-A, 36000 Guanajuato, Gto. ☎ **473/2-5251.** Fax 473/2-4739. 20 units. TV. $25 double. CB, MC, V.

Only 2 blocks beyond the Museo Alhóndiga, this four-story (no elevator) hotel is a good, clean, economical choice. The carpeted rooms have small tile bathrooms with showers, and most have a double and a single bed. The hotel restaurant is next door.

✪ **Hotel Embajadoras.** Parque Embajadoras, 36000 Guanajuato, Gto. ☎ **473/2-0081** or 473/2-4464. Fax 473/2-4760. 27 units. TV TEL. $45 double. AE, MC, V. Free parking.

This is a good choice if you have a car and don't want to stay far from downtown. It's on the tree-lined street heading toward Paseo Madero 5 blocks from the Jardín Unión. The rooms are spread out around a central patio, one side of which is a restaurant. Rooms, all of which have red-tile floors, are small, quiet, clean, and plainly furnished. Covered walkways with chairs link the rooms. A good, reasonably priced restaurant/bar takes care of meals.

WHERE TO DINE

If you find yourself hungry in the Mercado Hidalgo area, stop and try one of the many inexpensive market stalls inside or outside to the left of the huge mercado edifice. Observe the sign that says (in Spanish): "Avoid disappointment, ask to see the price list!"

EXPENSIVE

✪ **Casa del Conde de la Valenciana.** Carretera, Guanajuato-Dolores km 5, opposite La Valenciana church. ☎ **473/2-2550.** Main courses $7–$20. MC, V. Mon–Sat 10:30am–6pm. MEXICAN/INTERNATIONAL.

Dine in what was once the home of the count of La Valenciana, who also built the beautiful church (a national treasure) across the street. For an appetizer, try one of the fresh salads, and for a main course one of Mexico's finely prepared specialties, such as crepes huitlacoche or enchiladas suizas. The shady patio is so relaxing that most tourists linger over coffee and dessert far longer than they intended. If you want to shop after eating, there's a wonderful furniture/decorative arts shop as well as a FONART branch here.

MODERATE

✪ **La Hacienda de Marfil.** Arcos de Guadalupe 3, Marfil. ☎ **473/3-1148.** Main courses $8–$10. AE, CB, MC, V. Tues–Sun 1:20–6:30pm. MEXICAN NOUVELLE/FRENCH.

In the Marfil area outside of Guanajuato proper, and next to the Casa de Espíritus Alegres (see "Where to Stay," above), this stylish and shady patio restaurant attracts a sophisticated clientele who come for leisurely, unrushed dining. The menu changes every 3 months, but typical dishes are trout in almond sauce, squash blossom crepes, and fillet Roquefort. You can also order steaks and fine fresh salads with a choice of dressings (not usually available in Mexico). It's best to get there by cab.

Tasca de Los Santos. Plaza de la Paz 28. ☎ **473/2-2320.** Breakfast $3–$4.50; main courses $8–$10. AE, MC, V. Daily 8am–midnight. SPANISH/REGIONAL.

This is one of Guanajuato's snazzier restaurants, with a completely à la carte menu. The food, service, and heavy Spanish decor are pleasant. Paella is a house specialty. The restaurant also serves chicken in white-wine sauce and beef *a la andaluza.* You can order wine by the bottle or glass.

INEXPENSIVE

Café El Retiro. Sopeña 12. ☎ **473/2-0622.** Breakfast $2–$3; main courses $2–$6; comida corrida $3.50. AE, MC, V. Daily 8am–11pm (comida corrida served 1–5pm). Bar closes at 2am. MEXICAN.

Sooner or later, everyone—local, student, or visitor—winds up at El Retiro, which recently expanded into the building next door. The best inexpensive lunch in town is served here. From the à la carte menu, you can choose from a variety of antojitos such as tacos and enchiladas or a quarter chicken. El Retiro is half a block south of the Jardín Unión, catercorner to the Teatro Juárez.

✪ Truco 7. Truco 7. ☎ **473/2-8374.** Breakfast $1.75–$3; comida corrida $3; main courses $3–$5. No credit cards. Daily 8:30am–11:30pm (comida corrida served 2–4pm). MEXICAN.

With its economical prices and warm, colorful atmosphere, this place is very popular. It's a good place for a snack, a coffee, or a full meal. The three dining rooms are small and a bit crowded yet nicely decorated with leather *equipal* tables and chairs, paintings by local artists, and photographs taken by the owner. The restaurant is housed in an 18th-century structure originally built for members of the Valenciana silver family. calle Truco, a short street south of the basilica, runs between the Jardín Unión and the Plaza de la Paz.

GUANAJUATO AFTER DARK

If long ago city planners had known the **Jardín Unión** was going to be so popular, they might have made it larger. This tiny triangular plaza, shaded by Indian laurel trees, is the true heart of and best hangout in the city. No other spot in town rivals its benches and sidewalk restaurants. The quality of the food is less important than the viewing perch, but all the restaurants serve a variety of coffees over which you can linger. The best place to eat and drink on the plaza is the **Santa Fe Hotel** restaurant. Other nearby gathering spots include the ever-popular Café El Retiro and Truco 7, listed above. A hangout for the young literati is the **Café Dada** on the Plaza del Baratillo.

You can catch some worthwhile **theater,** for free, in Plazuela de San Roque at 8pm on any Sunday when the university is in session. Students perform short theatrical pieces known as *entremeses* (literally "intermissions"). These are usually costumed period pieces that rely more on action than dialogue, so you don't need to understand too much Spanish to get the point. The costumes are great and look curiously appropriate in this plazuela.

Of the more conventional nightspots, the two most popular aren't difficult to find; they're across the street from each other at the Jardín Unión and can be heard from a block away. One is a disco and the other has live rock or jazz bands. Another place to try is **La Dama de las Camelias,** Sopeña 32, an unpretentious second-floor bar that

The Redolent Mexican Cantina

If you're curious about Mexican cantinas, swinging saloon doors and all, Guanajuato is a good place to do your field work. You should know, however, that most of these are *men-only* drinking dives.

The town's favorite son is José Alfredo Jiménez, the undisputed master of *ranchera* music. This is the quintessential drinking music that drives most non-Mexicans screaming from the building (one long lament punctuated by classic Mexican yelps). But after downing a few *copitas* you may warm up to it, and after asking about Jiménez, you'll probably get a few more on the house. Around the Jardín Unión there are a couple of cantinas that aren't bad; the editor of this guide and I enjoyed a few shots at one called **El Incendio** ("Fire"), Cantarranas 15. Unlike most cantinas, this place welcomes women. The barkeep was a good talker, and the colorful wall murals held icons of Mexican culture—María Félix on one, and glancing at her from the opposite side, the love-sick Agustín Lara. We had our choice of beer, tequila or mezcal, and all the good-natured conversation we could handle. El Incendio opens at 10am and closes at 4am.

You may be surprised to see an open urinal at the end of the bar. While this is a standard feature in cantinas and part of the, er, authentic flavor, you still may wish to opt for a stool at the opposite end.

doesn't get going until late in the evening. The music is all classic recordings of danzón, mambo, son cubano, and salsa, and the decor is inspired by the Altamira cave paintings in Spain. The bar opens at 8pm and closes at 4am.

ALONG HIGHWAY 45 FROM GUANAJUATO TO ZACATECAS

On your way to Zacatecas, you'll pass through León, Mexico's leather and shoe capital, with thousands of shoe stores lining its streets. Unfortunately, uncontrolled growth has begotten an ugly city, which stands in stark contrast to clean Aguascalientes, beautiful Zacatecas, or historic Guanajuato. There's an international airport in León. From Guanajuato, you have a choice of a fast, inexpensive toll road or a free road to León. The drive takes 15 to 45 minutes, depending on which route you take.

Aguascalientes (population 514,000), 84 miles south of Zacatecas, means "hot waters"; the city is, as expected, famous for its hot springs. The Spanish founded it in 1575 as a place of protection and rest along the silver highway between Mexico City, Guanajuato, and Zacatecas, as well as a center of food cultivation for the mining region. Today Aguascalientes is known for its copper mining, embroidery, and knitwear. In the streets around the cathedral and the Plaza Principal, you'll note several stores selling the products of these industries.

With growth, the city has lost some of its colonial charm, although the people here are still friendly and relaxed. The main plaza, around which are several moderately priced hotels and restaurants, dates from the colonial era, and it's a pleasant place to stroll. The main tourist attraction in Aguascalientes is the **José Guadalupe Posada Museum** on the Plaza Encino. Posada's fanciful depictions of skeleton figures have recently gained popularity with the increased interest in Day of the Dead celebrations. If you enjoy these, you will like the museum. Posada was a 19th-century engraver and writer of popular literature.

The biggest fair in Mexico, the **Feria de San Marcos,** is held here annually from April 19 to May 10. Festivities include industrial expositions, fireworks, cultural events, rodeos, and bullfights with renowned bullfighters from all over the world.

3 Zacatecas

392 miles NW of Mexico City; 117 miles NW of San Luis Potosí; 197 miles NE of Guadalajara; 186 miles SE of Durango

Zacatecas, like Guanajuato, owes its existence and beauty to the wealth of silver extracted from its mines. The farthest flung of the silver cities, it is a true jewel in the rough. High over the town's center looms a steep mountain accessible by cable car. From there you can gaze over the city and beyond to the wild and desolate surroundings. The scene makes you realize what a frontier town Zacatecas was, and, after you have been in town for a few days, it makes you appreciate its present sophistication all the more. In this city out in the middle of nowhere, you find some startlingly good art museums, beautiful architecture, and wonderful restaurants. There also seems to be a high degree of civic pride, to judge from the fact that they have gone to the enormous trouble of hiding all the power and telephone cables. This adds greatly to the picturesque beauty of the town and makes a simple stroll about town delightful.

ESSENTIALS

GETTING THERE & DEPARTING **By Plane** Mexicana (☎ **800/531-7921** or 492/2-7429; 492/5-0352 at the airport) flies to Zacatecas from Chicago, Denver, and Los Angeles. **Taesa** (☎ **800/328-2372,** 492/4-0050 or 492/2-2555) has a flight from Los Angeles. Seats on any of these planes during Christmastime are hard to come by; native Zacatecans fly home in large numbers for the holidays. From points within Mexico, Mexicana flies nonstop to Zacatecas from Morelia, Mexico City, and Tijuana. Nonstop service is also available on Taesa from Ciudad Juárez, Guadalajara, Mexico City, Morelia, and Tijuana.

Arriving: Transportation from the airport, 18 miles north of Zacatecas, is about $12 by taxi. **Aero Transportes** (☎ **492/2-5946**) provides minibus transportation to and from the airport ($4.50); allow 30 minutes for the ride.

By Car From the south you can take Highway 45D, a toll road in various spots all the way from Querétaro through Irapuato, León, and Aguascalientes. It's a tad expensive, at about $10, but fast. Highway 54 heads northeast to Saltillo and Monterrey (a 5- to 6-hr. drive) and southeast to Guadalajara (a 4-hr. drive). Highway 40/49 heads to Torreón (4 hr.), Highway 45 to Durango (4 hr.).

By Bus Almost a dozen bus companies provide service in and out of Zacatecas. The sheer number of buses coming and going is a great convenience. I don't bother buying tickets ahead of time, nor do I get departure schedules unless I am planning to travel to the border or somewhere equally far away. Ticket sellers and the staff at the information booth are friendly and will tell you which bus line will have the next departure for your destination.

Arriving: The Central Camionera (bus station) is on a hilltop a bit out of town, about $3 by taxi. Frequent **Red Ruta 8** buses, which go into central Zacatecas, can be found in front of the station.

VISITOR INFORMATION Downtown on Hidalgo, across from the cathedral, is a one-room **Infotur office;** it's open Monday through Saturday from 9am to 2pm and 4 to 7pm.

CITY LAYOUT Understanding traffic circulation in the middle of town requires an advanced degree in chaos theory. I either walk or let the cab drivers handle it. The city's main axis is Hidalgo. From the main square (**Plaza de Armas**) it goes 8 blocks southeast to the Sierra de Alica Park and Hotel Camino Real (changing names as it goes), and in the opposite direction it reaches another 8 blocks to the Rafael Coronel

Zacatecas

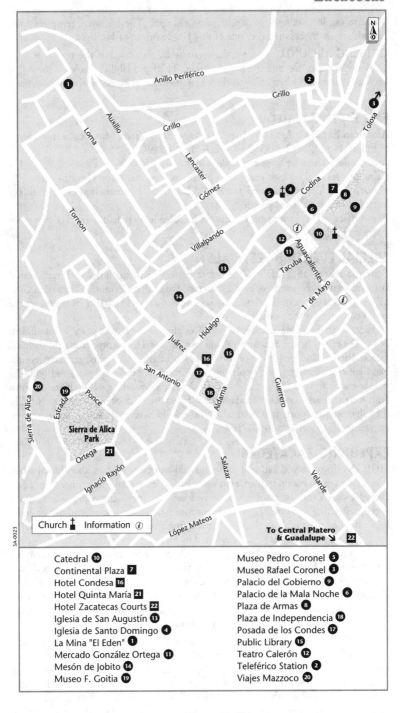

Church ✝ Information ⓘ

Catedral ❿
Continental Plaza 🄷
Hotel Condesa 🄸
Hotel Quinta María 🄴
Hotel Zacatecas Courts 🄼
Iglesia de San Augustín ⓭
Iglesia de Santo Domingo ❹
La Mina "El Eden" ❶
Mercado González Ortega ⓫
Mesón de Jobito ⓮
Museo F. Goitia ⓳

Museo Pedro Coronel ❺
Museo Rafael Coronel ❸
Palacio del Gobierno ❾
Palacio de la Mala Noche ❻
Plaza de Armas ❽
Plaza de Independencia ⓲
Posada de los Condes ⓱
Public Library ⓯
Teatro Calerón ⓲
Teleférico Station ❷
Viajes Mazzoco ⓴

205

Museum (again making a couple of name changes). The historical center of town extends several blocks on either side of this 1-mile stretch of Hidalgo.

GETTING AROUND   I love walking around Zacatecas, but the terrain is hilly. Cabs are inexpensive and readily available. Their availability declines somewhat between 2 and 4pm when office workers snag them to get home for the midafternoon meal.

FAST FACTS: ZACATECAS

American Express   American Express is handled by **Viajes Mazzoco,** a travel agent at Enlace 115 (☎ **492/2-5559** or 492/2-5159; fax 492/2-5559).

Area Code   The telephone area code is **492.**

Climate   It's cool enough year-round to require a sweater or other warm wrap.

Elevation   The city is situated at a lofty 8,200 feet. The air is always crisp and cool but a tad thin for a lot of people.

Post Office   The correo (post office) is at Allende 111, half a block down from avenida Hidalgo.

SPECIAL EVENTS & FESTIVALS

During Semana Santa (Holy Week before Easter) Zacatecas hosts an **international cultural festival** the town hopes will soon rival the similar Cervantino Festival in Guanajuato. Painters, poets, dancers, musicians, actors, and other artists from around the world converge on the town.

The annual **Feria de Zacatecas,** which celebrates the day the city was founded, begins the Friday before September 8 and lasts for 2 weeks, incorporating the national Fiestas Patrias (Independence celebration). Cockfights, bullfights, sporting events, band concerts, and general hoopla prevail. Famous bullfighters come, and bullfight tickets go for around $4; buses leave from downtown for the gigantic Plaza de Toros (and for the nearby cockpit) on days when fights are held. Sports events are held in the Olympic-size sports stadium and in the equally huge gymnasium; there are even car races at the racetrack outside town.

EXPLORING ZACATECAS

SIGHTS   In town you can visit museums and churches, tour an **abandoned silver mine,** ride a cable car up to the **Cerro de la Bufa,** perhaps take in a concert, and partake of an old Zacatecas tradition called *callejoneadas,* in which people on a Saturday night go strolling and singing, to the accompaniment of tamborines and drums and a burro ladened with mezcal, through the winding streets and alleyways (*callejones*) of the city. Zacatecas remains largely neglected by foreign tourists, though it is very popular with Mexicans. Consequently, there is little descriptive material in English at the various sights. If you don't speak Spanish, you might want to get a bilingual tour guide. Try contacting **Viajes Mazzoco** (see American Express, above, in "Fast Facts"). They have several tours that you can choose from and get a fixed price. Some of the tours take you around the city, others take you to **nearby ruins** or to some of the old towns near Zacatecas, such as **Jerez** or **Fresnillo.**

SHOPPING   **Zacatecan handcrafts** include stone and wood carvings, leather work, thread-pulled designs (drawn work) on textiles, and silver work. Examples of most of this work can be found in shops inside the old **Mercado González Ortega** on Hidalgo, next to the cathedral. This was once the municipal market but has been remodeled. It is well worth seeing. There are a few other stores on Hidalgo and Tacuba that sell crafts and antiques. Occasionally, Huichol Indians will sell their crafts around the Plaza Independencia. Of all its handcrafts, Zacatecas is best known for its stone carvers. Many architects and builders from the United States come to Zacatecas when they need fancy stonework for a fountain or doorway, etc. You can see impressive stonework when walking about town.

A Stroll Around Town

The **Plaza de Armas,** the town's main square on avenida Hidalgo, is where you'll find the **cathedral** with its famous facade. Nowhere in Mexico is there anything like this; the incredible amount of relief in the carving—4 inches and more—and wealth of detail create the impression that you're not looking at stone but some softer material. The cathedral took 23 years to build (1729 to 1752), and the final tower wasn't completed until 1904.

To the left of the cathedral, on the Plaza de Armas, is the 18th-century **Palacio de Gobierno,** where viceregal-era governors lived. By the time of Mexico's revolt against Spain in 1810, it was owned by Don Miguel de Rivera (Count of Santiago de la Laguna). Since 1834, it's been a government building; inside is a modern **mural** (1970) by Antonio Pintor Rodríguez showing the history of Zacatecas. It doesn't exactly present a rosy-colored view of the march of history. It's more of a bottom-up view; notice how the mural ties into the stone carving at the bottom, as if to argue that historical events are percolations rising from the stone and soil substrata, passing through the lives of those that toil closest to the earth, eventually giving shape to society's leaders. To the left of the Palacio de Gobierno is the **Residencia de Gobernadores,** with its ornate stone facade; the state governor lived here until 1950. Another building to observe is the **Palacio de Mala Noche** ("Palace of the Bad Night") facing the Palacio de Gobierno from across the square, to the left of the Continental Plaza Hotel. Its name comes from the mine that brought wealth to its original owner, Manuel de Rétegui, a philanthropic Spaniard. In case you're thinking that such fine stonework is becoming a lost art, look at the hotel's facade, which was done within the last 40 years. Throughout the downtown area, you'll see fine stone carving and ironwork, a hallmark of Zacatecas. If you are in the Plaza de Armas (or below it) before 11 in the morning, you will probably see men riding small burros that carry two or four small jugs—these guys are selling the fresh, unfermented juice of the maguey, known as *agua miel.* Flag one of the men down and try some. I am quite fond of it. It is usually all gone by noon.

South of the Palacio de la Mala Noche on avenida Hidalgo, opposite of the right side of the cathedral, is the 19th-century **Mercado Jesús González Ortega,** a striking combination of stone and elegant ironwork. Formerly the main market, it is now a great little shopping center. Between the mercado and the cathedral is the Plaza Francisco Goitia, the venue for frequent open-air artistic performances. Walking down Hidalgo, on the right you'll pass the **Teatro Calderón** (inaugurated first in 1836 and again in 1891 after a fire). A stately building with lovely stained-glass windows, it is also a favorite spot for people to sit and watch passersby. Scenes from the movie *The Old Gringo,* the film adapted from a book by Carlos Fuentes and starring Jane Fonda and Gregory Peck, were filmed here. The opera star Ángela Peralta sang here several times in the 1800s, and Plácido Domingo sang here in 1990. Zacatecas has a flourishing music school and there are always performers on tour; you might be able to catch a concert here. Look inside for announcements and a free monthly publication called *Agenda Cultural.*

Continue on Hidalgo, cross Juárez, and mount the hill to **Sierra de Alica Park** (the street changes names up the hill and becomes avenida Gral. Jesús González Ortega). The **equestrian statue** (1898) portrays none other than General González Ortega himself, hero of the Battle of Calpulálpan. Behind it is a gazebo with marvelous acoustics and a pleasant, shady park that at night is a romantic spot for young couples.

Beginning at Alica Park and extending southward, the famous **Aqueduct of Zacatecas** looms over the street. The wealth of this mining city at the end of the 18th century allowed it to undertake such impressive public works. Water passed along the aqueduct to a large cistern downtown.

A RIDE UP CERRO DE LA BUFA

The cable car ride to the top of Cerro de la Bufa is a lot of fun. To get to the cable car station from the Plaza de Armas, you must climb one of the streets or alleys that lead up the hill that faces the cathedral. But first, glance up to see if the cars are running; if it's windy, they won't be. The first cross street will be Villalpando; go right and make a left when you get to the Callejón (alley) de García. It's a bit of a climb. Here, you can take the *teleférico* (cable car; ☎ **492/2-5694**) on a sky ride over Zacatecas to the Cerro de la Bufa. The view from the top is best in the late afternoon/early evening when the sun is low in the sky, but if you intend to ride the cable car down, you can't stay too late. It operates only from 10am to 6pm; there's a fairly easy walk down if you want to stay later. The cost for a ride is 60¢ one way and $1.20 round-trip.

Up on Cerro de la Bufa, beside the Museo de la Toma de Zacatecas (see below) is the beautiful church **La Capilla de la Virgen del Patrocinio,** patron of Zacatecas. At the very top of the hill is an observatory used for meteorological purposes. Around the far side of the hill is the **Mausoleo de los Hombres Ilustres de Zacatecas,** the mausoleum from which many of the city's important revolutionary fighters still keep watch over their town below.

CHURCHES

Many of Zacatecas's churches are notable. **San Agustín** underwent construction in 1613, but its dedication had to wait until 1782. It has been a Catholic church, then a Protestant church (sadly stripped of its elaborate architectural ornamentation), a casino, a hotel, and tenement housing. Today it's an enormous, beautiful shell used for art exhibitions, conferences, and storage and display of pieces of its past glory. The state's **natural history museum** is also housed here. Note the mosaics of carved-stone chunks crammed into the archways and other niches. These pieces formerly decorated the church's ramparts, but now no one knows quite where. Other parts of the interior contain stonework that reveals how beautiful the exterior must have been. The church is 5 blocks south of the cathedral; walk past the Hotel Posada de la Moneda and turn right on the next street. The church is open Monday through Saturday from 10am to 2pm and 4 to 7pm, and on Sunday from 10am to 5pm. Admission is free.

To the right of the Museo Pedro Coronel is the **Iglesia de Santo Domingo,** completed in 1749, with its characteristic pink-stone facade. It was built by the Jesuits; after their expulsion, the Dominicans assumed responsibility and have taken care of it until today. Inside are stunning gilded altarpieces. During a surge of modernization, the baroque main altarpiece (retable), was replaced with the neoclassical masterpiece you see today. It, too, is stunning, but many still mourn the loss of the original.

Four miles from Zacatecas proper is the **Convent of Guadalupe,** the most famous church in the region. See "A Side Trip to Nearby Guadalupe," below, for details.

Museum Admissions

Unlike the rest of Mexico where museum admission is usually free on Sunday, museums are never gratis in Zacatecas. The Museo Pedro Coronel is closed on Thursday, while most others are closed on Monday.

MUSEUMS

La Mina "El Eden." Cerro Grillo. ☎ **492/2-3002.** Admission $1.50 (includes train and tour). Daily 11am–6:30pm.

Opened in 1586, this mine was excavated by hand by Indians forced into slavery by the Spanish. The Indians (mainly Caxcanes) began working in the mine at the age of 10 or 12 and lived to about 36 years of age. Accidents, tuberculosis, or silicosis caused their early deaths. The mine was extremely rich, yielding gold, copper, zinc, iron, and lead in addition to silver, but it was closed after only 60 years when an attempt to use explosives resulted in an inundation of water in the lower levels.

The back entrance to the mine is just a block from the lower cable-car station. You can visit it after you descend from Cerro de la Bufa. I prefer this entrance because you get tours of only three or four people, while tours leaving from the front are with 20 to 30 people and descend via a small train. For directions on getting to the front entrance, see "El Malacate" below, under "Zacatecas After Dark." The tour guides are quite good. This is one of the few places in Mexico where the guides provide good historical and social context and don't simply recite a litany of factoids. Unfortunately, there were no English-speaking guides. If they follow my advice, this will have changed. The tour is fun even for those who don't speak Spanish.

Museo F. Goitia. Enrique Estrada 102, Col. Sierra de Alica. ☎ **492/2-0211.** Admission $1.50. Tues–Sat 10am–1:30pm and 5–7:30pm; Sun 10am–4pm. Walk 7 short blocks south of the cathedral on Hidalgo, cross Juárez, and continue up the hill. Turn right on Manuel Ponce (look for the aqueduct) and walk 2 more short blocks. Look for the imposing white "palace" behind the park.

These days, I don't expect anyone to believe what they read about modern art, and since my credentials as a critic are nil, I'll be brief. I was surprised by this small museum and the work of Goitia and his Zacatecan comrades. I walked in expecting it to be a display of regional chauvinism. But to the contrary, I found the works to be moving, serious, and full of meaning. Goitia (1882–1960) is famous in Mexico; the others I had not heard of. The brothers Rafael and Pedro Coronel amassed great collections that became the basis for two highly touted museums. The others include Julio Relas, and José Kuri Breña.

Here is another little tidbit to test your sense of incredulity. It is said that the graceful marble stairway in the main hallway was constructed so that one may walk down its steps in perfect rhythm while humming the "Triumphal March" from Aïda.

✪ **Museo Pedro Coronel.** Plaza de Santo Domingo. ☎ **492/2-8021.** Admission $1.25. Fri–Wed 10am–2pm and 4–7pm. Closed Thurs. Facing the cathedral, walk left to the next street, De Veyna, and turn left and walk 1 block up to Plaza de Santo Domingo and the museum.

Pedro Coronel, in addition to being an artist, was a collector, and his collection shows him to be a man of inspired tastes. He acquired works from all over the world, but the strongest parts of the collection are the works of European modern masters (Dalí, Picasso, Miró, Kandinsky, Braque, Rouault, and the gang), pre-Columbian Mesoamerica, and West Africa. All but a few of the pieces of modern art are illuminating. Many were from early in the careers of the artists, and there is a seminal character in them that points toward the paths these artists would later take. This museum is not large; after a while you drift into the Mesoamerican room. Beautiful stuff, and seeing it so quickly after the modern art gets your mind working out strange connections between the two. There is no filler here. All of the pre-Columbian pieces are outstanding. The same can be said of the African material, but in this case the connections with modern art are real and not imagined.

✪ **Museo Rafael Coronel.** Calle Chevano, between Juan de Tolosa and Vergel Nuevo. ☎ **492/2-8116.** Admission $1.25. Thurs–Tues 10am–2pm and 4–7pm; Sun 10am–5pm. Facing the cathedral, walk left up Hidalgo to the Founder's Fountain (about 2 blocks), then take the left fork (Calle Abasolo) 2 more short blocks; at the large yellow-ocher building and traffic triangle, take the right fork. You'll spot the large, old temple ahead.

First stroll through the tranquil gardens and ruins of the former Convento de San Francisco, filled with trailing blossoms and verdant foliage and framed by decaying arches and the open sky. A small wing contains Coronel's drawings on paper. Once you step inside the mask museum, you'll be dazzled by the sheer number of fantastic masks, 4,500 of them, from all over Mexico; they're so exotic they look as if they could be from all over the world. There are entire walls filled with bizarre demons with curling 3-foot-long horns and noses; red devils; animals and unidentifiable creatures spitting snakes, pigs, or rats; conquistadors—anything the mind can conjure up. The masks, both antique and contemporary, are festooned with all manner of materials from human hair and animal fur, fabric, plant fibers, and bones to metal screening, steel wool, sequins, plastic, and glitter.

The amazing marionette museum is a great place to bring children. There are entire dioramas showing a bullfight, battling armies, and even a vision of hell. These marionettes are some of the hundreds created during the last century by the famous Rosete-Aranda family of Huamantla, Tlaxcala, where there is also a puppet museum.

Also in the museum, to the left after you enter, is the Ruth Rivera room, where some of Diego Rivera's drawings are on display. Ruth Rivera is the daughter of Diego Rivera and the wife of Rafael Coronel. The museum also has a delightful ground-floor cafe for coffee and pastries and a small gift shop.

Museo de la Toma de Zacatecas. Cerro de la Bufa. ☎ **492/2-8066.** Admission 60¢. Tues–Sun 10am–5pm. Taxis from the center of town are $2.50. Take the teleférico to Cerro de la Bufa (see above) and the museum.

The Museum of the Capture of Zacatecas displays pictures, a few exhibits, and a lot of blow-ups of contemporary newspaper accounts describing the battle between the Federales and the Revolucionarios in the hills surrounding Zacatecas in June 1914. This was a pivotal battle in the Mexican Revolution and one of Pancho Villa's greatest victories. This museum, however, will interest only Spanish-speaking history buffs.

A SIDE TRIP TO NEARBY GUADALUPE

The most famous religious edifice in the region, aside from the cathedral, is the **Convento de Guadalupe** in Guadalupe, only about 4 miles east of Zacatecas on Highways 45/49. A taxi to Guadalupe runs about $6. Transportes de Guadalupe buses go to Guadalupe from the Central Camionera in Zacatecas, or there's a Ruta 13 bus to Guadalupe at López Mateos and Salazar just up from the Hotel Gallery. The bus stops a block from the convent. It leaves about every 15 minutes or so and costs 50¢ for the 20-minute ride. If you're driving, look for a redbrick church and steeple and turn right just past it onto calle Independencia.

Convento de Guadalupe/Museo Virreinal de Guadalupe. Jardín Juárez, Ote., Guadalupe. ☎ **492/3-2089** or 492/3-2386. Admission $1.75; free on Sun. Tues–Sun 10am–4:30pm.

The convent dates from 1707, and most of it now houses the Museo de Arte Virreinal de Guadalupe and the adjoining Museo Regional de la Historia (see below). Inside the convent proper, every wall seems to be covered by paintings; a series of huge paintings on the ground floor describes the life of St. Francis of Assisi, another on the floor above describes the life of Christ.

Remember that the public was not meant to see the grounds, the paintings, or the cells where the Franciscan monks spent their spare time. You may catch a glimpse of the brown-robed monks through a slatted wooden door; today part of the building is still in use as a college of instruction in the Franciscan order. The third Franciscan monastery established in the New World, the convent educated missionaries and sent them northward into what is now northern Mexico and the southwestern United States as part of the cultural conquest by the Spaniards. The Dominican order, also important in the Conquest, appears in the artwork of the convent as well, but the brown-robed Franciscans are the more familiar figures. The three knots of their sashes signify their vows of obedience, penitence, and poverty—the occasional fourth knot signifies the additional vow of silence.

The chapel to the left of the main building (as you face the convent from the front court/park) is called the Capilla de Napoles. It must have taken a king's ransom in gold to decorate it; the gold ranges in quality from 6 karat on the lower walls up to 22 karat in the dome above. Guides are available for a tour or to open the chapel, which is visible from either the organ loft or the ground floor—be sure to tip the guide for opening the doors and turning on the lights.

Museo Regional de la Historia. Jardín Juárez, Guadalupe. ☎ **492/3-2386** or 492/3-2089. Free admission. Tues–Sun 10am–4:30pm.

This museum, to the right side of the convent, contains fine examples of carriages and antique cars that were collected from all over Mexico and that formerly belonged to ex-presidents and famous historical figures.

Centro Platero de Zacatecas. Exhacienda de Bernardez, Guadalupe. ☎ **492/2-1007.** Free admission. Mon–Fri 10am–6pm; Sat 10am–2pm.

Since Zacatecas ranks first in Mexico in the production of silver and fourth in gold, it seems only fitting that the art of metalworking is being reborn here. Young silversmiths are learning the trade in an old hacienda that once belonged to the counts of Laguna, located in the Fraccionamiento Lomas near the golf course. Most of the unusual jewelry designs are taken from the balconies and other architectural ironwork in Zacatecas; after you've seen them, you'll view Zacatecas's buildings with new eyes. The jewelry is sold at the school, and there's an equally large selection at the Centro Comercial "El Mercado," next to the cathedral in central Zacatecas. The school is about a mile north of the highway, zigzagging past newly constructed upscale homes on streets that don't yet have name signs. Take a cab.

WHERE TO STAY
EXPENSIVE

Hotel Quinta Real. Av. Rayón 434, 98000 Zacatecas, Zac. ☎ **01-800/3-6015** in Mexico, or 492/2-9104. Fax 492/2-8440. 49 suites. MINIBAR TV TEL. $135 master suite; $145 suite with whirlpool. AE, CB, DISC, MC, V. Free guarded parking.

Mexico is full of hotels made from converted colonial mansions, convents, and haciendas, but how many have risen from bullrings? And yet, it's the beauty, not the novelty, that makes this hotel so great. It has won several design awards, undoubtedly because the architects knew enough to leave this beautiful old bullring intact and keep the hotel small enough to be unobtrusive. The entrance to the hotel is framed by the few graceful arches that remain of the town's colonial aqueduct. Inside the lobby you can survey the whole arena with its arches and stepped levels. Across to the other side is the restaurant, below it a bar, and to the left are shops. The rooms have been built along the outside of the bullring and their windows open up to a small courtyard.

These rooms are large with luxurious bathrooms and come furnished with an armoire concealing the TV, a Queen Anne writing desk, and a couch.

Dining/Diversions: An outdoor restaurant with umbrella-shaded tables uses part of the tiers of the old bullfighting ring. The formal indoor restaurant is plush and sophisticated (see "Where to Dine," below). A bar on the lower level occupies the former bull shoots, and graffiti from this era remains on the rock walls.

Amenities: Laundry and room service, boutiques, valet parking, tour desk; whirlpool bathtubs in several rooms.

MODERATE

Continental Plaza. Av. Hidalgo 703, Col. Centro, 98000 Zacatecas, Zac. ☎ **800/ 882-6684** in the U.S., or 492/2-6183. Fax 492/2-9054. 115 units. A/C TV TEL. $82 double. MC, V. Free secured parking.

Here, you'll find a very comfortable hotel with the best location in town, right on the Plaza de Armas. The lobby holds a popular bar and good restaurant serving an excellent breakfast buffet. This is a popular hotel with Mexican tourists and businesspeople. The spacious, heated rooms on six floors are carpeted and well furnished. Rooms in the back are very quiet; rooms in the front are very sunny and have marvelous views of the cathedral and Cerro de la Bufa. Those on the third or fourth floor are shielded from some of the sound that occurs when Saturday night *callejoneadas* arrive at the Plaza de Armas between 11pm and 1am. All rooms come equipped with TVs broadcasting four U.S. channels; some have king-size beds, and others have two double beds. The tap water is purified.

Mesón de Jobito. Jardín Juárez 143, 98000 Zacatecas, Zac. ☎/fax **492/4-1722.** 31 units. TV TEL. $100 standard double. AE, MC, V. Parking on street.

A new hotel in a historic edifice, the two-story (no elevator) Mesón de Jobito easily competes in quality with the Continental Plaza, but it's more intimate. The hotel is built from an old *vecindad*, a traditional form of housing for the lower classes, and has the perfect amount of old ramshackle quality to it. But the rooms are quite a contrast—large, carpeted, and nicely furnished with queen- or king-size beds, large bathrooms, and in-room safes. The hotel is only about 4 blocks from the cathedral; look for the signs leading to it from the traffic light by the cathedral. The elegant Restaurante El Mesonero serves international cuisine at all three meals; there's soft music performed live in the evenings.

INEXPENSIVE

Hotel Posada de los Condes. Av. Juárez 107, 98000 Zacatecas, Zac. ☎ **492/2-1093.** 57 units. TV TEL. $21 double. No credit cards.

This budget hotel is clean, comfortable, and nondescript. Hot water is plentiful between the hours of 7am and noon. Rooms are not large, but they aren't drafty either, and the beds come with plenty of blankets. The hotel caters to a lot of families. It's located near the busy market streets in an interesting part of town.

Motel Zacatecas Courts. López Velarde 602, 98000 Zacatecas, Zac. ☎ **492/2-0328.** Fax 492/2-1225. 92 units. TV TEL. $20 double. AE, MC, V. Free enclosed parking.

This clean but somewhat worn modern-style hotel has carpeting, hot water 24 hours a day, and laundry and dry-cleaning services. Adjacent to the hotel are a travel agency and pharmacy. The clean, cheerful restaurant has economical meals and is open daily from 7am to 10:30pm. This is a great deal for those driving a car. It is a bit removed from the interesting parts of the city, but within walking distance.

WHERE TO DINE

Between the Plaza Independencia and López Mateos runs calle Ventura Salazar, which is lined with taco and snack shops, just fine for a quick bite at ridiculously low prices. The food market is on the north side of the Plaza Independencia bounded on the left side of the market by the Callejón del Tráfico, a narrow walkway to the left of the market entrance.

Café Nevería Acrópolis. Av. Hidalgo and Plazuela Candelario Huizar (beside the cathedral). ☎ **492/2-1284.** Breakfast $3.50–$4; main courses $3–$5.50; sandwiches $1.50–$2.50. MC, V. Daily 8:30am–10pm. MEXICAN.

This restaurant-cafe with a soda fountain is a popular meeting spot where people get together to talk over a cup of coffee. The kitchen does itself credit with its enchiladas. Along the wall are photos and signatures of famous people, including Gregory Peck and Jane Fonda, who stayed in Zacatecas for the filming of *The Old Gringo*. This cafe is a great place for a late-afternoon sightseeing break with tea or coffee and a slab of heavily iced cake.

Hotel Quinta Real. Av. Rayón 434. ☎ **492/2-9104.** Breakfast $5–$8; main courses $9–$13. AE, CB, DISC, MC, V. Daily 7am–11pm. REGIONAL/INTERNATIONAL.

White linen tablecloths, chairs covered with tapestry, high-beamed ceilings, and plants everywhere create an elegant but comfortable ambiance at this restaurant. Tables are at multiple levels conforming to the tiers of the old bullring, within which the hotel was built. Diners can gaze out at the twinkling lights in the courtyard's potted trees and the illuminated aqueduct that gracefully arches high above. An inventive menu features all sorts of dishes, including red snapper au poblana, with poblano peppers on top. For dessert, try *cajeta* (a very sweet dessert made from goat's milk), crêpes suzette, or chocolate mousse. Even if you don't eat here, drop by for a drink or canapés just to enjoy the unusual setting. Located at the southeast end of Hidalgo/Ortega.

La Cantera Musical Fonda y Bar. Tacuba 2. Centro Comercial "El Mercado." ☎ **492/2-8828.** Breakfast $1.50–$5; lunch $2.50–$9; dinner $3–$8. AE, CB, MC, V. Daily 8am–11pm. MEXICAN/REGIONAL.

Locals consider La Cantera one of the best Zacatecan-style restaurants in town. Against the background of Mexican music, Mexican art, handcrafted tiles, and an arched brick ceiling, colorfully dressed women press and fry masa into tortillas. The flavorful pozole rojo is loaded with chunks of pork and hominy; other dishes are also good. The restaurant is below the Mercado González Ortega by the cathedral.

✪ **La Cuija.** Tacuba T-5, Centro Comercial "El Mercado." ☎ **492/2-8275.** Main courses $6–$10. MC, V. Daily 1pm–midnight. MEXICAN.

This very stylish restaurant under the Centro Comercial has a peaceful setting in an elegant colonnade. Appetizers are referred to as "something to open the mouth," and the quesadillas de flor de calabaza are especially good reasons for doing so. The succulent *lomo zacatecano*—broiled pork with a delicate red-chile sauce—is a favorite dish. The pastas are fresh-tasting and an interesting change from Mexican fare. They sell a good wine produced in the family's vineyards. Friday and Saturday nights a guitar trio plays.

ZACATECAS AFTER DARK

The *Callejoneada Zacatecana* could be the best way to tour the city's quaint and picturesque back streets and alleys. It is a traditional walk through the city's *callejones* (the little curving alleys, byways, and plazas), accompanied by music and dancing and a burro carrying mezcal, on Saturdays beginning around 9pm (8pm in cold weather). Be sure to ask if there will be one while you're in town; call **Viajes Mazzoco** (☎ 492/2-8954) or ask at the lobby of your hotel. Or, if you want a free tour, tag along to a group as it marches through the streets—they're hard to miss with the drums and horns and a flower-bedecked burro laden with barrels of mezcal.

El Malacate. Mina El Eden, Calle Dovali. ☎ **492/2-3727.** Cover $6.

Disco music in a mine deep inside the earth—does "Disco Inferno" ring a bell? Whose life could be considered complete without having made the scene here? Call in advance to reserve a table since it's very popular. The entrance is at the end of calle Dovali. From Hidalgo, walk up Juárez, which turns into Torreón, and just past the Seguro Social building on avenida Torreón, you'll find Dovali; turn right. Take a cab if you don't want to be so bushed that you can't boogie. The club is open Thursday through Sunday from 9:30pm to 2am.

4 San Luis Potosí

261 miles NW of Mexico City; 216 miles NE of Guadalajara

San Luis Potosí, set more than a mile high in central Mexico's high-plains region, is among the most picturesque and prosperous mining cities of Mexico. It is the largest and most urban of the silver cities, with half a million inhabitants, but you would never know it if you stayed in the historic central district. It has rich colonial architecture and is known for the great plazas scattered about. Capital of the state of the same name, San Luis Potosí was named for Louis IX, saintly king of France, and "Potosí," the Quechua word for "richness," borrowed from the incredibly rich Potosí silver mines of Bolivia, which San Luis's mines were thought to rival. San Luis was formally founded in 1583 by Spaniards Fray Magdalena and Captain Caldera on the site of the Chichimec town of Tangamanga; the indigenous people had been living on this spot for 3 centuries before the Spaniards arrived.

The Spaniards came in search of silver and found it, mostly at a small town called San Pedro, 25 miles from San Luis Potosí. But San Luis's mineral springs made it a better place to settle than San Pedro, so this became the mining center. As a state capital, San Luis Potosí exudes prosperity and sophistication, much the way Morelia does. People make great use of their plazas as social centers, and there are many areas in the central district that are cordoned off for the use of the pedestrians only.

The city has in fact twice been the capital of Mexico—in 1863 and 1867—when Benito Juárez led the fight against European intervention, governing the country from the Palacio de Gobierno (on Plaza de Armas). From this palace he pronounced the death sentence on Maximilian and his two generals. During the Mexican Revolution, the "Plan of San Luis" was proclaimed here.

Today San Luis Potosí lives on industry rather than silver. Everything from automobiles to mezcal are produced in the factories ringing the city, but fortunately the colonial center has been preserved intact.

ESSENTIALS

GETTING THERE & DEPARTING   By Plane   The only direct flights from the United States are from San Antonio on Aerolitoral (a subsidiary of Aeromexico) and **Aeromar** (☎ 800-627-0207 in the U.S.). The latter has one nonstop flight a week. Domestic flights are handled by Aero California, Aeromar, and Aerolitoral. For transportation to the airport from all downtown hotels ($9), call **AeroTaxi** (☎ **48/11-0165** or 48/11-0167).

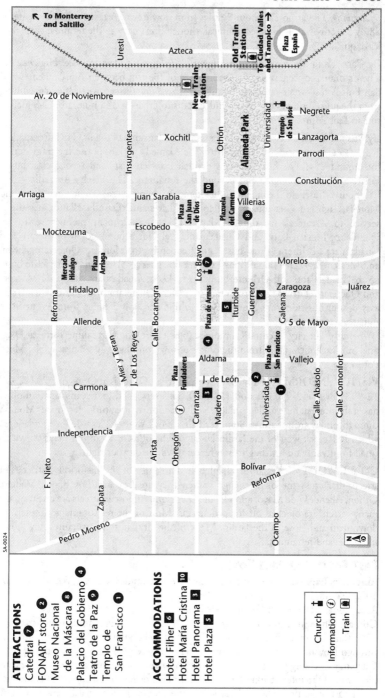

San Luis Potosí

To Monterrey and Saltillo

Uresti
Azteca
Old Train Station
To Ciudad Valles and Tampico
Plaza España

New Train Station

Av. 20 de Noviembre

Xochitl
Othón
Universidad
Negrete
Templo de San José
Lanzagorta
Parrodi

Alameda Park

Insurgentes

Constitución

Arriaga

Juan Sarabia
Plaza San Juan de Dios
Plazuela del Carmen
Villerias 9
8
10

Moctezuma

Escobedo

Mercado Hidalgo
Plaza Arriaga
Los Bravo 7
Morelos

Reforma

Hidalgo

Calle Bocanegra

Plaza de Armas
Iturbide
5
Guerrero 6
Zaragoza
Juárez
Galeana

Allende
4
5 de Mayo

Mier y Terán
J. de Los Reyes

Carmona

Plaza Fundadores
Aldama
J. de León
Plaza de San Francisco 2
Vallejo
Universidad
1
Calle Abasolo
Calle Comonfort

3
Madero
Carranza

Independencia

Arista
Obregón

Bolívar
Reforma

F. Nieto

Zapata

Ocampo

Pedro Moreno

SA-0024

N

Church
Information (i)
Train

215

Arriving: The airport is about 7 miles from downtown. A taxi to the city center is $8. A colectivo van is more economical, though don't tarry in the terminal since they leave quickly.

By Car   From Mexico City, take Highway 57; from Guadalajara, take Highway 80. There's dramatic scenery on the second half of the trip between Aguascalientes and San Luis Potosí—hair-raising hills and scenic *pueblitos* (little towns). If you're coming from the north, it takes between 6 and 7 hours to drive the 335 miles from Monterrey to San Luis Potosí.

By Bus   The large Central Camionera is on the outskirts of town. City buses marked "CENTRAL" go to the bus station from the Alameda park opposite the train station for around 25¢. The bus station is divided between first- and second-class buses. First-class buses are at the end beyond the restaurant. The **Flecha Amarilla** group has hourly buses to León and Querétaro, 16 buses a day to Mexico City and Morelia, eight to Guanajuato, and four to Pátzcuaro. **Estrella Blanca** has direct service to Zacatecas six times a day. **ETN** offers frequent premier service to Querétaro, Mexico City, and Guadalajara. **Del Norte** buses go to Querétaro and Guadalajara. **Primera Plus** buses go frequently to Morelia, Querétaro, León, and Mexico City. The **Tamaulipas Primera** line goes to Matehuala, while **Elite** buses go to Guadalajara, and **Oriente** buses go to León, Guadalajara, Lagos de Moreno, and Querétaro. **Futura** buses run often to Saltillo, Querétaro, and Mexico City. It's an easy 8-hour bus ride from Monterrey or Saltillo and only 3 hours from Zacatecas or Aguascalientes.

Arriving: The city's Central Camionera (bus station), on Guadalupe Torres at Diagonal Sur, is about 2 miles from the center of town on Highway 57 next to the Motel Potosí.

VISITOR INFORMATION   The **State Tourism Office** is at Obregón 520 (☎ **48/ 12-9939** or 48/12-9943; fax 48/12-6769). This very good tourist information office has a helpful staff, excellent maps, and descriptive literature. It's open Monday through Friday from 8am to 8pm. It's half a block west of Plaza de los Fundadores, which is 1 block west of the Jardín Hidalgo. The office is in an old mansion with a small front yard and a wrought-iron fence; it will be on your right.

CITY LAYOUT   The Jardín Hidalgo is the center of the historical district. The streets that cross the plaza change names; they are Carranza/Los Bravo, Madero/ Othon, Allende/5 de Mayo, and Hidalgo/Zaragoza. Almost all streets are one way, and many streets are blocked off for pedestrians. Most of the restaurants and hotels are downtown and close to the Jardín. Many of the city's historic structures now house museums and restaurants.

FAST FACTS: SAN LUIS POTOSÍ

American Express   The local representative is **Grandes Viajes,** avenida Carranza 1077 (☎ **48/17-6004;** fax 48/11-1166).

Area Code   The telephone area code is **48.**

Climate   It's warm and pleasant year-round here—the average annual temperature is 67°F. Rain is rare, with an average rainfall of 14 inches; the rainy season is from April through November, and the coolest weather is between November and March.

Currency Exchange   The best rates are to be had from the grouping of casa de cambios around the intersection of Morelos and Julián de los Reyes, about 3 blocks north and 1 east of Jardín Hidalgo. They keep better hours and have hardly any wait compared to banks. All are open on weekends, Saturdays at least.

EXPLORING SAN LUIS POTOSÍ
A Stroll Around the Historic Center

I delight in walking around San Luis. The city has more area designated for pedestrian use only than anywhere else in Mexico. The center of town is the **Jardín Hidalgo,** a large plaza dating from the mid-1700s and shaded by magnolia and flamboyan trees; before that it was a bullring. After the plaza was laid out, the **Palacio de Gobierno** was begun. What you see of this building today has been much repaired, restored, and added to through the centuries—the back and the south facade were redone as recently as 1973. The front of the building retains much of the original 18th-century decoration, at least on the lower floors.

The **bandstand** in the center of the plaza was built in 1947 (although in colonial style), using the pink stone famous to the region. You'll see the stone throughout San Luis. The band usually plays here on Thursday and Sunday evenings, free, beginning around 7:30 or 8pm.

Across the plaza from the Government Palace is the **cathedral.** The original building had only a single bell tower, so the one on the left was built in 1910 to match, although today the newer tower looks to be the older. The **Palacio Municipal,** on the north side of the cathedral, was built in 1850 by the Count of Monterrey and was loaded with great wealth—paintings and sculpture—little of which has survived the city's stormy history. When the count died in 1890, the palace was taken over by the bishop, and in 1921 by the city government. Since that year it has been San Luis's city hall, peaceful for many years until it was firebombed on January 1, 1986, because of political differences. It has all been restored and functions again with business as usual.

The area south of the Jardín Hidalgo is a grid of narrow streets lined with graceful and, for the most part, old mansions that haven't been modernized. These low, elaborate ancient homes are built in the Spanish style, each containing a lush central garden courtyard. It's well worth a stroll down here to peek through the delicate iron traceries that cover the windows, and if you're lucky you can catch glimpses of cool, aristocratic rooms lined with gilt and velvet, looking as they have for almost a century.

Heading north out of the Jardín Hidalgo, stroll along **calle Hidalgo.** This street is reserved for pedestrians, and it's a treat to walk from the jardín almost all the way to the city's central market.

Southeast of the Jardín Hidalgo is one of the city's most famous squares, **Plazuela del Carmen,** named for the **Templo del Carmen** church. From the jardín, walk east along Madero-Othón to Escobedo and the plazuela. The entire area you see was once part of the lush grounds of the Carmelite monastery, built in the 17th century. The church survives from that time and is perhaps the Potosinos' favorite place of worship, but the convent has been destroyed. The beautiful **Teatro de la Paz** now stands on the site, having been built there in 1889.

Attached to the Teatro de la Paz and entered to the right of the theater's main entrance, the **Sala German Gedovius** (☎ 48/12-2698) has four galleries for exhibitions of international and local art. It's open Tuesday through Sunday from 10am to 2pm and 4 to 6pm.

The square is a fine place to take a rest by the fountain before heading on a few blocks east to get to the shady and cool **Alameda,** the city's largest downtown park. All around the sides of the park are vendors selling handcrafts, fruits, and all manner of snacks. Just across Negrete is the magnificent **Templo de San José,** with lots of ornate gold decorations, huge religious paintings, and *El Señor de los Trabajos,* a miracle-working statue with many retablos testifying to the wonders it has performed.

PLAZAS

San Luis Potosí has more plazas than any other colonial city in Mexico. The two most famous ones are mentioned above. **Plaza de San Francisco** (also called Plaza de Guerrero) is south of the Palacio de Gobierno along Aldama, between Guerrero and Galeana. This shady square—lush with ivy, iris, vine-covered trees, and royal palms—takes its name from the huge monastery of the Franciscan order at the south side of the plaza. The church on the west side, the **Iglesia de San Francisco,** is dated 1799 and is really worth visiting. It boasts beautiful stained-glass scenes all around the dome; a carved, pink-stone altar; a statue of the Virgin surrounded by angels and golden rays; other lovely statues and paintings; and a spectacular crystal chandelier, shaped like a sailing ship, hanging from the center of the dome. This is the favorite for weddings in San Luis society.

Another square with a church to visit is **Plaza de los Fundadores** ("Founders' Square"), at the intersection of Obregón and Aldama (northwest of the Jardín Hidalgo). Take a peek through the baroque doorway of the **Loreto Chapel,** dating from the 16th century, and the neighboring headquarters of the **Compañía de Jesús,** the Jesuit order. In the chapel is a magnificent golden sunburst over the altar, a reminder of past glories.

MUSEUMS

Casa de la Cultura. Av. V. Carranza 1815. ☎ **48/13-2247.** Free admission. Tues–Fri 10am–2pm and 4–6pm; Sat 10am–2pm and 6–8pm. Take a cab or any of the city buses running west on Carranza.

Somewhat removed from the city center, this museum is housed in a splendid neo-classical building constructed at the turn of this century and is surrounded by large landscaped gardens. There are works of art, historical pieces, handcrafts, and a collection of archaeological items. Adjoining is the Center of Historical and Geographical Studies. All kinds of national and international cultural events are held here.

✪ **Museo Nacional de la Máscara.** Villerías 2. ☎ **48/12-3025.** Admission $2. Tues–Fri 10am–2pm and 4–6pm; Sat–Sun 10am–2pm; tours in Spanish are available. From the Jardín Hidalgo (Plaza de Armas), walk east along Madero-Othón to Escobedo and the Plazuela del Carmen. The museum is south, just off the plaza.

Just across from the Teatro de la Paz, the National Mask Museum merits a look just for the sake of seeing the 19th-century building it is housed in—not to mention the wonderful exposition of masks. It's loaded with regional dance masks from all over the country. In addition to its permanent and temporary exhibits, it offers lectures and workshops on mask making, theater, painting, movies, and history, and it hosts a national mask contest at Carnaval (Mardi Gras) time.

Museo Regional de Culturas Populares. Exhacienda de Teneria in Parque Tangamanga. ☎ **48/17-2976.** Free admission. Tues–Sun 9am–4pm. Take a taxi, or the Ruta 32 bus from behind the Del Carmen church.

Near the center of this large and well-kept urban park is the new home of this small gem of a museum housed in a 19th-century hacienda. Previously it was located on the Plaza de San Francisco where FONART, the government crafts store, is now. The exhibits of Potosino crafts are stunning: ceramics, inlaid wood, papier-mâché "sculptures," basketry, musical instruments, masks, lacy altars made of wax, and local designs in weaving and rebozos. To get there take a cab.

SHOPPING

The best one-stop shopping in San Luis is at the **FONART** store (☎ **48/12-7521**) on the Plaza de San Francisco. The building was originally part of the Convent of San

Francisco, founded in 1590. Today, it houses the offices of the Casa de la Cultura, and, on the ground floor, a branch of FONART, the government-operated crafts store. This one is especially well stocked with some of the country's best crafts. It's open Monday through Saturday from 10am to 2pm and 4 to 7pm. Another place to try is the state-run store, **La Casa del Artesano** (no phone) at Carranza 540, 5 blocks west of Jardín Hidalgo. The store carries examples of every kind of craft made in the state. Each room in the store is dedicated to the crafts of one of the cultural/climatic zones of the state. The store is open Monday through Saturday from 10am to 2pm and 4 to 8pm.

Several blocks along the pedestrian calle Hidalgo from the Jardín Hidalgo you'll find the city's **Mercado Hidalgo,** a mammoth building devoted mostly to food, but also carrying some baskets, rebozos, and straw furniture. While here, be sure to try some queso de tuna, a specialty of the region. Although called a "cheese," it's a sweet paste—something like dried figs or dates with a molasses or burned-sugar taste—made from the fruit of the prickly pear cactus. It's delicious and comes in pieces of varying sizes.

But the walk along Hidalgo is itself an introduction to the city's commercial life. Hardware stores, craftspeople's shops, shoe stores, groceries, and taverns all crowd the street. Past the Mercado Hidalgo is another big market, the Mercado República.

WHERE TO STAY

The most luxurious and expensive hotels in San Luis are on the outskirts of town off the highway leading to Mexico City. Most of their customers are businesspeople and conventioneers. I don't include them here because they are far from where the tourist interests are and there is nothing to distinguish them. The best of these, however, are the Real de Minas and the María Dolores. There are no luxury hotels in the middle of town.

Hotel Filher. Av. Universidad 375 (at the corner of Zaragoza), 78000 San Luis Potosí, S.L.P. ☎ **48/12-1562.** Fax 48/12-1564. 50 units. FAN TV TEL. $21 double. DISC, MC, V. Parking 2 blocks away $1.

This bright cheerful place was refurbished last year. Rooms are arranged around a four-story central courtyard (no elevator). They are large, clean, bright, and have modern furnishings, good mattresses, and tile floors. There is plenty of hot water, but it can take up to 5 minutes to heat up. Just leave the hot-water tap on for a while before you need it. There is a restaurant bar on the first floor.

Hotel María Cristina. Juan Sarabia 110, 78000 San Luis Potosí, S.L.P. ☎ **48/12-9408.** Fax 48/12-8823. 75 units. FAN TV TEL. $32 double. AE, MC, V. Guarded parking $1.50.

The María Cristina is in a narrow eight-story building. Furnishings are nondescript but perfectly comfortable, but the rooms can be a little dark. The rooftop pool is a plus after a long drive. The parking garage is cramped. You can get here from the Jardín Hidalgo by walking 3 blocks east on Othón and turning left onto Juan Sarabia; the hotel is on the right, reached by a flight of stairs up to the lobby.

✪ **Hotel Panorama.** Venustiano Carranza 315. 78000 San Luis Potosí, S.L.P. ☎ **48/12-1777.** Fax 48/12-4591. 127 units. FAN TV TEL. $42 double. AE, DC, MC, V. Free secured parking.

This is my favorite hotel in San Luis. It's in a modern 14-story building, and you can count on a large, comfortable room with a view. The external wall is solid glass with a heavy drapery to block it out. If the weather is warm, avoid a room on the west side of the building. There are two good restaurants and a swimming pool on the premises. It's just off the Plaza de los Fundadores, 2 blocks from Jardín Hidalgo and within walking distance of restaurants and museums.

Hotel Plaza. Jardín Hidalgo 22, 78000 San Luis Potosí, S.L.P. ☎ **48/12-4631.** 28 units. $16 double. No credit cards. Discounts are sometimes available. Free parking (guarded parking for 6 cars).

The lobby and staircase of this old, two-story colonial mansion show sighs of having seen better times—but it's a certain sense of faded glory that I find attractive. There are 2 rooms in the front that have balconies overlooking the main square. These have character. Otherwise the rooms are dark, unattractive, and without colonial atmosphere, but they are economical. The hotel's location is its biggest attraction.

WHERE TO DINE

San Luis has many good restaurants. Jardín Hidalgo and Plaza de los Fundadores both feature popular, everyday restaurants that do a credible job with standard fare and offer the standard midday meal: *comida corrida* or *menu del día.* These will be easy to spot; one is called **Posada del Virrey,** and the other **La Parroquia.** Below are a few restaurants that Potosinos would go to if they wanted to splurge a little.

✪ **El Callejón de San Francisco.** Callejón de Lozada 1. ☎ **48/12-4508.** Main courses $4–$8. AE, MC, V. Daily 1pm–1am. MEXICAN.

This is my favorite place in town. If the weather isn't too chilly, dine at night on the rooftop terrace with the beautiful backdrop of San Francisco's brightly lit bell towers and cupolas. I always hesitate to use the description "romantic," but here it fits to a T. If it is a tad too chilly, ask the owner for a *jorongo* (ho-*rong*-o), a traditional woolen wrap for the shoulders; he keeps a stack of them for the use of his customers. Downstairs is beautifully decorated and perfectly lit. *Curios,* objects such as old movie posters and an old elevator cage, are everywhere. The food is excellent. You might try the chiles ventilla or the pechuga Doña Luz. The restaurant is off the Plaza San Francisco to the right of the church.

La Corriente Restaurant Bar. Carranza 700. ☎ **48/12-9304.** Breakfast $4; main courses $5–$10. AE, MC, V. Daily 8am–midnight. REGIONAL.

Here you can get a number of regional specialties—much of the menu is the Mexican equivalent of down-home country cooking. I like their chamorro pibil, while the puntas al chipotle will do if you want to try a hearty country-style meat. Quesadillas de huitlacoche are wonderful. At nighttime, however, they offer a large selection of antojitos, which I have a real passion for. Tables are scattered about an interior patio and rooms off to the side. The restaurant is also a juice bar and offers large, extravagant combinations of blended fruits, which are very delicious and filling.

Restaurant Orizatlán. Pascual M. Hernández 240. ☎ **48/14-6786.** Breakfast $4; main courses $5–$7. AE. HUASTECAN.

A very colorful restaurant specializing in the traditional Huastecan cooking of eastern San Luis Potosí. If you are hungry, try the *parrillada a la Huasteca,* which is a large sampling of typical dishes, including portions of the zacahuil, Mexico's largest tamal. The waiter will keep the Huastecan enchiladas coming until you beg them to desist. More cautious eaters can order à la carte. After dinner, the restaurant serves its home-style after-dinner cordials made from several fruits; the *jobito* (a small fruit that tastes somewhat like a crab apple) is always the first flavor served. At night you can see some traditional Huastecan dancing. Eight blocks south of Jardín Hidalgo on Zaragoza, turn left when you get to Jardín Colón, about 100 feet down.

5 On the Road: From Texas to the Silver Cities

While the easiest way to experience the highlights of colonial Mexico may be to fly into Mexico City or a heartland airport, driving is still the best way to discover the real Mexico. Most people who drive into Mexico follow the southward "central route" from Nuevo Laredo at the Texas border through Monterrey, a sprawling city that is a gateway to mainland Mexico; Real de Catorce, a fascinating ghost town; and on towards San Luis Potosí. Here are some notes to guide you through the first leg of this journey:

MONTERREY   Mexico's third-largest city, Monterrey, is the first major stop on a southbound drive. Its setting is spectacular, but the city itself is primarily a commercial and industrial center. The best reason to stop in Monterrey is to see the **Museo de Arte Contemporáneo de Monterrey (MARCO),** on the Gran Plaza, at Zuazua and Ocampo (☎ **83/42-4901** or 83/42-8455).

The touristic heart of the city is centered on both the modern **Gran Plaza** and the adjoining **Zona Rosa,** a pedestrian-only shopping-and-restaurant area between Zaragoza and Morelos. **avenida Colón** is the main market street.

Since this is one of Mexico's three largest cities, accommodations are relatively high priced compared to a provincial town. Your best bets for value are the **Colonial Hotel,** Hidalgo Ote. 475 (☎ **83/43-6791**), and **El Paso Autel,** Zaragoza 130 Nte. (☎ **83/40-0690**). For luxury the **Camino Real** is among the best (☎ **83/42-2040**). For meals, check out **La Puntada,** avenida Hidalgo Ote. 123 (☎ **83/40-6985**), which has cheap breakfasts and good Mexican food; **Restaurant Luisiana,** Plaza Hidalgo (☎ **83/43-1561**), more expensive with lots of beef and seafood dishes; **El Rey del Cabrito,** corner of Dr. Coss and Constitución (☎ **83/45-3232**), which specializes in *cabrito* (roast kid), a northern Mexico tradition; or **Sanborn's,** Escobedo 920, (☎ **83/43-1834**), a Mexican chain of variety stores with restaurants that you'll learn to rely on in your Mexican travels.

SPOOKED ON THE WAY TO SAN LUIS

The ghost town of **Real de Catorce** awaits you along the road toward San Luis. Take the bypass around Saltillo and barrel on down Highway 57 toward San Luis Potosí. You'll pass through a barren desert of scrubby grass, cactus, and Joshua trees. Fill up your gas tank at every opportunity.

Matehuala is a tidy town with a good central market and several adequate hotels in town and on the highway. **El Mesquite Restaurant,** on the highway before you enter Matehuala, offers cabrito that's wonderfully flavored, not greasy and not goaty tasting.

There is one fascinating stop along the long, dull road from Saltillo to San Luis Potosí; 140 miles south of Saltillo you'll reach the ghost town of **Real de Catorce,** one of Mexico's most unusual places—like an 18th-century town preserved in a time capsule and hidden in the mountains. After the discovery of silver in 1773, Real de Catorce became one of Mexico's top three silver-producing towns by the early 1800s, with a population of over 40,000. Streets lined with mansions owned by wealthy mine owners sprouted side by side along with an opera house and a mint. The Mexican Revolution brought the downfall of the town; the mines were flooded, and townspeople fled to safety elsewhere. They never returned, although many descendants retain ownership and in recent years a few mines have reopened. Catorce is finally experiencing a renaissance of sorts and many structures are in the process of being restored. The latest population census attributes almost 11,000 people to this town, but locals guess that only around 2,000 people live in the immediate area. I had no idea the Mexican census counts ghosts.

Gas Caution

Fill up with gas in Matehuala—there's no gas in Catorce.

A visit here is a must if you can spare the time. Photographers, historians, lovers of the unusual in Mexico, and people who don't mind a touch of uncertainty in their travels will count this among the high points of a trip south of the border.

On the northern edge of Matehuala there's a sign on Highway 57 that is the Spanish equivalent of "turn here for ghost town." Although it's only 38 miles from the turn-off from Highway 57 to Real de Catorce, it takes 1 to 1½ hours to drive on a well-maintained but teeth-jarring cobblestone road that winds up to 9,000 feet in the mountains, passing an onyx quarry and several tiny, crumbling adobe-walled mining villages. You'll know you've arrived at Catorce when you reach the tunnel, 2 miles long and the only entrance into the town. Since it's one way, young men at both ends regulate traffic with walkie-talkies; there's a small fee for this service. Usually there is little traffic, but during past busy festival seasons (such as Oct 2) stalled cars and ensuing traffic jams have resulted in a few deaths from fumes. After passing through the tunnel, take the narrow, high street to the right, up into the town.

So what will you find once you emerge from the tunnel? A neat mountaintop town of mostly closed-up, crumbling rock-walled and stucco buildings, some of them mansions, with cactus and brush growing on the rooflines; a church that attracts 25,000 penitents every October 2; a mint that is sometimes open for tours; a stone cock-fighting arena; a fascinating cemetery; a small museum; and a few stores selling food, mining equipment, and Huichol Indian clothing and folk art. In winter, bring heavy clothes—the hotels have no heat. Hiking boots are useful, and you can inquire about renting a horse.

ACCOMMODATIONS   Although the town is off the beaten track, the small hotels sometimes fill up by nightfall. The **Vista** tries hard, and though each room has a bathroom, rooms are still humble. Find it after driving through town toward the cemetery. It has a restaurant, but no written menu. **El Real,** in a three-story restored town house, has pleasingly rustic rooms with private bathrooms and a cozy restaurant with wildly varying food preparation and service. Several people traveling together are often allowed to share a room meant for two to four people; sometimes these folks are a bit rowdy. Since the hotel's overnight guard often stays at **El Real II,** there's no control when noisy guests get out of hand. The facade of an old mansion was preserved, but the interior was gutted to make the stylish rooms and a plant-filled courtyard. The inattentive management is the same as at the El Real. Doubles in these hotels run around $35 to $40 a night. One phone (☎/fax **488/2-3733**) serves the whole town and you can try to make a reservation by fax. Best times to try are around 9am and 5pm weekdays. The phone may be continuously busy since people line up to use it, so keep trying. On weekends, denizens of Mexico City make a mad dash for Catorce, so to beat a possible crowd, arrange to arrive by 3pm on a Thursday or Friday. Sunday through Thursday or Friday morning there should be rooms available. On any day, though, if you arrive by 3pm and there are no vacancies, you'll still have time to look around briefly and return to the highway before dark. If you can't arrive by 3pm, spend the night at Matehuala, then get an early start the next day.

From here it's on to the Silver Cities through San Luis Potosí, or blast down Highway 57 all the way to Mexico City.

Tarascan Country

7

West of Mexico City and southeast of Guadalajara lies the state of Michoacán (meech-oh-ah-*kahn*), the homeland of more than 200,000 Tarascan Indians (properly known as the Purépecha). The land is mountainous in the east, north, and center, but it drops to a broad lowland plain that meets the Pacific in the south and west. The state gets more rain and is consequently greener than its neighbors Jalisco and Guanajuato. It is considered by many Mexicans to be one of the most beautiful states in their country; yet it remains relatively unexplored by foreign tourists.

Michoacán's impressive sights make it worth traveling there. High in the mountains, in the extreme northeastern part of the state, a small miracle occurs ritualistically every year: An isolated patch of forest becomes the meeting place for millions of monarch butterflies, some of which come from as far away as Canada. During the peak season the tree limbs bend under the cumulative weight of the monarchs, and the undulation of so many wings creates a dazzling spectacle.

Across the entire northern half of the state, including the monarchs' camping grounds, is a belt of great geothermal energy that has produced geysers and hot springs, many of which have been made into bathing spots. (Just the place to end up after hiking up and down a mountain in search of butterflies.) In the center of Tarascan Country, surrounding the highland lakes, are many vibrant indigenous communities. They're well known throughout the country for their handcrafts and their syncretic celebrations honoring their ancestors on the Day of the Dead. Farther west and south is the famous volcano, Paricutín, the only major volcano born in modern times (1943).

The two most important cities in Tarascan Country are Morelia and Pátzcuaro, which offer the visitor two contrasting visions of the colonial past. Morelia is a city built of stone, displaying clean-cut, sober, geometric lines and monumental proportions; Pátzcuaro, meanwhile, is composed of adobe, crooked rooflines, and a haphazard layout. The former city is proud of its Spanish heritage; the other remains rooted in its Indian origins.

In the Classic and early Postclassic periods, this entire area came under the influence of the central Mexican cities of Teotihuacán and Tula, as evidenced by the ruins at Tingambato. At some later date, the Purépecha arrived—from where, we don't know. Their language is unlike any of Mexico; the closest linguistic connection is with native peoples in Ecuador. They settled here and formed either an empire or a confederation of cities. The Purépecha successfully defended their lands from the expansionist Aztec and were the only civilized people in the Mexican highlands who did not pay tribute to the Aztec emperor. The ceremonial structures of the Purépecha are raised platforms with structures combining circles and rectangles. These are known as *yácatas,* the best examples of which are found in the old Purépecha capital, Tzintzuntzan.

In the history of the conquest and conversion of the Purépecha, two men represent the extremes of Spanish ambivalence toward the Indians. One was Nuño de Guzmán, a man so cruel and driven by greed that his crimes, condemned even by his fellow conquistadors, eventually earned him a prison cell in Spain. The other was Vasco de Quiroga, a man of education, who joined the church and arrived in Mexico late in life. Appointed as the first bishop of these people, he sought to put in place an almost-utopian society of cooperative efforts. He organized and instructed each village in the practice of specific crafts, and to this day, his distribution of crafts among the different villages is followed.

EXPLORING TARASCAN COUNTRY It takes only an hour or two to travel from one major town to another, and public transportation is frequent. You should plan no less than a day in **Morelia** (more if you plan to see the butterflies) and a minimum of 2 days in **Pátzcuaro. Uruapan,** another important city, is an easy day-trip from Pátzcuaro, though you may want to stay longer to be able to visit the **Paricutín volcano.** During Easter week or on Day of the Dead (which actually lasts 2 days, Nov 1 to 2), the Plazas Grandes in Pátzcuaro and Uruapan overflow with regional crafts. The Easter-week processions and other traditional customs in Pátzcuaro are exceptional. Reserve rooms well in advance for these holidays.

1 Morelia

195 miles NW of Mexico City; 228 miles SE of Guadalajara

The Spanish founded Morelia in 1541 and christened it Valladolid. The name was later changed to honor the revolutionary hero José María Morelos, who was born here.

Morelia's collection of original colonial buildings adds a touch of old-world Spanish elegance. The adjective most frequently employed to describe Morelia seems to be "aristocratic." In the last 10 years, however, street vendors have occupied so many of the plazas, stone arcades, and other public spaces that one can hardly move around in them, much less gain a decent visual perspective. Most of these vendors came from Mexico City after the horrendous earthquake there. Selling is what they know, and the public appears willing to buy what they sell. Cries of protest from civic groups and store owners' associations are constantly heard, but the politics around this issue are delicate.

ESSENTIALS

GETTING THERE & DEPARTING **By Plane** **Mexicana** (☎ 800/531-7921 or 43/24-3808) has flights to and from U.S. cities: San Francisco, San Jose, Los Angeles, and Chicago. These are either one-stop or nonstop, depending on the destination and day of the flight. Mexicana also flies direct to Zacatecas, León, and Guadalajara. **Aeromexico/Aerolitoral** (☎ 800/237-6639, 43/24-2424, or 43/24-3604) flies to/from Mexico City, Guadalajara, Querétaro, Tepic, and Tijuana with connections to U.S. destinations. **Taesa** (☎ 800/328-2372, 43/13-4105) has flights to Mexico City, Tijuana, Guadalajara, and Zacatecas with connections to domestic and international flights.

Arriving: **Aeropuerto Francisco J. Mújica** is a 45-minute drive from the city center on km 27 of the Carretera Morelia-Zinapécuaro. Taxis meet each flight. **Budget** has a car-rental office there (☎ **800/527-0700** in the U.S. and Canada or 43/13-3399).

By Car   With the **new toll highway** running between Mexico City and Guadalajara, the trip to Morelia from either city, formerly a tedious 4- to 5-hour trip, now takes only 3 hours. From Mexico City the road goes to Toluca, then to Atlacomulco, Marvatío, and Zinapécuaro. From Guadalajara it goes through La Barca (northeast of Lake Chapala). Coming from either direction, you will see the very large Lake Cuitzeo; then look for the intersection with Highway 43 and turn south. **Highway 43 North** is a fairly direct and straight route from San Miguel de Allende (2½ hr.) and from Guanajuato (2 hr.). Between Pátzcuaro and Morelia there is the four-lane **Highway 120;** the trip takes about 40 minutes. (Midway, you'll see a turnoff for Tupátaro and Cuanajo, covered in "Side Trips from Pátzcuaro," below.) **Highway 15** (the long route) runs west from Mexico City and east and south from Guadalajara. Both sections of Highway 15 are mountainous and slow going but with beautiful vistas.

By Bus   The **Central Camionera** bus station is at Eduardo Ruíz and Valentín Gómez Farías, 7 blocks northwest of the cathedral. First-class and deluxe bus service to and from Morelia is excellent. There are several major bus lines offering many departures at different levels of service. **Flecha Amarilla** probably has the most buses (42 per day to Mexico alone). **ETN** has the fanciest, most expensive service (extra wide and roomy seats and free beverages). If you have problems finding what you want, there's an information desk in the station.

VISITOR INFORMATION   The **Tourist Information Office** is in a former Jesuit monastery, the Palacio Clavijero, at the corner of Madero and Nigromante (☎ **43/ 13-2654;** fax 43/12-9816). The office is open daily from 9am to 9pm.

CITY LAYOUT   The heart of the city is the **cathedral,** with the Plaza de Armas on its left and the Plaza Melchor Ocampo on its right. The two-way street running east-west in front of the cathedral is **avenida Madero,** the city's main street. It meets the lovely colonial aqueduct and the modern fountain **Las Tarascas** a half mile east of the cathedral. This segment of Madero, along with several blocks to either side, is the old part of town (see "Other Attractions," below.) From the fountain, the **aqueduct** heads southwest toward what has become the fashionable part of town.

GETTING AROUND   Taxis are a bargain here. Still, you should settle the fare before you enter the cab.

FAST FACTS: Morelia

American Express   The local representative is the **Lopsa Travel Agency,** in the Servi Center, avenida del Campestre and Artilleros del 47 no. 1520 (☎ **43/15-3211;** fax 43/14-7716).

Area Code   The telephone area code is **43.**

Climate   Morelia can be a bit chilly mornings and evenings, especially from November through February.

Elevation   Morelia sits at 6,368 feet.

Newspapers   The local paper, *La Voz de Michoacán,* has a "What's New in Morelia This Week" page that appears every Monday and lists all kinds of interesting cultural events.

Population   Morelia has 484,000 residents.

Post Office/Telegraph Office   Both are in the Palacio Federal, on the corner of Madero and Serapio Rendón, 5 blocks east of the cathedral.

EXPLORING MORELIA

SPECIAL EVENTS   In March **the International Guitar Festival** attracts musicians from all over the world. In May the city holds **The International Organ Festival** (corresponding to the variable feast day of Corpus Christi). The cathedral has perhaps the largest pipe organ in this hemisphere—if you like organ music, consider attending this festival. In July there is the **International Festival of Music.** September is the month of the *fiestas patrias;* on **Independence Day** (Sept 16) and **Morelos's Birthday** (Sept 30) there are large fireworks displays (*castillos*), parades, and a good deal of celebrating.

A STROLL THROUGH THE COLONIAL CENTER

Downtown Morelia, its architecture having largely retained its colonial feel, is a good town for walking. One comes across interesting details on just about any street. To avoid the crowds of street vendors, you'll either have to get up early or do your strolling in the dark. The best times are in the morning before 9 or in the evening after 9—but, of course, during these times, you can't get into museums and other public buildings (see "Other Attractions," below).

The walk outlined below could take a whole day if you don't skip any parts. The museums open at 9am; you'll find a lot of places closed on Mondays, holidays, and during the midafternoon between 2 and 4pm.

The place to begin the tour is the **cathedral.** Notice how the main street widens in front of it, and a cross street lines up with the front of the building. The city builders very consciously sought to accentuate the city's churches by creating open spaces that would allow distant perspectives. You'll find this with many other churches in town. The cathedral took the place of an earlier one; the one that stands today was not started until 1640, and it took 104 years to build. It was to incorporate the finest features of the different styles of religious architecture already extant in the city, including plateresque, mannerist, and a native style of baroque unusually characterized by sobriety and restraint—qualities that came naturally to Morelianos. The cathedral's impressive size and monumental proportions were an absolute necessity to place it at the top of the hierarchy of the city's temples and to make plain Morelia's superiority to rival Pátzcuaro. The Italian architect who designed it worked closely with all the different authorities of Morelia's sizable religious community, and he did a masterful job in balancing the different architectural elements in the facade, handling the proportions of the towers, and in the placement of the cupola. In my opinion, it's the most beautiful cathedral in Mexico. The inside is magnificent: things to look for include the beautifully worked organ with 4,600 pipes (see "Special Events," above); the silver baptismal font where Mexico's first emperor, Agustín de Iturbide, was supposedly baptized; and the elegant choir with carved-wood stalls.

Across the street (Madero) from the cathedral is a two-story building with fanciful, Oriental-style decorations on top: This is the **Palacio del Gobierno,** built in 1732 as a seminary. The government palace now contains grand murals depicting the history of Michoacán and Mexico. Some were done by a well-known local artist, Alfredo Zalce.

Next, continue down Madero east for 2 blocks and then turn right; in the next block you will come across the **church and convent of San Francisco,** which faces a plaza. This and San Agustín are the two oldest religious buildings in Morelia. Both drew on the Spanish renaissance architectural style known as plateresque (which was already antiquated by that time) because they wanted to accentuate Morelia's Spanish inheritance to contrast it with Pátzcuaro's more Indian style. The convent is quite striking; it has the elegant, Moorish-style windows on the second floor, a common feature of Mudéjar architecture in Spain. The interior courtyard, unlike any in Morelia,

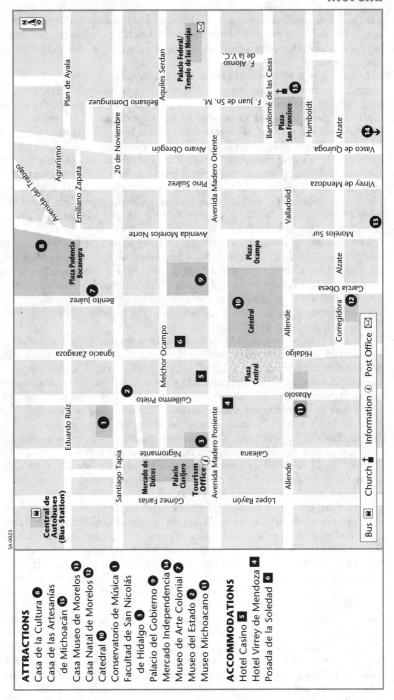

SA-0025

Central de Autobuses (Bus Station)

Plan de Ayala

Agrarismo

Aquiles Serdan

Belisario Domínguez

Palacio Federal/ Templo de las Monjas

F. Alonso de la V.C.

Bartolomé de las Casas

Plaza San Francisco

Humboldt

F. Juan de Sn. M.

Alzate

Avenida Madero Oriente

Alvaro Obregón

Vasco de Quiroga

Pino Suárez

Emiliano Zapata

20 de Noviembre

Avenida del Trabajo

Avenida Morelos Norte

Virrey de Mendoza

Valladolid

Morelos Sur

Plaza Pudencia Bocanegra

Benito Juárez

Plaza Ocampo

Melchor Ocampo

Catedral

García Obesa

Alzate

Ignacio Zaragoza

Allende

Corregidora

Eduardo Ruiz

Guillermo Prieto

Hidalgo

Plaza Central

Abasolo

Santiago Tapia

Mercado de Dulces

Palacio Clavijero

Tourism Office *i*

Nigromante

Avenida Madero Poniente

Galeana

Gómez Farías

López Rayón

Allende

ATTRACTIONS

Casa de la Cultura **8**
Casa de las Artesanías de Michoacán **15**
Casa Museo de Morelos **13**
Casa Natal de Morelos **12**
Catedral **10**
Conservatorio de Música **1**
Facultad de San Nicolás de Hidalgo **3**
Palacio del Gobierno **9**
Mercado Independencia **14**
Museo de Arte Colonial **7**
Museo del Estado **2**
Museo Michoacano **11**

ACCOMMODATIONS

Hotel Casino **5**
Hotel Virrey de Mendoza **4**
Posada de la Soledad **6**

Bus ■   Church ✝ ■   Information *i*   Post Office ⊠

227

has a wonderful medieval feel to it. Instead of being broad and open with light arches, it is closed and heavily buttressed with columns set closely together. The ex-convent now houses a local **handcrafts museum** and the best shopping in Morelia (see "Shopping," below).

Morelia's **city market** is 5 blocks south of San Francisco in a large, plain warehouselike structure. It's much like other Mexican city markets and a good place to observe details of local life. If you're going to walk as far as the market, you should also check out the **church and ex-convent of the Capuchinas.** It's a precious little baroque church with a guilded, highly ornate retablo inside. To get there from San Francisco, cross the plaza that is in front of the church and turn left (calle Vasco de Quiroga). (If you want to skip the market, instead of turning left, go straight down the street that lines up with the front of San Francisco. Turn left at the second intersection on calle Morelos Sur; 1½ blocks down on your left is the Casa Museo de Morelos. See below.) The **Templo de Capuchinas** is 5 blocks down, slightly downhill. You'll come across a shaded plaza that fronts a church. That's it. The market is 1 block to the left; it's easy to find.

From the market, backtrack to the church and keep going 2 blocks farther west to Morelos Sur. Turn right (uphill) and after 1 long block, look for the **Casa Museo de Morelos,** Morelos Sur 323 (☎ **43/13-2651**) on your right. This is where José María Morelos lived as an adult. It's a grand house with furniture and personal effects that belonged to the hero and a period kitchen. For history buffs, there is an exhibition of his four campaigns against Spanish royalist forces. The museum is open daily from 9am to 7pm; admission costs $1.25.

The next place to see is the **Museo Regional Michoacano,** at the intersection of Allende and Abasolo (☎ **43/12-0407**). To get there, walk back uphill towards Madero, turn left when you get to the plaza Melchor Ocampo, and walk through the stone arcades that are behind the cathedral. At the end of the arcades and across the street, catercorner to the Plaza de Armas, is this museum. It provides a colorful view of the state from prehistoric times to Mexico's Cardenist period of the 1930s. The building, finished in 1775, was originally owned by Isidor Huarte, father of Ana Huarte (Emperor Iturbide's wife). The museum is open Tuesday through Saturday from 9am to 7pm and Sunday from 9am to 4pm. Admission is $1.75.

If you would like to take a break, sit at one of the outdoor cafes under the stone arches facing the front of the cathedral. Here you can take refreshment and watch people pass by; this is exactly what the locals do here.

From there, go west on Madero for 1 block until you get to the corner of Nigromante, where, on the right corner, you'll find the **College of San Nicolás de Hidalgo,** a beautiful colonial-era building that claims to house the oldest university in the New World. Founded in Pátzcuaro in 1540, it was moved to Valladolid (present-day Morelia) in 1580 and incorporated into the University of Michoacán in 1917. The church that you see on the other corner is another one of Morelia's oldest churches, the Iglesia de la Companía de Jesús, built by the Jesuits. There is a **tourist information office** right next door; the large colonial building beside it is the former Jesuit convent. Now it houses government offices and is called **Palacio Clavijero.** The interior courtyard is the most photographed in all Morelia. When you see it, you'll know why. To enter the building, walk down Nigromante until you come to the door. Afterwards, continue down the street to the little park. Facing the park is the **Conservatorio de las Rosas,** a former convent for Dominican nuns. In 1785, it became a music school for boys, and it is now the home of the internationally acclaimed **Morelia Boys Choir.** The choir practices on weekday afternoons. If you would like to hear them in concert, you can ask for information inside.

Catercorner from the conservatory is the **Museo del Estado,** at the junction of Santiago Tapia and Guillermo Prieto (☎ **43/13-0629**). Exhibits include a display of the archaeology and history of the area and an intact 19th-century apothecary shop. The museum is open Monday, Tuesday, Thursday, and Friday from 9am to 2pm and 4 to 8pm; Wednesday, Saturday, Sunday, and holidays from 9am to 2pm and 4 to 7pm. Admission is free. Look for or ask about concerts and other goings-on here.

For another interesting museum, continue east on Santiago Tapia 2 blocks to Benito Juárez and turn north (left) to the **Museo de Arte Colonial,** av. Benito Juárez 240 (☎ **43/13-9260**). In a well-restored colonial mansion, it possesses a large collection of religious art from the 16th to the 18th centuries. One section of the museum displays Christ figures made from the paste of corn stalks. This was a pre-Columbian artistic technique among the Purépecha, and the missionaries soon had their Indian converts using it to create Christ figures. If you've been to La Parroquia in San Miguel Allende, you will have already seen an example of this. The Christ figure there came from Pátzcuaro. The museum is open Tuesday through Sunday from 10am to 2pm and 5 to 8pm.

To learn about local cultural events, cross the small street to the north (around the corner to the right from the museum) and turn left onto the next street (avenida Morelos Norte). Follow the high wrought-iron fence, which encloses a whimsical, contemporary sculpture made from machine parts, to reach the entrance of the **Casa de la Cultura.** This cultural complex (☎ **43/13-1320**) includes a mask museum, an open-air cafe, and several art galleries. It's open daily from 10am to 8pm, with no admission charge. Posters in the entrance announce events taking place here and at other locations in town.

OTHER ATTRACTIONS

If you enjoy morning walks, try going east on Madero from the cathedral. In a couple of blocks, you'll reach the **Templo de las Monjas** ("Nuns' Temple"), a lovely old church with a unique twin facade and B-shaped floor plan. Beside it is the massive **Palacio Federal,** which houses, among many other official bureaus, the post and telegraph offices. Continue and you'll reach the **aqueduct** and the **Las Tarascas fountain.** There, starting from one of the arches of the aqueduct, is a broad stone walkway, lined with trees and stone benches, that leads to the **church of San Diego.** The most ornate church in Morelia, San Diego is also known as **El Santuario de Guadalupe.** The distance from the cathedral to San Diego is a little more than a mile. You can take a taxi back or, if you still feel like walking, you can return by crossing the large plaza to the right of the church, passing by the equestrian statue of Morelos, going under the aqueduct, and entering the park known as **El Bosque.** Inside the park are a couple of interesting buildings that are now museums. West of the park there is a middle-class neighborhood. What you want to do is continue west and work your way back to Madero. If you get turned around here, note that if you're walking on level ground you're parallel to or heading towards Madero; if you're walking downhill, you're heading away from it.

SHOPPING

Casa de las Artesanías. Exconvento de San Francisco, Plaza Valladolid. ☎ **43/12-1248.**

This is one of the best crafts shops in Mexico. In the showroom on the right as you enter on the first floor, you'll find an array of objects, including fantastic carved-wood furniture, 6-foot-tall ceramic pots, beautiful handwoven clothing, embroidered scenes of daily life, wood masks, lacquerware from Pátzcuaro and Uruapan, cross-stitch embroidery from Tarecuato, waist-loomed table runners (used for mufflers) and carved-pine furniture from Cuanajo, woodwork and guitars from Paracho, and close-woven hats from the Isla de Jarácuaro. Straight ahead in the fabulous interior court-yard are showcases laden with the best regional crafts. Upstairs, individual villages have sales outlets for fabric, wood carving, weaving, copper, and the like. Everything on display is for sale at reasonable prices. Upstairs in a living crafts museum, workers create and display their art. The shop is open daily from 9am to 8pm; admission is free.

Mercado de Dulces. Beside the Palacio Clavijero, along Valentín Gómez Farías.

This delightful jumble of shops, west on Madero from the cathedral and north on Nigromante, sells *cubitos de ate* (candied fruit wedges), jelly candies, honey, goat's milk, strawberry jam, and *chongos* (a combination of milk, sugar, cinnamon, and honey that squeaks when you bite into it). Upstairs is a shop with all kinds of regional *artesanías* and hundreds of picture postcards from all over Michoacán. The mercado is open daily from 7am to 10pm.

WHERE TO STAY
EXPENSIVE

✪ **Villa Montaña.** Patzimba 201, 58090 Morelia, Mich. ☎ **800/223-6510** in the U.S., 800/44-UTELL in Canada, 43/14-0231, or 43/14-0179. Fax 43/15-1423. 64 units. TV TEL. $150 double standard; $200–$225 double suite. AE, MC, V.

Above the hustle and bustle, on the Santa María Ridge overlooking Morelia, this inn breathes beauty and tranquillity. Rooms are distributed among a small complex of buildings separated by gardens and connected by footpaths. Set on a hillside, the buildings are at different levels; this, as well as the placement of the entrances, allows for privacy. It's no wonder Villa Montaña is a member of the "Small Luxury Hotels of the World." There are no rough edges to this hotel; all the details are handled perfectly, including excellent food and attentive service. This hotel is so popular with repeat guests that it's almost always full around the Days of the Dead (Nov 1 and 2), Christmas, and most of February.

Dining/Diversions: One restaurant serves delicious meals facing an inner court-yard with views of the city. Romantic soloists or trios perform most evenings. It's open daily from 7:30am to 11pm. There is an adjoining bar.

Amenities: Laundry and room service, tour desk (for seeing monarch butterflies or other regional sights), concierge, lending library, in-room massage and hairstyling, heated swimming pool, tennis court.

MODERATE

Hotel Casino. Portal Hidalgo 229, 58000 Morelia, Mich. ☎ **800-528-1234** in the U.S., or 43/13-1328. Fax 43/12-1252. E-mail: casino@infosel.net.mx. 53 units. TV TEL. $58 double. AE, MC, V.

This fine old hotel features several structural and decorative touches—beams, chan-deliers, and columns—along with an excellent location—across the street from the cathedral. All the rooms in back are quiet; some rooms in front come with a balcony and view of the cathedral. Rooms are immaculate and have wall-to-wall carpeting. The hotel is a member of the Best Western chain. You cannot reserve a suite using the toll-free number—only standard rooms. The on-site restaurant in the covered courtyard is good. The staff can provide good tourist information and can connect you with a tour to see the monarchs.

Hotel Virrey de Mendoza. Madero Pte. 310, 58000 Morelia, Mich. ☎ **43/12-4940.** Fax 43/12-6719. 70 units. TV TEL. $81 double. AE, CB, DISC, MC, V. Valet parking.

On the main plaza, this recently renovated hotel exudes colonial elegance. The lobby is exquisite, with billowing fresh-flower arrangements and an inviting sitting area under an impressive stained-glass canopy. Rooms are comfortable and have a lot of character. All rooms have bathtubs—a luxury in Mexico—and many have writing desks. Oriental carpets and armoires (which hide TVs) add to the charm. For the sake of quiet, avoid a room facing Madero and interior rooms on the second floor that catch noise from the lobby. Interior rooms on the upper floors are perfect. There's a restaurant and bar on the first floor.

Posada de la Soledad. Ignacio Zaragoza 90, 58000 Morelia, Mich. ☎ **43/12-1888.** 67 units. TV TEL. $45–$53 double. AE, CB, DC, MC, V. Free parking.

The building was constructed in 1719 as the home and carriage house of a rich Spaniard. The original ambiance is carried on to this day in the hotel's lovely court-yards, where antique carriages are parked under the stone arches. Some rooms have fireplaces, tubs in addition to showers, and small balconies. Standard rooms are small, and some can be a little drafty. The price difference has to do with whether the room is off the front or the back patio. Rooms are carpeted, and most come plainly furnished, with one or two double beds and colonial-style furniture. Bathrooms vary in size and quality; in my last room the hot and cold taps were switched. To reach the hotel from the cathedral, walk 1 block west on Madero to Zaragoza; turn right and you'll find the hotel on the right, near Ocampo.

WHERE TO DINE
✪ **El Anzuelo.** Av. Camelinas 3180. ☎ **43/14-8339.** Main courses $5–$9. No credit cards. Tues–Sun noon–5:30pm. SEAFOOD.

This simple outdoor restaurant in the modern, fashionable part of town serves delicious food prepared with great care. They make the perfect Mexican seafood cocktail and have wonderful ceviche. After either of those as a starter, you might order salt-water or freshwater fish cooked in a variety of styles, or prime beef, which they also do well. The owners are meticulous (they insist on boiling the fish before making ceviche); every year they win the cleanliness award granted by the municipality to the best-run restaurant in the city. El Anzuelo is open only in the afternoon. On Sunday they offer paella; the place gets very crowded. To get there take a taxi.

Las Mercedes Restaurant. León Guzmán 47. ☎ **43/2-6113.** Main courses $8–$12. AE, MC, V. Mon–Sat 1:30pm–midnight; Sun 1:30–6pm. INTERNATIONAL.

In this peaceful inner courtyard stuffed with palms, flowers, and succulents in tubs and pots, one can dine on pasta, crepes with piñones and pistachios, beef brochette, and various seafood and meat offerings. Pastel-clothed tables are set with charming hand-painted ceramic plates; wine is presented in a translucent, handblown fluted green glass. A plate of small tacos is automatically brought while diners make their choices. Homemade bread also arrives with a small tub of herb-flavored butter. To get here from the cathedral, walk 4 short blocks west on Madero. Turn right on León Guzmán and look for a small sign on the left over the door.

✪ **Las Trojes.** Juan Sebastián Bach 51. ☎ **43/14-7344.** Main courses $7–$10. AE, CB, DISC, MC, V. Mon–Sat 1pm–midnight; Sun 1–6pm. MEXICAN.

A *troje* (or *troxe*) is the traditional dwelling of the Purépechan Indians. It is made of wood planks and can be of varying sizes, some approaching the size of barns. This restaurant is made of seven trojes joined together, with the addition of some large glass windows. The place is gorgeous. Choose from among several cuts of meat, including filet mignon, *cecina* (beef or pork sliced thin, spiced, and dried), chicken stuffed with cheese en brochette, and whitefish—the famous specialty that comes from the region's lakes. Vegetarians can try the *champiñones al ajillo* (mushrooms in garlic). You'll need a taxi to get here from the historic center.

Las Viandas de San José. Álvaro Obregón 263 at Emiliano Zapata. ☎ **43/12-3728.** Breakfast $2.65–$3.50; main courses $5–$7; comida corrida $4. No credit cards. Daily 8am–11pm. REGIONAL.

Dining is a pleasure under the arcades or adjacent rooms of this mansion, built around an interior patio. Service is gracious, and the menu offers intriguing regional specialties such as *uchepos* (fresh corn tamales) and *corundas* (little triangular-shaped tamales with hot sauce and cream); bone-marrow soup; rabbit in wine sauce; chicken *placero* with enchiladas; and 11 different fish dishes, including Pátzcuaro whitefish. Beef and chicken prepared home-style round out the menu. You can't go wrong with the huge comida corrida. To find Las Viandas from the cathedral, walk 3 blocks east on Madero Oriente and turn left on Álvaro Obregón. Walk straight for 3 blocks; it's on the corner opposite the Iglesia de San José.

MORELIA AFTER DARK

Aside from discos and hotel bars, Morelia doesn't have a lot of nightlife. The most popular disco at present is called **Siglo XVIII** (☎ 43/24-0747). The music is played loud—mostly American and Mexican pop, modern disco, and *rock en español.* It fills up with a young crowd that stays out on the dance floor. Friday nights there's a $12 cover for men and a $6 cover for women, and that includes free drinks and pizza. It's on Cerrada Turismo 20 and bulevar García de León.

There is also a club called **Peña Bola Suriana** (☎ 43/12-4641), 1 block off the Plaza de Armas, by the Museo Regional Michoacano, where you can hear live Mexican and South American folk music. Tuesday is free, Wednesday there's a $1 cover, and Thursday through Saturday it costs $3. The cover is charged when you pay your bill, not when you enter. The music is played in an open courtyard. The club is open between 8pm and midnight.

In the early evening, Morelia's **sidewalk cafes** become nightspots after dark. Hot coffee and cold beer are served to a lively, predominantly college-age crowd.

MICHOACÁN'S MONARCH MIGRATION

A visit to the winter nesting grounds of the monarch butterfly high in the mountains of Michoacán—a very long day-trip from Morelia—is a stirring experience. The monarchs gently make their way down from Canada for the winter; the best time to see them is from November through February. Take one of the **tours** offered by a number of travel agents in Morelia. Companies in Morelia offer the butterfly expedition frequently during peak months for about $30 to $45. The tour takes about 10 to 12 hours by van. In many cases, a hotel can get you signed up for a tour, but check on the price first. You might want to try **Auto Turismo de Michoacán** (☎ 43/12-4987 or 43/2-6810), or **AMEG** (☎ 43/12-0234). Monarch tours generally leave at 10am and return at 7:30pm; tours require a minimum of five people.

In the tiny, unpaved village of **El Rosario,** the brilliant butterflies flutter in a blizzard of orange and black. At the nearby **El Rosario Sanctuary** (admission $3; open daily from 10am to 5 or 6pm), a guide (whom you should tip a few dollars) accompanies each group of visitors along the loop trail (about an hour's steep walk at high altitude). It's worth the time, effort, and expense to get here, where you'll be enveloped by millions of monarchs. Hold still and you can hear the unequaled soft sounds of almost a billion butterfly wings—this is one of the few places where you can experience such magic.

At the high point of the trail, the branches of the tall pine trees bow under their burden of butterflies. For folks unable to tackle the walk, monarchs are also visible around the parking lot. There's also a comprehensive video show at the nearby information center, as well as snacks, soft drinks, and toilets.

BY CAR   If you wish to drive your own car, just follow the main roads to the towns described above. Zitácuaro is on Highway 15 between Toluca and Morelia. Ejido members (farmers who own the land on which the butterflies descend) take visitors the final distance in a truck from the parking lot at Ocampo to the reserve.

TOURS ORIGINATING ELSEWHERE   Travel agencies from **San Miguel de Allende** often have monarch tours. See the section on San Miguel de Allende in chapter 6 for details.

2 Pátzcuaro

231 miles NW of Mexico City; 178 miles SE of Guadalajara; 43 miles SW of Morelia

I have a thing for Pátzcuaro; there is something comforting to me about strolling along its streets and taking in its views. During the rainy season, when low clouds roll in and blow through the tall trees of the plaza, and water drips from low-slung tile roofs, a wonderfully sweet melancholy hangs about the place.

Except for the paved streets, little has changed about Pátzcuaro's appearance since colonial times. You'll have the feeling of traveling centuries back in time. The city is remarkably well preserved and without modern eyesores or traffic lights. The adobe walls are painted the traditional white with a bottom border in dark red.

Pátzcuaro's deep Indian roots are still very apparent. The Tarascan language is heard frequently, especially in the central market. Though distinct regional costumes are seldom seen today, Indian women still braid their hair with ribbons and wear bright blue rebozos. Women from several villages wear a new addition to local dress, a distinctive cross-point stitched apron. The town is well known for Lake Pátzcuaro, one of the world's highest at 7,250 feet, where fishermen snare delicious whitefish with nets delicate in texture and wide-winged in shape—the nets look like butterflies.

ESSENTIALS

GETTING THERE & DEPARTING   By Car   See "Getting There & Departing" under "Morelia," above, for information from Mexico City, Guadalajara, San Miguel de Allende, and Morelia. From Morelia there are two routes to Pátzcuaro; the fastest is the new four-lane **Highway 120,** which passes near Tiripetío and Tupátaro/Cuanajo (see "Side Trips from Pátzcuaro," below). The longer route via **Highway 15** takes about an hour and passes near the pottery-making village of Capula and then through Quiroga, where you follow signs to Pátzcuaro and Tzintzuntzan (see "Side Trips from Pátzcuaro," below).

By Bus   The bus station is on the outskirts of Pátzcuaro, 5 minutes by taxi. If you're going anywhere outside of Michoacán, it's usually best to go to Morelia first. There are buses to Morelia every 10 minutes. There are some exceptions: a couple of **Pegaso** first-class buses run nonstop from Pátzcuaro to Mexico City, and **ETN** has some nonstop buses to Guadalajara. From Pátzcuaro to Tocuaro and Erongarícuaro: **Occidente** buses make the 30- to 40-minute trip every 20 minutes. To Tupátaro and Cuanajo: Buses of the **Herradura de Plata** line run hourly between 7am and 9pm. To Tzintzuntzan: Frequent buses of the **Galeana** and **Occidente** lines labeled QUIROGA go frequently to Tzintzuntzan (40 min.). To Santa Clara del Cobre: Frequent buses labeled ARIO DE ROSALES pass first through Santa Clara del Cobre (the so-called

"Copper Capital" of Mexico), a 30-minute drive from Pátzcuaro. Occidente or Galeana buses are among the several buses that go there. To Ihuatzio: Frequent mini-vans and buses pass by the Plaza Chica in Pátzcuaro en route to Ihuatzio.

VISITOR INFORMATION   The **State Tourism Office,** Portal Allende 50 on the Plaza Grande (☎ 434/2-1214), is open Monday through Saturday from 9am to 2pm and 4 to 7pm and Sundays from 9am to 2pm only. Although you might not find someone who speaks English, the staff will try to be helpful, and you can pick up useful maps and brochures.

CITY LAYOUT   In a way, Pátzcuaro has two town centers, both of them plazas a block apart from each other. **Plaza Grande,** also called Plaza Principal or Plaza Don Vasco de Quiroga, is a picturesque and tranquil plaza with a fountain and a statue of Vasco de Quiroga. The square is flanked by hotels, shops, and restaurants in colonial-era buildings. **Plaza Chica,** also known as Plaza de San Agustín or Plaza Gertrudis Bocanegra, flows into the market, and around it swirls the commercial life of Pátzcuaro. Plaza Chica is north of Plaza Grande.

GETTING AROUND   With the exception of Lake Pátzcuaro, the lookout, and hotels on Lázaro Cárdenas, everything is within easy walking distance from almost any hotel in Pátzcuaro. Taxis are cheap. Although the lake is over a mile from town, buses make the run every 15 minutes from both the Plaza Grande and the Plaza Chica, going all the way to the pier (the *embarcadero* or *muelle*), passing by the train station and all the places I name on avenida Lázaro Cárdenas (formerly avenida de las Américas).

FAST FACTS: PÁTZCUARO

Area Code   The telephone area code is **434.**

Climate   The climate is delightful most of the year, but occasional blustery days bring swirls of dust and a chill of air across the lake, causing everyone to retreat indoors. From October through April, it's cold enough for a heavy sweater, especially in the morning and evening. Few hotels have fireplaces or any source of heat in the rooms.

Elevation   Pátzcuaro sits at an altitude of 7,250 feet.

Post Office   The correo is located half a block north of Plaza Chica, on the right side of the street.

SPECIAL EVENTS

The island of **Janitzio** has achieved international celebrity for the candlelight vigil that local residents hold at the cemetery during the nights of November 1 and 2, the Days of the Dead. **Tzintzuntzan** also hosts popular festivities, including folkloric dances in the main plaza and in the nearby *yácatas* (pre-Hispanic ruins), concerts in the church, and decorations in the cemetery. If you want to avoid the crowds, however, skip Janitzio and Tzintzuntzan and go to one of the smaller **lakeside villages or other islands** on the lake that also have extraordinary rituals. The tourism office (see "Visitor Information," above) has a schedule of events for the entire area and publishes an explanatory booklet, *Días de los Muertos.*

During the week celebrating **Days of the Dead,** the Plaza Grande in Pátzcuaro is loaded with regional crafts brought by artisans and vendors from all over Michoacán.

Easter week, beginning the Friday before Palm Sunday, is special here, too. Most activity centers around the basilica. There are processions involving the surrounding villages almost nightly, and in Tzintzuntzan there's a reenactment of the betrayal of Christ and a ceremonial washing of the feet. Although written in 1947, Frances Toor's

Pátzcuaro

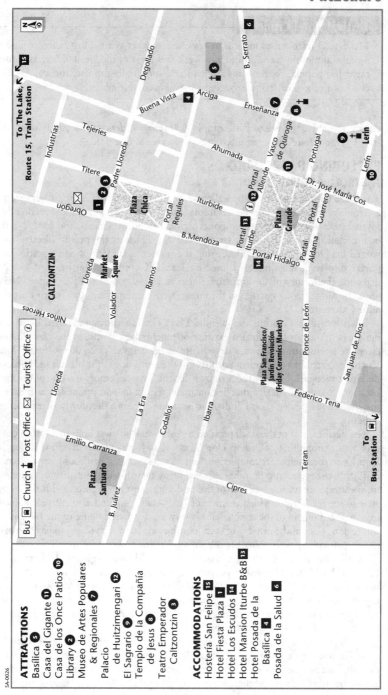

ATTRACTIONS
Basílica **5**
Casa del Gigante **11**
Casa de los Once Patios **10**
Library **2**
Museo de Artes Populares
& Regionales **7**
Palacio
de Huitzimengari **12**
El Sagrario **9**
Templo de la Compañía
de Jesús **8**
Teatro Emperador
Caltzontzin **3**

ACCOMMODATIONS
Hostería San Felipe **15**
Hotel Fiesta Plaza **1**
Hotel Los Escudos **14**
Hotel Mansion Iturbe B&B **13**
Hotel Posada de la
Basílica **4**
Posada de la Salud **6**

235

Festival Hotel Crunch

Make hotel reservations months in advance for either event. Most hotels require a 3-night minimum stay during Holy Week and Days of the Dead. There are some other less popular festivals in Pátzcuaro and surrounding towns, and you should check with the tourist office to see if any will occur during your visit.

---

description of Holy Week in Pátzcuaro, in *A Treasury of Mexican Folkways* (Crown), is still largely accurate and good preparation for a visit at that time.

EXPLORING PÁTZCUARO
A STROLL AROUND TOWN

The **Plaza Chica,** crisscrossed by walkways, contains a statue of Gertrudis Bocanegra, a heroine of Mexican independence. Immediately west of Plaza Chica, the **market** has myriad stalls with vendors selling pottery, copper, rebozos, serapes, and food. North of the market across the street, facing the Plaza Chica, is the **public library,** also named for Doña Bocanegra. Occupying the former monastery of San Agustín, the library displays a huge mural painted by Juan O'Gorman (the artist's first mural) depicting the history of the area from Tarascan legends up to the Revolution. Next door, the former living quarters of the monks were converted into the **Teatro Emperador Caltzontzin.**

Just 1 long block south is the splendid **Plaza Grande,** surrounded by colonial-era buildings. It's a vast, tree-shaded expanse of roughly kept lawns; in the center is an elaborate **stone fountain** with a large figure of the beloved Vasco de Quiroga, "Tata Vasco," depicted in a benevolent posture. On the north side of the plaza is the **Palacio de Huitziméngari,** built by the Spaniards for the Tarascan emperor—one of the rare occasions in colonial Mexico that demonstrated respect for and equitable treatment of the indigenous people. Local Indian artisans now occupy the slowly deteriorating building.

The **basilica,** east of the small plaza on top of a small hill, was built in the 16th century at the prompting of Bishop Don Vasco. It was inaugurated in 1554, although Don Vasco died before its completion, and was designated a basilica by papal decree in 1907. Now reconstructed, it has survived many catastrophes, human and natural—from earthquakes to the civil war of the mid-19th century. Be sure to visit the main altar to see the **Virgin,** which is made of "corn-stalk pulp and a mucilage obtained from a prized orchid of the region." She is very much a sacred figure to the Indians of this region, who on the 8th day of each month come from the villages to pay homage to her, particularly petitioning her miraculous healing power.

Two blocks to the south of the basilica is the **Museo Regional de Pátzcuaro** (☎ **434/2-1029**). It's housed in yet another beautiful colonial building (1540), originally Don Vasco's College of San Nicolás. The rooms, filled with fine examples of regional, popular art such as crafts and costumes, are located off the central courtyard. The museum is open Tuesday through Saturday from 9am to 7pm and Sunday from 9am to 3pm. Admission is $4; free on Sunday.

Of the many old churches in Pátzcuaro, one of the most interesting is the **Templo de la Compañía de Jesús,** just south of the museum. This church was Don Vasco's cathedral before the basilica and afterward was given to the Jesuits. The buildings across the street from the church were once part of the complex, containing the hospital, soup kitchen, and living quarters for religious scholars.

The **Casa de los Once Patios** (House of Eleven Patios), located between José María Cos and Enseñanza, is one of the most outstanding architectural achievements of the colonial period. Formerly a convent belonging to the Catherine nuns, today it houses the **Casa de las Artesanías de Michoacán,** with every type of local artistry for sale (see "Shopping," below).

SHOPPING

Pátzcuaro is one of Mexico's best shopping towns: It has terrific textiles, copper, wood carving, lacquerwork, and straw weavings made in the region. Most shops are on the **Plaza Grande** and the streets leading from it to the **Plaza Chica,** the place of choice for copper vendors. There are also a couple of shops on the street facing the basilica. If you're really interested in investigating a particular craft, you should find out which village or villages specialize in it and then go there. Tzintzuntzan, Ihuatzio, Cuanajo, Tupátaro, and Santa Clara del Cobre all have particular crafts (see "Side Trips from Pátzcuaro," below).

✪ **Casa de las Artesanías de Michoacán/House of the Eleven Patios.** Calle Lerin between José Cos and Enseñanza. No phone.

Housed in a former convent (see "A Stroll Around Town," above), this is the best one-stop shopping in the village. Small shops here sell much of what's produced in the region—textile arts, pottery and ceramic dishes, lacquerwork, paintings, wood carvings, jewelry, copper work, and musical instruments, including the famous Paracho guitars. Most of the shops are open daily from 9am to 2pm and 4 to 7pm.

✪ **Comunidad de Santa Cruz.** José María Cos 3. No phone.

Berta Servín Barriga is the helpful powerhouse behind this cooperative. Women of the farming community of nearby Santa Cruz, where she lives, send their embroidery work to be sold here. Scenes of village life are embroidered on colorful cloth panels ranging from 3 by 5 inches to 20 by 40 inches, plus tablecloths and clothing. Ask Berta or her daughter Esther to explain the events in each festive scene. There's no sign, but the shop's next to Mantas Típicas (see below), near the corner of Lerin. The shop is open Monday through Friday from 10am to 8pm and Saturday and Sunday from 10am to 5pm.

Diseño Artesano. José Cos 1. No phone.

Owner Esperanza Sepúlveda designs one-of-a-kind clothing using locally made fabrics. It's on the west side of the Plaza Grande and open daily from 10am to 3pm and 4:30 to 8pm.

✪ **Friday Pottery Market.** Plaza San Francisco, Ponce de León at Federico Teña. No phone.

Early each Friday morning this plaza, 1 block west of the Plaza Grande, fills with sellers of various styles of regionally made pottery, most of it not for sale in Pátzcuaro on other days. This is a market for locals, and few tourists seem to be in the know. Prices are *cheap.*

✪ **Galería de Arte Iturbe.** Portal Morelos 59. ☎ **434/2-0368.**

If you are an art aficionado, you'll be impressed by this powerful collection of works by Michoacán artists. There's also a small selection of folk art and books on Mexican art. Enter either through the Hotel Iturbe (go all the way to the back) or on calle Iturbe off the Plaza Grande. The gallery is open daily from 10am to 8pm.

✪ **Galería del Arcángel.** Corner of Enseñanza and Vasco de Quiroga. ☎/fax **434/ 2-1724.**

Across from the Museo Regional, this store ("the Archangel's Gallery") offers a fine collection of quality regional pottery and hand-carved furniture, plus some of the best crafts from other parts of Mexico. It's open daily from 9am to 7pm.

✪ **Mantas Típicas.** José Cos 5. ☎ **434/2-1324.** Fax 434/2-0527.

A factory outlet for the company's textile mill, this is one of several textile outlets on the Plaza Grande. Shelves are laden with colorful foot-loomed tablecloths, napkins, bedspreads, and bolts of fabric. It's at the corner of Lerin. Open daily from 9am to 7pm.

Market Plaza. West of Plaza Chica.

The House of the Eleven Patios (see above) should be your first stop, this your second. The entire plaza fronting the food market is filled with covered stalls selling crafts, clothing, rugs, rebozos, and more. Locally knitted sweaters are a good buy. Streets surrounding the plaza churn with exuberant sellers of fresh vegetables and caged birds.

Palacio Huitziméngari. Plaza Grande.

On the north side of the Plaza Grande, in a decaying building, there are a few shops run by folk from neighboring towns. The majority of the merchandise is pottery and wood carvings.

WHERE TO STAY

Hostería de San Felipe. Av. Lázaro Cárdenas 321 (Apdo. Postal 209), 61600 Pátzcuaro, Mich. ☎ **434/2-1298.** 11 units. TV, TEL. $47 double. CB, DC, MC, V. Free parking.

Located off Highway 14 as you come into town, this motel is very clean, quiet, and comfortable. It's a good choice if you're driving, since it's a long walk to the town center. Rooms are in back and arranged around a green lawn; each has a fireplace, wall-to-wall carpeting, and dark-wood ceilings. Its tranquillity makes this place ideal for a long-term stay.

✪ **Hotel Fiesta Plaza.** Plaza Bocanegra 24, 61600 Pátzcuaro, Mich. ☎ **434/2-2515** or 434/2-2516. Fax 434/2-2515. 60 units. TV TEL. $35–$42 double. MC, V. Free parking.

Fiesta Plaza has three stories of rooms along three sides of an open courtyard (no elevator). This is a new, attractive building, with pine columns, wrought-iron banisters, and wide arcades with attractive sitting areas. The comfortable rooms have tile floors, pine furniture, carpets, and small tile bathrooms. All have windows opening onto the courtyard, which are furnished with tables and chairs. A restaurant/bar is to the right as you enter. The hotel faces the north side of the Plaza Chica.

Hotel Los Escudos. Portal Hidalgo 73, 61600 Pátzcuaro, Mich. ☎ **434/2-0138** or 434/ 2-1290. Fax 434/2-0207. 30 units. TV. $37 double. MC, V. Parking $2.

This hotel is in a mansion on the west side of Plaza Grande, the birthplace of Gertrudis Bocanegra. It's a great location, and the courtyard captures some of the colonial feel of the original house. Renovation, however, has drained it of some of its original charms while adding to its comforts. Rooms are decorated with plush red or blue carpeting, red drapes, lace curtains, and scenes of an earlier Pátzcuaro painted on the walls. Some rooms have fireplaces, while others have private balconies overlooking the plaza. There's an excellent restaurant off the lobby.

Pátzcuaro Hotel Crunch

During Easter Week and Days of the Dead, Pátzcuaro's hotels fill up; visitors should be aware of two inexpensive hotels that face Santa Clara's main plaza: **The Hotel Oasis,** Portal Allende 144 (☎ 434/3-0040), the better of the two; and **Hotel Real del Cobre,** Portal Hidalgo 19 (☎ 434/3-0205), which has a restaurant.

○ **Hotel Mansión Iturbe Bed and Breakfast.** Portal Morelos 59, 61600 Pátzcuaro, Mich. ☎ **434/2-0368.** Reservations by fax in Morelia 43/13-4593 or E-mail: pazcuaro@ mail.giga.com. www.proturmich.com/mansioniturbe. 15 units. $63 double; $81 suite. All rates include breakfast. AE, MC, V. Free parking.

Located on the north side of the Plaza Grande, this 17th-century building has been through several incarnations. It was formerly a home (upstairs) and a commercial outlet (first floor); it had a stable (in back) for muleteers. Today the ground floor (where the shops once traded) holds Doña Paca, the hotel's excellent restaurant (see "Where to Dine," below). The Viejo Gaucho (see "Pátzcuaro After Dark," below), the local venue for evening music, is located in the stable area. The owners have worked hard to keep the original feel of this colonial house, with all its eccentric touches and time-worn charms. Rooms are on the second floor and have the original plank flooring; heavy, dark Spanish-style wooden furniture; deep-red drapes; and plaid bedspreads. Bathrooms are large. Hot water is slow to come but plenty hot when it finally arrives. Rates include a welcome drink, full breakfast with delicious cappuccino or coffee, 2-hour use of a bicycle, and a free daily paper; in addition, the 4th night is free. Instant coffee and hot water are available in the lobby early in the morning before the restaurant opens. A package deal like this is hard to beat in Pátzcuaro.

○ **Hotel Posada de la Basílica.** Arciga 6, 61600 Pátzcuaro, Mich. ☎ **434/2-1108.** Fax 434/2-0659. 12 units. TV. $42 double. Children under 12 stay free in parents' room. MC, V. Free enclosed parking.

A mansion transformed into a hotel, this appealing colonial-style inn across from the basilica surrounds a lovely patio. The sunny rooms have wonderful views, red curtains, heavy Spanish-style furniture, and little brick fireplaces. The hotel's restaurant, whose tables are decorated with regional pottery, is open for breakfast and lunch. Service is slow, but there's a fabulous view of the mountains, the tile rooftops, and the lake. The hotel is opposite the basilica, at the corner of Arciga and La Paz.

Posada de la Salud. Serrato 9, 61600 Pátzcuaro, Mich. ☎ **434/2-0058.** 15 units. $20 double. Street parking available.

This posada offers two tiers of exceptionally quiet rooms built around an attractive courtyard. All rooms have beautiful beds with carved wooden headboards and matching desks. Two rooms have fireplaces. The inn is a good bargain. It's on the southeast side of the basilica, a long half block up on the right.

WHERE TO DINE

Restaurants open late and close early in Pátzcuaro, so don't plan on hot coffee if you're up early, but do plan ahead for late-evening hunger pangs. For inexpensive eats, try the tamal and atole vendors in front of the basilica and by the market. Even more prolific are the pushcart taco stands that line up near Plaza Chica and the market in the mornings, dispensing tacos with meat from various, unidentified cow parts (don't worry which parts; the tacos are great). You can also get steamy cups of atole, hot *corundas*, and huge tamales sold by housewives. The corundas are one street food you can eat safely, and these are fresher and more delicious than those served in restaurants. Breakfast will cost a pittance here: $1 or less.

In the evenings, Plaza Chica is filled with small sidewalk restaurants selling another specialty: Pátzcuaro chicken with simple enchiladas and heaps of fried potatoes and carrots. You can also get *buñuelos*, which drip with honey. **Café Botafumeiro,** a coffee shop on the southwest corner of Plaza Grande, offers a variety of excellent Uruapan coffees and hot chocolate by the cup or kilo.

⭐ **El Patio.** Plaza Grande 19. ☎ **434/2-0484.** Breakfast $4; main courses $5–$8; comida corrida $4.50. MC, V. Daily 8am–10pm (comida corrida served 1:30–4pm). MEXICAN.

High ceilings, good lighting, and paintings of local scenes make this a pleasant place to dine. El Patio is on the south side of Plaza Grande and offers delicious, inexpensive meals. Hot bread and butter are served with dishes like carne asada. The three-course comida corrida is delicious and plentiful. For soup try the sopa tarasca. If you want something special, try the *trucha salmonada al vino blanco* (trout in white-wine sauce).

⭐ **Restaurant Doña Paca.** Hotel Iturbe, Portal Morelos 59. ☎ **434/2-3628.** Breakfast $2.50–$5; main courses $4.50–$8. AE, MC, V. Daily 8am–9pm. MEXICAN/ REGIONAL.

This is one of the best places for regional Michoacán cuisine. Warmly inviting, with leather equipal chairs, beamed ceilings, French doors facing the portals and Plaza Grande, and photos of old Pátzcuaro decorating the walls, it's a good place to linger. You can also have your meals served outdoors under the arcade. Try the trout served *al gusto* (as you like it) with a choice of cilantro (marvelous), garlic, or other herbs, or the chicken in mango sauce. This is one of the few places featuring *churipo,* a regional beef and vegetable stew served with corundas—but make sure it's available before tempting your taste buds. For a tasty dessert, try a buñuelo topped with delicious coconut yogurt. Margarita Arriaga, the English-speaking owner, prides herself on her coffee, with good reason. The cappuccino is surely the best in Mexico. The wonderful hot chocolate comes in a big cup frothed to a puffy frenzy.

WHERE TO DINE NEARBY

The traditional place to dine on whitefish is at one of the many restaurants lining the road to the lake. For an economical meal, wander down to the little open-air restaurants on the wharf (embarcadero), where señoras fry up delicious fish while you watch. Fish, garnishes, and a soft drink cost $7 to $10. The restaurants are open daily from 8am to 6pm.

Camino Real. Carretera Patz-Tzurumutaro. No phone. Main courses $4–$9; comida corrida $4. No credit cards. Daily 7am–10pm. MEXICAN.

Locals claim that this hard-to-find restaurant serves the best food in town. The chilaquiles, a hearty breakfast dish with eggs and tortillas, will keep you going for hours. The chicken and fish dishes are also delicious, and the comida corrida is a four-course feast. Service is good even when the restaurant is full. Camino Real is about a mile outside of town on the road to Morelia (Highway 14), shortly before the turnoff to Tzintzuntzan-Quiroga and beside the Pemex station.

Restaurant Las Redes. Av. Lázaro Cárdenas 6. ☎ **434/2-1275.** Main courses $3–$7; comida corrida $4.50–$5. No credit cards. Daily 9am–8pm (comida corrida served 1–8pm). On the road to the wharf. MEXICAN.

Local residents gather at this rustic restaurant on the road to the wharf for the comida corrida, which comes with soup, rice, fish or meat, frijoles, and coffee. The restaurant is famous for its *pescado blanco* (whitefish).

PÁTZCUARO AFTER DARK

Generally speaking, Pátzcuaro closes down before 10pm, so bring a good book or plan to rest up for the remainder of your travels.

Even so, late-night music lovers can go to **Viejo Gaucho** for performances that include Mexican trios and soloists that perform traditional and nueva trova. The small restaurant serves empanadas, pastas, soups, pizza, steaks, hamburgers, beer, and mixed drinks. It's in the Hotel Iturbe, Portal Morelos 59 (☎ **434/2-3627**), but the entry is on calle Iturbe. It's open Wednesday through Sunday from 8pm to midnight. Music starts between 8:30 and 9pm. After the music starts, there's a cover charge of $3 to $5.

SIDE TRIPS FROM PÁTZCUARO

EL ESTRIBO: A SCENIC OVERLOOK   For a good view of the town and the lake, head for the lookout at El Estribo, 2 miles from town on the hill to the west. Driving from the main square on calle Ponce de León, following the signs, will take 10 to 15 minutes. Walking will take you about 45 minutes, as it's up a steep hill. Once you reach the gazebo, you can climb the more than 400 steps to the very summit of the hill for a bird's-eye view. The gazebo area is great for a picnic; there are barbecue pits and sometimes a couple selling soft drinks and beer.

THE ISLAND VILLAGE OF JANITZIO   No visit to Pátzcuaro would be complete without a trip on the lake, preferably across to the island village of Janitzio, dominated by a hilltop statue of José María Morelos. The village church is famous for the annual **Day of the Dead** ceremony, held at midnight on November 1, when villagers climb to the churchyard carrying lighted candles in memory of their dead relatives and then spend the night in graveside vigil. The long day begins October 30 and lasts through November 2.

The most economical way to get to Janitzio is by colectivo launch, which makes the trip when enough people have gathered to go, about every 20 to 30 minutes from about 7:30am to 6pm. Round-trip fare is $2 for those age 5 and up; children under 5 are free. A private boat costs $33 round-trip; a trip to three islands costs $35. The **ticket office** (☎ **434/2-0681**) is open daily from 8am to 6pm.

At the ticket office on the pier (embarcadero), a map of the lake posted on the wall details all the boat trips possible around the lake to various islands and lakeshore towns. Launches will take you wherever you want to go. Up to 20 people can split the cost.

TZINTZUNTZAN: TARASCAN RUINS & HANDCRAFTS   Tzintzuntzan (tzeen-*tzoon*-tzahn) is an ancient village 10 miles from Pátzcuaro on the road to Quiroga (see "By Bus" under "Getting There & Departing," above). In earlier centuries, Tzintzuntzan was the capital of a Tarascan empire that controlled more than 100 towns and villages. On a hill on the right before you enter town, pyramids upon pyramids remind visitors of the town's glorious (and bloody) past. Today the village is known for its straw handcrafts—mobiles, baskets, and figures (skeletons, airplanes, reindeer, turkeys, and the like)—as well as its pottery and woven goods. The **old market** is now housed in a neocolonial building. Across from the basket market are several open-air **wood-carving workshops** full of photogenic, life-size, wooden saints and other figures.

During the week of February 1, the whole village honors **Nuestro Señor del Rescate** (Our Lord of the Rescue) with religious processions. The village also takes part in Holy Week celebrations.

SANTA CLARA DEL COBRE: COPPER SMITHERY   Although the copper mines that existed here during pre-Conquest times have disappeared, local artisans still make copper vessels using the ages-old method of hammering pieces out by hand. The streets of the village are lined with shops, and little boys pounce on visitors to direct them to stores (where they will get a commission). The **Museo del Cobre** (Copper Museum), half a block from the main plaza at Morelos and Piño Suárez, is a fine introduction to the local work and its quality and varied styles. A sales showroom to the left as you enter features the work of 77 local craftsmen. Admission is free; the museum is open daily from 10am to 3pm and 5 to 7pm.

The **National Copper Fair** is held here each August, which coincides on August 12 with the **Festival of Our Lady of Santa Clara de Asis,** and on August 15 with the **Festival of the Virgin of the Sacred Patroness,** with folk dancing and parades.

To get here from Pátzcuaro, take a bus from the Central Camionera (see "By Bus" under "Getting There & Departing," above). Buses back to Pátzcuaro run every few minutes or so from the plaza. Cabs crammed full of people head back to Pátzcuaro for the same price as the bus.

TOCUARO & ERONGARÍCUARO: MASKS & A COLONIAL CONVENT

Tocuaro, a village of mask carvers, and Erongarícuaro, noted for its colonial center and furniture factory, are both within easy reach of Pátzcuaro. Both are on the same road skirting the lake.

To get to **Tocuaro,** take the Erongarícuaro bus from Pátzcuaro's bus station to the Tocuaro stop. Then walk 3 or 4 blocks from the highway, where the bus lets you off. As you stroll the streets, villagers will ask you if you're interested in masks and invite you to their homes. When you want to return, simply go back to the highway and flag down a bus.

A few miles farther is **Erongarícaro,** formerly known for its textiles. It has an ex-convent and church built by Franciscans in the 16th century. There's a small American-run factory of expensive **art furniture** decorated with the likenesses of Frida Kahlo, plump Botero-inspired figures, and forms that recall Gauguin or Picasso, among others. The owners do not offer tours or have a factory outlet in town.

TUPÁTARO & CUANAJO: A HISTORIC CHURCH & HAND-CARVED FURNITURE

The turnoff into both of these colonial-era villages is approximately 20 miles northwest of Pátzcuaro off Highway 120 on the way to Morelia (see "Getting There & Departing," above). If you would like an in-depth view of village life, **Francisco Castilleja** (☎ 434/4-0167), who lives in Erongarícuaro, conducts tours of the villages explaining something of their daily life, customs, and beliefs. His tours leave from the Mansión Iturbe weekdays at 10am. The cost depends on the size of the group.

The narrow paved road passes first through tiny **Tupátaro** (population 600), which in Tarascan means "place of tule of Chuspata" (*tule* being a reed).

Just opposite the small main plaza is the **Templo del Señor Santiago Tupátaro,** unique in Mexico for its 18th-century painted ceiling. Restored in 1994 thanks to a civilian program, it's still a parish church but is overseen by the Institute of Anthropology and History (INAH). The church was built in 1775 after the miraculous discovery of a crucifix formed in a pine tree. Indian artists, anonymous today, brilliantly painted the entire wood-plank ceiling with scenes of the life and death of Christ and Mary. The magnificent gilt retablo, still intact behind the altar, features Solomonic columns and paintings. In the center of the retablo is Santiago (St. James), and above him the face of the Eternal Father. The sign of the dove crowns the retablo.

When visitors arrive at the church, electric lights are switched on to illuminate the fabulous colors of the ceiling and the retablo. There's no admission charge, but photography is not permitted. The church is open daily from 8am to 8pm. Days of religious significance here include the Tuesday of Carnaval week and July 25, which honors Santiago (St. James). Across the plaza, a small cafe serves soft drinks and snacks and sells regional crafts.

Five miles farther is **Cuanajo** (population 8,000), a village devoted to hand-carved pine furniture and weaving. On the road as you enter, and around the pleasant, tree-shaded main plaza, you'll see storefronts with **colorful furniture** inside and on the street. Among the myriad subjects carved into furniture are parrots, plants, the sun, moon, and faces; the pieces are then painted in fabulous combinations of color. Furniture is also sold at a **cooperative** on the main plaza. Here, too, you'll find soft-spoken women who weave exquisite tapestries and thin belts on waist looms. Motifs featured in their handsome tapestries include birds, people, and plants. Everything is for sale. It's open daily from 9am to 6pm.

Festival days in Cuanajo include March 8 and September 8, both of which honor the patron saint Virgin María de la Natividad. These are solemn occasions when neighboring villages make processions carrying figures of the holy Virgin.

IHUATZIO: TULE FIGURES & PRE-HISPANIC ARCHITECTURE This little lakeside village is renowned for its **weavers of tule figures**—fanciful animals such as elephants, pigs, and bulls all made from a reed that grows on the edge of the lake—and for a rather spread-out assembly of pre-Hispanic buildings. The turnoff to Ihuatzio is on a paved road a short distance from the outskirts of Pátzcuaro on the road to Tzintzuntzan.

ZIRAHUÉN: A PRISTINE LAKE To visit one of the few lakes in Mexico that remains more or less in its natural state, make the trip to **Zirahuén,** about 7 miles west of Pátzcuaro on the road to Uruapan. With no regular bus service, it will be difficult to get to Zirahuén without a car. Lakeside restaurants serve fish (though inspect it carefully—by look and by smell—for cleanliness).

URUAPAN: HANDCRAFTS & BASE FOR VOLCANO VISITS

Uruapan, Michoacán, 38 miles west of Pátzcuaro and an hour away, has long been known for its **lacquered boxes and trays.** Although this city of 217,000 people has few tourist attractions of its own, it makes a good base for several interesting side trips, the most famous of which is to the **Paricutín volcano** and the lava-covered church and village near **Angahuán.** If you leave Pátzcuaro early and change buses in Uruapan for Angahuán, you can see Uruapan and Angahuán in a day. Otherwise you may wish to spend the night in Uruapan and start for Angahuán early the next day. See "Angahuán, Paricutín Volcano & a Church Buried in Lava," below.

ESSENTIALS The **tourist office** (☎ 452/3-6172) is in the shopping area below the Hotel Plaza, just off the main plaza. It's open Monday through Saturday from 9am to 2pm and 4 to 7pm.

The main plaza, **Jardín Morelos,** is actually a very long rectangle running east to west, with the churches and La Huatapera Museum on the north side and the Hotel Victoria on the south. Everything you need is within a block or two of the square, including the market, which is behind the churches.

Uruapan's main square is 20 blocks from the bus station. Minivans labeled CENTRO and CENTRAL (central bus station) circulate from the street in front of the bus station to the south side of the main plaza all day.

WHERE TO STAY & DINE If you want to spend the night in Uruapan, consider three hotels by the main plaza: The inexpensive but clean **Hotel Villa de Flores,** Emiliano Carranza 15 (☎ 452/4-2800), and the slightly more expensive **Hotel Nuevo Hotel Alameda,** av. 5 de Febrero 11 (☎ 452/3-3635). The best hotel downtown and near the plaza is the **Hotel Plaza Uruapan,** Ocampo 64 (☎ 452/3-3980). All have restaurants, plus there are numerous good restaurants on or near the plaza.

EXPLORING URUAPAN Uruapan's main plaza fills with artisans and sellers of crafts from around the state before and during **Easter week.** There's an unbelievable array of wares, all neatly displayed.

The **market,** opposite the monument in the middle of the main square, has copper, cross-point blouses and tablecloths, hats, huaraches, caged birds, fresh vegetables, and lots of cookshops.

La Huatapera, attached to the cathedral on the main square, is a fabulous museum of regional crafts. It is housed in a former hospital built in 1533 by Fray Juan de

San Miguel, a Franciscan. It's open Tuesday through Sunday from 9:30am to 1:30pm and 3:30 to 6pm. Admission is free.

For the finest in foot-loomed, brilliantly colored tablecloths, napkins, and other beautifully made **textiles,** take a taxi to **Telares Uruapan** (☎ **452/4-0677** or 452/4-6135), in the Antigua Fábrica de San Pedro. Call in advance, and the English-speaking owners may give you a tour of the factory, which contains fascinating turn-of-the-century machinery.

When you enter the **Parque Nacional Eduardo Ruíz,** a botanical garden 8 blocks west of the main plaza, you'll feel like you're deep in the tropics. This multiacre, semi-tropical paradise includes jungle paths, deep ravines, rushing water, and clear water-falls. Children pester visitors, offering to be their guides, but you'll enjoy touring more with only a map (25¢). The garden is open daily from 8am to 6pm, and there is a small admission fee. Buses marked PARQUE leave from in front of the telegraph office on the main square and stop at the park.

OUTSIDE URUAPAN   A bus marked TZARÁRACUA, which can be caught from Uruapan's Central Camionera (the only bus station), goes to the impressive **waterfall at Tzaráracua,** 6 miles from the main plaza. The Río Cupatitzio originates as a bub-bling spring in the national park and then forms a cascade on its way to the Pacific. A trip to Tzaráracua and to the national park can be made in a day, even in an afternoon. The falls are reached down a steep pathway. To get back to Uruapan, pick up the bus where it dropped you off.

Often called Mexico's **"Guitar Capital"** for its fine handmade guitars, **Paracho** is a 30-minute bus ride from Uruapan's Central Camionera bus station. Take the Flecha Amarilla or Servicios Coordinados lines. Paracho is a small village; the bus drops you off and picks you up in the same place.

ANGAHUÁN, PARICUTÍN VOLCANO & A CHURCH BURIED IN LAVA

Twenty-one miles from Uruapan, **Angahuán** is the village from which to launch trips to **Paricutín volcano,** which began an extended eruption in 1943 that would eventu-ally bury portions of the village in lava. **Autotransportes Galeana** buses leave every 30 minutes from Uruapan's Central Camionera for the hour-long trip. To return, pick up the bus where it dropped you off.

ERUPTION   If you don't know the tale of Paricutín's volcanic blast, stop by the plaza in Angahuán and take a look at the carved wooden door of a nearby house that faces the church, around the stone fence to the right, two doors down. Etched in pic-tures and words, the story of the volcano tells how a local man was plowing his corn-field in the valley on February 20, 1943, when at 3pm, the ground began to boil. At first he tried to plug it up; when that proved impossible, he decided to flee. By that evening, rocks, smoke, and fire were spitting out of the ground. Some villagers fled that very night; others days later. The volcano was active for 9 years, continually spewing, until March 6, 1952, when it ceased as suddenly as it had begun.

GUIDES   When tourists arrive in Angahuán, they are besieged by guides ready to take them on horseback to see the half-buried **Church of San Juan Parangaricutiro,** which looms silently in the lava, and to the crater of the volcano. Though a horse is not necessary, a guide is advisable.

The road to the volcano—not at all obvious (nor indicated) in the village—is a few blocks to the left of the plaza, with the church to the right. About half a mile down the road from Angahuán toward old San Juan and the old lava flow is a state-run **lodge/restaurant** with bathrooms (the only ones in the area) and a stone patio with a good view of the church and volcanic cone. Unless there's an abundance of hikers or

To Angahuan

Paque Nacional Eduardo Ruíz

Mercado de Artesanías

To Paricutín Volcano

Plaza Alameda

Mercado de Antojitos
La Huatápera Museum

Templo de San Francisco

Bus Station

Bus ▣ Train ⊢⊢⊢⊢

La Tzararacua ↓

SA-0027

riders headed for the church, orient yourself here; once you're down in the woods, the church is not visible and you're confronted with a maze of unmarked trails in every direction. The walk to the church takes about an hour or so. There you can climb over the lava to the bell tower and see the mighty gray volcano in the distance.

CLIMBING THE VOLCANO   Those who want to climb the volcano should allow at least 8 hours from Angahuán. The round-trip is about 14 miles. *Take plenty of food and water: There is none available along the way.* The hike is mostly flat, with some steeper rises toward the end. Climbing the steep crater itself takes only about 40 minutes for those who exercise regularly, but count on more time to walk around the crater's rim on top (1 to 2 miles) to enjoy the spectacular view.

By horse, the trip to the church and volcano takes about 6 or 7 hours and costs $20 to $30, plus tip. The asking price for a horse to the volcano is $15 to $20 per animal, and you must also pay that amount for the guide's horse. It's possible to bargain the price down to a total of $25 (for two horses and a guide). However, don't be surprised when, a few kilometers into the ride, the guide asks for a tip to be paid at the end of the trip. A good guide will climb to the top of the crater with you, point out various interesting features, including steaming fumeroles, and provide riding instructions and a good history of the area. Acting as a guide to the volcano is one of the few opportunities to earn money for the conspicuously poor Angahuán villagers. Just withhold payment until the ride is over and services are delivered as promised.

Plan to spend an entire day for the trip from Uruapan, the ride to the foot of the volcano, the short climb, the return to Angahuán, and the trip back to Uruapan.

8 Guadalajara

Guadalajara may not be the largest city in Mexico (with five million people, it's a very distant second to Mexico City), but as the homeland of mariachi music, the *jarabe tapatío* (the Mexican hat dance), and tequila, it is considered one of the most Mexican of cities. Despite its size, Guadalajara is easy to get to know, and the people are very friendly and helpful. And unlike in Mexico City, visitors here can enjoy big-city pleasures without the metropolis-size hassles.

And what's an authentic Mexican city without shopping or history? The handcrafts and decorative arts here are perhaps the best in Mexico. Shoppers can browse through the very sophisticated shops of Tlaquepaque, which offer an immense variety of beautiful merchandise, as well as the market and workshops in Tonalá, which also offer a lot of variety, but at bargain prices.

The historic center of Guadalajara is a wonderful place to amble about among plazas, fountains, churches, and old convents. The relatively new Plaza Tapatía, which doubled the amount of public space in the downtown area, has helped enliven this part of town.

While in Guadalajara, you will undoubtedly come across the word *tapatío* (or *tapatía*). In the early days, people from the area were known to trade in threes (three of this for three of that), called tapatíos. Gradually the locals came to be called tapatíos too, and the word now signifies "Guadalajaran" when referring to a thing, person, or manner of doing something.

1 Orientation

GETTING THERE

BY PLANE   Guadalajara's international airport is a 25- to 45-minute ride from the city. Taxi and colectivo (shared ride) tickets to Guadalajara or Chapala are sold in front of the airport and are priced by zone. Local taxis are the only transport from town to the airport (around $7 to the center of town).

If you're flying out of Guadalajara, you'll be required to check in at least 1½ hours before takeoff for international flights, and at least 1 hour before takeoff for domestic flights.

Major Airlines   See chapter 3, "Planning a Trip to Mexico," for a list of toll numbers of international airlines serving Mexico. Local numbers for airlines currently flying to Guadalajara from points abroad are: **Aeromar** (☎ 3/615-8509), **Aeromexico** (☎ 3/669-0202), **American**

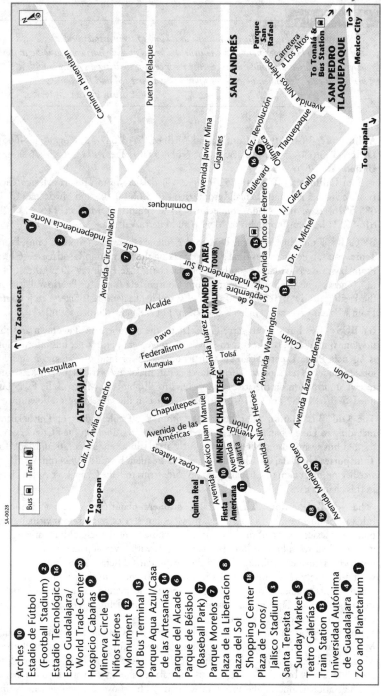

SA-0028

Bus ◨ Train ◨

To Zacatecas ↖

To Zapopan ←

**To Tonalá &
Bus Station** →

To Mexico City →

To Chapala →

SAN ANDRÉS

SAN PEDRO
TLAQUEPAQUE

Parque
San
Rafael

Carretera
a Los Altos

Camino a Huentitjan

Puerto Melaque

Avenida Independencia Norte

Avenida Circunvalación

Avenida Javier Mina

Gigantes

Dominiques

Calz. Revolución

Buleyard

O. Tlaquepaque

Avenida Niños Héroes

J.J. Glez Gallo

Dr. R. Michel

Alcalde

Pavo

Federalismo

Munguia

Mezquitan

Calz. M. Ávila Camacho

Chapultepec

Avenida de las
Américas

López Mateos

Quinta Real ■

Fiesta ■
Americana

Avenida México Juan Manuel

Avenida Juárez

Avenida Vallarta

Avenida
Union

Avenida Niños Héroes

Tolsá

Avenida Washington

Colón

Avenida Lázaro Cárdenas

Avenida Moreno Otero

Colón

EXPANDED
AREA
(WALKING
TOUR)

6 de
séptiembre

Calz. Independencia Sur

Avenida Cinco de Febrero

ATEMAJAC

MINERVA/CHAPULTEPEC

247

Impressions

The men [of Guadalajara] are handsome and cling to their attractive charro outfits and extremely large sombreros. At one time the brims of their hats were so wide that they were declared a public nuisance. Any man caught wearing a sombrero with a brim that extended much beyond his shoulders was arrested and fined.
                                                             —Burton Holmes, Mexico, 1939

Airlines (☎ 3/616-4090), **Continental Airlines** (☎ 3/647-4251 or 3/647-4605), **Delta** (☎ 3/630-3530), **Mexicana** (☎ 3/688-5526), **Taesa** (☎ 3/615-9761), and **United** (☎ 3/616-9489).

Aero California (☎ 3/616-2525) serves Guadalajara from Tijuana, Mexico City, Los Mochis, La Paz, and Puebla; **Aeromexico** (☎ 3/669-0202) and **Mexicana** (☎ 3/688-5526) have flights and connections to all points in Mexico; **Taesa** (☎ 3/615-9761) has nonstop flights to Mexico and Puerto Vallarta.

BY CAR   From Nogales on the U.S. border, follow Highway 15 south (21 hr.). From **Tepic,** you can decrease this time a little by taking the toll road to Guadalajara (6 hr.). From **Barra de Navidad** or southeast on the coast, take Highway 80 northeast (4½ hr.). There's a new toll road running from **Compostela** (north of Puerto Vallarta on the Pacific) nearly to **Tequila** (30 miles west of Guadalajara) that takes 4 to 5 hours. From **Mexico City,** take Highway 90 (7½ hr.) or the new toll road (5 hr.).

BY BUS   Two bus stations serve Guadalajara: the old one near downtown and the new one 6 miles out, on the way to Tonalá. A convenient place to get bus information is **Agencia Plaza Tapatía,** Calzada Independencia 254, a kind of "bus-ticket agency" located under Plaza Tapatía. There, travelers can make reservations, buy tickets, and receive information on the six main bus lines to all points in Mexico. The **ETN** bus line (☎ **3/614-8875** or 3/614-2479) has an office in the Hotel Carlton downtown.

The Old Bus Station   For bus trips within a 60-mile radius of Guadalajara, including to Lake Chapala, Ajijic, Jocotepec, Mazamitla, and San Juan Cosalá, go to the old bus terminal on Niños Héroes off Calzada Independencia Sur and look for **Transportes Guadalajara-Chapala,** which has frequent bus and *combi* (minivan) service beginning at 6am to Chapala (see also "Side Trips to Lake Chapala & Ajijic," later in this chapter).

The New Bus Station   The Central Camionera, about 6 miles and a 35-minute ride east of downtown toward Tonalá, provides bus service to and from virtually any point in Mexico. None of the buses at this terminal is of the school-bus variety. The new terminal resembles an international airport, with seven separate buildings connected by a covered walkway. Each building contains different lines, both first- and second-class service, for different destinations, so you must go to each one to find the line that suits you best. I recommend getting your information and buying your ticket from the Agencia Tapatía, mentioned above. Taxis are plentiful, and the ride to the downtown area should cost about $4.

Buses go to Puerto Vallarta (6 hr.), Lagos de Moreno, Colima, Manzanillo (2½ hr.), Mexico City (8 hr.), and to Aguascalientes; Zacatecas, Tuxcueca, La Manzanilla, and Mazamitla; Talpa and Macota; San Juan del Lago; Morelia and León. If you wish to travel Mexico by bus, this bus station in Guadalajara should get you on your way.

The station is one of the nicest in Mexico, with a host of amenities, including shuttle buses between terminals, restaurants, gift shops, luggage storage (*guarda equipaje*), liquor stores, long-distance telephones, and hotel information. There's also a large budget hotel next door.

VISITOR INFORMATION

The **State of Jalisco Tourist Information Office** is at calle Morelos 102 (☎ **3/ 658-0049** or 3/658-2222; fax 3/613-0335) in the Plaza Tapatía, at the crossroads of Paseo Degollado and Paraje del Rincón del Diablo. It's open Monday through Friday from 9am to 8pm and Saturday, Sunday, and festival days from 9am to 1pm. This is one of the most efficient and informative tourism offices in the country. They have a supply of maps as well as a monthly calendar of cultural events in the city.

CITY LAYOUT

Guadalajara may be big, but it's not hard to get to know. Of course, visitors will find that some areas are much more interesting than others. Probably the most important is the **historic downtown area.** Due west from there is the fashionable part of town, from **Chapultepec to Minerva Circle.** This is the prime hotel and restaurant zone. The main artery connecting downtown to Chapultepec/Minerva Circle is avenida Vallarta. Southwest from town is **Plaza del Sol,** Guadalajara's big shopping center with several clothing stores. To the southeast of downtown are **Tlaquepaque** and **Tonalá,** which are heaven for shoppers seeking handcrafts.

NEIGHBORHOODS IN BRIEF

Centro Histórico   The heart of the city contains the five main plazas, the cathedral, and several colonial buildings. This is where the action is—here you'll find museums, which house many of the masterpieces of the famous Mexican muralist, Jose Clemente Orozco, theaters, restaurants, hotels, clubs, and the largest covered market in Latin America all linked by wide boulevards and pedestrian-only streets. The historic center is bounded on the east and west by Avenidas 16 de Septiembre/ Alcalde and Prosperidad (across Calzada Independencia), and north and south by avenida Hidalgo and calle Morelos.

Parque Agua Azul   This enormous city park 20 blocks south of the Centro Histórico has a children's area and rubber-wheeled train. Nearby are the state crafts shop, performing-arts theaters, and the anthropology museum.

Chapultepec   This fashionable neighborhood with many shops and restaurants is 25 blocks west of the Centro Histórico, around the intersection of avenida Vallarta and avenida Chapultepec.

Minerva Circle   The Minerva Circle and fountain is a mile farther west beyond Chapultepec and is at the confluence of Avenidas Vallarta and López Mateos and Circunvalación Washington. It lends its name to the surrounding area ("La Minerva") known for its deluxe hotels and fine restaurants. It's a 15-minute taxi ride from the Centro ($3.50).

Plaza Del Sol   The largest shopping center in the city lies south of Minerva Circle and about 50 blocks southwest of the Centro Histórico, near the intersection of Avenidas López Mateos and Mariano Otero. This is the place to shop for clothing. Next to the shopping center is the Hotel President Inter-Continental.

Zapopan   Founded in 1542 as a separate village, Zapopan is now a full-fledged suburb of Guadalajara, 20 minutes northwest of the Plaza Tapatía via avenida Ávila Camacho. It's noted for its 18th-century basilica and the revered 16th-century image of the Virgin of Zapopan, made of corn paste and honored every October 12. The city's fashionable country club is just south of Zapopan.

Tlaquepaque   Seven miles southeast of the Centro Histórico (20 min. by taxi) is this village of erstwhile mansions turned into shops, which front pedestrian-only streets and plazas. This and Tonalá are the places to shop for handcrafts.

Tonalá   Four miles beyond Tlaquepaque is this village of over 400 artists who work in metal, clay, glass, and paper. A huge street market is held on Thursday and Sunday.

2 Getting Around

BY TAXI   Cabs in Guadalajara are not terribly expensive—maybe it's because there are so many around. A lot of hotels post general cab prices somewhere or you can simply ask at the desk before you take a cab ride. Also, agree on a price with the driver before setting out.

BY CAR   Keep in mind several main arteries. The **Periférico** is a loop around the city that connects with most other highways entering the city. Traffic on the Periférico is slow, filled with trucks, and has only two lanes. Several important freeway-style thoroughfares crisscross the city. **González Gallo** leads south from the town center and connects with the road to Tonalá and Tlaquepaque; it also leads straight to Lake Chapala. **Highway 15** from Tepic intersects with both **avenida Vallarta** and Calzada Lázaro Cárdenas. Vallarta then proceeds straight downtown. **Cárdenas** crosses the whole city and intersects the road to Chapala and to Tlaquepaque and Tonalá.

BY BUS & COLECTIVO   The city has a rapid-transit system called the **Tren Ligero,** which is not of much use to the visitor. The *Par Vial* (electric buses) will get you into the fashionable west side from downtown and back again. Those bearing the sign "PAR VIAL" run a rectangular route going east along Independencia/Hidalgo, passing the Mercado Libertad, and going as far west as the Minerva Circle, where they turn back east on Vallarta/Juárez and pass by the Plaza de Armas on their run east.

There are six varieties of city buses that run many of the same routes while offering different grades of service. The best are **Línea Turquesa buses,** which are colored pale turquoise and have the distinguishing letters "TUR" on the side; they run several routes around the city. These are air-conditioned, have padded seats, and best of all, carry only as many passengers as there are seats; they are worth the additional price. Once they've picked up passengers in the Centro Histórico, only a few stops remain until they reach their final destination, making them a relatively fast mode of public transportation. Frequent **TUR** buses also run between the Centro Histórico, Tlaquepaque, Central Camionera (new bus station), Tonalá, and Zapopan. Some of these go to Tonalá and not Zapopan, or Zapopan but not Tonalá. For more information on Tlaquepaque and Tonalá, see "Shopping," below.

Many buses run north-south along the Calzada Independencia (not to be confused with calle Independencia), but the **"San Juan de Dios–Estación"** bus goes between the points you are likely to want—San Juan de Dios church, next to the Mercado Libertad, and the railroad station (*estación*) past Parque Agua Azul. This bus is the best option because the others on Calzada Independencia have longer routes (out to the suburbs, for instance) and thus tend to be heavily crowded at all times. Fares are generally 40 cents; exact change is not necessary.

Colectivos are minivans that run throughout the city day and night, picking up and discharging passengers at fixed and unfixed points. There are no printed schedules, and routes and fixed pickup points change frequently. However, locals know the routes by heart and can tell you where and how to use these minivans if you tell them where you want to go. Fares are generally 40 cents.

FAST FACTS: Guadalajara

American Express   The local office is at Av. Vallarta 2440, Plaza los Arcos (☎ **3/615-8910**); it's open Monday through Friday from 9am to 6pm and Saturday from 9am to noon.

Area Code   The telephone area code is **3.**

Bookstores   Gonvil, a popular chain of bookstores, has a branch across from Plaza de los Hombres Ilustres on avenida Hidalgo and another a few blocks south at Av. 16 de Septiembre 118 (Alcalde becomes 16 de Septiembre south of the cathedral). **Sanborn's,** at the corner of Juárez and 16 de Septiembre, always has an excellent selection of English-language magazines, newspapers, and books.

Climate & Dress   Guadalajara has a mild, pleasant, and dry climate year-round. Evenings during the months from November through March require a sweater. The warmest months, April and May, are hot and dry. From June through September, it's rainy and a bit cooler. Guadalajara is as sophisticated and at least as formal as Mexico City. Dress is conservative; attention-getting sportswear (short shorts, halters, and the like) is out of place here, but knee-length shorts, skirts, slacks, and blouses for women, or slacks, Bermudas, and shirts for men, are appropriate except for a few formal restaurants or events.

Consulates   The largest American consular offices in the world are here, at Progreso 175 (☎ **3/825-2998** or 3/825-2700). The offices are open Monday through Friday from 8am to 4:30pm. Other consulates include the Canadian consulate: Hotel Fiesta Americana, Local 31 (☎ **3/615-6215**); the British consulate: Eulogio Parra 2539, Oficina 12 (☎ **3/616-0629**); and the Australian consulate: López Cotilla 2030 (☎ **3/615-7418**).

Currency Exchange   The best rates are to be found 2 blocks south of the Plaza de Armas, on López Cotilla street between the streets Corona and Maestranza. There must be a dozen casas de cambio on this one block. All have their rates posted, which are better than most banks in town and without the hassle.

Hospitals   For medical emergencies, there's the **Hospital México-Americano,** Cólomos 2110 (☎ **3/642-7152**).

Luggage Storage/Lockers   You can store luggage in the main bus station, the Central Camionera, and at the Guadalajara airport.

Newspapers/Magazines   The Hotel Fénix, on the corner of Corona and López Cotilla, sells English-language newspapers, magazines, and maps. It's also a good place to buy Guadalajara's newspaper in English, the *Colony Reporter,* published every Saturday.

Police   Tourists should fist try to contact the Jalisco tourist information office in Plaza Tapatía, listed under Vistor Information (☎ **3/658-0049**). If they can't reach this office, they should call the municipal police at ☎ **3/617-6060.**

Post Office   The main post office (correo) is at the corner of Carranza and calle Independencia, about 4 blocks northeast of the cathedral. Standing in the plaza behind the cathedral and facing the Degollado Theater, walk to the left and turn left on Carranza; walk past the Hotel Mendoza, cross calle Independencia, and look for the post office on the left side.

Safety   Crimes against tourists and foreign students in Guadalajara generally take the form of pickpocketing and purse snatching. Criminals usually work in teams and target travelers in busy places such as outdoor restaurants; they will wait until their victims set something down, then one will create a distraction while the other discreetly lifts the prize. There have been reports of purse snatching, usually against unaccompanied women at night, and rarely in places with crowds. Downtown is relatively safe. A similar crime, most common at night and in places with few people, is necklace snatching, where the assailant will grab hold of a necklace, especially if it has a gold chain, and pull hard, hoping it will break.

Spanish Classes   Foreigners can study Spanish at the **Foreign Student Study Center,** University of Guadalajara, calle Guanajuato 1047 (Apdo. Postal 12130), 44100 Guadalajara, Jalisco (☎ **3/853-2150;** fax 3/653-0040).

3 Where to Stay

If you're looking for good hotels at moderate prices, read on. I've selected a couple of moderate hotels in the historic center, the Calinda Roma and Mendoza, and one in nearby Agua Azul. All three of these offer pretty much the same services including laundry and room service. The Carlton is a little bigger and fancier than the other two, but doesn't offer the convenience of being right downtown. The deluxe hotels are farther out, in the west and southwest parts of town—about 15 minutes away by taxi. Guadalajara's luxury hotels are all quite modern, though the Quinta Real employs traditional architecture. As for value, there are few good hotels in the inexpensive category. Both moderate and expensive hotels reflect their big-city location: They are more expensive and sophisticated than most of their counterparts in the smaller provincial capitals.

DOWNTOWN/CENTRO HISTÓRICO
MODERATE

Calinda Roma. Juárez 170, 44100 Guadalajara, Jal. ☎ **800/228-5151** in the U.S., 01-800/900-0000 in Mexico, or 3/614-8650. Fax 3/614-2629. 174 units. A/C MINIBAR TV TEL. $74–$80 double. AE, DC, MC, V. Free secured parking.

Completely renovated in 1993, this is a comfortable, modern hotel within walking distance of all Centro Histórico sights and restaurants. The rooms are carpeted, have modern furniture and comfortable mattresses, and are well lit. They also have large bathrooms, and some even come with exercise bicycles. The hotel offers a small section just for women travelers. There's an excellent restaurant and bar in the lobby, and you can relax on the rooftop garden and pool. For those who don't want to relax, there's a business center here as well. The hotel is at the corner of Juárez and Degollado. Ask for a room that doesn't face Juárez.

Hotel de Mendoza. Carranza 16, 44100 Guadalajara, Jal. ☎ **800-221-6509** in the U.S., or 3/613-4646. Fax 3/613-7310. mexplaza.com.mx/dmendoza. 110 units. A/C TV TEL. $82 double. AE, DC, MC, V. Secured parking $1.25 daily.

Two blocks from the cathedral, this colonial-style hotel is popular with visitors for its location and quiet, staid atmosphere. Rooms have wall-to-wall carpeting, and some have a tub and a shower. The big decision here is deciding between a room facing the street or one facing an interior court with a swimming pool. The hotel is behind the Palacio de Gobierno. There is one restaurant called La Forja.

INEXPENSIVE

✪ **Hotel San Francisco Plaza.** Degollado 267, 44100 Guadalajara, Jal. ☎ **3/ 613-8954** or 3/613-8971. Fax 3/613-3257. 76 units. A/C TV TEL. $26–$32 double. AE, CB, MC, V. Free parking.

This hotel facing a tiny square near Prisciliano Sánchez is a great value. All rooms are ample and attractive, with comfortable beds but small bathrooms. And, since over the past year the management has been in the process of replacing mattresses and furniture, the rooms don't feel so old. The price difference is based on whether the room comes with one double or king-size bed or two double beds. Avoid getting a room along Sánchez street, where many trucks and buses pass. The English-speaking staff is friendly and helpful. A good, inexpensive restaurant off the lobby is open daily from 8am to 10pm. To get here from the Plaza de Armas, walk 5 blocks south on 16 de Septiembre, turn left onto Sánchez, and walk 2 blocks to Degollado and the hotel.

AGUA AZUL
MODERATE

Carlton Hotel. Av. Niños Héroes 125 and 16 de Septiembre, 44190 Guadalajara, Jal. ☎ **3/ 614-7272.** Fax 3/613-5539. 201 units. A/C TV TEL. $80 standard double. Ask about weekend discounts. AE, DC, MC, V. Parking $2 daily.

The Carlton is near Agua Azul Park, not far from the historic center. The well-furnished rooms are spacious. All come with hair dryers and remote-control TV with channels in English. Master suites have a large living-room area; junior suites have a small sitting area. Each of the fifth-floor executive suites includes terry robes, continental breakfast, afternoon coffee and pastries, and an open bar in the early evening. The 10th floor is reserved for nonsmokers. You'll save money by purchasing a package for this hotel through a travel agent in the United States.

The Carlton has an indoor/outdoor restaurant facing the large pool that serves all meals. Diversions include two bars, a disco, and a live-music nightclub here. The hotel also offers a small, fully equipped fitness center.

MINERVA CIRCLE
VERY EXPENSIVE

✪ **Quinta Real.** Av. Mexico 2727, 44680 Guadalajara, Jal. ☎ **800/445-4565** in the U.S. and Canada, or 3/615-0000. Fax 3/630-1797. 78 suites. A/C MINIBAR TV TEL. $205 master suite; $230 grand-class suite. AE, DC, MC, V. Free secured parking.

This chain of hotels specializes in creating extremely elegant settings that are suggestive of Mexico's past. You won't find a glass skyscraper here—the hotel is built of cut stone, wood beam, and ceramic tile. The rooms, which are distributed among a couple of four-story buildings amidst lush, beautiful grounds, create a warm, intimate feel not found in most modern hotels. The casual but sophisticated restaurant and bar attract a clientele with similar qualities. The hotel is host to numerous business meetings and is frequently full. Guest rooms are all different: Eight have brick cupolas, some have balconies, several have scallop-shaped headboards, and four are equipped with a whirlpool bathtub in the bathroom. All have antique decorative touches, large, fully equipped bathrooms with tub/shower combinations, remote-control TV with U.S. channels, and king-size beds. The hotel is 2 blocks from the Minerva Circle on avenida Mexico at López Mateos. Make sure to ask for a room that doesn't face López Mateos.

Dining/Diversions: An inviting restaurant just off the lobby has both terrace and indoor dining. The adjacent bar is open until 2am.

Amenities: Concierge, laundry and dry cleaning, massage by reservation, rental video players, travel agency. There's also a small heated pool.

EXPENSIVE

✪ **Fiesta Americana.** Aurelio Aceves 225, Glorieta Minerva, 44100 Guadalajara, Jal. ☎ **800/343-7821** in the U.S., or 3/825-3434. Fax 3/630-3671. www.fiestamexico. com. 399 units. A/C MINIBAR TV TEL. $120 double; $125 Fiesta Club. AE, DC, MC, V. Free secured parking.

A 22-story luxury hotel on a grand scale, the Fiesta Americana caters to the exacting demands of business and holiday travelers. Located 40 blocks from the Centro Histórico, it's a bustling hotel with a 14-story lobby and popular lobby bar that features occasional live entertainment. The rooms are spacious. All have TVs with U.S. channels. The 27 exclusive Fiesta Club rooms and three suites on the 12th and 14th floors come with special amenities (see below). One room is equipped for guests with disabilities. The lowest rates quoted above are for weekends.

Dining/Diversions: Two restaurants, one lobby bar.

Amenities: Laundry, dry cleaning, room service, travel agency, heated rooftop swimming pool, two lighted tennis courts, fitness room, business center, purified tap water. Fiesta Club guests have access to club floors, separate check-in and checkout, concierge, remote-control TV, continental breakfast and afternoon wine and hors d'oeuvres daily, as well as business services such as secretaries, fax, copy machine, and conference room.

PLAZA DEL SOL
VERY EXPENSIVE

Hotel Presidente Inter-Continental. Av. López Mateos Sur y Moctezuma, 45050 Guadalajara, Jal. ☎ **800/327-0200** in the U.S. and Canada, or 3/678-1234. Fax 3/678-1222. 414 units. A/C MINIBAR TV TEL. $175 double; $355 suite; $395 Club floors. AE, DC, MC, V. Free parking.

Located at the Plaza del Sol (about 50 blocks southwest of the Centro Histórico), the city's largest and fanciest shopping center, the elegant 14-story Presidente Inter-Continental caters to a very affluent set. Glass elevators whisk visitors up and down the towering lobby, and guest rooms are as stylish as the hotel's public areas. Rooms vary in size but all are decorated with natural wood furniture and have a tub/shower combination. Four key-only floors are reserved for Club guests who receive special amenities (see below). Nonsmoking rooms are on the 11th floor.

Dining/Diversions: The three on-site restaurants range from fine dining and Mexican specialties to poolside snacks. There's also a lobby bar and a cantina.

Amenities: Laundry, dry cleaning, room service, beauty shop, travel agency, car rental, business center with bilingual secretarial services, 24-hour doctor. Club guests receive a daily newspaper, continental breakfast, and evening cocktails in the club's separate lounge. There's a swimming pool on the 12th floor, gym, and separate sauna for men and women.

A NEARBY SPA

✪ **Río Caliente Spa.** Primavera Forest, La Primavera, Jal. No phone. (Reservations: Spa Vacations Limited, P.O. Box 897 Millbrae, CA 94030; ☎ **650/615-9543;** fax 650/615-0601.) 48 units. Patio area: $170 double. Pool area: $194 double. Rates include all meals. Discounts Apr 15–Dec 15; 10-night packages available. No credit cards.

Word of mouth keeps this popular and very casual spa busy. Situated at an elevation of 5,550 feet, along the hills of the Primavera Forest and a thermal water river, this unique spa is both rugged and serene. Temperatures average 80°F year-round.

Individual rooms are clustered in two areas. The simply furnished rooms near the activity area are smaller and cost less than the newer and more stylish rooms with patios near the river and pool. All rooms, however, have one double and one single bed, fireplace, full-length mirror, in-room safe-deposit box, desk, chest, and bedside reading lamps. Water is purified in the pools and kitchen, and jars of fresh purified water are supplied daily in each room. Additional spa programs vary throughout the year; they might include special instructors for Spanish and nutrition, and electro-acupuncture face-lifts at an extra cost. A doctor is available daily. Huichol Indians sell crafts on Sunday. Arranged pickup from the airport is available upon request for around $35 one way, or you can take a taxi for around $45 one way. If you're driving, follow avenida Vallarta west, which becomes Highway 15 with signs to Nogales. Go straight for almost 10½ miles and pass the village called La Venta del Astillero. Take the next left after La Venta and follow the rough road through the village of La Primavera for almost 5 miles. Keep bearing left through the forest until you see the hotel's sign on the left. There's no phone at the spa; reservations must be made through the United States.

Dining/Diversions: The self-serve vegetarian meals are taken in the cozy dining room. There's an activities room with nightly video movies or satellite TV, plus bingo and a library.

Amenities: Guests have a choice of two public outdoor thermal pools, as well as two private pools and sunning areas (separate for men and women). There's an outdoor bubbling whirlpool on the patio level. Among the services available at extra cost are massage, mud wrap, antistress and antiaging therapies, live-cell therapy, horseback riding, and sightseeing and shopping excursions. Included in the cost, besides meals, are daily guided hikes, yoga and pool exercises, and use of scented steam room with natural steam from an underground river.

4 Where to Dine

Guadalajara is an excellent city for both fine dining and common restaurants. Most of the restaurants are downtown, in the Chapultepec/Minerva section west of town, or in Tlaquepaque. Standard fare that is distinctly Guadalajaran includes *birria*—a hearty dish of lamb, pork, or goat meat in a tasty chicken-and-tomato broth. Restaurants around El Parián in Tlaquepaque serve birria every day. Another local specialty is the *lonche* or *torta*—a sandwich made from a scooped-out *bolillo* (a large roll) filled with a variety of meats and topped with sour cream, avocado, onions, and chiles. An especially well-known one is *torta ahogada* with a spicy pork filling. Also, there is the Jalisco-style *pozole,* a chicken-and-hominy soup to which you add lime juice, onion, and chile.

CENTRO HISTÓRICO
MODERATE

Fonda San Miguel. Donato Guerra 25. ☎ **3/613-0809.** Breakfast $5; main courses $7–$12. AE, MC, V. Sun–Tues 8am–6pm; Wed–Sat 8am–midnight. MEXICAN.

My favorite way to enjoy a good meal in Mexico is to have it in a beautiful courtyard of a colonial building. I feel this wonderful contrast between the bright and noisy street outside, and the quiet and shaded courtyard inside. And if there is a fountain, all the better. The surroundings make me feel perfectly at leisure. I can't think of a more splendid way of taking advantage of Mexico's wonderful climate and colonial past simultaneously. This particular restaurant is in a lovely two-story ex-convent with stone arches and with plaster walls painted in muted tones of orange and yellow.

For main courses, try the chile en nogada if it's in season, or perhaps a traditional mole poblano. The appetizers here are very good, and it's easy to fill up on them. Handmade tortillas and banana bread come with the meal.

Molino Rojo. Hotel Francés, Maestranza 35. ☎ **3/613-1190.** Main courses $5–$7. AE, MC, V. Daily 7:30am–10pm. INTERNATIONAL.

I can't recommend the Hotel Francés as a place to stay because of the nightly disco racket, but the off-lobby restaurant of the hotel, with its international menu, is a pleasant change from more traditional Mexican restaurants downtown. The decor matches that of the hotel—simple and bland—and looks about 30 years old. The only thing to engage the eye is a large reproduction of a famous portrait of Sor Juana, a leading literary figure and nun in Mexico during the colonial period. To engage the palate, try the spaghetti primavera (natural carrot-and-spinach pasta with fresh vegetables and Parmesan cheese), the Tampiqueña plate, or something resoundingly American like the club sandwich. From the Plaza de Armas, walk 1 block east on Moreno to Maestranza and turn right. The hotel and restaurant are on the left.

INEXPENSIVE

✪ **Café Madrid.** Juárez 264. ☎ **3/614-9504.** Breakfast $2–$4; main courses $3–$6. No credit cards. Daily 7:30am–10:30pm. MEXICAN.

Here's a wonderful cafe that has become a gathering place for many local folk. In the morning, you can enjoy great coffee and good Mexican breakfasts while watching people come in and greet each other and the staff by name, and chat over breakfast, coffee, and cigarettes. It's obviously an institution of many years, and change comes slowly. It's very informal yet the waiters wear white jackets with black bow ties, not because the cafe has pretensions, but because that's what they were wearing 20 years ago. There's a bright room in front with a small lunch counter and large windows, and another in the back with a mural entitled *Ciudad de Mujeres* ("City of Women"), in which the city is supposed to be Madrid. The afternoon and evening meals are good to take here, too; you can't go wrong with any of the traditional Mexican dishes. From the Plaza de Armas, walk 1 block on Corona to Juárez and turn right; the cafe is on the right.

La Chata Restaurant. Corona 126. ☎ **3/613-0588.** Breakfast $2–$4; main courses $3–$5. No credit cards. Daily 8am–11:30pm. REGIONAL.

This downtown restaurant is most popular in the evening for its à la carte menu—a great place to get soup, a Mexican-style sandwich, and guacamole salad. The restaurant's kitchen is in front; probably to lure passersby with the aroma of the cooking. Women with bandannas on their heads are busy stirring, chopping, and frying, while locals slip around the cooking island to a large, brightly colored dining room. Most of them frequent La Chata for Tapatían fare such as *pozole* (chicken-and-hominy soup) or a *torta ahogada* (a spicy pork sandwich). To find La Chata from the Plaza de Armas, walk 1½ blocks south on Corona; it's on the right between Juárez and López Cotilla.

Sanborn's. Juárez at 16 de Septiembre. ☎ **3/613-6264.** Breakfast $3–$4; main courses $4–$8. AE, MC, V. Daily 7:30am–1am. INTERNATIONAL.

On one side of the intersection is Sanborn's restaurant and on the other is its coffee shop, which offers a more limited menu. Both places are popular and can be crowded almost any time of day. Like other branches of this Mexican chain, this restaurant features waitresses in festive dresses. The varied menu features everything from tacos and hotcakes to steaks and sandwiches. One of their most popular dishes is enchiladas suizas. After eating, check out the section filled with drugstore items, English-language books and magazines, and gifts; Sanborn's is always well stocked. To find it from the Plaza de Armas, walk 1 block south on 16 de Septiembre to Juárez; it's on the left corner.

CHAPULTEPEC/MINERVA CIRCLE
EXPENSIVE

✪ **Recco.** Libertad 1981. ☎ **3/825-0724.** Main courses $10–$14. AE, MC, V. Daily 1–11:30pm. ITALIAN/CONTINENTAL.

Owned by Luigi Cupurro and housed in an old mansion, this fashionable restaurant rates high with locals. Dining rooms, all decked out in cloth-covered tables and cushioned chairs, are lit too brightly to be intimate, but the service and food are good. For starters you could try small portions of pasta, seafood, and carpaccio, or perhaps pâté and prosciutto and cantaloupe. Among main courses, you'll find pepper steak, charcoal-broiled trout, and veal with fettuccine. To reach the restaurant from the main plaza, take the Par Vial to Chapultepec and Vallarta. At Vallarta turn left on Chapultepec for 2 blocks to Libertad and turn left again. You'll see it on the right less than half a block down.

✪ **Suéhiro.** La Paz 1701. ☎ **3/826-0094** or 3/826-3122. Reservations recommended. Main courses $12–$20. AE, MC, V. Mon–Sat 1:30–5:30pm and 7:30–11:30pm; Sun 1:30–7:30pm. JAPANESE.

Guadalajarans love this taste of Japan in their city and have made it a popular place. Dishes are wonderfully flavored and cooked. Teppanyaki is the specialty, but the menu also offers a wide selection of tempura. If you want just sushi, you can dine in the separate sushi bar, where the selection is large, fresh, delicious, and prepared right in front of you. The restaurant is about 13 blocks beyond the Parque de la Revolución and avenida Enrique Díaz de León. If you don't want to take a taxi, you can ride the Par Vial from avenida Hidalgo to Chapultepec. Get off at Chapultepec and turn left (south) on Chapultepec for 3 blocks and turn left (east) on La Paz for about 3 blocks; it's on the right.

MODERATE

✪ **La Destilería.** Av. México 2916, corner of Nelson, Fracc. Terranova. ☎ **3/640-3440** or 3/640-3110. Main courses $6–$15. AE, DISC, MC, V. Mon–Sat 1pm–midnight; Sun 1–6pm. MEXICAN.

"The Distillery" is a popular, modern restaurant that has a playful take on the traditions involved in making tequila. But it's really the food that brings people here. Waiters clad in distillery uniforms and hard hats serve such specialties as *molcajete de la casa*—steaming fajitas, *rajas* (chile strips), cheese, onion, and avocado in a large, sizzling three-legged stone bowl. Steak with chipotle sauce or avocado sauce is memorable, as is the fish fillet in parsley sauce. The dessert menu is aptly named *los pecados* ("the sins"); and the temptation to order one is hard to resist. This is one of those places that is almost sure to please everyone. And while waiting for your food, you can examine the restaurant's collection of old photographs, memorabilia from historic distilleries, and large, rustic distilling equipment. It's 5 blocks northwest of the Fuente Minerva and about 2½ miles west of the Centro Histórico.

✪ **La Trattoría Pomodoro Ristorante.** Niños Héroes 3051. ☎ **3/622-1817.** Pasta $3–$5; chicken, beef, and seafood $5–$7. AE, MC, V. Daily 1pm–midnight. Free parking. ITALIAN.

Sooner or later, visitors to Guadalajara seem to learn about the good food at this popular restaurant. Service is friendly and swift, and the newly decorated restaurant is refreshing, with natural wood chairs, cushioned seats, and linen-clad tables. A large span of windows looks out onto Niños Héroes. There's separate seating for smokers and nonsmokers. For starters, you might want to sample the antipasto bar or the shrimp in white-wine cream sauce with chiles. As a main course, the fettuccine Alfredo is excellent. The superb salad bar and garlic bread are included in the price of main courses.

✪ **Modern Art Café.** Av. Américas 1939, corner Av. Patria, Col. Agraria, Zapopan. ☎ **3/636-6141** or 3/636-2999. Breakfast $3.75–$6; main courses $9–$12. AE, DISC, MC, V. Mon–Fri 8am–12:30am; Sat–Sun 9am–12:30am. CONTINENTAL.

Though removed from downtown sightseeing, many people seek out this restaurant (formerly called Café Pablo Picasso) for its festive atmosphere and food. Pass the small gift shop on the left as you enter and step down to the light and airy restaurant with a wood-fired pizza oven at one end. Paintings line the walls. The bar area near the front has tiny drink-size tables with high stools—they amount to a good test of one's sobriety. House specialties include a vibrant gazpacho, and *solomillo*, a variation on steak tartare. It's at the corner of calle Patria, diagonally across from the Plaza Patria shopping center. Take a taxi.

INEXPENSIVE

✪ **Los Itacates Restaurant.** Chapultepec Nte. 110. ☎ **3/825-1106** or 3/825-9551. Breakfast $2.50–$5; tacos 50¢; main courses $3–$6. MC, V. Mon–Sat 8am–11pm; Sun 8am–7pm. MEXICAN.

Locals can't say enough about how great the Mexican food is here. The place is packed during the hour of the *comida* (meal time). The atmosphere is festive, with colorfully painted chairs and table coverings. You can choose to dine outdoors at sidewalk tables or in one of the three interior rooms. Specialties include pozole, *sopa médula* (bone-marrow soup), *lomo adobado* (baked pork), and chiles rellenos. The chicken Itacates is a quarter of a chicken, two cheese enchiladas, potatoes, and rice. To find the restaurant, take the Par Vial west on Independence/Hidalgo. Get off at Chapultepec and walk to the right (north) on Chapultepec about 3 blocks. It's on the right.

TLAQUEPAQUE
EXPENSIVE

✪ **"Restaurant with No Name."** Madero 80. ☎ **3/635-4520** or 3/635-9677. Breakfast $4–$7; main courses $11–$20. AE, DISC, MC, V. Daily 8:30am–10pm. HAUTE MEXICAN.

The food and service here are excellent. You dine alfresco in a cool, shaded patio that has the informal feel of a Mexican country house; vegetation is allowed to grow pretty much at will, with a little coaxing to get it to form green canopies; peacocks strut around unruffled by the goings-on. This place could also be called Restaurant with No Menu; the waiters will recite the full list of dishes in English or Spanish and you can interrupt with questions at any time. I don't feel comfortable without text on a page, and it was a little off-putting at first, but it quickly became a game I had going on with the waiter, and he was very impressive in his knowledge of how dishes were prepared and in backing up or jumping forward from any spot. If you like something rich and strong-flavored, try the pork in a three-chile sauce (rich, dried chiles, not hot ones), an excellent milder dish would be the "no-name chicken" cooked in onions, green peppers, and a buttery sauce, served with rice. A trio plays music in midafternoon. To get here, face the main plaza (with the church to your right) and walk on Madero to the right for 1½ blocks; the restaurant is on the right, between Independencia and Constitución.

MODERATE

Casa Fuerte. 224-A Independencia. ☎ **3/639-6481.** Main courses $5–$9. AE, DISC, MC, V. Daily noon–8pm. MEXICAN/INTERNATIONAL.

Clothing designer Irene Pulos has turned her former showroom into this popular and charming patio restaurant. The setting says colorful Mexico: pastel walls and waiters sporting bold Pulos-designed vests. Imaginatively prepared menu items include shrimp in tamarindo juice, grilled brochette with banana, fresh vegetable salads, steaks, and fajitas. The restaurant's tucked in a town house among the row of shops on Independencia.

✪ **Mariscos Progreso.** Progreso 80. ☎ **3/657-4995.** Main courses $6–$12. AE, MC, V. Daily 11am–7pm. SEAFOOD/MEXICAN.

In a large, open patio shaded by trees, waiters bustle between the tables carrying large platters of delicious seafood. Mexicans do a wonderful job with seafood, and this popular restaurant does the tradition proud. Charcoal-grilled, Mexican-style, is the specialty here, but they'll cook it a variety of ways. Sometimes there can be quite a bit of *ambiente* with Mariachis adding to the commotion. At other times, the crowd thins and quiets down and one can rest from the exertions of shopping with a cold drink. To get here, walk 2 blocks south on Madero, cross Juárez (one of the streets that borders El Parián), and look for this corner restaurant on the right.

5 Exploring Guadalajara

SPECIAL EVENTS

The Jalisco State Band puts on free concerts in the Plaza de Armas usually every Tuesday, Thursday, and Sunday starting at about 7pm.

During September, when Mexicans celebrate independence from Spain, Guadalajara goes all out with a full month of festivities. Look for poster-size calendars listing attractions that include performances in theaters all over the city. On **September 15,** the Governor's Palace fills with well-dressed guests; they and the massive crowd in the park below await the governor's reenactment of the traditional *grito* (shout for independence) at 11pm. The grito commemorates Fr. Miguel Hidalgo de Costilla's pronouncement that initiated the Mexican War of Independence in 1810. The celebration features live music on a street stage, spontaneous dancing, joyous shouting of *"¡Viva México!"* and fireworks. For a couple of days after the **September 16** parade, the park in front of the Degollado Theater resembles a country fair and Mexican market, with games of chance, stuffed-animal prizes, cotton candy, and candied apples. Live entertainment in the park stretches well into the night.

In October is another monthlong event, **Fiestas de Octubre,** which originally began with the procession of Our Lady of Zapopan. Now, the fiesta simply and proudly celebrates Guadalajara and Jalisco. The celebration kicks off with an enormous parade, usually on the 1st Sunday (or possibly Sat) of the month. Festivities include performing arts, rodeos (*charreadas*), bullfights, art exhibits, regional dancing, a food fair, and a Day of Nations incorporating all the consulates in Guadalajara. Many of the displays and events take place in the **Benito Juárez Auditorium.**

On **October 12,** around dawn, the small, dark figure of Our Lady of Zapopan begins her 5-hour ride from the Cathedral of Guadalajara to the suburban Cathedral of Zapopan. The original icon dates from the mid-1500s; the procession began 200 years later. Today, crowds spend the night all along the route and vie for position as the Virgin approaches (in a gleaming new car pulled along with ropes by a team of the Virgin's caretakers). During the months before October 12, the figure visits churches all over the city. During that time, you will likely see neighborhoods decorated with paper streamers and banners honoring the passing of the figure to the next church.

The last 2 weeks in February are marked by a series of cultural events before the beginning of Lent.

WALKING TOUR
Downtown Guadalajara

Start: Plaza de Armas.
Finish: Mercado Libertad.
Time: Approximately 3 hours, not including museum and shopping stops.
Best Times: After 10am, when museums are open.
Worst Times: Mondays or holidays, when the museums are closed.

Guadalajara has a lovely downtown area with lots of open plazas. The founding fathers put four of them around the cathedral in the shape of a Latin cross. Later, a long swath of land was cleared to connect the cathedral to the Hospicio Cabañas, creating what is now known as **Plaza Tapatía.**

Start your tour in the plaza beside the main cathedral on avenida Alcalde, between avenida Hidalgo and calle Morelos, in the charming:

1. Plaza de Armas. This square has wrought-iron benches and walkways that lead like spokes to the ornate, French-made bandstand in its center. The bandstand was a gift to the city from the dictator Porfirio Díaz in the 1890s. Díaz made a name for himself by fighting the French invasion forces in the 1860s, but when he became head of the country, he expressed nothing but admiration for them. When Díaz was chased into exile by the Mexican Revolution, he chose to live in Paris where he is now buried. The wrought-iron figures on the bandstand are the female representations of the four seasons, and their loose form of dress scandalized conservative Guadalajaran society. French or not, Guadalajarans would not allow such corruption of morals and dressed the figures in something more modest. The dictator, recognizing when it's best to let the people have their way, said nothing.

Facing the plaza is the:

2. Palacio del Gobierno. This handsome palace was built in 1774 with a mixture of Spanish and Moorish elements, a popular style at the time. Inside the central courtyard, above the beautiful staircase to the right, is a spectacular mural of Hidalgo by the modern Mexican master José Clemente Orozco (1883–1949), in which the Father of Independence appears high overhead, bearing directly down on the viewer and looking as implacable as a force of nature. Orozco achieved this effect through the dramatic use of proportion and perspective that are the earmarks of his work. He was a native of Guadalajara. On one of the adjacent walls is another mural showing quite a contrast in treatment. It is a satire on the prevailing fanaticisms in Orozco's day and is called *The Carnival of Ideologies.*

Returning to the front entrance, turn right and walk to the:

3. Catedral. Begun in 1561, the unusual facade is actually an amalgam of several architectural styles, including Renaissance, neoclassical, and a touch of Gothic. An 1818 earthquake destroyed the original large towers; their replacements were designed by architect Manuel Gómez Ibarra, who was given broad instructions of how they were to look by the bishop of the time. The bishop had a vision of a Gothic cathedral when looking down at his dinner plate. Unfortunately, history doesn't record what the bishop had for dinner or the kind of china he used.

Walking Tour—Downtown Guadalajara

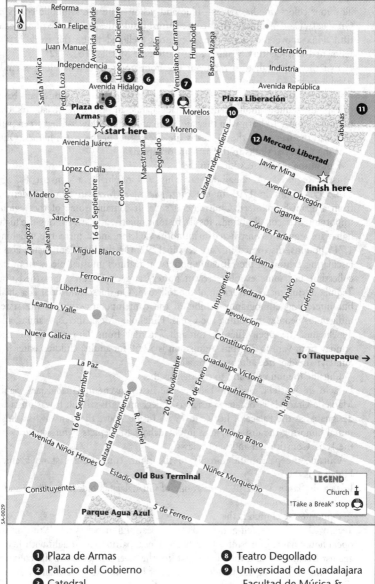

1. Plaza de Armas
2. Palacio del Gobierno
3. Catedral
4. Rotonda de los Hombres Ilustres
5. Museo Regional de Guadalajara
6. Palacio de Justicia
7. Iglesia de Santa María de Gracia
8. Teatro Degollado
9. Universidad de Guadalajara Facultad de Música & Iglesia de San Agustín
10. Quetzalcoatl Fountain
11. Hospicio Cabañas
12. Mercado Libertad

LEGEND

✝ Church

"Take a Break" stop

SA-0029

The roof colors on the towers—blue and yellow—are the symbolic colors of Guadalajara and are on the city's coat of arms. Inside, the cathedral is quite beautiful; look above the sacristy for a painting believed to be the work of the renowned 17th-century Spanish artist Bartolomé Murillo (1617–82).

Exit the cathedral, turn right out the front doors, and walk along avenida Alcalde to the:

4. Rotonda de los Hombres Ilustres. Sixteen gleaming-white columns, sans bases or capitals, stand as monuments to Guadalajara's, and the state of Jalisco's, distinguished sons. To learn who they are, stroll around the flower-filled green park and read the names on the 11 nearly life-size statues of the state's heroes. Only 4 of the 93 burial vaults in the park are occupied.

East of the plaza, cross Liceo to the:

5. Museo Regional de Guadalajara. This was originally a convent (☎ 3/ 614-9957), built in 1701 in the *churrigueresque* (Mexican baroque, derived from a Spanish architect, Churriguera) style. It contains some of the region's important archaeological finds, fossils, historic objects, and art. Among the highlights are a giant reconstructed mammoth's skeleton and a meteorite weighing 1,715 pounds, discovered in Zacatecas in 1792. On the first floor there's also a fascinating exhibit of pre-Hispanic pottery; it features unusual pieces from the collection and some exquisite recent pottery and clay figures unearthed near Tequila during the construction of the toll road. On the second floor is a small but interesting ethnography exhibit of the contemporary dress of the state's indigenous peoples, including the Coras, Huicholes, Mexicaneros, Nahuas, and Tepehuanes. It's open Tuesday through Saturday from 9am to 6:45pm and Sunday from 9am to 2:45pm. Admission is $2.50 for adults; children enter free Sunday; Tuesday free admission for all .

Outside the museum and to the right is the:

6. Palacio de Justicia. Built in 1588 as the first convent in Guadalajara, Santa María de Gracia later became a teachers college and girls school. It was officially designated as the Palace of Justice in 1952. Inside, above the stairway, is a huge mural honoring the justice system in Guadalajara; it depicts Benito Juárez with the 1857 Constitution and reform laws.

Outside the palace and directly to the right, continuing east on avenida Hidalgo, is the:

7. Iglesia de Santa María de Gracia, one of Guadalajara's oldest churches, and a convent next door.

Opposite the church is the:

8. Teatro Degollado (deh-goh-*yah*-doh), a beautiful neoclassical 19th-century opera house named for Santos Degollado, a local patriot who fought with Juárez against Maximilian and the French. Notice the seven muses above the columns in the theater's triangular facade. The theater hosts varied performances during the year, including the excellent Ballet Folklórico on Sunday at 10am. (The Degollado Theater is linked to the cathedral by Plaza Libertad.) It's open Monday through Friday from 10am to 2pm.

To the right of the theater, on the opposite side of the plaza from the Iglesia de Santa María de Gracia, is the:

9. University of Guadalajara School of Music and San Agustín Church. The church has continuous services, and sometimes the music school is open to the public. Continuing east on the plaza, be sure to notice the spectacular fountain behind the Teatro Degollado; it depicts Mexican history in low relief. You'll next pass the charming children's fountain, followed by the unusual sculpture of a tree with lions. Nearby are stone slabs engraved with text from Charles V proclaiming Guadalajara's inalienable right to be recognized as a city.

The plaza opens into a huge pedestrian expanse called Plaza Tapatía, now framed by department stores and offices, and dominated by the:

10. Quetzalcoatl Fountain. This towering abstract sculpture-fountain represents the mythical plumed serpent Quetzalcoatl, which figures so prominently in Mexican legend, ancient culture, and religion. The smaller pieces represent the serpent and birds; the centerpiece is the serpent's fire.

TAKE A BREAK   Take a breather at one of the small ice-cream shops or fast-food restaurants along the plaza, or hang tight for a moment, until you get to the Hospicio (no. 11 on the tour). It has a small cafeteria that serves hot dogs, sandwiches, cake, soft drinks, coffee, and snacks.

At the far end of the plaza, you'll spot the:

11. Hospicio Cabañas. Formerly called the Cabañas Orphanage and known today as the Instituto Cultural Cabañas (☎ **3/617-4322**), this impressive structure is a creation of the famous Mexican architect Manuel Tolsá. From 1829 until 1980, it housed homeless children. Today it's a thriving cultural center offering art shows and classes. The main building has a fine dome, and the walls and ceiling are covered by murals painted in 1929 by Orozco. Orozco's powerful painting in the dome, *Man of Fire,* is said to represent the spirit of humanity projecting itself toward the infinite. Other rooms hold additional Orozco works, as well as excellent temporary displays. A contemporary art exhibit in the south wing features fascinating and unusual paintings by Javier Arévalo. The institute's own Ballet Folklórico performs here every Wednesday at 8:30pm. To the left of the entrance is a bookstore.

Now for a change of pace, turn left out the front entrance of the Cabañas and look for a stairway that leads down to the:

12. Mercado Libertad, Guadalajara's gigantic covered central market, said to be the largest in Latin America. This site has been a market plaza since the 1500s; the present buildings date from the early 1950s. This is a great place to buy leather goods, pottery, baskets, rugs, kitchen utensils, and just about anything else (see "Shopping," below).

OTHER ATTRACTIONS

At the **Parque Agua Azul** (Blue Water Park), the plants, trees, shrubbery, statues, and fountains create a perfect refuge from the bustling city. Many people come here, near the former bus station at the south end of Calzada Independencia, to exercise early in the morning. The park is open daily from 7am to 6pm. Admission for adults is $1; children 50¢.

Across Independencia, catercorner from a small flower market in a small one-story rock building, is the **Museo Arqueología del Occidente de Mexico.** It houses a fine collection of pre-Hispanic pottery from Jalisco, Nayarit, and Colima and is well worth your time. The museum is open Tuesday through Sunday from 10am to 2pm and 4 to 7pm. There's a small admission charge.

The state-run **Casa de las Artesanías** (☎ **3/619-4664**) is just past the park entrance at the crossroads of Calzada Independencia and Gallo (for details, see "Shopping," below).

✪ **Museo de las Artes de la Universidad de Guadalajara.** Juárez 975. ☎ **3/625-7553.** Admission $2. Tues–Sat 10am–8pm; Sun and holidays noon–8pm. To reach the museum, take the Par Vial west on Independencia/Hidalgo. Get off after it makes the right turn onto Vallarta/Juárez. From the bus stop on Juárez, walk back (east) 2 or 3 blocks; it's on the right opposite the University of Guadalajara. It's about an 11-block walk from Alcalde/16 de Septiembre, straight west on Juárez, and 4 blocks beyond the Parque Revolución, which will be on your left.

This 5-year-old museum promises to be one of the most exciting in the country. An early show featured contemporary artists from all over the Americas. Several rooms house the university's collection, consisting mainly of Mexican and Jaliscan artists. There is always a traveling exhibition. Originally constructed as a primary school in 1914, this beautiful building holds bold Orozco murals: on one wall of the auditorium and the cupola above are *Man, Creator and Rebel* and *The People and Their False Leaders*.

✪ **Museo de la Ciudad.** Independencia 684 at M. Barcena. ☎ **3/658-2531.** Admission 50¢. Wed–Sat 10am–5:30pm; Sun 10am–2:30pm.

This fine museum in a wonderful old stone convent, opened in 1992, chronicles Guadalajara's fascinating past. The eight rooms, beginning on the right and proceeding in chronological order, cover the years just before the city's founding by 63 Spanish families to the present. Unusual artifacts, including rare Spanish armaments and equestrian paraphernalia, give a sense of what day-to-day life was like in Guadalajara's past. As you browse, dust off your Spanish and read the explanations, which give details not otherwise noted in the displays.

6 Shopping

Mexican markets present great opportunities for gathering impressions of a community and its members. The mammoth **Mercado Libertad** (see "Walking Tour: Downtown Guadalajara," stop no. 12, above) is no exception. You'll find vendors of food, produce, crafts (baskets, puppets, wood carvings, pottery, dance costumes), clothing, cheap watches, and household wares. Although it opens at 7am, the market doesn't get in full swing until around 10am.

Another stop worth making is in Agua Azul at the government-run **Casa de las Artesanías.** It's at the intersection of Calzada Independencia and Gallo, Gallo 20 (☎ **3/619-4664**). Here you'll find two floors of pottery, silver jewelry, dance masks, and regional clothing from around the state and the country, and often a great selection of colorful nativity scenes (*natividades*). As you enter, on the right are museum displays showing crafts and regional costumes from the state of Jalisco. The craft store is open Monday through Friday from 10am to 6pm, Saturday from 10am to 5pm, and Sunday from 11am to 3pm.

If you find yourself admiring the traditional charro outfits, there are several places in Guadalajara that can get you duded up, but it won't be cheap: There are a couple of stores on Juárez by the Hotel Calinda Roma, and a shop called **El Charro** in Plaza del Sol. The **Plaza del Sol** area also has some clothing boutiques.

SHOPPING IN TLAQUEPAQUE & TONALÁ

Almost everyone who comes to Guadalajara for the shopping has Tlaquepaque and Tonalá in mind. These two villages, now suburbs of Guadalajara, are traditional pottery and glassblowing centers.

TLAQUEPAQUE (TLAH-KEH-*PAH*-KEH)

Located about 20-minutes from downtown, Tlaquepaque has over the years become a fashionable center for shopping and has attracted talented designers in a variety of fields. It has the best shopping for handcrafts and the decorative arts in all of Mexico. Even though it's a suburb of a large city, there is a cozy, small-town feel to Tlaquepaque, and since the town is compact, it's a pleasure to shop here. You don't get

Shopping Tip

If you're going to Tonalá and Tlaquepaque, you may want to postpone your buying spree until then.

hassled, and there are some excellent restaurants (see Dining, above), or you can eat some simple fare at El Parián, a circular building in the middle of town housing a number of small eateries. The quality of the merchandise is high; and you don't see a lot of junk. You can find bargains here, and most things are reasonably priced, but this place isn't by any means a bargain-hunter's paradise. For that, try Tonalá (see below).

A taxi from downtown Guadalajara will cost you about $4. You can also take one of the deluxe **Turquesa buses** that make a fairly quick run from downtown to Tlaquepaque and Tonalá (see "Getting Around," above). Look for buses numbered 275 A or B. They leave every 10 minutes from the corner of Alcalde and Independencia in front of the cathedral ($1).

If you're having trouble finding any particular place in town, go to the **Tlaquepaque Tourism Office** in the Presidencia Municipal (opposite El Parián), calle Guillermo Prieto 80 (☎ **3/635-1503** or 3/635-0596); it's open Monday through Friday from 9am to 3pm and Saturday from 9am to 1pm. Most stores in Tlaquepaque close in the afternoon between 2 and 4pm and stay open in the evening until 7 or 8pm. Most are either closed or have reduced hours on Sunday.

While you're in Tlaquepaque, you might want to check out the **Regional Ceramics Museum,** Independencia 237 (☎ **3/35-5404**). Here you can learn something about traditional Jalisco pottery as produced in Tlaquepaque and Tonalá. There are high-quality examples dating back several generations. Note the cross-hatch design known as *petatillo* on some of the pieces; it's one of the region's oldest traditional motifs. Look for the wonderful old kitchen and dining room, complete with pots, utensils, and dishes. The museum is open Tuesday through Saturday from 10am to 4pm and Sunday from 10am to 1pm. There is also the Museo Nacional de Cerámica in Tonalá (see below.)

Across the street from the museum is **La Rosa de Cristal,** a glassblowing factory. From 10am to 2pm Monday through Friday, the public is invited to the rear patio to watch as a dozen men and boys heat glass bottles and jars on the end of hollow steel poles. After some furious glassblowing, the boys run across the room, narrowly missing spectators and fellow workers as they swing the red-hot glass within an inch of a man who sits oblivious to it all, placidly rolling an elaborate jug out of another chunk of heated glass. Nonchalantly, but at the precise moment the glass is thrust into his face, the old man will put aside his own task just long enough to clip off the end of the boy's vase. He then drops the clippers and returns once more to business as the youth charges across the room to reheat the vase in the furnace.

The following list of favorite Tlaquepaque shops will give you an idea of what to expect. But this is just a small fraction of what you'll find here, so the best thing might be to just follow your nose. The main shopping is along **Independencia,** a pedestrian-only street that starts at El Parián. You can go door to door visiting the shops on Independencia working your way to the end, and then work your way back towards El Parián along calle Juárez, another good shopping street, 1 block north. And there are some other good stores not on these streets.

Agustín Parra. Independencia 158. ☎ **3/657-8530.**

So you bought an old hacienda and are trying to restore its chapel—where do you go? This is where. Parra is famous for his baroque sculpture, religious art, gold-leaf picture frames and furniture, and large, traditional retablos such as the one on display here.

Bazar Hecht. Juárez 162. ☎ **3/657-0316.**

One of the village's longtime favorite stores, here you'll find wood objects, handmade furniture, and a few antiques. Open Monday through Saturday from 10am to 2:30pm and 3:30 to 7pm.

Casa Canela. Independencia 258, near Calle Cruz Verde. ☎ **3/635-3717.**

Step inside this grand mansion and discover one of the most elegant stores in Tlaque-paque. Browse through the rooms of decorative arts, one or which displays an imaginative use of Mexican and Guatemalan textiles on Equipal furniture. Open Monday through Friday from 10am to 2pm and 3 to 7pm, Saturday from 10am to 6pm, and Sunday from 11am to 3pm.

Ken Edwards. Madero 70. ☎ **3/635-5456.**

Ken was among the first artisans to produce high-fired, lead-free stoneware in Tonalá, and his blue-on-blue pottery is now sold all over Mexico. This showroom has a fine selection of his work, which is not usually seen in such size or quantity elsewhere. There's a section of seconds for bargain hunting. The shop is next door to the "Restaurant With No Name." Open Monday to Saturday from 10:30am to 7pm. His factory is in Tonalá.

Sergio Bustamante. Independencia 236 at Cruz Verde. ☎ **3/639-5519.**

Sergio Bustamante's imaginative and original brass, ceramic, and papier-mâché sculptures are among the most sought after in Mexico—as well as the most copied. He also has many designs in silver jewelry. This is an exquisite gallery showcasing his work. Open Monday through Saturday from 10am to 7pm and Sunday from 11am to 4pm.

Tierra Tlaquepaque. Independencia 156. ☎ **3/635-9770.**

Here you'll find unusual, rustic, but finely finished pottery and wood sculptures and table textiles and decorative objects. Open Monday through Saturday from 10am to 7pm, Sunday from 11am to 5pm.

Tete Arte y Diseño. Juárez 173. ☎ **3/635-7347.**

Here you'll find large architectural decorative objects mixed in with the pottery, antiques, glassware, and paintings, all thrown together. Open Monday through Saturday from 10am to 7pm.

TONALÁ: A TRADITION OF POTTERY MAKING

Tonalá is a pleasant, unpretentious village not far from Tlaquepaque. Of the two, you might find Tonalá easier on the wallet. The streets were paved only recently, and there aren't any pedestrian-only thoroughfares yet. The village has been a center of pottery making since pre-Hispanic times; half of the more than 400 artists who reside here produce high- and low-temperature pottery in different colors, with a dozen different finishes. Other local artists also work with forged iron, cantera stone, brass and copper, marble, miniatures, papier-mâché, textiles, blown glass, and gesso.

Market days are Thursday and Sunday: You can expect blocks and blocks of stalls of locally manufactured pottery and glassware and all kinds of other crafts. "Herb-men" sell multicolored dried medicinal herbs from wheelbarrows; magicians entertain crowds with sleight-of-hand; and craftspeople spread their colorful wares on the plaza's sidewalks. Lovers of handblown Mexican glass and folksy ceramics will wish they had a truck to haul home the gorgeous and inexpensive handmade items available here.

The many local shops are open here other days as well, allowing you to browse without having to negotiate the crowds.

The Tonalá Tourism Office (☎ 3/683-1740; fax 3/683-0590) is in the Artesanos building set back a bit from the road at Atonaltecas 140 Sur (the main street leading into Tonalá) at Matamoros. It offers free walking tours Monday, Tuesday, Wednesday, and Friday at 9am and 2pm and Saturday at 9am and 1pm. These include visits to artisans' workshops (where you'll see ceramics, stoneware, blown glass, papier-mâché, and the like). Tours last between 3 and 4 hours and require a minimum of five people. Hours are Monday through Friday from 9am to 3pm and Saturday from 9am to 1pm. Visitors can request an English-speaking guide. Also in Tonalá, catercorner from the church, you'll see a small tourism information kiosk that's staffed on market days and provides maps and useful information.

Tonalá is also the home of the **Museo Nacional de Cerámica,** Constitución 104, between Hidalgo and Morelos (☎ 3/683-0494). The museum occupies a huge two-story mansion and displays work from Jalisco and pottery from all over the country. There's a large shop in the front on the right as you enter. The museum is open Tuesday through Friday from 10am to 5pm and Saturday and Sunday from 10am to 2pm. A fee of $8.50 per camera will be charged for use of any video or still cameras.

If you feel hunger pangs coming on, try **Los Geranios** (☎ 3/683-0010) at Hidalgo 71, next to El Bazar de Sermel. It's closed on Saturdays and the rest of the week it's open only from 11am to 5pm. Try the fish with almonds and mushrooms or the pork baked in orange sauce with baked potato and vegetables. Or you can try something quick like nachos. To get here, face the church on the plaza, walk to the right, and turn on Hidalgo for about half a block; look on the left for a pretty stained-glass sign with red flowers.

7 Guadalajara After Dark

FOLKLORIC BALLET

Ballet Folklórico de la Universidad de Guadalajara. Degollado Theater, Plaza Tapatía. ☎ **3/626-9280** or 3/614-4773, ext. 144 or 143. Tickets $3–$12.

This wonderful dance company, acclaimed as the finest folklórico company in all of Mexico, is pure Jalisco. For more than a decade it has been performing at the Degollado Theater. Performances are on Sunday at 10am.

Ballet Folklórico Nacional del Instituto Cultural Cabañas. At the far end of the Plaza Tapatía. ☎ **3/618-6003.** Tickets $6–$8.

Performances are every Wednesday at 8:30pm at the theater of the Instituto Cultural Cabañas.

MARIACHIS

If you're in Guadalajara for any time at all, chances are you'll happen upon some mariachis. They may, however, not do mariachi music much credit, and really talented performances have to be sought out (see "La Feria," below). But if what you're really interested in is the flavor and atmosphere of the music, you can go to ✪ **El Parián** in Tlaquepaque, where mariachis serenade diners under the archways, or you can go to **Plaza de los Mariachis,** down by the San Juan de Dios Church and the Mercado Libertad at the junction of Calzada Independencia and avenida Juárez/calle Javier Mina. Every evening colorfully dressed mariachis, sometimes a little tipsy, play for money (if they can get it). Otherwise they'll just play for free. Enjoy a meal, snack, or soft drink here or just soak up the ambiance. Ask the price before you request a song.

THE CLUB & MUSIC SCENE

✪ **Restaurant/Bar Copenhagen 77.** Marcos Castellanos 140-Z. ☎ **3/826-1787.** No cover. Restaurant Mon–Sat noon–12:30am; jazz 8:30pm–12:30am.

This dark, snug little jazz den with upholstered walls and wood trim is the perfect setting for listening to jazz. The house band is led by the pianist Carlos de la Torre, who plays with an elegant and economic style in his interpretations of bebop, modern, and Latin jazz. This is nothing like the denatured jazz you're apt to here in a dentist's office—this is the real stuff; and this club has attracted a number of jazz heavyweights who come to relax and sit in with the band. The club is near the Parque de la Revolución, on your left as you walk down López Cotilla. You can just have drinks or you can order from the small but well-thought-out menu; the specialty is paella.

El Cubilete. Gral. Río Seco 9. ☎ **3/658-0406.** Mon–Sat 2pm–2am; Mon–Thurs boleros; Fri–Sat salsa 10pm–2am. $4 cover on weekends.

El Cubilete ("the dice cup") is a small, old-style club in one of the oldest neighborhoods in Guadalajara—Las nueve esquinas (the nine corners). In the afternoon it's piano and violin; at night on weekends, it's a full band playing salsa and merengue led by the very talented Rosalia, a Cuban singer who is famous here for her style. El Cubilete serves drinks and regional foods including birria, tortas ahogadas, and carne asada.

La Feria. Corona 291. ☎ **3/613-7150** or 3/613-1812. Daily noon–3am. Variety show at 3:30 and 10pm. Call for reservations.

To get a good sampling of local color, check out this multilevel restaurant-bar with a stage in the middle. The afternoon and nighttime shows include a variety of very impressive singers accompanied by a mariachi band, and there's also a charro who performs rope tricks, and some Ballet Folklórico dancers. The afternoon's entertainment ends by getting the whole restaurant involved in a game of Lotería—a Mexican bingo game. At night, some of the audience gets up on stage for dancing or drinking contests. When I was there, the audience was entirely Mexican. The owner promised a free margarita to anyone who shows a Frommer's book. Hold him to it. The menu is standard Mexican with emphasis on grilled meats. La Feria is downtown, 5 blocks south of the Plaza de Armas.

Rock-cocó. Pedro Moreno 532. ☎ **3/613-5632** or 3/614-3034. Wed, Fri, Sat 10pm–3am. $5 cover for men, $4 for women. Wed open bar, $10 cover for men, free for women.

And now for something completely different. The name of this club, in English or Spanish, is a play on the word rococo, a later, decadent form of baroque; and it couldn't be more appropriate. It's an amazing club that occupies an 18th-century ex-convent for Capuchin nuns. It has two stories of rooms and galleries that open to a courtyard with a graceful stairway of stone and wrought iron. Set in the wall above the stairway is a small stage with a red velvet curtain. This is for the nightly show by some variety of circus performers. When I was there, it was a trapeze artist. The decor, as you might imagine, is baroque. The DJ plays rock, pop, and rock en español. There are four bars distributed among the several rooms.

8 Side Trips to Lake Chapala & Ajijic

LAKE CHAPALA & ITS PICTURE-PERFECT LAKESIDE TOWNS

26 miles S of Guadalajara

Mexico's largest lake and the area surrounding it have long been popular with foreigners because of the near-perfect climate, gorgeous scenery, and several charming little lakeshore towns such as Chapala, Ajijic, and Jocotepec, each with a distinct ambiance. There's a large permanent expatriate community of around 4,000 people living in settlements along the shoreline and in the villages stretching all the way from Chapala to Jocotepec. When you first see it, you might think you've come upon the ocean. It's a stunning sight, ringed by high, forested mountains and fishing villages.

Note: The year-round climate is so pleasant that few hotels offer air-conditioning and only a handful have fans; neither is necessary.

ESSENTIALS

GETTING THERE & DEPARTING   By Car   Those driving will be able to enjoy the lake and the surrounding towns more fully, although there is intravillage bus service. From Guadalajara, drive to Lake Chapala via the new four-lane Highway 15/80. Leave Guadalajara via avenida González Gallo, which intersects with Calzada Independencia just before Agua Azul Park. Going south on Independencia, turn left onto Gallo and follow it all the way out of town past the airport, where it becomes Highway 15/80 (signs may also call it Highway 44). This is the main road to Chapala. The first view of the lake isn't until just outside of the town of Chapala.

The highway from Guadalajara leads directly into Chapala and becomes Madero, which leads straight to Chapala's pier, *malecón* (waterfront walkway and street), and small shopping and restaurant area. The one traffic light in town (a block before the pier) is the turning point (right) to Ajijic, San Antonio, San Juan Cosalá, and Jocotepec. Chapala's main plaza is 3 blocks north of the pier, and the central food market flanks the park's back side.

By Bus   Buses to Chapala (a 45-minute ride) leave from Guadalajara's old Central Camionera; Transportes Guadalajara-Chapala serves the route. Buses and minibuses run every half hour to Chapala and every hour to Jocotepec.

In Chapala, the bus station is about 7 blocks north of the lake pier. There are buses every half hour for Jocotepec. To get to Ajijic and San Juan Cosalá from Chapala, walk toward the lake (left out of the front of the station) and look for the local buses lined up on the opposite side of the street. These buses travel between Chapala and San Juan Cosalá. The last bus back to Guadalajara from Chapala is at 9pm.

VISITOR INFORMATION   The Jalisco State Information Office in Chapala is at Aquiles Serdán 26 (☎ 376/5-3141). Serdán is a narrow side street going toward the lake, 1 block before the correo (post office). The office is open Monday through Friday from 9am to 6pm and Saturday and Sunday from 10am to 6pm. The staff is willing to help and although they don't have a lot of information at their disposal, you can try to get a map from them.

FAST FACTS   The **area code** for the whole northern lakeshore (Chapala, Ajijic, San Juan Cosalá, and Jocotepec) is **376.**

Several outlets offer communications services, including fax, telephone, mail, and messages. **Centro de Mensajes Mexicano-Americano** is the local affiliate for UPS. They also have 24-hour telephone message and fax-receiving service, court-approved translation ability, and secretarial service. It's at Hidalgo 236 (Apdo. Postal 872), 45900 Chapala, Jalisco (☎ and fax **376/5-2102**), and it's open Monday through Friday from 10am to 6pm and Saturday from 10am to 2pm. Almost next door, **Aero Flash,** Hidalgo 236 (☎ **376/5-3696;** fax 376/5-3063), has a 24-hour fax service and specializes in package mailing. It's the local Federal Express office. The post office is on Hidalgo, 2 blocks from the intersection of Madero. Enter down the hill and in back. It's open Monday through Friday from 9am to 1pm and 3 to 6pm and Saturday from 9am to 1pm.

A good local bookstore is **Libros y Revistas,** at Madero 230 (☎ **376/5-2021**).

CHAPALA: AN OLD LAKE RESORT

Chapala, founded in 1538, is the district's business and administrative center as well as the oldest resort town on Lake Chapala. Much of the town's prosperity is derived from the retiree community, primarily Americans and Canadians, who live on the outskirts and come into Chapala to change money, buy groceries, and check the stock ticker. Except on weekends, when throngs of visitors fill the area around the pier and lake's edge, the town of 36,000 can be a pretty sleepy place. There are a couple of hotels in Chapala, but Ajijic is the preferable place to stay in the area. Good restaurants on the lake include Cozumel and Mariscos Guicho.

AJIJIC: A QUIET FISHING & ARTIST VILLAGE

Ajijic (ah-hee-*heek*), another lakeside village, is a quiet place of mostly fishermen, artists, and retirees. As you reach Ajijic, the highway becomes a wide, tree-lined boulevard through La Floresta, a wealthy residential district. The LA FLORESTA sign signals you've entered Ajijic, but the central village is about a mile farther on the left. To reach Ajijic's main street, Colón (which changes to Morelos), turn left when you see the SIX (corner grocery) sign on the left. Colón/Morelos leads straight past the main plaza and ends at the lake and the popular Restaurant La Posada Ajijic. The cobblestoned streets and arts-and-crafts stores give the town a quaint atmosphere. (See "Essentials," above, for bus information to Ajijic.)

The **Clínica Ajijic** (☎ 376/6-0662; for emergencies 376/6-0875 or 376/6-0500) is on the main highway at the corner of Javier and Mina and has a two-bed emergency section with oxygen and electrocardiogram, ambulance, and five doctors with different specialties. Their 16-bed hospital opened in 1993. The pharmacy there is available after hours for emergencies.

Línea Profesional (☎ 376/6-0187; fax 376/6-0066) is a locally owned car-rental agency in Ajijic. Make reservations as soon as you can, as cars are often all booked.

Exploring Ajijic

In La Floresta, immediately after the modern sculpture on the left, you'll see a cluster of buildings, one of which is marked ARTESANÍAS. **The state-owned crafts shop** (☎ 376/6-0548) has a good selection of pottery from all over Mexico as well as local crafts such as pottery, glassware, rugs, and wall tapestries. The shop is open Monday through Saturday from 10am to 6pm and Sunday from 10am to 2pm.

Ajijic has long been a center for weavers, although there now seem to be very few compared to the past. Shopping is only fair; the best streets are Colón and those leading immediately off of it for a block or so. You'll find designer clothing and decorative accessories such as hand-loomed fabrics made into pillows and bedspreads, furniture, and pottery, but no single item in abundance.

As for performing arts in the region, productions of the Lakeside Little Theater are usually announced in the local paper or on the bulletin board at the Nueva Posada Ajijic (see "Where to Stay," below).

Meeting local foreign residents is easy; just go to the popular hangouts: the Restaurant Posada Ajijic, La Nueva Posada Ajijic, the Rose Café, and Los Veleros Restaurant and Sports Bar.

Where to Stay

La Laguna Bed and Brunch. Zaragoza 29, 45900 Ajijic, Jal. ☎ **376/6-1174** or 376/6-1186. Fax 376/6-1188. E-mail: 104164.2603@compuserve.com. 4 units. $30 double (including brunch). No credit cards.

The rooms in this small inn are handsomely furnished: king-size beds with bright loomed bedspreads, thick tile floors, and fireplaces. Breakfast/brunch is served

Monday through Saturday from 8:30am to noon, Sunday from 9am to noon. You dine in a lovely glassed-in dining room facing the back patio, and your meal begins with fruit and apple-bran muffins followed by a choice of eggs. Nonguests can also have brunch ($4 to $5). To find La Laguna from the main highway, turn left on Colón and left again on the first street. It's 1½ blocks down on the left behind the Laguna Ajijic Real Estate Office (which faces the main highway).

✪ **La Nueva Posada.** Donato Guerra no. 9 (Apdo. Postal 30), 45900 Ajijic, Jal. ☎ **376/ 6-1444.** Fax 376/6-1344. E-mail: nuevaposada@laguna.com.mx. 16 units. TV, TEL. $50–$60 double. Rates include full breakfast. MC, V. Free parking.

This new posada was built by Michael and Elena Eager, the former owners of the popular Posada Ajijic (now a restaurant and bar under different ownership). Modeled after a gracious, traditional-style hacienda, La Nueva Posada looks a lot more expensive than it is. French doors, marble bathrooms, a wine cellar, and a small swimming pool are just some of the amenities. An elegant dining room looks gloriously out onto the view. Original paintings hang in all the color-coordinated rooms and public areas. Three rooms are equipped for people with disabilities. Some rooms overlook the lake, others have intimate patios, but the former will experience less disturbance from the after-hours kitchen crew. A paperback-exchange library is at the reception area. The hotel's restaurant, La Rusa, and casual bar (see "Where to Dine," below) are among the most popular meeting places in the village. There's live music most evenings and some afternoons. The Eagers' new venture is as popular as (if completely different from) their previous hostelry, and La Nueva Posada is often booked up way in advance for holidays. The hotel is east of the Plaza at the lakeshore corner of Independencia/ Constitución and Donato Guerra. You'll see the hotel's blue facade on the right by the lake.

✪ **Los Artistas B&B.** Constitución 105, 45900 Ajijic, Jal. ☎ **376/6-1027.** Fax 376/ 6-1762. E-mail: artistas@laguna.com.mx. 6 units. $40–$55 double (including breakfast). No credit cards.

One of Ajijic's loveliest homes also affords one of the best, most relaxing lodging values in Mexico. The inn has a beautiful garden setting with a swimming pool. All rooms but one have a private entry, and all are colorfully decorated, but completely different in size and arrangement. Guests have use of the pool and run of downstairs, which includes a comfortable living room with stereo and the dining room. Breakfast is served inside or out by the pool and patio. The inn is 5½ blocks east of the main square between Aldama and J. Álvarez. You'll see the name on a small tile plaque on the brick wall beside the iron gate.

Where to Dine

✪ **La Rusa.** Donato Guerra no. 9. ☎ **376/6-1444** and 376/6-1344. Reservations recommended Dec–Apr. Breakfast $3.50–$5; lunch $4.75–$8; dinner main courses $5–$12; Sun brunch $5–$6.50. MC, V. Mon–Sat 8am–9pm; Sun 9am–8pm (Sun brunch served 9am–1pm). INTERNATIONAL.

The dining and drinking area of La Nueva Posada gets it right, whether in the equipales-furnished bar, the elegant dining room with garden and lake view, or the garden. La Rusa continues to be a popular dining spot with locals and tapatíos alike. The lunch menu is simple: crepes, sandwiches, and salads. The dinner menu, printed on a large poster, has a dozen meat, seafood, and chicken main courses, plus soup, salad, and dessert. The Sunday brunch, which includes wine, offers an entirely different selection. There's live music on Friday and Saturday. To reach the restaurant from the Ajijic plaza, walk toward the lake on Colón, turn left on

Ajijic

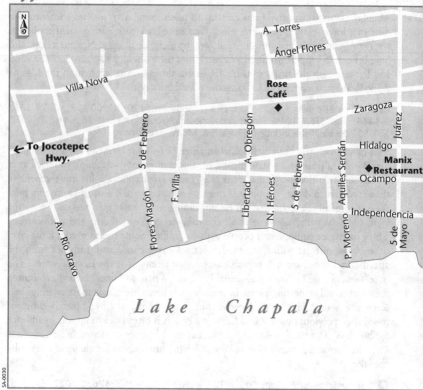

Independencia/16 de Septiembre, and look for Donato Guerra. Turn right; La Rusa is on the right by the lake.

✪ **Los Telares.** Morelos 6. ☎ **376/6-0428.** Pasta $7–$9; main courses $9–$14. CB, DISC, MC, V. Sun–Thurs noon–9pm; Fri–Sat noon–11pm. ITALIAN/INTERNATIONAL.

Sophisticated but casual, this fashionable dining establishment opened in 1994. Dining tables set with handwoven cloths and napkins are arranged around an open courtyard. There is a nonsmoking section. The pottery was made exclusively for the restaurant by Ken Edwards of Tlaquepaque, and prints of well-known international artists decorate the walls. Vegetables and herbs are grown organically in the restaurant's garden, and breads are made fresh daily. Main courses include fillet of sea bass in a smooth tamarindo sauce and Pacific prawns in key lime sauce. Try the outrageously rich and fresh fettuccine Alfredo. Los Telares is almost at the end of Colón/Morelos near the corner of Independencia/16 de Septiembre.

✪ **Manix Restaurant.** Ocampo 57. ☎ **376/6-0061.** Comida corrida $9–$10. MC, V. Mon–Sat 1–9pm. INTERNATIONAL.

This is one of my favorite restaurants in Mexico, and it has nothing to do with the 1970s TV show. I can always count on a delicious meal that's politely served in a pleasant, serene setting. The restaurant includes a nonsmoking section. Rainbow-colored napkins brighten the dark carved-wood furniture. There are usually two different international meals daily. Seafood, beef, and sometimes chicken cordon bleu, osso

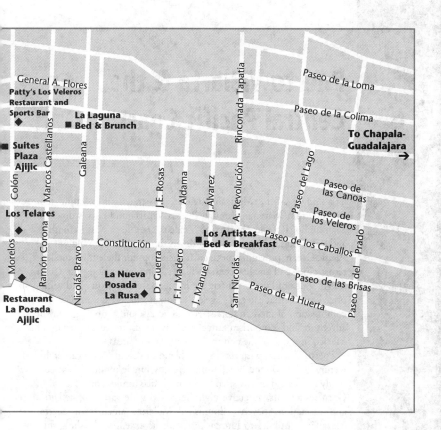

buco, or chicken Parmesan are served. Servings are generous and each meal comes with soup or salad and dessert. To get here from the plaza, turn your back to the church, walk straight ahead on Colón for 2 blocks, and turn right on Ocampo; the restaurant is down the street on the right, but the sign is obscured by the lone tree on the street.

Restaurant la Posada Ajijic. Morelos and Independencia. ☎ **376/6-0744.** Sandwiches $2.75–$4; main courses $3.90–$8. AE, MC, V. Sun–Thurs noon–9pm; Fri–Sat noon–1:30am. MEXICAN/INTERNATIONAL.

Formerly managed by the owners of La Nueva Posada, this restaurant facing the lake has reopened with graceful Mexican decor and good service. The menu covers traditional fare, including soups, salads, sandwiches, and more filling Mexican specialties, as well as imaginatively prepared main courses. The bar, opposite the restaurant, is a favorite Ajijic hangout. The restaurant is at the end of Colón/Morelos; you enter through the back by the lake, where there's parking.

9

Puerto Vallarta & the Central Pacific Coast

It's known as the Mexican Riviera: the stretch of coastline that extends from Mazatlán through Puerto Vallarta and curves down to Manzanillo. It's a lovely part of Mexico. The Sierra Madre foothills and palm-studded jungles sweep down to meet the deep blue of the Pacific Ocean, providing spectacular backdrops for these three modern resort cities and smaller coastal villages. Tiny coves along the Costa Alegre south of Puerto Vallarta are home to unique luxury and value-priced resorts that cater to travelers seeking seclusion and privacy. The combination of modern hotels, easy air access, and a growing array of adventure and ecotourism attractions have transformed this region of Mexico into one of the country's premier resort areas.

Puerto Vallarta, with its singular blend of colonial Mexican architecture and gold-sand beaches bordered by jungle mountains, is currently the second most visited resort in Mexico (trailing only Cancún). Great restaurants, an active nightlife, and a wide variety of activities and attractions haven't diminished Vallarta's small-town charm. Mazatlán continues to lure visitors with its exceptional fishing, historic downtown, and new championship golf facilities. Manzanillo is surprisingly relaxed, even though it's one of Mexico's most vibrant commercial ports, and it offers great fishing and exceptional value.

Villages such as San Blas, Bucerías, Barra de Navidad, and Melaque are still laid-back, almost undiscovered, and—except for the new, superluxurious Grand Bay Hotel—relatively inexpensive. Excursions to these smaller villages make easy day-trips or extended stays and are starkly different from bustling resort towns. Several villages are so close together that you can easily visit them all before heading home.

1 Puerto Vallarta

620 miles NW of Mexico City; 260 miles W of Guadalajara; 175 miles NW of Manzanillo; 300 miles SE of Mazatlán; 112 miles SW of Tepic

Puerto Vallarta is accustomed to seducing visitors. With a winning combination of stunning geography, a charming colonial village, and a genuine sense of welcome offered by local residents, it has become the second most popular beach destination in Mexico, with the highest percentage of repeat visitors in the country.

Vallarta's Banderas Bay, Mexico's largest natural bay, forms a protective barrier that to me feels as comforting as a gentle embrace. The cobblestone village, where picturesque images greet you at every turn, is nestled right in the heart of the curved center of the bay. A river runs down from the Sierra Madre mountains, bringing with it constant, cool breezes. The main waterfront street, or *malecón,* is graced with public sculptures and bordered by lively restaurants, shops, and bars. The malecón is a magnet for both residents and visitors, who stroll the broad walkway and take in the simplicity of an ocean breeze, a multihued sunset, or a moonlit, perfect wave.

Luxury hotels and shopping centers are concentrated on the outskirts of the original town, a fact that has allowed Vallarta to grow to a sizable city of 250,000 without sacrificing its charms. The city today is an ideal mix of modern services, infrastructure, and attractions with the authenticity of a colonial Mexican village.

The town began as a port for processing silver brought down from the Sierra Madre mountain mines, and evolved into an agricultural village. Its geography kept it isolated until it played an important role in launching a distinguished film career. The town's big break came when John Huston filmed Tennessee Williams's *Night of the Iguana,* starring Richard Burton, Ava Gardner, and Deborah Kerr, in Vallarta in the early 1960s. Elizabeth Taylor came along for the filming, and the scandalous romance between Burton and Taylor (both were married to other people at the time) became headline news, catapulting Puerto Vallarta into the global spotlight. The stars and director were charmed by Vallarta's simple innocence. Huston, Taylor, and Burton all bought homes in the area, and they returned for years and years. The tiny seaside village grew rapidly when a good highway and airport were added, maturing into the tourist resort it is today.

A considerable colony of Americans and Canadians has taken up permanent residence here, myself among them. If I sound partial to Vallarta, I am. Captivated by its unique magic, I've chosen to make my home here for the past 7 years.

ESSENTIALS

GETTING THERE & DEPARTING   By Plane   For a list of international carriers serving Mexico, see chapter 3, "Planning a Trip to Mexico." Some local numbers of international carriers serving Puerto Vallarta: **Alaska Airlines** (☎ 322/1-1350 or 322/1-1352), **American Airlines** (☎ 322/1-1972, 322/1-1799, or 322/1-1032), **America West** (☎ 322/1-1333), **Continental** (☎ 322/1-1025 or 322/1-1096), and **Delta** (☎ 322/1-1919 or 322/1-1734).

From other points in Mexico, **Aeromexico** (☎ 322/4-2777 or 322/1-1055) flies from Aguascalientes, Guadalajara, La Paz, León, Mexico City, and Tijuana. **Mexicana** (☎ 322/4-8900, 322/1-1266, or 322/1-0243) has direct or nonstop flights from Guadalajara, Mazatlán, Los Cabos, and Mexico City.

By Car   The coastal **Highway 200** is the only choice between Mazatlán to the north (6 hr. away) or Manzanillo to the south (3½ to 4 hr.). The 8-hour journey from Guadalajara through Tepic can be shortened to 5 to 6 hours by taking Highway 15A from Chapalilla to Compostela (this bypasses Tepic and saves 2 hr.), then continuing south on Highway 200 to Puerto Vallarta.

By Bus   A new bus station, **Central Camionera de Puerto Vallarta,** opened in early 1998 and has centralized bus travel in and out of Puerto Vallarta. Located just north of the airport, approximately 7 miles from downtown, it offers ticketing, long-distance telephone and fax service, restaurants, overnight guarded parking, baggage storage, and local transportation into town. A large, marble-floored waiting area offers ample seating in air-conditioned comfort. Most major first-class bus lines operate from here, with transportation to points throughout Mexico including Mazatlán, Tepic, Manzanillo, Guadalajara, and Mexico City. Taxis into town cost approximately $3.50 and are readily available; public buses have a regular stop in front of the arrivals hall, operating from 7am to 11pm.

ORIENTATION   Arriving by Plane   The airport is close to the north end of town near the Marina Vallarta, about 6 miles from downtown. **Transportes Terrestres** minivan (colectivo) and **Aeromovil** taxis make the trip. Costs for both are determined by zones—clearly posted at the respective ticket booths. **Colectivo** fares are $3, $4.50, $5.50, and $7 (for the farthest zone, the southern Hotel Zone). Colectivos to town run only when they fill up, so you may have to wait a bit to obtain transportation. **Airport taxis** are federally licensed taxis that operate exclusively to provide transportation from the airport. Their fares are almost three times as high as city (yellow) taxis. A trip to downtown Puerto Vallarta costs $8, whereas a return trip using a city taxi will only cost $3. Yellow cabs are restricted to picking up passengers leaving the airport.

VISITOR INFORMATION   The **State Tourism Office,** at Juárez and Independencia (☎ **322/2-0242,** 322/3-0844, or 322/3-0744; fax 322/2-0243), is in a corner of the white Presidencia Municipal building (city hall) on the north end of the main square. In addition to offering a collection of promotional brochures for local activities and services, they can also assist with specific questions—there's always an English-speaking person on staff. This is also the office of the tourist police. It's open Monday through Friday from 9am to 5pm and Saturday from 9am to 2pm.

CITY LAYOUT   The seaside promenade (the malecón) borders the street **Paseo Díaz Ordaz,** which runs north to south through the central downtown area. From the waterfront, the town stretches back into the hills a half a dozen blocks. The areas bordering the **Río Cuale** are the oldest parts of town—the original Puerto Vallarta. The area immediately south of the river, called **Olas Altas** after its main street, is now home to a growing selection of sidewalk cafes, fine restaurants, espresso bars, and hip nightclubs, many with live music. Once you're in the center of town, you'll find nearly everything within walking distance both north and south of the river. A **Tourism Trolley** (50¢) runs a loop around this zone, circling about every 20 minutes, with pickup on the western edge of the central plaza. The two sections of downtown are linked by **bridges** on Insurgentes (northbound traffic) and Ignacio Vallarta (southbound traffic).

Beyond downtown, Puerto Vallarta has grown along the beach to the north and south. **Nuevo Vallarta,** a planned resort, is north of the airport, across the Ameca River in the state of Nayarit (about 8 miles north of downtown). It also has hotels, condominiums, and a yacht marina, but very little in the way of restaurants, shopping, or other attractions. Most hotels there are all-inclusive, and guests usually plan to travel the distance into Puerto Vallarta (about an $8 cab ride) for anything other than poolside or beach action—however, these hotels do enjoy some of the finest beaches in the bay. There is regularly scheduled public bus service for about 50¢, which runs until 10pm.

Marina Vallarta, a resort city within a city, is at the northern edge of the Hotel Zone not far from the airport—you pass it on the right as you come into town from the airport. It boasts the most modern luxury hotels plus condominiums and residential homes, a huge marina with 450 yacht slips, a golf course, restaurants and bars, a water park, and several shopping plazas. Here, you're on a peninsula facing the open ocean and in a completely separate world from the rest of Puerto Vallarta.

Linking downtown to the airport is **avenida Francisco Medina Ascencio** (formerly called **avenida de las Palmas**). Along this main thoroughfare are many luxury hotels (in an area called the **Zona Hotelera,** or Hotel Zone), plus several shopping centers with casual restaurants.

Bucerías, a small beachfront village of cobblestone streets, villas, and small hotels, is farther north along Banderas Bay, 19 miles beyond the airport. Past Bucerías is **Punta de Mita.** A new beach club, **Los Veneros,** has recently opened there, and a

Puerta Vallarta: Hotel Zone & Beaches

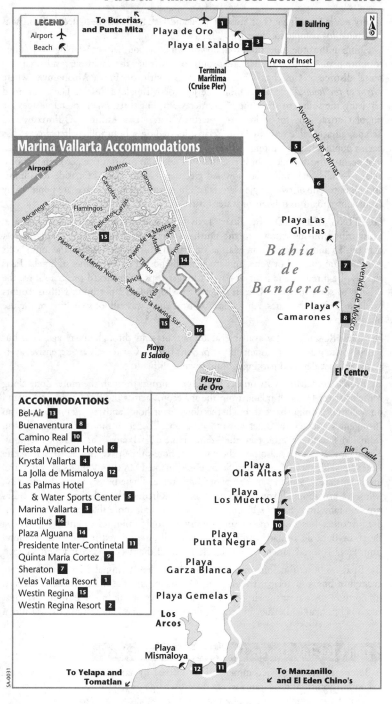

LEGEND
Airport ✈
Beach ⚲

To Bucerias, and Punta Mita

Playa de Oro
Playa el Salado

■ Bullring

Terminal Marítima (Cruise Pier)

Area of Inset

Avenida de las palmas

Marina Vallarta Accommodations

Airport

Albatros
Gaviotas
Garzas
Pelicanos
Garzas
Flamingos
Bocanegra
Paseo de la Marina
Popa
Proa
Paseo de la Marina Norte
Timon
Ancla
Vela
Paseo de la Marina Sur

Playa El Salado

Playa de Oro

Playa Las Glorias

Bahía de Banderas

Avenida de México

Playa Camarones

El Centro

Río Cuale

Playa Olas Altas

Playa Los Muertos

Playa Punta Negra

Playa Garza Blanca

Playa Gemelas

Los Arcos

Playa Mismaloya

ACCOMMODATIONS
Bel-Air **13**
Buenaventura **8**
Camino Real **10**
Fiesta American Hotel **6**
Krystal Vallarta **4**
La Jolla de Mismaloya **12**
Las Palmas Hotel
   & Water Sports Center **5**
Marina Vallarta **3**
Mautilus **16**
Plaza Alguana **14**
Presidente Inter-Continetal **11**
Quinta Maria Cortez **9**
Sheraton **7**
Velas Vallarta Resort **1**
Westin Regina **15**
Westin Regina Resort **2**

To Yelapa and Tomatlan

To Manzanillo and El Eden Chino's

SA-0031

luxury resort featuring a Four Seasons hotel and Jack Nicklaus–designed golf course is scheduled for completion in early 1999.

Going in the other direction from downtown is the southern coastal highway, home to more luxury hotels. Immediately south of town lies the exclusive residential and rental district of **Conchas Chinas**. Six miles south, on **Playa Mismaloya** (where *Night of the Iguana* was filmed), lies the Jolla de Mismaloya Resort. There's no road servicing the southern shoreline of Banderas Bay, but three small coastal villages are popular attractions for visitors to Puerto Vallarta: **Las Ánimas, Quimixto,** and **Yelapa,** all accessible only by boat. Yelapa, located on a beautiful sheltered cove, has been a popular haven for long-term ex-pat visitors and artists, due to its seclusion, natural beauty, and simplicity of life. Offering a selection of primitive accommodations, Yelapa—which has only solar-powered electricity—also offers beachside restaurants and hikes to one of two jungle waterfalls. Quimixto and Las Ánimas are popular day excursions aboard tour boats or water taxis.

GETTING AROUND   By Taxi   Taxis are plentiful and relatively inexpensive. Most trips from downtown to the northern Hotel Zone and Marina Vallarta cost between $5 and $6; to or from Marina Vallarta to Mismaloya Beach to the south costs $9. Rates are charged by zone, and are generally posted in the lobbies of hotels. Taxis can also be hired by the hour or day for longer trips, when you'd prefer to leave the driving to someone else. Rates run between $10 and $12 per hour, with discounts available for full-day rates. At publication time there was talk of switching to the use of meters.

By Car   Rental cars are available at the airport and through travel agencies, but unless you're planning a distant side trip, don't bother. Car rentals are expensive, averaging $60 per day, and parking around town is difficult.

By Bus & Colectivo   City buses run from the airport through the Hotel Zone along Morelos street (1 block inland from the malecón), across the Río Cuale, and inland on Vallarta, looping back through the downtown hotel and restaurant districts on Insurgentes and several other downtown streets. To get to the northern hotel strip from old Puerto Vallarta, take the "Zona Hoteles," "Ixtapa," or "Aeropuerto" bus. These same buses may also post the names of hotels they pass such as Krystal, Fiesta Americana, Sheraton, and others. Some buses, marked MARINA VALLARTA, will travel inside this area, stopping at the major hotels there. These buses, costing about 30¢, will serve just about all your transportation needs frequently and inexpensively. Buses run generally from 6am to 11pm, and it's rare to wait more than a few minutes for one. Another bus route travels south every 10 to 15 minutes to either Mismaloya Beach or Boca de Tomatlán (the destination will be indicated in the front window) from Plaza Lázaro Cárdenas, a few blocks south of the river at Cárdenas and Suárez.

By Boat   The cruise ship pier (*muelle*), also called Terminal Marítima, is where **excursion boats** to Yelapa, Las Ánimas, Quimixto, and the Marietas Islands depart. It's north of town near the airport and an inexpensive taxi or bus ride from town. Just take any bus marked IXTAPA and tell the driver to let you off at the Terminal Marítima.

Don't Let Taxi Drivers Steer You the Wrong Way

Beware of restaurant recommendations offered by taxi drivers—many receive a commission from restaurants where they discharge passengers. Be especially wary if a driver tries to talk you out of a restaurant you've already selected.

Water taxis offering direct transportation to Yelapa, Las Ánimas, and Quimixto leave at 10:30am, 11am, and 3:30pm from the pier at Los Muertos Beach (south of downtown) on Rodolfo Rodríguez next to the Hotel Marsol. Another water taxi departs at 11am from the beachfront pier at the northern edge of the malecón. A round-trip ticket to Yelapa (the farthest point) costs $12.

FAST FACTS: Puerto Vallarta

American Express   The local office is located in town at Morelos 660, at the corner of Abasolo (☎ **01-800/0-0555** in Mexico, or 322/3-2955). It's open Monday through Friday from 9am to 6pm and Saturday from 9am to 1pm.

Area Code   The telephone area code is **322.**

Climate   It's warm all year, with tropical temperatures; however, evenings in the winter months can turn quite cool. Summers are sunny, but with an increase in humidity during the rainy season, between May and October. Rains come almost every afternoon in June and July but are usually brief and strong—just enough to cool off the air for evening activities. September is the month in which heat and humidity are least comfortable.

Consumer Assistance   Tourists with complaints about taxis, stores, or other matters should contact **PROFECO,** the consumer protection office (☎ **322/50000,** 322/50018, or 322/2-2554).

Currency Exchange   Banks are found throughout downtown, and also in the other prime shopping areas of Vallarta. Most banks are open from 9am to 5pm Monday through Friday, with partial-day hours on Saturday. ATMs are commonly found throughout Vallarta, including on the central plaza downtown.

Embassies/Consulates   Both the U.S. and Canadian consulates maintain offices here, in the building on the southern border of the central plaza (you'll see the U.S. and Canadian flags). The **U.S. Consular Agency** office (☎ **322/2-0069;** 322/3-0074, 24 hours a day for emergencies) is open Monday through Friday from 10am to 2pm. The **Canadian Consulate** (☎ **322/2-5398** or 322/30858; emergencies 01-800-706-2900, 24 hours) is open Monday through Friday from 9am to 5pm.

Emergencies   **Police Emergency** ☎ 060; **local police** ☎ 322/2-0123; **Tourist Protection** ☎ 01-800-90-392; **Intensive Care Ambulance** ☎ 322/5-0386; **Ameri-Med Urgent Care** (U.S.-standards health care service) ☎ 322/1-0023 or 322/1-0024; **Red Cross** ☎ 322/2-1533.

Newspapers & Magazines   The following publications are excellent sources for local information: *Vallarta Today,* a daily English-language newspaper (☎ **322/4-2829**) and the quarterly city magazine *Vallarta Lifestyles* (☎ **322/1-0106**). Both are available for sale at area newsstands.

Pharmacies (late night)   **CMQ Farmacia,** Basilio Badillo 365, is open 24 hours (☎ **322/2-3572**).

Post Office   The post office (correo) is at Juárez 628 (☎ **322/2-1888**). It's open Monday through Friday from 9am to 7:30pm, Saturday from 9am to 1pm.

Safety   Puerto Vallarta enjoys a very low crime rate throughout the city. Public Transportation is perfectly safe to use, and Tourist Police (dressed in white safari uniforms with white hats) are available to answer questions, give directions, and offer assistance. Most crime or encounters with the police are linked to using or purchasing drugs–simply don't do it here (see chapter 3, "Planning a Trip to Mexico").

SPECIAL EVENTS

Each November, **Fiestas del Mar** (SeaFest) is celebrated with a Gourmet Dining Festival, International Boat Show, art exhibitions, tennis tournaments, regattas, and more. Dates vary; call the Tourism Board (☎ **888/384-6822** from the U.S.) for dates and schedule. **Santa Cecilia,** the patron saint of mariachis, is honored on November 23. Different mariachi groups take turns playing in the cathedral. From December 1 through December 12, the ✪ **Festival of the Virgin of Guadalupe**—Mexico's patron saint—is celebrated in one of the most authentic displays of culture and community in Mexico. Each business, neighborhood, association, or group makes a pilgrimage (called *peregrinaciones*) to the cathedral, where offerings are exchanged for a brief blessing by the priest. These processions, especially those offered by hotels, often include floats, Aztec dancers, and mariachis, and are followed by fireworks. Hotels frequently invite guests to participate in the walk to the church. It's an event not to be missed.

BEACHES, ACTIVITIES & EXCURSIONS

Travel agencies can provide information on what to see and do in Puerto Vallarta and can arrange tours, fishing, and other activities. Most hotels have a tour desk on-site. Of the many travel agencies in town, I highly recommend **Tukari Servicios Turísticos,** km 2.5 bulevar Francisco Medina Ascencio, Edif. Marbella, Depto. 502 (☎ **322/4-7177** or 322/4-7178; fax 322/4-2350). Another good source for information is **Xplora Adventours** (☎ **322/30661**), located in the **Sierra Madre** shop on the malecón. They have books of all locally available tours with photos, explanations, and costs.

THE BEACHES

For years, beaches were Puerto Vallarta's main attraction. Although more visitors are exploring more of the surrounding geography, the sands are still a powerful draw. Over 26 miles of beaches extend around the broad Bay of Banderas, ranging from action-packed party spots to secluded coves accessible only by boat.

IN TOWN   The easiest to reach is **Playa Los Muertos** (also known as Playa Olas Altas or Playa del Sol), just off calle Olas Altas, south of the Río Cuale. The water is rough here, but the wide beach is home to a wide array of palapa restaurants with food, beverage, and beach-chair service. On the southern end of this beach is a section known as "Blue Chairs"—the most popular gay beach. Vendors stroll the length of Los Muertos, and beach volleyball, parasailing, and jet skiing are all popular pastimes. The **Hotel Zone** is also known for its broad, smooth beaches, accessible primarily through the associated hotel lobbies.

SOUTH OF TOWN   **Playa Mismaloya** is in a beautiful sheltered cove about 6 miles south of town along Highway 200. The water here is clear and beautiful, ideal for snorkeling off the beach. Entrance to the public beach is just to the left of the Mismaloya hotel. Colorful palapa restaurants dot the small beach and rent beach chairs for sunning. You can also stake out a table under a palapa for the day. Using a restaurant's table and palapa is a reciprocal arrangement—they let you be comfortable, and you buy your drinks, snacks, and lunch there. *Night of the Iguana* was filmed at Mismaloya. La Jolla de Mismaloya Resort and Spa recently opened a restaurant on the restored film set—**La Noche de la Iguana Set Restaurant,** open daily from noon to

11pm. The movie runs continuously in a room below the restaurant, and still photographs from it hang in the restaurant. The restaurant is accessible by land on the point framing the south side of the cove. La Jolla de Mismaloya Resort and Spa is to the right of the public beach, and restaurants there are available to outsiders as well. The beach at **Boca de Tomatlán,** just down the road, is similar in setup to Mismaloya, but without a large resort looming in the backdrop.

  Las Ánimas, Quimixto, and **Yelapa** beaches offer a true sense of seclusion; they are accessible only by boat (see "Getting Around," above for information about water-taxi service). These are each larger than Mismaloya, offer intriguing hikes to jungle waterfalls, and are similarly set up with restaurants fronting a wide beach. Overnight stays are only available at Yelapa (see "Side Trips from Puerto Vallarta," below).

NORTH OF TOWN   The entire northern coastline from Bucerías to Punta de Mita is a succession of sandy coves alternating with rocky inlets. For years the beaches to the north, with their long, clean breaks, have been the favored locale for surfers. The broad sandy stretches at **Playa Anclote, Playa Piedras Blancas,** and **Playa Destiladeras,** along with their palapa restaurants, have made them favorites with local residents looking for a quick but meaningful getaway from town. Recently opened, the **Las Veneros Beach Club** is located on one of the finest stretches of beach in the area, with luxury facilities and casual yet elegant dining. There are two infinity pools (one adults only), a marble bathroom and changing area, lockers, showers, towel service, an artisan center and mini–shopping arcade, plus mountain bikes and horses available for riding on trails or the beach. They also have surfboards and kayaks available for rent. Day admission with the use of all facilities is $10; food and beverage consumption costs extra. Special packages including transportation are also available; call ☎ **322/1-0088** for more information.

Organized Tours

BOAT TOURS   Puerto Vallarta offers a number of different boat trips, including sunset cruises and trips for snorkeling, swimming, and diving. They generally travel one of two routes: to the **Marietas Islands,** about a 30- to 45-minute boat ride off the northern shore of Banderas Bay, or to **Yelapa, Las Ánimas,** or **Quimixto** along the southern shore. The trips to the southern beaches make a stop at **Los Arcos,** an island rock formation south of Puerto Vallarta, for snorkeling. When comparing all of these boat cruises, note that some include lunch, while most provide music and an open bar on board. Most leave around 9:30am, stop for 45 minutes of snorkeling, and arrive at the beach destination around noon for a 2½-hour stay before returning around 3pm. At Quimixto and Yelapa, visitors can take a half-hour hike to a jungle waterfall or rent a horse for the ride. Prices range from $20 for a sunset cruise or a trip to one of the beaches with open bar to $50 for an all-day outing with open bar and meals.

  One boat, the **Marigalante** (☎ **322/3-0309**), is an exact replica of Columbus's ship the *Santa Maria,* built in honor of the 500-year anniversary of his voyage to the Americas. It features a daytime "pirate's cruise" complete with treasure hunt. Sunset dinner cruises are also available, for $50.

  One of the best trips is the new tour to **Caletas,** the cove where John Huston made his home for years. **Vallarta Adventures** (☎ **322/1-0657** or 322/1-0658; www. vallarta-adventures.com) holds the exclusive lease on this private cove, and has done an excellent job of restoring Huston's former home, adding exceptional day-spa facilities, and landscaping the beach, which is wonderful for snorkeling. The quality facilities, combined with the relative privacy this excursion offers, has made it one of the most popular, at $50 per person. They also offer an evening cruise, complete with dinner and show (see "Puerto Vallarta After Dark," below.)

Travel agencies have tickets and information on all cruises. If you prefer to spend a longer time at Yelapa or Las Ánimas without taking time for snorkeling and cruise entertainment, note the information about travel by water taxis, above, under "Getting Around."

From mid- to late November through March, **whale-watching tours** are offered to view and photograph migrating humpback whales. Any travel agency can arrange whale-watching trips, or you can contact **Open Air Expeditions,** Guerrero 339 (☎/fax 322/2-3310; E-mail: openair@vivamexico.com). They offer ecologically oriented tours (up to eight people) in small boats, for $55, as well as other nature-oriented trips, including lagoon kayaking and bird watching, and ocean kayaking to Los Arcos. **Vallarta Adventures** (☎ 322/1-0657 or 322/1-0658) offers whale watching on their tours to the Marietas Islands aboard large catamaran boats, including lunch, time at a private beach, and a more festive than educational ambiance. The cost is $50.

DIVING   Underwater enthusiasts from beginner to expert can arrange scuba diving at **Chico's Dive Shop,** a PADI five-star dive center located at Díaz Ordaz 770-5, near Carlos O'Brian's (☎ 322/2-1895). Dives take place at Los Arcos, the Marietas Islands, Quimixto Coves, or the offshore El Morro and Chimo reefs, and certification courses are also available. Chico's also has branches at the Marriott, Vidafel, Villa del Palmar, Camino Real, and Continental Plaza hotels. **Vallarta Adventures** (☎322/1-0657 or 322/1-0658; www.vallarta-adventures.com) is also a five-star PADI dive center and offers similar dive trips. In addition, they have an overnight, six-tank dive to the Corbeteños and El Morro reefs, plus dives offshore the Marías Islands, for $380.

LAND TOURS   **Tukari Tours** travel agency can arrange bird-watching trips to the fertile birding grounds near **San Blas,** 3 to 4 hours north of Puerto Vallarta in the state of Nayarit; shopping trips to **Tlaquepaque and Tonalá** (6 hr. inland near Guadalajara); or a day-trip to **Rancho Altamira,** a 50-acre, hilltop, working ranch for a barbecue lunch and horseback riding, then a stroll through **El Tuito,** a small nearby colonial-era village. They can also arrange an unforgettable morning at **Terra Noble Art & Healing Center** (☎322/3-0308; www.terranoble.com.mx), a mountaintop day spa and center for the arts where participants can get a massage or treatment, work in clay and paint, and have lunch in a heavenly setting overlooking the bay.

Hotel travel desks and travel agencies, including Tukari, can also book the ever-popular **Tropical Tour** or **Jungle Tour** ($18 each), basically an orientation to the area. These tours are really expanded city tours that include a drive through the workers' village of Pitillal, the posh neighborhood of Conchas Chinas, the cathedral, the market, the Taylor-Burton houses, and lunch at a jungle restaurant. Any stop for shopping usually means the driver picks up commission for what you buy.

The **Sierra Madre Expedition** is another excellent tour offered by **Vallarta Adventures** (☎ 322/1-0657 or 322/1-0658). This daily excursion travels in special Mercedes all-terrain vehicles north of Puerto Vallarta through jungle trails, stopping at a small town, into a forest for a brief nature walk, and winding up on a beach for lunch and swimming. The outing, which costs $60, is worthwhile because it takes tourists into scenery that would otherwise be off-limits.

Ecotours de México, Ignacio L. Vallarta 243, Col. Emiliano Zapata (☎/fax 322/2-6606 and 322/4-7551; E-mail: 74174.2424@compuserve.com), offers popular Puerto Vallarta tours, as well as some unusual outings. Among these are an 8-day nature excursion north of Puerto Vallarta into the Huichol Indian area of Nayarit that includes bird watching at the Isabel Island sanctuary and a journey to the monarch butterfly sanctuary in the state of Michoacán, a neighbor state to Jalisco.

Every Thursday and Friday in high season (from late Nov through Easter), the **International Friendship Club** (☎ 322/2-5466), offers a **Private Home Tour** of four private villas in town for a donation of $25 per person, with proceeds donated to local charities. Tour arrangements begin at 10am at the Hotel Molina de Agua (avenida Ignacio L. Vallarta no. 130, adjacent to the southbound bridge over the Río Cuale) where you can buy breakfast while you wait for the group to gather—and arrive early, because this tour sells out quickly! The tour departs at 11am and lasts approximately 2½ hours.

An **Artist's Studio Tour** starts from Galería Pacífico, 109 Insurgentes (☎ **322/ 2-1982**), every Monday from 10am to 2pm. Gary Thompson, owner/curator of Galería Pacífico, gives an overview of the Puerto Vallarta and Latin American art scene before guiding the group to the working studios of between six and eight artists. The cost is $22; call in advance for reservations.

You can also tour the **Taylor/Burton villas** (Casa Kimberley; ☎ **322/2-1336**), located at 445 calle Zaragoza. Tours of the two houses owned by Elizabeth Taylor and Richard Burton cost $5; just ring the bell between 9am and 6pm, and if the manager is available, she will take you through the house.

HORSEBACK-RIDING TOURS Guided horseback rides can be arranged through travel agents or directly through one of the local ranches. The two best are **Rancho El Charro,** avenida Francisco Villa 895 (☎ **322/4-0114** or 329/2-0122), and **Rancho Ojo de Agua,** Cerrado de Cardenal 227, Fracc. Las Aralias (☎/fax **322/ 4-0607**). Both of these ranches are located about a 10-minute taxi ride north of downtown, toward the Sierra Madre foothills. The morning or sunset rides last 2 to 3 hours and take you up into the mountains overlooking the ocean and town. The cost is $36. They also have their own comfortable base camp for serious riders who want to stay out overnight. Each Tuesday, Rancho El Charro offers an exclusive **Botanical Horseback Safari** from 9:30am to 2pm. The price of $50 includes lunch, and advance reservations are required.

For a unique getaway, try **Horseback on Mexico's** Hacienda Trail from Sea to Sierra Madre, several 3- to 7-day journeys by horseback into the mountains. Trips are offered from November 1 through April 30; there's a 4-person minimum and a 15-person maximum. The cost of $250 per person per day includes food, horses, camping en route, and stays in centuries-old haciendas. They can arrange hotels in Puerto Vallarta and provide complete details on the quality of horses and accommodations. For details, contact Pam Aguirre of Rancho El Charro. Cash only.

✪ **SPORTS TOURS** **Bike Mex,** calle Guerrero 361 (☎ **322/3-1834** or 322/ 3-1680), offers expert guided biking and hiking tours up the Río Cuale canyon and to outlying areas. Bike trips cost around $30 to $40 for 4 hours and include bike, helmet, gloves, water, snacks, lunch, and an English-speaking guide. Trips start at around 7:30 or 8am. Make arrangements a day ahead. An advanced bike trip leaves at 7:30am, climbing for 2 hours to an elevation of 3,000 feet, with lunch at a ranch, and continuing to some hot springs for a rest, followed by more biking to the remote town of Los Llanitos. This tour costs around $50 and takes 7 or 8 hours. Other bicycle trips, such as along the beachfront of Punta Mita, are also available. Guided **hiking tours** are also available along the same routes, priced around $30, depending on the route.

New in Puerto Vallarta are individual or group surfing tours. **Surf Mex,** calle Guerrero 351 (☎ **322/3-1680**), (sister company to Bike Mex), can arrange a day of surfing at a variety of places 1 to 1½ hours north of Puerto Vallarta in the state of Nayarit. Trips are suitable for both experienced and novice surfers.

Hot-Air Balloon Tours, Morelos 36 at Corona (☎ **322/3-2002**), offers two hot-air balloon trips a day at 7am and at 4:30pm (weather permitting) for $130 to $155 per person. The balloons glide along the coast, over beaches, jungle, and farmland, ending with a round of champagne.

A STROLL THROUGH TOWN

Puerto Vallarta's cobblestone streets are a pleasure to explore; they're full of tiny shops, rows of windows edged with curling wrought iron, and vistas of red-tile roofs and the sea. Start with a walk up and down the malecón, the seafront boulevard.

Among the sights you shouldn't miss is the **municipal building,** on the main square (next to the tourism office), which has a large Manuel Lepe mural inside in its stairwell. Nearby, up Independencia, sits the **cathedral,** topped with its curious crown, (a replica of the one worn by Empress Carlotta during her brief reign); on its steps, women sell colorful herbs and spices to cure common ailments. Here Richard Burton and Elizabeth Taylor were married the first time—she in a Mexican wedding dress, he in a Mexican charro outfit.

Three blocks south of the church, head uphill on Libertad, lined with small shops and pretty upper windows, to the municipal market by the river. After exploring the market, cross the bridge to the island in the river; sometimes a painter is at work on its banks. Walk down the center of the island toward the sea and you'll come to the tiny **Museo Río Cuale,** which has a small but impressive permanent exhibit of pre-Columbian figurines. It's open Monday through Saturday from 10am to 4pm. Admission is free, and an English-language tour is offered daily at 2pm.

Retrace your steps back to the market and Libertad and climb up steep Miramar to Zaragoza. At the top is a magnificent view over rooftops to the sea. Up Zaragoza to the right 2 blocks is the famous **pink arched bridge** that once connected Richard Burton's and Elizabeth Taylor's houses. This area, known as **"Gringo Gulch,"** is where many Americans have houses.

OUTDOOR ACTIVITIES

WATERSKIING & PARASAILING Waterskiing, parasailing, and other water sports are available at many beaches along the Bay of Banderas. The best known for water-sports equipment rental is **Teresa's Water Sports Center** at the Las Palmas Hotel (avenida Fco. Medina Ascencio km 2.5, Hotel Zone; ☎ **322/4-0650**) beach. Windsurfers, Hobie Cats, Waverunners, banana boats, and waterskiing are all available here, for hourly, half-day, or full-day rentals.

SAILING   **Sail Vallarta,** Club de Tenis Puesta del Sol, Local 7-B, Marina Vallarta (☎ **322/1-0096;** fax 322/1-0097), offers a diverse variety of sailing vessels for hire. A group day-sail, including crew, use of snorkeling equipment, drinks and food, and music, plus a stop at a beach for swimming and lunch, costs $50. Most trips include a crew, but you can make arrangements to sail yourself or one of their smaller boats. Prices vary for full boat charters, depending on the vessel and amount of time desired.

SWIMMING WITH DOLPHINS Ever been kissed by a dolphin? Take advantage of a unique and absolutely memorable opportunity to swim with Pacific bottlenose dolphins in a clear lagoon. **Dolphin Adventure** (☎ **322/1-0657** or 322/1-0658; www.vallarta-adventures.com) operates an interactive dolphin-research facility, which allows limited numbers of people to swim with their dolphins Monday through Saturday at scheduled times. Cost for the swim is $130, with advanced reservations required. If they're booked, there is also the **Dolphin Encounter** ($65), at the same facility, which allows you to touch and learn about these dolphins, though not actually enter the water with them. I give this my highest recommendation—these dolphins are well cared for, happy, and spirited, and the program is geared for education and interaction, not entertainment or amusement. Highly recommended for children.

FISHING A fishing trip can be arranged through travel agencies or through the **Cooperativo de Pescadores** (Fishing Cooperative) (☎ **322/2-1202**) on the malecón,

ATTRACTIONS
Catedral **5**
Gringo Gulch
  (neighborhood) **4**
Main Square **6**
Río Cuale **7**
Terra Noble Center
  for the Arts **1**
Villas **3**
ACCOMMODATIONS
Hotel Cuatro Vientos **2**
Hotel Los Arcos **9**
Hotel Molina de Aqua **8**

Bahia de Banderas

Playa Los Muertos
Pier (water taxi)

north of the Río Cuale, next door to the Rosita Hotel and across from McDonald's. Fishing charters cost $200 to $300 a day for four to eight people. Price varies with the size of the boat. Although the posted price at the fishing cooperative is the same as through travel agencies, you may be able to negotiate a lower price at the cooperative. Major credit cards are accepted. It's open Monday through Saturday from 7am to 2pm, but make arrangements a day ahead. You can also arrange fishing trips at the Marina Vallarta docks, or by calling **Cheforo's Fleet** (☎ **322/2-6899**). Fishing trips generally include equipment and bait, but drinks, snacks, and lunch are optional, so check to see what the price includes.

GOLF   Puerto Vallarta has two long-standing golf courses, with the new **Four Seasons,** Jack Nicklaus course scheduled to open in late 1998. The Joe Finger–designed course at the **Marina Vallarta Golf Club** (☎ **322/1-0073**) is an 18-hole, par-74, private course that winds through the Marina Vallarta peninsula with ocean views. It's for members only, but most of the luxury hotels in Puerto Vallarta have memberships that their guests can use. It offers a bar, restaurant, golf pro, and pro shop. The greens fees are $70 to $90 in high season (depending on the type of membership your hotel has); $50 to $65 during low season. Fees include golf cart, caddy, range balls, and tax. Club rentals, lessons, and special packages are also available.

North of town in the state of Nayarit, about 10 miles beyond Puerto Vallarta, is the 18-hole, par-72 **Los Flamingos Club de Golf** (☎ **329/8-0606** or 329/8-0280). The older of the two courses, it's open to the public and has beautiful jungle vegetation, but is not as well maintained. It's open from 7am to 5:30pm daily, with a bar (no restaurant) and full pro shop. The greens fee is $43; add $25 for use of a golf cart, $9 for a caddy, and $14 for club rental. A free shuttle service is available from downtown Puerto Vallarta; call for pickup times and locations.

TENNIS Many hotels in Puerto Vallarta offer excellent tennis facilities, many with clay courts. There are also two full-service tennis clubs. The **Continental Plaza Tennis Club** (☎ 322/4-0123), located at the Continental Plaza hotel in the Hotel Zone, offers indoor and outdoor courts (including a clay court), full pro shop, lessons, clinics, and partner matchups. The **Iguana Tennis Center** (☎ 322/1-0683), located on the main highway, just south of the entrance to Marina Vallarta, offers covered courts, clinics, pro shop, and child care.

BULLFIGHTS Bullfights are held from December through April beginning at 5pm on Wednesday afternoons, at the bullring "La Paloma," across the highway from the town pier. Tickets can be arranged through travel agencies and cost around $20.

SHOPPING

Shopping in Puerto Vallarta is generally concentrated in small, eclectic, and independent shops rather than impersonal malls. You can find excellent-quality **folk art**, original **clothing** designs, and fine home accessories at great prices. Vallarta is known for having the most diverse and impressive selection of **contemporary Mexican art** available outside of Mexico City. There is also an abundance of tacky T-shirts and the ubiquitous **silver jewelry.**

There are a few key areas where the best shopping is concentrated: central downtown, the Marina Vallarta malecón, the popular mercados, and on the beach—where the merchandise comes to you. Some of the more attractive shops are found 1 to 2 blocks in **back of the malecón.** Start at the intersection of Corona and Morelos streets—interesting shops are found in all directions from here. **Marina Vallarta** does offer two shopping plazas with an increasing selection of shops—Plaza Marina and Neptuno Plaza, both located on the main highway coming from the airport into town. However, the most interesting shops are found around the marina boardwalk, or *marina malecón.*

Puerto Vallarta's **municipal market** is just north of the Río Cuale where Libertad and A. Rodríguez meet. The mercado sells clothes, jewelry, serapes, shawls, leather accessories and suitcases, papier-mâché parrots, stuffed frogs and armadillos, and, of course, T-shirts. Be sure to do some comparison shopping, and definitely bargain before buying. The market is open daily from 8am to 8pm. An outdoor market is found along Río Cuale island, between the two bridges. Stalls sell crafts, gifts, folk art, and clothing.

Along any public beach, it's more than likely that you'll be approached by walking **vendors** selling merchandise that ranges from silver jewelry to rugs, T-shirts to masks. "Almost free!" they'll call out, in seemingly relentless efforts to attract your attention. If you're too relaxed to think of shopping in town, this can be an entertaining alternative for picking up a few souvenirs, and remember: bargaining is expected. The most reputable beach vendors are concentrated at Los Muertos beach, in front of the El Dorado and La Palapa restaurants (calle Pulpito). *Note:* most of the silver sold on the beach is actually alpaca, a lesser-quality silver metal (even though many pieces are still stamped with the designation "9.5," supposedly indicating that it is true silver). The prices for silver on the beach are much lower, as is the quality. If you're looking for a more lasting piece of jewelry, you're better off in a true silver shop.

In most of the better quality shops and galleries, shipping, packing, and delivery services to Puerto Vallarta hotels are available.

Art of the Huichol Indians

Puerto Vallarta offers the best selection of Huichol art in Mexico. Descendants of the Aztecs, the Huichol Indians are one of the last remaining indigenous cultures in the world that has remained true to its ancient traditions, customs, language, and habitat. The Huichol live in adobe structures in the high Sierras (4,600 ft. elevation) north and east of Puerto Vallarta. Due to the decreasing fertility (and therefore, productivity) of the land surrounding their villages, they have come to depend more on the sale of their artwork for sustenance.

Huichol art is characterized by colorful, symbolic yarn "paintings," which are based on visions experienced during spiritual ceremonies. They also create fascinating masks and bowls decorated in colorful beads, using the same symbolic and mythological imagery inspired by their visions. Huichol Indians may also be seen on the streets of Vallarta—they are easy to spot, dressed in white clothing embroidered with colorful designs; men frequently wear wide-brimmed, highly decorated hats as well. A number of fine Huichol galleries are located in downtown Puerto Vallarta (see individual listings under "Crafts, Decorative & Folk Art," below).

A notable place for learning more about the Huicholes is **Huichol Collection** (Morelos 490, across from the sea-horse statue on the malecón; ☎ **322/3-2141**). Not only does this shop offer an extensive selection of Huichol art in all price ranges, but it also has a replica of a Huichol adobe hut, informational displays explaining more about their fascinating ways of life and beliefs, and usually, a Huichol Indian at work, creating art. The Huichol Collection donates a portion of all sales proceeds to projects, identified by the village elders, that help them retain their self-sufficiency.

CONTEMPORARY ART   Known for sustaining one of the stronger art communities in Latin America, Puerto Vallarta has an impressive selection of fine galleries featuring quality original works of art. The several dozen galleries get together to offer art walks almost every Friday evening between November and April, a social highlight of Vallarta during high season.

Galería Dante. Basilio Badillo 269. ☎ **322/2-2477.** Fax 322/2-6284. E-mail: dante@acnet.net.

This gallery in a villa showcases contemporary sculptures and classical reproductions of Italian, Greek, and art-deco bronzes. Featured original sculptures include works by Victor Villareal, Jonas Gutierrez, and the marine life of Octavio González, all set against a backdrop of gardens and fountains. Located on the "calle de los Cafés," the gallery's open daily during the winter from 10am to 2pm and from 6 to 9pm. Summer hours are 10am to 2pm. Viewings by appointment are also welcome.

✪ **Galería Pacífico.** Insurgentes 109, 2nd floor, opposite Le Bistro Jazz Café on the Río Cuale. ☎ **322/2-1982.** www.ArtMexico.com.

A leading gallery of contemporary Mexican art in Vallarta and within Mexico, it offers a wide selection of sculptures and paintings in various media, by midrange masters to up-and-coming artists. Limited-edition graphics by masters are available as are art posters. Affable owner/curator Gary Thompson brings 22 years of experience in Latin American art to help you in making your selection. Open Monday through Saturday from 10am to 9pm. This gallery also organizes the Artist's Studio Tour (see "Organized Tours," above

Galería Rosas Blancas. Juárez 523. ☎ **322/2-1168.**

A new and notable addition to Puerto Vallarta's gallery community, owner Marcella Alegre features contemporary painters from throughout Mexico in this gallery, adjacent to her folk-art store, Querubines (see "Crafts, Decorative & Folk Art," below). The downstairs courtyard exhibition space showcases a featured artist, while the upstairs offers a sampling of the artists represented here, most of whom reside in Mexico City. Adjacent is a shop selling art supplies and books on Mexican art in English and Spanish. Open Monday through Saturday from 9am to 9pm.

Galería Uno. Morelos 561 at Corona. ☎ **322/2-0908.**

One of Vallarta's first galleries, this features an excellent selection of contemporary paintings by Latin American artists, plus a variety of posters and prints. Set in a classic adobe building with open courtyard, it's also a casual, *salón*-styled gathering place for friends of owner Jan Lavender and her partner Martina Goldberg. Open Monday through Saturday from 10am to 8pm.

Arte de las Americas (☎ **322/1-1985**) at the Marina Vallarta (between La Taberna and the Yacht Club) is an arm of Galería Uno; it exhibits some of the same artists. Open Monday through Saturday from 10am to 10pm.

CLOTHING

Vallarta's single true department store is **Lans,** Juárez 867 (☎ **322/3-2899**), offering a wide selection of name-brand clothing, accessories, footwear, cosmetics, and home furnishings. Along with the nationally popular **ACA Joe, Carlos 'n' Charlie's,** and **Bye-Bye** brands, Vallarta offers several distinctive shops featuring original designs.

✪ **Laura López Labra Designs.** Basilio Badillo 324. ☎ **322/2-3099.**

The most comfortable clothing you'll ever enjoy—LLL designs are all white (or natural) in color, and 100% cotton or lace. Laura's fine gauze fabrics float in her designs of seductive skirts, romantic dresses, blouses, beachwear, and baby-dolls. Men's offerings include cotton drawstring pants and lightweight shirts. Personalized wedding dresses are also available. It's open Monday through Saturday from 10am to 2pm and 5 to 9pm. No credit cards.

Nina & June. Hidalgo 227-8, 2nd floor; 3 blocks south of Guadalupe church. ☎ **322/2-3099.**

Featured items here are the unique jewelry designed by award-winning New York artist June Rosen López, and the exclusive line of handwoven clothing designed by her sister, Nina. The shop also carries exquisite accessories and clothing made by others. Open Monday through Saturday from 10am to 8pm, Sundays 11am to 5pm. MasterCard and Visa are accepted.

CRAFTS, DECORATIVE & FOLK ART

Alfarería Tlaquepaque. Av. México 1100. ☎ **322/3-2121.** www.at.com.mx.

Opened in 1953, this is Vallarta's original source for Mexican ceramics and decorative crafts, all at excellent prices. Talavera pottery, blue glassware, bird cages, baskets, and wood furniture are just a few of the many items found in this warehouse-style store. Open Monday through Saturday from 9am to 9pm.

Galería Indígena. Juárez 270, between Guerrero and Zaragoza. ☎/fax **322/2-3007.**

This is a large shop featuring silver, Oaxaca pottery and wood carvings, lacquer chests, dance masks, pre-Hispanic pottery reproductions, and Huichol Indian art.

A second-floor gallery features changing exhibitions of contemporary art. It's open Monday through Saturday from 10am to 3pm and 5 to 9pm.

✪ **La Tienda.** Rodolfo Gómez 122, near Los Muertos beach. ☎ **322/2-1535.**

Fine decorative objects for the home, including unique furniture, antiques, glassware, and pewter. Outstanding selection of rustic candlesticks and beeswax candles, both in a variety of sizes. It's open Monday through Saturday from 10am to 2pm and 4 to 10pm. A second, smaller location is on "restaurant row," Basilio Badillo 276, with the same hours.

✪ **Lucy's CuCu Cabaña and Zoo.** Basilio Badillo 295. No phone.

Owners Lucy and Gil Givens have assembled one of the most entertaining, eclectic, and memorable collections of Mexican folk art—about 70% of which is animal-themed. Each summer they travel and personally select the handmade works, made by over 100 indigenous artists and artisans. Items include metal sculptures, Oaxacan wooden animals, retablos (alters), and fine Talavera ceramics. Five percent of all sales goes to benefit the Puerto Vallarta Animal Protection Association, organized by the Givenses. It's open Monday through Saturday from 10am to 2pm and 6 to 10pm. Closed May 15 to October 15.

Olinala Gallery. Cárdenas 274. ☎ **322/2-4995.**

Two floors of fine indigenous Mexican crafts and folk art, including an impressive collection of museum-quality masks and Huichol beaded art. It's open Monday through Saturday from 10am to 2pm and 5 to 9pm.

Puerco Azul. Marina Vallarta malecón, Marina Las Palmas II. ☎ **322/1-1985.**

A whimsical shop with original folk art with a colorful, contemporary design. Pigs and other animals are a central theme (the name means "Blue Pig"). The collection includes ceramics, dinnerware, furniture, jewelry, and paintings. Open Monday through Saturday from 10am to 10pm, Sunday 10am to 4pm.

✪ **Querubines.** Juárez 501A (corner with Galena, behind Planet Hollywood). ☎ **322/2-2988.**

My personal favorite for the finest-quality artisan works from throughout Mexico. Owner Marcella García Alegre personally travels across the country to hand-select items for this shop, which include exceptional, artistic silver jewelry, embroidered and handwoven clothing, bolts of foot-loomed fabric, glassware, pewter frames and trays, high-quality wool rugs, straw bags, and Panama hats. It's open Monday through Sunday from 10am to 6pm.

HOME FURNISHINGS & GIFTS

Sierra Madre. Paseo Díaz Ordaz 732 (malecón). ☎ **322/3-0661.**

Ecologically themed gifts, clothing, and artwork. Frameable posters by noted photographer Patricio Robles Gil, founder of the Sierra Madre Foundation. A percentage of all sales goes to support regional ecological preservation projects. Open daily from 9am to 10pm.

TEQUILA

La Casa del Tequila. Morelos 589. ☎ **322/2-2000.**

An extensive selection of premium tequilas, plus information and tastings to help guide you to an informed selection. Also, cigars from Cuba and Veracruz, regional bulk coffees, books, tequila glassware, humidors, and other tequila-drinking and cigar-smoking accessories. In the back, there's a garden patio with cafe and bar for enjoying espresso drinks, pastries, sandwiches, and, of course, tequila drinks. Open daily from 8am to 10pm.

WHERE TO STAY

Beyond a varied selection of hotels, Puerto Vallarta has many other types of accommodations. Oceanfront or marina-view condominiums or elegant private villas are also available; both can offer a better value and more ample space for families or small groups. For more information on short-term rentals, contact **Bill Taylor Real Estate,** International Yachting Center, Royal Pacific Yacht Club, Local 1, calle Timóm s/n, Marina Vallarta (☎ **322/1-0923** or 322/1-1085; fax and voice mail 322/1-1564; www.TristarRentals.com), or **Brock Squire y Asociados** (☎**322/3-0055**) for more information and listings of available properties. Prices start at $50 a night for non-beachfront condos and go to $1,000 for penthouse condos or private villas.

The following listings of the hotels are provided in directional order, moving south along Banderas Bay from the airport.

MARINA VALLARTA

Marina Vallarta is the most modern and deluxe area of hotel development in Puerto Vallarta. Located a mile south of the airport, and just north of the Maritime (cruise-ship) Terminal, it's a planned development whose centerpiece is a 450-slip modern marina. The boardwalk surrounding the marina is filled with excellent restaurants, bars, galleries, and shops. A stay here is a world apart from the quaintness of downtown Puerto Vallarta.

The hotels reviewed below are located on the beachfront of the peninsula. The beaches here are much less attractive than beaches in other parts of the bay; the sand is darker and firmly packed, and, during certain times of the year, also quite rocky. The hotels in this zone have more than made up for this shortfall, however—they offer dazzling designs of oversized pool areas with exotic landscaping. Still, if you're longing for a beautiful beach, try one of the southern hotel options. This area is better for families, or for those looking for lots of centralized activity. Marina Vallarta is also home to an 18-hole golf course designed by Joe Finger, and the Vidafel Waterpark, with water slides and tubes, pools, inner-tube canal, and snack-bar facilities. Open to the public daily from 11am to 7pm, it costs $13 for adults, $7 for kids.

Because of traffic, more than distance, a taxi from the Marina to downtown takes 20 to 30 minutes.

✪ **Velas Vallarta Grand Suite Resort.** Paseo de la Marina s/n, Marina Vallarta, 48354 Puerto Vallarta, Jal. ☎ **800/659-8477** in the U.S. and Canada, or 322/1-0091. Fax 322/1-0755. velasv@pvnet.com.mx. 361 units. A/C TV TEL. High season $180–$650 double. Low season $130–$450 double. AE, DC, MC, V. Free indoor parking.

Velas Vallarta is an excellent choice, especially for families, as each suite offers a full-size, fully equipped kitchen, ample living and dining areas, separate bedroom(s), and a large balcony with seating. The apartments are tastefully decorated with light-wood furnishings, cool terrazzo floors, bright fabrics, and marble tub/shower-combination bathrooms. This property is actually part hotel, part full-ownership condominiums, which means each suite is the size of a true residential unit, offering the feeling of a home away from home. The suites all have partial ocean views, as they face onto a central area where three free-form swimming pools, complete with bridges and waterfalls, meander through tropical gardens. A full range of services—including restaurants, minimarket, deli, tennis courts, spa, and boutiques—means you'd never need to leave the place if you didn't want to. The Marina Golf Club is across the street, and special packages are available to Velas guests.

Dining/Diversions: An excellent and elegant Italian restaurant, **Andrea,** offers indoor or terrace dining and has an exhibition kitchen. The beachfront restaurant, **La Ribera,** offers casual, international fare. Both are open for breakfast, lunch, and dinner. There's a nightly happy hour at the **Lobby Bar,** which also features a weekly fashion show. Poolside, there's the Aquabar swim-up bar, which also serves light fare.

Amenities: Beachfront with water-sports rental equipment, fitness center with sauna and massage service, minimarket, deli, boutique, beauty salon, activities program for children and adults, four lighted tennis courts, bicycle rentals, golf privileges at Marina Vallarta Golf Club, laundry, room service, car rental, concierge, travel agency.

✪ **Westin Regina Resort.** Paseo de la Marina Sur 205, Marina Vallarta, 48321 Puerto Vallarta, Jal. ☎ **800/228-3000** in the U.S., or 322/1-110. Fax 322/1-1141. 280 units. A/C MINIBAR TV TEL. High season $125–$195 double; $295–$495 suite. Low season $115–165 double; $245–$415 suite. AE, DC, MC, V. Free parking.

Stunning architecture and vibrant colors are the hallmark of this award-winning property, considered Puerto Vallarta's finest. Though the grounds are large—over 21 acres with 850 feet of beachfront—the warm service and gracious hospitality is more befitting of an intimate resort. The central free-form pool is spectacular, with hundreds of tall palms surrounding it. Hammocks are strung between the palms closest to the beach, where there's also an elaborate wooden playground for kids. Rooms are contemporary in style, brightly colored in textured fabrics with oversized wood furnishings, tile floors, original art, tub/shower-combination bathrooms, and in-room safes. Balconies have panoramic views. Eight junior suites have Jacuzzis, and the five grand suites and presidential suite are two-level, with ample living areas. Two floors of rooms are designated as their Royal Beach Club, with VIP services including private concierge, continental breakfast, newspaper, cocktails, and canapés. The fitness center here is one of the most modern, well-equipped facilities of its kind in Vallarta.

Dining/Diversions: Two restaurants serve all three meals; **Garibaldi** specializes in seafood and nouveau Mexican cuisine, and offers outdoor, beachfront dining, or indoor dining under a giant palapa. **El Palmar** offers international cuisine and an exceptional Sunday brunch buffet. Two poolside bars also offer snacks and sandwiches; and the **La Cascada Lobby Bar,** overlooking the pool and beach, features live music during its nightly happy hour.

Amenities: Ocean-side pool; full-service, state-of-the-art health club with treadmills, Stairmasters, resistance equipment, sauna, steam room, solarium, whirlpool, three grass tennis courts (lighted for night play), massage services, and salon; golf privileges at Marina Vallarta Golf Club; Kid's Club; laundry; 24-hour room service; travel agency; car rental; shopping arcade.

THE HOTEL ZONE TO DOWNTOWN

The main street running between the airport and town is named avenida Francisco Medina Ascencio, but is commonly referred to as avenida de las Palmas, for the stately palm trees that line the dividing strip. The hotels built along this road were the result of the tourism boom that Vallarta enjoyed in the early 1980s, and most have been exceptionally well maintained. All offer excellent, wide beachfronts with generally tranquil waters for swimming. From here it's a quick taxi or bus ride into downtown Vallarta.

Expensive

Fiesta Americana Puerto Vallarta. Bulevar Fco. Medina Ascencio km 2.5, 48300 Puerto Vallarta, Jal. ☎ **800/FIESTA-1** in the U.S., or 322/4-2010. Fax 322/4-2108. 223 units. A/C MINIBAR TV TEL. High season $170–$250 double; $250–$500 suite. Low season $130–$170 double; $220–$400 suite. AE, DC, MC, V. Limited free parking.

The Fiesta Americana's enormous, three-story, thatched palapa lobby is a landmark in the Hotel Zone. With an abundance of plants, splashing fountains, constant breezes, and comfortable sitting areas, the lobby has a casual South Seas feel to it. The nine-story, terra-cotta–colored building embraces a large plaza with a pool facing the beach. Marble-trimmed rooms, in neutral tones with pastel accents, come with attractive carved headboards and comfortable rattan and wicker furniture. All have private balconies with ocean views.

Dining/Diversions: The hotel's three restaurants include two for casual dining and one, **La Hacienda,** for fine dining featuring excellent Mexican cuisine. There's live music nightly in the lobby bar. **Friday López** is a popular karaoke and sports bar, located on the highway at the entrance to this hotel. It's open from 10:30pm to 3am.

Amenities: Large pool with cushioned lounges and towel service, pool activities, and children's activities in high season; laundry, room service, travel agency, boutiques, beauty shop.

Moderate

✪ **Los Cuatro Vientos.** Matamoros 520, 48350 Puerto Vallarta, Jal. ☎ **322/2-0161.** Fax 322/2-2831. 13 units. $55 double. Rates include continental breakfast. Ask about low-season discounts. No credit cards.

This quiet, secluded inn is set on a hillside overlooking Banderas Bay and features rooms built around a small central patio and pool. A flight of stairs takes you to the second-floor patio, pool, flowering trees, and the cozy Chez Elena restaurant, open in the evenings. The cheerful, spotless, and differently colored rooms have fans, small tiled bathrooms, brick ceilings, red-tile floors, and glass-louvered windows. Each is decorated with simple Mexican furnishings, folk art, and antiques. The whole rooftop, with a panoramic view of the city, is great for sunning, and it's the best place in the city for drinks at sunset. Continental breakfast is served on the terrace for guests only from 8 to 10:30am.

The hotel offers a weeklong "Women's Getaway" package offered several times a year. The program includes cultural discussions, exercise classes, hikes, some meals, and optional massages, facials, manicures, and pedicures. From the central plaza, the hotel is 2 blocks east on Iturbide; then 3 blocks north on Matamoros; but it's a steep walk with lots of stairs.

DOWNTOWN: SOUTH OF THE RÍO CUALE TO LOS MUERTOS BEACH

This part of town has recently undergone a renaissance, and economically priced hotels offering excellent values are the rule here. Several blocks off the beach you can find numerous budget hotels and inns offering clean, simply furnished rooms at true bargain prices; most will discount long-term stays. The neighborhood is older, but very friendly and generally safe. Most of Vallarta's nightlife activity is now centered in this area.

Hotel Molino de Agua. Vallarta 130 (Apdo. Postal 54), 48380 Puerto Vallarta, Jal. ☎ **322/2-1957.** Fax 322/2-6056. E-mail: aramal@tag.acnet.net. 53 units, including apts., bungalows, and suites. A/C. High season: apts $111; bungalows $93; suites $150. Low season: Rms $83; bungalows $68; suites $111 (All double). AE, V, MC. Free secured parking.

This complex beside the river and ocean has a mix of stone and stucco-walled bungalows and small beachfront buildings, which are spread among winding walkways and lush tropical gardens with fruit trees. It's adjacent to the Río Cuale to your right, just over the southbound bridge. Although the hotel is centrally located on a main street, its big trees and open spaces lend it tranquillity. The individual bungalows, with private patios, are located in the gardens, between the entrance and the ocean. They are simply furnished with a bed, wooden desk and chair, Mexican tile floors, beamed ceilings, and beautiful tile bathrooms. Rooms and suites in the two small two- and three-story buildings on the beach have double beds and private terraces.

Facilities include the casual **Aquarena** restaurant, and the poolside garden restaurant/bar, **The Lion's Court.** There's a whirlpool beside the beachside pool and another pool beside the Lion's Court restaurant.

✪ **Hotel Playa Los Arcos.** Olas Altas 380, 48380 Puerto Vallarta, Jal. ☎ **800/ 221-6509** in the U.S., or 322/2-1583. Fax 322/2-2418. 185 units. A/C TEL TV. High season $69–$82 double; $105 suite. Low season $48–$60 double; $76 suite. AE, MC, V.

With a stellar location in the heart of Los Muertos beach, in the midst of the Olas Altas sidewalk-cafe action, and close to downtown, this is one of Vallarta's perennially popular hotels, and a personal favorite of mine. The four-story structure is in a U shape, facing the ocean, with a swimming pool in the courtyard. Rooms with private balconies overlook the pool, while the 10 suites have ocean views and kitchenettes. The standard rooms are small but pleasantly decorated and immaculate, with carved wooden furniture painted pale pink. On the premises are a palapa beachside bar with occasional live entertainment, a coffee shop, and the popular Maximilian's gourmet restaurant. It's 7 blocks south of the river.

SOUTH TO MISMALOYA

✪ **Camino Real.** Carreterra Barra de Navidad, km 3.5, Playa Las Estacas, Puerto Vallarta Jal. C.P. 48300. ☎ **800/722-6466** or 322/1-5000. Fax 322/1-6000. 348 units. A/C MINIBAR TV TEL. High season $170–$250 double; $480–$1050 suite. Low season $130–$199 double; $400–$950 suite. AE, DC, MC, V.

The original luxury hotel in Puerto Vallarta, the Camino Real has retained its place as a premier property here despite newer arrivals. Scores of loyal guests think only of staying here, and its free monthly classical concerts (held the 1st Thurs of each month) have earned an integrated place in the local community. It unquestionably has the nicest beach of any Vallarta hotel, with soft white sand in a private cove. Set apart from other properties, with a lush mountain backdrop, it retains the exclusivity that made it popular from the beginning—yet it's only a 5- to 10-minute ride to town. The hotel consists of two buildings: the 250-room main hotel, which curves gently with the shape of the Playa Las Estacas, and a newer 11-story Camino Real Club tower, also facing the beach and ocean. An ample pool fronts the main building. Standard rooms in the main building are large, some with sliding doors opening onto the beach and others with balconies. The 2-story Presidential suite in the main building has a large private pool. Royal Beach Club rooms from the sixth floor up feature balconies with whirlpool tubs. The top floor is divided among six two-bedroom Fiesta Suites, each with a private swimming pool. All rooms are accented with the vibrant colors of Mexico and come with in-room safe-deposit boxes.

Dining/Diversions: There are three restaurants: **La Noria** serves a casual, international menu and buffet for all three meals. Open for dinner only are **La Finestra,** offering Italian cuisine and seafood, and the elegant, award-winning **La Perla,** a classic gourmet favorite. Royal Beach Club guests enjoy a complimentary full buffet breakfast on a beautiful open-air patio beside the ocean. Live bands frequently entertain in the lobby bar in the evening, with dancing on weekends. Adjacent is a specialty cantina serving a broad selection of premium tequilas.

Amenities: Two swimming pools; beach palapas with chair, towel, and dining service; two lighted grass tennis courts; health club with weights; boutiques and convenience store. Royal Beach Club guests enjoy separate check-in and concierge, daily complimentary breakfast, and evening cocktails and hors d'oeuvres. Laundry; 24-hour room service; travel agency; car rental; children's program December, July, and August.

✪ **Quinta María Cortez.** Sagitario 132, Playa Conchas Chinas, Puerto Vallarta, C.P. 48300. ☎ **888/640-8100** in the U.S., or phone/fax 322/1-53-17. 6 units. MINIBAR TEL. High season $120–$160 double. Low season $75–$135 double. Rates include breakfast. Discounts for long-term stays. AE, MC, V.

An eclectic, sophisticated, and imaginative B&B on the beach, this is Puerto Vallarta's most original place to stay—and one of Mexico's most unique inns. Six large suites, uniquely decorated in antiques, whimsical curios, and original art, all feature private bathroom, and most include kitchenette and balcony. Sunny terraces, a small pool, and a central gathering area with fireplace and palapa-topped dining area (where breakfast is served) occupy different levels of this seven-story house. Located on a beautiful cove on Conchas Chinas beach, the rocks just offshore form tranquil tide pools, perfect for wading and snuggling. A terrace fronting the beach supports Roman columns draped in ivy and accommodates chairs for taking in the sunset.

For years, this intimate inn was owned and run by a legendary Vallarta resident and Texan named Silver, who welcomed celebrity guests and allowed the house to be used as a location for fashion shoots and several films, including *Revenge,* starring Kevin Costner. The new owners have lovingly maintained its singular sense of style while significantly upgrading amenities and remodeling common areas in 1997. The Quinta María wins my highest recommendation (in fact, I enjoyed living here for a few years, when it accepted long-term stays) and the raves of the editor of this book, but admittedly it's not for everyone. There's no air-conditioning, and all the rooms are very open—part of the expansive penthouse suite is completely open to the view of sun and stars above. Breakfast is served under the midlevel thatched-roof area, overlooking the pool and ocean below. Those who love it return year after year, charmed by this remarkable place. Not appropriate for children.

Presidente Inter-Continental. Carr. Barra de Navidad, km 8.5, Puerto Vallarta C.P. 48300. ☎ **800/327-0200** or 322/8-0508. Fax 322/8-0146. www.interconti.com. 139 units. A/C TV TEL. High season $330–$360 double; $420–$650 suite. Low season $250–$300 double; $320–$550 suite. Rates are all-inclusive. AE, DC, MC, V. Limited free parking.

With its over-the-top concept of all-inclusive (meals, drinks, everything), it'll be hard to find a reason to leave this exquisite hotel, located 20 minutes south of downtown Puerto Vallarta. Backed by a jungle mountain landscape and fronted by a beautiful white-sand beach, the 11-story building is draped in flowering bougainvillea. Deluxe rooms all have large furnished balconies with ocean views, tile floors, white wood furnishings, and muted colored textiles. Marble tub/shower-combination bathrooms are extra large with separate vanity area. The 19 suites have in-room Jacuzzis; the three Master suites have two separate bedrooms and Jacuzzis; the Presidential suite has its own swimming pool. A large mosaic pool with swim-up bar is on a terrace overlooking the beach, adjacent to the two grass tennis courts and health club. Guests aren't limited to buffet dining, but can order à la carte from a selection of two restaurants, plus enjoy premium drinks at their choice of bars. It's a top choice for honeymooners looking for romantic seclusion.

Dining/Diversions: El Coral restaurant serves à la carte, international gourmet cuisine; the more casual, terrace restaurant **El Caribeño** offers three meals daily with choice of menu or buffet dining. A poolside restaurant/bar offers light fare and drinks.

The lobby Sunset Bar has a terrific ocean view with live music in the evenings. There are also two theme nights every week; one, a Mexican Fiesta, the second, a poolside barbecue, both with live music.

Amenities: Beachfront pool with water-sports equipment for rent; lighted tennis courts; fitness room with sauna and steam; full adults' activities program; year-round Kid's Club; game room; laundry and valet; travel agency; tobacco shop; car rental.

WHERE TO DINE

Puerto Vallarta boasts a notable dining scene, with over 200 restaurants serving cuisines from around the world, in addition to fresh seafood and regional dishes. Chefs from France, Switzerland, Germany, Italy, and Argentina have come for visits and then stayed on to open restaurants of their own. In celebration of the diversity of dining experiences available, Vallarta's culinary community hosts a 2-week-long Gourmet Dining Festival as part of its annual SeaFest each November.

Nonetheless, dining is not limited to high-end options—there are plenty of small, family-owned restaurants, local Mexican kitchens, and vegetarian cafes. Vallarta also has its branches of the imported world food-and-fun chains: Hard Rock Cafe, Planet Hollywood, and even Hooters. I won't bother to review these restaurants, as the consistency and decor are so familiar. Of the cheap, local spots, one of the long-standing favorites for inexpensive light meals and fresh fruit drinks is **Tutifruti,** Morelos 552 (☎ 322/2-1068). It's open Monday through Saturday from 8am to 10pm. No credit cards. The new favorite for cheap eats is **Archi's,** serving only (great) char-grilled burgers and homemade fries in a surfer-inspired atmosphere. It's located at Morelos 199 at Pípila, behind Carlos O'Brian's (☎ 322/2-43-83).

MARINA VALLARTA

Porto Bello. Marina Sol, Local no. 7 (Marina Vallarta malecón). ☎ **322/1-0003.** Reservations recommended. Main courses $6–$21. AE, MC, V. Daily noon–11pm. ITALIAN.

One of the first restaurants in the marina, this remains a favorite here, as Canadian owners Mario Nuñes and Maurizio Pellegrini prepare consistently flavorful Italian dishes based on old family recipes. Their signature dish is fusilli Porto Bello, prepared with olive oil, artichokes, black olives, basil, and a generous helping of Parmesan cheese. Another favorite is veal scaloppini in a white-wine cream sauce, with mushrooms and shrimp. Ample seating on the ivy-covered terrace, situated alongside the marina, provides diners with views of the elegant yachts. Indoor dining is air-conditioned.

HOTEL ZONE TO DOWNTOWN
Expensive
✪ **Café des Artistes.** Guadalupe Sánchez 740. ☎ **322/2-3228** or 322/2-3229. Reservations recommended. Main courses $12–$25. AE, MC, V. Daily 6–11:30pm. FRENCH/NOUVELLE MEXICAN.

This restaurant is both a culinary and visual delight. Chef Theirry Blouet is a master at making his plates look as stunning as they taste. He uses his French culinary training to use local herbs and spices to delicately draw out the flavor of regional seafood, fine cuts of beef, and poultry. Signature dishes include his creamy pumpkin-and-prawn soup, and roasted duck in a honey-and-soy sauce. The menu changes every 6 months to take advantage of seasonal items. Save room for dessert—Chef Theirry began his career as a pastry chef. Each corner of each of the creatively decorated rooms serves up stunning works of art, painted murals, and elegant bowls of fresh flowers. An outdoor terraced garden—decked in candles—is the most romantic place to dine, and live flute and piano music plays in the background from 8 to 11:30pm. Both chef and restaurant have been the recipients of numerous culinary awards and competitions—an evening at Café des Artistes is considered Vallarta's top gourmet-dining experience.

✪ **Chef Roger.** A. Rodríguez 267. ☎ **322/2-5900.** Reservations recommended. Main courses $10–$15. AE, MC, V. Mon–Sat 6:30–11pm. INTERNATIONAL/SWISS.

This sophisticated little dinner-only restaurant has developed a strong following since it opened in 1989, due to Swiss-born chef and owner Roger Dreir. A European-trained chef, he's combined elements of the cuisines of Europe and Mexico to create a highly personal style of cooking. Guests enjoy their meals on the patio or in one of the adjoining dining rooms. There are five or six daily specials using market-fresh ingredients; these might include such interesting combinations as crepes huitlacoche, red snapper fillet with bananas and almonds, or breaded crepes stuffed with spinach and goat cheese in a red-pepper sauce. His freshly made pâtés and terrines are especially notable. The restaurant is catercorner from the municipal market between Matamoros and Hidalgo.

Moderate

✪ **La Dolce Vita.** Paseo Díaz Ordaz no. 674, Centro. ☎ **322/2-3852.** Main courses $4–$10; wine and mixed drinks $2–$5. AE, MC, V. Daily noon–2am. ITALIAN.

This locally popular eatery eminently combines good food, a casually upbeat atmosphere, attentive service, and great entertainment. Overlooking the malecón, La Dolce Vita offers excellent views and prime people-watching through its oversized windows and second-floor balcony. Despite its prime location and superb food, its prices remain more than reasonable. Owned by an engaging group of Italian friends, the food is authentic in preparation and flavor, from the thin crust, brick-oven pizzas to savory homemade pastas—my favorite is the Braccio de Fiero, topped with spinach, black olives, and fresh tomatoes. Sultry jazz by "The Sweet Life" (the house band) plays Thursday through Sunday evenings.

Las Palomas. Paseo Díaz Ordaz 594. ☎ **322/2-3675.** Breakfast $1.50–$4.50; lunch $3–$12; main courses $6–$20. AE, MC, V. Daily 7am–11pm. MEXICAN.

One of Puerto Vallarta's first restaurants, this is the power-breakfast place of choice for local movers and shakers—and a generally popular hangout for everyone else throughout the day. Authentic in atmosphere and menu, it's one of Puerto Vallarta's few genuine Mexican restaurants, with the atmosphere of a gracious home. Breakfast is the best value here, with mugs of steaming coffee spiced with cinnamon poured as soon as you're seated. Try the classic huevos rancheros or *chilaquiles* (tortilla strips, fried and topped with a red or green spicy sauce, cream, cheese, and fried eggs). Lunch and dinner offer other traditional Mexican specialties, plus a selection of stuffed crepes. The best place for checking out the malecón and watching the sun set while sipping an icy margarita is in the spacious bar or new, upstairs terrace.

✪ **Rito's Baci.** Domínguez 181. ☎ **322/2-6448.** Pasta $4.50–$7.50; salads and sandwiches $3–$6.50; pizza $10–$13.50. MC, V. Daily 1–11:30pm. ITALIAN.

If the food weren't reason enough to come here (and it definitely is!) then Rito himself would be, with his gentle, devoted way of caring for every detail of this cozy *tratorria*. His grandfather emigrated from Italy, so the recipes and tradition of Italian food come naturally to him. So does his passion for food—obvious as he describes the specialties, which include lasagna (vegetarian, *verde*, or meat-filled), ravioli stuffed with spinach and ricotta cheese, spaghetti with garlic, anchovy and lemon zest, or a side of homemade Italian sausage. Everything, in fact, is made by hand from fresh ingredients. Pizza-lovers favor the Piedmonte, with that famous sausage and mushrooms, and the Horacio, a cheeseless pizza with tomatoes, oregano, and basil. Sandwiches come hot or cold; but arrive hungry, as they're a two-handed operation. Because Rito offers home and hotel delivery, I enjoy his food more than any other restaurant in town! It's 1½ blocks off the malecón, on Josefa de Domínguez between Morelos and Juárez.

SOUTH OF THE RÍO CUALE TO OLAS ALTAS

South of the river is the most condensed restaurant area, with the street Basilio Badillo nicknamed "Restaurant Row." A second main dining drag has emerged along calle Olas Altas, where you can find all variety of food types and price categories. Its wide sidewalks lined with cafes are concentrated with espresso bars, generally open from 7am to midnight.

Moderate

✪ **Adobe Café.** Badillo 252. ☎ **322/2-6720** or 322/3-1925. Main courses $9–$15. AE, MC, V. Wed–Mon 6–11pm. Closed Aug–Sept. INTERNATIONAL.

Adobe Café offers a classically chic atmosphere in which to enjoy innovative cuisine based on traditional Mexican specialties. The Santa Fe–style decor with rustic wood accents provides a serene backdrop, and tables are comfortably large for enjoying a leisurely meal. Waiters possess that ideal skill of being attentive without being intrusive. The menu features imaginative dishes, including grilled jumbo shrimp battered in coconut and served with homemade apple sauce, penne pasta with Italian sausage in a creamy tequila sauce, and tenderloin of beef stuffed with huitlacoche (Mexican truffles) in a cheese sauce—to name just a few specialties. Owner Rodolfo Choperena is almost always on hand, which accounts for the consistently fine food and service. Adobe Café is located at the corner of Calles Basilio Badillo and Ignacio Vallarta, opposite Los Pibes restaurant, on the "Calles de los Cafés," or Restaurant Row.

Archie's Wok. Francisco Rodríguez 130, ½ block from the Los Muertos pier. ☎ **322/2-0411.** Main courses $6–$12. AE, MC, V. Mon–Sat 2–11pm. ASIAN/SEAFOOD.

Since 1986, Archie's has been legendary in Puerto Vallarta for serving original cuisine influenced by the intriguing flavors of Thailand, China, and the Philippines. "Archie" was Hollywood director John Huston's private chef during the years he spent in the area. Today his wife Cindy continues his legacy as she welcomes guests to this tranquil retreat. Their Thai Mai Tai and other tropical drinks are made from only fresh fruit and juices, and they are a good way to kick off a meal here, as are the Filipino spring rolls, consistently crispy and delicious. The popular Singapore Fish Fillet features lightly battered fillet strips in a sweet-and-sour sauce, while the Thai Garlic Shrimp are prepared with fresh garlic, ginger, cilantro, and black pepper. Vegetarians have plenty of options, including the Broccoli, Tofu & Cashew Stir-Fry in a black-bean–and-sherry sauce. Finish things off with the signature Spice Islands coffee or a slice of lime cheese pie. Thursday through Saturday from 8 to 11pm, live classical guitar and flute set the atmosphere in Archie's Oriental garden.

El Palomar de los González. Aguacate 425. ☎ **322/2-0795** or 322/2-2795. Main courses $8–$16. MC, V. Daily 6–11pm. INTERNATIONAL/SEAFOOD.

The atmosphere and view are the principal attractions, one of the most romantic restaurants in town. This popular restaurant is located in a hillside villa, with sweeping views of the town and bay. The former González family home has remained much as it was when they lived here; only now, tables deck the balconies and border the pool for guests to enjoy dining under the stars. The menu offers traditional international fare, including fish, steaks, and jumbo shrimp, prepared grilled, with several choices of sauces. Specialty coffees, served flaming at your table, or their excellent bananas flambé, make for a delightful end to the meal. Generally, there's a trio on the premises serenading couples.

La Palapa. Pulpito 103. ☎ **322/2-5225.** Breakfast $1.50–$3; main courses $4–$20; salad or sandwiches $3–$8. AE, V, MC. Daily 8am–11pm. SEAFOOD/MEXICAN.

This colorfully decorated, open-air and palapa-roofed restaurant on the beach is a decades-old local favorite. Enjoy a tropical breakfast by the sea, lunch on the beach, cocktails at sunset, or a romantic dinner—at night they set cloth-covered tables in the sand. Once a rather rustic restaurant with mediocre food, owner Alberto Pérez has done an outstanding job of re-creating the menu, upgrading the atmosphere, and generally turning his family's restaurant into one of the true dining gems of Vallarta. Seafood is the specialty, with featured dishes including grilled shrimp in a *guajillo* (chile)–and-mango sauce, poached red snapper with fresh cilantro sauce, and a sublime crab soup served in a coconut shell. There's acoustic guitar and vocals nightly from 8 to 11pm, generally performed by Alberto himself—his talent as a musician equals that as a restaurateur.

Inexpensive

Café de Olla. Basilio Badillo 168. ☎ **322/3-1626.** Main courses $2.50–$6.50. No credit cards. High season Tues–Sun 10am–11pm. Low season Tues–Sun noon–11pm. Closed Sept 15–Oct 15. MEXICAN/STEAKS.

This small, inviting place gets high marks from both locals and tourists for its homestyle Mexican food. You'll find large portions of *carne asada* (grilled flank steak), plus sopes, Oaxaca-style tamales, and a great *plato mexicano*. Breakfasts are also a traditional treat, with ample portions. It's 6 blocks south of the Vallarta bridge near the corner of Olas Altas.

✪ **Fajita Republic.** Piño Suárez 321. ☎ **322/2-3131.** Main courses $3.75–$12. No credit cards. Daily 1–11pm. MEXICAN/STEAKS.

Lines for a table are already common at this great new addition to Vallarta dining. Fajita Republic has hit on a winning recipe: delicious food, ample portions, welcoming atmosphere, and low prices. The specialty is, of course, fajitas, grilled to perfection in every variety: steak, chicken, shrimp, combo, and vegetarian. All come with a generous tray of salsas and toppings. This "tropical grill" also serves sumptuous BBQ ribs, Mexican *molcajetes* with incredibly tender strips of marinated beef fillet, and grilled shrimp. Starters include fresh guacamole served in a giant spoon. Try a Fajita Rita Mango Margarita—or one of their other spirited temptations—served in oversized mugs or by the pitcher. Partners Fernando and Carlos have created a casual, fun, and festive atmosphere in a garden of mango and palm trees. Located between V. Carranza and Basilio Badillo, 1 block north of Olas Altas.

JUNGLE RESTAURANTS

One of the unique attractions of Puerto Vallarta is its "jungle restaurants," located to the south of town, toward Mismaloya. Each offers open-air dining in a magnificent tropical setting by the sea or beside a mountain river. A stop for swimming and lunch is included in the many varieties of "Jungle" or "Tropical" tours (see "Organized Tours," above). If you travel on your own, a taxi is the best transportation, as they are all located quite a distance from the main highway. Taxis are usually waiting for return patrons. The restaurants up the hill from the entrance to Mismaloya are **Chino's Paraíso** (☎ **322/3-0102;** open daily noon to 5pm) and **El Edén** (no phone; open daily 11am to 6pm). Both are located up the mountain road at km 6.5 Highway 200, and feature mediocre restaurants in beautiful natural settings of clear streams and tropical jungle. El Edén, further up the road from Chino's, was the site of several key scenes in *The Predator,* starring Arnold Schwarzenegger. Both are somewhat unkempt, and during summer months, swimming in the river here can be dangerous—flash floods come without warning and take several lives each year.

Just past Boca de Tomatlán, at km 20 Highway 200, is **Chico's Paradise** (☎ 322/2-0747 or 322/3-0413) which offers spectacular views of massive rocks—some marked with petroglyphs—and the surrounding jungle and mountains. There are natural pools and waterfalls for swimming, plus a small mercado selling pricey, touristy trinkets. The menu features excellent seafood (the seafood platter for two is excellent, with lobster, clams, giant shrimp, crab, and fish fillet) as well as Mexican dishes. The quality is quite good, and the portions are generous, although prices are higher than in town—remember, you're paying for the setting.

The newest and most recommendable of the jungle restaurants is ✪ **El Nogalito** (☎ 322/1-5225; open daily noon to 5:30pm). Located beside a clear jungle stream, this exceptionally clean, beautifully landscaped ranch serves lunch, beverages, and snacks on a shady terrace in a very relaxing atmosphere. There are also several hiking routes that depart from the grounds. If you're accompanied by one of El Nogalito's guides, they'll point out the native plants, birds, and wildlife of the area. To find it, a taxi can easily take you, or, travel to Punta Negra, just about 5 miles south of downtown Puerto Vallarta. There's a well-marked sign that leads up Calzada del Cedro, a dirt road, to the ranch. **Tukari Tours** (☎ 322/4-7177; see "Organized Tours," above) also takes groups there regularly. It's much closer to town than the other jungle restaurants mentioned above.

PUERTO VALLARTA AFTER DARK

Puerto Vallarta's spirited nightlife reflects the town's dual nature: part resort, part colonial Mexican town. The emphasis is on live music. The malecón, which used to be lined with restaurants, is now known more for its selection of hip dance clubs and a few more relaxed options, all of which look out over the ocean. You can first walk along the broad walkway by the water's edge and check out the action at the various clubs, which extend from Carlos O'Brian's on the north end to Star's and Hooters just off the central plaza.

Marina Vallarta has its own array of clubs, with a more upscale, indoor, air-conditioned atmosphere. South of the Cuale River, the Olas Altas zone literally buzzes with action pouring out of its wide selection of small cafes and clubs with every type of live music and entertainment imaginable. In this zone, there's also an active gay and lesbian club scene.

PERFORMING ARTS

Truth be told, there's a limited selection of cultural nightlife beyond the **Mexican Fiesta;** however, the 1998 winter season saw several theater productions meet with both critical and commercial success. Check listings in the daily English-language newspaper, *Vallarta Today,* upon arrival, to see what may be on the schedule during your stay.

Also, the first Thursday of every month, the Camino Real hosts a **free cultural concert,** which is open to the public. Concert pianists, nationally renowned bolero singers, and flamenco guitarists have been a few of the well-received performances. Following the concert, which begins promptly at 9pm, a complimentary cocktail reception is held. Call the Camino Real at ☎ 322/1-5000 for upcoming events.

FIESTA NIGHTS

Major hotels in Puerto Vallarta feature frequent fiestas for tourists—open-bar, Mexican buffet dinner, and live-entertainment extravaganzas. Some are fairly authentic and good introductions for first-time travelers to Mexico; others can be a bit cheesy. Shows are usually held outdoors but move indoors when necessary.

Krystal Vallarta Hotel. Av. de las Palmas, north of downtown off the airport road. ☎ **322/ 2-1459.** Cover $35.

One of the best Fiesta Nights is hosted by the Krystal Vallarta on Tuesday and Saturday at 7pm. These things are difficult to quantify, but Krystal's program is probably less tacky than most of its hotel counterparts.

Rhythms of the Night (Cruise to Caletas). Departs from Terminal Marítima. ☎ **322/ 1-0657** or 322/1-0658. www.vallarta-adventures.com. $50, includes boat cruise, dinner, open bar, and entertainment.

An unforgettable evening under the stars at John Huston's former home at the pristine cove called Las Caletas. The smooth, fast Vallarta Adventure catamaran travels here, entertaining guests along the way, until you're greeted at the dock by tiki torches and native drummers. There's no electricity here—you'll dine by the light of the multitude of candles, the stars, and the moon. The buffet dinner is delicious—steak, seafood, and generous vegetarian options. Everything is first class. The show, set to the music of native bamboo flutes and guitars, showcases the indigenous dances of the region. Departs at 6pm, returns by 11pm.

THE CLUB & MUSIC SCENE
Restaurant/Bars
✪ **Carlos O'Brian's.** Paseo Díaz Ordaz 786 (the malecón), at Pípila. ☎ **322/2-1444** or 322/2-4065. AE, DISC, MC, V. No cover.

Vallarta's most famed nightspot, it was once the only place you'd think of going for an evening of revelry. Although the competition is stiffer, COB's still packs them in—especially the 20-something set. Late at night, the scene resembles a college party. Although it would be easy to dismiss the food served in a place with such a rowdy reputation, I swear, it's very good—they're famous for their ribs. It's open daily from 11am to 2am. Happy hour is from 6 to 8pm.

Hard Rock Cafe. Díaz Ordaz at Abasolo. ☎ **322/2-5532.** No cover. AE, MC, V.

The Hard Rock Cafe offers up good food from 11am to midnight. Thursday through Tuesday nights, live music to dance to (usually rock 'n' roll) begins at 10:30pm and continues until the crowd leaves.

Rock, Jazz, & Blues
✪ **Club Roxy.** Ignacio Vallarta 217. ☎ **322/3-2404.** No cover. AE, MC, V.

Currently the most popular live-music club in Vallarta, Club Roxy features a hot house band led by club owner Pico, playing a mix of reggae, blues, rock, and anything by Santana. Live music jams between 10pm and 2am Monday through Saturday nights. It's south of the river between Madero and Cárdenas. Hours are nightly from 6pm to 2am.

Cuiza. Isla Río Cuale no. 3, below the southbound bridge. ☎ **322/2-5646.** No cover. AE, MC, V.

Although a notable restaurant in its own right, Cuiza has gathered a following for its nightly live jazz, performed by locally popular Beverly and Willow from 9pm to 1am. The large bar serves infused vodkas and other innovative cocktails.

✪ **El Faro Lighthouse Bar.** Royal Pacific Yacht Club, Marina Vallarta. ☎ **322/1-0541** or 322/1-0542. No cover. AE, MC, V.

El Faro is a circular cocktail lounge at the top of the Marina lighthouse and one of Vallarta's only romantic nightspots. Live or recorded jazz plays, and conversation is manageable. Drop by at twilight for the magnificent panoramic views. Open every evening from 4pm to midnight.

Mariachi Loco. Lázaro Cárdenas 254, at Ignacio Vallarta. ☎ **322/3-2205.** No cover. AE, DC, MC, V.

OK, so it's not rock, jazz, or blues, but this live and lively mariachi club also features singers belting out boleros and ranchero classics. By 10pm it gets going, with the mariachi show beginning at 11pm—the mariachis stroll and play as guests join in impromptu singing. After midnight the mariachis play for pay, which is around $3.50 for each song. It's open daily from 11am to 2am.

DANCE CLUBS & DISCOS

A few of Vallarta's clubs or discos charge admission, but generally you'll just pay for drinks—$3 for a margarita, $2 for a beer, more for a whiskey and mixed drinks. Keep an eye out for the discount passes that are frequently available in hotels, restaurants, and other tourist spots. Most clubs are open from 10pm to 4am.

Christine. In the Krystal Vallarta Hotel, north of downtown off Av. Fco. Medina Ascencio. ☎ **322/4-0202.** Cover $10. AE, DC, MC, V.

Proving that "disco lives," this dazzling club still packs a crowd with an opening laser-light show, pumped-in dry ice and oxygen, flashing lights, and a dozen large-screen video panels. The sound system is truly amazing, and the mix of music can get anyone dancing. Open nightly from 10pm to 4am; the light show begins at 11pm. *Note:* No shorts (for men, of course), tennis shoes, or thongs.

Collage. Calle Proa s/n, Marina Vallarta. ☎ **322/1-0505** or 322/1-0861. Cover varies with entertainment. AE, MC, V.

A multilevel monster of nighttime entertainment, including Champs pool salon, Captain America's video arcade, Bowl Vallarta, and the always-packed Crazy Worm Disco Bar, with frequent live entertainment. Open 10am to 6am, it's easily visible from the main highway, just past the entrance to Marina Vallarta.

J & B Salsa Club. Av. Fco. Medina Ascencio. Km 2.5 (Hotel Zone). ☎ **322/4-4616.** Cover $5. MC, V.

This is the locally popular place to go for dancing to Latin music—the dancing here is hot! Fridays, Saturdays and holidays they feature live bands. Open from 9pm to 6am.

Zoo. Paseo Díaz Ordaz 630 (the malecón). ☎ **322/2-49-45.** No cover (except peak weeks), AE, MC, V.

Your chance to be an animal and get wild at night. The Zoo even has cages to dance in if you're feeling unleashed. This popular club has a terrific sound system, and a great variety of dance music, including techno, reggae, and rap. Every hour's a happy hour here with two-for-one drinks. Open 10am until the wee hours.

A SPORTS BAR & A STRIP JOINT

Micky's No Name Cafe & Comedy Club. Morelos 460 (malecón) at Mina. ☎ **322/ 3-2508.** Cover for Comedy Club performances only; varies according to performer. MC, V.

With a multitude of TVs and enough sports memorabilia to start a minimuseum, Micky offers a great venue for catching your favorite game, with all NBA, NHL, NFL, MLB, and PPV sporting events broadcast. (He also serves great BBQ ribs and USDA imported steaks). New in 1998, the Jokes R Us Comedy Club opened in the upstairs level, featuring top comedians from "The Tonight Show," "Saturday Night Live," HBO, and Las Vegas. Comedy shows begin at 9pm nightly. The bar opens at 11am and closes at midnight.

Q'eros. Bulevar Fco. Medina Ascencio, in front of Plaza Genovesa. ☎ **322/2-4367.** $5 cover. MC, V.

Adult nightclub featuring exotic dancers, private shows, striptease. Open nightly 9pm to 6am.

GAY & LESBIAN CLUBS

Vallarta has a vibrant gay community with a wide variety of clubs and nightlife options, including special bay cruises and evening excursions to nearby ranches. The free **Southside PV Guide,** Piño Suárez 583 (☎ **322/3-0277**), specializes in gay-friendly listings. The two top clubs are:

Club Paco Paco. Ignacio L. Vallarta 278. ☎ **322/2-1899.** www.pacopaco.com. Cover $3.50, which includes a drink. (Cover applies at 10pm or before the first show, whichever is first.)

This combination disco, cantina, and rooftop bar also hosts a spectacular "Trasvesty" show every Friday, Saturday, and Sunday night at 1:30am. The club is open from noon to 6am daily and is air-conditioned. **Paco's Ranch,** located around the corner at V. Carranza 239, has nightly specials including Western night on Tuesdays and Leather night on Thursdays. A nightly "Ranch Hand's Show" performs at 8:30pm and 12:30 and 3am. This club, which can be accessed from Club Paco Paco, is open from 8pm to 6am. Cover is the same at both clubs.

Los Balcones. Juárez 182. ☎ **322/2-4671.** No cover. MC, V.

One of the original gay clubs in town, this bilevel club with several dance floors and an excellent sound system earned a few chuckles when it was listed as one of the most romantic spots in Vallarta by *Brides* magazine. Air-conditioned, it's open from 9pm to 4am and posts nightly specials.

SIDE TRIPS FROM PUERTO VALLARTA

YELAPA: A PICTURESQUE SANDY COVE   To visit a cove straight from a tropical fantasy, you need only take a 45-minute trip by boat across the bay. Yelapa has no electricity, no cars, not even any roads—it's accessible only by boat. Its tranquillity, natural beauty, and seclusion have made it a popular home for numerous artists and writers (looking for inspiration) and a few ex-pats (looking to escape the stress of the rest of the world). To get there, travel either by excursion boat or inexpensive water taxi (see "Getting Around Puerto Vallarta," above). You can spend an enjoyable day, but a longer stay is definitely recommended—and provides a completely different perspective of the place.

Once you're in Yelapa, you can lie in the sun, swim, snorkel, and eat fresh grilled crayfish or seafood at a restaurant right on the beach. You can also have your picture taken with an iguana (for $1 a shot), tour this tiny town, or hike up a river to see one of two waterfalls. The closest to town is about a 30-minute walk from the beach. *Note:* If you use a local guide, agree on a price before you start out. There's also horseback riding, sailing, guided bird-watching, and fishing trips available.

For overnight accommodations, local residents frequently rent rooms, and there's also the very clean, rustic **Hotel Lagunita** (☎ **329/8-0554;** E-mail: lagunita@pnet. puerto.net.mx.). With 27 individual bungalows and cottages (all with private bathroom, and a few hours of power daily), plus a freshwater pool and an amicable restaurant/bar, this is the most accommodating place for most visitors. Rates run $30 to $50 per night, depending on the cabaña and the time of year.

BUCERÍAS: AN UP AND COMING COASTAL VILLAGE Only 11 miles north of the Puerto Vallarta airport, Bucerías (boo-sayr-*ee*-ahs, meaning "place of the divers") is a small coastal fishing village of 10,000 people in Nayarit State on Banderas Bay. It's caught on as an alternative to Puerto Vallarta for those who find the pace of life there too invasive. Bucerías offers a seemingly contradictory mix of accommodations—trailer-park spaces and exclusive villa rentals tend to dominate, although there is also a small selection of hotels.

To reach the town center by car, turn left when you see all the roadside oyster stands and go straight ahead 1 block to the main plaza. The beach, with a lineup of restaurants, is half a block farther. You'll see cobblestone streets leading from the highway to the beach and hints of the villas and town homes behind high walls. Bucerías has already been discovered by second-home owners and by about 1,500 transplanted Americans as a peaceful getaway; tourists have discovered its relaxed pace as well.

If you are taking the bus to Bucerías, get off the bus when you see the roadside oyster stands; immediately beyond the stands, minivans and taxis to and from Bucerías line up on the shaded, divided street that leads to the beach. To get here from Puerto Vallarta via public transportation, take a minivan or bus marked BUCERÍAS (they run from 6am to midnight). The last minivan stop is Bucerías's town square.

Exploring Bucerías Come here for a day-trip from Puerto Vallarta just to enjoy the long, wide, and uncrowded beach, along with the fresh seafood served at the beach-front restaurants or at one of the unusually great cafes listed below. If you are inclined to stay a few days, you can relax inexpensively and explore more of Bucerías. Sunday is street-market day, but it doesn't get going until around noon, in keeping with Bucerías's casual pace.

A Place to Stay Several small hotels and condominiums rent rooms here. **Los Pericos Travel** in Bucerías (☎ **329/8-0601** or 329/8-0061; fax 329/8-0601) will book accommodations, including villas, houses, and condos. Call ahead or ask in Bucerías for directions to their office, which is open Monday through Friday from 9am to 2pm and 4 to 7pm, and Saturday from 9am to 2pm.

Posada Olas Altas. Calle Héroes de Nacozari s/n, 63732 Bucerías, Nay. ☎ **329/8-0407.** 24 units. FAN. $12–$18 double. No credit cards. Free parking on the street.

Fronting the highway and just down (left) from the roadside food stands, this is the ideal inexpensive place to stay while getting to know the area. Owners Arnulfo Sánchez and his wife Rosalina Ortega have created cheery and clean rooms with concrete floors and blue-iron doors and window frames. Bathrooms have doors and walls but no ceiling separating them from the rest of the room. Most rooms have a single and double bed or two doubles, and one room on the roof has both a king-size bed and a double bed. There's no hot water unless you ask for it (the room price is the same with or without it). An inexpensive lobby restaurant is open Monday through Saturday from 7am to 7pm and Sunday from 7am to 2pm.

Great Places to Eat Besides those mentioned below, there are many seafood restaurants fronting the beach. Find one that looks good to you and settle in for a tasty seafood meal.

Cafe Magaña. Lázaro Cárdenas 500. ☎ **329/8-0303.** Main courses $4–$10. No credit cards. Daily 4:30–11pm. Closed in June. BBQ RIBS.

Famous for its BBQ ribs and chicken, Cafe Magaña gives you a choice of 10 original sauces, all homemade. Flavors have mythological names, and contain creative ingredients like ginger, garlic, oranges, apples, cinnamon, and chiles. The sauces have been such a hit that British owner Jeff Rafferty now offers them bottled and for sale. This casual, colorful cafe—with one wall covered in news clippings and whimsical hats hung about the ceiling—also features TV sports and an occasional live band. It also serves as the unofficial neighborhood communication center, with Internet access, fax, and long-distance services. It's located directly across from the Bucerías Trailer Park.

✪ **Mark's.** Lázaro Cárdenas 56. ☎ **329/8-0303.** Pasta $6–$7; main courses $7–$10. MC, V. High season Wed–Mon noon–11pm. Low Season Wed–Mon 5:30–11pm. PASTA/ STEAK/SEAFOOD.

It's worth a special trip to Bucerías just to eat at this covered-patio restaurant. The most popular American hangout in town, Mark's offers a great assortment of thin-crust pizzas and flat bread, baked in their brick oven and seasoned with fresh herbs grown in the garden. In fact, everything from the shrimp in angel-hair pasta to the pesto-crusted fish fillet and grilled pork tenderloin with mango basil sauce has a wonderfully fresh taste. Mark's is only half a block from the beach. The restaurant has a boutique and live jazz music every weekend during high season.

From the highway, turn left just after the bridge where there's a small sign for Mark's. Then double-back left at the next street (it's immediately after you turn left) and turn right at the next corner. Mark's is on the right, the block before the ocean.

SAN BLAS: FOR BIRD-WATCHERS & SURFERS San Blas is a rather ugly Pacific Coast fishing village of 10,000 people in Nayarit State, but it's one of the country's premier birding spots. Birding enthusiasts come often and stay long. Surfers do too, since some of Mexico's best surfing waters are at Las Islitas Beach.

Only 150 miles from Puerto Vallarta, San Blas is an easy 3½-hour trip, along a new, two-lane, paved highway that starts at Las Varas off Highway 200 (a sign announces Las Varas), goes through the villages of Santa Cruz and Aticama, then connects with the two-lane highway into San Blas. Signs are few, so if you're driving, keep asking directions. Buses depart from Puerto Vallarta's new central bus station (1km north of Puerto Vallarta's airport) and travel regularly to San Blas.

As you enter the village, you'll be on avenida Juárez, the principal street, which leads to the main plaza on the right. At its far end sits the old church, with a new church next to it. Across the street from the church is the bus station, and on the other side of the churches is the market. After you pass the square, the first one-way street to your left is Batallón, an important street that passes a bakery, a medical clinic, several hotels, and Los Cocos Trailer Park and ends up at Borrego Beach, with its many outdoor fish restaurants. Nearly everything is within walking distance, and there are public buses that go to the farther beaches—Matanchen and Los Cocos—on their way to Santa Cruz, the next village to the south.

Exploring San Blas Like Acapulco, San Blas was once a very important port for New Spain's trade with the Philippines, and the town was fortified against pirates. Ruins of the fortifications, complete with cannons, the old church, and houses all overgrown with jungle, are still visible atop La Contadura Hill. The fort settlement was destroyed during the struggle for independence in 1811 and has been in ruins ever since. Also, it was from San Blas that Fr. Junípero Serra set out to establish missions in California in the 18th century.

The view from La Contadura is definitely worth the walk there—a panorama of coconut plantations, coastline, town, and the lighthouse at Playa del Rey. To reach the ruins from San Blas, head east on avenida Juárez about half a mile, as if going out of town. Just before the bridge, take the stone path that winds up the hill to your right.

Beaches & Water Sports   One of the closest beaches is **Borrego Beach;** to reach it, head south from the town plaza on Batallón until it ends.

Half a mile past the settlement is a dirt road to **Las Islitas Beach,** a magnificent stretch of sand extending for miles with a few beach-shack restaurants. This is a famous surfing beach with mile-long waves, especially during September and October, when storms create the biggest swells. If you don't have a surfboard, you can usually rent one from one of the local surfers. The bodysurfing at Islitas is good, too. A taxi to Islitas will cost about $5 from downtown San Blas.

Jungle Cruise to Tovara Springs   Almost the moment you hit San Blas, you'll be approached by a guide offering a boat ride into the jungle. This is one of Mexico's unique tropical experiences. To make the most of it, find a guide who will leave at 6:30 or 7am, since the first boat on the river encounters the most birds and the Tovara River is like glass early in the morning, unruffled by breezes. Around 9am, boatloads of groups start arriving, and the serenity evaporates like the morning mist.

The cost is about $40 for a boatload of one to four people for the 3- to 4-hour trip from the bridge at the edge of town on Juárez. It's less (about $30) for the shorter, 2-hour trip from the embarcadero near Matanchen Bay, out of town. Either way, you won't regret taking the early morning cruise through shady mangrove mazes and tunnels, past tropical birds and cane fields to the beautiful natural springs, **La Tovara,** where you can swim. There's a restaurant here, too, but it's much more costly than what's available in town.

Note: The guide may also offer to take you to "The Plantation," which refers to pineapple and banana plantations on a hill outside of town. The additional cost of this trip is not worth it for most people.

Bird Watching   As many as 300 species of birds have been sighted around San Blas, one of the highest counts in the Western Hemisphere. Birding is best from mid-October through April. Birders and hikers should go to the **Hotel Garza Canela** (☎ **328/5-0307** or 328/5-0480) in San Blas (see "A Place to Stay & Dine," below) to buy a copy of the booklet *Where to Find Birds in San Blas, Nayarit,* by Rosalind Novick and Lan Sing Wu. With maps and directions, it details all the best birding spots and walks, including hikes to some lovely waterfalls where you can swim. Ask the staff at Hotel Garza Canela which bilingual guide they currently recommend, and they'll put you in touch with this person. A day's tour will cost around $100, which can be divided among the participants.

A Place to Stay & Dine   There aren't many good accommodations and dining options in San Blas. The ✪ **Hotel Garza Canela** (☎ **328/5-0307,** 328/5-0480, 328/ 5-0112), is the former Hotel Las Brisas, although the owners are the same. It is still one of the most comfortable places to stay on the coast. A block inland from the waterfront and nestled among pretty gardens of palms, hibiscus, and other tropical plants are the cottagelike fourplexes and other buildings of this resort. You'll find a tranquil ambiance, two pools (one for toddlers), and the best restaurant/bar in town. Pets are welcome. The 45 rooms and minisuites ($69 double; $80 suite; breakfast included) are modern, bright, airy, and immaculate, with well-screened windows, fans, and air-conditioning. Several rooms have kitchens and come with king-size beds; otherwise, most have two double beds, and a few have an extra single bed. Each room has an in-room safe-deposit box. The hotel's **El Delfín** restaurant (main courses $6 to $12; open daily 8am to 10am and 1 to 9pm) serves the best food in San Blas in an air-conditioned dining room with soft lights, soft music, and comfortable captain's chairs. Try the exquisite shrimp with creamy chipotle pepper sauce. The spaghetti dishes include pasta with shrimp in lime, roasted garlic, and basil sauce. The homemade soups and desserts are also quite good. Find the hotel and restaurant on calle Paredes Sur 106. To get here, walk south from the square on Batallón about 6 blocks, turn right on Campeche across from the Marino Inn, then turn left on the next street, Paredes Sur. The hotel, which accepts major credit cards, has a fax (328/5-0308) and toll-free telephone number from within Mexico (☎ **800/71-32313**).

2 Mazatlán

674 miles NW of Mexico City; 314 miles NW of Guadalajara; 976 miles SE of Mexicali

Casual, lively, and sporting a lifestyle that revolves around the sea, Mazatlán is one of Mexico's best value-priced resorts. It's still a mecca for sportfishers in search of sailfish and marlin at reasonable prices. But these days, Mazatlán is better known as a world-class beach resort, due to its 17 miles of inviting sandy beaches extending northward from the original old city, complemented by new golf and marina facilities. Hotels, restaurants, shops, and clubs cozy up to those beaches as this city of 500,000 grows to accommodate its yearly influx of one million visitors.

Mazatlán is also a traditional commercial port city and boasts the largest shrimping fleet in Latin America. A 20-block historic area called Old Mazatlán dates from the 19th century (see "Architectural Highlights," below). Its seaside walkway (*malecón*) is the longest in Mexico, at 15 miles, and street musicians are known to play along its borders for tips. Famous for its annual Carnaval revelry, it's also got a reputation for playful nightlife.

ESSENTIALS

GETTING THERE   By Plane   There are numerous direct or nonstop flights to Mazatlán, most from the west coast of the United States. See chapter 3, "Planning a Trip to Mexico," for a list of international carriers serving Mexico. From the United States, **Aeromexico** (☎ **800/237-6639** in the U.S.) flies from Los Angeles, Atlanta, Phoenix, San Antonio, and Tucson. **Mexicana** (☎ **800/531-7921** in the U.S.) has service from Chicago, Denver, Los Angeles, Miami, San Antonio, and San Francisco. **Delta** (☎ **800-221-1212** in the U.S., or 69/14-41-56) and **Aero California** (☎ **800/237-6225** in the U.S.) fly from Los Angeles, and **Continental** (☎ **800/231-0856** in the U.S., or 01-800/525-0280 in Mexico) has service from Houston. **Alaska Airlines** (☎ **800-252-7522** or 69/85-2730) services San Francisco and Los Angeles. From elsewhere in Mexico, **Aero California** (☎ **69/13-2042,** 69/16-2190, or 69/16-2191 at the airport) also flies in from Tijuana, Guadalajara, and Mexico City. **Aeromexico** (☎ **69/13-1111**) has flights to Mazatlán from Mexico City, Los Mochis, Durango, Monterrey, Guadalajara, Tijuana, and León. **Mexicana** (☎ **69/82-7722** or 69/82-7381) offers service from Mexico City, Guadalajara, Monterrey, and Los Cabos. Check with a travel agent for the latest **charter flights.**

By Bus   First-class and deluxe buses depart almost hourly for Guadalajara and Mexico City and with more limited frequency to other points within Mexico.

By Car   To reach Mazatlán from the United States, take **International Highway 15** from Nogales, Arizona, to Culiacán. At Culiacán you change to the four-lane **tollway**—while it costs about $70, it is really the only road considered safe and in drivable condition. If you take the tollway, total trip time from the United States to Mazatlán is about 10 hours. Consider an overnight stop, as driving at night in Mexico can be hazardous.

By Ferry   Passenger ferries operated by SEMATUR run between Mazatlán and La Paz, Baja California. The ferry leaves daily at 3pm for cars, with Thursdays reserved

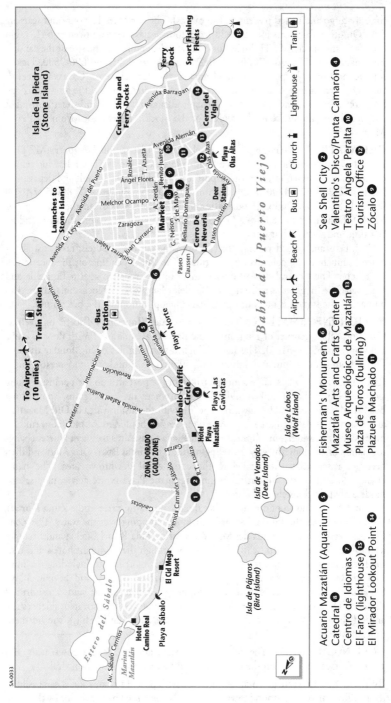

Mazatlán Area

Bahía del Puerto Viejo

Isla de la Piedra (Stone Island)

Cruise Ship and Ferry Docks

Ferry Dock

Sport Fishing Fleets

Avenida Barragan

Cerro del Vigía

Playa Olas Altas

Avenida Alemán

Olas Altas

Rosales
T. Azueta
Ángel Flores
Avenida del Puerto
Avenida G. Leyva

Launches to Stone Island

Melchor Ocampo

Deer Statue

A. Serdán

B. de Mayo

Market

Zaragoza

G. Nelson

Belisario Domínguez

Cerro De La Neveria

Gutiérrez Nájera

Paseo Claussen

Inzunztares

Train Station

To Airport (10 miles)

Bus Station

Paseo Clausen

Playa Norte

Avenida del Mar

Reforma

Revolución

Internacional

Avenida Rafael Buelna

Carretera

Sábalo Traffic Circle

Playa Las Gaviotas

Hotel Playa Mazatlán

Carzas

R.T. Loaiza

ZONA DORADO (GOLD ZONE)

Avenida Camarón Sábalo

Gaviotas

Av. Sábalo Cerritos

Marina Mazatlán

Hotel Camino Real

Playa Sábalo

El Cid Mega Resort

Estero del Sábalo

Isla de Pájaros (Bird Island)

Isla de Venados (Deer Island)

Isla de Lobos (Wolf Island)

Bahía del Puerto Viejo

Airport ✈   Beach ⚓   Bus 🚌   Church ✝   Lighthouse 🗼   Train 🚆

Acuario Mazatlán (Aquarium) 5	Sea Shell City 2
Catedral 8	Valentino's Disco/Punta Camarón 4
Centro de Idiomas 7	Teatro Ángela Peralta 10
El Faro (lighthouse) 15	Tourism Office 12
El Mirador Lookout Point 14	Zócalo 9
Fisherman's Monument 6	
Mazatlán Arts and Crafts Center 1	
Museo Arqueológico de Mazatlán 13	
Plaza de Toros (bullring) 3	
Plazuela Machado 11	

SA-0033

307

for only cargo and seated passengers (no cabins). The trip takes 18 hours and seats are $20. On other days seats are also $20, with tourist-class service priced at $41, cabin class $62, and special at $82. Prices for cars vary, depending on the size of the car. For information call ☎ 69/81-7020; toll-free within Mexico, 91/800/696-9600. Tickets for the ferry must be purchased in advance at the ferry office on Carnaval street or through travel agents; MasterCard and Visa are accepted. To find the ferry office, go south on Olas Altas and turn left on Alemán; Carnaval is the second street; turn right and you'll find the office in the middle of the block. Ferries return from La Paz to Mazatlán daily.

ORIENTATION   Arriving   The Rafael Beulna International Airport (MZT) is located 17 miles southeast of the hotel-and-resort area of town. The following rental-car companies have counters in the airport, open during flight arrivals and departures: **Hertz** (☎ 800/527-0700 in the U.S., or 69/850845), **Budget** (☎ 800/527-0700 in the U.S., or 69/826363), and **National** (☎ 800/328-4567 in the U.S., or 69/82400). Daily rates run $45 to $75, desirable if you want to explore the surrounding coastline and villages, but not essential.

Both taxis and colectivo minivans run from the airport to hotels; taxis cost about twice as much as the colectivo, which runs $3 to $8, depending on the location of your hotel. The **Central de Autobuses** (main bus terminal) is at Río Tamazula and Chachalacas. To get there from avenida del Mar, walk 3 blocks inland on Río Tamazula; the station is on your right. Taxis line up in front of the bus station.

VISITOR INFORMATION   The City and State Tourism Office is on avenida Camarón Sábalo (corner of Tiburón) in the Ban Rural building, fourth floor (☎ 69/16-5160; fax 69/16-5166). The staff is English-speaking. It's open Monday through Friday from 8am to 3pm and 4:30pm to 7:30pm, and Saturday from 9am to 1pm.

CITY LAYOUT   Mazatlán extends north from the port area on the peninsula along avenida Gabriel Leyva and avenida Barragan, where the cruise ships, sportfishing boats, and ferries dock. The downtown begins with the historic area of **Old Mazatlán** and **Playa Olas Altas** to the south. A curving seaside boulevard, or **malecón,** runs 17 miles along the waterfront, all the way from **Playa Olas Altas** to **Playa Norte,** changing names often along the way. Traveling north, it begins as Paseo Olas Altas and then becomes Paseo Claussen parallel to the commercial downtown area. The name changes to avenida del Mar at the beginning of the Playa Norte area, where several moderately priced hotels are located.

About 4 miles north of downtown lies the Sábalo traffic circle in the **Zona Dorada** (Gold Zone) near the **Punta Camarón** rocky outcropping over the water. The Zona Dorada begins where avenida del Mar intersects avenida Rafael Buelna and becomes **avenida Camarón Sábalo,** which leads north through the abundant hotels and fast-food restaurants of the tourist zone. From here, the resort hotels, including the huge El Cid Resort complex, continue to spread northward along and beyond **Playa Sábalo.** The new **Marina Mazatlán** development has changed the landscape north of the Zona Dorada considerably, as hotels, condo complexes, and private residences rise around the new marina. North of here is **Los Cerritos** (Little Hills), the northern limit of Mazatlán.

GETTING AROUND   The downtown transportation center for buses, taxis, and *pulmonías* (see below) is on the central Plaza Principal, facing the cathedral.

By Taxi   Eco Taxis are green-and-white cabs with posted set fares. Taxis can easily be flagged from anywhere around town, and can also be rented by the day or by the hour. Agree on a price in advance.

By Pulmonía   These Jeep-type open-air vehicles carry up to three passengers. *Pulmonías* (literally "pneumonias") have surreylike tops and open sides to let in the breezes. As a rule, they're slightly cheaper than taxis, but you should also still settle on a price before boarding.

By Bus   Buses, some with air-conditioning, cover most of the city and are relatively easy to use. The "Sábalo Centro" line runs from the Gold Zone along the waterfront to downtown near the market and the central plaza; at avenida Miguel Alemán the buses turn and head south to Olas Altas. The "Cerritos-Juárez" line starts near the train station, cuts across town to the malecón beside the Gold Zone, and heads north to Cerritos and back. The "Sábalo Cocos" line runs through the Gold Zone, heads inland to the bus station and on to downtown (also stopping at the market) by a back route (instead of the waterfront). The "Playa Sur" line goes to the area where the sport-fishing and tour boats depart. Buses run daily from 6am to 11pm.

FAST FACTS: MAZATLÁN

American Express   The office is on avenida Camarón Sábalo in the Centro Comercial Balboa shopping center, Loc. 4 and 16 (☎ 69/14-1337), between the traffic circle and the El Cid Resort; it's open Monday through Friday from 9am to 5pm and Saturday from 9am to noon.

Area Code   The telephone area code for Mazatlán is **69.**

Banks   Foreign currency is exchanged at most banks Monday through Friday from 9 to noon, although banks are generally open until 6pm, and some have limited hours on Saturday.

Climate   As the northernmost major beach resort on the mainland, Mazatlán can be cooler in summer than the resorts farther south. The wettest month is September.

Post Office   The correo is downtown on the east side of the main plaza, on Benito Juárez just off Angel Flores.

Spanish Classes   Spanish-language classes begin every Monday at the **Centro de Idiomas,** 3 blocks west of the cathedral near 21 de Marzo and Canizales. In addition to small group (maximum six students) and individual instruction, the language center offers a homestay program and a person-to-person program that matches students with local people of similar interests and vocations. On Friday at 7pm, the center holds free Spanish and English conversation groups open to both visitors and locals. The school also offers special tours for those enrolled in its programs, including a once-a-month walking tour of Old Mazatlán. For more information call or write Dixie Davis, Belisario Domínguez 1908, Mazatlán, Sin. (☎ 69/82-2053; fax 69/85-5606).

Telephones   Most telephone numbers for the Gold Zone, from the Hotel Camino Real south to the Hotel Playa Mazatlán, begin with a 1. Numbers in downtown and along avenida del Mar begin with an 8.

ACTIVITIES ON & OFF THE BEACH

To orient yourself, take a walk up and enjoy the panoramic view from **El Faro,** the famous lighthouse on the point at the south end of town. It's the second-highest lighthouse in the world (only Gibraltar is higher), towering 447 feet over the harbor. Begin at the end of Paseo Centenario near the sportfishing docks. There's a refreshment stand at the foot of the hill. Allow about 45 minutes for the climb. The view is nearly as spectacular from the top of **Cerro del Vigía** (Lookout Hill), which is accessible by car from Paseo Olas Altas.

BEACHES At the western edge of downtown is the rocky and pebbly **Playa Olas Altas,** a lovely stretch of pounding surf, although not suitable for swimming. Around a rocky promontory to the north of Olas Altas is **Playa Norte,** several miles of good sand beach.

At the Sábalo traffic circle, Punta Camarón juts into the water, and on either side of the point is **Playa Las Gaviotas.** Farther north, **Playa Sábalo** is perhaps the very best beach in Mazatlán. The next point jutting into the water is Punta Sábalo, beyond which you'll find a bridge over the channel that flows in and out of a lagoon. Beyond the marina lie even more beaches stretching all the way to Los Cerritos. Remember that all beaches in Mexico are public property, so feel free to wander where you like.

Mazatlán is one of the only resorts in Mexico that permits surfing at town beaches. The waves are best at **Los Pinos,** north of the fort—known in surfing circles as "the Cannon"—as well as at Playa Los Gaviotas and Playa Los Sábalos.

Another good beach, one that makes an enjoyable outing, is on the ocean side of **Isla de la Piedra** (Stone Island). From the center of town, board a "Circunvalación" or "Playa Sur" bus from the north side of the Plaza Principal for the ride to the boat landing, called Embarcadero—Isla de la Piedra. Small motorboats make the 5-minute trip to the island every 15 minutes or so from 7am to 7pm for a modest price. When you arrive on the island, walk through the sleepy little village to the ocean side, where the pale-sand beaches, bordered by coconut groves, stretch for miles. On Sunday afternoons, the palapa restaurants on the shore have music and dancing, attracting families and young people; on other days the beach is almost empty. **Carmelita's** has delicious fish called *lisamacho;* it's grilled over an open fire and served slightly blackened with fresh, hot corn tortillas and salsa.

CRUISES & BOAT RENTALS The **Fiesta Cruise** runs a large double-decker boat every morning at 11am, leaving from the south beach near the lighthouse. The 3-hour cruise takes in the harbor and bay; bilingual guides explain the marine life while a marimba band plays. Tickets cost $15 per person (children 5 to 8 pay half price). Purchase tickets through a major hotel or travel agency or call ☎ **69/85-2237.**

Amphibious boats heading for Isla de Venados (Deer Island), one of three big islands off the coast, leave from the beaches of the **El Cid Resort** (☎ **69/13-3333,** ext. 3341) throughout the day. When you buy your $8.50 round-trip ticket, you can rent snorkeling gear.

DEEP-SEA FISHING It's slightly cheaper to enjoy deep-sea fishing in Mazatlán than in other parts of Mexico, and if you request it (please do!), your captain will practice "catch and release." Rates are around $180 per day for a 24-foot *panga* for up to three persons; $265 per day for a 38-foot cruiser for up to four persons; and $300 per day for a 36-foot cruiser for up to 10 passengers; rates do not include fishing licenses and gratuities. Try the **Star Fleet** (☎ **69/82-2665** or 69/82-3878; fax 69/82-5155), the **Aries Fleet** (☎ **800/633-3085** in the U.S. and Canada, or 69/16-3468), or **Mike Mexemins's Faro Fleet** (☎ **69/81-2824** or 69/81-5988). Locals suggest making fishing reservations for October through January at least a month in advance; at the very least, do it the minute you arrive in town. **Mexico Sportsman,** in San Antonio, Texas (☎/fax **210/494-9916**), makes advance arrangements for a variety of fishing excursions from Mazatlán, providing anglers with complete information about cost; length of time fishing; kind of boat, line, and tackle used; and whether or not bait, drinks, and lunch are included—all at prices as good as you'll get on-site in Mazatlán.

OTHER WATER SPORTS Among the best places to rent water-sports equipment, from snorkeling gear to Hobie Cats, are the Aqua Sport Center at the **El Cid Resort** (☎ **69/13-3333**) and the Ocean Sport Center at the **Hotel Camino Real** (☎ **69/ 13-1111**).

TENNIS, GOLF & OTHER OUTDOOR SPORTS   Mazatlán has more than 100 tennis courts. Try those at the **El Cid Resort,** on Camarón Sábalo (☎ **69/13-3333**), though hotel guests have priority; and the **Racquet Club Gaviotas, Ibis,** and **Río Bravo** in the Golden Zone (☎ **69/13-5939**). Many larger hotels in Mazatlán also have courts.

As for **golf,** try the 18-hole course at the **El Cid Resort** (☎ **69/13-3333**), designed by Robert Trent Jones. Another 9 holes are being added, under the guidance of Lee Treviño. It's open to the public, but preference is given to hotel guests and tee times book up quickly. Other options are the new 18-hole **Marina Mazatlán** course next door (☎ **69/16-4672**) or the 9-hole course at the **Club Campestre Mazatlán** (☎ **69/80-0202, 69/88-0988,** open to the public), on Highway 15 on the outskirts of downtown.

In addition to its worldwide reputation for year-round sportfishing, Mazatlán is known for good **hunting,** principally duck and dove. For information about transportation, guides, equipment, and licenses, call the **Aviles Brothers** (☎ **69/81-3728**) or the **tourism office** (☎ **69/81-5837** or 69/81-5838).

You can rent horses for **horseback riding** on Isla de la Piedra for $12 per hour.

SPECTATOR SPORTS   There's a bullring (Plaza de Toros) on Rafael Buelna, about a mile from the Golden Zone. From December through early April, **bullfights** are held every Sunday and on holidays at 4pm; locals recommend arriving by 2pm. Tickets range from $8 for general admission (ask for the shady side—*la sombra*) to $25 for the front of the shaded section; tickets can be purchased in advance at most travel agencies and tour desks.

Mexican **rodeos,** or *charreadas,* are held at the Lienzo Charro (bullring) of the Asociación de Charros de Mazatlán (☎ **69/83-3154**) each Sunday at 4pm. Tickets go on sale Sunday morning at 10am and are about $5, but depend on the group that's showing. Tickets are also available through most major hotels and travel agencies.

At Playa Olas Altas, daring **cliff divers** take to the rock ledges of **El Mirador** and plunge into the shallow, pounding surf below. The divers perform sporadically during the day as tour buses arrive near their perch and sometimes dive with torches at 7pm. After the dive, they collect donations from spectators.

SPECIAL EVENTS IN NEARBY VILLAGES   On the weekend of the 1st Sunday in October, **Rosario,** a small town 45 minutes south on Highway 15 known for the gold altar screen of its colonial church, holds a **festival honoring Our Lady of the Rosary.** Games, music, dances, processions, and festive foods mark the event. From May 1 to 10, Rosario holds its **Spring Festival.**

In mid-October, the village of **Escuinapa,** south of Rosario on Highway 15, holds a **Mango Festival.**

EXPLORING MAZATLÁN
MUSEUMS

Museo Arqueológico de Mazatlán. Sixto Osuna 76, a block in from Paseo Olas Altas. ☎ **69/85-3502.** Admission $1. Tues–Sun 10am–1pm and 4–7pm.

This small but attractive archaeological museum exhibits both pre-Hispanic artifacts and a permanent contemporary-art exhibit. To get here from Olas Altas, walk inland on Sixto Osuna 1½ blocks; the museum is on your right. Art exhibits are sometimes held in the Casa de la Cultura across the street from the museum.

Acuario Mazatlán. Av. de los Deportes 111, half a block off Av. del Mar. ☎ **69/81-7815** or 69/81-7817. Admission $3.75 adults, $1.90 children 3–14. Daily 9:30am–6:30pm; sea lions, birds, and fish fed at almost hourly shows 10:30am–5pm.

Mazatlán's Carnaval: A Weeklong Party

The week before Lent (usually in Feb) is Mazatlán's famous Carnaval, or Mardi Gras. People come from all over the country and abroad for this flamboyant celebration. Parades, special shows, the coronation of the Carnaval queen, and many other extravaganzas take place all over town (for event information, check at major hotels or the tourism office and look for posters). Every night during Carnaval week, all along the Olas Altas oceanfront drive in the southern part of town, music fills the street with roving mariachi groups, the local traditional *bandas sinaloenses* (sporting lots of brass instruments), and electrified bands set up under tarpaulin shades. The crowd increases each day, until the last night (Shrove Tuesday), when the malecón is packed with musicians, dancers, and people out for a good time. The following day, Ash Wednesday, the party is over. People receive crosses of ashes on their foreheads at church, and Lent begins.

If you plan to be in Mazatlán for Carnaval, spring break, or Semana Santa (Holy Week), be sure to make reservations several months in advance. Hotels fill up, and prices usually rise, too.

Children and adults alike interested in the sea will love the Mazatlán Aquarium. With over 300 species of fish, including sharks, eels, and sea horses, it is one of the largest and best in Mexico. Next to the aquarium there's a playground and small zoo in a botanical garden.

ARCHITECTURAL HIGHLIGHTS

Two blocks south of the central plaza stands the lovely and historic **Teatro Ángela Peralta** (☎ 69/82-4447), which, in 1989, celebrated its first full season since being recently renovated. The theater was named for one of the world's great divas, who, along with the director and 30 members of the opera, died in Mazatlán of cholera in the 1863 epidemic. Some city tours make a stop at the theater; if you're visiting on your own, ask the guard if you can go in. The theater is open daily from 8:30am to 7pm; the fee for touring the building is 75¢. For information on scheduled performances, call or check at the box office at the theater.

The 20-block historic area near the theater, including the small square **Plazuela Machado** (bordered by Frías, Constitución, Carnaval, and Sixto Osuna), is packed with beautiful old buildings and rows of colorful town houses trimmed with wrought iron and carved stone; many buildings have recently been restored. Small galleries are beginning to move into the area, as the neighborhood becomes the center of Mazatlán's artistic community. Check out the **town houses** on Libertad between Domínguez and Carnaval and the two lavish **mansions** on Ocampo at Domínguez and at Carnaval. For a rest stop, try the **Café Pacífico** (decorated with historic pictures of Mazatlán) on the Plazuela Machado.

The **Plaza Principal,** also called Plaza Revolución, is the heart of the city, filled with vendors, shoe-shine stands, and people of all ages out for a stroll. At its center is a Victorian-style, wrought-iron bandstand with a diner-type restaurant underneath. Be sure to take a look at the **cathedral** with its unusual yellow-tiled twin steeples and partially tiled facade. It's on the corner of calle 21 de Marzo and Nelson.

ORGANIZED TOURS

In addition to **city tours** (3 hr. for $12), there are excursions to many colorful and interesting villages nearby, such as Concordia or Copala (see below). Some towns date from the Spanish conquest during the 16th century; others are modest farming or fishing villages. Information and reservations are available at any travel agency or major hotel, and all accept American Express, MasterCard, and Visa.

COPALA-CONCORDIA   This popular countryside tour stops at several mountain villages where furniture and other items are crafted. Copala is a historic mining village with a Spanish-colonial church. Lunch is included in the $33 tour, also known as the "Mountain Tour." For more about Copala, see "Road Trips from Mazatlán," below.

MAZATLÁN JUNGLE TOUR   Some might say that David Pérez's "Jungle Tour" is misnamed, but it's still worth doing. It consists of a 1½-hour boat ride past a Mexican navy base, Mazatlán's shrimp fleet and packing plants, and into the mangrove swamps to Stone Island. There's a 3-hour stop at a pristine beach that has what could be the world's largest sand dollars. Horseback rides on the beach are $5 for a half-hour ride. After the beach stop, feast on *pescado zarandeado* (fish cooked over coconut husks, green mangrove, and charcoal). Tours last from 9am to 3:30pm and cost $33 per person. Days vary, so call ☎/fax **69/14-1444** or 69/14-0451 for dates and reservations. American Express, MasterCard, and Visa are accepted.

WHERE TO STAY

The hotels in downtown Mazatlán are generally older and less expensive than those along the beachfront heading north. As a rule, room rates rise the farther north you go from downtown. The three major areas to stay are Olas Altas and downtown, the Playa Norte (North Beach), and the Zona Dorada.

THE ZONA DORADA

The Gold Zone is an elegant arc of gold sand linked by a palm-lined boulevard and bordered by dazzling hotels and a sprinkling of elaborate beach houses. A bonus here is the sunset view, unique because of the three islands just offshore which seem to melt gradually into the fading colors of evening. Many hotels along this beach cut their prices from May through September.

El Cid Mega Resort. Camarón Sábalo (between Rodolfo T. Loaiza and Calzada Campeador), 82100 Mazatlán, Sin. ☎ **800/525-1925** in the U.S., or 69/13-3333. Fax 69/14-1311. www.elcid.com. E-mail: sales@elcid.com. 1,320 units. A/C MINIBAR TV TEL. High season $80–$100 double; $250 junior suite; $450–$700 suite. Low season $94 double; $220 junior suite; $350 suite AE, DC, MC, V.

Mega is the operative word here. If you like your hotels large, imposing, and with every service and convenience you can think of, El Cid's your place in Mazatlán. This resort has changed the face of accommodations and added the modern edge to this resort. Both a hotel and residential development, El Cid has three beachfront buildings, private villas, and an 18-hole golf course on 900 acres. The main 17-story beachfront tower is called **Castilla;** there's also the 25-story, all-suite **El Moro Tower** and the lower-rise, lower priced **Granada** (near the golf course). Although there are multiple variations of rooms, most are heavily detailed in marble, and feature private balconies and contemporary, upscale furnishings.

Mazatlán Hotel Crunch

Mazatlán hotels fill up quickly during Carnaval and Easter week; some of the choicest rooms are reserved a year in advance, and room rates generally rise 30% to 40%. High season in Mazatlán, as in the rest of Mexico, is December 20 through Easter; low season begins the day after Easter and extends to December 20.

Dining/Diversions: With six restaurants, eight bars, and a glitzy disco, you never even need to leave this resort during your stay. Mexican specialties rule in the dining arena, but the **La Concha** seafood restaurant is a favorite as well.

Amenities: Whatever you can think of in terms of land and water sports, plus a "Mega Kids Club," lavish gardens, eight swimming pools (including one saltwater pool), 14 tennis courts, a marina, and complete fitness center are among the many services offered to pamper guests. There's also a shopping arcade, travel agency, salon services, business center, laundry, and baby-sitting.

✪ **Hotel Camino Real.** Punta de Sábalo s/n, 82100 Mazatlán, Sin. ☎ **800/722-6466** or 69/13-1111. Fax 69/14-0311. 169 units. A/C MINIBAR TV TEL. High season $130–$150 double; $190 junior suite. AE, DC, MC, V.

Long considered the grande dame of Mazatlán's hotels, the Camino Real continues to be the best choice for those seeking seclusion amid luxurious surroundings. Considered to have the best location in Mazatlán, it's set on a rocky cliff overlooking the sea. A purple-and-pink color scheme covers the marble-floored hallways and rooms, which have bathtubs and showers, large closets, and vanity tables. Junior suites have king-size beds and comfy couches. The hotel is about a 10-minute drive from the heart of the Gold Zone. The higher rates mentioned above are for rooms with an ocean view; other rooms have a marina view.

Dining/Diversions: Two restaurants serve all three meals and a lobby bar is open from 9am to midnight.

Amenities: The pool is very small, but the beach edges a small cove perfect for swimming. There are two tennis courts, room service, travel agency, and a boutique.

Pueblo Bonito. Av. Camarón Sábalo 2121 (Apdo. Postal 6), 82110 Mazatlán, Sin. ☎ **800/937-9567** or 619/275-4500 in the U.S., 800/69-990 toll-free within Mexico, or 69/14-3700. Fax 69/14-1723. 250 units. A/C TV TEL. $140 junior suite; $170 1-bedroom suite for 2 adults and 2 children. MC, V. Free guarded parking.

Many regard the Pueblo Bonito as the best hotel in Mazatlán, with good reason. The suites all have kitchens, seating areas, and nice architectural touches such as curved ceilings, arched windows, and tiled floors. The grounds are gorgeous—peacocks and flamingos stroll over lush lawns, a waterfall cascades into a large pool, and a row of palapas lines the beachfront. Suites are available as time shares or hotel rooms.

Dining/Diversions: There are three good restaurants on the property. The Mexican restaurant, **Las Palomas,** features a popular Sunday brunch. **Angelo's Continental** restaurant adds live piano music to its menu of attractions (see "Where to Dine," below). **Cilantro's** offers casual fare and snacks.

Amenities: Two large pools, equipped gym, sauna, massage, Jacuzzi, room and laundry service, sightseeing desk, boutiques, hairdressers.

PLAYA NORTE

The waterfront between the downtown and the Gold Zone is Mazatlán's original tourist strip. Moderately priced hotels and motels line the street across from the beach, where taco and souvenir vendors set up shop on weekends. Señor Frog's, Mazatlán's most famous restaurant, is in this neighborhood, as is the bus station. From May through September many hotels along this beach cut their prices.

Moderate

Hotel Playa Mazatlán. Av. Rodolfo Loaiza 202 (Apdo. Postal 207), 82110 Mazatlán, Sin. ☎ **800/762-5816** in the U.S., 69/13-1120, or 69/13-4455. Fax 69/14-0366. 423 units. A/C TV TEL. $82 double with garden view; $98 double with ocean view. AE, MC, V. Free guarded parking.

The most happening place on the beginning stretch of the Gold Zone, the Hotel Playa Mazatlán is enduringly popular with families, tour groups, and dozens of regulars who return annually for winter vacations or spring break. The quietest rooms are in the three-story section around an interior lawn; those by the terrace restaurant and beach can be very noisy. The hotel hosts Mexican fiestas and fireworks displays and has several fast-food stands on the grounds.

Dining/Diversions: Two restaurants serve the hotel in high season; one is open during the remainder of the year. There's both a pool bar and one near the main restaurant. The very popular **Fiesta Mexicana** is featured 3 nights a week in the third-floor nightclub.

Amenities: Three pools and two outdoor whirlpools, equipped gym, laundry and room service, boutique, small gift shop/pharmacy, tour desk.

✪ **Days Inn Suites Don Pelayo.** Av. del Mar 1111 (Apdo. Postal 1088), 82000 Mazatlán, Sin. ☎ **800/325-2525** in the U.S., 69/83-2221, or 69/83-1888. Fax 69/84-0799. 168 units. A/C TV TEL. $55 double. AE, CB, DC, MC, V. Free enclosed parking.

Following a total refurbishing in 1994 and 1995, the Don Pelayo is the top choice among budget inns, located on the North Beach at the edge of the malecón. The waterfront rooms have small balconies; all rooms have a king-size bed or two double beds, satellite TV, and central air-conditioning (without individual controls). The lighting and furnishings are gradually being improved. Suites have minibars and kitchenettes. Facilities include a restaurant, bar, two pools, and tennis courts. The hotel is very popular with families. This past year the pool was enlarged and a new wading pool was added.

Inexpensive

Apartments Fiesta. Ibis 502 at Río de la Plata, 82110 Mazatlán, Sin. ☎ **69/13-5355.** Phone/fax 69/13-1764. 7 units. 2 units with A/C; all units have FAN. $200–$400 per month; $75–$110 per week; $25 double per night. No credit cards.

A real find for long-term stays, the bright-blue–and-orange Fiesta has one- and two-bedroom apartments, all with kitchens, clustered around a small courtyard. Each apartment is decorated differently with a variety of wooden tables, chairs, and beds. The proprietors, Yolanda and Francisco Olivera, are very accommodating hosts. They don't take reservations far in advance and prefer that you call a week before you plan to visit. The complex is 2 blocks inland from Camarón Sábalo, an easy walk from the beach.

DOWNTOWN SEAFRONT/PLAYA OLAS ALTAS

The old section of Mazatlán is spread around a picturesque beach a short walk from downtown. It was here that movie stars used to come in the '50s and '60s for sun and surf. The hotels where they stayed are still here; they seem to whisper of their former glory. All the hotels are right on the waterfront and their seaside rooms have private balconies with beautiful views of the cove and the sunset. There are a few nice seafront restaurants along here, too, which are open from early until late, making it easy to dine near your hotel.

✪ **Hotel La Siesta.** Av. Olas Altas 11 Sur, 82000 Mazatlán, Sin. ☎ **69/81-2640** or 69/81-2334. Fax 69/13-7476. 57 units. A/C TEL. $30 double; $32 triple. AE, MC, V.

A fresh coat of tan paint makes the Siesta blend into its surroundings among the old mansions of Mazatlán. Inside, three levels of green-and-white railings surround a central courtyard. The rooms facing the ocean have balconies opening to sea breezes, pounding waves, and the roar of traffic. Guest rooms at the back of the hotel are quieter but less charming. All rooms have two beds, white walls with arched ceilings, a small table and chair, good lighting, and dependably hot water. There's a jug of purified water on each level. TVs cost extra. The courtyard houses the popular **El Shrimp Bucket** restaurant, where live marimbas and recorded music play until 10pm. This is one of the most popular hotels in Old Mazatlán and fills up quickly. Reservations are strongly advised. To get here from the deer statue on Olas Altas, go right 1 block.

WHERE TO DINE

Mazatlán boasts one of the largest shrimp fleets in the world and is a great town for seafood. A cheap-eats treat is to stop in one of the many *loncherías* scattered throughout the downtown area. Here you can get a *torta* (a sandwich on a small French roll) stuffed with a variety of meats, cheeses, tomatoes, onions, and chiles for around $2.

THE ZONA DORADO

Expensive

Angelo's. In the Hotel Pueblo Bonito, Camarón Sábalo 2121. ☎ **69/14-3700.** Reservations required. Main courses $8–$30. AE, CB, MC, V. Daily 7am–noon and 6pm–midnight. ITALIAN.

Even locals consider this hotel restaurant one of the best in town, as much for its ambiance as for its food. Beveled glass doors open to a soothing dining room gleaming with brass, polished wood, and crystal chandeliers. A pianist plays in the background as formally dressed waiters present menus featuring homemade pastas; shrimp dishes, including a superb scampi; and a large selection of imported wines.

✪ **Señor Pepper's.** Av. Camarón Sábalo 2121. ☎ **69/14-0101.** Main courses $8–$22; specials $8–$12. MC, V. Daily 6pm–midnight; bar open daily 6pm–2am. INTER-NATIONAL.

This restaurant, which manages to be both elegant and casual, serves the best steaks in Mazatlán. Potted plants, candlelight, and lots of polished crystal, silver, and brass give the dining room a romantic feeling, and some nights it seems as if all the diners are old friends. The Sonoran beef steaks are grilled over mesquite and served in staggering portions; lobster and shrimp are also big hits. The restaurant has a nightly special including appetizer, steak or seafood, vegetables, soup or salad; there is a complimentary appetizer for those only having drinks at the bar.

Moderate

Terraza Playa. In the Hotel Playa Mazatlán, R.T. Loaiza 202. ☎ **69/13-4455.** Breakfast $2.80–$5; Mexican plates $5–$9; seafood and meat $8–$18. AE, MC, V. Daily 6am–midnight. MEXICAN/SEAFOOD.

During the day, diners view the sea, beach, swimmers, sunbathers, and Isla de Venados (Deer Island). After sundown, they must be content with the stars overhead (in the completely open section) and the surging sounds of the waves as a backdrop to the live music presented nightly from 7pm to midnight. There's also a dance floor. Dine here and enjoy front-row seats to the hotel's free weekly fireworks shows, on Tuesday, Wednesday, and Saturday.

Inexpensive

Jungle Juice. Las Garzas and Laguna. ☎ **69/13-3315.** Breakfast $2–$4; main courses $4.50–$12. MC, V. Restaurant daily 7am–1am. Bar daily 6pm–1am. MEXICAN/STEAKS/SEAFOOD.

After last year's remodeling, the patio is now much more comfortable, and an upstairs bar with a definite Mexican flair gives this partially open-air restaurant a festive touch. Grilled meats and lobster are the specialties of this place, which has evolved from a juice-and-smoothie joint to a full-fledged grill and bar. Smoothies and many kinds of juices are still considered its specialties, as are vegetarian plates and meat dishes grilled over mesquite on the patio. This casual spot also serves good breakfasts and makes a nice stop after shopping in the Gold Zone. Look for daily specials on the blackboard. To get here from Pastelería Panamá on Sábalo, turn right on Las Garzas; it's a block down on your right. (Heading north on Loaiza, Las Garzas and the Pastelería Panamá are on the right after the Sábalo traffic circle but before the Mazatlán Arts and Crafts Center.)

DOWNTOWN & PLAYA NORTE
Moderate

Bahía Mariscos. Mariano Escobedo 203. ☎ **69/81-2645.** Main courses $5–$15. MC, V. High season daily 11am–9pm. Low season daily 11am–7pm. SEAFOOD.

A charming old town house in Olas Altas has been transformed into this delightful restaurant specializing in bountiful seafood lunches. The *campechana bahía* is a delicious medley of shrimp, octopus, oysters, and calamari, and the fried whole fish is the best you'll find in the city. To get here from El Shrimp Bucket (at M. Escobedo and Olas Altas), walk south 1 block and turn left on Escobedo; the restaurant is on your left.

✪ **Copa de Leche.** Olas Altas 1220 A Sur. ☎ **69/82-5753.** Fax 69/81-3897. Breakfast $3–$5; main courses $4.60–$14; soup $2–$4.50. AE, MC, V. Daily 7am–11pm. MEXICAN.

This shaded sidewalk cafe on the waterfront at Playa Olas Altas feels like Mazatlán must have in the 1930s. The food is consistently as good as the ocean view. The menu includes *pechugas en nogada,* chicken breast in a pecan-and-pomegranate sauce; shrimp in a tamarind sauce; traditional *alambre* barbecue (beef cooked with onion, peppers, mushrooms, ham, and bacon); wonderful seafood soup loaded with squid, shrimp, and chunks of fish; and great shrimp with chipotle sauce: Inside the cafe, there's updated Mexican decor; the bar is an old wooden boat, and the dining tables are covered with linen cloths. To get here from El Shrimp Bucket (at M. Escobedo and Olas Altas), turn south and walk half a block down Olas Altas; the cafe is on your left.

✪ **Doney.** Mariano Escobedo 610. ☎ **69/81-2651.** Soup or salad $2–$8; main courses $4–$9; Mexican plate $2.95–$6. AE, MC, V. Daily 8am–10:30pm (comida corrida served noon–4pm). MEXICAN.

This tried-and-true favorite, in a converted colonial home immediately south of the plaza, is regarded by many locals as the best moderately priced restaurant downtown. The mood is serene under the brick domes covering the interior courtyard. Inside, stained glass, handsome woodwork, and old sepia photographs add a turn-of-the-century flavor, especially when piano music fills the air. The large bilingual menu includes what some claim are the best apple pie and lemon meringue pie in town, in addition to a broad selection of traditional Mexican home-styled cooking. From the plaza with the city hall on your left, walk 1 block down Ángel Flores then turn left on Cinco de Mayo; the restaurant is at the end of the block at Escobedo.

✪ **Señor Frog's.** North Beach malecón, Av. del Mar. ☎ **69/85-1110** or 69/82-1925. Main courses $7–$15. AE, MC, V. Daily noon–1:30am. MEXICAN.

A sign over the door says JUST ANOTHER BAR AND GRILL, but once inside, you'll know it's another of the Anderson chain's infamous understatements. The decor is delightfully wacky, the food great, and the loud music even better. With an atmosphere this friendly and lively, revelers have been known to dance on the tables late into the night. The food is among the best in town. Try the tasty ribs, Caesar salad, or mango crepes. The restaurant is on the waterfront drive at Playa Norte next to the Frankie Oh! disco.

El Shrimp Bucket. In the Hotel La Siesta, Av. Olas Altas 11 at Escobedo. ☎ **69/81-6350** or 69/82-8019. Mexican plates $4.50–$9; seafood and steak $9–$16.50. AE, CB, DISC, MC, V. Daily 6am–midnight. MEXICAN/SEAFOOD.

A total remodeling in March 1998 rejuvenated the somewhat weary El Shrimp Bucket, making it once again one of the most popular restaurants in town. You can sample great shrimp in the air-conditioned dining room or under umbrellas in the center courtyard. The marimbas start up around 7pm. For wining, dining, and dancing, this is a great place for a splurge. El Shrimp Bucket is on Olas Altas at the corner of Escobedo.

SHOPPING

Most stores are open Monday through Saturday from 9 or 10am to 6 or 8pm. Very few close for lunch, and many stores are open on Sunday afternoon.

La Zona Dorada is the best area for shopping. For a huge selection of handcrafts from all over Mexico, visit the **Mazatlán Arts and Crafts Center** (☎ **69/13-5022**), at calle Gaviotas and Loaiza, open from 10am to 6pm. Shops throughout the Gold Zone have a good selection of name-brand clothing, fabrics, silver jewelry, leather, art, and Mexican crafts.

The **Centro Mercado** in Old Mazatlán is another kind of shopping experience. Here you'll find women selling freshly gathered shrimp under colorful umbrellas; open-air food stalls; and indoor shops stacked with pottery, clothing, and crafts (mostly of lesser quality). Small galleries and shops are beginning to appear in Old Mazatlán; one of the nicest is **NidArt Galería,** on avenida Libertad and Carnaval (☎ **69/81-0002**).

La Gran Plaza is a large shopping mall just 3 blocks inland from the waterfront on avenida de los Deportes. The plaza has a large supermarket, department stores, and specialty shops and is a good place for buying basic supplies.

MAZATLÁN AFTER DARK

A free **fireworks** show is held every Sunday, beginning at 8pm, on the beach fronting the Hotel Playa Mazatlán, R. T. Loaiza 202, in the Golden Zone (☎ **69/13-4444** or 69/13-5320). The display is visible from the beach or from the hotel's Terraza Playa restaurant.

The same hotel also presents an excellent **Fiesta Mexicana,** complete with buffet, open bar, folkloric dancing, and live music. Fiestas are presented on Tuesday, Thursday, and Saturday year-round beginning at 7pm; try to arrive by 6pm to get a good table. Tickets are $25.

CLUBS & BARS

Café Pacífico. Frías and Constitución. ☎ **69/81-3972.** No cover. AE, MC, V.

If you're staying downtown or prefer a quiet atmosphere, this bodega-like bar in a restored historic building on Plazuela Machado is a pleasant place to spend some time. The doors are inset with stained glass, and the thick roof beams and walls are decorated with braided garlic, dried peppers, and old photographs. Open daily from 10am to 2am.

Joe's Oyster Bar. Loaiza 100, on the beachfront at Los Sabalos Hotel. ☎ **69/83-5333.** No cover. AE, MC, V.

Beer, burgers, fresh oysters, and high-volume dance music are the house specialties at this casual, open-air disco. Open daily from 11am to 2am.

✪ **Valentino's.** Punta Camarón, near the Camarón Sábalo traffic circle. ☎ **69/84-1666** and 69/84-2465. Cover $5–$8. AE, MC, V.

Dramatically perched on a rocky outcropping overlooking the sea, this all-white, Moorish-looking building houses one of the area's most popular discos. There's a good high-tech light show complete with green laser beams. For a break from the pulsating dance floor, there are pool tables in another room and some (relatively) quiet areas for talking. Open daily from 9pm to 4am.

ROAD TRIPS FROM MAZATLÁN
TEACAPÁN: ABUNDANT WILDLIFE & A RUSTIC VILLAGE

Teacapán is the quintessential Mexican fishing village. It's just 2 hours south of Mazatlán (82 miles) at the tip of an isolated peninsula that extends 18 miles down a coastline of pristine beaches. Mangrove lagoons and canals border its other side. Palm and mango groves, cattle ranches, and an occasional cluster of houses dot the peninsula, which ends at the Boca de Teacapán, a natural marina separating the states of Sinaloa and Nayarit. Shrimping boats line the beach at the edge of the marina, which is backed by the worn houses and dirt streets of town.

Bird-watchers hire local fishermen to take them out around the lagoons, where they can see herons, flamingos, Canadian ducks, and countless other species of birds. Inland, the sparsely populated land is a haven for deer, ocelot, and wild boars. There's talk of making the entire peninsula into an ecological preserve, and thus far, residents have resisted attempts by developers to turn the area into a large-scale resort. For now, visitors are treated to the ultimate peaceful refuge.

GETTING THERE   By Car   To reach Teacapán, drive south from Mazatlán on the highway to Escuinapa. There are no signs marking the right turn for the road to Teacapán; ask for directions in Escuinapa.

By Bus   Autotransportes Escuinapa has several second-class buses daily to Escuinapa; from there you can transfer to Teacapán. The second-class bus station is located directly behind the first-class station across the lot where the buses park.

Where to Stay

Rancho Los Ángeles. km 25 Carretera Escuinapa-Teacapán. ☎ **695/3-2550**. (Reservations: Palmas 1-B, Colonia Los Pinos, 82000 Mazatlán, Sin.; ☎/fax 69/81-7867). 27 rms, 1 bungalow, 13 cabins. A/C or FAN. $40 double on the waterfront; $120 for the 3-bedroom bungalow; $30 double by the main street. AE.

Dr. Ernesto Rivera Gúzman and his sons have created this small resort at the edge of the sea in the midst of coconut groves. The best rooms are in the hacienda-style building with terraces and a clean blue pool beside a long beach. The single rustic bungalow is a few feet from the main building, while other rooms are in a motel-like structure beside the main road to town. There are newly built cabins on the beach and a trailer park for 40 trailers. Boat tours and horseback riding are available. The hotel's small restaurant serves meals on the patio by the pool.

COPALA: AN OLD SILVER TOWN

Popular tours from Mazatlán stop here for lunch only, but Copala is well worth an overnight stay. The town was founded in 1565; from the late 1880s to the early 1900s it was the center of the region's silver-mining boom. When the mines closed, the town became nearly deserted. Today, it's a National Historic Landmark with 600 full-time residents and a part-time community of retired Canadian and U.S. citizens devoted to Copala's picturesque solitude.

Every building in town is painted white, and most have red-tile roofs splashed with fuchsia-colored bougainvillea. Cobblestone streets wind from the entrance to town up slight hills to the main plaza and the Cathedral of San José, built in 1610. The town bustles around noon, when the tour buses arrive and visitors stroll the streets surrounded by small boys selling geodes extracted from the local hills. By 3pm, most of the outsiders have left, and you can wander the streets in peace and visit the century-old cemetery, the ruins of old haciendas, and the neighborhoods of white villas. The town's burros, roosters, and dogs provide the main background noise, and few cars clatter up the streets.

GETTING THERE   Organized tours go to Copala and Concordia (see "Organized Tours," above). Copala is an easy 2-hour drive from Mazatlán, but it is only served by one bus a day, a second-class Autotransportes Concordia bus that departs from the second-class bus station located directly behind the first-class bus station. The fare is $3.50; check the schedule carefully before departing so you don't get stranded in Copala, where there are few places to spend the night. (You may be able to talk one of the tour-bus drivers into giving you a lift back to Mazatlán for a small fee.)

Where to Stay & Dine

Daniel's. At the entrance to town. ☎ **69/86-5736.** 10 units. $25 double (including breakfast).

Daniel's restaurant is Copala's best-known landmark, revered for the sublime banana-cream coconut pie served with nearly every meal. Owner Daniel Garrison restored his uncle's turn-of-the-century home into the restaurant, set against a backdrop of the Sierra Madre foothills. The restaurant fills with guests at lunch, and later in the day it becomes the favored hangout of local expatriates. To the side of the restaurant is a small hotel housing large guest rooms with bathrooms, comfortable beds, fans, and windows looking out to the countryside. Daniel's also offers Copala tours from Mazatlán; call the number listed above or check at the Hotel San Diego in Mazatlán for information. Daniel's is less than a 10-minute walk from town.

RANCHO LAS MORAS

Just 30 minutes northeast of Mazatlán, a deserted agave ranch and tequila distillery has been transformed into a gorgeous guest ranch. The 3,000-acre ranch is a refuge for both humans and animals, from miniature horses to exotic pure-white peacocks. A small white chapel sits atop a slight ridge overlooking the property, while the Sierra Madre rises in the background. The original stables, hacienda, and tequila-factory buildings have been restored with loving attention to detail, and several new casitas are filled with classic Mexican touches. Drop-in visits are not allowed, but tour groups and individuals are welcome to visit the ranch for lunch or a horseback ride, with advance reservations arranged through the Mazatlán office, avenida Camarón Sábalo 204, Suite 6, 82110 Mazatlán, Sinaloa (☎ **800/400-3333** or 69/16-5044; fax 69/16-5045). Rates include three meals and airport transfers, and start at $125 per person, per night, depending on room and season. Cash only, and there are no phones, TVs, or "anything like that."

The ranch is a peaceful, completely secluded hideaway with accommodations that make you feel like you're staying in a luxurious private home. The 11 casitas have air-conditioning and fans, kitchens and bathrooms tiled in bright yellows and blues, upholstered equipal chairs and couches in the living rooms, and carved wooden armoires and dressers in the bedrooms. Each casita has a large porch, where guinea hens tend to roost in the window boxes among blooming flowers. The chef prepares superb regional Mexican cuisine with breads baked daily in a wood-burning beehive oven. Guests are welcome to ride the horses as long as they wish, up the mountain foothills and into towns that still lack automobiles and electricity. There's a pool and tennis courts, and plenty of space to roam in complete solitude.

3 The Costa Alegre: Puerto Vallarta to Barra de Navidad

Costa Alegre, the "happy coast," is the 145-mile stretch of tropical jungle bordering the ocean that runs along Highway 200 between Puerto Vallarta to the north and Manzanillo to the south. Along the way, the two-lane road has turnoffs toward pristine bays and an eclectic array of accommodations that range from rustic to sumptuous. Considered one of Mexico's great undiscovered treasures, this area is becoming a favored hideaway for publicity-fatigued celebrities and those in search of natural seclusion. The area is sometimes referred to as **Costa Careyes** (Turtle Coast), after the first deluxe resort to be located here.) Stops along the Costa Alegre can be an enjoyable day-trip from either Puerto Vallarta or Manzanillo, or an ultimate destination in itself.

ALONG THE TURTLE COAST

CRUZ DE LORETO: A LUXURY ECO-RETREAT   A cross between *Out of Africa* and *Blue Lagoon*, the ✪ **Hotelito Desconocido** (☎ 329/8-5209; fax 329/8-5109), located an hour and a half south of Puerto Vallarta, is ideal for making a pampered escape from it all. This elegantly rustic resort (literally, "unknown hotel") comprises 21 rooms and 9 suites in private bungalows. Each guest room is tastefully decorated with antiques, luxury linens, and an abundance of candles, all inspired by the owner, an Italian fashion designer with a passion for Mexico. Bathrooms are exotic, with cobblestone shower floors and bamboo walls, and private porches provide views of the water and of surrounding palm trees and tropical vegetation. The air is cooled by ceiling fans, and water is solar-heated. Private bungalows sit atop pilings over a clear lagoon that borders an exquisite Pacific beach. Take a private rowboat or a short walk to the *hotelito's* restaurant and bar, where gourmet meals are prepared three times daily.

A small, private beach club with pool offers an alternative to the rather aggressive ocean waters here. Facilities and activities include a fitness room with steam bath, kayaking, windsurfing, horseback riding, mountain bikes, turtle-reserve tours, and billiards. What service lacks in polished professionalism is made up for in enthusiasm.

Be warned: There are no phones, no electricity, no neighboring restaurants, nightclubs, or shopping—only delicious tranquillity for those in search of seclusion. High-season rates are $310 to $390, meals and activities included; low-season, $150 to $200. American Express, MasterCard, and Visa are accepted. The hotel is located at Playa de Mismaloya sin numero, Cruz de Loreto, Tomatlán Jalisco. For reservations call ☎ **800/223-6510** (www.puerto-vallarta.com/hotelito; E-Mail: hotelito@pvnet.com.mx). Check prices when you call for reservations, as rates seem to change every other week.

To get to Cruz de Loreto, take Highway 200 out of Puerto Vallarta. The turnoff is clearly marked, after which you proceed along a bumpy, dirt road another 5 or 6 miles, which takes about 45 minutes.

✪ **LAS ALAMANDAS: AN EXCLUSIVE LUXURY RESORT**   Almost equidistant between Manzanillo (1½ hr.) and Puerto Vallarta (1¾ hr.), a small sign points in the direction of the ocean to Las Alamandas. The dirt road winds for about a mile through a poor village to the guardhouse of **Las Alamandas** (☎ **800/223-6510** in the U.S., or 328/5-5500), part of a 1,500-acre estate and set on 70 acres against low hills. The small cluster of buildings that make up this resort almost spreads to the wide, clean beach. The resort is the most exclusive in Mexico, and its architecture, a blend of Mediterranean, Mexican, and southwestern United States, has been featured in

Architectural Digest, Condé Nast Traveler, and *Vogue.* The furnishings are a stunning blend of Mexican handcrafted furniture, pottery and folk art, and sofa beds and pillows covered in bright textiles from Mexico and Guatemala. While exquisite, the furnishings still achieve a relaxed feel. Only 20 guests can be accommodated at any one time, so the threat of crowds is nonexistent.

All the villas are spacious and have high-pitched tiled roofs, cool tiled floors, and tiled verandas with ocean views. The five villas have several bedrooms (each with its own bathroom) and can be rented separately or as a whole house; preference for reservations is given to guests who rent whole villas. Some villas are on the beach, while some are set back from the beach across a cobblestone plaza.

One restaurant serves all meals. All rooms have TVs with VCRs, but there's no television reception from the outside. Amenities include a weight room, 60-foot swimming pool, lighted tennis court, horses, hiking trails, fishing, boat tours to Río San Nicolás for birding, mountain bikes, and boogie boards. A private 3,000-foot paved landing strip capable of accommodating a King Air turbo prop is on the premises; make advance arrangements for landing. Transportation in the hotel's van to and from Manzanillo ($180 one way) and Puerto Vallarta ($180 one way) can be arranged when you reserve your room. Las Alamandas is located on Highway 200, Manzanillo–Puerto Vallarta (☎ **328/5-5500;** fax 328/5-5027). For information and reservations, call ☎ **800/223-6510** in the United States. High-season rates are $390 to $599 for one room; $1,449 to $2,248 for a whole villa. Low-season, $290 to $420 for one room; $1,010 to $1,520 for a whole villa. American Express, MasterCard, and Visa are accepted.

CAREYES   The resorts **Club Med Playa Blanca** and **Hotel Bel-Air Costa Careyes** are roughly 100 miles south of Puerto Vallarta. They're about a 2-hour drive north of Manzanillo on Highway 200 but only about a 1-hour drive from the Manzanillo airport. If you haven't arranged for transportation through either hotel, taxis from the Manzanillo airport charge around $90 one way for the trip. There are car rentals at both the Manzanillo and Puerto Vallarta airports. While these resorts are completely self-contained, a car is useful for exploring the coast—Barra de Navidad and other resorts, for example—but the hotels can also make such touring arrangements.

Club Med Playa Blanca. Cihuatlan, Careyes, Jal. ☎ **800/258-2633** in the U.S. and Canada, 335/1-0001, or 335/1-0002. Fax 335/1-0004. 295 units. A/C. Weekly all-inclusive, $955 single (no roommate); $865 per person double. Air-inclusive rates also available. AE, DC, MC, V. Closed May–Nov.

On a beautiful cove separated by grand bluffs from the Hotel Bel-Air Costa Careyes, this sienna-colored hotel spills up, around, and down a lovely, lushly landscaped hillside to the beach. Rooms are large and bright and have two full beds. A room with a king-size bed is available upon advance request.

This Club Med has always been popular with active singles and young couples, as the extensive, innovative program of activities would indicate. No facilities are available for children. Numerous special-interest activities are included in the prices. You can avail yourself of the circus workshop and learn to fly from a high trapeze, jump on a trampoline, juggle, and walk the high-wire. There is a PADI scuba-certification class for beginning divers (extra charge), but no exploration dives. Usually there are twice-daily boat excursions that include snorkeling and a picnic at a nearby secluded beach.

Other special-interest activities are offered at an additional charge, among them intensive horseback riding, with 2½ hours of daily ring instruction including lessons in dressage and jumping. There are daily opportunities for excursions to nearby Bird Island (a natural habitat for nesting boobies), out into the ocean for deep-sea fishing, and to nearby Manzanillo, Barra de Navidad, and more. Massage is available as well as arts-and-crafts workshops, with a small charge for materials.

Dining/Diversions: The main dining room, above the bar and pool, is open for all three buffet-style meals and features Mexican and continental food. **El Pelicano,** on the beach, serves extended breakfast and lunch buffets; for two people or more, seafood dinners are served at the table. **El Zapata,** also on the beach, serves steaks. Bars include one by the pool, a disco bar, and a beach bar. The staff provides evening entertainment in a combination of shows and games that involve guests, and there's disco dancing every night.

Amenities: One Olympic-size pool; six tennis courts (four lit for night play); equipment for sailing, kayaking, snorkeling, archery, volleyball, basketball, Ping-Pong, bocce, and billiards; fitness center with aerobics and calisthenics; in-room safes; irons and ironing boards available; token-operated washers and dryers; infirmary; telephone messages are posted.

✪ **Hotel Bel-Air Costa Careyes.** Km 53.5 Hwy. 200, Careyes, Jal. (APDO. Postal 24; Zihuatlan, Jal. 48970) ☎ **800/457-7676** in the U.S. and Canada, or 335/1-0000. Fax 335/1-0100. 51 units and suites. A/C MINIBAR TV TEL. High season $215 double; $340–$385 suite. Low season $195 double; $310–$325 suite. AE, MC, V.

The old Hotel Costa Careyes was gutted to create this totally luxurious hotel in a secluded setting facing the ocean. The first glimpse you see as you step into the breezy open "lobby" is the expansive grass and garden-filled lawn shaded by enormous palm trees leading to the ocean and free-form pool. It's both rustic and sophisticated, with the room facades awash in scrubbed pastels forming a U around the center lawn. Earthy but elegant Mexican tiles and decorative accents give each spacious room a dramatically luxurious feel, from the colony shutters to the white-tile floors, handsome loomed bedspreads, and colorful pillows. Some rooms have balconies; all have ocean views, robes and hair dryers, and small refrigerators. Twenty rooms have private pools. The hotel is a member of the Small Luxury Hotels of the World group.

The hotel offers a number of special-interest activities for guests. Named after the hawksbill turtle ("carey" in Spanish), the hotel, with a staff biologist, sponsors a "save the turtle" program in which guests can participate between July and December. You can also arrange a birding expedition to nearby Bird Island, a natural habitat for nesting boobies between July and September. Fishing and boat tours to nearby beaches are also available, as are horseback excursions and riding lessons at the equestrian center. Polo clubs from around the world converge here for polo season, December through April.

Dining/Diversions: Two restaurant/bars, both casually chic and with international menus, serve all meals in an open setting beside the beach and pool. "Just for Kids" is a program of activities for children. A movie theater provides evening entertainment, and there's a library well stocked with reading material.

Amenities: The resort has a large, free-form pool by the ocean and a fully equipped, state-of-the-art spa with massage, loofah scrub, wax, hot and cold plunge, steam and sauna, and weight equipment. Guests also have privileges at the superexclusive El Tamarindo Resort, 25 miles south, where there's a fabulous mountaintop golf course overlooking the ocean. El Tamarindo was damaged during the 1996 hurricane and is still only minimally open, but the golf course is open and in great shape. Laundry, purified tap water, room service, and helicopter or limo transportation from the Manzanillo airport can be arranged at an additional price.

TENACATITA BAY   Located 60 minutes (33 miles) north of Manzanillo airport, this jewel of a bay is accessed by a 5-mile dirt road, passing through a small village set among banana and coconut palms. Sandy, serene beaches are tucked into coves around the bay, and dolphins playing along the beachfront are a common sight; a coastal lagoon is filled with exotic birds. Swimming and snorkeling are good here, and the bay is a popular stop for luxury yachts cruising down the coast. Just south of the entrance to Tenacatita is a sign directing you to the area's accommodations, the all-inclusive **Blue Bay Los Ángeles Locos** and **Punta Serena** resorts, as well as the exclusive **El Tamarindo.** There is no commercial or shopping area, and dining options outside of your hotel are limited to a restaurant or two that may emerge during the winter months (high season). Relax, that's what you're here for.

Blue Bay Village Los Ángeles Locos. Km 20 Carretera Federal 200, Tenacatita, 48989 Municipio de la Huerta, Jal. ☎ **800/BLUE BAY** in the U.S., 335/1-5020, or 335/1-5100. Fax 335/1-5050. www.BlueBayResorts.com. E-Mail: LAL@bluebayresorts.com. 205 units. A/C TV TEL. High season $190 double. Low season $130–$150 double. Rates are all-inclusive. AE, DC, MC, V.

Set on a 3-mile stretch of sandy beach, Blue Bay Village Los Ángeles Locos concentrates an abundance of activities and entertainment in the midst of the seclusion of Tenacatita Bay. Water sports, tennis, horseback riding, an extensive activities program, and an ample selection of dining and entertainment options offer guests excellent value. It's a good choice for families and groups of friends. All rooms have ocean views, with either balconies or terraces. The three-story hotel is basic in its decor and amenities, but clean and comfortable. The attraction here is the wide array of activities on-site.

Two restaurants and a snack bar offer the option of ample buffets or à la carte dining. **La Trattoria** is set into a bluff overlooking the beach and bay, featuring specialty Italian cuisine. Three bars mean unlimited drinks almost anytime you feel the urge. There are nightly shows and entertainment. La Largata Disco is a little on the dark and smoky side, but can really rock, depending on the crowd—it's basically the only option on the bay.

A large pool for adults and one for kids are adjacent to the beach. Also included in the price of your stay are tennis (three courts), a Jungle River–cruise excursion, basketball court, exercise room, activities program, kids' club, horseback riding, windsurfing, kayaks, Hobie cats, and pool tables. Laundry, Massage services, travel agency, baby-sitting, and car rental are available for an extra charge.

✪ **Punta Serena.** Km 20 Carretera Federal 200, Tenacatita, 48989 Municipio de la Huerta, Jal. ☎ **800/551-2558** in the U.S., or 335/1-5100. Fax 335/1-5050. www. PuntaSerena.com. E-Mail: info@puntaserena.com. 24 smoke-free units. A/C. High season $135–$145. Low season $100–$125 double. Rates are all-inclusive. AE, DC, MC, V.

Punta Serena is a refuge for relaxation and renewal. Set on a mountain overlooking this virgin bay, it's an adults-only holistic resort with a complete offering of services to either put you into a total state of relaxation, or awaken some new energy inside. There seems to be a natural balance of positive energy here, with the lulling sound of the surf complimenting the serene atmosphere.

Punta Serena is one of the only resorts in Mexico truly geared for spiritual renewal, and does an excellent job of offering enough without making nonenthusiasts feel uncomfortable. Yoga, tai chi, and chi kung classes, native Aztec *Temazcal* (sweat lodge) ceremonies, and guided meditation sessions are offered with a daily-changing schedule. Too much introspection for your taste? Of course, it's also perfectly OK to simply immerse yourself in a mindless read while lolling in one of the two hot tubs that are nestled into the side of the cliff overlooking the Pacific blue below.

All rooms and suites are set in two-story bungalows, with ocean views and either balconies or large terraces with hammocks. Smoke-free and spacious, the rooms are very basic but both comforting and comfortable. One open-air restaurant serves three meals daily featuring excellent buffets of healthful selections, fresh juices, and vegetarian cuisine—it's the one buffet that I've ever really enjoyed. Palapa-topped, it has a stunning view of the bay, and a constant breeze. Yes, drinks are served with meals, also included in your stay.

There are cliff-side hot tubs, a small but striking pool, and a private beach—one of the only allowable nude (optional) beaches in Mexico. Take a massage in the open-air massage area, or a more private room. A library and video corner are part of the common areas, and there's a sauna and small but well-equipped gym. Guests have access to the facilities at the neighboring Blue Bay Village, if things get too quiet.

BARRA DE NAVIDAD & MELAQUE

Only 30 minutes north of Manzanillo's airport by car, or 1½ hours by bus north of downtown (65 miles), this pair of modest beach villages (only 3 miles apart) has been attracting vacationers for decades. Barra has a few bricked or cobblestone streets, good budget hotels and restaurants, and funky beach charm, all next to the superluxurious Grand Bay Hotel located on a bluff across the inlet from Barra. Melaque has a lineup of budget hotels both on and off the beach, fewer restaurants, and no funky charm, though the beach is as wide and more beautiful than Barra's. Both villages appeal to those looking for quaint, quiet and inexpensive hideaways, rather than modern, sophisticated destinations. The Grand Bay Hotel, with its five-star quality and 27-hole golf course, provides a whole new dimension to vacationing in Barra.

In the 17th century, Barra de Navidad was a harbor for the Spanish fleet, and it was from here that galleons first set off in 1564 to find China. Located on a gorgeous crescent-shaped bay with curious rock outcroppings, Barra de Navidad and neighboring Melaque are connected by a continuous beach on the same wide bay and boast an easy pace. It's safe to say that the only time Barra and Melaque hotels are full is during Easter and Christmas weeks. **Barra de Navidad** has the most charm, most tree-shaded streets, best restaurants, most stores, and the best conviviality among locals and tourists. Barra is very laid-back; there's definitely nothing flashy about it, which is something faithful returnees adore. Other than the new Grand Bay Hotel on the cliff across the waterway in what is called Isla Navidad (although it's not on an island), nothing is new or modern. But there's a bright edge to Barra now, with more good restaurants; a small, growing, nightlife; new paint and restored buildings after the 1996 earthquake; and streets that are being bricked little by little. **Melaque,** on the other hand, is larger, rather sun-baked, treeless, and lacking in attractions. It does, however, have plenty of cheap hotels available for longer stays and a few restaurants. Although the beach between the two is continuous, Melaque's beach, with deep sand, is more beautiful than Barra's, where the sand is rather packed down due to the particular wave action Barra receives.

Although the main part of the long-awaited **Isla de Navidad Resort** project is finished across the narrow inlet from Barra's main pier, the area's pace hasn't quickened as fast as expected. But the fabulous 27-hole golf course is complete, and the superluxurious Grand Bay Hotel is finished. Golf-course homes are ready, and hillside homes and condominiums are following. .

ESSENTIALS Getting There Buses from Manzanillo frequently run the route up the coast along Highway 200 on their way to Puerto Vallarta and Guadalajara. Most stop in the central villages of both Barra de Navidad and Melaque. From the

Manzanillo airport, it's only around 30 minutes to Barra. Puerto Vallarta is a 3-hour (by car) to 5-hour (by bus) ride north on Highway 200 from Barra. From Manzanillo, the highway twists through some of the Pacific Coast's most beautiful mountains covered in oak and coconut palm and acres of banana plantations.

VISITOR INFORMATION   The **tourism office** for both Barra de Navidad and Melaque is in Barra on Jalisco 67 between Veracruz and Mazatlán (☎/fax **335/ 5-5100**). The office is open Monday through Friday from 9am to 5pm. The **Travel Agency Isla Navidad Tours** at Veracruz 204-A (☎ **335/5-5665** or 335/5-5666; fax 335/5-5667), can handle arrangements for plane tickets and sells ETN (deluxe) bus tickets from Manzanillo to Puerto Vallarta and Guadalajara. It's open Monday through Saturday from 9am to 8pm. American Express, MasterCard, and Visa are accepted.

ORIENTATION   In Barra, the main beachfront street, **Legazpi,** is lined with hotels and restaurants. From the bus station, beachfront hotels are 2 blocks straight ahead across the central plaza. Two blocks behind the bus station and to the right is the lagoon side, with its main street, **Morelos/Veracruz,** and more hotels and restaurants. Few streets are marked, but 10 minutes of wandering will acquaint you with the village's entire layout.

ACTIVITIES ON & OFF THE BEACH   Swimming and enjoying the attractive beach and views of the bay take up most tourists' time. Hiring a small boat for a coastal ride or to go fishing can be done in two ways. Go toward the malecón on calle Veracruz until you reach the tiny boatmen's cooperative with fixed prices posted on the wall. You can also walk two buildings farther to the water taxi ramp. The inexpensive water taxi is the best option for going to Colimilla (5 min. away) or across the inlet (3 min.) to the Grand Bay Hotel. The water taxis make the rounds regularly, so if you're at Colimilla, all you have to do is wait and a water taxi will be along shortly. At the Cooperative, a 30-minute **tour around the lagoon** costs $12, and a tour out on the sea costs $25. **Sportfishing** is $125 for up to four people for half a day in a small *panga* (open fiberglass boat like they use for the water taxis). **Waterskiing** costs $15 per hour.

Unusual **area tours, house, condo, and apartment rentals,** and **sports- equipment rental** can be arranged through **The Crazy Cactus,** Jalisco 8 (☎/fax **335/ 5-6099**), operated by Trayce Ross and located half a block inland from the town church on Legazpi. She rents bicycles, boogie boards, snorkeling equipment, life jackets, kayaks, and mopeds. Among the unique Crazy Cactus tours is one along the coast to lagoons and mangroves and another to nearby small towns for market days and shopping. She also arranges horseback riding near Melaque. (The store may be closed from May through Oct.) **Paraíso Pacífico Tours,** Veracruz 94 (☎ **335/ 5-6319;** fax 335/5-5237), operated by Mari Blanca Pérez, offers up-to-date maps of both Barra and Melaque; a good lineup of nearby boat excursions for snorkeling, diving, and sunning at beaches north near Tenacatita; horseback riding near Melaque; an interesting trip to Bird Island near Chamela to see nesting boobies; shopping tours to Manzanillo; a daylong trip to Colima City; a day-trip to a village devoted to marble mining and making huaraches (leather sandals); a very long day-trip to Guadalajara and Tlaquepaque; sunset cruises; and fishing (a half day for $128 in a *panga* or $300 in a yacht).

For **golf,** the Grand Bay Hotel's beautiful and challenging 27-hole, 7,053-yard, par- 72 course is open to the public. Hotel guests pay greens fees of $65 for 18 holes, or $80 for 27 holes, while nonguests pay $80 and $100, respectively; the prices include

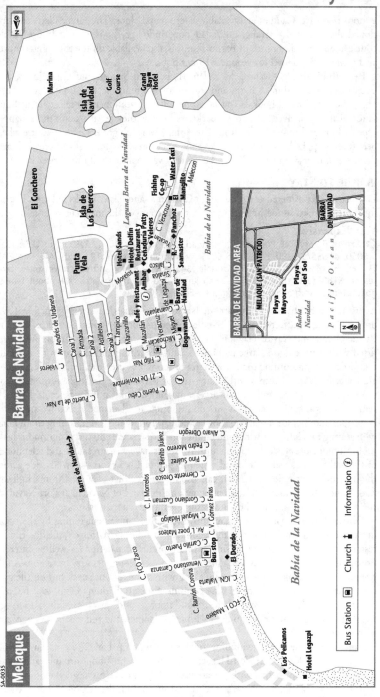

Barra de Navidad

Melaque

Marina

Isla de Navidad

Golf Course

Grand Bay Hotel

El Conchero

Isla de Los Puercos

Laguna Barra de Navidad

Punta Vela

Hotel Sands

Hotel Delfín

Restaurant Y

Cenaduría Patty

Water Taxi

Fishing Co-op

El Manglito

Malecon

C. Veracruz

C. Pancho?

Veleros

Seamaster

Bahía de la Navidad

Morelos

C. Yucatán

Jalisco

Sinaloa

Café y Restaurant Ambar

C. Guanajuato

C. Veracruz de Legazpi

Barra de Navidad

Bogavante

C. Miguel

C. Michoacán

Av. Andrés de Urdaneta

C. Veleros

Canal 1

C. Armada

Canal 2

C. Astilleros

Canal 3

C. Tampico

C. Manzanillo

C. Mazatlán

Filip Nas

C. 21 De Noviembre

C. Puerto Cebu

C. Puerto de la Nav.

Barra de Navidad →

C. J. Morelos

C. FCO Zarco

C. Benito Juárez

C. Clemente Orozco

C. Pedro Moreno

C. Pino Suárez

C. Alvaro Obregón

C. Gordiano Guzmán

C. Miguel Hidalgo

Av. L. pez Mateos

C. V. Gómez Farías

C. Carrillo Puerto

Bus stop

El Dorado

Venustiano Carranza

C. IGN. Vallarta

C. Ramón Corona

C. FCO. Madero

Bahía de la Navidad

Los Pelícanos

Hotel Legazpi

| Bus Station ▣ | Church ✝ | Information ⓘ |

BARRA DE NAVIDAD AREA

BARRA DE NAVIDAD

MELAQUE (SAN PATRICIO)

Playa Mayorca

Playa del Sol

Bahía Navidad

Pacific Ocean

SA-0035

a motorized cart. Caddies are available as are rental clubs. The Crazy Cactus (mentioned above) can also arrange golf at El Tamarindo's gorgeous, mountaintop, 9-hole course about 20 miles north of Barra. Tennis is also available on the three grass courts at the Grand Bay Hotel for around $18 per hour.

Beer Bob's Books, avenida Mazatlán 61, between Sinaloa and Guanajuato, is a book-lovers' institution in Barra and sort of a community service Bob does for fun. His policy of "leave a book if you take one" allows vacationers to select from thousands of neatly shelved trade paperbacks, as long as they leave a book in exchange. Open Monday through Friday from 1 to 4pm. (Beer Bob got his name because when beer was cheap, he kept a cooler stocked and book-browsers could sip and read. When the price of beer went up, Bob put the cooler away, but he's still called Beer Bob.)

WHERE TO STAY

Low season is considered any time except Christmas and Easter weeks in Barra. Except for those 2 weeks, it doesn't hurt to ask for a discount at the inexpensive hotels.

Very Expensive

✪ **Grand Bay Hotel.** Puerto de la Navidad, Col. ☎ **888/80-GRAND** in the U.S., 335/5-5050, or 335/5-6390. Fax 335/5-6071. www.grandbay.com. 191 units. A/C MINIBAR TV TEL. High season $279–$364 double; $450–$650 junior and executive suites. Low season $180–$225 double; $527–$645 junior and executive suites. Ask about tennis, golf, fishing, and honeymoon packages. AE, DC, MC, V.

Across the yacht channel from Barra de Navidad, this luxurious hotel opened in 1997 on 1,200 acres next to the hotel's 27-hole golf course. It overlooks the village, bay, the Pacific Ocean, and Navidad lagoon. The hotel's very large rooms are sumptuously outfitted with marble floors, large bathrooms, and beautiful hand-carved wood furnishings. Prices vary according to view and size of room, but even the more modest rooms are large. Each room comes with a king-size or two double beds, glass-top desk, in-room security box, bathrobes, hair dryers, magnified makeup mirrors, cable TV with remote control, ceiling fans plus air-conditioning, and balcony. Executive suites are enormous and include a separate shower and bathtub, living room, dining room table with seating for eight, bar with butler's kitchen and separate entry, and enormous bedroom. Junior suites lack the dining area. All suites have a steam sauna and telephones in the bathroom as well as a sound system. The hotel is a short water-taxi ride across the inlet from Barra de Navidad; it can also be reached by paved road from Highway 200. Although the hotel bills itself as being on the Island of Navidad at Port Navidad, the port is the marina, and the hotel is on a peninsula, not an island.

Dining/Diversions: Three restaurants offer either convenient dining by the pool, in a casual restaurant overlooking the lagoon, or fine dining. **Alfonso's,** the fine-dining restaurant, features Mexican cuisine with European preparation as well as international dishes. There's a lobby bar and swim-up pool bar—hours vary by season. A full restaurant is available at the golf club, along with a convenient snack hut on the golf course serving snacks and drinks. The **Club de Niños** (Children's Club) is a specially outfitted, brightly colored area on the ground floor set aside just for children up to age 11. A special staff entertains children with crafts, games, and other activities between 9am and 6pm.

Amenities: One main swimming pool with swim-up bar; 27-hole, par-72 golf course designed by Robert Von Hagge; golf club with pro shop, driving range, and restaurant; 150-slip marina with private yacht club; three lighted, grass tennis courts with stadium seating. The hotel's beach is narrow and on the lagoon. A better beach is opposite the hotel on the bay in Barra de Navidad. A full spa is scheduled to open in late 1999. 24-hour concierge, room service, boutique, beauty salon, high chairs, cribs, and complimentary round-trip transportation between the Manzanillo airport and the hotel. Fishing, boat tours, and other excursions can be arranged.

Inexpensive

✪ **Hotel Barra de Navidad.** Legazpi 250, 48987 Barra de Navidad, Jal. ☎ **335/5-5122.** Fax 335/5-5303. 60 units. FAN. $42–$45 double. MC, V.

At the northern end of Legazpi, this popular and comfortable hotel on the beach has friendly management and some rooms with fine balconies overlooking the beach and bay. Other, less-expensive rooms afford only a street view. A nice swimming pool is on the street level to the right of the lobby.

Hotel Delfín. Morelos 23, 48987 Barra de Navidad, Jal. ☎ **335/5-5068.** Fax 335/5-6020. 25 rms, 3 apts. FAN. High season $28 double. Ask about low-season discounts. MC, V. Free parking in the front.

One of Barra's better-maintained hotels, the four-story (no elevator) Delfín is on the landward side of the lagoon. It offers pleasant, basic, well-cared-for, and well-lit rooms. Each has red-tile floors and either a double, two double, or two single beds. The tiny courtyard, with a small pool and lounge chairs, is shaded by an enormous rubber tree. From the fourth floor there's a view of the lagoon. A breakfast buffet is served from 8:30 to 10:30am on the second-level terrace, and dinner is served between 6 and 10:30pm (see "Where to Dine," below).

Hotel Sands. Morelos 24, 48987 Barra de Navidad, Jal. ☎ and fax: **335/5-5018.** 36/16-2859. 45 units. FAN. High season $35 double. Low season $27 double. Rates include breakfast and parking. (Discounts for stays of 1 week or more.) MC, V.

The colonial-style Sands, catercorner from the Hotel Delfín (see above) on the lagoon side at Jalisco, offers small but homey rooms with red-tile floors and windows with both screens and glass. Bathrooms have just been remodeled with new tiles and fixtures. Lower rooms look onto a public walkway and wide courtyard; upstairs rooms are brighter. Twelve rooms (suites or bungalows) have air-conditioning and kitchenette facilities. In back there is a pool with a Jacuzzi overlooking the lagoon beach, and water-sports equipment is available for rent. The hotel is known for its high-season happy hour from 2 to 6pm at the pool terrace bar beside the lagoon. On weekends from 9pm to 4am, an adjacent patio "disco" hosts live mariachi music for dancing and libations. Breakfast is served from 7:30am to noon. There's tennis, a 24-hour watchman, fishing trips can be arranged, and tours are available to nearby beaches.

WHERE TO DINE

Café y Restaurant Ambar. Av. Veracruz 101-A. No phone. Breakfast $2.80–$4.50; crepes $4–$7; main courses $4–$12. Daily 8am–11pm (happy hour 1pm–midnight). Closed Sept. CREPES/VEGETARIAN/MEXICAN.

At the corner of Veracruz and Jalisco, opposite the Restaurant y Ceñaduría Patty, you'll find this cozy thatched-roof, upstairs restaurant open to the breezes. The crepes are named after towns in France; the delicious crepe Paris, for example, is filled with chicken, potatoes, spinach, and green sauce. International specialties include pepper steak in a wine or mushroom sauce, mixed brochettes, quiche, and Greek salad. For something lighter, try a seafood or fruit salad.

✪ **El Manglito.** Veracruz, near the Fishing Cooperative. No phone. Main courses $4–$8. Daily 9am–11pm. SEAFOOD/INTERNATIONAL.

Located on the placid lagoon, with a view of the palatial Grand Bay Hotel, El Manglito serves home-style Mexican food and enjoys a growing number of repeat diners. The whole fried fish accompanied by drawn garlic butter, boiled vegetables, rice, and french fries is a crowd-pleaser. Other enticements include boiled shrimp, chicken in orange sauce, and shrimp salad.

Hotel Delfín. Morelos 23. ☎ **335/5-5068.** Breakfast buffet $3.25–$3.75; fixed-price dinner $4–$5; main courses $2.85–$5. MC, V. Daily 8:30am–10:30am and 6–10:30pm. BREAKFAST/INTERNATIONAL.

The second-story terrace of this small hotel is a pleasant place to begin the day in Barra. The self-serve buffet offers an assortment of fresh fruit, juices, granola, yogurt, milk, pastries, and unlimited coffee. Eggs, and the delicious banana pancakes—for which the restaurant is known—are made to order and included in the buffet price. For dinner, you can choose from the à la carte menu or opt for the fixed-price menu. The latter includes salad, rice or potatoes, a main course usually with an international twist, and coffee or tea.

✪ **Restaurant Bar Ramón.** Legazpi 260. ☎ **335/5-6485.** Breakfast $2–$4; main courses $3–$7. Daily 7am–11pm. SEAFOOD/MEXICAN.

Ramón ran the excellent restaurant in the Hotel Barra de Navidad until the rent went up. Then he staked out a new place under two giant, peaked, thatched-palapa roofs across the street from the hotel. Now it seems like everybody eats at Ramón's, where the chips and fresh salsa arrive unbidden, service is prompt and friendly, and the food is especially good. Try the fresh fish with french fries or any of the daily specials that might feature vegetable soup or chicken fried steak.

Seamaster. Legazpi at Yucatán. No phone. Daily noon–11pm. SEAFOOD/INTERNATIONAL.

This cheery and colorful restaurant on the beach facing the ocean is a great place for sunsets and margaritas or a meal any time. Specialties include steamed shrimp (peeled or unpeeled), fried calamari, barbecue chicken, ribs and steak, plus chicken wings, hamburgers, and other sandwiches. Service is excellent.

BARRA DE NAVIDAD AFTER DARK   When dusk arrives, visitors and locals alike find a cool spot to sit outside, sip cocktails, and chat. Many outdoor restaurants and stores in Barra fill the bill for this relaxing way to end the day, adding extra tables and chairs to accommodate drop-ins. It's very friendly.

During high season there is always happy hour from 2 to 6pm at the **Hotel Sands** poolside/lagoon-side bar. **Sunset Bar and Restaurant,** facing the bay, at the corner of Legazpi and Jalisco, is a favorite for sunset watching, and afterwards for dancing to live or taped music. In the same vein, **Chips Restaurant,** on the second floor facing the ocean at the corner of Yucatán and Legazpi near the southern end of the malecón, has an excellent sunset vista. Live music follows the last rays of light, and patrons stay for hours.

At the **Disco El Galleón,** in the Hotel Sands on calle Morelos, cushioned benches and cement tables encircle the round dance floor. It's all open-air, but garden walls restrict air flow and there are a few fans. It serves drinks only. Admission is $4, and it's open on Friday and Saturday from 9pm to 2am.

A VISIT TO MELAQUE (SAN PATRICIO)

For a change of scenery, you may want to wander over to Melaque (also known as San Patricio), 3 miles from Barra on the same bay. You can walk on the beach from Barra or take one of the frequent local buses from the bus station near the main square in Barra. The bus is marked MELAQUE. To return to Barra, take the bus marked CIHUATLÁN.

Melaque's pace is even more laid-back than Barra's, and though it's a larger village, it seems smaller. It has fewer restaurants and less to do. It has more hotels or "bungalows," as they are usually called here, but few with the charm of those in Barra. If Barra hotels are full on a holiday weekend, then Melaque would be a second choice for accommodations. The paved road ends where the town begins. A few yachts bob in the harbor, and the palm-lined beach is gorgeous.

If you come by bus from Barra, you can exit the bus anywhere in town or stay on until the last stop, which is the bus station in the middle of town, a block from the beach. Restaurants and hotels line the beach; it's impossible to get lost, but some orientation will help. Coming into town from the main road, you'll be on the town's main street, **avenida López Mateos.** You'll pass the main square on the way to the waterfront, where there's a trailer park. The street going left (southeast) along the bay is **avenida Gómez Farías;** the one going right (northwest) is avenida Miguel Ochoa López.

WHERE TO EAT   At the north end of Melaque beach is **Los Pelicanos.** Friendly ex-Pennsylvanian Phil Garcia, along with spouse Trine, prepares meals like you might find at home. During high season there might be pork roast and mashed potatoes along with the usual seafood specialties. Year-round you can find burritos, nachos, and hamburgers. The tender fried squid is delectable with one of Phil's savory sauces. Order lobster 24 hours in advance. Many Barra guests come here to stake a place on the beach and use the restaurant as headquarters for sipping and nipping. It's peaceful to watch the pelicans bobbing just in front of this restaurant. The restaurant is at the far end of the bay before the **Hotel Legazpi** (☎ 335/5-5397), which by the way is a pleasant place to stay. The restaurant is open daily from 9am to 7pm.

In addition to the Los Pelicanos, there are many rustic **palapa restaurants** in town on the beach and farther along the bay at the end of the beach. You can settle in on the beach and use one of the restaurants as your base for drinking and dining.

4 Manzanillo

160 miles SE of Puerto Vallarta; 167 SW of Guadalajara; 40 miles SE of Barra de Navidad

One of Mexico's most vibrant commercial ports, Manzanillo has also developed, somewhat paradoxically, as a serene resort. Luxury properties, a diversity of sporting activities, and several interesting side trips within a few hours' drive make it popular for travelers looking for a mix of seclusion and exploration.

The geography surrounding Manzanillo is one of its principal attractions: emerald tropical mountains and the cobalt blue of the Pacific Ocean. The two most popular pastimes are golf, with courses that showcase the view, and sportfishing. Sailfish run almost year-round and are the featured catch in a pair of annual tournaments held each November.

Manzanillo is at the southern end of the unspoiled Costa Alegre, which begins in Puerto Vallarta to the north. This stretch of coast is in the process of being discovered as one of Mexico's seaside treasures, with tropical-fruit plantations and jungle landscape bordering the coastal highway. Within an hour or two's drive north from Manzanillo, pristine beaches are tucked into isolated bays along with a handful of exclusive, secluded, and very unique resorts. (See Section 3, above, for more information on Costa Alegre.) In addition to the beach attractions along the Costa Alegre, excellent, well-maintained roads connect Manzanillo to the colonial cities of Guadalajara and Colima.

Manzanillo itself is fairly neatly divided into two zones: the downtown commercial port and the understated resort zone to the north. The downtown zone is dominated by its busy harbor and rail connections to Mexico's interior. A recent beautification program has added more landscaping and parks to this district. A visit to the town's waterfront zócalo provides a glimpse into local life. Most resort hotels and the golf course are located north of town where two golden sand bays are separated by the Santiago Peninsula.

ESSENTIALS

GETTING THERE & DEPARTING   **By Plane**   **Aeromexico** and its sister airline, **Aerolitoral** (☎ **800/237-6639;** 333/3-2424 at the airport) as well as **Mexicana** (☎ **800/531-7921;** 333/3-2323 at the airport) offer flights to and from Mexico City, Guadalajara, Monterrey, and to connecting cities in the United States and Canada. **America West** (☎ **800/235-9292**) flies from Phoenix, and **Aero California** (☎ **800/237-6225** or 333/4-1414) has flights from Los Angeles. Ask a travel agent about the numerous charters that operate in winter from the States.

The **Playa de Oro International Airport** is 25 miles (45 min.) northwest of town. The colectivo-van airport service is available from the airport, with returns arranged by your hotel. Reservations for return trips should be arranged 1 day in advance. The colectivo fare is based on zones and ranges from $6 to $8 to most hotels. Private taxi service between the airport and downtown area is around $20. The following rental-car companies have counters in the airport, open during flight arrivals and departures: **Avis** (☎ **800/331-1212** or 333/3-0194), **Budget** (☎ **800/527-0700** or 333/3-1445), and **AutoRent** (☎ **333/32580**); they will also deliver a car to your hotel. Daily rates run $45 to $75, desirable only if you plan on exploring surrounding cities and the Costa Alegre beaches.

By Car   **Coastal Highway 200** leads from Acapulco and Puerto Vallarta. From Guadalajara, take Highway 54 through Colima (outside Colima you can switch to a toll road, which is faster but less scenic, into Manzanillo).

By Bus   Buses run to Barra de Navidad (1½ hr. north), Puerto Vallarta (5 hr. north), Colima (1½ hr.), and Guadalajara (4½ hr.), with deluxe service and numerous daily departures. Manzanillo's **Central Camionera** (bus station) is about 12 long blocks east of town. If you follow Hidalgo east, the Camionera will be on your right.

VISITOR INFORMATION   The **tourism office** (☎ **333/3-2277** or 333/3-2264; fax 333/31426) in Manzanillo is on the Costera Miguel de la Madrid 4960, km 8.5. It's open Monday through Friday from 9am to 3:30pm.

CITY LAYOUT   The town lies at one end of a 7-mile-long beach facing Manzanillo Bay. The beach has four sections—**Playa Las Brisas, Playa Azul, Playa Salahua,** and **Playa Las Hadas.** The northern terminus of the beaches is the high, rocky, **Santiago Peninsula.** Santiago is 7 miles from downtown; it's the site of many beautiful homes and the best hotel in the area, Las Hadas, as well as the **Mantarraya Golf Course** owned by Las Hadas. The peninsula juts out into the bay separating Manzanillo Bay from Santiago Bay. The beach, **Playa Las Hadas,** is on the south side of the peninsula facing Manzanillo Bay, and **Playa Audiencia** is on the north side facing Santiago Bay. There's also the town of Santiago, which is opposite the turnoff to Las Hadas.

Motorist Advisory: Carjackings

Motorists planning to follow Highway 200 south from Manzanillo toward Lázaro Cárdenas and Ixtapa should be aware of reports of random bus and motorist hijackings on that route, especially around Playa Azul. Before heading in that direction, ask locals and the tourism office about the current state of affairs.

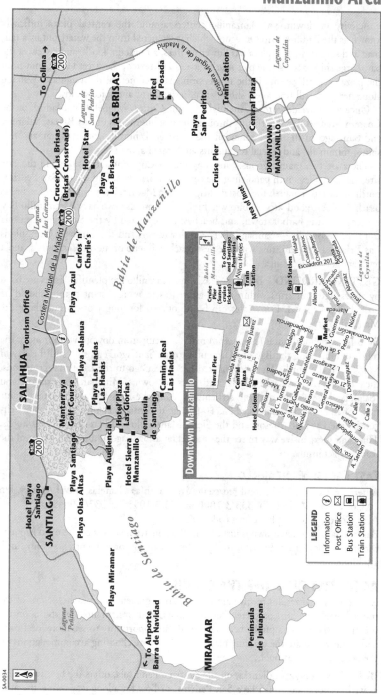

Manzanillo Area

To Colima → MEX 200

LAS BRISAS

Laguna de la Madrid

Laguna de Cuyutlan

Costera Miguel de la Madrid

Hotel La Posada

Train Station

Central Plaza

DOWNTOWN MANZANILLO

Playa San Pedrito

Cruise Pier

Area of Inset

Laguna de San Pedrito

Hotel Star

Crucero Las Brisas (Brisas Crossroads)

Playa Las Brisas

Bahía de Manzanillo

Carlos 'n Charlie's

Playa Azul

Laguna de las Garzas

SALAHUA Tourism Office

Costera Miguel de la Madrid

Playa Salahua

MEX 200

Playa Las Hadas Las Hadas

Camino Real Las Hadas

Mantarraya Golf Course

Hotel Plaza Las Glorias

Península de Santiago

Playa Audiencia

Hotel Sierra Manzanillo

MEX 200

Playa Santiago

SANTIAGO

Hotel Playa Santiago

Playa Olas Altas

Playa Miramar

Bahía de Santiago

Laguna Peñitas

← To Airporte Barra de Navidad

MIRAMAR

Península de Juluapan

SA-0034

N

Downtown Manzanillo

Bahía de Manzanillo

Cruise Pier (inset: cruise tickets)

To Colima and Santiago Peninsula

Niños Héroes

Train Station

Bus Station

Escuadron 201

Hidalgo

Cuauhtémoc

Juarez Chavaztepec

Aptda Colorada

Laguna de Cuyutlan

Gral. Amado Nervo

Gral. Cueto

Jesús Ataraz

Alameda

Naval Pier

Avenida Morelos

Central Plaza

21 de Marzo

Benito Juarez

Bocanegra

México

Coliuas

Hotel Colonial

Allende

Independencia

Hidalgo

Allende

5 de Mayo

V. Guerrero

Market

Circunvalación

Pedro Núñez

Camillo Puerto

Cuauhtémoc

Zaragoza

I. Zaragoza

México

Gral. Gral. Anaya

B. Dominguez

Pino Suárez

G. G. Torres Quintero

Nicolás Bravo

M. Galindo

General Anaya

E. Zapata

Calle 1

Calle 2

Corregidora

Fco. Villa

E. Zapata

A. Serdan

LEGEND

ⓘ Information

✉ Post Office

🚌 Bus Station

🚉 Train Station

333

Activity in downtown Manzanillo centers around the **central plaza,** officially known as the Jardín Álvaro Obregón, which is separated from the waterfront by a railroad and shipyards. The plaza has flowering trees, a fountain, kiosk, and a view of the bay. Large ships dock at the pier nearby. **avenida México,** the street leading out from the plaza's central gazebo, is the town's principal commercial thoroughfare. Walking along here you will find a few shops, small restaurants, and juice stands.

Once you leave downtown, the highway (the Costera Miguel de la Madrid, or the **Costera Madrid,** for short) runs through the neighborhoods of **Las Brisas, Salahua,** and **Santiago** to the hotel zones on the Santiago Peninsula and at Miramar. Shell shops, minimalls, and several restaurants are located along the way.

There are two main lagoons: One, **Laguna de Cuyutlán,** almost behind the city, stretches for miles south paralleling the coast; and the other, **Laguna de San Pedrito,** north of the city, parallels the Costera Miguel de la Madrid; it's behind Playa Las Brisas beach. Both are good sites for bird watching. There are also two bays: **Manzanillo Bay** encompasses the harbor, town, and beaches; it's separated by the Santiago Peninsula from the second bay—Santiago. Between downtown and the Santiago Peninsula is **Las Brisas,** a flat peninsula with the best beach, a lineup of inexpensive hotels, and a few very good restaurants.

GETTING AROUND   By Taxi   Taxis in Manzanillo are plentiful. Fares are fixed by zones; rates for trips within town, as well as to more distant points, should be posted at your hotel. Daily rates can be negotiated for longer drives outside of the Manzanillo area.

By Bus   The local buses (*camionetas*) make a circuit from downtown in front of the train station, along the Bay of Manzanillo to the Santiago Peninsula and the Bay of Santiago to the north. The ones marked LAS BRISAS go to the Las Brisas crossroads, then to the Las Brisas Peninsula, and back to town; "Miramar," "Santiago," and "Salahua" buses go to outlying settlements along the bays and to most restaurants mentioned below. Buses marked LAS HADAS go to Santiago Peninsula and make a circuit by the Las Hadas resort and the Sierra Manzanillo and Plaza Las Glorias hotels. This is an inexpensive way to see the coast as far as Santiago and to take a tour of the Santiago Peninsula.

FAST FACTS: MANZANILLO

American Express   The local representative is **Bahías Gemelas Travel Agency,** km 10 Costera M. Madrid (☎ **333/3-1000** or 333/3-1053; fax 333/3-0649).

Area Code   The telephone area code is **333.**

Bank   Banamex downtown is just off the plaza on avenida México; it's open Monday through Friday from 9:30am to 5pm but changes foreign currency only until 12:30pm.

ACTIVITIES ON & OFF THE BEACH

Activities in Manzanillo revolve around the area's golden-sand beaches. Most of the resort hotels here are completely self-contained, with restaurants and sports on the premises. Manzanillo's public beaches provide an opportunity to see more local color and scenery, and are the daytime playground for those choosing accommodations off the beach or without pools.

BEACHES   Playa Audiencia, on the Santiago Peninsula, offers the best swimming as well as snorkeling, but **Playa San Pedrito,** shallow for a long way out, is the most popular beach because it's much closer to the downtown area. **Playa Las Brisas** is an optimal combination of proximity and good swimming. **Playa Miramar,** on the Bahía de Santiago past the Santiago Peninsula, is popular with bodysurfers, windsurfers, and boogie boarders, and is accessible by local bus from town. The major part of **Playa Azul** drops off sharply, but is noted for its wide stretch of golden sand.

BIRD WATCHING There are several lagoons along the coast good for bird watching. As you go from Manzanillo up past Las Brisas to Santiago, you'll pass **Laguna de Las Garzas** (Lagoon of the Herons), also known as **Laguna de San Pedrito,** where you can see many white pelicans and huge herons fishing in the water. They nest here in December and January. Directly behind downtown is the **Laguna de Cuyutlán** (follow the signs to Cuyutlán), where birds can usually be found in abundance; species vary between summer and winter.

DIVING **Susan Dearing,** who conducts diving expeditions and classes, pioneered diving in Manzanillo and has come up with some unusually intriguing underwater scenery. Many locations are so close to shore that there's no need for a boat. Close-in dives include the jetty with coral growing on the rocks at 45 feet, and a nearby sunken frigate downed in 1959 at 28 feet. Divers can see abundant sea life, including coral reefs, sea horses, giant puffer fish, and moray eels. A one-tank dive requiring a boat costs $50 per person with a three-person minimum, or two tanks for $70. Offshore dives cost $50 per person. Dearing is certified in scuba (YMCA and CMAS) and life-saving and CPR by the Red Cross, and offers divers certification (PADI, YMCA, NAUI, CMAS, and SSI) in very intensive courses of various durations. She offers a 10% discount on your certification when you mention you read about her in a *Frommer's* guide. Students who dive with her after her certification course are entitled to discounted dive prices. For reservations, contact her directly at ☎/fax **333/3-0642,** cellular 335/8-0327, E-Mail: scubamex@bay.net.mx; or at the spa at the **Hotel Sierra** (☎ **333/3-2000,** ext. 250). Her mailing address is Apdo. Postal 295, Santiago, 28861 Colima, Mexico. MasterCard and Visa are accepted.

ESCORTED TOURS Because Manzanillo is so spread out, you might consider a city tour. Reputable local tour companies include **Viajes Lujo,** avenida México 143-2, 28200 Manzanillo, Colima (☎ **333/2-2919;** fax 333/2-4075), and **Bahías Gemelas Travel Agency,** (American Express representative ☎ **333/3-1000;** fax 333/3-0649). Tours can be scheduled at flexible times, with a half-day city tour costing around $20. Other tours include **Colima, Guadalajara,** and **Barra de Navidad** ($40), which includes a stop at a banana-and-coconut plantation.

FISHING Manzanillo is famous for its fishing, particularly sailfish. Marlin and sailfish are abundant year-round. Winter is best for dolphin fish and dorado (mahimahi), and in summer wahoo and rooster fish are in greater supply. The international sailfish competition is held around the November-20 holiday and the national sailfish competition is in November before Thanksgiving. Fishing can be arranged through travel agencies or directly at the **fishermen's cooperative** (☎ **333/2-1031**), located downtown where the fishing boats are moored. You can call from 7am to 6pm. A fishing boat is approximately $190 for a 5-hour fishing trip.

GOLF The 18-hole **La Mantarraya Golf Course,** rated by *Golf Digest* as one of the world's top 100 courses, is now also open to nonguests as well as guests of Las Hadas. Greens fees are $45 for 18 holes, cart and gear extra. Reserve in advance. In addition, the fabulous Von Hagge–designed, 27-hole golf course associated with the **Grand Bay Hotel** in Barra de Navidad is open to the public. The greens fees are: $80/$100 for 18/27 holes for guests of Grand Bay, $100/$120 for nonguests, including a motorized cart. Barra is about a 1- to 1½-hour drive north of Manzanillo on Highway 200. (See "Costa Alegre to Barra de Navidad," above.)

SHOPPING   A selection of shops carry Mexican crafts and clothing, mainly from nearby Guadalajara, one of Mexico's artisan centers. Almost all are downtown on the streets near the central plaza. The new **Plaza Manzanillo** is an American-style mall on the road to Santiago, and there's a traditional **"tianguis" market** in front of the entrance to **Club Maeva** with crafts from around Mexico. Most resort hotels also have boutiques or shopping arcades.

SUNSET CRUISES   For a sunset cruise, buy tickets from a travel agent or downtown at **La Perlita Dock** (across from the train station) fronting the harbor. Tickets go on sale at La Perlita daily from 10am to 2pm and 4 to 7pm and cost around $15. The trips vary in their combinations of drinks, music, and entertainment, and last 1½ to 2 hours.

WHERE TO STAY

The strip of coastline on which Manzanillo is located can be divided into three areas: **downtown,** with its shops, markets, and continual activity; **Las Brisas,** the hotel-lined beach area immediately to the north of the city; and **Santiago,** both the name of a town and peninsula, now virtually a suburb situated even farther north at the end of Playa Azul. Transportation by either bus or taxi makes all three areas fairly convenient to each other. Reservations are recommended for hotels during the Easter, Christmas, and New Year's holidays.

DOWNTOWN

Hotel Colonial. Av. México 100 and González Bocanegra, 28200 Manzanillo, Col. ☎ 333/2-1080 or 333/2-1134. 37 units. A/C (25 rms) FAN (12 rms). $19–$21 double. V, MC.

An old favorite, this three-story colonial-style hotel is very consistent. It still offers the same beautiful blue-and-yellow tile, colonial-style carved doors, and windows in the lobby and restaurant. Rooms are decorated with minimal furniture, red-tile floors, and basic comforts, with the highest rates for rooms with air-conditioning. A restaurant/bar is located in the central courtyard. The hotel is 1 block inland from the main plaza at the corner of Juárez and Galindo.

LAS BRISAS

Hotel La Posada. Av. Lázaro Cárdenas 201, Las Brisas (Apdo. Postal 135), 28200 Manzanillo, Col. ☎/fax **333/3-1899.** 24 units. FAN. High season $72 double. Low season $48 double. Rates include breakfast. AE, MC, V.

Another longtime favorite of travelers-in-the-know, this small inn has a shocking-pink stucco facade with a large arch that leads to a broad tiled patio right on the beautiful beach. The rooms have exposed-brick walls and simple furnishings with Mexican decorative accents. The atmosphere here is casual and informal—you can help yourself to beer and soft drinks all day long and at the end of your stay, owner Bart Varelmann (a native of Ohio) counts the bottle caps you deposited in a bowl labeled with your room number. All three meals are served in the dining room or out by the pool. If a nonguest wants to come for a meal, breakfast is served between 8 and 11am and costs around $7; lunch and dinner (sandwiches) are served between 1:30 and 8pm and cost about the same. During low season the restaurant is open only from 8am to 3pm. Or stop by for a drink at sunset; the bar's open until 9pm all year. It's located at the end of Las Brisas Peninsula, closest to downtown; on the local "Las Brisas" bus route.

Hotel Star. Av. Lázaro Cárdenas 1313, 28200 Manzanillo, Col. ☎ **333/3-2560** or 333/3-1980. 41 units. A/C FAN. $24 double; $31 suite; $60 bungalow. CB, MC, V.

In a row of modest hotels, the Hotel Star stands out for its tidy appearance and careful management. It features a two-story sunny complex facing a courtyard and a pool by the beach. Rooms are comfortable but sparsely decorated with rattan furniture. The higher-priced rooms, including the two suites, have air-conditioning and TV. One suite has a kitchen.

SANTIAGO

Three miles north of Las Brisas is the wide Santiago Peninsula. The settlement of Salahua is on the highway at one end where you enter the peninsula to reach the hotels Las Hadas, Plaza Las Glorias, and Sierra Manzanillo, as well as the Mantarraya Golf Course. Buses from town marked LAS HADAS pass by these hotels in the interior of the peninsula every 20 minutes. Past the Salahua turnoff and at the end of the settlement of Santiago, an obscure road on the left is marked ZONA DE PLAYAS and leads to the hotels on the other side of the peninsula, including Hotels Marlyn and Playa de Santiago.

Very Expensive

✪ **Camino Real Las Hadas.** Av. de los Riscos s/n, Santiago Peninsula, 28200 Manzanillo, Col. ☎ **800/722-6466** in the U.S. and Canada, or 333/4-0000. 236 units. A/C MINIBAR TV TEL. High season $252–$386 double; $360–$927 suite; $320–$386 Camino Real Club. AE, DC, MC, V.

Manzanillo and Las Hadas are, to many people, synonymous. The signature property of Manzanillo, Las Hadas was featured in the movie *10*—along with Bo Derek, of course. Featuring Moorish-style architecture, this elegant white resort is built on the beach and into the side of the rocky peninsula. A member of the exclusive "Leading Hotels of the World" group, it was the brainchild of the Bolivian millionaire Antenor Patino. The rooms are built around the hillside overlooking the bay, and are connected by cobbled lanes lined with colorful flowers and palms. Covered, motorized carts are on call for transportation within the property. Though it's a large resort, it maintains an air of seclusion since rooms are spread out among the meticulously landscaped grounds. The six types of accommodations are categorized by views, room size, and extra amenities. Understated, elegant, and spacious, the rooms have white-marble floors, sitting areas, and comfortably furnished balconies. Robes and in-room security boxes are standard. Camino Real Club rooms are on the upper tier and have great bay views; nine Club rooms have private pools.

Dining/Diversions: Of this resort's four restaurants, the most famous is elegant **Legazpi,** open in high season from 6pm to midnight (see "Where to Dine," below). Special theme nights at the hotel feature patio dining; Italian, Mexican, and Mariachi-themed nights are available at a cost of $45 per person. There are five lounges and bars with live entertainment somewhere on the property almost every evening, plus the disco, **Le Cartouche,** open nightly in high season from 10pm to 2am. Hours and restaurants may vary during low season.

Amenities: Club Las Hadas includes La Mantarraya, the hotel's 18-hole, par-71 golf course designed by Pete and Roy Dye; two pools; shade tents on the beach; 10 tennis courts (eight hard-surface, two clay); marina for 70 vessels and water sports—scuba diving, snorkeling, sailing, and trimaran cruises. Camino Real Club guests have an exclusive pool and reserved lounge chairs at the pool and beach. Laundry, room service, shopping arcade, travel agency, beauty and barber shops, child care (special children's activities in high season). Camino Real Club guests have rapid check-in, continental breakfast, cocktails, concierge, preferred restaurant reservations, and late checkout.

Hotel Sierra Manzanillo. Av. La Audiencia 1, Los Riscos, 28200 Manzanillo, Col. ☎ **800/448-5028** in the U.S., or 333/3-2000. Fax 333/3-2272. 350 units. A/C MINIBAR TV TEL. High season $305 double; $345–$375 suite. Low season $240–$255 double; $275–$300 suite. AE, MC, V.

Opened in 1990, this all-inclusive hotel has 21 floors overlooking La Audiencia beach, with a full program of activities, dining, and entertainment. Its excellent kids program makes it a top choice for families. Architecturally, it mimics the white Moorish style that has become so popular in Manzanillo. Inside, it's palatial in scale and covered in a sea of pale-gray marble. Room decor picks up the pale-gray theme with washed gray armoires that conceal the TV and minibar. Most standard rooms have two double beds or a king-size bed plus a small table, chairs, and desk. Several rooms at the end of most floors are small, with one double bed, small porthole-size windows, no balcony, and no view. Most rooms, however, have balconies and either ocean or hillside views. The 10 gorgeous honeymoon suites are carpeted and have sculpted shell-shaped headboards, king-size beds, and chaise lounges. Junior suites have a sitting area with couch, and large bathrooms.

Dining/Diversions: Seven restaurant and bar areas cover all meals and styles from casual to elegant, and rotate in their offerings of nightly music and entertainment.

Amenities: Grand pool on the beach plus children's pool; four lit tennis courts; health club with exercise equipment, scheduled aerobics, hot tub, and separate sauna and steam rooms for men and women. Scuba-diving lessons are given in the pool and excellent scuba-diving sites are within swimming distance of the shore. Laundry, room service, hair dryers, beauty salon with massage available, travel agency, 24-hour currency exchange.

Moderate

Hotel Plaza Las Glorias. Av. de Tesoro s/n, Santiago Peninsula. 28200 Manzanillo, Col. ☎ **800/342-AMIGO** in the U.S., or 333/4-1098. Fax 333/3-1395. 103 units. A/C TV TEL. $75 double. AE, MC, V.

The sunset-colored walls of this pueblolike hotel ramble over a hillside on Santiago Peninsula. From the restaurant on top and from most rooms is a broad vista of other red-tiled rooftops and either the palm-filled golf course or the bay. It's one of Manzanillo's undiscovered resorts, known more to wealthy Mexicans than to Americans. Originally conceived as private condominiums, the quarters were designed for living; each accommodation is spacious, stylishly furnished, and very comfortable. Each unit has a huge living room; a small kitchen/bar; one, two, or three large bedrooms with tile or brick floors; large Mexican-tiled bathrooms; huge closets; and large furnished private patios with views. A few rooms can be partitioned off and rented by the bedroom only. Water is purified in the tap and each room has a key-locked security box. Try to get a room on the restaurant-and-pool level to avoid climbing stairs to get to your room. A hillside rail elevator goes from top to bottom, but doesn't stop in between. Package rates are available.

Dining/Diversions: La Plazuela restaurant, a casual and informal restaurant shaped like a half moon, is beside the pool and fronts the bay side to capture both the views and breezes. It's open for all three meals. Live musicians often serenade diners.

Amenities: One pool on the restaurant level and game area; beach club on Las Brisas beach, where there's a pool and small restaurant; transportation to the beach club from the main hotel in the morning with return transportation in the afternoon. Laundry, room service, boutique, elevator from bottom of property to top, babysitters arranged with advance notice.

Inexpensive

Hotel Playa de Santiago. Santiago Peninsula (Apdo. Postal 147), 28860 Manzanillo, Col. ☎ **333/3-0055** or 333/3-0270. Fax 333/3-0344. 61 units. FAN TEL. $42 double. AE, MC, V. Free parking.

This is one of those 1960s-era hotels aimed at the jet set who've since migrated to Plaza Las Glorias and Las Hadas. You get the essence of glamour at a fraction of the price, and the hotel is on a small beach. Rooms in the main hotel building are small and clean with nearly up-to-date furnishings, tile floors, tiny closets, and balconies facing the ocean. The restaurant/bar is positioned for its views. Both a pool and tennis courts are on the property.

WHERE TO DINE

BOTANEROS   *Botaneros* are a variation on the cantina and a tradition throughout Mexico—although infrequently seen in resort towns. For the price of a beer or soft drink, they serve delicious complimentary snacks—ceviche, soup, shark stew, pickled pigs' feet, tacos, and the list goes on. The more you drink, the more the food appears. Bring a group of four or more and watch the platters arrive. It's customary to order at least two drinks and to tip the waitress well. Sometimes, roving musicians come in to serenade; you pay per song, so settle on the price in advance. Besides the one below, there's also **El Menudazo** on the way to Santiago. Most are open daily from noon to 8pm and all charge about the same for a beer or soft drink.

El Último Tren. Niños Héroes. Beer or soft drink $2. Daily noon–8pm. DRINKS/SNACKS.

Among the cheeriest of the botaneros, El Último Tren (The Last Train) is covered by a grand palapa with ceiling fans to stir up the breeze. There's enough of a family feel to the place to bring older children, although technically they aren't allowed. It's not far from downtown proper, on the right, several blocks past the train station. Women's rest rooms are named *máquinas* (cars) and the men's room is a *garrotero* (signalman). Whatever that means.

DOWNTOWN

Cafetería/Nevería Chantilly. Juárez and Madero (across from the plaza). ☎ **333/2-0194.** Breakfast $3–$3.50; main courses $2–$6; comida corrida $3.50. No credit cards. Sun–Fri 7am–10pm (comida corrida served 1–4pm). MEXICAN.

Join locals at this informal corner cafe facing the plaza. The large menu includes club sandwiches, hamburgers, *carne asada a la tampequeña,* enchiladas, fish, shrimp, and vegetable salads. The full comida corrida is a real value—it might begin with fresh-fruit cocktail, followed by soup, rice, the main course, dessert, and coffee.

LAS BRISAS

In addition to Willy's, below, the **Hotel La Posada** (see "Where to Stay," above) offers breakfast to nonguests at its beachside restaurant; it's also a great place to mingle with other tourists and enjoy the sunset and cocktails.

✪ **Willy's.** Las Brisas crossroads. ☎ **333/3-1794.** Reservations required. Main courses $8–$15. AE, MC, V. Daily 6pm–2am. SEAFOOD/INTERNATIONAL.

You're in for a treat at Willy's, one of Manzanillo's most popular restaurants. It's breezy, casual, and small, with perhaps 13 tables inside and 10 more on the narrow balcony over the bay. Among the grilled specialties are shrimp imperial wrapped in bacon, red-snapper tarragon, dorado basil, sea bass with mango and ginger, homemade pâté, and coconut flan. The food has flair and wins over locals and tourists alike.

If you double back left at the Las Brisas crossroads, you'll find Willy's on the right, down a short side street that leads to the ocean.

SANTIAGO ROAD

The restaurants below are on the Costera Madrid between downtown and the Santiago Peninsula, including the Salahua area.

Benedetti's Pizza. Av. del Mar 1, Las Brisas. ☎ **333/4-0141.** Pizza $3–$12; main courses $3.75–$6.50. AE, MC, V. Daily 9am–midnight. PIZZA.

Since there are several branches in town (some are called Giovanni's Pizza), you'll probably find a Benedetti's not far from where you are staying. The variety isn't extensive, but the pies are quite good; add some chimichurri sauce to enhance the flavor. They specialize in seafood pizza such as smoked oyster and anchovy pizza. In addition to pizza, you can select from pastas, sandwiches, burgers, fajitas, salads, Mexican soups, cheesecake, and apple pie. This branch is on the Costera Madrid, on the left just after the Las Brisas turn; across from the Coca Cola plant.

Bigotes III. Puesta del Sol 3. ☎ **333/3-1236.** Main courses $6–$14. MC, V. Daily noon–10pm. SEAFOOD.

Locals flock to this large, breezy restaurant (named "Mustache") by the water for the good food and festive atmosphere. Strolling singers serenade diners, who are rewarded with large portions of grilled seafood. To find Bigotes, follow the Costera de la Madrid from downtown past the Las Brisas turnoff. It's behind the Penas Coloradas Social Club across from the beach.

Manolo's Norteño Campestre. Km 11.5 Costera Salahua. ☎ **333/3-0475.** Main courses $5–$18.50. AE, MC, V. Daily 1–11pm. INTERNATIONAL/STEAK/SEAFOOD.

Manolo's offers excellent dining in a tropical garden setting. Owners Manuel and Juanita López and family serve diners. They cater to American tastes with a "safe" salad that is included with dinner. Among the popular entrees are Fillet of Fish Manolo on a bed of spinach with melted cheese Florentine-style and frogs' legs in brandy batter. Most people can't leave without first being tempted by the fresh coconut pie or homemade pecan pie. Coming from downtown, Manolo's is on the right, about 3 blocks before the turn to Las Hadas.

SANTIAGO PENINSULA

✪ **Legazpi.** Camino Real Las Hadas hotel, Santiago Peninsula. ☎ **333/4-0000.** Main courses $25–$55. AE, MC, V. High season 6pm–midnight; Low season closed. INTERNATIONAL.

A top choice in Manzanillo for sheer elegance, gracious service, and outstanding food. The candlelit tables, covered in pale-pink and white, are set with silver and flowers, and a pianist plays softly in the background. Enormous bell-shaped windows on two sides show off the sparkling bay below. Meals begin with a basket of warm breads, and courses are interspersed with servings of fresh-fruit sorbet. The sophisticated menu includes prosciutto with melon marinated in port wine, crayfish bisque, broiled salmon, roast duck, lobster, or veal, and flaming desserts from crepes to Irish coffee.

MANZANILLO AFTER DARK

Nightlife in Manzanillo is much less exuberant than in other Mexican resorts, but there are a few options. Due to the mainly seasonal demand, clubs and bars tend to change from year to year. Check with your concierge for current hot spots. Perennial favorites include **Carlos 'n' Charlie's,** km 5 Costera Madrid (☎ **333/3-1150**), always a good choice for both food and fun. In the evening during high season, there may be a required minimum order/cover if you come just to drink and dance, but the "cover" includes three drinks. Another longtime favorite is **Le Cartouche Disco** (☎ **333/ 3-0000**) at Las Hadas resort, the most opulent option for nightlife and dancing. It opens at 10pm and has a cover charge of around $20. **El Bar de Felix** (☎ **333/ 4-1444**), between Salahua and Las Brisas by the Avis rental-car office, is open Tuesday through Sunday from 9pm to 2am and doesn't charge a cover. Some area clubs have a dress code prohibiting shorts or sandals, principally applying to men.

A SIDE TRIP TO COLIMA & ITS VOLCANO

The city of Colima makes for an interesting and accessible day-trip from Manzanillo. It's just about an hour's drive along a well-maintained, four-lane highway to this charming, colonial city and the capital of Colima State. Well-preserved colonial buildings such as the city's cathedral, originally built in 1527, and the **Palacio de Gobierno,** with its murals depicting Mexican history, are key attractions in the city's center.

Colima has several interesting museums, including the **Museo de las Culturas del Occidente,** which displays an impressive, permanent collection of pre-Columbian pottery and artifacts. The **Casa de la Cultura** hosts changing exhibitions of contemporary art, plus offers free art, music, and dance classes.

Two imposing volcanoes (one still active) border the town. The **Volcán de Fuego,** still active, is located 15 miles to the north, next to the taller, extinct **Nevado de Colima.** Popular day-tours to Colima will often include a visit to two newly opened archaeological sites, **El Chanal** and **La Campana.**

10

Acapulco & the Southern Pacific Coast

It was along this stretch of coastline that Mexico first achieved recognition for having some of the finest beaches in the world. Stretches of blue coves complement the tropical jungles of the adjacent coastal mountains, making for a spectacular setting. Over the years, a diverse selection of resorts has evolved. Each is distinct, yet together they offer an idyllic place for all types of travelers.

The region encompasses the country's oldest resort, **Acapulco;** its newest, the **Bahías de Huatulco;** and the pair of complementary beach vacation spots, modern **Ixtapa** and simplistic **Zihuatanejo,** a centuries-old fishing village. Between Acapulco and Huatulco lie the small, laid-back coastal villages of **Puerto Escondido** and **Puerto Ángel,** both exquisite bays bordered by relaxed communities.

Acapulco still trades on bright lights and big-city glamour, even if the Hollywood celebrities that brought it recognition have largely moved on. The largest and most decadent of Mexican resorts, Acapulco leapt into the international spotlight in the late 1930s when movie stars made it their playground. Tourists followed, and suddenly the city was the place to see and be seen. Though increasingly challenged by other Mexican seaside resorts, Acapulco still appeals to those who favor nocturnal attractions with glitz and excitement.

Only a 4-hour drive north of Acapulco, the resort city Ixtapa and the seaside village Zihuatanejo began attracting travelers in the mid-1970s. This pair offers the best of Mexico back to back—sophisticated high-rise hotels as well as the color and pace of a traditional village.

South of Acapulco, the Bahías de Huatulco mega-resort encompasses a total of nine planned bays on an undeveloped portion of Oaxaca's coast.

Coastal towns in two Mexican states, **Guerrero** and **Oaxaca,** are covered in this chapter. The region is graced with stunning coastline and lush mountainous terrain. Outside the urban centers, paved roads are few, and the two states remain among Mexico's poorest, despite decades of tourist dollars (and many other currencies).

EXPLORING THE SOUTHERN PACIFIC COAST Most travelers to this part of Mexico have one thing on their minds: the beach! They tend to settle in a single destination and relax—or party, if in Acapulco. Each of the beach towns detailed here—Ixtapa and Zihuatanejo in the north, Acapulco and the Oaxacan resorts of Puerto Escondido and Huatulco southeast along the coast—is a holiday resort capable of satisfying your sand and surf needs for at least a few days, or even a week or more. If you've more time and wanderlust, several coastal resorts could be combined into a single trip, or you may choose to mix coastal with colonial, say, by combining visits to Puerto Escondido and Oaxaca City.

The resorts have distinct personalities—you get the requisite beach wherever you go, whether you choose a city that offers virtually every luxury imaginable or a sleepy town providing little more than basic (but charming) seaside relaxation.

Acapulco City has the best airline connections, the broadest range of late-night entertainment, ultrasophisticated dining, and a wide range of accommodations, from hillside villas and luxury resort hotels to modest inns on the beach and in the old center of Acapulco. The many beaches are generally wide and clean, but the ocean itself is polluted, though cleaner than in past days. Acapulco is also a good launching pad for side trips to colonial **Taxco** (Mexico's "Silver Capital"; see chapter 5), only 2½ hours away using the toll road, and to Ixtapa/Zihuatanejo.

Ixtapa and Zihuatanejo offer beach-bound tourist attractions, but on a smaller, newer, and less hectic scale than Acapulco. Their excellent beaches front clean ocean waters. Many people fly into Acapulco (where air service is better), spend a few days there, then make the 4- to 5-hour trip (by rental car or bus) to Ixtapa/Zihuatanejo.

Puerto Escondido, noted for its stellar surf break, laid-back village ambiance, attractive and inexpensive inns, plus nearby nature excursions, is by itself a worthy travel destination and exceptional value. It's a 6-hour drive south of Acapulco on coastal Highway 200. Most people choose to fly there, however, rather than drive or take a bus from Acapulco.

The small village of **Puerto Ángel,** just 50 miles south of Puerto Escondido and 30 miles north of the Bays of Huatulco, could be planned as a day-trip from either of those destinations. It might also serve as a quiet place to relax for several days, providing you care little for nightlife or grand hotels; nothing of the sort exists there. Though dining is limited, a couple of hotels in Puerto Ángel serve notable food, and a few beachside restaurants serve fresh fish. Enjoying nearly deserted beaches near the village will no doubt be your primary activity.

Huatulco, 80 miles south of Puerto Escondido, with an 18-hole golf course and a handful of resort hotels, appeals to the luxury traveler. There aren't many activities besides golfing, boat tours of the nine Huatulco Bays, and a couple of nature excursions that are actually nearer to Puerto Escondido. But the setting is beautiful and relaxing, and that's why most vacationers venture here.

1 Acapulco

229 miles S of Mexico City; 170 miles SW of Taxco; 612 miles SE of Guadalajara; 158 miles SE of Ixtapa/Zihuatanejo; 470 miles NW of Huatulco

Acapulco is like a diva—maybe a little past her prime, perhaps with her makeup smeared, but still able to sing a sultry song and captivate an audience.

The energy in Acapulco is nonstop, 24 hours a day. Acapulco Bay is an adult playground filled with water-skiers wearing tanga swimsuits and darkly tanned, mirror-shaded studs on WaveRunners. Golf and tennis are also played with intensity, but the real participant sport is the nightlife that has made this city famous for decades. When there was a definitive jet set, they came to Acapulco—filmed it, sang about it, wrote about it, and lived it.

It's not hard to understand why: The view of Acapulco Bay, framed by mountains and beaches, is breathtaking day or night.

Today, 80% of Acapulco's visitors come from within Mexico, most by way of the express toll road that links it with the capital city. International travelers began to reject Acapulco when it became clear that its development came at the expense of the cleanliness of the bay and surrounding areas. Since the early 1990s, a program called "ACA-Limpia" ("Clean Acapulco") has cleaned up the water, where whales have been sighted recently for the first time in years, and has also spruced up the Costera. Millions of dollars have been spent in this effort, along with an equivalent sum on trying to clean up the city's image. Still, I can't help but feel these efforts are, at best, superficial—not unlike the boat that skims the top of the bay each morning to remove debris and oil film.

In November of 1997, Hurricane Pauline blew through Acapulco, giving TV film crews and photojournalists numerous opportunities to capture images of the storm's damage as well as of the clear disparity of classes here. Within a week, the entire tourist zone was cleaned up and polished to perfection. Outlying areas took longer to receive the same treatment. Too many politicians have too much at stake in Acapulco to have let the town's tourism suffer any more.

Still, Acapulco has never claimed to be a town for ecotourists or Peace Corps wanna-bes. It is the place for those who want to have dinner at midnight, dance until dawn, and sleep all day on a sun-soaked beach. Acapulco remains the grande dame of resorts, with the allure of being the ultimate, extravagant party town. Where else do bronzed men dive from cliffs into the sea at sunset, and where else does the sun shine 360 days a year?

ESSENTIALS

GETTING THERE & DEPARTING   **By Plane**   See chapter 3, "Planning a Trip to Mexico," for information on flying from the United States or Canada to Acapulco. Local numbers for major airlines with nonstop or direct service to Acapulco are: **Aeromexico** (☎ 74/85-1600), **American** (☎ 74/66-9232 for reservations), **Continental** (☎ 74/66-9063), **Mexicana** (☎ 74/66-9121 or 74/84-6890), and **Taesa** (☎ 74/66-9067 for reservations, or 74/86-4576).

Within Mexico, **Aeromexico** flies from Guadalajara, Mexico City, Puebla, Toluca, and Tijuana; **Mexicana** flies from Mexico City; and **Taesa** flies from Laredo, Mexico City, and Guadalajara. The regional carrier Check with a travel agent about **charter flights.**

The airport (ACA) is 14 miles southeast of town, over the hills east of the bay. Private **taxis** are the fastest option, running about $15 to downtown Acapulco. The major **rental-car** agencies all have booths at the airport. **Transportes Terrestres** has desks at the front of the airport where you can buy tickets for minivan colectivo transportation into town ($3 to $8). Return service to the airport must be reserved through your hotel.

By Car   From Mexico City, you can take Highway 95 south or the curvy toll-free Highway 95 south (6 hr.). You could also take Highway 95D, the scenic, 4 to 6–lane toll highway (3½ hr.) that costs around $42 one way. The free road from Taxco is in good condition; you'll save around $40 in tolls from there through Chilpancingo to Acapulco. From points north or south along the coast, the only choice is Highway 200.

By Bus   From the **Ejido/Central Camionera station** in Acapulco, **Turistar, Estrella de Oro,** and **Estrella Blanca** have almost hourly service for the 5- to 7-hour trip to Mexico City and daily service to Ixtapa and Zihuatanejo. Buses also travel to other points in Mexico including Chilpancingo, Cuernavaca, Iguala, Manzanillo, Puerto Vallarta, and Taxco.

The **Ejido/Central Camionera** station in Acapulco is on the far northern end of the bay and north of downtown (Old Acapulco) at Ejido 47. It's far from the hotels;

Important Car & Bus Travel Warning

Car robberies and bus hijackings on Highway 200 south of Acapulco on the way to Puerto Escondido and Huatulco are frequent and make this an unsafe route for both bus and car travel, even though occasional military checkpoints have been installed. If you're going to either place from Acapulco, it's safer to fly; flight routing will take you from Acapulco to Mexico City and then to Puerto Escondido or Huatulco.

however, it has the widest array of bus lines served from one terminal and the widest array of routes of any Acapulco bus station; it also has a hotel-reservation service.

VISITOR INFORMATION The **State of Guerrero Tourism Office** operates the **Procuraduría del Turista** on street level in front of the **International** (Convention) **Center** (☎ **74/84-4583** or 74/84-4416)—set far back from the main avenida Alemán, down a lengthy walkway with fountains. It offers maps and information about the city and state and is open daily from 8am to 10pm.

CITY LAYOUT Acapulco stretches for more than 4 miles around the huge bay; trying to take it all in by foot is impractical. The tourist areas are roughly divided into three sections: **Old Acapulco** (Acapulco Viejo) is the original town that attracted the jet set of the 1950s and 1960s—and today it looks like it's locked in that era. It's home to the true downtown section of town. The second section is known as the Hotel Zone (Zona Hotelera) that follows the main boulevard, **Costera Miguel Alemán** (the Costera), as it runs east following the outline of the bay from downtown. This is where the main boulevard is lined with towering hotels, restaurants, shopping centers, and strips of open-air beach bars. At the far eastern end of the Costera lie the golf course and the International Center (Convention Center). **avenida Cuauhtémoc** is the major artery inland, running roughly parallel to the Costera. The third major area begins just beyond the Hyatt Regency Hotel, where the Costera changes its name to **Carretera Escénica** (Scenic Highway), which continues all the way to the airport. Along this section of the road the hotels are their most lavish, and extravagant private villas, gourmet restaurants, and glamorous nightclubs are built into the hillside, offering dazzling views. The area fronting the beach in this zone is called **Acapulco Diamante,** Acapulco's most desirable address.

Street names and numbers in Acapulco can be confusing and hard to find—many streets either are not well marked or change names unexpectedly. Fortunately, there's seldom a reason to be far from the Costera, so it's hard to get lost. Street numbers on the Costera do not follow logic, so don't assume that similar numbers will necessarily be close together.

GETTING AROUND **By Taxi** Taxis are more plentiful than tacos in Acapulco, and practically as inexpensive, but always establish the price with the driver before starting out. Hotel taxis may charge three times the rate of a taxi hailed on the street.

By Bus Even though the city has a confusing street layout, it's amazingly easy and inexpensive to use city buses. Two kinds of buses run along the Costera: pastel color-coded buses and regular "school buses." The difference is the price: New air-conditioned tourist buses (Aca Tur Bus) are 65¢; old buses, 30¢. Covered bus stops are located all along the Costera, with handy maps on the walls showing bus routes to major sights and hotels.

The best place near the zócalo to catch a bus is next to Sanborn's, 2 blocks east. "Caleta Directo" or "Base-Caleta" buses will take you to the Hornos, Caleta, and

Caletilla beaches along the Costera. Some buses return along the same route; others go around the peninsula and return to the Costera.

For expeditions to more distant destinations, there are buses to **Puerto Marqués** to the east (marked PUERTO MARQUÉS–BASE) and **Pie de la Cuesta** to the west (marked ZÓCALO–PIE DE LA CUESTA). Be sure to verify the time and place of the last bus back if you hop one of these.

By Car   Rental cars are available both at the airport and at hotel desks along the Costera. Unless you plan on exploring outlying areas, you're better off taking taxis or using the easy and inexpensive public bus station around town. Traffic can get tangled, and it's much easier to leave the driving to someone else.

FAST FACTS: Acapulco

American Express   The main office is in the "Gran Plaza" shopping center at Costera Alemán 1628 (☎ 74/69-1166).

Area Code   The telephone area code is **74.**

Climate   Acapulco boasts sunshine 360 days a year, with average daytime temperatures of 80°F. Humidity varies, with approximately 59 inches of rain per year. June through October is the rainy season, though July and August are relatively dry. Tropical showers are brief and usually occur at night.

Consular Agents   The **United States** has an agent at the Hotel Club del Sol on Costera Alemán at R. Católicos (☎ 74/84-0300 or 74/69-0556), across from the Hotel Acapulco Plaza; it's open Monday through Friday from 10am to 2pm. The **Canadian** representative is also at the Hotel Club del Sol (☎ 74/84-1305) and is open Monday through Friday from 9am to 1pm. The **United Kingdom** has an agent at the Las Brisas Hotel on Carretera Escénica near the airport (☎ 74/84-1650 or 74/84-6605); it's open Monday through Friday from 9am to 6pm. Most other countries in the European Union also have consulate offices in Acapulco. The following are the newly installed telephone numbers for consular agencies:

    Austria (☎ 74/82-5551 or 74/83-2979); **Finland** (☎ 74/84-7874 or 74/84-7875); **France** (☎ 74/82-3394 or 74/82-1229); **Germany** (☎ 74/62-0183); **Italy** (☎ 74/81-2533 or 74/83-3875); **Netherlands** (☎ 74/86-6179 or 74/86-8210); **Norway** (☎ 74/84-3525); **Spain** (☎ 74/86-2491 or 74/86-7205); **Sweden** (☎ 74/85-2935).

    Note that telephone numbers are still changing after Hurricane Pauline, and the whole process is going to take some time. The most reliable source for telephone numbers in Acapulco is the **Procuraduría de Turista** at ☎ 74/84-4583.

Currency Exchange   Numerous banks are located along the Costera and are open Monday through Friday from 9am to 6pm and Saturday from 10am to 1:30pm. They, and their automatic tellers, generally have the best rates. Casas de cambio (currency exchange booths) along the street may have better exchange rates than hotels.

Parking   It is illegal to park on the Costera at any time.

Post Office   The **central post office** (correo) is on the Costera, no. 215 near the zócalo and Sanborn's (☎ 74/82-1249). Other branches are located in the Estrella de Oro bus station on Cuauhtémoc, inland from the Acapulco Ritz Hotel, and on the Costera near Caleta Beach.

Safety   Pay close attention to warning flags posted on Acapulco beaches: Riptides claim a few lives every year. Red or black flags mean stay out of the water, yellow flags signify caution, and white or green flags mean it's safe to swim.

As is the case anywhere, tourists are vulnerable to thieves. This is especially true when shopping in a market, lying on the beach, wearing jewelry, or visibly carrying a camera, purse, or bulging wallet. Pay attention to joggers coming from both directions—one may knock you down, then rob you. To dissuade would-be thieves, purchase a waterproof plastic tube on a string to wear around your neck at the beach—it's big enough for a few bills and your room key. Street vendors and hotel variety shops sell them.

Telephone Numbers   As mentioned above, the area code for Acapulco is 74, different from the old code (748).

Tourist Police   If you see policemen in uniforms of white and light blue, they belong to a special corps of English-speaking police who assist tourists.

ACTIVITIES ON & OFF THE BEACH

Great beaches and water sports abound in Acapulco. It's also pleasant to take a walk early in the day (before it gets too hot) around the **zócalo,** called Plaza Álvarez. Visit the **cathedral**—the bulbous blue onionlike domes are reminiscent of a Russian Orthodox church, though it was actually designed as a movie theater! From the church, turn east along the side street going off at a right angle (calle Carranza, which doesn't have a marker) to find an arcade with newsstands and shops.

The hill behind the cathedral provides an unparalleled view of Acapulco. Take a taxi up to the top of the hill from the main plaza, following the signs leading to **La Mirador** (lookout point).

City tours, day-trips to Taxco, cruises, and other excursions and activities are offered through local travel agencies. Taxco is about a 3-hour drive inland from Acapulco (see chapter 5 for more information).

THE BEACHES   Here's the rundown, from west to east around the bay. **Playa la Angosta** is a small, sheltered, and often-deserted cove just around the bend from **La Quebrada** (where the cliff divers perform).

South of downtown on the Peninsula de las Playas lie the beaches **Caleta** and **Caletilla.** They're separated by a small outcropping of land that contains the new aquarium and water park, **Mágico Mundo Marino.** You'll find thatch-roofed restaurants, water-sports equipment for rent, and brightly painted boats that ferry passengers to **Roqueta Island.** You can rent beach chairs and umbrellas for the day. Mexican families favor these beaches because they're close to several inexpensive hotels. In the late afternoon, fishermen pull their colorful boats up on the sand; you can buy the fresh catch of the day and, occasionally, oysters on the half shell.

Pleasure boats dock at **Playa Manzanillo,** just south of the zócalo. Charter fishing trips sail from here. In the old days, the downtown beaches—Manzanillo, Honda, Caleta, and Caletilla—were the focal point of Acapulco. Today the beaches and the resort developments stretch along the 4-mile length of the shore.

East of the zócalo, the major beaches are **Hornos** (near Papagayo Park), **Hornitos, Condesa,** and **Icacos,** followed by the naval base (La Base) and **Punta del Guitarrón.** After Punta del Guitarrón, the road climbs to the legendary Las Brisas hotel, where many of the 300 *casitas* (bungalow-type rooms) have their own swimming pools (the hotel has 250 total pools). Past Las Brisas, the road continues to **Puerto Marqués** and **Punta Diamante,** about 12 miles from the zócalo. The fabulous Acapulco Princess and Pierre Marqués hotels dominate the landscape.

Acapulco Bay Area

Acapulco Region

Attractions:
Catedral
Centro Acapulco (Convention Center)
Cliff Divers
Mágico Mundo Marino
Jai Lai Frontón Stadium
Plaza de Toros

Zócalo/Plaza Álvarez
Fort San Diego/Museo Histórico
de Acapulco

SA-0036

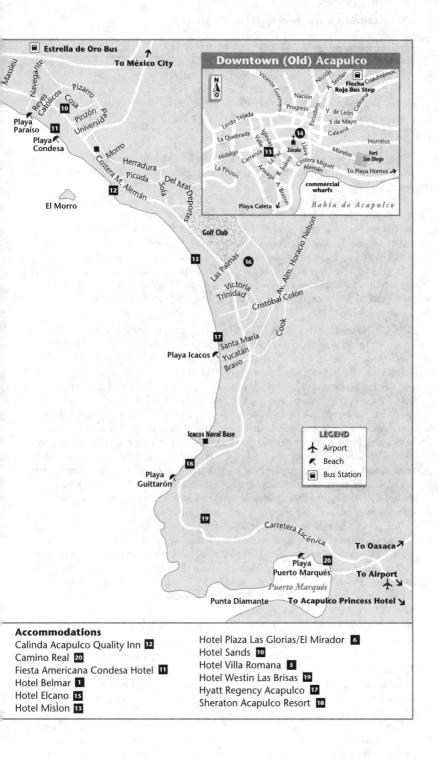

Downtown (Old) Acapulco

To México City
Estrella de Oro Bus

Massieu
Navegante
Reyes Católicos
Cosa
Pizarro
Pinzón
Universid
Pez
Morro
Herradura
Picuda
Sola
Del Mar
Deportes
Costera M. Alemán

Playa Paraíso
Playa Condesa
El Morro

Flecha Roja Bus Stop
Vicente Guerrero
Nicolás
A. Serdan
Cuauhtémoc
Galeana
Nación
Progreso
Escudero
V. de León
5 de Mayo
Lerdo Tejada
La Quebrada
Iglesias
Valle
La Paz
Llave
Zócalo
Costera Miguel Alemán
Galeana
Hornitos
Fort San Diego
La Pinzón
Hidalgo
Carranza
Arteaga
A. Breton
B. Juárez
Morelos
To Playa Hornos
commercial wharfs
Playa Caleta
Bahía de Acapulco

Golf Club
Las Palmas
Victoria
Trinidad
Cristóbal Colón
Av. Alm. Horacio Nelson
Cook
Santa María
Yucatán
Bravo
Playa Icacos

Icacos Naval Base

Playa Guittarón

LEGEND
✈ Airport
🏖 Beach
🚌 Bus Station

Carretera Escénica
To Oaxaca
Playa Puerto Marqués
Puerto Marqués
To Airport
Punta Diamante
To Acapulco Princess Hotel

Accommodations

Calinda Acapulco Quality Inn **12**
Camino Real **20**
Fiesta Americana Condesa Hotel **11**
Hotel Belmar **1**
Hotel Elcano **15**
Hotel Mислòn **13**

Hotel Plaza Las Glorias/El Mirador **6**
Hotel Sands **10**
Hotel Villa Romana **5**
Hotel Westin Las Brisas **19**
Hyatt Regency Acapulco **17**
Sheraton Acapulco Resort **18**

Tide Warning

Each year in Acapulco at least one or two unwary swimmers drown because of deadly riptides and undertow (see "Safety" in "Fast Facts," above). Swim only in Acapulco Bay or Puerto Marqués Bay—but be careful of the undertow no matter where you go.

The bay of Puerto Marqués is an attractive area for **swimming.** The water is calm, the bay sheltered, and waterskiing can be arranged. Past the bay lie **Revolcadero Beach** and a fascinating jungle lagoon.

Other beaches are difficult to reach without a car. **La Pie de la Cuesta** is 8 miles west of town (buses that regularly run along the Costera leave every 5 or 10 min.). You can't swim here, but it's a great spot for checking out big waves and the spectacular sunset, especially over coco locos (drinks served in a fresh coconut with the top whacked off) at one of the rustic beachfront restaurants hung with hammocks.

If driving, continue west along the peninsula, passing **Coyuca Lagoon** on your right, until you have almost reached the small air base at the tip. Along the way, you'll be invited to park near different sections of beach by various private entrepreneurs, mostly small boys.

BAY CRUISES & ROQUETA ISLAND   A boat deck bobbing in the ocean is a great spot for viewing the entire bay, and Acapulco has virtually every kind of boat to choose from—yachts, huge catamarans, and trimarans, single- and double-decker. Cruises are offered morning, afternoon, and evening. Some offer buffets, open bars, and live music; others just snacks, drinks, and taped music. Prices range from $20 to $60. Cruise operators come and go, and their phone numbers change so frequently from year to year that it's pointless to list them here; to find out what cruises are currently operated, contact any Acapulco travel agency or hotel tour desk. They usually have a scrapbook with pictures and brochures so you can get a good idea about what a cruise entails before booking it. Basically, you should choose your cruise on the basis of what you are willing to pay and the services you are looking to receive—the higher priced cruises offer better-quality drinks and snacks (if provided) and take place aboard newer, cleaner boats. Ask your hotel concierge or travel agent to explain the differences in the available boats and for recommendations.

Boats from Caletilla Beach to **Roqueta Island**—a good place to snorkel, sunbathe, hike to a lighthouse, visit a small zoo, or have lunch—leave every half hour from 10am until the last one returns at 5pm. There are also glass-bottom boat options where you circle the bay looking down at a few fish, then a diver swims down to a statue of a Madonna. Purchase tickets (approximately $3.75) directly from any boat that's loading or at a discount from the **information booth** on Caletilla Beach (☎ 74/82-2389).

WATER SPORTS & BOAT RENTALS   An hour of **waterskiing** can cost as little as $30 or as much as $60. Caletilla Beach, Puerto Marqués Bay, and Coyuca Lagoon have waterskiing facilities. There's also the **Water Skiing Club** located at Costera Alemán no. 100 (☎ 74/82-2034).

Scuba diving costs $40 for 1½ hours of instruction if you book directly with the instructor on Caleta Beach. It costs $45 to $55 if you make arrangements through a hotel or travel agency. Dive trips start around $50 per person for one dive.

Boat rentals are the least expensive on Caletilla Beach, where an information booth rents inner tubes, small boats, canoes, paddleboats, and beach chairs; it can also arrange waterskiing and scuba diving (see "Bay Cruises & Roqueta Island," above).

For **deep-sea fishing** excursions, go to the pale-pink building of the boat cooperative opposite the zócalo. Charter fishing trips run from $120 to $150 for 7 hours, tackle and bait included. Book a day in advance through the **boat cooperative** (☎ **74/82-1099**). Credit cards aren't accepted and ice, drinks, and lunch are extra. The boats leave at 7am and return at 2pm. If you book through a travel agent or hotel, fishing trips start around $200 to $280 for four people. Fishing license, food, and drinks are extra.

Parasailing, though not free from risk (the occasional thrill-seeker has collided with a palm tree or even a building), can be brilliant. The pleasure of floating high over the bay hanging from a parachute towed by a motorboat is yours for $35. Most parachute rides operate on Condesa Beach.

GOLF, TENNIS, RIDING & BULLFIGHTS A round of 18 holes of **golf** at the Acapulco Princess Hotel (☎ **74/69-1000**) is $62 for guests and $82 for nonguests; American Express, Visa, and MasterCard are accepted. Tee-times begin at 7:30am, and reservations should be made 1 day in advance. Club rental is $21. At the **Club de Golf Acapulco,** off the Costera next to the Convention Center (☎ **74/84-0781**) you can play 9 holes for $40, with equipment renting for $12.

Tennis at one of the tennis clubs open to the public goes for about $11 an hour. One option is the **Club de Golf Acapulco** (☎ **74/84-0781**), open daily from 7am to 7pm. Singles costs $12 per hour; doubles, $18. Many of the hotels along the Costera have tennis facilities for their guests.

Horseback-riding tours on the beach are available through the **Lienzo Charro "México Real,"** near the Acapulco Princess Hotel. Two-hour rides depart at 9:30am, 11:30am, and 3:30pm daily and cost $40, including two beers or soft drinks. There is no phone; you have to go directly to the beach near the Acapulco Princess Hotel.

Traditionally called the **Fiesta Brava, bullfights** are held during Acapulco's winter season at a ring up the hill from Caletilla Beach. Tickets purchased through travel agencies cost around $40 and usually include transportation to and from your hotel. The festivities begin each Sunday in winter at 5:30pm.

MUSEUMS & WATER PARKS The original **Fuerte de San Diego,** Costera Alemán, east of the zócalo, was built in 1616 to protect the town from pirate attacks. At that time, the port reaped considerable wealth from trade with the Philippine Islands (which, like Mexico, were part of the Spanish empire). The fort you see today was rebuilt after extensive earthquake damage in 1776. The structure houses the **Museo Histórico de Acapulco** (Acapulco Historical Museum), filled with exhibits that tell the fascinating story of Acapulco, from its role as a port for conquest of the

---

Death-Defying Divers

High divers perform at La Quebrada each day at 7:30, 8:30, 9:30, and 10:30pm for a $4 admission. From a spotlighted ledge on the cliffs, in view of the lobby bar and restaurant terraces of the **Hotel Plaza Las Glorias/El Mirador,** divers holding torches plunge into the roaring surf 130 feet below—after wisely praying at a small shrine nearby. To the applause of the crowd, divers climb up the rocks and accept congratulations and gifts of money from onlookers.

You can watch from the hotel's terraces for a cover charge, which is an obligatory $9 drink. You could get around the cover by having dinner at the hotel's **La Perla restaurant.** The buffet is $20 to $25. Reservations (☎ **74/83-1155**) are recommended during the high season.

Americas to a center for Catholic proselytization campaigns and trade with the Orient. Other exhibits chronicle Acapulco's pre-Hispanic past, the coming of the conquistadors, complete with Spanish armor, and subsequent Spanish imperial activity. Temporary shows are also held here.

To reach the fort, follow Costera Alemán past old Acapulco and the zócalo; the fort is on a hill on the right. The museum is open Tuesday to Sunday from 10:30am to 4:40pm, but the best time to go is in the morning, since the "air-conditioning" is minimal. The $2.50 admission is waived on Sunday.

The **Centro Internacional de Convivencia Infantil (CICI),** Costera Alemán, at Colón (☎ 74/84-8033), is a sea-life and water park east of the Convention Center with swimming pools that feature waves, water slides, and water toboggans. The park is open daily from 10am to 6pm. **Dolphin shows** at noon, 2:30, and 5pm are in English and Spanish. Bird shows are at 11:15am, 1:15, and 3:45pm. Amenities include a cafeteria and rest rooms. Admission is $5 for adults and $3 for children. Children under 2 are admitted free.

SHOPPING

Acapulco is perhaps not the best place to buy Mexican crafts, but it does have a few interesting shops. The best are the **Mercado Parazal** (often called the **Mercado de Artesanías**) on calle Velázquez de León near Cinco de Mayo in the downtown zócalo area (when you see Sanborn's, turn right and walk behind it for several blocks, asking directions). Stall after covered stall of curios from around the country, including silver, embroidered cotton clothing, rugs, pottery, and papier-mâché, are here. As they wait for patrons, artists paint ceramics with village folk scenes. The market's a pleasant place to spend a morning or afternoon.

Shopkeepers aren't pushy, but they'll test your bargaining mettle. The starting price will be steep, and inching the price down may take more time than you have. As always, acting uninterested often brings down prices in a hurry. Before buying silver here, examine it carefully and be sure it has ".925" stamped on the back (this signifies that the silver is 92.5% pure). The market is open daily from 9am to 8pm.

For a familiar department store with fixed prices, try **Artesanías Finas de Acapulco** (☎ 74/84-8039), called AFA-ACA for short. Tour guides bring their groups to this mammoth air-conditioned store. Merchandise includes a mix of mass-produced, tacky junk along with some fairly good folk art among the clothes, marble-top furniture, saddles, luggage, jewelry, pottery, papier-mâché, and more. The store is open Monday through Saturday from 9am to 7:30pm and Sunday from 9am to 2pm. To find it, go east on the Costera until you see the Hotel Romano Days Inn on the seaward side and Baby-O disco on the landward side. Take avenida Horacio Nelson, the street between Baby-O and the Hotel El Tropicana. On the right, half a block up, is AFA-ACA. **Sanborn's** is another good department store.

The Costera Alemán is crowded with boutiques selling resort wear. These stores have ample attractive summer clothing at prices lower than those you generally pay in the United States. If you find a sale, you can stock up on incredible bargains. One of the nicest air-conditioned shopping centers on the Costera is **Plaza Bahía**, Costera Alemán 125 (☎ 74/85-6939 or 74/85-6992), which has four stories of shops, movie theaters, a bowling alley, and small fast-food restaurants. The center is located just west of the Acapulco Plaza Hotel. The bowling alley, **Bol Bahía** (☎ 74/85-0970 or 74/85-6446), is open daily from 11am to 2am.

WHERE TO STAY

Descriptions below begin with the very expensive resorts south of town (nearest the airport) and continue along the famous main avenue, Costera Miguel Alemán, to the less-expensive hotels north of town in what is considered the zócalo (downtown or "Old Acapulco" part of the city). Especially in the "very expensive" and "expensive" categories, inquire about promotional rates or check airlines to see what air and hotel packages are available. During Christmas and Easter weeks, some hotels double their normal rates.

Private, ultrasecluded villas are available for rent all over the hills south of town; renting one of these luxurious and palatial homes makes an unforgettable Acapulco vacation alternative.

SOUTH OF TOWN

Some of Acapulco's most exclusive and famous hotels, restaurants, and villas are nestled in the steep forested hillsides south of town, between the naval base and Puerto Marquéz. The **Hotel Camino Real** is on Playa Guitarrón, the **Sheraton** on a secluded cove, the superexclusive **Acapulco Princess** faces the open ocean, and next to it is the enormous **Vidafel** resort. All of these are several miles from the heart of Acapulco.

Very Expensive

Acapulco Princess. El Revolcadero Beach, 39868 Acapulco, Gro. ☎ **800/223-1818** in the U.S., or 74/69-1000. Fax 74/69-1017. 1,020 units. A/C TV TEL. High season (including breakfast and dinner) $305–$450 double; $415–$675 suite. AE, DC, MC, V. Free parking.

The first luxury hotel most people see upon arriving in Acapulco is the 480-acre Acapulco Princess on El Revolcadero Beach (just off the road to the airport). Removed from the Manhattan-like skyscraper hotels downtown, the Princess complex, framed by the fabulously groomed and palm-dotted golf course, recalls a great Aztec ceremonial center. Its pyramidal buildings dominate the flat surrounding land.

Within the spacious complex of buildings is a self-contained tropical-paradise: waterfalls, fountains, and pools interspersed with tropical trees, flowers, shrubs, swans, peacocks, and flamingos. Though the beach is long, inviting, and beautifully maintained, swimming in the open ocean here is generally unsafe. Public spaces, including the enormous lobby, are striking. Guest rooms at the Acapulco Princess are big, bright, and luxurious, with marble floors and balconies.

During high season, prices include two meals. During low season, children within a certain age group may share a room with two adults at no extra charge. Ask about special packages that may include unlimited golf and daytime tennis, and other perks.

Dining/Diversions: Seven restaurants in all (some subject to seasonal closings); in general, all are excellent. There is elegant indoor dining and covered outdoor dining. Bars include **Laguna** and **La Cascada,** where mariachis often entertain; **La Palma** and **La Palapa** by the beach; and **Grotto,** the swim-up bar. **Tiffany's** is the trendy disco that gets going late and stays open until early morning. Garden theme parties, with regional music and dancing, are often held.

Amenities: Five free-form swimming pools, a saltwater lagoon with water slide, two 18-hole golf courses, nine outdoor tennis courts (all lighted), and two indoor courts with stadium seating. Fishing and other water sports can be arranged with the hotel's travel agency. The Princess also features a barber and beauty shop with massage, a fitness center with aerobics, boutiques, a flower shop, laundry and room service, baby-sitters, cribs, and wheelchairs.

✪ **Camino Real Acapulco Diamante.** km 14 Carretera Escénica, Calle Bajacatita, Pichilingue, 39887 Acapulco, Gro. ☎ **800/7-CAMINO** in the U.S. and Canada, or 74/66-1010. Fax 74/66-1111. 156 units. A/C MINIBAR TV TEL. High season $155 double; $380 junior suite. Ask about low-season and midweek discounts and "The Little Rascals Club" for children. AE, MC, V.

Opened in 1993, this is one of Acapulco's finest hotels, tucked in a secluded location on 81 acres, part of the enormous Acapulco Diamante project. From the Carretera Escénica, you wind down a handsome brick road to the hotel's location overlooking Puerto Marquéz Bay. The lobby has an enormous terrace facing the water. Elevators whisk you to all but the outside terrace levels. Spacious rooms have small sitting areas, cool marble floors, and elegant, minimalist furnishings. Each room has a ceiling fan in addition to air-conditioning and a safe-deposit box in the closet.

This relaxing, self-contained resort is an ideal choice if you already know Acapulco and don't need to explore much.

Dining/Diversions: La Vela is a formal, outdoor seafood grill overlooking the bay. The semiformal **Cabo Diamante** features both Mexican and international food. The open-air lobby bar facing the bay is a great place to be for evening cocktails.

Amenities: Trilevel pool, tennis court, beauty and barber shops, and shopping arcade. The health club offers aerobics, massage, and complete workout equipment. Room and laundry service, travel agency, car rental.

✪ **Westin Las Brisas.** Apdo. Postal 281, Carretera Escénica, Las Brisas, 39868 Acapulco, Gro. ☎ **800/228-3000** in the U.S., or 74/84-1580. Fax 74/84-2269. 267 units. A/C MINIBAR TV TEL. High season $210 double; $250 Royal Beach Club; $481–$1,250 suite. Low season $170 double; $200 Royal Beach Club; $375–$1,138 suite. $15 per day service charge extra (in lieu of all tips). Rates include continental breakfast. AE, DC, MC, V.

The Westin Las Brisas is often considered the finest hotel in Acapulco. Perched on a hillside overlooking the bay, Las Brisas is known for its tiered pink stucco facade, an Acapulco trademark. If you stay here, you ought to like pink because the color scheme extends to 175 pink Jeeps rented exclusively to Las Brisas guests. The hotel is a community unto itself: The elegantly simple, marble-floored rooms are like separate villas sculpted from a terraced hillside, and each has a private (or semiprivate) swimming pool with a panoramic bay view. Spacious Regency Club rooms at the apex of the property have private pools and fabulous views of the lights of all Acapulco twinkling across the bay. Altogether, there are 300 casitas and 250 swimming pools. Although its location on the airport road southeast of the bay means that Las Brisas is a distance from the center of town, guests tend to find this an advantage rather than a drawback. Plus, here you are close to the hottest nightclubs in Acapulco.

Dining: Complimentary breakfast of fruit, rolls, and coffee served to each room daily. **Bella Vista** is the reservations-only (but now open to the public) panoramic-view restaurant, open 7 to 11pm daily. **El Mexicano Restaurant** on a terrace open to the stars receives guests Saturday through Thursday evenings from 5 to 11pm. **La Concha Beach Club** offers seafood daily from 12:30 to 4:30pm. **The Deli Shop** is open from 11am to 7pm daily.

Amenities: Private or shared pools with each room, with fresh floating flowers daily; private La Concha Beach Club at the bottom of the hill has both fresh- and salt-water pools—the hotel provides transportation; five tennis courts; pink Jeeps for rent. Travel agency and gas station, express checkout with advance notice, 24-hour shuttle transportation around the resort, laundry and room service, beauty and barber shops.

Expensive

Sheraton Acapulco Resort. Costera Guitarrón 110, 39359 Acapulco, Gro. ☎ **800/325-3535** in the U.S., or 74/81-2222. Fax 74/84-3760. 220 units. A/C MINIBAR TV TEL. High season $180–$235 double. Ask about "Sure Saver" and weekend rates. AE, DC, MC, V. Parking $8 daily.

Secluded and tranquil, and completely invisible from the scenic highway, this hotel is nestled in a landscaped ravine with a waterfall and wonderful bay view. The 17 multistoried units descend to a small beach beside the pool. Each building unit has an elevator, allowing visitors to come and go directly to the rooms from the lobby. Rooms recently have been redecorated and have travertine tile floors, rattan furniture, and come with a private or shared balcony, purified tap water, and safe-deposit boxes. Some have a separate living room and kitchenette. The 32 Sheraton Club rooms have added amenities. All rooms have remote-control TV and tub/shower combinations. The hotel is located between La Base and Las Brisas, off the Carretera Escénica at Playa Guitarrón at the eastern end of the bay.

Dining/Diversions: Besides a restaurant with kosher service, there's the newly refurbished **La Bahía Restaurant,** with a magnificent semicircular bay view, elegantly set tables, and international cuisine. The **Lobby Bar** offers live piano music nightly and a bay view. The famous **Jorongo Bar** of the Sheraton María Cristina in Mexico City is re-created here with its cantina atmosphere, live trio music, and regional food specialties. Restaurants and bars are seasonal and not all may remain open during low season.

Amenities: Beach, two swimming pools, two wheelchair-accessible rooms, 20 non-smoking guest rooms, boutiques, beauty shops, small gym with sauna, steam room, and massage. The hotel has a tennis membership at the Club Brittanica and provides guests with free transportation. Laundry and room service, travel agency, car rental; scheduled shuttle service to and from town may be offered.

Costera Hotel Zone

These hotels are all found along the main boulevard, Costera Alemán, extending from the Convention Center (Centro Internacional) in the east to Papagayo Park, just before reaching Old Acapulco. One of the most familiar images of Acapulco is that of the twinkling lights of these hotels as they stretch for miles along Acapulco Bay.

Expensive

Fiesta Americana Condesa Acapulco. Costera Miguel Alemán 97, 39300 Acapulco, Gro. ☎ **800/223-2332** in the U.S., or 74/84-2355. Fax 74/84-1828. 500 units. A/C MINIBAR TV TEL. High season $155–$180 double; $195 suite. Low season $125–$140 double; $160 suite. Ask about "Fiesta Break" packages that combine hotel, sightseeing, and air travel. AE, DC, MC, V.

Once the Condesa del Mar, the Fiesta Americana Condesa Acapulco is one of Acapulco's long-standing favorite deluxe hotels. The 18-story hotel towers above Condesa Beach, just east up the hill from the Glorieta Diana. The attractive and very comfortable rooms each have a private terrace with an ocean view. The more expensive rooms have the best bay views, and all have purified tap water.

Dining/Diversions: The newly opened **Trattoria** restaurant serves Italian specialties in a casual atmosphere. Coffee shop, poolside restaurant, and lobby bar with live entertainment most nights.

Amenities: The dramatic adults-only swimming pool is perched atop a hill with the land dropping off toward the bay, affording swimmers the finest pool view of Acapulco in the city. Smaller pool for children. Two wheelchair-accessible rooms, beauty shop, boutiques, pharmacy, laundry and room service, travel agency.

Hotel Elcano. Costera Alemán 75, 39690 Acapulco, Gro. ☎ **800/222-7692** in the U.S., or 74/84-1950. Fax 74/84-2230. 180 units. A/C TV TEL. $190 studio and standard room; $210 junior suite; $300 master suite. Ask about promotional discounts. AE, DC, MC, V.

If you knew the old Elcano, you'll see that the completely new one is nothing like it. Completely gutted during 2 years of renovation, this formerly frumpy hotel now sports a lobby swathed in Caribbean blue and white and rooms with trendy navy-and-white tile. All have tub/shower combinations and ceiling fans in addition to the central air-conditioning. Their very large junior suites, all located on corners, have two queen-size beds and huge closets. Studios are quite small, with king-size beds and small sinks outside the bathroom area. In the studios, a small portion of the TV armoire serves as a closet. The studios don't have balconies, but full sliding doors open to let in the breezes. All rooms have purified tap water and in-room safe-deposit boxes.

Dining: The informal and excellent **Bambuco** restaurant is by the pool and beach and is open from 7am to 11pm daily. Appetizers such as fried calamari serve two or three. Daily specials, priced at $14, might include lamb with apples and salad, or the house specialty, charbroiled fish with a selection of sauces. At breakfast, it's hard to avoid the waffles stuffed with fruit and nuts. The more formal **Victoria** is on an outdoor terrace overlooking the pool and beach and is open from 6 to 11pm daily.

Amenities: One beachside pool, workout room, gift shop, boutiques, travel agency, beauty shop, massages, video-game room, room and laundry service, travel agency.

✪ Hyatt Regency Acapulco. Costera Miguel Alemán 666, 39869 Acapulco, Gro. ☎ **800/233-1234** in the U.S. and Canada, or 74/69-1234. Fax 74/84-3087. 645 units. A/C TV TEL. High season $130–$243 double; $280 Regency Club; $525–$2,680 suite. Low season $85–$128 double; $200 Regency Club; $370–$1,630 suite. AE, DC, MC, V.

The Hyatt is one of the most modern of Acapulco's hotels, and its lobby is a sophisticated oasis in this mainly dated destination. Several years of remodeling and a multi-million-dollar face-lift have given it an edge over even pricier options, especially in amenities and common areas. Its free-form pool fronts a broad stretch of beautiful beach, one of the most inviting in Acapulco. The sleek lobby has an inviting sitting/bar area that features live music every evening. Room decor is stylish with rich greens and deep blues. All rooms are large, with sizable balconies overlooking the pool and ocean, and come with security boxes and purified tap water. Robes, hair dryers, and remote-control TVs are standard in deluxe rooms and the Regency Club. Regency Club guests receive complimentary continental breakfast and afternoon canapés, separate check-in and checkout, and a paperback-exchange library. This hotel caters to a Jewish clientele with a full-service Kosher restaurant, on-premises synagogue, and a special Sabbath elevator for those observing kosher traditions and holidays.

Dining/Diversions: Four restaurants including the **Zapata Villa & Co. Cantina,** featuring Mexican specialties and mariachi music; the landmark seafood-specialty restaurant, **El Pescador;** and the poolside **El Isleno,** featuring full kosher service from December through April.

Amenities: A large, shaded free-form pool, laundry, room service, concierge, travel agency, car rental, direct-dial telephone, gift shops, boutiques. Synagogue services are held on the premises.

Moderate

Calinda Acapulco Quality Inn. Costera Miguel Alemán 1260, 39300 Acapulco, Gro. ☎ **800/228-5151** in the U.S., or 74/84-0410. Fax 74/84-4676. 357 units. A/C TV TEL. Year-round $110 double. Numerous discount rates apply to senior citizens, government and military employees, corporations, and travel clubs such as AAA. AE, DC, MC, V.

You'll see this tall cylindrical tower rising at the eastern edge of Condesa Beach. Each room has a view, usually of the bay. The guest rooms, though not exceptionally furnished, are large and comfortable; most have two double beds. Package prices are available; otherwise the hotel is overpriced for what is offered. Three restaurants offer everything from poolside snacks to informal indoor dining. For cocktails, the lobby-bar party gets going around 6pm and shuts down at 1am; there's a happy hour from 4 to 9pm when drinks are two-for-one, and live music plays from 9pm to 1am. Laundry and room service and a travel agency round out the routine services. There's a swimming pool, several lobby boutiques, a pharmacy, beauty shop, two wheelchair-accessible rooms, and four nonsmoking floors.

Hotel Sands. Costera Alemán 178, 39690 Acapulco, Gro. ☎ **74/84-2260.** Fax 74/84-1053. 93 units. A/C TV TEL. $55 double all year except Christmas, Easter, and other major Mexican holidays. MC, V.

Nestled on the inland side opposite the giant resort hotels, away from the din of Costera traffic, is this unpretentious and comfortable hotel. From the street, you enter the hotel lobby through a stand of umbrella palms and a pretty garden restaurant. The rooms are light and airy in the style of a good modern motel, with fairly fancy furniture and wall-to-wall carpeting. The Sands has four swimming pools (one for children), a squash court, and volleyball and Ping-Pong areas. The rates here are more than reasonable, the accommodations satisfactory, and the location opposite the Acapulco Plaza Hotel excellent.

DOWNTOWN (ON LA QUEBRADA) AND OLD ACAPULCO BEACHES

Numerous budget-quality hotels dot the streets fanning out from the zócalo (Acapulco's official and original downtown). They're among the best values in Acapulco, but be sure to check your room first to see that it has the basic comforts you require. Several in this area are found close to the beaches of Caleta and Caletilla, or on the back side of the hilly peninsula, at Playa La Angosta. These were the standards of luxury in the 1950s, and many have gorgeous views of the city and bay.

Expensive

✪ **Plaza Las Glorias/El Mirador.** Quebrada 74, Acapulco, 39300 Gro. ☎ **800/ 342-AMIGO** in the U.S., or 74/83-1221. Fax 74/82-4564. 130 units. A/C TV TEL. High season $105 double. AE, MC, V. Parking on street.

One of the landmarks of "Old Acapulco," the former El Mirador Hotel overlooks the famous cove where the cliff divers perform. Renovated with lush tropical landscaping and lots of handsome Mexican tile, this romantic hotel offers attractively furnished rooms with double or queen-size beds, minifridge and wet bar, and large bathrooms with marble counters. Most have a separate living-room area, and all are accented with handsome Saltillo tile and other Mexican decorative touches. Ask for a room with a balcony (there are 42) and ocean view (95 rooms).

Dining/Diversions: The evening buffet ($21 to $25) offers great views of the cliff-diving show, but the coffee shop has mediocre food and slow service. The large and breezy lobby bar is a favorite spot to relax as day fades into night on the beautiful cove and bay.

Amenities: Three pools, protected cove with good snorkeling, saltwater pool reached via mountainside elevator, room service for breakfast and lunch, laundry service, travel agency.

Inexpensive

Hotel Belmar. Gran Vía Tropical and Av. de las Cumbres, 39360 Acapulco, Gro. ☎ **74/ 83-8098** or phone/Fax 74/82-1526. 72 units. Year-round (except Easter week) $31 double. No credit cards.

Two pools and shady patios fill the grassy lawn in front of this hotel. Built in the 1950s, the Belmar's an ideal place to spread out and unwind. The hotel features large, breezy rooms, enormous balconies, and relaxing views. Although the majority of the rooms are air-conditioned, a few have fans only. There's a comfortable restaurant/bar open for breakfast and lunch. Dust from an adjacent unpaved street can be a problem here, however.

Hotel Lindavista. Playa Caleta s/n (Apdo. Postal 3), 39300 Acapulco, Gro. ☎ **74/82-2783** or 74/82-5414. Fax 74/82-2783. 43 units. $50 double with fan; $62.50 double with A/C. Rates include breakfast. Ask for a discount. AE, MC, V. Free parking.

The old-fashioned Lindavista snuggles into the hillside above Caleta Beach. Older American and Mexican couples are drawn to the well-kept rooms, beautiful views, and slow pace of the area here. Most rooms have air-conditioning; those that don't have fans. The hotel has a small pool and a terrace restaurant/bar. Cozy as the Lindavista is, the quoted prices are probably higher than merited—negotiate a discount or ask about their packages for a stay of several nights. Coming from Caleta Beach, you'll find the hotel up the hill to the left of the Hotel Caleta.

✪ **Hotel Misión.** Felipe Valle 12, 39300 Acapulco, Gro. ☎ **74/82-3643**, Fax 74/82-2076. 27 units. $27 double. No credit cards.

Enter this hotel's plant-filled brick courtyard, shaded by an enormous mango tree, and you'll retreat into an earlier, more peaceful Acapulco. This tranquil 19th-century hotel lies 2 blocks inland from the Costera and the zócalo. The original L-shaped building is at least a century old. The freshly painted rooms have colonial touches, such as colorful tile and wrought iron, and come simply furnished with a fan and one or two beds with good mattresses. Unfortunately, the promised hot water seldom appears—be prepared for cold showers. Breakfast is served on the patio. On Thursday beginning at 3pm, an elaborate pozole spread is cooked out on the patio—bowls of the regional specialty and accompanying botana plate cost around $5.

Hotel Villa Romana. Av. López Mateos 185, Fracc. Las Playas, 39300 Acapulco, Gro. ☎ **74/82-3995**. 9 units. A/C. High season $35 double. Low season $31 double. MC, V.

With terraces facing the sparkling Playa la Angosta, this is one of the most comfortable inns in the area, ideal for a long stay. Some rooms are tiled and others carpeted; all have small kitchens with refrigerators. There is a small plant-filled terrace on the second floor with tables and chairs and a fourth-floor pool with a splendid view of the bay.

WHERE TO DINE

Dining out in Acapulco can be one of the best experiences you can have in Mexico—whether you're in a bathing suit enjoying a hamburger on the beach or seated at a candlelit table with the glittering bay spread out before you.

A deluxe establishment in Acapulco may not be much more expensive than a mass-market restaurant. The proliferation of U.S. franchise restaurants (Subway, Shakey's Pizza, Tony Roma's) has increased competition in Acapulco, and even the more expensive places have reduced prices in response.

The restaurants listed below are good values with good food. If it's a romantic place you're looking for, you won't have to look far, since Acapulco fairly brims over with such inviting places.

SOUTH OF TOWN: LAS BRISAS AREA
Very Expensive
✪ **Madeiras.** Carretera Escénica 33. ☎ **74/84-4378.** Reservations required. $30 fixed-price 4-course meal. AE, MC, V. Daily 7–11pm. MEXICAN/CONTINENTAL.

Enjoy an elegant meal and a fabulous view of glittering Acapulco Bay at night at Madeiras, east of town on the scenic highway before the Las Brisas hotel. The several small dining areas have ceiling fans and are open to the evening breezes. If you arrive before your table is ready, have a drink in the comfortable lounge. A long-standing favorite of Mexico City's elite, dress tends toward fashionable tropical attire. Menu selections include roast quail stuffed with tropical fruits, and fish cooked in orange sauce. Other preferred dishes include filet mignon, beef Stroganoff, and frogs' legs in garlic and white wine. They offer an ample selection of reasonably priced national wines, plus imported labels as well.

✪ **Restaurant Miramar.** Plaza La Vista, Carretera Escénica. ☎ **74/84-7874.** Reservations required. Main courses $20–$30; desserts $5–$9. AE, DISC, MC, V. Daily 6:30pm–midnight. Closed Sun during the low season. ITALIAN/FRENCH/MEXICAN.

The Miramar is about as formal as Acapulco restaurants get, and with the view of the bay and outstanding food, the dining experience is something special. Waiters in black suits and ties are quietly solicitous, allowing you to soak in the view between courses. The menu is as refined as the service, offering familiar continental classics such as duck in orange sauce, coq au vin, and tournedos Rossini, all exquisitely presented. But save room for a dessert as memorable as the main courses. Dress up a bit for dining here. The Miramar is in the La Vista complex near the Las Brisas hotel.

Spicey. Carretera Escénica. ☎ **74/81-1380** or 74/81-0470. Reservations recommended on weekends. Main courses $15–$30. AE, CB, DC, DISC, MC, V. Daily 7–11:30pm. Valet parking available. CREATIVE CUISINE.

For original food with a flair, you can't beat this trendy new restaurant in the Las Brisas area, next to Kookaburas. Diners (in cool attire on the dressy side of casual) can enjoy the air-conditioning indoors or the completely open rooftop terrace with a sweeping view of the bay. To begin, try the shrimp Spicey, in a fresh coconut batter with an orange-marmalade-and-mustard sauce. Among the main courses, the grilled veal chop in pineapple and papaya chutney is a winner, as is the beef tenderloin, prepared Thai- or Santa Fe–style, or blackened. The chiles rellenos in mango sauce win raves.

COSTERA HOTEL ZONE
Expensive

Dino's. Costera Alemán s/n. ☎ **74/84-0037.** Reservations recommended. Main courses $10–$20. AE, DC, MC, V. Daily 9am–midnight. NORTHERN ITALIAN.

A popular dining spot for years, Dino's has secured its reputation with a combination of good food and service at respectable prices. From the second-story dining room, there's a modest bay view between high-rise hotels. The restaurant is famous for its fettuccine Alfredo, which waiters prepare with fanfare, often table-side. Other main courses include broiled seafood and steak, all of which come with baked potato, vegetables, and Dino's special oven-baked bread. A new menu features daily specials like tortellini in marinara sauce and *gnocchi al pesto,* as well as vegetarian main courses like fettuccine primavera. A nightly $20 special includes a welcome cocktail, salad, entree, dessert, and coffee.

El Olvido. Diana Circle, Plaza Marbella. ☎ **74/81-0203,** 74/81-0256, 74/81-0214, or 74/81-0240. Main courses $15–$45. AE, DC, MC, V. Daily 6pm–2am. NOUVELLE MEXICAN.

Once in the door of this handsome terrace restaurant, you'll almost forget that it's tucked in a shopping mall—you have all the glittering bay-view ambiance of the posh Las Brisas restaurants without the taxi ride. The menu is one of the most sophisticated in the city. It's expensive, but each dish is delightful, not only in presentation but taste. Start with one of the 12 house-specialty drinks such as Olvido, made with tequila, rum, Cointreau (orange-flavored liquor), tomato juice, and lime juice. Soups include a delicious cold melon and thick black-bean and sausage. Among the innovative entrees are quail with honey and pasilla chiles and thick sea bass with a mild sauce of cilantro and avocado. For dessert try the chocolate fondue or the guanabana (a tropical fruit) mousse in a rich zapote negro (black-colored tropical fruit) sauce.

El Olvido is in the shopping center fronted by the Aca-Joe clothing store on Diana Circle. Walk into the passage to the left of Aca-Joe and bear left; it's at the far back.

Moderate

✪ **El Cabrito.** Costera Alemán 1480. ☎ **74/84-7711.** Breakfast (served until noon) $3–$5; main courses $4–$8. AE, MC, V. Daily 8am–1am. NORTHERN MEXICAN.

With its arched adobe decor, waitresses in embroidered dresses, and location in the heart of the Costera, this restaurant targets tourists. But its authentic and well-prepared specialties attract Mexicans in the know—a comforting stamp of approval. Among its specialties are *cabrito al pastor* (roasted goat), charro beans, northern-style steaks, and burritos de machaca. Regional specialties from other areas include Jalisco-style birria and mole Oaxaca-style. Dine inside or outside on the patio facing the Costera. It's on the ocean side of the Costera opposite the Hard Rock Cafe, and south of the Convention Center.

Su Casa/La Margarita. Av. Anahuac 110. ☎ **74/84-4350** or 74/84-1261. Fax 74/84-0803. Reservations recommended. Main courses $8–$18. AE, MC, V. Daily 6pm–midnight. INTERNATIONAL.

Relaxed elegance and terrific food at moderate prices are what you get at Su Casa, a delightful restaurant with some of the best food in the city. Owners Shelly and Ángel Herrera created this pleasant and breezy open-air restaurant on the patio of their hill-side home overlooking the city. Both are experts in the kitchen and stay on hand nightly to greet guests on their patio. The menu changes often, so each time you go there's something new to try—ask about off-the-menu specials. Some items are standard, such as the unusual chile con carne, which is served both as a main dish and as an appetizer. Also served daily are shrimp à la patrona in garlic; grilled fish, steak, and chicken; and flaming *fillet al Madrazo,* a delightful brochette first marinated in tropical juices. Most entrees come with garnishes of cooked banana or pineapple, and often with a baked potato or rice. The margaritas are big and delicious. Su Casa is the hot-pink building on the hillside above the Convention Center.

DOWNTOWN: THE ZÓCALO AREA

The old downtown area of Acapulco is loaded with simple, inexpensive restaurants serving up tasty eats. It's easy to pay more elsewhere in Acapulco and not get such consistently good food as what you'll find at the restaurants in this part of town. To explore this area, start right at the zócalo and stroll west along Juárez. After about 3 blocks you'll come to Azueta, lined with small seafood cafes and street-side stands.

Moderate

✪ **Mariscos Pipo.** Almirante Breton 3. ☎ **74/82-2237.** Main courses $5–$11. AE, MC, V. Daily noon–8pm. SEAFOOD.

Check out the photographs of Old Acapulco on the walls while relaxing in the airy dining room of this place, decorated with hanging nets, fish, glass buoys, and shell lanterns. The English-language menu lists a wide array of seafood, including ceviche, lobster, octopus, crayfish, and baby-shark quesadillas. This local favorite is 5 blocks west of the zócalo on Breton, just off the Costera. Another branch, open daily from 1 to 9pm, is at Costera M. Alemán and Canadá (☎ **74/84-0165**).

Inexpensive

Cafe Los Amigos. Av. de la Paz 10 at Ignacio Ramírez. No phone. Breakfast $2.50; sandwiches $1.75–$3; fresh-fruit drinks $1.25; daily specials $3–$5. No credit cards. Daily 9am–10pm. MEXICAN/INTERNATIONAL.

With umbrella-covered tables on one of the coolest and shadiest sections of the zócalo, this little restaurant is especially popular for breakfast, with specials that include a great fresh-fruit salad with mango, pineapple, and cantaloupe, and coffee refills. Other specials include fish fingers, empanadas, breaded chicken, and burgers and fries. Fruit drinks, including fresh mango juice, come in schooner-size glasses. To find the restaurant, enter the zócalo from the Costera and walk toward the kiosk. On the left, about midway into the zócalo, you'll see a wide, shady passageway that leads onto avenida de la Paz and the umbrella-covered tables under the huge shady tree.

✪ **El Amigo Miguel.** Juárez 31, at Azueta. ☎ **74/83-6981.** Main courses $3–$8. AE, MC, V. Daily 10am–9pm. MEXICAN/SEAFOOD.

Locals know that El Amigo Miguel is a standout among downtown seafood restaurants—you can easily pay more but not eat better elsewhere. Fresh seafood reigns here; the large open-air dining room, 3 blocks west of the zócalo, is usually brimming with seafood lovers. Try the delicious *camarones borrachos* (drunken shrimp) in a delicious sauce made with beer, applesauce, ketchup, mustard, and bits of fresh bacon—its whole tastes nothing like the individual ingredients. The *filete Miguel* is red-snapper fillet stuffed with seafood and covered in a wonderful poblano-pepper sauce. To accommodate the crowds, El Amigo II is open directly across the street.

DINING WITH A VIEW

Restaurants with unparalleled views of Acapulco include **Madeiras** and **Miramar** in the Las Brisas area, **Bambuco** at the Hotel Elcano, **Su Casa** on a hill above the Convention Center, **La Bahía Restaurant** at the Sheraton Hotel, and the **Bella Vista Restaurant** (now open to the public) at the Las Brisas hotel.

ACAPULCO AFTER DARK

SPECIAL ATTRACTIONS   "Gran Noche Mexicana," performed by the **Acapulco Ballet Folklórico,** is held in the plaza of the Convention Center every Tuesday, Thursday, and Saturday night at 8pm. With dinner and open bar, the show costs $45; general admission (including three drinks) is $20. Call for reservations (☎ **74/84-7050**) or consult a local travel agency.

Another excellent **Mexican fiesta/folkloric dance show,** which includes *voladores* (flying pole dancers) from Papantla, is found at Marbella Plaza near the Continental Plaza Hotel on the Costera on Monday, Wednesday, and Friday at 7pm. The $35 fee covers the show, buffet, open bar, taxes, and gratuities. Make reservations through a travel agency.

Many major hotels also host Mexican fiestas and other theme nights that include dinner and entertainment. Local travel agencies will have information.

NIGHTCLUBS & DISCOS   Acapulco is even more famous for its nightclub scene than for its beaches. Because clubs open and close with regularity, it's extremely difficult to give specific and accurate recommendations. Some general tips will help. Every club seems to have a cover charge of around $20 in high season and $10 in low season; drinks can cost anywhere from $2.50 to $7.

Many periodically waive their cover charge or offer some other promotion to attract customers. Another trend is to have a higher cover charge but an open bar. Call the disco or look for promotional materials displayed in hotel reception areas, at travel desks or concierge booths, and in local publications.

The high-rise hotels have their own bars, and sometimes discos. Informal lobby or poolside cocktail bars often offer live entertainment to enjoy for the price of drinks.

THE BEACH BAR ZONE   Prefer a little fresh air with your nightlife? The young and hip crowd is favoring the growing number of open-air oceanfront dance clubs

Shorts Short

When the managers of local discos say no shorts, they mean no shorts for men; they welcome (no doubt encourage) them for women.

along Costera Alemán, most featuring techno or alternative rock. There's a concentration between the Fiesta Americana and Continental Plaza hotels. These clubs are an earlier and more casual option to the glitzy discos, and include the jamming **Disco Beach, Tabu** and the pirate-themed **Barbaroja.** These mainly offer open bar with cover charge (around $10) options. Ladies frequently drink for free with a lesser charge. Men may pay more, but then, this is where the young and tanned beach babes are. . . .

Baby-0. Costera Alemán. ☎ **74/84-7474.** Cover $15–$20.

Baby-O can be very selective about whom they allow in when it's crowded. Your chances of getting in here are directly proportional to how young, pretty, and female you are. Your next best shot is to be older and swathed in glittering riches. Across from the Romano Days Inn, this intimate disco has a small dance floor surrounded by several tiers of tables and sculpted, cavelike walls. It even has a hot tub and breakfast area. Drinks run $4 to $5. Open from 11pm to 5am.

Carlos 'n Charlie's. Costera Alemán 999. ☎ **74/84-1285** or 74/84-0039. No cover.

For fun, danceable music, and good food all at the same time, you can't go wrong with this branch of the Carlos Anderson chain. It's always packed. Come early and get a seat on the terrace overlooking the Costera. It's a great place to go for late dinner and a few drinks before going to one of the "true" Acapulco clubs. It's located east of the Diana traffic circle, across the street from the El Presidente Hotel and the Fiesta Americana Condesa. Open nightly from 6:30pm to 2am.

Extravaganzza. Carretera Escénica. ☎ **74/84-7154** or 74/84-7164. Cover $15–$20.

Venture into this snazzy chrome-and-neon extravaganza, perched on the side of the mountain, for a true Acapulco-nightlife experience. Located between Los Rancheros Restaurant and La Vista Shopping Center, you can't miss the neon lights. The plush, dim interior dazzles patrons with a sunken dance floor and panoramic view of the lights of Acapulco Bay. The door attendants wear tuxedos, so don't expect to be admitted in grunge wear—tight and slinky is the norm for ladies, no shorts for gentlemen. It opens nightly at 10:30pm; fireworks rock the usually full house at 3am. Call to find out if reservations are needed.

Fantasy. Carretera Escénica. ☎ **74/84-6727** or 74/84-6764. Cover $15–$20.

This club has a fantastic bay view and occasionally waives the cover charge. It's particularly popular with the moneyed Mexico City set, and musically it caters to patrons in their midtwenties to midthirties. Periodically during the evening the club projects a laser show across the bay. The dress code does not permit shorts, jeans, T-shirts, or sandals. Reservations are recommended. Located in the La Vista Shopping Center, it's open nightly from 10:30pm to 4am.

Hard Rock Cafe. Costera Alemán 37. ☎ **74/84-0077.** Cover for live music $5–$15, depending on the band.

If you like your music loud, your food trendy, and your entertainment *à la internationale,* you'll feel at home in Acapulco's branch of this chain bent on world domination.

Elvis memorabilia greets you in the entry area, and among other numerous framed or encased mementos is the Beatles gold record for "Can't Buy Me Love." There's a bandstand for the live music and a small dance floor. It's on the seaward side toward the southern end of the Costera, south of the Convention Center and opposite El Cabrito. It's open daily from noon to 2am. There's live music Wednesday through Monday from 11:30pm to 1:30am.

News. Costera Alemán. ☎ **74/84-5902.** Cover (including open bar) $20.

The booths and love seats ringing the vast dance floor can seat 1,200, so this disco doubles as a concert hall. While high-tech, it's also laid-back and user-friendly, with no dress code. Across the street from the Hyatt Regency Acapulco, it's open nightly from 10:30pm to 4am.

2 Northward to Zihuatanejo & Ixtapa

360 miles SW of Mexico City; 353 miles SE of Manzanillo; 158 miles NW of Acapulco

The side-by-side beach resorts of Ixtapa and Zihuatanejo share a common geography, but in character, they couldn't be more different. Ixtapa is a model of modern infrastructure, services, and luxury hotels, while Zihuatanejo is the quintessential Mexican fishing village. For travelers, this offers an agreeable contrast and the best of both worlds. Those who want creature comforts should opt for Ixtapa and take advantage of well-appointed rooms in a setting of great natural beauty. You can easily and quickly make the four-mile trip into Zihuatanejo for a sampling of the simple life of this pueblo by the sea. Those who prefer a more rustic retreat, however, tend to settle in Zihuatanejo—unless, of course, they want a livelier pace at night.

The area, with a backdrop of the Sierra Madre mountains and a foreground of Pacific waters, provides a full range of ways to pass the days. Scuba diving, deep-sea fishing, bay cruises to remote beaches, and golf are among the favorite activities.

This dual destination is the choice for the traveler looking for a little of everything, where you can sample each end of the spectrum from fashionable indulgence to unpretentious simplicity.

ESSENTIALS

GETTING THERE & DEPARTING   By Plane   These destinations tend to be even more seasonal than most resorts in Mexico, and most of the U.S.-based airlines suspend flights between Easter and Thanksgiving. See chapter 3, "Planning a Trip to Mexico," for information on flying to Ixtapa/Zihuatanejo from the United States and Canada. Both **Aeromexico** and **Mexicana** fly daily into Ixtapa via Mexico City and Guadalajara. Here are the local numbers of some international carriers: **Aeromexico** (☎ **755/4-2018,** 755/4-2022, or 755/4-2019), **Mexicana** (☎ **755/3-2208,** 755/3-2209, or 755/4-2227), and **Northwest** (☎ **5/207-0515** in Mexico City).

Ask your travel agent about charter flights, which are becoming the most efficient and least expensive way to get here.

Arriving: The Ixtapa-Zihuatanejo airport is 15 minutes (about 7 miles) south of Zihuatanejo. **Taxi** fares range from $10 to $15. **Transportes Terrestres** colectivo minivans transport travelers to hotels in Zihuatanejo, Ixtapa, and Club Med; tickets are sold just outside the baggage-claim area and run between $6 and $8. There are several car-rental agencies with booths in the airport. These include **Dollar Car Rental** (☎ **800/800-4000** in the U.S., or 755/4-2314) and **Hertz** (☎ **800/654-3131** in the U.S., or 755/4-2590).

Motorist Advisory

Motorists planning to follow Highway 200 northwest up the coast from Ixtapa or Zihuatanejo toward Lázaro Cárdenas and Manzanillo should be aware of reports of car and bus hijackings on that route, especially around Playa Azul, with bus holdups more common than car. Before heading in that direction, ask locals and the tourism office about the status of the route when you are there, and don't drive at night. According to tourism officials, police and military patrols of the highway have been increased, and the number of incidents has decreased dramatically.

Taxis are the single option for returning to the airport from town; they charge from $5.50 to $10 one way.

By Car From Mexico City, the shortest route is Highway 15 to Toluca, then Highway 130/134 the rest of the way, though on the latter, highway gas stations are few and far between. The other route is the four-lane Highway 95D to Iguala, then Highway 51 west to Highway 134.

From Acapulco or Manzanillo, the only choice is the coastal highway, Highway 200. The ocean views along the winding, mountain-edged drive from Manzanillo can be spectacular.

By Bus There are two bus terminals in Zihuatanejo: the **Central de Autobuses,** from which most lines operate, and the **Estrella de Oro** station, on Paseo del Palmar near the market and within walking distance of downtown hotels.

At the **Central de Autobuses,** several companies offer daily service to Acapulco, Puerto Escondido, Huatulco, Manzanillo, Puerto Vallarta, and other cities. First-class **Estrella de Oro** runs daily buses to Acapulco. Advance tickets with seat assignments can be purchased at **Turismo Caleta** in the La Puerta shopping center in Ixtapa, next to the tourism office (☎ **755/4-2175**).

The trip from Mexico City to Zihuatanejo takes 5 hours (bypassing Acapulco); from Acapulco, 4 to 5 hours. From Zihuatanejo, it's 6 or 7 hours to Manzanillo, and an additional 6 to Puerto Vallarta, which doesn't include time spent waiting for buses.

Arriving: In Zihuatanejo, the **Estrella de Oro** bus station, on Paseo del Palmar at Morelos, is a few blocks beyond the market and is within walking distance of some of the suggested downtown hotels. The clean, warehouselike **Central de Autobuses** is a mile or so farther out, opposite the Pemex station and IMSS Hospital on Paseo Zihuatanejo at Paseo la Boquita. Taxis wait in front of the stations.

VISITOR INFORMATION The **State Tourism Office** (☎ **888/248-7037** from the U.S. or 800/711-1526 toll-free inside Mexico; ☎/fax 755/3-1967 or 755/3-1968) is in the **La Puerta** shopping center in Ixtapa across from the Presidente Inter-Continental Hotel; it's open Monday through Friday from 9am to 7pm and on Saturday from 10am to 2pm. The **Zihuatanejo Tourism Office** (☎/fax **755/4-2001,** ext. 120; www.cdnet.com.mx/ixtapa/fondomix; E-mail: fondomixto@cdnet.com.mx.) is on the main square by the basketball court at Álvarez; it's open Monday through Friday from 9am to 8pm.

Note: According to recent regulations, time-share sales booths in both towns must be clearly marked according to business names and cannot carry signs claiming to be tourist-information centers.

CITY LAYOUT The fishing village and resort of **Zihuatanejo** spreads out around the beautiful Bay of Zihuatanejo, framed by downtown to the north and a beautiful long beach and the Sierra foothills to the east. The heart of Zihuatanejo is the waterfront walkway **Paseo del Pescador** (also called the **Malecón**), bordering the

Municipal Beach. The town centerpiece is, rather than a plaza as in most Mexican villages, Zihuatanejo's **basketball court,** which fronts the beach. It's a useful point of reference for directions. The main thoroughfare for cars is **Juan Álvarez,** a block behind the Malecón. Sections of several of the main streets are designated as *zona peatonal* (pedestrian zone, blocked off to cars). The area is zigzagged, however, and seems to block parts of streets haphazardly.

A cement-and-sand walkway runs from the Malecón in downtown Zihuatanejo along the water to Playa Madera, making it much easier to walk between the two points. The walkway is lit at night. Access to Playa La Ropa ("clothing beach") is via the main road, **Camino a Playa La Ropa.** Playa La Ropa and Playa Las Gatas are connected by road and boat.

A good highway connects "Zihua," as the resort is often called, to **Ixtapa,** 4 miles to the northwest. The 18-hole **Ixtapa Golf Club** marks the beginning of the inland side of Ixtapa. Tall hotels line Ixtapa's wide beach, **Playa Palmar,** against a backdrop of lush palm groves and mountains. Access is by the main street, **bulevar Ixtapa.** On the opposite side of the main boulevard lies a large expanse of small shopping plazas (many of the shops are air-conditioned) and restaurants. At the far end of bulevar Ixtapa, **Marina Ixtapa** has excellent restaurants, private yacht slips, and an 18-hole golf course. Condominiums and private homes surround the marina and golf course, and more developments of exclusive residential areas are rising in the hillsides past the marina en route to Playa Quieta and Playa Linda.

GETTING AROUND   **Taxi** rates are reasonable between Ixtapa and Zihuatanejo, but from midnight to 5am rates increase by 50%. The average fare between Ixtapa and Zihuatanejo is $3.25. A **shuttle bus** goes back and forth between Zihuatanejo and Ixtapa every 10 or 15 minutes from 5am to 11pm daily. In Zihuatanejo it stops near the corner of Morelos/Paseo Zihuatanejo and Juárez, about 3 blocks north of the market. In Ixtapa it makes numerous stops along bulevar Ixtapa.

Special note: The highway leading from Zihuatanejo to Ixtapa is now a broad, four-lane highway, which makes driving between the towns easier and faster than ever. Street signs are becoming more common in Zihuatanejo, and good signs now lead you in and out of both towns. However, both locations have an area called the "Zona Hotelera" (Hotel Zone), so if you're trying to reach Ixtapa's Hotel Zone, you may be confused by signs in Zihuatanejo pointing to that village's own Hotel Zone.

FAST FACTS: ZIHUATANEJO & IXTAPA

American Express   The main office is in the commercial promenade of the Krystal Ixtapa Hotel (☎ **755/3-0853;** fax 755/3-1206). They're open Monday through Saturday from 9am to 6pm.

Area Code   The telephone area code changed to **755** in 1995 (it was 753).

Banks   Ixtapa's main bank is **Bancomer,** in the La Puerta Centro shopping center. Zihuatanejo has four banks, but the most centrally located is **Banamex,** Cuauhtémoc 4. Banks change money during normal business hours, which are now generally 9am to 6pm Monday through Friday and Saturday from 9am to 1pm. Automatic tellers and currency exchanges are available during these and other hours.

Climate   Summer is hot and humid, though tempered by sea breezes and brief showers; September is the peak of the tropical rainy season, with showers concentrated in the late afternoons.

ACTIVITIES ON & OFF THE BEACH

The **Museo de Arqueología** de la Costa Grande traces the history of the Costa Grande (the area from Acapulco to Ixtapa/Zihuatanejo) from its significance in pre-Hispanic times, when it was known as Cihuatlán, through the colonial era. Most of the museum's pottery and stone artifacts depict evidence of extensive trade with far-off cultures and regions, including the Toltec and Teotihuacán cultures near Mexico City, the Olmec culture on both the Pacific and Gulf coasts, and areas known today as the states of Nayarit, Michoacán, and San Luis Potosí. Area indigenous groups paid the Aztecs tribute items, including cotton *tilmas* (capes) and *cacao* (chocolate), representations of which can be seen here. The museum, near Guerrero at the east end of Paseo del Pescador, easily merits the half hour or less it takes to stroll through; information is in Spanish. Admission is $1, and it's open Tuesday through Sunday from 10am to 5pm.

THE BEACHES **In Zihuatanejo** At Zihuatanejo's town beach, **Playa Municipal,** the local fishermen pull their colorful boats up onto the sand, making for a fine photo-op. Small shops and restaurants line the waterfront, making this also a great spot to people-watch and to absorb the flavor of daily village life. The municipal beach is protected from the main surge of the Pacific.

Zihuatanejo has three other beaches of note: Madera, La Ropa, and Las Gatas. **Playa Madera** ("Wood Beach"), just east of Playa Municipal, is open to the surf but generally peaceful. A number of attractive budget lodgings overlook this area from the hillside.

South of Playa Madera is Zihuatanejo's largest and most beautiful beach, **Playa La Ropa,** a long sweep of sand with a great view of the sunset. (The name "Playa La Ropa" comes from an old tale that tells of the sinking of a *galeón* during a big storm. The silk clothing that it was carrying back from the Philippines all washed ashore on this beach, hence the name.) Some lovely small hotels and restaurants nestle into the hills; palm groves edge the shoreline. Although it's also open to the Pacific, waves are usually gentle. A taxi from town costs $2.

The pretty, secluded **Playa Las Gatas** ("Cats Beach") can be seen across the bay from Playa Ropa and Zihuatanejo. The small coral reef just offshore makes it a good location for snorkeling and diving, and open-air seafood restaurants on the beach make it an appealing lunch spot. Small launches with shade run to Las Gatas from the Zihuatanejo town pier, a 10-minute trip; the captains will take you across whenever you wish between 8am and 4pm. Usually the last boat back leaves Las Gatas at 4:30pm, but check to be sure. Snorkeling and water-sports gear can be rented at the beach.

In Ixtapa Ixtapa's main beach, **Playa Palmar,** is a lovely white-sand arc on the edge of the Hotel Zone, with dramatic rock formations silhouetted in the sea. The surf here can be rough; use caution and never swim when a red flag is posted.

Several of the nicest beaches in the area are essentially closed to the public, as lavish resort developments rope them off exclusively for their guests. Although by law all Mexican beaches are open to the public, it is a common practice for hotels to create artificial "barriers" (such as rocks or dunes) to preclude entrance to their beaches. **Playa Quieta,** on the mainland across from Isla Ixtapa, has been largely claimed by Club Med and Qualton Club. The remaining piece of beach was once the launching point for boats to the Isla Ixtapa, but it is gradually being taken over by a private development. Isla Ixtapa-bound boats now leave from the jetty on **Playa Linda,** about 8 miles north of Ixtapa. Inexpensive water taxis here ferry passengers to Isla Ixtapa. Playa Linda is the primary out-of-town beach, with water-sports equipment and horse rentals available. **Playa las Cuatas,** a pretty beach and cove a few miles north of Ixtapa, and **Playa Majahua,** an isolated beach just west of Zihuatanejo, are both being transformed into resort complexes. Lovely **Playa Vista Hermosa** is framed by striking rock formations and bordered by the Westin Brisas Hotel high on the hill.

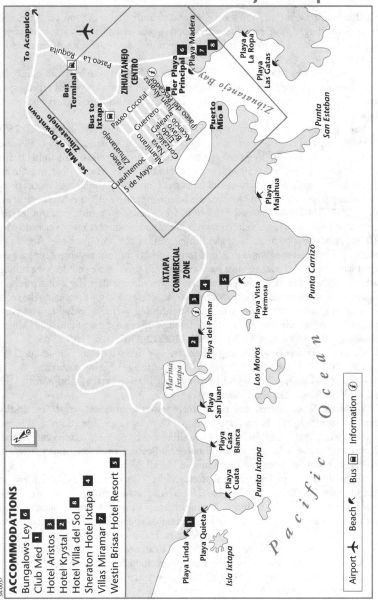

To Acapulco

Paseo La Roqueta

Bus Terminal

ZIHUATANEJO CENTRO

Bus to Ixtapa

See Map of Downtown Zihuatanejo

Paseo Cocotal

Paseo del Pescador

Pier Playa Principal

Playa Madera

Playa La Ropa

Playa Las Gatas

Juan Álvarez

Nicolás Bravo

Ascencio

Galeana

Ejido

González

Guerrero

Nava

Alamirano

Cuauhtémoc

5 de Mayo

paseo Zihuatanejo

Puerto Mío

Zihuatanejo Bay

Playa Majahua

Punta San Esteban

IXTAPA COMMERCIAL ZONE

Playa del Palmar

Playa Vista Hermosa

Punta Carrizo

Marina Ixtapa

Los Moros

Playa San Juan

Playa Casa Blanca

Punta Ixtapa

Playa Cuata

Playa Quieta

Playa Linda

Isla Ixtapa

Pacific Ocean

ACCOMMODATIONS

Bungalows Ley 6
Club Med 1
Hotel Aristos 3
Hotel Krystal 2
Hotel Villa del Sol 8
Sheraton Hotel Ixtapa 4
Villas Miramar 7
Westin Brisas Hotel Resort 5

SA-0037

Airport ✈   Beach ⚓   Bus ◼   Information 𝒊

WATER SPORTS & BOAT TRIPS   Probably the most popular boat trip is to **Isla Ixtapa** for snorkeling and lunch at El Marlin restaurant. Though you can book this outing as a tour through local travel agencies, you can also go on your own from Zihuatanejo by following the directions to Playa Linda above and taking a boat from there. Boats leave at 11:30am for Isla Ixtapa and return around 4pm. Along the way, you'll pass dramatic rock formations and the **Los Moros de Los Péricos islands,** known for the great variety of birds that nest on the rocky points jutting out into the blue Pacific.

On Isla Ixtapa you'll find good snorkeling and a nature trail with some birds and animals. Snorkeling, diving, and other water-sports gear is available for rent on the island. Be sure to catch the last water taxi back at 4pm, but double-check that time before you go.

Day-trips to **Los Moros de Los Péricos islands** for **bird watching** can usually be arranged through local travel agencies, though it would probably be less expensive to rent a boat with a guide at Playa Linda. The islands are offshore from Ixtapa's main beach.

Sunset cruises on the trimaran *TriStar*, arranged through **Yates del Sol** (☎ 755/4-3589), depart from the town pier at Puerto Mío. The sunset cruise costs $40 and includes an open bar. But they don't just cruise out at dusk. An all-day trip to Isla Ixtapa on this yacht begins at 10:30am, costs $60, and includes an open bar and lunch. Schedules and special trips vary, so call for current information and about special trips.

Fishing trips can be arranged with the **boat cooperative** at the Zihuatanejo town pier (☎ 755/4-2056) and cost $130 to $250, depending on boat size, trip length, and so on (most trips last about 6 hr.; no credit cards are accepted). The price includes 10 soft drinks and 10 beers, bait, and fishing gear. Lunch is on your own. You'll pay more for a trip arranged through a local travel agency; the least expensive trips are on small launches called *pangas;* most have shade. Both small-game and deep-sea fishing are offered, and the fishing here rivals that of Mazatlán or Baja. Trips that combine fishing with a visit to near-deserted ocean beaches that extend for miles along the coast from Zihuatanejo can also be arranged. Sportfishing packages including air transportation and hotels can be arranged through **Mexico Sportsman,** 202 Milam Building, San Antonio, TX 78205 (☎ 210/212-4567; fax 210/212-4568). San Lushinsky at **Ixtapa Sport-fishing Charters,** 33 Olde Mill Run, Stroudsburg, PA 18360 (☎ 717/424-8323; fax 717/424-1016), is another fishing outfitter.

Boating and fishing expeditions from the new **Marina Ixtapa,** a bit north of the Ixtapa Hotel Zone, can also be arranged.

Sailboats, Windsurfers, and other **water-sports equipment** rentals are usually available at various stands on Playa La Ropa, Playa las Gatas, Isla Ixtapa, and at the main beach, Playa Palmar, in Ixtapa. **Parasailing** can be done at La Ropa and Palmar. **Kayaks** are available for rent at the **Zihuatanejo Scuba Center** (see below), hotels in Ixtapa, and some water-sports operations on Playa La Ropa.

Scuba-diving trips are arranged through the **Zihuatanejo Scuba Center,** on Cuauhtémoc 3 (☎/fax 755/4-2147). Fees start at around $70 for two dives, including all equipment and lunch. Marine biologist and dive instructor Juan Barnard speaks excellent English and is very knowledgeable about the area, which has nearly 30 different dive sites, including walls and caves. He's also known as a very fun guide. They have added a small hotel, **Hotel Paraiso Real,** on La Ropa Beach (see "Where to Stay," below). Diving takes place year-round, though the water is clearest May through December, when visibility is 100 feet or better. The nearest decompression chamber is in Acapulco. Advance reservations for dives are advised during Christmas and Easter.

Surfing is particularly good at **Petacalco Beach** north of Ixtapa.

LAND SPORTS & ACTIVITIES   In Ixtapa, the **Club de Golf Ixtapa** (☎ 755/3-1062 or 755/3-1163) in front of the Sheraton Hotel has an 18-hole course designed by Robert Trent Jones, Jr. Bring your own clubs or rent them here. The greens fee is $45, caddies cost $16, and electric carts $25. Tee-offs begin at 7am, but they don't take reservations. The **Marina Ixtapa Golf Course** (☎ 755/3-1410; fax 755/3-0825), designed by Robert von Hagge, has 18 challenging holes. The greens fee is $85 with cart and caddie. Tee-off is at 7am. Call for reservations 24 hours in advance.

To polish your **tennis** game in Zihuatanejo, try the **Hotel Villa del Sol** at Playa La Ropa (☎ **755/4-2239** or 755/4-3239). In Ixtapa, the **Club de Golf Ixtapa** (☎ **755/ 3-1062** or 755/3-1163) and the **Marina Ixtapa Golf Course** (☎ **755/3-1410;** fax 755/3-0825) both have lit courts and both rent equipment. Fees are $10 per hour day-time, $12 per hour at night. Call for reservations. In addition, the **Dorado Pacífico** and several other hotels on the main beach of Ixtapa have courts.

For horseback riding, **Rancho Playa Linda** (☎ **755/4-3085**) offers guided trail rides from the Playa Linda beach (about 8 miles north of Ixtapa). Guided rides begin at 8:30, 9:45, and 11am, noon, 3, 4, and 5pm. Groups of three or more riders can arrange their own tour, which is especially nice a little later in the evening around sunset (though you'll need mosquito repellent in the evening). Riders can chose to trace along the beach to the mouth of the river and back through coconut plantations, or hug the beach for the whole ride (which usually lasts 1 to 1½ hr.). The fee is around $12, cash only. Travel agencies in either town can arrange your trip but will charge a bit more for transportation. Reservations are suggested in the high season.

A **countryside tour** of fishing villages, coconut and mango plantations, and the **Barra de Potosí Lagoon,** which is 14 miles south of Zihuatanejo and known for its tropical birds, is available through local travel agencies for $25 to $30. The tour typi-cally lasts 5½ hours and includes lunch and time for swimming.

For **off-the-beaten-track tours,** contact Alex León Piñeda, the friendly and knowl-edgeable owner of **Fw4 Tours** in the Los Patios Center in Ixtapa (☎ **755/3-1442;** fax 755/3-2014). His countryside tour ($33) goes to coconut and banana plantations, small villages of traditional brick makers and palm thatch huts, and to the beach at La Saladita, where fishermen and visitors together prepare a lunch of fresh lobster, dorado, or snapper.

SHOPPING
ZIHUATANEJO

Like other resorts in Mexico, Zihuatanejo has its quota of T-shirt and souvenir shops, but it's becoming a better place to buy Mexican crafts, folk art, and jewelry. The **artisan's market** on calle Cinco de Mayo is a good place to start your shopping before moving on to specialty shops. The **municipal market** on avenida Benito Juárez (about 5 blocks inland from the waterfront) is also good, especially the stands specializing in huaraches, hammocks, and baskets. The market area sprawls over several blocks and is well worth an early-morning visit. Spreading inland from the water-front some 3 or 4 blocks are numerous small shops worth exploring. Besides the places listed below, check out **Alberto's** at Cuauhtémoc 15 and **Ruby's** at Cuauhtémoc 7 for jewelry.

Shops are generally open Monday through Saturday from 10am to 2pm and 4 to 8pm; many of the better shops close on Sunday, but some smaller souvenir stands stay open, though hours vary.

Boutique D'Xochitl. Ejido at Cuauhtémoc. ☎ **755/4-2131.**

Light crinkle-cotton clothing that's perfect for tropical climates. Hours are Monday through Saturday from 9am to 9pm and Sunday from 11am to 9pm.

Casa Marina. Paseo del Pescador 9. ☎ **755/4-2373.**

This small complex extends from the waterfront to Álvarez near Cinco de Mayo and houses four shops, each specializing in handcrafted wares from all over Mexico. Items include handsome rugs, textiles, masks, colorful wood carvings, and silver jewelry. Café Marina, the small coffee shop in the complex, has shelves and shelves of used paperback books in several languages for sale. It's open daily from 9am to 9pm during the high season and from 10am to 2pm and 4 to 8pm during the rest of the year.

Coco Cabaña Collectibles. Guerrero and Álvarez. ☎ **755/4-2518.**

Located next to Coconuts Restaurant, this impressive shop is filled with carefully selected crafts and folk art from all across the country, including fine Oaxacan wood carvings. Owner Pat Cummings once ran a gallery in New York, and the inventory reveals her discriminating eye. If you make a purchase, she'll cash your dollars at the going rate. Her shop's opposite the Hotel Citali and is open Monday through Saturday from 10am to 2pm and 6 to 10pm; it's closed during August and September.

Galería Maya. Bravo 31. ☎ **755/4-3606.**

This small folk-art store is packed with Guatemalan jackets, *santos* (carved saints), silver, painted wooden fish from Guerrero, tin mirror frames, masks, lacquered gourds, rain sticks, and embroidered T-shirts. It's open Monday through Saturday from 10am to 2pm and 6 to 9pm.

Arte Mexicano Nopal. Álvarez 13-B. ☎ **755/4-7530.**

You'll wish you owned a nearby beach house after browsing through this handsome collection of handcrafted furniture; of course, you can always ship your purchases home. Smaller items include wooden and gourd masks and wicker baskets in bright colors. The store is across the street from the Hotel Ávila and is open Monday through Saturday from 10am to 2:30pm and 5 to 9:30pm.

IXTAPA

Shopping gets better in Ixtapa every year as several fine folk-art shops spring up. On several plazas, air-conditioned shops carry fashionable resort wear and contemporary art, as well as T-shirts and jewelry. Brand-name sportswear is sold at the shops **Ferroni, Bye-Bye, Aca Joe,** and **Navale.** All of these shops are within the same area on bulevar Ixtapa, across from the beachside hotels, and most are open from 9am to 2pm and 4 to 9pm, including Sunday.

La Fuente. Los Patios Center on Bulevar Ixtapa. ☎ **755/3-0812.**

This terrific shop carries gorgeous Talavera pottery, wicker tables in the form of jaguars, handblown glassware, masks, tin mirrors and frames, hand-embroidered clothing from Chiapas, and wood and papier-mâché miniatures. It's open daily from 9am to 10pm during the high season and daily 10am to 2pm and 5 to 9pm for the low season.

WHERE TO STAY

Accommodations in Ixtapa and Playa Madera are dominated by larger, more expensive hotels, including many of the principle chains. There are only a few choices in the budget and moderate price ranges. If you're looking for lower-priced rooms, Zihuatanejo will offer the best selections and the best values. Many long-term guests in Ixtapa and Zihuatanejo search out apartments and condos to rent. Information on rentals, as well as hotel reservations and personalized service, are available from Julia Ortíz Bautista at **Job Representatives,** Villas del Pacífico, Edificio C, Dept. 01, 40880 Zihuatanejo, Guerrero (☎/fax **755/4-4374**).

IXTAPA
Very Expensive

Sheraton Ixtapa. Bulevar Ixtapa, 40880 Ixtapa, Gro. ☎ **800/325-3535** in the U.S. and Canada, 755/3-1858, or 755/3-4858. Fax 755/3-2438. 331 units. A/C MINIBAR TV TEL. High season $230 double; $330 junior suite; $580 master suite. Low season $170 double; $250–$320 suite. AE, DC, MC, V. Free parking.

This grand, resort-style hotel has large, handsomely furnished public areas facing the beach; it's an inviting place to sip a drink and people-watch. Rooms are as nice as the public areas. Most have balconies with views of either the ocean or the mountains. Thirty-six rooms on the fifth floor are nonsmoking. Rooms equipped for travelers with disabilities are available.

Dining/Diversions: There are four restaurants, a nightclub, and a Wednesday-night Mexican fiesta with buffet and live entertainment outdoors.

Amenities: One beachside pool, four tennis courts, a fitness room, beauty and barber shop, boutiques, pharmacy/gift shop, room and laundry service, travel agency, concierge, car rental.

○ **Westin Brisas Resort.** Bulevar Ixtapa, 40880 Ixtapa, Gro. ☎ **800/228-3000** in the U.S., or 755/3-2121. Fax 755/3-0751. 447 units. A/C MINIBAR TV TEL. High season $265 deluxe; $306 Royal Beach Club; $1,230 suite. Low season $155 single or double; $195 Royal Beach Club; $1,000 suite. AE, CB, DC, MC, V. Free parking.

Set above the high-rise hotels of Ixtapa on its own rocky promontory, the Westin is a cut above the others. The austere but luxurious public areas, all in stone and stucco, are bathed in sweeping breezes. A minimalist luxury also characterizes the rooms, which have Mexican-tile floors and grand, private, and plant-decorated patios with hammocks and lounges. All rooms face the hotel's cove and private beach. The six master suites come with private pools. Water is purified in your tap. The 16th floor is reserved as a nonsmoking floor, and three rooms on the 18th floor are equipped for travelers with disabilities.

Dining/Diversions: Five restaurants, from elegant indoor dining to casual open-air restaurants, allow you to relax entirely; you might never even go out for a meal. The airy lobby bar is one of the most popular places to enjoy sunset cocktails while a soothing trio croons romantic Mexican songs.

Amenities: Shopping arcade, barber and beauty shop, four swimming pools (one for children), four lit tennis courts with pro on request, elevator to secluded beach, laundry and room service, travel agency, car rental, massage, baby-sitting.

Expensive

Krystal. Bulevar Ixtapa s/n, 40880 Ixtapa, Gro. ☎ **800/231-9860** in the U.S., or 755/3-0333. Fax 755/3-0216. 254 units. A/C MINIBAR TV TEL. High season $188 double; $238–$264 suite. Low season $150 double; $195–$240 suite. 2 children under 12 stay free in parents' room. AE, DC, MC, V. Free parking.

Krystal hotels are known in Mexico for quality service and rooms. This one is no exception. This large, V-shaped hotel has ample grounds and a pool area. Each spacious and nicely furnished room has a balcony with an ocean view, game table, and tile bathrooms. Master suites have large, furnished triangular-shaped balconies. Some rates include a daily breakfast buffet. The eighth floor is nonsmoking, and there's one room equipped for travelers with disabilities.

Dining/Diversions: Among the hotel's five restaurants is the superelegant, evening-only **Bogart's.** There's live music nightly in the lobby bar. The **Krystal's** famed Cristine Disco, which originated in Cancún, is the one and only true nightclub in the area.

Amenities: Swimming pool, two tennis courts, racquetball court, gym with sauna, beauty and barber shop, massage, laundry, room service, travel agency, car rental.

○ **Villa del Lago.** Retorno Alondras 244 (Apdo. Postal 127), 40880 Ixtapa, Gro. ☎ **755/3-1482.** Fax 755/3-1422. 7 units. A/C TEL. High season $115–$160 double. Low season $85–$130 double. Rates include breakfast and wine and cheese. AE, MC, V. Street parking available.

Architect Raúl Esponda has transformed his private villa into a luxurious and secluded bed-and-breakfast overlooking the Ixtapa golf course. The best room is the trilevel master suite, with a sunken tiled shower, huge bedroom with great views of the golf course, and a large living room and private terrace. Other rooms are smaller but still delightful, decorated with fine folk art and carved furnishings. Breakfast is served on the terrace; get up early enough and you'll probably spot the two resident alligators sunning in the golf course's lake, or a giant gray heron perched in a nearby palm. The lounge chairs by the swimming pool are a perfect reading spot (check out the well-stocked library) or place to judge the swings of the local golfers. The staff of five keeps a watchful eye over the guests, anticipating their whims and needs. Reasonable golf, tennis, and meal packages are available. Advance reservations are a good idea, since regular guests sometimes claim the entire villa for weeks at a time.

Dining/Diversions: Formal dining room for breakfast; lunch and dinner are available on request for both guests and nonguests. They serve either in the living room or on the terrace. TV room with satellite service and a good video library. Family room stocked with games and books. Well-stocked honor bar by the pool.

Amenities: Swimming pool, transportation to Ixtapa's Hotel Zone.

ZIHUATANEJO

The more economical hotels are in Zihuatanejo. The term "bungalow" is used loosely in Zihuatanejo, as it is elsewhere in Mexico. Thus a bungalow may be an individual unit with a kitchen and bedroom, or a mere bedroom. It may be hotel-like in a two-story building with multiple units, some of which have kitchens. It may be cozy or rustic, and there may or may not be a patio or balcony.

Playa Madera and Playa La Ropa, separated from each other only by a craggy shoreline, are both accessible by road. Prices here tend to be higher than those in town, but some people find that the beautiful and tranquil setting is worth the extra cost. The town is just 5 to 20 minutes away, depending on whether you walk or take a taxi.

In Town

✪ **Apartamentos Amueblados Valle.** Vincente Guerrero 14, 40880 Zihuatanejo, Gro. ☎ **755/4-2084.** Fax 755/4-3220. 8 units. TV. High season $45 1-bedroom apt; $65 2-bedroom apt. Low season $35 1-bedroom apt; $50 2-bedroom apt. No credit cards.

Here you can rent a well-furnished apartment for the price of an inexpensive hotel room. Five one-bedroom apartments accommodate up to three people; the three two-bedroom apartments can fit four comfortably. Each apartment is different, but all are clean and airy, with ceiling fans, private balconies, and kitchenettes. Maid service is provided daily. There's a paperback-book exchange in the office. Guadalupe Rodríguez, the owner, can often find cheaper apartments elsewhere for guests who want to stay several months. Reserve well in advance during high season. It's on Guerrero about 2 blocks in from the waterfront between Ejido and N. Bravo.

Hotel Ávila. Juan Álvarez 8, 40880 Zihuatanejo, Gro. ☎ **755/4-2010.** Fax 755/4-3299. 27 units. A/C TV. High season $60–$70 double. Low season $35–$40 double. AE, MC, V. Street parking is available.

This hotel's rooms are expensive for what you get; essentially you're paying for location. Eighteen rooms have private balconies facing town, but no ocean view. The rest share a terrace facing the sea. There's a restaurant/bar off the lobby, with tables spread-ing across the sidewalk and onto the beach. With your back to the water at the basketball court, turn right; the Ávila is on your left.

Downtown Zihuatanejo

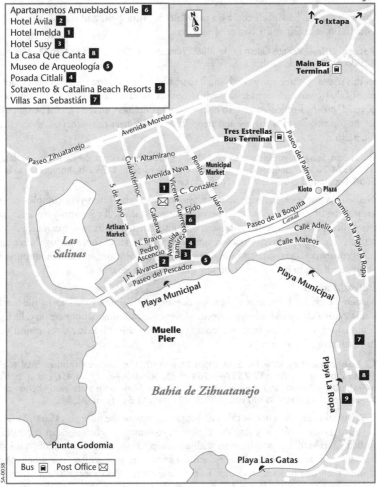

Apartamentos Amueblados Valle **6**
Hotel Ávila **2**
Hotel Imelda **1**
Hotel Susy **3**
La Casa Que Canta **8**
Museo de Arqueología **5**
Posada Citlali **4**
Sotavento & Catalina Beach Resorts **9**
Villas San Sebastián **7**

To Ixtapa

Main Bus Terminal

Avenida Morelos

Tres Estrellas Bus Terminal

Paseo Zihuatanejo

C. I. Altamirano

Cuauhtémoc

Avenida Nava

Benito Juárez

Municipal Market

Paseo del Palmar

Kioto   Plaza

C. González

Ejido

Vicente Guerrero

Caleana

5 de Mayo

Artisan's Market

Paseo de la Boquita

Canal

Camino a la playa la Ropa

Calle Adelita

Calle Mateos

Las Salinas

N. Bravo
Pedro Ascencio

Avenida Ramírez

J.N. Álvarez

Paseo del Pescador

Playa Municipal

Playa Municipal

Muelle Pier

Playa La Ropa

Bahía de Zihuatanejo

Punta Godomia

Bus   Post Office

Playa Las Gatas

SA-0038

Hotel Imelda. Catalina González 11, 40880 Zihuatanejo, Gro. ☎ **755/4-7662;** fax 755/4-3199. 44 units. A/C TV. High season $44 double. Low-season discounts. No credit cards. Free enclosed parking.

Despite its proximity to the market area, this hotel is well maintained and remarkably quiet. Each room has a tile floor and tile bathroom (no shower curtain), a large closet, louvered windows without screens, and two or three double beds. There's a long lap pool and a cheerful restaurant, Rancho Grande, which offers an inexpensive comida corrida. To get here from the museum, walk inland 4 blocks and turn left on González; the Imelda is on your right between Cuauhtémoc and Vicente Guerrero.

Hotel Susy. Juan Álvarez 3 (at Guerrero), 40880 Zihuatanejo, Gro. ☎ **755/4-2339.** 20 units. TV. High season $30 double. Low season $20 double. MC, V.

Consistently clean, with lots of plants along a shaded walkway set back from the street, this two-story hotel offers small rooms with fans and louvered glass windows with screens. Upper-floor rooms have balconies overlooking the street. Facing away from the water at the basketball court on the Malecón, turn right and walk 2 blocks; the hotel is on your left at the corner of Guerrero.

Posada Citlali. Vicente Guerrero 3, 40880 Zihuatanejo, Gro. ☎ **755/4-2043**. 19 units. $25 double. No credit cards.

In this pleasant, three-story hotel, small rooms with fans are arranged around a shaded plant-filled courtyard decked out with comfortable rockers and equipale (leather-covered) chairs. Bottled water is in help-yourself containers on the patio. The stairway to the top two floors is narrow and steep. The hotel is near the corner of Álvarez and Guerrero.

Villas San Sebastián. Bulevar Escénico Playa La Ropa (across from the Dolphins Fountain). ☎ **755/4-2084**. 7 units. A/C. High season $135 1-bedroom; $195 2-bedroom. Low season $60 1-bedroom; $110 2-bedroom. No credit cards.

Nestled on the mountainside above Playa La Ropa, this seven-villa complex offers great views of Zihuatanejo's bay. The villas surround tropical vegetation and a central swimming pool. Each comes complete with kitchenette and its own spacious, private terrace. The personalized service is one reason these villas come so highly recommended; owner Luis Valle, whose family dates back decades in this community, is always available to help guests with any questions or needs.

Playa Madera

Madera Beach is a 15-minute walk along the street, a 10-minute walk along the beach pathway, or a cheap taxi ride from town. Most of the accommodations are on calle Eva S. de López Mateos, the road overlooking the beach. Most hotels are set against the hill and have steep stairways.

✪ **Bungalows Ley.** Calle Eva S. de López Mateos s/n, Playa Madera (Apdo. Postal 466), 40880 Zihuatanejo, Gro. ☎ **755/4-4563** or 755/4-4087, Fax 755/4-4563. 8 units. TV. $40 double with fan, $45 double with A/C; $70 for 2-bedroom suite with kitchen and fan for up to 4 persons, $100 with A/C; $120 for up to 6 persons. AE, MC, V.

No two suites are the same at this small complex, one of the nicest on Playa Madera. If you're traveling with a group, you may want to splurge on the most expensive suite (called Club Madero), which comes with a rooftop terrace with tiled hot tub, outdoor bar and grill, and a spectacular view. All the rooms are immaculate; the simplest are studios with one bed and a kitchen in the same room. Most rooms have terraces or balconies just above the beach. Clients praise the management. To find the complex, follow Mateos to the right up a slight hill; it's on your left.

Villas Miramar. Calle Adelita, Lote 78, Playa Madera (Apdo. Postal 211), 40880 Zihuatanejo, Gro. ☎ **755/4-2106** or 755/4-3350. Fax 755/4-2149. 18 units. A/C, TEL. High season $70 suite for 1 or 2, $92 with ocean view; $110 2-bedroom suite. Low season $50 suite for 1 or 2, $55 with ocean view; $85 2-bedroom suite. AE, MC, V. Free parking.

Some of these elegant suites are built around a beautiful, shady patio that doubles as a restaurant. Those across the street center around a lovely pool and have private balconies and sea views. Parking is enclosed. To find Villas Miramar, follow the road leading south out of town towards Playa La Ropa, then take the first right after the traffic circle, then left on Adelita.

Playa La Ropa

Some travelers consider Playa La Ropa to be the most beautiful of Zihuatanejo's beaches. It's a 20- to 25-minute walk south of town on the east side of the bay or a $2 taxi ride. In addition to the selections below, consider trying the **Hotel Paraiso Real** (☎/fax **755/4-2147**), on La Ropa Beach. It has 20 rooms, and no children under 12 are allowed. Rates are $65 to $80 and they accept American Express, MasterCard, and Visa.

✪ **La Casa Que Canta.** Camino Escénico a la Playa La Ropa, 40880 Zihuatanejo, Gro. ☎ **888/523-5050** in the U.S., 755/4-2722, or 755/4-2782. 24 suites. A/C MINIBAR. High season $280–$490 double. Low season $220–$385 double. AE, MC, V. No children under 16.

La Casa Que Canta ("The House that Sings") opened in 1992, and in looks alone, it's a very special hotel. Located on a mountainside overlooking Zihuatanejo Bay, it was designed with striking molded-adobe architecture. Rooms, all with handsome natural-tile floors, are individually decorated in unusual painted Michoacán furniture, antiques, and stretched-leather equipales, with hand-loomed fabrics used throughout. All units have large, beautifully furnished terraces with bay views. Hammocks under the thatched-roof terraces, supported by rough-hewn vigas, are perfectly placed for watching yachts sail in and out of the harbor. The four categories of rooms are all spacious; there are three terrace suites, four deluxe suites, nine grand suites, and two private-pool suites. Rooms meander up and down the hillside, and while no stairs are extensive, there are no elevators. La Casa Que Canta is a member of the "Small Luxury Hotels of the World" group. Technically it's not on Playa La Ropa; it's on the road leading there. The closest stretch of beach (still not yet Playa La Ropa) is down a steep hill.

Dining/Diversions: There's a small restaurant/bar on a shaded terrace overlooking the bay.

Amenities: Freshwater pool on the main terrace, saltwater pool on the bottom level, laundry and room service.

✪ **Sotavento and Catalina Beach Resorts.** Playa La Ropa, 40880 Zihuatanejo, Gro. ☎ **755/4-2032.** Fax 755/4-2975. 109 units. TEL in 85 units. $37–$65 standard room; $75–$95 bungalow or terrace room. AE, CB, DC, MC, V.

Perched high on the hill, close to each other and managed together by the same owners, these two attractive hotels were among the first in the area and retain the slow-paced, gracious mood of Zihuatanejo's early days as a little-known hideaway. While the terrace rooms of the Sotavento are only average in decoration, they are spacious and offer spectacular panoramic views of the bay and Playa La Ropa below. Best of all is the large, shared ocean-view terrace, equipped with hammocks and a chaise lounge for each room—great for sunning and sunset watching. The Catalina has recently remodeled many of its rooms with Mexican tile, wrought iron, and other handcrafted touches; these also have lovely terraces with ocean views and come with two queen-size beds. Between them the two hotels cover eight stories climbing the slope and two restaurants and bars. Ask to see at least a couple of rooms first, as they can vary quite a bit in furnishings and price. Also keep in mind the walk down many steps to the beach (depending on the room level). Although there's no air-conditioning, it's compensated for by the ceiling fans and sea breezes. There's no swimming pool. To get here, take the highway south of Zihuatanejo about a mile, turn right at the hotels' sign, and follow the road to the hotels.

WHERE TO DINE
IXTAPA
Very Expensive
Villa de la Selva. Paseo de la Roca. ☎ **755/3-0362.** Reservations recommended during high season. Main courses $11–$28. AE, MC, V. Daily 6–11pm. MEXICAN/CONTINENTAL.

Clinging to the edge of a cliff overlooking the sea, this elegant restaurant enjoys the most spectacular sea and sunset view in Ixtapa. The elegant candlelit tables are arranged on three terraces; try to come early in hopes of getting one of the best vistas, especially on the lower terrace. The cuisine is delicious and classically rich: Filet Villa de la Selva is red snapper topped with shrimp and hollandaise sauce. The cold avocado soup or hot lobster bisque makes a good beginning; finish with chocolate mousse or bananas Singapore.

Expensive

✪ **Beccofino.** Marina Ixtapa. ☎ **755/3-1770.** Breakfast $4–$6; pastas $8–$15; main courses $8–$18. AE, MC, V. Daily 9:30am–midnight. NORTHERN ITALIAN.

This restaurant is a standout in Mexico. Owner Ángelo Rolly Pavia serves up the flavorful northern Italian specialties he grew up knowing and loving. The breezy marina location has a menu that includes dishes with pastas of all shapes and sizes. Ravioli, a house specialty, comes stuffed with seafood in season. The garlic bread is terrific, and there's an extensive wine list.

Moderate

Golden Cookie Shop. Los Patios Center. ☎ **755/3-0310.** Breakfast $3–$4; sandwiches $3–$5; main courses $3–$8. MC, V. Daily 8am–5pm for the restaurant and 8am–9pm for takeout. PASTRIES/INTERNATIONAL.

Although the name is misleading—there are more than cookies here—Golden Cookie's freshly baked goods beg for a detour, and the coffee menu is the most extensive in town. The large sandwiches, made with fresh soft bread, come with a choice of sliced deli meats. Chicken curry is among the other specialty items. To get to the shop, walk to the rear of the shopping center as you face Mac's Prime Rib; walk up the stairs, turn left, and you'll see the restaurant on your right. They have a new air-conditioned area, reserved for nonsmokers.

ZIHUATANEJO

Zihuatanejo's **central market,** located on avenida Benito Juárez (about 5 blocks inland from the waterfront), will whet your appetite for cheap and tasty food. It's best at breakfast and lunch because the market activity winds down in the afternoon. Look for what's hot and fresh. The market area is one of the best on this coast for shopping and people watching.

Two excellent **bakeries** should quell cravings for something freshly baked. Try **El Buen Gusto,** at Guerrero 4, a half a block inland from the museum (☎ 755/4-3231), where you'll find banana bread, French bread, doughnuts, and cakes. It's open daily from 7:30am to 10pm. For more fresh-baked bread aroma, head for **Panadería Francesa,** González 15, between Cuauhtémoc and Guerrero (☎ 755/4-4520). Here you can buy sweet pastries or grab a long baguette or loaf of whole-wheat bread for picnic supplies. It's open daily from 7am to 9pm.

Expensive

El Patio. Cinco de Mayo 3 at Álvarez. ☎ **755/4-3019.** Breakfast $3–$5; Mexican platters $5–$11; seafood $7–$18. AE, MC, V. Daily 9am–2pm and 3–11pm. SEAFOOD/MEXICAN.

Casually elegant, this romantic patio restaurant is decorated with baskets and flickering candles. Whatever you crave, you're likely to find it here, whether it's fajitas, steak, chicken, chiles rellenos, green or red enchiladas, or lobster in garlic sauce. You can also order hamburgers and salads. In the evenings, musicians often play Latin American favorites. It's a block inland from Álvarez and next to the church.

✪ **Restaurant Paul's.** Benito Juárez s/n. ☎ **755/4-6528.** Main courses $7–$18. MC, V. Mon–Sat noon–2am. INTERNATIONAL/SEAFOOD.

This is sure to be the only place in town that serves fresh artichokes as an appetizer, and their fish fillet is covered with a smooth, delicately flavored shrimp-and-dill sauce. The pasta comes topped with a pile of shrimp and fish in a light cream sauce, and the pork chops and beef medaillons are thick and juicy. They also offer vegetarian main courses such as pasta with fresh artichoke hearts and sun-dried tomatoes. Paul's new location is on Benito Juárez, half a block from the Bancomer and Serfin banks on the same block as the number 1 notary. Taxi drivers all know how to get there.

Moderate

Casa Elvira. Paseo del Pescador. ☎ **755/4-2061.** Main courses $3.50–$10. MC, V. Daily noon–10:30pm. MEXICAN/SEAFOOD.

Casa Elvira almost always has a crowd, drawn to its neat, clean atmosphere and wide selection of low-cost lunches and dinners on the bilingual menu. House specialties are snapper (or whatever fish is in season) and lobster; the restaurant also serves meat dishes and chicken mole. The most expensive seafood platter includes lobster, red snapper, and jumbo butterfly shrimp. Facing the water and the basketball court, turn right; Casa Elvira is on the west end of the waterfront near the town pier.

✪ **Coconuts.** Augustín Ramírez 1 (at Vicente Guerrero). ☎ 755/4-2518 or 755/4-7980. E-mail: coconuts@cdnet.com.mx. Main courses $8–$20. AE, MC, V. High season daily 6pm–11pm. Closed during rainy season. INTERNATIONAL/SEAFOOD.

This popular restaurant set in a tropical garden was the former weigh-in station for Zihua's coconut industry in the late 1800s—it's the oldest building in town. Fresh is the operative word on this creative, seafood-heavy menu. Chef Patricia Cummings checks what's fresh at the market, then uses only top-quality ingredients to prepare notable dishes like seafood pâté and grilled fillet of snapper Coconuts. Their Bananas Flambé has earned a following of its own, with good reason. Expect friendly, efficient service here.

La Bocana. Álvarez 13. ☎ **755/4-3545.** Breakfast $3–$4; main courses $5–$19. MC, V. Daily 8am–11pm. MEXICAN/SEAFOOD.

One of Zihuatanejo's favorite seafood restaurants, La Bocana is known for its huge *plato de mariscos*—a seafood platter that feeds two to four people. It comes heaped with lobster, crayfish, shrimp, fish fillet, rice, and salad. Most fish is prepared with a heavy hand on the butter and oil. Mariachis and marimba bands come and go on Sunday. It's on the main street near the town plaza.

Inexpensive

Casa Puntarenas. Calle Noria, Colonia Lázaro Cárdenas. No phone. Soup $1.50; main courses $2.75–$5. No credit cards. Daily 6:30–9pm. MEXICAN/SEAFOOD.

A modest spot with a tin roof and nine wooden tables, Puntarenas is one of the best spots in town for fried whole fish served with toasted bolillos (crusty, white-bread miniloaves), sliced tomatoes, onions, and avocado. The chiles rellenos are mild and stuffed with plenty of cheese; the meat dishes are less flavorful. To get to Puntarenas from the pier, turn left on Álvarez and cross the footbridge on your left. Turn right after you cross the bridge; the restaurant is on your left.

La Sirena Gorda. Paseo del Pescador. ☎ **755/4-2687.** Breakfast $2–$4; main courses $3–$6. MC, V. Thurs–Tues 7am–10pm. MEXICAN.

For the best inexpensive breakfast in town, head to La Sirena Gorda for a variety of eggs and omelets, or hotcakes with bacon, as well as fruit with granola and yogurt. For lunch or dinner try the house specialty, seafood tacos with fish prepared to taste like machaca or carnitas or covered with mole. There's always a short list of daily specials, such as blackened red snapper, steak, or fish kebabs. Patrons enjoy the casual sidewalk-cafe atmosphere. To get here from the basketball court, face the water and walk to the right; La Sirena Gorda is on your right just before the town pier.

Nueva Zelanda. Cuauhtémoc 23 at Ejido. ☎ **755/4-2340.** Tortas $2–$3.50; enchiladas $2–$4; fruit-and-milk *licuados* (milkshakes) $1.50; cappuccino $1.25. No credit cards. Daily 8am–10pm. MEXICAN.

One of the most popular places in town, this clean open-air snack shop welcomes diners with rich cappuccinos sprinkled with cinnamon and pancakes with real maple syrup. But the mainstays of the menu are tortas and enchiladas.

You'll find Nueva Zelanda by walking 3 blocks inland from the waterfront on Cuauhtémoc; the restaurant is on your right. There's a second location (☎ **755/3-0838**) in Ixtapa in the back section of the Los Patios shopping center.

✪ Ruben's. Calle Adelita s/n. ☎ **755/4-4617.** Burgers $2.25–$3.25; vegetables $1.50; ice cream $1. No credit cards. Daily 6–11pm. BURGERS/VEGETABLES.

The choices are easy here—you can order either a big juicy burger made from top sirloin beef grilled over mesquite, or a foil-wrapped packet of baked potatoes, chayote, zucchini, or sweet corn. Homemade ice cream plus beer and soda fill out the menu, which is posted on the wall by the kitchen. It's kind of a do-it-yourself place: Guests snare a waitress and order, grab their own drinks from the cooler, and tally their own tabs. Rolls of paper towels hang over the tables on the open porch and shaded terrace. Ruben's is a popular fixture in the Playa Madera neighborhood, though the customers come from all over town. To get here from Mateos, turn right on Adelita; Ruben's is on your right.

Playa Madera & Playa La Ropa

Kon-Tiki. Camino a Playa La Ropa. ☎ **755/4-2471.** Pizza $7–$18. No credit cards. Daily 1pm–midnight; happy hour 6–7pm. PIZZA.

In the air-conditioned dining room on a cliff overlooking the bay, enjoy 13 types of pizzas—and a stunning view. The vegetarian is topped with beans, peanuts, onions, mushrooms, bell peppers, garlic, pineapples, and avocado. There's also a big-screen sports-video bar here, open the same hours.

La Perla. Playa La Ropa. ☎ **755/4-2700.** Breakfast $2.50–$5; main courses $6–$11. AE, MC, V. Daily 9am–10pm; breakfast served 10am–noon. SEAFOOD.

There are many palapa-style restaurants on Playa La Ropa, but La Perla, with tables under the trees and thatched roof, is the most popular, and a Zihua tradition. The long stretch of pale sand in either direction and array of wooden chairs under palapas combine with decent food to make La Perla a favorite with visitors. The "fillet of fish La Perla" is wrapped in foil with tomatoes, onions, and cheese. It's near the southern end of La Ropa Beach. Take the right fork in the road; there's a sign in the parking lot.

IXTAPA & ZIHUATANEJO AFTER DARK

With an exception or two, Zihuatanejo nightlife dies down around 11pm or midnight. For a good selection of clubs, discos, hotel fiestas, special events, and fun watering holes with live music and dancing, head for Ixtapa. Just keep in mind that the shuttle bus stops at 11pm, and a taxi ride back to Zihuatanejo after midnight costs 50% more than the regular price. During off-season (after Easter or before Christmas) hours vary: Some places are open only on weekends, while others are closed completely.

THE CLUB & MUSIC SCENE

Many discos and dance clubs stay open until the last customers leave, so closing hours are dependent upon revelers. Most discos have a ladies night at least once a week—admission and drinks are free for women, making it easy for men to buy them a drink.

Carlos 'n' Charlie's. Bulevar Ixtapa (just north of the Best Western Posada Real), Ixtapa. ☎ **755/3-0085.** Cover (including drink tokens) after 9pm for dancing $5 (only on Sat during the off-season).

Knee-deep in nostalgia, bric-a-brac, silly sayings, and photos from the Mexican Revolution, this restaurant-cum-nightclub offers party ambiance and good food. The eclectic menu includes iguana in season (with Alka-Seltzer and aspirin on the house). Out back by the beach is an open-air section (partly shaded) with a raised wooden platform called the "pier" for "pier-dancing" at night. The recorded rock and roll mixes with sounds of the ocean surf. The restaurant is open daily from noon to midnight; pier dancing is nightly from 9pm to 3am.

Christine. In the Hotel Krystal, Bulevar Ixtapa, Ixtapa. ☎ **755/3-0456.** Cover $7.50. AE, MC, V.

This glitzy street-side disco is famous for its midnight light show, which features classical music played on a mega–sound system. A semicircle of tables in tiers overlooks the dance floor. No tennis shoes, sandals, or shorts are allowed, and reservations are advised during high season. It's open nightly during high season from 10:30pm to the wee hours; the light show is at midnight. (Off-season hours vary.)

Señor Frog's. Bulevar Ixtapa in the La Puerta Center, Ixtapa. ☎ **755/3-0272.** No Cover.

A companion restaurant to Carlos 'n' Charlie's, Señor Frog's has several dining sections and a warehouselike bar with raised dance floors. Rock and roll plays from large speakers, sometimes prompting even dinner patrons to shimmy by their tables between courses. The restaurant is open daily from 6pm to midnight; the bar is open until 3am.

HOTEL FIESTAS & THEME NIGHTS

Many hotels hold Mexican fiestas and other special events that include dinner, drinks, live music, and entertainment for a fixed price ($30 to $40). The **Sheraton Ixtapa** (☎ 755/3-1858) is famous for its Wednesday-night fiesta; good Mexican fiestas are also held by the **Krystal Hotel** (☎ 755/3-0333) and **Dorado Pacífico** (☎ 755/3-2025) in Ixtapa and the **Villa del Sol** (☎ 755/4-2239) on Playa La Ropa in Zihuatanejo. The Sheraton Ixtapa is the only one that offers these in the off-season. The **Westin Brisas Ixtapa** (☎ 755/3-2121) and the Sheraton Ixtapa also put on theme nights featuring the cuisine and music of different countries. Call for reservations (travel agencies also sell tickets) and be sure you understand what the fixed price covers (drinks, tax, and tip are not always included).

A TRIP TO TRONCONES: A SLEEPY FISHING VILLAGE

Twenty miles northwest of Ixtapa, the tiny fishing hamlet of Troncones, with its long beaches, has become a favorite escape for visitors to Ixtapa and Zihuatanejo. There's not much to do but stroll the empty beach, swim in the sea, and savor the fresh seafood at one of the fishermen's-shack restaurants or at The Mako (see below). But who needs more? If you do, horse rentals can be arranged, and hotel owners can provide information on hiking in the jungle and to nearby caves. Joining a fiesta in the teeny fishing village of **Troncones** (population 250), is a highlight for many guests.

There are no direct telephone lines yet to Troncones. The phones listed below are cellular, and the fax lines are in Ixtapa or Zihuatanejo. No public buses serve this area, so you'll have to join a tour or hire a taxi to take you there. For about $20, the driver will take you and return at the hour you request to bring you back to town. If you're driving, follow the highway northwest through Ixtapa, past the Marina Ixtapa and continue past the Ciudad Altamirano turnoff. Mark your odometer at the turnoff because 14 kilometers ahead is the sign pointing left to El Burro Borracho. Turn there and continue 3.5 kilometers until you reach the ocean, and turn left. El Burro Borracho is the last restaurant on the right. From that location you can get directions to the rest of the inns.

WHERE TO STAY

All of the lodgings mentioned below may offer discounts on rentals of as much as 50% in low season.

Casa Canela. Los Troncones, Guerrero, 6 miles north of Ixtapa on Hwy. 200. ☎ **755/ 7-0777.** Fax 755/4-3296. 2-bedroom house (3 bathrooms). High season $90 per day for the house; $535 per week. Rates include continental breakfast. No credit cards.

On the opposite side of the road from El Burro Borracho, Anita Lapointe also offers this complete house, with two bedrooms, three bathrooms, a kitchen, porch, garden, and satellite TV. The house sleeps up to six people. The beach is just across the road.

Casa de la Tortuga B&B. Troncones, 12 miles north of Ixtapa on Hwy. 200. ☎ **755/ 7-0732.** Fax 755/3-2417. (Reservations: write Apdo. Postal 37, 40880 Zihuatanejo, Gro.) 6 units. High season $55–$100 double. Rates include full breakfast. No credit cards.

Dewey and Karolyn MacMillan, a young American couple, recently renovated their isolated paradise on the beach at Troncones using Mexican tiles and creating a garden setting. Casa Tortuga is a six-bedroom home with four bathrooms, a dining room, kitchen, laundry, pool, TV and VCR, plus a book and video library. Rooms are available for rent separately, or the entire place can be rented as a vacation home that will sleep up to 12 people. A palapa-covered bar is just steps from the beach and ocean.

Casa Ki. Los Troncones, Guerrero, 6 miles north of Ixtapa on Hwy. 200. ☎ **755/7-0992.** Fax 755/3-2417 or 755/4-3296. 3 units. $75 double. Rates include breakfast. No credit cards.

Ed and Ellen Weston offer these three bungalows in a garden setting right on the beach. Each has a king-size bed, private bathroom, and porch with a hammock to while away some relaxing hours. They pay extra attention to the health and well-being of the guests and have all the facilities for people traveling with small children: babysitters, cribs, high-chairs, etc.

La Puesta del Sol. Los Troncones, Guerrero, 6 miles north of Ixtapa on Hwy. 200. **755/ 7-0503,** or 213/467-4495 in the U.S. 2 units. $60–$80 double. CB, DC for prepayment in the U.S. No credit cards at the hotel.

Next to El Burro Borracho, Malury Wells maintains this small inn with two large separate units on the beach. One has a kitchenette. In either room, you have a choice of a king-size or single bed. Guests use the El Burro Borracho restaurant.

The Mako. Los Troncones, Guerrero, 6 miles north of Ixtapa on Hwy. 200. ☎ **755/3-0809.** Fax 755/4-3296. E-mail: burro@cdnet.com. 3 bungalows, 5 RV spaces. High season $55 double. Low season $30 double. RV space $10–$15. Rates include continental breakfast. No credit cards.

Owner Anita Lapointe oversees three rustic stone bungalows, all with private bathroom, king-size bed, and a hammock on the porch. In addition, guests can use the fully equipped kitchen, library, and satellite TV. Boogie boards and kayaks are available for rent. Five full-hookup RV spaces and a place to camp are available as well. Local artisans from Troncones provide The Mako with hand-embroidered dresses and blouses, lace, and other locally made art. The beachfront restaurant is the one recommended for the area.

WHERE TO DINE

The Mako. Troncones Beach. ☎ **755/3-0809.** Main courses $3–$11. No credit cards. Daily 8am–9pm. AMERICAN/SEAFOOD.

This casual beachfront restaurant is not your ordinary beach-shack restaurant—it offers fish, shrimp, and lobster as well as steak and grilled meat. Specialties include shrimp tacos, filet mignon with mashed potatoes and mushroom gravy, the "ultimate" hamburger, barbecue pork ribs, and grilled chicken breast with tamarindo chipotle sauce. You can kick back with a frosty margarita, iced cappuccino, glass of wine, or cold beer.

If you are only spending the day in Troncones, you can use the beach and this restaurant as headquarters and have the taxi return for you at your requested time.

3 Puerto Escondido

230 miles SE of Acapulco; 150 miles NW of Salina Cruz; 50 miles NW of Puerto Ángel

Puerto Escondido (*pwer*-toe es-con-*dee*-do)—or simply "Puerto," as the locals call it— is a place for those whose priorities include the dimensions of the surf break (big), the temperature of a beer (cold), and the degree of the sun (OTA—beach-speak for "Optimal Tanning Angle"). Time is measured and the pace is slow for the young and very hip crowd that comes here.

Puerto Escondido is ranked as one of the world's top surf sites. It's been dismissed as a place of former hippies and dropouts, but my theory is that those who favor "Puerto" are just trying to keep the place true to its name (*escondido* means "hidden"), and a great thing to themselves. I consider it the best overall beach value in Mexico, from hotels to dining.

People come from the United States, Canada, and Europe to stay for weeks and even months, easily and inexpensively. Expats have migrated here from Los Cabos, Acapulco, and Puerto Vallarta seeking what originally attracted them to their former homes—stellar beaches, friendly locals, and inexpensive prices. Added pleasures include an absence of beach vendors and time-share sales, an abundance of English spoken, and incredibly great live music.

It's a real place, not a produced resort. European travelers make up a significant number of the visitors, and it's common to hear various dialects in the conversational air. Solo travelers will probably make new friends within an hour of arriving, if they choose. No doubt about it: There are still scores of surfers here, lured by the best surf in Mexico, but espresso cafes and jazz music are just as ubiquitous. What a combo!

GETTING THERE & DEPARTING   By Plane   AeroMorelos and **Aerovega** (☎ 958/2-0151) have several flights daily between Oaxaca and Puerto Escondido flying a small plane. The Aerovega flights leave at 7am to Oaxaca, returning at 8am. Prices are about $55 each way. Tickets for both these lines can be handled by **Rodimar Travel** (see below). **Mexicana** (☎ 800/531-7921 in the U.S., 958/2-0098, or 958/ 2-0302) flies to Puerto Escondido 6 days per week from Los Angeles, Miami, San Antonio, and San Francisco, connecting through Mexico City.

If flights to Puerto Escondido are booked, you have the option (possibly less expensive) of flying into the Huatulco airport via scheduled or charter flights. This is an especially viable option if your destination is Puerto Ángel, which lies between Puerto

Escondido and Huatulco but is closer to the Huatulco airport. A taxi will cost $25 from Huatulco to Puerto Ángel or $45 between Huatulco and Puerto Escondido. There is frequent bus service between the three destinations.

Arriving: The **airport** (PXM) is about 2½ miles north of the center of town near Playa Bacocho. Prices for the collective **minibus** to hotels are posted: $3.25 per person. **Aerotransportes Terrestres** sells colectivo transportation tickets to the airport through **Rodimar Travel** on Perez Gasga St. (the pedestrian-only zone) next to Hotel Casa Blanca (☎ **958/2-1551;** fax 958/2-0737). They will pick you up at your hotel.

By Car   From Oaxaca, Highway 175 via Pochutla is the least bumpy road. The 150-mile trip takes 5 to 6 hours. Highway 200 from Acapulco is also a good road and should take about 5 hours to travel. However, this stretch of road has been plagued with car and bus hijackings and robberies in recent years—travel only during the daytime.

From Salina Cruz to Puerto Escondido is a 4-hour drive, past the Bahías de Huatulco and the turnoff for Puerto Ángel. The road is paved but can be rutty in the rainy season. The trip from Huatulco to Puerto Escondido takes just under 2 hours.

By Bus   Buses are frequent between Acapulco and Oaxaca and south along the coast to and from Huatulco and Pochutla, the transit hub for Puerto Ángel. Puerto Escondido's several bus stations are all within a 3-block area. For Gacela and Estrella Blanca, the station is just north of the coastal highway where Pérez Gasga crosses it. First-class buses go from here to Pochutla (1 hr.), Huatulco, Acapulco, Zihuatanejo, and Mexico City (11 hr.). A block north at Hidalgo and Primera Poniente is Transportes Oaxaca Istmo, in a small restaurant. Several buses leave daily for Pochutla, Salina Cruz (5 hr.), or Oaxaca (10 hr. via Salina Cruz). The terminal for Líneas Unidas, Estrella del Valle, and Oaxaca Pacífico is 2 blocks farther down on Hidalgo, just past Oriente 3. They service Oaxaca via Pochutla. At Primera Norte 207, Cristóbal Colón buses serve Salina Cruz, Tuxtla Gutiérrez, San Cristóbal de las Casas, and Oaxaca.

Arriving: Minibuses from Pochutla or Huatulco will let you off anywhere en route, including the spot where Pérez Gasga leads down to the pedestrians-only zone.

VISITOR INFORMATION   The **State Tourist Office, SEDETUR** (☎ **958/ 2-0175**), is about a half mile from the airport at the corner of Carretera Costera and bulevar Benito Juárez. It's open Monday through Friday from 9am to 2pm and 5 to 8pm and Saturday from 10am to 1pm. A kiosk at the airport is open for incoming flights, and another, near the west end of the paved tourist zone, is open Monday through Saturday from 9am to 2pm and 5 to 8pm.

CITY LAYOUT   Looking out on the Bahía Principal and its beach, to your left you'll see the eastern end of the bay, consisting of a small beach, **Playa Marinero,** followed by rocks jutting into the sea. Beyond this is **Playa Zicatela,** unmistakably the main surfing beach. Zicatela Beach has restaurants, bungalows, surf shops, and hotels, well back from the shoreline. The western side of the bay, to your right, is about a mile long, with a lighthouse and low green hills descending to meet a long stretch of fine sand. Beaches on this end are not quite as accessible by land, but hotels are overcoming this difficulty by constructing beach clubs reached by steep private roads and Jeep shuttles.

The town of Puerto Escondido has roughly an east-west orientation, with the long Zicatela Beach turning sharply southeast. Residential areas behind (east of) Zicatela Beach tend to have unpaved streets; the older town (with paved streets) is north of the Carretera Costera (Highway 200). The streets are numbered, with avenida Oaxaca the dividing line between east (oriente) and west (poniente), and avenida Hidalgo the divider between north (norte) and south (sur).

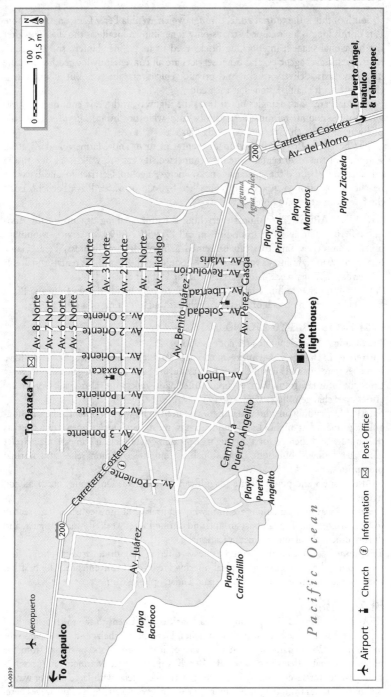

South of this is the **tourist zone,** through which avenida Pérez Gasga makes a loop. Part of this loop is a paved pedestrians-only zone, known locally as the *Adoquin,* after the hexagonal-shaped, interlocking bricks used in its paving. Hotels, shops, restaurants, bars, travel agencies, and other services are all conveniently located here. In the morning, taxis, delivery trucks, and private vehicles are allowed. But at noon it is closed off, with chains fastened at each end.

avenida Pérez Gasga angles down from the highway at the east end; on the west, where the Adoquin terminates, it climbs in a wide northward curve to cross the highway, after which it becomes avenida Oaxaca.

The beaches—Playa Principal in the center of town and Marinero and Zicatela, southeast of the town center—are interconnected. It's easy to walk from one to the other, crossing behind the separating rocks. Puerto Ángelito, Carrizalillo, and Bacocho beaches are west of town and can be reached by road or water. Playa Bacocho hosts the few more-expensive hotels.

GETTING AROUND　Almost everything is within walking distance of the Adoquin. **Taxis** are inexpensive around town; call ☎ **958/2-0990** for service. Mountain bikes, motorcycles, and cars can be rented at **Arrendadora Express,** Pérez Gasga 605-E, on your right just as you enter the Adoquin on the east. Bikes rentals run about $7 per day, $37 per week. Motorcycles rent for $52 per day.

Though it's easy to hire a boat, it is possible to walk beside the sea from the Playa Principal to the tiny beach of Puerto Ángelito, though it's a bit of a hike.

FAST FACTS: PUERTO ESCONDIDO

Area Code　The telephone area code is **958.**

Currency Exchange　Banamex, Bancomer, Bancrear, and Banco Bital all have branches in town, and all will change money during business hours, generally Monday through Saturday from 9am to 6pm. Automatic tellers are also available, as are currency-exchange offices.

Safety　Depending on who you talk to, you need to be wary of potential beach muggings, primarily at night. Local residents say most incidents happen after tourists overindulge and then go for a midnight stroll along the beach. It's an easy place to let your guard down, but don't carry valuables, and use common sense and normal precautions.

Also, respect the power of the magnificent waves here. Drownings occur all too frequently.

Seasons　Season designations are somewhat arbitrary, but most consider high season to be mid-December to January, around and during Easter week, July and August, and during other school and business vacations.

Telephones　There are numerous businesses offering long-distance telephone service, many along the Adoquin with several offering credit-card convenience. The best bet remains the purchase and use of a prepaid Ladatel phone card.

BEACH TIME

BEACHES　**Playa Principal** and **Playa Marinero,** adjacent to the town center and on a deep bay, are the best swimming beaches. Here, beach chairs and sun shades rent for about $1.25, a charge which may be waived if you order food or drinks from the restaurants that offer them. **Zicatela Beach** adjoins Playa Marinero and extends southeasterly for several miles. The surfing part of Zicatela, with large curling waves, is about 1½ miles from the town center. Due to the size and strength of the waves here, it's not a swimming beach, and only experienced surfers should attempt to ride Zicatela's powerful waves.

Ecotours & Other Adventurous Explorations

The **Turismo Rodimar Travel Agency,** on the landward side just inside the Adoquin (☎ **958/2-0734** or 958/2-0737; open daily 7:30am to 10pm), is an excellent source of information and can arrange all types of tours and travel. Manager Gaudencio Díaz speaks English. He can arrange individualized tours or formal ones such as **Michael Malone's Hidden Voyages Ecotours.** Malone, a Canadian ornithologist, takes you on a dawn or sunset trip to **Manialtepec Lagoon,** a bird-filled mangrove lagoon about 12 miles northwest of Puerto Escondido. The cost is $25 to $30 and includes a stop on a secluded beach for a swim. Probably the best all-day tour is to **Chacahua Lagoon National Park** about 42 miles west, at a cost of $30. These are true ecotours—small groups treading lightly. You visit a beautiful sandy spit of beach and the lagoon, which has incredible bird life and flowers including black orchids. Locals provide fresh barbecued fish on the beach. If you know Spanish and get information from the tourism office, it's possible to stay overnight under a small palapa, but bring plenty of insect repellent. If no agency-led tour is available, ask at the tourism office for the names of a couple of locals who also lead these trips.

An interesting and slightly out-of-the-ordinary excursion is **Jorge Perez's Aventura Submarina,** located "on the strip" (Zicatela Beach, calle del Morro s/n, in the Acuario building near the Cafecito; ☎ **958/2-1026**). Jorge, who speaks fluent English and is a certified scuba-dive instructor, guides individuals or small groups of qualified divers along the Coco trench, just offshore. He also arranges surface activities such as deep-sea fishing, surfing, trips to lesser-known yet nearby swimming beaches, and dirt-bike tours into the mountains. If you want to write ahead, contact him at Apdo. Postal 159, Puerto Escondido, 71980 Oaxaca.

Fishermen keep their colorful *pangas* (small boats) on the beach beside the Adoquin. A **fisherman's tour** around the coastline in this boat costs about $35, but a ride to Zicatela or Puerto Ángelito beaches is only $3. Most hotels offer or will gladly arrange tours to meet your needs.

Barter with one of the fishermen on the main beach for a ride to **Puerto Ángelito** and other small coves just west of town, where the swimming is safe and the pace calmer than in town. You'll find palapas, hammock rentals, and snorkeling equipment. The clear blue water is perfect for snorkeling. Enjoy fresh fish, tamales, and other Mexican dishes cooked right at the beach by local entrepreneurs. **Playa Bacocho** is on a shallow cove farther to the northwest and is best reached by taxi or boat, rather than walking.

SURFING   Zicatela Beach, 1½ miles southeast of Puerto Escondido's town center, is a world-class surf spot. A surfing competition in August, and Fiesta Puerto Escondido, held for at least 10 days each November, celebrate Puerto Escondido's renowned waves. The tourism office can supply exact dates and details. Beginning surfers often start out at Playa Marinero before graduating to Zicatela's awesome waves.

NESTING RIDLEY TURTLES   The beaches around Puerto Escondido and Puerto Ángel are nesting grounds for the endangered Ridley turtle. During the summer months, tourists can sometimes see the turtles laying eggs or observe the hatchlings trekking to the sea.

Escobilla Beach near Puerto Escondido and **Barra de la Cruz Beach** near Puerto Ángel seem to be favored among other nesting grounds for the Ridley turtle. In 1991 the Mexican government established the Centro Mexicano la Tortuga, known locally as the **Turtle Museum,** for the study and life enhancement of the turtle. On view are examples of all species of marine turtles living in Mexico, plus six species of freshwater turtles and two species of land turtles. The center is located on **Mazunte Beach,** near the town of the same name. Hours are 9am to 5pm daily, and entry is $2.25. Buses go to Mazunte from Puerto Ángel about every half hour, and a taxi ride is around $5. You can fit this in with a trip to Zipolite Beach, the next one closer to Puerto Ángel.

SHOPPING

The Adoquin sports a row of tourist shops selling straw hats, postcards, and Puerto Escondido T-shirts, plus a few excellent shops featuring Guatemalan, Oaxacan, and Balinese clothing and art. You can also get a tattoo, or rent surfboards and boogie boards here. Interspersed among the shops, hotels, restaurants, and bars are pharmacies and minimarkets for basic necessities. Some highlights along the Adoquin include:

Artesanía. Av. Pérez Gasga 707. ☎ **958/2-1331.**

High-quality clothing, bags, and jewelry from Guatemala and Chiapas.

La Luna. Av. Pérez Gasga s/n.

Jewelry, Batik surf wear, and Balinese art.

1000 Hamacas. Av. Pérez Gasga s/n.

The name, which means "1,000 hammocks," says it all. Custom-made, all colors—it's the favored way to take a siesta here.

Un Tigre Azul. Av. Pérez Gasga s/n. ☎ **958/2-1871.**

The only true art gallery in town with quality works of art and a cafe-bar upstairs. Open Monday through Saturday from 9am to 2pm and 6pm to 1am.

Also of interest:

Bazaar Santa Fe. Hotel Santa Fe lobby, Calle del Morro s/n. ☎ **958/2-0170.**

Antiques, including vintage Oaxacan embroidered clothing, vintage jewelry, and religious artifacts. American Express, MasterCard, and Visa are accepted.

Iguana Verde. Calle del Morro s/n.

One-of-a-kind collectibles and Mexican momentos including Day of the Dead skeletons, hand-loomed rugs, straw hats, pewter candlesticks, and unique artisania. Open daily from 9am to 2pm.

WHERE TO STAY
MODERATE

Best Western Posada Real. Av. Benito Juárez 1, Fracc. Bacocho, 71980 Puerto Escondido, Oax. ☎ **800/528-1234** in the U.S., 958/2-0133, or 958/2-0237. Fax 958/2-0192. 100 units. A/C TV TEL. High season $110 double. Low season $85 double. AE, DC,MC, V.

Set on a cliff top overlooking the beach, the expanse of manicured lawn that backs the hotel is one of the most popular places in town for a sunset cocktail. A large heated swimming pool, two restaurants, and lobby bar round out the amenities on the main level. The clean but smallish standard rooms are less enticing than the hotel grounds. A big plus here is their Coco's Beach Club, with a half-mile stretch of soft-sand beach, large swimming pool, kid's playground, and bar with swing-style chairs and live music. A shuttle service (or a lengthy walk down a set of stairs) will take you there. This is a great place for families, and it's open to the public ($4 cover for nonguests). The hotel is located only 5 minutes from the airport and about the same from Puerto Escondido's tourist zone. Travel agency, car rental, gift shop, and laundry on-site.

✪ **Hotel Santa Fe.** Calle del Morro (Apdo. Postal 96), 71980 Puerto Escondido, Oax. ☎ **958/2-0170** or 958/2-0266. Fax 958/2-0260. 69 units. A/C TV TEL. High season $76.50 double; $91 bungalow. Low season $52 double. AE, MC, V. Free parking.

If Puerto Escondido is the best beach value in Mexico, then the Santa Fe is without a doubt one of the best hotel values in Mexico. It's got a winning combination of unique Spanish-colonial style, a welcoming staff, and clean, comfortable rooms. The hotel has grown up over the years with the surfers who came to Puerto in the 1960s and 1970s. Here, they can enjoy the comfort they've grown accustomed to with the nostalgia they're looking for in a return visit—which many do. It's located a half a mile southeast of the town center, off Highway 200, at the curve in the road where Marinero and Zicatela beaches join—a prime sunset-watching spot. The three-story hacienda-style buildings have clay-tiled stairs, archways, and blooming bougainvillea, surrounding two courtyard swimming pools (one is a lap pool). The ample but simple rooms feature large tile bathrooms, colonial furnishings, handwoven fabrics, Guerrero pottery lamps, and both air-conditioning and ceiling fans. Most have a balcony or terrace, with ocean views on upper floors. Bungalows are next to the hotel, and each comes equipped with a living room, a kitchen, and a bedroom with two double beds. The Santa Fe Restaurant is one of the best on the southern Pacific coast. There's also a tour service, boutique, in-room massage, laundry, baby-sitting service, and security boxes.

✪ **Paraíso Escondido.** Calle Union 10, 71980 Puerto Escondido, Oax. ☎ **958/2-0444.** 20 units. A/C. $50 double. No credit cards.

This eclectic inn is hidden up a shady street a couple of short blocks from the main beach. A curious array of Mexican folk art, masks, religious art, and paintings on the walls make this an exercise in Mexican magic realism, in addition to a tranquil place to stay. An inviting pool is surrounded by gardens, Adirondack chairs, and a fountain, with a commanding view of the bay. The rooms each have one double and one twin bed, built-in desks, plus a cozy balcony with French doors. Each has a slightly different accent in decor, and all are very clean. The restaurant lacks the ambiance of the rest of the property and serves breakfast and dinner only. There's limited free parking available in front of the hotel.

INEXPENSIVE

Bungalows & Cabañas Acuario. Calle del Morro s/n, 71980 Puerto Escondido, Oax. ☎ **958/2-0357** or 958/2-1027. 40 units. TV. High season $19 double; $38 bungalow. Low season $16 double; $30 bungalow. No credit cards.

Facing Zicatela beach, this surfer's sanctuary offers clean, cheap accommodations, plus an on-site gym and surf shop. The two-story hotel and bungalows surround a pool shaded by a few great palms. Rooms are small and basic, but bungalows offer the addition of fundamental kitchen facilities. The cabañas are more open and have hammocks. There's parking, public telephones, and money exchange, plus a dive shop, pharmacy, and vegetarian restaurant in the adjoining commercial area. The well-equipped gym costs an extra $1.50 per day, $20 per month.

Castillo de Los Reyes. Av. Pérez Gasga s/n, 71980 Puerto Escondido, Oax. ☎ **958/2-0442.** 17 units. High season $15 double. Low season $10 double.

Don Fernando, the proprietor at Castillo de Los Reyes, has a gift for making his guests feel at home. Guests chat around tables on a shady patio near the office. Most of the clean, bright, white-walled rooms have a special touch—perhaps a gourd mask or carved coconut hanging over the bed. There's hot water, and the rooms are shaded from the sun by palms and cooled by fans. The "castle" is on your left as you ascend the hill on Pérez Gasga, after leaving the Adoquin (you can also enter Pérez Gasga off Highway 200).

Hotel Casa Blanca. Av. Pérez Gasga 905, 71980 Puerto Escondido, Oax. ☎ **958/2-0168.** 21 units. TV. $25 double. MC, V.

If you want to be in the heart of the Adoquin, this is your best bet for excellent value and clean, ample accommodations. A courtyard pool and adjacent palapa restaurant make a great place to hide away and enjoy a margarita or a book from the hotel's exchange rack. The bright, clean, and simply furnished rooms offer a choice of bed combinations, but all have at least two beds and a fan. The best rooms have a balcony overlooking the action in the street below, but light sleepers have an option of rooms in the back. Some rooms can sleep up to five ($60), and a few have A/C.

✪ **Hotel Flor de María.** Playa Marinero, 71980 Puerto Escondido, Oax. ☎/fax **958/ 2-0536.** 24 units. $35 double.

Though not right on the beach, this is a real find. The Canadians María and Lino Francato built their cheery three-story hotel facing the ocean, which you can see from the rooftop. Built around a garden courtyard, each room is colorfully decorated with beautiful trompe l'oeil still lifes and landscapes painted by Lino. Some rooms have windows facing the outdoors, some face the courtyard. All have double beds with orthopedic mattresses and small safes. On the roof there are, in addition to the great view, a small pool, shaded hammock terrace, and an open-air bar (open 5 to 9pm during high season) with a TV that receives American channels—all in all, a great place to be for sunset. I highly recommend the first-floor restaurant (see "Where to Dine," below). Ask about off-season discounts for long-term stays. The hotel is a third of a mile from the Adoquin and 200 feet up a sandy road from Marinero Beach on an unnamed street at the eastern end of the beach.

WHERE TO DINE
MODERATE

✪ **Art & Harry's.** Av. Morro s/n. No phone. Seafood $3.50–$12; steaks $9–$11. No credit cards. Daily 10am–10pm. SEAFOOD/STEAKS.

Located about three-quarters of a mile southeast of the Hotel Santa Fe on the road fronting Zicatela Beach, this robust watering hole is great for taking in the sunset, especially if you're having a monster shrimp cocktail or savoring fork-tender pieces of budget- and diet-bursting grilled beef. Late afternoon and early evening here amount to a portrait of Puerto Escondido. You sit peacefully watching surfers and tourists, the sun as it dips into the ocean, and the resident cat.

✪ **Cabo Blanco, "Where Legends are Born."** Calle del Morro s/n. ☎ **958/2-0337.** Breakfast $1.50–$5; main courses $1.50–$15. MC, V. Open daily Nov-May 8am–2pm and 6pm–2am. Closed June-Oct. INTERNATIONAL.

The local crowd at this beachfront restaurant craves Gary's special sauces that top his grilled fish, shrimp, steak, and rib dinners. Favorites include his dill-Dijon mustard, wine-fennel, and Thai curry sauces. But you can't count on them, because Gary buys what's fresh, then creates from there. If the great food isn't enough, an added bonus is that Cabo Blanco turns into the hottest live-music bar on Zicatela beach each Thursday and Saturday after 11pm. Gary's wife Roxana and an all-babe team of bartendresses keep the crowd well served but behaving. For breakfast, they cater to surfers on a budget and serve up fresh veggie and fruit juices.

La Galería. Av. Pérez Gasga. No phone. Breakfast $1.25–$3; main courses $3–$7.50. No credit cards. Daily 8am–midnight. INTERNATIONAL/SEAFOOD.

At the east end of the Adoquin, La Galería has a satisfying range of eats in a cool, creative setting. Dark-wood beams tower above, and contemporary works by local artists grace the walls while jazz music plays. Specialties are homemade pastas and brick-oven pizzas, but burgers and steaks are also available. Cappuccino and espresso, plus desserts such as baked pineapples, finish the meal.

✪ **Restaurant Santa Fe.** In the Hotel Santa Fe, Calle del Morro s/n. ☎ **958/ 2-0170.** Breakfast $2–$4; main courses $4–$12. AE, MC, V. Daily 7am–10:30pm. INTERNATIONAL.

The atmosphere here is classic and casual, with great views of the sunset and the waves on Zicatela Beach. Big pots of palms are scattered around, and fresh flowers grace the tables, all beneath a lofty palapa roof. The shrimp dishes are a bargain for the rest of the world, though at $12, a little higher-priced than the rest of town. Their perfectly grilled tuna, served with homemade french-fried potatoes and whole-grain bread, is an incredible meal deal at under $5. A Roquefort salad on the side ($3) is a perfect complement. Vegetarian dishes are reasonably priced and creative, adapting traditional Mexican and Italian dishes. A favorite is the house specialty, chiles rellenos: mild green peppers stuffed with cheese, raisins, and nuts, baked in a mild red-chile sauce and served with brown rice, beans, and salad. The bar offers an excellent selection of tequilas.

INEXPENSIVE

Bananas. Av. Pérez Gasga s/n. ☎ **958/2-0005.** Breakfast $2–$2.75; sandwiches $1.75–$3; breakfast buffet $3. MC, V. Daily 7:30am–1am. MEXICAN.

You'll see this bamboo-and-thatch-roofed, two-story restaurant/bar at the eastern entrance to the Adoquin. Breakfast includes fresh yogurt, crepes, and fresh-fruit drinks. A range of light appetizers includes quesadillas with potato or squash flowers, tacos, and stuffed tortillas. Happy hour is every night from 6 to 8pm, with live music in high season.

Carmen's La Patisserie. Playa Marinero. ☎ **958/2-0005.** Pastries 50¢–$1.25; sandwiches $1.75–$2.25. No credit cards. Mon–Sat 7am–3pm; Sun 7am–noon. FRENCH PASTRY/ SANDWICHES/COFFEE.

Carmen is the proprietor of this tiny but excellent cafe/bakery with a steady and loyal clientele. Carmen's baked goods are unforgettable. By 8am on one weekday, there was only one mango creme roll left, and other items were disappearing fast. The coffee is perhaps the best in town. Taped international music provides a soothing background, and a paperback exchange is another reason to linger. Fruit, granola, and sandwiches (croissant or whole-wheat) round out the menu. Carmen also provides space for an English-speaking AA group here. La Patisserie is across the street from the Hotel Flor de María.

✪ **El Cafecito.** Calle del Morro s/n, Playa Zicatela. No phone. Pastries 50¢–$1.25; main entrees $1.75–$4.75. No credit cards. Wed–Mon 6am–10pm. FRENCH PASTRY/ SEAFOOD/VEGETARIAN/COFFEE.

Carmen's second shop opened a few years ago on Zicatela Beach, with a motto of "Big waves, strong coffee!" Featuring all of the attractions of La Patisserie (above), it's now also open for dinner. A palapa roof tops a relaxed, oceanfront setting with wicker chairs and Oaxacan cloth–topped tables. Giant shrimp dinners are under $5, with creative daily specials always a sure bet. An oversized mug of cappuccino is $1.

María's Restaurant. In the Hotel Flor de María, Playa Marinero. ☎ **958/2-0536.** Breakfast $2.50; main courses $3–$8. No credit cards. Daily 8–11:30am, noon–2pm, and 5–10pm. INTERNATIONAL.

Locally popular meals are served in the first-floor open-air dining room of this hotel near the beach. The menu changes daily and features specials such as María Francato's fresh homemade pasta dishes. María's is a third of a mile from the Adoquin and 200 feet up a sandy road from Marinero Beach on an unnamed street at the eastern end of the beach.

PUERTO ESCONDIDO AFTER DARK

Sunset-watching is a ritual to plan your days around, and good lookout points abound. Watch the surfers at Zicatela from the **Los Tres Osos** restaurant or practice your wave-speak with them at **Art and Harry's Bar and Grill,** both about a quarter of the way down the beach near the end of current development. For another great sunset spot, head to the **Hotel Santa Fe** at the junction of Zicatela and Marinero beaches or the rooftop bar of **Hotel Flor de María.** Sun-worshippers might want to hop in a cab or walk half an hour or so west to the **Hotel Posada Real.** The hotel's cliff-top lawn is a perfect sunset perch. Or climb down the cliff side (or take the hotel's shuttle bus) to the pool-and-restaurant complex on the beach below.

When it comes to bars and clubs, Puerto has a nightlife that will satisfy anyone dedicated to late nights and good music. **Tequila Sunrise** charges a small cover to its open and spacious disco that plays Latino, reggae, and salsa from its location above a rocky cove. It's a half a block from the Adoquin on avenida Marina Nacional.

There's an ample selection of clubs along the Adoquin. The **Bucanero Bar and Grill** is one of the newest, with a good-sized bar and outdoor patio fronting Playa Principal. Both **The Blue Iguana** and **Rayos X** cater to a younger surf crowd with alternative and techno tunes. **Montezuma's Revenge** has live bands, usually playing contemporary Latin American music. And the popular daytime restaurant **Bananas** turns into a hot TV sports bar after appetites are satisfied. Pool and Ping-Pong tables add sport to the place. **El Tubo** is an open-air beachside disco just west of Restaurant Alicia on the Adoquin.

Out on Zicatela, don't miss **Cabo Blanco** (see "Where to Dine," above) and its live music played by a collection of local musicians who truly jam together. **María Sabina** is a cavernous club, located on the second floor along with a restaurant, pool hall, and bowling alley.

Most nightspots are open until 3am or until the customers leave.

A TRIP TO PUERTO ÁNGEL: BACKPACKING BEACH HAVEN

Fifty miles southeast of Puerto Escondido, and 30 miles northwest of the Bays of Huatulco, is the tiny fishing port of **Puerto Ángel** (*pwer*-toe *ahn*-hel). Puerto Ángel, with its beautiful beaches, unpaved streets, and budget hotels, is popular with the international backpacking set and those seeking an inexpensive and restful vacation. In November of 1997, Hurricane Paulina blew through Puerto Ángel, taking most of the palm-tree tops with her and leaving damaged roads and structures in her wake. Repairs will be slower in coming than in the other, wealthier southern resort areas. It may be until the year 2000 before Puerto Ángel recovers the simple beauty that made it such an alluring place to vacation. Nonetheless, it still retains its tranquil atmosphere, small, beautiful bay, and several inlets that offer peaceful swimming and good snorkeling. The village follows a slow and simple way of life: Fishermen leave very early in the morning and return with their catch by late forenoon. Taxis make up most of the traffic, and the bus from Pochutla passes every half hour or so.

Important Travel Note

Highway 200 north to Acapulco has had numerous problems with car and bus hijackings; if you go, you would be wise to fly. Traveling south to Puerto Ángel and Huatulco, on this road only during the day.

ESSENTIALS

GETTING THERE & DEPARTING   By Car   North or south from Highway 200, take coastal Highway 175 inland to Puerto Ángel. The road will be well marked with signs to Puerto Ángel. From either Huatulco or Puerto Escondido, the trip should take about an hour.

By Taxi   Taxis are a readily available option that can take you to Puerto Ángel or Zipolite Beach for a reasonable price, or to the Huatulco airport or Puerto Escondido.

By Bus   There are no direct buses from Puerto Escondido or Huatulco to Puerto Ángel; however, numerous buses leave Puerto Escondido and Huatulco for Pochutla, 7 miles north of Puerto Ángel, where you can transfer for the short ride to the village. If you arrive at Pochutla from either Huatulco or Puerto Escondido, you may be dropped at one of several bus stations that line the main street; if so, walk 1 or 2 blocks toward the large sign reading POSADA DON JOSÉ. The buses to Puerto Ángel are in the lot just before the sign. Ask for the "amarillos" buses (to Puerto Ángel). These buses originate in Huatulco, drop passengers in Pochutla, and depart for Puerto Ángel every 20 or 30 minutes.

ORIENTATION   The town center is only about 4 blocks long, oriented more or less east-west. There are few signs in the village giving directions, and off the main street much of Puerto Ángel is a narrow sand-and-dirt path. The navy base is toward the far (west) end of town, just before the creek-crossing toward Playa Panteón (Cemetery Beach).

Puerto Ángel has several public (LADATEL) telephones that use the readily accessible prepaid phone cards. In addition, a **TelMex office** (☎ **958/4-3055;** fax 958/ 4-3103) is just past the turnoff to La Buena Vista, across from the Casa de Huéspedes Anahi. It's open daily from 9am to 9:30pm. They will accept messages for pickup (Spanish only) and accept incoming faxes for $1 per fax.

If you want to stash your belongings while you look for lodgings, **Gambusino's Travel Agency** offers luggage storage for $1.25 during their office hours (Mon through Sat from 10:30am to 2pm and 4 to 6pm). It's about half a block up the street opposite the pier.

The closest bank is **Bancomer** in Pochutla, which will change money Monday through Friday from 9am to 6pm and Saturday from 9am to 1pm.

The **post office** (correo), open Monday through Friday from 9am to 3:30pm, is on the curve as you enter town.

BEACHES, WATER SPORTS & BOAT TRIPS

The golden sands of Puerto Ángel and peaceful village life are the attractions here, so in terms of "where to hit the beach," we'll begin with Playa Principal in the central village. You can't miss it: The beach lies between the Mexican navy base and the pier that plays host to the local fishing fleet. Near the pier, fishermen pull their colorful boats on the beach and unload their catch in the late morning while trucks wait to haul it off to processing plants in Veracruz. The rest of the beach seems light years from the world of work and purpose, and except on Mexican holidays, it's relatively deserted.

It's important to note that Pacific Coast currents deposit trash on Puerto Ángel beaches. The locals do a fairly good job of keeping it picked up, but the currents are constant.

Playa Panteón is the main swimming and snorkeling beach. "Cemetery beach," ominous as that sounds, is about a 15-minute walk from the town center, straight through town on the main street that skirts the beach. You'll see the *panteón* (cemetery) on the right.

In Playa Panteón, some of the palapa restaurants and a few of the hotels rent snorkeling and scuba gear and can arrange boat trips, but all tend to be rather expensive. Check the quality and condition of gear—particularly scuba gear—that you're renting.

Playa Zipolite (*see*-poh-lee-tay) and its village are 3.7 miles down a paved road from Puerto Ángel. Taxis charge around $4.50 (taxis are relatively expensive here), or you can catch a colectivo on the main street in the town center and share the cost.

Zipolite is well known as a good surf break and as a nude beach. Although public nudity (including topless sunbathing) is technically against the law throughout Mexico, it's allowed here—one of only a handful of beaches in Mexico. This sort of open-mindedness has attracted an increasing number of young European travelers here over other coastal resorts. Most sunbathers concentrate beyond a large rock outcropping at the far end of the beach. Police will occasionally patrol the area, but they are much more intent on searching out illegal drug use rather than au natural sunbathers—as throughout Mexico, the purchase, sale, or use of drugs is definitely against the law, no matter what the local custom may be (see "Fast Facts: Mexico," in chapter 3). The ocean and currents here are quite strong (of course, that's why the surf is so good!) and because of this, a number of drownings have occurred over the years—know your limits. There are places to tie up a hammock, and a few palapa restaurants for a light lunch and a cold beer.

Hotels in Playa Zipolite are basic and rustic; most are made with rugged walls and palapa roofs. Prices range from $10 to $35 a night, with the highest prices being charged on Mexican holidays.

Traveling north on Highway 175, you'll come to another hot surf break and a beach of spectacular beauty, **Playa San Augustinillo.** One of the pleasures of a lengthy stay in Puerto Ángel is discovering the many hidden beaches nearby and spending the day there. Local boatmen can give details and quote rates for this service, or ask at your hotel.

WHERE TO STAY

Two areas in Puerto Ángel have accommodations: Playa Principal in the tiny town, and Playa Panteón, the beach area beyond the village center. Between Playa Panteón and town are numerous bungalow and guest-house setups with budget accommodations. During the high season—December, January, around Easter, and July and August—rates can go up, and you should reserve well in advance.

Hotel La Cabaña de Puerto Ángel. Apdo. Postal 22, 70902 Pochutla, Oax. ☎ **958/ 4-0026.** 23 units. Year-round $20 double. No credit cards.

Covered in vines and plants, with lots of shade, this hacienda-style hotel has sunny rooms with louvered windows and screens, ceiling fans, and double beds. The rooftop patio is a pleasant place to sunbathe peacefully. The hotel is on Playa Panteón on the landward side of the road, just steps from the beach and several restaurants.

La Buena Vista. Apdo. Postal 48, 70902 Puerto Ángel, Oax. ☎/fax **958/4-3104.** 18 units. $32 double. No credit cards.

To find La Buena Vista, follow the road through town; you'll see a sign on the right pointing to the hotel. It's on a hillside, so to get to the lobby/patio you follow the sign, taking a left at Casa de Huéspedes Alex, after which you climb a flight of stairs. Once there, you'll discover why this hotel's name means "good view," with the bay and village in the distance. The rooms, each with a natural tile floor, a fan, one or two double beds, and well-screened windows, are simply furnished with Mexican accents. On the upper floor is a small, reasonably priced restaurant with bay views. It's open for breakfast from 7:30 to 11am and for dinner from 6 to 10pm.

✪ **Posada Cañon Devata.** Calle Cañon del Vata (Apdo. Postal 10), 70902 Puerto Ángel, Oax. ☎/fax **958/4-3048.** E-mail: lopez@spin.com.mx. 10 rms, 4 bungalows (only 1 without bathroom). $22–$29 double; $35–$40 bungalow or El Cielo room for 2. No credit cards. Closed May–June.

One of the most inviting places in Puerto Ángel is a 3-minute walk almost straight up from Playa Panteón. Americans Suzanne and Mateo López run this ecologically sound, homey, cool, green, and wooded oasis in a narrow canyon. All water is recycled for the benefit of the resident plants and critters. Rooms—completely remodeled in early 1998—are agreeably rustic-chic, with fans, beds covered in Guatemalan tie-dyed cloth, and Mateo's paintings hanging from the walls (the paintings are for sale). The patio restaurant serves delicious food, featuring home-baked bread and the posada's own organically grown vegetables. Don't miss climbing to the appropriately named El Cielo to see the bay bathed in the light of the setting sun, and be sure to enjoy the happy hour from 5pm until dark. Mateo also offers fishing and snorkeling trips.

   To find it, walk just past the Hotel Cabaña del Puerto Ángel to the point at which the road more or less ends; turn right and go down the sandy path to an area with a few parked cars. Walk across the tiny bridge on your right and follow the stairs on the left until you reach the restaurant, where someone should be around to rent rooms and serve food.

WHERE TO DINE

In addition to the restaurants below and those mentioned under "Where to Stay," above, there are four or five palapa-topped restaurants on the main beach in town as well as on Playa Panteón that are all similar in price, menu, and service. Breakfasts generally cost $2.25 to $4.50, and meat or seafood plates run $3.50 to $11. Watch for overbilling in these restaurants.

✪ **Restaurant Cañon Devata.** At Posada Cañon Devata, Calle Cañon Devata. ☎ **958/4-3048.** Breakfast $2–$4.50; sandwiches $3.50; dinner $6.25. No credit cards. Daily 7:30am–4pm and 7–8:30pm. Closed May–June. VEGETARIAN.

It's always a few degrees cooler under the thatched palapa here in the middle of the canyon area. Fresh flowers on the thick wooden tables set the mood. Guests enjoy some of the healthiest cooking around, mainly vegetarian dishes with occasional fish specialties. The restaurant is in the hotel by the same name, on the right, past the Hotel Cabaña de Puerto Ángel.

Villa Florencia. Bulevar Virgilio Uribe. ☎ **958/4-3044.** Breakfast $1.85–$2.25; pasta dishes $3.50–$5; pizzas $4–$6. AE, MC, V. Daily 7am–10pm. ITALIAN.

One of the best restaurants in town is Lulu and Walter Pelliconi's delightful slice of Italy. Their generous servings are prepared in a spotlessly clean kitchen that contains a purifier for all water used on the premises. Pasta products are imported from Italy, and the chefs use only extra-virgin olive oil. The restaurant is located near the pier and the bus drop-off in the central village.

4 Bahías de Huatulco

40 miles SE of Puerto Ángel; 425 miles SE of Acapulco

Pristine beaches and jungle landscapes can make for an idyllic retreat from the stress of daily life—when viewed from a luxury hotel balcony, even better. Huatulco is for those who want to enjoy the beauty of nature during the day, then retreat to sumptuous comfort by night. Leisurely, slow-paced, and still relatively untouched, the Bays of Huatulco enjoy the most modern infrastructure on Mexico's Pacific coast.

Undeveloped stretches of pure white sands and isolated coves lie in wait for the promised growth of Huatulco, but it's not catching on as rapidly as Cancún, the previous resort planned by Mexico's Tourism Development arm. The FONATUR development of the Bahías de Huatulco is an ambitious but staged-in development project that aims to cover 52,000 acres of land, with over 40,000 acres to remain ecological preserves. The small communities of locals have been transplanted from the coast into Crucecita. The area is distinctly divided into three sections: **Santa Cruz, Crucecita,** and **Tangolunda Bay** (see "City Layout," below).

It's not that Huatulco doesn't have what it takes to attract visitors; it just hasn't developed a true personality of its own yet. There's little to do here in the way of nightlife, or even dining outside of hotels. But if you're drawn to snorkeling, diving, boat cruises to virgin bays, and simple relaxation, Huatulco fills the bill. With nine bays encompassing 36 beaches and countless inlets and coves, the clear blue waters and golden beaches are attracting an increasing number of visitors to Huatulco each year.

ESSENTIALS

GETTING THERE   By Plane   Aeromexico (☎ 800/237-6639, from the U.S.; 01-800/133-4000 or 958/1-0329 from within Mexico) offers service from Dallas, Guadalajara, Houston, Miami, and New York via Mexico City daily. Three times daily **Mexicana** flights (☎ 800/531-7921 from the U.S.; 958/7-0223 or 958/1-9007 at the airport) connect Huatulco with Cancún, Chicago, Guadalajara, Los Angeles, Miami, San Antonio, San Francisco, San Jose, and Toronto by way of Mexico City. **AeroMorelos** (☎ 800/237-6639 from the U.S.) has direct flights from Oaxaca 5 days per week, and via Puerto Escondido 3 days per week. **Continental** (☎ 800/525-0120 from the U.S., or 958/1-9028) flies from Houston several times a week.

From Huatulco's international airport (HUX), about 12 miles northwest of the Bahías de Huatulco, private **taxis** charge $10 to Crucecita, $12 to Santa Cruz, and $15 to Tangolunda. **Transportes Terrestres colectivo** minibus fares range from $6 to $10 per person.

Budget (☎ 800/527-0700 from the U.S., or 958/1-0036), **Dollar** (☎ 800/800-4000 from the U.S., 958/1-9004, or 958/1-9017), and **Hertz** (☎ 800/654-3131 from the U.S., or 958/7-0751) all have offices at the airport that are open for flight arrivals. Daily rates run around $50 for a VW sedan, $75 for a VW Golf, and $75 for a Jeep Tracker. Dollar also has rental offices at the Royal Maeva, Sheraton, and downtown. Because this destination is so spread out and has excellent roads, you may want to consider a rental car, at least for a day or two, to explore the area.

By Car   The coastal Highway 200 leads to Huatulco (via Pochutla) from the north and is generally in good condition. The drive from Puerto Escondido is just under 2 hours. Allow at least 6 hours for the trip from Oaxaca City on mountainous Highway 175.

By Bus   Reaching Huatulco by bus has become easier. There are three bus stations in Crucecita, but none in Santa Cruz or Tangolunda. The stations in Crucecita are all

Important Travel Note

The stretch of Highway 200 north between Huatulco and Acapulco has been sub-jected to numerous bus hijackings and occasional car robberies; only drive during the day, and if you have a choice, fly.

---

within a few blocks of one another. The **Gacela and Estrella Blanca** station is at the corner of Gardenia and Palma Real with service to Acapulco, Mexico City, Puerto Escondido, and Pochutla. The **Cristóbal Colón** station (☎ 958/7-0261) is at the corner of Gardenia and Ocotillo, 4 blocks from the Plaza Principal. They service des-tinations throughout Mexico, including Oaxaca, Puerto Escondido, and Pochutla. The **Estrella del Valle** station services Oaxaca, and is located on Jasmin, between Sabali and Carrizal.

If you arrive by bus, you'll be dropped off in Crucecita.

VISITOR INFORMATION   The **State Tourism Office** (Oficina del Turismo; ☎ **958/7-1542;** fax 958/7-1541; E-Mail: sedetur6@oaxaca-travel.gob.mx) is located in the Plaza San Miguel in Santa Cruz at the corner of Santa Cruz and Monte Albán. It offers very friendly, helpful service, and is open Monday through Friday from 9am to 3pm and 6 to 9pm, and Saturday from 9am to 1pm.

CITY LAYOUT   The resort area is called Bahías de Huatulco and includes all nine bays. The town of Santa María de Huatulco, the original settlement in this area, is 17 miles inland. **Santa Cruz Huatulco,** usually called Santa Cruz, was the first area on the coast to be developed. It has a pretty central park with a bandstand kiosk, an artisan's market by the park, a few hotels and restaurants, and a marina where bay tours and fishing trips set sail. **Juárez** is Santa Cruz's main street, about only 4 blocks long in all, anchored at one end by the Hotel Castillo Huatulco and at the other by the Meigas Binniguenda hotel. Opposite the Hotel Castillo is the marina, and beyond it are restaurants housed in new colonial-style buildings facing the beach. The area's banks are on Juárez. It's impossible to get lost; you can take in almost everything at a glance.

A mile and a half inland from Santa Cruz is **Crucecita,** a planned city that sprang up in 1985 centered on a lovely grassy plaza edged with flowering hedges. It's the res-idential area for the resorts, with neighborhoods of new stucco homes mixed with small apartment complexes. Most of the area's less expensive hotels and restaurants are here.

Until other bays are developed, **Tangolunda Bay,** 3 miles east, is the focal point of development for the nine bays. Gradually, half the bays will have resorts. For now, Tangolunda has the 18-hole golf course, as well as the Club Med, Quinta Real, Sher-aton Huatulco, Royal Maeva, Casa del Mar, and Zaachila hotels, among others. Small strip centers with a few restaurants occupy each end of Tangolunda Bay. **Chahue Bay,** between Tangolunda and Santa Cruz, is a small bay with a marina under construction as well as houses and hotels.

GETTING AROUND   It's too far to walk between any of the three destinations of Crucecita, Santa Cruz, and Tangolunda, but **taxis** are inexpensive and readily avail-able. The fare between Santa Cruz and Tangolunda is roughly $2; between Santa Cruz and Crucecita, $1.25; between Crucecita and Tangolunda, $2.75.

There is **minibus service** between towns. In Santa Cruz, catch the bus across the street from Castillo Huatulco; in Tangolunda, in front of the Caribbean Village; and in Crucecita, catercorner from the Hotel Grifer.

FAST FACTS: BAHÍAS DE HUATULCO

Area Code   The area code is **958.**

Banks   All three areas have banks with automatic tellers; including the main Mexican banks, Banamex and Bancomer. They can change money during business hours, which are from 9am to 6pm Monday through Friday and 9am to 1pm on Saturday.

Taxis   In Crucecita there's a taxi stand opposite the Hotel Grifer and another on the Plaza Principal. Taxis are readily available in Santa Cruz and Tangolunda through your hotel. They can also be rented by the hour (about $10 per hour) or for the day, should you want to make a more thorough exploration of the area.

BEACHES, WATER SPORTS & OTHER THINGS TO DO

BEACHES   A section of the beach at Santa Cruz (away from the small boats) is an inviting sunning spot. Several restaurants are on the beach, and palapa umbrellas are found down to the water's edge. The most popular is **Tipsy's** (☎ **958/7-0576**), with full beach bar and restaurant service, lounge chairs, towel service, and showers. All kinds of water-sports equipment is available for rent here, including kayaks ($10 per hour); snorkeling equipment, catamarans, jet skis ($62 per hour); banana boats; and there's even waterskiing ($50 per hr.). They're open from 10am to 8pm Tuesday through Friday and 9am to 11pm Saturday and Sunday. They accept American Express, MasterCard, and Visa.

For about $6 one way, pangas from the marina in Santa Cruz will ferry you to **La Entrega Beach,** also in Santa Cruz bay. There you'll find a row of palapa restaurants, all with beach chairs out front. Find an empty one and use that restaurant for your refreshment needs in return. A snorkel equipment–rental booth is about midway down the beach, and there's some fairly good snorkeling on the end away from where the boats arrive.

Between Santa Cruz and Tangolunda bays is **Chahúe Bay.** A beach club here has palapas, beach volleyball, and refreshments for an entrance fee of about $1.25. However, a strong undertow makes this a dangerous place for swimming.

Tangolunda Bay beach, fronting the best hotels, is wide and beautiful. Theoretically all beaches in Mexico are public; however, nonguests at Tangolunda hotels may have difficulty being allowed to enter the hotel to get to the beach.

BAY CRUISES/TOURS   Huatulco's major attraction is the coastline, that magnificent stretch of pristine bays bordered by an odd blend of cactus and jungle vegetation at the water's edge. The only way to really grasp its beauty is by taking a cruise of the bays, stopping at Chahue or **Maguey Bay** for a dip in the crystal-clear water and a fish lunch from one of the palapas on the beach.

One way to arrange a bay tour is to go to the **boat-owners' cooperative** in the red-and-yellow tin shack at the entrance to the marina. Prices are posted here, and you can buy tickets for definite times for sightseeing, snorkeling, or fishing. Besides La Entrega Beach, there are other beaches farther away that are noted for good offshore snorkeling. These beaches, however, have no food or toilet facilities, so bring your own provisions. Boatmen at the cooperative will arrange to return to get you at an appointed time. Prices run about $67 for 2 to 3 hours.

Another option is to join one of the organized bay cruises, such as aboard the *Tequila,* complete with guide, drinks, and on-board entertainment. These can easily be arranged through any travel agency and cost about $30 per person, with an extra charge of $6 for snorkeling-equipment rental.

In Crucecita, **Shuatur Tours** (Plaza Oaxaca, Local no. 20, ☎ /fax **958/7-0734**) offers bay tours; tours to Puerto Ángel, Puerto Escondido, and associated beaches; an ecotour on the Río Copalito (7 hr.); or an all-day tour to a coffee plantation.

An especially popular option is the daylong trip to **Oaxaca City** and **Monte Alban.** The trip includes round-trip airfare on Aerocaribe, lunch, entrance to the archaeological sight of Monte Alban, and a tour of the architectural highlights of Oaxaca City, and costs $110. It's available through any travel agency, or through the **Aerocaribe** office at ☎958/7-1220.

GOLF & TENNIS   The 18-hole, par-72 **Tangolunda Golf Course** (☎ 958/ 1-0037) is adjacent to Tangolunda Bay and has tennis courts as well. The greens fee is $35 and carts cost about the same. Tennis courts are also available at the **Sheraton** hotel (☎ 958/1-0055).

SHOPPING   Shopping in the area is limited, and concentrated in both the Santa Cruz Market, by the marina in Santa Cruz, and the Crucecita Market, on Guamuchil, half a block from the plaza in Crucecita. Also in Crucecita is the Plaza Oaxaca, adjacent to the central plaza, with clothing shops including **Carlos 'n' Charlie's** (☎ 958/ 7-0698) for official T-shirts of the same name; **Poco Loco Club** (☎ 958/7-0279) for casual sportswear; **Mic Mac** (☎ 958/7-0565), featuring beachwear, bathing suits and, souvenirs; and **Sideout** (☎ 958/7-0254) for active wear. **Coconuts** (☎ 958/ 7-0057) has English-language magazines, books, and music. Several strip shopping centers in Tangolunda Bay offer a selection of crafts and Oaxacan goods, but are pricier than the markets.

WHERE TO STAY

Moderate- and budget-priced hotels in Santa Cruz and Crucecita are generally higher in price compared to similar hotels in other Mexican beach resorts, where the luxury beach hotels have comparable rates. Low-season rates refer to the months of August through November only.

VERY EXPENSIVE

✪ **Quinta Real.** Bulevar Benito Juárez Lt. no. 2, Bahía de Tangolunda, 70989 Huatulco, Oax. ☎ **888/561-2817** or 800/445-4565 in the U.S., 958/1-0428, or 958/1-0430. Fax 958/1-0429. 28 units. A/C MINIBAR TV TEL. High season $265 Master Suite; $350 Grand Class Suite; $400 with private pool. Low season $175 Master Suite; $240 Grand Class Suite; $280 with private pool. AE, DC, MC, V.

Double Moorish domes mark this romantic and relaxed hotel with a richly appointed cream-and-white decor and complete attention to detail. From the gentle reception at a private desk to the luxurious beach club below, they emphasize excellence in service. The small groupings of suites built into the gently downward sloping hill to Tangolunda Bay offer privacy as well as spectacular views of the ocean and golf course next door. Interiors are elegant and comfortable, with stylish Mexican furniture, wood-beamed ceilings, marble tub/shower-combination bathrooms with Jacuzzi tubs, and detailed finishings including original works of art and telescopes in many of the suites. Balconies have overstuffed seating and floors have stone inlays. Eight Grand Class Suites and the Presidential Suite have ultraprivate pools of their own. The Presidential Suite has two separate full-sized bedrooms, a spacious open-air living/dining area with seating for eight, a bar, and a palapa-topped terrace. The Quinta Real is perfect for weddings, honeymoons, or small corporate retreats.

Dining/Diversions: The restaurant serves nouvelle international cuisine with signature dishes that include lobster medaillons in a pink crab sauce, Oaxacan grilled beef tenderloin in a black-bean sauce, and shrimp marinated in cinnamon with pineapple. It's open for breakfast, lunch, and dinner. The bar extends over a terrace with a stunning view, and has comfy sofas and cowhide-covered chaises.

Amenities: Beach Club with two pools (one a children's pool) and a restaurant and bar, plus shade palapas on the beach and chair and towel service. All suites have bathrobes, hair dryers, in-room safe-deposit boxes. Laundry and room service and in-room massage are available.

MODERATE

Hotel Meigas Binniguenda. Bulevar Benito Juárez s/n (Apdo. Postal 175), 70989 Santa Cruz de Huatulco, Oax. ☎ **958/7-0077.** Fax 958/7-0284. 165 units. A/C MINIBAR TV TEL. High season $160 double, all-inclusive. Low season $75 double, room only. AE, MC, V.

This was Huatulco's first hotel, and it retains the Mexican charm and comfort that made it memorable. A new addition has more than doubled the hotel's original size. Rooms have Mexican-tile floors, foot-loomed bedspreads, and colonial-style furniture; French doors open onto tiny wrought-iron balconies overlooking Juárez or the pool and gardens. TVs receive Mexican channels plus HBO. There's a nice shady area around the hotel's beautiful, original pool in back of the lobby. A large, palapa-topped restaurant with seating for 300 separates this pool from the new, larger one. The hotel is away from the marina at the far end of Juárez, only a few blocks from the water. They offer free transportation every hour to the beach club at Santa Cruz Bay. They now have in-room safe-deposit boxes, plus complete travel-agency services.

Royal Maeva. Bulevar Benito Juárez s/n, Bahía de Tangolunda, 70989 Huatulco, Oax. ☎ **800/GO-MAEVA** in the U.S., or 958/1-0000. Fax 958/1-0020. 312 units. A/C TV TEL. High season $210 double, all-inclusive; $100 per night surcharge for suites. Low season $185 double. Children under 12 stay free in parents' room. AE, MC, V.

With all meals, drinks, entertainment, tips, and a slew of activities included in the price, Maeva is a value-packed experience in Huatulco. It caters to adults of all ages (married and single) who enjoy a mix of activities and relaxation. An excellent kids' activity program makes it probably the best option in the area for families. Three restaurants serve a variety of meals, located at various points around the expansive property, with both buffet and à la carte options, as well as changing theme nights. Four bars serve drinks until 2am nightly. Rooms have tile floors and Oaxacan wood trim, large tub/shower-combination bathrooms, and ample balconies, all with views of Tangolunda Bay. There's also a full gym, large free-form pool, four lighted tennis courts, and a complete beachfront water-sports center.

INEXPENSIVE

✪ **Hotel Las Palmas.** Av. Guamuchil 206, 70989 Bahías de Huatulco, Oax. ☎ **958/ 7-0060.** Fax 958/7-0057. 25 units. TV. High season $25 double. Low season $22 double. AE, MC, V. Free parking.

The central location and accommodating staff are an added benefit to the clean, bright rooms at Las Palmas. Located a half a block from the main plaza, it's also connected to the popular Sabor de Oaxaca restaurant (see "Where to Dine", below). Ten new suites have air-conditioning. Room interiors have tile floors, cotton textured bedspreads, tiles showers, and cable TV. Tobacco shop, travel-agency services, and a public telephone are available.

WHERE TO DINE

Outside of the hotels, the best choices are in Crucecita and on the beach in Santa Cruz.

✪ **El Sabor de Oaxaca.** Av. Guamuchil 206, Crucecita. ☎ **958/7-0060.** Fax 958/ 7-0057. Main dishes $2–$10. AE, MC, V. Daily 7am–midnight. OAXACAN.

This is the best place in the area to enjoy authentic and richly flavorful Oaxacan food, among the best of traditional Mexican cuisine. This restaurant is a local favorite, as well as catering to the quality standards of tourists. Among the most popular items are their Mixed Grill for Two, with a Oaxacan beef fillet, tender pork tenderloin *chorizo* (a zesty Mexican sausage), and pork ribs; and the Oaxacan Special for Two, offering a generous sampling of the best of the menu with tamales, Oaxacan cheese, pork mole, and more. Generous breakfasts are just $2.25 and include eggs, bacon, ham, beans, toast, and fresh orange juice. There's a colorful decor and lively jazz music, and special group events are happily arranged.

Oaxacan Nights. Bulevar Benito Juárez s/n (across from Royal Maeva), Tangolunda Bay. ☎ **958/1-0001.** Dinner and show $20; show only, $10; extra charge for beverages. AE, MC, V. Thurs–Sat 9pm–11:30pm. OAXACAN.

The colorful, traditional folkloric dances of Oaxaca are performed in an open-air courtyard, reminiscent of an old hacienda despite being located in a modern strip mall. The dancers clearly enjoy performing this traditional ballet under the direction of owner Celicia Flores Ramirez (wife of Don Willo Porfirio, of local restaurant fame). The dinner that accompanies the show is a generous, flavorful sampling of traditional Oaxacan fare including a tamale, sope, Oaxacan cheese, grilled fillet, pork enchilada, and a chile relleno. You may choose to order off the menu of the adjoining Don Porfiro's. Groups are welcome.

Restaurant Avalos Doña Celia. Santa Cruz Bay. ☎ **958/7-0128.** Breakfast $3–$6; seafood $5–$10. No credit cards. Daily 8:30am–10pm. SEAFOOD.

Doña Celia, an original Huatulco resident, chose to stay in business in the same area where she started her little thatch-roofed restaurant years ago. Now she's in a new building at the end of Santa Cruz's beach, serving the same good eats. Among her specialties are *filete empapelado,* a foil-wrapped fish baked with tomato, onion, and cilantro; and *filete almendrado,* a fish fillet covered with hotcake batter, beer, and almonds. The ceviche is terrific (one order is plenty for two). The *Platillo a la Huatulqueño* (shrimp and young octopus fried in olive oil with chile and onion and served over white rice) should satisfy any seafood lover. The ambiance is basic, and it could be cleaner, but the food is the reason for its popularity.

Restaurante María Sabina. Flamboyan 15, Crucecita. ☎ **958/7-1039.** Main courses $2.75–$17; regional $3–$7; seafood $6–$11. AE, MC, V. Daily 7am–midnight. SEAFOOD/OAXACAN.

This popular restaurant is on the far side of the Plaza Principal. The staff is super-attentive, and owner Jaime Negrete presides over the big, open grill where the tantalizing aroma of grilled steak, ribs, chicken, and fresh fish drifts throughout the cafe. Almost always full, this is where carnivores feed. The lengthy menu also features Oaxacan dishes.

HUATULCO AFTER DARK

There's a limited but lively selection of dance clubs available. Ever-present in Mexican resorts, **Carlos 'n' Charlie's** (☎ **958/7-0005**), located just off the plaza in Crucecita, is the best bet for earlier dancing and revelry. Open 4pm to 3am.

Magic Circus (☎ **958/7-0017**), located in Santa Cruz, is the area's most popular disco. It opens at 9pm and closes when the last dance is danced. **Poison** (☎ **958/ 7-1530**) is the top spot for very late nights, with open-air dancing on the beachfront of Santa Cruz bay. Located next to the Marina Hotel on the beach, it's open until 5am and plays techno and rock.

11

The Southernmost States: Oaxaca & Chiapas

Oaxaca and Chiapas have the largest populations of indigenous peoples in Mexico. But these Indians aren't hidden somewhere on a distant reservation; they lead normal lives and you'll see them everywhere—on buses, in marketplaces and plazas, in banks and offices. The southern part of Mexico is its most Indian—what sets Oaxaca and Chiapas apart from the rest of the country. Not coincidentally, these two states are renowned for the beauty and variety of their arts and crafts. In Oaxaca, most of the native art is produced in the central region of the state: near the city of Oaxaca, a jewel of colonial architecture set in a highland valley surrounded by mountains. On one of those mountains lie the ruins of an ancient ceremonial center, Monte Albán, which offer not only a commanding view of the whole valley but an intriguing collection of buildings and artifacts whose design is far different from those of the Maya to the east or the many cultures of central Mexico to the northwest.

In Chiapas, the two areas that hold the most interest are the eastern lowland jungles and the central highlands. In the former are the famous ruins of Palenque, a city that dates from the classic age of Maya civilization. These ruins look unspeakably old, and the surrounding jungle seems poised to reclaim them should ever their caretakers falter in their duties. Deeper into the interior, for those willing to make the trek, are the sites of Yaxchilán and Bonampak. The central highlands are just as dramatic, but easier to enjoy. Of particular interest are the colonial city of San Cristóbal de las Casas and surrounding Indian villages. The Indians here cling so tenaciously to their beliefs and traditions that this area was once considerably better known to anthropologists than tourists. Knowing anthropologists, I suspect this was also due in some measure to the beauty and agreeable climate of San Cristóbal.

Lately, political violence in this area—a massacre in Acteal, near San Cristóbal, and killings in the Ocosingo area, which lies between Palenque and San Cristóbal—have attracted international attention. No foreigners were attacked in these events, and no restrictions were placed on travel to Palenque or the San Cristóbal region. I toured the area a month after the events took place, and saw little disruption of the day-to-day affairs of the local people. The State Department has not issued a travel advisory for the region, but before you go, get the most current information you can by checking the State Department Web site www.travel.state.gov.

EXPLORING OAXACA & CHIAPAS

Airline and bus service to this area have improved a lot in the last few years. Most people arrive and depart through Oaxaca, Villahermosa, Tuxtla Gutiérrez, and now even San Cristóbal or Palenque. A common way of entering the region from the Palenque side is to go through Villahermosa in the neighboring state of Tabasco, and if you're there for any considerable time, it's worth your while to check out the **Parque-Museo La Venta.** Half park, half museum, it displays artifacts from the mother of all Mesoamerican cultures—the Olmec. These artifacts—including some of the famous giant, monolithic heads—come from the nearby site of La Venta and were brought here and displayed in something akin to their original surroundings.

Palenque can be seen in a day. A couple of worthwhile side trips would add a day or two, and if you plan on going to **Bonampak** and **Yaxchilán,** add 2 full days. **Oaxaca City** and **San Cristóbal** and their respective neighborhoods have so much to offer that I would consider 4 days in either place the minimum; a week, more realistic. If you are considering traveling to Oaxaca and Chiapas but want to include some beach time, keep in mind that Oaxaca's coastal resorts—including Puerto Escondido and Puerto Ángel—are not far away. See chapter 10 for more information.

1 Oaxaca City

325 miles SE of Mexico City; 144 miles SE of Tehuacán; 168 miles NE of Puerto Escondido

What you see today when you walk through the old parts of Oaxaca (wa-*hah*-kah) is largely the product of three centuries of colonial society. You'll notice that most of the city is dressed in a beautiful green limestone, which sets it apart from other colonial cities. You'll see heavily buttressed and decidedly stout churches and monasteries, but note the absence of lofty bell towers. During colonial times, the city endured several violent earthquakes, and, rather than defy nature, the builders adopted their own colonial style with lower, thicker arches and towers and massive walls.

The central valley of Oaxaca was an important and populous region in pre-Hispanic times. Olmec influence reached the area sometime around 1200 B.C.; by 800 B.C. the Zapotecs (the original builders of Monte Albán) occupied the valley, and their culture flourished about the same time as Teotihuacán. Trade between this valley and the valleys of Cholula and Mexico intensified and remained important into the Postclassic age right up to the Conquest. There was also trade with the Maya to the east. In early Postclassic times, the Mixtec appeared in the region and through war and conquest gained ascendancy over much of the Zapotec homeland, until both peoples were humbled by the Aztecs, and later the Spaniards. To this day, however, the two principal ethnic groups in Oaxaca remain the Zapotec and Mixtec.

The city of Oaxaca, originally called Antequera, was founded just a few years after the vanquishing of the Aztec; most of the surrounding valley was granted to Hernán Cortés for his services to the crown. For the three centuries of colonial rule, the region remained calm.

In the years following Mexico's independence, there was more or less continuous upheaval. From the 1830s to the 1860s, two factions, the Liberals and Conservatives, fought for control of Mexico's destiny; eventually the French intervened on the side of the Conservatives. One man, a Zapotec Indian from Oaxaca, led the resistance against the French and played the deciding role in shaping Mexico's future. He was Benito Juárez, and his handiwork is known to history as "La Reforma."

Juárez was born in the village of Guelatao and "adopted" by a wealthy Oaxacan family who clothed, educated, and taught him Spanish in return for his services as a houseboy. He fell in love with the daughter of his benefactor and promised he would become rich and famous and return to marry her. He managed all three, achieving legendary status along the way. Juárez attended law school, was the governor of the state of Oaxaca (1847–52), and became president of the Republic in 1861. Juárez is revered throughout Mexico as a national hero.

ESSENTIALS

GETTING THERE & DEPARTING **By Plane** **Mexicana** (☎ 800/531-7921 in the U.S., 951/6-7352, or 951/6-8414) and **Aeromexico** (☎ 800/237-6639 in the U.S., or 951/6-1066) have several flights daily to and from Mexico City. **Aerocaribe** (affiliated with Mexicana, ☎ 951/6-0229 or 951/6-0266) flies once a day to Tuxtla Gutiérrez, Villahermosa, Mérida, and Cancún. **Aviacsa** (☎ 01-800/006-2200 inside Mexico, or 951/4-5187) flies once a day to Tuxtla Gutiérrez. **Aerovega** (☎ 951/6-4982 or 951/6-2777) flies a 6-passenger twin-engine Aero-Commander from Puerto Escondido and Bahías de Huatulco once daily (twice if there are enough passengers). Arrangements for AeroVega are made at the Monte Albán Hotel facing the Alameda (next to the zócalo).

Inexpensive transportation from hotels in town to the airport can be arranged by **Transportes Aeropuerto Oaxaca** (☎ 951/4-4350), located a few doors from the Hotel Monte Albán on the Alameda. They don't accept phone reservations, so drop by Monday through Saturday from 9am to 2pm or 5 to 8pm to buy your ticket. And since the office is closed on Sunday, buy tickets on Saturday if you plan to leave on Monday. The cost is $2 from downtown hotels and around $4 from outlying hotels—more if you have more than two suitcases and one small carry-on.

By Car It's an easy 5-hour drive from Mexico City via the toll road, which opened in late 1994. It begins at Cuacnoapalan, about 50 miles southeast of Puebla, and runs south, terminating in Oaxaca; the one-way toll is $16. For adventurous souls, the old federal highway still winds through the mountains and offers spectacular views; it takes 9 to 10 hours.

By Bus On long trips to and from Oaxaca, be sure to ask if your potential bus is *con escalas* (with stops), *directo* (fewer stops), or *sin escalas* (no stops). Almost all first-class buses to/from Mexico City take the superhighway toll road (*autopista*), which takes 6 hours. A couple still take the old highway (9 hr.). You should ask when you buy your ticket. During special holidays, you need to reserve a seat. All the native Oaxaqueños I know living outside the state like to return for the Days of the Dead and Holy Week and Christmas.

ADO (Autobuses del Oriente) and its affiliates handle almost all of the first-class and deluxe bus service. These buses leave from the **ADO station** on Calzada Niños Héroes. There are at least 50 buses a day to Mexico City's TAPO (East) and Central del Norte (North) stations. Departures for other destinations include Tuxtla Gutiérrez (five a day); San Cristóbal de las Casas (two overnight buses); Puebla (10 a day); Tehuacán (four a day); Tapachula (one a day); Veracruz (three a day); Villahermosa (two a day); and Huatulco, Pochutla, and Puerto Escondido on the coast (two a day, stopping at all three towns). These last buses take 9 hours to reach Puerto Escondido because they go by way of Huatulco; for a faster trip, see below.

For some destinations you have the choice between first-class and deluxe (*de lujo*). Deluxe service offers more leg room, coffee or sodas, nonstop service, and perhaps better movies, and in the really deluxe buses, wider seats. When you walk through the station's main door, the passage to the buses will be straight in front of you. The long counter to the right of this sells first-class tickets (don't worry about the different company names—it's all the same), and the shorter counter to the left sells deluxe.

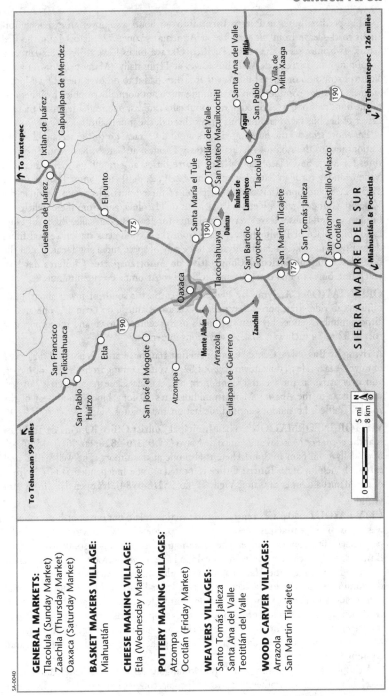

Oaxaca Area

To Tuxtepec ↑

To Tehuantepec 126 miles ↓

To Tehuacan 99 miles ↖

Ixtlan de Juárez

Calpulalpan de Mendez

Guelatao de Juárez

El Punto

175

Santa Ana del Valle

Villa de Mitla Xaaga

Mitla

San Pablo

Yagul

Teotitlán del Valle

San Mateo Macuilxochitl

Tlacolula

Santa María el Tule

Ruinas de Lambityeco

190

San Martín Tilcajete

San Tomás Jalieza

San Antonio Castillo Velasco Ocotlán

Miahuatlán & Pochutla ↓

Tlacochahuaya

Dainzu

San Bartolo Coyotepec

175

San Francisco Telixtlahuaca

San Pablo Huitzo

Etla

190

San José el Mogote

Atzompa

Oaxaca

Monte Albán

Arrazola

Cuilapan de Guerrero

Zaachila

SIERRA MADRE DEL SUR

N

5 mi
8 km

0

SA-0040

GENERAL MARKETS:
Tlacolula (Sunday Market)
Zaachila (Thursday Market)
Oaxaca (Saturday Market)

BASKET MAKERS VILLAGE:
Miahuatlán

CHEESE MAKING VILLAGE:
Etla (Wednesday Market)

POTTERY MAKING VILLAGES:
Atzompa
Ocotlán (Friday Market)

WEAVERS VILLAGES:
Santo Tomás Jalieza
Santa Ana del Valle
Teotitlán del Valle

WOOD CARVER VILLAGES:
Arrazola
San Martín Tilcajete

403

The speediest buses to **Puerto Escondido**—6 hours away over an extremely tortuous road—leave from the terminal at Armenta y López 721 across from the Red Cross. Two lines serve the route. **Pacífico Oaxaca** buses leave daily at 8:30am and 10:30pm. One **Estrella de Valle** bus leaves at 11pm daily. (Many people who go to Puerto Escondido on these buses say that if they had it to do over, they'd fly. Motion sickness is a huge consideration even among those not normally troubled by it because of the hundreds of curves through the mountains; at least one reader reported that the driver of her bus raced another bus driver through the mountains!)

For short trips to the outlying villages around Oaxaca, go to the second-class bus station next to the Abastos Market. **Fletes y Pasajes,** at Gate 9, has frequent departures for Mitla and Tlacolula. **Valle de Norte** buses, at gate 29, go to Teotitlán del Valle Monday through Saturday at 11am, 12:30, 2, 3:30, and 5pm. They return at 12:30, 2, 5, and 6pm (but double-check all of these hours). To get to Teotitlán del Valle on a Sunday, take a Fletes y Pasajes bus to Tlacolula, and from there (where the bus lets you off) buses leave every 20 minutes for Teotitlán del Valle. Buses for Guelatao (birthplace of Benito Juárez) leave from the second-class station several times daily. Buy your tickets a day in advance to be sure of space and a good seat. Under the breathless name of **Sociedad Cooperativa de Autotransportes Chóferes del Sur,** you'll find buses to Etla every 40 minutes, and to Atzompa every 30 minutes.

ORIENTATION   Arriving by Plane   The airport is south of town; about a 20-minute cab ride. Transportes Aeropuerto Oaxaca, Alameda de León 1A, operates an airport minibus service between the hotels in the center of town and the airport at a cost of $2 to $4 each way. Make reservations in person.

Arriving by Bus   The Central Camionera first-class bus station is north of the center of town. A taxi ride to downtown is about $2. If you're coming from the Pacific Coast, you may arrive at the Central Camionera de Segunda Clase (second-class bus terminal) next to the Abastos Market buildings. It's 10 long blocks southwest of the zócalo. Traffic is horrendous around the station and Abastos Market.

VISITOR INFORMATION   The **Municipal Tourist Office** (Oficina de Turismo) is at the corner of Morelos and Cinco de Mayo (☎ **951/6-4828;** fax 951/6-1550); it's open daily from 8am to 8pm. There is also one at the airport. The well-staffed and extremely helpful **State Tourist Office** is located at calle Independencia 607 in front of the Alameda (corner of García Vigil; ☎/fax **951/6-0984**). It's open daily from 9am to 8pm.

CITY LAYOUT   Oaxaca's central historic section is laid out on a north-south, east-west grid. The central east-west axis is Independencia. When streets cross Independencia, their names change. The same is true for the north-south axis, Alcalá/Bustamante. The city's center is the **zócalo,** a large square surrounded by stone archways, and next to it is the **Alameda,** a smaller plaza attached to the northwest part of the zócalo. Oaxaca's cathedral faces the Alameda, its Palacio del Gobierno the zócalo. A few blocks to the north is the **Plaza de Santo Domingo.** The area between these two open spaces holds most of historic district's shops, hotels, and restaurants. Two of the streets that run from Santo Domingo toward the zócalo—Alcalá and Cinco de Maya—are in part blocked off to traffic, making the stroll from the zócalo to Santo Domingo very pleasant.

A couple of blocks northeast of Santo Domingo is Parque Paseo Juárez, also known as **El Llano.** This is another place where people congregate, groups practice dance steps, children learn to skate, and joggers run and stretch.

GETTING AROUND   By Taxi   Colectivos depart for nearby villages from calle Mercadores, on the south side of the Abastos Market. You can negotiate rides to the ruins based on the number of people in your group. The average cost is around $10 per hour, which can be shared with up to five people. A regular taxi stand is along Independencia at the north side of the Alameda, while another is on calle Murguía just south of the Hotel Camino Real. An honest, careful, and dependable English-speaking driver, **Tomás Ramírez,** can be found here, or reached at his home at ☎ **951/1-5061.**

By Bus   Buses to the outlying villages of Guelatao, Teotitlán del Valle, Tlacolula, and Mitla leave from the second-class station just north of the Abastos Market (see "Getting There & Departing," above, for details).

FAST FACTS: Oaxaca

American Express   The office, in **Viajes Micsa,** is at Valdivieso and Hidalgo (northeast corner of the zócalo; ☎ **951/6-2700;** fax 951/6-7475). American Express office hours are Monday through Friday from 9am to 2pm and 4 to 6pm and on Saturday from 9am to 1pm. However, the travel agency is open Monday through Friday from 9am to 8pm and Saturday from 9am to 6pm. Here you will find both their travel agency and financial services office.

Area Code   The telephone area code is **951.**

Consulates   Several consulates can be contacted through **Grupo Consular,** upstairs at Hidalgo 817 no. 4 (☎ **951/4-2744**). The **U.S. Consular Agency** is at Alcalá 201 (☎/fax **951/6-4272** or 951/4-3054). Hours are Monday through Friday from 9am to 1pm.

Currency Exchange   Oaxaca is one of those places in Mexico where traveler's checks don't buy as many pesos as does cash, but the difference is small. There is a cluster of casas de cambio on the streets that intersect at the northeast corner of the zócalo—Alcalá and Valdivieso. These places have their rates posted, have hardly any lines, and keep better hours than banks. Some of these places exchange Canadian dollars.

E-mail   There are a number of places that offer E-mail access. The outfit that has the best rates and is most savvy about technical aspects is **Terrán Multimedia y Sistemas.** They are at avenida Morelos 600, second floor (☎ **951/6-8292**). They are also set up to make calls through the Internet, and this comes out much cheaper than regular long-distance rates—but often response time is slow. Their hours are Monday through Friday from 9:30am to 7pm and Saturday from 10am to 2pm.

Newspapers/Magazines   The English newspapers the *News* and the *Times,* both published in Mexico City, are sold at major newsstands. The monthly giveaway *Oaxaca Times,* published in English, is available at the tourist offices and many hotels. Another monthly, the trilingual *OAXACA* (English, Spanish, and French), is widely available.

Post Office   The *correo* (main post office) is at the corner of Independencia and Alameda Park. It is open Monday through Friday from 8am to 7pm and Saturday from 9am to 1pm.

Safety   By most standards, Oaxaca is a very safe town. Three years ago, the government opened an agency to help tourists who have been robbed or feel they have been cheated. This agency, CEPROTUR, has compiled data for 2½ years. The average number of crimes against tourists has been 334 per year. Almost all of this was purse or camera snatching or pickpocketing. The number of violent crimes barely made it to double digits. Excluding the large bus tours (where tourists are so closely shepherded that there is virtually no opportunity to rob them), the number of tourists who visit Oaxaca every year is over 60,000. You do the math. Most of the theft happens in crowded areas such as the markets. A common method is to discreetly slice open a tourist's backpack; another method is to distract someone who has set down a bag while a partner makes away with it. Should you lose any documents or things that might be covered by insurance, contact **CEPROTUR,** calle Alcalá 607, interior 13 at Plaza Santo Domingo (☎ **951/6-7280**). They will document your losses and facilitate the bureaucratic process.

Shipping   Oaxaca is a shoppers' delight, and it's hard to resist accumulating huge quantities of pottery, rugs, and other heavy goods that must be sent home. Many shops can arrange shipping, but if your goods have come from the markets and villages, you'll need to ship them yourself. The first rule of shipping is this: You must have a receipt. That means carrying a notebook and asking merchants to write out a receipt for you when you shop. All shipped items must be stamped *"hecho en México"* (made in Mexico). **Mexicana** airlines has a cargo office at Libres 617 (☎ **951/5-3711**), open Monday through Saturday from 9am to 8pm, and it can ship your goods to any gateway cities in the United States that have U.S. Customs offices. Mexicana requires *eight copies* of your receipts and charges a hefty fee in 20-kilo increments. Don't ship unless you absolutely must; remember that you're allowed two checked suitcases on an international flight. Some companies ship overland, which is cheaper. **Mexpost** (☎ **951/6-1291**), in the post office, is affiliated with UPS. They ask for a purchase slip and proof of origin. Items are shipped at customer's risk.

SPECIAL EVENTS & FESTIVALS

Oaxaca is famous for its colorful, exuberant, tradition-filled festivals. The most important ones are ✪ **Holy Week,** the **Guelaguetza** in July, **Días de los Muertos** in November, and the **Night of the Radishes** and **Christmas** in December. Make hotel reservations at least 2 months in advance if you plan to visit during these times.

At festival time in Oaxaca, sidewalk stands are set up in the market areas and near the cathedral to sell *buñuelos,* a large, thin, crisp, sweet snack food that costs about 75¢. It is the custom to serve buñuelos in cracked or otherwise flawed dishes, and after you've finished eating them, you smash the crockery on the sidewalk for good luck. Don't be timid! You can wash down the buñuelos with hot *ponche* (a favorite of mine) or atole for about 60¢ each.

Note: If you want to come for Christmas or the Guelaguetza but rooms and transportation are booked, you may want to consider using **Sanborn's Tours** for both festivals. Contact them at 2015 S. 10th St., McAllen, TX 78502 (☎ **800/395-8482**). **Remarkable Journeys,** P.O. Box 31855, Houston, TX 77231-1855 (☎ **800/856-1993** in the U.S., or 713/721-2517; fax 713/728-8334), also organizes trips that arrive in time for the Night of the Radishes.

For more activities, see "Oaxaca After Dark" and "Road Trips from Oaxaca" at the end of this section.

HOLY WEEK   During Holy Week, figurines made of palm leaves are sold on the streets. On Palm Sunday (the Sunday before Easter) there are colorful parades, and on the following Thursday, Oaxaca residents follow the Procession of the Seven Churches. Hundreds of the pious move from church to church, taking communion in each one to ensure a prosperous year. The next day, Good Friday, many of the barrios have *"Encuentros,"* where groups depart separately from the church, carrying relics through the neighborhoods, then "encountering" each other back at the church. Throughout the week each church sponsors concerts, fireworks, fairs, and other entertainment.

FIESTA GUELAGUETZA   On the Mondays following the last two weekends in July, you can witness the Fiesta Guelaguetza, or Feast of Monday of the Hill. In the villages, a *guelaguetza* (literally, a gift) is held by a family in need of the means to hold a wedding or other obligatory community celebration. Gifts are catalogued and will be repaid in kind at other guelaguetzas. In Oaxaca the custom of a guelaguetza, which includes elaborately staged regional dancing, has been a civic celebration since 1974, when the stadium was built.

During these last 2 weeks in July, there are fairs and exhibits, and regional dances are performed in the stadium on the Cerro del Fortín each Monday (about 10am to 1pm). It's a marvelous spectacle of color, costumes, music, and dance in which the dancers toss small candies or other treats to the crowd as a form of guelaguetza or gift. Some 350 different *huipils* (women's long overblouses) and dresses can be seen during the performance, as the villages of the seven regions of Oaxaca present their traditional dances. Admission ranges from free (in Section C) to $50 to $75 (in Section A), and tickets must be reserved in advance through the State Tourism Office (no later than May). A travel agency may be able to help you. I recommend Sections 5 and 6 in Palco A for the best seating in the Cerro del Fortín stadium. The ticket color matches the color of your seat. You will be sitting in strong sunlight, so wear a hat and long sleeves.

On the Sunday nights before the Guelaguetza, university students present an excellent program in the Plaza de la Danza at the Soledad church. The production is called the Bani Stui Gulal and is an abbreviated history of the Oaxaca valley. The program begins at 9pm, but since the event is free and seating is limited, you should get there quite early.

DÍAS DE LOS MUERTOS   This Mexican festival (Nov 1 and 2) has garnered worldwide media attention. It is celebrated across Oaxaca with more enthusiasm than in most of Mexico, which says quite a bit. Markets brim with marigolds—the flower of mortality—and every household fills an altar with these flowers and the dead's favorite dishes, drinks, and cigarettes. People visit relatives and friends, and anyone who visits is offered food. This is also the time to pay one's respects at the graveyard. Try to take one of the nocturnal cemetery tours offered around this time. An excellent one is offered out of **Casa Arnel** (☎ **951/5-2856;** fax 951/3-6285). It leaves for the village of Xoxo (pronounced *"ho*-ho") around 8pm on October 31, taking flowers and candles to be placed on tombs that have no visitors, and returns about 11:30pm. Cost is $15.50. Visits to other villages take place on the nights of November 1 and 2.

Another common form of celebrating is for young men to dress up in macabre outfits and frolic in the streets in Carnaval-like fashion.

DECEMBER FESTIVALS   The December Festivals begin on the 12th with the **festival of the Virgin de Guadalupe** and continue on the 16th with a *calenda,* or procession, to many of the older churches in the barrios, all accompanied by dancing and costumes. Festivities continue on the 18th with the **Fiesta de la Soledad** in honor of the Virgen de la Soledad, patroness of Oaxaca state. On that night there is a cascade of fire from a "castle" erected for the occasion in Plaza de la Soledad. December 23 is the ✪ **Night of the Radishes,** when Oaxaqueños build fantastic sculptures out of enormous radishes (the most prized vegetable cultivated during the colonial period), as well as flowers and corn husks. Displays on three sides of the zócalo are set up from 3pm on. By 6pm, when the show officially opens, lines to see the amazing figures are 4 blocks long. It's well organized and overseen by a heavy police presence. On December 24, around 8:30pm, each Oaxacan church organizes a procession with music, floats, enormous papier-mâché dancing figures (*carros alegóricos*), and crowds bearing candles, all of which converge on the zócalo.

NEW YEAR'S EVE   The new year is rung in with the **Petition of the Cross,** where villagers from all over come to the forlorn chapel on the hill near Tlacolula (about 22 miles southeast of Oaxaca, near Mitla) to light candles and to express their wishes for the coming new year. This they do through mock bargaining, with sticks and stones that represent livestock and produce. They also bring tiny symbolic representations of their farms and fields to aid them in their petitions for a prosperous year.

EXPLORING OAXACA

There is so much sightseeing to do inside and outside Oaxaca and so much to claim your attention that you have to be sure to allow some idle time for enjoying the zócalo. It is completely closed off to traffic (the mark of a highly civilized people), and here you can relax while getting a feel for the town and a good glimpse of Oaxacan society. I recommend going there in the late afternoon and taking a seat at the outdoor cafe with the best perspective of the cathedral. You can get a beer or order a bowl of the traditional drink of Oaxaca: chocolate. The afternoon light filters through the shiny green leaves of the laurel trees and illuminates the green limestone of the cathedral, making it seem even greener. There is always a crowd of people about. As dusk comes you can witness a flag-lowering ceremony performed by a small drill corps with much pomp and circumstance. Then either the marimba or the municipal band strikes up in the central bandstand for the evening's entertainment. Taken as a whole it is as quaint as quaint gets.

Inside the city there are museums worth close attention, some interesting churches, and colorful markets. Outside town there are the famous ruins of Monte Albán, the ruins at Mitla, and area villages known for their arts and crafts. It is sometimes best to check these out on market day; see "Shopping Splendor: Oaxaca's Market Villages," later in this chapter.

MUSEUMS

✪ **Museo Regional de Oaxaca.** Gurrión at Alcalá. ☎ **951/6-2991.** Admission $2; free Sun and holidays. Tues–Fri 10am–6pm; Sat, Sun, and holidays 10am–5pm.

Next to the Santo Domingo Church (6 blocks north of the zócalo), this museum is housed in a former Dominican convent—one of the greatest of colonial Mexico. The courtyard is astonishingly beautiful and imposing—exactly what you might expect from a Dominican monastery. The exterior walls are massive, which is why the building has withstood so many earthquakes. It was built early in the colonial period, largely completed by the early 1600s. The Mexican government did some extensive and painstaking renovation on it last year. The result is magnificent. The Santo Domingo Church also bears visiting (see below).

The museum's most treasured possessions are the artifacts from Monte Albán's Tomb 7, which were discovered in 1932. The tomb contained 12 to 14 corpses and some 500 pieces of jewelry and art, making use of almost 8 pounds of gold and turquoise, conch shell, amber, and obsidian. This is part of a larger collection of artifacts from Monte Albán, which you would do well to see before going up to the ruins. In the many ceramics and carvings you can see definite Olmec and Teotihuacan influences, but most display a style that is distinctly different from either culture. There are other rooms dedicated to an ethnographic exhibit of the region's customs, dress, religion, and cultural life, and there is another on colonial-age sculpture.

1990

BANCO NACIONAL DE OBRAS Y SERVICIOS PUBLICOS

S.N.C.

SERVICIOS PUBLICOS

SNC

SECRETARIA DE HACIENDA Y CREDITO PUBLICO

SUBSECRETARIA DE INGRESOS

Folio

A 0002005

BANCO NACIONAL DE OBRAS Y SERVICIOS PUBLICOS, S.N.C.

AV. JAVIER BARROS SIERRA No. 515 COL. LOMAS DE SANTA FE DEL. ALVARO OBREGON C.P. 01219 MEXICO, D.F. TEL. 5270-1200 (CONMUTADOR)

mejoracontinua@capufe.gob.mx

RF 0387063

BAN**BRAS**
BANCO NACIONAL DE OBRAS Y SERVICIOS PÚBLICOS, S.N.C.

Nº: 000000015   Carril: 262A
10/02/2006 16:11:07
Categoria : 1A

BAN**BRAS**
BANCO NACIONAL DE OBRAS Y SERVICIOS PÚBLICOS, S.N.C.

Total   ## 0004.31 Pesos
Modo pago   : Efectivo M.N.

BAN**BRAS**
BANCO NACIONAL DE OBRAS Y SERVICIOS PÚBLICOS, S.N.C.

0028.69 Pesos

0033.00 Pesos

Downtown Oaxaca

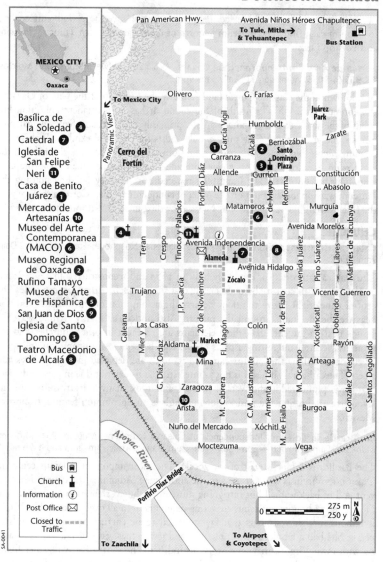

Basílica de
  la Soledad **4**
Catedral **7**
Iglesia de
  San Felipe
  Neri **11**
Casa de Benito
  Juárez **1**
Mercado de
  Artesanías **10**
Museo del Arte
  Contemporanea
  (MACO) **6**
Museo Regional
  de Oaxaca **2**
Rufino Tamayo
  Museo de Arte
  Pre Hispánica **5**
San Juan de Dios **9**
Iglesia de Santo
  Domingo **3**
Teatro Macedonio
  de Alcalá **8**

MEXICO CITY
Oaxaca

Pan American Hwy.
Avenida Niños Héroes Chapultepec
To Tule, Mitla →
& Tehuantepec
Bus Station
To Mexico City
Olivero
G. Farías
Juárez Park
García Vigil
Humboldt
Zarate
Berriozábal
Alcalá
Santo Domingo Plaza
Carranza
Porfirio Díaz
Cerro del Fortín
Panoramic View
Allende
Gurrion
Constitución
N. Bravo
5 de Mayo
Reforma
L. Abasolo
Matamoros
Murguía
Tinoco y Palacios
Crespo
Teran
Avenida Morelos
Avenida Independencia
Alameda
Avenida Hidalgo
Zócalo
Avenida Juárez
Pino Suárez
Libres
Mártires de Tacubaya
Trujano
J.P. García
20 de Noviembre
Colón
M. de Fiallo
Vicente Guerrero
Xicoténcatl
Doblando
Galeana
Mier y
Las Casas
Fl. Magón
M. de Fiallo
Rayón
Arteaga
González Ortega
Santos Degollado
Aldama
Market
Mina
G. Díaz Ordaz
Zaragoza
Arista
M. Cabrera
C.M. Bustamante
Armenta y Lópes
M. Ocampo
Burgoa
Nuño del Mercado
Xóchitl
M. de Fiallo
Vega
Moctezuma
Atoyac River
Porfirio Díaz Bridge
To Zaachila ↓
To Airport & Coyotepec ↘

Bus
Church
Information
Post Office
Closed to Traffic

0   275 m
     250 y
N

SA-0041

⊕ Rufino Tamayo Museo de Arte Pre-Hispánico. Av. Morelos 503. ☎ **951/6-4750.** Admission $2. Wed–Mon 10am–7pm. Closed Tues and holidays. Open all day (no midday break) Dec 17–30.

The artifacts displayed in this museum were chosen "solely for the aesthetic rank of the works, their beauty, power, and originality." The result is one of the most important collections of pre-Hispanic art in Mexico. The collection was amassed over a 20-year period by the famed Mexican artist Rufino Tamayo, born in Oaxaca. The artifacts range from the Preclassic period up to the Aztecs, from far northwest Nayarit to southeastern Chiapas: terra-cotta figurines, scenes of daily life, lots of female fertility figures, Olmec and Totonac sculpture from the Gulf Coast, and Zapotec long-nosed god figures. The works are beautifully displayed to give you an appreciation for the variety of styles in pre-Columbian Mexico. Plaques in Spanish give the period, culture, and location of each find. The museum is north of the zócalo between Tinoco y Palacios and Porfirio Díaz.

Museo de Arte Contemporáneo de Oaxaca. Alcalá 202, between Murgía and Morelos. ☎ **951/4-1055.** Admission $1. Daily 9am–9pm.

Also known as the Casa de Cortés (and formerly the Museum of the City of Oaxaca), this museum is 2½ blocks north of the zócalo. It has no permanent collection but exhibits the work of contemporary artists, primarily from Oaxaca State (which produces some great artists). The museum also hosts international exhibits. If there's an opening night, join the crowd; concerts and other cultural events are also held on the main patio. A second patio has a cafe and cinema club. A fine, small bookstore is to your right as you enter. The beautifully restored 16th-century building housing the museum was supposedly built on the order of conqueror Hernán Cortés after receiving the title of Marqués of the Valley of Oaxaca (he died in Spain without ever seeing it).

CHURCHES

Catedral de Oaxaca. Fronting the Parque Alameda. No phone. Free admission. Daily 7am–9pm.

The Oaxaca cathedral was originally built in 1553 and reconstructed in 1773. It has an elaborate 18th-century baroque facade that shows much of the Oaxacan style. The central panel right above the door depicts the assumption of the Virgin. Note the heavy, elaborate frame around the picture. Also notice the highly stylized wavelike clouds next to the cherubs—these elements are repeated in other churches and are some of the most interesting aspects of Oaxacan baroque. An uncommon and quite lovely detail is how the Virgin's cape and its folds are depicted in angular lines and facets. The cathedral's interior is not as interesting as its exterior due in part to the fact that it was plundered in the Wars of Reform, and it lost many of its treasures. Still, its layout is curious, and the position of the choir is an uncommon feature in most of Mexico.

Basílica de la Soledad. Independencia at Galeana. No phone. Museum 25¢. Museum, Mon–Sat 10am–2pm and 4–6pm; Sun 11am–2pm. Basílica, daily 7am–2pm and 4–9pm.

The Basílica is 7 blocks west of the zócalo. The most important religious center in Oaxaca, its Virgin is the patroness of the entire state. Adjoining the church is a convent and in back a small but intriguing museum. A huge celebration on and around December 18 honors this saint, attracting penitents from all over Oaxaca. The Virgin is famous for her vestments that are supposed to be encrusted with thousands of pearls. She had a fabulous crown of silver and jewels that was stolen a few years ago. As with most Virgins, there is a story behind her. The short of it is that her figure (actually just her hands and face) were found in a box that was transported by a burro of unknown origin. For more details ask any local person—everyone in Oaxaca knows the story. The church was built on the spot where the Virgin revealed herself and where the burro sat and refused to rise. This was next to an outcropping of rock—now behind iron bars to protect it—that you can still see immediately to your right along the wall as you enter the church.

The concave facade of the church projecting forward from the building and towers is unique in Mexico's religious architecture. It resembles something of the retablos that you find behind the altar. The interior is most impressive, too, but I really liked the museum, which is a curious blend of pieces—some museum-quality and others trinkets of little value that might have come from my grandmother's attic. Everything is displayed in seemingly random order. The Basílica's upper plaza is an outdoor patio/theater (Plaza de la Danza), with stone and concrete step/seats; here spectators view the famous Bani Stui Gulal (see "Fiesta Guelaguetza" under "Festivals," above).

When visiting the Basílica, it is traditional to eat ice cream; there are several vendors in the smaller and lower plaza in front of the church. Next to these are vendors of religious objects and icons, should you want to pick up a memento.

☉ **Iglesia de Santo Domingo.** Corner of Gurrión and Alcalá. No phone. Free admission. Daily 7am–2pm and 4–11pm.

There are 27 churches in Oaxaca, but none equals this in interior splendor. The interior makes up for the rather uninspired facade that offers little to appreciate, aside from the proverb about judging books by their covers. The church was started in the 1550s by Dominican friars and finished a century later; it contains the work of all the best artists of that period. The walls and ceiling are covered with ornate plaster statues and flowers, and are extravagantly gilded. The sun shines through the yellow stained-glass window, casting a golden glow over the whole interior. There is a large gilded rosary chapel to the right as you enter. If you are there around 11am Monday through Saturday, you are likely to hear the lovely sound of the gift-shop operator singing her devotions in the Rosario chapel. It is worth timing your visit for this.

Iglesia de San Felipe Neri. Tinoco y Palacios at Independencia. No phone. Free admission. Daily 8am–11pm.

This church, 2½ blocks northeast of the zócalo, was built in 1636 and displays all the architectural opulence of that period: The altar and nave are covered with ornately carved and gilded wood, and the walls are frescoed—ornate but not overpowering. In the west transept/chapel is a small figure of St. Martha and the dragon; the faithful have bedecked her with ribbons, praying that she assist them in vanquishing their woes (often a spouse).

San Juan de Dios. 20 de Noviembre s/n, corner of Aldama and Arteaga. No phone. Free admission. Daily 6am–11pm.

This is the earliest church in Oaxaca, built in 1521 or 1522 of adobe and thatch. The present structure was begun during the mid-1600s, and included a convent and hospital (where the 20 de Noviembre Market is now). Although the exterior is nothing special, the interior has an ornate altar and Urbano Olivera paintings on the ceiling. A glass shrine to the Virgin near the entrance and one dedicated to Christ (off to the right) are especially revered by Oaxaqueños. Because it's by the market, 1 block west and 2 blocks south of the zócalo, many of the people who visit the church are villagers who've come in to buy and sell. There's an interesting guitar mass on Sunday at 1pm.

MORE ATTRACTIONS

Teatro Macedonio de Alcalá. Independencia at Armenta y López. No phone. Open only for events.

This beautiful 1903 belle époque theater, 2 blocks east of the zócalo, holds 1,300 people and is still used for concerts and performances in the evening. Peek through the doors to see the marble stairway and Louis XV vestibule. A list of events is sometimes posted on the doors.

Cerro del Fortín. Díaz Ordaz at Calle Delmonte. No phone.

To take all this sightseeing in at a glance, those with cars can drive to this hill at the west of town for a panoramic view of the city, especially good just before sunset. Recognize the hill by the statue of Benito Juárez and a stadium built to hold 15,000 spectators. The annual Fiesta Guelaguetza is held here. You can also walk to the hill. Head up Díaz Ordaz/Crespo and look for the Escaleras del Fortín (Stairway to the Fortress) shortly after you cross calle Delmonte; the 180-plus steps (interrupted by risers) are a challenge, but the view is worth it.

SPANISH & ART CLASSES

The **Instituto Cultural Oaxaca A.C.,** avenida Juárez 909 (Apdo. Postal 340), 68000 Oaxaca, Oaxaca (☎ **951/5-3404;** fax 951/5-3728; E-mail: inscuoax@antequera. com), offers Spanish classes for foreigners, classes on Mexican music and Latin dance, and workshops with Mexican artisans: weavers, potters, and cooks. There are also lectures emphasizing Oaxaca's history, archaeology, anthropology, and botany. Although the normal course length is 4 weeks, arrangements can be made for as short a period as a week, and the institute will arrange inexpensive housing with local families. The institute itself is housed in a lovely old hacienda next to the Pan American Highway. Even a short time at the institute will give you a better understanding of both the language and Oaxaca.

The **Instituto de Comunicación y Cultura,** Alcalá 307-12, 68000 Oaxaca, Oaxaca (☎/fax **951/6-3443;** E-mail: info@iccoax.com), has provided group or private Spanish instruction to many satisfied students. They can also arrange for homestays with Mexican families.

SHOPPING

Oaxaca and the surrounding villages are wonderful hunting grounds for handcrafted pottery, wood carvings, and weavings. And the hunt itself may be the best part. Specialties include the shiny **black pottery** for which Oaxaca is famous, **woolen textiles** with the deep reds and purples produced using the natural dye *cochineal,* and highly imaginative **wood carvings.**

For market days in outlying villages and directions to the crafts villages of importance, see "Road Trips from Oaxaca," below.

ARTS & CRAFTS

The area around **Plaza Santo Domingo** and the streets of **Alcalá and Cinco de Mayo** are fertile grounds for shopping. Some of the shops listed below are in this area. There is also the **20 de Noviembre market,** south of the zócalo.

Artesanías e Industrias Populares del Estado de Oaxaca (ARIPO). García Vigil 809. ☎ **951/4-4030.** E-mail: aripod@oaxaca.gob.mx.

ARIPO is a government store with a broader range of goods than most stores. English is spoken. It is located 2 blocks farther up the hill beyond the Benito Juárez house. You can hear looms working in the back as you browse through the handcrafts expertly displayed in the many rooms. There's a good supply of masks, baskets, clothing, furniture, and cutlery. They will ship anywhere. Open Monday through Saturday from 9am to 7pm, at the corner of Vigil and Cosijopi.

Arte y Tradición. García Vigil 406. ☎ **951/6-3552.**

Four blocks north of the zócalo, a brightly painted doorway leads into this attractive arcade of shops with an open patio in the center. Each shop functions as a cooperative, with articles on consignment from the various villages, such as Teotitlán del Valle and Arrazola. Individuals from these villages are on hand to explain the crafts (weaving, wood carving, and the like) as practiced by their townspeople. You'll also find an excellent restaurant serving authentic Oaxacan cuisine, the Belaguetza Travel Agency, and a small bookstore. The English-speaking manager, Judith Reyes, is a real dynamo and has tremendous pride in her Mixtec heritage. The store is open daily from 9am to 8pm, although the individual shop hours may vary.

Holiday Inn - Express

O Kot lam

Artist - Rudolpho Morales

Francisco Toledo

Pottery - La vasida → Tierra Que madra

Turist walk way
| Plaza las vergina

Pendant le temps de l'Égypte ancienne, ils ne jouaient pas les instruments tout le temps comme maintenant. Il avait certain moment où l'on utilise certains instruments. Dans une scène de militaire (sur un

Casa Víctor. Porfirio Díaz 111. ☎ **951/6-1174.**

This art shop in a 17th-century monastery is managed by Sr. Ramón Fosado, who goes to the villages himself in search of the best native art. He speaks English and is very pleasant. If you're shopping for serapes and blankets, be sure to stop at Casa Víctor to do a little research. The quality of these goods varies, but the friendly staff here is willing to tell you about the differences in materials (wool versus synthetic), dyes (natural and chemical), and designs. You should also scout around and compare the various products in the open markets. Open Monday through Saturday from 9am to 2pm and 4 to 8pm.

FONART. Crespo 114. ☎ **951/6-5764.**

Oaxaca's branch of this government-supported chain, featuring a wide selection of native crafts from all over Mexico, is on Crespo at Morelas. The name stands for "Fondo Nacional para el Fomento de las Artesanías." Prices are fixed, and the store is open Monday through Saturday from 9am to 2pm and 4 to 7pm. It's open Sundays during Christmastime.

Galería Arte de Oaxaca. Murgía 105. ☎/fax **951/4-0910** or 951/4-1532.

Owner Nancy Mayagoitia represents some of the state's leading contemporary artists. It's open Monday through Friday from 11am to 3pm and 5 to 9pm, and Saturday from 11am to 3pm. You'll find it 2 blocks north and 1 block east of the zócalo.

Galería Quetzalli. Constitución 104. ☎ **951/4-2606.**

A modest-looking art gallery behind the Church of Santo Domingo and next to Los Pacos restaurant, Galería Quetzalli represents some of the big names in Mexican art—Francisco Toledo, José Villalobos—and some up-and-coming artists. Hours are Monday through Saturday from 10am to 2pm and 5 to 8pm.

✪ **La Mano Mágica.** Alcalá 203. ☎ **951/6-4275.**

This gallery of contemporary and popular art is across from the city museum. The name means "magic hand," and it's a true celebration of Oaxacan artistic creativity. Fine exhibits of paintings by local artists occupy the front room. The back rooms are full of regional folk art by the area's best artisans—folks who carry on inherited artistic traditions in their village homes. Pieces are personally selected by owners Mary Jane and Arnulfo Mendoza (don't miss his weavings). They can help you ship what you buy here anywhere in the world via DHL courier service. Located between Morelos and Matamoros opposite the Museum of Contemporary Art/MACO (House of Cortés), it's open Monday through Saturday from 10am to 2:30pm and 3:30 to 7pm.

Mercado de Artesanías. J. P. García at Zaragoza.

If the crafts section of the Benito Juárez and 20 de Noviembre markets (mentioned under "City Markets" below) leaves you wanting, this is a good place to get an overview of Oaxaca's folk arts, particularly textiles. Women and men weave rugs, belts, huipils, serapes, and bags on looms and display their finest work. Ask the artisans where they're from, and you'll get an idea of which villages you'd like to visit. Located 1 block south and 1 block west of the 20 de Noviembre Market and 4 blocks south and 2 blocks west of the zócalo, it's open daily from 10am to 4pm.

CHOCOLATE & MOLE

Frothy hot chocolate is a traditional drink in Mexico, and especially in Oaxaca. Most of the chocolate here is made from cacao beans grown in nearby Tabasco. The chocolate is mixed with almonds and cinnamon. You can see it sold in the market in the form of hard cakes or tablets. The drink is prepared with either water or milk (water is more traditional and is quite good), and it is considered essential to have a thick head of foam.

Mole (*moh*-lay), of which there are several varieties, is another Oaxacan tradition. Most moles are used as sauces poured over chicken or turkey or used to flavor foods such as tamales. The black mole is what Oaxaca is most famous for, and one of its many ingredients is chocolate. You can find black and red mole in the market. Establishments that sell fresh chocolate often also grind and mix the ingredients for mole and sell it as a paste. These kinds of mole keep very well.

Chocolate Mayordomo. 20 de Noviembre at Mina. ☎ **951/6-1619** or 951/6-0246.

This corner store by the market is actually a large operation with another outlet across the street on Mina and several others throughout the city. All sell several varieties of chocolate (all of these are for either cooking or making hot chocolate, not for eating) and mole as well. Here you'll find shelves of boxed chocolate—traditional with almonds and cinnamon for mixing with water, a slightly sweeter version for milk, one with vanilla for American and European tastes, and pure unsweetened for cooking. Most of these are sold in the traditional form and in a more convenient tablet form. A half-kilo of chocolate costs around $1.50; gift boxes of plastic-wrapped fresh black or red mole are also found here for $2.50 per kilo. They make excellent gifts for friends back home. Ask general manager Salvador Flores about chocolate—you'll learn a lot! The store is open daily from 8am to 8:30pm.

CITY MARKETS

Mercado Abastos. Across the railroad tracks and just south of the second-class bus station.

The Abastos Market is open daily but most active on Saturday, when Indians from the villages come to town to sell and shop. You'll see huge mounds of dried chiles, herbs, vegetables, crafts, bread, and even burros for sale at this bustling market.

✪ **Benito Juárez Market.** Bordered by Las Casas, Cabrera, Aldama, and 20 de Noviembre.

One block south of the zócalo, this covered market is big and busy every day, especially so on Saturday, when the area around it becomes an open street market, teeming with vendors of chiles, parrots, talismans, food, spices, cloth, dresses, blankets, and more. And in Mexico there is always a festive attitude about market day. The bulk of the produce trade has been relocated to a new building called the Abastos Market (see above).

20 de Noviembre Market. Bordered by Aldama, Cabrera, Mina, and 20 de Noviembre.

This market occupies an entire block (except for Juan de Dios church) just across Aldama from the Benito Juárez market. This was once the site of the church's hospital and convent. Food, arts and crafts, and cooking stalls predominate.

WHERE TO STAY

If you're going to Oaxaca during any of the high tourist periods—Easter, July, November, and December—make reservations. You probably will not have any difficulties during the rest of the year, but the unknown factor in this equation is the large tour operators.

EXPENSIVE

✪ **Hotel Camino Real.** Cinco de Mayo 300, 68000 Oaxaca, Oax. ☎ **800/722-6466** in the U.S., or 951/6-0611. Fax 951/6-0732. 91 units. FAN TV TEL. $175 double standard rooms; $200 superior rooms; $245 Club rooms. Children under 12 stay free in parents' room. AE, MC, V.

A magnificent hotel in a 16th-century, landmark convent, this is the place to cloister yourself when in Oaxaca. The original Santa Catalina convent was very large, which allowed for a spacious hotel. The Camino Real chain of hotels has made a specialty out of renovating and managing these sorts of properties, and it does a great job here. The hotel has the perfect mix of new and old. Several beautiful courtyards with age-old walls bring to mind the original purpose of the building. The rooms, however, do not; there is in fact nothing in them to evoke thoughts of a nun's quarters. All are large, well furnished and with all the conveniences you would expect in a hotel of this caliber (no small feat given the constraints imposed by the 16th-century infrastructure). Exterior rooms come with double-paned windows to keep out noise. The location is great: between the zócalo and the Plaza de Santo Domingo.

Dining/Diversions: Dining can be inside or outside in a courtyard. There are two bars. On Sunday there's a lavish brunch. The breakfast buffet changes daily but always includes Oaxacan specialties. On Friday evenings the hotel hosts a Guelaguetza, a great regional dance show and dinner buffet.

Amenities: Laundry and room service, travel agency, swimming pool.

MODERATE

Casa Colonial Bed and Breakfast. División Oriente, corner Negrete (Apdo. Postal 640), 68000 Oaxaca, Oax. ☎ **800/758-1697** in the U.S., or 951/6-5280. Fax 951/6-7232. 12 units. $86 double. Rates include breakfast. No credit cards. Free parking.

The casual and comfortable setting of this B&B and the attention of its gracious hosts promptly set you at ease here. All the rooms open up to large garden with tall Jacaranda trees. The way they are furnished and decorated bring to mind a charming, earlier time. You'll feel very much at home here. Owners Jane and Thornton Robison are very knowledgeable about Oaxaca and lead specialty tours to surrounding villages. There is a *sala*, or living room, full of books about Mexico, and the dining room has both a large family-style table and smaller individual tables. Breakfast is substantial: It includes fresh fruit, yogurt, hot cereal, eggs any style, bacon, juice, and coffee. To reach the hotel from the zócalo, walk 1 block north on García Vigil, then turn left on Independencia for 6 blocks. Just pass La Soledad church, angle right for a couple of blocks; the Casa will be on your left. There is no sign; just look for a green house with purple trim.

✪ **Hostal de la Noria.** Av. Hidalgo 918, 68000 Oaxaca, Oax. ☎ **800/528-1234** in the U.S., or 951/4-7844. Fax 951/6-3992. 43 units. TV TEL. High season $95 double. Low season $75 double. AE, DC, MC, V.

Behind this gracious colonial-era facade is one the city's newest hotels, complete with a handsome courtyard restaurant, elegant bar, and three stories (no elevator) of large rooms. Pastel-yellow walls with lavender accent trim around the wooden doors lead to rooms overlooking both the interior courtyard or exterior streets. Rooms are large, with high ceilings, carpeting, handsome wardrobes for clothing, and remote-control TV. Some bathrooms have a tub/shower combination. The hotel, which is affiliated with Best Western, is 2 blocks east of the zócalo at the corner of Fiallo/Reforma.

Hotel Victoria. Lomas del Fortín 1, 68070 Oaxaca, Oax. ☎ **800/448-8355** in the U.S., or 951/5-2633. Fax 951/5-2411. 151 units. TV TEL. $85 double standard; $110 villa; $135 suite. AE, MC, V. Free parking.

Spread out over immaculate grounds on a hillside above the city, Hotel Victoria offers the best view in town. You can enjoy this view from a room or suite in one of the main buildings, or you can stay in one of the secluded villas with its own terrace. There is an indoor/outdoor dining area next to a large swimming pool that also offers a view. Rooms are large, carpeted, and furnished in a modern style. This hotel is not for people who mind climbing stairs.

✪ **Marqués del Valle.** Portal de Claveria s/n, 68000 Oaxaca, Oax. ☎ **951/6-3677** or 951/6-6294. Fax 951/6-9961. 95 units. TV TEL. $55 double. AE, DC, MC, V.

Right on the zócalo, this five-story hotel is for people who want to be in the middle of things. About half the rooms have been remodeled/refurnished, making all the difference. The plaza is usually not very noisy except for Sunday-afternoon band concerts. An interior room would solve this problem. Rooms with French doors facing the plaza have a grand view. *A tip:* Walk-in customers get lower hotel rates than those who reserve ahead.

INEXPENSIVE

Calesa Real. García Vigil 306, 68000 Oaxaca, Oax. ☎ **951/6-5544.** Fax 951/6-7232. 77 units. FAN TV TEL. $50 double. AE, MC, V. Free secured parking.

The Calesa Real is in a colonial-style building 3½ blocks north of the zócalo. It does a lot of business with large tour groups. The spacious rooms have comfortable, plain furnishings. One of the nicest features here is a small pool in a cool courtyard. Eight of the rooms on the first floor have French doors opening to the pool area; others on the second and third floors have small balconies. A second-story terrace and restaurant overlook the pool. The hotel is between Bravo and Matamoros.

Hotel Antonio's. Independencia 601, 68000 Oaxaca, Oax. ☎ **951/6-7227.** Fax 951/6-3672. 15 units. TV. $25 double. No credit cards.

Opened in 1991, this comfortable and conveniently located hotel was converted from an old two-story town house, with a lovely interior patio surrounded by an arcaded walkway. A small, colorful, and cozy restaurant occupies the patio. Rooms are cramped. Each has a tile floor, colonial-style pine furniture, some with two double beds, and a small tile bathroom. Wall hooks solve the storage problem in rooms without closets. It's located 1½ blocks west of the cathedral, at the corner of Porfirio Díaz and Independencia.

✪ **Hotel Casa Arnel.** Aldama 404, Col. Jalatlaco, 68080 Oaxaca, Oax. ☎ **951/5-2856.** Fax 951/3-6285. E-mail: casa.arnel@spersaoaxaca.com.mx. 40 units, 22 with bathroom. $14 double without bathroom; $19 with bathroom; apartment $350–$400 monthly. No credit cards. Parking ($2.25 daily).

Not far from the bus station, this favorite budget hotel is slightly removed from the city center but still within walking distance of most sights. It's a great hotel for those traveling with kids. The Cruz family lives here, with a kid of their own, and there is a shady tropical garden where the pet parrots and Pascual, the duck and hotel mascot, are always around. There is also a roof-top terrace for those wishing to admire the view and soak up some sun. The rooms are plain but clean and comfortable; some share a bathroom among four rooms. Across the street in the new wing are three additional rooms with double beds and private bathrooms, plus four furnished, full-service apartments with fully equipped kitchens. Breakfast and dinner, at extra cost (around $3), are served on the family patio. At other times the patio is a mingling place for guests, who come from all over the world.

At Christmas the family involves guests in the traditional Mexican Christmas celebrations known as *posadas* (akin to "caroling" in the U.S.), which are held during the 12 nights before Christmas. There is also an elaborate room-size nativity scene, and a festive Christmas Eve dinner—all at no charge to Arnel guests. It's something special;

many guests return every Christmas. The hotel also acts as a travel agent and can make tour, bus, and airline arrangements. To get to the hotel, turn right out the front door of the first-class bus station, go 2 blocks, and turn right onto Aldama. Casa Arnel is 7 blocks ahead on your left across from the Iglesia San Matias Jalatlaco.

Hotel Gala. Bustamante 103, 68000 Oaxaca, Oax. ☎ **951/4-2251.** Fax 951/6-3660. 36 units. FAN TV TEL. $44 double. AE, MC, V.

The Gala, a favorite of Mexican tourists, is a good value for the money. There are three stories of rooms with no elevator. The rooms are carpeted and have coordinated furnishings and firm mattresses. Some rooms have windows overlooking Bustamante, and others have windows on the hall. Though some rooms have minuscule bathrooms, and in most cases there's not a lot of room for luggage, it's otherwise a very comfortable and excellently located hotel. The hotel restaurant is to the right of the front door. The Gala is half a block south of the zócalo near the corner of Bustamante and Guerrero.

Hotel Principal. Cinco de Mayo 208, 68000 Oaxaca, Oax. ☎/fax **951/6-2535.** 16 units. $30 double. No credit cards.

The Principal, 1 block east and 2½ blocks north of the zócalo, is a longtime favorite of budget travelers, and for good reason. The location—near shops, museums, and restaurants—is great; rooms are clean and filled with sunlight. Six upstairs rooms have balconies. Make reservations in advance, since the hotel is often full.

✪ **Las Golondrinas.** Tinoco y Palacios 411, 68000 Oaxaca, Oax. ☎ **951/4-3298.** Fax 951/4-2126. 25 units. $30 double. No credit cards.

This charming one-story hotel is situated amid rambling patios with roses, fuchsia, bougainvillea, and mature banana trees. Owned and personally managed by Guillermina and Jorge Velasco, Las Golondrinas ("The Swallows") is a very popular hotel. The 24 simply furnished rooms, with windows and doors opening onto courtyards, all have tile floors and a small desk and chairs. The suite, with one bed, has unpainted pine furniture, a sunny shuttered window, and a largish bathroom. Breakfast (nonguests welcome) is served between 8 and 10am in a small tile-covered cafe in a garden setting (for an additional charge of $3.25). The hotel is 6½ blocks north of the zócalo between Allende and Bravo.

WHERE TO DINE

Oaxacan cooking has a great reputation in Mexico. It is a highland style of cooking, but it includes more ingredients from the lowlands than central Mexican cooking. Moles are what the state is best known for, but these should not be confused with the kinds of mole and pipian of central Mexico. Street foods include *tasajo*, a thin cut of beef; *cecina*, a thin cut of pork; Oaxacan tamales; and *tlayudas*—12-inch" tortillas, slightly dried, on which you put a number of toppings. To see a magnificent array of local foods, walk through the Abastos Market on Saturday; the quantity and variety are remarkable. You will hear women shouting "tlayuda, tlayuda," so you can taste one yourself. Oaxaca is also known for pozole Mixteco, a different version of the hearty soup, which includes chicken and red mole sauce.

For a snack or light breakfast, pick up your fill of pastries, cookies, sweet rolls, and breads from the large **Panificadora Bamby,** at the corner of Morelos and García Vigil, 2 blocks north of the zócalo. It's open daily from 7am to 9pm.

MODERATE

✪ **El Naranjo.** Trujano 203. ☎ **951/4-1878.** Main courses $4–$8. AE, MC, V. Daily 1–10pm. OAXACAN/MEXICAN.

El Naranjo is my favorite restaurant in the city. The emphasis here is on Oaxacan specialties. The owner and cook Iliana de la Vega prepares dishes that she grew up cooking and eating. She has added some others and made alterations, such as reducing the fat, to bring out more of the flavors of the vegetables, herbs, and chiles. Also, she is meticulous in the preparation of her dishes. If you have a craving for a fresh salad but have been reluctant to dig into one, this is your chance—all the salad greens are dipped in antimicrobial solution. I recommend the Caesar salad. For a main dish you can try the featured mole of the day. For an especially exotic flavor try the fish cooked in the leaves of hoja santa with a spicy *guajillo* sauce or the strong taste of an ancho chile stuffed with goat cheese. A milder flavor would be the poblano chile stuffed with squash blossoms. The restaurant occupies the roofed courtyard of a colonial house half a block from the southwest corner of the zócalo.

La Casa de la Abuela. Av. Hidalgo 616 alto. ☎ **951/6-3544.** Main courses $5–$9. MC, V. Daily 1–9:30pm. MEXICAN/REGIONAL.

This upstairs restaurant overlooks both the zócalo and the Alameda. It is a peaceful, bright, and lovely place to dine. "Grandmother's house," as the name translates, serves many regional dishes such as huge tlayuda tortillas, empanadas with many local sauces, black-bean soup, tamales, mole coloradito, *caldo de gato* ("cat's stew") made with beef and pork, and much more. The entrance is a few steps west of the zócalo.

Restaurant del Vitral. Guerrero 201. ☎ **951/6-3124.** Main courses $5.50–$11.50. AE, DISC, MC, V. Daily 1–11pm. MEXICAN/INTERNATIONAL/REGIONAL.

Dinner here seems vaguely Victorian. The restaurant is in the second floor of a mansion of the Porfiriate era, when opulence and decoration were the hallmarks of fashion and architects were giving a Mexican expression to Victorian design. The restaurant follows suit in its colors and table settings. The interesting menu features cold cucumber-and-avocado soup or a tomato soup with cheese, chile pasilla and epazote, an assortment of U.S. cuts of beef, chicken Kiev, duck with honey and cognac, chateaubriand for two, and regional specialties such as mole coloradito. The restaurant is only a block east of the zócalo, at the corner of Armenta y López.

INEXPENSIVE

✪ **Doña Elpidia.** Miguel Cabrera 413. ☎ **951/6-4292.** Fixed-price lunch $4.50. No credit cards. Daily 1–5pm. REGIONAL.

The phrase "home-style cooking" is bandied about a lot, but in this case it really means something. Doña Elpidia is virtually an institution in Oaxaca. For the traveler it means having a meal just like what would be served as the main dinner in a well-run Mexican home. Finding this place is not hard; it's 5½ blocks south of the zócalo, between Arista and Nuño del Mercado. Look for a small sign saying only RESTAURANT." A chalk board with the day's meal will be in front of you as you enter. You will find some tables behind the overgrown garden. There is also indoor dining. The comida corrida includes a basket of bread, an appetizer, vegetable or pasta soup, rice, a meat or enchilada course, and a dessert. Beer and other beverages are sold.

Gecko Coffee Shop. Cinco de Mayo 412. ☎ **951/4-8024.** Sandwiches $2; desserts $1–$1.50; coffee 75¢; chocolate $1.25. No credit cards. Mon–Sat 9:30am–8pm. PASTRIES/SANDWICHES/CHOCOLATE/COFFEE.

Less than half a block south of the Santo Domingo Church is this little, habit-forming gem. A variety of delicious sandwiches and pastries is served along with hot chocolate and coffee either in a small dining room or in the more ample patio. Here you have peace and quiet to sip, snack, and read or write the postcards you've been toting around. And when you finally tear yourself away, a gallery, small bookstore, and the wonderful Instituto Welte (of Oaxacan studies) are just off the patio.

Restaurant El Mesón. Av. Hidalgo 805 at Valdivieso. ☎ **951/6-2729.** Breakfast and lunch buffet $3.50; comida corrida $2; Mexican specialties $1.50–$6. No credit cards. Daily 8am–1am (breakfast buffet 8am–noon, lunch buffet noon–6pm, and comida corrida noon–4:30pm). MEXICAN/REGIONAL.

At the entrance of El Mesón, you see women patting out fresh tortillas. I imagine that this is their hook. During the day this is mostly a comida corrida place for working folk. At night it's a good taquería. The menu and prices are printed on a sheet the waitress gives you; just check off what you want and present it to the waitress. The food is good and reasonably priced. What's more, the all-you-can-eat buffets include fresh fruit, and at lunch fresh salads are added, plus a variety of main courses. The comida corrida is a shortened version of the lunch buffet. Taco prices are per order (usually two tacos). Besides the large range of tacos, they serve some *especialidades* such as tamal Oaxaqueño (for which Oaxaca is known), pozole, and *puntas de filete albañil* ("bricklayer" beef tips). It's right next to the zócalo.

Restaurant Las Quince Letras. Abasolo 300. ☎ **951/4-3769.** Breakfast $2–$4; main courses $4–$5.75; comida corrida $4. No credit cards. Daily 8am–9pm. MEXICAN/REGIONAL.

Look for a bright-blue entryway with the restaurant's name painted vertically in white. Though it has only one small dining room, and it's a bit off the well-worn path, the restaurant has a loyal following of foreigners who appreciate value and good food. Parties larger than one get complimentary *memelitas* while they decide what to order. Memelitas are akin to sopes: a fried masa patty topped with meat, cream or salsa, and shredded cheese. The sopa azteca is a delicious, hearty dish. The tasajo, prepared several ways, is cooked in a wonderful marinade. If you order the filling botana oaxaqueña, the dozen different enticements leave barely enough room for a light dessert. The restaurant is 7½ blocks northeast of the zócalo, just past the corner of Juárez.

OAXACA AFTER DARK

If you are interested in seeing something of the region's traditional dance, you can check out the small-scale **Guelaguetza,** performed at the Hotel Camino Real on Friday from 7 to 10pm by a group of highly professional dancers. The cost of $30 per person includes a buffet and elaborate show. The Hotel Monte Albán presents more reasonably priced folk dances daily from 8:30 to 10pm, costing $5 for the show alone. Dinner and drinks are extra. Buy your ticket the day before; when you enter, you'll find your name card placed at your reserved seat.

Concerts and dance programs are offered all year long at the **Teatro Macedonio de Alcalá,** at Independencia and Armenta y López. Schedules are often posted by the front doors of the theater. In the early evening hours, the **zócalo** is a happening place, with all sorts of people out and about. The municipal brass band and the marimba players perform free concerts on alternating nights.

Most music and socializing taper off at 9pm. If you are still in the mood for music and perhaps want to go dancing, here are some options.

MUSIC & DANCE CLUBS

Bar Sagrario. Valdivieso 120. ☎ **951/4-0303.** $6 minimum consumption on weekends. Music nightly 9pm–2am.

This place gets a variety of bands, usually two per night that alternate sets. The owner likes to have acoustic guitar duos playing *trova contemporanea,* which resembles a cross between Gypsy Kings and José Feliciano. The duo I saw was very talented in both their playing and singing. Then there was a trio comprising keyboards, bass, and singer that played some well-known *grupera* cover tunes, easy and fun to dance to. The establishment is a tall and narrow three-story affair built around a small dance floor. The first story is a bar, the second a pizzeria, the third a restaurant.

Disco Tequila Rock. Porfirio Díaz 102. ☎ **951/5-1500.** Thurs $1.25 cover; free Fri; Sat $4. No credit cards. Thurs–Sat 10pm–3am.

The most popular disco in town, Tequila Rock caters to a crowd in their twenties and thirties. The decor is modern and the music shifts between Mexican pop, European dance music, and American disco. It is next to the Hotel Posada de los Ángeles.

El Sol y La Luna. Reforma 502. ☎ **951/4-8069.** $2.50–$4 cover. MC, V. Mon–Sat 9:30pm–1am.

This is a lovely little place with a small patio and three adjoining rooms. The club, in business for 20 years, starts serving food around 7pm. The food is good— mostly pizzas, crepes, and steaks (the pizzas are quite good). The music can be just about anything. I saw a wonderful jazz quintet that did a number of Charlie Parker's blues and be-bop tunes with excellent arrangements. Two nights earlier it was an Argentine group that played tangos. The week before it was a Jarocho band from Veracruz.

La Candela. Allende no. 211 ☎ **951/4-1254.** $2.50 cover on weekdays; $3 on weekends. No credit cards. Music nightly 10:30pm–2am.

This salsa-and-latino music club is simply laid out—a no-frills kind of place. Not terribly big, it does have a large, smooth dance floor. People come here to dance. It's very casual and friendly. The eight-piece house band plays salsa, merengue, and even cha-cha-cha with a lot of gusto. Occasionally there's a jazz band. It's a block from the Plaza Santo Domingo.

La Cumbancha. Netzahualcoyotl 218. ☎ **951/5-6573.** $4 cover Fri–Sat; free Thurs. No credit cards. Thurs–Sat 10pm–2am.

Cumbancha is a Cuban word that encapsulates the philosophical position laid out in the old song verse "Enjoy yourself, it's later than you think." This place is roomy, with a high ceiling and a large dance floor, and when I was here, it had a very tight nine-piece band. This place is about 4 blocks from the ADO bus station, and 2 blocks north of Calzada Niños Héroes.

Restaurant El Marqués. Portal de Claverías. ☎ **951/4-4803.** $4.50 minimum consumption. MC, V. Music nightly 9:30pm–1am.

This place is right on the zócalo, and you can get a pretty good idea of the music from outside. The four-piece house band plays very well: their repertoire contains some Colombian music not generally performed by this style of band. The minimum can be met with food or drink purchases.

ROAD TRIPS FROM OAXACA

Monte Albán and **Mitla** are the two most important archaeological sites near Oaxaca; several smaller ruins are also interesting. There are day-trips one can make to a number of interesting villages. The tourist office will give you a map detailing the nearby villages where beautiful handcrafts are made. The visits are fun excursions by car or bus. If you want to make a longer trip to one of Oaxaca's seaside resorts, see "By Bus" under "Getting There & Departing," in this chapter and chapter 10, "Acapulco & the Southern Pacific Coast."

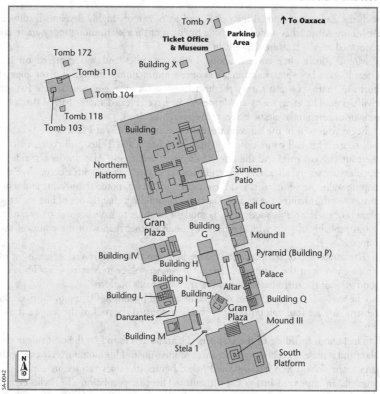

MONTE ALBÁN: RUINS WITH A VIEW

If I had been the priest-king of a large Indian nation in search of the perfect site on which to build a ceremonial center, this is the place I would have picked. It is situated on a mountain that rises from the middle of the valley floor, or rather, divides two valleys. And from here you can see a great distance to the nearest mountains.

For some 1,500 years prior to 500 B.C., village-dwelling peoples of mysterious origins inhabited the Oaxaca valleys. Between 800 and 500 B.C., a new ceramic style appeared, presumably produced by an influx of new peoples, now called Zapotec. Around 500 B.C. these peoples began the monumental exercise of leveling the top of a mountain, where they would build the magnificent city we know today as Monte Albán (*mohn*-teh ahl-*bahn*).

Very little of the original structures can be seen; they've been either obscured beneath newer constructions or recycled in other configurations, their stones reused. The Danzantes friezes (see below), however, date from this period.

An elite center of Zapotec culture, Monte Albán was also influenced by contemporary cultures outside the valley of Mexico. You can see Olmec influence in the early sculptures; more recent masks and sculptures reflect contact with the Maya. When Monte Albán was at its zenith in A.D. 300, architectural ideas were borrowed from Teotihuacán. By around A.D. 800, the significance of Monte Albán in Zapotec society began to wane. Although most likely never completely abandoned, it became a mere shell of its former grandeur. Around the beginning of the 13th century, Monte Albán was appropriated by the Mixtecs. The Mixtecs, who had long coexisted in the area with the Zapotecs, imposed their own, and by now more highly developed, culture. At Monte Albán, they added very little building of their own, though they are today renowned for the treasure they left in Tomb 7.

Monte Albán once covered about 15 square miles and was centered on the Great Plaza, a large grassy area that was once a mountaintop. From this plaza, aligned north to south, you can survey the lush Oaxacan valley, a gorgeous setting for any civilization. The excavations at Monte Albán have revealed more than 170 tombs, numerous ceremonial altars, stelae, pyramids, and palaces.

Begin your tour of the ruins on the eastern side of the **Great Plaza** at the I-shaped ball court. This ball court differs slightly from Maya and Toltec ball courts in that there are no goal rings and the sides of the court are sloped. Also on the east side of the plaza are several altars and pyramids that were once covered with stucco. Note the sloping walls, the wide stairs, and the ramps, typical of Zapotec architecture and reminiscent of the architecture of Teotihuacán. The building, slightly out of line with the plaza (not on the north-south axis), is thought by some to have been an observatory; it was probably aligned with the heavenly bodies rather than with the points of the compass.

The south side of the plaza has a large platform that bore several stelae, most of which are now in the National Museum of Anthropology in Mexico City. There's a good view of the surrounding area from the top of this platform.

The west side has more ceremonial platforms and pyramids. On top of the pyramid substructure are four columns that probably supported the roof of the temple at one time.

The famous **Building of the Dancers** (Danzantes) is found on the west side of the plaza and is the earliest known structure at Monte Albán. This building is covered with large stone slabs carved into distorted naked figures (the ones you see are copies; the originals are protected in the site museum). There is speculation as to who carved these figures and what they represent, although a distinct resemblance to the Olmec "baby faces" seen at La Venta, in Tabasco State, certainly exists. The distorted bodies and pained expressions of the faces might connote disease. Clear examples of figures representing childbirth, dwarfism, and infantilism are visible. Because of the fluid movement represented in the figures, they became known as the Danzantes, though this is merely a modern label for these ancient and mysterious carvings.

The **Northern Platform** is a maze of temples and palaces interwoven with subterranean tunnels and sanctuaries. Take time to wander here, for there are numerous reliefs, glyphs, paintings, and friezes along the lintels and jambs as well as the walls.

Leaving the Great Plaza, head north to the **cemetery** and **tombs.** Of the tombs so far excavated, the most famous is **Tomb 7,** to the east of the cemetery. Inside some 500 pieces of jewelry made of gold, amber, and turquoise, and art objects of silver, alabaster, and bone, were discovered. This amazing collection is on display at the Regional Museum of Oaxaca.

If you have a day to spend at Monte Albán, be sure to visit some of the tombs, for they contain magnificent glyphs, paintings, and stone carvings of gods, goddesses, birds, and serpents. Two especially intriguing tombs are Tombs 104 and 105, guarded but entered via ladders; the guards are usually helpful about pointing out areas of special interest. Ignore the vendors hawking "original" artifacts, supposedly found at the site—if they were real, these guys would hardly need to wander around in the midday sun trying to sell them!

As you enter the site, you'll see an on-site museum, a shop with guidebooks to the ruins, a cafe, and a craft shop. I recommend purchasing a guidebook. Admission to the ruins is $4; free on Sunday and holidays. The site is open daily from 8am to 5pm.

Shopping Splendor: Oaxaca's Market Villages

You could spend a full week in Oaxaca just visiting the various markets held in nearby villages. Each has its specialty—cheese, produce, livestock, weaving, and pottery—and unique character. Market days in the villages are as follows:

Day	Market
Wednesday	**Etla,** known for its cheese; 9½ miles north.
Thursday	**Zaachila,** ruins and agriculture; 11 miles southwest.
	Ejutla, agriculture; 40 miles south.
Friday	**Ocotlán,** pottery, textiles, and food; 18½ miles south.
Saturday	**Oaxaca,** Abastos Market.
Sunday	**Tlacolula,** agriculture and crafts (visit the chapel as well); 19½ miles southeast.

You can get to any of these craft villages by taking a bus from the second-class bus station, 8 blocks west of the zócalo on Trujano. On market days these buses are crammed with passengers. If you get off a bus between destinations—say, at Dainzú on the way to Mitla or at Cuilapan on the way to Zaachila—but want to continue to the next place, return to the highway and hail a passing bus.

It's also possible to take a colectivo taxi to the villages that don't have bus service. To find a colectivo, head to the south end of the Abastos Market. On calle Mercaderos you'll see dozens of parked maroon-and-white colectivo taxis. The town each one serves is written on the door, trunk, or windshield. There are also posted metal signs for destinations. They fill up relatively fast and are an economical way to reach the villages. Be sure to go early; by afternoon the colectivos don't fill up as fast and you'll have to wait.

Tours to all the markets as well as the craft villages and ruins can easily be arranged through **Tours Arnel,** at Hotel Casa Arnel, Aldama 404 (☎ **951/ 5-2856**), or **Belaguetza,** at Arte y Tradición, García Vigil 406 (☎ **951/6-3552**). There are, of course, many tour agencies in Oaxaca, but these both offer friendly, personal, English-speaking guide service at competitive prices. Three- to 4-hour tours to Monte Albán or Mitla will cost about $9 per person (plus site entry). Other villages can be included at minimal cost.

Many of these historical and/or craft villages have, in the past several years, developed some truly fine small municipal museums. **San José El Mogote,** site of one of the very earliest pre-Hispanic village-dweller groups, has a display of carvings and statues found in and around the town and a display model of an old hacienda and details of its produce and social organization. **Teotitlán del Valle** is another with such a municipal museum; it features displays on the weaving process. Ask at the State Tourism Office (north side of the Alameda on Independencia) for more information on these and others.

Licensed guides charge $13.50 per person for a walking tour. Video-camera permits cost $5.50.

To get to Monte Albán, take a bus from the Hotel Mesón del Ángel, Mina 518, at Mier y Terán. Autobuses Turísticos makes seven runs daily, leaving at 8:30, 9:30, 10:30, and 11:30am and 12:30, 1:30, and 3:30pm. Return service leaves the ruins at

11am, noon, and 1, 2, 3, 4, and 5:30pm. The round-trip fare is $2. The ride takes half an hour, and your scheduled return time is 2 hours after arrival. It's possible to take a later return for an additional $1; inform the driver of your intent (but you won't be guaranteed a seat). During high season there are usually additional buses.

THE ROAD TO MITLA: RUINS & RUG WEAVERS

East of Oaxaca, the Pan American Highway to Mitla rolls past several important archaeological sites, markets, and craft villages. En route you can visit the famous El Tule tree; the church at Tlacochahuaya; the ruins at Dainzú, Lambityeco, and Yagul; the weaver's village of Teotitlán del Valle; and the Saturday-market village of Tlacolula.

Without a car, it's impossible to cover all these destinations in a single day, and by car the route makes for a very long day. On a Sunday, you could combine the Tlacolula market with all the archaeological sites, which have free admission on Sunday. Save the weaving village of Teotitlán del Valle and the church of Tlacochahuaya for another day.

The Fletes y Pasajes bus line runs buses every 20 minutes from 6am to 8pm to Mitla from the second-class terminal. The terminal is 8 long blocks west of the zócalo on Trujano. The trip takes 75 minutes each way. The driver will stop at any point along the way; let him know in advance.

SANTA MARÍA DEL TULE'S 2,000-YEAR-OLD TREE   Santa María del Tule is a small town (8 miles outside Oaxaca) filled with turkeys, children, and rug vendors. The town is famous for the immense **El Tule Tree,** an *ahuehuete* (Montezuma cypress) in a churchyard just off the main road. Now 2,004 years old and counting, the enormous tree is still growing, as is evidenced by the foliage, but pollution and a sinking groundwater level pose a serious threat. The entire region around Santa María del Tule was once marshland; in fact, the word *tule* means "reed." A private foundation has been established in an effort to provide protection for this lone survivor. Beyond El Tule is agricultural country; at siesta time you'll see whole families resting in the shade of giant cacti. You can see the tree from outside the churchyard fence, or pay $1.50 to go inside, close to the tree.

The **Iglesia de San Jerónimo Tlacochahuaya** is a fine example of how the Spanish borrowed from Zapotec architectural design. Inside you'll see how church leaders artistically melded the two cultures. Note the elaborately carved altar and the crucified Christ fashioned from ground dried corn cobs. Also, don't miss the still-functional organ (which dates to 1620) in the choir loft. The church is open from 10am to 2pm and 4 to 6pm. It's on the right side of the road, past El Tule Tree, and 14 miles from Oaxaca.

The Mitla bus will drop you off at the road leading into town. You can either hitch a ride with locals or walk the distance.

DAINZÚ'S ZAPOTEC RUINS   Sixteen miles from Oaxaca, this site (first excavated in the 1960s) dates from sometime between 700 and 600 B.C. Increasingly sophisticated building continued until about A.D. 300. One of the major buildings was constructed against a west-facing hill; incorporated into the lower portion of this building were 35 **carvings** resembling Monte Albán's Danzantes. These carvings are now housed in a protective shed; a caretaker will unlock it for interested parties. There is a partially reconstructed ball court. The site provides an outstanding view of the valley. Admission is $2.

Dainzú (dine-*zoo*), beautiful in the afternoon sun, lies less than a mile south of Highway 190, at the end of a mostly paved road. Look for a sign 16 miles from Oaxaca.

LAMBITYECO'S RAIN GOD   On the south side of Highway 190, a few miles east of the turnoff to Dainzú, is the small archaeological site of Lambityeco. Part of a much larger site containing more than 200 mounds, it is thought to have been inhabited as of about 600 B.C., although the fully studied part belongs to the period following the decline of Monte Albán. Of particular interest are the two beautifully executed and preserved **stucco masks** of the rain god Cocijo. A Lambityeco product was salt, distilled from saline groundwaters nearby. Admission is $1.50; $5.50 for use of your video camera.

TEOTITLÁN DEL VALLE'S BEAUTIFUL RUGS   This town is famous for weaving; its products can be found in the shops in Oaxaca, but if you're serious about **rug shopping,** there's a lot of pleasure in buying them at the source and meeting the weavers in the process. Most weavers sell out of their homes and give demonstrations. The prices are considerably lower than in Oaxaca, and here you have the opportunity to visit weavers in their homes.

The church in town is well worth a visit, as is the community museum opposite the artisan's market and adjacent to the church. The museum has an interesting exhibit of the natural dye–making, using herbs, plants, and cochineal.

For a bite to eat, consider the **Restaurant Tlaminalli,** av. Juárez 39 (☎ 952/ 4-4157), run by six lovely Zapotec sisters who serve authentic Oaxacan cuisine. Its reputation as a shrine of Oaxacan cooking brings in lots of foreigners; my last meal there, however, was only average. Prices on the à la carte menu seem a bit steep at $2 for soup and $5 for a smallish main course. It's on the main street as you approach the main part of town, in a redbrick building on the right with black wrought-iron window covers. It's open Monday through Friday from 1 to 4pm. A bit farther on, there's another nice restaurant on the left where the main street intersects with the town center.

Direct buses make the run between Oaxaca and Teotitlán from the second-class bus station. If you're coming from or going to Mitla, you'll have to hitch or walk from the highway crossroads.

TLACOLULA' S FINE MARKET & UNIQUE CHAPEL   Located about 19 miles from Oaxaca, southeast on the road to Mitla, Tlacolula is famous for its **market** and **Dominican chapel,** which is considered by many to be the most beautiful of the Dominican churches in the Americas. The wrought-iron gates, the choir loft, and the wrought-iron pulpit, considered unique in Mexico, are worth a look, as are the frescoes and paintings in relief. A few years ago a secret passage was found, leading to a room that contained valuable silver religious pieces. The silver was hidden during the Revolution of 1916, when there was a tide of antireligious sentiment; the articles are now back in the church.

Sunday is market day in Tlacolula, with rows of textiles fluttering in the breeze and aisle after aisle of pottery and baskets.

YAGUL'S ZAPOTEC FORTRESS   Yagul was a fortress city on a hill overlooking the valley. It's 20 miles southeast of Oaxaca, about half a mile off the road to Mitla. There's a small sign indicating the turnoff to the left; go up the paved road to the site. The setting is spectacular, and because the ruins are not as fully reconstructed as those at Monte Albán, you're likely to have the place to yourself. It's a good place for a picnic lunch.

The city was divided into two sections: the fortress at the top of a hill and the area of palaces lower down. The center of the palace complex is the plaza, surrounded by four temples. In the center is a ceremonial platform, under which is the **Triple Tomb.**

The door of the tomb is a large stone slab decorated on both sides with beautiful hieroglyphs. The tomb may or may not be open for viewing.

Look for the beautifully restored **ball court,** typical of Zapotec ball courts. North of the plaza is the incredible **palace** structure built for the chiefs of the city. It's a maze of huge rooms with six patios, decorated with painted stucco and stone mosaics. Visible here and there are ceremonial mounds and tombs decorated in the same geometric patterns found in Mitla. This is one of the most interesting palaces in the area. The panoramic view of the valley from the fortress is worth the rather exhausting climb.

Admission is $1.25; free on Sunday and holidays. Still cameras are free, but use of a video camera will cost you $4.15. Save your receipt—it will serve for any other sites visited the same day. The site is open daily from 8am to 5:30pm, but be prepared to blow all of 11¢ for parking.

It's just a few miles farther southeast to Mitla. The turnoff comes at a very obvious fork in the road.

MITLA'S LARGE ZAPOTEC & MIXTEC SITE   Mitla is 2¾ miles from the highway, and the turnoff terminates at the **ruins** by the church. If you've come here by bus, it's about half a mile up the road from the dusty town square to the ruins; if you want to hire a cab, there are some available in the square.

Mitla was settled by the Zapotecs around 600 B.C. but became a Mixtec bastion in the late 10th century. This city was still flourishing at the time of the Spanish Conquest, and many of the buildings were used through the 16th century.

The **town of Mitla** (population 10,000) is often bypassed by tour groups, but is worth a visit. The University of the Americas maintains the **Museum of Zapotec Art** (previously known as the Frissell collection) in town. It contains some outstanding Zapotec and Mixtec relics. Admission is $1.50. Be sure to look at the Leigh collection, which contains some real treasures. The museum is housed in a beautiful old hacienda. On a back patio is the excellent **Restaurant La Sorpresa,** av. Juárez 2 (☎ **952/ 8-0194**), a pleasant place to relax. You can dine on the patio daily between 9am and 5pm. Breakfast starts at $3.50; the daily lunch special costs $5.50 and includes soup, salad, a main course, and dessert. The lunch special is truly delicious and a good value.

You can easily see the most important buildings in an hour. Mixtec architecture is based on a quadrangle surrounded on three or four sides by patios and chambers, usually rectangular in shape. The chambers have a low roof, which is excellent for defense but makes the rooms dark and close. The stone buildings are inlaid with small cut stones to form geometric patterns.

There are five groups of buildings divided by the Mitla River. The most important buildings are on the east side of the ravine. The **Group of the Columns** consists of two quadrangles, connected at the corners with palaces. The building to the north has a long chamber with six columns and many rooms decorated with geometric designs. The most common motif is the zigzag pattern, the same one seen repeatedly on the Mitla blankets. Human or animal images are rare in Mixtec art. In fact, only one **frieze** has been found (in the Group of the Church, on the north patio). Here you'll see a series of figures painted with their name glyphs.

Admission to the site is $1.50; free on Sunday and holidays. Use of a video camera costs $4.25. Entrance to the museum is included in the price. It's open daily from 8am to 5pm.

Outside the ruins you'll be hounded by vendors. The moment you step out of a car or taxi, every able-bodied woman and child for 10 miles around will come charging over with shrill cries and a basket full of bargains—heavily embroidered belts, small pieces of pottery, fake archaeological relics, and cheap earrings. Offer to pay half the price the vendors ask. There's a modern handcrafts market near the ruins, but prices are lower in town.

In Mitla and on the highway going south, you'll find **mezcal outlets** (*expendios de mezcal*), factory outlets for little distilleries that produce the fiery cactus *aguardiente* (literally, "fire water"). To be authentic, a bottle of mezcal must have a **worm** in the bottom. The liquor is surprisingly cheap, the bottle labels are colorful, and the taste is unique. It is not unlike tequila—mix a shot of mezcal with a glass of grapefruit or pomegranate juice and you've got a cocktail that will make you forget the heat, even in Mitla. Eat the worm at your own risk!

SOUTH OF MONTE ALBÁN: ARRAZOLA, CUILAPAN & ZAACHILA

ARRAZOLA: WOOD-CARVING CAPITAL Arrazola lies in the foothills of Monte Albán, about 15 miles southwest of Oaxaca. The tiny town's most famous resident is **Manuel Jiménez,** the septuagenarian grandfather of the resurgence in wood-carving-as-folk-art. Jiménez's polar bears, anteaters, and rabbits carved from copal wood are shown in galleries throughout the world; his home is a mecca of sorts for folk-art collectors. Now the town is full of other carvers, all making fanciful creatures painted in bright, festive colors. Among those who should be sought out are **Antonio and Ramiro Aragon;** their delicate and imaginative work ranks them alongside Jiménez. Little boys will greet you at the outskirts of town offering to guide you to individual homes for a small tip. Following them is a good way to know the town, and after a bit you can take your leave of them.

If you're driving to Arrazola, take the road out of Oaxaca City that goes to Monte Albán, then take the left fork after crossing the Atoyac River and follow the signs for Zaachila. Turn right after the town of Xoxo and you will soon be there. There are no road signs, but other travelers along the way will direct you. The bus from the second-class station in Oaxaca will let you off at the side of the road to Arrazola where it meets the highway. From there, it's a pleasant 3½-mile walk to the town, past a few homes. The occupants of these homes are wood-carvers who will invite you in for a look at their work. To return, colectivo taxis make the run to Zaachila and Oaxaca for around $2, which can be shared.

CUILAPAN'S DOMINICAN MONASTERY Cuilapan (kwi-*lap*-an) is about 10 miles southwest of Oaxaca. The Dominican friars inaugurated their second **monastery** here in 1550. However, parts of the convent and church were never completed due to political complications in the late 16th century. The roof of the monastery has fallen in, but the cloister and the church remain. The church is being restored and is still used today. There are three naves with lofty arches, large stone columns, and many frescoes. It is open daily from 10am till 6pm; entry is $5.50, plus $4 for a video camera. The monastery is visible on the right a short distance from the main road to Zaachila, and there's a sign as well. The bus from the second-class station stops within a few hundred feet of the church.

ZAACHILA: MARKET TOWN WITH MIXTEC TOMBS Farther on from Cuilapan, 15 miles southwest of Oaxaca, Zaachila (za-*chee*-la) has a **Thursday market;** baskets and pottery are sold for local household use, and the produce market is always full. Also take note of the interesting livestock section and a *mercado de madera* (wood market) just as you enter town.

Behind the church is the entrance to a small **archaeological site** containing several mounds and platforms and two quite interesting tombs. Artifacts found there now reside in the National Museum of Anthropology in Mexico City, but Tomb 1 contains carvings worth seeing.

At the time of the Spanish Conquest, Zaachila was the last surviving city of the Zapotec rulers. When Cortés marched on the city, the Zapotecs offered no resistance, instead forming an alliance with him, which outraged the Mixtecs, who invaded Zaachila shortly afterward. The site and tombs are open daily from 9am till 4pm, and the entrance fee is $1.50.

To return to Oaxaca, your best option is to line up with locals to take one of the colectivo taxis on the main street across from the market.

SOUTH ALONG HIGHWAY 175

SAN BARTOLO COYOTEPEC'S POTTERY   San Bartolo is the home of the **black pottery** you will have seen in all the stores in Oaxaca. It's also one of several little villages named Coyotepec in the area. Buses frequently operate between Oaxaca and this village, 23 miles south on Highway 175. In 1953, a native woman named Doña Rosa invented the technique of smoking the pottery during firing to make it black and rubbing the fired pieces with a piece of quartz to produce a sheen. Doña Rosa died in 1979, but her son, **Valente Nieto Real,** carries on the tradition. It is almost a spiritual experience to watch Valente change a lump of coarse clay into a work of living art with only two crude plates used as a potter's wheel. The family's home/factory is a few blocks off the main road; you'll see the sign as you enter town. It's open daily from 9am to 5:30pm.

Black pottery is sold at many shops on the little plaza or in the artists' homes. Villagers who make pottery often place a piece of their work near their front door, by the gate, or on the street. It's their way of inviting prospective buyers to come in.

SAN MARTÍN TILCAJETE: WOOD-CARVING CENTER   San Martín Tilcajete is a recent addition to the tour of folk-art towns. Located about 10 miles south of San Bartolo Coyotepec, San Martín is noted, as is Arrazola, for its **wood-carvers** and their fantastical, brightly painted animals and dragons. The **Sosa and Hernández families** are especially prolific, and you can easily spend half a day wandering from house to house to see the amazing collections of hot-pink rabbits, 4-foot-long bright-blue twisting snakes, and two-headed Dalmatians.

OCOTLÁN: MARKET TOWN & THE AGUILAR POTTERS   One of the best **markets** in the area is held on Friday in Ocotlán de Morelos, 35 miles south of Oaxaca on Highway 175. The variety of goods includes modern dishware and cutlery, hand-molded earthenware jugs, polyester dresses, finely woven cotton or wool *rebozos* (scarves), hand-dyed and tooled leather, and electronics, as well as produce. You won't find a more varied selection except in Oaxaca. On other than market days, you can always visit Ocotlán's most famous potters, the noted **Aguilar family:** Josefina, Guillermina, and Irena. On the right, just at the outskirts of Ocotlán, their row of home-workshops is distinguished by pottery pieces stuck up on the fence and the roof. Their work, often figures of daily life, is colorful, sometimes humorous, and highly prized by collectors. Visitors are welcome daily.

NORTH OF OAXACA

GUELATAO: BIRTHPLACE OF BENITO JUÁREZ   High in the mountains north of Oaxaca, this lovely town has become a living monument to its favorite son, Benito Juárez. Although usually peaceful, the town comes to life on **Juárez's birthday** (Mar 21). The museum, statues, and plaza all attest to the town's obvious devotion to the patriot.

To get here, a second-class bus departs from Oaxaca's first-class station six times daily. There are also several departures from the second-class station. The trip will take at least 2 hours, through gorgeous mountain scenery. Buses return to Oaxaca every 2 hours until 8pm.

EN ROUTE TO SAN CRISTÓBAL DE LAS CASAS

Tuxtla Gutiérrez, the boomtown capital of the wild, mountainous state of Chiapas, is west of San Cristóbal on Highway 190. If you need to stop for a night's rest, try the large, comfortable **Hotel Bonampak Tuxtla** (bulevar Domínguez 180; ☎ **961/3-2050**) on the outskirts of town, or the less-expensive but sometimes loud **Gran Hotel Humberto** (av. Central 180; ☎ **961/2-2080**) right downtown. No trip to Tuxtla is complete without a meal at ✪ **Las Pichanchas** (avenida Central Ote. 837; ☎ **961/2-5351**), a colorful restaurant devoted to the regional food and drink of Chiapas. If you've got some time to spare, check out Tuxtla's fine **zoo** (ZOOMAT). On the highway to San Cristóbal 10 minutes outside of Tuxtla, you get a good view of majestic canyon walls rising from a wide river. This is the **Sumidero Canyon,** and a boat trip through it makes for a fun outing. Boats leave from a dock where Highway 190 crosses the river and another in **Chiapa de Corzo,** a pleasant town just off the highway a couple of minutes down the road. A boat leaves when enough people are present. Cost per person is about $7; the trip takes 2 hours. You can get to Chiapa de Corzo from Tuxtla by colectivo. One leaves every 10 minutes from the corner of calles 3 Oriente and 3 Sur.

2 San Cristóbal de las Casas

143 miles SW of Palenque; 50 miles E of Tuxtla Gutiérrez; 46 miles NW of Comitán; 104 miles NW of Cuauhtémoc; 282 miles E of Oaxaca

San Cristóbal (population 90,000) is a colonial town of plastered stone or adobe walls and red-tile roofs. It lies in a lovely valley, nearly 7,000 feet high. Part of the town's name is derived from the 16th-century bishop Fray Bartolomé de las Casas, who sought to protect native peoples from exploitation. The area is home to a large population of Indians who speak Mayan languages such as Tzotzil or Tzeltal. San Cristóbal is the major market center for these Indians, who trek down from the surrounding mountains. Some groups, such as the Lacandóns (who number only about 450) seldom come into town; they live so far off in the forests of eastern Chiapas that it takes 6 days on horseback to get to their territory.

Probably the most visible among the local indigenous groups are the **Chamula.** The men wear baggy thigh-length trousers and white or black serapes, while the women wear blue rebozos, gathered white blouses with embroidered trim, and black wool wraparound skirts.

Another local Indian group is the **Zinacantecan,** whose male population dresses in light-pink overshirts with colorful trim and tassels and sometimes short pants. Hat ribbons (now a rare sight) are tied on married men, while ribbons dangle loosely from the hats of bachelors and community leaders. The Zinacantecan women wear beautiful, brightly colored woven shawls along with black wool skirts. You may also see **Tenejapa** men clad in knee-length black tunics and flat straw hats and Tenejapa women dressed in beautiful reddish and rust-colored *huipils.* Women of all groups are barefooted, while men wear handmade sandals or cowboy boots.

There are several Indian villages within reach of San Cristóbal by road: Chamula, with its weavers and highly unorthodox church; Zinacantán, whose residents practice a unique religion; Tenejapa, **San Andrés,** and **Magdalena,** known for brocaded textiles; **Amatenango del Valle,** a town of potters; and **Aguacatenango,** known for embroidery. Most of these "villages" consist of little more than a church and the

San Cristóbal de las Casas

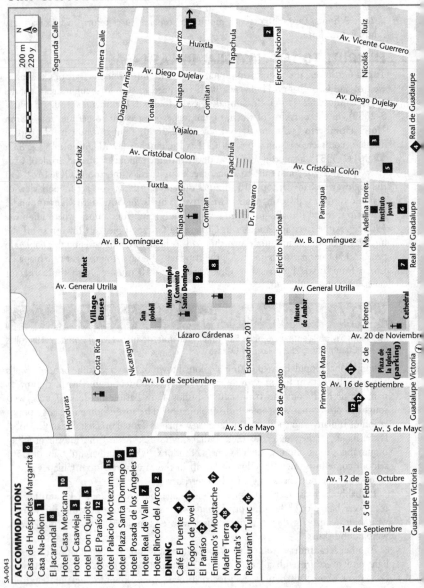

municipal government building, with homes scattered for miles around and a general gathering only for church and market days (usually Sun).

Evangelical Protestant missionaries recently have converted large numbers of indigenous peoples, and in some villages new converts find themselves expelled from their homelands; in Chamula, for example, as many as 30,000 people have been expelled. Many of these people, called *expulsados* (expelled ones), have taken up residence in new villages on the outskirts of San Cristóbal de las Casas. They still wear their traditional dress. Other villages, such as Tenejapa, allow the Protestant church to exist, and villagers to attend it without prejudice.

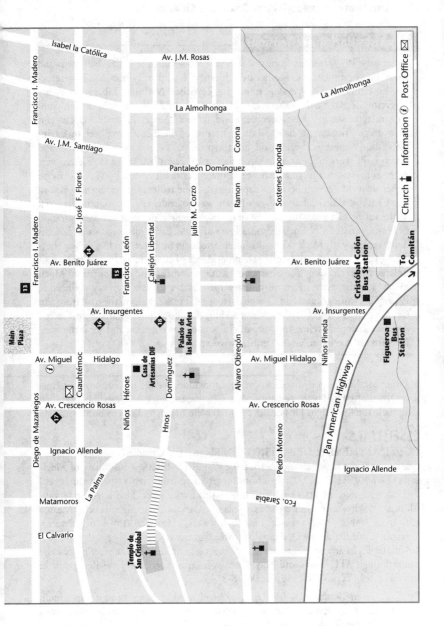

Although the influx of tourists is increasing and the influence of outsiders (including Mexicans) is inevitably chipping away at the culture, the Indians aren't really interested in acting or looking like the foreigners in their midst. They may steal glances at tourists or even stare curiously, but mainly they pay little attention to outsiders.

You'll hear the word *ladino* here; it refers to non-Indian Mexicans or people who have taken up modern ways, changed their dress, dropped their Indian traditions and language, and decided to live in town. It may be used derogatorily or descriptively, depending on who is using the term and how.

Zapatista Uprising & Tensions

In January 1994, Indians from this area rebelled against the ladino-led towns and Mexican government over health care, education, land distribution, and representative government. Their organization, the **Zapatista National Liberation Army (Ejercito Zapatista de Liberacion Nacional, or EZLN),** and its leader, Subcomandante Marcos, have become world famous. Since the revolt, discussions between government officials and the leadership of the EZLN have been on-again-off-again. Progress has been made, but the principal issues remain unresolved, and tension still exists in the area. In December of 1997 and January of 1998 there were more killings, but they may have been more the result of local political division rather than the tension between Zapatistas and the national government. I was in San Cristóbal shortly afterwards, and there was no evidence of tension in the town or the valley. Life was normal. The only visible signs I found of the confrontation were the initials EZLN painted on a few walls, and little Subcomandante Marcos dolls, replete with black ski masks, offered for sale by street vendors (a very hot-selling item, by the way). Locals gave no evidence of concern. Tourists were present in large numbers. Only the newspapers made an issue of the confrontation. Much to my surprise, there were no military road blocks on the highway connecting Palenque, Ocosingo, and San Cristóbal; troops did make stops on the road from San Cristóbal to Oaxaca, but they were checking for illegal immigrants from Central America. Before traveling to Chiapas, check your news sources and see if the State Department has issued any advisories: **www.state.gov.**

Other local lingo you should know about includes *Jovel,* San Cristóbal's original name, used often by businesses; and *coleto,* meaning someone or something from San Cristóbal. You'll see signs for tamales coletos, coleto bread, and coleto breakfast.

ESSENTIALS

GETTING THERE & DEPARTING   By Plane   San Cristóbal's airport offers service through one major airline: **Aerocaribe** (☎ 961/2-0020), a subsidiary of **Mexicana** (☎ 800/531-7921). There is nonstop service to/from Tuxtla (four flights/week) and Palenque (four flights/week). To/from Mérida (twice a week) has one-stop service. All other destinations require changing planes: Cancún (four flights/week), Mexico City (four flights/week), Oaxaca (four flights/week), Huatulco (three flights/week), Veracruz (three flights/week), Acapulco (three flights/week).

Charter-flight arrangements or flight changes on any airline in another city can be made through **ATC Tours and Travel,** across from El Fogón de Jovel Restaurant in San Cristóbal (☎ 967/8-2550; fax 967/8-3145).

By Car   From Tuxtla, a 1½-hour trip, the road winds through beautiful mountain country. The road between Palenque and San Cristóbal de las Casas is adventurous and provides jungle scenery, but portions of it may be heavily potholed, washed out, or have dangerous dips; the trip takes about 5 hours.

Arriving: To get to the main plaza if you're arriving from Oaxaca/Tuxtla, turn left on avenida Insurgentes (there's a traffic light); if you're coming from Palenque/Ocosingo, turn right.

By Taxi   Taxis from Tuxtla Gutiérrez to San Cristóbal leave from both the airport and the Cristóbal Colón bus station.

By Bus   The two bus stations in town are directly across the Pan American Highway from each other. The smaller one belongs to **Transportes Rodolfo Figueroa (TRF),** which provides first-class service to/from Tuxtla (every 40 min.) and Palenque (four buses/day with a stop in Ocosingo—cheaper than the competition). For other destinations go to the large station run by **ADO** and its affiliates Cristóbal Colon and Maya de Oro. This company offers service to/from Tuxtla (12 buses/day), Palenque (almost every hour) and several other destinations: Mérida (two buses/day), Villahermosa (two buses/day), Oaxaca (two buses/day), Puerto Escondido (two buses/day).

Arriving: The main plaza is 9 blocks north up avenida Insurgentes (a 10-min. walk slightly uphill). Cabs are cheap and plentiful.

VISITOR INFORMATION   The **Municipal Tourism Office** (☎ 967/8-0660, ext. 126; fax 967/8-0135), on the main square in the town hall, across the street from the cathedral, is well organized and has a friendly, helpful staff. The office keeps convenient hours: Monday through Saturday from 9am to 8pm and Sunday from 9am to 2pm. Check the bulletin board here for apartments, shared rides, cultural events, and local tours. Or try the **State Tourism Office** across the main plaza, at av. Hidalgo 2 (☎ 967/8-6570); it's open Monday through Friday from 9am to 9pm, Saturday from 9am to 8:30pm, and Sunday from 9am to 2pm. Both offices are helpful, but the state office is open an hour later and usually isn't as busy.

CITY LAYOUT   San Cristóbal is laid out on a grid; the main north-south axis is **Insurgentes/Utrilla** and the east-west being **Mazariegos/Madero.** All streets change names when they cross either of these streets. **Real de Guadalupe** seems to have become a main drag for tourism-related businesses. The market is 9 blocks north along Utrilla. From the market, minibuses (colectivos) trundle to outlying villages.

Take note that this town has at least three streets named "Domínguez" and two streets named "Flores." There's Hermanos Domínguez, Belisário Domínguez, and Pantaleón Domínguez, and María Adelina Flores and Dr. José Flores.

GETTING AROUND   Most of the sights and shopping in San Cristóbal are within walking distance of the plaza.

Urbano buses—minibuses—take residents to and from town and the outlying neighborhoods. All buses pass by the market and central plaza on their way through town. Utrilla and avenida 16 de Septiembre are the two main arteries; all buses use the market area as the last stop. Any bus on Utrilla will take you to the market.

Colectivos to outlying villages depart from the public market at avenida Utrilla. Buses late in the day are usually very crowded. Always check to see when the last or next-to-last bus returns from wherever you're going, then take the one before that—those last buses sometimes don't materialize, and you might be stranded. I speak from experience!

Rental cars come in handy for trips to the outlying villages and may be worth the expense when shared by a group, but keep in mind that insurance is invalid on unpaved roads. There's a **Budget** rental-car office here at av. Mazariegos 36 (☎ 800/527-0700 in the U.S. and Canada, or 967/8-3100). You'll save money by arranging the rental from your home country; otherwise, a day's rental with insurance will cost $62 for a VW Beetle with manual transmission, the cheapest car available. Office hours are Monday through Sunday from 8am to 1pm and 5 to 8pm.

Bicycles are another option for getting around the city; a day's rental is about $12, and bike tours are offered at **Los Pinqüinos,** av. Cinco de Mayo 10-B (no phone); open daily from 9:15am to 2:30pm and 4 to 7pm.

FAST FACTS: San Cristóbal de las Casas

Area Code   The telephone area code is **967**.

Books   *Living Maya* by Walter Morris, with photography by Jeffrey Fox, is the best book to read to understand the culture, art, and traditions around San Cristóbal de las Casas, as well as the unsolved social, economic, and political problems that gave rise to the 1994 Chiapas Indian uprising. *The People of the Bat: Mayan Tales and Dreams from Zinacantán,* by Robert M. Laughlin, is a priceless collection of beliefs from that village near San Cristóbal. Another good book with a completely different view of today's Maya is *The Heart of the Sky,* by Peter Canby, who traveled among the Maya to chronicle their struggles (written before the Zapatista uprising).

Bookstore   For a wide selection of new and used books and reading material in English, go to **La Pared,** av. Hidalgo 2 (☎ **967/8-6367**), next to the state tourism office. The owner, Dana Gay, is very helpful and informed. Or try Librería Soluna, Real de Guadalupe 13B and Insurgentes 27. These stores have a good number of books in English as well.

Bulletin Boards   Since San Cristóbal is a cultural crossroads for travelers from all over the world, several places maintain bulletin boards with information on Spanish classes, local specialty tours, rooms or houses to rent, rides needed, etc. These include boards at the Tourism Office, Café el Puente, Mi Tierra, and Na Bolom.

Climate   San Cristóbal can be cold day or night year-round, especially during the winter. Most hotels are not heated, although some have fireplaces. There is always a possibility of rain, but I would particularly avoid going to San Cristóbal from late August to late October.

Currency Exchange   There are at least five casas de cambio on Real de Guadalupe near the main square and a couple under the colonnade facing the square. Most are open until 8pm and some are open Sunday.

E-mail   The **Cyberc@fe** is in the little concourse that cuts through the block that is just east of the main square. Look for the entrance on either Real de Guadalupe or Francisco Madero (☎ **967/8-7488**). It is the largest Internet cafe I have seen in Mexico. They have several well-connected machines and a few other toys besides.

Homestays   Café el Puente (see "Where to Dine," below), besides being a gathering place, restaurant, and telephone center, can also arrange homestays.

Parking   If your hotel does not have parking, use the underground public lot (*estacionamiento*) located in front of the cathedral, just off the main square on 16 de Septiembre. Entry is from calle 5 de Febrero.

Photography Warning   Photographers should be very cautious about when, where, and at whom or what they point their cameras. In San Cristóbal, taking a photograph of even a chile pepper can be a risky undertaking; local people just do not like having people take pictures. Especially in the San Cristóbal market, people who think they or their possessions are being photographed may angrily pelt photographers with whatever object is at hand—rocks or rotten fruit. Be respectful and ask first. You might even try offering a small amount of money in exchange for taking a picture. Young handcraft vendors will sometimes offer to be photographed for money.

Post Office   The post office (correo) is at Crescencio Rosas and Cuauhtémoc, a block south and west of the main square. It's open Monday through Friday from 8am to 7pm and Saturday from 9am to 1pm.

Spanish Classes   The **Centro Bilingue,** at the Centro Cultural El Puente, Real de Guadalupe 55, 29250 San Cristóbal de las Casas, Chiapas (☎ **800/303-4983** in the U.S., or phone/fax 967/8-3723), offers classes in Spanish. The **Instituto Jovel,** María Adelina Flores 21 (Apdo. Postal 62), 29250 San Cristóbal de las Casas, Chiapas (☎/fax **967/8-4069**), gets high marks for its Spanish courses. It also offers courses in weaving and cooking. Both schools can arrange homestays for their students.

Telephone   **Centro el Puente** at the Café el Puente, Real de Guadalupe 55 (☎/fax **967/8-1911**), offers telephone and fax service at reasonable prices. Besides sending faxes, they'll receive faxes and hold them for you. The telephone service is open Monday through Saturday from 9am to 2pm and 5 to 9pm.

SPECIAL EVENTS IN & NEAR SAN CRISTÓBAL

In nearby Chamula, **Carnaval,** the big annual festival that takes place days before Lent, is a fascinating mingling of the Christian pre-Lenten ceremonies and the ancient Maya celebration of the five "lost days" at the end of the 360-day Maya agricultural cycle. Around noon on Shrove Tuesday, groups of village elders run across patches of burning grass as a purification rite. Macho residents then run through the streets with a bull. During Carnaval, roads are closed in town and buses drop visitors at the outskirts.

Nearby villages (except Zinacantán) also have celebrations during this time, although they're perhaps not as dramatic. Visiting these villages, especially on the Sunday before Lent, will round out your impression of Carnaval in all its regional varieties. In Tenejapa, the celebrants are still active during the Thursday market after Ash Wednesday.

During Easter and the week after, when the annual **Feria de Primavera** (Spring Festival) is held, San Cristóbal is ablaze with lights and excitement and gets hordes of visitors. Activities include carnival rides, food stalls, handcraft shops, parades, and band concerts. Hotel rooms are scarce and more expensive.

Another spectacle is staged July 22 to 25, the dates of the annual **Fiesta of San Cristóbal,** honoring the town's patron saint. The steps up to San Cristóbal church are lit with torches at night. Pilgrimages to the church begin several days earlier, and on the night of the 24th, there's an all-night vigil.

For the **Día de Guadalupe,** on December 12, honoring Mexico's patron saint, the streets are gaily decorated, and food stalls line the streets leading to the church honoring her, high on a hill.

Photography Rules in the Villages

In villages outside of San Cristóbal, there are strict rules about photography. To ensure proper respect by outsiders, villages around San Cristóbal, especially Chamula and Zinacantán, require visitors to go to the municipal building upon arrival and sign an agreement (written in Spanish) not to take photographs. The penalty for disobeying these regulations is stiff: confiscation of your camera and perhaps even a lengthy stay in jail. And they mean it!

EXPLORING SAN CRISTÓBAL

San Cristóbal, with its beautiful scenery, clean air, and mountain hikes, draws many visitors. However, the town's biggest attraction is its colorful, centuries-old indigenous culture. The Chiapanecan Maya, attired in their beautifully crafted native garb, surround tourists in San Cristóbal, but most travelers take at least one trip to the outlying villages to get a close-up of Maya life.

ATTRACTIONS IN TOWN

Catedral. 20 de Noviembre at Guadalupe Victoria. No phone. Free admission. Daily 7am–6pm.

San Cristóbal's main cathedral was built in the 1500s and boasts fine timber work and a very fancy pulpit.

Museo de Ambar. Plaza Silvan, Utrilla 10. ☎ **967/8-3507.** Free admission. Daily 9:30am–7pm. From the plaza, walk 2½ blocks north on Utrilla (going toward the market); the museum will be on your left.

Seen from the street, this place looks like just another store, but pass through the small shop area and you'll find the long, narrow museum a fascinating place to browse. It's the only museum in Mexico devoted to amber, a fossilized resin thousands of years old mined in Chiapas near Simojovel. Owner José Luis Coría Torres has assembled more than 250 sculpted amber pieces as well as a rare collection of amber with insects trapped inside and amber fused with fossils. Amber jewelry and other objects are also for sale.

Museo Templo y Convento Santo Domingo. Av. 20 de Noviembre. ☎ **967/8-1609.** Church, free. Museum, $2. Museum open Tues–Sun 10am–5pm.

Inside the front door of the carved-stone plateresque facade, there's a beautiful gilded wooden altarpiece built in 1560, walls with saints, and gilt-framed paintings. Attached to the church is the former Convent of Santo Domingo, which houses a small museum about San Cristóbal and Chiapas. The museum, housed on three floors, has changing exhibits and often shows cultural films. It's 5 blocks north of the zócalo.

✪ **Casa Na-Bolom.** Av. Vicente Guerrero 3, 29200 San Cristóbal de las Casas, Chi. ☎ **967/8-1418.** Fax 967/8-5586. $3 group tour and film *La Reina de la Selva*, (in Spanish) is available Tues–Sun at 11:30am, and another (in English) at 4:30pm. The extensive library devoted to Maya studies is open Mon–Thurs 9am–3pm; Fri 9–11am. The Artisanía Lacandon gift shop is open Tues–Sun 10am–2pm and 4–7pm. Leave the square on Real de Guadalupe, walk 4 blocks to Av. Vicente Guerrero, and turn left; Na-Bolom is 5½ blocks up Guerrero.

If you're interested in the anthropology of this region, you'll want to visit this house-museum. Stay here if you can. The house, built as a seminary in 1891, became the headquarters of anthropologists Frans and Trudy Blom in 1951 and the gathering place of outsiders interested in studying the region. Frans Blom led many early archaeological studies in Mexico, and Trudy was noted for her photographs of the Lacandón Indians and her efforts to save them and their forest homeland. A room at Na-Bolom contains a selection of her Lacandón photographs, and postcards of the photographs are on sale in the gift shop. A tour of the home includes the displays of pre-Hispanic artifacts collected by Frans Blom; the cozy library with its numerous volumes about the region and the Maya; and the gardens Trudy Blom started for the ongoing reforestation of the Lacandón jungle. *La Reina de la Selva* is an excellent 50-minute film on the Bloms, the Lacandóns, and Na-Bolom. Trudy Blom died in 1993, but Na-Bolom continues to operate as a nonprofit public trust.

The 12 guest rooms, named for surrounding villages, are decorated with local objects and textiles. All rooms have fireplaces and private bathrooms. Prices for rooms (including breakfast) are $35 single and $45 double.

Even if you're not a guest here you can come for a meal, usually a delicious assortment of vegetarian and other dishes. Just be sure to make a reservation at least 2½ hours in advance and be on time. The colorful dining room has one large table, and the eclectic mix of travelers sometimes makes for interesting conversation. Breakfast costs $4, lunch and dinner $5 each. Following breakfast between 8 and 10am, tours to San Juan Chamula and Zinacantán are offered by a guide not affiliated with the house. (See "Nearby Maya Villages & Countryside," below.)

Palacio de las Bellas Artes. Av. Hidalgo, 4 blocks south of the plaza. No phone.

Be sure to check out this building if you are interested in the arts. It periodically hosts dance events, art shows, and other performances. The schedule of events is usually posted on the door if the Bellas Artes is not open. There's a public library next door.

Templo de San Cristóbal. Exit the zócalo on Av. Hidalgo and turn right onto the 3rd street (Hermanos Domínguez); at the end of the street are the temple steps.

For the best view of San Cristóbal, climb the seemingly endless steps to this church and *mirador* (lookout point). A visit here requires stamina. By the way, there are 22 more churches in town, some of which also demand strenuous climbs.

HORSEBACK RIDING

The **Casa de Huéspedes Margarita** and **Hotel Real del Valle** (see "Where to Stay," below) can arrange horseback rides for around $15 for a day, including a guide. Reserve your steed at least a day in advance. A horse-riding excursion might go to San Juan Chamula, to nearby caves, or just up into the hills.

NEARBY MAYA VILLAGES & COUNTRYSIDE

The Indian communities around San Cristóbal are fascinating worlds unto themselves. If you are unfamiliar with these indigenous cultures, you will understand and appreciate more of what you see by visiting them with a guide, at least for a first foray out into the villages. Guides are acquainted with members of the communities and are viewed with less suspicion than newcomers. These communities have their own laws and customs—and visitors' ignorance is no excuse. Should something happen, the state and federal authorities will not intervene except in case of a serious crime. There are three guides who go to the neighboring villages.

Pepe leaves from Na-Bolom (see "Attractions in Town," above) for daily trips to San Juan Chamula and Zinacantán at 10am if there is a minimum of five people. Minivan transportation and a knowledgeable guide are included in the $10 per-person price. The tour returns to San Cristóbal between 2 and 3pm.

Another tour is led by a very opinionated mestiza woman, **Mercedes Hernández Gómez.** Mercedes, a largely self-trained ethnographer, is extremely well informed about the history and folkways of the villages. She explains (in English) the religious significance of what you see in the churches, where shamans try to cure Indian patients of various maladies. She also facilitates tourists' firsthand contact with Indians. Her group goes by minivan to the village or villages she has selected; normally tours return to the plaza at about 2:30pm. You can meet her near the kiosk in the main plaza at 9am (she will be carrying an umbrella). The tour costs $10 per person.

Two additional guides, **Alex and Raul,** can be found in front of the cathedral at 9am. They give tours of the Indian villages (also for $10 per person) in both English and Spanish.

For excursions farther afield, see "Road Trips from San Cristóbal" at the end of this section.

CHAMULA & ZINACANTÁN   A side trip to the village of San Juan Chamula will really get you into the spirit of life around San Cristóbal. Sunday, when the market is in full swing, is the best day to go for shopping; but other days, when you'll be unimpeded by anxious children selling their crafts, are better for seeing the village and church. Colectivos to San Juan Chamula leave the municipal market in San Cristóbal about every half hour. Don't expect anyone in these vans to speak English or Spanish, and the driver may be around 11 or 12 years old and barely able to see over the steering wheel.

The village, 5 miles northeast of San Cristóbal, is the **Chamula cultural and ceremonial center.** Activity centers around the huge church, the plaza, and the municipal building. Each year, a new group of citizens is chosen to live in the municipal center as caretakers of the saints, settlers of disputes, and enforcers of village rules. As in other nearby villages, on Sunday local leaders wear their leadership costumes with beautifully woven straw hats loaded with colorful ribbons befitting their high position. They solemnly sit together in a long line somewhere around the central square. Chamula is typical of other villages in that men are often away working in the "hot lands" harvesting coffee or cacao, while women stay home to tend the sheep, the children, the cornfields, and the fires. It's almost always the women's and children's work to gather sticks for fires, and you see them along roadsides bent under the weight.

Don't leave Chamula without seeing the **church interior.** As you step from bright sunlight into the candlelit interior, it will take a few minutes for your eyes to adjust. The tile floor is covered in pine needles scattered amid a meandering sea of lit candles. Saints line the walls, and before them people are often kneeling and praying aloud while passing around bottles of Pepsi Cola. Shamans are often on hand, passing eggs over sick people or using live or dead chickens in a curing ritual. The statues of saints are similar to those you might see in any Mexican Catholic church, but they take on another meaning to the Chamulas that has no similarity to the traditional Catholic saints other than in name. Visitors can walk carefully through the church to see the saints or stand quietly in the background and observe.

Carnaval, which takes place just before Lent, is the big annual festival. The Chamulas are not a very wealthy people, as their economy is based on agriculture, but the women are the region's best wool weavers, producing finished pieces for themselves and for other villages.

In Zinacantán, a wealthier village than Chamula, you must sign a rigid form promising *not to take any photographs* before you are allowed to see the two side-by-side **sanctuaries.** Once permission is granted and you have paid a small fee, an escort will usually show you the church, or you may be allowed to see it on your own. Floors may be covered in pine needles here, too, and the rooms are brightly sunlit. The experience is an altogether different one from that of Chamula.

AMATENANGO DEL VALLE   About an hour's ride south of San Cristóbal is Amatenango, a town known mostly for its **women potters.** You'll see their work in San Cristóbal—small animals, jars, and large water jugs—but in the village, you can visit the potters in their homes. Just walk down the dirt streets. Villagers will lean over the walls of family compounds and invite you in to select from their inventory. You may even see them firing the pieces under piles of wood in the open courtyard or painting them with color derived from rusty iron water. The women wear beautiful red-and-yellow *huipils,* but if you want to take a photograph, you'll have to pay.

To get here, take a colectivo from the market in San Cristóbal, but before it lets you off, be sure to ask about the return-trip schedule.

AGUACATENANGO   Located 10 miles south of Amatenango, this village is known for its **embroidery.** If you've visited San Cristóbal shops before arriving here, you'll recognize the white-on-white or black-on-black floral patterns on dresses and blouses for sale. The locals' own regional blouses, however, are quite different.

TENEJAPA   The **weavers** of Tenejapa make some of the most beautiful and expensive work you'll see in the region. The best time to visit is on market day (Sun and Thurs, though Sun is best). The weavers of Tenejapa taught the weavers of San Andrés and Magdalena—which accounts for the similarity in their designs and colors. To get to Tenejapa, try either to find a colectivo in the very last row by the market or hire a taxi. On Tenejapa's main street, several stores sell locally woven regional clothing, and you can bargain for the price.

THE HUITEPEC CLOUD FOREST   **Pronatura,** a private nonprofit ecological organization, offers environmentally sensitive tours of the cloud forest. The forest is a haven for **migratory birds,** and more than 100 bird species and 600 plant species have been discovered here. Guided tours are Tuesday through Sunday from 9am to noon at a cost of $18 per group (up to eight people). Make reservations a day in advance. Their office is at av. Benito Juárez 11-B (☎ **967/8-5000**). To reach the reserve on your own, drive on the road to Chamula; the turnoff is at km 3.5. The reserve is open Tuesday through Sunday from 9am to 4pm.

SHOPPING

Many Indian villages near San Cristóbal are noted for their weaving, embroidery, brocade work, leather, and pottery, making the area one of the best in the country for shopping. The craftspeople make and sell beautiful woolen shawls, indigo-dyed skirts, colorful native shirts, and magnificently woven *huipils,* all of which often come in vivid geometric patterns. Working in leather, they are artisans of the highest caliber, making sandals and men's handbags. There's a proliferation of tie-dyed *jaspe* from Guatemala, which comes in bolts and is made into clothing, as well as other textiles from that country. There are numerous shops up and down the streets leading to the market. calle Real de Guadalupe has more shops than any other street.

CRAFTS

Casa de Artesanías DIF. Niños Héroes at Hidalgo. ☎ **967/8-1180.**

Crafts are sold in a fine showroom in one of the city's old houses. Here you'll find such quality products as lined woolen vests and jackets, pillow covers, amber jewelry, and more. In back is a fine little museum showing costumes worn by villagers who live near San Cristóbal. Open Tuesday through Saturday from 9am to 2pm and 5 to 8pm.

Central Market. Av. Utrilla. No phone.

The market buildings and the surrounding streets offer just about anything you need. The market in San Cristóbal is open every morning except Sunday (when each village has its own local market), and you'll probably enjoy observing the sellers as much as the things they sell. See the "Photography Warning" in "Fast Facts," above, regarding photography here. The mercado is north of the Santo Domingo church, about 9 blocks from the zócalo.

El Encuentro. Calle Real de Guadalupe 63-A. ☎ **967/8-3698.**

You should find some of your best bargains here—at a minimum you'll think the price is fair. The shop carries many regional ritual items, such as new and used men's ceremonial hats, false saints, and iron rooftop adornments, plus many huipils and other textiles. It's open Monday through Saturday from 9am to 8pm and is found between Dujelay and Guerrero.

La Alborada, Centro Desarrollo Comunitario DIF. Barrio María Auxiliadora. No phone.

At this government-sponsored school, young men and women from surrounding villages come to learn how to hook Persian-style rugs, weave fabric on foot looms, sew, make furniture, construct a house, cook, make leather shoes and bags, forge iron, and grow vegetables and trees for reforestation. Probably the most interesting crafts for the general tourist are the rug making and weaving. Artisans from Temoaya in Mexico State learned rug making from Persians, who came to teach this skill in the 1970s. The Temoaya artisans in turn traveled to San Cristóbal to teach the craft to area students, who have since taught others. The beautiful rug designs are taken from brocaded and woven designs used to decorate regional costumes. Visitors should stop at the entrance and ask for an escort. You can visit all the various areas and see students at work or simply go straight to the weavers. There's a small sales outlet at the entrance selling newly loomed fabric by the meter, leather bags, rugs, and baskets made at another school in the highlands. La Alborada is in a far southern suburb of the city off the highway to Comitán, to the right. To get here take the "María Auxiliadora" urbano bus from the market. Ask the driver to let you off at La Alborada. The same bus makes the return trip, passing through the town center and ending its route at the market.

La Galería. Hidalgo 3. ☎ **967/8-1547.**

This lovely gallery beneath a cafe has expositions by well-known national and international painters. Also for sale are the paintings and greeting cards by Kiki, the owner, a German artist who has found her niche in San Cristóbal. There are some Oaxacan rugs and pottery, plus unusual silver jewelry. Open daily from 10am to 9pm

TEXTILE SHOPS
Kun Kun SC. Real de Mexicanos 21. ☎ **967/8-1417.**

The name means "little by little." This cooperative society to aid local native artisans sells mostly ceramic tiles, weavings, and pottery. The weavings are made of locally produced wool that has been spun, dyed, and woven by members. Kun Kun holds workshops for artisans on such things as working with floor looms, which you can watch when visiting the store. The tiles are wonderful. Also, if you're interested, ask about classes in using a back-strap loom.

Plaza de Santo Domingo. Av. Utrilla.

The plazas around this church and the nearby Templo de Caridad are filled with women in native garb selling their wares. Here you'll find women from Chamula weaving belts or embroidering, surrounded by piles of loomed woolen textiles from their village. More and more Guatemalan shawls, belts, and bags are included in their inventory. There are also some excellent buys in Chiapanecan-made wool vests, jackets, rugs, and shawls similar to those in Sna Jolobil (see below), if you take the time to look and bargain. Vendors arrive between 9 and 10am and begin to leave around 3pm.

Sna Jolobil. Calzada Lázaro Cárdenas 42 (Plaza Santo Domingo). ☎ **967/8-2646.**

Meaning "weaver's house" in the Mayan language, this place is located in the former convent (monastery) of Santo Domingo, next to the Templo de Santo Domingo between Navarro and Nicaragua. This cooperative store is operated by groups of Tzotzil and Tzeltal craftspeople and has about 3,000 members who contribute products, help in running the store, and share in the moderate profits. Their works are simply beautiful; prices are set and high—as is the quality. Be sure to take a look. Open Monday through Saturday from 9am to 2pm and 4 to 6pm; credit cards are accepted.

Tzontehuitz. Real de Guadalupe 74. ☎/fax **967/8-3158.**

About 3½ blocks from the plaza, this shop is one of the best on calle Real de Guadalupe, near the corner of Diego Dujelay. Owner Janet Giacobone specializes in her own textile designs and weavings. Some of her work is loomed in Guatemala, but you can also watch weavers using foot looms in the courtyard. Hours are Monday through Saturday from 9am to 2pm and 4 to 7pm.

Unión Regional de Artesanías de los Altos (also known as J'pas Joloviletic). Av. Utrilla 43. ☎ **967/8-2848.**

Another cooperative of weavers, this one is smaller than Sna Jolobil (see above) and not as sophisticated in its approach to potential shoppers. It sells blouses, textiles, pillow covers, vests, sashes, napkins, baskets, and purses. It's near the market and worth looking around. Open Monday through Saturday from 9am to 2pm and 4 to 7pm, and Sunday from 9am to 1pm.

WHERE TO STAY

Keep in mind that among the most interesting places to stay in San Cristóbal is the ex-seminary–turned–hotel-museum; see **Casa Na-Bolom** in "Attractions in Town," above, for details.

For really low-cost accommodations, there are basic but acceptable *hospedajes* and *posadas*, which charge about $6 for a single and $8 to $12 for a double. Usually these places are unadvertised; if you're interested in a very cheap place to stay, ask around in a restaurant or cafe, and you're sure to find one, or go to the tourist office, which often displays notices of new *hospedajes* on the metal flip rack in the office. Some of the best economical offerings are on calle Real de Guadalupe, east of the main square.

VERY EXPENSIVE

✪ **El Jacarandal.** Comitán 7, 29200 San Cristóbal de las Casas, Chi. ☎/fax **967/8-1065.** 4 units. $160 per person for double occupancy, includes all meals, drinks, activities. No credit cards.

El Jacarandal is the home of Nancy and Percy Wood—who choose to entertain guests and, in so doing, elevate the practice to a form of high art. This is not merely a lodging. You can stay here for a week without ever having to look for outside entertainment. The owners keep a stable of horses for the use of their guests and like to go for morning rides. They also enjoy showing their guests the Indian villages, the Huitepec cloud forest, and the Maya ruins that are not far from the city, or simply letting the guests lounge around a bit or do some exploring on their own. Meals are not to be missed. Fidelia the cook is most able, and on many occasions local anthropologists, environmentalists, or prominent citizens drop in for a bite and a chat. The house and grounds themselves are lovely; sometimes it's hard to tear yourself away. From the patio where breakfast is taken, the garden and trees present a lovely foreground of green to the background of red-tile roofs and church cupolas, and behind everything else, the mountains. The rooms come with one or two beds. Accommodations are gracious and engaging, as is everything in the house.

MODERATE

✪ **Hotel Casa Mexicana.** 28 de Agosto 1, 29200 San Cristóbal de las Casas, Chi. ☎ **967/8-1348.** Fax 967/8-2627. E-mail: Hcasamex@mail.internet.com.mx. 52 units. TV TEL. $57 double. AE, MC, V. Free secure parking.

This lovely hotel—created from a large mansion, with a grand exterior—is a conveniently located deluxe addition to the San Cristóbal scene. The entryway reveals a lovely courtyard and fountain. The carpeted rooms have excellent reading lights, electric heaters for those chilly nights, and either one or two double beds with handsome carved headboards. Guests are welcome to use the sauna, and inexpensive massages can be arranged. The hotel handles a lot of large tour groups; it can be quiet and peaceful one day and full and bustling the next. It is 4 blocks north of the main plaza at the corner of Utrilla and Agosto/Eje Nacional.

Hotel Casavieja. Ma. Adelina Flores 27, 29200 San Cristóbal de las Casas, Chi. ☎/fax **967/8-5223** or 967/8-0385. 40 units. TV TEL. $55 double. AE, MC, V. Free parking.

The Casavieja is one of the choice hotels in San Cristóbal. Originally built in 1740, restoration and new construction have faithfully replicated the original design and detail complete with wood-beam ceilings. The size and beautiful furnishings of the carpeted rooms, plus the welcome heaters, create an ideal cozy nest. The hotel's stylish restaurant, Doña Rita, faces the interior courtyard with tables on the patio or inside and offers reasonable prices, but service is slow. Fifteen rooms across the street house the tour groups, which in the past have created lots of noise in this otherwise tranquil hotel. The hotel is 3½ blocks northeast of the plaza between Cristóbal Colón and Diego Dujelay.

✪ **Hotel Rincón del Arco.** Ejército Nacional 66, 29200 San Cristóbal de las Casas, Chi. ☎ **967/8-1313.** Fax 967/8-1568. 36 units. TV TEL. $42 double. MC, V. Free parking.

This well-run hotel has comfortable rooms at a good price. The original section of this former colonial-era home is built around a small interior patio and dates from 1650. Rooms in this part are spacious with tall ceilings and carpet over hardwood floors. The adjacent new section faces a large grassy yard with a view of the mountains. These rooms are nicely furnished and come with beds covered in thick handsome bedspreads made in the family factory. Some are furnished in antiques, others in colonial style. Some have small balconies; all have fireplaces. In fact, if this hotel were a bit closer to the plaza, the rooms would be much more expensive. Consider it a value. Owner José Antonio Hernández is eager to make your stay a good one. There's a restaurant just behind the lobby. The hotel offers special discounted prices to students, but make arrangements in advance and be able to show university identification. The hotel is 8 blocks northeast of the main plaza at the corners of Ejército Nacional and V. Guerrero.

INEXPENSIVE

Casa de Huéspedes Margarita. Real de Guadalupe 34, 29200 San Cristóbal de las Casas, Chi. ☎/fax **967/8-0957.** 24 units, none with bathroom. $7.50 single; $10 double. AE, MC, V.

This inexpensive place offers rooms arranged around a courtyard where the young backpackers congregate. The rooms have sagging mattresses and bare light bulbs hanging from the ceiling; the shared bathrooms are only fair. Margarita's also has horse rentals and offers tours to the nearby ruins and to the Sumidero Canyon near Tuxtla Gutiérrez. You'll find this lodging 1½ blocks east of the plaza between avenida B. Domínguez and Colón.

Hotel Don Quijote. Colón 7, 29200 San Cristóbal de las Casas, Chi. ☎ **967/8-0920.** Fax 967/8-0346. 24 units. TV. $25 double. MC, V. Free secured parking 1 block away.

The small rooms here are crowded with furniture and closets are small, but the rooms are well lit, carpeted, and coordinated with warm, beautiful textiles handwoven in the family factory. All have two double beds with lamps over them, private tiled bathrooms, and plenty of hot water. It's 2½ blocks east of the plaza, near the corner of Colón.

✪ **Hotel El Paraíso.** Av. 5 de Febrero 19, 29200 San Cristóbal de las Casas, Chi. ☎ **967/8-0085.** 13 units. TEL. $35 double. AE, MC, V.

This is a safe haven from busloads of tour groups. Rooms, which have patchwork bedcovers and reading lights, are lovely but small; some even have a ladder to a loft holding a second bed. The entire hotel is decorated in terra-cotta and blue, with beautiful wooden columns and beams supporting the roof. The restaurant may be the best in town.

Hotel Palacio de Moctezuma. Juárez 16, 29200 San Cristóbal de las Casas, Chi. ☎ **967/8-0352** or 967/8-1142. Fax 967/8-1536. 42 units. TV TEL. $24 double. No credit cards. Free limited parking.

Near the plaza, this three-story hotel is filled with bougainvillea and geraniums. Freshcut flowers tucked around tile fountains are a hallmark of this hotel. The rooms have coordinated drapes and bedspreads, red carpeting, and modern tiled showers. Alas, they are very cold in winter. Two suites have a TV and refrigerator. Overstuffed couches face a large fireplace in the lobby bar, and the cozy restaurant looks out on the interior courtyard. On the third floor is a solarium with comfortable tables and chairs and great city views. The hotel is 3½ blocks southeast of the main plaza at the corner of Juárez and León.

Hotel Plaza Santo Domingo. Utrilla 35, 29200 San Cristóbal de las Casas, Chi. ☎ **967/8-1927.** Fax 967/8-6514. 30 units. TV TEL. $20 double. MC, V. Limited parking.

This hotel, established in 1992, is ideally situated—close to the Santo Domingo Church, near the bustling market area. Rooms are nicely furnished and carpeted. Each comes with a small closet and small desk below the TV, which is set high on the wall. Bathrooms are trimmed in blue-and-white tile, and the sink area is conveniently placed outside the shower area. A large and pleasant indoor dining room is off the lobby, along with a smaller patio dining area and a large bar. This is one of the few places near Santo Domingo and the market where you can get a good meal and use clean rest rooms.

Hotel Posada de los Ángeles. Calle Francisco Madero 17, 29200 San Cristóbal de las Casas, Chi. ☎ **967/8-1173** or 967/8-4371. Fax 967/8-2581. 20 units. TV TEL. $32 double. AE, MC, V.

Vaulted ceilings and skylights make this three-story hotel seem much larger and brighter than many others in the city. Rooms have either two single or two double beds, and the bathrooms are large, modern, and immaculately clean; windows open onto a pretty courtyard with a fountain. The rooftop sundeck is a great siesta spot.

✪ **Hotel Real de Valle.** Real de Guadalupe 14, 29200 San Cristóbal de las Casas, Chi. ☎ **967/8-0680.** Fax 967/8-3955. 36 units. $20 double. No credit cards.

The 24 new rooms in the back three-story section have new bathrooms, big closets, and a brown-and-cream decor. In addition to a rooftop solarium, you'll find a small cafeteria and an upstairs dining room with a big double fireplace.

WHERE TO DINE

San Cristóbal is not known for its cuisine, but you can eat well at several restaurants. **El Fogon de Jovel,** below, is the place to try typical Chiapanecan fare. Also, if you are interested, you might come across some local dishes, including tamales, *butifarra* (a type of sausage), and *pox* (pronounced "posh," it's a distilled sugar-and-corn drink similar to aguardiente). For baked goods, try the **Panadería Mercantil** at Mazariegos 17 (☎ **967/8-0307**). It's open Monday through Saturday from 8am to 9:30pm and Sunday from 9am to 9pm.

MODERATE

El Fogón de Jovel. 16 de Septiembre 11. ☎ **967/8-1153**. Main courses $4–$8. No credit cards. Daily 12:30–10pm. CHIAPANECAN.

The waiters here wear local costumes, and walls are hung with Guatemalan and Chiapanecan prints and folk art. Each dish and regional drink is explained on the menu, which is available in English. A basket of warm handmade tortillas with six filling condiments arrives before the meal. Among the specialties are corn soup, Chiapas-style mole, pork or chicken in adobo (a delicious rich chile sauce), and pipián, a dish of savory chile-and-tomato sauce served over chicken. For a unique dessert try the *changleta*, which is half of a sweetened, baked chayote—so delicious you may want two. Cooking classes for small groups can be arranged, but make reservations well in advance. The restaurant is only a block northwest of the plaza at the corner of Guadalupe Victoria/Real de Guadalupe and 16 de Septiembre.

✪ **El Paraíso.** Av. 5 de Febrero 19 (in the Hotel El Paraíso). ☎ **967/8-0085**. Breakfast $2.25–$3.25; main courses $4–$12. AE, MC, V. INTERNATIONAL

This is my favorite restaurant in San Cristóbal; just about anything is good here except for the Swiss rarebit. The cuts of meat are especially tender, the margaritas especially dangerous (one is all it takes). Specialties include the Swiss cheese fondue for two, the Eden salad, and the brochette. This small, quiet restaurant is where locals go for a splurge. It's two blocks from the main plaza.

Madre Tierra. Insurgentes 19. ☎ **967/8-4297**. Main courses $2–$6; comida corrida $6. No credit cards. Restaurant daily 8am–9:45pm (comida corrida served after noon). Bakery Mon–Sat 9am–8pm; Sun 9am–noon. INTERNATIONAL/VEGETARIAN.

For vegetarians and nonvegetarians alike, Madre Tierra is a good place for a cappuccino and pastry or an entire meal. The comida corrida is very filling, or try the chicken curry, lasagna, and fresh salads. The bakery specializes in whole-wheat breads, pastries, pizza by the slice, quiche, grains, granola, and dried fruit. The restaurant serves the bakery's goods and other delicious fare in an old mansion with wood-plank floors, long windows looking onto the street, and tables covered in colorful Guatemalan jaspe. Madre Tierra is 3½ blocks south of the plaza.

INEXPENSIVE

Café el Puente. Real de Guadalupe 55. No phone. Breakfast $1.75–$2.50; soups and salads $1–$2; pastries 75¢–$2. Mon–Sat 7am–11pm. MEXICAN/AMERICAN.

Ex-Californian Bill English has turned an old mansion into a cafe/cultural center where tourists and locals can converse, take Spanish classes, arrange a homestay, leave a message on the bulletin board, and send and receive faxes. How's that for a one-stop place? The cafe takes up the main part of the building and a weaver's shop and travel agency are to the side. Movies are presented nightly in an interior patio and meeting room. It's the kind of place you return to often: for fresh waffles and coffee in the morning, for an inexpensive lunch or dinner of brown rice and vegetables. The long bulletin board is well worth checking out if you're looking for a ride, a place to stay, or information on out-of-the-way destinations. It's 2½ blocks east of the plaza between Dujelay and Cristóbal Colón.

Emiliano's Moustache. Crescencio Rosas 7. ☎ **967/8-7246**. Comida corrida $2.50; taco plates $4–$6; main courses $3–$6. No credit cards. Daily 8am–midnight. MEXICAN/TACOS.

Like any right-thinking tourist, I initially avoided this place on account of its unpromising name and some cartoonlike charro figures by the door. But a conversation with some local folk overruled my prejudice and tickled my sense of irony. Sure enough, when I went in, the place was crowded with *Coletos* enjoying the restaurant's highly popular comida corrida and delicious tacos, and there was not a foreigner in sight. The daily menu is posted by the door for inspection; if it isn't appealing, you can choose from a menu of taco plates (a mixture of fillings cooked together and served with tortillas and a variety of hot sauces). Any Mexican will be quick to confess that Mexico is a nation of *taqueros:* A good taco is much appreciated. Here, you can pick from the menu of taco plates, which are quite filling, or ask for an order of traditional tacos such as tacos al pastor.

Normita's. Av. Juárez 6 at Dr. Jose Flores. No phone. Breakfast $2–$2.50; comida corrida $3.25; pozole $2; tacos $1. No credit cards. Daily 7am–11pm (comida corrida served 1:30–7pm). MEXICAN.

Normita's is famous for its pozole, a hearty chicken-and-hominy soup to which you add a variety of things. It also offers cheap, dependable, short-order Mexican mainstays. It's an informal "peoples" restaurant; the open kitchen takes up one corner of the room and tables are scattered in front of a large paper mural of a fall forest scene from some faraway place. It's 2 blocks southeast of the plaza.

Restaurant Tuluc. Insurgentes 5. ☎ **967/8-2090.** Breakfast $1.50–$2.50; main course $3–$4; comida corrida $3. No credit cards. Daily 7am–10pm (comida corrida served 1–5pm). MEXICAN/INTERNATIONAL.

A real bargain with its popular comida corrida, Tuluc also has that rarity of rarities in Mexico: a nonsmoking section. The house specialty is the filete Tuluc, a beef fillet wrapped around spinach and cheese served with fried potatoes and green beans. The Chiapaneco breakfast is a filling quartet of juice, toast, two Chiapanecan tamales, and your choice of tea, coffee, cappuccino, or hot chocolate. Tuluc is 1½ blocks south of the plaza between Cuauhtémoc and Francisco Léon.

COFFEEHOUSES

Since Chiapas-grown coffee is highly regarded, it's natural to find a proliferation of coffeehouses here. Most are concealed in the nooks and crannies of San Cristóbal's side streets. Try **Cafe La Selva,** Crescencio Rosas 9 (☎ 967/8-7244), for coffee served in all its varieties and brewed from organic beans (and well known for its baked goods), open daily from 9am to 11pm. Or for the more traditional style cafe where locals meet to talk over the day's news, try **Café San Cristóbal,** Cuauhtémoc 1 (☎ 967/8-3861), open Monday through Saturday from 9am to 10pm and Sunday from 9am to 9pm.

SAN CRISTÓBAL AFTER DARK

San Cristóbal is blessed with a wide variety of nightlife species, both resident and migrating. There is a lot of live music, which is surprisingly good and varied. The bars/restaurants are cheap—none charges a cover, only one charges a minimum tab. And they are easy to get to: You can hit all the places mentioned below without setting foot in a cab. Weekends are best, but any night is good.

El Cocodrilo. Plaza 31 de Marzo. ☎ **967/8-0871.** MC, V. Live music nightly.

El Cocodrilo, in the Hotel Santa Clara on the main plaza, is a good place to start the evening off. The band begins to play at 9. They do a lot of cover tunes of the Beatles and Santana, but they put their own stamp on the music. A typical thing they might do is play a rock 'n' roll standard to a reggae beat and mix in some funk riffs. The live music shuts down at 11pm.

La Margarita. Real de Guadalupe 34. No phone. No credit cards. Live music daily.

Starting at 9:30 you can catch flamenco at this popular restaurant bar, a block and a half from the plaza. The band consists of two guitarists, congas, and bass. It plays flamenco-style music with a lot of flare, if not all the passion of real flamenco. As the night progresses, they might get into some Latin jazz. You can't go wrong here unless you are in the mood to dance. The live music ends between 11:30 and midnight.

Las Velas. Madero 14. ☎ **967/8-7584.** $2.50 minimum tab. No credit cards. Live music nightly. ROCK/REGGAE/ROCK EN ESPAÑOL.

Bands here play with a rougher edge than the one at El Cocodrilo. Some get into Latin beats and "rock en Español," which is increasingly gaining a foothold all over the world. The place is designed in a way that guarantees it to be crowded. The cost of admission if you are male is to be frisked for weapons, but this is more for setting the ambiance than actual security. All the locals I spoke with said nothing has ever happened here or at any other of the bars that would warrant such a practice. Las Velas appeals to a younger crowd than most of these places. Live music between 11pm–1am.

Latino's. Mazarriegos 19. ☎ **967/8-2083.** No credit cards.

A large dance floor and a really impressive nine-piece house band playing salsa and merengue are an invitation to dance. This was the best band I heard in San Cristóbal. The place fills up on weekends with people of all ages, and everybody dances. Live music Mon–Sat 10pm–2am.

Madre Tierra. Insurgentes 19 (above the restaurant). ☎ **967/8-4297.** No credit cards. BLUES/ROCK.

This would be the place to close out an evening. Here both the crowd and the band are looser than at other places. One comes here more for the society and the bohemian setting than the music. The band specializes in blues, reggae, rock—just about anything that has a slow, steady bass line, and a solid down beat. The place is unpretentious, the music is loud, and the mostly young crowd friendly. It closes when the last person leaves—sometimes around 6 o'clock in the morning. Open nightly.

ROAD TRIPS FROM SAN CRISTÓBAL

Several individuals in town offer excursions to nearby villages (see "Nearby Maya Villages & Countryside," above) and those farther away. Strangely, except where noted otherwise, the cost of the trip includes a driver but does not necessarily include either a bilingual guide or guided information of any kind. You pay extra for those services, so if you want to be informed while taking a tour, be sure to ask if the tour is merely transportation or if it includes a knowledgeable guide as well.

RUINS OF TONINÁ   The Maya ruins of Toniná ("house of rocks") are 2 hours from San Cristóbal and 8½ miles east of Ocosingo. Dating from the Classic period, the terraced site covers an area of at least 9 square miles. Extensive excavations are under way here during the dry season.

As early as A.D. 350, Toniná emerged as a separate dynastic center of the Maya and has the distinction of having the last recorded date of the long count yet found (A.D. 909) on a small stone monument. The date signifies the end of the Classic period. Another stone discovered here, dated A.D. 711, depicts the captured King Kan-Xul of Palenque (the younger brother of Chan-Bahlum and the son of King Pacal); the portrait shows him with his arm tied by a rope but still wearing his royal headdress. Recently a huge stucco panel was unearthed picturing the Lord of Death holding Kan-Xul's head, confirming long-held suspicions that the king died at Toniná.

At the moment there are no signs to guide visitors through the site, so you're on your own. The caretaker can also show you around (in Spanish), after which a tip is appreciated. Ask at the **Casa de Huéspedes Margarita** in San Cristóbal (see "Where to Stay," above) about guided trips to Toniná (four-person minimum). The trip

Chiapas Highlands

To Misol–Ha & Palenque ↖

Tila
Tumbalá
Agua Azul

← To Pichucalco & Villahermosa

195

Huitiupán
Simojovel
Yajalón
Chilón
El Bosque
Bachajón
Temo
Jitotol
Pantelhó
Bochil
Chalchihuitán
Magdalenas
Ocosingo
Soyaló
San Pedro Chenalhó
Cancuc
Toniná
San Andrés Larráinzar
Mitontic
Abasolo
Ixtapa
Tenejapa
Oxchuc
Zinacantán
San Juan Chamula △ Tzontehuitz
Huitepec
Altamirano
← To Chiapa de Corzo & Tuxtla Gutiérrez
San Cristóbal de las Casas
El Arcotete
Huixtán
Ecatepec
Grutas de San Cristóbal
Chanal
Villa de Chiapilla
190
Teopisca
Amatenango del Valle
→ To Comitán
0   12.5 mi. / 20 km
N
↓ To Las Rosas & Venustiano Carranza

SA-0044

includes the services of a bilingual driver, a tour of the site, lunch, and a swim in the river. From November through February, you'll see thousands of swallows swarming near the ruins.

You can go on your own by bus to Ocosingo and from there take a taxi to the ruins, but have the taxi wait for your return. The ruins are open daily from 8am to 5pm; admission is $2.

PALENQUE, BONAMPAK & YAXCHILÁN   Many visitors to San Cristóbal want to visit the ruins of Palenque near Villahermosa and the Bonampak and Yaxchilán ruins on Mexico's border with Guatemala. A trip to Palenque can be accomplished in a long day-trip from San Cristóbal, but I don't recommend it because Palenque really should be savored. Bonampak and Yaxchilán are easier to see from Palenque.

For arranging these trips from San Cristóbal, I highly recommend **ATC Tours and Travel,** located across from El Fogón restaurant, calle 5 de Febrero 15 at the corner of 16 de Septiembre (☎ **967/8-2550;** fax 967/8-3145). The agency has bilingual guides and good vehicles. See the Palenque section, below, for details on Bonampak and camping overnight at Yaxchilán; see "Outdoor Sports, Adventure Travel & Wilderness Trips" in chapter 3 for other ATC regional tours focusing on birds and orchids, textiles, hiking, and camping.

If you're considering a day-trip to the archaeological site of Palenque using ATC (mentioned above) or a similar travel agency, here's how your tour will be arranged. You start at 7 or 8am and within 3 hours reach the Agua Azul waterfalls, where there's a 1½-hour stop to swim. From there it's another 1½-hour drive to Palenque. You'll have about 2 hours to see the site. If your group agrees, you can skip the swim and have more time at Palenque. It'll be a minimum 16-hour day and cost about $80 per person with a minimum of four people traveling.

CHINCULTIC RUINS, COMITÁN & MONTEBELLO NATIONAL PARK

Almost 100 miles southeast of San Cristóbal, near the border of Guatemala, is the Chincultic archaeological site and Montebello National Park, with **16 multicolored lakes** and exuberant pine-forest vegetation. Forty-six miles from San Cristóbal is Comitán, a pretty hillside town of 40,000 inhabitants known for its flower cultivation and a sugarcane-based liquor called *comitecho*. It's also the last big town along the Pan American Highway before the Guatemalan border.

The Chincultic ruins, a late Classic site, have barely been excavated, but the main **acropolis,** set high up against a cliff, is magnificent to see from below and worth the walk up for the view. After passing through the gate, you'll see the trail ahead; it passes ruins on both sides. Steep stairs leading up the mountain to the acropolis are flanked by more unexcavated tree-covered ruins. From there, you can gaze upon the distant Montebello Lakes and miles of cornfields and forest. The paved road to the lakes passes six lakes, all different colors and sizes, ringed by cool pine forests; most have parking lots and lookouts. The paved road ends at a small restaurant. The lakes are best seen on a sunny day, when their famous brilliant colors are optimal.

Most travel agencies in San Cristóbal offer a daylong trip that includes the lakes, the ruins, lunch in Comitán, and a stop in the pottery-making village of Amatenango del Valle. If you're driving, follow Highway 190 south from San Cristóbal through the pretty village of Teopisca and then through Comitán; turn left at La Trintaria, where there's a sign to the lakes. After the Trintaria turnoff and before you reach the lakes, there's a sign pointing left down a narrow dirt road to the Chincultic ruins.

3 Palenque

89 miles SE of Villahermosa; 143 miles NE of San Cristóbal

The ruins of Palenque look out over the jungle from a tall ridge, which projects from the base of steep mountains also swathed in jungle. It is a dramatic sight colored by the mysterious and ancient feel of the ruins themselves. The temples here are in the classic style with tall, high-pitched roofs crowned with elaborate combs. Inside many are representations in stone and plaster of the rulers and their gods, which give evidence of a cosmology that is and perhaps will remain impenetrable to our understanding. This is one of the grand archaeological sites of Mexico.

Five miles from the ruins is the town of Palenque. There you can find lodging and food and make travel arrangements. Transportation between the town and ruins is cheap and convenient.

ESSENTIALS

GETTING THERE & DEPARTING   By Plane   The new airport has service to various destinations via **Aerocaribe** (☎ 934/5-0618): Cancún (five flights/week); Mérida (two nonstop flights/week); San Cristóbal (four nonstop flights/week); Tuxtla (five flights/week—two nonstop). There is one flight per week to Oaxaca with a stop in Tuxtla, and two flights per week requiring a change of planes. Mexico City (five flights/week) requires changing planes. Aerocaribe is a subsidiary of **Mexicana** (☎ 800/531-7921).

By Car   The 143-mile trip from San Cristóbal to Palenque takes 5 to 6 hours and passes through lush jungle and mountain scenery. Take it easy, though, since potholes and other hindrances occur. Highway 186 from Villahermosa is in good condition,

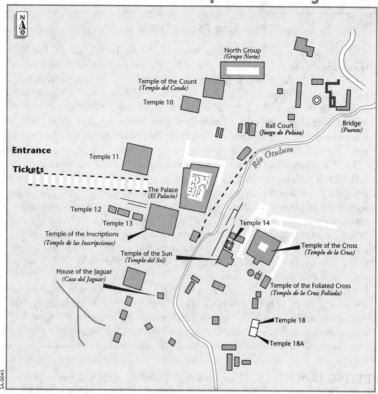

and the trip from there should take about 2 hours. Expect military roadblocks and cursory inspection of your travel credentials and perhaps your vehicle.

By Bus The two first-class bus stations are about a block apart from each other. Both are on Palenque's main street between the main square and the turnoff for the ruins. The smaller company, **Transportes Rodolfo Figueroa,** offers good first-class bus service to/from San Cristóbal and Tuxtla (four/day—5 hr. to San Cristóbal, 6½ to Tuxtla). Cristóbal Colon offers service to those destinations as well as to Campeche (six/day, 5 hr.), Villahermosa (nine/day, 2 hr.), and Mérida (two/day, 9 hr.).

VISITOR INFORMATION The **State Tourism Office** (☎/fax **934/5-0356**) is a block before the main square, where avenida Juárez intersects Abasolo. The office is open Monday through Saturday from 8:30am to 9pm.

CITY LAYOUT At one end of avenida Juárez, the main street, is the **main plaza,** at the other is the impossible-to-miss **Maya statue.** To the right of the statue is the entrance to La Cañada, to the left is the road to the ruins, straight ahead past the statue is the airport and the highway to Villahermosa. The distance between the main square and the monument is a half mile.

La Cañada, a restaurant-and-hotel zone, is a small area tucked into the rain forest. Here, you'll find shaded, unpaved streets, a few small hotels and restaurants, and stands of artists who carve and paint. Aside from the main plaza area, this is the best location for travelers without cars, since the town is within a few blocks and the buses that run to the ruins pass by La Cañada.

King Pacal's Tomb

The great stone hieroglyphic panels found inside the **Temple of the Inscriptions** contain the dynastic family tree of King Pacal (most of the panels are in the National Anthropological Museum in Mexico City). The temple is famous for the tomb, or crypt, of Pacal that the archaeologist Alberto Ruz Lhuller discovered in its depths in 1952. Ruz's discovery of the tomb is considered by Mayanist scholars to be among a handful of great discoveries in the Maya world. Ruz's own grave site is opposite the Temple of the Inscriptions, on the left as you enter the park.

Pacal began building the temple less than a decade before he died at age 80 in A.D. 683. It took Ruz and his crew four seasons of digging to clear out the rubble designed to conceal the crypt containing the remains of King Pacal. The crypt itself is 80 feet below the floor of the temple and was covered by a monolithic sepulchral slab 12½ feet long and 7 feet wide, engraved with a depiction of Pacal falling backwards from the land of the living into the underworld. Four men and a woman were left at the entrance to the crypt when it was sealed so that they could accompany Pacal on his journey through the underworld. Unless you're claustrophobic, you should definitely visit the tomb. The way down is lighted, but the steps can be slippery due to condensed humidity. Carved inscriptions on the sides of the crypt (which visitors can't see) show the ritual of the funerary rites carried out at the time of Pacal's death and portray the lineage of Pacal's ancestors, complete with family portraits.

GETTING AROUND   The cheapest way to get back and forth from the ruins is on the white **VW buses,** which depart from the terminal at avenidas Juárez and Allende every 10 minutes from 6am to 6pm. The buses pass La Cañada and hotels along the road to the ruins, but they may not stop if they're full. Roads are not good, making these buses the best method for getting to the ruins.

FAST FACTS   The telephone area code is **934.** As for the **climate,** Palenque's high humidity is downright oppressive in the summer, especially after rain showers. During the winter, the damp air can be chilly in the evenings. Rain gear is important any time of year.

EXPLORING PALENQUE

The real reason for being here is the ruins; although they can be toured in a morning, many people savor Palenque for days. There are no must-see sights in town. The La Cañada area west of town (see "City Layout," above) is a pleasant spot for a leisurely lunch and for browsing through Maya reproductions made by local artists.

PARQUE NACIONAL PALENQUE

The archaeological site of Palenque underwent several changes in 1994, which culminated in the opening of a new **museum/visitor center** on the highway to the ruins. The complex includes a large parking lot, a refreshment stand serving snacks and drinks, and several shops. The museum, although not large, is worth the time it takes to see it; it's open Tuesday through Sunday from 10am to 5pm. It contains well-chosen and artistically displayed exhibits, including the jade contents of recently excavated tombs. (The museum was robbed in 1996, but most of the jade pieces have been recovered.) Explanatory texts, in both Spanish and English, explain the life and times of the magnificent city of Palenque. New pieces are constantly being added as they are uncovered in ongoing excavations.

The **main entrance,** about a mile beyond the museum, is at the top of a hill at the end of the paved highway. There, you'll find a large parking lot, a refreshment stand, a ticket booth, and several shops. Among the vendors selling souvenirs by the parking lot are Lacandón Indians wearing white tunics and hawking bows and arrows.

Admission to the ruins is $2; free on Sunday. There's a $4 charge for each video camera used. Parking at the main entrance and at the visitor center is free. The site and visitor-center shops are open daily from 8am to 4:45pm; King Pacal's crypt is open daily from 10am to 4pm.

TOURING THE RUINS   Pottery found during the excavations shows that people lived in this area as early as 300 B.C. During the Classic period (A.D. 300 to 900), the ancient Maya city of Palenque was a ceremonial center for the high priests; the civilization peaked at around A.D. 600 to 700.

When John Stephens visited the site in the 1840s, the cleared ruins you see today were buried under centuries of accumulated earth and a thick canopy of jungle. The dense jungle surrounding the cleared portion still covers yet unexplored temples, which are easily discernible in the forest even to the untrained eye. But be careful not to drift too far from the main paths. Recently there have been two incidents where a single tourist went into the rain forest to inspect unreconstructed temples and was assaulted.

Of all the ruins in Mexico open to the public, this is the most haunting because of its majesty and sense of the past. Scholars have unearthed names of the rulers and their family histories, putting visitors on a first-name basis with these ancient people etched in stone. Read about it in *A Forest of Kings,* by Linda Schele and David Friedel (William Morrow, 1990).

As you enter the ruins from the entrance, the building on your right is the **Temple of the Inscriptions,** named for the great stone hieroglyphic panels found inside. Just to your right as you face the Temple of the Inscriptions is **Temple 13,** which is receiving considerable attention from archaeologists. Recently, the burial of another richly adorned personage was discovered here, accompanied in death by an adult female and an adolescent. These remains are still being studied, but the treasures are on display in the museum.

When you're back on the main pathway, the building directly in front of you will be the **Palace,** with its unique watchtower. A pathway between the Palace and the Temple of the Inscriptions leads to the **Temple of the Sun, Temple of the Foliated Cross, Temple of the Cross,** and **Temple 14.** This group of temples, now cleared and in various stages of reconstruction, was built by Pacal's son, Chan-Bahlum, who is usually shown on inscriptions as having six toes. Chan-Bahlum's plaster mask was found in Temple 14 next to the Temple of the Sun. Archaeologists have recently begun probing the depths of the Temple of the Sun in search of **Chan-Bahlum's tomb.** Little remains of this temple's exterior carving. Inside, however, behind a fence, a carving of Chan-Bahlum shows him ascending the throne in A.D. 690. The panels, which are still in place, depict Chan-Bahlum's version of his historic link to the throne.

The North Group, to the left of the Palace, is also undergoing restoration. Included in this area are the **Ball Court** and **the Temple of the Count,** so named because Count Waldeck camped there in the 19th century. The explorer John Stephens camped in the Palace when it was completely tree- and vine-covered, spending sleepless nights fighting off mosquitoes. At least three tombs, complete with offerings for the underworld journey, have been found here. The lineage of at least 12 kings has been deciphered from inscriptions left at this marvelous site.

Just past the North Group is a small building (once a museum) now used for storing the artifacts found during the restorations. It is closed to the public. To the right of the building, a stone bridge crosses the river, leading to a pathway down the hillside to the new museum. The path is lined with rocks and has steps in the steepest areas, leading past the **Cascada Motiepa,** a beautiful waterfall that creates a series of pools perfect for cooling weary feet. Benches are placed along the way as rest areas, and some small temples have been reconstructed near the base of the trail. In the early morning and evening, you may hear monkeys crashing through the thick foliage by the path; if you keep noise to a minimum, you may spot wild parrots as well. Walking downhill (by far the best way to go), it will take you about 20 minutes to reach the main highway. The path ends at the paved road across from the museum. The colectivos going back to the village will stop here if you wave them down.

WHERE TO STAY

The fanciest hotel in town (the Hotel Misión Park Inn Palenque) gets too many complaints for me to recommend it. And with the recent addition of some upscale hotels, it faces a lot of competition. Transportation to and from the ruins is easy from just about any hotel and should not be of concern when choosing one.

MODERATE

✪ **Chan-Kah Ruinas.** Km 30 Carretera Palenque, 29960 Palenque, Chi. ☎ **934/ 5-1100.** Fax 934/5-0820. 72 units. A/C or FAN. $75 double. AE, MC, V. Free parking.

This hotel is a collection of comfortable, roomy bungalows that offer privacy, quiet, and the surroundings of a tropical forest. Some are air-conditioned, some are not. The grounds are beautifully laid out around a stream, and there is a large, inviting pool with rock floor. The hotel is on the road to the ruins midway between the ruins and the town. Christmas prices may be higher than those quoted here, and you may be quoted a higher price if you reserve a room in advance from the United States.

Hotel Ciudad Real. Carretera a Pakal-Na, 29960 Palenque, Chi. (reservations made in San Cristóbal). ☎ **967/8-0187.** E-mail: 103144.2762@compuserve.com. 72 units. A/C TV TEL. $80 double. AE, DC, DISC, MC, V. Free secured parking.

This is your best bet for creature comforts and modern convenience. The hotel is on the highway to the airport. The rooms are large, well lit, and comfortably furnished. Facilities include a pool, bar, restaurant, and travel agency.

Hotel Maya Tucan. Carretera Palenque, 29960 Palenque, Chi. ☎ **934/5-0290.** Fax 934/ 5-0337. 60 units. A/C TV TEL. $53 double. AE, MC, V. Free secured parking.

Get a room in back and you will have a view of the hotel's natural pond. All rooms come with double beds. They are adequate in size and cheerfully decorated. The A/C is quiet and gets the job done. Facilities include pool, restaurant, bar, and sometimes a discotheque—when large tour groups are present (which might bear asking about before checking in). The grounds are well kept in a tropical fashion, and scarlet macaws kept by the hotel fly about the parking lot. The Maya Toucan is a stone's throw from the Ciudad Real on the highway to the airport.

Hotel Maya Tulipanes. Calle Merle Green 6, 29960 Palenque, Chi. ☎ **934/5-0201.** Fax 934/5-1004. 50 units. A/C TV TEL. $49 double. AE, MC, V. Free parking.

This hotel tries hard to remind you why you have come to Palenque—Maya statues, carvings, and paintings fill the hallways and public areas in this rambling, overgrown, but comfortable two-story hotel. And because the hotel is in the Cañada, it has a definite tropical-forest feel; the dark shade is a cool respite from the sun's glare. Rooms vary from section to section, so ask to see rooms in different parts of the hotel. A new addition to the hotel is a small pool.

INEXPENSIVE

Hotel Casa de Pakal. Av. Juárez 10, 29960 Palenque, Chi. ☎ **934/5-0443**. 15 units. A/C. $22 double. AE, MC, V.

This bright, relatively new four-story hotel might be the best bargain in town if you don't have a car. The air-conditioning is strong and quiet. The rooms are a little small but far brighter and cleaner than those at nearby establishments, and they come with one double and one single bed covered with chenille spreads. A good restaurant is on the premises. The hotel is a half block east of the main plaza.

Hotel Kashlan. Cinco de Mayo 105, 29960 Palenque, Chi. ☎ **934/5-0297**. Fax 934/5-0309. 59 units. A/C or FAN. $20–$31 double. No credit cards.

This is the closest hotel to the bus station and is a dependable establishment. The clean rooms have interior windows opening onto the hall, marble-square floors, nice bedspreads, tile bathrooms, small vanities, and luggage racks. Show owner Ada Luz Navarro your Frommer's book and you'll receive a discount. Higher prices are for rooms with air-conditioning (there are 29, and some of the new ones are quite comfortable); ceiling fans (in 30 rooms) are powerful. The hotel restaurant features vegetarian food. Trips around the region, including to Agua Azul and Misol Ha, can also be arranged at the hotel.

WHERE TO DINE

avenida Juárez is lined with many small restaurants, none of which is exceptional. There are a couple in the main plaza, some on the road to the ruins, and a couple in the Cañada that I do like.

MODERATE

✪ **La Chiapaneca.** Carretera Palenque Ruinas. ☎ **934/5-0363**. Main courses $7–$9. AE, MC, V. Daily 8am–noon. MEXICAN.

Palenque's traditional best restaurant continues to serve top-notch regional cuisine in a pleasant tropical setting. Though it has a thatched roof, the dining room is large and refined. The pollo Palenque (chicken with potatoes in a tomato-and-onion sauce) is a soothing choice; save room for the flan. Mexican wines are served by the bottle. La Chiapaneca is about a 20-minute walk from the Maya statue toward the ruins.

La Selva. Km 0.5 Carretera Palenque Ruinas. ☎ **934/5-0363**. Main courses $4–$17. AE, MC, V. Daily 8am–noon. MEXICAN/INTERNATIONAL.

La Selva (jungle) offers fine dining in a large, outdoor space under a beautiful thatched roof and beside well-tended gardens. The menu includes seafood, freshwater fish, steaks, and enchiladas. The most expensive thing on the menu, and something you find very rarely, is Pigua—a freshwater lobster that is caught in the large rivers of southeast Mexico. These can get quite large—the size of small regular lobsters. I especially liked the fish stuffed with shrimp or the mole enchiladas.

INEXPENSIVE

Chan-Kah Centro. Juárez 2. ☎ **934/5-0318**. Breakfast $2.25–$3; comida corrida $3–$4; main courses $4–$7. AE, MC, V. Daily 7am–11pm. MEXICAN.

This attractive hotel restaurant is the most peaceful place to eat in town. The waiters are extremely attentive, and the food is fairly well prepared (avoid the tough beef, though). The second-story bar overlooks the main plaza—you can have your meal served there. The restaurant is on the west side of the main plaza at the corner of Independencia and Juárez.

La Cañada. Prolongacion Av. Hidalgo 12. ☎ **934/5-0102.** Main courses $5–$9. No credit cards. Daily 7am–10pm. MEXICAN.

This palapa restaurant tucked into the jungle is one of the best in town, though it never seems crowded. Though the dining room has a dirt floor, the place is spotless, the service attentive, and the food good, if not exceptional. Try one of the local specialties such as pollo mexicano or bean soup. This restaurant is in the Hotel La Cañada.

○ **Restaurant Maya.** Av. Independencia s/n. ☎ **934/5-0042.** Breakfast $3–$4; main courses $4–$5. No credit cards. Daily 7am–11pm. MEXICAN/STEAKS.

The most popular place in town among tourists and locals, Restaurant Maya is opposite the northeast corner of the main plaza near the post office. Breezy and open, it's managed by a solicitous family. At breakfast, there are free refills of very good coffee. Try the tamales or any of the other local dishes or traditional Mexican fare.

ROAD TRIPS FROM PALENQUE
SPECTACULAR WATERFALLS AT AGUA AZUL & CASCADA DE MISOL HA
The most popular excursion from Palenque is a day-trip to the Misol Ha waterfall and Agua Azul. Misol Ha is about 12 miles from Palenque off the road to Ocosingo. Visitors swim in the waters below the falls and scramble up slippery paths to smaller falls beside the large one, which drops about 90 feet before spraying its mist on the waters below. There's a small restaurant run by the ejido cooperative that owns the site. Entrance costs around $1.25. Approximately 24 miles beyond Misol Ha on the same road are the **Agua Azul waterfalls,** a truly spectacular series of beautiful cascades tumbling into a wide river. Seeing both is a full-day trip. Visitors can picnic and relax (bring something to sprawl on), swim, or clamber over the slippery cascades and go upstream for a look at the jungle encroaching the water. Agua Azul is prettiest after 3 or 4 consecutive dry days; heavy rains can make the water very murky. Check with guides or other travelers about the water quality before you decide to go. Cost to enter is around $3. Trips can be arranged through **Viajes Shivalva Tours, Viajes Toniná** (see "Bonampak & Yaxchilán," below), or the **Hotel Kashlan.** Another way to go is to take a **special colectivo** from the same company that runs colectivos to the ruins. You can find them on Juárez by the main plaza. They make the trip to Agua Azul and the Cascada de Misol Ha every day, with two round-trips beginning at 10am; the last van departs Agua Azul for Palenque at 6:30pm. Be sure to check this with the drivers. They may wait until six or eight people want to go, or decide to make only one trip.

BONAMPAK & YAXCHILÁN: RUINS & RUGGED ADVENTURE   Intrepid travelers may wish to consider the 2-day excursion to the Maya ruins of Bonampak and Yaxchilán. The ruins of Bonampak, southeast of Palenque on the Guatemalan border, were discovered in 1946. The **mural** discovered on the interior walls of one of the buildings is the greatest battle painting of pre-Hispanic Mexico. Reproductions of the vivid murals found here are on view in the Regional Archaeology Museum in Villahermosa.

You can fly or drive to Bonampak. Several tour companies offer a 2-day (minimum) tour by four-wheel–drive vehicle to within 4½ miles of Bonampak. You must walk the rest of the way to the ruins. After camping overnight, you continue by river to the extensive ruins of the great Maya city, Yaxchilán, famous for its highly ornamented buildings. Bring rain gear, boots, a flashlight, and bug repellent. All tours include meals but vary in price ($80 to $120 per person); some take far too many people for comfort (the 7-hr. road trip can be unbearable).

The two most reputable tour operators in Palenque are Viajes Shivalva and Viajes Toniná. **Viajes Shivalva** is at calle Merle Green 1 (Apdo. Postal 237), 29960 Palenque, Chi. (☎ **934/5-0411;** fax 934/5-0392). Office hours are Monday through Friday from 7am to 3pm. A branch office is now open a block from the zócalo (main plaza) at the corner of Juárez and Abasolo (across the hall from the State Tourism Office). It's open Monday through Saturday from 9am to 9pm (☎ **934/5-0822**). **Viajes Toniná** is at calle Juárez 105 (☎ **934/5-0384**).

Information about **ATC Tours and Travel** can be obtained at their office in San Cristóbal de las Casas. This agency has a large number of clients (and thus the best chance of making a group) and offers a large number of tours. Among its offerings is a 1-day trip to the ruins of Tikal in Guatemala for five people; another tour takes in Yaxchilán, Bonampak, and Tikal with a minimum of four people. Though rustic, they have the only permanent overnight accommodations at Yaxchilán at their Posada del Río Usumacinta. Their headquarters are in San Cristóbal (see "San Cristóbal de las Casas," above). See also "Outdoor Sports, Adventure Travel & Wilderness Trips" in chapter 3 for U.S. companies offering this trip.

12 Cancún

Can over 2,000,000 people a year be wrong? The sheer number of annual travelers to Cancún underscores the magnetic appeal of this resort on Mexico's eastern coast.

Cancún is home to an impressive array of hotels set alongside translucent turquoise water and blinding white sand—all bordered by mangrove jungles. It is the peak of Caribbean splendor with the added lure of ancient cultures evident in all directions. As the showcase of Mexico to the world, Cancún is the unrivaled favorite place for travelers to this country—Mexico's calling card of breathtaking natural beauty and the depth of its thousand-year-old history.

But Cancún is also a modern mega-resort. Even a traveler feeling apprehensive about visiting foreign soil will feel completely at home and at ease here. English is spoken, dollars are accepted, roads are well paved and lawns are manicured. Malls are the mode for shopping and dining, and you would swear some hotels are larger than a small town. Travelers feel comfortable in Cancún. You do not need to spend a day getting your bearings, as you immediately see familiar names for dining, shopping, nightclubbing, and sleeping.

You may have heard that in 1974 a Mexican government computer analyst picked Cancún for tourism development for its ideal mix of elements to attract travelers—he was right on. It's actually an island, a 14-mile long sliver of land connected to the Mexican mainland by two bridges and separated from it by an expansive lagoon. (Cancún means Golden Snake in the Mayan language.)

In addition to attractions of its own, Cancún is a convenient distance from the traditional, less-expensive resorts of **Isla Mujeres, Playa del Carmen,** and **Cozumel.** The **Maya ruins** at Tulum, Chichén-Itzá, and Cobá are within driving distance.

You will run out of vacation days before you run out of things to do in Cancún. Snorkeling, jet skiing, jungle tours, and visits to ancient Maya ruins or modern ecological theme parks are among the most popular diversions. There are a dozen malls with name-brand and duty-free (better-than-U.S.-priced European goods) shops, plus over 350 restaurants and nightclubs. Over 20,000 hotel rooms in the area offer something for every taste and every budget.

Cancún's luxury hotels have pools so spectacular you may find it tempting to remain poolside, but don't. Put aside some time to simply gaze into the water the color of a dream and wriggle your toes in the powdery fine, absolutely white sand. This is, after all, what put Cancún on the map.

1 Orientation

GETTING THERE

BY PLANE Several airlines connect Cancún with other Mexican and Central American cities. **Aeromexico** (☎ 800/237-6639 in the U.S., 91/800-90999 toll-free within Mexico, or 98/84-1186 in Cancún) offers direct service from Atlanta, Houston, Miami, New Orleans, and New York, plus connecting service via Mexico City from Dallas, Los Angeles, and San Diego. **Mexicana** (☎ 800/531-7921 from the U.S., 91/800-36654 toll-free within Mexico, 98/86-0123, or 98/86-0124 in Cancún) flies in from Chicago, Denver, Guadalajara, Los Angeles, San Antonio, San Francisco, and San Jose via Mexico City, with nonstop service from Miami and New York. Regional carriers **Aerocozumel** (☎ 98/84-2000, affiliated with Mexicana) fly from Cozumel, Havana, Mexico City, and other points within Mexico. The regional airline **Aviateca** (☎ 800/327-9832 in the U.S.; 98/84-3938) flies from Cancún to Mérida, Villahermosa, Tuxtla Gutiérrez, Guatemala City, and Flores (near Tikal). **Taesa** (☎ 800/328-2372 in the U.S.; 98/87-4314) has flights from Tijuana, Chetumal, Mérida, and other cities within Mexico.

You'll want to confirm departure times for flights back to the States; here are the Cancún airport numbers of the major international carriers: **American** (☎ 98/84-0129), **Continental** (☎ 98/86-0006), and **Northwest** (☎ 98/86-0044 or 98/86-0046).

Most major **car-rental firms** have outlets at the airport, so if you're renting a car, consider picking it up and dropping it off at the airport to save on airport-transportation costs. Another way to save money is to arrange for the rental before you leave your home country. If you rent on the spot after arrival, the daily cost of a rental car will be around $65 to $75 for a VW Beetle. Major rental services include **Avis** (☎ 800/331-1212 in the U.S., or 98/86-0238); **Budget** (☎ 800/527-0700 in the U.S., or 98/84-5011); **Dollar** (☎ 800/800-4000 or 98/86-0159); **National** (☎ 800/328-4567 in the U.S., or 98/86-4493); and **Hertz** (☎ 800/654-3131 in the U.S. and Canada, or 98/84-4692). The Hotel Zone is about a 15-minute drive from the airport along wide, well-paved roads.

Rates for a **taxi** cost around $20 to $25, depending on your destination. Special **vans** (colectivos) run from Cancún's international airport into town. Tickets are purchased as you exit the building and cost about $8. There's expensive minibus transportation from the airport to the Puerto Juárez passenger ferry that takes you to Isla Mujeres. The least expensive way to get to the ferry is to take the colectivo to the bus station in downtown Cancún and from there bargain for a taxi.

There is no colectivo service returning to the airport from Ciudad Cancún or the Zona Hotelera, so you'll have to hire a taxi. Ask at your hotel what the fare should be.

BY CAR From Mérida or Campeche, take Highway 180 east to Cancún. This is mostly a winding, two-lane road, which branches off into the express toll road 180D between Izamal and Nuevo Xcan. Nuevo Xcan is approximately 26 miles from Cancún. Mérida is about 52 miles, and it takes about 3½ hours to drive between the two cities.

BY BUS Cancún's **bus terminal** (☎ 98/84-4804 or 98/84-4352) is in downtown Ciudad Cancún at the intersection of Avenidas Tulum and Uxmal. All out-of-town buses arrive here. Buses run to Playa del Carmen, Tulum, Chichén-Itzá and other nearby beach and archaeological zones, as well as to other points within Mexico. Greenline buses offer packages (*paquetes*) to popular nearby destinations. The package to Chichén-Itzá departs at 9am and includes the round-trip air-conditioned bus ride, with video, for the 3-hour trip, entry to the ruins, 2 hours at the ruins, lunch, a brief stop for shopping, and a visit to a cenote. The tour returns to Cancún by 5pm. The trip to Xcaret (which is much cheaper than the same trip offered at the Xcaret terminal office), includes round-trip transportation and entry to the park; the tours depart daily at 9 and 10am and return at 5pm. Package trips to Cozumel depart at 8, 9, and 10am (returning at 5pm) and include round-trip, air-conditioned bus transportation to and from Playa del Carmen and the ferry ticket to and from Cozumel.

VISITOR INFORMATION

The State Tourism Office (☎ 98/84-8073) is centrally located downtown on the east side of avenida Tulum 26 next to Banco Inverlat, immediately left of the Ayuntamiento Benito Juárez building between Avenidas Cobá and Uxmal. It's open daily from 9am to 9pm. A second tourist information office, the **Fondo Mixto of Cancún** (☎ **98/84-3238** or 98/84-3438), is located on avenida Cobá at avenida Tulum, next to Pizza Rolandi, and is open Monday through Friday from 9am to 9pm. Hotels and their rates are listed at each office, as are ferry schedules.

Pick up free copies of the monthly *Cancún Tips* booklet and a seasonal tabloid of the same name. Both are useful and have fine maps. The publications are owned by the same people who own the Captain's Cove restaurants, a couple of sightseeing boats, and time-share hotels, so the information (though good) is not completely unbiased.

CITY LAYOUT

There are two Cancúns: **Isla Cancún** (Cancún Island) and **Ciudad Cancún** (Cancún City). The latter, on the mainland, has restaurants, shops, and less-expensive hotels, as well as all the other establishments that make life function—pharmacies, dentists, automotive shops, banks, travel and airline agencies, car-rental firms—all within an area about 9 blocks square. The city's main thoroughfare is **avenida Tulum.** Heading south, avenida Tulum becomes the highway to the airport and to Tulum and Chetumal on farther south; heading north, it intersects the highway to Mérida and the road to Puerto Juárez and the Isla Mujeres ferries.

The famed **Zona Hotelera** (alternately called the **Zona Turística**) stretches out along Isla Cancún, a sandy strip 14 miles long, shaped like a "7." It's now joined by bridges to the mainland at the north and south ends. avenida Cobá from Cancún City becomes Paseo Kukulkán, the island's main traffic artery. Cancún's international airport is just inland from the south end of the island.

FINDING AN ADDRESS The street-numbering system is left over from Cancún's early days. Addresses are still given by the number of the building lot and by the *manzana* (block) or *supermanzana* (group of city blocks). The city is still relatively small, and the downtown section can easily be covered on foot.

On the island, addresses are given by kilometer number on Paseo Kukulkán or by reference to some well-known location.

2 Getting Around

BY TAXI Taxi prices in Cancún are clearly set by zone, although keeping track of what's in which zone can take some doing. Within the downtown area the cost is about $1; within any other zone, about $2 per cab ride (not per person). Between zones runs around $3, and if you cross two zones, that'll cost $3.50. Settle on a price in advance, or check at your hotel, where destinations and prices are generally posted.

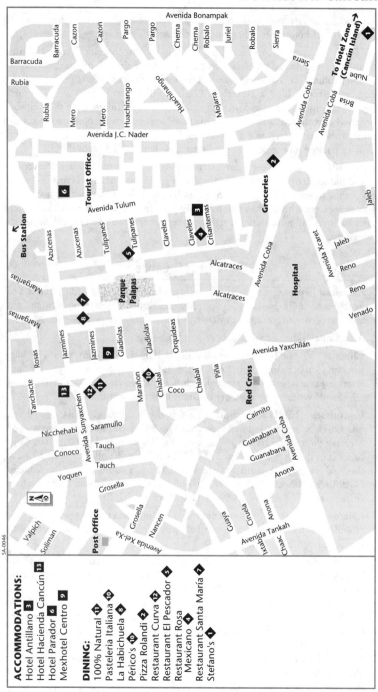

Downtown Cancún

Avenida Bonampak

Barracuda · Cazon · Cazon · Pargo · Pargo · Cherna · Cherna · Robalo · Juriel · Robalo · Sierra

Barracuda

Rubia

To Hotel Zone (Cancún Island)

Nube · Brisa · Sierra

Avenida Cobá · Avenida Cobá · Avenida Cobá

Rubia · Mero · Mero · Huachinango · Huachinango · Mojarra

Avenida J.C. Nader

Tourist Office

Jaleb · Avenida Xcaret · Jaleb

Groceries

Avenida Tulum

Bus Station

Azucenas · Azucenas · Tulipanes · Tulipanes · Claveles · Claveles · Crisantemas

Reno · Reno · Venado

Alcatraces

Avenida Coba

Hospital

Parque Palapas

Alcatraces

Margaritas · Margaritas

Rosas · Jazmines · Jazmines · Gladiolas · Gladiolas · Orquideas

Avenida Yaxchilán

Tanchacte · Marañon · Chiabal · Coco · Chiabal · Piña

Red Cross

Nicchehabi · Saramullo · Caimito

Conoco · Tauch · Guanabana

Avenida Sunyaxchen · Tauch · Guanabana

Avenida Coba

Yoquen · Grosella · Anona

Valpich · Soliman

Post Office

Grosella · Nancen · Guaya · Ciruela · Anona · Avenida Tankah

Avenida Xel-Xa · Ixtabad · Chaac

SA-0046

ACCOMMODATIONS:
Hotel Antillano **3**
Hotel Hacienda Cancún **13**
Hotel Parador **6**
Mexhotel Centro **9**

DINING:
100% Natural **11**
Pastelería Italiana **10**
La Habichuela **8**
Périco's **10**
Pizza Rolandi **2**
Restaurant Curva **12**
Restaurant El Pescador **5**
Restaurant Rosa Mexicano **4**
Restaurant Santa María **7**
Stefano's **1**

Trips to the airport from most zones cost $8. Taxis can also be rented by the hour for about $10 per hour for travel around the city and Hotel Zone.

BY BUS   In town, almost everything is within walking distance. Ruta 1 and Ruta 2 ("Hoteles") city buses travel frequently from the mainland to the beaches along avenida Tulum (the main street) and all the way to Punta Nizuc at the far end of the Zona Hotelera on Isla Cancún. Ruta 8 buses go to Puerto Juárez/Punta Sam for ferries to Isla Mujeres. They stop on the east side of avenida Tulum. Both these city buses operate between 6am and midnight daily. Beware of private buses along the same route; they charge far more than the public ones. The public buses have the fare amount painted on the front; at publication the fare was 2.5 pesos (30¢).

BY MOPED   Mopeds are a dangerous way to cruise around through the very congested traffic. Rentals start at $25 for a day. A credit-card voucher is required as security for the moped. You should receive a crash helmet (it's the law) and instructions on how to lock the wheels when you park. Read the fine print on the back of the rental agreement regarding liability for repairs or replacement in case of accident, theft, or vandalism.

FAST FACTS: Cancún

American Express   The local office is at avenida Tulum 208 and Agua (☎ **98/ 84-1999** or 98/84-5441) and is open Monday through Friday from 9am to 2pm and 4 to 6pm, and Saturday from 9am to 1pm. It's 1 block past the Plaza México.

Area Code   The telephone area code is **98.**

Climate   It's hot but not overwhelmingly humid. The rainy season is May through October. August through October is the hurricane season, which brings erratic weather. November through February can be cloudy, windy, somewhat rainy, and even cool, so a sweater is handy, as is rain protection.

Consulates   The **U.S.** Consular Agent is in the Playa Caracol 2, 3rd level, no. 320-323, km 8.5 bulevar Kukulkán (☎ **98/83-0272**). The office is open Monday through Friday from 9am to 2pm and 3 to 6pm. The **Canadian** Consulate is in the Plaza México 312 (☎ **98/84-3716**). The office is open Monday through Friday from 10am to 2pm. The **UK** has a consular office in Cancún (☎ **98/85-1166,** ext. 462; fax: 98/85-1225). Irish, Australian, and New Zealand citizens should be referred to their embassies in Mexico City.

Crime   Car break-ins are just about the only crime, and they happen frequently, especially around the shopping centers in the Zona Hotelera. VW Beetles and Golfs are frequent targets.

Currency Exchange   Most banks are downtown along avenida Tulum and are usually open Monday through Friday from 9:30am to 5pm, and many now have automatic teller machines for after-hour cash withdrawals. In the Hotel Zone you'll find banks in the Plaza Kukulkán and next to the convention center. There are also many *casas de cambio* (exchange houses). Downtown merchants are eager to change cash dollars, but island stores don't offer good exchange rates. Avoid changing money at the airport as you arrive, especially at the first exchange booth you see—its rates are less favorable than any in town or others farther inside the airport concourse.

Drugstores   Next to the Hotel Caribe Internacional, **Farmacia Canto,** avenida Yaxchilán 36, at Sunyaxchen (☎ **98/84-9330**), is open 24 hours. American Express, MasterCard, and Visa are accepted.

Emergencies To report an emergency dial ☎ **06,** which is supposed to be similar to 911 in the United States. For first aid, the **Cruz Roja** (Red Cross; ☎ **98/84-1616**) is open 24 hours on avenida Yaxchilán between Avenidas Xcaret and Labná, next to the Telemex building. **Total Assist,** a small nine-room emergency hospital with English-speaking doctors at Claveles 5, SM 22, at avenida Tulum (☎ **98/84-1058** or 98/84-1092), is also open 24 hours. American Express, MasterCard, and Visa are accepted. Desk staff may have limited English. *Urgencias* means "Emergencies."

Luggage Storage/Lockers Hotels will generally tag and store excess luggage while you travel elsewhere.

Newspapers/Magazines For English-language newspapers and books, go to **Fama** on avenida Tulum between Tulipanes and Claveles (☎ **98/84-6586**); open daily from 8am to 10pm. American Express, MasterCard, and Visa are accepted.

Police To reach the **police** (Seguridad Pública), dial ☎ **98/84-1913** or 98/84-2342. The *Procuraduria del Consumidor* (consumer protection agency) is opposite the Social Security Hospital at avenida Cobá 10 (☎ **98/84-2634** or 98/84-2701).

Post Office The **main post office** is at the intersection of Avenidas Sunyaxchen and Xel-Ha (☎ **98/84-1418**). It's open Monday through Friday from 8am to 7pm and Saturday from 9am to 1pm.

Safety There is very little crime in Cancún. People in general are safe late at night in touristed areas; just use ordinary common sense. As at any other beach resort, don't take money or valuables to the beach. See "Crime," above.

Swimming on the Caribbean side presents a danger from undertow. See "The Beaches" in "Beaches & Water Sports," below, for flag warnings.

Seasons Technically, high season is December 15 to Easter; low season is May through November, when prices are reduced 10% to 30%. Some hotels are starting to charge high-season rates between July and September when travel is high for Mexican national, European, and school-holiday visitors. There's a short low season in January just after the Christmas–New Year's holiday.

Telephones The phone system for Cancún changed in 1992. The area code is now **98** (it was 988). All local numbers now have six digits instead of five; all numbers begin with 8. If a number is written 988/4-1234, when in Cancún you must dial 84-1234.

3 Where to Stay

Island hotels are stacked along the beach like dominoes, with almost all offering clean, modern facilities available from numerous chains. Extravagance is the byword in the more recently built hotels, many of which are awash in a sea of marble and glass. Some hotels, however, while exclusive, affect a more relaxed attitude. The water is placid on the upper end of the island facing Bahía de Mujeres, while beaches lining the long side of the island facing the Caribbean are subject to choppier water and crashing waves on windy days (for more information on swimming safety, see "Beaches & Water Sports," later in this chapter). Be aware that the farther you go south on the island, the longer it takes (20 to 30 min. in traffic) to get back to the "action spots," which are primarily between the Plaza Flamingo and Punta Cancún on the island and along avenida Tulum on the mainland. On Cancún Island, almost all major hotel chains are represented, so this list can be viewed as a representative summary, with a select number of notable places to stay. Ciudad Cancún offers independently owned, smaller, and less-expensive stays. Prices are lower during the off-season (Apr through Nov).

The hotel listings in this chapter begin on Cancún Island and finish in Cancún City, where bargain lodgings are available. Parking is available at all island hotels.

CANCÚN ISLAND
VERY EXPENSIVE

✪ **Caesar Park Beach & Golf Resort.** Km 17 Paseo Kukulcán, Retorno Lacandones, 77500 Cancún, Q. Roo. ☎ **800/228-3000** in the U.S., or 98/81-8000. Fax 98/81-8080. 427 units. A/C MINIBAR TV TEL. High-season standard rooms $275–$350 double; Royal Beach Club $300–$485 double; $375–$500 suite. Low-season standard rooms $200–$300; Royal Beach Club $370–$290; $550–$350 suite. AE, DC, MC, V.

A true resort in every sense of the word, the Caesar Park, which is affiliated with the Westin chain and is a member of the Leading Hotels of the World, opened in 1994 on 250 acres of prime Cancún beachfront property with two restaurants, seven interconnected pools, an 18-hole par-72 golf course across the street, and a location that gives every room a sea view. Like the sprawling resort, rooms are grandly spacious and immaculately decorated in an austere Japanese style. Marble floors and bathrooms throughout are softened with area rugs and pastel furnishings. All rooms have sea views and some have both sea and lagoon views. Other amenities in each luxurious room include robes, house shoes, hair dryers, and safe-deposit boxes. Suites have coffeemakers. Royal Beach Club guests enjoy nightly cocktails and each Tuesday a manager's cocktail party on the patio. The elegant Royal Beach Club rooms are set off from the main hotel in two- and three-story buildings (no elevators) and have their own check-in and concierge service.

Dining: Spices Restaurant serves the cuisines of Mexico, Argentina, and Italy, while **Serenita** offers selections of Japanese and seafood cuisine.

Amenities: 18-hole, par-72 golf course; seven interconnected swimming pools with a swim-up bar; two whirlpools; two lighted tennis courts; water-sports center; large fully equipped gym with daily aerobics; massage; sauna. A Kids Club is part of the gym program. Greens fee is $75 for 18 holes for guests and $100 for nonguests; carts cost $22. Laundry and room service, ice machine on each floor, concierge, tour desk, beauty salon, gift shop and boutiques, golf clinic, car rental.

✪ **Camino Real Cancún.** Av. Kukulkán, 77500 Punta Cancún (Apdo. Postal 14), Cancún, Q. Roo. ☎ **800/722-6466** in the U.S., or 98/83-0100. Fax 98/83-1730. 381 units. A/C MINIBAR TV TEL. High season $265–$415 double; Camino Real Club $220–$305 double; $1,600 suite. Low season $185–$305 double; Camino Real Club $200 double; $1,320 suite. AE, DC, MC, V. Daily fee for guarded parking adjacent to hotel.

▮ Important Note on Hotel Prices

Cancún's hotels, even in budget and moderately priced hotels, generally set their rates in dollars, so they are immune to any swings in the peso. Travel agents and wholesalers always have air/hotel packages available, with Sunday papers often advertising inventory-clearing packages. There are also several all-inclusive properties in Cancún, which allow you to have a fixed-cost vacation, if this is desirable. Note that the price quoted to you when you call a hotel's reservation number from the United States may not include Cancún's 12% tax. Prices can vary considerably at different times of the year, so it pays to consult a travel agent or shop around.

Isla Cancún (Zona Hotelera)

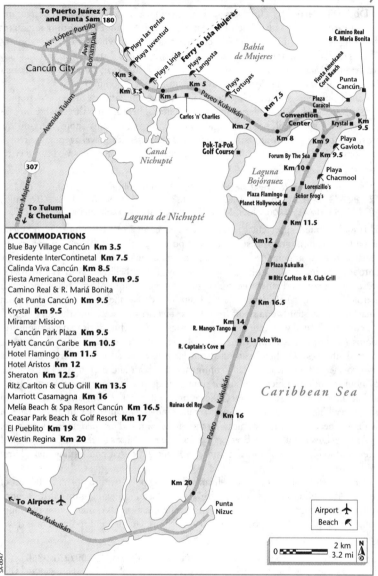

ACCOMMODATIONS

Blue Bay Village Cancún **Km 3.5**
Presidente InterContinetal **Km 7.5**
Calinda Viva Cancún **Km 8.5**
Fiesta Americana Coral Beach **Km 9.5**
Camino Real & R. Mariá Bonita
   (at Punta Cancún) **Km 9.5**
Krystal **Km 9.5**
Miramar Mission
   Cancún Park Plaza **Km 9.5**
Hyatt Cancún Caribe **Km 10.5**
Hotel Flamingo **Km 11.5**
Hotel Aristos **Km 12**
Sheraton **Km 12.5**
Ritz Carlton & Club Grill **Km 13.5**
Marriott Casamagna **Km 16**
Melía Beach & Spa Resort Cancún **Km 16.5**
Ceasar Park Beach & Golf Resort **Km 17**
El Pueblito **Km 19**
Westin Regina **Km 20**

On 4 acres right at the tip of Punta Cancún, the Camino Real is among the island's most appealing places to stay. The rooms are elegantly outfitted with pink breccia-marble floors, tropical high-backed raffia easy chairs, and drapes and spreads in soft pastel colors. Some rooms in the new 18-story Camino Real Club have elegant Mexican decor, while standard rooms in this section are much like rooms in the rest of the resort. Master suites have expansive views, large dining tables with four chairs, and hot tubs on the balconies. Camino Real Club guests receive a complimentary full breakfast daily in the Beach Club lobby, as well as complimentary cocktails and snacks there each evening. Lower priced rooms have lagoon views.

Dining/Diversions: Three restaurants include a seafood-specialties restaurant; indoor casual dining with flame-broiled meat; and an elegant evening-only restaurant featuring Mexican cuisine. There's a children's menu at the more casual restaurants. There's an Italian night on Wednesday and a Mexican Grill Party on Friday. The lobby bar features Mexican music nightly from 5:30 to 7:30pm, and the sea-view **Azucar Disco** swings into action Monday through Saturday at 9:30pm.

Amenities: Freshwater pool; private saltwater lagoon with sea turtles and tropical fish; private beach; sailing pier; water-sports center. There are also three lighted tennis courts, beach volleyball, boutiques, gift shops, barber and beauty shops, state-of-the-art fitness center with steam bath, laundry and room service, travel agency, car rental, in-room safe-deposit boxes, baby-sitting (with advance notice), medical service, 24-hour room service, and massages.

✪ **Fiesta Americana Coral Beach.** Km 9.5 Paseo Kukulkán, 77500 Cancún, Q. Roo. ☎ **800/343-7821** in the U.S., or 98/83-2900. Fax 98/83-3173. 602 units. A/C MINIBAR TV TEL. High season $405 double. Low season $260 double. AE, DC, MC, V.

This sophisticated, spectacular hotel, which opened in 1991, has a lot to recommend it: perfect location, gracious service, grand public areas, a full range of water sports, beach activities, and indoor tennis. It's enormous in a Mexican way and grandly European in its lavish public halls and lobby. It's embellished with elegant dark-green granite from France, deep-red granite from South Africa, black-and-green marble from Guatemala, beige marble from Mexico, a canopy of stained glass from Guadalajara, and hardwood floors from Texas. The elegance seeps into the guest rooms, which are decorated with more marble, area rugs, and tasteful Mexican decorations. All rooms have balconies facing the ocean. Master suites have double vanities, dressing room, bathrobes, whirlpool bathtubs, and large terraces; all rooms have hair dryers. Two concierge floors feature daily continental breakfast and evening cocktails, and a 24-hour reception-cashier. Two junior suites are equipped for guests with disabilities.

The hotel's great Punta Cancún location (opposite the convention center, and within walking distance of shopping centers and restaurants) has the advantage of facing the beach to the north, meaning the surf is calm and just perfect for swimming.

Dining/Diversions: The five-star **La Jolla** serves Mexican fare, the **Coral Reef** offers seafood and international cuisine, and there's a casual pool dining area. There are five bars.

Amenities: A 660-foot-long free-form swimming pool; swim-up bars; 1,000 feet of beach; three indoor tennis courts with stadium seating; gymnasium with weights, sauna, and massage; water-sport rentals on the beach; business center; tennis pro shop; fashion and spa boutiques; beauty and barber shops; laundry and room service; travel agency; car rental; massage.

Krystal Cancún. Km 7.5 Paseo Kukulkán, 77500 Cancún, Q. Roo. ☎ **800/231-9860** in the U.S., or 98/83-1133. Fax 98/83-1790. 322 units. A/C MINIBAR TV TEL. High season $210–$450 double. Low season $140–$170 double. AE, DC, MC, V.

The Krystal Cancún lies on Punta Cancún along with the Camino Real and the Hyatt Regency, near the Convention Center, shops, restaurants, and clubs. The Krystal uses lots of cool marble in its decor. The guest rooms, in two buildings, have an option of bed configurations, with drapes and spreads in earthy tones, and water views. The hotel's tap water is purified, and there are ice machines on every floor. The presidential suites have Jacuzzis. Club Krystal rooms come with in-room safe-deposit boxes, complimentary continental breakfast, and evening canapés and drinks; guests in those rooms also have access to the Club Lounge, a rooftop sun lounge with a whirlpool and concierge service.

Dining/Diversions: Among the hotel's four restaurants are two that have gained countrywide recognition for fine cuisine—**Bogart's,** a chic dining room with a Moroccan "Casablanca" theme, and the luxurious **Hacienda El Mortero,** a replica of a colonial hacienda featuring Mexican cuisine. The hotel also hosts theme nights throughout the week. In the evening there's live entertainment in the lobby bar. **Christine's,** one of the most popular discos in town, is open nightly.

Amenities: Swimming pool complex overlooking the Caribbean and a beach with fairly safe swimming; pharmacy; barber and beauty shop; boutiques and a silver shop; two tennis courts with an on-duty tennis pro; a racquetball court; a dive shop; and a fitness club with whirlpool, sauna, and massage facilities; laundry, room service, travel agency, car and moped rental.

✪ **Ritz-Carlton Hotel.** Retorno del Rey, off Km 13.5 Paseo Kukulkán, 77500 Cancún, Q. Roo. ☎ **800/241-3333** in the U.S. and Canada, or 98/85-0808. Fax 98/85-1015. 369 units. A/C MINIBAR TV TEL. High season $329–$369 double; $425–$4,000 suite. Low season $220–$250 double; $275–$3,200 suite. AE, MC, V. Free guarded parking.

On 7½ acres, the nine-story Ritz-Carlton has set the standard for excellence in Cancún and in Mexico. It is easily the island's most elegant hotel and a member of Leading Hotels of the World. The hotel has won countless recognitions and accolades for its impeccable service and stunning decor of stained glass, marble, and lush carpets. Fresh flowers are found throughout the property.

The spacious guest rooms are as sumptuous as the public areas. All rooms have safe-deposit boxes, electronic locks, and twice-daily maid service. Suites are large, and some have a private dressing area, two TVs, balconies, and 1½ bathrooms. In all rooms marble bathrooms have telephones, separate tubs and showers, lighted makeup mirrors, scales, robes, and hair dryers. Floors 8 and 9 are for Ritz-Carlton Club members and offer guests special amenities, including five minimeals a day. The hotel fronts a 1,200-foot white-sand beach, and all rooms overlook the ocean, pool, and tropical gardens. Special packages for golfing, spa, and weekend getaways are worth exploring.

Dining/Diversions: Of the five exceedingly stylish restaurants, **The Club Grill,** a fashionable English pub, is one of the best restaurants in the city (See "Where to Dine," below), offering grilled specialties, nightly entertainment, and a dance floor. The **Caribe Bar and Grill** is open for snacks during pool hours. The **Lobby Lounge** opens at 5pm daily offering tea and, later, live music between 7:30 and 11pm. This bar was the original home of proper tequila tastings, and features one of the world's most extensive menus of fine tequilas, plus Cuban cigars.

Amenities: On the beach, deluxe cabanas for two, with thickly cushioned lounges, are available just in front of the two connecting swimming pools (heated during the winter months) with Jacuzzi. For play, there are three lighted tennis courts and a fully equipped gym with Universal weight training and cardiovascular equipment, personal trainers, steam, sauna, and massage service. A Ritz Kids program offers supervised activities for children. Rounding out the offerings are a pharmacy/gift shop, exclusive shopping arcade, and beauty and barber shops. Laundry and dry cleaning, 24-hour room service, travel agency, and concierge are also available.

EXPENSIVE

Blue Bay Village Cancún. Km 3.5 Paseo Kukulkán, 77500 Cancún, Q. Roo. ☎ **800/BLUE-BAY** in the U.S., or 98/83-1725. Fax 98/83-1724. 220 units. A/C TV TEL. High season $280 double. Low season $180 double. Rates are all-inclusive. AE, DC, MC, V.

Blue Bay Village Cancún is a spirited yet relaxing all-inclusive resort for adults only. Surrounded by acres of tropical gardens, it's ideally located at the northern end of the Hotel Zone close to the major shopping plazas, restaurants and nightlife, and where the waters are calm for swimming. Comfortable, clean, and modern, guests have a choice of rooms in two sections: the central building features 72 rooms decorated in rustic wood, the main lobby, administrative offices, restaurants and Tequila Sunrise bar. The remaining nine buildings offer guests 148 rooms, featuring traditional Mexican decor with laguna, garden, and ocean views available. Nonsmoking rooms and wheelchair-accessible rooms are available upon request. All rooms feature satellite TV, private bathrooms with showers, and safe-deposit boxes. Blue Bay allows guests to use the amenities and facilities at their sister resort, the Blue Bay Club and Marina, located just outside of Ciudad Cancún, near the ferry to Isla Mujeres. There's a free bus and boat shuttle service provided between both Blue Bay resorts.

Keeping guests active is the obvious objective here, with two swimming pools, four Jacuzzis, windsurfing, kayaks, catamarans, boogie boards, complimentary snorkeling and scuba lessons in the swimming pool, a marina, an exercise room with daily aerobics classes, tennis court, bicycles, and a game room with pool and Ping-Pong tables.

All meals and drinks are included with the room price, served at one of four restaurants. Among them, **El Embarcadero** is an ocean-view restaurant serving buffet-style international cuisine. **La Largata** features natural, healthful breakfasts and a "snack bar" menu during the day, then an à la carte Italian menu for dinner. Their four bars include a video bar and disco. In addition, there are theme-night dinners, nightly shows, and live entertainment in their outdoor theater with capacity for 150 guests.

Marriott Casamagna. Km 20 Paseo Kukulkán, 77500 Cancún, Q. Roo. ☎ **800/228-9290** in the U.S., or 98/81-2000. Fax 98/81-2071. 443 units. A/C MINIBAR TV TEL. High season $225–$270 double; $350–$695 suite. Low season $135–$165 double; $300–$550 suite. Ask about available packages. AE, CB, DC, MC, V.

Luxury is this hotel's hallmark. Entering through a half circle of Roman columns, you pass through a long, domed foyer to a wide, lavishly marbled 44-foot-high lobby filled with plants. The lobby expands in three directions with wide, Mexican cantera-stone arches branching off outdoors, where columns vanish into shallow pools like Roman baths. Guest rooms have contemporary furnishings, tiled floors, and ceiling fans; most have balconies. All suites occupy corners and have enormous terraces, ocean views, and TVs in both the living room and the bedroom. All rooms have been remodeled.

Dining/Diversions: The hotel has four restaurants: La Capilla overlooks the pool and ocean and features an international menu; Las Isla serves light snacks and beverages poolside; the Bahia Club offers the same fare, only served on the beach; and the recently remodeled Mikado offers Japanese and Thai cuisine. The lobby bar features nightly mariachi music.

Amenities: Beach; swimming pool; two lighted tennis courts; health club with saunas, whirlpool, aerobics, and juice bar; beauty and barber shop; massage and facials available; laundry and room service; travel agency; car rental.

Presidente Inter-Continental Cancún. Km 7.5 Paseo Kukulkán, 77500 Cancún, Q. Roo. ☎ **800/327-0200** in the U.S., or 98/83-0200. Fax 98/83-2515. 298 units. A/C TV TEL. High season $215–$485 double. Low season $155–$450 double. AE, MC, V.

On the island's best beach facing the placid Bahia de Mujeres, the Presidente's location is tops. Cool and spacious, the Presidente sports a postmodern design with lavish marble and wicker accents and a strong use of color. Guests have a choice of two double beds or one king-size bed. All rooms have private balconies, tastefully simple unfinished pine furniture, and in-room safes. Sixteen rooms on the first floor have patios with outdoor whirlpool tubs. The club floors offer robes, magnified makeup mirrors, complimentary continental breakfast, evening drinks and canapés, 1 hour free use of the tennis court, complimentary use of the fitness club, and use of a private key-activated elevator. Two rooms are available for guests with disabilities and two floors are reserved for nonsmokers. The expansive pool has a pyramid-shaped waterfall, and is surrounded by cushioned lounge chairs. Coming from Cancún City, you'll reach the Presidente on the left side of the street before you get to Punta Cancún—it's behind the golf course and next to million-dollar homes.

Dining: The fine-dining **Mediterraneo** restaurant features foods from France, Greece, Italy, Spain, and Morocco. **El Caribeño,** a three-level palapa restaurant by the beach and pool, serves all meals. **Frutas y Flores** is a family-style coffee shop.

Amenities: Two landscaped swimming pools with a waterfall; whirlpools; fitness center; a great beach fronting the calm Bahía de Mujeres; lighted tennis courts; watersports equipment rental; marina; laundry and room service; travel agency; car rental.

Westin Regina Cancún. Km 20 Paseo Kukulkán, 77500 Cancún, Q. Roo. ☎ **800/ 228-3000** in the U.S., or 98/85-0086. Fax 98/85-0779. 385 units. A/C MINIBAR TV TEL. High season $245–$300 single or double. Low season $180–$220 single or double. AE, MC, V.

The strikingly austere but grand and beautiful architecture, immediately impressive with its elegant use of stone and marble, is the stamp of leading Latin American architect Ricardo Legorreta. The hotel is divided into two sections, the main hotel and the more exclusive six-story hot-pink tower section. Standard rooms are unusually large and beautifully furnished with cool, contemporary furniture. Those on the sixth floor have balconies and first-floor rooms have terraces. Rooms in the tower all have ocean or lagoon views, oodles of marble, furniture with Olinalá lacquer accents, Berber carpet area rugs, oak tables and chairs, and marble terraces with lounge chairs. Bear in mind that this hotel is a 15- to 20-minute ride from the "action" strip that lies between the Plaza Flamingo and Punta Cancún. Buses stop in front and taxis are readily available.

Dining/Diversions: Two restaurants—**Arrecifes** for elegant dining and **El Palmar** for casual dining, plus two bars, keep guests satisfied.

Amenities: Five swimming pools; three whirlpools; beach; two lighted tennis courts; gymnasium with Stairmaster, bicycle, weights, aerobics, sauna, steam, and massage; pharmacy/gifts; boutiques; beauty and barber shop; laundry and room service; baby-sitting; concierge; travel agency; car rental; purified tap water; and ice machine on each floor.

MODERATE

Calinda Viva Cancún. Km 8.5 Paseo Kukulkán, 77500 Cancún, Q. Roo. ☎ **800/221-2222** in the U.S., or 98/83-0800. Fax 98/83-2087. 210 units. A/C TV TEL. High season $145–$185 double. Low season $135 double. AE, MC, V.

From the street, this hotel looks like a blockhouse, but on the ocean side you'll find a small but pretty patio garden and Cancún's best beach for safe swimming. Its location is ideal, close to all the shops and restaurants clustered near Punta Cancún and the Convention Center. You have a choice of rooms with either lagoon or ocean view. The rooms are large and undistinguished in decor, but comfortable with marble floors and either two double beds or a king-size bed. Facilities include one swimming pool for adults and one for children, two lighted tennis courts, water-sports equipment rental, and a marina. The main restaurant is open for all meals. Two others, both beside the pool, serve drinks and light meals. They're joined by three bars.

Flamingo Cancún. Km 11.5 Paseo Kukulkán, 77500 Cancún, Q. Roo. ☎ **98/83-1544.** Fax 98/83-1029. 220 units. A/C TV TEL. High season $160 double. Low season $118 double. AE, MC, V. Free, unguarded parking across the street in the Plaza Flamingos.

The Flamingo seems to have been inspired by the dramatic, slope-sided architecture of the Camino Real, but the Flamingo is considerably smaller. The clean, comfortable, and modern guest rooms form a courtyard facing the swimming pool. A colorful open-air restaurant faces the pool, where guests lounge with a view of the Caribbean. The Flamingo is in the heart of the island hotel district, opposite the Flamingo Shopping Center and close to other hotels, shopping centers, and restaurants. A restaurant and snack bar are both open daily, and a lobby bar and pool bar offer libations.

Miramar Misión Cancún Park Plaza. Km 9.5 Paseo Kukulkán, 77500 Cancún, Q. Roo. ☎ **800/215-1333** in the U.S., or 98/83-1755. Fax 98/83-1136. 300 units. A/C MINIBAR TV TEL. $145 double. AE, DC, MC, V.

Each of the ingeniously designed rooms has partial views of the lagoon and ocean. Public spaces throughout the hotel have lots of dark wood, cream-beige stucco, red tile, and pastel accents. The big swimming pool is next to the beach. Rooms are on the small side but comfortable, with bamboo furniture offset by pastel-colored cushions and bedspreads; bathrooms have polished limestone vanities. In-room amenities include hair dryers and safe-deposit boxes.

Three restaurants serve cuisine of Mexico and the United States. There's live music nightly in the lobby bar, and a bar by the pool serves guests during pool hours. A nightclub also has live music for dancing from 9pm to 4am Tuesday through Sunday.

INEXPENSIVE

El Pueblito. Km 19.5 Paseo Kukulkán, 77500 Cancún, Q. Roo. ☎ **98/85-0422** or 98/85-0797. Fax 98/85-0422. 239 units. A/C TV TEL. High season $155 double. Low season $95–$130. AE, DC, MC, V.

Dwarfed by its ostentatious neighbors, El Pueblito nevertheless has several three-story buildings (no elevators) terraced in a V-shape down a gentle hillside toward the sea. A meandering swimming pool with waterfalls runs between the two series of buildings. Rooms have just been repainted and restyled with modern rattan furnishings, travertine marble floors, and large bathrooms. Many have balconies facing the pool or sea. Three restaurants and two bars are on the grounds. Minigolf and a water style make this an ideal place for families with children. The hotel is located towards the southern end of the island past the Caesar Park Resort.

Hotel Aristos. Km 12 Paseo Kukulkán (Apdo. Postal 450), 77500 Cancún, Q. Roo. ☎ **800/527-4786** in the U.S., or 98/83-0011. 244 units. A/C TV TEL. High season $100–$130 double. Low season $85 double. All-inclusive option for 3 meals and drinks, add $36 daily. AE, MC, V. Free, unguarded parking.

This was one of the island's first hotels. Rooms are neat and cool, with red-tile floors, small balconies, and yellow Formica furniture. All rooms face either the Caribbean or the paseo and lagoon; the best views (and no noise from the paseo) face the Caribbean side. The hotel has one restaurant and several bars and offers room and laundry service, a travel agency, and baby-sitting service. The central pool overlooks the ocean with a wide stretch of beach one level below the pool and lobby. You'll also find a marina with water-sports equipment and two lighted tennis courts. Beware of spring break here, when the hotel blares loud music poolside all day.

CANCÚN CITY
INEXPENSIVE

Hotel Antillano. Claveles 1 in the corner of Tulum, 77500 Cancún, Q. Roo. ☎ **98/84-1532.** Fax 98/84-1878. 48 units. A/C TV TEL. High season $60 double. Low season $40 double. MC, V.

A quiet and very clean choice, Hotel Antillano is close to the Ciudad Cancún bus terminal. Rooms overlook either avenida Tulum, the side streets, or the interior lawn and pool, with the latter being the most desirable since they are quieter. Each room has nicely coordinated furnishings, one or two double beds, a sink area separate from the bathroom, red-tile floors, and a small TV. There's a small bar to one side of the reception area and a travel agency in the lobby. The hotel offers guests use of its beach club on the island. Baby-sitting can be arranged. To find it from Tulum, walk west on Claveles a half block; it's opposite the Restaurant Rosa Mexicana. Parking is on the street.

Hotel Hacienda Cancún. Sunyaxchen 39-40, 77500 Cancún, Q. Roo. ☎ **98/84-3672.** Fax 98/84-1208. 40 units. A/C MINIBAR TV TEL. $35 double. AE, MC, V.

This extremely pleasing little hotel is another great value. The facade has been remodeled to look like a "hacienda" and all rooms were refurbished in 1997. The guest rooms are clean and plainly furnished but very comfortable, and all have two double beds and windows (but no views). There's a nice small pool and cafe under a shaded palapa in the back. The hotel is also a member of the Imperial Las Perlas beach club in the Zona Hotelera. To find it from avenida Yaxchilán, turn west on Sunyaxchen; it's on your right next to the Hotel Caribe International, opposite 100% Natural. Parking is on the street.

Hotel Parador. Tulum 26, 77500 Cancún, Q. Roo. ☎ **98/84-1043** or 98/84-1310. Fax 98/84-9712. 66 units. A/C TV TEL. High season $45 double. Low season $35 double. Ask about promotional rates. MC, V.

One of the most popular downtown hotels, the three-story Parador is conveniently located. Guest rooms are arranged around two long, narrow garden courtyards leading back to a pool (with separate children's pool) and grassy sunning area. The rooms are modern, each with two double beds, a shower, and cable TV. Help yourself to bottled drinking water in the hall. There's a restaurant/bar, plus it's next to Pop's restaurant, almost at the corner of Uxmal. Street parking is limited.

✪ Mexhotel Centro. Yaxchilán 31, SM 22, Cancún, Q. Roo. ☎ **98/84-3078.** Fax 888/594-6835 in the U.S. or 98/84-3478. 80 units. A/C TV TEL. High season $80 double. Low season $60 double. AE, MC, V.

The nicest hotel in Ciudad Cancún, the Mexhotel Centro has the warmth and style of a small hacienda when entering from the back; on the street side, it's been incorporated into a small shopping mall. The three stories of rooms (with elevator) front a lovely palm-shaded pool area with comfortable tables and chairs and a restaurant. Standard rooms are extra clean with muted decor, two double beds framed with wrought-iron headboards, large tile bathrooms with separate sink, desks, and over-bed reading lights. Although prices may seem high for the location, free privileges at the beach and pool facilities at its sister resort in the Hotel Zone make it a great bargain. The hotel is between Jazmines and Gladiolas catercorner from Perico's.

4 Where to Dine

The restaurant scene in Cancún is dominated by the known names of U.S.–based franchise chains—which really need no introduction. These include Hard Rock Cafe, Planet Hollywood, All Star Cafe, Rainforest Cafe, Tony Roma's, TGI Fridays, Ruth's Chris Steak House, and the gamut of fast-food burger places. The restaurants listed here are either locally owned, one-of-a-kind restaurants, or exceptional selections at area hotels.

CANCÚN ISLAND
VERY EXPENSIVE

✪ Club Grill. Ritz-Carlton Hotel, Km 13.5 Paseo Kukulkán. ☎ **98/85-0808.** Reser-vations required. Main courses $30–$50. AE, DC, MC, V. Tues–Sun 6–11pm. INTERNATIONAL.

Cancún's most elegant and stylish restaurant is also its best. Even rival restaurateurs give it an envious thumbs up. The gracious service starts as you enter the anteroom with its comfortable couches and chairs and selection of fine tequilas and Cuban cigars. It continues into the candlelit dining room with padded side chairs and tables shimmering with silver and crystal. Under the trained eye of chef de cuisine John Patrick Gray, elegant plates of peppered scallops, truffles, and potatoes in tequila sauce, grilled lamb, or mixed grill arrive without feeling rushed after the appetizer. The restaurant has both smoking and nonsmoking sections (a rarity in Mexico). A band plays romantic music for dancing from 8pm on. This is the place for that truly special night out. Dress code enforced. Gentlemen must wear long pants; no sandals for ladies or tennis shoes for gentlemen.

EXPENSIVE

Captain's Cove. Km 15 Paseo Kukulkán. ☎ **98/85-0016.** Main courses $16–$20; breakfast buffet $6.95. AE, MC, V. Daily 7am–11pm. INTERNATIONAL.

Though it sits almost at the end of Paseo Kukulkán, far from everything, the Captain's Cove continues to pack customers into its several dining levels. Diners face big open windows overlooking the lagoon and Royal Yacht Club Marina. During breakfast there's an all-you-can-eat buffet. Main courses of steak and seafood are the norm at lunch and dinner, and there's a menu catering especially to children. For dessert there are flaming coffees, crepes, and key lime pie. The restaurant is on the lagoon side opposite the Omni Hotel.

✪ **La Dolce Vita.** Km 14.6 Av. Kukulkán. ☎ **98/85-0150** or 98/85-0161. Reservations required for dinner. Main courses $10–$21. MC, V. Daily noon–midnight. ITALIAN.

Prepare to dine on some the best Italian food in Mexico. Now at its new location on the lagoon, and opposite the Marriott Casamagna, the casually elegant La Dolce Vita is even more pleasant and popular than its old garden location downtown. Appetizers include pâté of quail liver and carpaccio in vinaigrette, or watercress salad. You can order such pastas as green tagliolini with lobster medaillons, linguine with clams or seafood, or rigatoni Mexican-style (with chorizo, mushrooms, and chives) as an appetizer for half-price or as a main course for full-price. Other main courses include veal with morels, fresh salmon with cream sauce, scampi, and various fish.

La Fisheria. Playa Caracol, 2nd floor. ☎ **98/83-1395.** Main courses $6.50–$21. AE, MC, V. Daily 11am–11:30pm. SEAFOOD.

Patrons find a lot to choose from at this restaurant overlooking bulevar Kukulkán and the lagoon. The expansive menu offers shark fingers with a jalapeño dip, grouper fillet stuffed with seafood in a lobster sauce, Acapulco-style ceviche (in a tomato sauce), New England clam chowder, steamed mussels, grilled red snapper with pasta—you get the idea. The menu changes daily, but there's always *tikin xik*, that great Yucatecan grilled fish marinated in achiote sauce. And for those not inclined toward seafood, a wood-burning oven pizza might do, or perhaps one of the grilled chicken or beef dishes.

✪ **Lorenzillo's.** Km 10.5 Av. Kukulkán. ☎ **98/83-1254.** Main courses $8–$50. AE, MC, V. Daily 10am–11:30pm. SEAFOOD.

Live lobster is the overwhelming favorite here, and selecting your "dinner" out of the giant lobster tank is part of the appeal. Lorenzillo's sits on the lagoon under a giant palapa roof. A dock leads down to the main dining area, and when that's packed (which is often), a wharf-side bar handles the overflow. In addition to lobster—which comes grilled, steamed, or stuffed—good bets are the shrimp stuffed with cheese and wrapped in bacon, the Admiral's fillet coated in toasted almonds and a light mustard sauce, or the seafood-stuffed squid. Desserts include the tempting Martinique: Belgian chocolate with hazelnuts, almonds, and pecans, served with vanilla ice cream.

Mango Tango. Km 14.2 Paseo Kukulkán, opposite the Ritz-Carlton. ☎ **98/85-0303.** Main courses $6–$16; dinner show $25–$35. AE, MC, V. Daily 2pm–2am. INTERNATIONAL.

Mango Tango's made a name for itself with its floor shows (see "Cancún After Dark," below), but its kitchen is deserving of attention as well. Try the peel-your-own shrimp, Argentine-style grilled meat with chimichuri sauce, and other grilled specialties. The Mango Tango Salad has shrimp, chicken, avocado, red onion, tomato, and mushrooms on mango slices. Entrees includes Mango Tango rice with seafood and fried bananas. The Creole gumbo comes with lobster, shrimp, and squid.

✪ **María Bonita.** Hotel Camino Real, Punta Cancún. ☎ **98/83-0100,** ext. 8060 or 8061. Main courses $10–$25. AE, DC, MC, V. Daily 6:30–11:30pm. REGIONAL/ MEXICAN/NOUVELLE MEXICAN.

Enjoy Mexico at its very best—its music, food, and atmosphere—in a stylish setting that captures the essence of Mexico with every bite and glance. Overlooking the water, the interior is divided by cuisine—La Cantina Jalisco includes an open colorful Mexican kitchen (with pots and pans on the wall) and Tequila bar (with more than 50 different tequilas); the Salon Michoacán in the center features food from that state's cuisine; and the Patio Oaxaca is on the lower level. The menu includes foods from these three states, as well as the best of Mexico's other cuisines, as excellently prepared as you'll find them anywhere, with a few international dishes thrown in for variety. While you dine, you'll be serenaded by duets, marimba music, jarocho, and the ever-enchanting mariachis. The different peppers used in sauces and preparation are explained on the front of the menu, and each dish is marked for its heat quotient (from zero chiles to two chiles). A nice starter is the Mitlan salad, which has Oaxaca cheese slices (the state is known for its excellent cheese) dribbled with a little olive oil and a coriander dressing. The stuffed chile "La Doña"—a poblano pepper (mildly hot) filled with lobster and huitlacoche, in a cream sauce—comes as either an appetizer or a main course and is wonderful. The restaurant is to the left of the hotel entrance and is entered from the street.

Savio's. Playa Caracol. ☎ **98/83-2085.** Main courses $8.25–$20. AE, MC, V. Daily 10am–midnight. ITALIAN.

Savio's, in stylish black and white with tile floors and green marble-topped tables, is on two levels, and faces Paseo Kukulkán through two stories of awning-shaded windows. Its bar is always crowded with patrons sipping everything from cappuccino to imported beer. Repeat diners look forward to large fresh salads and richly flavored, subtly herbed Italian dishes. The ravioli stuffed with ricotta and spinach is served in a delicious tomato sauce.

CANCÚN CITY
EXPENSIVE

La Habichuela. Margaritas 25. ☎ **98/84-3158.** Reservations recommended in high season. Main courses $8–$30. AE, DC, MC, V. Daily 1pm–midnight. GOURMET SEAFOOD/BEEF/ MEXICAN.

In a garden setting with tables covered in pink-and-white linens and soft music playing in the background, this restaurant is ideal for a romantic evening. For an all-out culinary adventure, try *habichuela* (string bean) soup; shrimp in any number of sauces including Jamaican tamarindo, tequila, and a ginger and mushroom combination; and the Maya coffee with xtabentun (a strong, sweet, anise-based liquor). The grilled seafood and steaks are excellent as well, but this is a good place to try a Mexican specialty such as enchiladas Suizas or *tampiqueña*-style (thinly sliced, marinated and grilled) beef. For something totally new, try the "Cocobichuela," which is lobster and shrimp in a curry sauce served in a coconut shell and topped with fruit.

✪ **Périco's.** Yaxchilán 61. ☎ **98/84-3152.** Main courses $9–$20. AE, MC, V. Daily 1pm–1am. MEXICAN/SEAFOOD/STEAKS.

Périco's has colorful murals that almost dance off the walls, a bar area overhung with baskets and saddles for bar stools, colorfully bedecked leather tables and chairs, and accommodating waiters; it's always booming and festive. The extensive menu offers well-prepared steak, seafood, and traditional Mexican dishes for moderate rates (except lobster). This is a place not only to eat and drink but to let loose and join in the fun, so don't be surprised if everybody drops their forks and dons huge Mexican sombreros to bob and snake in a conga dance around the dining room. It's fun whether or not you join in. There's marimba music from 7:30 to 10:30pm, and mariachis from 10:30pm to midnight. This is a popular spot, so expect a crowd.

MODERATE

✪ **Restaurant El Pescador.** Tulipanes 28, off Av. Tulum. ☎ **98/84-2673.** Fax 98/84-3639 or 98/85-0505. Main courses $9–$35; Mexican plates $5–$9. AE, MC, V. Daily 11am–11pm. SEAFOOD.

There's often a line at this restaurant, which serves well-prepared fresh seafood in its street-side patio and upstairs venue overlooking Tulipanes. Feast on shrimp cocktail, conch, octopus, Créole-style shrimp (camarones à la criolla), charcoal-broiled lobster, and stone crabs. *Zarzuela* is a combination seafood plate cooked in white wine and garlic. There's a Mexican specialty menu as well. Another branch, **La Mesa del Pescador,** is in the Plaza Kukulkán on Cancún Island and is open the same hours, but is more expensive.

Restaurant Rosa Mexicano. Claveles 4. ☎ **98/84-6313.** Reservations recommended for parties of 6 or more. Main courses $6–$12; lobster $20. AE, MC, V. Daily 5–11pm. MEXICAN HAUTE.

This beautiful little place has candlelit tables and a plant-filled patio in back, and it's almost always packed. Colorful paper banners and piñatas hang from the ceiling, efficient waiters wear bow ties and cummerbunds color-themed to the Mexican flag, and a trio plays romantic Mexican music nightly. The menu features "refined" Mexican specialties. Try the *pollo almendro,* which is chicken covered in a cream sauce sprinkled with ground almonds, or the pork baked in a banana leaf with a sauce of oranges, lime, chile ancho, and garlic. The steak tampiqueño is a huge platter that comes with guacamole salad, quesadillas, beans, salad, and rice.

INEXPENSIVE

Pizza Rolandi. Cobá 12. ☎ **98/84-4047.** Pasta $5–$8; pizza and main courses $4–$9. AE, MC, V. Daily 12:30pm–midnight. ITALIAN.

At this shaded outdoor patio restaurant you can choose from almost two dozen different wood-oven pizzas and a full selection of spaghetti, calzones, and Italian-style chicken and beef and desserts. There's a full bar list as well. There's another Pizza Rolandi in Isla Mujeres at 110 avenida Hidalgo (☎ **98/704-30**) with the same food and prices. It's open Monday through Sunday from 11am to 11pm.

✪ **Restaurant Curva.** Av. Yaxchilán at Sunyaxchen. No phone. Breakfast $1.75–$2.50; comida corrida $2.50–$3. No credit cards. Mon–Sat 9am–5pm. MEXICAN.

It's worth the wait for a seat at one of the six tables in this tiny and spotless storefront cafe. You'll join young office workers and students for an inexpensive home-style lunch. The daily comida includes soup, rice, beans, and meat. There's usually a choice of main courses, such as beef tips, pozole, pollo adobado (a red sauce of achiote seed and otherspices), and pollo frito (fried). Lingering is not appreciated during lunchtime.

✪ **Restaurant Los Almendros.** Av. Bonampak and Sayil. ☎ **98/87-1332.** Main courses $4–$6. Daily 11am–10pm. AE, V, MC. YUCATECAN.

To steep yourself in Yucatecan cuisine, head directly to this large, colorful, and air-conditioned restaurant. Many readers have written to say they ate here almost exclusively, since the food and service are good and the illustrated menu, with color pictures of dishes, makes ordering easy. Some of the regional specialties include lime soup, *poc chuc* (a marinated, barbecue-style pork), chicken or pork *pibil* (a sweet and spicy, shredded meat), and such appetizers as *panuchos* (soft fried tortillas with refried beans and either shredded turkey or pork pibil—a type of barbeque sauce on top). The combinado Yucateco is a sampler of four typically Yucatecan main courses: chicken, poc chuc, sausage, and *escabeche* (onions marinated in vinegar and sour orange). A second location opened in 1994 on Cancún Island on Paseo Kukulkán across from the Convention Center. The downtown location is opposite the bullring.

Restaurante Santa María. Azucenas at Parque Palapas. ☎ **98/84-3158.** Main courses $3.50–$9; tacos 75¢–$5. No credit cards. Daily 5–10pm. MEXICAN.

The open-air Santa María restaurant is a clean, gaily decked-out place to sample authentic Mexican food. It's cool and breezy with patio dining that's open on two sides and is furnished with leather tables and chairs covered in multicolored cloths. A bowl of frijoles de olla and an order of beefsteak tacos will fill you up for a low price. You may want to try the tortilla soup or enchiladas, or go for one of the grilled U.S.–cut steaks, order of fajitas, ribs, or grilled seafood, all of which arrive with a baked potato.

Stefano's. Bonampak 177. ☎ **98/87-9964.** Main courses $4–$6; pizza $4.75–$6.75. AE, MC, V. Wed–Mon 2pm–midnight. ITALIAN/PIZZA/PASTA.

Tourists are beginning to find Stefano's, which serves Italian food with a few Mexican accents. On the menu you'll find a huitlacoche-and-shrimp pizza; rigatoni in tequila sauce; and seafood with chile peppers, nestled proudly alongside the Stefano special pizza, made with fresh tomato, cheese, and pesto; and calzones stuffed with spinach, mozzarella, and tomato sauce. For dessert the ricotta strudel is something out of the ordinary, or else try the tiramisu. There are lots of different coffees and mixed drinks, as well. New decor and ambiance, plus a new wine list.

COFFEE & PASTRIES

Pasteleria Italiana. Av. Yaxchilán 67, SM 25, near Sunyaxchen. ☎ **98/84-0796.** Pastries $1.75–$2.25; ice cream $2; coffee $1–$2. AE. Mon–Sat 9am–11pm; Sun 1–9pm. COFFEE/PASTRIES/ICE CREAM.

More like a casual neighborhood coffeehouse than a place aimed at tourists, this shady little respite has been doing business here since 1977. You'll spot it by the white awning that covers the small outdoor, plant-filled table area. Inside are refrigerated cases of tarts and scrumptious-looking cakes, ready to be carried away in their entirety or by the piece. The coffeehouse is in the same block as Périco's, between Maraño and Chiabal.

5 Beaches & Water Sports

THE BEACHES   The best stretches of beach are dominated by the big hotels. All of Mexico's beaches are public property, so you can use the beach of any hotel by walking through the lobby. Be especially careful on beaches fronting the open Caribbean, where the undertow is quite strong. By contrast, the waters of Mujeres Bay (Bahía de Mujeres) at the north end of the island are usually calm. Get to know Cancún's water-safety pennant system, and make sure to check the flag at any beach or hotel before entering the water. Here's how it goes:

- White — Excellent
- Green — Normal conditions (safe)
- Yellow — Changeable, uncertain (use caution)
- Black or red — Unsafe; use the swimming pool instead!

In the Caribbean, storms can arrive and conditions can change from safe to unsafe in a matter of minutes, so be alert: If you see dark clouds heading your way, make your way to shore and wait until the storm passes.

Playa Tortuga (Turtle Beach), Playa Langosta, Playa Linda, and Playa Las Perlas are some of the public beaches. At most beaches, in addition to swimming you can rent a sailboard and take lessons, ride a Parasail, or partake in a variety of water sports. There's a small but beautiful portion of public beach on Playa Caracol, by the Xcaret Terminal. Both of these face the calm waters of Bahía de Mujeres and for that reason are preferable to those facing the Caribbean.

WATER SPORTS Many beachside hotels offer water-sports concessions that include rental of rubber rafts, kayaks, and snorkeling equipment. On the calm Nichupte Lagoon are outlets for renting **sailboats, water jets, Windsurfers,** and **water skis.** Prices vary and are often negotiable, so check around.

For windsurfing, go to the Playa Tortuga public beach, where there's a **Windsurfing School** (☎ 98/84-2023) with equipment for rent.

DEEP-SEA FISHING You can arrange a day of **deep-sea fishing** at one of the numerous piers or travel agencies for around $200 to $360 for 4 hours, $420 for 6 hours, and $520 for 8 hours for up to four people. Marinas will sometimes assist in putting a group together. Charters include a captain, a first mate, bait, gear, and beverages. Rates are lower if you depart from Isla Mujeres or from Cozumel island.

SNORKELING AND SCUBA Known for its shallow reefs, dazzling color and diversity of life, Cancún is one of the best places in the world for beginning **scuba diving.** Punta Nizuc, the northern tip of the Great Meso American Reef (Gran Aricife Mayan) begins in Cancún. This is the largest reef in the western hemisphere, and one of the largest in the world. In addition to the sea life present along this reef system, several sunken boats add a variety of dive options. Inland, a series of caverns and wellsprings, known as *cenotes,* are fascinating venues for the more experienced diver. Drift diving is the norm here, with popular dives going to the reefs at **El Garrafón** and **the Cave of the Sleeping Sharks.**

Resort courses that teach the basics of diving—enough to make shallow dives and slowly ease your way into this underwater world of unimaginable beauty—are offered in a variety of hotels. Scuba trips run around $60 for two-tank dives at nearby reefs, $100 and up for locations farther out. **Scuba Cancún,** km 5 Paseo Kukulkán, on the lagoon side (☎ 98/83-1011; fax 98/84-2336; open 8:30am to 10pm, phone reservations also available in the evenings from 7:30 to 10:30pm using the fax line), offers a 4-hour resort course for $88. Full certification takes 4 to 5 days and costs around $325. The largest operator is **Aquaworld** (☎ 98/85-2288 or 98/83-3007, located across from the Meliá Cancún at km 15.2 Kukulcán), offering resort courses and diving from their man-made anchored dive platform, **Paradise Island.** Their **Sub See Explorer** provides nondivers with a look at life beneath the sea. **Scuba Cancún** also offers diving trips to 20 nearby reefs, including Cuevones at 30 feet and the open ocean at 30 to 60 feet (offered in good weather only). The average dive is around 35 feet. One-tank dives cost $45, and two-tank dives cost $60. Discounts apply if you bring your own equipment. Dives usually start around 9am and return by 2:15pm. Snorkeling trips cost $25 and leave every afternoon after 2pm for shallow reefs about a 20-minute boat ride away.

Besides **snorkeling** at **Garrafón National Park** (see "Boating Excursions," below), travel agencies offer an all-day excursion to the natural wildlife habitat of **Isla Contoy,** which usually includes time for snorkeling. This island, located an hour and a half past Isla Mujeres, is a major nesting area for birds, and is a treat for true nature lovers. Only two boats hold permits for excursions there, which depart at 9am and return by 5pm. The price of $60 includes drinks and snorkeling equipment.

6 Excursions & Organized Tours

Cancún's beaches beckon visitors here to the lucid waters for pure relaxation. But they also invite play, in a lively variety of ways. The options for exploring beyond your beach chair are many. To start, I highly recommend **Perfect Host,** km 20 avenida Kukulkán, in the Hotel Westin Regina (☎ **98/87-5537;** fax 98/87-5541). The company has investigated every provider of tour services in the region, and offers unbiased advise tailored to your expectations. With so many offering similar tour routes, they can help you match the service and price to the level of organization and amenities you're looking for. The most popular, according to manager Andrés Brakke, are the routes south to **Tulum** and **Xel-Ha** or **Xcaret,** the route west to the ruins of **Chichén-Itzá,** a boat cruise over to the nearby **Isla Mujeres,** and the **Jungle Cruise** (by WaveRunner), exploring Cancún's lagoon and reefs.

Day-trips are the most popular way to explore the seaside ruins of **Tulum** and the ecological theme parks of **Xcaret** and **Xel-Ha,** detailed below. Besides these, see also "Road Trips from Cancún" at the end of this chapter for suggestions on getting to the ruins of **Chichén-Itzá, Cobá, El Eden,** a 500,000-acre private biological reserve northwest of Cancún, and the two-million-acre **Sian Ka'an Biosphere Reserve** south of Cancún and Tulum. Each can be explored as a day trip or seen in a more extended stay.

The popular Jungle Cruise is offered by several companies and takes you by jet ski or WaveRunner through Cancún's lagoon and mangrove estuaries out into the Caribbean Sea and a shallow reef. The excursion runs about 2½ hours driving your own boat, and is priced from $35 to $40, with snorkeling and beverages included. Some of the motorized miniboats seat one person behind the other, others seat you side-by-side.

Day tours to Chichén-Itzá cost $52, including transportation, admission, guide, and buffet lunch. The special "Sound & Light" tour that includes the evening light show and buffet dinner costs $70, and returns at 11pm. See also "Road Trips from Cancún," at the end of this chapter, for more details on getting to these ruins.

XCARET: A DEVELOPED NATURE PARK   Six and a half miles south of Playa del Carmen (and 50 miles south of Cancún) is the turnoff to Xcaret (pronounced *ish*-car-et), a specially built ecological and archaeological theme park that is one of the area's most popular tourist attractions, designed as a place to spend the day. Xcaret has become almost a reason in itself to visit Cancún. It's as close to Disneyland as is found in Mexico, with a myriad of attractions in one location, most participatory. It's open Monday through Saturday from 8:30am to 8:30pm and Sunday from 8:30am to 5:30pm. Everywhere you look in Cancún are signs advertising Xcaret, or someone handing you a leaflet about it. They even have their own bus terminal to take tourists from Cancún at regular intervals, and they've added an evening extravaganza.

Xcaret may celebrate Mother Nature, but its builders rearranged quite a bit of her handiwork in completing it. If you're looking for a place to escape the commercialism of Cancún, this may not be it; it's expensive and may even be very crowded, thus diminishing the advertised "natural" experience. Children, however, love it, and the jungle setting and palm-lined beaches are beautiful. Once past the entrance booths (built to resemble small Maya temples) you'll find pathways that meander around bathing coves, the snorkeling lagoon, and the remains of a group of Maya temples. You'll have access to swimming beaches with canoes and pedal boats; limestone tunnels to snorkel through; marked palm-lined pathways; a wild-bird breeding aviary; a charro exhibition; horseback riding; scuba diving; a botanical garden and nursery; a sea turtle nursery where the turtles are released after their 1st year; a pavilion showcasing regional butterflies; a tropical aquarium where visitors can touch underwater creatures such as manta rays, starfish, and octopi; and a "Dolphinarium" where visitors swim with the dolphins for an extra charge of $80. The opportunity to swim with the dolphins is limited in number each day, and no reservations are taken—it's strictly a first-come, first-serve basis. There is also a visitor center with lockers, first aid, and gifts. Visitors aren't allowed to bring in food or drinks, so you're limited to the rather high-priced restaurants on site. No personal radios are allowed, and you must remove all suntan lotion if you swim in the lagoon, as the chemicals in lotion will poison the lagoon habitat.

The price of $35 per person entitles you to all the facilities—boats, life jackets, and snorkeling equipment for the underwater tunnel and lagoon, and lounge chairs and other facilities. Other attractions, such as horseback riding, scuba diving, and the Dolphin Swim, cost extra. However, there may be more visitors than equipment (such as beach chairs), so bring a beach towel and your own snorkeling gear. Travel agencies in Cancún offer Xcaret as a day trip (departing at 8am and returning at 6pm) that includes transportation and admission plus guide, for $50. You can also buy a ticket to the park at the **Xcaret Terminal** (☎ **98/83-0654** or 98/83-3143) next to the Hotel Fiesta Americana Coral Beach on Cancún Island. Xcaret's nine colorfully painted buses transport people to and from Cancún. "Xcaret Day and Night" includes round-trip transportation from Cancún, a charreada festival, lighted pathways to Maya ruins, dinner, and folkloric show for a price of $69 for adults and $45 for children 5 to 11; 5 and under are free. Xcaret buses leave its terminal at 9 and 10am daily, with the "Day and Night" tour returning at 9:30pm.

TULUM Another popular day-excursion combines a visit to the ruins at Tulum with the ecological water park, Xel-Ha. Ancient Tulum is the only Maya ruin by the sea. It is a stunning site, poised on a rocky hill overlooking the transparent, turquoise Caribbean sea. Not the largest or most important of the Maya ruins in this area, it is still memorable due to its location and the intriguing carvings and reliefs that decorate the well-preserved structures. The site dates back to between the 12th and 16th centuries A.D., in the Postclassic period. "Tulum" means fence, trench, or wall, and is the name given to this site due to the wall surrounding it on three sides. Its ancient name is believed to have been *Záma,* a derivative of the Maya word for morning, associated with the dawn. Sunrise at Tulum is very dramatic. The wall is believed to have been constructed after the original buildings to protect the interior religious altars from a growing number of invaders. It is considered to have been principally a place of worship, with members of upper classes later taking residence there due to its protective wall. Between the two most dramatic structures—the Castle and the Temple of the Wind—lies Tulum Cove. A small inlet with a beach of fine, white sand, it was a point of departure for Maya trading vessels in ancient times. Today, it's a playground for tourists. Entrance to the site without a tour is $2; use of video camera requires a $4 permit.

XEL-HA: SNORKELING & SWIMMING   The Caribbean coast of the Yucatán is carved by the sea into hundreds of small *caletas* (coves) that form the perfect habitat for tropical marine life, both flora and fauna. Many caletas remain undiscovered and pristine along the coast, but Xel-Ha, 8 miles south of Akumal, is enjoyed daily by throngs of snorkelers and scuba divers who come to luxuriate in its warm waters and swim among its brilliant fish. Xel-Ha (shell-*hah*) is a swimmers' paradise, with no threat of undertow or pollution. It's a beautiful, completely calm cove that's a perfect place to bring kids for their first snorkeling experience (experienced snorkelers may be disappointed—the crowds here seem to have driven out the living coral and a lot of the fish; you can find more abundant marine life and avoid an admission charge by going to Akumal, among other spots).

The entrance to Xel-Ha (☎ **98/84-9412**) is half a mile from the highway. Admission is $15 per adult and $7 for children 5 to 12 (children under 5 are free), and includes use of inner tubes, life vest, and shuttle train to the river. It's open daily from 8:30am to 5:30pm, and offers free parking with admission.

Once in the 10-acre park, you can rent snorkeling equipment and an underwater camera—but you may also bring your own. Food and beverage service, changing rooms, showers, and other facilities are all available. For nonsnorkelers, platforms have been constructed that allow decent sea-life viewing. When you swim, be careful to observe the "swim here" and "no swimming" signs. (The greatest variety of fish can be seen right near the ropes marking off the no-swimming areas, and near any groups of rocks.)

Just south of the Xel-Ha turnoff on the west side of the highway, don't miss the **Maya ruins** of ancient Xel-Ha. You'll likely be the only one there as you walk over limestone rocks and through the tangle of trees, vines, and palms. There is a huge, deep, dark cenote to one side and a temple palace with tumbled-down columns, a jaguar group, and a conserved temple group. A covered palapa on one pyramid guards a partially preserved mural. Admission is $2.50.

Xel-Ha is close to the ruins at **Tulum** (see above). It's a good place for a dip when you've finished climbing these Maya ruins. You can even make the short 8-mile hop north from Tulum to Xel-Ha by bus. When you get off at the junction for Tulum, ask the restaurant owner when the next buses come by, otherwise you may have to wait as long as 2 hours on the highway.

BOATING EXCURSIONS   The island of **Isla Mujeres,** just 10 miles offshore, is one of the most pleasant day-trips from Cancún. At one end is **El Garrafón National Underwater Park,** which is excellent for snorkeling. And at the other end is the captivating village with small shops, restaurants, and hotels, and **Playa Norte,** the island's best beach. (See chapter 13 for more on Isla Mujeres.) If you're looking for relaxation and can spare the time, Isla Mujeres is worth several days.

There are four ways to get there: by frequent **public ferry** from Puerto Juárez, which takes between 20 and 45 minutes; by a **shuttle boat** from Playa Linda or Playa Tortuga (an hour-long ride) but with irregular service; by the **Watertaxi** (also with limited service), next to the Xcaret Terminal; and by one of the daylong **pleasure-boat trips,** most of which leave from the Playa Linda pier. The cost of the public ferry from Puerto Juárez is the least expensive, and a very convenient way to travel there.

The inexpensive Puerto Juárez **public ferries** are just a few miles from downtown Cancún. From Cancún City, take the Ruta 8 bus on avenida Tulum to Puerto Juárez; the ferry docks in downtown Isla Mujeres by all the shops, restaurants, hotels, and

Norte beach. You'll need a taxi to go to Garrafón Park at the other end of the island. You can stay as long as you like on the island (even overnight) and return by ferry, but be sure to ask about the time of the last returning ferry—don't depend on the posted hours. (For more details and a shuttle schedule see chapter 13.)

Pleasure-boat cruises to Isla Mujeres are a favorite pastime here. Modern motor yachts, catamarans, trimarans, and even old-time sloops—more than 25 boats a day—take swimmers, sunners, snorkelers, and shoppers out into the translucent waters. Some tours include a snorkeling stop at Garrafón, lunch on the beach, and a short time for shopping in downtown Isla Mujeres. Most leave at 9:30 or 10am, last about 5 or 6 hours, and include continental breakfast, lunch, and rental of snorkel gear. Others, particularly the sunset and night cruises, go to beaches away from town for pseudo-pirate shows, and include a lobster dinner or Mexican buffet. If you want to actually see Isla Mujeres, go on a morning cruise, or go on your own using the public ferry at Puerto Juárez mentioned above. Prices for the day cruises run around $45 per person.

Other excursions go to the **reefs** in glass-bottom boats, so you can have a near-scuba-diving experience and see many colorful fish. However, the reefs are a distance from shore and impossible to reach on windy days with choppy seas. They've also suffered from overuse and their condition is far from pristine. The glass-bottomed **Nautibus** ($25 adults, $12.40 children; ☎ **98/83-3552** or 98/83-2119; American Express, MasterCard, and Visa accepted) has been around for years. The morning and afternoon trips in a glass-bottom boat from the Playa Pier to the Chitale coral reef to see colorful fish take about 1 hour and 20 minutes, with around 50 minutes of it consumed going to and from the reef. The **Atlantis Submarine** takes you even closer to the subaquatic action. Departures are variable, depending on weather conditions. Prices range from $44 to $65, depending on the length of the trip. Still other boat excursions visit **Isla Contoy,** a **national bird sanctuary** that's well worth the time. If you are planning to spend time in Isla Mujeres, the Contoy trip is easier and more pleasurable to take from there.

The operators and names of boats offering excursions change often. To find out what's available when you're there, check with a local travel agent or hotel tour desk, for they should have a wide range of options. You can also go to the Playa Linda Pier either a day ahead or the day of your intended outing and buy your own ticket for trips on the Nautibus or to Isla Mujeres. If you go on the day of your trip, arrive at the pier around 8:45am since most boats leave by 9 or 9:30am.

7 Outdoor Activities & Other Attractions

OUTDOOR ACTIVITIES

DOLPHIN SWIMS   On Isla Mujeres, you have the opportunity to swim with dolphins, at **Dolphin Discovery** (☎ **98/83-0779**). Each session is one hour, with an educational introduction followed by 30 minutes of swim time. Price is $119, with transportation to Isla Mujeres an additional $15. Advanced reservations are required, as capacity is limited each day.

GOLF & TENNIS   The 18-hole **Club de Golf Cancún** (☎ **98/83-0871**), also known as the Pok-Ta-Pok Club, was designed by Robert Trent Jones, Sr., and is located on the northern leg of the island. Greens fees run $100 per 18 holes, with clubs renting for $18 and a caddy at $20 per bag. The club is open daily; American Express, MasterCard, and Visa are accepted. It also has tennis courts available for play. The Melía Cancún offers an 18-hole, par-54 executive course, and the Caesar Park

Cancún also has its own championship 18-hole, par-72 course designed around the "Ruinas Del Rey." It's open daily from 6am to 6pm.

HORSEBACK RIDING Rancho Loma Bonita (☎ 98/87-5465 or 98/87-5423) is Cancún's most popular option for horseback riding. Five-hour packages are available that include 2 hours of riding to caves, cenotes, lagoons, Maya ruins, and along the Caribbean coast, plus a Donkey Polo game and some time for relaxing on the beach. Located about 30 minutes south, the price of $45 includes transportation to the ranch, riding, soft drinks, and lunch, plus guide and insurance.

IN-LINE SKATING You can rent in-line skates outside Plaza Las Glorias Hotel and in front of Playa Caracol, where the valet parking is located. The jogging track that runs parallel to avenida Kukulcán along the hotel zone is well maintained and safe.

OTHER ATTRACTIONS

RUINAS EL REY Cancún has its own **Maya ruins.** It's a small site and not impressive compared to ruins at Tulum, Cobá, or Chichén-Itzá. The Maya fishermen built this small ceremonial center and settlement very early in the history of Maya culture. It was then abandoned, to be resettled later near the end of the Postclassic period, not long before the arrival of the conquistadors. The platforms of numerous small temples are visible amid the banana plants, papayas, and wildflowers. A new golf course has been built around the ruins, but there is a separate entrance for sightseers. You'll find the ruins about 13 miles from town, at the southern reaches of the Zona Hotelera, almost to Punta Nizuc. Look for the Caesar's Palace hotel on the left (east), then the ruins on the right (west). Admission is $4.50 (free on Sun and holidays); the hours are daily from 8am to 5pm.

A MUSEUM To the right side of the entrance to the Cancún Convention Center is the **Museo Arqueológico de Cancún** (☎ 98/83-0305), a small but interesting museum with relics from archaeological sites around the state. Admission is $1.75 (free on Sun and holidays); the hours are Tuesday through Saturday from 9am to 7pm and Sunday from 10am to 5pm.

BULLFIGHTS Cancún has a small **bullring** (☎ 98/84-8372) near the northern (town) end of Paseo Kukulkán opposite the Restaurant Los Almendros. Bullfights are held every Wednesday at 3:30pm during the winter tourist season. There are usually four bulls, and the spectacle begins with a folkloric dance exhibition, followed by a performance of the Charros. Travel agencies in Cancún sell tickets: $32 for adults and children over 12; $15 for children 6 to 12; under 6 are free.

8 Shopping

Cancún is known throughout Mexico as having the most diverse array of shops that cater to a large number of international tourists. Where tourists arriving from the United States may find apparel more expensive in Cancún, the selection is much broader than in other Mexican resorts. There are numerous duty-free shops that offer excellent value on European goods.

Handcrafts and other *artesanía* works are more limited and more expensive in Cancún than in other regions of Mexico, but they are available here. There are several **open-air crafts markets** easily visible on avenida Tulum in Cancún City and near the convention center in the Hotel Zone. One of the biggest is **Coral Negro,** located at avenida Kukulcán km 9.5 (☎ 98/83-0758), open daily from 7am.

The main venue for shopping in Cancún is the **mall,** not quite as grand as its U.S. counterpart, but coming close to the experience. All of Cancún's malls are air-conditioned, sleek, and sophisticated, with most located on avenida Kukulkán between km 7 and km 12—Plaza Lagunas, Costa Brava, La Mansión, Mayfair, Plaza Terramar, Playa Caracol, Plaza Flamingo, Plaza Kukulcán, and the newest, Forum by the Sea. Everything from fine crystal and silver to designer clothing and decorative objects can be found with numerous restaurants and clubs interspersed. Stores are generally open daily from 10am to 8 or 10pm. Stores in malls near the Convention Center generally stay open all day, but some—especially in malls farther out—close between 2 and 4pm. Here's a brief rundown on the malls and some of the shops each contain.

Inside the **Plaza Kukulkán** (☎ 98/85-2200) you'll find a branch of Banco Serfin, OK Maguey Cantina Grill, a movie theater with U.S. movies, Tikal, a shop with Guatemalan textile clothing, several crafts stores, a liquor store, a bathing-suit specialty store, a record and tape outlet, all leather goods including shoes and sandals, and another store specializing in silver from Taxco. In the food court are a number of U.S. franchise restaurants including Ruth's Chris Steakhouse, plus one featuring specialty coffee. For entertainment, it has a bowling alley, Q-Zar laser game pavilion, and video game arcade. There's indoor parking for 1,000 cars.

Planet Hollywood anchors the **Plaza Flamingo,** but inside you'll also pass branches of Bancrecer, Denny's, Subway Sandwiches, and La Casa del Habana for Cuban cigars.

The long-standing **Playa Caracol** holds Cartier jewelry, Aca Joe, Guess, Señor Frog clothing, Waterford crystal, Samsonite luggage, Thomas Moore Travel, Gucci, Fuji film, Mr. Papa's, and La Fisheria restaurant.

Mayfair Plaza/Centro Comercio Mayfair is the oldest, with an open-bricked center that's lively with people sitting in open-air restaurants and bars such as Tequila Sunrise, Fat Tuesday, El Mexicano (a dinner-show restaurant), Pizza Hut, and several stores selling silver, leather, and crafts.

The newest and largest of the malls is the entertainment-oriented **Forum by the Sea,** avenida Kukulkán km 9 (☎ 98/83-4425). Shops include Tommy Hilfiger and Aca Joe, but most people come here for the food and fun, choosing from Hard Rock Cafe, Rainforest Cafe, Santa Fe Beer Factory, and an extensive food court. It's open from 10am to midnight, with bars open later.

9 Cancún After Dark

One of Cancún's principal draws is its active nightlife. The two hottest centers of action are the **Centro Comercio Mayfair** and the new **Forum by the Sea,** both on the island near Punta Cancún. Hotels also compete with happy-hour entertainment and special drink prices to entice visitors and guests from other resorts—lobby bar–hopping at sunset is one great way to plan next year's vacation.

THE CLUB & MUSIC SCENE   Clubbing in Cancún, still called discoing here, is a favorite part of the vacation experience, and can go on each night until the sun rises over that incredibly blue sea. Several of the big hotels have nightclubs, usually a disco, or entertain in their lobby bars with live music. At discos, expect to pay a cover charge of $10 to $20 per person, and $5 to $8 for a drink. Some of the higher-priced discos include an open bar or live entertainment.

Numerous restaurants, such as **Carlos 'n' Charlie's, Planet Hollywood, Hard Rock Cafe, All Star Cafe, Señor Frog, TGIFriday's,** and **Iguana Wana,** double as nighttime party spots; the first four offer wildish fun at a fraction of the prices of more costly discos.

The most refined and upscale of all Cancún's nightly gathering spots is the **Lobby Lounge** at the **Ritz-Carlton Hotel** (☎ **98/85-0808**), with live dance music and a list of over 120 premium tequilas.

Azúcar Bar Caribeño (☎ **98/83-0441**), adjacent to the Hotel Camino Real, offers spicy tropical dancing of the salsa, meringue, and bolero kind, with bands from Cuba, Jamaica, and the Dominican Republic; it's open Monday through Saturday from 9:30pm to 4am.

La Boom, km 3.5 bulevar Kukulkán (☎ **98/83-1152**), has two sections: On one side is a video bar, and on the other is a bilevel disco with cranking music. Both sides offer air-conditioning. Each night special client-getting attractions are offered, like no cover, free bar, ladies' night, or bikini night. It's popular with people in their early twenties. It's open nightly from 8pm to 6am. A sound-and-light show begins at 11:30pm in the disco.

Carlos 'n' Charlie's, km 4.5 Paseo Kukulkán (☎ **98/83-0846**), is a reliable place to find both good food and packed frat house–level entertainment in the evenings. There's a dance floor to go along with the live music that starts nightly around 9pm. A cover charge kicks in if you're not planning to eat. It's open daily from noon to 2am.

With taped music, **Carlos O'Brian's,** Tulum 107, SM 22 (☎ **98/84-1659**), is only slightly tamer then other Carlos Anderson restaurants/nightspots in town (Señor Frog and Carlos 'n' Charlie's are two others). It's open daily from 11am to 12:30am.

Christine's, at the Hotel Krystal on the island (☎ **98/83-1793**), is where disco lives. Although the music is more hip and alternative, the laser-light shows, infused oxygen, and large video screens take you back to the glitz style of high disco. The dress code permits no shorts or jeans. It opens at 9:30pm nightly. American Express, MasterCard, and Visa are accepted.

Dady'O, km 9.5 Paseo Kukulkán (☎ **98/83-3333**), is another rave—highly favored, with frequent long lines. It opens nightly at 9:30pm.

Dady Rock Bar and Grill, km 9.5 Paseo Kukulkán (☎ **98/83-1626**), the offspring of Dady'O, opens early (7pm) and goes as long as any other nightspot, offering a new twist on entertainment with a combination of live bands and DJ-orchestrated music, along with an open bar, full meals, a buffet, and dancing.

Hard Rock Cafe, in Plaza Lagunas Mall and Forum by the Sea (☎ **98/83-3269** or 98/83-2024), entertains with a live band at 10:30pm Thursday through Tuesday nights. Other hours you'll get your share of lively recorded music to munch by—the menu combines the most popular foods from American and Mexican cultures. It's open daily from 11am to 2am.

Planet Hollywood, Flamingo Shopping Center, km 11 Paseo Kukulkán (☎ **98/85-3044**), is the trendy brainchild of Sylvester Stallone, Bruce Willis, and Arnold Schwarzenegger. It's both a restaurant and nighttime music/dance spot with megadecibel live music. It's open daily from 11am to 2am. American Express, MasterCard, and Visa are accepted.

THE PERFORMING ARTS   Nightly performances of the **Ballet Folklórico de Cancún** (☎ **98/83-0199,** ext. 193 or 194), are held at the Cancún Convention Center. Tickets are sold between 8am and 9pm at a booth just as you enter the Convention Center. You can go for dinner and the show. Dinner-show guests pay around $48, and arrive at 6:30pm for drinks, which is followed by dinner at 7pm, and the show at 8pm. The price includes an open bar, dinner, show, tax, and tip. Several hotels host **Mexican fiesta nights,** including a buffet dinner and a folkloric dance show; admission, including dinner, ranges from $35 to $50. A Ballet Folklórico appears

Monday through Saturday nights in a 1¼-hour show at the **Continental Villas Plaza** (☎ **98/85-1444,** ext. 5690). The **Hyatt Regency Cancún** (☎ **98/83-1234**) has a dinner, folkloric show, and mariachi fiesta Tuesday through Sunday nights during the high season, as does the **Camino Real** (☎ **98/83-1200**). In the Costa Blanca shopping center, **El Mexicano** restaurant (☎ **98/84-4207;** American Express, MasterCard, and Visa accepted) hosts a tropical dinner show every night as well as live music for dancing. The entertainment alternates each night with mariachis entertaining off-and-on from 7 to 11pm and a folkloric show from 8 to 9:30pm.

You can also get in the party mood at **Mango Tango,** km 14 Paseo Kukulkán (☎ **98/85-0303**), a lagoon-side restaurant/dinner-show establishment. Diners can choose from two levels, one nearer the music and the other overlooking it all. Music is loud and varied. The 1-hour-and-20-minute dinner show begins at 8pm nightly and costs $25 to $35. At 9:30pm live reggae music begins and there's no cover. If you want to enjoy the show without a meal, just order a drink and be seated at an upper-level table and order a drink. It's opposite the Jack Tar Village.

For something that mingles tourists with the locals, head for the downtown **Parque de las Palapas** (the main park) for *Noches Caribeños,* where live tropical music is provided at no charge for anyone who wants to listen and dance. Performances begin at 7:30pm on Fridays.

SPORTS WAGERING   This form of entertainment seems to be sweeping Mexico's resorts. TV screens mounted around the room of **LF Caliente** (☎ **98/83-3704**), at the Fiesta Americana Hotel, show all the action in racetrack, football, soccer, and so on in a bar/lounge setting.

10 Road Trips from Cancún

Outside of Cancún lie the many wonders of the Yucatán Peninsula; you'll find details in chapter 13. Cancún can be a perfect base for day- or overnight trips or the starting point for a longer exploration. Any travel agency or hotel tour desk in Cancún can book these tours, or you can elect to do them on your own via local bus or rental car. The Maya ruins to the south at **Tulum** or **Cobá** should be your first goal, then perhaps the *caleta* (cove) of **Xel-Ha** or the day trip to **Xcaret.** If you're going south, consider staying a night or two on the island of **Cozumel** or at one of the budget resorts on the **Tulum coast** or **Punta Allen,** south of the Tulum ruins. **Isla Mujeres** is an easy day trip off mainland Cancún (see chapter 13).

About 80 miles south of Cancún begins the **Sian Ka'an Biosphere Reserve,** a 1.3 million-acre area set aside in 1986 to preserve a region of tropical forests, savannas, mangroves, canals, lagoons, bays, cenotes, and coral reefs, all of which are home to hundreds of birds and land and marine animals (see chapter 13 for details). The Friends of Sian Ka'an, a nonprofit group based in Cancún, offers biologist-escorted day-trips (weather permitting) from the **Cabañas Ana y José** just south of the Tulum ruins. Trips take place on Monday, Tuesday, Friday, and Saturday for $50 per person using their vehicle or $40 per person if you drive yourself. The price includes chips and soft drinks, round-trip van transportation to the reserve from the Cabañas, a guided boat/birding trip through one of the reserve's lagoons, and use of binoculars. Tours can accommodate up to 19 people. Trips start from the Cabañas at 9:30am and return there around 2:30pm. For reservations, contact Amigos de Sian Ka'an, Cobá 5, Plaza America (☎ **98/84-9583;** fax 98/87-3080) in Cancún. Office hours are 9am to 3pm and 6 to 8pm.

Although I don't recommend it, by driving fast or catching the right buses, you can go inland to **Chichén-Itzá,** explore the ruins, and return in a day, but it's much better to spend at least 2 days seeing Chichén-Itzá, Mérida, and Uxmal. See chapter 14 for transportation details and further information on these destinations.

Reserva Ecológica El Eden, established in 1990, is a privately owned 500,000-acre reserve dedicated to research for biological conservation in Mexico. Only 30 miles northwest of Cancún, it takes around 2 hours to reach the center of this reserve deep in the jungle. It's intended as an overnight (or more) excursion for people who want to know more about the biological diversity of the peninsula. Within the reserve, or near to it, are found marine grasslands, mangrove swamps, rain forests, savannas, wetlands, and sand dunes, as well as evidence of archaeological sites and at least 205 different species of birds, plus orchids, bromeliads, and cacti. Among the local animals are spider monkey, jaguar, cougar, deer, and ocelot. The "ecoscientific" tours offered include naturalist-led bird watching, animal tracking, star gazing, spotlight surveys for nocturnal wildlife, and exploration of cenotes and Maya ruins. Comfortable, basic accommodations are provided. Tours include transportation from Cancún, 1 or 2 nights accommodation at La Savanna Research Station, meals, nightly cocktail, guided nature walks, and tours. The tours cost $235 to $315 depending on the length of stay, with a fee of $90 per extra night. Contact Reserva Ecológica El Eden, Apdo. Postal 770, 77500 Cancún, Quintana Roo (☎/fax **98/80-5032; maya.ucr.edu/pril/ el_eden/Front.html**; E-mail: mlazcano@Cancún.rce.com.mx.)

13

Isla Mujeres, Cozumel & the Caribbean Coast

A Mexican friend of mine reminded me that the Mayas never settled in Cancún. "The original inhabitants always choose the best places to live," he reasoned, pointing to neighboring Cozumel, Tulum, Isla Mujeres, and other sites along the Yucatán coastline. Each of these holds remnants of ancient settlements in addition to many modern attractions.

In fact, those who shun the highly stylized, rather Americanized ways of Cancún will find that these and other stops in the Yucatán offer abundant natural pleasures, authentic experiences, and a relaxed charm. They're so close to the easy air access of Cancún, yet miles away in mood and matter.

The **Quintana Roo** coast, dubbed the Costa Turquesa (Turquoise Coast) or the Tulum Corridor as far as Tulum, stretches south from Cancún all the way to Chetumal. It's 230 miles of powdery white-sand beaches, scrubby jungle, and crystal-clear lagoons full of coral and colorful fish. Along this coastline—and the islands off the peninsula— are a few places worthy of being designated "resorts," as well as a handful of inexpensive hideaways. Some treasured spots on both the Punta Allen Peninsula and the Majahual Peninsula also merit travelers' attention. This whole coastal region is rapidly evolving, and it offers more and more options for a wider range of travelers.

Many travelers become acquainted with these areas through an initial stay in Cancún, and day-trips that take them sailing over to Isla Mujeres, venturing down the Caribbean coast to Tulum, or exploring the reefs off Cozumel. Their next trip often becomes a closer concentration of one or more of these smaller towns.

Points west of Cancún, such as Chichén-Itzá and Mérida, are detailed in chapter 14.

EXPLORING MEXICO'S CARIBBEAN

ISLA MUJERES   A day trip to Isla Mujeres on a party boat is one of the most popular excursions from Cancún. This fish-shaped island is located just 8 miles northeast of Cancún. It's a quick boat ride away, allowing ample time to get a taste of the peaceful pace of life here. But to fully explore the small village of shops and cafes, relax at the broad, tranquil Playa Norte, or snorkel or dive El Garrafón Reef, (a national underwater park), more time is needed. Overnight accommodations range from rustic to offbeat chic on this small island where relaxation rules.

Passenger ferries go to Isla Mujeres from Puerto Juárez near Cancún, and car ferries leave from Punta Sam, also near Cancún. More expensive passenger ferries, with less frequent departures, leave from the Playa Linda pier on Cancún Island.

COZUMEL   Mexico's principal Caribbean island, Cozumel is known as one of the world's top-five dive destinations. It has also earned the dubious honor of being one of the world's top cruise ports of call. This allows hundreds of thousands each year to get a glimpse of the beauty of the place, but crowds clog the shops, streets, and restaurants from morning to midafternoon. Apart from diving and shopping, favored pastimes include fishing and exploring ruins on the island. For those staying in Cozumel, the ruins, cenote diving, and the beach villages of the mainland are a quick ferry ride away. Cozumel has a few luxury resorts, numerous hotels that cater to divers with special packages, plus many inexpensive places to stay.

A car/passenger ferry runs between Puerto Morelos (south of Cancún) and Cozumel. Passenger ferries also run between Playa del Carmen and Cozumel, the preferred way to go if you aren't flying directly from your home base.

THE COSTA TURQUESA   Signs pointing to brand-new, expensive resort developments are found all along Highway 307 from Cancún south to **Tulum,** a stretch known both as the "Tulum Corridor," referring to the distance from Cancún to Tulum, and as the "Costa Turquesa," south from Cancún to Chetumal on the Belize border. The character of Corridor is changing, but there are still plenty of small, beachfront hideaways, bargain bungalows, and luxury retreats a short distance from the highway. South of Tulum, almost 100 miles of this coast have been set aside as the Sian Ka'an Biosphere Reserve.

A trip down the coast is a great way to spend a day of a vacation centered in Cancún. The most popular agency-led tours out of Cancún are to the ruins of Tulum, followed by a stop at Xel-Ha for swimming and/or snorkeling in the beautiful clear lagoon, and to the ecological/archaeological theme park of Xcaret.

The Costa Turquesa is best experienced in a car (see chapter 12, "Cancún," for information on rentals). Highway 307 south of Cancún has just been expanded to four broad lanes between Cancún and the Playa del Carmen turnoff. It is bordered by jungle on both sides, except where there are beaches and beach settlements.

Here are some **drive times from Cancún:** Puerto Morelos (port for the car ferry to Cozumel and a sleepy beachside town), 45 minutes; Playa del Carmen (the very hip beachside village), 1 hour; Xcaret Lagoon and Paamul, 1¼ hours; Akumal, 1¾ hours; Xel-Ha and Tulum, around 2 hours; and Chetumal, about 5 hours.

THE PUNTA ALLEN & MAJAHUAL PENINSULAS   These two areas will appeal to people looking for totally off-the-beaten-track travel, and/or for world-class adventure sports. **Punta Allen's** saltwater fly-fishing is extraordinary, and the **Chinchorro Banks,** 22 miles off Majahual's little village of Xcalak, is perhaps the last example of a pristine Caribbean reef—the diving is spectacular. Both places are hard to get to, have beautiful beaches, are overrun by exotic bird life and jungle flora, and have a few laid-back, rustic inns to stay at.

THE RÍO BEC RUIN ROUTE   Between Lago Bacalar and Escárcega, in Campeche State, is the Río Bec ruin route, where several "new" sites are open to the public and others are available with special permission.

CHETUMAL   Though Chetumal is the capital of Quintana Roo State, it's best to think of it as a gateway to Guatemala, Belize, the several ruins near the city, and the excellent diving and fishing to be had off the Xcalak Peninsula. In 1995 a fantastic museum opened in Chetumal, and the reexcavation of many of the ruins near

The Yucatán Peninsula

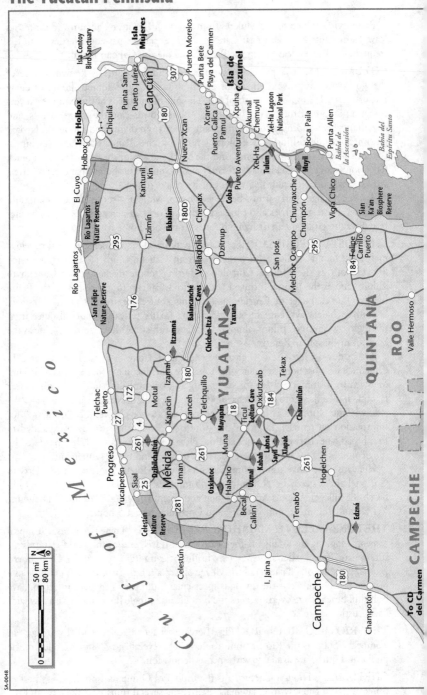

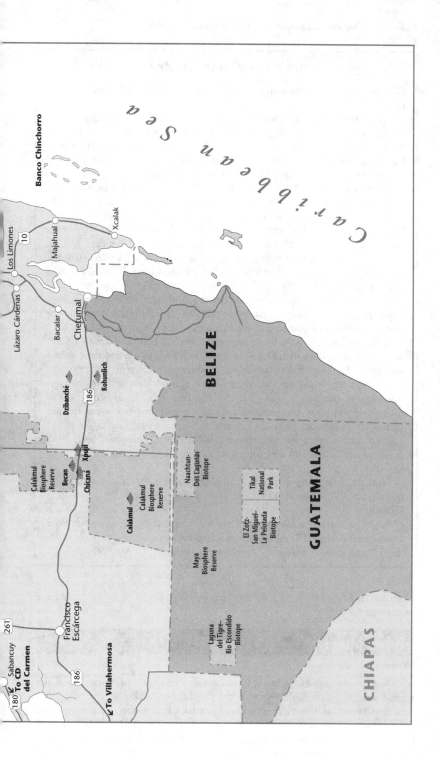

On the Road in the Yucatán

Here are a few things to keep in mind if you're planning to hit the road and explore the Yucatán.

Exchanging money is easiest in Cancún, Isla Mujeres, Playa del Carmen, and Cozumel, with many smaller resorts along the coast operating on a cash-only basis. And though Isla Mujeres and Cozumel are breezy enough to keep them at bay, everywhere else on this coast, **mosquitoes** are numerous, so bring plenty of mosquito repellent that has DEET as the main ingredient.

The best way to see the Yucatán is **by car.** It's one of the most pleasant parts of the country for a driving vacation. The jungle- and beach-lined roads, while narrow, straight, and without shoulders, are generally in good condition and have little traffic. The section with the most traffic—the stretch from Cancún to Puerto Morelos—has just been widened to four lanes, with a shoulder.

The four-lane toll road between Cancún and Mérida is complete. Costing around $20 one way, it cuts the trip from 5 to around 4 hours. The old two-lane free road is still in fine shape and passes through numerous villages with many speed-control bumps (*topes*)—this route is much more interesting. New directional signs seem to lead motorists to the toll road (*cuota*) and don't mention the free road (*libre*), so if you want to use it, ask locals for directions.

Traffic can become quite heavy on certain stretches from Cancún to Tulum, and drivers go too fast. A stalled or stopped car is hard to see, and there are no shoulders for pulling off the roadway. Follow these precautions for a safe journey: Never turn left while on the highway (it's against Mexican law anyway). Always go to the next road on the right and turn around and come back to the turnoff you want. Occasionally, a specially constructed right-hand turnoff, such as at Xcaret and Playa del Carmen, allows motorists to pull off to the right in order to cross the road when traffic has passed. There have been many accidents and fatalities on this road, so use caution. After Tulum, traffic is much lighter.

Be aware of the **long distances** in the Yucatán. Mérida, for instance, is 400 miles from Villahermosa, 125 miles from Campeche, and 200 miles from Cancún.

Note: Gas stations are found in all major towns, but they're only open from around 8am to around 7pm in smaller villages. If you're planning to rent a car to travel the area, see "Car Rentals" in chapter 3, "Planning a Trip to Mexico."

Chetumal may be a reason for a detour there, but Lago Bacalar is the preferred place to stay near Chetumal.

1 Isla Mujeres

10 miles N of Cancún

Isla Mujeres—the Island of Women: Was this really a place where 17th-century pirates stashed their women for safekeeping as they headed out to plunder and pillage? Or does the name of this tiny sliver of an island date back even further, to the time of the Maya, who possibly considered it a sanctuary for sacred virgins? A legacy of stony statues of women and shrines to Ixchel, their fertility goddess, was discovered by Spanish conquistadors upon their arrival.

Whatever its history, Isla Mujeres today is a serene respite from the nonstop glitz and action of Cancún, easily viewed across a narrow channel. Just 5 miles long and 2½ miles wide, it's known as the best value in the Caribbean, assuming you prefer your vacation laid-back and heavy on relaxation.

The streets have been paved in bricks and many original Caribbean-style clapboard houses remain, adding a colorful and authentic reminder of the island's past. Sun-tanned visitors hang out in open-air cafes and stroll streets lined with frantic souvenir vendors. Calling out for attention to their bargain-priced wares, they give a carnival atmosphere to the hours when tour-boat traffic is at its peak.

Days in "Isla"—as the locals call it—can alternate between adventurous activity and absolute repose. Trips to the Isla Contoy bird sanctuary are popular, as are the excellent diving, fishing, and snorkeling. In the evenings most people find the slow, relaxing pace one of the island's biggest draws. It is then that the island is bathed in a cool breeze, perfect for casual open-air dining and drinking in small street-side restaurants. Most people pack it in as early as 9 or 10pm, when most of the businesses close. Restless night owls, however, will find kindred souls at a few bars on Playa Norte that stay open late.

ESSENTIALS

GETTING THERE & DEPARTING   **Puerto Juárez,** just north of Cancún, is the dock for the passenger ferries to Isla Mujeres. The *Caribbean Queen* makes the 45-minute trip many times daily, and costs just under $2. The newer *Caribbean Express* makes the trip in 20 minutes and costs about $3, running every hour on the half hour between 6:30am and 8:30pm. Pay at the ticket office, or if the ferry is about to leave, you can pay aboard.

Taxi fares are now posted by the street where the taxis park; be sure to check the rate before agreeing to a taxi. Moped and bicycle rentals are also readily available as you depart the ferry boat.

Isla Mujeres is so small that a vehicle isn't necessary, but if you're taking one, you'll use the **Punta Sam** port a little beyond Puerto Juárez. The ferry runs the 40-minute trip five or six times daily all year except in bad weather (check with the tourist office in Cancún for a current schedule). Cars should arrive an hour in advance of the ferry departure to register for a place in line and pay the posted fee, which varies depending on weight and type of vehicle.

There are also ferries to Isla Mujeres from the **Playa Linda** pier in Cancún, but they're less frequent and more expensive than those from Puerto Juárez. The Playa Linda ferries simply don't run if there isn't a crowd. A new **Water Taxi** (☎ **988/6-4270** or 988/6-4847) to Isla Mujeres operates from Playa Caracol, between the Fiesta Americana Coral Beach Hotel and the Xcaret terminal on the island, with prices about the same as those from Playa Linda, about four times the cost of the public ferries from Puerto Juárez. Scheduled departures are 9 and 11am and 1 and 3pm with returns from Isla Mujeres at 10am, noon, 2pm, and 5pm. Adult fares are $13.50, kids 3 to 12 are half-price, and those under 3 ride free.

To get to either Puerto Juárez or Punta Sam **from Cancún,** take any Ruta 8 city bus from avenida Tulum. If you're coming from Mérida, you can either fly to Cancún and then proceed to Puerto Juárez, or you can take a bus directly from the Mérida bus station to Puerto Juárez. **From Cozumel,** you can either fly to Cancún (there are daily flights) or take a ferry to Playa del Carmen (see the Cozumel section below for details), where you can travel to Puerto Juárez.

Arriving: Ferries arrive at the dock in the center of town. Most hotels are close by. Tricycle taxis are the least expensive and most fun way to get to your hotel; you and your luggage pile in the open carriage compartment while the "driver" peddles through the streets. Regular taxis are always lined up in a parking lot to the right of the pier, with their rates posted.

VISITOR INFORMATION The **City Tourist Office** (☎/fax **987/7-0316**) is on the second floor of the Plaza Isla Mujeres. You'll find it at the northern end of Juárez, between López Mateos and Matamoros. It's open Monday through Friday from 9am to 2:30pm and 7 to 9pm. Also look for *Islander,* a free publication with history, local information, advertisements, and list of events (if any).

ISLAND LAYOUT Isla Mujeres is about 5 miles long and 2½ miles wide, with the town located at the northern tip of the island. The **ferry docks** are right at the center of town, within walking distance of most hotels, restaurants, and shops. The street running along the waterfront is **Rueda Medina,** commonly called the **malecón.** The **market** (Mercado Municipal) is by the post office on **calle Guerrero,** an inland street at the north edge of town, which, like most streets in the town, is unmarked.

GETTING AROUND A popular form of transportation on Isla Mujeres is the electric **golf cart,** available for rent at many hotels for $10 per hour or $50 per day. They don't go more than 20 miles per hour, so don't expect to speed around the island, but they're fun. Anyway, on Isla Mujeres you aren't there to hurry. Many people enjoy touring the island by "moto," the local sobriquet for motorized bikes and scooters. Fully automatic versions are available for around $25 to $30 per day or $6 per hour. They come with seats for one person, but some are large enough for two. There's only one main road with a couple of offshoots, so you won't get lost. Be aware that the rental price does not include insurance, and any injury to yourself or the vehicle will come out of your pocket. **Bicycles** are also available for rent at some hotels for $5 per day.

Fast Facts: Isla Mujeres

Area Code The area code of Isla Mujeres is **987.** The first digit for all telephone numbers on the island has been changed from 2 to 7.

Hospital The **Hospital de la Armada** is on Medina at Ojon P. Blanco (☎ **987/7-0017**). It's half a mile south of the town center.

Post Office/Telegraph Office The correo is on calle Guerrero, by the market.

Telephone Ladatel phones accepting coins and prepaid phone cards are found at the plaza and throughout town.

Tourist Seasons Isla Mujeres's tourist season (when hotel rates are higher) is a bit different from that of other places in Mexico. High season runs December through May, a month longer than in Cancún; some hotels raise their rates in August and some hotels raise their rates beginning in mid-November. Low season is June through mid-November.

BEACHES & WATER SPORTS

THE BEACHES The most popular beach in town used to be called Playa Cocoteros ("Cocos" for short). Then, in 1988, Hurricane Gilbert destroyed the coconut palms on the beach. Gradually, the name has changed to **Playa Norte,** referring to the long stretch of beach that extends around the northern tip of the island, to your left as you get off the boat. This is a truly splendid beach—a wide stretch of fine white sand and calm, translucent, turquoise-blue water. Topless sunbathing is allowed here. The beach is easily reached on foot from the ferry and from all downtown hotels. Water-sports equipment, beach umbrellas, and lounge chairs are available for rent. Those in front of restaurants usually cost nothing if you use the restaurant as your headquarters for drinks and food. New palms are sprouting all over Playa Norte, and it won't be long until it will be deserving of its previous name.

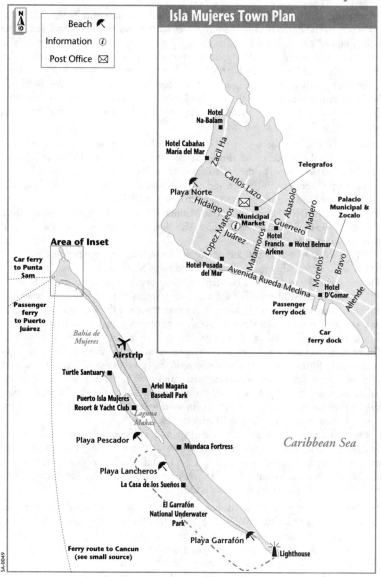

Isla Mujeres Town Plan

Beach

Information ⓘ

Post Office ✉

Area of Inset

Car ferry to Punta Sam

Passenger ferry to Puerto Juárez

Hotel Na-Balam

Hotel Cabañas María del Mar

Zacil Ha

Carlos Lazo

Telegrafos

Playa Norte

Hidalgo

Palacio Municipal & Zocalo

Abasolo

Madero

Municipal Market

Guerrero

López Mateos

Juárez

Matamoros

Hotel Francis Arlene

Hotel Belmar

Hotel Posada del Mar

Avenida Rueda Medina

Morelos

Bravo

Hotel D'Gomar

Allende

Passenger ferry dock

Car ferry dock

Bahia de Mujeres

Airstrip

Turtle Sanctuary

Ariel Magaña Baseball Park

Puerto Isla Mujeres Resort & Yacht Club

Laguna Makax

Playa Pescador

Mundaca Fortress

Caribbean Sea

Playa Lancheros

La Casa de los Sueños

El Garrafón National Underwater Park

Ferry route to Cancun (see small source)

Playa Garrafón

Lighthouse

SA-0049

Garrafón National Park is known best as a snorkeling area, but there is a nice stretch of beach on either side of the park. **Playa Lancheros** is on the Caribbean side of Laguna Makax. Local buses go to Lancheros, then turn inland and return downtown. The beach at Playa Lancheros is nice, but the few restaurants there are high-priced.

WATER SPORTS   Swimming   Wide Playa Norte is the best swimming beach, with Playa Lancheros second. There are no lifeguards on duty on Isla Mujeres, and the system of water-safety flags used in Cancún and Cozumel isn't used here.

Snorkeling   By far the most popular place to snorkel is **Garrafón National Park,** at the southern end of the island, where you'll see numerous schools of colorful fish. The well-equipped park has beach chairs, changing rooms, rental lockers, showers, and a snack bar. Admission is $2. Also good for snorkeling is the **Manchones Reef,** which is just offshore and reached by boat, where a bronze cross was installed in 1994.

Another excellent location is around the lighthouse (*el faro*) in the **Bahía de Mujeres** at the southern tip of the island, where the water is about 6 feet deep. Boatmen will take you for around $10 per person if you have your own snorkeling equipment or $15 more if you use theirs.

Diving   Several dive shops have opened on the island, most offering the same trips. The traditional dive center is **Buzos de México,** on Rueda Medina at Morelos (☎ 987/7-0131), next to the boat cooperative. Dive instructor Carlos Gutiérrez, speaks English, French, and Italian and offers certification (5 to 6 days for $350), and resort courses ($80 with three dives), and makes sure all dives are led by certified dive masters. **Bahía Dive Shop,** on Rueda Medina 166 across from the car-ferry dock (☎ 987/7-0340), is a full-service shop with dive equipment for sale and rent and resort and certification classes.

All 30- to 40-foot dives cost $45 to $65 for a two-tank trip; equipment rental costs $15. Cuevas de los Tiburones (Caves of the Sleeping Sharks) is Isla's most famous dive site and costs $70 to $80 for a two-tank dive at a depth of 70 to 80 feet (only advisable for experienced divers). There are actually two places to see the sleeping sharks: the Cuevas de Tiburones and La Punta. A storm collapsed the arch that was featured in a Jacques Cousteau film showing the sleeping sharks, but the caves are still there. Sharks have no gills, and so must constantly move to receive the oxygen they need. (Remember the line in *Annie Hall* equating relationships to sharks: "They must constantly move forward or die"?) The phenomenon here is that the high salinity and lack of carbon monoxide in the caves, combined with strong and steady currents, allow the sharks to receive the oxygen they need without moving. Your chance of actually seeing sleeping sharks, by the way, is about one in four; fewer sharks are present than in the past. The best time to see them is January through March.

Other dive sites include a wreck 9 km (14.4 miles) offshore; Banderas reef, between Isla Mujeres and Cancún, where there's always a strong current; Tabos reef on the eastern shore; and Manchones reef, 1 km (1.6 miles) off the southeastern tip of the island, where the water is 15 to 35 feet deep. The best season for diving is from June through August, when the water is calm.

Fishing   To arrange a day of fishing, ask at the **Sociedad Cooperativa Turística** (boatmen's cooperative; ☎ 987/7-0274) or the travel agency mentioned below, under "A Visit to Isla Contoy." The cost can be shared with four to six others and includes lunch and drinks. All year you'll find bonito, mackerel, kingfish, and amberjack. Sailfish and sharks (hammerhead, bull, nurse, lemon, and tiger) are in good supply in April and May. In winter, larger grouper and jewfish are prevalent. Four hours of fishing close to shore costs around $120; 8 hours farther out goes for $240. The cooperative is open Monday through Saturday from 8am to 1pm and 5 to 8pm, and Sunday from 7:30 to 10am and 6 to 8pm.

MORE ATTRACTIONS
A TURTLE SANCTUARY   A worthwhile outing on the island is to this reserve dedicated to preserving Caribbean sea turtles and to educating the public about them.

As few as 20 years ago fishermen converged on the island nightly from May through September waiting for these monster-size turtles to lumber ashore to deposit their Ping Pong ball-shaped eggs. Totally vulnerable once they begin laying their eggs, and exhausted when they finished, the turtles were easily captured and slaughtered for their highly prized meat, shell, and eggs. Then a concerned fisherman, Gonzalez Cahle Maldonado, began convincing others to spare at least the eggs, which he protected. It was a start. Following his lead, the fishing secretariat founded this **Centro de Investigaciones** 10 years ago; it's funded by both the government and private donations. Since then at least 28,000 turtles have been released and every year local school-children participate in the event, thus planting the notion of protecting the turtles for a new generation of islanders.

Six different species of sea turtles nest on Isla Mujeres. An adult green turtle, the most abundant species, measures 4 to 5 feet in length and can weigh as much as 450 pounds when grown. At the center, visitors walk through the indoor and outdoor turtle pool areas, watching the creatures paddling around. The turtles are separated by age, from newly hatched up to 1 year. Besides protecting the turtles that nest on Isla Mujeres of their own accord, the program also calls for capturing the turtles at sea and bringing them to enclosed compounds to mate and later to be freed to nest on Isla Mujeres. They are tagged and then released. While in the care of the center these guests receive a high-protein diet and reportedly grow faster than in the wild. People who come here usually end up staying at least an hour, especially if they opt for the guided tour, which enhances a visit. The permanent shelter has large wall paintings of all the sea turtles of the area. The sanctuary is on a piece of land separated from the island by Bahía de Mujeres and Laguna Makax; you'll need a taxi to get there. Admission is $1; the shelter is open daily from 9am to 5pm.

A MAYA RUIN   Just beyond the lighthouse, at the southern end of the island, is a pile of stones that formed a small Maya pyramid before Hurricane Gilbert struck. Believed to have been an observatory built to the moon goddess Ixchel, it's been reduced to a rocky heap. The location, on a lofty bluff overlooking the sea, is still worth seeing. If you're at Garrafón National Park and want to walk, it's not too far. Turn right from Garrafón. When you see the lighthouse, turn toward it down the rocky path.

A PIRATE'S FORTRESS   The Fortress of Mundaca is about 2½ miles in the same direction as Garrafón, about half a mile to the left. The fortress was built by the pirate Mundaca Marecheaga, who in the early 19th century arrived at Isla Mujeres and proceeded to set up a blissful paradise in a pretty, shady spot while making money from selling slaves to Cuba and Belize. Island lore also says he decided to settle down and build this hacienda after being captivated by the charms of an island girl. However she reputedly spurned his affections and left with another man, leaving him heartbroken and alone on Isla Mujeres.

A VISIT TO ISLA CONTOY   If at all possible, plan to visit this pristine uninhab-ited island, 19 miles by boat from Isla Mujeres, that was set aside as a national wildlife reserve in 1981. The oddly shaped 3.8-mile-long island is covered in lush vegetation and harbors 70 species of birds as well as a host of marine and animal life. Bird species that nest on the island include pelicans, brown boobies, frigates, egrets, terns, and cor-morants. Flocks of flamingos arrive in April. June, July, and August are good months to spot turtles that bury their eggs in the sand at night. Most excursions troll for fish (which will be your lunch), anchor en route for a snorkeling expedition, and skirt the island at a leisurely pace for close viewing of the birds without disturbing the habitat, then pull ashore. While the captain prepares lunch, visitors can swim, sun, follow the nature trails, and visit the fine nature museum. For a while the island was closed to visitors, but it's reopened now after rules for its use and safety were agreed to by fishermen and those bringing visitors. The trip from Isla Mujeres takes a minimum of

1½ hours one way, more if the waves are choppy. Because of the tight-knit boatmen's cooperative, prices for this excursion are the same everywhere: $30. You can buy a ticket at the **Sociedad Cooperativa Turística** (☎ 987/7-0274) on avenida Rueda Medina, next to Mexico Divers and Las Brisas restaurant, or at one of several travel agencies, such as **La Isleña,** on Morelos between Medina and Juárez (☎ 987/7-0036). La Isleña is open daily from 7am to 9pm and is a good source for tourist information. Contoy trips leave at 8:30am and return around 4pm.

Three types of boats go to Contoy. Small boats have one motor and seat eight or nine people. Medium-size boats have two motors and hold 10. Large boats have a toilet and hold 16 passengers. Most boats have a sun cover. The first two types are being phased out in favor of larger, better boats. Boat captains should respect the cooperative's regulations regarding capacity and should have enough life jackets to go around. Snorkeling equipment is usually included in the price, but double-check that before heading out.

SHOPPING

Shopping is a casual activity here. There are only a few shops of any sophistication. Otherwise you are bombarded by shop owners, especially on Hidalgo, selling Saltillo rugs, onyx, silver, Guatemalan clothing, blown glassware, masks, folk art, beach paraphernalia, and T-shirts in abundance. Prices are also lower than in Cancún or Cozumel, but with the overeager sellers, bargaining is necessary to achieve a satisfactory price.

WHERE TO STAY

There are plenty of hotels in all price ranges on Isla Mujeres. Rates are at their peak during high season, which is the most expensive and most crowded time to go. Elizabeth Wenger of **Four Seasons Travel** in Montello, Wisconsin (☎ 800/552-4550 or 608/297-2332) specializes in Mexico travel and especially books a lot of hotels in Isla Mujeres. Her service is invaluable in high season when hotel occupancy is high.

VERY EXPENSIVE

✪ **La Casa de los Sueños.** Carretera Garrafón s/n, 77400 Isla Mujeres, Q. Roo. ☎ **800/551-2558** in the U.S., or 987/7-0651. Fax 987/7-0708. www.lossuenos.com. E-mail: info@lossuenos.com. 9 units. A/C FAN TV. High season $200–$290 double. Low season $120–$250 double. Rates include breakfast. AE, MC, V.

This "house of dreams" is easily Isla Mujeres' most sophisticated property, originally built as a private residence. Lucky for us, it opened in early 1998 as an upscale, adults-only B&B. Its location on the southern end of the island, adjacent to El Garrafón National Park, makes it ideal for snorkeling or diving enthusiasts. The excellent design features vivid colors and sculpted architecture, with a large, open interior courtyard, tropical gardens, and an infinity pool that melts into the cool Caribbean waters. All rooms have balconies or terraces and face west, offering stunning views of the sunset and the night lights of Cancún. In addition, the rooms—which have names like "Serenity," "Passion," and "Love"—also have satellite TV, large, marble bathrooms, and luxury amenities. There's a small beach, palapa-shaded lounge area, private boat dock, and complimentary use of snorkeling equipment, kayaks, and bicycles for sightseeing around the island. A full American breakfast is included in the room price, and bar service and light lunches are also available. Geared to a healthful, stress-free vacation, the B&B forbids smoking and encourages casual dress and no shoes. Meditation areas and daily massage services are also available. Private boat transportation from Cancún to the B&B's dock can be arranged on request.

Dining/Diversions: The well-equipped kitchen and dining area serves breakfast, included in the rates, plus light lunches. There's also an outdoor palapa bar for refreshments.

Amenities: Swimming pool, meditation areas, massage service, free use of bicycles, private beach, boat dock, diving, and snorkeling available.

Puerto Isla Mujeres Resort & Yacht Club. Puerto de Abrigo Laguna Macax, 77400 Isla Mujeres, Q. Roo. ☎ **800/960-ISLA** in the U.S., 987/7-0413, 987/7-0330, or 98/83-1228 in Cancún. (Reservation address: Km 4.5 Paseo Kukulcán, 77500 Cancún, Q. Roo.) 25 units. A/C MINIBAR TV TEL. High season $265 suite. Low season $135 suite. Villas $190–$375. Rates include transportation from Cancún's offices in Playa Linda and daily continental breakfast. AE, MC, V.

The concept here—an exclusive glide-up yachting/sailing resort—is new not only to Isla Mujeres, but to all of Mexico. Facing an undeveloped portion of the glass-smooth, mangrove-edged Macax Lagoon, Puerto Isla Mujeres is a collection of modern suites and villas with sloping white-stucco walls and red-tile roofs spread across spacious palm-filled grounds. Beautifully designed with Scandinavian and Mediterranean elements, guest quarters feature tile, wood-beam ceilings, natural wood and marble accents, televisions with VCR, stereos with CD changer, and living areas. Villas have two bedrooms upstairs with a full bathroom and a small bathroom downstairs with a shower. Each villa also features a small stylish kitchen area with dishwasher, microwave, refrigerator, and coffeemaker. A whirlpool is on the upper patio off the master bedroom. Since weather is of consideration to the boating crowd, nightly turn-down service leaves the next day's weather forecast on the pillow beside the requisite chocolate. The beach club, with refreshments, is a water-taxi ride across the lagoon on a beautiful stretch of beach. A staff biologist can answer questions about birds and water life on Isla Mujeres. Even though the resort opened in 1995, more suites and villas were already on the drawing board.

Dining: Two excellent restaurants, one indoor and one outdoors by the pool, gourmet deli, small grocery store.

Amenities: Nearby beach club, free-form swimming pool with swim-up bar. Transportation is offered from the Cancún office at Playa Linda by boat to Isla Mujeres, plus there's a full-service marina with 60 slips for 30- to 60-foot vessels, short- and long-term dockage, fueling station, charter yachts and sailboats, and sailing school. Mopeds, golf carts, bicycles, and water-sports equipment for rent, and video and CD library. Laundry and room service.

EXPENSIVE

Hotel Na Balam. Zacil Ha 118, 77400 Isla Mujeres, Q. Roo. ☎ **987/7-0279.** Fax 987/7-0446. E-mail: nabalam@cancun.rce.com.mx. 31 units. A/C FAN. High season $125 suite. Low season $86 suite. AE, MC, V. Free unguarded parking.

This popular, two-story hotel near the end of Norte Beach has comfortable rooms on a quiet, ideally located portion of the beach. Rooms are in three sections, with some facing the beach and others across the street in a garden setting where there's a swimming pool. All rooms have either a patio or a balcony. Each fashionably furnished and spacious suite contains two double beds, a seating area, and folk-art decorations. Though other rooms are newer, the older section is well-kept, with a bottom-floor patio facing the peaceful palm-filled sandy inner yard and Norte Beach. From Tuesday through Thursday yoga lessons are offered; ask about the time and price. The restaurant, **Zacil-Ha,** is one of the island's most popular (see "Where to Dine," below). To find the hotel from the pier, walk 5 blocks to López Mateos; turn right and walk

4 blocks to Lazo (the last street). Turn left and walk to the sandy road parallel to the beach and turn right. The hotel is half a block farther.

Dining/Diversions: Zazil-Ha restaurant serves Mexican cuisine, seafood, and health food; two bars—one adjacent to the restaurant and one on the beach.

Amenities: Swimming pool and beach; diving and snorkeling trips available; mopeds, golf carts, and bicycles for rent; library, rec room with TV and VCR, and Ping-Pong tables. Salon services including manicures, pedicures, massages and facials, along with yoga classes.

MODERATE

Hotel Cabañas María del Mar. Av. Carlos Lazo 1, 77400 Isla Mujeres, Q. Roo. ☎ **800/ 223-5695** in the U.S., or 987/7-0179. Fax 987/7-0213 or 987/7-0156. 56 units. A/C. High season $70–$75 double. Low season $45–$50 double. Rates include continental breakfast. MC, V.

A good choice, the Cabañas María del Mar is located on Playa Norte, a half block from the Hotel Nabalam. There are three completely different sections to this hotel. The older two-story section behind the reception area and beyond the garden offers nicely outfitted rooms facing the beach, all with two single or double beds, refrigerators, and balconies with ocean views. Eleven single-story cabañas closer to the reception and pool are rather dark and are the lowest priced. The newest addition, **El Castillo,** is across the street and built over and beside Buho's restaurant. It contains all "deluxe" rooms, but some are larger than others; the five rooms on the ground floor all have large patios. Upstairs rooms have small balconies. Most have one double bed. All have ocean views, blue-and-white tile floors, and tile lavatories, and are outfitted in colonial-style furniture. There's a small pool in the garden. The owners also have a bus for tours and a boat for rent, as well as golf-cart and moto (motorized bikes or scooters) rental.

To get here from the pier, walk left 1 block, then turn right on Matamoros. After 4 blocks, turn left on Lazo, the last street. The hotel is at the end of the block.

○ **Hotel Posada del Mar.** Av. Rueda Medina 15, 77400 Isla Mujeres, Q. Roo. ☎ **800/ 544-3005** in the U.S., or 987/7-0044. Fax 987/7-0266. www.iminet.com/mexico/ posada.htm. E-mail: hposada@cancun.rce.com.mx. 40 units. A/C TEL. High season $54–$64 double. Low season $32–$36 double. AE, MC, V.

Attractively furnished, quiet, and comfortable, this long-established hotel faces the water and a wide beach 3 blocks north of the ferry pier, and it has one of the few swimming pools on the island. The very spacious rooms are in either a three-story building or one-story bungalow units. For the spacious quality of the rooms and the location, this is among the best values on the island. A wide, seldom-used but appealing stretch of Playa Norte is across the street. An extremely appealing casual palapa-style bar and a lovely pool are set on the back lawn, and the popular restaurant **Pinguino** (see "Where to Dine," below) is by the sidewalk at the front of the property. From the pier, go left for 4 blocks; the hotel is on the right.

INEXPENSIVE

○ **Hotel Belmar.** Av. Hidalgo 110, 74000 Isla Mujeres, Q. Roo. ☎ **987/7-0430.** Fax 987/7-0429. 11 units. A/C TV TEL. High season $56 double. Low season $28–$45 double. AE, MC, V.

Situated above Pizza Rolandi (consider the restaurant noise), this hotel is run by the same people who serve up those wood-oven pizzas. Each of the simple but stylish rooms comes with two twin or double beds and handsome tile accents. Prices are high for no views, but the rooms are very pleasant. On the other hand, this is one of the few island hotels with televisions (bringing in U.S. channels) in the room. There is a large suite with Jacuzzi and a patio. The hotel is between Madero and Abasolo, 3½ blocks from the passenger-ferry pier.

Hotel D'Gomar. Rueda Medina 50, 77400 Isla Mujeres, Q. Roo. ☎ **987/7-0541.** 16 units. High season $30–$35 double. Low season $20–$25 double. No credit cards.

You can hardly beat this hotel for comfort at reasonable prices. Rooms, with rattan furniture, all have two double beds, pink walls and drapes, and a wall of windows with great breezes and picture views. The higher prices are for air-conditioning, which is hardly needed with fantastic breezes and ceiling fans. Manager Manuel Serano says, "We make friends of all our clients." The only drawback is that there are five stories and no elevator. But it's conveniently located catercorner (look right) from the ferry pier, with exceptional rooftop views. The name of the hotel is the most visible sign on the "skyline."

Hotel Francis Arlene. Guerrero 7, 77400 Isla Mujeres, Q. Roo. ☎/fax **987/7-0310;** 98/ 84-3302 in Cancún. 26 units. A/C (20 rms) or FAN. High season $41–$46 double. Low season $37–$42 double. No credit cards.

The Magaña family operates this neat little two-story inn behind the family home, which is built around a small shady courtyard. You'll notice the tidy cream-and-white facade of the building from the street. Rooms are clean and comfortable, with tile floors and all-tile bathrooms, and soap and towels laid out on your bed. Each downstairs room has a refrigerator and stove; each upstairs room comes with a refrigerator and toaster. All have either a balcony or a patio. Rates are substantially better if quoted in pesos and are reflected above. In dollars they are 15% to 20% higher. It's 5½ blocks inland from the ferry pier, between Abasolo and Matamoros.

WHERE TO DINE

The **Municipal Market,** next door to the telegraph office and post office on avenida Guerrero, has several little cookshops operated by obliging and hard-working women. At the **Panadería La Reyna,** at Madero and Juárez, you can pick up inexpensive sweet bread, muffins, cookies, and yogurt. It's open Monday through Saturday from 7am to 9:30pm.

As in the rest of Mexico, a **cocina economica** restaurant literally means "economic kitchen." Usually aimed at the local population, these are great places to find good food at rock-bottom prices. That's especially so on Isla Mujeres, where you'll find several.

MODERATE

✪ **Las Palapas Chimbo's.** Norte Beach. No phone. Breakfast $2–$3; sandwiches and fruit $2–$3.50; seafood $5–$8. No credit cards. Daily 8am–6pm. SEAFOOD.

If you're looking for a beachside palapa-covered restaurant where you can wiggle your toes in the sand while relishing fresh seafood, this is the best of them. Locals recommend it as their favorite on Norte Beach. Try the delicious fried fish (a whole one), which comes with rice, beans, and tortillas. You'll notice the bandstand and dance floor that's been added to the middle of the restaurant, and especially the sex-hunk posters all over the ceiling—that is, when you aren't gazing at the beach and the Caribbean. Chimbo's becomes a disco at night, and draws a motley crew of drinkers and dancers (see "Isla Mujeres After Dark," below). To find it from the pier, walk left to the end of the malecón, then right onto the Playa Norte; it's about half a block on the right.

✪ **Pinguino.** In the Hotel Posada del Mar, Av. Rueda Medina 15. ☎ **987/7-0300.** Breakfast $2–$3; main courses $3.75–$6.75; daily special $6. AE, MC, V. Daily 7:30am–10pm; bar open to midnight. MEXICAN/SEAFOOD.

The best seats on the waterfront are on the deck of this restaurant/bar, especially in late evening when islanders and tourists arrive to dance and party. This is the place to feast on lobster—you'll get a beautifully presented, large, sublimely fresh lobster tail with a choice of butter, garlic, and secret sauces. Breakfasts include fresh fruit, yogurt, and granola or sizable platters of eggs, served with homemade wheat bread. Pinguino is in front of the hotel, 3 blocks west of the ferry pier.

✪ **Zacil-Ha.** At the Hotel Na Balam, Norte Beach. ☎ **987/7-0279.** Breakfast $3.50–$4.50; main courses $6–$9. AE, MC, V. Daily 7:30am–10pm; closed 10:30–12:30pm, 3:30–7pm. INTERNATIONAL.

At this restaurant you can enjoy some of the island's best food while sitting among the palms and gardens at tables on the sand. The serene environment is enhanced by the food—terrific pasta with garlic, shrimp in tequila sauce, fajitas, seafood pasta, and delicious mole enchiladas. Main courses come with vegetable and rice. Between the set hours for meals you can have all sorts of enticing food, such as blender vegetable and fruit drinks, tacos and sandwiches, ceviche, and terrific nachos. It's likely you'll stake this place out for several meals before you leave. It's at the end of Playa Norte and almost at the end of calle Zacil-Ha.

INEXPENSIVE

✪ **Cafecito.** Calle Matamoros 42 Corner of Juárez. ☎ **987/7-0438.** Coffee drinks $1–$3; crepes $1.75–$3.75; breakfast $2–$4; main courses $4.75–$7. No credit cards. Mon–Wed and Fri–Sat 8am–2pm and 6:30–10:30pm; Thurs and Sun 8am–2pm. CREPES/ICE CREAM/COFFEE/FRUIT DRINKS.

Sabina and Luis Rivera own this cute, Caribbean-blue corner restaurant where you can begin the day with flavorful coffee and a croissant and cream cheese, or end it with a hot-fudge sundae. Terrific crepes are served with yogurt, ice cream, fresh fruit, or chocolate sauces, as well as ham and cheese. The two-page ice-cream menu satisfies most any craving, even one for waffles with ice cream and fruit. The three-course fixed-price dinner starts with soup, then a main course such as fish or curried shrimp with rice and salad, followed by dessert. It's 4 blocks from the pier at the corner of Juárez and Matamoros.

✪ **Chen Huaye.** Bravo 6. No phone. Breakfast $2–$3.50; main courses $1.75–$5. No credit cards. Wed–Mon 9am–11pm. YUCATECAN MEXICAN/HOME COOKING.

The Juanito Tago Trego family owns this large lunchroom where tourists and locals find a variety of pleasing dishes at equally pleasing prices. Light meals include empanadas, Yucatecan salubites, panucos, and quesadillas. The *tamal costado*, a tamal stuffed with chicken pieces and baked in a banana leaf, is a daily special. Main courses might include breaded pork chops, chicken in adobado, or fried chicken. The name, by the way, is Maya for "only here." It's between Guerrero and Juárez; you'll recognize it by the wagon wheel in front.

Cocina Económica Carmelita. calle Juárez 14. ☎ **987/7-0136.** Meal of the day $3. No credit cards. Daily noon–3pm; Dec–Mar also open for dinner, 4–8pm. MEXICAN/HOME COOKING.

Few tourists find their way to this tiny restaurant, open only for lunch. But locals know they can get a filling, inexpensive, home-cooked meal prepared by Carmelita in the back kitchen and served by her husband at the three cloth-covered tables in the front room of their home. Two or three comida corridas are available each day and are served until they run out. They begin with black-bean soup and include a fruit water drink. Common selections include paella or *cochinita pibil,* and fish-stuffed chiles; Sunday is pozole day. It's 2 blocks from the passenger-ferry pier, between Bravo and Allende.

ISLA MUJERES AFTER DARK

Those in a party mood by day's end might want to start out at the beach bar of the **Hotel Na Balam** on Playa Norte, which hosts a crowd until around midnight. On Saturday and Sunday there's live music here between 4 and 7pm. **Las Palapas Chimbo's** restaurant on the beach becomes a jammin' dance joint with a live band from 9pm until whenever. Farther along the same stretch of beach, **Buho's,** the restaurant/beach bar of the Cabañas María del Mar has its moments as a popular, low-key hangout. **Pinguino** in the Hotel Posada del Mar offers a convivial late-night hangout. There are two places to be: the restaurant/bar, where the manager, Miguel, whips up some potent concoctions and the band plays nightly during high season from 9pm to midnight; and the more tranquil but totally delightful poolside bar with swings under a giant palapa.

2 Cozumel

44 miles SE of Cancún

Cozumel is the original Caribbean destination in Mexico, a top cruise-ship port of call in the Americas, and one of the world's top-five dive destinations. Despite all this acclaim, Cozumel remains a laid-back, ocean-oriented village, infused with a mix of Maya and Mexican authenticity.

The largest island in the Mexican Caribbean, it is located just 12 miles offshore from Playa del Carmen, a 45-minute, $5 ferry ride away. The name comes from the Maya word *Cuzamil,* meaning "land of the swallows." Today, it remains the home of two species of birds found nowhere else: the Cozumel vireo and the Cozumel thrasher. Only 3% developed, this 28-mile long, 11-mile wide island still has vast stretches of pristine jungle and uninhabited shoreline.

The only town is San Miguel de Cozumel, usually called just San Miguel. On the island, you'll find a mix of all the necessities for a good vacation: excellent snorkeling and scuba places, sailing and water sports, expensive resorts and modest hotels, elegant restaurants and taco shops, and even a Maya ruin or two. Due to the influx of cruise visitors, shopping is extensive, with many duty-free stores selling jewelry, perfumes and designer wares. If after a while you do get restless, the ancient Maya city of **Tulum,** the lagoons of **Xel-Ha** and **Xcaret,** or the nearby village of **Playa del Carmen** provide convenient and interesting excursions.

During pre-Hispanic times the island was one of three important ceremonial centers (Izamal and Chichén-Itzá were the other two). Maya women would travel the 12 miles by boat to the island at least once in their life to worship the goddess of fertility, Ixchel. More than 40 sites around the island containing shrines remain today, and archaeologists still uncover the small dolls regularly offered in the fertility ceremony.

Salt and honey, trade products produced on the island, further linked Cozumel with the mainland; they were brought ashore at the ruins we know today as Tulum. The site was occupied when Hernán Cortés landed here in 1519. Before his own boat docked, Cortés's men sacked the town and took the chief's wife and children captive. According to Bernal Díaz del Castillo's account, everything was returned. Diego de Landa's account says Cortés converted the Indians and replaced their sacred Maya figures with a cross and a statue of Mary in the main temple at Cozumel. After the Spanish Conquest the island was an important port; but foreign diseases decimated the population, and by 1570 it was almost uninhabited.

The inhabitants returned later, but the War of the Castes in the 1800s severely curtailed Cozumel's trade. Cozumel continued on its economic roller coaster, and after the Caste War it again took its place as a commercial seaport. In the mid-1950s Cozumel's fame as a diving destination began to grow, and real development of the island as the site for a vacation resort evolved along with Cancún, beginning in the mid-1970s.

ESSENTIALS
GETTING THERE & DEPARTING

BY PLANE **Aerocozumel,** a Mexicana affiliate, has numerous flights to and from Cancún and Mérida. **Mexicana** flies from Mexico City. **Taesa** flies from Cancún, Chetumal, and Mérida.

Here are some telephone numbers for confirming departures to and from Cozumel: **Aerocozumel** (☎ **987/2-3456,** or 988/4-2002 in Cancún), **Continental** (☎ **800/ 231-0856** in the U.S.; 987/2-0847 in Cozumel), and **Mexicana** (☎ **800/531-7921** in the U.S.; 800/50-220-00 in Mexico; 987/2-0157 or 987/2-2945 at the airport; fax 987/2-2945).

Only **colectivo** vans are available from the airport into town, costing around $5 to $6. Taxis from town to the airport will run $8 to $12.

BY FERRY Passenger ferries to Cozumel depart from Playa del Carmen on the mainland daily, with scheduled service. There is also a car ferry from Puerto Morelos. You can catch a bus to Playa del Carmen from Cancún.

The **Water Jet Service** (☎ **987/2-1508** or 987/2-1588), makes the trip between Cozumel and Playa del Carmen in 45 minutes. It costs $5 one way and is enclosed and air-conditioned, with cushioned seats, bar service, and video entertainment. Departures are almost hourly from 5am to 11pm. In Playa del Carmen, the ferry dock is 1½ blocks from the main square and from the bus drop-off point. Tickets are also sold in booths at the main pier in Cozumel. Since schedules change frequently, be sure to double-check them at the docks, especially the time of the last ferry back, if that's the one you intend to use. Storage lockers are available at the Cozumel dock for $2 per day. From Cozumel to Playa del Carmen, the ferry runs approximately every hour or hour and a half between 4am and 10pm, also at a cost of $5 one way.

For those who are considering a **car ferry,** the first thing to know is that you're better off without a car in Cozumel; parking is difficult. A solution is to drive to Playa del Carmen, find a reliable place to leave your car, and take the passenger ferry. If you do want to take your car over, the terminus in **Puerto Morelos** (☎ **987/1-0008**) is the largest establishment in town, and is very easy to find. The car-ferry schedule is complicated and may change, so double-check it before arriving in Puerto Morelos. On Monday, the ferry leaves at 6am, 9:30am, and 6pm; on Tuesday at 10am and 3 and 8pm; from Wednesday through Sunday one daily departure with varying hours. The crossing takes approximately 3 hours.

Cargo takes precedence over cars. Officials suggest that camper drivers stay overnight in the parking lot to be first in line for tickets. In any case, *always arrive at least 3 hours in advance of the ferry's departure to purchase a ticket and to get in line.*

Since passenger-boat service between Playa del Carmen and Cozumel is so fast and frequent, I don't recommend that foot passengers bother with this boat.

When returning to Puerto Morelos from Cozumel, the ferry departs from the international cruise-ship pier daily. Get in line about 3 hours before departure, and

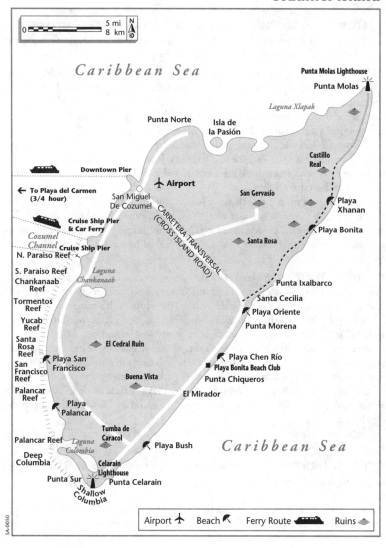

Map legend: Airport ✈ Beach ⚓ Ferry Route 🚢 Ruins ◈

Labels on map:
- Caribbean Sea
- Punta Molas Lighthouse
- Punta Molas
- Laguna Xlapak
- Punta Norte
- Isla de la Pasión
- Castillo Real
- Downtown Pier
- ← To Playa del Carmen (3/4 hour)
- Airport
- San Miguel De Cozumel
- San Gervasio
- Playa Xhanan
- Cruise Ship Pier & Car Ferry
- Cozumel Channel
- Cruise Ship Pier
- N. Paraíso Reef
- Playa Bonita
- CARRETERA TRANSVERSAL (CROSS ISLAND ROAD)
- Santa Rosa
- S. Paraíso Reef
- Chankanaab Reef
- Laguna Chankanaab
- Punta Ixalbarco
- Tormentos Reef
- Santa Cecilia
- Yucab Reef
- Playa Oriente
- Punta Morena
- Santa Rosa Reef
- San Francisco Reef
- El Cedral Ruin
- Playa San Francisco
- Playa Chen Río
- Playa Bonita Beach Club
- Buena Vista
- Punta Chiqueros
- Palancar Reef
- Playa Palancar
- El Mirador
- Palancar Reef
- Laguna Colombia
- Tumba de Caracol
- Playa Bush
- Caribbean Sea
- Deep Columbia
- Celarain Lighthouse
- Punta Sur
- Shallow Columbia
- Punta Celarain

SA-0050

double-check the schedule by calling ☎ **987/2-0950.** The fare is $45 for a car and $5 per passenger.

ORIENTATION

ARRIVING   Cozumel's **airport** is immediately north of downtown. Aero Transportes colectivo vans at the airport provide transportation into town and to the north or south hotel zone. Buy your ticket as you exit the terminal. Cozumel now has two **cruise ferry docks,** with a third under controversial construction. The newest one, **Puerto Maya,** about a mile south of the older one (dubbed the **International Pier**) also stirred controversy because it was built over North Paradise Reef—the reef with the best shore diving and snorkeling possibilities. Dive operators, the town, and ecological preservation activists from around the world protested the building of this pier, without success.

VISITOR INFORMATION   The **State Tourism Office** (☎/fax **987/2-0972** or 987/2-0218) is on the second floor of the Plaza del Sol commercial building facing the central plaza and is open daily from 8:30am to 3pm.

CITY LAYOUT   San Miguel's main waterfront street is called **avenida Rafael Melgar,** running along the western shore of the island. Passenger ferries dock right in the center, opposite the main plaza and Melgar. Car ferries dock south of town at the International Pier near the hotels Sol Caribe and La Ceiba. Cruise ships dock at the International Pier and at the New Puerto Maya Pier.

The town is laid out on a grid, with avenidas running north and south, calles running east and west. The exception is **avenida Juárez,** which runs right from the passenger-ferry dock through the main square and inland. Juárez divides the town into northern and southern halves.

Heading inland from the dock along Juárez, you'll find that the avenidas you cross are numbered by fives: 5a av., 10a av., 15a av. If you turn left and head north, calles are numbered evenly: 2a Norte, 4a Norte, 6a Norte. Turning right from Juárez heads you south, where the streets are numbered: 1a Sur (also called Adolfo Salas), 3a Sur, 5a Sur.

ISLAND LAYOUT   The island is cut in half by one road, which runs past the airport and the ruins of San Gervasio to the almost uninhabited southern coast of the island. The northern part of the island has no paved roads. It's scattered with small, badly ruined Maya sites, from the age when "Cuzamil" was a land sacred to the moon goddess Ixchel. San Gervasio is accessible by motor scooter and car.

Most inexpensive hotels are in the town of San Miguel. Moderate to expensive accommodations are north and south of town. Many cater to divers. Beyond the hotels to the south is **Chankanaab National Park,** centered on the beautiful lagoon of the same name. Beyond Chankanaab are **Playa Palancar** and, offshore, the **Palancar Reef** (*arrecife*). At the southern tip of the island are **Punta Celarain** and the lighthouse.

The eastern, seaward shore of the island is mostly surf beach, beautiful for walking but dangerous for swimming.

GETTING AROUND   You can walk to most destinations in town. However, getting to outlying hotels and beaches, including the Chankanaab Lagoon, requires a taxi.

Car rentals are as expensive here as they are in other parts of Mexico. International agencies have counters in the airport, or rentals can be arranged by your hotel tour desk or any local travel agency. See "By Car" under "Getting Around" in chapter 3 for specifics.

Moped rentals are all over the village and cost about $25 for 24 hours, but terms and prices vary. Carefully inspect the actual moped you'll be renting to see that all the gizmos are in good shape: horn, light, starter, seat, mirror. And be sure to note all damage to the moped on the rental agreement. Most important, read the fine print on the back of the rental agreement, which states that you are not insured, are responsible

Street Smarts

North/south streets have the right of way, and these drivers don't slow down.

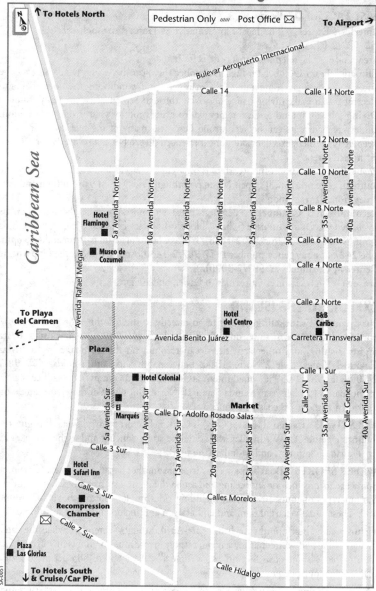

San Miguel de Cozumel

for paying any damage to the bike (or for all of it if it's stolen or demolished), and must stay on paved roads. It's illegal to ride a moped without a helmet (subject to a $25 fine).

Taxis: Here are a few sample fares: Island tour: $30; town to southern hotel zone: $4 to $8; town to northern hotels: $3 to $5; to Chankanaab from town: $6. Call ☎ **987/2-0236** for taxi pickup.

FAST FACTS: COZUMEL

American Express The local representative is **Fiesta Cozumel,** calle 11 no. 598 (☎ **987/2-0725**).

Area Code The telephone area code is **987.**

Climate From October through December there can be strong winds all over the Yucatán, as well as some rain. In Cozumel, wind conditions in November and December can make diving dangerous. May through September is the rainy season.

Diving If you intend to dive, remember to bring proof of your diver's certification. Underwater currents can be very strong here, and many of the reef drops are quite steep, making them excellent sites for experienced divers, but can be overly challenging for novice divers.

Post Office The post office (*correo*) is on avenida Rafael Melgar at calle 7 Sur, at the southern edge of town; it's open Monday through Friday from 9am to 6pm and Saturday from 9am to noon.

Recompression Chamber There are three recompression chambers (*cámara de recompresión*). One is on calle 5 Sur, 1 block off Melgar between Melgar and avenida 5 Sur (☎ **987/2-2387** or 987/2-1848). Normal hours are 8am to 1pm and 4 to 8pm. The 24-hour **emergency** number is ☎ **987/2-1430.** Another one is the **Hyperbaric Center of Cozumel** (☎ **987/2-3070**).

Seasons High season is Christmas to Easter, and August.

EXPLORING THE ISLAND

For **diving** and **snorkeling** it's best to go directly to the recommended shops below. For **island tours, ruins tours** on and off the island, **glass-bottom boat tours, fiesta nights, fishing,** and other activities, I can recommend the travel agency **InterMar Cozumel Viajes,** calle 2 Norte, 101-B between 5th and 10th avenidas. (☎ **987/ 2-1098;** fax 987/2-0895; E-mail intermar@cozumel.czm.com.mx). The office is close to the main plaza between avenida 5 and 10 Norte. But many of these you can do on your own without purchasing a tour.

A FESTIVAL **Carnaval** (Mardi Gras) is Cozumel's most colorful fiesta. It begins the Thursday before Ash Wednesday with daytime street dancing and nighttime parades on Thursday, Saturday, and Monday (the best).

WATER SPORTS **Boat Trips** Boat trips are another popular pastime at Cozumel. Some excursions include snorkeling and scuba diving or a stop at a beach with lunch. Various types of tours are offered, including rides in glass-bottom boats for around $30. These usually start at 9am and end at 1pm and include beer and soft drinks.

Fishing The best months for fishing are April through September, when the catch includes blue and white marlin, sailfish, tarpon, swordfish, dorado, wahoo, tuna, and red snapper. Fishing costs $450 for six people all day or $80 to $85 per person for a half day for four people.

✪ **Scuba Diving** Cozumel is Mexico's dive capital, and one of the world's premier dive destinations. Various establishments on the island rent scuba gear—tanks, regulator with pressure gauge, buoyancy compensator, weight belts, mask, snorkel, and fins. Many will also arrange a half-day expedition in a boat, complete with lunch, for a set price—usually around $40. Sign up the day before if you're interested. A two-tank morning dive costs around $50; some shops are now offering an additional afternoon one-tank dive for $9 for those who took the morning dives, or $25 for a one-tank dive. However, if you're a dedicated diver, you may save by buying a diving package that includes air transportation, hotel, and usually two dives a day. Cozumel is such a popular dive destination it has over 60 dive operators and three recompression chambers on the island (see "Fast Facts: Cozumel," above).

The underwater wonders of the famous **Palancar Reef** are offshore from the beach of the same name. From the car-ferry pier south to Punta Celarain are more than 20 miles of offshore reefs. In the famous blue depths, divers find caves and canyons, small and large colorful fish, and an enormous variety of sea coral. The **Santa Rosa Reef** is famous for its depth, sea life, coral, and sponges. **San Francisco Reef,** off the beach by the same name south of town, has a drop-off wall, but it's still fairly shallow and the sea life is fascinating. The **Chankanaab Reef,** where divers are joined by schools of tropical fish, is close to the shore by the national park of the same name. It's shallow and good for novice divers. Next after Chankanaab going south on the eastern road, **Yucab Reef** has beautiful coral.

Numerous vessels on the island operate daily diving and snorkeling tours, so if you aren't traveling on a prearranged dive package, the best plan is to shop around and sign up for one of those. Of Cozumel's many dive shops, two are among the top: Bill Horn's **Aqua Safari,** in front of the Aqua Safari Inn and next to the Vista del Mar Hotel on Melgar at calle 5 (☎ **987/2-0101;** fax 987/2-0661) and in the Hotel Plaza Las Glorias (☎ **987/2-3362** or 987/2-2422), is a PADI five-star instructor center, has full equipment and parts, a good selection of books, and its own pier just across the street. They're on the Internet at www.aquasafari.com. **Dive House,** on the main plaza (☎ **987/2-1953;** fax 987/2-0368), offers PADI and NAUI SSI instruction. Both shops offer morning and night dives, and afternoon snorkeling trips. Aqua Safari is one of the oldest dive shops in Cozumel. For private, independent dive instruction, I can recommend **Sheena Mulshaw, Divemaster** (☎ **984/1-1978**).

You can save money by renting your gear at a beach shop, such as the two mentioned above, and diving from shore. The shops at the Plaza Las Glorias and La Ceiba hotels are good for shore diving. It costs about $6 to rent one tank and weights; extra charges apply for regulator, BC, mask, and fins. The dives from shore are only worthwhile from San Francisco beach, Chankanaab, and La Ceiba beach. Even then it's a lot of work to haul your own gear. The sites are much better in the depths offshore, and it really is a lot easier to take a boat.

A new twist in underwater Yucatán is **cenote diving** and **snorkeling.** The peninsula's underground *cenotes* (say-*noh*-tehs) or sinkholes, which were sacred to the Maya, lead to a vast system of underground caverns. Here, the gently flowing water is so clear, divers appear to be floating on air through caves that look just like those on dry land, complete with stalactites and stalagmites, plus tropical fish, eels, and turtles. The caverns were formed millions of years ago during the last two glacial eras, but only in recent years has this other world been opened to certified divers. The experienced cave divers/owners of **Yucatech Expeditions** (☎/fax **987/2-5659;** fax 987/2-1417; E-mail: yucatech@cozumel.czm.com.mx), offer this unique experience five times weekly from Playa del Carmen (you take the ferry with your gear and they meet you with vans there). Cenotes are 30 to 45 minutes from Playa and a dive in each cenote lasts around 45 minutes. Snorkelers paddle around the cenotes, while divers explore the depths. Dives are within the daylight zone, about 130 feet into the caverns and no more than 60 feet deep. There's plenty of natural light. Company owner German Yañez Mendoza, inspects diving credentials carefully and has a list of requirements divers must meet before cave diving is permitted. They also offer the equivalent of a resort course in cave diving and a full cave-diving course. A snorkeling trip to two cenotes runs around $65, while a two-cenote dive costs around $130, including transportation from Cozumel, tanks, weights, food, and drinks (beers only after the dives).

Snorkeling Anyone who can swim can snorkel. Rental of the snorkel (breathing pipe), goggles, and flippers should cost only about $4 for half a day; a 2-hour snorkeling trip costs $15. The brilliantly colored tropical fish provide a dazzling show. **Chankanaab Park** is one of the best places to go on your own for an abundant fish show.

Agency-arranged **snorkeling excursions** cost around $40 for a 10am-to-3pm trip that includes snorkeling at three different reefs, lunch, beer, and soft drinks. Two-hour snorkeling trips through the dive shops recommended above last 2 hours, cost $15, and usually leave around 2:30pm.

Windsurfing One of Mexico's top windsurfing champions, **Raul de Lille,** offers windsurfing classes and equipment rentals at the beach in front of Sol Cabañas del Caribe, on the north side. For information call ☎ **987/2-0017;** fax 987/2-1942.

A TOUR OF THE ISLAND

Travel agencies can book you on a group tour of the island for around $35, depending on whether the tour includes lunch and a stop for snorkeling. A taxi driver charges $60 for a 4-hour tour. A 4-hour horseback tour of the island's interior to the ruins and jungle costs $60; call **Rancho Buenavista** (☎ **987/2-1537** or 987/2-4374). The trip leaves from the Neptuno Disco (call for schedule information), or the InterMar Viajes travel agency mentioned above. You can also easily rent a moped or car for half a day to take you around; see "Getting Around," above.

North of town, along avenida Rafael Melgar (which becomes Carretera Pilar), you'll pass a yacht marina and a string of Cozumel's first hotels as well as some new condominiums. A few of the hotels have nice beaches. This road ends just past the hotels; you can backtrack to the transversal road that cuts across the island from west (the town side) to east and links up with the eastern highway that brings you back to town.

The more interesting route begins by going south of town on Melgar (which becomes Costera Sur or Carretera a Chankanaab) past the Hotel Barracuda and Sol Caribe. After about 3 miles you'll see a sign pointing left down an unpaved road a short distance to the Rancho San Manuel, where you can rent horses. There are only seven horses here, but a guide and soft drink are included in the price. Rides cost $20 per hour. It's open daily from 8am to 4pm.

About 5 miles south of town you'll come to the Crowne Princess and La Ceiba hotels and also the car-ferry dock for ferries to Puerto Morelos. Go snorkeling out in the water by the Hotel La Ceiba and you might spot a sunken airplane, put there for an underwater movie. Offshore, from here to the tip of the island at Punta Celarain 20 miles away, is the Underwater National Park, so designated to protect the reef from damage by visitors. Dive masters warn not to touch or destroy the underwater growth.

CHANKANAAB NATIONAL PARK This lagoon and botanical garden is a mile past the big hotels and 5½ miles south of town. Known as a natural aquarium, it has long been famous for the color and variety of its sea life. The intrusion of sightseers began to ruin the marine habitat, so now visitors must swim and snorkel in the open sea, not in the lagoon. The beach is wide and beautiful, with plenty of shady thatched umbrellas to sit under, and the snorkeling is good—lots of colorful fish. Arrive early to stake out a chair and palapa before the cruise-ship visitors arrive. There are rest rooms, lockers, a gift shop, several snack huts, a restaurant, and a snorkeling-gear-rental palapa.

Surrounding the lagoon, the botanical garden, with shady paths, has 352 species of tropical and subtropical plants from 22 countries and 451 species from Cozumel. Several Maya structures have been re-created within the gardens to give visitors an idea of

Maya life in a jungle setting. There's a small natural-history museum as well. Admission to the park costs $3; it's open daily from 8am to 5pm.

THE BEACHES

Ten miles past the Chankanaab National Park, you'll come to Playa San Francisco and, south of it, Playa Palancar. Besides the beach at Chankanaab Lagoon, they're the best on Cozumel. Food (usually overpriced) and equipment rentals are available. On the east side of the island, the Playa Bonita Beach Club, near Playa Chiqueros, has watersports and windsurfing-equipment rentals. The restaurant is open daily from 10am to 5pm.

PUNTA CELARAIN   After Playa San Francisco, you plow through the jungle on a straight road for miles until you're 17½ miles from town. Finally, though, you emerge near the southern reaches of the island on the east coast. The lighthouse you see in the distance is at Punta Celarain, the island's southernmost tip. The sand track is unsuitable for motorbikes, but in a car you can drive to the lighthouse in about 25 minutes.

THE EASTERN SHORE   The road along the east coast of the island is wonderful. There are views of the sea, the rocky shore, and the pounding surf. On the land side are little farms and forests. Exotic birds take flight as you approach, and monstrous (but harmless) iguanas skitter off into the undergrowth.

Most of the east coast is unsafe for swimming because the surf can create a deadly undertow. There are always cars pulled off along the road here, with the occupants spending the day on the golden beach dotted with limestone formations, but not in the churning waters. Three restaurants catering to tourists are along this part of the coast, complete with sombrero-clad iguanas for a picture companion.

Halfway up the east coast, the paved eastern road meets the paved transversal road (which passes the ruins of San Gervasio) back to town, 9½ miles away. The east-coast road ends when it turns into the transversal, petering out to a narrow track of sandy road by a nice restaurant in front of the Chen Río Beach; vehicles, even motorbikes, will get stuck on the sand road. If you're a bird-watcher, leave your vehicle on the highway here and walk straight down the sandy road. Go slowly and quietly and at the least you'll spot many herons and egrets in the lagoon on the left that parallels the path. Much farther on are Maya ruins.

MORE ATTRACTIONS

MAYA RUINS   One of the most popular island excursions is to **San Gervasio** (100 B.C. to A.D. 1600). A road leads there from the airport, or you can continue on the eastern part of the island following the paved transversal road. The worn sign to the ruins is easy to miss, but the turnoff (left) is about halfway between town and the eastern coast. Stop at the entrance gate and pay the $1 road-use fee. Go straight ahead over the potholed road to the ruins about 2 miles farther and pay the $3.50 to enter; camera permits cost $4 for each still or video camera you want to bring in. A small tourist center at the entrance has cold drinks and snacks for sale.

When it comes to Cozumel's Maya remains, getting there is most of the fun, and you should do it for the mystique and for the trip, not for the size or scale of the ruins. The buildings, though preserved, are crudely made and would not be much of a tourist attraction if they were not the island's only cleared and accessible ruins. More significant than beautiful, the site was once an important ceremonial center where the Maya gathered, coming even from the mainland. The important deity here was Ixchel, known as the goddess of weaving, women, childbirth, pilgrims, the moon, and medicine. Although you won't see any representations of her at San Gervasio today, Bruce

Hunter, in his *Guide to Ancient Maya Ruins,* writes that priests hid behind a large pottery statue of her and became the voice of the goddess speaking to pilgrims and answering their petitions. She was the wife of Itzamná, sun god, and as such, preeminent among all Maya gods.

Tour guides charge $10 for a tour for one to six people. A better option is to find a copy of the green booklet *San Gervasio,* sold at local checkout counters or bookstores, and tour the site on your own. Seeing it takes 30 minutes. Taxi drivers offer a tour to the ruins for about $25; the driver will wait for you outside the ruins.

PARQUE ARQUEOLÓGICO This park contains reproductions of many of Mexico's important archaeological treasures, including the 4-foot-high Olmec head and the Chaac-Mool seen in Chichén-Itzá. A Maya couple demonstrate the lifestyle of the Maya in a *nah,* or thatch-roofed oval home. The park is a nice addition to the island's cultural attractions and is well worth visiting, but wear bug repellent before you begin exploring. The park is open daily from 8am to 6pm; admission is $1.50. To get there, turn left on the unmarked road across from the International Pier, off Costera Sur just south of the La Ceiba hotel, then left on avenida 65 Sur and follow the signs.

A HISTORY MUSEUM The **Museo de la Isla de Cozumel,** on avenida Melgar between calles 4 and 6 Norte (☎ **987/2-1475**), is more than just a nice place to spend a rainy hour. On the first floor an excellent exhibit showcases endangered species, the origin of the island, and its present-day topography and plant and animal life, including an explanation of coral formation. Upstairs, showrooms feature the history of the town, artifacts from the island's pre-Hispanic sites, and colonial-era cannons, swords, and ship paraphernalia. It's open daily from 9am to 5pm. Admission is $3; guided tours in English are free. There's a rooftop restaurant open long hours.

TRIPS TO THE MAINLAND
PLAYA DEL CARMEN & XCARET

Going on your own to the nearby seaside village of **Playa del Carmen** and the **Xcaret** nature park is as easy as a quick ferry ride from Cozumel (for ferry information, see "Getting There & Departing," above.) Playa del Carmen is covered in detail later in this chapter; Xcaret, in chapter 12. Cozumel travel agencies offer an Xcaret tour that includes the ferry fee, transportation to the park, and the admission fee for $45.

CHICHÉN-ITZÁ, TULUM & COBÁ

Travel agencies can arrange day-trips to the fascinating ruins of **Chichén-Itzá** either by air or by bus. Departure times vary depending on which transportation you choose. Since the ruins of **Tulum,** overlooking the Caribbean, and **Cobá,** in a dense jungle setting, are closer, they cost less to visit. They are a complete architectural contrast to Chichén-Itzá: Coba is a grandiose archeological zone within a remote jungle setting, while Tulum is much smaller in actual dimensions. A trip to Coba and Tulum, both of which have had less restorative attention given them than Chichén-Itzá, begins at 9am and returns around 6pm. See chapter 14 for further details on Chichén-Itzá.

SHOPPING

Shopping has evolved from the ubiquitous T-shirt shops into stores that feature expensive resort wear, silver, and better decorative and folk art. Most stores are on avenida Melgar; the best shops for high-quality Mexican folk art are Los Cinco Soles, Talavera, and Playa del Ángel. Prices for sarapes, T-shirts, and the like are normally less expensive on the side streets off Melgar.

If you want to pick up some Mexican tapes and CDs, head to **Discoteca Hollywood,** at Juárez 421 (☎ **987/2-4090**); it's open Monday through Saturday from 9am to 10pm. Self-billed as the "Paradise of the Cassette," this store stocks a large selection.

WHERE TO STAY

Cozumel's hotels are in three separate locations: in the **central town,** and to the **north** and **south** of town. The older resorts, most of which are expensive, line beaches and coral and limestone outcroppings north and south of town; the more budget-oriented inns are in the central village. *Note:* The **central reservations number** for many (not all) of the island's hotels is ☎ **800/327-2254** in the U.S. and Canada. As an alternative to a hotel, **Cozumel Vacation Villas and Condos,** av. 10 Sur no. 124, 77600 Cozumel, Quintana Roo (☎ **800/224-5551** in the U.S., 987/2-0729, or 987/2-1375; E-mail: info@ cozumel-villas.com), offers a wide range of accommodations and prices.

Because Cozumel is principally a destination for divers, there are numerous options that cater to this specialty market. Some are for serious no-frills divers who only want a good bed and a hot shower for after the dive. These hotels usually don't have a pool or restaurant. There are others that are a little more upscale, often on the beach, that offer complete dive services in addition to rooms and facilities. The remaining properties are for divers traveling with nondivers.

HOTELS NORTH OF TOWN

I'll start with the northernmost hotels going through town, and move onward to the end of the southern hotel zone. Like beaches south of town, those along the northern shore appear sporadically and some hotels have enclosed them with retaining walls. **Carretera Santa Pilar** is the name of Melgar's northern extension, so just take Melgar north and all the hotels are lined up in close proximity to each other on the Santa Pilar Beach a short distance from town and the airport.

Very Expensive

Hotel El Cozumeleño Beach Resort. Km 4.5 Carretera Santa Pilar (Apdo. Postal 53), 77600 Cozumel, Q. Roo. ☎ **987/2-0050** or 987/2-0049. Fax 987/2-0381. 100 units. A/C TV TEL. High season $200–$280 double. Low season $140–$220 double. Rates are all-inclusive. AE, MC, V.

The Cozumeleño all-inclusive resort is a five-story hotel (with elevator) on one of the nicest stretches of coral-free beach on the island. The expansive marble-floored lobby scattered with groupings of pastel chairs and couches is a popular gathering place. The glassed-in dining room looks out onto the Caribbean, as do all the spacious and nicely furnished guest rooms. The beach here is rocky, but their pleasant free-form pool and surrounding areas compensate with extensive gardens, a hot tub, and shade palapas.

Dining/Diversions: Two restaurants, one by the beach and pool and the other indoors, serve all three meals. A karaoke bar provides music to drink by.

Amenities: Palm-shaded pool, children's pool, tennis court, water-sports equipment, 19-hole miniature golf course, game room, gym, diving center, laundry and room service, travel agency, auto and moped rental.

Expensive

Playa Azul. Km 4 Carretera Pilar, 77600 Cozumel, Q. Roo. ☎ **987/2-0199** or 987/2-0043. Fax 987/2-0110. E-Mail: playazul@cozumel.czm.com.mx. 30 units. A/C TEL. High season $110–$170 double. Low season $70–$130 double. MC, V.

This boutique hotel caters to divers and offers extra-clean, extremely spacious rooms, most with large balconies or terraces overlooking their white, sandy beach. Under new management, the hotel has recently been completely renovated, and offers new common services and facilities, including a second-floor lobby with pool table and video room, plus a library. The beachfront pool has cushioned lounges. There are shade palapas on the beach, plus a private dock for dive boat pickups. All rooms have either king-size or two double beds, with suites offering two convertible single sofas in the separate living-room area. In-room safe-deposit boxes and extra-large bathrooms are added features. All rooms are simply furnished, with tile floors. The friendly, on-site management assures top service.

Dining/Diversions: The **Playa Azul** restaurant specializes in seafood and Mexican cuisine and offers indoor or patio dining; there's room service available from 7am to 11pm. The beachfront palapa bar is open from 9am to 6pm.

Amenities: Beachfront pool with water-sports equipment, atrium lounge with video room and satellite TV, laundry, dry cleaning, gift shop, room service, scooter and car rental, massage service available.

Sol Cabañas del Caribe. Km 4.5 Carretera Santa Pilar (Apdo. Postal 9), 77600 Cozumel, Q. Roo. ☎ **888/341-5993** in the U.S., 987/2-0017, or 987/2-0072. Fax 987/2-1599. E-mail: paradisu@cozumel.czm.com.mz. 49 units. A/C. High season $168 double. Low season $69 double. Dive and honeymoon packages available. AE, MC, V. Free parking.

Built in two sections, the hotel gives you two choices of room styles. Standard rooms in the two-story section adjacent to the lobby are smallish (but very nice) and decorated in Southwestern shades of apricot and blue. All have small sitting areas and either a porch or balcony facing the beach and pool. The one-story bungalow/cabaña section has a similar decor, but rooms are larger and have patios on the beach.

Dining/Diversions: The main restaurant is in a glassed-in terrace on the beach, and there's a poolside spot for snacks.

Amenities: Swimming pool; water-sports equipment for rent, including sailboats, jet skis, and diving, snorkeling, and windsurfing equipment; pharmacy; gift shop; travel agency.

IN TOWN
Very Expensive

✪ **Hotel Plaza Las Glorias.** Km 1.5 Av. Rafael Melgar, 77600 Cozumel, Q. Roo. ☎ **800/342-AMIGO** in the U.S., or 987/2-2000. Fax 987/2-1937. 170 units. A/C MINIBAR TV TEL. High season $252 double. Low season $168 double. AE, MC, V.

An all-suite hotel, this one offers the top-notch amenities of the expensive hotels farther out, but it's within 5 blocks of town. Beyond the expansive, lively lobby bar is the pool, with a swim-up bar, a multilevel deck, a shored-up beach, and the ocean. Most of the large, pleasantly furnished rooms all have marble floors, separate sunken living rooms, and balconies with views. Standard in-room amenities include hair dryers, purified tap water, and in-room safe-deposit boxes.

Dining/Diversions: There's usually a buffet at breakfast and dinner. The main restaurant features different specialties nightly. Palapa dining outside serves all meals (weather permitting), and the popular lobby bar features a large-screen TV that brings in major sports events. In high season there's often live entertainment (soft music) there as well and a happy hour with two-for-one drinks between 5 and 7pm.

Amenities: Swimming pool with Jacuzzi and swim-up bar by the beach, diving pier, organized pool games, recreational director, travel agency, concierge, laundry and room service, travel agency, car rental, shopping arcade, and fully equipped dive shop with PADI and NAUI certification available.

Moderate

Hotel Colonial. Av. 5 Sur no. 9 (Apdo. Postal 286), 77600 Cozumel, Q. Roo. ☎ **987/ 202-11**. Fax 987/2-1387. 28 units. A/C TV TEL. High season $54 studio; $64 suite. Low season $43–$47; $50–$55 suite. AE, MC, V.

Across the street from the El Marqués hotel is a collection of shops and this pleasant three-story hotel, with an elevator. It's a good deal for the money, especially if you like to spread out. The lobby is far back past the shops. You get a quiet, spacious, furnished studio or a one-bedroom apartment with red tile floors on the first floor; second- and third-floor rooms have kitchenettes. The street is closed to traffic. From the plaza, walk half a block south on avenida 5 Sur; the hotel is on the left.

Inexpensive

✪ **Hotel del Centró.** Av. Juárez 501, 77600 Cozumel, Q. Roo. ☎ **987/2-5471.** Fax 987/2-0299. 24 units. A/C TV. High season $45 double. Low season $35 double. Suite w/kitchen $70. Discounts for weekly stays. MC, V.

Although this new, surprisingly stylish hotel is located 6 long blocks from the waterfront, it's a great bargain and one of the most attractive locations in town. The rooms are small, but modern and extra-clean, with decorative details, TV, and two double beds. Several suites with kitchenettes are also available. The rooms surround a garden courtyard with an oval pool framed by comfortable lounge chairs and a restaurant/bar.

✪ **Hotel Flamingo.** Calle 6 Norte no. 81, 77600 Cozumel, Q. Roo. ☎ **800/806-1601** or 987/2-1264. Fax 987/2-6006. www.hotelflamingo.com. E-mail: dive@hotelflamingo. com. 22 units. TV. High season $35–$50 double. Low season $30–$40 double. Penthouse $99–$129. MC, V. Street parking available.

Completely remodeled in 1997, the Flamingo offers the best value in Cozumel, and caters to serious divers looking for extra-clean, basic accommodations. The Flamingo offers three floors of quiet rooms, a grassy inner courtyard, rooftop terrace, and very helpful new management. Second- and third-story rooms are spacious. All have white tile floors and new bathroom fixtures; 15 rooms have A/C and some have mini-refrigerators. Rooms in the front of the building have balconies overlooking the street. All have two double beds and cable TV. The penthouse suite has a full kitchen and sleeps up to six. Trade paperbacks are by the reception desk and a TV and complimentary coffee in the lobby are for guests. Special dive packages are available, and Spanish lessons are taught at the hotel. To find it, walk 5 blocks north on Melgar from the plaza and turn right on calle 6; the hotel is on the left between Melgar and avenida 5.

Hotel Safari Inn. Av. Melgar at Calle 5 Sur (Apdo. Postal 41), 77600 Cozumel, Q. Roo. ☎ **987/2-0101.** Fax 987/2-0661. E-Mail: dive@aquasafari.com. 12 units. A/C. $40 double. MC, V.

This pleasant budget hotel has a great location for divers: It's in town, above and behind the Aqua Safari Dive Shop. Natural colors and stucco pervade the interior of this three-story (no elevator) establishment. The huge rooms come with firm beds, built-in sofas, and tiled floors. The hotel caters to divers and offers some good dive packages through its dive shop Aqua Safari, one of the most reputable on the island. To find it from the pier, turn right (south) and walk 3½ blocks on Melgar; the hotel is on your left facing the Caribbean at the corner of calle 5 Sur.

SOUTH OF TOWN

The best beaches are south of town, but not all the best ones have hotels on them. Each hotel has either a swimming pool, a tiny cove, a dock, or all three. You'll be able to swim, sun, and relax at any of these hotels, and most are diver-oriented. **Costera Sur,** also called **Carretera a Chankanaab,** is the southern extension of Melgar, so just follow Melgar south through town to reach these hotels, which are, generally speaking, farther apart than those north of town, and a more-expensive cab ride.

Very Expensive

✪ **Presidente Inter-Continental Cozumel.** Km 6 Costera Sur, 77600 Cozumel, Q.
Roo. ☎ **800/327-0200** in the U.S., or 987/2-0322. Fax 987/2-1360. 253 units.
A/C MINIBAR TV TEL. High season $240–$400 double. Low season $180–$330 double.
Discounts and packages available. AE, DC, MC, V. Free parking.

Without a doubt, this is Cozumel's finest hotel in terms of style, on-site amenities, and
excellence in service. Palatial in scale, it still retains a feeling of conviviality. The
common areas display a masterful combination of marble with hot-pink stucco and
stone. Located near the Chankanaab Lagoon, the hotel is surrounded by shady palms
and spread out on a beautiful beach with no close neighbors. Rates vary widely,
depending on your view and time of year you travel, even within seasons. There are
four categories of rooms—some have balconies and garden views, while very spacious
rooms come with balconies and ocean views. Deluxe beachfront rooms are the top
choice, with expansive private patios and direct access to the beach on the ground
floor; on the second floor there are balconies with ocean views. These deluxe rooms
exude luxury; other rooms may be disappointing by comparison. Nonsmoking rooms
are all on the fourth level, and two rooms are set aside for guests with disabilities.

Dining/Diversions: The **Arrecife** restaurant serves international specialties and is
open daily from 6pm to midnight. **Caribeño,** by the pool and beach, is open from
7am to 7pm. There are three bars, including a pool bar, plus 24-hour room service.
They offer a special in-room dining option for deluxe beach-front rooms, and will set
up your service on your private patio for a romantic dinner, complete with serenading
trio.

Amenities: Swimming pool, two tennis courts, water-sports equipment rental, dive
shop and dive-boat pier, children's activities program, pharmacy, boutiques, laundry
and room service, travel agency, car and motorbike rental.

Expensive

La Ceiba Beach Hotel. Km 4.5 Costera Sur (Apdo. Postal 284), 77600 Cozumel, Q. Roo.
☎ **800/877-4383** in the U.S., or 987/2-0844. Fax 987/2-0065. 113 units. A/C MINIBAR
TV TEL. High season $145–$180 double. Low season $96–$120 double. Diving packages
available. AE, MC, V. Free parking.

Across from the Crown Paradisse Sol Caribe, on the beach side of the road, La Ceiba
is named for the lofty and majestic tropical tree that was sacred to the Maya. It's a popular hotel with divers, and the large lobby seems to always be bustling with guests. The
guest rooms, while not necessarily outfitted in the latest style, are nicely furnished,
large, and comfortable; all have ocean views and balconies. The swimming pool is only
steps from the beach.

The emphasis here is on water sports, particularly scuba diving, and if this is your
passion, be sure to ask about the special dive packages when you call for reservations.
Diving is available right from the hotel beachfront.

Dining/Diversions: The **Galleon Bar/Restaurant,** off the lobby, has walls shaped
like an old ship and is open for all meals. **Chopaloca,** by the beach, is open daily from
early morning until almost midnight.

Amenities: Small, rectangular swimming pool and hot tub by the beach with outdoor Jacuzzi; tennis court; gym and sauna; water sports; dive shop and dive-boat pier;
roped-off area for snorkeling; laundry and room service; travel agency.

WHERE TO DINE

To tide yourself over, try **Zermatt** (☎ 987/2-1384), a terrific little bakery on avenida
5 at Calle 4 Norte. On Calle 2 Norte, half a block in from the waterfront, is the

Panificadora Cozumel, excellent for a do-it-yourself breakfast or for picnic supplies. It's open from 6am to 9pm daily.

VERY EXPENSIVE

✪ **Café del Puerto.** Av. Melgar 3. ☎ **987/2-0316.** Reservations recommended. Main courses $15–$35. AE, MC, V. Daily 5pm–11pm. INTERNATIONAL.

For a romantic dinner with a sunset view, try this restaurant. After being greeted at the door, you can climb the spiral staircase to the main dining room or continue to a higher loft, overlooking the rest of the dining room. Soft piano music echoes in the background. The service is polished and polite, and the menu is sophisticated, with dishes like mustard steak flambé, shrimp brochette with bacon and pineapple, and prime rib. From the pier, cross the street and turn left on Melgar; it's almost immediately on your right.

Pepe's Grill. Av. Rafael Melgar at Salas. ☎ **987/2-0213.** Reservations recommended. Main courses $15–$30; children's menu $6.50. AE, MC, V. Daily 5–11:30pm. GRILLED SPECIALTIES.

Pepe's started the grilled-food tradition in Cozumel and continues as a popular trendsetter, with low lights, soft music, solicitous waiters, and excellent food; the perpetual crowd is here for a reason. The menu is extensive, with flame-broiled specialties such as beef fillet Singapore and shrimp Bahamas. The children's menu offers breaded shrimp and fried chicken. For dessert try the cajeta (a thick sauce similar to caramel) crepes.

MODERATE

El Moro. 75 bis Norte 124. ☎ **987/2-3029.** Main courses $4–$12; margaritas $3; beer $1.25. MC, V. Fri–Wed 1–11pm. REGIONAL.

Crowds flock to El Moro for its wonderfully prepared food and service, but not the decor, which is orange, orange, orange, and Formica. And it's away from everything; a taxi is a must, costing around $1.50 one way. But you won't care as soon as you taste anything (and especially if you sip on one of their giant, wallop-packing margaritas). The pollo Ticuleño, a specialty from the town of Ticul, is a rib-sticking, delicious, layered plate of smooth tomato sauce, mashed potatoes, crispy baked corn tortilla, and batter-fried chicken breast, all topped with shredded cheese and green peas. Besides the regional food, other specialties of Mexico come out of the kitchen piping hot, such as enchiladas and seafood prepared many ways, plus grilled steaks, sandwiches, and, of course, nachos. El Moro is 12½ blocks inland from Melgar between calles 2 and 4 Norte.

La Choza. Salas 198 at Av. 10 Sur. ☎ **987/2-0958.** Breakfast $2.80; main courses $8–$16. AE, MC, V. Daily 7:30am–11pm. YUCATECAN.

The filled tables looking out the big open-air windows on the corner of Salas and avenida 10 Sur announce that this is a favorite of both tourists and locals. It looks like a big Maya house with white stucco walls and a thatched roof. Platters of chiles stuffed with shrimp, *pollo en relleno negro* (chicken in a blackened pepper sauce), *puerco entometado* (pork stew), and beefsteak in a poblano pepper sauce are among the truly authentic specialties.

✪ **La Veranda.** Calle 4 Norte. ☎ **987/2-4132.** Reservations recommended in high season. Main courses $6–$16. MC, V. Daily 6pm–1am. SEAFOOD/INTERNATIONAL.

Nothing here is quite what you expect. La Veranda is in a new building that's architecturally like the old island frame houses with cutout wood trim. It's a stylish restaurant with cloth-covered tables, good service, and terrific crispy fresh salads, curried chicken, large seafood platters, roast-beef sandwiches, fajitas, stir-fried vegetables, steaks, and an enormous Mexican combo including roasted chicken, rice, beans, guacamole, an enchilada, and a quesadilla. You can dine inside or on the veranda or patio in back overlooking the shaded garden. In the main room, casual couches and conversational areas are conducive to leisurely drinking, chatting, card playing, backgammon, or watching ESPN, CNN, WGN Chicago, or sporting events. (The television is played at low volume.) The gracious owners Anibal and Mercedes de Iturbide are almost always on hand. To get there from the plaza, turn left (north) on avenida 5 Norte, walk 2 blocks, and turn right on calle 4 Norte; it's behind Zermatt bakery, on your right midway up the block.

✪ Lobster House (Cabaña del Pescador). Carretera Pilar, Km 4. No phone. Lobster sold by weight $10–$30. No credit cards. Daily 6–10:30pm. LOBSTER.

If you do something well, then concentrate on that and forget the rest. This is the obvious rule to live by here, as the only item on this menu is their lobster dinner, served one way—steamed with a side of rice, vegetables, and bread. It's a flavorful meal, perfectly seasoned, and flawlessly cooked—why bother with anything else when you've achieved perfection? The price of dinner is determined by the weight of the lobster you select, with side dishes provided at no charge. Dark wooden tables lit with candles add to the inviting atmosphere, surrounded by tropical gardens, fountains and a small pond, complete with ducks. Owner Fernando adds to the welcoming feeling here, and will even send next door to his brother's restaurant, El Guacamayo, if you simply must have something other than lobster. The Lobster House is located across from the Playa Azul hotel.

✪ Prima. Calle Salas 109. ☎ **987/2-4242.** Pizzas $5–$14; pastas $5–$15; calzones $3.75–$5.25. AE, MC, V. Daily 4–11pm. ITALIAN.

One of the few good Italian restaurants in Mexico, Prima gets better every year. Everything is fresh—the pastas, calzones, vegetables, and sourdough pizza. Owner Albert Domínguez grows most of the vegetables in his hydroponic garden on the island. The menu changes daily and might include shrimp scampi, fettuccine with pesto, and lobster or crab ravioli with cream sauce. The fettuccine Alfredo is wonderful, as are the puff-pastry garlic "bread" and crispy house salad. Dining is upstairs on the breezy terrace. Next door is **Habanas Co.** with cigars and liquors. To get to either place from the pier turn right (south) on Melgar and walk 2 blocks to calle 5 Sur and turn left. Prima is visible on your left between Avenidas 5 and 10 Sur. Hotel delivery is available.

INEXPENSIVE

✪ Café Caribe. Av. 10 Sur 215. ☎ **987/2-3621.** Coffee and pastries $1.50–$4. No credit cards. Mon–Sat 7am–1pm and 6–10:30pm. PASTRIES/COFFEE.

This cute little cafe behind a facade of fuchsia and dark green may become your favorite place to start the day, finish it, or spend time in between. You'll find ice cream, milk shakes, fresh cheesecake and carrot cake, waffles, bagels, croissants, and biscuits filled with cheese and cream, ham and cheese, or butter and marmalade. Nine different coffees are served, including Cuban, cappuccino, espresso, and Irish. To get there from the plaza turn right (south) on avenida 5 Sur, walk 1 block and turn left on calle Salas, then right on avenida 10; it's on your left.

Coco's. Av. 5 Sur no. 180, at the corner of Calle Salas. ☎ **987/2-0241.** Breakfast $3–$5.75. No credit cards. Tues–Sun 7am–noon. Closed the last 2 weeks of Sept through the 1st week of Oct. MEXICAN/AMERICAN.

Tended by owners Terri and Daniel Ocejo, Coco's is clean and welcoming to the tourist, right down to the free coffee refills. Plan to indulge in Stateside favorites like hash browns, cornflakes and bananas, gigantic blueberry muffins, cinnamon rolls, and cream stuffed rolls. Mexican specialties include huevos rancheros, huevos Mexicana, and eggs scrambled with chiles and covered with melted cheese. A gift section at the front includes gourmet coffee, local honey, bottles of hot pepper, chocolate, rompope, and vanilla. To get there from the plaza turn right (south) on avenida 5 Sur. Coco's is on your right beside the entrance to the Hotel El Marqués.

Comida Casera Toñita. Calle Salas 265, between Calles 10 and 15 Norte. ☎ **987/2-0401.** Breakfast $1.75–$3; main courses $3.75–$5; daily specials $3; fruit drinks $1.75. No credit cards. Mon–Sat 8am–6pm. HOME-STYLE YUCATECAN.

The owners have taken the living room of their home and made it into a comfortable dining room, complete with filled bookshelves and classical music playing in the background. Whole fried fish, fish fillet, fried chicken, and beefsteak prepared as you wish are on the regular menu. Daily specials give you a chance to taste authentic regional food, including a *pollo a la naranja* (orange chicken), chicken mole, pollo en escabeche, and pork chops with achiote seasoning. Their sopa de Lima is one of the best in all of the Yucatán Peninsula, but their pozole is consistently over salted. To reach Toñita, walk south from the plaza on avenida 5 Sur for 1 block, then turn left on calle Salas and walk east 1½ blocks; the restaurant is on your left.

Natural. Calle Rosado Salas 352. ☎ **987/2-5560.** Breakfast $1.75–$3.25; salads $1.75–$3; sandwiches $1.55–$3; fruit and vegetable juices 95¢–$1.55; coffee 75¢. No credit cards. Mon–Sat 7am–6pm. FRUIT/PASTRIES.

The sweet smell of fruit will greet you as you enter Frutas Selecta. Downstairs is a grocery store specializing in fresh fruit, and upstairs is the sleek and cheery restaurant with windows on two sides. Juices, licuados, "the best coffee in town," yogurt, veggie sandwiches, a salad bar, fruit shakes, baked potatoes with a variety of toppings, and pastries are served. From the plaza, turn right and walk 1 block south on avenida 5 Sur, then turn left on calle Salas and walk 3 blocks east. It's on your right between 15 and 20 Norte.

COZUMEL AFTER DARK

Cozumel is a town frequented by divers and other actively inclined visitors who play hard all day and wind down at night. People sit in outdoor cafes around the zócalo (plaza) enjoying the cool night breezes until the restaurants close. **Carlos 'n' Charlie's, Planet Hollywood,** the **All-Star Cafe,** and the **Hard Rock Cafe,** all located along Melgar, are among the liveliest and most predictable places in town. **Joe's Lobster Pub** on avenida 5 between Juárez and calle 2 Norte, is the most happening place for live music, with reggae and salsa their specialty. The other hot spot is **Raga,** with live and recorded reggae, rock, and dance music. It's located on avenida Rosado Salas, at 10 avenida Sur. Other specialty bars include the **Hog's Breath Saloon,** imported from Key West and located on the main highway across from the International Pier; and **Scruffy Murphy's** Irish Pub, across from the La Ceibe hotel.

3 Puerto Morelos & Environs

21 miles S of Cancún

Puerto Morelos remains a small and tranquil fishing town, with not a whole lot going on after dark. It's excellent for diving, snorkeling, and fishing, and for simply lying on the beach. Puerto Morelos was once important for the Maya: It was the spot where women departed on their pilgrimages to Cozumel, in order to pay homage to the goddess of fertility, and it was a key trading point with Cozumel and other islands. Today, most people come to Puerto Morelos in order to take the car ferry to Cozumel, several hours away. The building boom in this area that was stalled following Hurricane Gilbert has been resumed.

ESSENTIALS

GETTING THERE   By Bus   Buses from Cancún's bus station going to Tulum and Playa del Carmen usually stop here, but be sure to ask in Cancún if your bus makes the Puerto Morelos stop.

By Car   Drive south from Cancún along Highway 307 to the km 31 marker, then turn east toward Puerto Morelos.

By the Puerto Morelos–Cozumel Car Ferry   The dock (☎ **987/1-0008**), the largest establishment in town, is very easy to find. Look to the Cozumel section above for details on the car-ferry schedule, but several points bear repeating here: The car-ferry schedule is complicated and may change, so double-check it before arriving. And always arrive at least 3 hours in advance of the ferry's departure to purchase a ticket and to get in line.

ORIENTATION   On the highway, near the Puerto Morelos junction, you'll see a gas station with public phones (including Ladatel phones that accept prepaid phone cards) and a supermarket on the right.

EXPLORING IN & AROUND PUERTO MORELOS

Puerto Morelos is attracting more and more people who seek seaside relaxation without the crowds and high prices. Its beaches are as beautiful as any along the coast, but they don't look like it because the deposits of seaweed and other wave-brought debris mar the visual appeal. Also, except for **Los Pelicanos,** there are no seaside restaurants selling drinks and food and no thatched beach umbrellas. Though the village is attracting more resort development now, and other businesses are popping up too, you make your own fun here, which is precisely its appeal to some people. For diving and fishing, try **Sub Aqua Explorers** (☎ **987/1-0078;** fax 987/1-0027). More than 15 dive sites are nearby and many are close to shore. A two-tank dive costs around $60, and night dives, $55. Two hours of fishing costs around $80 and snorkeling excursions run around $5.

If you are traveling by car, there are a couple of worthwhile stops along Highway 307 on the way to Puerto Morelos from Cancún. **Croco Cun,** a zoological park where crocodiles are raised, is one of the most interesting attractions in the area—don't be put off by the comical name. Though far from grand, the park has exhibits of crocodiles in all stages of development, as well as animals of nearly all the species that once roamed the Yucatán Peninsula. The snake exhibit is fascinating, though it may make you think twice about roaming in the jungle. The rattlesnakes and boa constrictors are particularly intimidating, and the tarantulas are downright enormous. Children enjoy the guides' enthusiastic tours and are entranced by the spider monkeys and wild pigs. Wear plenty of bug repellent and allow an hour or two for the tour, followed by a cool drink in the restaurant. Croco Cun is open daily from 8:30am to 5:30pm. Admission is $5; free for children under 6. The park is at km 31 on Highway 307.

About half a mile before Puerto Morelos is a 150-acre **Jardín Botánico,** opened in 1990 and named after Dr. Alfredo Barrera, a biologist who studied the selva (a common geographical term meaning "tropical evergreen broadleaf forest"). A natural, protected showcase for native plants and animals, it's open Tuesday through Sunday from 9am to 4pm. Admission is $3.75.

The park is divided into six parts: an **epiphyte area** (plants that grow on others); **Maya ruins;** an **ethnographic area,** with a furnished hut and typical garden; a **chiclero**

The Yucatán's Upper Caribbean Coast

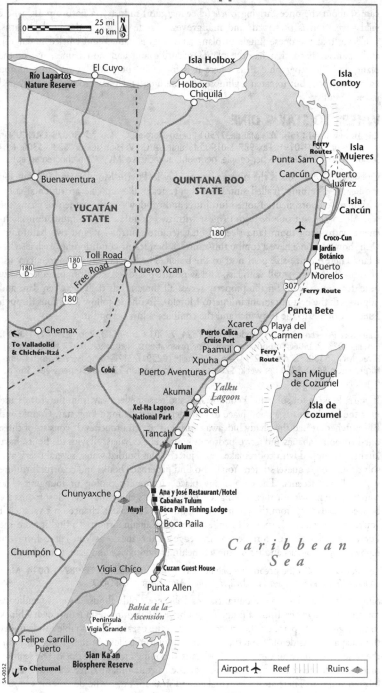

25 mi
40 km

N

Isla Holbox

Río Lagartos
Nature Reserve

El Cuyo

Isla Contoy

Holbox
Chiquilá

Ferry
Routes

Isla
Mujeres

Punta Sam

Cancún

Puerto
Juárez

QUINTANA ROO
STATE

Buenaventura

Isla
Cancún

YUCATÁN
STATE

180

Croco-Cun

Jardín
Botánico

180
D

Toll Road

180
D

Puerto
Morelos

180
D

Free Road

Nuevo Xcan

307

Ferry Route

180

Punta Bete

180

Chemax

To Valladolid
& Chichén-Itzá

Xcaret

Playa del
Carmen

Puerto Calica
Cruise Port

Cobá

Paamul

Ferry
Route

Xpuha

Puerto Aventuras

San Miguel
de Cozumel

Akumal

Yalku
Lagoon

Xel-Ha Lagoon
National Park

Xcacel

Isla de
Cozumel

Tancah

Tulum

Ana y José Restaurant/Hotel

Chunyaxche

Cabañas Tulum

Boca Paila Fishing Lodge

Muyil

Boca Paila

Chumpón

Caribbean
Sea

Vigía Chíco

Cuzan Guest House

Punta Allen

Bahía de la
Ascensión

Felipe Carrillo
Puerto

Península
Vigía Grande

To Chetumal

Sian Ka'an
Biosphere Reserve

Airport ✈   Reef |||| Ruins 〰

SA-0052

517

camp, about the once-thriving *chicle* (chewing gum) industry; a **nature park,** where wild vegetation is preserved; and **mangroves.** Wandering along the marked paths, you'll see that the dense jungle of plants and trees is named and labeled in English and Spanish. Each sign has the plant's scientific and common names, use of the plant, and the geographic areas where it is found in the wild. It's rich in bird and animal life, too, but to catch a glimpse of something you'll have to move quietly and listen carefully.

WHERE TO STAY & DINE

Caribbean Reef Club. Villa Marina, 77501 Puerto Morelos, Q. Roo. ☎ **800/3-CANCUN** in the U.S., or 987/1-0191. Fax 987/1-0190. 45 units. A/C TV. High season $280–$300. Low season $220–$240. Price is per couple, per night, all-inclusive. MC, V. No children accepted.

Opened in 1991, this is the nicest place to stay in Puerto Morelos, and it's right on the beach. The units (called suites but they're really like upscale apartments) come with marble floors, neutral-toned furniture, and windows on the garden all facing the sea. All come with one bedroom (most with two double beds), combination kitchenette with living room (and sleeper sofa), remote-control TV, and two bathrooms with showers (some have a combo tub/shower). Besides air-conditioning, each also has a fan. There's a nice-size pool next to the beach. The hotel offers complimentary use of snorkeling gear, small sailboats, and windsurf boards. A comfortable and breezy beachfront restaurant on the property serves all three meals daily between 8am and 10pm—it's the best restaurant in Puerto Morelos. To find it, follow directions through Puerto Morelos to the ferry pier and the complex is just beyond it.

Cabañas Puerto Morelos. Apdo. Postal 1524, 77501 Cancún, Q. Roo. ☎ **987/1-0004.** E-mail: 102312.3506@compuserve.com. (For reservations: Niki Seach, 7912 NE Ochoa, Elk River, MN 55330; ☎/fax 612/441-7630; E-mail: 102301.2317@compuserve.com.) 4 units. High season $450–$750 per week; $70 per night. Low season $275–$450 per week; $50 per night. No credit cards.

If you're looking for something comfortable and reasonable, away from the crowds and near the beach, this is a good place to consider, especially for a long stay. Connie and Bill Butcher created this shady hideaway with lots of extra touches. It consists of three one-bedroom cabañas and a two-bedroom house. The cabañas, all with tile floors, have kitchens equipped with coffeemakers and juicers, plus bottled water, several beers, and soft drinks to get guests started. You'll also find paperback books and colorful furniture with folk-art accents. There's a shady place outside for dining or lounging. The Butchers are known for their willingness to help guests enjoy the area. Most rooms are booked in advance from the United States, but you can take a chance on a vacancy if you're in the area. This spot is 12 miles from the Cancún airport. To find it from the Puerto Morelos zócalo, turn left at the edge of the zócalo as you come from the highway. Go 3 blocks and it's on the left behind a white wall and gate. Ring the bell.

Los Pelicanos. On the ocean side behind and right of the zócalo. ☎ **987/1-0014.** Main courses $5.50–$16; lobster $25. MC, V. Daily 10am–11pm. SEAFOOD.

Since this village has few restaurants, Los Pelicanos holds almost a captive audience for central village beachside dining. You'll notice the inviting restaurant down a block to the right of the plaza on the street paralleling the ocean. Select a table inside under the palapa or outside on the terrace (wear mosquito repellent in the evenings). From the terrace you have an easy view of pelicans swooping around the dock. The seafood menu has all the usual offerings, from ceviche to conch made three ways to shrimp, lobster, and fish. There are grilled chicken and steak for those who don't want seafood.

Sea Turtles of the Yucatán

At least four species of endangered marine turtles nest on the beaches of Quintana Roo: the **loggerhead, green, hawksbill,** and **leatherback** varieties. Of these, the leatherback is almost nonexistent, and the loggerhead is the most abundant.

Most turtles return to the beach of their birth to lay their eggs, as often as three times in a season. Strolling along the beach late at night in search of giant turtles (prime egg-laying hours are between 10pm and 3am) is a special experience that will make you feel closer to the Yucatán's environment. It may take you a while to get used to the darkness, but don't use your flashlight—lights of any kind repel the turtles. Laying the eggs is tough work. A female will dig nonstop with back flippers for more than an hour; the exercise leaves her head and legs flushed. Depositing the 100 or more eggs takes only minutes, then she makes the nest invisible by laboriously covering it with sand and disappears into the sea. Each soft-shelled egg looks like a Ping-Pong ball.

Hatchlings scurry to the sea 45 days later, but successful incubation depends on the temperature and depth of the nest. When conditions are right, the hatch rates of fertile eggs are high; however, only 5% of those that do make it to the sea escape predators long enough to return.

Despite recent efforts to protect Mexico's turtles, the eggs are still considered an aphrodisiac, and there's a market for them; turtles are killed for their shells and meat as well. Since turtle life expectancy is more than 50 years, killing one turtle kills thousands more. Costly protection programs include tagging the female and catching the eggs as they are deposited and removing them to a protected area and nest of identical size and temperature.

EN ROUTE TO PLAYA DEL CARMEN

Heading south on Highway 307 from Puerto Morelos, it's only 20 miles to Playa del Carmen, so you'll be there in half an hour or less. However, you'll pass several small beach resorts en route. The two more-upscale places below are run by the reputable Turquoise Reef Group. And less than 3 miles before Playa del Carmen you'll pass several roads that head out to the relaxed, isolated small hotels at **Punta Bete,** which is the name of a beach—not a town. If you turn left and follow a small unpaved trail at the km 52 marker and PUNTA BETE sign, you'll find two small inexpensive groups of bungalows at the end of the trail and on a fine stretch of beach, which you'll have almost to yourself. Two of these are Spartan and inexpensive (yet comfortable) at $25 to $35 per double, with a few individual bungalows on the beach and a restaurant at each one. **Cabañas Bahía Xcalacoco,** (Apdo. Postal 176), 77710 Playa del Carmen, Quintana Roo, has two cabañas. **Cabañas Xcalacoco,** (Apdo. Postal 176), 77710 Playa del Carmen, Quintana Roo, has seven cabañas. There's no electricity, but all rooms have private bathrooms. There's another group of cabañas to the left of the Cabañas Xcalacoco, with nearly the same name, but the upkeep and service are undependable, and I don't recommend it.

If you come here between July and October, you can walk the beach at night to watch for **turtles** lumbering ashore to lay their eggs, or watch the eggs hatch and the tiny vulnerable turtles scurry to the ocean in the last 2 months.

WHERE TO STAY & DINE FARTHER ALONG HIGHWAY 307

Continuing on Highway 307, a few miles beyond the Punta Bete turnoff, you'll see a large sign on the left to the entrance to La Posada del Capitán Lafitte.

La Posada del Capitán Lafitte. Km 62 Carretera Cancún-Tulum, 77710 Playa del Carmen, Q. Roo. ☎ **800/538-6802** or 303/674-9615 in the U.S.; or 987/3-0214. Fax 987/3-0212. 62 units. High season $170 double. Low season $120 double. Rates at Christmas, New Year's, Thanksgiving, and part of Feb are higher. Minimum 3-night stay. Rates include breakfast and dinner. AE, MC, V. Free parking.

From the highway, drive a mile down a rough dirt road that heads towards the ocean. Here you can enjoy the feeling of being on a private, nearly deserted island, but enjoy all the amenities of a relaxing vacation. The numerous cabañas of Capitán Lafitte stretch out along a huge portion of powdery white beach with space enough between them to feel luxuriously separate from other guests. The one- and two-story white stucco bungalows are smallish but very comfortable, stylishly furnished, and equipped with tile floors, small tiled bathrooms, either two double or one king-size bed, and an oceanfront porch. Twenty-nine bungalows have A/C; the rest have fans. There's 24-hour electricity (a plus you learn to value on isolated stretches of this coast). If you wish, coffee can be served in the room as early as 6:30am. There's a turtle patrol in which guests can participate during summer on nearby beaches, where green and loggerhead turtles nest. Divers from North America make up a sizable portion of the clientele here, as well as repeat visitors who come annually just for the peace, quiet, beach, and relaxation.

Dining/Diversions: One restaurant takes care of all meals, and the chef will prepare your catch. There's also a poolside bar and swinging-chair bar.

Amenities: You'll find a large raised swimming pool and sunning deck, well-equipped game room, and excellent dive shop with PADI instruction. Laundry and room service, travel agency.

Shangri-La Caribe. Km 69.5 Carretera Cancún-Tulum (Apdo. Postal 253), Playa del Carmen, Q. Roo 77710. ☎ **800/538-6802** or 303/674-9615 in the U.S.; or 987/3-0611. Fax 987/3-0500. 85 units. High season $177 ocean-view double; $227 beachfront double. Low season $127 ocean-view double; $177 beachfront double. Rates include breakfast. AE, MC, V. (Book well in advance during high season.) Free parking.

After Punta Bete and La Posada del Capitán Lafitte—and only a mile or so before you reach Playa del Carmen on Highway 307—you'll see the Volkswagen Plant and a huge sign for the Shangri-La Caribe and another resort called Las Palapas. Turn left at the VW building, and you'll find the Shangri-La a mile straight ahead on a semipaved road. The two-story, high-domed, palapa-topped bungalows meander to the ocean linked by sidewalks and edged by tropical vegetation. Accommodations are quaint, but all come with two double beds, nice tile bathrooms, and an inviting hammock strung on the patio or balcony. Windows are screened, and a ceiling fan circulates the breeze. Prices get higher the closer you get to the beach and are higher for two-bedroom casas. Though you're very close to Playa del Carmen, hotel guests are the only ones using the beach, and the feeling is one of being many relaxing miles from civilization. You'll share this beachside retreat with lots of European vacationers, meaning topless sunbathing is the norm.

Dining/Diversions: One restaurant serves all three meals, and the bar is open long hours.

Amenities: The large inviting pool is surrounded by a sundeck, and there are horses for rent at $25 an hour. The absence of coral on the beach makes it an ideal place for windsurfing and swimming, less ideal for snorkeling. The **Cyan-Ha Diving Center** on the premises offers diving, snorkeling, and fishing trips, and equipment rental for these sports. May and June are best for fishing with abundant marlin, sailfish, and dorado. Car rental and bus or taxi tours to nearby lagoons and to Tulum, Cobá, and Chichén-Itzá.

4 Playa del Carmen

20 miles SW of Puerto Morelos; 44 miles SW of Cancún; 6.5 miles N of Xcaret; 8 miles N of Puerto Calica

Playa del Carmen has become, in my opinion, the ultimate Mexican beach vacation today. It's definitive *nuevo hip*, with an intriguing mix of smaller, eclectic accommodations and entertainment, set alongside amazing beach beauty. Already discovered by European travelers, this place sizzles with style.

Once this was little more than a very authentic launch for fishing boats and the Cozumel ferry. Playa now rivals Cozumel and her northern neighbor of Cancún in vacation appeal. Playa's location is the best on the Caribbean coast: It's an hour from the many flights arriving into Cancún's airport, a 45-minute ferry ride from Cozumel, and less than an hour to the Tulum ruins and other worthy coastal explorations.

Accommodations here are dominated by one-of-a-kind inns, B&Bs, and cabañas. Currently, almost 80% of the visitors here come from the European Union, which gives Playa an offbeat, global attitude. Snippits of conversation in various languages float in the constant sea breeze. Playa attracts a chic, young crowd that enjoys the growing number of coffee shops, reggae bars, and new-age vegetarian restaurants that are appearing along the pedestrian-only avenida 5.

A couple of larger resorts have joined the small guest houses. The Continental Plaza Playacar was the first major hotel to open here in 1991, followed by the Diamond Resort, Royal Maeva, and the Fisherman's Village. In addition, new sewage and water lines, telephone service, and more brick-paved streets have been added, but still, Playa's a small town undergoing substantial growth.

The wide, clear stretches of beach and calm, aquamarine water are the main draws here. The strong European influence means topless sunbathing (nominally against the law in Mexico) is a nonchalantly accepted practice, including leisurely topless strolling anywhere there's a beach.

Locals anticipate that Playa del Carmen won't remain a secret for long, and that a greater number of Americans soon will be strolling beside Europeans on the beach. Before all this changes the feel of Playa, book a trip now and enjoy this stylish, welcoming, easy-paced place.

ESSENTIALS
GETTING THERE & DEPARTING

BY CAR   The turnoff to Playa del Carmen from Highway 307 is plainly marked, and you'll arrive on the town's widest street, avenida Principal, also known as avenida Benito Juárez (not that there's a street sign to that effect).

BY THE PLAYA DEL CARMEN–COZUMEL PASSENGER FERRY   See "Getting There & Departing" in section 2, above, for details.

BY TAXI   Taxi fares from the Cancún airport are high—about $60 one-way, but they're the fastest, most immediate form of travel. Colectivos from the Cancún airport can reduce this to about $30. Returning to the airport, there is a service offering shared taxi rides for $14 per person. Check at your hotel or at the Caribe Maya restaurant on avenida 5 at calle 8 for information and reservations.

BY BUS   There are three bus stations in Playa del Carmen, all on avenida Principal (the main street): Transportes de Oriente, Playa Express, and ATS are half a block north of the plaza and avenida 5 on avenida Principal; Expreso Oriente is on the corner of avenida 5 and avenida Principal; and the ADO station is 4 blocks west of the plaza.

Buses travel to and from Cancún with regularity, as well as to Xcaret, Tulum, Cobá, Chetumal, Chichén-Itzá, and Mérida.

ORIENTATION

ARRIVING   The ferry dock in Playa del Carmen is 1½ blocks from the main square and within walking distance of hotels. Buses are along avenida Principal, a short distance from hotels, restaurants, and the ferry pier. Tricycle taxis are the only vehicles allowed between the bus stations and avenida 5 and the ferry. A number of these efficient taxis meet each bus and ferry and can transport you and your luggage to any hotel in town. The New Puerto Calica cruise pier is almost 8 miles south of Playa del Carmen; Playa taxis meet each ship.

CITY LAYOUT   Villagers know and use street names, but few street signs exist. The main street, avenida Principal, also known as avenida Benito Juárez, leads into town from Highway 307, crossing avenida 5, 1 block before it ends at the beach next to the main plaza, or zócalo. Traffic is diverted from avenida Principal at avenida 10. avenida 5 (5th Avenue), the other main artery (closed to traffic from avenida Principal to calle 6), leads to the ferry dock, 2 blocks from the zócalo; most restaurants and hotels are either on avenida 5, or a block or two off of it. The village's beautiful beach parallels avenida 5 and is only a block from it.

FAST FACTS: PLAYA DEL CARMEN

Area Code   The telephone area code is **987.**

Money Exchange   There are several major banks and branches in Playa, along with a collection of independent money-exchange houses. Several are located close to the pier, or along avenida 5 at calle 8.

Parking   Because of the pedestrian-only blocks and increasing population and popularity of Playa, parking close to hotels has become more difficult. The most accessible parking lot is the **Estacionamiento Mexico** at the corner of avenida Principal and avenida 10, open daily 24 hours; the fee is $1.25 per hour and $8 per day. There's also a 24-hour lot just a block from the pier, where you can leave your car while you cross over to Cozumel.

Post Office   The post office is on avenida Principal, 3 blocks north of the plaza, on the right past the Hotel Playa del Carmen and the launderette.

Seasons   High season is August and December to Easter. Low season is all other months, but November is becoming very popular.

Telephones   Most hotels have phones and faxes now; often both are on the same phone line. Ladatel phones are readily available, with numerous phones located along avenida 5. There's also **The Calling Station** on the street leading up from the ferry pier; a full-service phone center with air-conditioned booths, no surcharges, fax service, and a bulletin board where you can leave messages for friends. It's open Monday through Saturday from 8am to 11pm and Sunday from 9am to 10pm.

WHAT TO SEE & DO IN PLAYA

Playa is for relaxing. But beyond that, the island of **Cozumel** is a $5, 45-minute ferry ride away; **Tulum, Xel-Ha, Xcaret,** and **Xcalacoco** are easy excursions.

Avenida 5 is lined with dozens of trendy, small shops selling imported batik clothing, Guatemalan fabric clothing, premium tequilas, Cuban cigars, masks, pottery, hammocks, and a few T-shirts. There's even a couple of tattoo salons in the mix.

Reef diving can be arranged through **Tank-Ha Dive Center** (☎/fax **987/3-0302;** fax 987/3-1355; mayanriviera.com/diving/tankha E-mail tankha@playadelcarmen.

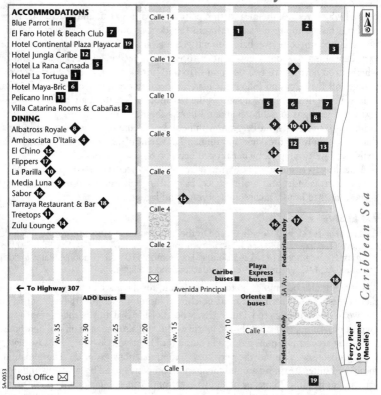

ACCOMMODATIONS
Blue Parrot Inn **3**
El Faro Hotel & Beach Club **7**
Hotel Continental Plaza Playacar **19**
Hotel Jungla Caribe **12**
Hotel La Rana Cansada **5**
Hotel La Tortuga **1**
Hotel Maya-Bric **6**
Pelicano Inn **13**
Villa Catarina Rooms & Cabañas **2**
DINING
Albatross Royale **8**
Ambasciata D'Italia **4**
El Chino **15**
Flippers **17**
La Parilla **10**
Media Luna **9**
Sabor **16**
Tarraya Restaurant & Bar **18**
Treetops **11**
Zulu Lounge **14**

Calle 14
Calle 12
Calle 10
Calle 8
Calle 6
Calle 4
Calle 2

Caribbean Sea

← To Highway 307
ADO buses ■
Caribe buses ■
Playa Express buses ■
Avenida Principal
Oriente buses ■
Post Office ✉

Av. 35
Av. 30
Av. 25
Av. 20
Av. 15
Av. 10
Calle 1
Calle 1

Pedestrians Only
5A AV.
Pedestrians Only
Ferry Pier to Cozumel (Muelle)

SA-0053

com). The friendly owner Alberto Leonard, came to Playa by way of Madrid, and is now offering cave and cenote diving excursions. You can also book his trips at the Hotel Maya Bric and at the Royal Albatros. Snorkeling trips cost $25 and include soft drinks and equipment. Two-tank dive trips are $55; resort courses are available for $65 with PDIC and PADI instructors. For **cavern diving,** see "Scuba Diving" under "Cozumel," above, where small groups meet in Playa del Carmen for this new one-of-a-kind experience.

An 18-hole championship **golf course** (☎ 987/3-0624), designed by Robert von Hagge, is open adjacent to the Continental Plaza Playacar. Greens fees are $99 (includes golf cart), caddie $20, club rental $20, and the price includes a cart and tax. Two **tennis** courts are also available at the club. If your hotel is a member of the golf club, greens fees may be reduced to as low as $20.

WHERE TO STAY
VERY EXPENSIVE

Continental Plaza Playacar. Km 62.5 Fracc. Playacar, 77710 Playa del Carmen, Q. Roo. ☎ **800/88-CONTI** in the U.S., or 987/3-0100. Fax 987/3-0105. 185 units. A/C MINIBAR TV TEL. High season $280–$485 double. Ask about off-season rates and special packages. AE, DC, MC, V.

The village's most upscale resort hotel opened in 1991 on 308 acres that spread out along the beach beyond the ferry pier. Almost 200 Maya ruins were found during development of the resort, many of which decorate the grounds and common areas. The entrance of this five-story, pale-pink hotel leads you through a wide marble lobby beyond which you see the meandering pool with swim-up bar, and beach. The large, nicely furnished rooms all have in-room safe-deposit boxes, purified tap water, tile floors, large bathrooms, wet bars with refrigerators, and balconies with sea views. Rates vary depending on your view—garden, ocean, parking lot, or brick wall—and on whether you have one or two bedrooms. To find it from the ferry pier, turn left when you get off the ferry and follow the road a short distance until you see the Playacar sign. If you're driving in, turn right at the last street before the main street dead-ends and you'll see signs to the hotel about 2 blocks ahead.

Dining/Diversions: La Pergola, with pool, beach, and ocean view, serves international food daily for breakfast and dinner. **La Sirena** is the poolside restaurant. The stylish and welcoming lobby bar is open between 6pm and 1am daily.

Amenities: Ocean-side pool with swim-up bar, water-sports equipment, one lit tennis court, laundry and room service, baby-sitting, gift shop and boutiques, travel agency, tours to nearby archaeological zones and lagoons.

EXPENSIVE

✪ **El Faro Hotel and Beach Club.** On the beach at Calle 10 Norte, 77710 Playa del Carmen, Q. Roo. ☎ **888/243-7413** from the U.S., or 987/3-0970. Fax 987/3-0968. 72 units. High season $145–$205 double. Low season $105–$175 double. Rates include breakfast. AE, MC, V. Limited, free guarded parking available.

This hotel is also becoming the town's landmark, for the graceful, swirling lighthouse that borders the northern edge of its beachfront location. El Faro ("the lighthouse") is the work of German Bernd Durrmeier, who explains that this is the only privately owned, official operating lighthouse in the world, and also the only official lighthouse with guest accommodations inside. He calls it the "Honeymoon Suite," because newlyweds probably won't mind the very cozy accommodations as much. The remaining rooms and suites are spread around the spacious property graced by tall palms and tropical gardens fronting 75 meters of sandy beachfront. A small but stunning pool (heated in winter months) has islands of palms inside, and is bordered by cushioned lounges and a palapa-topped bar for libations. The entire property has a cool, clean feel to it, with its white and cream stucco facade. The spacious rooms, in two-story buildings, have clay tile floors, marble bathrooms, and either one king or two double beds. Decor is quality Mexican folk art with rustic wood furnishings, and all units have ocean views, plus a large balcony or terrace. Rates vary according to the dominant view (garden, sea, or beachfront), size of the room, and the time of year. The property has many ecologically friendly extras that you can't see—the owners use solar heat and recycled water to maintain their exquisite gardens. The restaurant, supervised by a Swiss chef, is open from 7:30am to 6pm serving guests their choice of continental or American breakfast in the mornings, and tasty choices for lunch and snacks through-out the day. European spa services were in the process of being added. Above all, the exceptional standard of service and the warm hospitality is a winning and rare combination for this area.

Dining/Diversions: Beachfront restaurant serving Mexican and international cuisine. Open for breakfast and lunch, from 8am to 6pm. Palapa poolside bar is open 8am to 8pm.

Amenities: Swimming pool, beach, massage services, free guarded parking.

MODERATE

Albatros Royale. Calle 8 (Apdo. Postal 31), 77710 Playa del Carmen, Q. Roo. ☎ **800/ 538-6802** in the U.S. and Canada, or 987/3-0001. 31 units. High season $80 double. Low season $60 double. Rates include breakfast. AE, MC, V.

This "deluxe" sister hotel to the neighboring Pelicano Inn rises up on a narrow bit of land facing the beach. The two stories of rooms all have tile floors, tile bathrooms with marble vanities and showers, balconies or porches, and most have ocean views. Most have two double beds, but seven have queen-size beds. Breakfast is taken almost next door at the Pelicano Inn. To get here from the corner of avenida 5 and calle 8 (where you'll see the Rincón del Sol center) turn toward the water on calle 8; it's midway down the block on your left. Street parking is scarce.

Blue Parrot Inn. Calle 12 Norte and the beachfront (Apdo. Postal 64), 77710 Playa del Carmen, Q. Roo. ☎ **800/634-3547** from the U.S., or 987/3-0083. Telephone/fax 987/3-0049. 45 units. High season $65–$75 double; $125–$160 suite; $155–$175 villa. Low season $45–$55 double; $75–$105 suite; $100–$110 villa. AE, MC, V.

One of the original beachfront inns in Playa, the Blue Parrot has evolved along with the town, each year offering improvements and additions in rooms and services. It has arguably the best beach location, and its three bars and beachfront pool have made it a favorite place in town for evening entertainment. Rooms are clean and comfortable, though a bit worn, with white walls and very basic Mexican decor. Mattresses are on the thin side in some of the older units. Some rooms have small kitchenettes, and the beachfront villa sleeps up to eight people. Several of the newer units come with air-conditioning. A main restaurant serves fresh seafood and Mexican favorites, and a new Japanese restaurant recently opened, serves sushi as well. Live music plays every weekend in the on-site jazz club. There's also a dive center and massage service on the premises. Overall, it's a casual, friendly place to meet other visitors and indulge in the many pleasures of being on such an exquisite beach.

Dining/Diversions: Beachfront restaurant serving international and Mexican cuisine, open from 7am to midnight. There's also the World-Famous Beach Bar.

Amenities: Broad beachfront and pool, dive shop, plus snorkeling and ocean kayaking available. Some rooms have their own pools.

✪ Hotel Jungla Caribe. Av. 5 Norte at Calle 8 (Apdo. Postal 180), 77710 Playa del Carmen, Q. Roo. ☎ **987/3-0650.** 26 units. A/C TV. High season $60–$80 double; $100–$120 suite. Low season 30% off high-season prices. AE, MC, V.

Located right in the heart of 5th Avenue action, La Jungla is an inventive inn, with high-styled decor that mixes neoclassical with Robinson Crusoe. For the creativity and quality, it's an excellent value. Rolf Albrecht, the mastermind behind the hotel, envisioned a lot of space and comfort for guests, so even the standard rooms are expansive, with gray-and-black marble floors, the occasional Roman column, and large bathrooms. There's a catwalk to the "tower" section of suites. There's an attractive pool on the first level and an excellent restaurant infused with tropical plants that overlooks calle 8.

La Tortuga. no. 732 Av. 10, corner with Calle 12 and 14, 77710 Playa del Carmen, Q. Roo. ☎/fax **987/3-1484.** hotel_la_tortuga@bigfoot.com. 15 units. A/C MINIBAR TV TEL. High season $75–$80 double. Low season $65–$70 double. No credit cards.

This new and stylish inn is already enjoying success due to its clean, elegant rooms and quiet location. There's a small, central swimming pool, with a grassy area surrounding it to take in the sun. Rooms are decorated in a rustic Southwestern style with Mexican accents. The higher-priced rooms have private Jacuzzis; all have cable TV. Room service is available from the neighboring Tucan restaurant. The hotel is located 2 large blocks off the beach, on the main north/south avenue in town.

INEXPENSIVE

Hotel Maya-Bric. Av. 5 Norte, 77710 Playa del Carmen, Q. Roo. ☎/fax **987/3-0011.** 29 units. High season $45 double. Low season $30 double. MC, V. 6% commission charged for using credit cards. Free guarded parking.

Flowers and a colorful exterior will draw your eye to this two-story beachfront inn. Each of the well-kept rooms has recently been redecorated and has two double beds with fairly firm mattresses; some have ocean views. The buildings frame a small pool where guests gather for card games and conversation. The pool was repainted last year, with new landscaping added to the surrounding garden.

The Maya-Bric is well supervised and frequented by loyal guests who return annually. The gates are locked at night, and only guests are allowed to enter. A small restaurant by the office sometimes serves breakfast and snacks during the high season. Air-conditioning is being added to all rooms. The on-site dive shop, **Tank-Ha** (See "What to See & Do in Playa," above), rents diving and snorkeling gear and arranges trips to the reefs.

La Rana Cansada. Calle 10 no. 732, 77710 Playa del Carmen, Q. Roo. ☎/fax **987/3-0389.** 15 units. High season $55 double. Low season $25 double. No credit cards.

The "Tired Frog" is one of the most simply pleasant inns in the village, though it's a bit overpriced in high season. Behind an elegant hacienda-style wall and handsome iron gate, clean, plainly furnished rooms face an inner courtyard with a small snack bar under a large thatched palapa. Hammocks are strung on the covered porch outside the row of rooms. Some rooms have concrete ceilings and others a thatched roof, and all have well-screened doors and windows. New rooms are on the drawing board, as well as a small pool and breakfast service. Paperbacks are available at the front desk, and manager John Swartz is very accommodating with tips on seeing the area. It's 1½ blocks inland from the beach. To find it from the main plaza, walk 5 blocks north on avenida 5 and turn left on calle 10; the hotel is on the left.

Treetops. Calle 8 s/n, 77710 Playa del Carmen, Q. Roo. ☎/fax **987/3-0351.** E-mail: treetops@linux.pya.com.mx. 14 units. High season $45–$75 double. Low season $35–$55 double. Rates include continental breakfast. MC, V.

Set in a small patch of undisturbed jungle, with bungalows linked by stone pathways, this place is cooler than any in town and comes complete with its own cenote and swimming pool. The older bungalows (each a separate unit) are rustic but comfortable and come with small charms like thatched roofs and rock walls and unusual architecture—no two are alike. Two bungalows have kitchens. The new rooms, in a two-story fourplex, have a choice of air-conditioning or fan, refrigerators, and nice balconies or patios. The new air-conditioned **Safari Restaurant** is situated in the treetops above the pool. The restaurant offers a short menu of charcoal-broiled hot dogs and hamburgers (with U.S. beef), club sandwiches, homemade potato salad, Tex-Mex chili, and tacos. The **Safari Bar,** to the left after you enter, is a good place to go for an evening drink and to meet fellow travelers. The bar is open daily from 3pm to midnight. Happy hour is from 5 to 7pm. There's satellite TV broadcasting U.S. channels in the reception area and bar. From the avenida Principal, walk 4 blocks north on avenida 5, then turn right for half a block on calle 8; the hotel is on the left, half a block from the beach.

✪ Villa Catarina Rooms & Cabañas. Calle Privada Nte. between 12 and 14, 77710 Playa del Carmen, Q. Roo. ☎ **987/3-0970.** Fax 987/3-0968. 15 units. High season $55–$75 double. Low season $33–$45 double. No credit cards. Limited street parking available.

Hammocks are stretched in front of each of the stylishly rustic rooms and cabañas here, nestled in a grove of palms and fruit trees. Each of the clean, tastefully furnished rooms has one or two double beds on wooden bases, and brick floors. Some units have a small loft for reading and relaxing, others have palapa roofs or terraces. Furnishings and Mexican folk art decorations are very high quality, especially considering the room prices. Bathrooms are detailed with colorful tiles, and some of the larger rooms have sitting areas. There's good cross-ventilation through well-screened windows. Complimentary coffee is served every morning.

WHERE TO DINE

Restaurants are constantly opening and closing in Playa, so you may find many new ones besides those listed below.

EXPENSIVE

Ambasciata D'Italia. Av. 5 at Calle 12. No phone. Main courses $6–$20. No credit cards. Daily 6–11:30pm. ITALIAN.

The predominately Italian crowd filling the tables here is a telling sign that the food is authentic and delicious. Entrees cover a range of homemade pasta and northern Italian specialties, with seafood prominently featured. There's an admirable selection of wines and an exceptional espresso is served. The ambiance is lively and sophisticated.

Flippers. Av. 5 at Calle 4. No phone. Grilled specialties $7–$17; seafood platter $22. No credit cards. Daily 3–10:30pm. MEXICAN/GRILLED MEAT.

There's almost always something happening at Flippers, which stands out for its nautical theme, created by fishnets and ropes under a thatched palapa. There's an extensive bar list as well as a varied menu that includes grilled specialties from sea and land, plus hamburgers, poc-chuc, and beef tampiqueña. Happy hour, when drinks are two for the price of one, runs from 5 to 11pm, and live music draws a crowd most evenings between 7 and 10pm.

✪ **La Parrilla.** Av. 5 at Calle 8. ☎ **987/3-0687.** Main courses $6.25–$25. AE, MC, V. Daily noon–2am. MEXICAN/GRILLED MEATS.

The Rincón del Sol plaza is one of the prettiest buildings in Playa, and now it houses one of the most popular restaurants in town. The dining room is set in two levels above the street with the open kitchen in back. The aroma of grilling meat permeates the air. The huge chicken fajitas come with plenty of homemade tortillas and beans, and if you want to feast on lobster, this is one place to do it. The tables fill quickly in the evening, but there are smaller bar tables set out in the plaza's courtyards, where you can wait.

MODERATE

El Chino. Calle 4 at Av. 15. ☎ **987/3-0015.** Breakfast $2.25–$3.50; main courses $4–$9. No credit cards. Daily 8am–11pm. YUCATECAN/MEXICAN.

Despite its name, there's not a Chinese dish on the menu. But locals highly recommend this place. Though slightly off the popular avenida 5 row of restaurants, it has its own clean, cool ambiance, with tile floors and plastic-covered polished wood tables set below a huge palapa roof with whirring ceiling fans. The open-air side patio is good for evening meals. The standard breakfast menu applies, plus you can order fresh blended fruit drinks. Main courses include such regional favorites as poc chuc, chicken pibil, and Ticul-style fish, plus shrimp-stuffed fish and beef, chicken, and shrimp brochettes. Other selections are lobster and shrimp crepes, fajitas, and ceviche.

✪ **Media Luna.** Av. 5, corner of Calle 8. No phone. Breakfast $2.50–$5; main courses $2.50–$10. No credit cards. Daily 7:30am–11:30pm. INTERNATIONAL.

Few restaurants have such mouthwatering aromas coming from the kitchen. When you read the menu you'll know why. The spinach-and-mushroom breakfast crepes arrive with fabulous herb-, onion-, and garlic-flavored potatoes. Other crepes are filled with fresh fruit. For dinner there are savory Greek salads, black-bean quesadillas, giant shrimps with polenta, grilled shrimp salads, fresh grilled fish, and pastas with fresh herbs and sauces, plus other entrees featuring Indian, Italian, Mexican, and Chinese specialties. Decorated in muted textiles from Guatemala, it's a casual, inviting place, with sidewalk dining facing festive 5th Avenue and soft taped guitar music in the background.

Pelicano Inn. On the beach, at Calle 6. ☎ **987/3-0997.** Buffet breakfast $6; main courses $3–$30. AE, MC, V. Buffet breakfast daily 7–11am; lunch daily 11:30am–6pm (happy hour noon–1pm and 4–6pm). MEXICAN/AMERICAN.

Located on the beach, this is a good place to meet Americans who live here and while away some hours munching and people watching. The food is dependably good. The breakfast buffet is all you can eat, so arrive hungry. Apart from breakfast you have a choice of peel-your-own Cajun-flavored shrimp with U.S.-style tartar and shrimp sauce, hamburgers, hot dogs, quesadillas, pastries, ice cream, beer, wine, and coffee. From avenida Principal, walk 4 blocks north on avenida 5, turn right half a block on calle 8 to a marked Pelican Inn pathway, and turn right, or go to the beach and turn right; the hotel/restaurant is on the beach.

✪ **Zulu Lounge.** Av. 5, between Calles 6 and 8. ☎ **987/3-0056.** Main courses $4–$9. AE. Daily 5:30–11:30pm. THAI/ VEGETARIAN.

Inspired by Thai flavors and decor, this fetching restaurant offers a casual, relaxing space for dining on flavorful food. Broken tile-topped tables add a Mexican touch to the smartly decorated interior accented by bamboo and Thai fabrics. Asian jazz and techno recorded music underscores the hip ambiance, and plays a little louder in the back room, where there are a couple of pool tables and a few rooms for rent. Standard Thai favorites include pad Thai and vegetarian spring rolls. Their yellow curry is invitingly spicy. Most dishes are prepared with your choice of seafood, chicken, beef, or vegetarian. Full bar service and excellent espresso drinks are available.

INEXPENSIVE

Sabor. Av. 5 between Calles 2 and 4. No phone. Yogurt and granola $1.50–$2.75; sandwiches $2–$3; vegetarian plates $2.25–$4; pastries 95¢–$1.50. No credit cards. Daily 8am–11pm. BAKERY/HEALTH FOOD.

A patio that's always full of patrons attests to the popularity of this modest restaurant. The list of hot and cold drinks includes espresso and cappuccino, café frappe, hot chocolate, tea, and fruit and vegetable drinks, and Sabor now has Blue Bell ice cream (a favorite of Texans) and light vegetarian meals. Try a cup of something with a slice of pie and watch village life stroll by.

✪ **Tarraya Restaurant/Bar.** Calle 2 Norte at the beach. No phone. Main courses $4–$7; whole fish $5.75. No credit cards. Daily noon–9pm. SEAFOOD.

THE RESTAURANT THAT WAS BORN WITH THE TOWN, proclaims the sign. This is also the restaurant locals recommend as the best for seafood. Since it's right on the beach, with the water practically lapping at the foundations, and since the owners are fishermen, the fish is so fresh it's practically still wiggling. The wood hut doesn't look like much, but you can have fish fixed almost any way imaginable. If you haven't tried the Yucatecan specialty, Tik-n-xic fish, this would be a good place. It's opposite the basketball court.

PLAYA DEL CARMEN AFTER DARK

It seems like everyone in town is out on avenida 5 or Juárez across from the square until 10 or 11pm; there's pleasant strolling, meals and drinks at street-side cafes, huskers to watch and listen to, and shops to duck into. Later in the evening your choices move to the beach or to bars located mostly above street level: a **Señor Frog's** down by the ferry dock, dishing out its patented mix of thumping dance music, Jell-O shots, and frat-house antics; on the beach at 4th Street, the pirate ship–designed **Captain Tutils** has a large bar area, dance floor, and live entertainment nightly; the **Safari Bar** at the Treetops hotel always has a congenial crowd gathered around the bar and television until midnight; and then there's the beachside bar at the **Blue Parrot,** which seems to draw most of the European and American expatriate community with its sultry jazz music, has swings for bar stools, and stays open late (somewhere around 2 to 3am). **Pancho's Mexican Cafe,** one of Playa's most popular restaurants, is known for its oversized margaritas and lively, open-air ambiance. It's located on calle 12, just off of 5th Avenue. (They're also adding a second courtyard bar and have 40 rooms for rent in back of the original bar/restaurant.) **Espiral,** on 5th Avenue near the bus station, was the newest addition, playing recorded techno dance music.

5 Nature Parks & Resorts Along Highway 307

This section of the mainland coast between Playa del Carmen and Tulum is right on the front lines of the Caribbean Coast's transformation from idyllic backwater to developing tourist destination. South of Playa del Carmen along Highway 307 is a succession of new commercial nature parks, planned resort communities, and for now, anyway, a few rustic beach hideaways and unspoiled coves. From north to south, this section will cover Xcaret, Paamul, Xpuha, Puerto Aventuras, Akumal, and Xel-Ha. Puerto Calica, the new cruise-ship pier, is 2½ miles south of Xcaret and 8 miles south of Playa del Carmen.

Of the fledgling resorts south of Playa del Carmen, **Akumal** is one of the most attractive and complete, with moderately priced hotels and bungalows scattered among the graceful palms that line the beautiful, soft beach and gorgeous bay. **Puerto Aventuras** is a privately developed, growing resort city aimed at affluent travelers and private-condo owners. **Paamul** and **Xpuha** offer inexpensive inns on gorgeous beaches 2½ miles apart. If the offbeat beach life is what you're after, grab it now before it disappears. (Other little-known and inexpensive getaways can be found on the Punta Allen Peninsula south of Tulum, and the Majahual Peninsula south of Felipe Carrillo Puerto; see the following section for details.) Two water theme parks offer entertaining ways to spend the day immersed in the beauty of this region. One is centered around the crystal clear series of cenotes and lagoons at **Xel-Ha.** The other is the immensely popular park development of **Xcaret.** Popular day-trips from Cancún, they are open to anyone traveling along this coast. See "Excursions & Organized Tours," in chapter 12, for detailed information on Xel-Ha and Xcaret.

EN ROUTE SOUTH FROM PLAYA DEL CARMEN   The best way to travel this coast is in a rental car. Bus transportation from Playa del Carmen south exists but is not great. Buses depart fairly regularly from Playa headed toward Chetumal, stopping at every point of interest along the way; however, remember—it can be a long walk to the coast and to your final destination. There's also bus service to and from Cobá three times a day. Another option is to hire a car and driver; costs run around $10 to $12 per hour, or an all-day rate can be negotiated. Find a driver you like and whose English is good; remember, you'll be with him all day.

PAAMUL: A BEACH HIDEAWAY

About 10 miles south of Xcaret, 16 miles south of Cozumel, 62 miles southwest of Cancún, and half a mile east of the highway is Paamul (also written Pamul), which in

Maya means "a destroyed ruin." Turn when you see the Minisuper (a place to pick up reasonably priced snacks and drinks), which is also owned by the Cabañas Paamul (see below). At Paamul you can enjoy a beautiful beach and a safe cove for swimming; it's an idyllic place to leave the world behind. Thirty years ago the Martin family gave up coconut harvesting on this wide stretch of land, which includes a large shallow bay, gained title to the land, and established this comfortable out-of-the-way respite. They plan soon to build more rooms on the unoccupied portion of the bay.

Scuba Max (☎ **987/3-0667;** fax 987/4-1729) is a fully equipped, PADI-, NAUI-, and SSI-certified dive shop here, located next to the cabañas. Using three 38-foot boats, they take guests on dives 5 miles in either direction. If it's too choppy, the reefs in front of the hotel are also excellent. They also offer a night dive in Paamul, which is considered the best night dive in the Mexican Caribbean. The cost per dive is $30 to $35 if you have your own equipment plus $20 to $25 if you rent their gear. The snorkeling is also excellent in this protected bay and the one next to it.

WHERE TO STAY & DINE

✪ **Cabañas Paamul.** Km 85 Carretera Cancún-Tulum (Apdo. Postal 83), 77710 Playa del Carmen, Q. Roo. ☎ **99/25-9422** in Mérida. Fax 99/25-6913. (Reservations: Av. Colón 501-C, Depto. D-211 x 6 y 62, 97000 Mérida, Yuc.) 7 bungalows; 190 trailer spaces (all with full hookups). July–Aug and Dec–Feb $60 double. Mar–June and Sept–Nov $50 double. RV space with hookups $16 per day; $360 per month. No credit cards.

When you reach this isolated, relaxing hotel you'll see an extremely tidy lineup of mobile homes and beyond them a row of coral-and-white beachfront bungalows with covered porches, just steps away from the Caribbean. Despite the number of mobile homes (which are occupied more in winter than any other time), there's seldom a soul on the beautiful little beach. Each bungalow contains two double beds, tile floors, rattan furniture, ceiling fans, hot water, and 24-hour electricity. A large, breezy palapa-topped restaurant serves delicious food at more than reasonable prices. Saturdays the happy hour starts at 6pm with country music, and Sundays at 6pm there's a buffet dinner. Try the Pescado Paamul or Shrimp Paamul; both are wonderful baked medleys devised by the gracious owner Eloiza Zapata. For stays longer than a week, ask for a discount, which can sometimes be as much as 10%. The trailer park isn't what you might expect—some trailers have decks or patios and thatched palapa shade covers. Trailer guests have access to 12 showers and separate bathrooms for men and women. Laundry service is available nearby. Turtles nest here June through September. The Paamul turnoff is clearly marked on the highway; then it's almost a mile on a straight, narrow, paved-but-rutted road to the bungalows. Visitors not staying here are welcome to use the beach, though the owners request that they not bring in drinks and food and use the restaurant instead.

PUERTO AVENTURAS: A RESORT COMMUNITY

About 2½ miles south of Paamul (65 miles southwest of Cancún), you'll come to the new city-size development of Puerto Aventuras on Chakalal Bay. Though it's on 900 oceanfront acres, you don't see the ocean unless you walk through one of the three hotels. A complete resort, it includes a state-of-the-art marina, hotels, several restaurants, and multitudes of fashionable condominiums winding about the grounds and around the marina. The golf course has 9 holes open for play, plus there are numerous options for sportfishing. I don't recommend this resort for a vacation at this time because it's so far from anything, and there are better options along this coast. And, if you're touring this part of the world you won't see much of it by staying here. Architecturally sophisticated, it's like the island of Cancún without the crowds or nightlife.

It's targeted more as a resort community for Mexican nationals who've purchased condominiums here, than at foreign tourists who've come to experience the Yucatecan culture.

Even if you don't stay here, the **Museo CEDAM** on the grounds is worth a stop. CEDAM stands for Center for the Study of Aquatic Sports in Mexico, and the museum houses displays on the history of diving on this coast from pre-Hispanic times to the present. Besides dive-related memorabilia, there are displays of pre-Hispanic pottery, figures, copper bells found in the cenotes of Chichén-Itzá, shell fossils, and sunken-ship contents. It's open daily from 10am to 1pm and 2 to 6pm. Donations are requested. If you're hungry, there's a restaurant opposite the museum.

AKUMAL: A RESORT ON A LAGOON

Continuing south on Highway 307 a short distance, you'll come to Akumal, a small, modern, and ecologically oriented community built around and named after a beautiful lagoon. It's one of those places foreigners discover, explore, fall in love with, and return to live. Signs point the way in from the highway, and the white arched Akumal gateway is less than half a mile toward the sea. The resort complex here consists of five distinct establishments sharing the same wonderful, smooth palm-lined beach and the adjacent Half Moon Bay and Yalku Lagoon. The hotel's signs and white entrance arches are clearly visible from Highway 307. On the way in to Akumal, a visitor information and reception center (generally open afternoons, 2pm to 7pm) will assist you with help on where to stay and what to do in town. It's sponsored by a local real-estate office, and although the information may not be completely unbiased, I still found it to be a friendly and helpful service.

You don't have to be a guest to enjoy the beach, swim in the beautiful clear bay, and eat at the restaurants. It's an excellent place to spend the day while on a trip down the coast. Besides the excellent snorkeling, ask at the reception desk about **horseback rides on the beach.** Equipment rental for snorkeling and windsurfing are readily available. For **scuba diving,** two completely equipped dive shops with PADI-certified instructors serve the hotels and bungalows in this area. Both are located between the two hotels. There are almost 30 dive sites in the region (from 30 to 80 ft.), and two-tank dives cost around $65. Both shops offer resort courses as well as complete certification. **Lagoon snorkeling** is best on the left side of the lagoon, the side by the big circular restaurant and a bit farther out. **Fishing trips** can also be arranged through the dive shops. You're only 15 minutes from good fishing. Two hours (the minimum period) costs $100, and each additional hour is $35 for up to four people with two fishing lines.

WHERE TO STAY

Club Akumal Caribe/Hotel Villas Maya Club. Km 104 Carretera Cancún-Tulum (Hwy. 307). ☎ **987/5-9012.** (For reservations: P.O. Box 13326, El Paso, TX 79913; ☎ 800/351-1622 in the U.S., 800/343-1440 in Canada, or 915/584-3552.) 70 units. A/C. High season $90 bungalow; $110 hotel room; $140–$397 villa/condo. Low season $76 bungalow; $100 hotel room; $120–$233 villa. AE, MC, V for reservations only; "cash only" at the resort.

The white arches you drive under and the entrance are not impressive, but the lodging selection is. The 41 spacious **Villas Maya Bungalows** have beautiful tile floors and comfortable, nice furniture, all with fully equipped kitchens. The 21 rooms in the new three-story **beachfront hotel** are similarly furnished but with small kitchens (no stove), a king-size or two queen-size beds, pale tile floors, and stylish Mexican accents. The **Villas Flamingo** are four exquisitely designed and luxuriously (but comfortably) furnished two-story homes facing Half Moon Bay. Each has one, two, or three bedrooms; large living, dining, and kitchen areas; and a lovely furnished patio just steps from the beach. The hotel has its own pool separate from other facilities on the grounds. Akumal's setting is truly relaxing and there's a restaurant facing the beach and lagoon, plus a **grocery store** with all the common necessities. If you're traveling with children, ask about the **children's program** that functions during specific times of year (extra charge of $15 per child, per day; with prepay discounts available). The hotel has recently upgraded the decor in the rooms, and the pools, restaurant, and Kid's Club were all remodeled in late 1997.

WHERE TO DINE

La Buena Vida. Media Luna Bay, Akumal. ☎ **987/5-9060.** Main courses $3–$7.50. MC, V. Daily 11am–11:30pm. CASUAL MEXICAN AND GRILLED SPECIALTIES.

La Buena Vida is the town's most popular beachfront restaurant and bar, a laid-back place for passing the day and reveling in the otherwise tranquil Akumal nights. Tables on the beach are set for enjoying the casual and consistently good fare. Sandwiches, fish fillets, and chicken dishes are more popular items. The shrimp tacos come with generous servings of jumbo shrimp and freshly made guacamole. Lounge chairs and beach setups are an extra bonus for daytime patrons. A large, round bar with swing chairs and satellite TV serves as the locally favorite gathering place, where you catch up with the goings-on around town.

A CAVERN-TOUR/SCUBA-DIVING OPERATOR

On the right side of the road (if coming from Cancún) about 11½ miles south of Xcacel (and about 9 miles north of Tulum), is **Divers of the Hidden Worlds** (☎ **987/4-4081;** it's a cellular phone in Cancún). Experienced divers lead certified divers, snorkelers, and hikers on a variety of unusual trips, with two-tank dives ranging in price from $60 to $90, depending on the type of dive and location. Some require hiking in the jungle to dry caves, others have divers penetrating the underground world of watery caves with glass-clear water. Snorkelers investigate the *cenotes* (sinkholes leading to underground caves). Some dives are for more advanced divers, and some trips last all day, while others consume half a day. They also offer reef dives, resort courses, and cave-diving certification. They'll provide transportation from Cancún.

6 Tulum, Punta Allen & Sian Ka'an

Tulum (80 miles southwest of Cancún) and the Punta Allen Peninsula (110 miles southwest of Cancún at its tip) are the southernmost points many travelers reach in their wanderings down the Caribbean coast (although there is more to discover farther on). The walled Maya city of Tulum is a large Postclassic Maya site that dramatically overlooks the Caribbean. It's a natural beacon to visitors to Quintana Roo, and within a 2-hour drive from Cancún. Tour companies and public buses make the trip regularly from Cancún and Playa del Carmen. And for those who want to leave the modern world a long, long way behind, Punta Allen (which can take between 1½ to 3 hrs. to reach from Tulum, depending on the current road conditions) may be the ultimate. It's a place without the crowds, frenetic pace, or creature comforts of the resorts to the north—down here, the generator shuts down at 10pm (if there is one). What you will find is great fishing and snorkeling, the natural and archaeological riches of the Sian Ka'an Biosphere Reserve, and a chance to rest up at what truly feels like the end of the road. A few beach cabañas now offer reliable power, telephones, and hot showers.

ORIENTATION When traveling south of Highway 307, get your bearings on Tulum by thinking of it as several distinct areas: First, on your left will be the junction of Highway 307 and the old access road to the Tulum ruins (it no longer provides

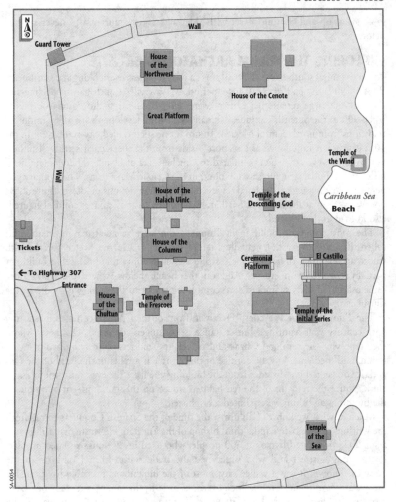

access); here you'll find two small hotels, two restaurants, and a Pemex gas station. Next, a few feet south of the old road on Highway 307, also on the left, is the new Tulum ruins access road, leading to a large parking lot. And a few feet farther along 307 is the left turn onto the road leading to the hotels and campgrounds south of the ruins.

This last road is the road south along the narrow **Punta Allen Peninsula** to **Boca Paila,** a portion of the **Sian Ka'an Biosphere Reserve,** and **Punta Allen,** a lobstering/fishing village at the tip's end. Though most of this 30-mile-long peninsular stretch of sandy, potholed road is uninhabited, there are several rustic inns along a fabulous beach south of the ruins.

Across the highway from the turnoff to the Punta Allen Peninsula on Highway 307 is the road to Cobá, another fascinating Maya city 40 miles inland. See "Cobá," below, for details.

Finally, south of the Punta Allen Road on Highway 307 is the **village of Tulum.** The highway here is lined with businesses, including bus stations, auto-repair shops, markets, and pharmacies. The village of Tulum, by the way, increasingly has the look of an up-and-coming place, with sidewalks and restaurants it's never sported before.

EXPLORING THE TULUM ARCHAEOLOGICAL SITE

Located 8 miles south of Xel-Ha, Tulum is a Maya fortress overlooking the Caribbean. By A.D. 900, the end of the Classic period, Maya civilization began to decline and most of the large ceremonial centers were deserted. During the Postclassic period (A.D. 900 to the Spanish Conquest), small rival states developed with a few imported traditions from north central Mexico. Tulum is one such walled city-state; built in the 10th century, it functioned as a seaport. Aside from the spectacular setting, Tulum is not an impressive city when compared to Chichén-Itzá or Uxmal. There are no magnificent pyramidal structures as are found in the Classic Maya ruins. The primary god here was the diving god, depicted on several buildings as an upside-down figure above doorways. Seen at the Palace at Sayil and Cobá, this curious, almost comical figure is also known as the bee god.

The most imposing building in Tulum is the large stone structure on the cliff called the **Castillo** (castle), actually a temple as well as a fortress, once covered with stucco and painted. In front of the Castillo are several unrestored palacelike buildings partially covered with stucco. And on the **beach** below, where the Maya once came ashore, tourists swim and sun, combining a visit to the ruins with a dip in the Caribbean.

The **Temple of the Frescoes,** directly in front of the Castillo, contains interesting 13th-century wall paintings, but entrance is no longer permitted. Distinctly Maya, they represent the rain god Chaac and Ixchel, the goddess of weaving, women, the moon, and medicine. On the cornice of this temple is a relief of the head of the rain god. If you get a slight distance from the building you'll see the eyes, nose, mouth, and chin. Notice the remains of the red-painted stucco on this building—at one time all the buildings at Tulum were painted a bright red.

Much of what we know of Tulum at the time of the Spanish Conquest comes from the writings of Diego de Landa, third bishop of the Yucatán. He wrote that Tulum was a small city inhabited by about 600 people, who lived in dwellings situated on platforms along a street and who supervised the trade traffic from Honduras to the Yucatán. Though it was a walled city, most of the inhabitants probably lived outside the walls, leaving the interior for governors, priestly hierarchy, and religious ceremonies. Tulum survived about 70 years after the Conquest, when it was finally abandoned.

Because of the excess of visitors this site receives, it is no longer possible to climb all of the ruins. In many cases, visitors are asked to remain behind roped-off areas to view them.

In late 1994 a new entrance to the ruins was constructed about a 10-minute walk from the archaeological site. Cars and buses enter a large parking lot; some of the public buses from Playa del Carmen go directly to the visitor center, where there are artisans' stands, a bookstore, a museum, a restaurant, several large rest rooms, and a ticket booth for Inter-Playa buses, which depart for Playa del Carmen and Cancún frequently between 7:40am and 4:40pm. After walking through the center, you pay the admission fee to the ruins ($2; free on Sun), and another fee ($1) if you choose to ride an open-air shuttle to the ruins and, if you're driving, another fee ($1) to park. You can easily walk, however. There's an additional charge of $4 for a permit to use a video camera at the site. Licensed guides have a stand by the path to the ruins and charge $20 for a 45-minute tour in English, French, or Spanish for up to four persons. They will point out many architectural details you might otherwise miss.

The Sian Ka'an Biosphere Reserve

Down the peninsula a few miles south of the Tulum ruins, you'll pass the guard-house of the Sian Ka'an Biosphere Reserve. The reserve is a tract of 1.3 million acres set aside in 1986 to preserve tropical forests, savannas, mangroves, coastal and marine habitats, and 70 miles of coastal reefs. The area is home to jaguars, pumas, ocelots, margays, jaguarundis, spider and howler monkeys, tapirs, white-lipped and collared peccaries, manatees, brocket and white-tailed deer, croco-diles, and green, loggerhead, hawksbill, and leatherback sea turtles. It also protects 366 species of birds—you might catch a glimpse of an ocellated turkey, a great curassow, a brilliantly colored parrot, a toucan or trogon, a white ibis, a roseate spoonbill, a jabiru (or wood stork), a flamingo, or one of 15 species of herons, egrets, and bitterns.

The park is separated into three parts: a "core zone" restricted to research; a "buffer zone," where visitors and families already living there have restricted use; and a "cooperation zone," which is outside the reserve but vital to its preserva-tion. If you drive on Highway 307 from Tulum to an imaginary line just below the Bahía (bay) of Espíritu Santo, all you see on the Caribbean side is the reserve; but except at the ruins of Muyil/Chunyaxche, there's no access. At least 22 archaeological sites have been charted within Sian Ka'an. The best place to sample the reserve is the Punta Allen Peninsula, part of the "buffer zone." The inns were already in place when the reserve was created. Of these, only the Cuzan Guest House (see "Where to Stay & Dine" under "The Punta Allen Peninsula," below) offers trips for birding. But bring your own binoculars and birding books and have at it—the bird life here is rich. At the Boca Paila bridge you can often find fishermen who'll take you into the lagoon on the landward side, where you can fish and see plenty of bird life; but it's unlikely the boatman will know bird names in English or Spanish. Birding is best just after dawn, especially during the April-to-July nesting season.

Day-trips to the Sian Ka'an are led by the Friends of Sian Ka'an from the Restaurant y Cabañas Ana y José just south of the Tulum ruins, on Monday, Tuesday, Friday, and Saturday for $50 per person using their vehicle or $40 per person if you drive yourself. Trips start from the Cabañas at 9:30am and return there around 2:30pm. For reservations, contact **Amigos de Sian Ka'an** (☎ **98/84-9583;** fax 98/87-3080) in Cancún. Or you may be able to book the tour once you've arrived at the Restaurant y Cabañas Ana y José (see "Where to Stay & Dine" under "The Punta Allen Peninsula," below) if the tour, limited to 19 people, isn't full.

WHERE TO STAY & DINE IN TULUM

There are three places to stay near the entrance to the Tulum ruins, at the old cross-roads entrance. The Hotel Acquario and Cabañas Cristinas are owned by the same family and offer an array of clean, comfortable accommodations in the broadest range of prices. The **Motel Crucero** is across the street. I much prefer the two-story **Hotel Acquario,** which offers 35 rooms, all with TV, air-conditioning, and ceiling fans, plus screened windows. The best rooms are a selection of newly redecorated rooms that face the street on the second floor. These are more modern and include in-room security boxes. Rates range from $37.50 to $75 a night per double during high season; and $19 to $50 in low season. There's even a small pool. The Acquario's ground-floor restau-rant and bar offers an eclectic mix of services for this remote part of Mexico: There's

E-mail and Internet access, *The New York Times* daily delivery, and excellent cappuccino. Basic needs are also met, including a small tobacco shop, public phones, and laundry service. Owner Felipe Ramíerez will supply details about the ruins or surrounding attractions, including locating area cenotes. Next door, their Cabañas Cristinas offers more basic, rustic accommodations, which are nonetheless very clean and comfortable. Each room comes with two double beds (or an equivalent combination), a bathroom with hot water, ceiling fans, and screened windows under a palapa roof. Rates are $22.50 double, cash only. They also have a mini supermarket for basic supplies, plus a restaurant with TV. For reservations, call ☎ **987/1-2194** or 987/1-2195. E-mail: tulum@cancun.rce.com.mx.

THE PUNTA ALLEN PENINSULA

About 3 miles south of the Tulum ruins on the Punta Allen Road, the pavement ends and the road becomes narrow and sandy, with many potholes during the rainy season. Beyond this point is a 30-mile-long peninsula called Punta Allen, split in two at a cut called Boca Paila, where a bridge connects the two parts of the peninsula and the Caribbean enters a large lagoon on the right. It's part of the far eastern edge of the 1.3-million-acre **Sian Ka'an Biosphere Reserve** (see above). Along this road you'll find several cabaña-type inns, all on beautiful beaches facing the Caribbean. Taxis from the ruins can take you to most of these; then you can find a ride back to the junction at the end of your stay.

EXPLORING THE PUNTA ALLEN PENINSULA

The natural environment is the peninsula's marquee attraction, whether your tastes run to relaxing on the beaches or going on bird-watching expeditions (these are available between June and Aug, with July being best). Sea turtles nest on its beaches from May through October. The turtles lumber ashore at night, usually between 10pm and 3am. *A note about provisions:* Since the Punta Allen Peninsula is rather remote and there are no stores, handy provisions to bring along include a flashlight, mosquito repellent, mosquito coils, water, and snacks. Most hotels along here charge for bottled water in your room and for meals. From October through December winds may be accompanied by nippy nights, so come prepared—some hotels don't have blankets.

Lodgings here vary in quality; some are simple but quite comfortable, while others are a lot like camping out. One or two have electricity for a few hours in the evening, but shut it off around 10pm, and there are no electrical outlets; most don't have hot water. The first one is half a mile south of the ruins, and the farthest is 30 miles down the peninsula.

The following hotels are listed in the order you'll find them as you drive south on the Punta Allen Road (from Tulum). To reach the first one you'll need to take the Punta Allen exit from Highway 307, then turn left when it intersects the coastal road. The rest of the hotels are to the right.

WHERE TO STAY & DINE

Restaurant y Cabañas Ana y José. Punta Allen Peninsula, Km 7 Carretera Punta Allen (Apdo. Postal 15), 77780 Tulum, Q. Roo. ☎ **987/1-2004** or 98/80-6022 in Cancún. E-mail: anayjose@cancun.rce.com.mx. 16 units. High season $60–$70 double. Low season $50–$60 double. No credit cards. Free unguarded parking.

This place started as a restaurant and blossomed into a comfortable inn on the beach. All rooms have tiled floors, one or two double beds, bathrooms with cold-water shower, patios or balconies, and electricity between 5:30 and 10:30pm. The rock-walled cabañas in front are a little larger, and some face the beautiful wide beach just a few yards off, but these are also the most expensive rooms. New rooms have been added on a second level in back. The only drawback is the lack of cross ventilation in some of the lower rooms in the back section, which can be extremely uncomfortable at night without electricity to power fans. The inn also offers bicycle and kayak rentals, trips through Maya canals and to little-known ruins, snorkeling, and dive trips. Biologist-led boat excursions, organized by the Friends of Sian Ka'an headquartered in Cancún, to the Sian Ka'an Biosphere Reserve begin here at 9:30am Monday, Tuesday, Friday, and Saturday (weather permitting) for $50 per person. (See "The Sian Ka'an Biosphere Reserve" box above, and "Road Trips from Cancún," in chapter 12, for details on making reservations for the Biosphere Reserve trip).

The excellent, screened-in restaurant, with sand floors under the palapa, offers modest prices and is open daily from 8am to 9pm. The hotel is 4 miles south of the Tulum ruins. Reservations are a must in high season, or arrive very early in the day, before it fills up.

Boca Paila Fishing Lodge. Km 25 Carretera Tulum–Punta Allen Apdo. Postal 59, 77600 Cozumel, Q. Roo. ☎ **987/2-5944** or 987/2-1176. Fax 987/2-0053. (For reservations contact Frontiers, P.O. Box 959, 100 Logan Rd., Wexford, PA 15090; ☎ 800/245-1950 in the U.S., or 412/935-1577; fax 412/935-5388.) 8 cabañas. High season (Dec 3–June 2) $2,150 per person double. Low season $1,750 per person double. Rates for 6 days and 7 nights, including all meals and a private boat and bonefishing guide for each cabaña. Ask about prices for a nonangler sharing a double with an angler. Nonfishing drop-in prices July–Sept, $210 per person double with 3 meals; $300 1 or 2 people for day of fishing with lunch but no overnight. No credit cards on-site; however, if prepaying while reserving with Frontiers, all major credit cards are accepted.

Easily a top contender for the nicest spot along this road, the white stucco cabañas offer friendly beachside comfort. Spread out on the beach and linked by a pleasant walkway, each individual unit has a mosquito-proof palapa roof, large tiled rooms comfortably furnished with two double beds, rattan furniture, hot water in the bathrooms, wall fans, 24-hour electricity, and a comfortable, screened porch. The Boca Paila attracts a clientele that comes for saltwater fly-fishing in the flats, mostly for bonefish. Prime fishing months are March through June. But when occupancy is low, nonfishing guests can be accommodated with advance notice. Overnight nonfishing rates are priced high as a discouragement to drop-ins. The lodge is about midway down the Punta Allen Peninsula, just before the Boca Paila bridge.

✪ Cuzan Guest House. Punta Allen. For reservations contact Apdo. Postal 24, 77200 Felipe Carrillo Puerto, Q. Roo. ☎ **983/4-0358;** fax 983/4-0383 in Felipe Carrillo Puerto). 8 units. $40–$65 double. All-inclusive 7-day fly-fishing package $1,599. Rates include all meals. No credit cards.

About 30 miles south of the Tulum ruins is the end of the peninsula and Punta Allen, the Yucatán's best-known lobstering and fishing village, planted on a palm-studded beach. Isolated and rustic, it's part Indiana Jones, part Robinson Crusoe, and certainly the most laid-back end of the line you'll find for a while. The small town has a lobster cooperative, a few streets with modest homes, and a lighthouse at the end of a narrow sand road dense with coconut palms and jungle on both sides. So it's a welcome sight to see the beachside Cuzan Guest House and its sign in English that reads STOP HERE FOR TOURIST INFORMATION. A stay here could well be the highlight of your trip, provided you're a flexible traveler.

Two rooms are simply furnished Maya-style oval stucco buildings with thatched roofs, concrete floors, hammocks, private bathrooms, and a combination of single and king beds with mosquito netting. Six more comfortable and spacious wooden huts, with thatched roofs and private bathrooms, offer ocean views from hammocks on the porch. These have two double beds each. A few other rooms or houses elsewhere in the village are sometimes available for rent, but these don't offer that special Cuzan experience and may suffer from loud village noises at night. Unfortunately, Cuzan's delightful thatched teepees disappeared during Hurricane Roxanne. There's solar-powered electricity at night, and plenty of hot water. The real charmer here is the sand-floored restaurant run by co-owner Sonja Lilvik, a Californian who makes you feel right at home. If it's lobster season, you may have lobster at every meal, always prepared with a deliciously different recipe. But you might also be treated to a pile of heavenly stone crabs or some other gift from the sea.

Sonja arranges fly-fishing trips for bonefish, permit, snook, and tarpon to the nearby saltwater flats and lagoons of Ascension Bay. The $25 per person boat tour of the coastline that she offers is a fascinating 3 hours of snorkeling, slipping in and out of mangrove-filled canals for bird watching, and skirting the edge of an island rookery loaded with frigate birds. November through March is frigate-bird mating season and the male frigate shows off his big billowy red breast pouch to impress potential mates. The all-day Robinson Crusoe Tour costs $100 per person and includes a boat excursion to remote islands, beaches, reefs, jungles, lagoons, and bird-watching areas. Or you can go kayaking along the coast or simply relax in a hammock on the beach.

7 Cobá Ruins

105 miles SW of Cancún

From the turnoff at the Tulum junction, you travel inland an hour or so to arrive at these mystical ruins jutting up from the forest floor.

The impressive Maya ruins at Cobá, deep in the jungle, are a worthy detour from your route south. You don't need to stay overnight to see the ruins, but there are a few hotels. The village is small and poor, gaining little from the visitors who pass through to see the ruins. Used clothing (especially for children) would be a welcome gift.

ESSENTIALS

GETTING THERE & DEPARTING **By Car** The road to Cobá begins in Tulum, across Highway 307 from the turnoff to the Punta Allen Peninsula. Turn right when you see the signs to Cobá and continue on that road for 40 miles. When you reach the village, proceed straight until you see the lake; when the road curves right, turn left. The entrance to the ruins is at the end of that road past some small restaurants. Cobá is also about a 3-hour drive south from Cancún.

By Bus Several buses a day leave Coba for Tulum and Playa del Carmen.

ORIENTATION The highway into Cobá becomes one main paved street through town, which passes El Bocadito restaurant and hotel on the right (see "Where to Stay & Dine," below) and goes a block to the lake. If you turn right at the lake you reach the Villas Arqueológicas a block farther. Turning left will lead you past a couple of primitive restaurants on the left facing the lake, and to the ruins, straight ahead, the equivalent of a block.

EXPLORING THE COBÁ RUINS

The Maya built many breathtaking cities in the Yucatán, but few were grander in scope than Cobá. However, much of the 42-square-mile site, on the shores of two lakes, is unexcavated. A 60-mile-long *sacbe* (a pre-Hispanic raised road or causeway) through the jungle linked Cobá to Yaxuná, once a large and important Maya center 30 miles south of Chichén-Itzá. It's the Maya's longest-known sacbe, and there are at least 50 or more shorter ones from here. An important city-state, Cobá, which means "water stirred by the wind," flourished between A.D. 632 (the oldest carved date found here) until after the founding of Chichén-Itzá, around 800. Then Cobá slowly faded

---

Keeping Your Cool in Cobá

Because of the heat, visit Cobá in the morning or after the heat of the day has passed. Mosquito repellent, drinking water, and comfortable shoes are imperative.

---

in importance and population until it was finally abandoned. Scholars believe Cobá was an important trade link between the Yucatán Caribbean coast and inland cities.

Once in the site, keep your bearings—it's very easy to get lost on the maze of dirt roads in the jungle. If you're into it, bring your bird and butterfly books; this is one of the best places to see both. Branching off from every labeled path you'll notice unofficial narrow paths into the jungle, used by locals as shortcuts through the ruins. These are good for scouting for birds, but be careful to remember the way back.

The **Grupo Cobá** boasts a large, impressive pyramid, the **Temple of the Church** (La Iglesia), which you'll find if you take the path bearing right after the entrance. Walking to it, notice the unexcavated mounds on the left. Though the urge to climb the temple is great, the view is better from El Castillo in the Nohoc Mul group farther back at the site.

From here, return back to the main path and turn right. You'll pass a sign pointing right to the ruined *juego de pelota* (ball court), but the path is obscure.

Continuing straight ahead on this path for 5 to 10 minutes, you'll come to a fork in the road. To the left and right you'll notice jungle-covered, unexcavated pyramids, and at one point you'll cross a raised portion crossing the pathway—this is the visible remains of the sacbe to Yaxuná. Throughout the area, intricately carved stelae stand by pathways, or lie forlornly in the jungle underbrush. Though protected by crude thatched roofs, most are so weather-worn as to be indiscernible.

The left fork leads to the **Nohoch Mul Group,** which contains **El Castillo,** the tallest pyramid in the Yucatán (rising even higher than the great El Castillo at Chichén-Itzá and the Pyramid of the Magician at Uxmal). So far, visitors are still permitted to climb to the top. From the magnificent lofty position you can see unexcavated jungle-covered pyramidal structures poking up through the forest all around. The right fork (more or less straight on) goes to the **Conjunto Las Pinturas.** Here, the main attraction is the **Pyramid of the Painted Lintel,** a small structure with traces of the original bright colors above the door. You can climb up to get a close look. Though maps of Cobá show ruins around two lakes, there are really only two excavated buildings to see after you enter the site.

Admission is $2; children under 12 enter free daily, and Sunday and holidays it's free to everyone. Camera permits are $4 for each video. The site is open daily from 8am to 5pm.

WHERE TO STAY & DINE

El Bocadito. Calle Principal, Cobá, Q. Roo. No phone. For reservations contact Apdo. Postal 56, 97780 Valladolid, Yuc. 8 units. $16–$21 double. No credit cards. Free unguarded parking.

El Bocadito, on the right as you enter town, could take advantage of being the only game in town besides the much more expensive Villas Arqueológicas, but it doesn't. Next to the hotel's restaurant of the same name, the rooms are arranged in two rows facing an open patio. They're simple, each with tile floors, two double beds, no bedspreads, a ceiling fan, and a washbasin separate from the toilet and cold-water shower cubicle. It's agreeable enough and always full by nightfall, so arrive no later than 3pm to secure a room.

The clean open-air restaurant offers good meals at reasonable prices, served by a friendly, efficient staff. Busloads of tour groups stop here at lunch (always a sign of

Wings & Stings

The mosquito and fly population is fierce, but Cobá is one of the best places along the coast for birding—go early in the morning.

approval). I enjoy the casual atmosphere of El Bocadito, and there's a bookstore and gift shop adjacent to the restaurant.

○ **Villas Arqueológicas Cobá.** Cobá, APDO.Postal 710, 77500, Cancun, Q. Roo. ☎ **800/258-2633** in the U.S., or 5/203-3086 in Mexico City. 44 units. A/C. $90 double (room only, including tax). Half board (choice of breakfast or lunch) available for an additional $12 per person; full board (3 meals) available for an extra $25 per person). Rates include all charges and taxes. AE, MC, V. Free guarded parking.

Operated by Club Med but nothing like a Club Med Village, this lovely lakeside hotel is a 5-minute walk from the ruins. The hotel has a French polish, and the restaurant is top-notch, though expensive. A room rate including meals is available. The rooms, built around a plant-filled courtyard and beautiful pool, are stylish and soothingly comfortable. The hotel also has a library on Mesoamerican archaeology (with books in French, English, and Spanish). Make reservations—this hotel fills with touring groups.

To find it, drive through town and turn right at the lake; the hotel is straight ahead on the right.

EN ROUTE TO FELIPE CARRILLO PUERTO: MUYIL & CHUNYAXCHE

From Tulum you continue along the main Highway 307 past the Cobá turnoff; it heads southwest through Tulum village. About 14 miles south of Tulum village are the ruins of **Muyil** (ca. A.D. 1 to 1540) at the settlement of **Chunyaxche,** on the left side. Although archaeologists have done extensive mapping and studies of the ruins, only a few of the more than 100 or so buildings, caves, and subterranean temples have been excavated; it's actually more historically significant than it is interesting, and for most people it may not be worth the time or admission price. Birding in the early morning, however, is quite worthwhile. New excavations take place off and on, so keep checking the progress. One of the objects of this research is to find evidence of an inland port, since canals link the site to the Caribbean 9 miles east of the Boca Paila cut.

Admission is $2; free for children under 12 and free for everyone on Sunday and festival days. It's open daily from 8am to 5pm.

The **Friends of Sian Ka'an** in Cancún (see box on "The Sian Ka'an Biosphere Reserve," above) organizes trips through the canals from Boca Paila. The **Restaurant y Cabañas Ana y José** south of the Tulum ruins (see listing under "Where to Stay & Dine" under "The Punta Allen Peninsula," above) also guide visitors here through the lagoons and canals.

After Muyil and Chunyaxche, Highway 307 cuts through 45 miles of jungle to Felipe Carrillo Puerto.

8 Felipe Carrillo Puerto

134 miles SW of Cancún

Felipe Carrillo Puerto (population 47,000) is a busy crossroads in the jungle along the road to Ciudad Chetumal. It has gas stations, a market, a small ice plant, a bus terminal, and a few modest hotels and restaurants.

Tank Check

Felipe Carrillo Puerto is the only place to buy **gasoline** between Tulum and Chetumal.

Since the main road intersects the road back to Mérida, Carrillo Puerto is the turning point for those making a "short circuit" of the Yucatán Peninsula. Highway 184 heads west from here to Ticul, Uxmal, Campeche, and Mérida.

As you pass through, consider its strange history: This was where the rebels in the War of the Castes took their stand, guided by the "Talking Crosses." Some remnants of that town (named Chan Santa Cruz) are still extant. Look for signs in town pointing the way.

ESSENTIALS

Coastal Highway 307 from Cancún leads directly here. There's frequent bus service south from Cancún and Playa del Carmen. The highway goes right through the town, becoming avenida Benito Juárez in town. Driving in from the north, you'll pass a traffic circle with a bust of the great Juárez. The town market is here. Small hotels and good restaurants are located on the highway as it goes through town.

The directions given above assume you'll be driving. If you arrive by bus, the **bus station** is right on the plaza. From there it's a 10-minute walk east down calle 67, past the cathedral and banks, to avenida Juárez. Turn left onto Juárez to find restaurants and hotels and the traffic circle, which I use as a reference point.

The telephone **area code** is **983. Banks** here don't exchange foreign currency.

9 Majahual, Xcalak & the Chinchorro Reef

In recent years, a tremendous amount of commercial attention has been focused on this remote part of Quintana Roo, with developments rumored to be going in both north of the Majahual turnoff and in the tiny village of Xcalak itself. Several small inns have also opened between Majahual and Xcalak. But the peninsula is still a little-known area, at least for the moment. A roll-with-the-punches kind of traveler will savor its rustic and remote appeal, especially those preferring this coast's offbeat offerings, divers looking for new underwater conquests, bird-lovers seeking an abundance of colorful tropical bird life, and anyone looking for quiet, beachfront relaxation. Your destination is the **Costa de Cocos Dive Resort** and the nearby fishing village of **Xcalak** near the end of the peninsula. Offshore reefs and the exceptional yet little-known Chinchorro Reef offer great diving possibilities. The village of Xcalak once had a population as large as 1,200 before the 1958 hurricane; now it has only 200 inhabitants. You'll pass many down-and-out places on the way, so the clean Costa de Cocos will stand out when you see it.

ARRIVING

BY CAR   Driving south from Felipe Carrillo Puerto, you'll come to the turnoff (left) onto Highway 10, 1½ miles after Limones, then it's a 30-mile drive to the coastal settlement of **Majahual** (mah-*hah*-wahl), and another 35 miles to the end of the peninsula and the tiny fishing village of Xcalak (eesh-*kah*-lahk). To orient you further, the turnoff from Highway 307 is 163 miles southwest of Cancún and 88 miles southwest of Tulum.

Driving from the turnoff at Highway 307 to Xcalak takes around 2 hours. At Majahual, where you turn right (south), there's a military guard station. Tell the guard your destination and continue on the new paved highway for 35 more miles, about half an hour. *Slow down at settlements. Residents aren't expecting much traffic, and dogs and children play on the road.*

BY PLANE   A new, 4,500-foot airstrip opened in early 1998, and regular, twice-weekly air service from Cancún was expected to be put in place. Check with the **State Tourism Office** in Chetumal (☎ **983/20855** or 983/25073) about the status of this service.

BY BUS   From Chetumal's bus station, two full-size **buses** daily go to Xcalak. There's combi (minivan) transportation from behind the Holiday Inn, but they cram in twice as many passengers as will fit comfortably and may carry a pig or goat on top as well.

BY FERRY   A year ago, ferry docks and two 20-car **ferries** (with passenger space) were being prepared to run between Chetumal and Xcalak, eliminating the tedious road trip through Limones and Majahual. Again, check with the **State Tourism Office** in Chetumal (☎ **983/2-0855** or 983/2-5073) about the status of this service. To date, there is only passenger service aboard a 30-passenger ferry that takes you 6 miles north of Xcalak; the cost is $5 each way.

DIVING THE CHINCHORRO REEF

The **Chinchorro Reef Underwater National Park** is a 24-mile-long, 8-mile-wide oval-shaped reef with a depth of 3 feet on the reef's interior to 3,000 feet on the exterior. Locals claim it's the last virgin reef system in the Caribbean. It's invisible from the ocean side; one of its diving attractions is the number of shipwrecks, at least 30 of them, along the reef's eastern side. One is on top of the reef. Divers have counted 40 cannons at one wreck site. On the west side are walls and coral gardens, but it's too rough to dive there.

Aventuras Chinchorro is the fully equipped dive shop for Sandwood Villas and Villa Caracol (see below) as well as for other establishments in the area. Local diving just offshore costs $45 per diver for a two-tank dive. Chinchorro Banks diving costs between $25 and $65 per person, depending on how long you stay, how far you go, and how many divers are in the group. Fishing and snorkeling excursions and trips into Belize can also be arranged, as well as rental of kayaks and horses. For diving reservations or for rooms at the above-mentioned inns, contact **Aventuras Chinchorro,** 812 Garland Ave., Nokomis, FL 34275 (☎ **800/480-4505** or 941/488-4505). Credit Cards are only accepted when prepaying reservations from the United States.

Important Note about Provisions

Since this is a remote part of the world, travelers should expect inconveniences. When things break down or food items run out, replacements are a long way off. You might arrive to find that the dive boat's broken, or that there's no beer, or that the generator powering the water pumps, toilets, and electricity is off for hours or days. Needless to say, a flashlight might come in handy. Bring a large quantity of strong mosquito repellent with DEET as a main ingredient—the mosquitoes are undaunted by anything else. You might want to stow a package or two of mosquito coils to burn at night. Your last chance for gas is at Felipe Carrillo Puerto, although if you're desperate, the tire repairman's family in Limones might sell you a liter or two. Look for the big tire leaning against the fence.

The Yucatán's Lower Caribbean Coast

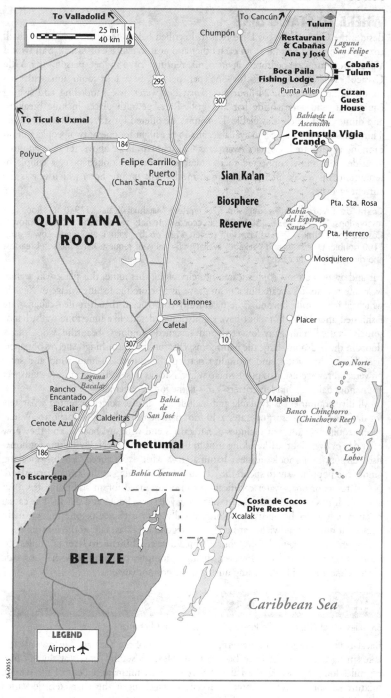

To Valladolid

0 — 25 mi / 40 km

N

To Cancún

Chumpón

Tulum

Restaurant & Cabañas Ana y José

Laguna San Felipe

Cabañas Tulum

Boca Paila Fishing Lodge

Punta Allen

Cuzan Guest House

To Ticul & Uxmal

Bahía de la Ascensión

Peninsula Vigia Grande

Polyuc

184

Felipe Carrillo Puerto (Chan Santa Cruz)

Sian Ka'an

Biosphere

Reserve

Pta. Sta. Rosa

Bahía del Espíritu Santo

Pta. Herrero

QUINTANA ROO

Mosquitero

Los Limones

Cafetal

Placer

307

10

Cayo Norte

Laguna Bacalar

Rancho Encantado

Bahía de San José

Bacalar

Cenote Azul

Calderitas

Majahual

Banco Chinchorro (Chinchorro Reef)

186

Chetumal

Cayo Lobos

To Escarcega

Bahía Chetumal

Costa de Cocos Dive Resort

Xcalak

BELIZE

Caribbean Sea

LEGEND

Airport

SA-0055

WHERE TO STAY & DINE

Besides the Costa de Cocos Dive Resort described below, there are two other small, cozy inns about half a mile from each other and near the village of Xcalak. **Sandwood Villas** are four two-bedroom apartments renting for $55 per person; the **Villa Caracol,** where rooms rent for $65 per person, is a four-room inn with air-conditioning, balconies, 24-hour electricity, hot water, free snorkeling and fishing equipment, and a beachside bar and grill. Rates at both places include breakfast and dinner, and lunch is available. Discounts are offered for stays of a week or more. Thirteen RV hookups are also available, at $15 per night for one or two people, but no camping is permitted. Contact **Aventuras Chinchorro,** listed above, for reservations.

Aside from those connected to the establishments mentioned here, a couple of restaurants in Xcalak offer good seafood meals—ask at your hotel which one is the current favorite.

Costa de Cocos Dive Resort. Km 52 Carretera Majahual–Xcalak, 77940, Q. Roo. (For reservations ☎ **800/538-6802.** E-mail: ccocos@gte.net; www.northcoast.com/~brown/ CostadeCocos.html.) 12 cabañas. High season $120 double with 1 or 2 beds. Low season $100 double. Dive rates and packages available; E-mail your request. Rates include breakfast and dinner. No credit cards.

Far and away the most sophisticated hostelry along this route, this place will seem a welcome respite. It's located in a palm grove just before the fishing village of Xcalak, which is half a mile beyond. The beautifully constructed thatch-roofed cabañas are fashioned after Maya huts, but have sophisticated details like limestone walls, handsomely crafted mahogany-louvered and screened windows, beautiful wood-plank floors in the bedroom, large tile bathrooms, comfortable furnishings, shelves of paperback books, hot water, and mosquito netting. They have 24-hour wind and solar power, and reverse-osmosis purified tap water. Nice as it is, it still won't hurt to inspect your shoes daily for hidden critters—this is the jungle, after all.

All dive equipment is available and included in dive packages or rented separately for day-guests. The resort operates a 40-foot dive boat for diving Chinchorro. Watersports equipment for rent includes ocean kayaks and windsurf boards, and they now offer day or overnight sea-kayaking trips to Belize, inside the reef. Fly-fishing for bonefish, tarpon, and snook inside Chatumal Bay with experienced, English-speaking guides is a popular way to spend the day, as is bird watching at their sanctuary island. NAUI resort or open-water certification can be arranged for an additional fee. Beer and soft drinks are sold at the resort, but bring your own liquor and snacks. The casual restaurant features home-style cooking, usually with a choice of one or two main courses at dinner, sandwiches at lunch, and regular breakfast fare in the morning.

Anytime the sea gets choppy, your planned dive at **Chinchorro Reef** (22 miles offshore) may be grounded. However, diving 5 minutes offshore from the Costa de Cocos Resort is highly rewarding during these postponements.

10 Lago Bacalar

65 miles SW of Felipe Carrillo Puerto; 23 miles NW of Chetumal

Bacalar offers another offbeat alternative in this part of the Yucatán. The crystal-clear lake spring-fed waters of Lake Bacalar form Mexico's second largest at slightly over 65 miles long. Known as the Lake of Seven Colors, mismanagement of the natural mixture of spring and seawater in recent years changed the characteristic varied deep-blue colors. It's still beautiful to gaze upon, and the colors range from crystal clear and pale-blue to deep blue-green and Caribbean turquoise. Spaniards fleeing coastal pirates used Maya pyramid stones to build a fort in Bacalar, which is now a modest museum. The area is very quiet—it's the perfect place to swim and relax. At least 130 species of birds have been spotted in the area. If you're in a car, take a detour through the village of Bacalar and down along the lakeshore drive. To find the lakeshore drive, go all the way past town on Highway 307, where you'll see a sign pointing left to the lake. When you turn left, that road is the lakeshore drive. You can double back along the drive from there to return to the highway. The Hotel Laguna is on the lakeshore drive. From here it's a 30-minute drive to Chetumal and to the Corozol Airport in Belize. Besides its location on Lago Bacalar, this area is also perfect for launching excursions into the Río Bec ruin route, described below.

ORIENTATION   If driving, signs into Bacalar are plainly visible from Highway 307. Buses going south from Cancún and Playa del Carmen stop here, and there are frequent buses from Chetumal.

WHERE TO STAY

Hotel Laguna. Costera de Bacalar 143, 77010 Lago Bacalar, Q. Roo. ☎ **983/2-3517** in Chetumal. 34 units. $30 double. $55 bungalow for 5 persons. No Credit Cards.

The Laguna is off the beaten path, so there are almost always rooms available, except in winter, when Canadians seem to fill the place. Rooms overlook the pool and have a lovely view of the lake. The water along the shore is very shallow, but you can dive from the hotel's dock into 30-foot water. The hotel's restaurant offers main courses costing about $4 to $8. It's open daily from 8am to 8pm. To find it, go through town toward Chetumal. Just at the edge of town you'll see a sign pointing left to the hotel and lakeshore drive.

✪ **Rancho Encantado Cottage Resort.** Km 3 Carretera Felipe Carrillo Puerto–Chetumal (Apdo. Postal 233), 77000 Chetumal, Q. Roo. ☎/fax **983/8-0427.** (For reservations contact P.O. Box 1256, Taos, NM 87571; ☎ 800/505-MAYA in the U.S.; fax 505/776-2102; www.encantado.com; E-mail: mpstarr@laplaza.org.) 12 casitas. Dec–Apr $150 double; May–Nov. $120 double; both including continental breakfast and dinner. Villa $1,100 week (discount for longer villa stays). Rates for casitas only, without food service, are $17.50 less per person. AE, MC, V.

What an Edenic, serene place in which to unwind! Rancho Encantado's immaculate white stucco individual casitas/cottages are spread out on a shady manicured lawn beside the smooth Lago Bacalar. Each spacious, sublimely comfortable, and beautifully kept room has mahogany-louvered windows, a shiny red-tile floor, mahogany dining table and chairs, a living room or sitting area, a porch with chairs, and hammocks strung between trees. All rooms are decorated with folk art, murals inspired by Maya ruins, foot-loomed pastel-colored bedspreads, and Zapotec rugs from Oaxaca. The newest rooms are the four waterfront casitas (rooms 9 through 12) with white stucco walls, thatched roofs, and fabulous hand-painted murals inspired by those at Bonampak. The owners' villa on the lake is also available several months a year.

An open-air conference center, with a soaring palapa roof, sits next to the water and near the restaurant. The large palapa-topped restaurant overlooks the lake and serves all three meals. There's no beef on the menu, but plenty of chicken, fish, vegetables, and fresh fruit. The honey here is from Rancho hives. You can swim from the hotel's dock, and kayaks and canoes are available for guest use. Orange, lime, mango, sapote, ceiba, banana, palm, and oak trees, wild orchids, and bromeliads on the expansive grounds make great bird shelter, attracting flocks of chattering parrots, turquoise-browed motmots, toucans, and at least 100 more species, many of which are easy to spot outside your room. Ask the manager, Luis Tellez, for a copy of the extensive birding list.

Tellez also keeps abreast of developments at the nearby archaeological sites and is the only source of current information before you reach the ruins. He's developed a lot of knowledge about the sites and leads several trips himself. Almost a dozen excursions are available through the hotel. Among them are day-trips to the **Río Bec** ruin route, an extended visit to **Calakmul,** a ruins visit and lunch with a local family (a guest favorite), outings to the **Majahual Peninsula,** and a riverboat trip to the Maya ruins of **Lamanai** deep in a Belizian forest. Mirabai Starr offers 8-day "Writing at the Ruins" workshops in January and June. *Note:* This is the only hotel offering guided trips to the Río Bec ruins, many of which are available only by special permit, which Tellez can obtain. Several ruins are easily reachable from the road, and others are so deep in the jungle that a guide is necessary to find them and a four-wheel-drive vehicle is a must. With advance notice, the hotel can arrange guides and the hotel has transportation. They also work with Río Bec specialist Serge Rìou (see "Touring the Ruins with a Guide," below). Excursions range in price from $55 to $115 per person, depending on the length and difficulty of the trip, and several have a three-person minimum. Groups interested in birding, yoga, archaeology, and the like are invited to bring a leader and use Rancho Encantado as a base. Special packages and excursions can be arranged in advance from the hotel's U.S. office. To find the Rancho, look for the hotel's sign on the left about 1 mile before Bacalar.

WHERE TO DINE

Besides the lakeside restaurant of **Rancho Encantado** (see above), you may enjoy the **Restaurant Cenote Azul,** a comfortable open-air thatched-roof restaurant on the edge of the beautiful Cenote Azul. In both places, main courses cost from $5 to $12. To get to Restaurant Cenote Azul, follow the highway to the south edge of town and turn left at the restaurant's sign; follow that road around to the restaurant. At Rancho Encantado you can swim in Lago Bacalar, and at the Restaurant Cenote you can take a dip in placid Cenote Azul, but without skin lotion of any kind, because it poisons the cenote.

SIDE TRIPS FROM BACALAR: THE RÍO BEC RUIN ROUTE

A few miles west of Bacalar begins the Yucatán's **southern ruin route,** generally called the Río Bec region, although other architectural styles are present. Until recently the region enjoyed little attention. However, all that is rapidly changing. Within the last several years, the Mexican government has spent millions of pesos to build a new highway, conserve previously excavated sites, and uncover heretofore unexcavated ruins.

This is an especially ruin-rich, but little-explored, part of the peninsula. With the opening in late 1994 of **Dzibanché** (an extensive "new" site), paved-road access to **Calakmul** in 1994, and the **Museo de la Cultura Maya** in 1995 in Chetumal, together with other "new sites" and discoveries at existing ruins, the region is poised to become the peninsula's newest tourist destination. With responsible guides, other jungle-surrounded but difficult-to-reach sites may also be available soon. A new four-lane highway leads from close to Bacalar for several miles before it becomes two lanes again; construction crews are continuing to work on widening the road even further. Tourist services (restaurants, hotels) are slowly being added along the route, but informed guides must be arranged before you arrive, and there are no visitor centers. Rancho Encantado trucks in water to the bathrooms at the ruins of Kohunlich, making them the only public rest rooms on the route. Part of what makes this area so special is the feeling of pioneering into unmarked land, and with that comes a bit of inconvenience. However, this area is definitely worth watching and visiting now.

BIRD AND ANIMAL LIFE   The fauna along the entire route is especially rich. Toucans fly across the highway, and orioles are extremely common. Gray fox, wild turkey, *tesquintle* (a bushy-tailed, plant-eating rodent), the raccoon-relative *coatimundi* (with its long tapered snout and tail), and armadillos will surely cross your path. At Calakmul a family of howler monkeys resides in the trees overlooking the parking area.

THE ROUTE'S STARTING POINT   The route begins just 9 miles from the edge of Bacalar where there's the turnoff from Highway 307 to Highway 186, which leads to the Río Bec ruin route as well as to Escarcega, Villahermosa, and Palenque. *A reminder:* On your return, if you are going back to Bacalar (or north on Highway 307), the guards at the government inspection station at the Reforma intersection will ask to see your travel papers (birth certificate or passport) and tourist permit. It is the intersection you pass after turning from Highway 186 north on Highway 307 toward Bacalar. You can divide your sightseeing into several day-trips. If you get an early start, many of the ruins mentioned below can be easily visited in a day from Bacalar. These sites will be changing, though, since swarms of laborers are still busy with further exploration.

Evidence shows that these ruins, especially Becán, were part of the **trade route** linking the Caribbean coast at Cobá to Edzná and the Gulf coast, and with Lamanai in Belize and beyond. Once this region was dense with Maya cities, cultivated fields, lakes, and an elaborate system of rivers that connected the region with Belize and Central America. Today many of these ancient cities hide under cover of jungle, which has overtaken the land from horizon to horizon.

FACILITIES, OR LACK THEREOF   There are no visitor facilities or refreshments at these sites, so bring your own water and food. However, in the village of Xpujil (just before the ruins of Xpujil), the **Restaurant Posada Calakmul** (☎ **983/2-9162**) is open daily from 6am to 1am. Under the watchful eye of Doña María Cabrera, it serves excellent home-style food and caters to ruins enthusiasts—hung about the room are photos and descriptions of little-known sites written by Río Bec specialist Serge Rìou (see below). The new **hotel rooms** behind the restaurant cost $20 for a double and are clean and comfortable, with tile floors, private bathrooms with hot water, good beds, and a small porch.

Because phone service is so limited in this area, note the number (☎ **983/2-8863**) for **Caseta Telefónica** in Xpujil Campeche, where residents make phone calls and where tourists can receive messages.

Near the entrance to the Chicanná ruins, on the north side of the road, is the new **Ramada Inn Eco Village,** km 144 Carretera Excarcega (☎ **981/6-2233** in Campeche for reservations; the hotel has no phone). Though the name suggests an ecological bent, approximately 20 acres of jungle were completely leveled to build an as yet unpaved parking lot for all the buses and cars that will one day come, a swimming pool, a restaurant, and 28 nicely furnished rooms in sets of two stories. Manicured lawns with flower beds and pathways link the rooms, which have a Polynesian architecture. There are no ecologically oriented tours. For the moment, the hotel attracts primarily bus tours and individual travelers. Electricity is generated between 6pm and 10am. Restaurant prices are high and don't include the 15% tax. A 15% service charge might also be added. Double rooms go for $100, including breakfast. American Express, MasterCard, and Visa are accepted.

Luis Tellez at Rancho Encantado, at Bacalar (see "Where to Stay," under "Lago Bacalar," above), is the best source of information about the status of these sites and any new ones. Entry to each site is $2 to $4, and all are free on Sunday. Informational signs at each building within the sites are in Mayan, Spanish, and English. Wear loads

Maya Construction Styles

Río Bec Style Found particularly in the states of Campeche and Quintana Roo, and south in Guatemala, the style takes its name from the ruins of Río Bec, located south of Xpuhil of Highway 186 between Chetumal and Escarcega. Río Bec architecture is characterized by roof combs, which adorn rooftops like latticework false fronts. Frequently, doorways are elaborate stonework mouths of Chaac, also called "monster mouths." Steep pyramids are frequently almost cone-shaped, with such narrow stairs leading to the top that they are difficult to climb. Examples of the Río Bec style are at Xpuhil, Becán, Chicaná, and Calakmul. Away from the traditional Río Bec area, roof combs also appear in several places such as Palenque, Uxmal, and Kabah.

Chenes Style The baroque examples of Maya architecture, Chenes buildings have facades that are elaborately embellished from top to bottom with separately cut stone pieces, often with many representations of Chaac, the Maya rain god. As with the Río Bec style, doorways are often open mouths of a fierce-looking Chaac with pointed teeth representing the "monster mouth" entrance to Xibalba, the Maya underworld. Though the Chenes heartland is in the states of Campeche and Quintana Roo, Yucatán's ruins also have excellent Chenes-style buildings. Good examples are the Nunnery Annex at Chichén-Itzá, and the high-up doorway on the Temple of the Magician at Uxmal, and at Kabah where 250 Chaac masks cover the stunning facade of the Codz Poop. Chenes, or "well-country" style, is the name given to a region that contains many wells or that features this type of architecture.

Puuc Style The name Puuc refers to a region, a culture, and an architectural style. The Yucatán's only hilly area, south of Mérida, is known as the *Puuc* (Maya for hills or mountains), and gives the architecture its name. Architecturally elaborate stonework, often in the style of mosaics, generally begins from the top of the door line to the roofline and includes many masks of Chaac, appearing with an elephant trunk[nd]like hook nose. In other places, these masks appear on the facade as well as ornamental corner ends of buildings. Puuc buildings are also embellished with a series of short stone columns, giving the buildings a beautiful, almost Greek appearance.

of mosquito repellent. The following list of sites is in order if you're driving from Bacalar or Chetumal.

For a map of this area, consult the Yucatán Peninsula map earlier in this chapter.

TOURING THE RUINS WITH A GUIDE If you're coming to this part of the Yucatán specifically to see the Río Bec ruins, the services of Serge Rìou, "Maya Lowland Specialist," will probably be indispensable to you. Several years ago young Mr. Rìou visited the Río Bec ruin route on a vacation from France. He fell so in love with the culture, romance, and history of the ruins that he returned to live and learn all that was possible about these little-known ruins. Living in Xpujil, he hiked the forests daily in search of ruins, worked with archaeologists on the trail of new sites, photographed the ruins, attended conferences of Maya specialists, and read everything he could find on Mexican archaeology. Today his encyclopedic knowledge of the nearby ruins makes him the most informed guide. He speaks excellent English and Spanish and charges around $75 to $100 per person a day to guide up to three people to a variety of sites. The higher price is for **Calakmul,** the farthest site from Chetumal. He can arrange necessary permits to unopened sites. You can contact him directly (Apdo. Postal 298, 77000 Chetumal, Q. Roo; ☎ 983/2-4514 or 983/2-1251) or arrange for his services through **Rancho Encantado** at Lago Bacalar (see "Where to Stay," under "Lago Bacalar," above), which has all the necessary types of vehicles, or contact him through the **Holiday Inn** in Chetumal (see "Where to Stay & Dine," under "Chetumal," below).

DZIBANCHÉ

Dzibanché (or Tzibanché) means "place where they write on wood." Exploration began here in 1993, and it opened to the public in late 1994. Scattered over 26 square miles (though only a small portion is excavated), it's both a Preclassic and a Postclassic site (A.D. 300 to 900) that was occupied for around 700 years.

TEMPLES & PLAZAS   Two enormous adjoining plazas have been cleared. The site shows influence from Río Bec, Petén, and Teotihuacán. The Temple of the Owl, on the Plaza de Xibalbá, has a miniature version of Teotihuacán-style *talud tablero* (slant and straight facade) architecture flanking the sides of the main stairway leading to the top with its lintel and entrance to an underground tomb. (Teotihuacán ruins are near Mexico City, but their influence was strong as far as Guatemala.) Despite centuries of an unforgiving wet climate, a wood lintel, in good condition and with a date carving, still supports a partially preserved corbeled arch on top of this building. Inside the temple, a tomb was discovered, making this the second known temple in Mexico built over an underground tomb (the first discovered is the Temple of Inscriptions at Palenque). A diagram of this temple shows interior steps leading from the top, then down inside the pyramid to ground level, just as at Palenque. The stairway is first reached by a deep, well-like drop that held remains of a sacrificial victim and which was sacked during pre-Hispanic times. Uncovered at different levels of the stairwell were a number of beautiful polychromed lidded vessels, one of which has an owl painted on the top handle, with its wings spreading onto the lid. White owls were messengers of the gods of the underworld in the Maya religion. This interior stairway isn't open to the public, but you can clearly see the lintel just behind the entrance to the tomb. Further exploration of the tomb awaits stabilization of interior walls.

Opposite the Temple of the Owl is the **Temple of the Cormorant,** so named after a polychromed drinking vessel found here picturing a cormorant. Here, too, archaeologists have found evidence of an interior tomb similar to the one in the Temple of the Owl, but excavations of it have not begun. Other magnificently preserved pottery pieces found during excavations include an incense burner with an almost three-dimensional figure of the diving god attached to the outside, and another incense burner with an elaborately dressed figure of the god Itzamná attached.

The site also incorporates another section of ruins called **Kinichná** (keen-eech-*nah*), which is about 1½ miles north and is reachable only by a rutted road that's impassable in the rainy season. There, an Olmec-style jade figure was found.

NO ROAD—YET   A formal road to these ruins has not been built, but there's a sign pointing to the right turn to Morocoy approximately 18 miles from the Highway 307 turnoff. You follow that paved road, which turns into an unpaved road, and pass the small settlement (not really a town) of Morocoy to another rough dirt road to the right (there's a sign to the ruins there), and follow it for about a mile to the ruin entrance. Ask at Rancho Encantado, near Bacalar (see "Where to Stay," under "Lago Bacalar," above), about the condition of the unpaved portion of road.

KOHUNLICH

Kohunlich (koh-*hoon*-leek), 26 miles from the intersection of Highways 186 and 307, dates from around A.D. 100 to 900. Turn left off the road, and the entrance is 5½ miles ahead. From the parking area you enter the grand parklike site, crossing a large and shady ceremonial area flanked by four large conserved pyramidal edifices. Continue walking, and just beyond this grouping you'll come to Kohunlich's famous **Pyramid of the Masks** under a thatched covering. The masks, actually enormous plaster faces, date from around A.D. 500 and are on the facade of the building. Sporting an elongated face and undulating lips, the masks show vestiges of blue and red paint. Note the carving on the pupils, which show a cosmic connection, possibly with the night sun that illuminated the underworld. It's speculated that masks covered much of the facade of this building, which is built in the Río Bec style with rounded corners, a false stairway, and a false temple on the top. At least one theory is that the masks are a composite of several rulers at Kohunlich. During recent excavations of buildings immediately to the left after you enter, two intact pre-Hispanic skeletons and five decapitated heads were uncovered that were once probably used in a ceremonial ritual. To the right after you enter (follow a shady path through the jungle) is another recently excavated plaza. It's thought to have housed elite citizens, due to the high quality of pottery found there and the fine architecture of the rooms. Scholars believe that Kohunlich became over-populated, leading to its decline. The bathrooms here are the only ones at any site on the route.

CHACAN BACAN

Chacan Bacan (chah-*kahn* bah-*kahn*), which dates from around 200 B.C., was first discovered in 1980 with excavation beginning in 1995. It's scheduled to open some time in 1999, with 30 to 40 buildings uncovered. The discovery of huge **Olmec-style heads** on its facade should make future digs exciting. The heads, showing from the middle of the skull forward, have helmetlike caps similar in style to the full multiton Olmec heads unearthed in Veracruz and Tabasco on Mexico's Gulf Coast, where the Olmecs originated. These heads are thought to be older than the figures at both Kohunlich and Balamkú. The exact size of the site hasn't been determined, but it's huge. In a densely forested setting, with thousands of tropical hardwood trees, plants, birds, and wild animals, it's been earmarked as an ecological/touristic center. Though not yet open to the public, it's about 50 miles and a 1½-hour drive from Bacalar. The turnoff (left) to it is at Caoba, where you follow a paved road for about 1½ miles, then turn left on an unmarked path. From the paved portion you can look left and see the uncovered pyramid protruding over the surrounding jungle. Ask Luis Tellez at Rancho Encantado at Lago Bacalar about the accessibility of this site.

XPUJIL

Xpujil (also spelled Xpuhil) means either "cattail" or "forest of kapok trees" and flourished between A.D. 400 and 900. Ahead on the left after you enter, you'll see a rectangular ceremonial platform 6½ feet high and 173 feet long holding three once-ornate buildings. These almost conical edifices resemble the towering ruins of Tikal in Guatemala and rest on a lower building with 12 rooms. Unfortunately, they are so ruined you can only ponder how it might have been. To the right after you enter are two newly uncovered structures, one of which is a large acropolis. From the highway, a small sign on the right points to the site that is just a few yards off the highway and 49 miles from Kohunlich.

BECÁN

Becán (bay-*kahn*), about 4½ miles beyond Xpujil and once surrounded by a moat, means "canyon filled by water" and dates from the early Classic to late Postclassic periods (600 B.C. to A.D. 1200). The moat, which isn't visible today, once had seven bridges leading to the seven cities that were pledged to Becán. Following jungle paths beyond the first visible group of ruins, you'll find at least two recently excavated **acropolises.** Though the site was abandoned by A.D. 850, ceramic remains indicate there may have been a population resurgence between A.D. 900 and 1000, and it was still used as a ceremonial site as late as A.D. 1200. Becán was a governmental and cer-emonial center with political sway over at least seven other cities in the area, including Chicanná, Hormiguero, and Payan.

To really understand this site, you need a good guide. But for starters, the first plaza group you see after you enter was the center of grand ceremonies. From the highway you see the backside of a pyramid (Temple 1) with two temples on top. From the highway you can see between the two pyramid-top temples to Temple 4, which is opposite Temple 1. When the high priest appeared through the mouth of the earth monster in the center of Temple 4 (which he reached via a hidden side stairway that's now partly exposed), he was visible from what is now the highway. It's thought that commoners had to watch ceremonies from outside the ceremonial plaza; thus the site was positioned for good viewing purposes. The backside of Temple 4 is believed to have been a civic plaza where rulers sat on stone benches while pronouncing judg-ments. The second plaza group dates from around A.D. 850 and has perfect twin towers on top, where there's a big platform. Under the platform are 10 rooms that are thought to be related to Xibalba (shee-*bahl*-bah), the underworld. Earth-monster faces probably covered this building (and they appeared on other buildings as well). Remains of at least one ball court have been unearthed. Becán is about 4½ miles beyond Xpujil and is visible on the right side of the highway, about half a mile down a rutted road.

CHICANNÁ

Slightly over a mile beyond Becán, on the left side of the highway, is Chicanná, which means "house of the mouth of snakes." Trees loaded with bromeliads shade the cen-tral square surrounded by five buildings. The most outstanding edifice features a monster-mouth doorway and an ornate stone facade with more superimposed masks. As you enter the mouth of the earth monster, note that you are walking on a platform which functions as the open jaw of the monster with stone teeth on both sides.

CALAKMUL

This area is both a massive Maya archaeological zone with at least 60 sites and a 178,699-acre rain forest designated in 1989 as the Calakmul Biosphere Reserve, which includes territory in both Mexico and Guatemala.

THE ARCHAEOLOGICAL ZONE   Since 1982, archaeologists have been exca-vating the ruins of Calakmul, which dates from 100 B.C. to A.D. 900. It's the largest of the area's 60 known sites. Nearly 7,000 buildings have been discovered and mapped. At its zenith at least 60,000 people may have lived around the site, but by the time of the Spanish Conquest of Mexico in 1519, there were fewer than 1,000 inhabitants. Discoveries include more stelae than any other site. By Building 13 is a stelae of a woman dating from A.D. 652. Of the buildings, Temple 3 is the best preserved. In it were found offerings of shells, beads, and polychromed tripod pottery. The tallest, at 178 feet, is Temple 2. From the top of it you can see the outline of the ruins of

El Mirador, 30 miles across the forest in Guatemala. Temple 4 charts the line of the sun from June 21, when it falls on the left (north) corner, to September 21 and March 21, when it lines up in the east behind the middle temple on the top of the building, to December 21, when it falls on the right (south) corner. Numerous jade pieces, includ-ing spectacular masks, were uncovered here, most of which are on display in the Museo Regional in Campeche. Temple 7 is largely unexcavated except for the top, where in 1984 the most outstanding jade mask yet to be found at Calakmul was uncovered. In *A Forest of Kings,* Linda Schele and David Freidel tell of wars between Calakmul, Tikal, and Naranjo (the latter two in Guatemala) and how Ah-Cacaw, king of Tikal (75 miles south of Calakmul) captured King Jaguar-Paw in A.D. 695 and later Lord Ox-Ha-Te Ixil Ahau, both of Calakmul. From January through May the site is open Tuesday through Sunday from 7am to 7pm. The site gets so wet during the rainy season, from June through October, that it's best not to go.

CALAKMUL BIOSPHERE RESERVE   Set aside in 1989, this is the peninsula's only high forest *selva,* a rain forest that annually records as much as 16 feet of rain. Among the plants are cactus, epiphytes, and orchids. Endangered animals include the white-lipped peccary, jaguar, and puma. So far, more than 250 species of birds have been recorded. At the moment there are no guided tours in the reserve, and no overnight stays or camping are permitted. But a hint of the region can be seen around the ruins. Howler monkeys are often peering down on visitors as they park their cars near the entrance to the ruins.

The turnoff on the left for Calakmul is located approximately 145 miles from the intersection of Highways 186 and 307, just before the village of Conhuas. There's a guard station there where you pay to enter the road/site. From the turnoff it's a 1½-hour drive on a paved, but very narrow and somewhat rutted road that may be difficult during the rainy season from May through October.

BALAMKÚ

Balamkú (bah-lahm-*koo*) was literally snatched from the incredibly destructive hands of looters by Instituto de Antropología e Historia (INAH) archaeologist Florentino García Cruz in October 1990. Amateur archaeologist and guide Serge Rìou was close behind him to photograph the site before looters hit one last time, destroying the head of one of the figures. An uncharted site at the time, it was saved by García, who had been alerted by locals that looters were working there.

Today it's open to the public, and though small, it's worth the time to see it since the facade of one building is among the most unusual on this route. When you reach the clearing, about 2 miles from the highway via a narrow dirt path through the jungle, there are two buildings, one on the right and one on the left. The right building is really three continuous, tall, but narrow, pyramids dating from around A.D. 700. The left building, which dates from around A.D. 400, holds the most interest because of the cross-legged figures resembling those found at Copan, in Hon-duras. Originally there were four of these regal figures (probably representing kings), seated on crocodiles or frogs above the entrance to the underworld, but looters destroyed two on each end and further disfigured the others.

A Driving Caution

Numerous curves in the road make seeing oncoming traffic (what little there is) dif-ficult, and there have been head-on collisions.

Still, enough remains to see the beauty; the whole concept of this building, with its molded stucco facade, is of life and death. On the head of each almost three-dimensional figure are the eyes, nose, and mouth of a jaguar figure, followed by the full face of the human figure, then a neck formed by the eyes and nose of another jaguar, and an Olmec-like face on the stomach, its neck decorated by a necklace, then the crossed legs of the figure seated upon a frog or crocodile. The earth monster is represented by a half-snake, half-crocodile animal, all symbols of death, water, and life. The May 1992 issue of *Mexico Desconocido* features the discovery of Balamkú written by Florentino García Cruz.

11 Chetumal

85 miles S of Felipe Carrillo Puerto; 23 miles S of Lago Bacalar

Quintana Roo became a state in 1974, and Chetumal (population 170,000) is its capital. While Quintana Roo was still a territory, it was a free-trade zone to encourage trade and immigration between neighboring Guatemala and Belize. The old part of town, down by the river (Río Hondo), has a Caribbean atmosphere and wooden buildings, but the newer parts are modern Mexican. There is lots of noise and heat, so your best plan would be not to stay—it's not a particularly interesting or friendly town. It is, however, worth a detour to see the wonderful **Museo de la Cultural Maya,** especially if your trip involves seeing the Río Bec ruin route described above.

ESSENTIALS
GETTING THERE & DEPARTING

BY PLANE **Aerocaribe** (Mexicana ☎ **983/2-6336** and 983/2-6675) has daily flights to and from Cancún and flights several times weekly between Chetumal and the ruins of Tikal in Guatemala. **Avio Quintana** (☎ **983/2-9692**) flies Monday through Friday to Cancún in a 19-passenger plane for around $50 one way.

BY CAR It's a 2½-hour ride from Felipe Carrillo Puerto. If you're heading to Belize, you'll need a passport and special auto insurance, which you can buy at the border. You can't take a rental car over the border, however.

To get to the ruins of Tikal in Guatemala you must first go through Belize to the border crossing at Ciudad Melchor de Mencos.

BY BUS The bus station of **Autotransportes del Caribe** (no telephone) is 20 blocks from the town center on Insurgentes at Niños Héroes. Buses go to Cancún, Tulum, Playa del Carmen, Puerto Morelos, Mérida, Campeche, Villahermosa, and Mexico City. **Omniturs del Caribe** (☎ **983/2-7889** or 983/2-8001) has deluxe buses to Mérida.

To Belize: Two companies make the run from Chetumal (through Corozal and Orange Walk) to Belize City. **Batty's Bus Service** runs 10 buses per day, and **Venus Bus Lines** (☎ **983/2-2132** in Corozal) has seven daily buses. Though it's a short distance from Chetumal to Corozal, it may take as much as 1½ hours, depending on how long it takes the bus to pass through Customs and Immigration (see "Onward from Chetumal," below, for more Customs information.)

To Limones, Majahual, and Xcalak: Two buses a day run between these destinations.

BY FERRY The docks are ready, but the new ferry was too big and ferry service has been delayed between Chetumal and the Xcalak/Majahual Peninsula. However, check with the **State Tourism Office** in Chetumal (☎ **983/20855;** fax 983/2-5073) about the status of this service. To date, there is only passenger service aboard a 30-passenger ferry that takes you 6 miles north of Xcalak; the cost is $5 each way.

VISITOR INFORMATION

The State Tourism Office (☎ **983/2-0266** or 983/2-0855; fax 983/2-5073 or 983/2-6097) is at avenida Hidalgo 22, at the corner of Carmen Ochoa.

ORIENTATION

The telephone **area code** is **983**. Chetumal has many "no left turn" streets, with hawk-eyed traffic policemen at each one. Be alert—they love to nail visitors and may even motion you into making a traffic or pedestrian violation, then issue a ticket, or take a bribe instead.

You'll arrive following Obregón into town. Niños Héroes is the other main cross street. When you reach it, turn left to find the hotels mentioned below.

A MAYA MUSEUM NOT TO MISS

Chetumal is really the gateway to Belize or to the Río Bec ruins, and not a touristi-cally interesting city. But it's worth a detour to Chetumal to see the **Museo de la Cultura Maya.** If you can arrange it, see the museum before you tour the Río Bec ruins, since it will all make more sense after getting it in perspective here.

✪ **Museo de la Cultura Maya.** Av. Héros s/n. ☎ **983/2-6838.** Admission $2 adults, $1 children. Tues–Thurs 9am–7pm; Fri–Sat 9am–8pm; Sun 9am–2pm. It's on the left between Colón and Gandhi, 8 blocks from Av. Obregón, past the Holiday Inn.

Sophisticated, impressive, and informative, this new museum unlocks the complex world of the Maya. Push a button and an illustrated description appears explaining the medicinal and domestic uses of plants with their Maya and scientific names, another describes the five social classes of the Maya by the way they dress, and yet another shows how the beauty signs of cranial deformation, crossed eyes, and facial scarifica-tion were achieved. An enormous screen flashes moving pictures taken from an air-plane flying over more than a dozen Maya sites from Mexico to Honduras. Another large television shows the architectural variety of Maya pyramids and how they were probably built. Then a walk on a glass floor takes you over representative ruins in the Maya world, clearly showing the variety of pyramidal shapes and particular sites. And, finally, one of the most impressive sections is the three-story stylized sacred ceiba tree, which the Maya believed represented the underworld (Xibalba) (on the bottom floor of the museum), earth (the middle floor of the museum), and the 13 heavens (the third floor of the museum). From this you'll have a better idea of the significance of the symbolism on the pyramids in the Maya world. Plan no less than 2 hours here. Even then, especially if your interest is high, you may want to take a break and return—there's a lot to see and learn. What a museum!

WHERE TO STAY & DINE

Hotel Nachancan. Calzada Veracruz 379, 77000 Chetumal, Q. Roo. ☎ **983/2-3232.** 20 units. A/C TV. $20 double; $28 suite. No credit cards.

Opposite the new market, this hotel offers rooms that are plain but clean and com-fortable. A restaurant is off the lobby. It's relatively convenient to the bus station, but not close enough to walk if you arrive by bus. It is, however, within walking distance of the Museo de la Cultura Maya. To find it from avenida Obregón, turn left on Calzada Veracruz and follow it for at least 10 blocks; the hotel will be on the right.

Hotel Holiday Inn Caribe. Niños Héroes 171, 77000 Chetumal, Q. Roo. ☎ **800/ 465-4329** in the U.S., or 983/2-1100. Fax 983/2-1676. 75 units. A/C TV TEL. $60–$85 double. AE, DC, MC, V. Free parking.

This modern hotel (formerly the Hotel Continental) across from the central market was remodeled in 1995 and became a Holiday Inn. The hotel has a good-size pool (a blessing in muggy Chetumal) and a good restaurant. The hotel is only 2 blocks from the Museo de la Cultura Maya. You can contact Río Bec specialist Serge Rìou through the travel agency here. To find it as you enter the town on Obregón, turn left on Niños Heroes, go 6 blocks and look for the hotel on the right, opposite the market.

ONWARD FROM CHETUMAL

From Chetumal you have several choices. The Maya ruins of Lamanai are an easy day trip into Belize if you have transportation (not a rental car); you can explore the Río Bec ruin route north of the city; and north of Bacalar you can cut diagonally across the peninsula to Mérida or retrace your steps to Cancún. You can take Highway 186 west to Escarcega, Villahermosa, and Palenque, but I don't recommend it and neither does the U.S. State Department: It's a long, hot, and lonely trip on a highway that is often riddled with potholes after you cross into Campeche state. Permanent ZONA DE DESLAVE signs warn motorists that parts of the roadbed are missing entirely or are so badly dipped they might cause an accident. Road conditions improve from time to time, but annual rains cause constant problems. And from time to time bandits have robbed travelers. At the Campeche state line there's a military guard post with drug-sniffing dogs; every vehicle is searched. A military guard post at the Reforma intersection just before Bacalar requires you to present the identification you used to enter Mexico (birth certificate or passport), plus your tourist permit. Other photo identification may be required, as well as information on where you're staying or where you're headed. The whole procedure should take only minutes.

14 Mérida & the Maya Cities

Ask most people about the Yucatán, and they think of Cancún and the Caribbean coast, Chichén-Itzá, and perhaps Uxmal. In fact, there's so much to do in the Yucatán, and such variety, that you'll find something different and exciting at every stop. One day you can be climbing a pyramid, another day descending into a cave or *cenote* (deep natural well), another day walking on a deserted beach (and dancing in the streets in Mérida that night), and the next day heading out in a small boat to pay a visit to a giant colony of pink flamingos. The Yucatecan people are warm and helpful, and their way of life is a fascinating mix of Mexican and Caribbean cultures—with a strong dose of Maya heritage.

The best way to see the Yucatán is by car. The terrain is flat, the highways and towns are laid out in a simple manner, there is little traffic on the highways, and the main roads are in great shape. Off the beaten path, the roads are narrow and rough, but hey—we're talking rental cars. Rentals are pricey compared to those in the United States, but some promotional deals are available (See "By Car" in the Mérida section below). Regular buses ply the roads between the main towns, and there are plenty of tour buses going to the ruins—but buses to out-of-the-way destinations are much less common than in the rest of Mexico. One giant bus company (ADO) controls almost all the first-class bus service. The key to comfortable bus travel is air-conditioning, and this is the main difference between first and second class.

Keep in mind that the Yucatán is *tierra caliente* (the hotlands). The coolest weather is from December through February; the hottest is from May through June when the air is still, and to a lesser degree from July through October, due to the rainy season. September and October can go either way. Never travel in this region without sunblock and mosquito repellent! High season is seldom as crowded in the interior of the peninsula as in Cancún, and most hotels have dropped the two-tiered pricing system. Even in the off-season, tourism from Europe is heavy from May through August (a fact that astounds most Yucatecans), and July and August are the traditional vacation months for Mexicans—when the residents of Mérida flock to the port of Progreso.

From the many available options, here's my pick of essential stops in Yucatán:

MÉRIDA   There's a lot to do in this vibrant and tropical-style colonial city; it's the place to buy hammocks, guayaberas, Panama hats, and native embroidered dresses called *huipils*.

CHICHÉN-ITZÁ & VALLADOLID   These two towns 25 miles apart are about midway between Mérida and Cancún. It's about 2 hours by car from Mérida to Chichén on the new toll road, or *autopista*. You can spend a day at the beautifully restored ruins, then stay at one of the nearby hotels—or drive 25 miles south to Valladolid, a quiet but charming colonial town with a pleasant central square. Valladolid features two eerie but accessible cenotes, and the spectacular ruins at Ekbalam are only 25 miles to the north. Also nearby is the Río Lagartos nature preserve, teeming with flamingoes and other native birds who shelter there.

CELESTÚN NATIONAL WILDLIFE REFUGE   This flamingo-sanctuary wetlands reserve is an offbeat sand-street fishing village on the Gulf coast, a 1½-hour drive from Mérida. Plan a long day, with a very early start. Travelers looking for solitude might find this a welcome respite for a week.

DZIBILCHALTÚN   This Maya site, now a national park, is located 9 miles north of Mérida along the Progreso Road. Here you'll find a number of pre-Hispanic structures, nature trails, and the new Museum of the Maya. Make this a half-day trip in the cool of the morning.

PROGRESO   A modern city and Gulf-coast beach escape 21 miles north of Mérida, Progreso has a beautiful oceanfront drive and a wide beach lined with coconut palms that's popular on the weekends. Plan a full-day trip if you like beaches, but there's not much else to see.

UXMAL   Smaller than Chichén, but architecturally more striking and mysterious. It's about 50 miles to the south of Mérida and can be seen in a day. Several other nearby sites comprise the Puuc route, and can be explored on the following day. It's also possible, though a bit rushed, to see Uxmal and the other ruins on a 1-day trip by special excursion bus from Mérida. Sunday is a good day to go, since admission is free to the archaeological sites.

CAMPECHE   This beautiful walled colonial city has been so meticulously restored that it's a delight just to stroll down the streets. Campeche is about 3 hours southwest of Mérida in the direction of Palenque; a full day should give you enough time to see its architectural highlights and museums.

1 Mérida: Gateway to the Maya Heartland

900 miles E of Mexico City; 200 miles W of Cancún

Mérida is the capital of the state of Yucatán and has been the dominant city in the region since the Spanish conquest. The colonial historic center is large but easy to navigate. Mérida is also the only city in the interior that has a nightlife to speak of, and it's more varied and authentic than Cancún's. People here know how to have a good time; there's something happening every night, making Mérida the preferred place to stay overnight while making day-trips to nearby attractions.

ESSENTIALS

GETTING THERE & DEPARTING   By Plane   Aeromexico (☎ 800/237-6639 in the U.S.) and **Mexicana** (☎ 800/531-7921 in the U.S.) have direct nonstop flights from Miami. **Aviateca** (☎ 800/) has a direct nonstop from Houston, as does **Continental** (☎800/231-0856), three times a week. Otherwise, you will have to get here through Cancún, Cozumel, or Mexico City. **Mexicana** (☎ 99/24-6633 or 99/24-6910) flies from Mexico City. **Aeromexico** (☎ 99/27-9277 or 99/27-9433) flies to and from Cancún and Mexico City. **Aerocaribe** (☎ 99/28-6786), a Mexicana affiliate, provides service to and from Cozumel, Cancún, Oaxaca, Tuxtla Gutiérrez,

San Cristóbal, Veracruz, Villahermosa, and points in Central America. **Taesa** (☎ **99/ 46-1826** at the airport) flies in from Monterrey and Mexico City. **Aviateca** (☎ **800/ 237-6639** in the U.S., or 99/46-1312) flies from Guatemala City. **Aviacsa** (☎ **99/ 26-9087**) provides service from Cancún, Monterrey, Villahermosa, Tuxtla Gutiérrez, Tapachula, Oaxaca, and Mexico City. Taxis to and from the city to the airport run about $6.

Arriving: Mérida's airport is 8 miles from the city center on the southwestern outskirts of town, where Highway 180 enters the city. Taxi tickets to town are sold outside the airport doors, under the covered walkway. A **colectivo** (group van or minibus) ticket is less expensive, but you'll need to wait for a group of five to assemble. Colectivos are $2; private taxis, $6.

City bus no. 79 ("Aviación") operates between the town center and the airport, but the buses do not have frequent service. Other city buses run along avenida Itzáes, just outside the airport precincts, heading for downtown.

By Car Highway 180 from Cancún, Chichén-Itzá, or Valladolid enters Mérida at calle 65, past the market and within 1 block of the Plaza Mayor. Highway 261 from Uxmal (via Muna and Uman) becomes avenida Itzáes; if you arrive by 261, turn right on calle 59 (first street after the zoo). If you arrive from Uxmal via Ticul and the ruins of Mayapán, you can get to Highway 180 into Mérida from the town of Kanasín.

A traffic loop or *periférico* encircles Mérida, making it possible to skirt the city and head for a nearby city or site. Directional signs are generally good into the city, but going around the city on the loop requires constant vigilance.

The federal highway (carretera federal) between Mérida and Cancún is labeled 180. The trip takes 5 to 6 hours, and the road is in decent shape. There is a new, four-lane divided **toll road** (known as the *cuota* or *autopista*) that parallels highway 180. It starts at the town of Kantunil, 35 miles east of Mérida. By avoiding small towns and a multitude of annoying speed bumps, the *autopista* cuts up to 2 hours from the journey between Mérida and Cancún; one-way tolls cost about $20. See "En Route to Uxmal," below, at the end of the Mérida section, for suggested routes from Mérida.

By Bus The first-class bus station, CAME, is on calle 70, between calles 69 and 71 (See "City Layout," below). When you get there you'll see the names and logos of a number of different bus lines—ADO, Premier, Expresso, Maya de Oro, Linea Dorada—these all belong to the same company. To buy a ticket, find your destination on the big board above the ticket counter and go to the ticket agent directly below it. The ticket agent might give you a couple of options with different prices for either first class or deluxe. The main difference between the two is that deluxe has more leg room; both are air-conditioned. Unless it's a really long ride, I choose the bus that has the most convenient departure time. Tickets can be purchased in advance.

To/from Chichén-Itzá: Four buses per day plus all the *de paso* buses. Also, check out tours operating from the hotels in Mérida and Valladolid.

To/from Valladolid and Cancún: There is a bus every hour.

To/from Playa del Carmen, Tulum, and Chetumal: There are 10 departures per day for Playa del Carmen, three for Tulum, four for Chetumal. **Caribe Express** is the only nonaffiliated, first-class bus line, and it has service to Chetumal four times per day. Buses leave from the second-class bus station (see below).

To/from Campeche: There is service to Campeche every hour between 6am and 10pm

To/from Palenque and San Cristóbal de las Casas: There is first-class service to Palenque twice daily.

For shorter trips, such as to Uxmal, go to the **second-class bus station,** next block over, on calle 68 between calles 69 and 71.

To/from Uxmal: four buses per day. The last departure from Uxmal leaves before the popular English version of the nightly sound-and-light show. You can hook up with various tour buses through most hotels or any travel agent/tour operator in town. There's also one bus per day that combines Uxmal with the other sites to the south (Kabah, Sayil, Labná, and Xlapak route—known as the Puuc route) and does the whole round-trip in a day. It stops for 2 hours at Uxmal and 30 minutes at each of the other sites. Tour-bus companies cover this route as well.

To/from Progreso, Dzibilchaltún, and Celestún: Buses to these places depart from the **Progreso Station** at calle 62 no. 524, between calles 65 and 67.

VISITOR INFORMATION   You'll find two sources of tourist information: one run by the city, the other by the state. Each has different materials. The principal **state office** is the downtown branch in the Teatro Peón Contreras, on calle 60 between calles 57 and 59 (☎ **99/24-9290**). It's open daily from 8am to 8pm, as are the information booths at the airport (☎ **99/46-1300**), the bus station, and on calle 62 next to the Palacio Municipal. Mérida's **visitor information office** is on calle 59 between 60 and 62 (☎ **99/23-0883**). Hours are from 9am to 2pm and from 4 to 8pm.

CITY LAYOUT   Mérida has the standard layout for towns in the Yucatán: Streets running north-south are even numbers, those running east-west are odd numbers. The numbering begins on the north and the east sides of town so that if you are walking on an odd-numbered street and the even numbers of the cross streets are increasing, then you know that you are heading west; likewise, if you are on an even-numbered street and are crossing streets with odd numbers that are increasing, then you know you are going south.

Another useful tip is that address numbers don't tell you anything about what cross street to look for, so you really can't be sure of where your destination is on the city grid. This is why in addition to an address, you will often see cross streets listed, usually like this: "calle 60 No. 549 x 71 y 73." The "x" is actually a multiplication sign— a short way of saying the word "por" (meaning "by") and "y" ("and"). Thus, you know that the place is on calle 60 between calles 71 and 73.

The center of town is the bright, busy **Plaza Mayor** (sometimes called the Plaza Principal but most often referred to simply as *el centro*). It's bordered by calles 60, 62, 61, and 63. The plaza always has a big, cheerful crowd in and around it, but it's really hopping on Sundays—when the city closes off the crossing streets to traffic, and the plaza becomes an instant festival. (See the section "Special Events Every Day of the Week," below.) Around the Plaza Mayor are the cathedral, the Palacio de Gobierno (state government headquarters), the Palacio Municipal, and the Casa de Montejo. Within a few blocks are several smaller plazas, the University of Yucatán, and the bustling market district.

Mérida's most fashionable district is the broad tree-lined boulevard called **Paseo de Montejo** and its surrounding neighborhood. The Paseo de Montejo begins 7 blocks northwest of the Plaza Mayor and runs north-south. There are a number of trendy restaurants and a few clubs here, some gorgeous mansions built during the boom times of the *henequén* industry, the new international hotels, and offices for various banks and airlines. Where the Paseo intersects avenida Colón you'll find the two fanciest hotels in town: the Hyatt and the Fiesta Americana.

GETTING AROUND   By Car   In general, reserve your car in advance from the United States to get the best weekly rates. During peak high season (Dec through Jan), you may be able to get a better price in Mérida than in Cancún; check prices for both. Rental cars are expensive, averaging $40 to $90 per day. If you want to rent for only a day or two, you can avoid the high cost of parking lots in Mérida. These *estacionamentos* charge one price for the night and double that if you leave your car for the following day. Many hotels offer free parking, but make sure they include daytime parking in the price. The local rental companies are very competitive and have promotional deals you can only get if you are there on the spot. When comparing, make sure it's apples to apples; ask if the price quote includes the IVA tax and insurance coverage (practically everybody offers unlimited free mileage). For tips on saving money on car rentals by renting in advance from your home country see "Getting Around," in chapter 3. Also, you may want to look into a special rental deal offered by Mayaland Tours if you stay at their hotels in Chichén-Itzá and Uxmal. Ask about pickup or drop-off in Cancún if your trip starts or ends there. For information contact **Mayaland Resorts,** avenida Colón 502, 97000 Mérida, Yucatán (☎ **800/235-4079** in the U.S., or 99/25-2122; fax 99/25-7022).

By Taxi   Taxis are easy to come by and are cheaper than in Cancún, but still expensive by Mexican standards.

By Bus   Bus travel within the heart of downtown isn't necessary since everything is within walking distance of the main plaza. However, to get to the large, shady Parque Centenario on the western outskirts of town a bus is available. Look for a white bus of the same name ("Centenario") on calle 64. Most buses on calle 59 go to Mérida's ambitious zoological park, or to the Museum of Natural History. "Central" buses stop at the bus station, and any bus marked MERCADO or CORREO (post office) will take you to the market district. For quick trips, take the Volkswagen minivans (usually painted white) that run out in several directions from the main plaza along simple routes. Known as combis, colectivos, or *peseros,* they're easy to spot along the side streets next to the plaza.

FAST FACTS: Mérida

American Express   The local office is located at Paseo de Montejo No. 492 (☎ **99/42-8200**).

Area Code   The telephone area code is **99.**

Bookstore   The **Librería Dante,** calle 60 at calle 57 (☎ **99/24-9522**), has a selection of English-language cultural-history books on Mexico. It's open Monday through Friday from 8am to 9:30pm, Saturday from 8am to 2pm and 5 to 9pm, and Sunday from 10am to 2pm and 4 to 8pm.

Climate   From November through February, the weather can be chilly and windy. In other months, it's just hot, especially during the day. Rain can occur anytime of year but usually occurs in the July-to-November rainy season and follows the pattern of afternoon tropical showers.

Complaints   Tourists who encounter **difficulties with public officials** such as police officers can call ☎ **01-800/0-0148** in Mexico to report incidents. If you have problems with customs officials at the airport report them to **SEDOCAM,** which is the Comptroller and Administrative Development Secretariat (☎ **01-800/0-0148** in Mexico).

Consulates   The **American consulate** is at Paseo de Montejo no. 453 and avenida Colón (☎ **99/25-5409** or 99/25-5011). The **British Vice-Consulate** is at calle 53 no. 498 at the corner of calle 58 (☎ **99/28-6152**). Office hours are 9am to 1pm. The vice-consul fields questions about travel to Belize as well as matters British.

Currency Exchange   Most banks in Mérida are a mess to deal with and do not offer outstanding exchange rates to offset the hassle. More times than not, casas de cambio in Mérida offer better rates and no wait. Try **Mérida Consultoria Finex** (☎ **99/24-1842**), open daily from 8am to 8pm. It is in the Parque Hidalgo, next door to the Caribe Hotel.

Hospitals   **Hospital O'Horan** is on avenida Itzáes at avenida Jacinto Canek (☎ **99/24-4111**), north of the Parque Centenario.

Post Office   Mérida's main post office (correo) is located in the midst of the market at the corner of calles 65 and 56. A branch office is located at the airport. Both are open Monday through Friday from 8am to 7pm and Saturday from 9am to noon.

Seasons   There are two high seasons: one in July and August when the weather is very hot and humid, and when Mexicans most commonly take their vacations; and another between November 15 and Easter Sunday, when northerners flock to the Yucatán to escape winter weather, and the weather is significantly cooler.

Spanish Classes   Maya scholars, Spanish teachers, and archaeologists from the United States are among the students at the Centro Idiomas del Sureste, calle 14 no. 106 at calle 25, Colonia México, 97000 Mérida, Yucatán (☎ **99/26-1155;** fax 99/26-9020). The school has two locations: in the Colonia México, a northern residential district, and on calle 66 at calle 57 in the downtown area. Students live with local families or in hotels; sessions running 2 weeks or longer are available for all levels of proficiency and areas of interest. For brochures and applications, contact Chloe Conaway de Pacheco, Directora.

Telephones   There are long-distance *casetas* at the airport, the bus station, at calle 57 corner with calle 60, calle 59, corner with calle 62, and at calle 60 between calles 55 and 53. To use the public Ladatel phones, buy a card from just about any newsstand or store. (To call long-distance from a Ladatel phone, you'll also need a separate long-distance card.) Also see "Telephone/Fax" in "Fast Facts: Mexico," in chapter 3.

SPECIAL EVENTS EVERY DAY OF THE WEEK
Many Mexican cities offer weekend concerts in the park, but Mérida surpasses them all with almost-daily public events, most of which are free and fun to watch.

SUNDAY   Each Sunday from 9am to 9pm, there's a fair called Domingo en Mérida ("Sunday in Mérida"). The main plaza and a section of calle 60 from el centro to Plaza Santa Lucía are blocked off from traffic. This was done by initiative of the municipal government, which wanted to get tourists to stay in the city longer, but the local populace quickly made the party its own. Parents come with their children to stroll around and take in the scene. There are booths selling food and drink along with a lively little flea market and used-book fair. There are children's art classes, educational booths, and concerts of all kinds. At 11am in front of the Palacio del Gobierno, musicians play everything from jazz to classical and folk music. Also at 11am, the police orchestra performs Yucatecan tunes at the Santa Lucía park. At 11:30am, you'll find bawdy comedy acts at the Parque Cepeda Peraza (Parque Hidalgo) on calle 60 at calle 59. There's a lull in midafternoon, and then the plaza fills up again as people walk around the plaza and visit with friends. Around 7pm in front of the Ayuntamiento, a large band starts playing mambos, rumbas, and cha-cha-chas with great enthusiasm; you may see a thousand people dancing there in the street. Then everyone is invited into the Ayuntamiento to see folk ballet dancers reenact a typical Yucatecan wedding. All events are free.

MONDAY   The City Hall Folklore Ballet and the Police Jaranera Band perform at 9pm in front of the Palacio Municipal. The music and dancing celebrate the

Vaquerías feast, which occurs after the branding of cattle on Yucatecan haciendas. Among the featured performers are dancers with trays of bottles or filled glasses on their heads—a sight to see. Admission is free.

TUESDAY The theme for the Tuesday entertainment, held at 9pm in Parque Santiago, on calle 59 at calle 72, is Musical Memories. Music includes popular South American and Mexican as well as North American songs from the 1940s. Admission is free.

WEDNESDAY At 9pm in the Teatro Peón Contreras on calle 60 at calle 57, the University of Yucatán Folklore Ballet presents "Yucatán and Its Roots." Admission is $5.

THURSDAY Typical Yucatecan music and dance are presented at the Serenata in Parque Santa Lucía at 9pm. Admission is free.

FRIDAY At 9pm on the patio of the University of Yucatán, calle 60 at calle 57, the University of Yucatán Folklore Ballet often performs typical regional dances from the Yucatán. Admission is free.

SATURDAY "Noche Mexicana" at the park at the beginning of Paseo de Montejo begins at 9pm. It features several performances of various kinds of traditional music and dance of Mexico. Some of the performers are amateurs who acquit themselves reasonably well; others are professional musicians and dancers who thoroughly know their craft. There are some food stands selling very good antojitos, as well as drinks and ice cream.

Also, on the evening of the 1st Friday of each month, Dennis LaFoy of the **Yucatán Trails Travel Agency** (☎ **99/28-2582**) invites the English-speaking community to a casual get-together. They usually gather at the Hotel Mérida Misión Park Plaza on calle 60, across from the Hotel Casa del Balam, but call Dennis to confirm the location.

EXPLORING MÉRIDA

In addition to the special events and festivals enumerated in the box above, Mérida has a number of attractions, most of which are within walking distance of each other in the downtown area.

WALKING TOUR
Mérida

Start: Plaza Mayor.
Finish: Palacio Cantón.
Time: Allow approximately 2 hours, not counting time for browsing or refreshment.
Best Times: Wednesday through Sunday before noon.
Worst Times: Monday, when the Anthropology Museum is closed; Tuesday when the Museo de Arte Contemporáneo is closed.

Downtown Mérida is a great example of a lowland colonial city. There is a casual, homey feel to the town. Buildings lack the severe baroque features that characterize central Mexico; most are finished in stucco and painted in tropical colors. Mérida's gardens add to this relaxed, tropical atmosphere. The gardeners here do not seek the kind of garden where all is exactly in its place and is obviously a display of the gardener's control over nature. Natural exuberance is the ideal, with plants growing in a wild profusion that disguises human intervention. A perfect example is the patio in the Palacio Montejo, which is one of our first stops. Mérida's plazas are a slightly different version of this aesthetic: Unlike the highland plazas, with their carefully sculpted trees and shrubs, Mérida's squares are typically built around giant laurel trees, surrounded by beds of native ornamentals. Usually you'll see a part of the plaza dedicated to a small, thoroughly manicured area or topiary showing that the gardener could work in the highland style, if he chose.

Begin this walk at the:

1. **Plaza Mayor.** It has had many names over the years; this one finally stuck for its simplicity. Simpler still is El Centro, which is how most people refer to it. Even when there's no formal event in progress, the park is full of people sitting on the benches talking with friends or taking a casual stroll. A plaza like El Centro is a great advantage for a big city such as Mérida; there's a personal feel to the place and a sense of community that combat the modern bustle of urban life. Notice the beautiful scale and composition of the major buildings surrounding the plaza. The most prominent of these is the:

2. **Cathedral.** Built between 1561 and 1598, it's celebrating its 400th anniversary with concerts and fiestas all the way into 1999. Much of the stone in the cathedral's walls came from the ruined buildings of Tihó, the former Maya city. This building, too, was once finished with stucco, and you can still see where it remains in places. People like the look of the unfinished walls, which show the cathedral's age. Notice how the two top levels of the bell towers are built off-center from their bases—an uncommon feature. Inside, decoration is sparse, with altars draped in fabric colorfully embroidered like a Maya woman's shift. The most notable feature is a picture over the right side door of Ah Kukum Tutul Xiú visiting the Montejo camp.

To the left of the main altar is a smaller shrine with a curious statue of Jesus, recovered from a burned-out church in the town of Ichmul. The figure was carved in the 1500s by a local artist from a miraculous tree that was hit by lightning and burst into flames—but did not char. The statue blistered as the flames destroyed the church it, but the figure of Jesus survived the fire. In 1645 it was moved to the cathedral in Mérida, where the locals named it Cristo de las Ampollas (Christ of the Blisters). Take a look in the side chapel (open from 8 to 11am and 4:30 to 7pm), which contains a life-size diorama of the Last Supper. The Mexican Jesus is covered with prayer crosses brought by supplicants asking for intercession.

To the right (south) of the cathedral is the:

3. **Museo de Arte Contemporáneo Ateneo de Yucatán (MACAY)** (☎ **99/ 28-3236**). The city's contemporary art museum is housed in the former seminary on the site of the archbishop's palace. The palace was torn down during the Mexican Revolution in 1915, but the remaining building is a stately architectural gem. Inside its two stories, built around a patio, 17 exhibition rooms show works by contemporary artists from the Yucatán and around the world. Nine of the rooms hold the museum's permanent collection while eight rooms showcase changing exhibits. One area includes a display of the building's history and Yucatecan embroidery. It's open Wednesday through Monday from 10am to 6pm (closed Tues). Admission $2.50; free on Sunday. On the south side of the Plaza Mayor is the:

4. **Palacio Montejo** (also called the Casa de Montejo). Conquering the Yucatán was the Montejo family business, begun by Francisco Montejo the Elder and continued by his son and his nephew, also named Francisco. Construction of the house started in 1542 under Francisco Montejo El Mozo, ("The Younger"; the elder Montejo's illegitimate son). Bordering the entrance is a politically incorrect

figure of the conqueror standing on the heads of the vanquished—borrowed, perhaps, from the pre-Hispanic custom of portraying victorious Maya kings treading on their defeated foes. The posture of the conquistador—and his expression of wide-eyed dismay—makes him less imposing than perhaps he would have wished. This building is now occupied by a bank, and you can enter the courtyard and see for yourself what a charming residence it must have been for the descendants of the Montejos, who lived here until as recently as the 1970s. If we continue circling the plaza in the same direction, on the west side, facing the cathedral is the:

5. **Palacio Municipal (City Hall).** This is more commonly known as the *Ayuntamiento,* with its charming clock tower, where you can look out over the plaza and see the hall that serves for public meetings of the city council. On the north side of the Plaza Mayor is the:

6. **Palacio de Gobierno,** dating from 1892. Large murals painted by the Meridiano artist Fernando Pacheco Castro between 1971 and 1973 decorate the interior walls. Scenes from Maya and Mexican history abound, and the painting over the stairway depicts the Maya spirit with ears of sacred corn: the "sunbeams of the gods." Nearby is a painting of the mustachioed Lázaro Cárdenas, who as president in 1938 expropriated 17 foreign oil companies and was hailed as a Mexican liberator. The palace is open Monday through Saturday from 8am to 8pm and Sunday from 9am to 5pm.

TAKE A BREAK   Revive your batteries with a cup of coffee and some pastries or a bolillo from the **Pan Montejo** on the southwest side of the plaza on the corner of calles 63 and 62. Add a glass of fresh orange or papaya juice from Jugos California next door, take a seat at the plaza, and enjoy the morning sun.

EXPLORING CALLE 60   Continuing north from the Plaza Mayor up calle 60, you'll see many of Mérida's old churches and little parks. Several stores catering to tourists along calle 60 sell gold-filigree jewelry, pottery, clothing, and folk art. A stroll along this street leads to the Parque Santa Ana and continues to the fashionable boulevard Paseo de Montejo and its Museo Regional de Antropología. On your right as you leave the northeast corner of the plaza, turn right on calle 61 for a block to the corner of calle 61 and calle 58 and the:

7. **Museo de la Ciudad.** Occupying a former convent and hospital, the museum collection relates the city's past in the form of photographs, drawings, and dioramas. It's open Tuesday through Saturday from 9am to 8pm and Sunday from 9am to 1pm. Admission is $2. Backtrack to calle 60; ahead on your right is the:

8. **Teatro Daniel de Ayala.** This theater offers a busy schedule of performing artists from around the world. Inquire within. A few steps beyond and across the street is the:

9. **Parque Cepeda Peraza** (also called the Parque Hidalgo). Named for the 19th-century general Manuel Cepeda Peraza, the *parque* was part of Montejo's original city plan. Small outdoor restaurants front hotels on the *parque,* making it a popular stopping-off place at any time of day.

TAKE A BREAK   Any of the several outdoor restaurants on the Parque Cepeda Peraza makes an inviting respite. My favorite is **Giorgio,** where you can claim a table and write postcards; barter for hammocks, amber jewelry, and baskets displayed by wandering artisans; or just watch the people go by. It's in front of the Gran Hotel.

Bordering Parque Cepeda Peraza across calle 59 is the:

10. **Iglesia de Jesús, or El Tercer Orden** (the Third Order). Built by the Jesuit order in 1618, this is the favorite spot in Mérida for getting hitched. You might come across a wedding in progress. The entire block on which the church stands belonged to the Jesuits, who are traditionally known as great educators, and their schools developed into the Universidad de Yucatán. Walk east on calle 59, 5 blocks past the Parque Cepeda Peraza and the church, and you'll see the former:

11. **Convento de la Mejorada.** This convent is a late-1600s work by the Franciscans. While here, go half a block farther on calle 59 to the Museo Regional de Artes Populares (see "More Attractions," below). Backtrack to calle 60 and turn north. Just beyond the church (Iglesia de Jesús) is the:

12. **Parque de la Madre** (also called the Parque Morelos). The park contains a modern statue of the Madonna and Child; the statue is a copy of the work by Renoir that stands in the Luxembourg Gardens in Paris. Beyond the Parque de la Madre and across the pedestrian way is:

13. **Teatro Peón Contreras.** This enormous beige edifice was designed by Italian architect Enrico Deserti in the early years of this century. In one corner you'll see a branch of the State Tourist Information Office facing the Parque de la Madre. The main theater entrance, with its Carrara marble staircase and frescoed dome, is a few steps farther. Domestic and international performers appear here frequently. On the west side of calle 60, at the corner of calle 57, is the:

14. **Universidad de Yucatán.** The university was founded in the 19th century by Felipe Carrillo Puerto with the help of General Cepeda Peraza. The founding is illustrated by a fresco (1961) by Manuel Lizama.

A block farther on your left, past the Hotel Mérida Misión Park Inn, is the:

15. **Parque Santa Lucía.** Surrounded by an arcade on the north and west sides, the park once was where visitors first alighted in Mérida after arriving in their stagecoaches. On Sunday, Parque Santa Lucía holds a used-book sale and small swap meet, and several evenings a week it hosts popular entertainment. On Thursday nights performers present Yucatecan songs and poems. A block west from the *parque* on calle 55 at the corner of calle 62 is:

16. **Biblioteca Cepeda Peraza.** This library was founded by the general in 1867. Head back to the Parque Santa Lucía. Facing the park is the ancient:

17. **Iglesia de Santa Lucía** (1575). To reach Paseo de Montejo, continue walking north on calle 60 to the:

18. **Parque Santa Ana,** 4 blocks up calle 60 from the Parque Santa Lucía. Turn right here on calle 47 for 1½ blocks; then turn left onto the broad, busy boulevard known as the:

19. **Paseo de Montejo.** This tree-lined thoroughfare has imposing banks, hotels, and several 19th-century mansions erected by *henequén* barons, generals, and other Yucatecan potentates. It's Mexico's humble version of the Champs-Elysées.

😊 **WINDING DOWN** Before or after tackling the Palacio Cantón (see below), stop for a break at the **Dulcería y Sorbetería Colón,** on Paseo de Montejo 1 block north of the Palacio between calles 39 and 41. Baked goods, ice cream, and candy are displayed in a long glass counter. Unfortunately, coffee and tea are not available.

At the corner of calle 43 is the:

20. **Palacio Cantón** (entrance on calle 43). This palace houses the **Museo Regional de Antropología** (Anthropology Museum; ☎ 99/23-0557). Designed and built

by Enrico Deserti, the architect who designed the Teatro Peón Contreras, this is the most impressive mansion on Paseo de Montejo and the only one open to the public. It was constructed between 1909 and 1911, during the last years of the Porfiriato as the home of General Francisco Cantón Rosado. The general enjoyed his palace for only 6 years before he died in 1917. The house was converted into a school and later became the official residence of the governor of the Yucatán.

The Palacio became an interregional museum covering not only the state of Yucatecas but also the rest of the peninsula and Mexico. Its exhibits include cosmology, a pre-Hispanic time computation and comparative timeline, musical instruments, weaving examples and designs, and stone carvings from all over the country.

On the right as you enter is a room used for changing exhibits, usually featuring "the piece of the month." After that are the permanent exhibits with captions mostly in Spanish. Starting with fossil mastodon teeth, the exhibits take you through the Yucatán's history, paying special attention to the daily life of its inhabitants. You'll see how the Maya tied boards to babies' heads in order to give them the slanting forehead that was then a mark of great beauty, and how they filed teeth to sharpen them or drilled teeth to implant jewels. Enlarged photos show the archaeological sites, and drawings illustrate the various styles of Maya houses and how they were constructed. The one of Mayapán, for instance, clearly shows the city's ancient walls. Even if you know only a little Spanish, the museum provides a good background for explorations of Maya sites. The museum is open Tuesday through Saturday from 8am to 8pm and Sunday from 8am to 2pm. Admission is $3; free on Sunday. There's a museum bookstore on the left as you enter.

ECOTOURS & ADVENTURE TRIPS

Recently there's been an explosion of companies that organize nature and adventure tours of the Yucatán Peninsula. One outfit with a long track record is **Ecoturismo Yucatán,** calle 3 no. 235, Col. Pensiones, 97219 Mérida, Yucatán. (☎ **99/25-2187;** fax 99/25-9047; www.imagenet.com.mx/EcoYuc/Home.html; E-mail: ecoyuc@ minter.cieamer.conacyt.mx). It is run by Alfonso and Roberta Escobedo, who can create an itinerary to meet just about any special and general interests you have for going to the Yucatán or southern Mexico. Alfonso has been creating adventure and nature tours for more than a dozen years.

Another specialty tour agency is **Yucatán Trails,** calle 62 no. 482 (☎ **99/28-2582**). Canadian Dennis LaFoy, well known and active in the English-speaking community, is a font of information and can arrange a variety of individualized tours or answer any questions about travel.

SHOPPING

Mérida is known for **hammocks, guayaberas** (lightweight men's shirts that are worn untucked), and **Panama hats.** And there are good buys in **baskets** made in the Yucatán and **pottery,** as well as crafts from all over Mexico, especially at the **central market.** Mérida is also the place to pick up prepared **achiote,** a pastelike mixture of ground achiote seeds (*annatto*), oregano, garlic, masa, and other spices used in Yucatecan cuisine. When mixed with sour orange to a soupy consistency, it makes a great marinade, especially on grilled meat and fish. It can be found bottled in this form. It's also the sauce that makes baked chicken and cochinita pibil.

Mérida's bustling **market district,** bounded by calles 63 to 69 and calles 62 to 54, is a few blocks southeast of the Plaza Mayor. The streets surrounding the market are as busy and crowded as the market itself. Heaps of prepared achiote are sold in the food section.

CRAFTS

Casa de las Artesanías. Calle 63 no. 513, between Calles 64 and 66. ☎ **99/28-6676.**

This store is in the front part of a restored monastery. Here you can find a wide selection of crafts from throughout Mexico. Stop by here before going to the various crafts markets to see what high-quality work looks like. The monastery's back courtyard is used as a gallery, with rotating exhibits on folk and fine arts. It's open Monday through Saturday from 9am to 8pm and Sunday from 9am to 1pm.

Crafts Market. In a separate building of the main market, Calle 67 at Calle 56.

Look for a large pale-green building behind the post office. Climb the steps and wade into the clamor and activity while browsing for leather goods, hammocks, Panama hats, Maya embroidered dresses, men's formal guayabera shirts, and craft items of all kinds.

Museo Regional de Artes Populares. Calle 59 no. 441, between Calles 50 and 48. No phone.

A branch of the Museo Nacional de Artes y Industrias Populares in Mexico City, this museum displays regional costumes and crafts in the front rooms. Upstairs is a large room full of crafts from all over Mexico, including filigree jewelry from Mérida, folk pottery, baskets, and wood carving from the Yucatán. Open Tuesday through Saturday from 8am to 8pm and Sunday from 9am to 2pm. Admission is free.

GUAYABERAS

Business suits are hot and uncomfortable in Mérida's soaking humidity, so businessmen, politicians, bankers, and bus drivers alike wear the guayabera, a loose-fitting shirt that buttons up, is decorated with narrow tucks, pockets, and sometimes embroidery and is worn over the pants rather than tucked in. Mérida is famous as the best place to buy guayaberas, which can be purchased for under $10 at the market or for over $50 custom-made by a tailor. A guayabera made of Japanese linen can set you back about $65. Most are made of cotton but can be had in various kinds of shirting material, and the traditional color is white. Connoisseurs have very definite opinions on color, the type of tucks that will run down the front, and about embroidery. Most shops display ready-to-wear shirts in several price ranges. Guayabera makers pride themselves on being innovators. I have yet to enter a shirtmaker's shop in Mérida that did not present its own updated version of the guayabera. When looking at guayaberas, here are few things to keep in mind. When Yucatecans say *seda,* they do not mean silk but polyester; *lino* is linen. Take a close look at the stitching and the way the tucks line up over the pockets, etc.; with guayaberas, the details are everything.

Jack Guayaberas. Calle 59 no. 507A. ☎ **99/28-6002.**

The craftsmanship here is very good, the place has a reputation to maintain, and some of the sales people can speak English. Prices are marked. This will give you a good basis of comparison should you want to hunt for a bargain. If they do not have the style and color of shirt you want, they will make it for you in about 3 hours. This shop also sells regular shirts and women's blouses. The shop is open Monday through Saturday from 10am to 8pm and Sunday from 10am to 2pm.

HAMMOCKS

I am an aficionado of hammocks, having slept in every variety across the length and breadth of Latin America. None is so comfortable as those of the Yucatán, which are woven with local cotton string in a fine mesh. For most of us, of course, the hammock is the equivalent of lawn furniture, something to relax in for an hour or so in the afternoon. But for the vast majority of Yucatecans, hammocks are their beds—what they sleep in at night. Many well-to-do Meridianos keep a bed just for show. I know a hotel owner who has 150 beds in his establishment, but will not sleep on a single one of them. He complains that when he does so he wakes up unrested and sore.

My advice to the hammock buyer is this: The woven part should be cotton, it should be made with fine string, and the strings should be so numerous that when you get in it and stretch out at an angle, the gaps between the strings remain small. Don't pay attention to the words used to describe the size of a hammock; they have become practically meaningless. Good hammocks don't cost a lot of money ($15 to $30). If you want a superior hammock, then ask for one made with *"hilo de crochet de cuatro cajas"* (the word crochet is also bandied about loosely). This should set you back about $80.

Nothing beats a tryout when you're shopping for this indispensable item; the two shops mentioned below will gladly hang a hammock for you to test drive. When it's up, look to see that there are no untied strings. You can also see what street vendors are offering, but you have to know what to look for—or they are likely to take advantage of you.

Hamacas El Aguacate. Calle 58 no. 604, corner with Calle 73. ☎ **99/28-6429.**

El Aguacate sells hammocks wholesale and retail. It has the greatest variety and is the place to get a really expensive hammock. A good hammock is their size no. 6 in cotton; it runs $26. The store is open Monday through Friday from 8am to 7pm and Saturday from 8am to 5pm. The store is about 6 blocks south of the main square.

Tejidos y Cordeles Nacionales. Calle 56 no. 516-B, between Calles 63 and 65. ☎ **99/28-5561.**

This place is near the municipal market. The only hammocks they sell are cotton, and they sell them on the basis of weight—a pretty good practice because hammock lengths are standard. The prices here are better than at El Aguacate, and the difference in quality is slight. My idea of a good hammock is one that weighs about 1½ kilos and runs about $18.

PANAMA HATS

Another useful and popular item is this soft, pliable hat made from the fibers of the jipijapa palm in several towns along Highway 180, especially Becal, in the neighboring state of Campeche. There's no need to journey all the way to Campeche, however, since Mérida sells the hats in abundance. They're just the thing to shade you from the fierce Yucatecan sun, and the hats can be rolled up and carried in a suitcase for the trip home.

Jipi hats come in three grades determined by the quality (pliability and fineness) of the fibers and closeness of the weave. The difference in weave is easily seen. A fine weave improves the shape of a hat. It has more body and regains its shape better. The best deals are in the Mercado and the *artesanías* market next to it; go from stall to stall until you find the specific shape and size of hat you are looking for.

WHERE TO STAY

Mérida is easier on the budget than Yucatán resort cities. Most hotels offer at least a few air-conditioned rooms, and some also have pools. You may find every room taken in July and August, when Mexicans vacation. In Mérida, free parking is a relative concept—for some hotels free parking means only at night; during the day there is a charge.

Mérida Accommodations & Dining

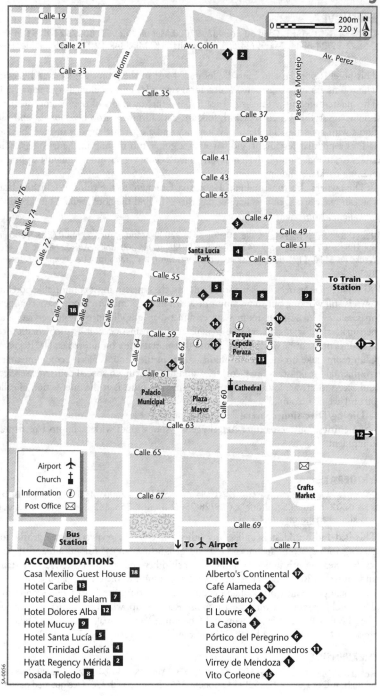

0 ‎ ‎ ‎ ‎ 200m
0 ‎ ‎ ‎ ‎ 220 y

N

Calle 19
Calle 21
Av. Colón
Calle 33
Reforma
Av. Perez
Calle 35
Paseo de Montejo
Calle 37
Calle 39
Calle 41
Calle 43
Calle 45
Calle 76
Calle 74
Calle 72
Calle 47
Calle 49
Calle 51
Santa Lucía Park
Calle 53
Calle 55
To Train Station
Calle 70
Calle 68
Calle 66
Calle 57
Calle 59
Calle 58
Calle 56
Calle 64
Calle 62
Parque Cepeda Peraza
Calle 61
Calle 60
Cathedral
Palacio Municipal
Plaza Mayor
Calle 63
Calle 65
Airport
Church
Information
Post Office
Calle 67
Crafts Market
Calle 69
Bus Station
To Airport
Calle 71

ACCOMMODATIONS
Casa Mexilio Guest House **18**
Hotel Caribe **13**
Hotel Casa del Balam **7**
Hotel Dolores Alba **12**
Hotel Mucuy **9**
Hotel Santa Lucía **5**
Hotel Trinidad Galería **4**
Hyatt Regency Mérida **2**
Posada Toledo **8**

DINING
Alberto's Continental **17**
Café Alameda **10**
Café Amaro **14**
El Louvre **16**
La Casona **3**
Pórtico del Peregrino **6**
Restaurant Los Almendros **11**
Virrey de Mendoza **1**
Vito Corleone **15**

SA-0056

EXPENSIVE

✪ **Casa del Balam.** Calle 60 no. 488, 97000 Mérida, Yuc. ☎ **800/624-8451** in the U.S., or 99/24-8844. Fax 99/24-5011. 57 units. A/C MINIBAR TV TEL. $85 double. Free parking.

This hotel is popular and centrally located. Most of the rooms are large and bright. The rooms are in two sections, which form two sides to the colonial-style courtyard. The quietest are in the three-story section and the top floors of the six-story section. Rooms are stylishly decorated with folk art, dark furniture, iron headboards, and tile floors with area rugs. There's a travel agency and a car-rental agency in the lobby, as well as a popular restaurant and bar with a guitar trio playing in the evenings. The tables scattered around the courtyard have become a favorite romantic spot for evening cocktails and appetizers.

The owners also run the hotel **Hacienda Chichén,** at the ruins of Chichén-Itzá; you can make arrangements here to stay there. To find the hotel, walk 2 blocks north on calle 60 from the main square.

Hyatt Regency Mérida. Calle 60 no. 344, 97000 Mérida, Yuc. ☎ **800/228-9000** in the U.S., 99/25-6722, or 99/42-0202. Fax 99/25-7002. 300 units. A/C MINIBAR TV TEL. Weekdays $110–$125 double. Ask about "supersaver rates"; rates may be cheaper if reserved from U.S.

At these prices perfection is the standard, and the fanciest, most comfortable hotel in town is still working out some minor details. The large, modern rooms have channels on satellite TV, 24-hour room service, direct-dial long-distance phone service, and personal safes. Trying to retrieve E-mail at the business center is problematic; ice machines may not be working; and room thermostats are a bit unpredictable. Regency Club rooms take up the top two floors; guests in these rooms receive complimentary continental breakfast, evening cocktails, and hors d'oeuvres; special concierge service; and access to private lounges and boardrooms. The hotel is at the intersection of calle 60 and avenida Colón.

Dining/Diversions: Several restaurants and bars.

Amenities: Business center, travel agency, shops, pool with swim-up bar, fitness equipment.

MODERATE

✪ **Casa Mexilio Guest House.** Calle 68 no. 495, 97000 Mérida, Yuc. ☎ **800/538-6802** in the U.S.; phone/fax 99/28-2505. 8 units. $55–$65 double. Rates include breakfast. Parking on street.

This bed-and-breakfast is unlike any other I know. The owners show a genius for playing with space in an unexpected and delightful manner. Rooms are at different levels—creating private spaces joined to each other and to rooftop terraces by stairs and cat walks. Rooms are large and comfortable; most of the central patio is taken up by a small pool and whirlpool and exuberant vegetation. Breakfast fare is wonderful. The hotel is connected with the Turquoise Reef Group, which runs inns on Mexico's Caribbean coast between Cancún and Chetumal. You can make reservations here for those inns. The hotel is 4 blocks west of the plaza between calles 57 and 59.

INEXPENSIVE

Hotel Caribe. calle 59 no. 500, 97000 Mérida, Yuc. ☎ **99/24-9022.** Fax 99/24-8733. 54 units. A/C or FAN TV TEL. $38–$42 double; $55 suite for 2 with A/C. Free guarded parking.

This hotel is very popular for several reasons. It is located back from the street on the Plaza Hidalgo; rooms are comfortable and quiet; and the prices are good. Like most hotels in Mexico, rooms are not lit brightly enough for American tastes. All rooms are built around a three-story, covered courtyard. From the top floor, where there's a small pool and sundeck, there are nice views of the cathedral and town. Most doubles and suites come with air-conditioning. Parking during the day is extra. To get to the hotel from the Plaza Mayor, walk a half block to the Parque Cepeda Peraza. The hotel is in the back right corner of the park.

Hotel Dolores Alba. Calle 63 no. 464, 97000 Mérida, Yuc. ☎ **99/28-5650.** Fax 99/28-3163. E-mail: asanchez@yucatan.com.mx. 46 units. A/C or FAN. $25–$28 double. Free guarded parking.

This is the perfect place to stay if you are traveling by car and are on a budget. The hotel is family-owned and -operated and was built from a converted Spanish colonial house. It has a large open court and a smaller courtyard with a clean pool, sundeck, and gardens. The rooms, half of which have air-conditioning, are decorated with local crafts. A small dining room opens for breakfast between 7 and 9am. The owners also operate the **Hotel Dolores Alba** outside Chichén-Itzá; you can make reservations at one hotel for the other. To find this hotel from the Plaza Mayor, walk east on calle 63 for 3½ blocks; it's between calles 52 and 54.

✪ **Hotel Mucuy.** Calle 57 no. 481, 97000 Mérida, Yuc. ☎ **99/28-5193.** Fax 99/23-7801. 22 units. FAN. $12 double.

This is half the price of other budget hotels listed here, and what separates it from the other $12 hotels in this city is the effort of the family that runs it. The Mucuy is named for a small dove said to bring good luck to places where it alights. Owners Alfredo and Ofelia Comín strive to make guests feel welcome with conveniences such as a communal refrigerator in the lobby, and for a small extra charge the use of a washer and dryer. This place stays pretty full, and reservations are not accepted. To find the hotel from the Plaza Mayor, walk 2 blocks north on calle 60, then turn right on calle 57 and go 1½ blocks; it's between calles 56 and 58.

Hotel Santa Lucía. Calle 55 no. 508, 97000 Mérida, Yuc. ☎/fax **99/28-2662.** 51 units. A/C (or FAN) TV TEL. $24 double. Free guarded parking nearby.

This small hotel opened in 1990. The rooms are in a three-story building with windows facing the inner hallways or the courtyard, which contains a long, inviting pool. Rooms are quiet but mattresses are thin. The management is very helpful, providing information on tours, restaurants, and sights. They also run the **Hotel San Clemente** in Valladolid. The hotel faces Parque Santa Lucía, just off calle 60.

Hotel Trinidad Galería. Calle 60 no. 456, 97000 Mérida, Yuc. ☎ **99/23-2463.** Fax 99/24-2319. 31 units. FAN. $20 double; $25 suite with A/C and TV. Limited free parking.

Once an enormous home, this rambling hotel offers its guests a small shaded pool, a communal refrigerator, a shared dining room, original art and antiques, and lots of relaxing nooks with comfortable furniture. Upstairs, a covered porch decorated with antiques and plants runs the length of the hotel, providing yet another place to read or converse. Rooms are rather dark and simply furnished, and most don't have windows, but the overall ambiance of the hotel is comparable to that of more expensive inns. To find the hotel from the Plaza Mayor, walk 5 blocks north on calle 60; it's at the corner of calle 51, 2 blocks north of the Santa Lucía Park.

Posada Toledo. Calle 58 no. 487, 97000 Mérida, Yuc. ☎ **99/23-1690.** Fax 99/23-2256. E-mail: hptoledo@pibilfinred.com.mx 23 units. A/C or FAN TEL. $40–$45 double. Free parking next door.

This colonial inn was once a private mansion. It's now a cross between a garden dripping with vines and a fading museum with beautifully kept antique furnishings. Two of the grandest rooms have been remodeled into a suite with ornate cornices and woodwork. Most rooms have no windows, but high ceilings, and appropriately creaky hardwood floors are standard. The highest rates are for air-conditioned rooms. The rooftop lounge area is excellent for viewing the city. Five rooms have TVs. To find the inn from the Plaza Mayor, walk 2 blocks north on calle 60, then right 1 block on calle 57 to calle 58; it's on the left.

WHERE TO DINE

Calle 62 between the Plaza Mayor and calle 57 contains a short string of small, budget food shops. To make your own breakfast, try the **Panificadora Montejo,** at the corner of calles 62 and 63 on the southwest corner of the Plaza Mayor. For those who can't start a day without fresh orange juice, juice bars have sprouted up all over Mérida, and several are on or near the Plaza Mayor.

EXPENSIVE

Alberto's Continental. Calle 64 no. 482. ☎ **99/28-5367.** Reservations recommended. Main courses $8–$19. Daily 1pm–11pm. LEBANESE/YUCATECAN/ITALIAN.

Created from a fine old town house, the large and elegantly furnished rooms are built around a plant- and tree-filled patio that's framed in Moorish arches. Cuban floor tiles from a bygone era, along with antique furniture and sideboards, create an old-world mood. The eclectic menu features Lebanese, Yucatecan, and Italian specialties. There's a sampler plate of four Lebanese favorites, plus traditional Yucatecan specialties, such as pollo pibil and fish Celestún (bass stuffed with shrimp). Polish off your selections with Turkish coffee. Alberto's is at the corner of calle 57.

MODERATE

✪ **La Casona.** Calle 60 no. 434. ☎ **99/23-8348.** Reservations recommended. Pasta courses $5–$9; meat courses $5–$12. Daily 1pm–midnight. ITALIAN/REGIONAL.

A gracious old Mérida house and its lush interior garden make a charming and romantic restaurant. The cuisine is Yucatecan and Italian, so you can choose among such dishes as pollo pibil, filet mignon with brandy and cream, linguini with mushrooms, and lasagna. The pollo en escabeche scored a hit on our latest visit. It's also a fine place to wind up the day sipping espresso or cappuccino. La Casona is 6 blocks north of the Plaza Mayor near the corner of calles 60 and 47. Free valet parking.

✪ **Los Almendros.** Calle 50A no. 493. ☎ **99/28-5459.** Main courses $4–$9; daily special $5–$8. Daily 9am–11pm. YUCATECAN.

For traditional home-style Yucatecan food, this is the place that comes to mind. It is practically an institution in Mérida. The colorful chairs and tables make for a festive mood. Ask to see the menu with color photographs of their dishes accompanied by descriptions in English. They are known for their poc chuc—grilled pork with marinated onions. To reach the restaurant from the Parque Cepeda Peraza, walk east on calle 59 for 5 blocks, then left on calle 50A; it's half a block on the left facing the Parque de la Mejorada.

✪ **Restaurante Pórtico del Peregrino.** Calle 57 no. 501. ☎ **99/28-6163.** Reservations recommended. Main courses $6–$10. Daily noon–11pm. MEXICAN/ INTERNATIONAL.

El Pórtico is a favorite place among locals and visitors alike. It exudes local charm and comfort with a distinctive Mérida flavor. The interior is a lovely garden with three dining areas—two air-conditioned rooms and a patio (one room is nonsmoking, a rarity in Mexico). The menu offers soup, fish fillet, grilled gulf shrimp, spaghetti, pollo pibil, baked eggplant with chicken and cheese, and coconut ice cream topped with Kahlúa. The restaurant is 2 blocks north of the main square between calles 60 and 62.

✪ **Virrey de Mendoza.** Calle 60 327. ☎ **99/25-3082.** Main courses $7–$10. Daily 12:30pm–11:30pm. Valet parking. YUCATECAN/MEXICAN.

Across the street from the Hyatt, Virrey is the most polished and contemporary restaurant in Mérida. The food and service are superb, while other essential matters— furniture, lighting, and surroundings—are all handled well. Try any of the Yucatecan specialties, like the pepper stuffed with crab; the filet mignon with cilantro, mushrooms, and olive oil; or the huitlacoche crepes. My one reservation is that Virrey (like most restaurants throughout the Yucatán) thinks very highly of gouda cheese and uses it in dishes that are better suited to stronger domestic cheeses.

INEXPENSIVE

Café Alameda. Calle 58 no. 474. ☎ **99/28-3635.** Breakfast $2.75–$3.25; main courses $3–$5. Open daily 7:30am–6pm. MIDDLE EASTERN/MEXICAN.

The trappings are simple and informal, and the trick here is figuring out the Spanish names for popular Middle Eastern dishes. Kibbe is "quebbe bola," not "quebbe cruda," hummus is "garbanza," and shish kebab is "alambre." I leave it to you to figure out what a spinach pie is called (and they're excellent). Café Alameda is a treat for vegetarians, and the umbrella-shaded tables on the patio are perfect for morning coffee and pastries. The cafe is 3 blocks north and 1 block east of the Plaza Mayor, between calles 57 and 59.

Café Amaro. Calle 59 no. 507 interior 6. ☎ **99/28-2451.** Breakfast $2–$3; main courses $3–$4.50. Mon–Sat 8:30am–11pm. REGIONAL/VEGETARIAN.

This restaurant serves food in a pleasant courtyard beneath the branches of a large orchid tree. Their *crema de calabacitas* (pumpkin) soup is delicious, as is the apple salad. The cafe is well known for its avocado pizza. There is also a limited menu of meat and chicken dishes; try the Yucatecan chicken. To find it from the Plaza Mayor, walk 1 block north on calle 60 and turn left on calle 59.

El Louvre. Calle 62 no. 499. ☎ **99/24-5073.** Main courses $2.75–$4; comida corrida $3.75. Daily 24 hours (comida corrida served 1–5pm). MEXICAN.

This big, open restaurant feeds everybody from farm workers to townspeople. There's also an English menu. The comida corrida might include beans with pork on Monday, pork stew on Tuesday, and so on, plus there are sandwiches, soups, and other full meals. From the Palacio Municipal, cross calle 61 and walk north on calle 62 a few steps; it's near the corner of calle 61.

Vito Corleone. Calle 59 no. 508 between Calles 60 and 62. ☎ **99/28-5777.** Main courses $2–$5. Daily 9:30am–11:30pm. PIZZA/SPAGHETTI.

Aside from the food, the most impressive aspect of this tiny pizza parlor is the interesting use of *ollas* (clay pots) embedded in the wall above the hand-painted tile oven. The oven's golden-yellow tiles are as handsome as those that decorate church domes. The tables by the sidewalk are the only bearable places to sit when it's warm, since the oven casts incredible heat. Another section upstairs in the back is also tolerable. The thin-crusted pizzas are smoky and savory, and on Thursdays there's a two-for-one pizza special. To find it from the Plaza Mayor, walk north on calle 60 1 block and turn left on calle 59; it's half a block ahead.

MÉRIDA AFTER DARK

For nighttime entertainment, see "Special Events Every Day of the Week," above, or check out the theaters included below.

Teatro Peón Contreras, at calles 60 and 57, and **Teatro Ayala,** on calle 60 at calle 61, both feature a wide range of performing artists from around the world. Stop in and see what's showing.

If nothing strikes your fancy, don't despair; Mérida has plenty of variety in its nightlife. Most of the discos are in the big hotels or on Paseo de Montejo. The most popular one at present is **Vatzya,** in the Fiesta Americana Hotel on the corner of calle 60 and avenida Colón (across from the Hyatt). For live music and entertainment, try one or more of the places listed below.

Ciudad Maya. Calle 84 no. 506, 11 blocks west of the Plaza Mayor. ☎ **99/24-3313.** $6 minimum.

Where else can you find a club that combines massive replicas of Maya architecture with a racy, Latin-style floor show featuring scantily clad Cuban dancers? This bar/restaurant has a Cuban floor show at 8 and 10pm; the six-member Cuban band puts Ricky Ricardo to shame, and costumes have the requisite big headdresses. There are two shows: "Streets of My Havana" and "Under the Mayan Sky"; call ahead to find out which is being performed. Between dance numbers, magicians and acrobats entertain the audience. Ciudad Maya serves drinks, steaks, and antojitos, but the main attraction is the show. One more note of interest: Meridianos regard the club as a family place—don't be surprised to see little kids there. Open from 1pm to 1am; there are no shows on Mondays.

El Trovador Bohemio. Calle 55 no. 504. ☎ **99/23-0385.** Cover $1.25.

It's hard to overstate the importance of *música de trio* in Mexican popular culture. Boleros may have been at their most popular in the 1940s and 1950s, but every new heartthrob in Mexican pop music feels compelled to release a new version of the classics at some point in his career. I like the originals best, and so do most Mexicans. If you know something of this music and are curious about it, El Trovador is your chance to hear how the music should be played. And if you understand colloquial Spanish, all the better; the language of boleros is vivid, passionate, and quite Mexican—definitely a unique cultural experience. El Trovador is small and dark, and everything is red, including diamond-tufted upholstered walls. The best time to go is Thursday through Saturday. This place faces the Santa Lucía Park. Open nightly from 9pm to 3am.

Pancho's. Calle 59 no. 509. ☎ **99/23-0949.** 3-drink minimum if you do not order food.

If you take this place seriously, you won't like it. Waiters in bandoliers and oversized sombreros, walls adorned with blow-ups of Revolution-era photos and assorted emblems of Mexican identity—Pancho's, which serves Tex-Mex, is a parody of the tourist attraction, a place for drinking beer and loosing the occasional *grito.* Live music is performed in the courtyard, beginning at 9 on most nights, 10:30 on Saturdays. The five-piece band is quite good with its large repertoire of cover tunes; they'll crank up salsa, rock, and jazz. Open nightly from 6pm to 3am.

ROAD TRIPS FROM MÉRIDA
CELESTÚN NATIONAL WILDLIFE REFUGE

This flamingo sanctuary and offbeat sand-street fishing village on the Gulf coast is a 90-minute drive from Mérida. To get here, take Highway 281 (a two-lane road) past numerous old *henequén* haciendas. **Autobuses de Occidente** schedules 10 buses per day bound for Celestún from the terminal at calles 50 and 67.

One telephone at the **Hotel Gutiérrez** (☎ **99/28-0419**) serves as the public phone for the entire village. You'll find a bank, two gas stations (but no unleaded gas), and a grocery store. Bus tickets are purchased at the end of the row of market stalls on the left side of the church. Celestún hotels don't furnish drinking water, so bring your own or buy it in town.

December 8 is the **Feast Day of the Virgen de Concepción,** the patron saint of the village. On the Sunday that falls nearest to July 15, a colorful procession carries Celestún's venerated figure of the Virgen de Concepción to meet the sacred figure of the Virgen de Asunción on the highway leading to Celestún. Returning to Celestún, they float away on decorated boats and later return to be ensconced at the church during a mass and celebration.

SEEING THE WATERFOWL   The town is on a narrow strip of land separated from the mainland by a lagoon. Crossing over the lagoon bridge, you'll find the 14,611-acre wildlife refuge spreading out on both sides without visible boundaries. You'll notice small boats moored on both sides waiting to take visitors to see the flamingos. In addition to flamingos, you will probably see frigate birds, pelicans, cranes, egrets, sandpipers, and other waterfowl feeding on shallow sandbars at any time of year. Of the 175 bird species that come here, some 99 are permanent residents. At least 15 duck species have also been counted. Flamingos are found here all year; nonbreeding flamingos remain year-round, and the larger group of breeding flamingoes takes off around April to nest on the upper Yucatán Peninsula east of Río Lagartos.

A 90-minute flamingo-sighting trip costs around $25 for four people or twice that much if you stay half a day. The best time to go is around 7am; the worst is midafternoon, when sudden storms come up. Be sure not to allow the boatmen to get close enough to frighten the birds; they've been known to do it for photographers, but it will eventually cause the birds to permanently abandon the habitat. Your tour will take you a short distance into the massive mangroves that line the lagoon to a sulfur pool, where the boatman kills the motor and poles in so you can experience the stillness and density of the jungle, feel the sultry air, and see other birds.

WHERE TO STAY   To find restaurants and hotels, follow the bridge road a few blocks to the end. On the last street, calle 12, paralleling the oceanfront, you'll find restaurants and hotels, all of which have decent rooms but marginal housekeeping standards. Always try to bargain for lower rates, which can go down by as much as 30% in the off-season.

Hotel María del Carmen. Calle 12 no. 111, 97367 Celestún, Yuc. ☎ **99/28-0152.** 9 units. FAN. $14 double.

Built in 1992, this three-story hotel on the beach stands out among Celestún's modest accommodations lineup. Spare but clean and large, each room has terrazzo floors, two double beds with sheets but no bedspread, screened windows (check screens for holes), and a small balcony or patio facing the ocean. Best of all, there's hot water in the bathrooms (not necessarily a hallmark of other Celestún hotels), but not always toilet seats. Lorenzo Saul Rodríguez and María del Carmen Gutiérrez own the hotel and are actively involved in local conservation efforts, particularly in protecting the sea turtles that nest on the beach in early summer. Look for the sign for Villa del Mar, the hotel's restaurant; the rooms are behind it across the parking area.

WHERE TO DINE   Calle 12 is home to several rustic seafood restaurants aside from the place listed below. All have irregular hours of operation.

✪ **Restaurant Celestún.** Calle 12 no. 101, on the waterfront. ☎ **99/16-2031.** Main courses $3.75–$7. Daily 10am–6pm (sometimes). SEAFOOD/MEXICAN.

I highly recommend this ocean-view restaurant, owned by Elda Cauich and Wenseslao Ojeda; the service is friendly and swift. Tables and chairs fill a long room that stretches from calle 12 to the beach. The house specialty is a delicious shrimp, crab, and squid omelet (called a *torta*). But if you're a fan of stone crabs (*manitas de cangrejo* on the menu), this is definitely the place to chow down. Trapped in the Gulf by Celestún fishermen, they come freshly cooked and seasoned with lime juice. Also popular during the fall season is *pulpo* (octopus). Other local specialties include *liza* (mullet) and *caviar de Celestún* (mullet eggs). To find the restaurant, follow the bridge road to the waterfront (calle 12); turn left and the restaurant is immediately on the right.

DZIBILCHALTÚN: MAYA RUINS

This Maya site, now a national park located 9 miles north of Mérida along the Progreso road and 4½ miles east off the highway, is worth a stop. Dzibilchaltún, which was founded around 500 B.C. and flourished around A.D. 750, was in decline long before the coming of the conquistadors but may have been occupied until A.D. 1600, almost 100 years after the arrival of the Spaniards. Since its discovery in 1941, more than 8,000 buildings have been mapped. The site, which was probably a center of commerce and religion, covers an area of almost 10 square miles with a central core of almost 65 acres. At least 12 *sacbeob* (causeways), the longest of which is 4,200 feet, have been unearthed. *Dzibilchaltún* means "place of the stone writing," and at least 25 stelae have been found, many of them reused in buildings constructed after the original ones were covered or destroyed.

Today, the most interesting buildings are grouped around the Cenote Xlacah, the sacred well, and include a complex of buildings around Structure 38, the **Central Group** of temples, the raised **causeways,** and the **Seven Dolls Group,** centered on the **Temple of the Seven Dolls.** It was beneath the floor of the temple that seven weird little dolls (now in the museum) showing a variety of diseases and birth defects were discovered. The Yucatán State Department of Ecology has added nature trails and published a booklet (in Spanish) of birds and plants seen at various points along the mapped trail. The booklet tells where in the park you are likely to see specific plants and birds.

The federal government has spent over a million pesos for the **Museum of the Maya** on the grounds of Dzibilchaltún. The museum, which opened in 1995, is a replica of a Maya village of houses, called *nah,* staffed by Maya demonstrating traditional cooking, gardening, and folk-art techniques.

To get to Dzibilchaltún by bus from Mérida, go to the Progreso bus station at calle 62 no. 524, between calles 65 and 67. There are five buses per day, Monday through Saturday, to the pueblo of Chanculob; it's a 1-kilometer (1.6-mile) walk to the ruins from there. On Sunday there are only three buses to Chanculob. The return bus schedule is posted at the ticket window by the ruins.

The site and nature trails are open daily from 8am to 5pm. Admission is $4; free on Sunday. Video-camera use costs $4.

PROGRESO: GULF COAST CITY

For another beach escape, go to Progreso, a modern city facing the Gulf less than an hour from Mérida. This is where Meridianos have their weekend houses and where they come in large numbers for the months of July and August. At other times there are no crowds, no traffic—just the sea. Here, the malecón, a beautiful oceanfront drive, borders a wide beach lined with coconut palms. The water here is not blue as on the Caribbean side, but it is clean. A long pier, or *muelle* (pronounced *mway*-yay), extends several miles into the bay to service oceangoing ships. Progreso is part-time home to some Americans and Canadians who come to escape northern winters.

Along or near the malecón are several restaurants and hotels, including **Le Saint Bonnet** (Malecón at calle 78; ☎ **993/5-2299**), where locals dine on fresh seafood; try the *pescado al ajillo* (fish cooked in garlic).

From Mérida, buses to Progreso leave the special bus station at calle 62 no. 524, between calles 65 and 67, every 15 minutes during the day, starting at 5am. The trip takes 45 minutes.

In Progreso, the bus station is about 4 blocks south of calle 19, or malecón, which runs along the beach.

EN ROUTE TO UXMAL

There are two routes to Uxmal, about 50 miles south of Mérida. The most direct is Highway 261 via Uman and Muna. From downtown, take calle 65 to avenida Itzáes and make a left. If you have the time and would like a more scenic route, try the meandering State Highway 18 (see below).

HIGHWAY 261: YAXCOPOIL & MUNA Ten miles beyond Uman along Highway 261 is Yaxcopoil (yash-koh-poe-*eel*), the tongue-twisting Maya name of a fascinating 19th-century hacienda on the right side of the road between Mérida and Uxmal. It's difficult to reach by bus.

This hacienda, dating from 1864, was originally a cattle ranch comprising over 23,000 acres. Around 1900, it was converted to growing *henequén* (for the manufacture of rope). Take half an hour to tour the house (which boasts 18-ft. ceilings and original furniture), factory, outbuildings, and museum. You'll see that such haciendas were the administrative, commercial, and social centers of vast private domains; they were almost little principalities carved out of the Yucatecan jungle. It's open Monday through Saturday from 8am to 6pm and Sunday from 9am to 1pm.

From Mérida via Uman, it's 20 miles to the Hacienda Yaxcopoil and 40 miles to Muna on Highway 261. Uxmal is 10 miles from Muna.

HIGHWAY 18: KANASÍN, ACANCEH, MAYAPÁN & TICUL Taking calle 67 east, head out of Mérida toward Kanasín (kahn-ah-*seen*) and Acanceh (ah-kahn-*keh*), for about 12 miles. When calle 67 ends, bear right, then go left at the next big intersection. Follow the wide divided highway with speed bumps. At Mérida's *periférico* (the road that circles the city), you'll see signs to Cancún. You can either cross the periférico and go straight into Kanasín or turn and follow the Cancún signs for a short distance and then follow the signs into Kanasín. In **Kanasín,** watch for signs that say CIRCULACIÓN or DESVIACIÓN. As in many Yucatán towns, you're being redirected to follow a one-way street through the urban area. Go past the market, church, and the main square on your left and continue straight out of town. The next village you come to, at km 10, is **San Antonio Tehuit,** an old *henequén* hacienda. At km 13 is **Tepich,** another hacienda-centered village, with those funny little *henequén*-cart tracks crisscrossing the main road. After Tepich comes **Petectunich** and finally **Acanceh.**

Across the street from and overlooking Acanceh's church is a partially restored pyramid. From Acanceh's main square, turn right (around the statue of a smiling deer) and head for **Tecoh** with its huge crumbling church (5½ miles farther along Highway 18) and Telchaquillo (7 miles farther). This route takes you past several old Yucatecan haciendas, each with a big house, chapel, factory with smokestack, and workers' houses.

Shortly after the village of Telchaquillo, a sign on the right side of the road will point to the entrance of the ruins of Mayapán.

THE RUINS OF MAYAPÁN

Founded, according to Maya lore, by the man-god Quetzalcoatl (*Kukulkán* in Maya) in about A.D. 1007, Mayapán ranked in importance with Chichén-Itzá and Uxmal and covered at least 2½ square miles. For more than 2 centuries, it was the capital of a Maya confederation of city-states that included Chichén and Uxmal. But before the year 1200, the rulers of Mayapán ended the confederation by attacking and conquering Chichén and by forcing the rulers of Uxmal to live as vassals in Mayapán. Eventually a successful revolt by the captive Maya rulers brought down Mayapán, which was abandoned during the mid-1400s.

After all this history, what you find at the site is a disappointment. There is some debate about why a city so powerful and important lacks more impressive architecture. Some believe this is evidence of social decay in the last years of Maya civilization.

The site is open daily from 8am to 5pm. Admission is $2; free on Sunday; use of a personal video camera is $4.

FROM MAYAPÁN TO TICUL   The road is a good one, but directional signs through the villages are almost nonexistent; stop and ask directions frequently. From Mayapán, continue along Highway 18 to **Tekit** (5 miles), turn right, and you'll come to **Mama** on a road as thrilling as a roller-coaster ride (4⅓ miles). Turn right again for Chapab (8 miles). After Chapab you reach Ticul (6¼ miles), the largest town in the region.

TICUL

Best known for the cottage industry of *huipil* embroidery and for the manufacture of ladies' dress shoes, Ticul isn't the most exciting stop on the Puuc route—but it's a convenient place to wash up and spend the night. It's also a center for large-size commercially produced pottery; most of the widely sold sienna-colored pottery painted with Maya designs comes from here. If it's a cloudy, humid day, the potters may not be working since part of the process requires sun-drying, but they still welcome visitors to purchase finished pieces.

One place worth a visit is **Arte Maya,** calle 23 no. 301, Carretera Ticul Muna (☎ **997/2-1095;** fax 997/2-0334). It is owned and operated by Luis Echeverría and Lourdes Castillo. This shop and gallery produces museum-quality art in alabaster, stone, jade, and ceramics. Much of the work is done as it was in Maya times; soft stone or ceramic is smoothed with the leaf of the siricote tree, and colors are derived from plant sources. If you buy from them, hang onto the written description of your purchase—their work looks so authentic that U.S. customs has delayed entry of people carrying their wares, thinking that they're smuggling real Maya artifacts into the States.

Ticul is only 12 miles northeast of Uxmal, so thrifty tourists stay here instead of the more expensive hotels at the ruins. Try the **Hotel Bougambillias Familiar,** calle 23 no. 291A, 97860 Ticul, Yucatán (☎ **997/2-0761**). This place, with 20 rooms ($12 to $15 double) is motel-like, with parking outside the rooms. The half-circle drive into the arched entrance is lined with plants and pottery from the owner's local factory. High windows don't let in much light, the rooms have saggy beds, and bathrooms come without shower curtains and toilet seats. But the cool tile floors and ready hot water are attractions. In back is the hotel's pretty restaurant, **Xux-Cab,** but it has a limited menu. To find the hotel, follow calle 23 through Ticul on the road to Muna. It's on the right before you leave town, past the Santa Elena turnoff.

FROM TICUL TO UXMAL

From Ticul to Uxmal, follow the main street (calle 23) west through town. Turn left at the sign to Santa Elena. It's 10 miles to Santa Elena; then, at Highway 261, cut back right for about 2 miles to Uxmal. The easiest route to follow is via Muna, but it's also longer and less picturesque. To go this way, drive straight through Ticul 14 miles to Muna. At Muna, turn left and head south on Highway 261 to Uxmal, 10 miles away.

A Side Trip: Spelunking in the Yaxnic Caves

Just outside the village of Yotolín (also spelled Yohtolín), between Ticul and Oxkutzcab (along Highway 184), are some impressive caves called Yaxnic (*yash-neek*), on the grounds of the old, private Hacienda Yotolín. Virtually undeveloped and full of colored stalactites and stalagmites, the caves are visited by means of a perilous descent in a basket let down on a rope.

Arranging this spelunking challenge takes more time and advance planning than most travelers have, but the thrill may be worth the extra work. Here's the procedure: Several days (or even weeks, if that's possible) before your intended cave descent, go to Yotolín and ask for the house of the *comisario,* a village elder. He will make the proper introductions to the hacienda owners, who in turn will tell you how to prepare for the experience.

---

2 The Beautiful Ruins of Uxmal

50 miles SW of Mérida; 12 miles W of Ticul; 12 miles S of Muna

One of the highlights of a vacation in the Yucatán, the ruins of Uxmal—noted for their rich geometric stone facades—are the most beautiful on the peninsula. Remains of an agricultural society indicate that the area was occupied possibly as early as 800 B.C. However, the great building period took place 1,000 years later, between A.D. 700 and 1000, during which time the population probably reached 25,000. Then Uxmal fell under the sway of the Xiú princes (who may have come from the Valley of Mexico) after the year 1000. In the 1440s, the Xiú conquered Mayapán, and not long afterward the glories of the Maya ended when the Spanish conquistadors arrived.

Close to Uxmal, four other sites—Sayil, Kabah, Xlapak, and Labná—are worth visiting. With Uxmal, these ruins are collectively known as the Puuc route, for the Puuc hills of this part of the Yucatán. See the "Puuc Maya Sites" section below if you want to explore these sites.

ESSENTIALS

GETTING THERE & DEPARTING   By Car   Two routes to Uxmal from Mérida, via Highway 261 or via State Highway 18, are described in "From Ticul to Uxmal," at the end of the Mérida section above. *Note:* There's no gasoline at Uxmal.

By Bus   See "Getting There & Departing" in "Mérida," above, for information about bus service between Mérida and Uxmal. To return, wait for the bus on the highway at the entrance to the ruins. To see the sound-and-light show, sign up with one of the tour operators in Mérida.

ORIENTATION   Uxmal consists of the archaeological site and its visitor center, five hotels, and a highway restaurant. The **visitor center,** open daily from 8am to 9pm, has a restaurant (with good coffee); toilets; a first-aid station; shops selling soft drinks, ice cream, film, batteries, and books; and a state-run **Casa de Artesanía.** There are no phones except at the hotels. The food at the hotel restaurants is iffy and expensive. Most public buses pick up and let off passengers on the highway at the entrance to the ruins. The site itself is open daily from 8am to 5pm. Admission to the archaeological site of Uxmal is $4, but a Sunday visit will save money since admission is free to Uxmal and other recommended sites nearby. There's a $4 charge for each video camera you bring in (save your receipt; it's good for other area sites on the same day). Parking costs $1.

Guides at the entrance of Uxmal give tours in a variety of languages and charge $20 for either a single person or a group. The guides frown on any unrelated individuals joining a group. As usual, they'd rather charge you as a solo visitor, but you can ask other English speakers if they'd like to join you in a tour and split the cost. As at other sites, the guides vary in quality, but you will see areas and architectural details you might otherwise miss.

A 45-minute **sound-and-light show** is staged each evening in Spanish for $3 at 7pm and in English for $4 at 9pm. The bus from Mérida is scheduled to leave near the end of the Spanish show; confirm the exact time with the driver. If you stay for the English show, the only return to Mérida is via an expensive taxi. After the impressive show, the chant *"Chaaac, Chaaac"* will echo in your mind for weeks.

A TOUR OF THE RUINS

THE PYRAMID OF THE MAGICIAN As you enter the ruins, note the *chultún,* or cistern, where Uxmal stored its water. Unlike most of the major Mayan sites, Uxmal has no river or cenote to supply freshwater—perhaps the most mystifying feature of what was once a large and populous city.

Just beyond the chultún, the remarkable Pyramid of the Magician (also called Pyramid of the Dwarf) looms majestically on the right. The name comes from a legend about a mystical dwarf who reached adulthood in a single day after being hatched from an egg, and who built this pyramid in 1 night. Beneath it are five temples, since it was common practice for the Maya to build new structures atop old ones as part of a prescribed ritual.

The pyramid is unique because of its rounded sides, height, steepness, and the doorway on the opposite (west) side near the top. The doorway's heavy ornamentation, a characteristic of the Chenes style, features 12 stylized masks of the rain god Chaac, and the doorway itself is a huge open-mouthed Chaac mask.

The steep and risky climb to the top is worth it for the view. From on top you can see Uxmal's entire layout. Next to the Pyramid of the Magician, to the west, is the Nunnery Quadrangle, and left of it is a partially restored ball court, south of which are several large complexes. The biggest building among them is the Governor's Palace, and behind it lies the massive, largely unrestored Great Pyramid. In the distance is the Dovecote (House of the Doves), a small building with a lacy roof comb (false front) that looks like the perfect apartment complex for pigeons. From this vantage point, note how Uxmal is unique among Maya sites for its use of huge terraces constructed to support the buildings; look closely and you'll see that the Governor's Palace is not on a natural hill but rather on a giant platform, like the nearby Nunnery Quadrangle.

THE NUNNERY QUADRANGLE The 16th-century Spanish historian Fray Diego López de Cogullado gave the building its name because it resembled a Spanish monastery. Possibly it was a military academy or a training school for princes, who may have lived in the 70-odd rooms. The buildings were constructed at different times: The northern one was first, then the southern, then the eastern, then the western. The western building has the most richly decorated facade, composed of intertwined stone snakes and numerous masks of the hook-nosed rain god Chaac.

The corbeled archway on the south was once the main entrance to the Nunnery complex; as you head toward it out of the quadrangle to the south, look above each doorway in that section for the motif of a Maya cottage, or *nah,* looking just like any number of cottages you'd see throughout the Yucatán today.

THE BALL COURT A small ball court is conserved to prevent further decay, but compare it later in your trip with the giant, magnificently restored court at Chichén-Itzá.

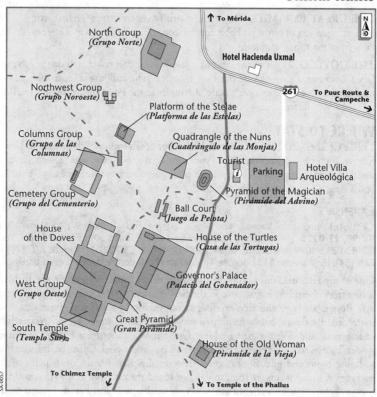

THE TURTLE HOUSE Up on the terrace south of the ball court is a little temple decorated with a colonnade motif on the facade and a border of turtles. Though it's small and simple, its harmony is one of the gems of Uxmal.

THE GOVERNOR'S PALACE In its size and intricate stonework, this rivals the Pyramid of the Magician as Uxmal's masterwork—an imposing three-level edifice with a 320-foot-long mosaic facade done in the Puuc style. *Puuc* means "hilly country," the name given to the hills nearby and thus to the predominant style of pre-Hispanic architecture found here. Uxmal has many examples of Puuc decoration, characterized by elaborate stonework from door tops to the roofline. Fray Cogullado, who named the Nunnery, also gave this building its name. The Governor's Palace may have been just that—the administrative center of the Xiú principality, which included the region around Uxmal. It probably had astrological significance as well. For years, scholars pondered why this building was constructed slightly turned from adjacent buildings. Originally they thought the strange alignment was because of the *sacbe* (ceremonial road) that starts at this building and ends 11 miles distant at the ancient city of Kabah. But recently scholars of archaeoastronomy (a relatively new science that studies the placement of archaeological sites in relation to the stars), discovered that the central doorway, which is larger than the others, is in perfect alignment with Venus.

Before you leave the Governor's Palace, note the elaborately stylized headdress patterned in stone over the central doorway. As you stand back from the building on the east side, note how the 103 stone masks of Chaac undulate across the facade like a serpent and end at the corners where there are columns of masks.

THE GREAT PYRAMID   A massive, partially restored nine-level structure, it has interesting motifs of birds, probably macaws, on its facade, as well as a huge mask. The view from the top is wonderful.

THE DOVECOTE   It wasn't built to house doves, but it could well do the job in its lacy roof comb, a kind of false front on a rooftop. The building is remarkable in that roof combs weren't a common feature of temples in the Puuc hills, although you'll see one (of a very different style) on El Mirador at Sayil.

WHERE TO STAY

Unlike Chichén-Itzá, which has several classes of hotels from which to choose, Uxmal has (with one exception) only one type: comfortable but expensive. If occupancy is low you might get a deal. Less expensive rooms are also available in nearby Ticul, but you'll need a car, as bus service is limited.

EXPENSIVE

✪ **Hotel Hacienda Uxmal.** Km 80 Carretera Mérida–Uxmal, 97840 Uxmal, Yuc. ☎ **99/23-0275.** (Reservations: Mayaland Resorts, Av. Colón 502, 97000 Mérida, Yuc.; ☎ 800/235-4079 in the U.S., or 99/25-2122; fax 99/25-7022.) 79 units. A/C (21) or FAN (54). High season $133 double. Low season $110 double. Free guarded parking.

One of my favorites, this is also the oldest hotel in Uxmal. Located on the highway across from the ruins, it was built as the headquarters for the archaeology staff years ago. Rooms are large and airy, exuding an impression of a well-kept yesteryear, with patterned tile floors, heavy furniture, and well-screened windows. All rooms have ceiling fans, and TVs are being added. Guest rooms surround a handsome central garden courtyard with towering royal palms, a bar, and a pool. Other facilities include a dining room and gift shop. A guitar trio usually plays on the open patio in the evenings. Checkout time is 1pm, so you can spend the morning at the ruins and take a swim before you hit the road again. It's on the highway just before you get to the entrance to the ruins.

Mayaland Resorts, owner of the hotel, offers tour packages that include discount car rental for the nights you spend in its hotels. Mayaland also has a transfer service between the hotel and Mérida for about $30 one way.

✪ **Villa Arqueológica.** Ruinas Uxmal, 97844 Uxmal, Yuc. ☎ **800/258-2633** in the U.S., or 99/28-0644. 43 units. A/C. $74 double. Free guarded parking.

This hotel is operated by Club Med but it is nothing more than a hotel. It offers a beautiful two-story layout around a plant-filled patio and a pool. At guests' disposal are a tennis court, a library, and an audiovisual show on the ruins in English, French, and Spanish. Each of the serene rooms has two oversize single beds. French-inspired meals are à la carte only. It's easy to find—follow the signs to the Uxmal ruins, then turn left to the hotel just before the parking lot at the Uxmal ruins.

INEXPENSIVE

Rancho Uxmal. Km 70 Carretera Mérida–Uxmal, 97840 Uxmal, Yuc. No local phone. (Reservations: Sr. Macario Cach Cabrera, calle 26 no. 156, 97860 Ticul, Yuc.; ☎ **99/49-0526** or 99/23-1576.) 20 units. A/C or FAN. $30–$36 double; $6 per person campsite. Free guarded parking.

This modest little hotel is an exception to the high-priced places near Uxmal, and it gets better every year. Air-conditioning has been added to 10 of the rooms, all of which have good screens, hot-water showers, and 24-hour electricity. The restaurant is good; a full meal of poc chuc, rice, beans, and tortillas costs about $5, and breakfast is $2.25 to $3. It's a long hike to the ruins from here, but the manager may help you flag down a passing bus or combi or even drive you himself if he has time. A primitive campground out back offers electrical hookups and use of a shower. The hotel is 2¼ miles north of the ruins on Highway 261.

WHERE TO DINE

Besides the hotel restaurants mentioned above and the restaurant at the visitor center, there are few other dining choices.

Café-Bar Nicte-Ha. In the Hotel Hacienda Uxmal. ☎ **99/23-0275.** Soups and salads $2–$5; main courses $5–$8; fixed-price lunch $9. Daily 1–8pm. MEXICAN.

This small restaurant attached to the Hotel Hacienda Uxmal is visible from the crossroads entrance to the ruins. The food is decent, though the prices tend to be high. If you eat here, take full advantage of the experience and spend a few hours by the pool near the cafe: Its use is free to customers. This is a favorite spot for bus tours that fill the place to overcrowding, so come early.

Las Palapas. Hwy. 261. No phone. Breakfast $3; comida corrida $3.75; soft drinks $1. Daily 9am–6pm (comida corrida served 1–4pm). MEXICAN/YUCATECAN.

Three miles north of the ruins on the road to Mérida, you'll find this pleasant restaurant with open-air walls and large thatched palapa roof. The amiable owner, María Cristina Choy, has the most reasonable dining prices around. Individual diners can sometimes become lost in the crowd if a busload of tourists arrives, but otherwise the service is fine and the food quite good. There's also a small gift shop with regional crafts and a few books.

THE PUUC MAYA ROUTE & VILLAGE OF OXKUTZCAB

South and east of Uxmal are several other Maya cities worth exploring. Though smaller in scale than either Uxmal or Chichén-Itzá, each contains gems of Maya architecture. The facade of masks on the Palace of Masks at **Kabah,** the enormous palace at **Sayil,** and the fantastic caverns of **Loltún** may be among the high points of your trip. Also along the way are the **Xlapak** and **Labná ruins** and the pretty village of **Oxkutzcab.**

The sites are open daily from 8am to 5pm. Admission is $2 each for Sayil, Kabah, and Labná; $1.25 for Xlapak; and $3 for Loltún. All except the caves of Loltún are free on Sunday. Use of a video camera at any time costs $4, but if you're visiting Uxmal in the same day, you pay only once for video permission and present your receipt as proof at each ruin. The sites are open daily from 8am to 5pm.

Kabah is 17 miles southeast of Uxmal. From there it's only a few miles to Sayil. Xlapak is almost walking distance (through the jungle) from Sayil, and Labná is just a bit farther east. A short drive beyond Labná brings you to the caves of Loltún. And Oxkutzcab is at the road's intersection with Highway 184, which can be followed west to Ticul or east all the way to Felipe Carrillo Puerto.

If you are driving, between Labná and Loltún you'll find a road and a sign pointing north to Tabí. A few feet west of this road is a narrow dry-weather track leading into the seemingly impenetrable jungle. A bit over a mile up this track, the jungle opens to the remains of the fabulous old *henequén*-producing **Hacienda Tabí.** The hewed-rock, two-story main house extends almost the length of a city block, with the living quarters above and storage and space for carriages below. In places it looks ready to collapse. Besides the house, you'll see the ruined chapel, remnants of tall chimneys, and broken machinery. Though not a formal public site, the caretaker will ask you to sign a guest book and allow you to wander around the hulking ruins, without climbing to the second story.

Ruins Tips

All these archaeological sites are currently undergoing excavation and reconstruction, and some buildings may be roped off when you visit. Photographers will find afternoon light the best.

If you aren't driving, a daily bus from Mérida goes to all these sites, with the exception of Loltún and Tabí. (See "By Bus" under "Getting There & Departing," in Mérida, above, for more details.)

PUUC MAYA SITES

KABAH   If you're off to Kabah, head southwest on Highway 261 to Santa Elena (8½ miles), then south to Kabah (8 miles). The ancient city of Kabah is on both sides along the highway. Make a right turn into the parking lot.

The most outstanding building at Kabah is the huge **Palace of Masks,** or *Codz Poop* ("rolled-up mat"), named for a motif in its decoration. You'll notice it first on the right up on a terrace. Its outstanding feature is the Chenes-style facade, completely covered in a repeated pattern of 250 masks of the rain god Chaac, each one with curling remnants of Chaac's elephant-trunklike nose. There's nothing like this facade in all of Maya architecture. For years, stone-carved parts of this building lay lined up in the weeds like pieces of a puzzle awaiting the master puzzle-maker to put them into place. Now workers are positioning the parts, including the broken roof comb, in place. Sculptures from this building are in the museums of anthropology in Mérida and Mexico City.

Once you've seen the Palace of Masks, you've seen the best of Kabah. But you should take a look at the other buildings. Just behind and to the left of the Codz Poop is the **Palace Group** (also called the East Group), with a fine Puuc-style colonnaded facade. Originally it had 32 rooms. On the front you see seven doors, two divided by columns, a common feature of Puuc architecture. Recent restoration has added a beautiful L-shaped colonnaded extension to the left front. Further restoration is under way at Kabah, so there may be more to see when you arrive.

Across the highway, a large, conical dirt-and-rubble mound (on your right) was once the **Great Temple,** or Teocalli. Past it is a **great arch,** which was much wider at one time and may have been a monumental gate into the city. A sacbe linked this arch to a point at Uxmal. Compare this corbeled arch to the one at Labná (below), which is in much better shape.

SAYIL   Just about 3 miles south of Kabah is the turnoff (left, which is east) to Sayil, Xlapak, Labná, Loltún, and Oxkutzcab. And 2½ miles along this road are the ruins of Sayil (which means "place of the ants").

Sayil is famous for **El Palacio.** This tremendous palace of over 100 rooms is impressive for its size alone, but what makes it a masterpiece of Maya architecture is the building's facade that stretches across three terraced levels. Its rows of columns give it a Minoan appearance. On the second level, notice the upside-down stone figure of the diving god of bees and honey over the doorway; the same motif was used at Tulum several centuries later. The top of El Palacio affords a great view of the Puuc hills. Sometimes it's difficult to tell which are hills and which are unrestored pyramids, since little temples peep out at unlikely places from the jungle. The large circular basin on the ground below the palace is an artificial catch basin for a *chultún* (cistern) because this region has no natural *cenotes* (wells) to catch rainwater.

In the jungle past El Palacio is **El Mirador,** a small temple with an oddly slotted roof comb. Beyond El Mirador, a crude **stela** (tall, carved stone) has a phallic idol carved on it in greatly exaggerated proportions.

XLAPAK   Xlapak (shla-*pahk*) is a small site with one building; it's 3½ miles down the road from Sayil. The **Palace** at Xlapak bears the masks of the rain god Chaac.

LABNÁ   Labná, which dates to between A.D. 600 and 900, is 18 miles from Uxmal and only 1¾ miles past Xlapak. Like other archaeological sites in the Yucatán, it's also undergoing significant restoration and conservation. Descriptive placards fronting the main buildings are in Spanish, English, and German.

The first thing you see on the left as you enter is **El Palacio,** a magnificent Puuc-style building much like the one at Sayil but in poorer condition. There is an enormous mask of Chaac over a doorway with big banded eyes, a huge snout nose, and jagged teeth around a small mouth that seems on the verge of speaking. Jutting out on one corner is a highly stylized serpent's mouth out from which pops a human head with an unexpectedly serene expression. From the front, you can gaze out to the enormous grassy interior grounds flanked by vestiges of unrestored buildings and jungle.

From El Palacio, you can walk across the interior grounds on a newly reconstructed sacbe leading to Labná's **corbeled arch,** famed for its ornamental beauty and for its representation of what many such arches must have looked like at other sites. This one has been extensively restored, although only remnants of the roof comb can be seen, and it was part of a more elaborate structure that is completely gone. Chaac's face is on the corners of one facade, and stylized Maya huts are fashioned in stone above the doorways.

You pass through the arch to **El Mirador,** or El Castillo, as the rubble-formed, pyramid-shaped structure is called. Towering on the top is a singular room crowned with a roof comb etched against the sky.

There's a refreshment/gift stand with rest rooms at the entrance.

LOLTÚN   The caverns of Loltún are 18½ miles past Labná on the way to Oxkutzcab, on the left side of the road. The fascinating caves, home of ancient Maya, were also used as a refuge and fortress during the War of the Castes (1847 to 1901). Inside, while you should examine the statuary, wall carvings and paintings, chultúns (cisterns), and other signs of Maya habitation, you'll note that the grandeur and beauty of the caverns alone are impressive. In front of the entrance is an enormous **stone phallus.** The cult of the phallic symbol originated south of Veracruz and appeared in the Yucatán between A.D. 200 and 500.

Tours lasting 1½ hours in Spanish are given daily at 9:30 and 11am and 12:30, 2, and 3pm and are included in the admission price. Before going on a tour, confirm these times at the information desk at Uxmal.

To return to Mérida from Loltún, drive the 4½ miles to Oxkutzcab and from there head northwest on Highway 184. It's 12 miles to Ticul, and (turning north onto Highway 261 at Muna) 65 miles to Mérida.

OXKUTZCAB

Oxkutzcab (ohsh-kootz-*kahb*), 7 miles from Loltún, is the heartland of the Yucatán's fruit-growing region. Oranges abound. The tidy village of 21,000, centered around a beautiful 16th-century church and the market, is worth a stop if for no other reason than to see the church and eat at Su Cabaña Suiza (see below) before heading back to Mérida, Uxmal, or Ticul.

During the last week in October and the first week in November is the **Orange Festival,** when the village turns exuberant with a carnival and orange displays in and around the central plaza.

A DINING DETOUR

✪ **Su Cabaña Suiza.** Calle 54 no. 101. ☎ **997/5-0457.** Main dishes $3.50; soft drinks or orange juice 75¢. Daily 7:30am–6:30pm. CHARCOAL-GRILLED MEAT/MEXICAN.

It's worth a trip from Loltún, Ticul, or Uxmal just to taste the delicious charcoal-grilled meat at this unpretentious restaurant draped in colorful plants. Park in the gravel courtyard, then take a seat at one of the metal tables either under the palapa roof or outdoors where caged birds sing. Señora María Antonia Puerto de Pacho runs the spotless place with an iron hand, and family members provide swift, friendly service. The primary menu items include filling portions of charcoal-grilled beef, pork, or chicken served with salad, rice, tortillas, and a bowl of delicious bean soup. But you can also find a few Yucatecan specialties, such as costillas entomatadas, escabeche, queso relleno, and pollo pibil. The restaurant is between calles 49 and 51 in a quiet neighborhood 3 blocks south of the main square.

3 The Spectacular Ruins of Chichén-Itzá

112 miles W of Cancún; 75 miles E of Mérida

The fabled pyramids and temples of Chichén-Itzá (no, it doesn't rhyme with chicken pizza; it's pronounced chee-*chin* eat-*zah*) are the Yucatán's best-known ancient monuments. The ruins are plenty hyped, but Chichén is truly worth seeing. Walking among these stone platforms and pyramids and ball courts gives an appreciation for this ancient civilization that cannot be had from reading books. It evokes a tremendous sense of wonder; the amount of open space surrounding the Pyramid of Kukulcán prompts you to ponder the kind of mass celebrations or rituals that occurred here a millennium ago. Remember that much of what is said about the Maya (especially by tour guides) is merely educated guessing; even the Mayan alphabet is still poorly understood by scholars.

This Postclassic Maya city was established by Itzáes perhaps sometime during the 9th century A.D. Linda Schele and David Friedel, in *A Forest of Kings* (Morrow, 1990), have cast doubt on the legend that Kukulkán (called Quetzalcoatl by the Toltecs—a name also associated with a legendary god) came here from the Toltec capital of Tula (in north-central Mexico), and, along with Putún Maya coastal traders, built a magnificent metropolis that combined the Maya Puuc style with Toltec motifs (the feathered serpent, warriors, eagles, and jaguars). Not so, say Schele and Friedel. Readings of Chichén's bas-reliefs and hieroglyphs fail to support that legend, they say, and instead show that Chichén-Itzá was a continuous Maya site influenced by association with the Toltecs but not by an invasion. Not all scholars, however, embrace this new thinking, so the idea of a Toltec invasion still holds sway.

Though it's possible to make a round-trip from Mérida to Chichén-Itzá in 1 day, it will be a long, tiring, and very rushed day. Try to spend at least 1 night at Chichén-Itzá (most hotels are actually in the nearby village of Pisté).

ESSENTIALS

GETTING THERE & DEPARTING   By Plane   Day-trips on charter flights from Cancún and Cozumel can be arranged by travel agents in the United States or in Cancún or Cozumel.

By Car   Chichén-Itzá is on the main Highway 180 between Mérida and Cancún. You can also take the *autopista.*

By Bus   From Mérida, there are four first-class **ADO** buses per day, plus a couple that go to Valladolid will stop here. And there are several second-class buses per day. If you go round-trip in a day (a 2½-hr. trip one way), take the 8:45am bus and reserve a seat on the return bus. *De paso* buses to Mérida leave hourly day and night, as do those to Valladolid and Cancún.

If coming by bus, you'll arrive in the village of Pisté, at the station next to the Pirámide Inn. From Pisté, there's a sidewalk to the archaeological zone, which is a mile or so east of the bus station.

ORIENTATION   The small town of **Pisté,** where most hotels and restaurants are located, is about a mile and a half from the ruins of Chichén-Itzá. Public buses from Mérida, Cancún, Valladolid, and elsewhere discharge passengers here. A few hotels are at the edge of the ruins, and one, the Hotel Dolores Alba (see "Where to Stay," below), is out of town about 1½ miles from the ruins on the road to Valladolid.

EXPLORING THE RUINS

The site occupies 4 square miles, and it takes a full, strenuous day (from 8am to noon and 2 to 5pm) to see all the ruins, which are open daily from 8am to 5pm. Service areas are open from 8am to 10pm. Admission is $4, free for children under 12, and free for all on Sunday and holidays. A permit to use your own video camera costs an additional $4. Parking is extra. *You can use your ticket to reenter on the same day, but you'll have to pay again for an additional day.* Chichén-Itzá's light-and-sound show is well worth seeing. The Spanish version is shown nightly at 7pm and costs $3.50; the English version is at 9pm and costs $4. The show may be offered in French and German as well. Ask at your hotel.

The large, modern visitor center, at the main entrance where you pay the admission charge, is beside the parking lot and consists of a museum, an auditorium, a restaurant, a bookstore, and rest rooms. You can see the site on your own or with a licensed guide who speaks either English or Spanish. These guides are usually waiting at the entrance and charge around $30 for one to six people. Although the guides frown on it, there's nothing wrong with your approaching a group of people who speak the same language and asking if they would like to share a guide with you. The guide, of course, would like to get $30 from you alone and $30 each from other individuals who don't know one another and still form a group. Be wary of some of the history guides spout—some of it is just plain out-of-date, but the architectural details they point out are enlightening.

There are actually two parts of Chichén-Itzá (which dates from around A.D. 600 to 900). There's the northern (new) zone, which shows distinct Toltec influence, and the southern (old) zone, which is mostly Puuc architecture.

EL CASTILLO   As you enter from the tourist center, the beautiful 75-foot El Castillo pyramid (also called the Pyramid of Kukulkán) will be straight ahead across a large open area. It was built with the Maya calendar in mind. There are 364 stairs plus a platform to equal 365 (days of the year); 52 panels on each side (which represent the 52-year cycle of the Maya calendar); and nine terraces on each side of the stairways (for a total of 18 terraces, which represents the 18-month Maya solar calendar). If this isn't proof enough of the mathematical precision of this temple, come for the **spring** or **fall equinox** (Mar 21 or Sept 21 between 3 and 5pm). On those days, the seven stairs of the northern stairway and the serpent-head carving at the base are touched with sunlight and become a "serpent" formed by the play of light and shadow. It appears to descend into the earth as the sun hits each stair from the top, ending with the serpent head. To the Maya this was a fertility symbol: The golden sun had entered the earth, meaning it was time to plant the corn.

El Castillo was built over an earlier structure. A narrow stairway at the western edge of the north staircase leads into the structure, where there is a sacrificial altar-throne—a red jaguar encrusted with jade. The stairway is open only at 11am and 3pm and is claustrophobic, usually crowded, humid, and uncomfortable. A visit early in the day is best. Photos of the figure are not allowed.

MAIN BALL COURT (JUEGO DE PELOTA)   Northwest of El Castillo is Chichén's main ball court, the largest and best preserved anywhere, and only one of nine ball courts built in this city. Carved on both walls of the ball court are scenes showing Maya figures dressed as ball players decked out in heavy protective padding. The carved scene also shows a headless player kneeling with blood shooting from the neck; the player is looked upon by another player holding the head.

Players on two teams tried to knock a hard rubber ball through one or the other of the two stone rings placed high on either wall, using only their elbows, knees, and hips (no hands). According to legend, the losing players paid for defeat with their lives. However, some experts say the victors were in fact the only appropriate sacrifices for the gods. One can only guess what the incentive for winning might be in such a case. Either way, the game must have been riveting, heightened by the perfect acoustics of the ball court.

THE NORTH TEMPLE   Temples are found at both ends of the ball court. The North Temple has sculptured pillars and more sculptures inside, as well as badly ruined murals. The acoustics of the ball court are so good that from the North Temple a person speaking can be heard clearly at the opposite end about 450 feet away.

TEMPLE OF JAGUARS   Near the southeastern corner of the main ball court is a small temple with serpent columns and carved panels showing warriors and jaguars. Up the flight of steps and inside the temple, a mural was found that chronicles a battle in a Maya village.

TEMPLE OF THE SKULLS (TZOMPANTLI)   To the right of the ball court is the Temple of the Skulls, with rows of skulls carved into the stone platform. When a sacrificial victim's head was cut off, it was impaled on a pole and displayed in a tidy row with others. Also carved into the stone are pictures of eagles tearing hearts from human victims. The word Tzompantli is not Maya but came from central Mexico. Reconstruction using scattered fragments may add a level to this platform and change the look of this structure by the time you visit.

PLATFORM OF THE EAGLES   Next to the Tzompantli, this small platform has reliefs showing eagles and jaguars clutching human hearts in their talons and claws, as well as a human head emerging from the mouth of a serpent.

PLATFORM OF VENUS   East of the Tzompantli and north of El Castillo near the road to the Sacred Cenote is the Platform of Venus. In Maya-Toltec lore, Venus was represented by a feathered monster or a feathered serpent with a human head in its mouth. It's also called the tomb of Chaac-Mool because a Chaac-Mool figure was discovered "buried" within the structure.

SACRED CENOTE   Follow the dirt road (actually an ancient sacbe, or causeway) that heads north from the Platform of Venus; after 5 minutes you'll come to the great natural well that may have given Chichén-Itzá (the Well of the Itzáes) its name. This well was used for ceremonial purposes, not for drinking water, and according to legend, sacrificial victims were drowned in this pool to honor the rain god Chaac. Anatomical research done early this century by Ernest A. Hooten showed that bones of both children and adults were found in the well. Judging from Hooten's evidence, they may have been outcasts, diseased, or feeble-minded.

Edward Thompson, who was the American consul in Mérida and a Harvard professor, purchased the ruins of Chichén early this century and explored the cenote with dredges and divers. His explorations exposed a fortune in gold and jade. Most of the

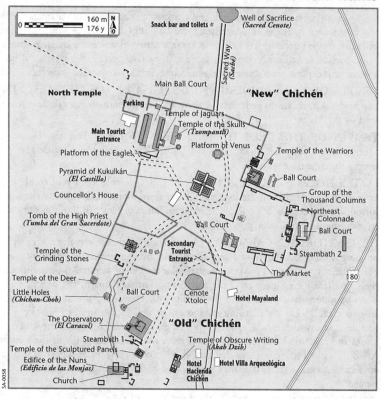

Map labels:

Well of Sacrifice (Sacred Cenote)

Snack bar and toilets

0 160 m / 176 y N

Sacred Way (Sacbé)

North Temple

Main Ball Court

"New" Chichén

Parking

Temple of Jaguars

Main Tourist Entrance

Temple of the Skulls (Tzompantli)

Platform of the Eagles

Platform of Venus

Temple of the Warriors

Pyramid of Kukulkán (El Castillo)

Ball Court

Councellor's House

Group of the Thousand Columns

Tomb of the High Priest (Tumba del Gran Sacerdote)

Northeast Colonnade

Ball Court

Ball Court

Temple of the Grinding Stones

Secondary Tourist Entrance

Steambath 2

Temple of the Deer

The Market

180

Little Holes (Chichan-Chob)

Ball Court

Cenote Xtoloc

Hotel Mayaland

The Observatory (El Caracol)

"Old" Chichén

Steambath 1

Temple of Obscure Writing (Akab Dzib)

Temple of the Sculptured Panels

Edificio de las Monjas (Edificio de las Monjas)

Hotel Hacienda Chichén

Hotel Villa Arqueológica

Church

SA-0058

riches wound up in Harvard's Peabody Museum of Archaeology and Ethnology—a matter that continues to disconcert Mexican classicists today. Later excavations in the 1960s unearthed more treasure, and studies of the recovered objects detail offerings from throughout the Yucatán and even farther away.

TEMPLE OF THE WARRIORS (TEMPLO DE LOS GUERREROS) Due east of El Castillo is one of the most impressive structures at Chichén: the Temple of the Warriors, named for the carvings of warriors marching along its walls. It's also called the Group of the Thousand Columns for the rows of broken pillars that flank it. During the recent restoration, hundreds more of the columns were rescued from the rubble and put in place, setting off the temple more magnificently than ever. A figure of Chaac-Mool sits at the top of the temple, surrounded by impressive columns carved in relief to look like enormous feathered serpents. South of the temple was a square building that archaeologists called the **Market** (Mercado); its central court is surrounded by a colonnade. Beyond the temple and the market in the jungle are mounds of rubble, parts of which are being reconstructed.

The main Mérida-Cancún highway once ran straight through the ruins of Chichén, and though it has now been diverted, you can still see the great swath it cut. South and west of the old highway's path are more impressive ruined buildings.

TOMB OF THE HIGH PRIEST (TUMBA DEL GRAN SACERDOTE) Past the refreshment stand to the right of the path is the Tomb of the High Priest, which stood atop a natural limestone cave in which skeletons and offerings were found, giving the temple its name.

The tomb has been reconstructed, and workers are unearthing other smaller temples in the area. As the work progresses, some buildings may be roped off and others will open to the public for the first time. It's fascinating to watch the archaeologists at work, meticulously numbering each stone as they take apart what appears to be a mound of rocks and then reassembling the stones into a recognizable structure.

TEMPLE OF THE GRINDING STONES (CASA DE LOS METATES)   This building, the next one on your right, is named after the concave corn-grinding stones used by the Maya.

TEMPLE OF THE DEER (TEMPLO DEL VENADO)   Past the House of Metates is this fairly tall though ruined building. The relief of a stag that gave the temple its name is long gone.

LITTLE HOLES (CHICHAN-CHOB)   This next temple has a roof comb with little holes, three masks of the rain god Chaac, three rooms, and a good view of the surrounding structures. It's one of the older buildings at Chichén, built in the Puuc style during the late Classic period.

OBSERVATORY (EL CARACOL)   Construction of the Observatory, a complex building with a circular tower, was carried out over centuries; the additions and modifications reflected the Maya's careful observation of celestial movements and their need for increasingly exact measurements. Through slits in the tower's walls, Maya astronomers could observe the cardinal directions and the approach of the all-important spring and autumn equinoxes, as well as the summer solstice. The temple's name, which means "snail," comes from a spiral staircase within the structure.

On the east side of El Caracol, a path leads north into the bush to the Cenote Xtoloc, a natural limestone well that provided the city's daily water supply. If you see any lizards sunning there, they may well be xtoloc, the lizard for which the cenote is named.

TEMPLE OF PANELS (TEMPLO DE LOS TABLEROS)   Just to the south of El Caracol are the ruins of a steam bath (*temazcalli*) and the Temple of Panels, named for the carved panels on top. This temple was once covered by a much larger structure, only traces of which remain.

EDIFICE OF THE NUNS (EDIFICIO DE LAS MONJAS)   If you've visited the Puuc sites of Kabah, Sayil, Labná, or Xlapak, the enormous nunnery here will remind you at once of the "palaces" at the other sites. Built in the late Classic period, the new edifice was constructed over an older one. Suspecting that this was so, Le Plongeon, an archaeologist working earlier in this century, put dynamite in between the two and blew away part of the exterior, thereby revealing the older structures within. You can still see the results of Le Plongeon's indelicate exploratory methods.

On the eastern side of the Edifice of the Nuns is an **annex (Anexo Este)** constructed in highly ornate Chenes style with Chaac masks and serpents.

THE CHURCH (LA IGLESIA)   Next to the annex is one of the oldest buildings at Chichén, absurdly named the Church. Masks of Chaac decorate two upper stories. Look closely and you'll see other pagan symbols among the crowd of Chaacs: an armadillo, a crab, a snail, and a tortoise. These represent the Maya gods called *bacah,* whose job it was to hold up the sky.

TEMPLE OF OBSCURE WRITING (AKAB DZIB)   Beloved of travel writers, this temple lies east of the Edifice of the Nuns. Above a door in one of the rooms are some Maya glyphs, which gave the temple its name, since the writings have yet to be deciphered. In other rooms, traces of red handprints are still visible. Reconstructed and expanded over the centuries, Akab Dzib may well be the oldest building at Chichén.

OLD CHICHÉN (CHICHÉN VIEJO)   For a look at more of Chichén's oldest buildings, constructed well before the time of Toltec influence, follow signs from the Edifice of the Nuns southwest into the bush to Old Chichén, about half a mile away. Be prepared for this trek with long trousers, insect repellent, and a local guide. The attractions here are the **Temple of the First Inscriptions** (Templo de los Inscripciones Iniciales), with the oldest inscriptions discovered at Chichén, and the restored **Temple of the Lintels** (Templo de los Dinteles), a fine Puuc building.

WHERE TO STAY

The expensive hotels in Chichén are all set in beautiful surroundings displaying the local flora's finery. All have toll-free numbers for reservations, which I recommend using. Some of these hotels do a lot of business with tour operators—they can be empty one day and full the next.

EXPENSIVE

Hacienda Chichén. Zona Arqueológica, 97751 Chichén-Itzá, Yuc. ☎/fax **985/1-0045.** (Reservations: Casa del Balam, calle 60 no. 488, 97000 Mérida, Yuc.; ☎ 800/624-8451 in the U.S., or 99/24-8844; fax 99/24-5011; http://www.wotw.com/casadelbalam.) 21 units. A/C FAN. $93 double. Free guarded parking.

This is the smallest and most private of the hotels at the ruins. It was a hacienda that in 1923 served as the headquarters for the Carnegie Institute's excavations. Several bungalows were built to house the staff; these are now the guest rooms. Each is simply furnished and decorated. They are separated from each other by a short distance and each has a porch from which you can enjoy the beautiful grounds. The main building belonged to the hacienda. It houses the terrace restaurant and the lobby, and has a pool beside it.

✪ **Hotel Mayaland.** Zona Arqueológica, 97751 Chichén-Itzá, Yuc. ☎ **985/1-0127.** (Reservations: Mayaland Resorts, Av. Colón 502, 97000 Mérida, Yuc.; ☎ 800/235-4079 in the U.S., or 99/25-2122; fax 99/25-7022.) 95 units. A/C TV. High season $133 double; $192 bungalow. Low season 10% off. Free guarded parking.

Glancing out the lobby doorway, you can't lose sight of the ruins; before you sits El Caracol (the observatory). Rooms in the main building are connected by a wide, tiled veranda, tiled bathrooms (with tubs), and colonial-style furnishings. Maya-inspired bungalows with beautifully carved furniture are tucked into the wooded grounds. The grounds are gorgeous, with huge trees and lush foliage— the hotel has had 75 years to get them in shape. There are three pools, a restaurant, a grill, and a buffet. Mayaland has a shuttle service between the hotel and Mérida for about $35 each way.

The Hotel Mayaland in the past has maintained car-rental offers that make the hotel a bargain. The official policy seems to be under revision, however, so you may want to ask about their offers.

Hotel Villa Arqueológica. Zona Arqueológica, 97751 Chichén-Itzá, Yuc. ☎ **800/ 258-2633** in the U.S.; 985/1-0034 , or 985/6-2830. 40 units. A/C. High season $110 double. Low season $70 double.

A lovely hotel built around a pool partially shaded by two large flamboyan trees and the background is formed by bougainvillea. The rooms are not large but are very comfortable. Each comes with a double and an oversized single bed. There are tennis courts, and the hotel's restaurant features international and Yucatecan food.

MODERATE

Stardust Inn. Calle 15A no. 34A, Carretera Mérida-Valladolid, 97751 Pisté, Yuc. ☎/fax **985/1-0122.** (Reservations: calle 81A no. 513, 97000 Mérida, Yuc.; ☎ 99/84-0072.) 57 units. A/C TV. $50 double. Free parking.

The two-story Stardust Inn is built around a pool and a shaded courtyard. Each of the comfortable rooms has a tile floor, a shower, nice towels, and one or two double beds or three single beds; check the condition of your mattress before selecting a room. During high season, there's a video bar/disco on the first floor; it's open during other times of the year if there are groups. If tranquillity is one of your priorities, ask if the disco is going to kick into gear before you rent a room. The very nice air-conditioned restaurant adjacent to the lobby and facing the highway serves all three meals and is open from 7:30am to 9:30pm.

INEXPENSIVE

Hotel Dolores Alba. Km 122 Carretera Mérida-Valladolid, Yuc. No phone. (Reservations: Hotel Dolores Alba, Calle 63 no. 464, 97000 Mérida, Yuc.; ☎ **99/28-5650;** fax 99/28-3163; E-mail: asanchez@yucatan.com.mx.) 30 units. A/C (or FAN). $22–$27 double. Free parking.

This place is of the motel variety, perfect if you come by car. It is a bargain for what you get: two pools (one of them unlike any I have ever seen), palapas and hammocks around the place for the benefit of the guests, and large and comfortable rooms. The restaurant serves good meals at moderate prices. Free transportation is provided to the ruins and the Caves of Balankanche during visiting hours, though you will have to take a taxi to get back. The hotel is on the highway 1½ miles east of the ruins (toward Valladolid).

Pirámide Inn. Km 118 Carretera Mérida Valladolid, 97751 Pisté, Yuc. ☎ **985/1-0115.** Fax 985/1-0114. 44 units. A/C or FAN. $27–$40 double.

Less than a mile from the ruins at the edge of Pisté, this hospitable inn has large motel-like rooms equipped with two double beds or one king-size bed. You might want to check your mattress for its sag factor before accepting the room. Hot water comes on between 5 and 9am and 5 and 9pm. Water is purified in the tap for drinking. There is a pool in the midst of landscaped gardens, which include the remains of a pyramid wall. Try to get a room in the back. If you're coming from Valladolid, it's on the left, and from Mérida look for it on the right.

Posada Novelo. Carretera Mérida-Valladolid, 97751 Pisté, Yuc. ☎/fax **985/1-0122.** 11 units. FAN. $12 double. Free parking in front.

Operated by the Stardust Inn next door, this hotel is in effect the budget wing of the main hotel. Rooms are attached in a row and linked by a covered walkway; all have one or two beds and are sparsely furnished but clean. Hot water is a rarity.

WHERE TO DINE

Reasonably priced meals are available at the restaurant in the visitor center at the ruins and at hotels in Pisté. Hotel restaurants near the ruins jump quite a bit in price. In Pisté, however, many places cater to large groups, which descend on them en masse for lunch after 1pm.

Cafetería Ruinas. In the Chichén-Itzá visitor center. No phone. Breakfast $4; sandwiches $4–$5; main courses $5–$8. Daily 9am–5pm. MEXICAN/ITALIAN.

Though it has the monopoly on food at the ruins, this cafeteria actually does a good job with such basic meals as enchiladas, spaghetti, and baked chicken. Eggs are cooked to order, as are burgers, and the coffee is very good. Sit outside at the tables farthest from the crowd and relax.

A Side Trip to the Grutas de Balankanche

The Grutas (Caves) de Balankanche are 3½ miles from Chichén-Itzá on the road to Valladolid and Cancún. Taxis will make the trip and wait, but they are also usually on hand when the tours let out. The entire excursion takes about half an hour, and the walk inside is hot and humid. The natural caves became wartime hideaways. You can still see traces of carving and incense burning, as well as an underground stream that served as the sanctuary's water supply. Outside, take time to meander through the botanical gardens, where most of the plants and trees are labeled with their common and scientific names.

The caves are open daily. Admission is $3. Use of your video camera will cost an additional $4. Children under 6 are not admitted. Guided tours in English are at 11am and 1 and 3pm, and in Spanish at 9am, noon, and 2 and 4pm. Tours go only if there is a minimum of six people and take up to 30 people at a time. Double-check these hours at the main entrance to the Chichén ruins.

La Fiesta. Carretera Mérida-Valladolid, Pisté. No phone. Main courses $4–$6; comida corrida $6.50. Daily 7am–9pm (comida corrida served 12:30–5pm). REGIONAL/MEXICAN.

With Maya motifs on the wall and colorful decorations, this is one of Pisté's long-established restaurants catering especially to tour groups. Though relatively expensive, the food is very good. You'll be quite satisfied unless you arrive when a tour group is being served, in which case service to individual diners may suffer. Going toward the ruins, La Fiesta is on the west end of town.

Puebla Maya. Carretera Mérida-Valladolid, Pisté. No phone. Fixed-price lunch buffet $7. Daily 1–5pm. MEXICAN.

Opposite the Pirámide Inn, the Puebla Maya looks just like its name, a Maya town with small white huts flanking a large open-walled palapa-topped center. Inside, however, you cross an artificial lagoon, planters drip with greenery, and live musicians play to the hundreds of tourists filling the tables. Service through the huge buffet is quick, so if you've been huffing around the ruins all morning, you have time to eat and relax before boarding the bus to wherever you're going. You can even swim in a lovely landscaped pool.

Restaurant Bar "Poxil." Calle 15 s/n, Carretera Mérida-Valladolid, Pisté. ☎ **985/1-0123.** Breakfast $3–$4; main courses $3–$5. Daily 7am–8pm. MEXICAN/REGIONAL.

A *poxil* is a Maya fruit somewhat akin to a guanábana. Although this place doesn't serve them, what is on the menu is good, though not gourmet, and the price is right. You will find the Poxil near the west entrance to town on the south side of the street.

4 Colonial Valladolid

25 miles E of Chichén-Itzá; 100 miles SW of Cancún

Valladolid (pronounced *bye*-ah-doh-*leed*) is a small, pleasant, colonial city halfway between Mérida and Cancún. The people here are friendly and informal, and, except for the heat, life is easy. The city's economy is based on commerce and small-scale manufacture. Valladolid boasts a large cenote in the center of town and another one 3 miles down the road to Chichén. A restoration project has reconstructed several rows of colonial housing in the neighborhood surrounding the convent of San Bernardino de Siena. Side trips to Holbox and Ekbalam (see below) can be mounted from

Valladolid, and you should consider staying here rather than at one of the more expensive hotels at Chichén.

ESSENTIALS

GETTING THERE & DEPARTING   By Car   From either Mérida or Cancún, you have two choices for getting to Valladolid: the toll road (*cuota*) or Highway 180. The cuota passes a few miles north of the city, and the exit is at the crossing of Highway 295 to Tizimín. Highway 180 takes significantly longer because it passes through a number of tiny villages and over their not-so-tiny speed bumps. Both 180 and 295 lead directly to the main square. Leaving is just as easy: From the main square, calle 41 turns into 180 east to Cancún; calle 39 heads to 180 west to Chichén Itzá and Mérida. To take the cuota to either Mérida or Cancún, take calle 40. (See "City Layout," below.)

By Bus   **Expresso de Oriente** has eight first-class buses per day to/from Mérida, nine buses to/from Cancún, three to/from Tulum, and three to/from Playa del Carmen. To secure a seat you can buy a ticket a day in advance. In addition, first-class buses make a stop in Valladolid while passing through (*de paso*) on the way to Cancún. To get to Chichén-Itzá you must take a second-class bus, which leaves every hour and sometimes on the half hour.

VISITOR INFORMATION   There is a small tourism office in the Palacio Municipal where you can get a map, but little else.

CITY LAYOUT   Valladolid has the standard layout for towns in the Yucatán: Streets running north-south are even numbers; those running east-west are odd numbers. The main plaza is bordered by calle 39 on the north, 41 on the south, 40 on the east, and 42 on the west. The plaza is named Parque Francisco Cantón Rosado, but everyone simply calls it El Centro. Valladolid has two bus stations at the corners of calles 39 and 46, and 37 and 54. For all practical purposes, they are interchangeable; departing buses pass by both stations. Taxis are easy to come by.

EXPLORING VALLADOLID

Before it became Valladolid, the city was a Maya settlement called Zací (zah-*kee*), which means "white hawk." There are two cenotes in the area, one of which is called **Cenote Zací**—located at the intersection of calles 39 and 36, in a small park in the middle of town. The walls and part of the roof of the cenote have been opened up, and a trail leads down close to the water. Caves, stalactites, and hanging vines contribute to a wild, prehistoric atmosphere. The park features a large palapa restaurant that is popular with local residents, plus three traditional Maya dwellings that house a small photograph collection and some historical materials on Valladolid. Admission is 50¢.

To the southwest of el centro is the Franciscan monastery of **San Bernardino de Siena** (1552). Most of the compound was built in the early 1600s; a large underground river is believed to pass under the convent and surrounding neighborhood, which is called Barrio Sisal. "Sisal" is, in this case, a corruption of the Mayan phrase *sis-ha*, meaning "cold water." The barrio has undergone extensive restoration and is a delight to behold.

Valladolid's **main square** is the social center of town and a thriving market for the prettiest Yucatecan dresses to be found anywhere. On its south side is the principle church, **La Parroquia de San Servacio.** Vallesoletanos, as the locals call themselves, believe that almost all cathedrals in Mexico point east, and they cherish a local legend to explain why theirs points north—but don't believe a word of it. On the east side of the plaza is the municipal building known modestly as El Ayuntamiento. Be sure to appreciate the four dramatic paintings outlining the history of the peninsula. In particular, note the first panel, featuring a horrified Maya priest as he foresees the arrival of Spanish galleons. On Sunday nights, from beneath the stone arches of the ayuntamiento, the municipal band plays *jaranas* and other traditional music of the region.

SHOPPING   The **Mercado de Artesanías de Valladolid** at the corner of calles 39 and 44 gives you a good idea of the local merchandise. Perhaps the main handcraft of the town is embroidered Maya dresses, which can be purchased here or from women around the main square. The latter also sell, of all things, Barbie doll–size Maya dresses! Just ask, *"¿Vestidos para Barbie?"* and out they come. The area around Valladolid is cattle country; the local leather goods are exceptional, and some of the best sandals and huaraches and leather goods are sold over the main plaza, above the municipal bazaar. An Indian named Juan Mac makes *alpargatas,* the traditional everyday footwear of the Maya, in his factory on calle 39, two doors south of the plaza; look for a doorway painted yellow. Most of his output is for locals, but he's happy to knock some out for travelers.

Valladolid also produces a highly prized **honey** made from the tzi-tzi-ché flower. You can find it and other goods at the **town market** on calle 32 between calles 35 and 37. The best time to see the market is Sunday morning.

WHERE TO STAY

Hotels (and restaurants) here are less expensive than the competition in Chichén. Occupancy rates are very high so you should make reservations.

Hotel El Mesón del Marqués. Calle 39 no. 203, 97780 Valladolid, Yuc. ☎ **985/6-3042** or 985/6-2073. Fax 985/6-2280. 73 units. A/C FAN TV TEL. $35 double. Free secured parking.

The Mesón del Marqués is a very comfortable and gracious hotel. The first courtyard surrounds a fountain and is draped in hanging plants and bougainvillea. This, the original house, mostly holds a good restaurant (see "Where to Dine," below). In back is another courtyard with plenty of greenery and a pool. There is always hot water, and most of the rooms are sheltered from city noise. It's on the north side of el centro, opposite the church.

Hotel María de la Luz. Calle 42 no. 193, 97780 Valladolid, Yuc. ☎/fax **985/6-2071,** or 985/6-2071. 41 units. A/C FAN TV. $20 double. Free secured parking.

The two stories at the María de la Luz are built around an inner swimming pool. The rooms have been refurbished with new tile floors and bathrooms and new mattresses; some have balconies overlooking the square. The wide interior space holds a restaurant that is quite comfortable and airy for most of the day—a popular place for breakfast. The hotel is on the west side of the main square.

WHERE TO DINE

Valladolid is not a center for haute-cuisine, but you should try some of the regional specialties. The lowest restaurant prices are found in the **Bazar Municipal,** a little arcade of shops beside the Hotel El Mesón del Marqués right on the main square.

Hostería del Marqués. Calle 39 no. 203. ☎ **985/6-2073.** Breakfast $3–$5; main courses 3.50–$7. Daily 7am–11:30pm. MEXICAN/YUCATECAN.

This is part of the Hotel El Mesón del Marqués, facing the main square. The patio is calm and cool for most of the day. The menu is extensive and features local specialties. If you are hungry, try the Yucatecan sampler. Any of the enchiladas are good. The guacamole was a hit on my last visit.

SIDE TRIPS FROM VALLADOLID

CENOTE DZITNUP The Cenote Dzitnup (also known as Cenote Xkeken), 2½ miles west of Valladolid off Highway 180, is worth a side trip, especially if you have time for a dip. Descend a short flight of rather perilous stone steps, and at the bottom, inside a beautiful cavern, is a natural pool of water so clear and blue it seems plucked from a dream. If you decide to take a swim, be sure you don't have creams or other chemicals on your skin, as they damage the habitat for the small fish and other organisms living there. Also, no alcohol, food, or smoking is allowed after you enter the cavern.

Admission is $1. The cenote is open daily from 8am to 5pm.

EKBALAM: RECENTLY EXCAVATED MAYA RUINS About 11 miles north of Valladolid, off the highway to Río Lagartos, is the spectacular site at Ekbalam, which means "star jaguar" in Mayan. Recently opened and largely unknown to tourists, the Ekbalam ruins are years away from complete renovation, but a must-see for travelers who have access to a rental car. Take calle 40 north out of Valladolid, to Highway 295; go 11 miles to the sign marking the Ekbalam turnoff. Follow a narrow, winding road through a small village, and watch the jungle for mounds that indicate the presence of undiscovered ruins leading to the main site. Ekbalam is 8 miles from the highway; the entrance fee is $1, plus $4 for each video camera. The site is open from 8am to 5pm every day; on our last visit, the custodians obligingly admitted us at 6pm to clamber on the main pyramid.

Built between 100 B.C. and A.D. 1200, the smaller buildings are architecturally unique—especially the large and perfectly restored **Caracol.** The principal buildings in the main group have been reconstructed beautifully, but the huge and imposing main pyramid will take years to complete. Flanked by two smaller pyramids, the central temple is 517 feet long and 200 feet wide, and though only a little more than 100 feet high, feels easily as tall as the biggest structures in Chichén and Uxmal. You can see the restoration work in progress: stones are carefully separated, numbered, and arranged, then reassembled by archaeologists from INAH, the national institute for anthropology. The caretaker/guide led us up the rocky, forested path to the summit, where we watched a full moon rise to illuminate the jungle for a radius of 35 miles. In the middle distanced, unrestored ruins loom to the north and the southwest, and you can spot the tallest structures at **Coba,** 30 miles to the southeast. Also plainly visible are the **raised causeways** of the Maya—the sacbeob that appear as raised lines in the forest vegetation. More than any of the better-known sites, Ekbalam at dusk excites a sense of mystery and awe at the scale of Maya civilization, and the utter ruin to which it came.

RÍO LAGARTOS NATURE RESERVE: NESTING FLAMINGOS

Some 50 miles north of Valladolid (25 miles north of Tizimín) on Highway 295 is Río Lagartos, a 118,000-acre refuge established in 1979 to protect the largest nesting population of flamingos in North America. Found in the park's dunes, mangrove swamps, and tropical forests are jaguars, ocelots, sea turtles, and at least 212 bird species (141 of which are permanent residents).

With flamingos, the earlier you get out to see them, the better. There was a hotel in Río Lagartos, but it was never any good and now is closed. One option is to stay the night in Tizimín, which is about 30 minutes away. The best place to stay there is **Hotel 49,** on calle 49 373-A (☎ 986/3-2136) by the main square. The owner can give you good advice about going to the nature preserve. There is not much to do in Tizimín unless you are there in the first 2 weeks of January when it holds the largest fair in the Yucatán. The prime fiesta day is January 6: the epiphany, known popularly as *Día de los Reyes*. The fiesta is celebrated with lots of music, carnival rides, etc.

SEEING THE RÍO LAGARTOS REFUGE   Río Lagartos is a small fishing village of around 3,000 people who make their living from the sea and from the occasional tourist who shows up to see the flamingos. Colorfully painted homes face the Malecón (the oceanfront street), and brightly painted boats dock along the same half-moon-shaped port.

If you arrive by car, you have the option of driving to the salt plant at Los Colorados and out over the flats to the shore of the lagoon, where you can get fairly close to a large colony. Otherwise, go straight to the dock area in Río Lagartos where you can hire a boat to the large flamingo colony for $75, which can be split among up to six people; the trip takes 4 to 6 hours. Or you can get a shorter trip to a closer colony for $20. Ask around for Filiberto Pat Zem, a reliable boatman who takes the time to give a good tour.

Although thousands of flamingos nest near here from April through August, it is prohibited by law to visit their nesting grounds. Flamingos need mud with particular ingredients (including a high salt content) in order to multiply, and this area's mud does the trick. Flamingos use their special bills to suck up the mud, and they have the unique ability to screen the contents they need from it. What you see on the boat trip is a mixture of flamingos, frigates, pelicans, herons in several colors, and ducks. Don't allow the boatman to frighten the birds into flight for your photographs; it causes the birds to eventually leave the habitat permanently.

15 Veracruz & the Gulf Coast

With its awesome natural beauty, growing array of true adventure excursions, and intriguing mix of historical and archaeological landmarks, the state of Veracruz is an ideal destination for travelers who have explored established Mexico and are in search of something different.

What Veracruz lacks is a developed tourism infrastructure, deluxe resorts, and attractive beaches—in other words, the key attributes that lure most travelers to coastal climes. But for the adventurous soul, this could be a refreshing change from the increasingly Americanized resort routine, and you'd be hard-pressed to match the diversity and desirability found in the area's geography.

Stretching from sea level to cloud forest mountains, Veracruz is home to Mexico's highest peak, the 18,513-foot Pico de Orizaba. Fertile volcanic slopes produce some of Mexico's finest coffee, and coastal waters harvest an abundance of seafood and shellfish. To date, tourism has been dominated by national visitors, but a growing number of international travelers are recognizing the virtues of this region, which has the added benefit of being arguably the best value in the country.

The region is studded with the archaeological ruins of the land's indigenous peoples. The **Huastec** occupied the area that extends from north of the Cazones River to Soto la Marina, including portions of Veracruz, Tamaulipas, and San Luis Potosí; the **Totonac** lived south of the Cazones River to the Papaloapan River, in mid- to upper Veracruz; and the **Olmec,** a civilization dating back 3,000 years, lived in an area encompassing Río Papaloapan to La Venta in southern Veracruz and northern Tabasco. **Pyramidal sites** dot the coast, some of which, like El Tajín and Zempoala, make for excellent off-the-beaten-track travel. At least 15% of the people in this region speak indigenous languages: Otomi is spoken around Puebla, spilling into Veracruz; Huasteco, a Mayan-linked language, is spoken in Tamaulipas and San Luis Potosí; and Nahuatl and Totonaco are used in both Puebla and Veracruz.

Most will at least begin their travels in the colonial port city of **Veracruz,** the first point of entrance for the Spanish conquest. To the south, **Catemaco** is known for its wild environs and white witchcraft. To the north and west, river rafting, mountain climbing, and hiking offer a serious adrenaline fix for the adventure-deprived. Museums and ruins will not only lead you through this unique land, but will take you on an exploration of different layers in time as well.

EXPLORING THE GULF COAST   Highlights of the Gulf Coast include Veracruz and the Zempoala ruins, the ruins of El Tajín, Jalapa, and Lake Catemaco. All are clustered within an hour or so of the city of Veracruz. Many people fly directly from the United States to Veracruz and base their exploration of the Gulf Coast from this city. Veracruz can be easily reached from Mexico City by plane, bus, or car, and is a natural base for side trips to **Jalapa,** the capital of the state, and to **Zempoala.** For more extensive exploration, you'll want to allow more time, as your schedule allows.

1 Veracruz City: Where Cortés Landed

145 miles E of Mexico City; 68 miles SE of Jalapa

Veracruz (vayr-ah-*croos*) is where traditional Mexico meets an exotic blend of Afro/Cuban/Caribbean influences. This mix has resulted in a melodic culture where strains of marimba music float on sea breezes and couples dance the samba and equally sultry *danzón* with regularity in the central plaza.

Cafes bordering the town square serve up freshly caught seafood and heftily brewed regional coffee. Where coffee is concerned, the ritual of how to drink it—one waiter serves the thick, black coffee; then you signal a second waiter and indicate how much hot milk should be added—is as important as knowing that only locally grown beans are acceptable.

Think of Veracruz as the gateway for foreign influence into Mexico. Its historical notoriety stems from the fact that Hernan Cortés first set foot on Mexican soil on this point in 1519.

Within 3 months, the conquistador had moved his forces 45 miles north to Quiauixtlan, a small Indian settlement known today as Villa Rica. Six years later, Cortés's forces resettled near the mouth of the Río Huitzilapan, at what is now Antigua (about 14 miles north of modern Veracruz). The ruins of several massive stone houses, including the House of Cortés (La Casa de Cortés), still stand there. In 1599, the settlement was moved south to the original landing site, and Villa Rica de la Vera Cruz ("Rich Town of the True Cross"), Cortés's christening of the town, became permanent.

Delegates of the Spanish crown shipped most of their gold and silver out of the port, and looting pirates periodically ransacked the town. The citizens defended themselves by constructing a high wall around the old town (around the Plaza de Armas) and a massive fort, San Juan de Ulúa, on what was then an island in the harbor (now connected to the mainland by a curving pier).

The town went on to be the site of numerous events of significant importance in Mexico's history, including the expulsion of the Spanish in 1825, three foreign invasions, and the drafting of the Mexican constitution.

Prior to the arrival of the Spaniards, it was a center of Olmec culture. All of these historic details can be better explained through the varied and impressive selection of museums—including the renowned Anthropological Museum in neighboring Jalapa. Also known as Xalapa, this university town is also the capital of Veracruz state, and the jalapeño capital of Mexico.

ESSENTIALS

GETTING THERE & DEPARTING   By Plane   Aeromexico (☎ **800/237-6639** from the U.S., 01-800/021-4000, or 29/35-0283; 29/34-1534 at the airport) flies direct from Mexico City and Houston, with connecting flights from Dallas, Houston, and Los Angeles. **Aerolitoral** (☎ **800/237-6639** from the U.S., or 29/35-0142), an Aeromexico affiliate, flies from Ciudad Juárez, McAllen and San Antonio (Texas),

Monterrey, Tampico, and Villahermosa. **Mexicana** (☎ **800/531-7921** from the U.S., or 29/32-2242; 29/38-0008 at the airport) flies to Veracruz from Mexico City five times daily and from Mérida twice daily, with connecting flights from Chicago, Denver, Los Angeles, Miami, New York, San Antonio, San Francisco, and San Jose. **Aerocaribe/Aerocozumel** (☎ **29/22-5212;** 29/22-5210 at the airport) flies from various locations in the Yucatán, Guatemala, Belize, and Cuba.

The **airport** (VER) is 2½ miles from the town center. Getting there by **taxi** costs about $10 to $12. Vans belonging to **Transportación Terrestre Aeropuerto** (☎ **29/ 37-8719**) meet every arriving flight. You can also arrange pickup from your hotel to the airport by calling this number. The fare to downtown is set by zone, and costs about $6 to $8. No public buses run from the airport into town.

Several major car-rental agencies have counters at the airport that are open for flight arrivals, as well as locations in downtown hotels. **Avis** (☎ **800/331-1212** or 29/ 31-1580), **Dollar** (☎ **800/800-4000** or 29/35-5231), and **National** (☎ **800/ 328-4567** or 29/31-7556) are some of the options. Renting a car to explore the small towns and ruins near Veracruz may be desirable, and the roads in this area are generally well maintained.

If you **arrive by plane,** don't linger long in the airport before getting to the colectivo minivans that await each flight: They fill up and leave, not returning until the next flight.

By Car   Veracruz is less than 2 hours away from Jalapa, via Highway 140 to the coastal Highway 180 and the toll road into Veracruz; or cut off before the coast at Puente Nacional and go south to Veracruz on toll-free Highway 146.

From Mexico City (6 hr.), Córdoba, or Orizaba, take Highway 150 to the coast and drive north on Highway 180 to Veracruz; it's not quite a 2-hour drive from the latter two cities.

By Bus   There are frequent buses from Jalapa, Orizaba, Córdoba, and Mexico City to Veracruz. From Veracruz's ADO station, **ADO** buses leave frequently for Orizaba, Córdoba, and San Andrés Tuxtla; buses to Jalapa leave every 30 minutes.

From the **Central Camionera,** frequent buses head from Veracruz to Mexico City, a 7-hour trip.

Arriving **by bus,** the Central Camionera (main bus station) is 20 or so blocks south of the town center on Díaz Mirón between Orizaba and Molina. Taxis wait in front of the terminal. "Díaz Mirón" buses go to and from the town center. Catch the outbound on Avenida Cinco de Mayo (2 blocks west of the Plaza de Armas).

VISITOR INFORMATION   The **tourism office** (☎ 29/32-1999), is downtown on the east side of the Plaza de Armas. The office is on the ground floor of the **Palacio Municipal** (City Hall) and is open daily from 9am to 9pm.

CITY LAYOUT   Parallel to the shoreline, the **malecón/bulevar Camacho** runs north and south; it goes into the town center and out to the beaches and resorts south of town. City life peaks around **Plaza de Armas,** 1 block west of the malecón. It's bounded by Lerdo and Zamora going east and west and by Independencia and Morelos going north and south. Most museums, restaurants, and hotels are either here or within a short walk.

GETTING AROUND   Taxis are plentiful and relatively cheap compared to those in other cities in Mexico. **City buses** are very cheap (25¢ to 40¢) and easy to use; they'll get you to and from the most important places in town. There are also old wooden trolley cars on wheels, called **tranvías,** that operate as part of the public

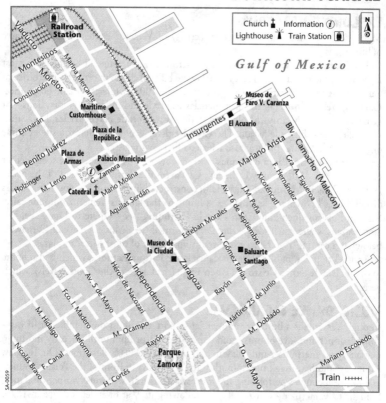

Downtown Veracruz

Church ⛪ Information ⓘ
Lighthouse 🗼 Train Station 🚉

Gulf of Mexico

transportation system. These sightseeing trolleys are open-air, rubber-wheeled replicas of those that ran on rails in Veracruz until the early 1980s. They leave from Insurgentes (corner of 16 de Septiembre, on the Malecón) every hour daily (unless the weather is bad) from 10am to 11:30pm, making an hour-long tour through town.

FAST FACTS: VERACRUZ

American Express   Viajes Olymar represents American Express. They have offices in Plaza Mocambo, Local A-18 (☎ 29/21-9923), as well as on Bulevar Camacho 2221, Col. Zaragoza (☎ 29/31-4636; fax 29/31-3169).

Area Code   The telephone area code is 29.

Climate   You'll find it hot and humid in summer and mild in spring, fall, and winter, with windy, sand-blowing *nortes* (northers) from November through March.

Consulate   The U.S. Consulate is located on Víctimas del 25 de Junio, no. 384, almost at the corner of Gómez Farías (☎ 29/31-0142). It's open Monday through Friday from 9am to 1pm. The British Consulate is found at Emparan 200, Apdo. Postal 724 (☎/fax 29/310955).

High Season   The peak tourist season falls in June, July, and August and then December through March. Veracruz is most popular with Mexican national tourism, as well as European tourism, rather than visitors from the United States or Canada.

Post Office   The correo (post office), located on Avenida de la República, near the Maritime Customs House, is open Monday through Friday from 8am to 8pm.

EXPLORING VERACRUZ

Much of the cultural and commercial activity of Veracruz centers around its three public plazas:

The **Plaza de la República** is a long, narrow plaza surrounded by the city's most important civic structures, most of which were built in the 19th century. The office of Customs, **Aduna Marítima,** was constructed in 1903, while the main post office, **Correo y Telegrafo,** is famed for its neoclassical style and the large, golden lions that grace its entrance. Nearby, the old train station, **Estacion de Ferrocarriles,** has a stunning yellow-and-blue tile facade. The **Civil Registry** is not only an exquisite example of period architecture, but was also Mexico's first civil registry.

The 16th-century **Plaza de Armas,** with its towering palm trees, is the social center of the city. The 18th-century cathedral, **La Parroquia,** borders one end of the plaza, while the **Palacio Municipal** (City Hall), constructed in 1627, graces another. A series of tall arches known as **Las Portales** is home to the famous Veracruz outdoor cafes, bars, and bistros, including **Gran Café la Parroquia** (see "Where to Dine," below). This plaza is where you'll see the *danzón* performed (see "Music, Dance & Carnaval", below) as a central stage replaces the traditional kiosk of most Mexican plazas.

Another popular, public place for dance is the **Parque Zamora,** which is also home to the **Igelsia de Santo Cristo del Buen Viaje** (the Christ of the Good Travels), which dates back to 1598.

MUSIC, DANCE & CARNAVAL

Though Veracruz is a bustling commercial seaport, it is most memorable for its easy-going manner and love of music and dance. From 1 or 2pm until the early morning, mariachi and marimba bands play in and around the Plaza de Armas. On Tuesday, Thursday, and Saturday from 8pm, the city band plays in front of the Palacio Municipal for local couples performing the *danzón,* a classical, sensuous two-person dance, brought to Veracruz by Cuban refugees following its War of Independence in 1879. Sunday evenings are also popular for *danzón* and salsa dancing in **Parque Zamora.** Up and down the Malecón and in the square, people gather to socialize, listen to music, or sell trinkets.

The **Ballet Tradicional de México** (☎ 29/31-0574 for reservations) performs at the Teatro J. Clavijero. Tickets cost $3.25 to $5. Check with the tourism office to verify schedules (see "Visitor Information," above). The ballet season is usually only during Easter time.

For the three days before Ash Wednesday, Veracruz explodes with Carnaval, one of the best in Mexico. Visitors flood in from Mexico City, packing the streets and hotels; those without rooms are content to live out of their cars. Indians, many of whom have walked a day's journey from their villages, spread their crafts on the sidewalks. Locals join the crowds in the music-filled streets.

Fabulous floats (*carros alegóricos,* "allegorical cars") are made with true Mexican flair—bright colors, papier-mâché figures, flowers, and live entertainment. Groups from neighboring villages dance in peacock- and pheasant-feathered headdresses. Draculas, drag queens, and women in sparkling dresses parade the streets. Most of the other activities center in the Plaza de Armas and begin around noon, lasting well into the night.

If you plan to be in Veracruz for the three days of Carnaval, reserve hotel space months in advance, as everything's jammed at this time. On the Sunday before Ash Wednes-day, the longest and most lavish of the Carnaval parades takes place on the Malecón. Parades on Monday and Tuesday are scaled-down versions of the Sunday parade (ask at the tourist office about the parade routes on Mon and Tues), and by Wednesday, it's all over.

THE TOP ATTRACTIONS

Fort of San Juan de Ulua. ☎ **29/38-5151.** Admission $2.50; free Sun. Tues–Sun 9am–5pm. Bus: "San Juan de Ulua" from the *parada* (stop) across from Calle Juárez on Avenida de la República. By car, drive across the bridge that heads north out of Plaza de Armas between Avenida de la República and Avenida Morelos, then turn right past the box storage and piers.

Built as a limestone-rock fortress to ward off pirate invasions, the structure became infamous instead as a prison noted for its extreme cruelty and for the famous people incarcerated there, among them Benito Juárez, who later led the reform movement from the fort and became one of Mexico's most revered presidents. English-speaking guides charge for tours at the entrance or you can go on your own. This was also the site of the eerie, alligator-infused scene in the movie *"Romancing the Stone"*.

Baluarte Santiago. At Fco. Canal between Gómez Farías and 16 de Septiembre. ☎ **29/31-1059.** Admission $1.75; free Sun and holidays. Tues–Sun 10am–4:30pm. From Plaza de Armas, walk 5 blocks south on Independencia, then turn left (east) onto Rayón and walk for 2 more blocks.

Built in 1636 as part of the city's fortifications against the pirates, this bulwark is all that's left of the old city walls and original nine forts. It's remarkable to see up close the type of construction used in those days—it's nothing if not solid. A collection of pre-Hispanic gold jewelry, recovered several years ago by a fisherman along the coast some miles north of Veracruz, is on permanent display.

City Museum. Zaragoza 397. ☎ **29/31-8410.** Admission 60¢. Tues–Sun 9am–3pm. From the Palacio Municipal, walk 4½ blocks south on Zaragoza; the museum is on the right.

This recently restored 120-year-old building was converted into the City Museum years ago. Twelve rooms on two levels off the beautiful interior courtyard display archaeological relics from pre-Columbian Gulf Coast sites. The collection is small compared to those of the museums in Jalapa and Villahermosa, but the exhibits are of interest. The Indian cultures represented here are the Olmec, the Totonac, and the Huastec. Several rooms display regional costumes and crafts.

El Acuario. Plaza Acuario Veracruz, Bulevar M. Ávila Camacho at Playón de Hornos. ☎ **29/32-7984.** Admission $1.80 adults, 60¢ children 2–12. Daily 10am–7pm. Buses marked MOCAMBO–BOCA DEL RÍO stop here. The Plaza Acuario Veracruzana is at the eastern edge of downtown where Bulevar Ávila Camacho meets Xicoténcatl. Walking along the Malecón, you'll find it about 15 blocks from the corner of the Malecón and Camacho.

Opened in fall 1992, the aquarium has become a major attraction in Veracruz. Located in a shopping center (where there are numerous restaurants), the aquarium is one of the largest of its kind in Latin America, with nine freshwater and 15 saltwater tanks featuring the marine life of the area and all of Mexico. The circular *gran pecera* (large tank) gives the illusion of being surrounded by the ocean and its inhabitants, including sharks.

Faro Venustiano Carranza Museum. Malecón between Xicoténcatl and Hernandez. No phone. Free admission. Tues–Sun 9am–4pm. The Faro (lighthouse) is a block west of the Pemex Tower on the Malecón, next to the Hotel Emporio. (The museum has been closed for repairs, but should be reopened by publication. If not, the temporary home of the displays has been the "Museo Histórico Naval" at the corner of Arista and Landero y Coss.)

This small museum is located on the second floor of the headquarters of the Third Naval Military Zone and the site of the port's second lighthouse. It's dedicated to

Venustiano Carranza, a leading figure in Mexico during the Revolutionary period, who became president in 1917. Carranza served as first chief of the "Constitutional-istic Army," and was assassinated in 1920 by killers vaguely linked to Álvaro Obregón, who sought to overthrow him. The museum consists of four rooms: Carranza's office/bedroom; two rooms of photographs showing Carranza at various stages of his life (including a facsimile of his autopsy report); and a room with a copy of the Constitution, a portrait of Carranza, and a diagram of the trajectory of the bullets that killed him.

MORE ATTRACTIONS

GUIDED BOAT TRIPS Guided boat tours of the harbor (most in Spanish only) pass many of the sights listed above, as well as many of the international tankers and ships docked in the port. Launches leave sporadically (depending on the weather and demand) from the dock in front of the Hotel Emporio. The cost is $2 for adults and $1 for children 2 to 8, plus a tip for the guide. If the group is small, the price may go up to $5 per adult.

BEACHES Veracruz has beaches, but this is not the key attraction here; the sand is grayish and hard-packed, and the Gulf water tends to be shallow. There are points all along the waterfront downtown where people swim, but the nearest true beach is at the **Villa del Mar,** an open-air terrace and palm-lined promenade with changing rooms and showers at the southern end of town. To get there, take the "Playa V. del Mar" bus, which travels south on Zaragoza. The trip takes 15 minutes.

About 5 miles south of Veracruz along the Gulf Coast is the beach of **Mocambo,** where boats, snorkeling equipment, and water skis can be rented. There are public pools at both Villa del Mar (entrance $1.50) and Mocambo (entrance $2) beaches.

A little farther past Mocambo at the mouth of the Jamapa River is **Boca del Río.** Both places can easily be reached by taking the buses that leave every 30 minutes (on the hour and half hour) from the corner of Serdán and Zaragoza near the municipal fish market. The bus stop is marked with the sign COSTA VERDE or BOCA DEL RÍO; the trip takes 30 minutes.

EXCURSIONS Veracruz is making a name for itself among adventure travelers. Popular day-trips include those to **La Antigua;** the Totonas ruins at **Zempoala;** the state capital and home of an excellent anthropology museum, **Jalapa;** the archaeological site at **El Tajín;** and **Lago Catemaco.** For prices and reservations, contact **VIP Tours** (☎ 29/22-3315 or 29/22-1918) or **Centro de Reservaciones de Veracruz** (☎ 29/35-6422).

For the more actively inclined, **river rafting, sportfishing, mountain climbing,** and **diving** are all excellent options here. **Veraventuras** runs a daily white-water rafting adventure down the Actopan River and to the thermal waters of the Carrizal Spa. The 9-hour tour, with lunch included, costs $65. Other trips take you down the Filobobos and La Antigua rivers. **Diving** centers around a series of reefs and corresponding shipwrecks south of town towards Boca del Río. Contact **Dorado Divers** (☎ 29/31-4305) for more details.

SHOPPING The **Veracruz** market (near the corner of Madero and Gonzáles Pages) is one of the most interesting in Mexico. It's possible to find just about anything here, from caged parrots to live iguanas with tethered feet and tied tails. You can shop for curios in little shops along the **malecón** opposite the Hotel Oriente and around the corner toward the pier. Here, the wares include more typical beachside junk: full shark's jaws, tacky shell art, ships in a jar, and the like.

WHERE TO STAY

Veracruz has a good assortment of hotels, with most concentrated in the more active, lively sections of town. This is a popular beach destination for Mexican nationals, and so the high tourist season is June through August, with a secondary period from December through March. Veracruz is also a favorite weekend spot for tourists from the capital city, and they frequently fill every means of transportation on Friday. The flow of people traveling back up into the mountains is reversed but equally heavy on Sunday. Weekdays, hotel rooms are generally occupied by business travelers.

EXPENSIVE

Fiesta Americana Veracruz. Bulevar Ávila Camacho and Camacho, 94299 Veracruz, Ver. ☎ **800/FIESTA-1** in the U.S., or 29/22-2228. Fax 29/22-5733. 233 units. A/C TV TEL. $105 double. AE, DC, MC, V. Free parking.

Veracruz's most modern and well-appointed hotel is targeted to a business clientele, but is also an excellent choice for more pampered vacations. Opened in 1996, the rooms are located along wide marble corridors on six floors. Spacious and decorated in muted colors, most rooms have either terraces or balconies with views that overlook the ocean or large, free-form pool. In-room amenities include hair dryers, safe-deposit boxes, satellite TV, and voice mail. Nonsmoking and wheelchair-accessible rooms are available. It's located along the Playa Costa de Oro, a long stretch of beach targeted for further development. A Fiesta Club Floor offers extra services, mainly to accommodate business travelers, for an extra charge.

Dining/Diversions: The poolside **Cafe Fiesta** offers daily breakfast buffets and casual fare, while the **El Delfin** features more formal dining and an international menu. There are also two bars.

Amenities: Two pools, three hot tubs, exercise room, golf-course access, travel agency, business center, salon services, room service, baby-sitting, laundry.

MODERATE

Emporio. Insurgentes Veracruzanos 210, 91700 Veracruz, Ver. ☎ **29/32-0020.** Fax 29/31-2261. 242 units. A/C TV TEL. $66 double. AE, MC, V. Free parking.

You can't beat the location of this longtime Veracruz favorite, just across from the malecón and Carranza Lighthouse. Built in 1952, this eight-story hotel has been continually updated and offers modern services with an intriguingly dated ambiance. The last major renovation took place in 1995, giving the whole property a more elegant feel to it. Rooms are large and bright, with white stucco walls, balconies with harbor or city views, marble bathrooms with combination shower/tubs, and a small sitting area. If you're not looking for beachfront, this hotel is an excellent bargain. Facilities include a grand, neoclassic lobby, three pools (one children's), a small business center, full gym with sauna, tennis courts, two restaurants, and two bars.

Hotel Calinda Quality Veracruz. Av. Independencia at Lerdo (Apdo. Postal 606), 91700 Veracruz, Ver. ☎ **800/228-5151** in the U.S., 29/31-2233, or 29/31-1124. Fax 29/31-5134. 116 units. A/C TV TEL. $60 double. AE, MC, V.

By far the best hotel on the Plaza de Armas, Hotel Calinda is a colonial-style hotel with the comfort of a modern hotel. The well-lit, carpeted rooms are spacious, and have just been completely remodeled (fall 1998). There's a restaurant on the second floor and a rooftop dining terrace with great views of the city and plaza.

Hotel Mocambo. Boca del Río (Apdo. Postal 263), 91700 Veracruz, Ver. ☎ **800/666-1986** in the U.S., or 29/22-0205. Fax 29/22-0212. 129 units. A/C TV TEL. $75 double. AE, DC, MC, V. Free parking.

The Mocambo, built in 1932, lies 9 miles southeast of the town center on one of Veracruz's finest stretches of beach. One of the city's first and best hotels, it has hosted presidents, movie stars, and governors. Never out of fashion, it has become a comfortable, stylish hotel with just the right amount of old-fashioned touches. Although a bit worn from time, recent renovations have maintained its stature as a top choice in Veracruz. It's a palatial property, with wide halls, terraces, a sauna, a Jacuzzi and four pools (two indoor), a tennis court, and a restaurant. Most rooms have sea views, but the cost of rooms varies depending on quality of view and the size of the room. At least 32 rooms have balconies. Inquire about cheaper (standard) rooms, since they might not be offered to you at first. Even if you choose another hotel for your stay, it's worth visiting either the Mocambo's beach (which is public) or its restaurant, **La Fragata.** If you're not driving, take the bus marked MOCAMBO from Zaragoza and Serdán by La Prosperidad restaurant; buses stopping at the hotel's front gate go into town.

INEXPENSIVE

Hotel Colonial. Plaza de la Constitución 117, 91700 Veracruz, Ver. ☎ **29/32-0193.** Fax 29/32-2465. 182 units. A/C TV TEL. $30–$38 double. AE, CB, DC, MC, V. Parking $2.50 daily.

The pleasant and ideally located Colonial has two sections: the older, with centrally controlled air-conditioning, and the newer, with individually controlled air-conditioning. Rooms are very bright and comfortable, with tile floors. Outside rooms have a small balcony overlooking the plaza; interior rooms are quieter. Hotel services include covered parking, an indoor pool on the second floor and a sidewalk cafe and bar. The Colonial is the only tourist-class hotel on the Plaza de Armas; there's an entrance on the plaza and another through the garage.

WHERE TO DINE

The restaurants under the portals that surround Plaza de Armas are the best spots for eating, drinking, and just hanging out. While more expensive than places a few blocks away, their prices are not outrageous, and represent a great value for those paying with dollars.

You'll quickly catch on that seafood and coffee are two dining rituals in Veracruz. Throughout the country one of the most popular preparations of fish is *Veracruzana,* denoting a tomato-based sauce infused with onions, olives, garlic, chiles, and other delicate seasonings. Veracruz claims its locally grown coffee is the best in Mexico.

On Landero y Coss between Arista and Serdán, the street level of the **municipal fish market** is swimming with little *ostionerías* (oyster bars) and shrimp stands. Take a stool, ask the price, and order. Look upstairs for more good places.

The **Paris** is a *panadería* and *pastelería* (bakery and pastry shop) that sells a very wide selection of Mexican rolls and pastries for 5¢ to 50¢. You can't miss the assortment and the smell at Avenida Cinco de Mayo at the corner of Molina.

MODERATE

Gran Café El Portal. Independencia at Zamora. ☎ **29/31-2759.** Main courses $3–$8; comida corrida $4.75–$5.75. No credit cards. Daily 6am–midnight. MEXICAN.

Catercorner from the Plaza de Armas, occupying the former home of the ever-popular Café la Parroquia (now on the Malecón), the Gran Café El Portal is actually a resumption of its original name, dating back to 1835. From the cavernous dining room, huge windows on two sides look onto the Plaza de Armas and Independencia, where a parade of strolling troubadours, harpists, roving marimba players, and shoe-shine men pass by. Elsewhere, old sepia photos of Veracruz decorate walls. Enjoy a coffee, an excellent comida corrida, or traditional Mexican cuisine such as crepes huitlacoche, tinga (a specialty of Puebla state), and grilled chicken. The comida corrida (an inexpensive, fixed-price lunch of several courses) fills the place with local regulars.

La Paella. Zamora 138. ☎ **29/32-0322.** Breakfast $1.45–$3; main courses $3–$8; comida corrida $3.75 Mon–Fri, $4.25 Sun. No credit cards. Daily 8:30am–10pm (comida corrida served 1–4pm). SPANISH.

Devotees of Spanish food will appreciate La Paella, where the four-course comida corrida is popular but portions are small, served almost tapas-style. Three courses include such Spanish specialties as crema bretona, paella valenciana, and *tortilla española* (potato omelet). The walls of this long and narrow cafe are adorned with bullfight posters. La Paella is right at the southeast corner of the Plaza de Armas, near the tourism office and next door to KFC—look for its very colonial-tiled facade.

INEXPENSIVE

Café Andrade. Calle Hernández y Hernández. No phone. Desserts $1–$2.50; sandwiches $1.70–$3. No credit cards. Daily 10am–8pm. COFFEE/SNACKS.

Take a break from touring, and enjoy a coffee here—it's served up six ways hot and three ways cold (also available by the kilo, in whole-bean or ground form). Light snacks include sandwiches, croissants, pies, and wonderful cookies from the village of Xico. It's 2½ blocks east of the Baluarte Santiago.

✪ **Gran Café de la Parroquia.** Av. Insurgentes s/n. No phone. Breakfast $2–$4; coffee $1–$1.50; main courses $3–$8. No credit cards. Daily 7am–1am. MEXICAN/COFFEE.

A trip to Veracruz without coffee at La Parroquia would be a crime, like going to New Orleans and not eating beignets. In 1994, the original La Parroquia moved from its longtime location opposite the Plaza de Armas to its current spot; nearly next door is a second branch facing the harbor 2 blocks before the Hotel Emporio. Bright and always busy, hopping with music (usually marimba) at almost any hour, this restaurant has customers who virtually own particular tables at the same time every day. Novice Parroquia patrons catch onto the ritual quickly. Two waiters scurry about with big aluminum kettles, one with thick black coffee and the other with hot milk. Order the rich *café lechera,* and you'll get a few fingers of coffee in the bottom of your glass. Then pick up your spoon and bang on the glass to call the waiter with the milk; La Parroquia is filled with the constant chime of banging spoons. Though the cafe is known for its coffee and pastries, main courses are also quite good—the menu is virtually unchanged for 20 years.

2 Exploring North of Veracruz: Ruins & a Great Museum

THE RUINS OF ZEMPOALA

On Highway 180, about 14 miles north of Veracruz, is the village of Antigua, on the river of the same name. It's not very well known today, but for 75 years, beginning in 1525, it was a seat of Spanish power. The village is known locally for its seafood restaurants and is especially festive on weekends.

About 25 miles north of Veracruz, past Antigua on the way to Jalapa, are the ruins at **Zempoala** (or Cempoala), surrounded by lush foliage and rich agricultural land. Though not as large as the site of El Tajín, they're still noteworthy.

Zempoala is a pre-Columbian ruin of the Totonacs. It flourished along with El Tajín during the Classic period (A.D. 300 to 900). Although Tajín was abandoned in the 13th century, Zempoala continued to thrive and was the capital of the Totonacs at the time of the Spanish Conquest. Zempoala means "place of the 20 waters," thus named for the many rivers that converged at the site. When the conquerors saw Zempoala for the first time, the whitewashed stucco walls glimmered like silver in the tropical sun, which of course brought Spaniards running. Though disappointed, the Spaniards still made friends, and this city of Totonac Indians became Cortés's first major ally. The Spaniards spent considerable time here, learning about the Totonacs' hatred of the Aztecs and about the Aztec Emperor Moctezuma, before heading overland to the Aztec capital of Tenochtitlán.

Most buildings at Zempoala date from the 14th and 15th centuries—quite late for pre-Columbian structures. Yet the town was in existence at least 1,500 years earlier. The Great Temple resembles the Temple of the Sun in Tenochtitlán, probably a result of Aztec influence during the 15th century. The Temple of the Little Faces is decorated with stuccoed faces in the walls and hieroglyphs painted on the lower sections. The Temple of Quetzalcoatl, the feathered serpent god, is square, and the Temple of Ehecatl, god of the wind, is, as usual, round.

Admission to the archaeological site is $2.50; it's open daily from 9am to 6pm. A permit to use your video camera costs $4. If you're going by car, driving time is 40 minutes north on Highway 180 through Cardel; the ruins of Zempoala are just north of Cardel. **Transportes Regionales Veracruzianas** (TRV) buses run hourly from Veracruz, taking riders on a gorgeous 1½-hour journey through tropical forests.

JALAPA: PEPPERS & SANTA ANNA

Capital of the state of Veracruz, Jalapa (65 miles northwest of Veracruz; pronounced ha-*lap*-a and spelled "Xalapa" by locals) is an interesting town to explore for a day or more. Although modern, the city is riddled with old, narrow, and winding streets. In addition to being the jalapeño-pepper capital of Mexico, Jalapa is the hometown of Antonio López de Santa Anna, whose various terms as president of Mexico spanned 22 years; his hacienda is now a museum southeast of town.

Earlier in the city's history, Cortés and his troops passed through nearby Xico on their way from the Gulf Coast to the Aztec capital of Tenochtitlán for the first time. Chroniclers of the Conquest described the hazards of the trip and particularly noted the onomatopoeic chipi chipi rain, a fine but pelting component of Jalapa life. Coffee plantations surround the city for miles around, so take time out for a cup of the excellent local java.

ESSENTIALS

GETTING THERE Veracruz, two hours south of Jalapa, has the closest major airport, although some charter flights use the small Jalapa airport. If you're driving from Veracruz, take Highway 180 to Cardel and then turn left (west) onto Highway 140 past the coffee plantations. From Mexico City, Puebla, Tlaxcala, or Papantla, dense fog is common and dangerous between Perote and Jalapa. On a clear day this drive might call to mind Switzerland, with spotted cows grazing on verdant hillside pastures. If you're coming from or going to the north, the trip by bus to or from Papantla takes either 4 or 6 hours depending on route.

The **bus station,** Caxa, is about 1½ miles east of the town center just off Calle 20 de Noviembre. Taxis are downstairs, and prices here are controlled. Tickets to the center of town cost around $1.75.

VISITOR INFORMATION The **State Tourism Office** is on the first floor of Bulevar Cristóbal Colón no. 5 Fracc. Jardines de las Ánimas. (☎ **28/12-8500,** ext. 130). Little English is spoken, but they have maps and literature. Hours are Monday through Friday from 8:30am to 9pm and Saturday from 9am to 1pm.

Jalapa Orientation

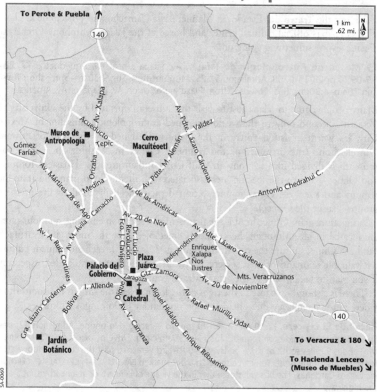

To Perote & Puebla

140

To Perote & Puebla
Av. Xalapa
Acueducto
Tepic
Museo de Antropología
Gómez Farías
Cerro Macuitéoetl
Av. Pdte. Lázaro Cárdenas
Valdez
Antonio Chedrahui C.
Av. Pdte. M. Alemán
Av. Mártires 28 de Ago
Orizaba
Medina
Av. M. Ávila Camacho
Av. de las Américas
Av. 20 de Nov
Dr. Lucio
Revolución
Fco. J. Clavijero
Independencia
Av. Pdte. Lázaro Cárdenas
Av. A. Ruiz Cortines
Plaza Juárez
Enríquez
Xalapa
Nos
Ilustres
Mts. Veracruzanos
Palacio del Gobierno
Gra. Lázaro Cárdenas
Bolívar
Zaragoza
Glz. Zamora
Av. 20 de Noviembre
I. Allende
Diebe
Catedral
Miguel Hidalgo
Av. Rafael Murillo Vidal
140
Jardín Botánico
Av. V. Carranza
Enrique Rébsamen
To Veracruz & 180
To Hacienda Lencero (Museo de Muebles)

0   1 km
     .62 mi.

SA-0060

CITY LAYOUT   Jalapa is a hilly town with streets seemingly resistant to any order. The center of town is the beautiful **Plaza Juárez,** where on a clear day the Pico de Orizaba is visible to the southwest. Facing and across the street (north) from the plaza is the Palacio Municipal (city hall), while just east is the Palacio del Gobierno (state offices). Across (north) from this is the cathedral. A tunnel runs under the park and connects Avenidas Zaragoza and Ávila Camacho, two of the main arteries that traverse the city, randomly changing both name and direction in the process.

GETTING AROUND   The recommended hotels and restaurants (see "Where to Stay" and "Where to Dine," below) are within easy walking distance of the central Plaza Juárez. Taxis in Jalapa are inexpensive, as are city buses.

FAST FACTS   The telephone **area code** is 28. The **climate** is humid and warm in summer and humid and chilly in winter. Year-round, be prepared for the light chipi chipi rain that comes and goes.

EXPLORING JALAPA

Artist José Chávez Morado painted a series of murals in the **Palacio de Gobierno** that are well worth seeing, as is the massive **cathedral,** with its disconcerting floor that inclines toward the altar. Walk through the streets and admire the blossoming bougainvillea, fruit trees, and flowers. Halfway between the mountains and the tropics, Jalapa has both coffee plantations and sultry breezes.

The **Agora,** a hangout for artists, students, and other urbane types, is just off the main park. This is the place to go for records, films, conversation, and concerts. Then check out the **Teatro del Estado,** at Manuel Ávila Camacho and Ignacio de la Llave. This is Jalapa's official cultural center and home of the Jalapa Symphony Orchestra. There's always something going on.

✪ **Museo de Antropología de Jalapa.** Av. Jalapa s/n at Av. Aqueducto. ☎ **28/ 15-0920** or 28/15-0708. Admission $1.25. Museum Tues–Sun 9:30am–5pm; shop Tues–Sun 10am–4:30pm. Bus: "Museo" from Plaza Juárez or on Av. Jalapa or Av. Américas.

Many people come to Jalapa just to visit this museum operated by the University of Veracruz. Second only to the world-renowned anthropological museum in Mexico City, it's worth a visit if you're in the vicinity. Designed by the firm of Edward Durrell Stone (the architect of the Kennedy Center in Washington, D.C.), the museum is divided into sections on Gulf Coast Indian groups—Huastec, Totonac, and Olmec—and to the specific sites associated with them. Good maps illustrate the regions and sites. An ethnographic section depicts the daily modern life of these groups (except the Olmec).

A signature giant Olmec head is the first item you see upon entering, and four more are located inside. Although the gigantic Olmec pieces are the most visible artifacts (and the Olmec culture the oldest, dating from 1500 B.C.), each subsequent culture left valuable remnants of their society. A visit here is highly recommended, especially if you plan to take in any of the actual sites in your travels.

There is a shop/bookstore to the right of the lobby. Near the shop is the auditorium where music recitals are often held at noon on Sunday ("Domingos Culturales").

Hacienda El Lencero. Km 9 on Hwy. 140 toward Veracruz. No phone. Admission $2; free Spanish-speaking guides on request. Tues–Sun 10am–5pm. Drive or take a taxi ($10 round-trip) about 9 miles south of town on Hwy. 140 toward Veracruz, past the country club; watch for the signs on the right. You can also catch a bus marked BANDERILLA–P. CRYSTAL–LENCERO on Av. Lázaro Cárdenas. The bus will stop either in the village of Lencero or at a nearby spot along the highway.

Known today as the Hacienda El Lencero, and occasionally the Museo de Muebles (Furniture Museum), this fabulous country estate 9 miles southeast of the town center was for 14 years (1842–56) the home of Antonio López de Santa Anna, the 11-time president of Mexico. Here he retreated from the world, though on occasion he opened his doors to receive notable visitors. Purchased by the state of Veracruz in 1981, the hacienda is one of the best museums of its kind in the country.

Rooms in the sprawling mansion are filled with furniture from Mexico, Europe, and Asia, illustrating the elegance found in Mexico during the 19th century. Among the notable pieces is the leader's bed, embellished with the national emblem of an eagle holding a snake in its beak. The carefully tended grounds are awash with flowers and shaded by ancient trees. Next to the grand house, the spacious servants' quarters, with a lovely, wide, covered patio facing a lake fed by a natural spring, have been converted into a restaurant that serves light snacks, pastries, and soft drinks.

SHOPPING

The **Casa de Artesanías** is now being used as a cultural center, so its emphasis has shifted from shopping for tourists to classes and concerts for locals. At **Paseo de la Laguna** (☎ **28/17-0804**), the quantity and quality of crafts varies, but you can usually pick up packaged Veracruz coffee, cans of jalapeño peppers, baskets from Papantla, and pottery from San Miguel Aguasuelos—all local products. It opens Monday through Friday from 9am to 1pm and 4 to 7pm and on Saturday from 9am to 3pm. It's on calle Dique, off Zaragoza, 6 blocks south of Plaza Juárez and near a lakeside park.

A good place to pick up something for yourself or a gift typical of the region is **Café Colón,** downtown at Primo Verdad 15. The staff roasts, grinds, and packages coffee here, and it's available for purchase ground or *en grano* (whole bean) by the kilo or partial kilo. Walk 2 blocks east from the Parque Juárez on Zaragoza, then north half a block on Primo Verdad. Café Colón is on the right.

WHERE TO STAY

✪ Mesón del Alférez. Sebastián Camacho 2, 91000 Jalapa, Ver. ☎ **28/18-6351.** Fax 28/12-4703. 20 units. TV TEL. $32.50 double; $52.50 suite. Rates include breakfast. AE, DC, MC, V. Free secured parking nearby.

The owners of the Posada del Cafeto (see below) also operate this wonderful hotel in the 1808 home of the former Spanish viceroy's representative. Rooms, named after historic Jalapa streets, are colonial in style, accented by bright colors and stone. Some rooms feature a cozy loft bedroom overlooking a living room. The dining room, Hostería La Candela, is located in what once was the private chapel, and is open from 7:30am to 10pm. To find the Mesón from the plaza, go 1 block east on Zaragoza to the corner of Sabastián Camacho; it's close to the Hotel Monroy. The entrance is actually on Zaragoza.

✪ Posada del Cafeto. Canovas 8 and 12, 91000 Jalapa, Ver. ☎ **28/17-0023.** Fax 28/12-0403. 29 units. TEL. $15–$28 double. AE, DC, MC, V. Free secured parking nearby.

A treat of a place for the serious coffee lover. This colorful and comfortable townhouse-turned-hotel opened in 1987 and was named for the coffee industry in the region; not surprisingly, coffee is amply available morning and evening. Room decor is brightly styled Mexican, with colorful bedspreads, royal-blue metal doors and window frames, white walls with painted flower designs, and Mexican-tile accents. Windows allow plenty of light (but also some cold in winter). Each room is slightly different: Some are small, but all come with two single beds, two doubles, or one of each. A small restaurant, open daily from 7am to 1pm and 5 to 10pm, serves coffee, pastries, fruit, and yogurt. From the Plaza Juárez, walk 4 blocks east on Zaragoza, then 1 block south where it bends. Canovas is the first street on your right, and the Posada is farther down on the right.

WHERE TO DINE

Almost every block in the downtown area is filled with a variety of restaurants. Callejón del Diamante is a narrow pedestrian street, 1½ blocks from Plaza Juárez, with half a dozen restaurants, **La Fonda** and **La Sopa El Mayab** among them. Prices are reasonable and most are open Monday through Saturday from 8am to 10pm. To find them, turn your back to the cathedral and walk left on Enríquez across Lucio 1 block; the Callejón will be on the left.

Restaurant la Casona del Beaterio. Zaragoza 20. ☎ **28/18-2119.** Breakfast $2–$5; main courses $2.50–$7; comida corrida $3.50. AE, MC, V. Mon 8am–11pm; Tues–Sat 8am–midnight; Sun 8:30am–10pm. MEXICAN.

This agreeable place near the zócalo offers good food and service and charming atmosphere. Tables and chairs are plain, but there are high-beamed ceilings, plants, and photos of old Jalapa on the walls. The menu lists a variety of chicken dishes, such as *pechuga maguey* (chicken breast in rich liquor). You can find La Casona on Zaragoza, 2 blocks east from Parque Juárez on the south side of the street; it's at the end of a row of restaurants. Live music Thursday through Sunday begins at 9pm.

Salon Don Quijote. Lucio 4. ☎ **28/17-3365.** Breakfast $2.50–$3.50; main courses $3–$6; comida corrida $3.50; paella (Sun only) $6. No credit cards. Daily 7am–10pm (comida corrida served 1–5:30pm). MEXICAN.

For years this restaurant, far back in the parking lot of the Hotel Mexico, has been serving the best comida corrida (fixed price, multicourse meal) downtown. It's half a block east of Plaza Juárez, facing the left side of the cathedral, notable for its stained-glass windows.

PAPANTLA & THE RUINS OF EL TAJÍN

The best reasons to visit **Papantla,** a city of 159,000, 140 miles northwest of Veracruz, are its proximity to the impressive ruins of **El Tajín** (el-ta-*heen*), the frequent shows of *voladores* (Indian dancers performing a ritualistic pole ceremony, signifying flight), and **festivities** held in the city around Corpus Christi Day. El Tajín ranks as one of Mexico's most important and mysterious archaeological sites. Vast excavation in recent years has uncovered unusual buildings, revealing still more of the site's rich history.

Papantla is the former vanilla capital of the world. Displayed at both entrances to the city is a large concrete vanilla bean with inscribed hieroglyphs, the symbol of the community and a representation of the hybrid nature of its history. Vanilla extract can be purchased here for about half of what it costs in the States. The long, slender, almost-black vanilla beans are also for sale, which you'll see fashioned into figures, flowers, or a dozen different designs.

ESSENTIALS

GETTING THERE **By Car** If you're driving from the south, Papantla is a 4- to 5-hour mountainous drive (subject to fog delays) from Jalapa, via Misantla, Martínez de la Torre, and finally Highway 180 on the coast. From Veracruz, Papantla is about 5 hours away along Highway 180.

By Bus There are two bus stations in Papantla. The **first-class station** (☎ 784/ 2-0218) is at the corner of Venustiano Carranza and Benito Juárez.

CITY LAYOUT Coming into town, you'll most likely arrive at the bottom of the hill. The landmark cathedral and blue facade of the Hotel El Tajín are at the top of the hill, and mark the center of town. In front of the cathedral is a shady zócalo (main square) that's bordered by hotels, markets, and restaurants.

GETTING AROUND Taxis are available around the central plaza, and city buses go to the ruins of El Tajín (see below). Almost everything worth seeing is within easy walking distance of the central plaza.

FAST FACTS The telephone **area code** is 784. The **climate** is sultry and rainy in summer, cold and rainy in winter; hotels are unheated.

SPECIAL EVENTS The **Feast of Corpus Christi,** the 9th Sunday after Easter, is part of a very special week in Papantla. Well-known Mexican entertainers perform, and the native voladores (see "The Ruins of El Tajín," below) make special appearances. Lodging is scarce during this week, so be sure to book ahead.

EXPLORING PAPANTLA & EL TAJÍN

In Papantla, the ceramic-tiled and shady zócalo is where couples and families sit while squirrels scavenge for food. The cathedral wall facing the square is covered with an artist's rendering in concrete of El Tajín (**a miniature, 3-D model of the archaeological site**). On top of a hill overlooking the city is an enormous statue of a *volador* (flying pole dancer).

THE RUINS OF EL TAJÍN Papantla's major attraction is the nearby ruins of El Tajín, a place of archaeological fascination. Of the 150 buildings identified at the site, 20 have been excavated and conserved, resurrecting their forms from what were grass-covered mounds. At least 17 ball courts have been found, though only five are visible.

Mural fragments led archaeologists to a Teotihuacán-influenced mural at the top of Building 11, which has since been restored.

The ruins at Tajín are divided into old (**Tajín Viejo**) and new sections (**Tajín Chico**). The most impressive structure, found in the old section, is the **Pyramid of the Niches,** one of the most unusual pre-Columbian structures in Mesoamerica. The unique stone-and-adobe pyramid has 365 recesses extending to all four sides of the building. The pyramid was formerly covered in red-painted stucco, the niches painted black. A similar but less dramatic structure exists near Cuetzalan, Puebla. Near the Pyramid of the Niches is a restored **ball court** with beautiful carved reliefs on the vertical playing sides depicting religious scenes and sacrifices.

Look for the **Temple of the Columns** in the new section. A stairway divides the columns, three on either side, each decorated with reliefs of priests and warriors and hieroglyphic dates. Many mounds are still unexcavated, but with the reconstruction that has been done so far, it's increasingly easier to visualize the ruins as a city. The view from atop one of the pyramids, overlooking the rich, green forests that are dotted with mounds and excavated buildings, is indeed impressive.

At the ruins, witnessing the *voladores* (fliers) is a memorable sight, and a traditional, solemn ceremony that dates back centuries. Local Totonac Indians perform this unusual ritual in honor of the four poles of the earth. They appear to be flying upside-down, circling a tall pole in a clearing near the museum. There's no set schedule for performances; the sounds of a slow-beating drum and flute signals that the voladores are preparing to perform. Five flyers, dressed in brightly colored ceremonial garments that include cone-shaped hats with ribbons and small round mirrors, climb the 90-foot pole to the top, where there is a square revolving platform. While four dancers perch on the four sides of the platform and attach themselves by the waist to a rope, the fifth stands and plays an instrument called a *chirimía,* used in rituals by the Toltecs and Olmecs. It consists of a small bamboo flute with a deerskin drum attached to it. The performer plays the three-holed flute with his left hand and beats the drum with his right hand.

When the time is right, the four fall backwards, suspended by the rope, and revolve 13 times before reaching the ground. The number 13 is neither arbitrary nor unlucky; it corresponds to the number of months in the Aztec calendar.

A small but impressive **museum** greets you as you approach the esplanade. Across from the museum is a small snack/gift shop, as well as a small restaurant. In a semi-circle facing the volador pole are several more gift shops. Admission to the site and museum is $2; it is free to all on Sunday. The fee for a personal video camera is $4. Use of a tripod oddly requires a permit from the **Instituto Nacional de Antropología e Historia (INAH)** in Mexico City. If you watch a performance of the voladores, one of them will collect an additional $2 from each spectator. The site is open daily from 9am to 5pm; the voladores soar Friday to Sunday at 11am and 4pm, although any time a tour bus arrives they are likely to perform.

To get to El Tajín from Papantla, look for buses marked CHOTE/TAJÍN, which run to El Tajín from beside the Juárez market (opposite the front of the church, at the corner of Reforma and 20 de Noviembre) regularly beginning at 7am. As an alternative, buses marked CHOTE pass more frequently and will leave you at the Chote crossroads; from there, wait for a bus for the short distance to El Tajín or take a taxi from there for around $5. From Veracruz, take Highway 180 to Papantla; from there, take Route 127, which is a back road to Poza Rica, going through Tajín.

SHOPPING   There are two principal markets in Papantla, both near the central plaza. **Mercado Juárez** is opposite the front door of the church. **Mercado Hidalgo** is a block or two down Reforma on the left, away from the plaza. The latter has a better selection of locally made baskets and regional clothing. In addition to vanilla, **Xanath,** a popular local liqueur, makes a good gift and costs around $13; another, **Vreez,** costs $11.

WHERE TO STAY

Hotel Premier. Enríquez 103, 93400 Papantla, Ver. ☎ **784/2-2700** or 784/2-1645. 20 units. A/C TV TEL. $30 double. MC, V. Free secured parking half a block away.

Opened in 1990, the Premier is a fine exception among Papantla's otherwise meager selection of hotels. Rooms are nicely furnished, with tile floors, bathrooms with showers, and some have small balconies overlooking the zócalo. Others toward the back are windowless and quiet and are reached through a tunnel-like hallway.

Tajín Hotel. Nuñez 104, 93400 Papantla, Ver. ☎ **784/2-0121,** 784/2-1623, or 784/ 2-0644. Fax 784/2-1062. 60 units. TV TEL. $20–$36 double. MC, V. Free secured parking half a block away.

Walk along the cathedral wall up the hill to the landmark El Tajín Hotel, the building with the bright-blue facade near the top. The rooms here are small and tidy and have either air-conditioning or a fan; some have king-size beds. The Restaurant Tajín in the hotel is clean and inexpensive (but the coffee is lamentable).

WHERE TO DINE

Mercado Juárez has numerous cookshops offering the delicious local specialty, *zacahuil* (a huge tamale cooked in a banana leaf), in the morning. Look around until you see a cook with a line of patrons—that's where you'll get the best zacahuil. Outside the market, rolling cart vendors sell steamy hot *atole,* a thick, sweet corn meal–based beverage with various flavorings.

Besides zacahuil, be sure to try delicious *molotes,* small football-shaped creations of fried dough that are served as appetizers.

Plaza Pardo. Enríquez 105-altos. ☎ **784/2-0059.** Breakfast $2–$4; sandwiches $2–$3; main courses $2.75–$5. No credit cards. Daily 7:30am–10:30pm.

This cheerful place, located across from the main plaza, is an old-fashioned ice-cream parlor with added dining service. Try the coconut (coco) or pecan (nuez) ice cream; the strawberry malts (malteadas de fresa) are exceptionally fresh and frothy. Full meals are available here morning to night.

If you love the Grand Canyon but aren't so thrilled about all the crowds; if you're interested in taking a train ride through remote, rugged lands; if you want see a wealth of diverse flora and fauna; or if you're curious about a land still populated by the indigenous people living pretty much the way they have for centuries, the Copper Canyon is the place to go. The *Barranca del Cobre* is not one canyon, but a network of canyons carved into the volcanic rock of the Sierra Tarahumara, a section of the Sierra Madre Occidental.

Hugging the rim of these canyons is the famed *Chihuahua al Pacífico* (Chihuahua to the Pacific) railway. Acclaimed as an engineering marvel, the 390-mile-long railroad has 39 bridges (the highest is more than 1,000 ft. above the Chinipas River; the longest is a third of a mile in length) and 86 tunnels (one over a mile long). It climbs from Los Mochis, at sea level, up to 8,000 feet through some of Mexico's most magnificent scenery—thick pine forests, jagged peaks, and shadowy canyons—before descending again to it's destination, the city of Chihuahua.

EXPLORING THE COPPER CANYON   Peak season for travel to the canyon is March through April and October through November. These months can be very crowded at the canyons. If you want to go in the off-season, try July or August. This is the rainy season, and, barring drought, you will see afternoon thunder showers (very pretty in the canyon land), vegetation will be green, water will be flowing, and temperatures will be comfortable up in the canyon rim, but hot down in the canyons. Early December or late February might be okay, but cold. May, June, and September are very hot and dry; January is the coldest month.

The Copper Canyon at peak season is not the place to do casual, unplanned, follow-your-nose kind of traveling unless you don't mind spending a night on someone's floor. At some of the stops, the number of hotel rooms is limited, and a hotel that is empty one day may be suddenly and completely packed by a tour the next. Overbooking is also a problem some travelers to the canyon have encountered.

With perseverance, however, it's possible to **plan your own trip,** choose train stops and hotels, obtain train tickets or buy them upon arrival in Los Mochis or Chihuahua (see "Buying a Ticket," below), and make your own hotel reservations. You could also travel in the off-season without hotel reservations and wing it. If you intend to purchase your own train ticket, avoid peak travel times and try to buy your ticket a day or two in advance, as the train may be booked to capacity. As a base for canyon travel, Creel (see "Stop 5: Creel," below), which has the most budget-priced hotels and affords some of the best side trips, is the most economical choice, and you don't have to have a train ticket to get there. Going through a **travel agent** who specializes in the Copper Canyon can remove a lot of the uncertainty and preparatory work for your trip (see "Travel Agents" in section 2, below).

Generally speaking, **Los Mochis,** the western terminus, is the preferred starting place for this trip: The most scenic part of the 12- to 15-hour journey comes between El Fuerte and Creel, and the chances of seeing it in good daylight are best if the trip begins in Los Mochis. If the train in the other direction, from Chihuahua to Los Mochis, runs on schedule (which it often doesn't), you'd also get daylight during the best part of the trip. Chihuahua is the more interesting of the two cities, but if you don't want to chance it, start in Los Mochis or El Fuerte. Recently, the ownership of the railroad entered private hands, and there is a small degree of uncertainty as to how this may change matters.

Making stops along the train trip to stay at lodges en route is a full-fledged adventure. Accommodations are comfortable but rustic; most don't have electricity (only lanterns), and only in Creel and El Fuerte are telephones to be found. Rooms have wood-burning stoves for heat in winter, and most, except where noted, have private bathrooms.

Be sure to start the journey with adequate funds, since *exchanging money outside of Creel is almost impossible;* even credit cards are only good at the expensive hotels. (I won't use a credit card at some of the hotels listed in this chapter because they use radio communication to the main office to confirm a card—hardly a closed system.) You could pass through the Copper Canyon in one long 15-hour day, spending a night in Chihuahua and another in Los Mochis, but you'd miss the larger part of the canyon experience. I'd recommend at least one or two overnight stops along the way.

Even the 4-night, 5-day trips planned by tour companies can seem too brief to some people. These allow for flying into either Chihuahua or Los Mochis, with 1 night in each city at the beginning and end of a trip, and 2 nights in the canyon, usually at El Divisadero. I suggest, for those who have the time, that you begin and end your trip in Chihuahua (taking the train twice), skip Los Mochis, and spend 2 nights (and a full day) in El Fuerte instead. This allows for overnighting at the five stops en route, or some variation of that. A trip like this takes about 10 days, but you'd have broader experience of the canyon.

If you spend a night en route, you'll have roughly 24 hours at each destination—usually enough time for one or two excursions. While every stop holds interest, Creel and Cerocahui offer the most possibilities. **Creel,** a rustic lumber town, offers the only economical lodgings in the canyon, as well as great hiking, overnight camping, and van tours.

Drivers from all canyon hotels await trains; if you don't have a reservation, you can ask a driver about room availability. The hotels are quite small, however, and often filled by groups, so it's almost imperative to make reservations in advance, especially in peak season.

For those wishing to see the canyons in slightly more comfort than that offered by the standard first-class train, the **South Orient Express** operates a single car at the end of the regular Chihuahua al Pacífico first-class train. Each way is (usually) $198. (See "Buying a Ticket" in section 2, "The Copper Canyon Train," below.)

1 Los Mochis

126 miles SW of Alamos; 50 miles SW of El Fuerte; 193 miles SE of Guaymas; 260 miles NW of Mazatlán

Los Mochis, in Sinaloa State, is a low-lying city of 350,000 founded in 1893 by Benjamin Johnson of Pennsylvania. Today it is a wealthy city in a fertile agricultural area but, aside from the enormous sugar mill at the northwestern end of town, there's not much of note. The city's architecture looks like small-town America, and the city's singular importance to the tourist is as a boarding point for the Chihuahua al Pacífico train. From the port at Topolobampo Bay nearby, you can also take a ferry to La Paz, in Baja California.

ESSENTIALS

GETTING THERE & DEPARTING **By Plane** **Aeromexico/Aerolitoral** (☎ **800/237-6639** in the U.S., or 68/15-2570 for reservations) has direct service from Phoenix, Chihuahua, Hermosillo, Mazatlán, and La Paz. **Aero California** (☎ **800/237-6225** in the U.S., or 68/15-2250) flies to and from Los Angeles, La Paz, Guadalajara, Mexico City, Culiacán, and Tijuana.

Arriving: The airport is 13 miles north of town; transportation by collective minivan or airport taxis.

By Train The **Chihuahua al Pacífico** (Copper Canyon train) runs between Los Mochis and Chihuahua once daily. It leaves Los Mochis at 6am (mountain/Los Mochis time). From Chihuahua it leaves at 7am and arrives in Los Mochis around 7pm (first-class fare either way is $30). Complete Copper Canyon train information can be found in section 2 of this chapter. The train station is about 3 miles from town. Taxis are available at the train station.

By Car **Coastal Highway 15** is well maintained in both directions leading into Los Mochis.

By Ferry The **SEMATUR ferry** from La Paz, Baja California Sur, to nearby Topolobampo leaves La Paz Monday through Saturday at 11am and arrives in Los Mochis at 7pm.

From Topolobampo the *SEMATUR* ferry to La Paz, Baja California Sur, leaves Monday through Saturday at 10pm and arrives in La Paz at 8am. Service ranges from seat only (Mon through Sat) to Cabina Especial (special cabin; Wed and Thurs only). For tickets and information, contact *SEMATUR* at the ferry pier in Topolobampo (☎ **68/62-0141;** fax 68/62-0035), or better yet call **Viajes Paotam** (☎ **68/15-1914** or 68/15-8262) in Los Mochis. Reservations are highly recommended, due both to the ferry's popularity and possible schedule changes. The vessel has restaurant and medical facilities, video movies, and a disco. It's 13 miles from the ferry to downtown Los Mochis.

Caution: Don't Be a Dope

It's no secret that clandestine farmlands in the Copper Canyon are used by marijuana farmers and that prominent names in the state are rumored to be linked to their activities. This has never affected any of my trips to the region. If you are hiking the backwoods and you happen upon a field of marijuana, simply leave the area.

If you arrive by ferry in Topolobampo, you'll have to bargain with waiting taxis for the fare to Los Mochis.

By Bus   Los Mochis is, however marginally, served by buses. Most are *de paso*—passing through. The first-class station is near Juárez at Degollado 200. From here, **Elite** buses go to and from Tijuana, Monterrey, Nogales, and Ciudad Juárez. **Auto-transportes Transpacíficos** (same station) serves Nogales, Tijuana, Mazatlán, Guadalajara, Querétaro, and Mexico City. A lot of travelers who arrive in Los Mochis prefer to go directly to El Fuerte, spend the night there, and then catch the train. There are two places to catch the bus to El Fuerte (1½ to 2 hr.). The first is at the **Mercado Independencia,** where the bus stops at the corner of Independencia and Degollado. The other is at the corner of Cuauhtémoc at Prieto, close to the Hotel America. Ask hotel desk clerks or the tourism office for a schedule. Buses, which run frequently throughout the day, are the school-bus variety, and the purser stows luggage in the back of the bus. Were it not for the numerous stops en route, the trip would take only an hour, as does a taxi to or from El Fuerte.

All bus stations are downtown within walking distance of the hotels.

VISITOR INFORMATION   The **City Tourist Office** is in a back corner of the State Government building at Cuauhtémoc and Allende (☎ **68/12-6640**) and has a helpful staff. The office is open Monday through Friday from 8am to 3pm.

CITY LAYOUT   Los Mochis contains no central plaza, and streets run northwest to southeast and southwest to northeast. To acquaint yourself with this city, use the **Hotel Santa Anita** (avenida Leyva at avenida Obregón) as an orientation point. The bus stations, hotels, and restaurants are within a few blocks of here.

Plaza Fiesta Las Palmas, at the corner of Obregón and Rosales, is the shopping mall and the main spot where people of all ages gather—an interesting slice of Mexican life. **Ley,** a large store, sells everything from groceries to clothes to TVs. Hotels, restaurants, and the Plaza Fiesta Las Palmas are all within walking distance of downtown.

FAST FACTS: LOS MOCHIS

American Express   The local representative is **Viajes Araceli,** avenida Álvaro Obregón 471-A Pte. (☎ **68/15-5780;** fax 68/15-8787).

Area Code   The telephone area code is **68.**

Currency Exchange   Changing money outside of Los Mochis is difficult, so stock up on pesos before boarding the train. Credit cards aren't accepted in most places in the canyons.

Time   The entire railroad operates on central time, even though Los Mochis is in the mountain time zone.

EXPLORING LOS MOCHIS

For most travelers, Los Mochis is a stopover en route to somewhere else. There isn't much of importance here, but the town is pleasant, and you can enjoy some of the best seafood in Mexico.

A city tour, hunting and fishing trips, and boat rides around **Topolobampo Bay** can be arranged through the **Viajes Flamingo** travel agency, on the ground floor of the Hotel Santa Anita (☎ **68/12-1613** or 68/12-1929); it's open Monday through Saturday from 8:30am to 1pm and 3 to 6:30pm. The boat ride is really just a spin in the bay and not especially noteworthy, although the bay is pretty and dolphins have been known to surface.

Topolobampo also has a nice **beach,** though the town itself isn't much. To get to Topolobampo, catch the bus at the corner of Obregón and Degollado, across from the Hotel Catalina.

WHERE TO STAY

Hotel América. Allende 655 Sur, 81200 Los Mochis, Sin. 81200. ☎ **68/12-1355** or 68/
12-1356. Fax 68/12-5983. 48 units. A/C TV TEL. $26 double. MC, V. Free enclosed parking.

The clean marble-floored lobby is an indication of how well this hotel is maintained.
The freshly painted rooms have tile floors and large windows facing the street. Rooms
away from the Allende side escape the noise of early-morning, muffler-challenged local
buses. On the second floor there's a sitting area, purified water, and an ice-making
machine. To get here from the Hotel Santa Anita, turn right out the front door. Turn
left on Obregón, continue 3 blocks and go right on Allende for 2 blocks; the hotel is
just past Cuauhtémoc, on your left.

✪ **Hotel Corintios.** Obregón 580 Pte., 81200 Los Mochis, Sin. ☎ **01-800-690-3000**
in Mexico, or 68/18-2300. Fax 68/18-2277. 42 units. A/C TV TEL. $52 double. Rates
include continental breakfast. AE, MC, V. Free parking.

Behind a campy Greek-columned entrance are two stories of rooms, which have ample
light, are carpeted, and adequate in size for two comfortable double beds and luggage.
The bathrooms have marble tub-showers, large towels, and purified water from the
tap. A complimentary continental breakfast is served in the small restaurant (open
from 7am to 10pm). For those catching the train to Chihuahua, fruit, juice, and coffee
are available before you catch your cab at 5:15am.

Hotel Santa Anita. Leyva at the corner of Hidalgo (Apdo. Postal 159), 81200 Los Mochis,
Sin. ☎ **800-896-8196** from the U.S. phone/fax 68/18-7046. 133 units. A/C TV TEL.
$100 double. AE, MC, V. Free parking.

The Santa Anita is completely remodeled and well kept. The rooms are nicely furnished, although some are small. All are carpeted and have comfortable beds, color
TVs with U.S. channels, and tap water purified for drinking. The hotel's excellent and
popular restaurant is just off the lobby. There are two bars, one with live music at least
1 day a week. Another special feature: Every morning at 5:20 a private hotel bus takes
guests to the *Chihuahua al Pacífico* train, which departs daily at 6am. That saves you
the $7 taxi ride. The hotel also provides pickup at the train station for guests, for a
small fee. The lobby travel agency, **Viajes Flamingo** (☎ **68/12-1613** or 68/12-1929),
is about the best in town; you can buy your train tickets here and find out about all
the other tourist activities in the area.

WHERE TO DINE

Besides the restaurants described below, the Hotel Santa Anita, mentioned above, has
a popular restaurant.

✪ **El Farallon.** Obregón corner with Ángel Flores. ☎ **68/12-1428.** Main courses $4.75–$9.
AE, MC, V. Daily 8am–midnight. SEAFOOD.

Locals consider El Farallon the best seafood restaurant in downtown. Go ahead and
splurge on giant shrimp in garlic and oil; you won't be disappointed. Or try the tender
fillets of fresh snapper, dorado, or halibut. And in the morning, although you could
order a conventional breakfast, most folks wouldn't dream of passing up the seafood.
To get here from the Santa Anita, turn right on Leyva and right again for 1 block on
Obregón. It's on your left at the corner of Obregón and Flores.

El Taquito. Leyva at Barrera. ☎ **68/12-8119.** Breakfast $2–$3.50; main courses $3–$6.
AE, DC, MC, V. Daily 24 hours. MEXICAN.

Any time of the day or night, El Taquito has its share of locals enjoying some of the
best food in town or lingering over cups of coffee. With orange booths and Formica
tables, the cafe looks like an American fast-food place. The tortilla soup comes in a

large bowl, and both breakfast and main-course portions are quite generous. From the Hotel Santa Anita, turn left on Leyva, cross Hidalgo and go 1 block. It's on your right.

Restaurante España. Obregón 525 Pte. ☎ **68/12-2221.** Breakfast $4–$6; main courses $7–$10. No credit cards. Daily 7am–11pm. STEAK/SEAFOOD.

This Spanish-style restaurant is a favorite among downtown professionals, who devour huge bowls of paella at noon on Thursday and Sunday. The decor is upscale for Los Mochis, with a splashing cascade fountain in the dining room and heavy, carved-wood tables and chairs. From the Hotel Santa Anita, turn right out the front door to Obregón, then right on Obregón for 1½ blocks. The restaurant is on your right.

2 The Copper Canyon Train

The name of the *Chihuahua al Pacífico* railway reflects the idea of linking arid, desert-like Chihuahua with the natural port of Topolobampo, a few miles west of Los Mochis. The American Albert Kinsey Owen, who invested in the railroad's building, envisioned it as the shortest route for goods from Kansas City to the Pacific.

The longest train stop where passengers can view the canyons is the 15-minute break at **El Divisadero**—barely enough time to dash to the canyon's edge for a look.

BUYING A TICKET   In Los Mochis, the railroad station (☎ **68/15-7775**) is about 3 miles from the center of town on avenida Onofre Serrano, a half mile past Bulevar Gaxiola. This is the station for the *Chihuahua al Pacífico* train, which runs between Los Mochis and Chihuahua simultaneously from both directions daily. The ticket window is supposed to stay open daily from 5am to 1pm, but it's best to go to the station early in the morning in case the window closes early. A one-way ticket in either direction in Primera Especial class costs $30, or double that if you want a round-trip ticket. There's a 10% extra charge for any stops you make en route.

There are three ways to get tickets. The first is from a local travel agency in Los Mochis or Creel. In Los Mochis I've had good luck using **Viajes Flamingo** at the Hotel Santa Anita. The second is at the train station a day ahead or on the day of travel. The third way, and the most reliable, is to go through a U.S. travel agency specializing in the Copper Canyon and selling air/train/hotel packages (not tickets alone). The least preferable option is to use a travel agent in Chihuahua; several agencies may end up selling the same seat, leaving unfortunate travelers to decide how to share it.

Travel Agents   A tour company specializing in the Copper Canyon area can save you many headaches. I highly recommend **Columbus Travel,** 900 Ridge Creek Lane, Bulverde, TX 78163-2872 (☎ **800/843-1060** or 830/885-2000; fax 830/885-2010).

Train Essentials

If you plan to stop off en route, you must tell the ticket agent at the time you purchase your ticket. You will have to plan in advance how long you will be staying at various stops. Once purchased, the ticket is good for those dates only and cannot be changed. A reserved seat is necessary, but your reserved seat number may be good only until your first stop; thereafter, when you reboard you'll have to take what's available. On one trip, conductors had my name on a list at each stop and had an assigned seat for me—but I wouldn't expect such efficiency every time. You can also buy a ticket for shorter distances along the way, enabling you to spend as much time as you like in any location; but if you're traveling during a peak season, it may mean you'll have to take your chances finding a seat when you reboard the train, or stand in any available space between cars, as many locals do.

Train Departure Times

From Los Mochis		From Chihuahua	
Los Mochis	6am (mountain time)	Chihuahua	7am
El Fuerte	7:25am	Creel	12:25pm
Bahuichivo/Cerocahui	12:15pm	El Divisadero	1:45pm
El Divisadero	1:30pm	Bahuichivo/Cerocahui	3:30pm
Creel	3:15pm	El Fuerte	6:15pm
Chihuahua (arrives)	8:50pm	Los Mochis (arrives)	7:50pm

Important note: The railroad runs on central time, although Los Mochis is on mountain time. This means that *if the train is scheduled to depart Los Mochis at 7am railway time, it pulls out at 6am local time.* Be aware of that when reading a printed schedule.

Another specialist in Copper Canyon travel is **The California Native,** 6701 W. 87th Place, Los Angeles, CA 90045 (☎ **800/926-1140** or 310/642-1140; fax 310/ 216-0400; www.calnative.com). Both organizations arrange group tours as well as individualized and special-interest trips in the Copper Canyon.

South Orient Express Car   The **South Orient Express,** 16800 Greenspoint Park Dr., Suite 245 North, Houston, TX 77060-2308 (☎ **800/659-7602** or 713/ 872-0190; fax 713/872-7123) provides a refurbished U.S. car at the back of the *Chihuahua al Pacífico* first-class train, at a premium price. If you are taking the South Orient Express car, you must purchase your ticket in advance—these tickets are not available at the train station.

WHAT TO PACK   While Los Mochis is warm year-round, Chihuahua can be blistering in summer, windy almost any time, and freezing or even snowy in winter. Both cities are wealthy, and people in Chihuahua in particular tend to dress up.

The canyon, of course, is blue-jeans and hiking-boot country, but pay special attention to the climate. From November through March it may snow; even in the bottom of the canyon, you may need a sweater. In the upper elevations, be prepared for freezing temperatures at night, even in spring and fall. Long johns and gloves are a must in winter. Sturdy shoes or hiking boots are essential anytime if you plan even minimal walking and hiking.

TRAVEL CONDITIONS   The first-class *Chihuahua al Pacífico* has adjustable cloth-covered seats, and it usually has air-conditioning in summer and heating in winter. There's no dining car, but sandwich plates and refreshments may be purchased from the porter. At many stops local food vendors come to you, selling an assortment of pies, tacos, empañadas, fruit, and soft drinks. Toilet paper and water may be in short supply; it's best to bring your own along with some favorite snacks.

The train stops frequently; the following are stops with hotels:

STOP 1: EL FUERTE

Though not yet in Copper Canyon proper, the train stops here first. El Fuerte, with cobblestone streets and handsome old colonial mansions, is a former silver-mining town about an hour and a half outside of Los Mochis. It's the prettiest town along the train route, well worth visiting for a night. The town has a beautiful plaza and bandstand, and historic houses around the square. I prefer to skip Los Mochis and start my train journey here. The train station is several miles from town. Taxis meet each train; join with others to get a group rate—otherwise the taxi charges per person.

EXPLORING THE TOWN   Here you're not yet in canyon country. The town is pretty and quaint; you can visit nearby villages, go bird watching, fish for black bass and trout, or hunt for duck and dove. Hotels can arrange guides and all equipment if notified in advance.

WHERE TO STAY & DINE   Besides the restaurants at the hotels mentioned here, there are inexpensive restaurants on or near the central plaza.

El Fuerte Lodge. Montesclaro 37, 81820 El Fuerte, Sin. ☎ **689/3-0226.** 21 units. A/C. $86 double. No credit cards.

Owner Robert Brand and his wife have taken one of the oldest homes in El Fuerte and turned it into a charming inn loaded with antiques and character. All 21 rooms have double or king beds, tiled bathrooms (with plenty of water pressure for great hot showers), and colonial furnishings that make you feel like you're staying in a museum. An excellent bilingual guide with knowledge of flora and fauna in the area leads trips to nearby villages. The hotel's restaurant menu includes plenty of dishes for those not yet accustomed to Mexican food, and is said to be the best in town. The gift shop/gallery has a wonderful display of paintings of the area and a great selection of Casas Grandes pottery. The hotel can prearrange motor transport from the Los Mochis airport for $98 one-way, getting you out into the country almost as soon as you land. Taxis from the El Fuerte bus or train stop will be awaiting reserved hotel patrons.

Hotel Posada Hidalgo. Hidalgo 101, 81820 El Fuerte, Sin. ☎ **800-896-8196** from the U.S., telephone/fax 689/3-0242, or 689/8-7046. (Reservations: the Hotel Santa Anita, Apdo. Postal 159, 81200 Los Mochis, Sin.) 54 units. A/C. $100 double. AE, MC, V.

This delightful hotel 4 blocks from the bus stop and 3 miles from the train station has two different parts. The mansion section, with open arcades around a central patio, belonged to silver grandees in the 18th century; there's even a steep carriage ramp from its days as a stagecoach stop. These rooms have high ceilings and hardwood floors, and they're less affected by the hotel's late-night, megadecibel disco. In the newer section, rooms are similarly decorated, each with two double beds; all open onto a shady court-yard with covered walkway. Meals at the hotel restaurant are expensive.

STOP 2: BAHUICHIVO & CEROCAHUI

This is the first train stop in canyon country. **Bahuichivo** consists mainly of the station and a few humble abodes. Your destination is the village of **Cerocahui** (elevation 5,550 ft.) in a valley about 6 miles from the train stop. Because of the rough, primitive road, the ride takes an hour before you can see the village, home to 600 people.

EXPLORING CEROCAHUI   Built around a mission church, Cerocahui consists of little more than rambling unpaved streets and a hundred or so houses. There is a wonderful view of the mountains, but you have to take an excursion to get real canyon vistas. In Cerocahui tourists are besieged by children vying to be their escorts to the waterfalls. Both hotels can arrange horseback rides to the falls and other lookout points and trips by truck to **Cerro Gallego,** a lookout high in the mountains around the town and worth the trip. It's possible to see the waterfall on arrival and schedule the Gallego trip for the next morning, have lunch, and still make the train. The **Urique** trip (see below) would require another day.

The **Paraíso del Oso** offers a trip to the mining town of Urique at the bottom of the Urique Canyon (one of several canyons that make up the Copper Canyon). You can go down and back in a day or schedule an overnight. The Urique day-trip costs $40 per person, minimum three people.

WHERE TO STAY & DINE   The Hotel Paraíso del Oso is about a mile short of the village. Another hotel, the Misión, is in Cerocahui.

Hotel Misión. Cerocahui. No phone. (Reservations: the Hotel Santa Anita, Apdo. Postal 159, 81200 Los Mochis, Sin.; ☎ **800-896-8196** from the U.S.) 34 units. $190 double. Rates include meals. AE, MC, V.

Established years ago in the village of Cerocahui, the Hotel Misión is the only lodging in town. Guest rooms have hot water, as well as electricity, until 11pm. The lobby/restaurant area surrounds a large rock fireplace where a local guitarist and singer sometimes entertains in the evenings. The food is usually good, and the ranch-style rooms, with tile floors, wood-burning stoves, and kerosene lanterns, are comfortable.

✪ **Paraíso del Oso.** A mile outside Cerocahui. ☎ **800-884-3107** in the U.S., or phone/fax 14/21-3372 in Chihuahua. (Reservations: Paraíso del Oso, P.O. Box 31089, El Paso, TX 79931.) 21 units. $130 double. Rates include all meals. MC, V.

Opened in 1990, Paraíso del Oso's rustic setting beside a stream is what you come to the canyon country for. It's at the foot of a mountain with a natural rock profile of a bear—hence the hotel's name, "Bear's Pardise." The food in this case is worth writing home about, and the immense night sky usually shines with an incredible blanket of stars. Each room has two double beds and pine-log furniture. There's no electricity, though the dining room has solar-powered lights. The emphasis here is on the cultural and natural history of the area, which can be experienced on foot or by guided horseback trips (the horses live here, too). There is a cash bar, a small but good library (with both novels and books on Mexican history), and topographical maps of the area.

STOPS 3 & 4: EL DIVISADERO

Stops 3 and 4 are just 2 miles apart. Stop 3 (coming from Los Mochis) in front of the **Hotel Posada Barrancas** is opposite the Mansión Tarahumara. Stop 4 is **El Divisadero** proper (elevation 9,000 ft.), where you'll find the Hotel Cabañas Divisadero-Barrancas, delicious taco stands at train time, and the most **spectacular view of the canyon** that you'll get if you are making no overnight stops en route. The train stops for only 15 minutes—just time enough to make a mad dash to the lookout and to make a hurried purchase or two from the Tarahumara Indians who appear at train time with beautiful baskets, homemade violins, and wood and cloth dolls.

Hotels can arrange various excursions, including visits to cave-dwelling Tarahumara, hiking, and horseback riding.

WHERE TO STAY & DINE   There is a handful of good hotels—none of them particularly cheap—with great settings at these stops, including the lovely Mansión Tarahumara.

Hotel Cabañas Divisadero-Barrancas. El Divisadero. No phone. E-mail: hoteldivisadero@infosel.net.mx (Reservations: av. Mirador 4516, Apdo. Postal 661, Col. Residencial Campestre, 31238 Chihuahua, Chih.; ☎ **14/16-5136;** fax 14/15-1199.) 50 units. $185 double. Rates include three meals. AE, MC, V (in Chihuahua).

This hotel's location on the edge of the canyon overlook provides the most spectacular view of any hotel in the canyon. As might be expected, the hotel is often filled with groups. The restaurant has a large picture window, perfect for hours of sitting and gazing at the canyon. The rooms are well appointed rustic, with foot-loomed, brightly colored bedspreads and matching curtains, two double beds, a fireplace, and 24-hour electricity.

Hotel Posada Barrancas Mirador. El Divisadero. No phone. (Reservations: the Hotel Santa Anita, Apdo. Postal 159, 81200 Los Mochis, Sin.; ☎ **800-896-8196** from the U.S.) 34 units. $210 double. Rates include meals. AE, MC, V.

Opened in 1993, the Mirador sits at the edge of the canyon, about 5 minutes up the mountain from its sister hotel, the Rancho (see below). The dramatic balconies in each room seem to hang right over the cliff's edge. All rooms have heavy wood furnishings, bold drapes and bedspreads, and individual heaters. Generous and tasty meals are served in the dining room/lounge by a huge fireplace.

Hotel Posada Barrancas Rancho. El Divisadero. No phone. (Reservations: the Hotel Santa Anita, Apdo. Postal 159, 81200 Los Mochis, Sin.; ☎ **800-896-8196** from the U.S.) 33 units. $95 double. Rates include meals. AE, MC, V.

The train stops right in front of this inn. Rooms are comfortable, each with two double beds and a body-warming, wood-burning iron stove. Like those in other lodges, meals are a communal affair in the cozy living/restaurant area, and the food is quite good. You can rent horses or hike to the Tarahumara caves and to the rim of the canyon, where a more expensive sister hotel, the Mirador (see above), has a beautiful restaurant/bar with a magnificent view.

✪ **Mansión Tarahumara.** El Divisadero. No phone. (Reservations: Mansion Tarahumara, Calle Juárez 1602-A, Col. Centro, 31000 Chihuahua, Chih.; ☎/fax **14/16-5444** or 14/15-4721.) 45 units. $105 double. Rates include three meals. MC V.

Like an enormous stone castle, the Mansión Tarahumara is perched on a hillside opposite the train stop at Posada Barrancas. A van meets the train and carries guests and luggage across the tracks to the hotel. This is among my favorite canyon lodges because of the gorgeous setting, rooms, and management's attention to their guests' comfort. Rock-walled, nicely furnished bungalows sit behind the castle. Each has a big fireplace, wall heater, two double beds, and windows facing the view.

The castle houses the restaurant, which has a lovely view from its big windows and a large area ideal for dancing or live entertainment, which the hotel sometimes schedules. Some nights a guitarist stops in for a sing-along after dinner. Besides the usual cave tours or horseback riding, the hotel can also arrange guided hiking to the bottom of the canyon or to Batopilas (see Batopilas description in "Stop 5: Creel," below).

STOP 5: CREEL

This rustic logging town with a handful of paved streets offers the only economical lodgings in the canyon, as well as some of the best side trips, especially hiking and overnight camping.

ESSENTIALS

GETTING THERE & DEPARTING By Train When you're ready to get off the train, keep a lookout for the station because the train stops here for only a few minutes. When you're ready to reboard, be sure to get to the station at least a few minutes in advance of the train. You'll need to be ready to jump on when you see it coming.

By Car From Chihuahua, follow the signs to La Junta (but don't go there), until you see signs to Hermosillo. Follow those signs until you see signs to Creel (left). The trip takes about 4 hours on a paved road.

By Bus With facilities next to the Hotel Korachi, Estrella Blanca serves Creel and Chihuahua every 2 hours from 6am to 5:30pm. Five direct buses make the trip in 4 hours; the three *de paso* buses take 5 hours. (See also "Getting to Batopilas" under "Nearby Excursions," below.)

ORIENTATION   The train station, around the corner from the Mission Store and the main plaza, is in the heart of the village and within walking distance of all lodgings except the Copper Canyon Sierra Lodge. Look for your hotel's van waiting at the station (unless you're staying at the Casa de Huéspedes Margarita, which is only 2 blocks away). There's one main street, **López Mateos,** and most everything is on it or within walking distance.

FAST FACTS   The telephone **area code** is **145. Electricity** is available 24 hours daily in all Creel hotels. The best sources of **information** are the Mission Store and the hotels. Several businesses and many of the hotels offer long-distance **telephone** service; look for signs proclaiming LARGA DISTANCIA or ask at your hotel. Creel sits at an **elevation** of 8,400 feet and has a **population** of around 6,000.

Exploring Creel

You'll occasionally see the Tarahumara as you walk around town, but mostly you'll see rugged logging types and tourists from around the world.

Several stores around Creel sell Tarahumara arts and crafts. The best is **Artesanías Misión** (Mission Crafts), which has quality merchandise at reasonable prices; all profits go to the Mission Hospital run by Father Verplancken, a Jesuit priest, and benefit the Tarahumara. Here you'll find dolls, pottery, woven purses and belts, drums, violins (an instrument inherited from the Spanish), bamboo flutes, bead necklaces, bows and arrows, cassettes of Tarahumara music, wood carvings, baskets, and heavy wool rugs, as well as an excellent supply of books and maps relating to the Tarahumara and the region. The shop's open Monday through Saturday from 9:30am to 1pm and 3 to 6pm, and Sunday from 9:30am to 1pm. It's beside the railroad tracks, on the main plaza.

Nearby Excursions

Close by are several canyons, waterfalls, a lake, hot springs, Tarahumara villages and cave dwellings, and an old Jesuit mission. Six miles north of town is an "ecotourism" complex called **San Ignacio de Arareko** (☎ **145/6-0120** or 145/6-0078). It has a lake, hiking and biking trails, horses, cabins, and a craft shop, all run by indigenous peoples of the *ejido* (communal area)—a pleasant change from the mestizo population's almost total control of tourism in Mexico. **Batopilas,** a fascinating 18th-century silver-mining village at the bottom of the canyon, requires an overnight jaunt. You can ask for information about these and other things to do at your hotel.

If you are **driving,** the partially paved road from Creel now makes possible a day-trip to the village of **El Divisadero** (see "Stops 3 & 4: El Divisadero," above, for details). The trip takes about an hour one way. Even the unpaved part is generally in good condition, although if you are traveling during or just after rains, it may not be. Ask about its condition before starting out.

ORGANIZED TOURS   Hotels offer organized tours. The **Motel Parador de la Montaña** has 10 different excursions, ranging from 2 to 10 hours and priced between $13 and $64 per person (four people minimum); they charge $55 per person (minimum four) for the Batopilas trip. The **Hotel Nuevo** and **Casa de Huéspedes Margarita** offer the most economical tours in town, priced around $14 for a daylong canyon-and-hot-springs tour. All tour availability depends on whether a group can be assembled; your best chance is at the Plaza Mexicana or the Parador de la Montaña, both of which cater to groups. The **Copper Canyon Sierra Lodge** arranges packages throughout Tarahumara land.

BATOPILAS   You can make an overnight side trip on your own from Creel to the silver-mining village of Batopilas, founded in 1708. It's 7 to 9 hours from Creel by bus

Going Solo: Not a Good Idea

Whether you go by foot, horseback, bus, or guided tour, if you're planning to do any strenuous hiking, rock climbing, or adventuring, I strongly recommend that you take along someone who knows the area. You're in the wilderness out here, and you can't count on anyone to come along and rescue you should an accident occur.

(school-bus type), considerably less by four-wheel-drive vehicle, along a narrow dirt road winding down through some of the most spectacular scenery in the Copper Canyon. In Batopilas, which lies beside a river at the bottom of a deep canyon, the weather is tropical, though it can get a bit chilly in the evenings. You can visit a beautiful little church and do several walks and a hike to **Misión Satevó** from there. The town itself seems stuck in an 18th-century time warp: The dry-goods store has the original shelving and cash register, cobblestone streets twist past whitewashed homes, miners and ranchers come and go on horseback, and the Tarahumara frequently visit. A considerable number of pigs, dogs, and flocks of goats roam at will—this is, after all, Chihuahua's goat-raising capital.

Getting to Batopilas　In Creel, take the **bus** from the Restaurant Herradero, on López Mateos s/n, three doors past the turnoff to Hotel Plaza Mexicana. It goes to Batopilas on Tuesday, Thursday, and Saturday, leaving Creel at 7am and arriving midafternoon. A Suburban-type **van** leaves on Monday, Wednesday, and Friday at 10:30am, also arriving about midafternoon. Both bus and van return the following day. There are no bathrooms, restaurants, or other conveniences of civilization along the way, but the bus may stop to allow passengers to stretch and find a bush. Tickets (for the bus) are sold at the restaurant.

Where to Stay & Dine in Batopilas　Batopilas has several little restaurants and inns. There are no telephones, though, so don't expect to make firm reservations. Information about the basic but comfortable, 10-room **Hotel Mary** (formerly Parador Batopilas) can be had at the Parador de la Montaña in Creel; its staff can tell you the likelihood of vacancies. All rooms share the hotel's four bathrooms and cost around $20 double per night. There are also the rustic **Hotel Batopilas** and **Hotel Las Palmeras** with five or six rooms each; if all else fails, you can probably find a family willing to let you stay in an extra room. Despite the paucity of accommodations options, 1 night probably isn't enough for a stay here, since you arrive midafternoon and must leave at 7am or 10:30am the next morning.

Restaurants are informal here, so bring along some snacks and bottled water to tide you over, though snacks are available at the general store. Upon arrival ask for directions to **Doña Mica's** (everyone knows her). She serves meals on her front porch surrounded by plants, but it's best to let her know in advance when to expect you. On short notice, however, she can probably rustle up some scrambled eggs.

The most expensive lodging choice is the **Copper Canyon Riverside Lodge** (no phone), owned by the same folks who own the Copper Canyon Sierra Lodge near Creel. Rooms are generally sold as part of a package that includes a few nights in both lodges, but if any rooms are available, they can be had for $250 per day, which includes all meals, guides, and transportation (see below). A restored 19th-century hacienda, this one-of-a-kind lodge sits among colonial-era buildings 1 short block from the rushing Batopilas River. All 14 rooms have large private bathrooms, electrical outlets, and kerosene lamps; most have balconies looking out onto the street. Interior courtyards, a parlor filled with antiques, and a library stocked with historical materials evoke a sense of a simpler past. Meals are generous and quite good; guests can prepare their own drinks from a self-serve bar. A resident guide provides information on the canyon and will point out and describe the area's attractions, and the guests decide what they want to do.

WHERE TO STAY

Though a small town, Creel has several places to stay because of its popularity with international tourists and loggers on business. Be sure to make reservations during high season.

Very Expensive

Copper Canyon Sierra Lodge. (Reservations: Copper Canyon Lodges, 2741 Paldan Dr., Auburn Hills, MI 48326; ☎ **800/776-3942** or 248/340-7230; fax 248/340-7212.) 14 units. $250 per person per night. Rates include meals, guides, transportation to/from lodge in Batopilas and to/from airport in Chihuahua). AE, DISC, MC, V.

Rooms are normally booked as part of an 8-day package ($2,250 per person, double occupancy; $2,500 single) that includes 4 nights at their lodge outside of Creel, 3 nights in Batopilas, transfers, guides, and meals at their hotels. Transportation to Batopilas is provided by suburbans, which come equipped with bucket seats and belt harnesses mounted on the roof for those who want to take in as much of the dramatic landscape as possible.

The Sierra Lodge is about 20 minutes (14 miles) southwest of Creel proper, this place has everything you hope for in a mountain lodge—rock walls, beamed ceilings, lantern lights, and wood-burning stoves. In other words, it has rustic charm and no electricity. Its out-of-town location is a great starting point from which to take guided or self-guided hikes and walks in the mountains to the Cusárare Waterfalls, cave paintings, and the present-day Tarahumara cave dwellings. Owner Skip McWilliams has a special reverence for the Tarahumara and has made an effort to become friends with those who live near the lodge. Tarahumara guides conduct tours to villages and into the canyons. Admittedly, there is usually a language barrier with guests, and the Tarahumara are shy, but hand gestures and friendliness go a long way. A resident bilingual guide provides personal service.

This is one hotel that definitely should be booked ahead of time from the United States; drop-ins are likely to find the hotel full. There are several options for getting to the lodge. Guests usually fly into Chihuahua on a Wednesday or Saturday and use the hotel's shuttle service to Creel and the lodge. The shuttle leaves the airport at 2:30pm. Guests can also opt to arrive by train from Los Mochis or Chihuahua.

Moderate

Best Western The Lodge at Creel (formerly Pensión Creel). Av. López Mateos 61, 33200 Creel, Chih. ☎ **800/528-1234** in the U.S.; 145/6-0071. Fax 145/6-0082. 27 units. TV. $88 double. MC, V.

The Lodge's cabins are painted Mennonite blue and furnished with double beds; some come with their own porch. Bathrooms sport tub/shower combinations, and each room has a coffee pot. There's a dining room where meals other than breakfast are served by arrangement. The lobby, next to the dining area, has a phone for guest use and a small gift shop. Three-night backpacking trips to the bottom of the canyon, among other tours, are offered for 4 to 10 people. The pensión is located 5 blocks west of the main plaza, just beyond the Parador de la Montaña. The Lodge's van meets all trains.

Hotel Nuevo. Francisco Villa 121, 33200 Creel, Chih. ☎ **145/6-0022**. Fax 145/6-0043. 40 units. $40-$80 double. AE, DC, DISC, MC, V. Free secured parking.

There are two hotel sections at the Nuevo—the older one across the tracks from the train station next to the restaurant and variety store, and newer log cabañas in back.

The higher-priced cabañas are carpeted and have TVs. All rooms have a heater or fireplace. There is a nice hotel restaurant open from 8:30am to 8pm, plus a small general store that sells local crafts as well as basic supplies. Ask at the store about rooms.

Motel Parador de la Montaña. Av. López Mateos s/n, 33200 Creel, Chih. ☎ **145/ 6-0075.** Fax 145/6-0085. (For reservations in Chihuahua, contact offices at calle Allende 114, 31300 Chihuahua, Chih. ☎ 14/10-4580; fax 14/15-3468.) 50 units. TEL, TV. $70 double. MC, V.

The largest hotel in town is the Parador de la Montaña, located 4 blocks west of the plaza. The comfortable rooms have two double beds, high wood-beamed ceilings, central heating, tiled bathroom, and very thin walls. Guests congregate in the restaurant, bar, and lobby with its roaring fireplace. The bar is the town's evening hot spot. The motel caters to groups, and offers some 10 overland tours, priced from $10 to $50. They also offer helicopter tours. The hotel can give you information about the Hotel Mary in Batopilas.

Inexpensive

✪ **Casa de Huéspedes Margarita.** Av. López Mateos 11, 33200 Creel, Chih. ☎/fax **145/ 6-0045.** 27 units (17 with bathroom). $4.50 sleeping bag space (10 spaces); $6 share in 4-bed dormitory; $25 double private room; $30 double private cabaña. Rates include breakfast and dinner. No credit cards.

With its youth-hostel atmosphere, this white house (with no sign) between the two churches on the main plaza is the most popular spot in town with international backpacking, student, and minimal-budget travelers. Yet it's also one of the cleanest hotels in the region. Rooms have pine details and tile floors and are decorated with frilly curtains and spreads; there is plenty of hot water and gas heat in each. Breakfasts and suppers are taken family-style around a big dining table. Nonguests can eat here, too—just let them know in advance ($2.50). Margarita is one of the best sources of information in the area, and does all she can to help budget travelers enjoy their stays.

✪ **Margarita's Plaza Mexicana.** Calle Chapultepec s/n, 33200 Creel, Chih. ☎/fax **145/ 6-0245.** 26 units. $45 double. Rates include 2 meals. No credit cards. Free parking.

Margarita has transformed an old town house into a charming inn filled with Tarahumara folk art. The rooms are gaily furnished with wood chairs and dressers from Michoacán and decorated with paintings of Tarahumara scenes. Gas wall heaters take the chill off winter nights. A mural depicting Semana Santa celebrations covers one wall in the large dining room, where guests take breakfast and dinner. Vegetables and salads are prepared with purified water. To get to the hotel, go 2 blocks west of the plaza on López Mateos, then half a block south on Chapultepec. Or just ask anyone.

WHERE TO DINE

Besides the restaurants mentioned below, there's also good food at Margarita's Casa de Huéspedes and the Motel Parador de la Montaña mentioned above.

El Caballo Bayo. Av. López Mateos 25. ☎ **145/6-0136.** Sandwiches $2.50–$3; steak dinners $8. No credit cards. Daily 2–10pm. AMERICAN.

Travelers who've grown weary of Mexican food and yearn for a taste of home will be happy to find this bright, clean restaurant with cheery tablecloths. The menu is Americana, with burgers and fries, club sandwiches, T-bone steaks from Chihuahua, and shrimp from Los Mochis. The restaurant is across the street from the Motel Parador de la Montaña.

Restaurant Las Rejas. In the Motel Parador de la Montaña, Av. López Mateos. ☎ **145/ 6-0075.** Breakfast, sandwiches, and hamburgers $1.50–$3; main courses $3–$6.50. No credit cards. Daily 7:30–11:30am and 12–10:30pm. INTERNATIONAL.

The largest and most popular restaurant in town serves full dinners, which might include soup, salad, steak, dessert, and coffee, or just a simple grilled half-chicken. There's full service from the cozy little attached bar, open all day and every evening until around midnight. With its hanging lanterns, high wood-beamed ceiling, huge fireplace, and friendly atmosphere, Las Rejas is worth a stop, though the food is pretty average. This is *the* gathering place for out-of-towners. It's 4 blocks west of the plaza.

3 Chihuahua

213 miles S of El Paso; 275 miles NW of Torreón

Chihuahua, a city of wide boulevards and handsome buildings, is the capital of the state of Chihuahua, the largest and richest in Mexico. The wealth comes from mining, timber, cattle raising, *maquiladoras* (assembly plants for export goods), and tourism—it's one of two major departure points for the Copper Canyon train. Population is booming in Chihuahua largely due to the manufacturing plants, and the city has lost much of its frontier feeling. In Chihuahua you'll find a modern university and several museums, including the house where Pancho Villa once lived.

ESSENTIALS

GETTING THERE & DEPARTING   By Plane   Aspen Mountain Air (☎ 800/ 877-3932 in the U.S., or 14/20-9154) started daily flights (using 30-passenger Dornier twin-prop aircraft) from El Paso and Dallas/Fort Worth to Chihuahua. (**Southwest Airlines,** ☎ 800/531-5601, serves El Paso from several U.S. cities.) **Aeromexico/Aerolitoral** (☎ 14/15-6303) fly direct from El Paso, Guadalajara, Hermosillo, Mexico City, Monterrey, Torreón, Tijuana, Culiacán, La Paz, and Los Mochis, with connecting flights from Los Angeles and San Antonio. **Transportes Aeropuerto** (☎ 14/20-3366) controls minivan service from the airport ($5 per person, $10 if it's an early flight). Taxis from town charge $15 for up to four people.

By Train   The *Chihuahua al Pacífico* (☎ 14/10-9059; fax 14/16-9059) leaves Chihuahua daily for its route through the Copper Canyon country to Los Mochis. (The complete train schedule and the train route are found in section 2 of this chapter.) The station in Chihuahua is 2 blocks behind the prison on 20 de Noviembre, near the intersection with Ocampo. The train is scheduled to leave promptly at 7am daily. To get there from the Plaza Principal and avenida Juárez, take a bus marked CERRO DE LA CRUZ. It lets you off 2 blocks from the station.

Public transportation is good if you are going to the station to buy tickets. However, for getting to the station for the early-morning train departure, it's best to arrange transportation through one of the travel agencies recommended under "Canyon Arrangements" in "Fast Facts: Chihuahua," below. They pick up clients taking the train each morning; taxis that early can be scarce.

By Car   Highway 45 leads south from Ciudad Juárez; **Highway 16** south from Ojinaga; and **Highway 49** north from Torreón. For the drive to Creel, see "Getting There & Departing" under "Stop 5: Creel," above.

By Bus   The Central Camionera **bus station** (also called the Terminal de Autobuses) is on the outskirts of the city, on avenida Juan Pablo II, 5 miles northeast of town en route to the airport. Buses leave hourly heading for major points inland and north and south on the coast. **Omnibus de México** has deluxe service to Ciudad Juárez at 8am and 6pm, Mexico City at 3:15pm, and Monterrey at 9:30pm. **Transportes Chihuahuenses,** the big local line, offers deluxe service leaving for Ciudad Juárez at 8am and 2pm.

For travel to Creel, look for the **Estrella Blanca** line. Buses leave every 2 hours from 6am to 6pm. Direct buses make the trip in 4 hours; *de paso* buses take 5.

Transportes del Norte and **Autobuses Estrella Blanca** also run buses hourly from the border through Chihuahua to points south. **Omnibus de México** has *real ejecutivo* (deluxe) service from Juárez, Mexico City, and Monterrey. **Futura/Turistar** also has deluxe service to Monterrey and Durango.

The Central Camionera (bus station) in Chihuahua is 5 miles northeast of the town center and west of the airport.

VISITOR INFORMATION   For basic tourist information, visit the **tourist information center** (☎ **14/10-1077** or 14/29-3300, ext. 4515 or 1061) on Libertad at Carranza in the Government Palace, just left of the altar and murals dedicated to Father Hidalgo. It's open Monday through Friday from 9am to 7pm and Saturday and Sunday from 10am to 2pm.

CITY LAYOUT   The town center is laid out around the **Plaza Principal,** bounded by Avenidas Libertad and Victoria (which run northeast to southwest) and avenida Independencia and calle 4 (which run northwest to southeast). The **cathedral** is at the southwest end of the plaza, and the city offices are on the northeast end. Standing on Independencia with the cathedral on your left, odd-numbered streets and blocks will be to your right, and even-numbered streets and blocks to your left.

GETTING AROUND   Local buses run along main arteries beginning at the central plaza. You can take taxis from the town center to most major sights. For early-morning transportation to the train station, it's best to make pickup arrangements with one of the travel agencies, since taxis are scarce at that hour.

FAST FACTS: CHIHUAHUA

American Express   The local representative is **Viajes Rojo y Casavantes,** with one agent in the Hotel San Francisco and a full office at Vicente Guerrero 1207 (☎ **14/15-4636;** fax 14/15-5384).

Area Code   The telephone area code is **14.**

Canyon Arrangements   If you wait to make canyon hotel reservations until you are in Chihuahua, consider using a local travel agent. I recommend **Turismo Al Mar,** calle Berna 2202, Colonia Mirador, 31270 Chihuahua, Chih. (☎ **14/16-5950;** fax 14/16-6589). You can buy train tickets yourself at the station, however, but do so before your day of departure.

Elevation   Chihuahua sits at 4,700 feet.

Population   Chihuahua has some 1,000,000 residents.

EXPLORING CHIHUAHUA

To see all Chihuahua's sights in 1 day, consider taking a 3-hour city tour with English-speaking guides available. Three recommended agencies are **Torres del Sol,** Independencia 116-2 (☎ **14/15-7380**) in the Hotel Palacio del Sol; **Turismo Al Mar** (see above); and **Viajes Rojo y Casavantes,** with one agent in the lobby of the Hotel San Francisco and a larger office at Vicente Guerrero 1207 (☎ **14/15-4636**). Any of these will pick you up at your hotel. A half-day city tour includes visits to the museums, the churches, the colonial aqueduct, the state capital building, the state penitentiary, and more. Cost is $16 per person (minimum of two) plus museum admission. A 7-hour trip to the Mennonite village near Cuauhtémoc costs about $32.50 per person, with a minimum of four people.

Chihuahua

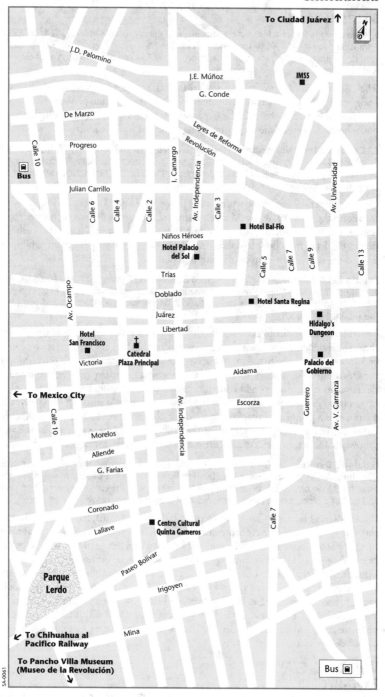

To Ciudad Juárez ↑

J.D. Palomino

J.E. Múñoz

G. Conde

IMSS

De Marzo

Leyes de Reforma

Progreso

Revolución

Calle 10

Bus

Julian Carrillo

Calle 6

Calle 4

Calle 2

I. Camargo

Av. Independencia

Calle 3

Av. Universidad

■ Hotel Bal-Flo

Niños Héroes

Hotel Palacio
del Sol ■

Calle 5

Calle 7

Calle 9

Calle 13

Trias

Doblado

Av. Ocampo

■ Hotel Santa Regina

Juárez

Libertad

■
Hidalgo's
Dungeon

Hotel
San Francisco
■

†
Catedral
Plaza Principal

Victoria

Aldama

Palacio del
Gobierno

← To Mexico City

Escorza

Guerrero

Av. V. Carranza

Calle 10

Morelos

Allende

Av. Independencia

G. Farias

Coronado

Calle 7

Lallave

■ Centro Cultural
Quinta Gameros

Paseo Bolívar

Parque
Lerdo

Irigoyen

↙ To Chihuahua al
Pacifico Railway

Mina

To Pancho Villa Museum
(Museo de la Revolución)
↓

Bus 🚌

SA-0061

631

SIGHTS IN TOWN

✪ Museo de la Revolución. Calle 10 no. 3014, at the corner of Mendez. ☎ **14/16-2958.** Admission $1. Mon–Sat 9am–1pm and 3–7pm; Sun 9am–5pm. Bus: "Colonia Dale" heads west down Juárez, turning south onto Ocampo, and will let you off on the corner of Ocampo and Mendez.

The "Revolution Museum" is Pancho Villa's house, where Luz Corral de Villa lived until her death in 1981. Exhibits include Villa's weapons, some personal effects, lots of period photos, and the 1922 Dodge in which he was shot in 1923, complete with bullet holes. It's one of the more interesting museums in the country.

✪ Centro Cultural Universitaria (Quinta Gameros). Paseo Bolívar 401. ☎ **14/16-6684.** Admission $1.50. Tues–Sun 10am–7pm. Heading away from the Plaza Principal with the cathedral on your right, walk 7 blocks on Independencia to Bolívar, turn right, and walk 1 more block; the museum's on the right.

Quinta Gameros is an exact replica of a neoclassical, French Second Empire–style mansion. Built in 1910 for Manuel Gameros, the mansion was converted to a museum in 1961. Pancho Villa used it briefly as a headquarters. Notice the wealth of decorative detail from floor to ceiling, inside and out. There are permanent exhibits of turn-of-the-century art nouveau furnishings, plus traveling exhibits.

Palacio del Gobierno. Av. Aldama between Guerrero and Carranza. ☎ **14/10-6324.** Free admission. Daily 8am–10pm. With the cathedral on your right, walk along Independencia 1 block, then turn left on Aldama and continue 2 long blocks; cross Guerrero and you'll find the entrance on the left.

The Palacio del Gobierno is a magnificent ornate structure dating in part from 1890; the original building, the Jesuit College, was built in 1718. A colorful, expressive mural encompasses the entire first floor of the large central courtyard and tells the history of the area around Chihuahua from the time of the first European visitation up through the Revolution. In the far-right corner, note the scene depicting Benito Juárez flanked by Abraham Lincoln and Simón Bolívar, liberator of South America. In the far-left rear courtyard is a plaque and altar commemorating the execution of Miguel Hidalgo, the father of Mexican independence, at 7am on July 30, 1811; the plaque marks the very spot where the hero was executed in the old building, and the mural portrays the scene.

Hidalgo's Dungeon. In the Palacio Federal, Av. Juárez at Guerrero. No phone. Admission 20¢. Tues–Sun 10am–6pm. From the Plaza Principal, walk on the pedestrian-only Calle Libertad for 3 long blocks, cross Guerrero, and turn left on it to the corner of Juárez. Turn right and go half a block; the entrance to the museum is on the right, below the post office.

Father Miguel Hidalgo y Costilla was a priest in Dolores, Guanajuato, when he started the War of Independence on September 15, 1810. Six months later he was captured by the Spanish, brought to Chihuahua, and thrown in a dungeon for 98 days, before being shot with his lieutenants, Allende, Aldama, and Jiménez. The four were beheaded, and their heads hung in iron cages for 9½ years on the four corners of the Alhóndiga granary in Guanajuato—as examples of the fate revolutionaries would meet. It was in this cell that Hidalgo lived on bread and water before his execution. The night before his death, he wrote a few words on the wall with a piece of charcoal to thank his guard and the warden for the good treatment they gave him. A bronze plaque commemorates his final message.

WHERE TO STAY
EXPENSIVE

Holiday Inn. Escudero 702, 31240 Chihuahua, Chih. ☎ **800/465-4329** in the U.S., or 14/14-3350. Fax 14/14-3313. 74 units. A/C TV TEL. $110 double. AE, CB, DC, MC, V. Free secured parking.

Visitors to Chihuahua rave about this Holiday Inn (formerly Villa Suites), citing its quiet location and excellent amenities as among the best in the city. All suites have a kitchenette with stove, refrigerator, and coffeemaker. The hotel's clubhouse contains an indoor heated swimming pool and fitness center. There's also a full restaurant and room service. Though it's outside the downtown area, this is a good spot to relax in luxury. The hotel is on Escudero between avenida Universidad and avenida de Montes.

✪ **Hotel San Francisco.** Victoria 409, 31000 Chihuahua, Chih. ☎ **800/847-2546** in the U.S., or 14/16-7550. Fax 14/15-3538. 146 units. A/C TV TEL. $120 double standard. AE, MC, V. Free covered parking.

The excellent location of this modern downtown hotel attracts repeat visitors. Locals and tourists alike use the hotel's lobby bar and restaurant, Degá, as a meeting place, and the atmosphere is always convivial (see "Where to Dine," below). The good-sized rooms are fashionably furnished, if a bit dimly lit. From the cathedral, walk to Victoria and turn right; the hotel is 1½ blocks down on your right, before avenida Ocampo.

MODERATE

✪ **Hotel Palacio del Sol.** Independencia 116, 31000 Chihuahua, Chih. ☎ **14/16-6000.** Fax 14/15-9947. 220 units. A/C TV TEL. $94 double standard; $115 single or double suites. AE, DC, MC, V. Free valet parking.

Well located, in the financial and commercial area of Chihuahua and close to the main square, the Palacio del Sol has 17 stories of rooms, which are well lit, carpeted, and have king-size beds, writing tables, and purified tap water. Nonsmoking and rooms equipped for visitors with disabilities are available. There is a good restaurant (24-hr. service), lobby bar, and bar featuring nightly live music. Leaving the cathedral, it is 3½ blocks to your left on Independencia.

INEXPENSIVE

Hotel Bal-Flo. Calle 5 no. 702, 31300 Chihuahua, Chih. ☎/fax **14/16-0335.** 91 units. A/C TV TEL. $25 double. MC, V. Free parking.

All rooms at the Bal-Flo are heated and carpeted. Some units have windows on the street; others open onto an air shaft. The proprietor, Sr. Baltazar Flores, speaks English and is quite helpful. The cafeteria, open daily from 7am to 11pm, serves good, inexpensive food. With the front of the cathedral to your left, walk 4 long blocks on Independencia, then right on Niños Héroes for 2 blocks; the hotel's on the left at calle 5.

Hotel Santa Regina. Calle 3 no. 102, 31000 Chihuahua, Chih. ☎ **14/15-3889.** Fax 14/10-1411. 100 units. A/C TV TEL. $28 double. AE, MC, V. Free parking.

The three-story Santa Regina has carpeted rooms (heated in winter) and TVs that receive U.S. channels. More than half the rooms have windows facing outside; others have windows on the hall. With the cathedral on your left, walk 2 blocks on Independencia to Doblado. Turn right for 2 more blocks, then left; the hotel is between Juárez and Doblado.

WHERE TO DINE

✪ **Club de los Parados.** av. Juárez 3901. ☎ **14/10-5335.** Steak dinners $10–$15. AE, MC, V. Daily 1–11pm. MEXICAN/STEAKS.

Opened by the wealthy cattle rancher Tony Vega in the 1950s, this club once hosted rugged, rich ranchers who needed a place to drink and dine sumptuously, yet casually. The restaurant is filled with photos of important historical figures from Chihuahua, including the actor Anthony Quinn, a local boy who hit the big time in Hollywood.

The adobe-style building houses a large dining room with a wood-burning fireplace and a separate private dining room. As might be expected, beef is the big draw here, especially the hefty steaks. The carne asada is served with superb guacamole. Reservations accepted.

Degá. In the Hotel San Francisco, Calle Victoria 409. ☎ **14/16-7550.** Breakfast $4–$7 (buffet $6); main courses $6–$13; Sun buffet $8. DC, MC, V. Daily 7am–11pm. MEXICAN/INTERNATIONAL.

The restaurant/cafeteria/bar at this popular downtown hotel draws both downtown workers and travelers. The breakfast buffet features superb made-to-order omelets. The plato mexicano comes with a tamal, chile relleno, beans, chips, and guacamole. Fish, charcoal-grilled chicken, barbecue, and salads are all reasonably priced. American breakfasts and burgers are included in the extensive menu. From the cathedral walk to Victoria and turn right; it's 1 block down on your right, before avenida Ocampo.

CHIHUAHUA AFTER DARK

Most nighttime action takes place in hotel lobby bars. At the **Hotel San Francisco** behind the cathedral, Victoria 409, there's live music Monday through Saturday, with happy hour from 5 to 8pm. The **Hotel Palacio del Sol,** at Independencia 500, has different live entertainment nightly in the lobby bar. The **Hostería 1900,** at Independencia 506, has live entertainment on weekends from 9:30pm to 2am and is popular with a young crowd, as is **Chihuahua Charlie's Bar and Grill** at avenida Juárez 3329.

ROAD TRIP: THE MENNONITE VILLAGE OF CUAUHTÉMOC

Two hours west of Chihuahua, this village makes an unusual side trip. Originally from northern Germany, the Mennonites became an official reformist religious sect under Menno Simons in the early 16th century. With a strict Bible-based philosophy governing their daily lives, prohibiting them from engaging in war and many aspects of popular culture, they emigrated to other lands rather than violate their beliefs.

The group of 5,000 that migrated to Cuauhtémoc from Canada in 1920 petitioned the Mexican government for permission to settle here and maintain their own community traditions. Cuauhtémoc was little more than a desert then, and Mexico was trying to develop its lands. The Mennonites have since transformed this desert into a productive and prosperous farming community, and they have become famous for their fine woodwork, embroidery, and delicious cheese, as well as other agricultural products.

Yet the community has assimilated to a considerable extent. Very few maintain their 16th-century customs, religion, dress, or language (a dialect of Old German). The traditional horses and buggies have largely been replaced by cars and pickup trucks, and an occasional satellite dish can be spotted. In recent years, a young woman from the Mennonite community was crowned Miss Chihuahua.

An all-day Mennonite tour to Cuauhtémoc allows you to meet the people and learn about their culture and history. It includes a visit to the Mennonite village and agricultural lands and cheese factory, plus lunch in a Mennonite home. The tour company mentioned in "Fast Facts: Chihuahua," above, can arrange such a tour.

Los Cabos & Baja California Sur

Southern Baja California is a land of supreme contrasts. In its geography and what it offers to travelers, there is a sharp mix of opposites that are not polarizing but oddly complementary. Hot desert and cool ocean; vast depths and great heights; manicured golf greens and colorful craggy mountains all exist in eclectic harmony. Not to be forgotten is the peculiar blending of Mexican and American cultures.

The Baja Peninsula is part of Mexico—and yet it is not. Attached to the mainland United States and separated from the rest of Mexico by the Sea of Cortés (Gulf of California), this peninsula extends almost 1,000 miles—longer than Italy. Desert terrain rises from both coasts: Whole forests of cardon cactus, spiky Joshua trees, and spindly ocotillo bushes populate this raw, untamed landscape where volcanoes once rumbled.

The overwhelming attraction of this seemingly uninviting landscape lies at its tip. There, a handful of unique towns and opportunities for exploration tempt visitors to a region known for centuries as "Land's End" (Finisterra). Baja is legendary as a haven for sportfishing and rugged adventure activities. And the spectrum of what you can do, both in the water as well as on land, continues to grow.

Golf has begun to rival sportfishing as Los Cabos's main draw, with five championship courses open for play. Sailing, kayaking, windsurfing, hiking, and whale watching, as well as the chance to explore ancient cave paintings and camp on isolated, wild beaches add even more reasons to visit.

The most popular destinations in Baja Sur are the twin towns at the peninsula's tip: Cabo San Lucas and San José del Cabo. Collectively they are known as Los Cabos (The Capes), but the contrasts continue. Cabo San Lucas is an extension of American-styled Southern California, with deep-sea fishing, ubiquitous golf courses, myriad shopping options, luxury accommodations, and a spirited nightlife. San José del Cabo, however, remains rooted in the traditions of a quaint Mexican town.

Eighteen miles of smooth highway known as the Corridor lies between the two Cabos. Major new resort and residential developments, including some of the world's finest golf courses, are springing up along this stretch of road. And what has always been here continues to beckon: dozens of pristine coves and inlets with a wealth of marine life just offshore.

Though it's the southern playground of the U.S. West Coast, Baja can seem like one of the least crowded corners of Mexico. Todos Santos, an outpost on the Pacific side of the coastal curve, just north of the tip, is beginning to draw travelers who find that Cabo San Lucas has outgrown them. La Paz, capital of Baja Sur, remains a lazy maritime port, with an interesting assortment of small hotels, inns, ecotours, and guest services.

The weather in this land of extremes can be unpredictable. It can be frying-pan hot in summer and cold and windy in winter—so windy that fishing and other nautical expeditions may have to be grounded for a few days. Though winter is often warm enough for water sports, bring a wet suit along if you're a serious diver or snorkeler, as well as a change of warm clothes for unexpectedly chilly weather at night.

Baja has earned a reputation for being much higher-priced than other Mexican resorts. New hotel construction is only now catching up with the tremendous boom in demand. Los Cabos will practically double its inventory of hotel rooms by the year 2000, which should help adjust prices of accommodations somewhat downward. The other factor is that, compared to mainland Mexico, there's little agriculture in Baja; most foodstuffs (and other daily required items) must be shipped in. U.S. dollars are the preferred currency here, and it's not uncommon to see price listings in dollars rather than pesos.

With over 20 miles separating the two Cabos and numerous attractions in between, you may want to rent a car, even if only for a day. Transportation by taxi tends to be pricey here, and if you are at all interested in exploring, a rental car is your most economical option.

Above all, try to take your time in Baja; it's a land of hidden treasures that takes patience to penetrate.

1 Los Cabos: Resorts, Water Sports & Golf

Los Cabos refers to the two towns at the tip of the rugged Baja Peninsula. The end of the line, San José del Cabo and Cabo San Lucas are separated not just by 22 miles but by distinct vibes. Cabo San Lucas mirrors an L.A. lifestyle, whereas San José del Cabo remains a typical and tranquil Mexican small town.

Great sportfishing centered attention on Los Cabos, and it remains a lure today. Once only accessible by water, it attracted a hearty community of cruisers, fishermen, divers, and adventurers dating back to the late 1940s. By the early 1980s, the Mexican government realized the growth potential of Los Cabos and began investing in new highways, airport facilities, golf courses, and modern marine facilities. Expanded airlift and the opening of Transpennisular Highway no. 1 in 1973 paved the wave for spectacular growth.

The most growth has emerged along the road that connects Cabo San Lucas and San José del Cabo. The Corridor, with its perilous cliff-top vistas, has been widened to four well-paved lanes—though it still has no nighttime lighting. The area's most deluxe resorts and renowned golf courses are found here, along with a collection of dramatic beaches and coves. The view is especially outstanding in January and February, when gray whales often spout close to shore.

Because of the distinctive character and attractions of each of these three areas, they are treated separately here. It is possible to stay in one and make day-trips to the other two.

Note: The one airport that serves both towns and the connecting corridor is 7½ miles northwest of San José del Cabo and 22 miles northeast of Cabo San Lucas.

SAN JOSÉ DEL CABO
122 miles SE of La Paz; 22 miles NE of Cabo San Lucas; 1,100 miles SE of Tijuana

San José del Cabo, with its pastel buildings and flowering trees lining the narrow streets, retains the air of a provincial Mexican town. Originally founded in 1730 by Jesuit missionaries, it remains the seat of the Los Cabos government and the center of its business community. The main square, adorned with a wrought-iron bandstand and shaded benches, faces the cathedral, which was built on the site of an early mission.

San José is becoming increasingly sophisticated, with a collection of noteworthy cafes and intriguing small shops adding European flavor to the central downtown area. This is the best choice for those who want to travel to this paradoxical landscape, but still be aware that you're in Mexico.

ESSENTIALS
GETTING THERE & DEPARTING   By Plane   Aerocalifornia (☎ **800/ 237-6225** in the U.S., 114/3-0848, or 114/3-3700) has nonstop or direct flights from Los Angeles, Tijuana, and Phoenix; **Aeromexico** (☎ **800/237-6639** in the U.S., or 114/2-0398) flies nonstop from San Diego, and has connecting flights from Houston, Dallas, New York, Tucson, Guadalajara, and Mexico City. **America West** (☎ **800/ 235-9292** in the U.S.) makes connecting flights through Phoenix; **Alaska Airlines** (☎ **800/426-0333** in the U.S., or 114/2-1015) flies from Los Angeles, San Diego, Seattle, and San Francisco; **Continental** (☎ **800/525-0280** in the U.S., or 114/ 2-38-40) flies from Houston; **Mexicana** (☎ **800/531-7921** in the U.S., 114/3-5352, or 114/353-53) has direct or connecting flights from Denver, Guadalajara, Los Angeles, Mexico City, Puerto Vallarta, and Mazatlán.

By Car   From La Paz, take Highway 1 south, a scenic route that winds through foothills and occasionally skirts the eastern coastline; the drive takes 3 to 4 hours. From La Paz, you can also take Highway 1 south just past the village of San Pedro, then take Highway 19 south (a less winding road than Highway 1) through Todos Santos to Cabo San Lucas, where you pick up Highway 1 east to San José del Cabo; this route takes 2 to 3 hours. From Cabo San Lucas, it's a half-hour drive.

By Bus   The **bus station** (Terminal de Autobuses) on Valerio González, a block east of Highway 1 (☎ **114/2-1100**), is open daily from 5:30am to 7pm, though buses can arrive and depart later. Buses between Cabo San Lucas and La Paz run almost hourly during the day. For points farther north you usually change buses in La Paz. The trip to Cabo San Lucas takes 40 minutes; to La Paz, 3 hours. Buses also go to Todos Santos on the Pacific, and the trip takes around 3 hours.

ORIENTATION   Arriving   Upon arrival at the airport, buy a ticket inside the building for a colectivo or a taxi, which can be shared by up to four passengers. Colectivo fares run about $3 and are only available from the airport. Taxis charge about $6 to San José. Time-share resorts have booths in the arrival/baggage area of this airport. The promoters hook visitors with a free ride to their hotel in return for listening to their spiel.

The major car-rental agencies all have counters at the airport, open during flight arrivals: **Avis** (☎ **800/331-1212** from the U.S., or 114/6-0201), **Budget** (☎ **800/ 527-0700** from the U.S., or 114/3-4190), **Hertz** (☎ **800/654-3131** from the U.S., or 114/2-0375), and **National** (☎ **800/328-4567** from the U.S., or 114/2-2424). Advance reservations are not always necessary.

If you arrive at the bus station, it's too far from the bus station to the hotels to walk with luggage. A taxi from the bus station to either area costs $2 to $4.

The Two Cabos & The Corridor

Cabo San Lucas
Playa El Medano
El Arco
SEE BELOW
Transpeninsular Highway
Golfo de California
Cabo Bello
Punta Cabeza de Ballena
Cabo del Sol
Playa Barco Varado km9.5
Playa de Las Vludes km11
Santa María's Bay km12
Chileno Beach km14
El Tule

CABO SAN LUCAS

A. López Mateos
Ildefonso Green
A. Mijares
Félix Ortega
Rosario Morales
Alikan
12 de Octubre
Morelos
Calle Juventud
M. Hidalgo
Matamoros
Abasolo
M. Ocampo
I. Zaragoza
A. Morelos
Leona Vicario
Narcizo Mendoza
A. Obregón
V. Carranza
Gómez Farías
16 de Septiembre
Cabo Inn
Revolución
20 de Noviembre
Libertad
16 de Septiembre
Niños Héroes
Cabo San Lucas
Constitución
5 de Mayo
Hotel Mar de Cortez
Guerrero
Fco. I. Madero
Iglesia de San Lucas
Main Square
Marina Blvd.
Plaza Las Glorias Hotel
J.O. de Domínguez
Siesta Suites
Marina
Market
Lázaro Cárdenas
Highway 1
To Airport & La Paz →
To San José del Cabo →
Meliá San Lucas
Playa Medano

Bahía de Cabo San Lucas

Solmar Suites

Land's End
Playa de Amor

Pacific Ocean

El Arco

SA-0062

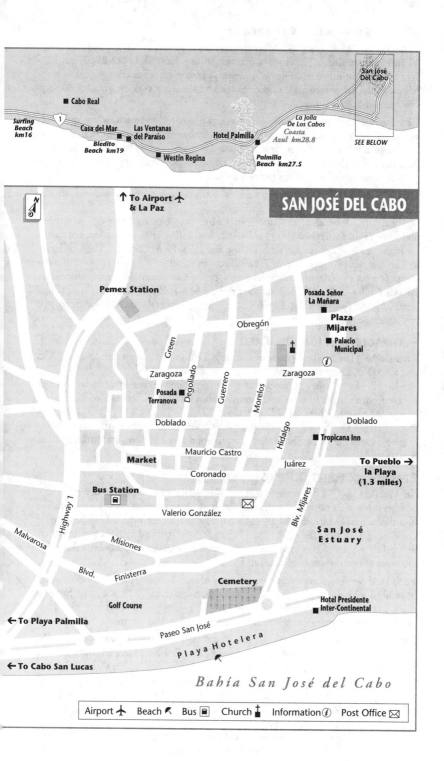

San José Del Cabo (inset)

Cabo Real

Surfing Beach km16

Casa del Mar

Bledito Beach km19

Las Ventanas del Paraíso

Westin Regina

Hotel Palmilla

Palmilla Beach km27.5

La Jolla De Los Cabos Coasta Azul km28.8

SEE BELOW

SAN JOSÉ DEL CABO

N

↑ To Airport ✈ & La Paz

Pemex Station

Posada Señor La Mañara

Obregón

Plaza Mijares

✝

■ Palacio Municipal

(i)

Zaragoza

Green

Degollado

Guerrero

Morelos

Zaragoza

Posada ■ Terranova

Doblado

Doblado

Hidalgo

■ Tropicana Inn

Market

Mauricio Castro

Juárez

Coronado

To Pueblo → la Playa (1.3 miles)

Bus Station

🚍

Valerio González

✉

Blv. Mijares

San José Estuary

Highway 1

Malvarosa

Misiones

Blvd.

Finisterra

Cemetery

Golf Course

Hotel Presidente Inter-Continental

← To Playa Palmilla

Paseo San José

← To Cabo San Lucas

Playa Hotelera

↖

Bahía San José del Cabo

Airport ✈   Beach ⬈   Bus 🚍   Church ✝   Information (i)   Post Office ✉

Visitor Information   The city tourist information office (☎ 114/2-2960, ext. 150) is in the old post-office building on Zaragoza at Mijares. It offers maps, local free publications, and other very basic information about the area. It's open Monday through Friday from 8am to 3pm.

City Layout   San José del Cabo consists of two zones: **downtown,** where the traditional and budget hotels are located, and the **hotel zone** along the beach.

Zaragoza is the main street leading from the highway into town; **Paseo San José** runs parallel to the beach and is the principal boulevard of this hotel zone. The mile-long **Bulevar Mijares** connects the two areas.

GETTING AROUND   There is no local bus service between downtown and the beach; a **taxi** is the only means of getting there.

For day-trips to **Cabo San Lucas,** catch a **bus** (see "Getting There & Departing," above) or a cab. **Tourcabos** (☎ 114/2-0982; fax 114/2-2050), in the Plaza Los Cabos on Paseo San José, offers a day tour to Cabo San Lucas for around $35. The tour leaves at 9am and returns around 4pm. Their office is in the Plaza Los Cabos across from the Fiesta Inn on the Malecón. Bicycles rent for $3 an hour and $15 a day from **Baja Bicycle Club** (☎ 114/2-2828), at the Brisa del Mar Trailer Park on the highway just south of town. Ask them about special offers; they also offer surfboards, boogie boards, and snorkel equipment.

FAST FACTS: SAN JOSÉ DEL CABO

Area Code   The local telephone area code is **114.** Calls between San José del Cabo and Cabo San Lucas are toll calls, so you must use the area code.

Banks   Banks exchange currency during business hours, generally Monday through Friday from 8:30am to 6pm and Saturday 9am to 2pm. There are two banks on Zaragoza between Morelos and Degollado.

Post Office   The correo, on Mijares at Valerio González on the south side of town, is open Monday through Friday from 8am to noon and 2 to 6pm, and Saturday from 8 to 11am.

BEACHES & SPORTS OUTINGS

San José del Cabo is a fine place to unwind, ride horses across the sand, play golf, shop, and absorb authentic Mexican flavor. Beach aficionados who want to explore the beautiful coves and beaches along the 22-mile coast between the two Cabos should consider renting a car for a day or so ($45 to $65 per day and up). Frequent bus service between San José del Cabo and Cabo San Lucas makes it possible to take in the pleasures of both towns (see "Getting There & Departing," above).

FESTIVALS   The feast of the patron saint of San José del Cabo is celebrated on **March 19** with a fair, music, dancing, feasting, horse races, and cockfights. **June 19** is the festival of the patron saint of San Bartolo, a village 62 miles north. **July 25** is the festival of the patron saint of Santiago, a village 34 miles north.

BEACHES   The nearest beach safe for swimming is **Pueblo la Playa** (also called "La Playita"), located about 2 miles east of town: From Bulevar Mijares, turn east at the small sign PUEBLO LA PLAYA and follow the dusty dirt road through cane fields and palms to a small village and beautiful beach where a number of *pangas* (skiffs) belonging to local fishermen are pulled ashore. The La Playita Resort and its adjacent restaurant (see "Where to Stay," below) offers the only formal sustenance on the beach. There are no shade palapas.

Estero San José, a nature reserve with at least 270 species of birds, is located between Pueblo la Playa and the Presidente Inter-Continental Hotel. The estuary is a protected ecological reserve. A building at the edge of the water is a small cultural

Swimming Safety

Although the area is ideal for water sports, occasional strong currents and undertow sometimes make swimming dangerous at **Playa Hotelera,** the town beach—check conditions before entering the surf. However, swimming is generally safe at **Pueblo la Playa** (see "Beaches," below).

---

center, with changing exhibitions such as revolutionary photos and geological artifacts. A $1 donation is suggested. Just beside it is a pathway to enter the estuary on foot.

A fine swimming beach with beautiful rock formations, **Playa Palmilla,** 5 miles west of San José, is located near the Spanish colonial-style Hotel Palmilla—an elegant place to stay or to eat lunch or dinner. To reach Playa Palmilla, take a taxi to the road that leads to the Hotel Palmilla grounds, then take the fork to the left (without entering the hotel grounds) and follow signs to Pepe's restaurant on the beach.

For a list of other nearby beaches worth exploring if you have a rental car, see "Outdoor Activities: Fishing, Golfing & More," under "Cabo San Lucas."

CRUISES Both daytime and sunset cruises are featured. Boats depart from Cabo San Lucas; the cruises vary in prices and offerings, but generally include music, open bar, and snacks for between $30 to $40 per person. Arrange cruises through a travel agency, or call **Xplora Adventours** (located in the Sierra Madre store, on the plaza; ☎ 114/2-3537 or 114/2-9000, ext. 9316.) Xplora handles all tour providers in the area and can give unbiased information on the full selection available.

LAND SPORTS Golf Los Cabos is rapidly becoming a major golf destination, with several new courses open and others under construction. The most economical greens fees are at the 9-hole **Club Campo de Golf San José** (☎ 114/2-0900 or 114/2-0905), on Paseo Finisterra across from the Howard Johnson Hotel. The course is open daily from 7am to 4pm (to 4:30pm in summer). Club guests can use the swimming pool. The greens fee is $15 for 9 holes. Carts cost $30. For more information about playing golf in Los Cabos, see "Golf" under "Cabo San Lucas," below.

Horseback Riding Horses can be rented near the Presidente Inter-Continental, Fiesta Inn, and Palmilla hotels at $15 to $20 per hour. Most people choose to ride on the beach.

Tennis You can play tennis at the two courts of the **Club Campo de Golf Los Cabos** (☎ 114/2-0900) for $10 an hour during the day, $20 an hour at night. Club guests can use the swimming pool. Tennis is also available at the Hotel Palmilla (two lit courts) and the Presidente Intercontinental (two lit courts).

WATER SPORTS Fishing The least expensive way to enjoy deep-sea fishing is to pair up with another angler and charter a *panga,* a 22-foot skiff used by local fishermen from Playa la Puebla. Several *panga* fleets offer 6-hour sportfishing trips, usually from 6am to noon, for $25 per hour (There's a 3-hr. minimum.) The cost can be divided between two or among three people. For information, contact the fisherman's cooperative in Pueblo la Playa, or **Victor's Aquatics** (☎ 800/521-2281 in the U.S., or 114/2-1092; fax 114/2-1093) at the Hotel Posada Real. Victor has a full fishing fleet with both *pangas* ($165 for 6 hr.) and cruisers ($380 to $450). Outfitters supply the boat and tackle, and the client buys the bait, drinks, and snacks.

Snorkeling/Diving Trips start around $50 per person and can be arranged through **Xplora Adventours,** (☎ 114/2-3537 or 114/2-9000, ext. 9316), the dive shop at the **Hotel Palmilla** (☎ 114/2-0582), or **Amigos del Mar** in Cabo San Lucas (☎ 114/3-0505).

Surfing **Playa Costa Azul,** at km 29 on Highway 1 just south of San José, is the most popular surfing beach in the area. There are a few bungalows available for rent here, or surfers can camp on the beach. Spectators can watch from the highway lookout point at the top of the hill south of Costa Azul.

Whale Watching From January through March, whales congregate offshore. Fishermen at Pueblo la Playa will take small groups out to see the whales; a 4-hour trip runs about $45 per person. Another option is **Tourcabos** (☎ 114/2-1982), which arranges whale watching for groups of four or more people; the 2-hour trip costs $50 per person.

SHOPPING

The town has a growing selection of unique design shops, hip boutiques, and collections of fine Mexican *artesanía,* clustered around **Bulevar Mijares** and **Zaragoza,** the main street. The municipal **market** on Mauricio Castro and Green sells edibles and utilitarian wares. Highlights include:

ADD. Zaragoza at Mijares. No phone.

This shop (the name is the initials for "Art, Design, and Decoration") sells creative home accessories and furnishings. Shipping is available.

Copal. Zaragoza 20. ☎ **114/2-3070.**

Traditional and contemporary Mexican housewares and home accessories are the specialties here.

Escape. Zaragoza, across from the cathedral. No phone.

Designer and casual sportswear and accessories, including Armani jeans, hand-tooled leather bags, belts, and a trendy selection of sunglasses.

Sierra Madre. Zaragoza, on the plaza. ☎ 114/2-3537.

Here you'll find nature-inspired gifts, books, and collectibles, with a conservationist theme. Xplora Adventours has a location inside the shop.

WHERE TO STAY

There's more demand than supply for hotel rooms in Baja Sur, so prices tend to be higher than equivalent accommodations in other parts of Mexico. San José has only a handful of budget hotels, so it's best to call ahead for reservations if you want economical accommodations. Accommodations in the beachfront hotel zone often offer package deals that bring room rates down to the moderate range, especially during summer months. Check with your travel agent.

Expensive

Hotel Presidente Inter-Continental. Bulevar Mijares s/n, 23400 San José del Cabo, B.C.S. ☎ **800/327-0200** in the U.S., or 114/2-0211. Fax 114/2-0232. 250 units. A/C TV TEL. $155 double standard room; $195 double oceanfront room; $210 double suite. Rates include all meals and many sports. AE, DC, MC, V.

Serenity, seclusion, and luxury are the hallmarks of the Presidente, set on a long stretch of beach next to the Estero San José. Low-rise, sand-colored buildings frame the beach and San José's largest swimming pool, which has a swim-up bar. If possible, splurge on a ground-floor oceanfront room with a terrace, preferably on the estuary side of the property. From your outdoor lounge chair, you'll be able to spot horseback riders trotting along the sand and white herons and egrets flying past the palms as the sun sets. The rooms have satellite TV and large bathrooms with hair dryers and makeup mirrors; suites include a separate sitting area.

Dining/Diversions: There's a palapa restaurant between the pool and beach with theme-night dinners; two indoor restaurants, one serving Mexican and one Italian cuisine; and a garden cafe, where dinner is served under the stars.

Amenities: The largest swimming pool in San José, as well as tennis, bicycles, golf clinics, and horseback riding. Laundry and room service, tour desk, and twice-daily shuttle to Cabo San Lucas for a fee.

Moderate

✪ **La Playita Resort.** Pueblo la Playa, Apdo. Postal 175, 23400 San José del Cabo, B.C.S. ☎ **888/288-8137** from the U.S., or phone/fax 114/2-4166. www.mexonline.com/playita/. 26 units. A/C TV. High season $82 double. Low season $60 double. AE, MC, V. Free parking.

Removed from even the slow pace of San José, this impeccably clean and friendly courtyard hotel is ideal for fishermen and rat-race escapees. Run by the warm and welcoming Karen Davis, it's the only hotel on San José's only beach that's safe for swimming. Just steps from the water and the lineup of fishing *pangas,* the two stories of sunlit rooms frame a patio with a swimming pool just large enough to allow you to swim laps. Each room is spacious, with high ceilings, high-quality if basic furnishings, screened windows, and nicely tiled bathrooms, plus cable TV. Two large suites on the second floor have small refrigerators. If you catch a big one, there's a fish freezer for storage. Services include coffee every morning and golf-cart shuttle to the beach. Next door, the hotel's La Playita Restaurant is open from 8am to 8pm and serves a great mix of seafood and standard favorites, plus occasional live jazz or tropical music. To find the hotel from Bulevar Mijares, follow the sign pointing to Puebla la Playa on a dirt road for about 2 miles to the beach. The hotel is on the left facing the water and at the edge of the tiny village of Puebla la Playa.

✪ **Tropicana Inn.** Bulevar Mijares 30, 23400 San José del Cabo, B.C.S. ☎ **114/2-0907** or 114/2-1580. Fax 114/2-1590. 40 units. A/C TV TEL. Dec 21–Apr 30 $77 double. May 1–Dec 20 $55 double. AE, MC, V. Free limited parking in back.

This handsome colonial-style hotel is a true oasis in sunny San José and a favorite hotel for repeat visitors. Set just behind (and adjacent to) the Tropicana Bar and Grill, it frames an attractive plant-filled courtyard with a graceful arcade bordering the rooms and inviting swimming pool. Each nicely furnished, medium-size room in the L-shaped building (which has a two- and a three-story wing) comes with Saltillo tile floors, two double beds, a window looking out on the courtyard, a brightly tiled bathroom with shower, coffee pot, and complimentary in-room coffee. Each morning, freshly brewed coffee, delicious sweet rolls, and fresh fruit are set out for the hotel guests. There's room service until 11pm from the adjacent Tropicana Bar and Grill (owned by the hotel). The inn is located behind the restaurant, a block south of the town square.

Inexpensive

Posada Señor La Mañana. Obregón 1, 23400 San José del Cabo, B.C.S. ☎/fax **114/2-1372.** E-mail: sr_manana@1cabonet.com.mx. 18 units. FAN. $32–$45 double. No credit cards.

Remodeled in 1995, this comfortable two-story guest house, set in a lush grove of fruit trees, offers cheery rooms with tile floors and new furniture. There's a small swimming pool, and guests have cooking privileges in a large fully equipped kitchen beside two spacious, breezy palapas. Ask about discounts and weekly rates. It's next to the Casa de la Cultura, behind the main square. A swimming pool has recently been added.

Posada Terranova. Degollado, 23400 San José del Cabo, B.C.S. ☎ **114/2-0534.** Fax 114/2-0902. 20 units. A/C TV. $50 double. AE, MC, V.

This is the nicest budget hotel in town. The terrace has a newly tiled floor, and the bright white rooms feature two double beds, tiled counters, bathrooms with brand new fixtures, TV, and powerful air-conditioning. One suite even has a small kitchen. The ground-floor restaurant (open daily from 7am to 10pm) has a front patio and an enclosed dining room and serves reasonably priced Mexican and American dishes. The posada is on Degollado, between Zaragoza and Doblado.

WHERE TO DINE
Expensive

Damiana. San José town plaza. ☎ **114/2-0499.** Reservations recommended during Christmas and Easter holidays. Main courses $12–$25. AE, MC, V. Daily 10:30am–10:30pm. SEAFOOD/MEXICAN.

This casually elegant restaurant in an 18th-century hacienda is decorated in the colors of a Mexican sunset: deep-orange walls, and tables and chairs clad in bright rose, lavender, and orange cloth. Mariachis play nightly from 8 to 9pm (mid-Dec through Mar) in the tropical courtyard, where candles flicker under the trees and the bougainvillea. For an appetizer, try the mushrooms diablo—a moderately zesty dish. For a main course, the ranchero shrimp in cactus sauce or grilled lobster tail are flavorful choices. You can also enjoy brunch almost until the dinner hour. There is an interior dining room, but the courtyard is the most romantic dining spot in Los Cabos. It's located on the east side of the town plaza.

✪ **Tequila.** M. Doblando s/n. ☎ **114/2-1155.** Main courses $10–$25. AE. Daily 11am–3pm and 6–10:30pm. MEXICAN/ASIAN.

The contemporary Mexican cuisine with a light and flavorful touch is the star attraction here, although the garden setting is lovely, with rustic *equipal* furniture and lanterns scattered among palms and giant mango trees. Start with a heavenly version of the traditional chiles en nogada, stuffed with couscous, raisins, and papaya and seasoned with cinnamon. Grilled tuna with ginger sauce arrive perfectly seared; the whole-grain bread, fresh and hot. Jazz music and attentive service complement the fine meal. An added touch: Cuban cigars and an excellent selection of tequilas are available.

Tropicana Bar and Grill. Bulevar Mijares 30. ☎ **114/2-1580.** Breakfast $4–$6; main courses $8–$20. AE, MC, V. Daily 8am–midnight. SEAFOOD/MEAT.

The Tropicana remains a popular mainstay, especially for tourists. The bar has a steady clientele day and night and often features special sporting events on satellite TV. The dining area is in a pretty garden (candlelit in the evening) with a tiled mural at one end. Cafe-styled sidewalk dining is also available. The menu is too extensive to lay claim to any specialty; it aims to please everyone. All meats and cheeses are imported, and dinners include thick steaks and shrimp fajitas. Paella is the Sunday special. The restaurant is 1 block south of the Plaza Mijares.

Zipper's. Playa Costa Azul just south of San José. No phone. Burgers and sandwiches $7–$10; main courses $7–$18. No credit cards. Daily 8am–10pm. BURGERS/MEXICAN/SEAFOOD.

Mike Posey and Tony Magdeleno own this popular, breezy hangout. Sitting at the far south end of the beach heading toward Cabo San Lucas and fronting the best surfing waters, it's become popular with gringos in search of American food and TV sports. Burgers have that back-home flavor—order one with a side of spicy, curly fries. Steaks, lobster, beer-batter shrimp, deli sandwiches, and Mexican combination plates round out the menu, which is printed with dollar prices.

Moderate

El Café Fiesta. Bulevar Mijares 14 at Zaragoza. ☎ **114/2-2808.** Breakfast $3–$6; main courses $3–$11. AE, MC, V. Daily 7am–10:30pm. VEGETARIAN/LIGHT MEXICAN.

On a shady edge of the Plaza Mijares, tables and chairs are set out under the trees and inside the largish dining room. Patrons enjoy a variety of hot and cold coffees, fruit-flavored margaritas, submarine sandwiches, platters of food with fresh whole-wheat pita bread and tortillas, and plenty of fresh fruits and salads. Chicken and beef fajitas are available for those who prefer meat.

SAN JOSÉ AFTER DARK

San José's nightlife revolves mainly around the restaurants and large hotels. Bulevar Mijares is the town's restaurant row, where you can wander until you find the restaurant or watering hole with the most appealing music. Several of the hotels have Mexican fiestas and other weekly theme nights that include a buffet (usually all-you-can-eat), drinks, live music, and entertainment for $25 to $35 per person.

Eclipse. Bulevar Mijares 38. Daily 11pm–4am.

This techno and alternative dance club is San José's only truly late-night option. There's usually no cover, though occasionally on weekends they charge an entrance fee of $15 that includes open bar. Recorded music only. It's open daily from 11pm to 4am.

Iguana Bar and Grill. Bulevar Mijares 24. ☎ **114/2-0266.** No cover.

This casual, lively open-air bar and restaurant is sheltered by a broad thatched roof and has a patio under the stars. Live music and dancing on Friday and Saturday get cranking around 9:30pm and can last until 2am. If you're hungry, the house specialty is barbecued ribs. The place is open daily from noon to 2am. Drinks run $3 to $5.

Tropicana Bar and Grill. Bulevar Mijares 30. ☎ **114/5-2684.** No cover.

This is definitely the most popular place in town. Patrons ensconce themselves in leather barrel chairs in the large bar, where, during the day, they tune in to American sports events on the big-screen TV. Come evening, guitarists play Mexican *boleros* and other traditional music from 6 to 11pm. After 9pm on some nights, a band plays Americanized rock and pop for those inclined to dance. The Tropicana is open daily from 7am to 1am. Drinks go for $3 and up.

THE CORRIDOR: BETWEEN THE TWO CABOS

The Corridor between the towns of San José del Cabo and Cabo San Lucas contains some of Mexico's most lavish resorts, designed as self-contained dream getaways. Most growth at the tip of the peninsula is occurring along the Corridor, which has been positioned to become a major international locale for championship golf. The three major resort areas are **Palmilla, Cabo Real,** and **Cabo del Sol,** each a self-enclosed community with golf courses, elegant hotels, and million-dollar homes.

If you plan to explore the region while staying at a Corridor hotel, you'll need a rental car for at least a day or two; cars are available at the hotels. Even if you're not staying here, the beaches and dining options are worth visiting. Hotels—all of which qualify as "very expensive" selections—are listed as you'll encounter them as you drive from San José to Cabo San Lucas. Rates listed are for the high season (winter); typically they'll be 20% lower in the summer. Golf and fishing packages are available at most resorts.

WHERE TO STAY

Casa del Mar. Km 19.5 on Hwy. 1, 23410 Cabo San Lucas, B.C.S. ☎ **800/221-8808** in the U.S., or 114/4-0030. Fax 114/4-0034. 56 units. A/C MINIBAR TV TEL. $365–$420 double. AE, MC, V.

A little-known treasure, this intimate resort is one of the best values along the Corridor. The hacienda-style building offers guests luxury accommodations in an intimate setting, as well as an on-site spa and nearby golf facilities. Located within the Cabo Real development, it's convenient to the 18-hole championship Cabo Real golf course. Gentle waterfalls lead to the adults-only pool area and a flowered path takes you further along, to the wide, sandy stretch of beach with a clear surf break. There's even a "quiet area" on the lawn for those looking for a siesta. Guest rooms have a clean, bright feel to them, with white marble floors, light wicker furnishings, and a large Jacuzzi tub, plus separate shower on the raised bathroom level. Each room features air-conditioning plus ceiling fan, sitting area, bathrobes, safe-deposit boxes, and cable TV. Balconies have oversized chairs, with a view of the ocean beyond the pool.

Dining/Diversions: Elegant restaurant—reminiscent of a formal dining room in a grand hacienda—serving international cuisine. The comfortable Lobby Bar serves an extensive selection of tequilas.

Amenities: Adults-only swimming pool and hot tub, plus pool bar; beach club with snack bar; two lit Astroturf tennis courts; Cabo Real Golf Club privileges; full service Avanti Spa, plus a small but well-equipped workout room; laundry and room service, gift shop, tour desk.

✪ **Hotel Palmilla.** Km 27.5 on Hwy. 1, 23400 San José del Cabo, B.C.S. ☎ **800/637-2226** in the U.S., or 114/4-5000. Fax 114/4-5100. www.palmillaresort.com. 130 units, 2 villas. A/C MINIBAR TV TEL. High season $450 double; $620–$1,150 suites and villas. Low season $230–$260 double; $335–$735 suites and villas. AE, DC, MC, V.

One of the most comfortably luxurious hotels in Mexico, the Palmilla is the grand dame of Los Cabos resorts. With a $12-million renovation completed in 1997, the rooms and facilities surpass even the newest luxe resorts built along the Corridor. Perched on a cliff top above the sea, the resort is a series of white buildings with red-tile roofs, towering palms, and flowering bougainvillea. Talavera vases, carved dressers and headboards, heavy-weave drapes and spreads, and bathrooms walled in hand-painted tiles give the rooms a colonial Mexico feeling. Private balconies have extra comfortable, overstuffed chairs. TVs have built-in VCRs with a wide selection of movies available at the concierge office. Standard amenities include bathrobes and fresh juice, coffee, and croissants delivered after your wake-up call. The hotel automatically adds a 15% service charge to all rates, which is included in the rates quoted above.

Dining/Diversions: The restaurant La Paloma has an outdoor terrace overlooking a small pool, plus a large dining room with gourmet exhibition kitchen. The Sunday brunch is as lavish as you could possibly imagine. Friday nights there's a special fiesta with entertainment and buffet dinner. There's also El Jardín, a pool snack bar, and the Neptuno Bar, known for both its views and margaritas.

Amenities: A large palm-shaded pool and 2 miles of beach, new fitness center with aerobic and weight-training equipment, two lit tennis courts, croquet court, two volleyball courts, horseback riding. Across the highway is the resort's championship golf course, designed by Robert Trent Jones II. The hotel has a small white chapel where weddings take place nearly every weekend. Hotel-owned fishing boats are available for guests. An on-premises dive shop rents equipment and can arrange diving and snorkeling expeditions. Laundry and room service, baby-sitting on request, tour desk, boutiques, hairstyling, car rental.

✪ **Las Ventanas al Paraíso.** Km 19.5 on Hwy. 1, 23400 San José del Cabo, B.C.S. ☎ **888/ 525-0483** in the U.S., or 114/4-0300. Fax 114/4-0301. 61 suites. A/C MINIBAR TV TEL. $485 double with partial ocean view; $500 double with full ocean view; $625 split-level suite with rooftop terrace. Special Spa and Golf packages available. AE, DC, MC, V. Complimentary valet parking.

No resort to date in Mexico has achieved this standard of luxury and attention to detail. Opened in late 1997, the architecture, with adobe structures and rough-hewn wood accents, provides a soothing complement to the desert landscape. The only burst of color comes from the dazzling windows (*ventanas*) of pebbled rainbow glass— handmade by regional artisans—that reflect the changing positions of the sun. Richly furnished, Mediterranean-style rooms are large (starting at 1,000 sq. ft.) and appointed with every conceivable amenity, from fireplaces to computerized telescopes for whale gazing in your own room. Fresh flowers and tequila setups welcome each guest, and room standards include satellite TV with VCRs, stereos with CD players, dual-line phones, and bathrobes. Sizable Jacuzzi tubs overlook the room but may be closed off for privacy. Larger suites offer pampering extras like rooftop terraces, sunken Jacuzzis on a private patio or a personal pool. The Spa, featured on the cover of *Travel & Leisure* (Mar 1998) is already known as the finest in Los Cabos. Only for those who want (and can afford) to be seriously spoiled.

Dining/Diversions: Ocean-view gourmet restaurant with wine cellar, specializing in seafood and nouvelle Mexican cuisine; adjoining terrace bar with live classical music; seaside casual-dining grill, plus fresh-juice bar.

Amenities: Deluxe European Spa with complete treatment and exercise facilities; access to adjoining championship Cabo Real golf course; availability of sportfishing and luxury yachts; 24-hour room service; water sports, tour services, boutique, car rental, shuttle services, laundry, and meeting rooms.

Westin Regina. km 22.5 on Hwy. 1, Apdo. Postal 145, 23400 San José del Cabo, B.C.S. ☎ **800/228-3000** in the U.S., or 114/2-9000. Fax 114/2-9010. 243 units. A/C MINIBAR TV TEL. $270 double with partial ocean view; $305 double with full ocean view; $370–$600 suite. Rates drop 20% in low season. AE, DC, MC, V.

Architecturally dramatic, the Westin Regina sits at the end of a long paved road atop a seaside cliff. Vivid terra-cotta, yellow, and pink walls rise against a landscape of sandstone, cacti, and palms, with fountains and gardens lining the long pathways from the lobby to the rooms. Electric carts carry guests and their luggage through the vast property. The rooms are gorgeous, with both air-conditioning and ceiling fans, private balconies, satellite TV, in-room safes, and walk-in showers separate from the bathtubs.

Dining/Diversions: Los Arrecifes restaurant is considered to be one of the most glamorous in Los Cabos. There are five other restaurants and two bars on the property.

Amenities: Three swimming pools, wide beachfront with beach club, full fitness center, and two tennis courts. The Palmilla and Cabo Real golf courses are nearby. Laundry and room service, Xplora Adventour services, boutique, gift shop, beauty and barber shop, business services.

WHERE TO DINE

Da Gorgio. Km 15 on Hwy. 1 at Misiones del Cabo. Breakfast $7–$12; pastas $9–$20. AE, MC, V. Daily 8am–midnight. ITALIAN.

The view surpasses the food at this cliff-top restaurant. Bar tables are set on small platforms scattered down the cliff side beside a rock-strewn waterfall and pond. Get here early if you want a prime sunset-watching spot, since demand is high for seats with an incomparable view of the sea and the rock arch at Land's End. Meals are served in an open-air dining room atop the cliff. The pastas and pizzas are good but not exceptional, and there's a lavish salad bar.

CABO SAN LUCAS
110 miles S of La Paz; 22 miles W of San José del Cabo; 1,120 miles SE of Tijuana

Although legendary for what lurks beneath the deep blue sea here, Cabo San Lucas is now drawing more people for its rich fairways and greens—and the world-class golf being played on them. The hundreds of new hotel rooms being added in this destination cater to a deluxe traveler getting away for a long weekend of sport and relaxation.

But playtime doesn't end when the sun goes down. The nightlife here is as hot as the desert in July. A collection of popular restaurants and bars, spread along Cabo's main street, stay open and active until the morning's first fishing charters head out to sea. Despite the growth in diversions, Cabo remains more or less a "one stoplight" town, with most everything located along the main strip, within easy walking distance.

If you're driving from La Paz, you'll pass through the village of Todos Santos, which has several restored historic buildings and makes a pleasant stop for a meal—try the Café Santa Fe, which draws diners from Los Cabos with its fresh fish and Italian cuisine.

ESSENTIALS
GETTING THERE & DEPARTING   By Plane   For arrival and departure information see "Getting There & Departing," above, under San José del Cabo. Local airline numbers are as follows: **Aerocalifornia (☎ 114/3-3700); **Alaska Airlines** (☎ 114/2-0959 at the airport); and **Mexicana** (☎ 114/3-5352, or 114/2-0606 at the airport).

By Car   From La Paz, take Highway 1 south past the village of San Pedro, then Highway 19 south through Todos Santos to Cabo San Lucas, a 2-hour drive.

By Bus   The **bus terminal** (☎ 114/3-0400) is on Héroes at Morelos; it is open daily from 6am to 9:30pm. Buses go to San José del Cabo about every hour between 6:30am and 8:30pm, and to La Paz every 90 minutes between 6am and 6pm.

Arriving   At the airport, either buy a ticket for a colectivo from the authorized transportation booth inside the building (about $10) or arrange for a rental car, the most economical way to explore the area. Private taxis can be shared by up to four people, and cost about $28 between San José and Cabo San Lucas.

It is not too far to walk with light luggage from the bus station to most of the budget hotels, but taxis are readily available.

VISITOR INFORMATION   The **Fondo Mixto de Los Cabos** functions as the information office in Cabo. It's on Madero between Hidalgo and Guerrero (☎ 114/3-4180; fax 114/3-2211). The English-language *Los Cabos Guide, Cabo Life, Baja Sun,* and *Gringo Gazette,* distributed free at most hotels and shops, have up-to-date information on new restaurants and clubs. *Note:* The many "visitor information" booths along the street are actually time-share sales booths, and their staffs will pitch a visit to their resort in exchange for discounted tours, rental cars, or other giveaways.

CITY LAYOUT   The small town spreads out north and west of the harbor of **Cabo San Lucas Bay,** edged by foothills and desert mountains to the west and south. The main street leading into town from the airport and San José del Cabo is **Lázaro Cárdenas;** as it nears the harbor, **Marina Boulevard** branches off from it and becomes the main artery that curves around the waterfront.

GETTING AROUND   Taxis are easily found and relatively inexpensive within Cabo, compared to the high cost of everything else.

For day-trips to San José del Cabo, catch a bus (see "Getting There & Departing," above) or a cab. You'll see car-rental specials advertised in town, but before signing on, be sure you understand the total price after insurance and taxes have been added. Rates can run between $40 and $75 per day, with insurance an extra $10 per day.

FAST FACTS: CABO SAN LUCAS

Area Code   The telephone area code was changed in 1993 from 684 to **114.** Calls between Cabo San Lucas and San José del Cabo are toll calls, so you must use the area code.

Beach Safety   Before swimming in the open water here, it's important to *check if the conditions are safe.* Undertows and large waves are common. **Medano Beach,** close to the marina and town, is the principle beach safe for swimming; it has several lively beachfront restaurant-bars. It's also easy to find water-sports equipment for rent here. The Hotel Melia Cabo San Lucas, on Medano Beach, has a roped-off swimming area to protect swimmers from jet skis and boats. Colored flags signaling swimming safety aren't generally used in Cabo and neither are lifeguards.

Currency Exchange   Banks exchange currency during normal business hours, generally Monday through Friday from 9am to 6pm and Saturday from 10am to 2pm. Currency-exchange booths, found all along Cabo's main tourist areas, aren't as competitive but they're more convenient.

Pharmacy   The largest drugstore in town, with a wide selection of toiletries as well as medicines, is **Farmacia Aramburo,** in Plaza Aramburo, on Cárdenas at Zaragoza; open daily from 7am to 9pm.

Post Office   The correo is at Cárdenas and Francisco Villa, on the highway to San José del Cabo, east of the bar El Squid Roe. It's open Monday through Friday from 9am to 1pm and 3 to 6pm, and Saturday from 9am to noon.

OUTDOOR ACTIVITIES: FISHING, GOLF & MORE

Although superb sportfishing put Cabo San Lucas on the map, there's more to do here than dropping your line and waiting for the Big One. For most cruises and excursions, try to make fishing reservations at least a day in advance; keep in mind that some trips require a minimum number of people. Most sports and outings can be arranged through a travel agency; fishing can also be arranged directly at one of the fishing-fleet offices at the far south end of the marina.

Besides fishing there's kayaking ($60 for a sunset kayak around the Arches rock formation) and boat trips to Los Arcos or uninhabited beaches. All-inclusive daytime or sunset cruises are provided on a variety of boats, including a replica of a pirate ship. Many of these trips include snorkeling; serious divers have great underwater venues to explore. Horseback riding to Los Arcos and to the Pacific (very popular at sunset) costs $50 for 2 hours.

Whale watching, between January and March, has become one of the most popular local activities. Guided ATV tours take you down dirt roads and through desert landscape to the old Cabo Lighthouse or an ancient Indian village. And then, of course, there's the challenge of world-class golf, now a major attraction of Los Cabos.

For a complete rundown of what's available, contact **Xplora Adventours** at ☎ **114/2-9000,** ext. 9316. They offer all tours from all local companies, rather than working with only a select few. Xplora has tour desks in the Westin Regina hotel, the Sierra Madre store on Lázaro Cárdenas, and at the Cabo Wabo Beach Club at Medano Beach.

FESTIVALS & EVENTS   The **Bisbee International Marlin Fishing Tournament** is held in October with a huge dollar prize for the winner. The **Senior Slam Golf**

Tournament, the richest jewel on the Senior PGA Tour, takes place in early spring each year.

ATV TRIPS   Expeditions on ATVs (all-terrain vehicles) to visit Cabo Falso, an 1890 lighthouse, and La Candelaria, an Indian pueblo in the mountains, are available through travel agencies. The 3-hour tour to **Cabo Falso** includes a stop at the beach, a look at some sea-turtle nests (without disturbing them) and the remains of a 1912 shipwreck, a ride over 500-foot sand dunes, and a visit to the lighthouse. Tours cost around $50 per person or $60 for two riding on one ATV. The vehicles are also available for rent at $35 for 3 hours.

La Candelaria is an isolated Indian village in the mountains 25 miles north of Cabo San Lucas. Described in *National Geographic,* the old pueblo is known for the white and black witchcraft still practiced here. Lush with palms, mango trees, and bamboo, the settlement is watered by an underground river that emerges at the pueblo. The return trip of the tour travels down a steep canyon, along a beach (giving you time to swim), and past giant-sea-turtle nesting grounds. Departing at 9am, the La Candelaria tour costs around $80 per person or $100 for two on the same ATV. A 440-pound weight limit per two-person vehicle applies to both tours.

BEACHES   All along the curving sweep of sand known as Medano Beach, on the east side of the bay, you can rent snorkeling gear, boats, WaveRunners ($35 per hr.), kayaks, pedal boats, and windsurf boards. You can also take windsurfing lessons. This is the town's main beach and is a great place for safe swimming as well as people watching from one of the many outdoor restaurants along its shore.

Beach aficionados may want to rent a car (see "Getting Around," above) and explore the five more remote beaches and coves between the two Cabos: Playas Palmilla, Chileno, Santa María, Barco Varado, and Vista del Arcos. Palmilla, Chileno, and Santa María are generally safe for swimming—but always be careful. The other beaches should not be considered safe. Experienced snorkelers may very well wish to check them out, but other visitors should go for the view only. Always check at a hotel or travel agency for directions and swimming conditions. Although a few travel agencies run snorkeling tours to some of these beaches, there's no public transportation: Your only option for beach exploring is to rent a car at a cost of $40 per day and up.

CRUISES   Glass-bottom boats leave from the town marina every 45 minutes daily between 9am and 4pm. They cost upwards of $6 for an hour tour past sea lions and pelicans to see the famous "El Arco" (Rock Arch) at Land's End, where the Pacific and the Sea of Cortés meet. Most boats make a brief stop at Playa de Amor or drop you off there if you ask; you can use your ticket to catch a later boat back (be sure to check what time the last boat departs).

There are a number of **daylong** and **sunset cruises,** on a variety of boats and catamarans. They vary in price—from $30 to $45 depending on the boat, duration of cruise, and amenities. A sunset cruise on the 42-foot catamaran *Pez Gato* (☎ 114/ 3-3797 or 114/3-2458) departs from the Hacienda Hotel dock at 5pm. The 2-hour cruise costs $35, which includes margaritas, beer, and sodas. Similar boats leave from the marina and the Plaza las Glorias hotel. Check with travel agencies or hotel tour desks.

GOLF   Los Cabos has become the golf mecca of Mexico, and though the courses are principally located along the Corridor, people look to Cabo San Lucas for information about this sport in Baja Sur. The Los Cabos golf master plan calls for a future total of 207 holes of golf. Fees listed below are for 18 holes of play, including golf cart, water, club service, and tax. Summer rates are about 25% lower, and many hotels offer special golf packages.

The 27-hole course at the **Palmilla Golf Club** (Palmilla resort; ☎ 800/386-2465 in the U.S., 114/2-1701, or 114/2-1708) was the first Jack Nicklaus Signature layout in Mexico, built in 1992 on 900 acres of dramatic oceanfront and desert. The course is a par-72 and measures a tough 6,939 yards, with greens fees of $115.50. Just a few miles away is another Jack Nicklaus Signature course, the 18-hole Ocean Course at **Cabo del Sol** (at the Cabo del Sol resort development in the Corridor; ☎ 800/386-2465 in the U.S.). The par-72, 7,100-yard course is known for its challenging three finishing holes. Fees are $132. The 18-hole, 6,945-yard, par-72 course at **Cabo Real** (by the Melia Cabo Real Hotel in the Corridor; ☎ 114/4-0232), was designed by Robert Trent Jones, Jr., and features holes that sit high on mesas overlooking the Sea of Cortés. Fees run $165 for 18 holes. Located in Cabo San Lucas is the 18-hole, par-72 course designed by Roy Dye at the **Cabo San Lucas Country Club** (☎ 800/854-2314 in the U.S., or 114/3-4653). The entire course overlooks the juncture of the Pacific Ocean and Sea of Cortés, including the famous Land's End rocks. It includes the 607-yard, par-5 7th hole—the longest hole in Mexico. Fees are $132. The most economical greens fees in the area are found at the 9-hole **Club Campo de Golf San José** (☎ 114/2-0900 or 114/2-0905), in San José del Cabo (see above). Green fees are just $15, carts an additional $30.

SNORKELING/DIVING   Several companies offer snorkeling; a 2-hour cruise to sites around El Arco costs $30, and a 4-hour trip to Santa María costs $55, including gear rental. Among the beaches visited on different trips are Playa de Amor, Santa María, Chileno, and Barco Varado. Snorkeling gear rents for $10 to $15. For scuba diving, contact **Amigos del Mar** (☎ 800/344-3349 in the U.S. or fax 213/545-1622 in the U.S.; 114/3-0505 or fax 114/3-0887 in Mexico) at the marina. Here diving specialist Ricardo Sevilla has the Cabo diving answers. Dives are made along the wall of a canyon in San Lucas Bay, where you can see a "sandfalls" that even Jacques Cousteau couldn't figure out—no one knows its source or cause. There are also scuba trips to Santa María Beach and places farther away, including the Gordo Banks and Cabo Pulmo. Dives start at $55 for a one-tank dive and $70 for two tanks; trips to the coral outcropping at Cabo Pulmo start at $115. Two hours from Cabo San Lucas, Cabo Pulmo is rated for beginners and up. Gordo Banks, for advanced divers, is an underwater mountain about 5 miles offshore with a black coral bottom and schools of game fish and manta rays. Resort courses cost $100 per person and open-water certification costs around $400. April through November is the best time to dive, although diving is busiest from October to mid-January—it's important to make reservations in advance if you're planning to dive then.

SPORTFISHING   Go to the town marina on the south side of the harbor. There, you'll find several fleet operators with offices near the docks. The best deals are offered by the *panga* **fleets,** where 5 hours of fishing for two or three people costs $150 to $200. To choose one, take a stroll around the marina and talk with the captains—you may arrive at an economical deal. Try **ABY Charters** (main office at the Giggling Marlin restaurant; ☎ 114/3-0831) or the **Picante Fleet** (☎ 114/3-2474), both of which are located at the sportfishing dock at the far south end of the marina. The going rate for a day on a fully equipped cruiser with captain and guide (many of the larger hotels, like the Solmar, have their own fleets) starts at around $350 for up to four people. These have bathrooms aboard. For deluxe trips with everything included aboard a 43-foot boat, you'll have to budget $1,400. (See also "Outdoor Sports, Adventure Travel & Wilderness Trips," in chapter 3, for companies that can arrange fishing in advance.)

The fishing really lives up to its reputation: Bringing in a 100-pound marlin is routine. Angling is good all year, though the catch varies with the season: Sailfish and wahoo are best from June through November; yellowfin tuna, from May through December; yellowtail, from January through April; black and blue marlin, July through December; and striped marlin are prevalent year-round.

The "catch and release" program is encouraged in Los Cabos. Anglers reel in their fish, which are tagged and released unharmed into the sea. The angler gets a certificate and the knowledge that there will still be billfish in the sea when he or she returns.

SURFING　Good surfing can be found from March through November all along the beaches west of town, and there's a famous right break at **Chileno Beach,** near the Cabo San Lucas Hotel east of town.

WHALE WATCHING　Whale-watching cruises are not to be missed when gray whales migrate to the Los Cabos area between January and March. The sportfishing boats, glass-bottom boats, and cruise catamarans all offer whale-watching trips ranging from $35 to $60 for a half-day trip. You can also spot the whales from shore; good whale-watching spots include the beach by the Solmar Suites hotel on the Pacific and the beaches and cliffs along the Corridor. The ultimate whale excursion is an all-day trip to **Magdalena Bay,** an hour's plane ride away. In a small skiff (*panga*) you get close enough to touch the whales. The cost for the 4-hour trip, including air transportation, is $320.

OTHER SPORTS　**Bicycles, boogie boards, snorkels, surfboards,** and **golf clubs** are available for rent at **Cabo Sports Center** in the Plaza Náutica on Bulevar Marina (☎ 114/3-4272); the center is open Monday through Saturday from 9am to 9pm and Sunday from 9am to 5pm.

You can rent **horses** at the Hacienda Hotel (☎ 114/3-0123) or the Melia San Lucas (☎ 114/3-0420) for around $20 to $30 per hour. They have guided beach rides and sunset tours to El Faro Viejo (the Old Lighthouse) for $30 to $45 per person and to the Pacific for sunset riding on the beach.

A Break from Sports: Exploring Cabo San Lucas

FESTIVALS & EVENTS　**October 12** is the festival of the patron saint of Todos Santos, a town about 65 miles north. **October 18** is the feast of the patron saint of Cabo San Lucas, celebrated with a fair, feasting, music, dancing, and other special events.

HISTORIC CABO SAN LUCAS　Sports and partying are Cabo's main attractions, but there are also a few cultural and historical points of interest. The stone **Iglesia de San Lucas** (Church of San Lucas) on Calle Cabo San Lucas close to the main plaza was established in 1730 by the Spanish missionary Nicolás Tamaral; a large bell in a stone archway commemorates the completion of the church in 1746. Tamaral was eventually killed by the Pericúe Indians, who reportedly resisted his demands that they practice monogamy. Buildings on the streets facing the main plaza are gradually being renovated to house restaurants and shops, and the picturesque neighborhood promises to have the strongest Mexican ambiance of any place in town.

DAY-TRIPS TO LA PAZ　Day-trips to the city of La Paz can be booked through a travel agency for around $80, including lunch and a tour of the countryside along the way. Usually there's a stop at the weaving shop of Fortunato Silva, who spins his own cotton and weaves it into wonderfully textured rugs and textiles.

SHOPPING　A popular tourist shopping stop is the **open-air market** on Plaza Papagayo on Bulevar Marina opposite the entrance to Pueblo Bonito. However, it mainly has trinkets and traditional souvenirs—little in the way of real craftwork.

Be sure to bargain. Most shops are on or within a block or two of Bulevar Marina and the plaza.

Casa Maya. Calle Morelos between Rev. and 20 de Noviembre. ☎ **114/3-3197.**

Unusual decorative items for the home, at excellent prices. Tin lamps, colored glass, and rustic wood furnishings.

Cuca's Blanket Factory. Cárdenas at Matamoros. ☎ **114/3-1913.**

This open-air stand sells the standard Mexican cotton and woolen blankets with an added attraction—you can design your own and have it ready the next day. Open daily from 9am to 9pm.

El Callejon. Vicente Guerrero s/n, at Cárdenas. ☎ **114/3-1139.**

This, the most eclectic shop in Los Cabos, features antiques, unique gifts, paintings, and home furnishings. The one-of-a-kind items are mostly made by local artists. It's open Monday through Saturday from 10am to 8pm. American Express is accepted.

Galería Gattamelata. Hacienda Rd. ☎ **114/3-1166.**

In the Medano Beach area, this handsome gallery specializes in antiques and colonial-style furniture. Open daily from 9am to 9pm.

Mamma Eli's. Calle Cabo San Lucas west of the plaza at Madero. ☎ **114/3-1616.**

One of the nicest shops in Los Cabos, Mamma Eli's has three levels packed with a high-quality selection of folk art, crafts, clothing, and furniture. Open Tuesday through Sunday from 9am to 1:30pm and 4 to 7pm.

Nupalli. Zaragoza s/n, corner of Lázaro Cárdenas. ☎/fax **114/3-5644** or 114/3-5645.

Exquisite, artistic jewelry and other decorative and fine arts. All are original, signed pieces by Mexican artists. The adjoining gallery features regional artists as well as contemporary Mexican masters. Owner Lia Esses's own jewelry designs are among the more creative pieces available. Open daily, 10:30am to 9:30pm.

Plaza Bonita. Bulevar Marina at Cárdenas.

This large terra-cotta colored plaza on the edge of the marina has been around since 1990 and is finally filling with successful businesses. **Libros** (☎ **114/3-1770**), at the front of the mall, is a bookstore with English-language novels and magazines and a good selection of books on Baja. A branch of **Dos Lunas** (☎ **114/3-1969**) sells colorful sportswear. **Cartes** (☎ **114/2-1770**) is filled with hand-painted ceramic vases and dishes, pewter frames, carved furniture, and handwoven textiles. Most shops in the plaza are open daily from 10am to 9pm.

Rostros de México. Cárdenas at Matamoros. No phone.

Walls of wooden masks and carved religious statues are the draw at this gallery—whose name means "Faces of Mexico." Open Monday through Saturday from 10am to 2pm and 4:30 to 9pm, Sunday from 10am to 2pm.

WHERE TO STAY

All hotel prices listed here are for the high season, in effect from November through Easter; summer rates are about 20% less. Several Cabo San Lucas hotels offer package deals that significantly lower the nightly rate; ask your travel agent for information.

Budget accommodations are scarce in Cabo San Lucas. The handful of inexpensive hostelries often have no vacancies, so it's wise to call ahead for reservations or to arrive early when other travelers are checking out.

Very Expensive

Melia San Lucas. Playa Medano, 23410 Cabo San Lucas, B.C.S. ☎ **800/336-3542** in the U.S., or 114/3-4444. Fax 114/3-0420. 150 units. A/C MINIBAR TV TEL. $266 double; $545 junior suite. Ask about golf and other packages and summer specials. AE, MC, V.

By far the most popular hotel in Cabo San Lucas, the Melia sits above Playa Medano within easy walking distance of town. A tall, peaked palapa covers the lobby, with its breathtaking view of El Arco in the distance. All rooms, furnished in wicker and white marble, have balconies with views of the ocean and the landscaped pool area. The entire property needs a little maintenance, but it remains popular due to its location. Satellite TV brings in U.S. channels. Each room has its own safe and coffeemaker. Rates above include tax and the hotel's mandatory 10% service charge.

Dining/Diversions: Three restaurants cover the dining spectrum from haute cuisine (where reservations are required) to seafood by the beach. Two bars, one of them swim-up, keep guests in beverages. There's live entertainment nightly in the lobby.

Amenities: Two heated pools (one children's pool); laundry and room service; boutique; hairstyling; tour desk; car rental; rentals of water-sport equipment, bicycles, and motor scooters; two lit tennis courts; nearby golf courses.

✪ **Solmar Suites.** Av. Solmar 1, 23410 Cabo San Lucas, B.C.S. ☎ **114/3-3535.** Fax 114/3-0410. (Reservations: Box 383, Pacific Palisades, CA 90272; ☎ **800/344-3349** or 310/459-9861; fax 310/454-3349.) 90 suites. A/C MINIBAR TV TEL. $200–$336 suite. AE, MC, V.

Set against sandstone cliffs at the very tip of the Baja Peninsula, the Solmar is beloved of those seeking seclusion, comfort, and easy access to Cabo's diversions. The suites are in two-story white stucco buildings along the edge of a broad beach and have either a king or two double beds, satellite TV, separate seating areas, and private balconies or patios on the sand. Guests gather by the pool and on the beach at sunset and all day long during the winter whale migration. Advance reservations are necessary almost year-round. A small time-share complex adjoins the Solmar; some units are available for nightly stays. Rates above include the hotel's mandatory 10% service charge.

Dining/Diversions: The restaurant, La Roca, serves excellent Mexican specialties and seafood and presents a Mexican fiesta on Saturday nights.

Amenities: The pool's swim-up bar faces the palapa-covered beach bar; lounge chairs are scattered in the sun and under mature palms. The Solmar has one of the best sportfishing fleets in Los Cabos, including the deluxe Solmar V used for long-range diving, fishing, and whale-watching expeditions.

Expensive

Plaza Las Glorias. Bulevar Marina s/n, 23410, Cabo San Lucas, B.C.S. ☎ **800/342-AMIGO** from the U.S., or 114/3-1220. Fax 114/3-1238. 287 units. A/C TV TEL. $190 double standard room. AE, MC, V.

If you've come to Cabo San Lucas to fish, you can't get any closer to the docks than the marina-front Plaza Las Glorias. This large, lively hotel caters to the active traveler and is situated above a shopping-and-dining arcade, offering exceptional views of the marina harbor and boats. Beyond the standard accommodations, there are also suites available with kitchens and private terraces with Jacuzzis. The hotel's style is decidedly Mediterranean, with muted desert colors and tile floors. On the second level, there's a large mosaic pool and bar on a terrace that borders the marina, adjacent to the lighthouse restaurant. A small boat shuttles guests to a private beach club near Los Arcos, with a restaurant, towel service, and shade palapas.

Dining/Diversions: Sea Food Mama's, in the marina lighthouse, specializes in what's brought in from the adjacent docks. There's also a pool snack bar, La Vela beach club restaurant, and a tequila-oriented lobby bar.

Amenities: Terrace-level swimming pool, private beach club with boat shuttle. Tour desk, car rental, laundry and room service also available.

Inexpensive

✪ **Cabo Inn.** 20 de Noviembre and Leona Vicario, 23410 Cabo San Lucas, B.C.S. ☎/fax **114/3-0819.** 20 units. A/C. $53 double; $300 double weekly. Street parking available.

This three-story hotel on a quiet street is a real find. It's a rare combination of low rates, extra-friendly management, and great, funky style—not to mention extra clean. Rooms are basic and very small; although this was a bordello in a prior incarnation, everything is new, from the mattresses to the minirefrigerators. Muted desert colors add a spark of personality, and rooms come with either two twin beds or one queen bed. The rooms surround a courtyard where you can enjoy satellite TV, a barbecue grill, and free coffee. The third floor has a palapa and hot tub with extra seating. A large fish freezer is available, as are kitchenettes in most rooms. The hotel's just 2 blocks from downtown and the marina. Next door, a lively restaurant will even deliver pitchers of margaritas and dinner to your room.

Hotel Mar De Cortez. Cárdenas at Guerrero, 23410 Cabo San Lucas, B.C.S. ☎ **114/ 3-0032.** (Reservations: 17561 Vierra Canyon Rd., Suite 99, Salinas, CA 93907; ☎ 800/ 347-8821; fax 408/663-1904.) 82 units. A/C. $42–$60 double. MC, V. Free parking.

In a great location, on Cárdenas 3 blocks from the marina in the center of town, this attractive two-story hotel arranged its Spanish-style white stucco building around a rambling, landscaped courtyard with a huge pool shaded by palm and banana trees. The front of the hotel houses shops and a travel agency. Each of the smaller rooms of the older section has dark-wood furniture and one double or two single beds, a desk, and a tiny front porch facing the courtyard. Those in the newer section have two double beds; suites have one king bed and a sleeper couch or two doubles and a sleeper couch. A semi-outdoor bar with a fireplace under its thatched roof for occasional cool winter nights is a pleasant gathering place. There's also a restaurant with a TV and a freezer for storing your fish. The place books up quickly; many patrons are regulars who return every year. Rates above include the hotel's mandatory 10% service charge.

Siesta Suites. Zapata at Hidalgo, 23410 Cabo San Lucas, B.C.S. ☎/fax **114/3-2773.** 20 suites (all with kitchenette). A/C FAN. $45–$55 double. No credit cards.

Reservations are a must at this immaculate small inn, which opened in early 1994. The rooms have white tile floors and white walls, kitchenettes with seating areas, refrigerators, and sinks. The mattresses are new and firm, and the bathrooms are large and sparkling clean. In 1997 the hotel added a fourth floor; its five rooms have two queen beds each. The accommodating proprietors offer free movies; a barbecue pit and outdoor patio table on the second floor; and a comfortable lobby with TV. They can also arrange fishing trips. Weekly and monthly rates are available. The hotel is 1½ blocks from the marina, where parking is available.

WHERE TO DINE

It's not uncommon to pay a lot for mediocre food in Cabo, so try to get a couple of unbiased recommendations before settling in for a meal. If people are only drinking and not dining, take that as a clue, since many seemingly popular places are long on party atmosphere but short on food. Prices decrease the farther you walk inland from the waterfront. Besides the restaurants mentioned below, dozens of good, clean taco stands and taco restaurants dot the downtown area. The absolute favorite with locals is **Manuel's Tamales,** a street stand selling these traditional treats of corn meal stuffed with meat or cheese, then steamed in a corn husk. He's always found on weekend nights on the corner of Cárdenas and Zaragoza, across from Planet Hollywood. These are truly the least expensive good eats in town. Streets to explore for other good restaurants include Hidalgo and Cárdenas, plus the Marina at the Plaza Bonita. The expected U.S. franchise chains (Kentucky Fried Chicken, Subway, Pizza Hut, etc.) proliferate downtown. Note that many restaurants automatically add the tip onto the bill.

Very Expensive

Casa Rafael's. Hacienda Rd. ☎ **114/3-0739.** Fax 114/316-79. Reservations suggested. Main courses $20–$45. AE, MC, V. Daily 6–10pm. INTERNATIONAL.

Looking for a little romance? If the ambiance here doesn't inspire it, the food most certainly will. Chef Willie Michel produces innovative specialties that have become a mainstay of repeat visitors to Los Cabos. Dine in one of the candlelit rooms and alcoves (air-conditioned) of this large house, or outside beside the small swimming pool. Piano music plays in the background while you enjoy a leisurely meal; the courses are timed not to rush you. To start, try the sublime smoked dorado pâté, or perhaps the hearts of palm with a raspberry vinaigrette dressing. House specialties—a tasty combination of selections from the meat, seafood, and pasta menus—include the chicken Parmesan Sonia and scampi with pasta. Steaks are made from black Angus cattle imported from the United States; the lamb comes from New England. The rich desserts may make you wish you'd seen them first—or then again maybe not. Wine and aperitif menus are extensive. *Note:* Menu prices do not include 10% tax or 10% tip. Recent additions include their popular Cigar Room, a piano bar, and the new "Ocean Room" for dining featuring a saltwater fish tank.

Casa Rafael's is also a lovely 11-room B&B (with rooms upstairs and downstairs). The air-conditioned rooms cost $120 to $145 and include breakfast. To find it, follow the Hacienda Road toward the ocean; when you top the hill, look left and turn left when you see the rosy-pink château with arched front and patio with caged birds and fountain.

Expensive

✪ **Nick-San.** Bulevar Marina, Plaza de la Danza, Local no. 2. ☎ **114/3-4484.** Main courses $12–$25; sushi $3 and up. MC, V. Tues–Sun 3–10:30pm. JAPANESE/SUSHI.

Exceptional Japanese cuisine and sushi are the specialties in this air-conditioned restaurant with a clean, minimalist decor. A rosewood sushi bar with royal-blue–tiled accents welcomes diners to watch the master sushi chef at work. An exhibition kitchen behind him demonstrates why this place has been honored with a special award for cleanliness.

Peacocks. Paseo del Pescador s/n, corner of Melia Hotel. ☎ **114/3-1858.** Main courses $15–$30. AE, MC, V. Daily 6–10:30pm. INTERNATIONAL.

One of Cabo's most exclusive patio-dining establishments, Peacocks emphasizes fresh seafood creatively prepared. Start off with the house pâté or a salad of feta cheese with cucumber, tomato, and onion. For a main course, try one of the pastas—linguini with grilled chicken and sun-dried tomatoes is a good choice. More filling entrees include steaks, shrimp, and lamb, all prepared several ways.

Moderate

✪ **La Dolce Vita.** M. Hidalgo y Zapata s/n. ☎ **114/3-4122.** Main courses $6–$9. No credit cards. Daily 6–midnight. Closed Sept. ITALIAN.

This Cabo version of the original Puerto Vallarta locale has once again transported authentic Italian thin-crust, brick-oven pizzas intact to Mexico. The food is some of the best you'll find in the Baja Peninsula, and the fact that 80% of their business is from local customers underscores the point. Partner Stefano (a dead-ringer for

Michaelangelo's *David*, albeit with pants) keeps the service attentive and welcoming and the food up to the high standards it's known for. The simple menu also features sumptuous pastas and calzones, plus great salads. This is the best late-night dining option.

✪ **Mi Casa.** Calle Cabo San Lucas at Madero. ☎ **114/3-1933.** Main courses $11–$20. MC, V. High season Mon–Sat 1–10pm. Low season Mon–Sat 5–10pm. MEXICAN/ NOUVELLE MEXICAN.

The building's vivid cobalt-blue facade is your first clue that this place celebrates Mexico; the menu confirms that impression. This is one of Cabo's finest gourmet Mexican restaurants. Traditional specialties such as *manchamanteles* (literally, "table-cloth stainers"), cochinita pibil, and chiles enogados are everyday menu staples. Fresh fish is prepared with delicious seasonings and recipes from throughout Mexico. Especially pleasant at night, the restaurant's tables, scattered around a large patio, are set with colorful cloths, traditional pottery, and glassware. It's across from the main plaza.

Inexpensive

✪ **Cafe Canela.** On the Marina boardwalk, below Plaza Las Glorias hotel. ☎ **114/3-3435.** Main courses $3–$6; coffee $1.75–$3.50. MC, V. Open daily, 7am–10pm. COFFEE/PASTRY/ LIGHT MEALS.

This cozy, tasty cafe and bistro is a welcome addition to the Cabo Marina boardwalk. Espresso drinks or a fruit smoothie and a muffin are good eye-openers for early risers. Enjoy a light meal or a tropical drink either inside or on the bustling waterfront terrace. The appealing menu also offers breakfast egg wraps, salads (curried chicken salad with fresh fruit), sandwiches (blue cheese quesadillas with smoked tuna and mango), and pastas, all reasonably priced. There's full bar service, also.

Felix Tacos. Hidalgo and Zapata s/n, across from Mama's Royal Cafe. Main courses $4–$8. Daily 1–10pm. MEXICAN.

At this tiny, friendly family-run place, you can sit on a stool and watch the preparation of some of the most delicious cheap eats in Los Cabos. Everything's fresh and homemade, including the corn tortillas and several different salsas. Fish tacos made with fresh dorado are superb.

✪ **Mama's Royale Cafe.** Hidalgo at Zapata. ☎ **114/3-4290.** Breakfast special $3; breakfast à la carte $2.50–$7; lunch $5–$8. Daily 7am–2:30pm. BREAKFAST/LUNCH/INTERNATIONAL.

What a great place to start the day. The shady patio decked with cloth-covered tables and the bright, inviting interior dining room are both comfortable places to settle in. And the food's just as appetizing. Spencer Moore presides over this dining mecca with well-prepared breakfast selections that include grilled Polish sausage, French toast stuffed with pecans and cream cheese and topped with pineapple, eggs Benedict, great hash browns, fruit crepes, and, of course, traditional breakfasts, plus free coffee refills. The lunch menu includes Mexican specialties such as enchiladas and quesadillas, fresh fish and shrimp, sandwiches, and burgers.

Pollo de Oro Rostizado. Cárdenas, by El Squid Roe. ☎ **114/3-0310.** Breakfast $3–$4; chicken $2.25–$6; ribs $2–$4; comida corrida $3–$4. Daily 7am–11pm. ROAST CHICKEN AND RIBS.

In the midst of glitzy prime real estate, this simple red-and-white wood-frame restaurant has been dishing out delicious roast chicken and rib plate meals and preparing box lunches for fisher folk for at least a decade. Platters of whatever you choose (a whole, half, or quarter chicken for example) are tasty and filling and come with rice, salad, and fresh corn tortillas. The green sauce, set at each table, is great dabbed on chicken. The daily comida corrida features chicken in mole sauce, chile rellenos, and steak ranchero. It's beside Squid Roe and opposite Plaza Bonita.

The Fish Company. Av. Guerrero at Zapata. ☎ **114/3-1405.** Breakfast $3–$4; main courses $4.50–$12. Daily 8:30am–10pm. MEXICAN/SEAFOOD.

Owner Miguel Olvera has his share of fans among local diners tired of high prices and small portions. His small restaurant has only a dozen or so cloth-covered tables, but they're nearly always full. Main courses usually come with rice or baked potato, beans, and tortillas. Fisher folk can have their catch prepared to eat there with all the same accompaniments for $5 per person. If you're tired of fish, the carne asada is great. The restaurant is half a block inland from Bulevar Marina and the Plaza Las Glorias Hotel.

CABO SAN LUCAS AFTER DARK

Cabo San Lucas is the nightlife capital of Baja and a contender within resort Mexico. After-dark fun is centered around the party ambiance and camaraderie found in the casual bars and restaurants on Bulevar Marina or facing the marina, rather than around a flashy disco scene. You can easily find a happy hour with live music and a place to dance or a Mexican fiesta with mariachis.

MEXICAN FIESTAS & THEME NIGHTS   Some of the larger hotels have weekly "Fiesta Nights," "Italian Nights," and other buffet-plus-entertainment theme nights that can be fun as well as a good buy. Check travel agencies and the following hotels: the **Solmar** (☎ 114/3-0022), the **Finisterra** (☎ 114/3-0000), the **Hacienda** (☎ 114/3-0123), and the **Melia San Lucas** (☎ 114/3-0420). Prices range from $16 (drinks, tax, and tips are extra) to $35 (which covers everything, including an open bar with national drinks).

SUNSET WATCHING   At twilight, check out Land's End, where the two seas meet, and watch the sun sink into the Pacific.

Whale Watcher's Bar. In the Hotel Finisterra. ☎ **114/3-3333.** Fax 114/305-90. AE, CB, DC, MC, V.

This is Los Cabo's premier place for sunset watching. Its location at Land's End—where the two seas meet—offers a truly world-class view of the sun sinking into the Pacific. The high terrace offers vistas of both sea and beach, as well as magical glimpses of whales from January to March. Mariachis play on Friday, Saturday, and Sunday from 5 to 8pm. The bar is open daily from noon to 11pm. "Whale margaritas" cost $4; beer, $3. There are two-for-one drinks during happy hour from 4 to 6pm.

HAPPY HOURS & HANGOUTS   If you shop around, you can usually find an *hora alegre* (happy hour) somewhere in town between noon and 7pm. On my last visit, the most popular places to drink and carouse until all hours were the Giggling Marlin, El Squid Roe, Rio Grill, and the Cabo Wabo Cantina.

El Squid Roe. Bulevar Marina, opposite Plaza Bonita. ☎ **114/3-0655.** No cover.

El Squid Roe is one of the late Carlos Anderson's inspirations, and it still attracts wild, fun-loving crowds with its two stories of nostalgic decor and eclectic food that's far better than you'd expect from such a party place. As fashionable as blue jeans, this is a place to see and see what can be seen—women's tops are known to be discarded with regularity here, as the dancing on tables moves into high gear. There's also a patio out back for dancing when the tables, chairs, and bar spots have all been taken. Open daily from noon to 3am.

Giggling Marlin. On Cárdenas at Zaragoza across from the marina. ☎ **114/3-0606.** No cover.

Live music alternates with recorded tunes to get the happy patrons dancing—and occasionally jumping up to dance on the tables and bar. A contraption of winches, ropes, and pulleys above a mattress provides entertainment as couples literally string each other up by the heels—just like a captured marlin. The food is only fair here; stick with nachos and drinks. There is live music Wednesday through Sunday from 9pm to midnight during high season. The Giggling Marlin is open daily from 8am to midnight; the bar stays open till 1am. Beer runs $1.75 to $2.50; schooner margaritas cost $4 to $6. Drinks are half-price during happy hour from 2 to 6pm.

Latitude 22+. Cárdenas. ☎ **114/3-1516.**

This raffish restaurant/bar never closes. License plates, signs, sports caps, and a 959-pound blue marlin are the backdrop for U.S. sports events that play on six TVs scattered among pool tables, dart boards, and assorted games. Foodstuffs from hamburgers to chicken-fried steak is offered, or you can have breakfast any time. Latitude 22+ is 1 block north of the town's only traffic light.

Río Grill Restaurant and Bar. Bulevar Marina 31-A at Guerrero. ☎ **114/3-1335.** No cover.

The curving bar in the middle of the room has a cozy neighborhood feeling, with tourists and locals taking advantage of the two-for-one "happy-hour" margaritas, served from 5 to 9pm. Soft music plays during dinner. From Thursday through Sunday live rhythm-and-blues and reggae bands play from 9:30pm to 12:30am. On Thursdays at 8:30pm, enthusiastic patrons partake in "Karaoke Kraziness." Río Grill is open daily from 7am to midnight.

Dancing

Cabo Wabo Cantina. Guerrero at Cárdenas. ☎ **114/3-1188.** Cover $15–$20 for live-music shows (includes 2 drinks); otherwise free.

Owned by the rock band Van Halen and its Mexican and American partners, this "cantina" packs in youthful crowds, especially when rumors fly that a surprise appearance by a vacationing musician is imminent. Live rock bands from the United States, Mexico, Europe, and Australia perform frequently on the well-equipped stage. When live music is absent, a disco-type sound system plays mostly rock but some alternative and techno as well. Overstuffed furniture frames the dance floor. For snacks, the "Taco-Wabo," just outside the club's entrance, stays up late, too. The cantina is open nightly from 8pm to 4am.

Kokomo. Bulevar Marina s/n. ☎ **114/3-0600.** No cover. AE, MC, V.

Lively and tropical in theme and spirit, Kokomo is gaining in popularity as a happening dance club. They also serve lunch and dinner, but the drinks are better than the food. A happy hour features two-for-one drinks daily from 4 to 8pm. Grab a table along the oversized windows looking out over Bulevar Marina for people watching. Open daily from 11am to 2am.

MEN'S CLUBS   Or, should they be called "ladies' clubs," since that's who's doing the dancing? In any event, there's now a selection of places in Cabo that offer so-called exotic dancing. **Lord Black** (☎ 114/3-5415), located on Bulevar Marina in the Plaza Náutica, features not only show girls, but sushi, too. **Showgirls 20** (☎ 114/3-5380) at the corner of Lázaro Cárdenas and Francisco Villa, calls itself a world-class cabaret. It also offers pool tables, satellite TVs, and private dancers.

Todos Santos: A Desert Oasis

42 miles N of Cabo San Lucas, on Highway 19

Having become known as "Bohemian Baja," Todos Santos is finding its way on the travel agendas of those looking for the latest, the trendiest, and the hippest of artist outposts. With local establishments like Hotel California and Café Santa Fe, you get the picture.

Todos Santos, an oasis in this desert landscape, enjoys an almost continuous water supply that stems from the peaks of the Sierra de la Laguna mountains. Just over an hour's drive up the Pacific coast from Cabo San Lucas, you'll know you're arriving when the arid coastal scenery is suddenly interrupted by the verdant groves of palms, mangos, avocados and papayas.

Over the last several hundred years, this town has alternated between boom and bust, roughly following the reliability of the water supply. Its most recent boom lasted from the mid-19th century until the 1950s, when the town prospered as a center of sugarcane production and developed a strong cultural influence. Many of the buildings now being restored and converted into galleries, studios, shops, and restaurants were built during this era.

In recent years, Todos Santos residents have turned to organic farming as a principal industry. The resulting produce has encouraged the development of more contemporary dining options, and a handful of excellent restaurants and cafes attract patrons from throughout southern Baja. Demand for the town's older colonial-style structures by artists, entrepreneurs, and foreign residents have resulted in a real-estate boom. New shops and cafes are continuously cropping up. For the casual visitor, Todos Santos can easily be explored in a day, but a few tranquil inns welcome charmed guests who want to stay a little longer.

FROM LOS CABOS TO THE EAST CAPE

The coastline of the Sea of Cortés north of San José has long been a favored destination of die-hard anglers, who fly their private planes to airstrips at out-of-the-way lodges. The coastline has experienced considerable development in the past few years, and hotels have expanded their services to please even those who never plan to set foot on a boat. Housing developments are appearing along the main road, but there's still plenty of space for adventurous campers to find secluded beaches.

A rough dirt road called the **Coastal Road** runs along the East Cape from San José to La Ribera, but it can take up to 4 hours to complete the 55-mile drive. Along this route you pass by **Cabo Pulmo,** where Baja's only coral reef lies just offshore. There are no major hotels, restaurants, or dive shops here, and most divers reach the reefs via dive boats from Los Cabos. The more efficient approach to the East Cape is to drive the paved **Highway 1** from San José north to dirt roads leading off the highway to resorts and communities at Punta Colorado, Buena Vista, Los Barriles, and Punta Pescadero. Public buses from San José stop at major intersections, where you'll need to catch a cab to the hotels. Most guests at the hotels take a cab from the airport and simply stay there.

WHERE TO STAY & DINE

Hotel Buenavista Beach Resort. Km 35 Hwy. S. Buenavista, (35 miles north of San José del Cabo; Apdo. Postal 574), 23000 La Paz, B.C.S. ☎ **112/2-1962** or 114/1-0033.

During the **Festival Fundidor** (Oct 10 through 14), celebrating the founding of the town in 1723, streets around the main plaza are filled with food, games, and wandering troubadours. Many of the shops and the Café Santa Fe are closed from the end of September through the festival. Todos Santos is a good stopover for those traveling between Cabo and La Paz; a day's visit can be arranged through tour companies in Los Cabos or done on your own with a rental car.

In Todos Santos, you can stay at **Hotel California,** Calle Juárez between Morelos and Marquez de León (☎ **114/5-0002;** fax 114/5-2333). Is this the namesake of the famous song by the Eagles? You'll get your answer when it's time to check out. Constructed in 1928, in part from planks salvaged from a shipwrecked Norwegian vessel, it's as upscale as you get in terms of local accommodations. Plain but very clean rooms—all refurbished—face either the street or a courtyard and small pool. It has 16 with fans and runs $45 for a double (cash only); reservations are a good idea in high season. The hotel restaurant serves breakfast, and other restaurants are nearby. A good choice is ✪ **Café Santa Fe,** calle Centenario 4 (☎ **114/5-0340**). Much of the attention Todos Santos is receiving these days can be directly attributed to this superb cafe. Owners Ezio and Paula Colombo have completely refurbished a large stucco house across from the plaza, creating several dining rooms and a lovely courtyard located beside a garden of hibiscus, bougainvillea, papaya trees, and herbs. The Italian cuisine emphasizes local produce and seafood; try the homemade ravioli stuffed with spinach and ricotta in a Gorgonzola sauce or the ravioli with lobster and shrimp. In high season the wait for a table at lunch can last for quite a while. Everything is prepared fresh when ordered, and reservations are recommended. Main courses run between $10 and $18. It's open Wednesday through Monday from noon to 9pm; closed September 29 to October 18.

(Reservations: 10166 35th St., Suite U, National City, CA 91950; ☎ 800/752-3555 or 619/425-1551; fax 619/425-1832.) 60 units. A/C. $125–$150 double. Rates include 3 meals daily. AE, MC, V.

Though the Buenavista has been around for nearly 2 decades, it's the most modern and luxurious place on the East Cape, thanks to additions, remodeling, and constant care. Tan buildings draped in bougainvillea are scattered down a slight slope toward the beach, with two rooms in each building. The rooms have one king or two double beds, brown-tiled bathrooms with showers, wood tables and chairs, and patios. Adjoining rooms are often used by families, who find the resort the perfect getaway for both grown-ups and kids. The excellent sportfishing fleet is a big attraction; there are also two swimming pools with swim-up bars, two hot tubs from thermal spring waters, volleyball courts, tours to the mountains, and horseback riding. Massages are available. The meal plan is a good idea, though there are a few other restaurants in the Buena Vista area.

Rancho Buena Vista. Hwy. 1 at Buena Vista, 35 miles north of San José del Cabo. No phone. (Reservations: P.O. Box 1408, Santa Maria, CA 93456; ☎ **800/258-8200** outside Calif., or 805/928-1719; fax 805/925-2990.) 55 units. A/C. $165 double. Rates include 3 meals daily.

A fishing resort with no pretensions, Rancho Buena Vista has several one-story bungalows spread about the grounds. The simple rooms have red-tiled floors, good showers, double beds, and small patios in front. Hammocks hang under palms and by the swimming pool, and the bar/restaurant is the center of the action. The hotel has an excellent deep-sea fishing fleet with its own dock and a private airstrip.

2 La Paz: Peaceful Port Town

110 miles N of Cabo San Lucas; 122 miles NW of San José del Cabo; 980 miles SE of Tijuana

La Paz means "peace," and it's not hard to imagine how this town got its name. Despite being an important port town with almost 200,000 inhabitants, it remains slow-paced, relaxed, and easygoing. You'll no doubt get into the lazy swing of things as you linger in an open-air cafe along La Paz's palm-fringed seaside boulevard. As both a port city and the capital of the state of Baja California Sur, it lacks the feeling of a tourist town, though there's plenty to do nearby. Many visitors use La Paz as a launching point for whale-watching and birding expeditions or sea kayaking, diving, or fishing trips. At Espíritu Santo and Los Islotes it's possible to swim with sea lions. Beaches line the Malecón (the main waterfront drive), and others are within a 20-mile radius. While this casual capital is enjoyable anytime, its carefree charm bursts into full bloom each February—La Paz has the biggest Carnaval celebration in Baja.

ESSENTIALS

GETTING THERE & DEPARTING By Plane Aerocalifornia (☎ **800/ 237-6225** in the U.S., or 112/5-1023) has flights to La Paz from Los Angeles, Tijuana, and Mexico City. **Aeromexico** (☎ **800/237-6639** in the U.S., 112/2-0091, 112/2-0093, or 112/2-1636) connects through Tucson and Los Angeles in the United States, as well as flying in from Mexico City, Guadalajara, Tijuana, and other points within Mexico.

By Car From San José del Cabo, Highway 1 north is the longer, more scenic route; you can travel a flatter and faster route by taking Highway 1 east to Cabo San Lucas, then Highway 19 north through Todos Santos. A little before San Pedro, Highway 19 rejoins Highway 1 north into La Paz; the trip takes 2 to 3 hours. From Loreto to the north, Highway 1 south is the only choice; the trip takes 4 to 5 hours.

By Bus The Central Camionera (main bus station) is at Jalisco and Héroes de la Independencia, about 25 blocks southwest of the center of town; it's open daily from 6am to 10pm. The bus lines serve La Paz with buses from the south (Los Cabos, 2½ to 3½ hr.) and north (as far as Tijuana). It's best to buy your ticket in person the day before, though reservations can be made over the phone.

To get to the station, catch the "Ruta INSS" city bus near the corner of Revolución and Degollado by the market. Taxis are available in front of the station.

To get to Pichilingue, the ferry pier, and close to outlying beaches, the Aguila line has a station, sometimes called the "beach bus station," on the Malecón at Alvaro Obregón and Cinco de Mayo (☎ **112/2-7898**). The station is open daily from 7am to 6pm, but buses to the ferry have shorter hours: every hour from 7am to 2pm and then again at 4 and 5pm.

Taking Your Car

Those planning to take their cars on the ferry to the Mexican mainland will be required to meet all the requirements listed in "By Car" (see "Getting There," in chapter 3), and all travelers going to the mainland need tourist cards. Tourism officials in La Paz say it's best to get your car permit and tourist card when you first cross the border at Tijuana, since the system is set up more efficiently there.

By Ferry Two *SEMATUR* car ferries serve La Paz from Topolobampo (the port for Los Mochis) Monday through Saturday at 10pm (a 10-hr. trip), and from Mazatlán Sunday through Friday at 3pm (an 18-hr. crossing). In La Paz, tickets are sold at the *SEMATUR* office at Cinco de Mayo no. 502.

The *SEMATUR* car ferry departs for Topolobampo Monday and Wednesday through Saturday at 11am and for Mazatlán Sunday through Friday at 3pm. The dock is at Pichilingue, 11 miles north of La Paz. Passengers pay one fee for themselves and another for their vehicles, with prices for cars varying, depending on the size of the car. Least expensive is Salon class with about 440 bus-type seats ($20 to Mazatlán) in one or more large rooms on the lower deck; these can become very crowded. Turista class ($41 to Mazatlán) is next providing a tiny room with four bunks, chair, sink, window, and individual bathrooms/showers down the hall. Cabina class ($62 to Mazatlán) is the best with a small room with one bunk, chair, table, window, and private bathroom. *Note:* All of these classes are not available all of the time, and ferry schedules change.

SEMATUR ferries are usually, but not always, equipped with a cafeteria and bar. Also, reserve as early as possible and confirm your reservation 24 hours before departure; you can pick up tickets at the port terminal ticket office as late as the morning of the day you are leaving. Ferry tickets are sold at the office at Cinco de Mayo no. 502 at Guillermo Pieta, 23000 La Paz, B.C.S. (☎ **112/5-3833** or 112/5-4666). The office is open daily from 8am to 6pm (☎ **112/2-9485;** fax 112/5-6588). Several tour agencies in town book reservations on the ferry, but it is best to buy your ticket in person at the ferry office. For information, you can also call ☎ **91/800/696-9600,** toll-free within Mexico.

Buses to Pichilingue depart from the "beach bus terminal" (☎ **112/2-7898**) on the Malecón at Independencia 10 times a day from 7am to 2:30pm.

ORIENTATION   Arriving by Plane   The airport is 11 miles northwest of town along the highway to Ciudad Constitución and Tijuana. Airport **colectivos** (minivans) run only from the airport to town, not vice versa. **Taxi** service is available as well.

By Bus   Buses arrive at the **Central Camionera,** about 25 blocks southwest of downtown. Taxis line up out front.

By Ferry   Buses line up in front of the ferry dock at Pichilingue to meet every arriving ferry. They stop at the "beach bus station" on the **Malecón at Independencia,** within walking distance of many downtown hotels if you're not encumbered with luggage. Taxis meet each ferry as well, and cost about $8 to downtown La Paz.

VISITOR INFORMATION   The most accessible visitor information office is on Álvaro Obregón across from the intersection with calle 16 de Septiembre (☎ **112/ 2-1199,** or 112/2-5939). It's open daily from 8am to 10pm. The extremely helpful staff speaks English and can supply information on La Paz, Los Cabos, and the rest of the region.

Another source of visitor information is **tourist services in the lobby of the Hotel Los Arcos** (☎ **112/1-5577** or 112/5-4794), open daily from 9am to 2pm and from 4 to 7pm. Jack and Jackie Velez have been operating this service for years as part of their sportfishing business and are extremely knowledgeable about the area. The English-speaking staff can help with everything from airline schedules to whale-watching trips, not to mention water sports, tours, and cruises.

CITY LAYOUT   Although La Paz sprawls well inland from the **Malecón** (the seaside boulevard, Paseo Alvaro Obregón), you'll probably spend most of your time in the older, more congenial downtown section within a few blocks of the waterfront. The main plaza, **Plaza Pública,** or **Jardín Velasco** as it's also called, is bounded by Madero,

Independencia, Revolución, and Cinco de Mayo. The plaza is centered on an iron kiosk where public concerts are held frequently in the evenings.

GETTING AROUND   Because most of what you'll need in town is located on the Malecón between the tourist information office and the Hotel Los Arcos or a few blocks inland from the waterfront, it's easy to get around La Paz on foot. There are public buses that go to some of the beaches north of town (see "Beaches & Sports," below), but to explore the many beaches within 50 miles of La Paz, your best bet is to rent a car. There are several car-rental agencies on the Malecón.

FESTIVALS & EVENTS   February features the biggest and best **Carnaval/Mardi Gras** in Baja. In **March** there's the Festival of the Whale. **May 3** features a festival celebrating the city's founding by Cortés in 1535. The annual marlin-fishing tournament is in **August,** with other fishing tournaments scheduled in **September** and **November.** And on **November 1 to 2,** the Days of the Dead, altars are on display at the Anthropology Museum.

FAST FACTS: LA PAZ

Area Code   The telephone area code is **112.** Phone numbers have recently gone through some changes, so call information if you have difficulty reaching a number.

Banks   Banks generally exchange currency during normal business hours: Monday through Friday from 9am to 6pm and Saturday from 10am to 2pm.

Marinas   La Paz has two marinas: **Marina de La Paz,** at the west end of the Malecón at Legaspi (☎ 112/5-2112) and **Marina Palmira,** south of town at km 2.5 on the Pichilingue Highway (☎ 112/16297).

Municipal Market   Three blocks inland at Degollado and Revolución de 1910, the public market sells mainly produce, meats, and utilitarian wares and is open Monday through Saturday from 6am to 6pm and Sunday from 6am to 1pm.

Parking   In high season, street parking may be hard to find in the downtown area, but there are several guarded lots, and side streets are less crowded overall.

Post Office   The correo is 3 blocks inland at Constitución and Revolución de 1910 and is open Monday through Friday from 8am to 1pm and 3pm to 6pm, and Saturday from 8am to 1pm.

BEACHES & SPORTS

La Paz combines the unselfconscious bustle of a small capital port city with beautiful, isolated beaches not far from town. Everything from whale watching and sea kayaking to beach tours, sunset cruises, and visits to the sea-lion colony can usually be arranged through travel agencies in major hotels or along the Malecón. These can also be arranged through agencies in the United States that specialize in Baja's natural history. (See "Outdoor Sports, Adventure Travel & Wilderness Trips," in chapter 3.)

BEACHES   Within a 10- to 45-minute drive from La Paz lie some of the loveliest beaches in Baja, many rivaling those of the Caribbean with their clear, turquoise water. The beach-lined **malecón** is the most convenient beach in town. More exclusive and nicer is the beach immediately north of town at **La Concha Beach Resort;** nonguests may use the hotel restaurant/bar and rent equipment for snorkeling, diving, skiing, and sailing. It's 6 miles north of town on the Pichilingue Highway at km 5.5. The other beaches are all farther north of town, but midweek you may have these far distant beaches to yourself.

At least 10 public buses from the "beach bus station" at Independencia on the Malecón depart from 8am to 2:30pm for beaches to the north. The buses stop at the small **Playa Coromuel** (3.1 miles), **Playa Camancito** (5 miles), **Playa Tesorso**

(8.9 miles), and **Pichilingue** (10.5 miles; from the ferry stop, walk north on the highway to the beach). Ask when the last bus will make the return trip. Both Pichilingue and Coromuel beaches have palapa-shaded bars or restaurants, which may not be open midweek. Other beaches have no shade, and no rentals of chairs or umbrellas, so you'll be sitting in the sun on whatever you brought, and most likely consuming food you packed.

The most beautiful of these outlying beaches is **Playa Tecolote,** found approximately 18 miles from La Paz on a paved road that ends there. The water is a heavenly cerulean blue. There are several restaurants, but service is limited midweek. To get to Playa Tecolote, take a bus as far as Pichilingue and from there a taxi the remaining 8 miles. Making arrangements for the taxi to return may be difficult. The road is paved as far as Playa Tecolote and Playa Balandra (18 miles), and turnoffs to these and other beaches are well marked.

For more information about beaches and maps, check at the tourist information office on the Malecón.

CRUISES   A fascinating cruise is to **Isla Espíritu Santo** and **Los Islotes** to visit the largest sea-lion colony in Baja, stunning rock formations, and remote beaches, with stops for snorkeling, swimming, and lunch. If conditions permit, you may even be able to snorkel beside the sea lions. Both boat and bus tours are available to **Puerto Balandra,** where pristine coves of crystal-blue water and ivory sand are framed by bold rock formations rising up like humpback whales. **Viajes Coromuel** at the Hotel Los Arcos (☎ **112/2-8006**), **Viajes Palmira** (☎ **112/2-4030**) on the Malecón across from Hotel Los Arcos, and other travel agencies can arrange these all-day trips, weather permitting, for $40 per person. Sometimes a minimum of four to six people is required.

SCUBA DIVING   Scuba-diving trips, best from June through September, can be arranged through **Fernando Aguilar's Baja Diving and Services** at Obregón 1665-2, (☎ **112/2-1826;** fax 112/2-8644). Diving sites include the sea-lion colony at Los Islotes, distant Cerralvo Island, the sunken ship *Salvatierra,* a 60-foot wall dive, several sea mounts (underwater mountains) and reefs, and a trip to see hammerhead sharks and manta rays. Rates start at $77 to $87 per person for an all-day outing and two-tank dive. They've recently added a sports lodge and beach resort, Club Hotel Cantamar, with 16 rooms and 2 suites. Rates run $65 per room, double, and $100 per suite. **Baja Expeditions,** Sonora 586 (☎ **112/5-3828;** fax 112/5-3829) in La Paz (see chapter 3 for information in the U.S. and Canada) runs live-aboard and single-day dive trips to the above-mentioned locations and other areas in the Sea of Cortés: $110 for a three-tank dive.

SEA KAYAKING   Kayaking has become extremely popular in the many bays and coves near La Paz. Many enthusiasts bring their own equipment. Kayaking trips can be arranged in advance with several companies from the United States (see "Outdoor Sports, Adventure Travel & Wilderness Trips," in chapter 3, for company descriptions). Locally, **Mar y Aventuras** (☎ **112/2-2744,** ext. 608, or 112/5-4794) also arranges kayaking trips.

SPORTFISHING   La Paz, justly famous for its sportfishing, attracts anglers from all over the world. Its waters are home to more than 850 species of fish. Here's a list of the most sought-after fish and when you can find them: black marlin, August through November; crevalle, January through October; dorado, June through December; roosterfish, snapper, and grouper, April through October; marlin, May through July; needlefish, May through September; sailfish, June through November; sierra, October through June; wahoo and yellowfin tuna, April through December; and yellowtail,

December through May. The most economical approach is to rent a *panga* (skiff) with guide and equipment for $125 for 3 hours, but you don't go very far out. Super *pangas,* which have a shade cover and comfortable seats, start at around $180 for two persons. Larger cruisers with bathrooms start at $240.

Sportfishing trips can be arranged locally through hotels and tour agencies. One of the best-known operations is **Jack Velez's Dorado Velez Fleet;** call him for reservations at the Hotel Los Arcos Fishing Desk (☎ **112/2-2744,** ext. 608) or write to him at Apdo. Postal 402, 23000 La Paz, B.C.S. Prices start at $140. Other operations include the **Mosquito Fleet** (☎ **818/541-1465** from the U.S., or 112/2-1674) and **Baja Fishing** (☎ **112/2-1313**). Ask what the price includes, since you may need to bring your own food and drinks. (See also "Outdoor Sports, Adventure Travel & Wilderness Trips," in chapter 3, for booking La Paz fishing from the United States.)

WHALE WATCHING   Between January and March (and sometimes as early as Dec), 3,000 to 5,000 gray whales migrate from the Bering Strait to the Pacific Coast of Baja. The main whale-watching spots are **Laguna San Ignacio** (on the Pacific near San Ignacio), **Magdalena Bay** (on the Pacific near Puerto López Mateos—about a 2-hr. drive from La Paz), and **Scammon's Lagoon** (near Guerrero Negro).

Though it is located across the peninsula on the Sea of Cortés, La Paz has the only major international airport in the area and thus has become the center of Baja's whale-watching excursions. Most tours originating in La Paz go to Magdalena Bay, where the whales give birth to their calves in calm waters. Several companies arrange whale-watching tours originating either in La Paz or other Baja towns or in the United States; 12-hour tours from La Paz start at around $100 per person, including breakfast, lunch, transportation, and an English-speaking guide. Make reservations at **Viajes Coromuel** at the Hotel Los Arcos travel desk (☎ **112/2-2744,** ext. 608, or 112/2-8006), or **Viajes Buendía Osório** (☎ **112/2-6544** or 112/5-0467). Most tours from the United States offer birding, sea kayaking, and other close-to-nature experiences during the same trip. (See "Outdoor Sports, Adventure Travel & Wilderness Trips," in chapter 3, for details.)

You can go whale watching without joining a tour by taking a bus from La Paz to Puerto López Mateos or San Carlos at Magdalena Bay (a 3-hr. ride) and hiring a boat there. It's a difficult trip to do in 1 day, but there are a few very modest hotels in San Carlos. Check at the La Paz tourist office for information.

A BREAK FROM THE BEACHES: EXPLORING LA PAZ

City tours of all the major sights are offered by most tour agencies. Tours last about 3 hours, include time for shopping, and cost $25 per person.

HISTORIC LA PAZ   When Cortés landed here on May 3, 1535, he named it Bahía Santa Cruz. It didn't stick. In April 1683, Eusebio Kino, a Spanish Jesuit priest, arrived and dubbed the place Nuestro Señora de la Paz (Our Lady of Peace). It wasn't until November 1, 1720, however, that a permanent mission was set up here by Jaime Bravo, another Jesuit priest. He used the same name as his immediate predecessor, calling it the Misión de Nuestro Señora de la Paz. The mission church stands on La Paz's main square on Revolución between Cinco de Mayo and Independencia, and today the city is called simply La Paz.

The Anthropology Museum. Altamirano and Cinco de Mayo. ☎ **112/2-0162.** Free admission (donations encouraged). Mon–Fri 8am–6pm; Sat 9am–2pm.

The museum features large, though faded, color photos of Baja's prehistoric cave paintings. There are also exhibits on various topics, including the geological history of the peninsula, fossils, missions, colonial history, and daily life. All information is in Spanish.

El Teatro de la Ciudad. Av. Navarro 700. ☎ **112/5-0486.**

The city theater is the city's cultural center, with performances by visiting and local artists. There's no extended calendar available, but performances include small ballet companies, experimental and popular theater, popular music, and an occasional classical concert or symphony.

Biblioteca de las Californias. In the Casa de Gobierno, across the plaza from the mission church on Madero between Cinco de Mayo and Independencia. Mon–Fri 8am–8pm.

The small collection of historical documents and books at the Library of the Californias is the most comprehensive in Baja. Free international films are sometimes shown in the evenings.

SHOPPING   La Paz has little in the way of folk art or other treasures from mainland Mexico. The dense cluster of streets behind the Hotel Perla between 16 de Septiembre and Degollado is full of small shops, some tacky, others quite upscale. Serdan from Degollado south offers dozens of sellers of dried spices, piñatas, and candy. Stores selling crafts, folk art, clothing, and handmade furniture and accessories lie mostly along the Malecón (Paseo Obregón) or a block or two in from the Malecón. The municipal market at Revolución and Degollado, however, has little of interest to visitors.

Antigua California. Paseo Álvaro Obregón 220 in the corner with Arreola. ☎ **112/5-5230.**

This shop manages to stay in business as others come and go and carries a good selection of folk art from throughout Mexico. It's open Monday through Saturday from 9:30am to 8:30pm and Sunday from 10am to 5pm. American Express, MasterCard, and Visa are accepted.

Artesanías Cuauhtémoc (The Weaver). Abasolo 3315 between Jalisco and Nayarit. ☎ **112/2-4575.**

If you like beautiful handwoven tablecloths, place mats, rugs, and other textiles, it's worth the long walk or taxi ride to this unique shop. Fortunato Silva, an elderly gentleman, weaves wonderfully textured cotton textiles from yarn he spins and dyes himself. He charges far less than what you'd pay for equivalent artistry in the United States. Open Monday through Saturday from 9am to 2pm and 4 to 6pm, and Sunday from 10am to 1pm. Cash only.

A DAY-TRIP TO EL ARCO

A day-trip by car or guided tour to Los Cabos at the southern tip of Baja California, where the Pacific Ocean meets the Sea of Cortés, will take you past dramatic scenery and many photogenic isolated beaches. A guided tour that includes lunch and a glass-bottom-boat tour to **El Arco** in Cabo San Lucas costs $45 to $60 per person and can be booked through most travel agencies. Most tours last from 7am to 6pm, and some include breakfast.

WHERE TO STAY
EXPENSIVE

La Concha Beach Resort. Km 5 Carretera Pichilingue, 23000 La Paz, B.C.S. ☎ **800/999-2252** or 112/1-6344. Fax 112/1-6218. 132 units, 12 condos/suites. A/C TEL. $85 double; $100–$195 suite or condo. AE, DC, MC, V. Free guarded parking.

Though 6 miles north of downtown La Paz, this resort's setting is perfect: on a curved beach ideal for swimming and water sports. All rooms face the water and have double beds, balconies or patios, and small tables and chairs. The only satellite TV available is in a large lounge, where movies are shown every evening. Condos with full kitchens and one or three bedrooms are also available on a nightly basis in the high-rise complex next door. The hotel offers scuba, fishing, and whale-watching packages.

Dining/Diversions: There are two bars. The Las Palmas restaurant serves seafood and Mexican and American classics. The La Palapa poolside bar is often the site of buffet dinners, brunch, and Mexican fiestas.

Amenities: Beachside pool, complete aquatic-sports center with WaveRunners, kayaks, and paddleboats; Beach Club with scuba program available, 18-hole golf course and tennis courts are under construction. Laundry and room service, tour desk, gift shop, free twice-daily shuttle to town.

MODERATE

✪ **Hotel Los Arcos.** Paseo Obregón 498 (Apdo. Postal 112), 23000 La Paz, B.C.S. ☎ **800/ 347-2252** or 714/450-9000 in the U.S., or 112/2-2744. Fax 112/5-4313. 121 units, 52 bungalows, 9 suites. A/C MINIBAR TV TEL. $75 double unit; $84 bungalows; $120 suite. AE, MC, V. Free guarded parking.

This three-story neocolonial-style hotel at the west end of the malecón, between Rosales and Allende, is the best place for downtown accommodations. Los Arcos is decidedly modern in its furnishings and amenities, which include room service, laundry, cafeteria, an upscale restaurant, bar with live music, travel agency, and a desk for fishing information. The hotel's rambling nooks and crannies are filled with fountains, plants, and even rocking chairs that lend lots of old-fashioned charm. Most rooms come with two double beds and a balcony overlooking the pool in the inner courtyard or the waterfront. Suites are more modern, in the same hotel building. South Pacific–style bungalows with thatched roofs and fireplaces are in the back part of the property, nestled into an appealing jungle garden shaded by large trees. The complex also offers two pools (one heated), a sauna, Ping-Pong tables, and a tourist information booth in the lobby. TVs carry U.S. channels.

INEXPENSIVE

Hotel Aquario's. Ramírez 1665, 23000 La Paz, B.C.S. ☎ **112/2-9266.** Fax 112/5-5713. 60 units. A/C TV TEL. $36 double. MC, V. Free parking.

This popular, well-maintained three-story motel frames a protected parking lot and pool. Each of the comfortable, clean rooms comes with a small balcony, one or two double beds, a table and two chairs, and a bathroom with a tub as well as a shower. Most rooms have just been upgraded, and the lobby and restaurant/bar, open daily from 7am to 11pm, were expanded last year. Laundry service is available. You'll find the hotel 6 blocks inland from the Malecón; take Degollado and then make a left on Ramírez.

WHERE TO DINE

Although La Paz is not known for culinary achievements, it has a growing assortment of small, pleasant restaurants that are good and reasonably priced. In addition to the usual seafood and Mexican dishes, you can find Italian, French, Spanish, Chinese, and even a growing selection of vegetarian offerings. Restaurants along the seaside Malecón tend to be more expensive than those a few blocks inland.

For baked goods try the *panadería* at Independencia and Domínguez and the *pastelería* at Altamirano and Bravo.

MODERATE

Bismark II. Degollado and Altamirano. ☎ **112/2-4854.** Breakfast $3–$4; main courses $4–$17. MC, V. Daily 7am–10pm. SEAFOOD/MEXICAN.

Bismark excels at seafood; you can order fish tacos, chile rellenos stuffed with lobster salad, marlin "meatballs" and paella, breaded oysters, or a sundae glass filled with ceviche or shrimp. Extremely fresh dorado, halibut, snapper, or whatever else is in season is prepared in a number of ways. Chips and a creamy dip are served while you wait. It's a good place to linger over a late lunch. The decor of pine walls and dark wood chairs are reminiscent of a country cafe. Walk 7 blocks inland on Degollado to Altamirano. The owners will call a cab for you if you wish.

El Moro Flair. In the Club El Moro, Pichilingue Hwy. km 2. (☎ 112/5-2828). Breakfast $3–$7; main courses $6–$13. Wed–Mon 8am–10pm. SEAFOOD/CONTINENTAL.

An auspicious way to start the day is with a breakfast of orange French toast or *huevos motuleños* (fried eggs served on soft corn tortillas, stuffed with melted cheese and ham, topped with tomato sauce) on El Moro's small patio looking out to sea. You might expect the pink-and-gray restaurant at this pseudo-Moorish private club to be outrageously expensive, but prices are quite reasonable and the setting is extravagant, with such fancy touches as individual French press coffeepots at each table. For dinner try the Caesar salad mixed table-side, the filet mignon and shrimp or fresh halibut Florentine, and flaming crêpes suzette. The restaurant is about a 15-minute walk along the waterfront toward Pichilingue.

✪ **Trattoria La Pazta.** Allende 36. ☎ **112/5-1195.** Main courses $5–$9. AE, MC, V. Wed–Mon 4–10pm. ITALIAN/SWISS.

The trendiest restaurant in town, La Pazta gleams with black lacquered tables and white tile; the aromas of garlic and espresso float in the air. The menu features local fresh seafood such as pasta with squid in wine and cream sauce, and crispy fried calamari. Lasagna is homemade, baked in a wood-fired oven. Choose from an extensive wine list to complement your meal. The restaurant is in front of the Hotel Mediterrane, 1 block inland from the Malecón.

LA PAZ AFTER DARK

A night in La Paz might logically begin in a cafe along the malecón as the sun sinks into the sea—have your camera ready.

A favorite ringside seat at dusk is a table at **La Terraza,** next to the Hotel Perla. La Terraza makes good schooner-sized margaritas. **Pelicanos Bar,** in the second story of the Hotel Los Arcos, has a good view of the waterfront and a clubby, cozy feel. **La Paz-Lapa** has live music on the weekends. The liveliest of all is **La Cabaña** nightclub in the Hotel Perla, featuring one or two bands Tuesday through Sunday playing Latin rhythms. It opens at 9:30pm, and there's a $8 minimum consumption requirement. An inexpensive alternative is to stroll along the Malecón and people-watch, stopping here and there for a drink or snack or to hear some wandering mariachis.

The poolside bar overlooking the beach at **La Concha Beach Resort,** km 5.5 Pichilingue Highway (☎ 112/2-6544), is the setting for Mexican fiestas at 7pm on Friday nights and barbecues at 6:30pm Saturday nights during holidays and busy tourist seasons. Cover is $15.

Appendix

A Telephones & Mail

USING THE TELEPHONES

Generally within a city, you will be dialing a five- or six-digit number. **To call long distance (abbreviated "lada") within Mexico,** you'll need to dial the national long distance code **01** prior to dialing a two- or three-digit area code. In total, Mexico's telephone numbers are eight digits in length. Mexico's area codes (*claves*) are usually listed in the front of telephone directories. Area codes are listed before all phone numbers in this book.

International long distance calls to the United States or Canada are accessed by dialing **001,** then the area code and seven-digit number. For other international dialing codes dial the operator at **04.**

For additional details on making calls in Mexico and to Mexico, see chapter 3, "Planning a Trip to Mexico."

POSTAL GLOSSARY
Airmail   **Correo Aéreo**
Customs   **Aduana**
General Delivery   **Lista de Correos**
Insurance (insured mail)   **Seguros**
Mailbox   **Buzón**
Money Order   **Giro Postale**
Parcel   **Paquete**
Post Office   **Oficina de Correos**
Post Office Box (abbreviation)   **Apdo. Postal**
Postal Service   **Correos**
Registered Mail   **Registrado**
Rubber Stamp   **Sello**
Special Delivery, Express   **Entrega Inmediata**
Stamp   **Estampilla** or **Timbre**

B Basic Vocabulary

Most Mexicans are very patient with foreigners who try to speak their language; it helps a lot to know a few basic phrases.

I've included a list of certain simple phrases for expressing basic needs, followed by some common menu items.

ENGLISH-SPANISH PHRASES

English	Spanish	Pronunciation
Good day	**Buenos días**	*bway*-nohss *dee*-ahss
How are you?	**¡Cómo está usted?**	*koh*-moh ess-*tah* oo-*sted*?
Very well	**Muy bien**	mwee byen
Thank you	**Gracias**	*grah*-see-ahss
You're welcome	**De nada**	day *nah*-dah
Goodbye	**Adiós**	ah-*dyohss*
Please	**Por favor**	pohr fah-*vohr*
Yes	**Sí**	see
No	**No**	noh
Excuse me	**Perdóneme**	pehr-*doh*-ney-may
Give me	**Déme**	*day*-may
Where is . . . ?	**¡Dónde está . . . ?**	*dohn*-day ess-*tah*?
the station	**la estación**	lah ess-tah-*seown*
a hotel	**un hotel**	oon oh-*tel*
a gas station	**una gasolinera**	*oon*-uh gah-so-lee-*nay*-rah
a restaurant	**un restaurante**	oon res-tow-*rahn*-tay
the toilet	**el baño**	el *bahn*-yoh
a good doctor	**un buen médico**	oon bwayn *may*-thee-co
the road to . . .	**el camino a/hacia**	el cah-*mee*-noh ah/ *ah*-see-ah
To the right	**A la derecha**	ah lah day-*reh*-chuh
To the left	**A la izquierda**	ah lah ees-ky-*ehr*-thah
Straight ahead	**Derecho**	day-*reh*-cho
I would like	**Quisiera**	key-see-*ehr*-ah
I want	**Quiero**	*kyehr*-oh
to eat.	**comer**	ko-*mayr*
a room.	**una habitación**	*oon*-nuh ha-bee-tah-*seown*
Do you have?	**¡Tiene usted?**	tyah-nay oos-*ted*?
a book.	**un libro**	oon *lee*-bro
a dictionary.	**un diccionario**	oon deek-seown-*ar*-eo
How much is it?	**¡Cuánto cuesta?**	*kwahn*-to *kwess*-tah?
When?	**¡Cuándo?**	*kwahn*-doh?
What?	**¡Qué?**	kay?
There is (Is there . . . ?)	**(¡)Hay (. . . ?)**	eye?
What is there?	**¡Qué hay?**	kay eye?
Yesterday	**Ayer**	ah-*yer*
Today	**Hoy**	oy
Tomorrow	**Mañana**	mahn-*yahn*-ah
Good	**Bueno**	*bway*-no
Bad	**Malo**	*mah*-lo
Better (best)	**(Lo) Mejor**	(loh) meh-*hor*
More	**Más**	mahs
Less	**Menos**	*may*-noss
No smoking	**Se prohíbe fumar**	say pro-*hee*-bay foo-*mahr*
Postcard	**Tarjeta postal**	tar-*hay*-ta pohs-*tahl*
Insect repellent	**Rapellante contra insectos**	rah-pey-*yahn*-te *cohn*-trah een-*sehk*-tos

MORE USEFUL PHRASES

English	Spanish	Pronunciation
Do you speak English?	¡Habla usted inglés?	*ah*-blah oo-*sted* een-*glays*?
Is there anyone here who speaks English?	¡Hay alguien aquí qué hable inglés?	eye *ahl*-ghee-en kay *ah*-blay een-*glays*?
I speak a little Spanish.	Hablo un poco de español.	*ah*-blow oon *poh*-koh day ess-pah-*nyol*
I don't understand Spanish very well.	No (lo) entiendo muy bien el español.	noh (loh) ehn-tee-*ehn*-do myee bee-ayn el ess-pah-*nyol*
The meal is good.	Me gusta la comida.	may *goo*-sta lah koh-*mee*-dah
What time is it?	¡Qué hora es?	kay *oar*-ah ess?
May I see your menu?	¡Puedo ver el menú (la carta)?	*puay*-tho veyr el may-*noo* (lah *car*-tah)?
The check please.	La cuenta por favor.	lah *quayn*-tah pohr fa-*vorh*
What do I owe you?	¡Cuánto lo debo?	*Kwahn*-toh loh *day*-boh?
What did you say?	¡Mande? (colloquial expression for American "Eh?")	*Mahn*-day?
More formal:	¡Cómo?	*Koh*-moh?
I want (to see)	Quiero (ver)	Key-*yehr*-oh vehr
a room	un cuarto (una habitación)	oon *kwar*-toh
for two persons.	para dos personas	*pahr*-ah doss pehr-*sohn*-as
with (without) bath.	con (sin) baño.	kohn (seen) *bah*-nyoh
We are staying here only . . .	Nos quedamos aquí solamente . . .	nohs kay-*dahm*-ohss ah-*key* sohl-ah-*mayn*-tay
one night.	una noche.	oon-ah *noh*-chay
one week.	una semana.	oon-ah say-*mahn*-ah
We are leaving	Partimos (Salimos)	Pahr-*tee*-mohss (sah-*lee*-mohss)
tomorrow.	mañana.	mahn-*nyan*-ah
Do you accept traveler's checks?	¡Acepta usted cheques de viajero?	Ah-*sayp*-tah oo-*sted* chay-kays day bee-ah-*hehr*-oh?
Is there a Laundromat near here?	¡Hay una lavandería cerca de aquí?	Eye *oon*-ah lah-*vahn*-day-ree-ah *sehr*-ka day ah-*key*?
Please send these clothes to the laundry.	Hágame el favor de mandar esta ropa a la lavandería.	*Ah*-ga-may el fah-*vhor* day mahn-*dahr* ays-tah *rho*-pah a lah lah-*vahn*-day-*ree*-ah

NUMBERS

1	**uno** (*ooh*-noh)		11	**once** (*ohn*-say)
2	**dos** (dohs)		12	**doce** (*doh*-say)
3	**tres** (trayss)		13	**trece** (*tray*-say)
4	**cuatro** (*kwah*-troh)		14	**catorce** (kah-*tor*-say)
5	**cinco** (*seen*-koh)		15	**quince** (*keen*-say)
6	**seis** (sayss)		16	**dieciseis** (de-*ess*-ee-sayss)
7	**siete** (*syeh*-tay)		17	**diecisiete** (de-*ess*-ee-*syeh*-tay)
8	**ocho** (*oh*-choh)		18	**dieciocho** (dee-*ess*-ee-*oh*-choh)
9	**nueve** (*nway*-bay)		19	**diecinueve** (dee-*ess*-ee-*nway*-bay)
10	**diez** (dee-ess)		20	**veinte** (*bayn*-tay)

30	**treinta** (*trayn*-tah)		90	**noventa** (noh-*ben*-tah)
40	**cuarenta** (kwah-*ren*-tah)		100	**cien** (see-*en*)
50	**cincuenta** (seen-*kwen*-tah)		200	**doscientos** (*dos*-se-en-tos)
60	**sesenta** (say-*sen*-tah)		500	**quinientos** (keen-ee-*ehn*-tos)
70	**setenta** (say-*ten*-tah)		1,000	**mil** (meal)
80	**ochenta** (oh-*chen*-tah)			

TRANSPORTATION TERMS

English	Spanish	Pronunciation
Airport	**Aeropuerto**	Ah-ay-row-*por*-tow
Flight	**Vuelo**	Boo-*ay*-low
Rental Car	**Arrendadora de Autos**	Ah-rain-da-dow-rah day autos
Bus	**Autobús**	ow-toh-*boos*
Bus or truck	**Camión**	ka-me-*ohn*
Lane	**Carril**	kah-*rreal*
Nonstop	**Directo**	dee-*reck*-toh
Baggage (claim area)	**Equipajes**	eh-key-*pah*-hays
Intercity	**Foraneo**	fohr-ah-*nay*-oh
Luggage storage area	**Guarda equipaje**	gwar-daheh-key-*pah*-hay
Arrival gates	**Llegadas**	yay-*gah*-dahs
Originates at this station	**Local**	loh-*kahl*
Originates elsewhere; stops if seats available	**De Paso**	day *pah*-soh
First class	**Primera**	pree-*mehr*-oh
Second class	**Segunda**	say-*goon*-dah
Nonstop	**Sin Escala**	seen ess-*kah*-lah
Baggage claim area	**Recibo de Equipajes**	ray-see-boh day eh-key-*pah*-hay
Waiting room	**Sala de Espera**	*Saw*-lah day ess-*pehr*-ah
Toilets	**Sanitarios**	Sahn-ee-tahr-*ee*-oss
Ticket window	**Taquilla**	tah-*key*-lah

C Menu Glossary

Achiote Small red seed of the annatto tree.

Achiote preparada A prepared paste found in Yucatán markets made of ground achiote, wheat and corn flour, cumin, cinnamon, salt, onion, garlic, and oregano. Mixed with juice of a sour orange or vinegar and put on broiled or charcoaled fish (tikin chick) and chicken.

Agua fresca Fruit-flavored water, usually watermelon, canteloupe, chia seed with lemon, hibiscus flour, or ground melon-seed mixture.

Antojito A Mexican snack, usually masa-based with a variety of toppings such as sausage, cheese, beans, and onions; also refers to tostadas, sopes, and garnachas.

Atole A thick, lightly sweet, warm drink made with finely ground rice or corn and usually flavored with vanilla.

Birria Lamb or goat meat cooked in a tomato broth, spiced with garlic, chiles, cumin, ginger, oregano, cloves, cinnamon, and thyme and garnished with onions, cilantro, and fresh lime juice to taste; a specialty of Jalisco state.

Botana A light snack—an antojito.

Buñuelos Round, thin, deep-fried crispy fritters dipped in sugar.

Cabrito   Grilled kid; a northern Mexican delicacy.

Carnitas   Pork that's been deep-cooked (not fried) in lard, then steamed and served with corn tortillas for tacos.

Ceviche   Fresh raw seafood marinated in fresh lime juice and garnished with chopped tomatoes, onions, chiles, and sometimes cilantro and served with crispy, fried whole corn tortillas.

Chayote   Vegetable pear or merleton, a type of spiny squash boiled and served as an accompaniment to meat dishes.

Chile en nogada   Poblano peppers stuffed with a mixture of ground pork and chicken, spices, raisins, and almonds, fried in a light batter and covered in a walnut and cream sauce.

Chiles rellenos   Poblano peppers usually stuffed with cheese, rolled in a batter, and baked; other stuffings include ground beef spiced with raisins.

Churro   Tube-shaped, breadlike fritter, dipped in sugar and sometimes filled with cajeta or chocolate.

Cochinita pibil   Pork wrapped in banana leaves, pit-baked, and served with a pibil sauce of achiote, sour orange, and spices; common in Yucatán.

Corunda   A triangular tamal wrapped in a corn leaf; a Michoacan specialty.

Enchilada   Tortilla dipped in a sauce and usually filled with chicken or white cheese and sometimes topped with tomato sauce and sour cream (enchiladas Suizas—Swiss enchiladas), or covered in a green sauce (enchiladas verdes), or topped with onions, sour cream, and guacamole (enchiladas Potosiños).

Epazote   Leaf of the wormseed plant, used in black beans and with cheese in quesadillas.

Escabeche   A lightly pickled sauce used in Yucatecan chicken stew.

Frijoles charros   Beans flavored with beer; a northern Mexican specialty.

Frijoles refritos   Pinto beans mashed and cooked with lard.

Garnachas   A thickish small circle of fried masa with pinched sides, topped with pork or chicken, onions, and avocado or sometimes chopped potatoes, and tomatoes, typical as a botana in Veracruz and Yucatán.

Gorditas   Thickish fried-corn tortillas, slit and stuffed with choice of cheese, beans, beef, chicken, with or without lettuce, tomato, and onion garnish.

Gusanos de maguey   Maguey worms, considered a delicacy, and delicious when charbroiled to a crisp and served with corn tortillas for tacos.

Horchata   Refreshing drink made of ground rice or melon seeds, ground almonds, and lightly sweetened.

Huevos Mexicanos   Eggs with onions, hot peppers, and tomatoes.

Huevos Motuleños   Eggs atop a tortilla, garnished with beans, peas, ham, sausage, and grated cheese; a Yucatecan specialty.

Huevos rancheros   Fried egg on top of a fried corn tortilla covered in a tomato sauce.

Huitlacoche   Sometimes spelled "cuitlacoche," mushroom-flavored black fungus that appears on corn in the rainy season; considered a delicacy.

Machaca   Shredded dried beef scrambled with eggs or as salad topping; a specialty of northern Mexico.

Manchamantel   Translated means "tablecloth stainer," a stew of chicken or pork with chiles, tomatoes, pineapple, bananas, and jícama. Sometimes listed as "mancha manteles."

Masa   Ground corn soaked in lime used as basis for tamales, corn tortillas, and soups.

Mixiote   Lamb baked in a chile sauce or chicken with carrots and potatoes, used as basis for tamales, corn tortillas, and soups

Pan de Muerto   Sweet or plain bread made around the Days of the Dead (Nov 1 to 2), in the form of mummies, dolls, or round with bone designs.

Pan dulce   Lightly sweetened bread in many configurations, usually served at breakfast or bought at any bakery.

Papadzules   Tortillas are stuffed with hard-boiled eggs and seeds (cucumber or sunflower) in a tomato sauce.

Pavo relleno negro   Stuffed turkey Yucatán-style, filled with chopped pork and beef, cooked in a rich, dark sauce.

Pibil   Pit-baked pork or chicken in a sauce of tomato, onion, mild red pepper, cilantro, and vinegar.

Pipian   Sauce made with ground pumpkin seeds, nuts, and mild peppers.

Poc chuc   Slices of pork with onion marinated in a tangy sour orange sauce and charcoal broiled; a Yucatecan specialty.

Pollo Calpulalpan   Chicken cooked in pulque; a specialty of Tlaxcala.

Pozole   A soup made with hominy and pork or chicken, in either a tomato-based broth Jalisco-style, or a white broth Nayarit-style, or green chile sauce Guerrero-style, and topped with choice of chopped white onion, lettuce or cabbage, radishes, oregano, red pepper, and cilantro.

Pulque   Drink made of fermented sap of the maguey plant; best in state of Hidalgo and around Mexico City.

Quesadilla   Flour tortillas stuffed with melted white cheese and lightly fried.

Queso relleno   "Stuffed cheese" is a mild yellow cheese stuffed with minced meat and spices; a Yucatecan specialty.

Rompope   Delicious Mexican eggnog, invented in Puebla, made with eggs, vanilla, sugar, and rum.

Salsa verde   A cooked sauce using the green tomatillo and puréed with mildly hot peppers, onions, garlic, and cilantro; on tables countrywide.

Sopa de calabaza   Soup made of chopped squash or pumpkin blossoms.

Sopa de lima   A tangy soup made with chicken broth and accented with fresh lime; popular in Yucatán.

Sopa seca   Not a soup at all, but a seasoned rice which translated means "dry soup."

Sopa Tarasca   A rib-sticking pinto bean–based soup, flavored with onions, garlic, tomatoes, chiles, and chicken broth and garnished with sour cream, white cheese, avocado chunks, and fried tortilla strips; a specialty of Michoacán state.

Sopa Tlalpeña   A hearty soup made with chunks of chicken, chopped carrots, zucchini, corn, onions, garlic, and cilantro.

Sopa Tlaxcalteca   A hearty tomato-based soup filled with cooked nopal cactus, cheese, cream, and avocado with crispy tortilla strips floating on top.

Sopa tortilla   A traditional chicken broth–based soup, seasoned with chiles, tomatoes, onion, and garlic, bobbing with crisp fried strips of corn tortillas.

Sope   Pronounced *"soh*-pay," a botana similar to a garnacha, except spread with refried beans and topped with crumbled cheese and onions.

Tacos al pasto   Thin slices of flavored pork roasted on a revolving cylinder dripping with onion slices and juice of fresh pineapple slices.

Tamal   Incorrectly called tamale (tamal singular, tamales plural); meat or sweet filling rolled with fresh masa, then wrapped in a corn husk or banana leaf and steamed; many varieties and sizes throughout the country.

Tepache   Drink made of fermented pineapple peelings and brown sugar.

Tikin xic Also seen on menus as "tikin chick," charbroiled fish brushed with achiote sauce.

Tinga A stew made with pork tenderloin, sausage, onions, garlic, tomatoes, chiles, and potatoes; popular on menus in Puebla and Hidalgo states.

Torta A sandwich, usually on bolillo bread, usually with sliced avocado, onions, tomatoes, with a choice of meat and often cheese.

Torta Ahogado A specialty of Lake Chapala is made with a scooped out roll, filled with beans and beef strips and seasoned with a tomato or chile sauce.

Tostadas Crispy fried corn tortillas topped with meat, onions, lettuce, tomatoes, cheese, avocados, and sometimes sour cream.

Venado Venison (deer) served perhaps as pipian de venado, steamed in banana leaves and served with a sauce of ground squash seeds.

Xtabentun (shtah-ben-*toon*) A Yucatán liquor made of fermented honey and flavored with anise. It comes *seco* (dry) or *crema* (sweet).

Zacahuil Pork leg tamal, packed in thick masa, wrapped in banana leaves, and pit-baked, sometimes pot-made with tomato and masa; specialty of mid- to upper Veracruz.

Index

684 Index

FROMMER'S® COMPLETE TRAVEL GUIDES
(Comprehensive guides with selections in all price ranges—from deluxe to budget)

Alaska
Amsterdam
Arizona
Atlanta
Australia
Austria
Bahamas
Barcelona, Madrid & Seville
Belgium, Holland & Luxembourg
Bermuda
Boston
Budapest & the Best of Hungary
California
Canada
Cancún, Cozumel & the Yucatán
Cape Cod, Nantucket & Martha's Vineyard
Caribbean
Caribbean Cruises & Ports of Call
Caribbean Ports of Call
Carolinas & Georgia
Chicago
China
Colorado
Costa Rica
Denver, Boulder & Colorado Springs
England
Europe
Florida

France
Germany
Greece
Hawaii
Hong Kong
Honolulu, Waikiki & Oahu
Ireland
Israel
Italy
Jamaica & Barbados
Japan
Las Vegas
London
Los Angeles
Maryland & Delaware
Maui
Mexico
Miami & the Keys
Montana & Wyoming
Montréal & Québec City
Munich & the Bavarian Alps
Nashville & Memphis
Nepal
New England
New Mexico
New Orleans
New York City
Nova Scotia, New Brunswick & Prince Edward Island
Oregon
Paris
Philadelphia & the Amish Country

Portugal
Prague & the Best of the Czech Republic
Provence & the Riviera
Puerto Rico
Rome
San Antonio & Austin
San Diego
San Francisco
Santa Fe, Taos & Albuquerque
Scandinavia
Scotland
Seattle & Portland
Singapore & Malaysia
South Pacific
Spain
Switzerland
Thailand
Tokyo
Toronto
Tuscany & Umbria
USA
Utah
Vancouver & Victoria
Vermont, New Hampshire & Maine
Vienna & the Danube Valley
Virgin Islands
Virginia
Walt Disney World & Orlando
Washington, D.C.
Washington State

FROMMER'S® DOLLAR-A-DAY GUIDES
(The ultimate guides to comfortable low-cost travel)

Australia from $50 a Day
California from $60 a Day
Caribbean from $60 a Day
England from $60 a Day
Europe from $50 a Day
Florida from $60 a Day
Greece from $50 a Day
Hawaii from $60 a Day
Ireland from $50 a Day

Israel from $45 a Day
Italy from $50 a Day
London from $70 a Day
New York from $75 a Day
New Zealand from $50 a Day
Paris from $70 a Day
San Francisco from $60 a Day
Washington, D.C., from $60 a Day

FROMMER'S® MEMORABLE WALKS

Chicago
London

New York
Paris

San Francisco

FROMMER'S® PORTABLE GUIDES

Acapulco, Ixtapa/
  Zihuatenejo
Bahamas
California Wine
  Country
Charleston & Savannah
Chicago

Dublin
Las Vegas
London
Maine Coast
New Orleans
New York City
Paris

Puerto Vallarta, Manzanillo
  & Guadalajara
San Francisco
Sydney
Tampa Bay & St. Petersburg
Venice
Washington, D.C.

FROMMER'S® NATIONAL PARK GUIDES

Grand Canyon
National Parks of the American West
Yellowstone & Grand Teton

Yosemite & Sequoia/
  Kings Canyon
Zion & Bryce Canyon

THE COMPLETE IDIOT'S TRAVEL GUIDES
(The ultimate user-friendly trip planners)

Cruise Vacations
Planning Your Trip to Europe
Hawaii

Las Vegas
Mexico's Beach Resorts
New Orleans

New York City
San Francisco
Walt Disney World

SPECIAL-INTEREST TITLES

The Civil War Trust's Official Guide to
  the Civil War Discovery Trail
Frommer's Caribbean Hideaways
Israel Past & Present
New York City with Kids
New York Times Weekends
Outside Magazine's Adventure Guide
  to New England
Outside Magazine's Adventure Guide
  to Northern California

Outside Magazine's Adventure Guide
  to the Pacific Northwest
Outside Magazine's Guide to Family Vacations
Places Rated Almanac
Retirement Places Rated
Washington, D.C., with Kids
Wonderful Weekends from Boston
Wonderful Weekends from New York City
Wonderful Weekends from San Francisco
Wonderful Weekends from Los Angeles

THE UNOFFICIAL GUIDES®
(Get the unbiased truth from these candid, value-conscious guides)

Atlanta
Branson, Missouri
Chicago
Cruises
Disneyland

Florida with Kids
The Great Smoky
  & Blue Ridge
  Mountains
Las Vegas

Miami & the Keys
Mini-Mickey
New Orleans
New York City
San Francisco

Skiing in the West
Walt Disney World
Walt Disney World
  Companion
Washington, D.C.

FROMMER'S® IRREVERENT GUIDES
(Wickedly honest guides for sophisticated travelers)

Amsterdam
Boston
Chicago

London
Manhattan

New Orleans
Paris

San Francisco
Walt Disney World
Washington, D.C.

FROMMER'S® DRIVING TOURS

America
Britain
California

Florida
France
Germany

Ireland
Italy
New England

Scotland
Spain
Western Europe

WHEREVER YOU TRAVEL, *H*ELP IS NEVER FAR AWAY.

From planning your trip to

providing travel assistance along

the way, American Express®

Travel Service Offices are

always there to help.

American Express Travel Service
Offices are found in central locations
throughout Mexico.

Travel

http://www.americanexpress.com/travel